SPECIAL INDIAN EDITION

OPERATIONS AND SUPPLY CHAIN MANAGEMENT

Fifteenth Edition

AF659996

SPECIAL INDIAN EDITION

OPERATIONS AND SUPPLY CHAIN MANAGEMENT

Fifteenth Edition

Richard B. Chase
University of Southern California

Ravi Shankar
Indian Institute of Technology Delhi

F. Robert Jacobs
Indiana University

McGraw Hill Education (India) Private Limited

Published by McGraw Hill Education (India) Private Limited
Registered Office: Anjana Complex No: 5/90 A, Butt Road, St. Thomas Mount, Chennai – 600016

Operations and Supply Chain Management, 15e Copyright © 2018, 2014, 2011, 2009, 2006 by McGraw Hill

Adaptation Copyright © 2019, by McGraw Hill Education (India) Private Limited
Published by arrangement with McGraw Hill LLC.

ALL RIGHTS RESERVED. NO PART OF THIS BOOK MAY BE REPRODUCED OR TRANSMITTED IN ANY FORM OR BY ANY MEANS, ELECTRONIC OR MECHANICAL, INCLUDING PHOTOCOPYING, RECORDING OR BY INFORMATION STORAGE AND RETRIEVAL SYTEMS, WITHOUT PERMISSION IN WRITING FROM MCGRAW HILL.

Special Indian Edition (SIE) 2019, 2014, 2010

Eighth reprint 2022

This edition can be exported from India only by the publishers,

Sales Territories: India, Pakistan, Nepal, Bangladesh, Sri Lanka and Bhutan

Fictious names of companies, products, people, characters and/or data that may be used herein (in case studies or in examples) are not intended to represent any real individual, company, product or event.

Print Edition
ISBN-13: 978-93-5316-117-0
ISBN-10: 93-5316-117-7

E-Book Edition
ISBN-13: 978-93-5316-118-7
ISBN-10: 93-5316-118-5

09 10 11 12 13 RAJ 26 25 24 23 22

Managing Director: *Lalit Singh*
Head of HED Portfolio: *Nikhil Wadhera*
Head—Production: *Pankaj Manohar*
Manager—Production: *Reji Kumar*

Information contained in this work has been obtained by McGraw Hill Education (India), from sources believed to be reliable. However, neither McGraw Hill Education (India) nor its authors guarantee the accuracy or completeness of any information published herein, and neither McGraw Hill Education (India) nor its authors shall be responsible for any errors, omissions, or damages arising out of use of this information. This work is published with the understanding that McGraw Hill Education (India) and its authors are supplying information but are not attempting to render engineering or other professional services. If such services are required, the assistance of an appropriate professional should be sought.

Typeset at The Composers, 260, C.A. Apt., Paschim Vihar, New Delhi 110063 and
Printed and bound in India at Rajkamal Electric Press, Plot No.2, Phase-IV, Kundli, Haryana.

Cover Designer: APS Compugraphics
Cover Image Source: Shutterstock

Visit us at: www.mheducation.co.in
Toll free in India: 1800 103 5875
Write to us at: info.india@mheducation.com
CIN: U80302TN2010PTC111532

SPECIAL INDIAN EDITION

OPERATIONS AND SUPPLY CHAIN MANAGEMENT

Fifteenth Edition

Richard B. Chase
University of Southern California

Ravi Shankar
Indian Institute of Technology Delhi

F. Robert Jacobs
Indiana University

McGraw Hill Education (India) Private Limited

Published by McGraw Hill Education (India) Private Limited
Registered Office: Anjana Complex No: 5/90 A, Butt Road, St. Thomas Mount, Chennai – 600016

Operations and Supply Chain Management, 15e Copyright © 2018, 2014, 2011, 2009, 2006 by McGraw Hill

Adaptation Copyright © 2019, by McGraw Hill Education (India) Private Limited
Published by arrangement with McGraw Hill LLC.

ALL RIGHTS RESERVED. NO PART OF THIS BOOK MAY BE REPRODUCED OR TRANSMITTED IN ANY FORM OR BY ANY MEANS, ELECTRONIC OR MECHANICAL, INCLUDING PHOTOCOPYING, RECORDING OR BY INFORMATION STORAGE AND RETRIEVAL SYTEMS, WITHOUT PERMISSION IN WRITING FROM MCGRAW HILL.

Special Indian Edition (SIE) 2019, 2014, 2010

Eighth reprint 2022

This edition can be exported from India only by the publishers,

Sales Territories: India, Pakistan, Nepal, Bangladesh, Sri Lanka and Bhutan

Fictious names of companies, products, people, characters and/or data that may be used herein (in case studies or in examples) are not intended to represent any real individual, company, product or event.

Print Edition
ISBN-13: 978-93-5316-117-0
ISBN-10: 93-5316-117-7

E-Book Edition
ISBN-13: 978-93-5316-118-7
ISBN-10: 93-5316-118-5

09 10 11 12 13 RAJ 26 25 24 23 22

Managing Director: *Lalit Singh*
Head of HED Portfolio: *Nikhil Wadhera*
Head—Production: *Pankaj Manohar*
Manager—Production: *Reji Kumar*

Information contained in this work has been obtained by McGraw Hill Education (India), from sources believed to be reliable. However, neither McGraw Hill Education (India) nor its authors guarantee the accuracy or completeness of any information published herein, and neither McGraw Hill Education (India) nor its authors shall be responsible for any errors, omissions, or damages arising out of use of this information. This work is published with the understanding that McGraw Hill Education (India) and its authors are supplying information but are not attempting to render engineering or other professional services. If such services are required, the assistance of an appropriate professional should be sought.

Typeset at The Composers, 260, C.A. Apt., Paschim Vihar, New Delhi 110063 and
Printed and bound in India at Rajkamal Electric Press, Plot No.2, Phase-IV, Kundli, Haryana.

Cover Designer: APS Compugraphics
Cover Image Source: Shutterstock

Visit us at: www.mheducation.co.in
Toll free in India: 1800 103 5875
Write to us at: info.india@mheducation.com
CIN: U80302TN2010PTC111532

To my wife, Harriet, and to our children
Laurie, Andy, Glenn, Robb, and Christine

To my wife, Poonam, and to our children
Pratyush and Snigdha

To my father, Forest

Preface

Operations and supply chain management (OSCM) is a key element in the improvement in productivity in business around the world. Establishing a *competitive advantage* through operations requires an understanding of how the operations and supply chain functions contribute to productivity growth. However, our intent in this book is to do more than just show you what companies are doing to create a competitive advantage in the marketplace by conveying to you a set of skills and tools that you can actually apply.

Hot topics in business today that relate to operations and supply chain management are reducing the cost of supply chain processes, integration and collaboration with customers and suppliers, sustainability, and minimizing the long-term cost of products and processes. These topics are studied in the book with up-to-date, high-level managerial material to clarify the "big picture" of what these topics are and why they are so important to business today.

A significant feature of this book is the organization of each chapter by concise learning objectives. Each objective relates to a block of knowledge that should be studied as a unit. The objectives are carried through the end-of-chapter material that includes Concept Connections, Discussion Questions, Objective Questions, and a Practice Exam. The material is organized to ease the understanding of each topic.

Success in OSCM requires a data-driven view of a firm's business. Every chapter in the book has *analytic* content that ties decisions to relevant data. Mathematical models are used to structure the data for making decisions. Given the facts that are supported by data, success in OSCM requires using a *strategy* that is consistent with the operations-related priorities of a firm. Different approaches can often be used, and usually trade-offs related to cost-and-flexibility-related criteria exist. Strategies are implemented through *processes* that define exactly how things are done. Processes are executed over and over again as the firm conducts business, so they must be designed to operate efficiently to minimize cost while meeting quality-related standards. Great managers are analytic in their approach to decision making; they understand and select the appropriate strategy, and then execute the strategy through great processes. We develop this pattern throughout the topics in this book.

The reality of global customers, global suppliers, and global supply chains has made the global firm recognize the importance of being both lean and green to ensure competitiveness. Applications that range from high-tech manufacturing to high-touch service are used in the balanced treatment of the traditional topics of the field. Success for companies today requires successfully managing the entire supply flow, from the sources of the firm, through the value-added process of the firm, and on to the customers of the firm.

Each chapter includes information about how operations and supply chain–related problems are solved. There are concise treatments of the many decisions that need to be made in designing, planning, and managing the operations of a business. Many spreadsheets are available from the book website to help clarify how these problems are quickly solved. We have indicated those spreadsheets with an Excel icon in the margin.

OSCM should appeal to individuals who want to be directly involved in making products or providing services. The entry-level operations specialist is the person who determines how best to design, supply, and run the processes. Senior operations managers are responsible for setting the strategic direction of the company from an operations and supply chain standpoint, deciding what technologies should be used and where facilities should be located, purchasing the resources needed, and managing the facilities that make the products or provide the services. OSCM is an interesting mix of managing people and applying sophisticated technology. The goal is to efficiently create wealth by supplying quality goods and services.

Features to aid in your understanding of the material include the following:

- OSCM at work boxes provide short overviews of how leading-edge companies are applying OSCM concepts today.
- Solved problems at the end of chapters to serve as models that can be reviewed prior to attempting problems.
- Key terms highlighted in the chapter with their definitions in the margin

- Concept Connections section in each chapter that summarizes the concepts in each learning objective, has definitions of the key terms, and lists the equations where appropriate.
- Discussion questions that are designed to review concepts and show their applicability in real-world settings. These are included in each chapter and organized by learning objectives.
- Objective questions at the end of chapters that cover each concept and problem. These are organized by the chapter learning objectives.
- Practice exam questions at the end of each chapter. These are special questions designed to require a deeper understanding of the material in the chapter. They are similar to the type of short-answer questions that might be given on a test.
- Answers to selected problems are in Appendix D.
- Topic-wise additional material accessible via QR code, which include Excel Spreadsheets, for the solved problems and other examples; video segments that illustrate the application of operations concepts
- Concepts strengthened according to Indian needs, which includes but not limited to, Sustainability in SCM, Demand Chain Management, Maintenance Management, Retail Operations, and Application of OSCM concepts to Indian IT among others.

Our aim is to cover the latest and the most important issues facing OSCM managers, as well as basic tools and techniques. We supply many examples of leading-edge companies and practices and have done our best to make the book an interesting read and give you a competitive advantage in your career.

We hope you enjoy it.

PLAN OF THE BOOK

This book is about methods to effectively produce and distribute the goods and services sold by a company. To develop a better understanding of the field, this book is organized into five major sections: Strategy, Products, and Capacity; Manufacturing and Service Processes; Supply Chain Processes; Supply and Demand Planning and Control; and Special Topics. In the following paragraphs, we quickly describe the major topics in the book.

Strategy and sustainability are important and recurring topics in the book. Any company must have a comprehensive business plan that is supported by a marketing strategy, operations strategy, and financial strategy. It is essential for a company to ensure that the three strategies support each other. Strategy is covered from a high-level view in Chapter 2 (Strategy), and more details that relate to economies of scale and learning are covered in Chapters 5 and 6.

The lifeline of the company is a steady stream of innovative products that are offered to the marketplace at the lowest cost possible. Design of Products and Services (Chapter 3) includes a view of how products are designed in the context of having to actually produce and distribute the product over its life cycle. The chapter includes material on how to manage and analyze the economic impact of a stream of products that are developed over time. Projects (Chapter 4) are used to implement change in a firm, be it a change in strategy, a new product introduction, or a new process.

The second section of the book, titled Manufacturing and Service Processes, focuses on the design of internal processes. Chapters 7 and 9 cover the unique characteristics of production and service processes. Important technical material that relates to design activities is covered in Chapters 8 (Facility Layout) and 10 (Waiting Line Analysis and Simulation).

Chapter 11, Process Design and Analysis, is a nuts-and-bolts chapter on process flow charting and static process analysis using some easily understood real-life examples.

An essential element of process design is quality. Six Sigma Quality is the topic of Chapter 12. Here we cover total quality management concepts, Six Sigma tools, and ISO 9000 and 14000. Technical details covering all the statistical aspects of quality are in Chapter 13 (Statistical Quality Control).

The third section of the book, titled Supply Chain Processes, expands our focus to the entire distribution system from the sourcing of material and other resources to the distribution of products and services. We discuss the concepts behind lean manufacturing and just-in-time processes in Chapter 14. These are ideas used by companies throughout the world and are key drivers for efficient and quick-responding supply systems. Many different transformation processes are needed to put together a supply chain. There are critical decisions such as: Where should we locate our facility? What equipment should we buy or lease? Should we outsource work or do it in-house? These are the topics of Chapters 15 and 16 that relate to sourcing, procurement, location of facilities, and distribution. All of these decisions have a direct financial impact on the firm.

Section Four, titled Supply and Demand Planning and Control, covers the techniques required to actually run the system. This is at the heart of OSCM. The basic building blocks are Forecasting (Chapter 18), Sales and Operations Planning

(Chapter 19), Inventory Management (Chapter 20), Material Requirements Planning (Chapter 21), and Workcenter Scheduling (Chapter 22). These daily processes are often partially automated with computer information systems. Coverage of Enterprise Resource Planning Systems is the topic of Chapter 17.

In the final section of the book, titled Special Topics, we show how the concepts in the book are applied to special business situations. Here we have selected two types of businesses, Health Care (Chapter 24) and Operations Consulting (Chapter 25). We know that many of you may be interested in working for hospitals and similar specialized care facilities, a growing segment of the world economy. In addition, we know that many of those interested in OSCM are also interested in consulting as a profession.

Making fact-based decisions is what OSCM is all about, so this book features extensive coverage of decision-making approaches and tools. One useful way to categorize decisions is by the length of the planning horizon, or the period of time that the decision maker must consider. For example, building a new plant would be a long-term decision that a firm would need to be happy with for 10 to 15 years into the future. At the other extreme, a decision about how much inventory for a particular item should be ordered for tomorrow typically has a much shorter planning horizon of a few months or, in many cases, only a few days. Such short-term decisions are usually automated using computer programs. In the intermediate term are decisions that a company needs to live with for only 3 to 12 months. Often these decisions correspond to yearly model changes and seasonal business cycles.

As you can see from this discussion, this material is all interrelated. A company's strategy dictates how operations are designed. The design of the operation dictates how it needs to be managed. Finally, because businesses are constantly being presented with new opportunities through new markets, products, and technologies, a business needs to be very good at managing change.

Acknowledgments

Many talented scholars have made major contributions to specific chapters in this edition of the book. We are pleased to thank the following individuals:

Rhonda Lummus of Indiana University, for her many ideas for improving the material in the book. Ronny Richardson of Kennesaw State University and Matthew Drake of Duquesne University, who have spent countless hours checking problems and improving Connect.

Chris Albright, Goker Aydin, Doug Blocher, Kyle Cattani, Seb Hesse, Ash Soni, Gilvan Souza, and Wayne Winston of the ODT department at the Kelley School of Business, Indiana University, for all the time spent discussing ideas.

Supplements are a great deal of work to write, and we appreciate the efforts that make teaching the course easier for everyone who uses the text. John Kros of East Carolina University created the Connect guided examples. P. Sundararaghavan of University of Toledo updated the test bank. Ronny Richardson of Kennesaw State University updated the PowerPoint decks and revised Smartbook.

We also want to thank former doctoral students who have contributed to the book over the years, including Mahesh Nagarajan, *University of British Columbia;* Hiroshi Ochiumi, Wayne Johannson, and Jason Niggley, *USC;* Douglas Stewart, *University of New Mexico;* Anderas Soteriou, *University of Cyprus;* Arvinder Loomba, *University of Northern Iowa;* Deborah Kellogg, *University of Colorado–Denver;* Blair Berkeley, *California State University–Los Angeles;* and Bill Youngdahl, *Thunderbird American Graduate School of International Management.*

We also want to thank the following individuals for their thoughtful reviews of the previous edition and suggestion for this text: Gladys Simpson, *Florida International University;* Scott Swenseth, *University of Nebraska;* Mohsen El Hafsi, *University of California Riverside;* Joel Wisner, *University of Nebraska;* Kim Roberts, *Athens State University;* Chris Kiscaden, *University of New Mexico;* Steven Yourstone, *University of New Mexico;* Mark Ippolito, *Indiana University;* Frank Armstrong, *Ferris State University* and *Lansing Community College.*

Thanks to the McGraw-Hill Education team who make this possible—Chuck Synovec, director; Michele Janicek, lead product developer; Trina Maurer, senior marketing manager; Kathryn Wright and Kristin Bradley, project managers; Mark Christianson, program manager; Sandy Ludovissy, senior buyer; Egzon Shaqiri, designer; and Melissa Homer and Jacob Sullivan, content licensing specialists.

Finally, I want to thank my past co-authors Dick Chase and Nick Aquilano for giving me the opportunity to work with them on their book for the past 16 years. I had the opportunity to work with Nick Aquilano on two editions of the book and with Dick Chase on six editions. Both Nick and Dick have now retired from writing the book, but they are still engaged in many creative activities. They have been an inspiration to me and are wonderful colleagues. Enjoy your retirement, you both deserve it.

F. Robert Jacobs

I would like to thank my mentors, colleagues, co-researchers, and well-wishers. They include Prof. Prem Vrat, Prof. Surendra S Yadav, Prof. S G Deshmukh, Prof. Manoj Kumar Tiwari, Prof. C. Rajendran, Prof. Sanjeev Swami, Prof. Pradeep Kumar, Dr. Navin K. Dev, Prof. Alok Choudhary, Prof. Alok Baveja, Prof. Christian Hicks, Prof. Jingxin Dong, Prof. Zach Zacharia, Prof. Dr. Hans Ziegler, and Prof. Shams Rahman, for their active support and help during various stages of my learning and growth. I was fortunate to have the opportunity to supervise many brilliant and hard working Ph.D. research scholars. Till date, 53 of them have either obtained their Ph.D. degrees or are about to do so. During academic interactions with them, I was able to learn many new aspects in OSCM. All of them have maintained an enduring academic relationship. I express my sincere thanks and good wishes to Prof. S Jharkharia, Prof. Ashish Agarwal, Prof. Shiri Vivek, Prof.

Tilak Raj, Dr. Akhilesh Barve, Prof. Rakesh Kumar Mudgal, Dr. Roma Mitra Debnath, Dr. Parikshit Charan, Dr. A Ramesh, Dr. Rohit Joshi, Prof. V C Pandey, Dr. Pravin Kumar, Dr. K K Bhattacharya, Dr. Muktesh Chander, Dr. Ajay Tomar, Dr. Sourish Acharia, Dr. Krishnendu Shaw, Dr. Devendra Choudhary, Dr. Arun Purohit, Dr. Pallab Biswas, Prashant Tuli, Ashish Kaushal, Rachita Gupta, Vijayta Fulzele, Mahamaya Mohanty, Devendra Pathak, Praveer Sinha, Veepan Kumar, Monika Sharma, Sushil Punia, Sonali Shankar, Bishal Dey Sarkar and Archana Roy.

For this Special Indian Edition, I would like to thank the McGraw Hill Education (India) team of Sachin Kumar, Anuj Srivastava, Taranpreet Kaur, Shivkant Singhal, Satinder Singh, Nikhil Wadhera, and Shalini Jha.

Last, but certainly not the least, I thank my family members, who once again let the life cycle of the book disrupt theirs.

Publisher and the author would also like to thank the following reviewers for providing their valuable suggestions and comments:

Dixit Garg	*National Institute of Technology Kurukshetra, Haryana*
Harish Venkatesh Rao	*International Management Institute, New Delhi, Delhi*
Rajesh Matai	*Birla Institute of Technology and Science, Pilani, Rajasthan*
Pravash Ghosh	*ICFAI Business School, Gurugram, Haryana*
Rajat Agrawal	*IIT Roorkee, Roorkee, Uttarakhand*
Gaurav Kabra	*Xavier Institute of Management Bhubaneswar, Bhubaneswar*
Rajesh Wasudeorao Raut	*Modern Institute of Business Management, Pune, Maharashtra*
Niraj Shirish Mankad	*FLAME School of Business, Pune, Maharashtra*
S. Purushothaman	*SRM Easwari Engineering College, Ramapuram, Chennai*
Pachayappan M	*Xavier Institute of Management and Entrepreneurship, Bengaluru, Karnataka*

Ravi Shankar

Note to Instructors

DISCUSSION OF FIFTEENTH EDITION REVISIONS

The revisions to the fifteenth edition are a refinement of major changes made in the last edition. Each chapter is organized around a short set of learning objectives. These learning objectives define the major sections of each chapter. A complete set of Discussion Questions together with Objective Questions, which include concepts and problems, are included.

The Objective Questions are available and many have both static versions (these are identical to the problem in the book) and scenario versions. In the scenario versions of the problem, the parameters have been changed, but the problem is essentially the same, thus allowing students to see different examples of the same problem. The instructor can select predefined or set up custom problem sets that students can complete. These are automatically graded with the results available in a spreadsheet that can be easily downloaded by the instructor. There are many options for how these problem sets can be used, such as allowing the students multiple tries, giving the students help, and timed exams.

In this edition, we have increased our focus on supply chain analytics. Supply chain analytics involve the analysis of data to better solve business problems. We recognize that this is not really a new concept because data has always been used to solve business problems. But what is new is the reality that there is so much more data now available for decision making.

In the past, most analysis involved the generation of standard and ad hoc reports that summarized the current state of the firm. Software allowed query and "drill down" analysis to the level of the individual transaction, useful features for understanding what happened in the past. Decision making was typically left to the decision maker, based on their judgment or simply because they were aware of the rules. The new "analytics" movement takes this to a new level using statistical analysis, forecasting to extrapolate what to expect in the future, and even optimization, possibly in real time, to support decisions.

In this edition, our goal is to capture this spirit of using integrated analytic and strategic criteria in making operations and supply chain decisions. We have done this in two major ways. First, we have reorganized the material in the book by integrating the strategic and analytic material. Next, we have refined our series of 11 Analytics Exercises spread throughout the chapters. In this edition, many small changes designed to increase clarity, simplify assumptions, and make the exercises better learning tools have been made.

These new Analytics Exercises use settings that are modern and familiar to students taking the course. They include Starbucks, cell phones, notebook computers, Taco Bell Restaurant, Toyota, a retail website-based company, and industrial products that are sourced from China/Taiwan and sold globally. The book has been reorganized into five major sections: Strategy, Products, and Capacity; Manufacturing and Service Processes; Supply Chain Processes; Supply and Demand Planning and Control; and Special Topics. Our strategy is to weave analytics into the managerial material so students see the important role of data analysis in making operations and supply chain management decisions.

In the first section, *Strategy, Products, and Capacity*, our chapters cover Strategy, the Design of Products and Services, Project Management, Strategic Capacity Management, and Learning Curves. The key themes of operations strategy, product design to support the strategy, and strategic capacity are a good foundation for learning about operations and supply chain management. Because most strategic plans are implemented using projects, we include this topic in the first section as well. In the project management chapter, we introduce a good amount of material on product design through examples and exercises, emphasizing the strategic importance of these projects to the success of the firm.

The second section, *Manufacturing and Service Processes*, gets into the nuts and bolts of operations management. The section introduces the ways manufacturing and service systems are organized and includes new Analytics Exercises for assembly line design and queuing. The Six Sigma and Statistical Quality Control chapters cover topics that would be appropriate for a green-belt program and include good coverage of the popular value-stream mapping technique.

The third section, *Supply Chain Processes*, discusses processes that source material for internal operations and then distribute products to the customers. The analytic models involved with location/transportation are included here. The topics are tied together in the Lean Supply Chain chapter, which now stresses the cost versus disruption risk trade-offs that are involved in such tactics as single sourcing and just-in-time inventory.

The fourth section, *Supply and Demand Planning and Control*, covers the techniques typically implemented in Enterprise Resource Planning Systems. These include Forecasting, Sales and Operations Planning, Inventory Management, Material Requirements Planning, and Workcenter Scheduling. We also include a chapter on the Theory of Constraints, a set of thought-provoking concepts.

Finally, the fifth section, titled *Special Topics*, covers two industries where operations and supply chain management concepts are being applied with great success. The first is health care, with the majority of our material on hospital and special care facilities. We also discuss operations consulting because this is an area where many of our students find jobs.

The following are a list of the major revisions in selected chapters:

- *Chapter 1* Introduction—The opening vignette has been changed to highlight "Efficiency at Southwest Airlines." Exhibit 1.4 the "Good-Services Continuum" has been changed to make it more relevant to today. A number of new key terms were added that relate to major concepts that define OSCM. These are from the timeline. Exhibit 1.7 has been updated and is now a comparison of Toyota, GM, and Ford.
- *Chapter 2* Strategy—The new opening vignette features the innovative car company Tesla Motors. Exhibit 2.2 "Formulating an Operations and Supply Chain Strategy" is new. A new definition of the key term *order winner* now indicates that there can be more than one order winner. Exhibit 2.4 "Risk Mitigation Strategies" has been updated.
- *Chapter 3* Design of Products and Services—The opening vignette has been updated. It still features IDEO but now captures their new process, Overlapping Thought Spaces. Tesla has been added as an example of an innovative and highly successful company. Exhibit 3.7 ("Process Alternatives for a Family Restaurant") has been updated to be more in tune with today. Exhibit 3.11 has been replaced with measures related to product development success, focusing on the terms: time-to-market, productivity, and quality. These terms have all been changed to keywords.
- *Chapter 4* Project Management—The opening vignette that describes how a Chinese construction company builds 30-story hotels in only 15 days has been updated.
- *Chapter 5* Strategic Capacity Management—The opening vignette has been updated. Rewrote Example 5.1 to explain how this planning example fits into a hierarchical planning process. Also, clarified some terminology.
- *Chapter 6* Learning Curves—The opening vignette has been updated.
- *Chapter 8* Facility Layout—The opening vignette has been updated. The description of assembly line task times is updated to reflect the usual focus on labor task time. Efficiency calculation is also updated to reflect this. The Retail Service Layout section is rewritten and updated to reflect current trends. The Analytic Exercise discussion questions have been updated for clarity.
- *Chapter 9* Service Processes—The opening vignette has been updated. Exhibit 9.4 is updated to reflect current thought. Updated material on service guarantees. Updated examples to reflect current times. The "Three Contrasting Service Design" section was extensively rewritten to reflect current thought.
- *Chapter 10* Waiting Line Analysis and Simulation—The opening vignette has been completely rewritten. The "Waiting Line Problem" section was rewritten. The new Exhibit 10.9 for multi-server (Model 3) analysis now includes many more values. This is needed to support the *Connect* scenario-based problems.
- *Chapter 11* Process Design and Analysis (title changed)—A new opening vignette has been added featuring Amazon Air Prime. In Example 11.2, the solution is rewritten and clarified. The material describing cycle time and flow time is rewritten and clarified. Object question 21 is rewritten to clarify assumptions.
- *Chapter 12* Sigma Quality—Here, a new case "Tesla's Quality Challenge" has been added. This replaced the old Toyota case.
- *Chapter 13* Statistical Quality Control—The notation for the standard deviation (Sc) for the c-chart was changed from Sp to Sc to prevent any confusion with Sp, the standard deviation for the p-chart. The "Hot Shot Plastics Company" has been changed to an analytics exercise. "Quality Management—Toyota" is also changed to an analytics exercise.
- *Chapter 14* Lean Supply Chains—The section that describes "minimized setup time" has been rewritten.
- *Chapter 15* Logistics, Distribution, and Transportation—The opening vignette has been rewritten to reflect the current status and thoughts related to the Panama Canal project. Many other updates have been made to make the material up-to-date. The OSCM at Work box about Boeing is rewritten.
- *Chapter 16* Global Sourcing and Procurement—Exhibit 16.6 has been rewritten and updated to current thought.

- *Chapter 17* Enterprise Resource Planning Systems—Updated OSCM at Work box titled Open Information Warehouse. Updated "Supply Chain Council" section to show current association with APICS.
- *Chapter 18* Forecasting—Changed the definition of MAPE and how it is calculated. It is the average of the percent errors associated with each forecast. This does not impact any problems, but it does impact the analytics exercise section (only slightly) at the end of the chapter.
- *Chapter 20* Inventory Management—The exhibits in Big10Sweaters have been updated to make them clearer.
- *Chapters 23* Theory of Constraints—Updated Eli Goldratt's Theory of Constraints section to reflect current thinking. The Lahey Clinical OSCM at Work box has been removed.
- *Chapter 24* Health Care—Exhibit 24.2 has been updated and Exhibit 24.6 has been replaced with better material. Exhibit 24.7 and the description of DRGs has been updated. Exhibit 24.8 has been removed and its material is inserted into the text.

F. Robert Jacobs
July 2016

ONLINE LEARNING CENTER (OLC)

The text website, our Online Learning Center (OLC), can be found at connect.mheducation.com. It includes material to help students succeed in the course. For students, the asset includes: Additional Student Resources.

The instructors' assets include a "Map to Harvard Cases", Solutions Manual, Framework PowerPoints, Author's Website, OM Videos, Data Files, Errata, Additional Student Resources and Instructor PowerPoints in addition to what the students receive.

ASSURANCE OF LEARNING READY

Many educational institutions today are focused on the notion of *assurance of learning,* an important element of some accreditation standards. *Operations and Supply Chain Management* is designed specifically to support your assurance of learning initiatives with a simple, yet powerful solution.

Each test bank question for *Operations and Supply Chain Management* maps to a specific chapter learning objective listed in the text. You can use our test bank software, EZ Test and EZ Test Online, to easily query for learning objectives that will directly relate to the learning objectives for your course. You can then use the reporting features of EZ Test to aggregate student results in a similar fashion, making the learning of data simple and easy.

Walkthrough

Chapter Opener

The following section highlights the key features developed to provide the student with the best overall text available. We hope these features give maximum support to learn, understand, and apply operations concepts.

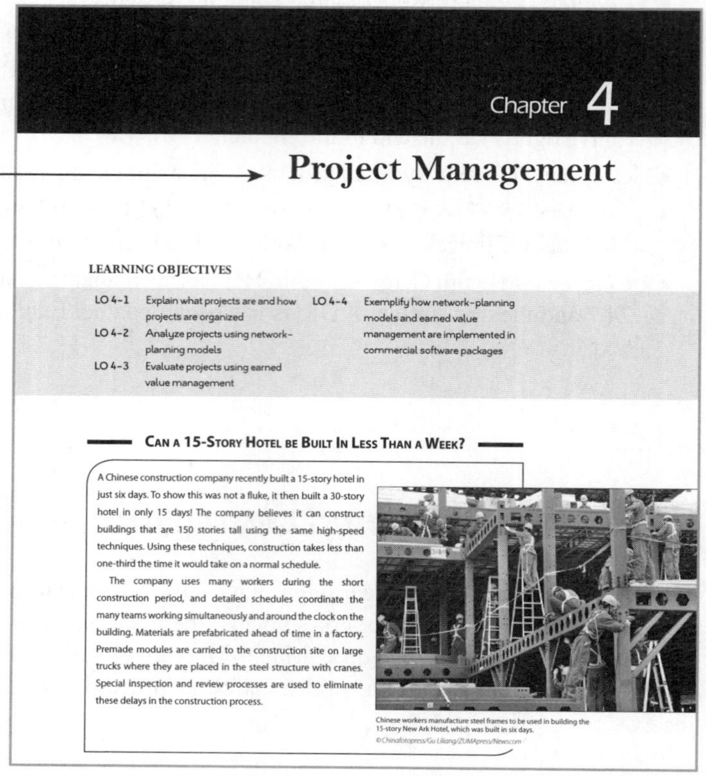
Chapter 4

Project Management

LEARNING OBJECTIVES

LO 4-1 Explain what projects are and how projects are organized

LO 4-2 Analyze projects using network-planning models

LO 4-3 Evaluate projects using earned value management

LO 4-4 Exemplify how network-planning models and earned value management are implemented in commercial software packages

CAN A 15-STORY HOTEL BE BUILT IN LESS THAN A WEEK?

A Chinese construction company recently built a 15-story hotel in just six days. To show this was not a fluke, it then built a 30-story hotel in only 15 days! The company believes it can construct buildings that are 150 stories tall using the same high-speed techniques. Using these techniques, construction takes less than one-third the time it would take on a normal schedule.

The company uses many workers during the short construction period, and detailed schedules coordinate the many teams working simultaneously and around the clock on the building. Materials are prefabricated ahead of time in a factory. Premade modules are carried to the construction site on large trucks where they are placed in the steel structure with cranes. Special inspection and review processes are used to eliminate these delays in the construction process.

Chinese workers manufacture steel frames to be used in building the 15-story New Ark Hotel, which was built in six days.

© Chinafotopress/Gu Liliang/ZUMApress/Newscom

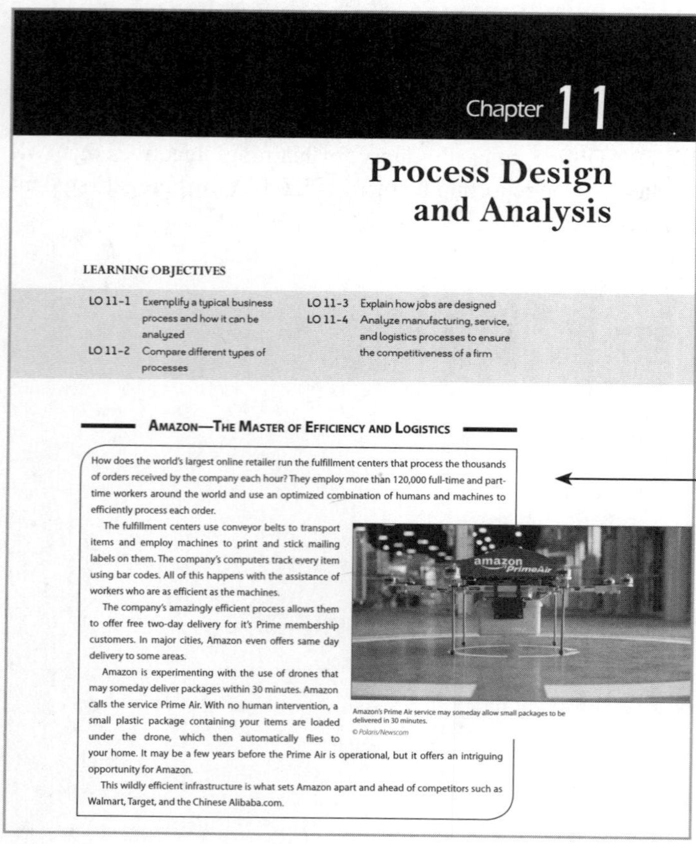
Chapter 11

Process Design and Analysis

LEARNING OBJECTIVES

LO 11-1 Exemplify a typical business process and how it can be analyzed

LO 11-2 Compare different types of processes

LO 11-3 Explain how jobs are designed

LO 11-4 Analyze manufacturing, service, and logistics processes to ensure the competitiveness of a firm

AMAZON—THE MASTER OF EFFICIENCY AND LOGISTICS

How does the world's largest online retailer run the fulfillment centers that process the thousands of orders received by the company each hour? They employ more than 120,000 full-time and part-time workers around the world and use an optimized combination of humans and machines to efficiently process each order.

The fulfillment centers use conveyor belts to transport items and employ machines to print and stick mailing labels on them. The company's computers track every item using bar codes. All of this happens with the assistance of workers who are as efficient as the machines.

The company's amazingly efficient process allows them to offer free two-day delivery for it's Prime membership customers. In major cities, Amazon even offers same day delivery to some areas.

Amazon is experimenting with the use of drones that may someday deliver packages within 30 minutes. Amazon calls the service Prime Air. With no human intervention, a small plastic package containing your items are loaded under the drone, which then automatically flies to your home. It may be a few years before the Prime Air is operational, but it offers an intriguing opportunity for Amazon.

This wildly efficient infrastructure is what sets Amazon apart and ahead of competitors such as Walmart, Target, and the Chinese Alibaba.com.

Amazon's Prime Air service may someday allow small packages to be delivered in 30 minutes.

© Polaris/Newscom

Opening Vignettes

Each chapter opens with a short vignette to set the stage and help pique students' interest in the material about to be studied. A few examples include:

- Boeing, Chapter 6
- United Parcel Service (UPS), Chapter 11
- Starbucks, Chapter 18

Walkthrough

OSCM at Work Boxes

The boxes provide examples or expansions of the topics presented by highlighting leading companies practicing new, breakthrough ways to run their operations. Examples include:

- Efficiency: It's the Details That Count, Chapter 1
- What's It Like Working on an Assembly Line?, Chapter 8
- J.D. Power and Associates Initial Quality Study of New Cars, Chapter 12
- Mr. Rounder Is On-Call at Hackensack University Medical Center, Chapter 24

OSCM AT WORK

Best Practices at LG Electronics India Ltd.

Best operations management practices of global leaders like typical Korean company LG Electronics, typical Japanese company Suzuki and many others are well reflected in their Indian counterpart. These companies have adapted to the concept of open, responsive and flexible approach towards developing operations and supply chain strategies. For example, in 1998, with an investment of around ₹500 crore, LG Electronics India Ltd. (LGEIL) has set up a world-class manufacturing facility for color televisions, washing machines, air-conditioners and microwave ovens at Greater Noida, very near to the capital city of India—Delhi. Production of eco-friendly refrigerators and PC monitor started here in the year 2001 [1].

LGEIL has developed many good practices to improve its operational strategies. For example, the Production, Sales and Inventory (PSI) plan and Rolling Sales Plan-review (RSP) are conducted daily, followed by on weekly and monthly basis, with an aim to increase the accuracy in planning activities of sales and production. To maintain a high quality six-sigma level and 100 PPM, it aims to reduce defects through modification in process using S.M.A.R.T. targets. Vendor performance-linked rating system, called as ABC system in LGEIL, identifies A-class as excellent vendors, B-class as Ok and C-class as "should-improve vendors." Open communication systems, such as pizza-lunch with MD helps LGEIL employees to share work-related issues with MD. Dosti tour is another concept used to improve team work in continuous improvement process. It provides a forum where an operator shows to his supervisor the job or process-related improvements to get acknowledgement and reward. [2] Like LG Electronics Korea, LGEIL has also launched its own codes of conduct by nurturing a "green partnership" with the first-tier suppliers in order to maintain high standards of environmentally-sound practice and product quality [3].

The goal of innovation is to introduce a positive change, to make someone or something better. LGEIL believes in open innovation culture, where employees at all levels are encouraged to create, implement and share their innovative ideas. It encourages various approaches to innovate the products, processes & systems, e.g. Six Sigma & TDR (Tear Down Re-engineering). Six-sigma, a statistical approach for product quality improvement, is used to optimize the existing processes by reducing the overall variation in the process. Through this, the root cause of the problem are identified and eliminated by means of statistical tools and techniques. The quality issues are identified at different stages like (i) incoming part issues from suppliers, (ii) assembly processes during manufacturing, (iii) product issues while actual usage by consumer. These issues are resolved by quality experts known as Six Sigma Black Belts certified by Korea HQ. These black belts follow DMAIC (Define, Measure, Analyse, Improve & Control) approach to eliminate the root causes of quality issues.

In order to focus on waste elimination, Lean Six Sigma drive has been initiated across the whole organisation of LGEIL. In the process, employees use value-stream-mapping to identify and eliminate the non-value-added activities to improve the level of prevailing processes through different statistical approaches. The idea behind using Six Sigma approach is to create value and eliminate waste.

In his foreword to a book authored by Dr. Yasho V. Verma – the then COO of LGEIL, Mr. Y.K. Kim, LG Electronics at Seoul writes, "LGEIL has often been benchmarked by other LG Electronics subsidiaries and also credited as a successful localization case... From planning and administration, to marketing and sales, to R&D, local Indian employees are actively engaged in all areas of business." [4]

Question

(1) What are the reasons of competitive advantages of LGEIL?

(2) Map the growth of LGEIL in consumer durables and electronics-goods in India in terms of product, brand, best practices in manufacturing and HR.

LO 15–1 SOLVED PROBLEM 1

Green Energy Technologies (GET) is planning to locate a new solar panel manufacturing plant in the southeastern United States to meet strongly growing demand in that market. It is considering three cities for this new plant: Montgomery, Alabama; Atlanta, Georgia; and Charleston, North Carolina. It has developed a list of important factors to consider in making its decision. After making site visits to each of the three cities, the facility location team has rated each of the cities as shown in the following table.

		City Ratings		
Factor	Max Points	Montgomery	Atlanta	Charleston
Availability of labor	60	55	52	48
Availability of technical skills	50	37	46	41
Transportation infrastructure	40	34	37	32
Warehousing availability/costs	40	30	33	28
Proximity to customers	35	22	27	25
Proximity to suppliers	25	25	22	20
Taxation structure	15	12	10	14
Quality of life	10	7	8	9
Climate	5	3	3	4

Based on this factor-rating system and the points assigned by the facility location team, which location appears to be the best choice?

Solution

The difficulty in applying a factor-rating system lies in the design of the system and the evaluation of each potential site on every factor. Once this is accomplished, evaluating the results is a simple matter of adding up the total points for each candidate location. Based on the ratings shown, the point totals are as follows.

Montgomery	225
Atlanta	238
Charleston	221

Based on the results of the rating system, Atlanta would appear to be the best choice.

LO 15–2 SOLVED PROBLEM 2

Industrial Packaging Solutions (IPS) is a manufacturer of corrugated fiberboard shipping boxes used by companies across the United States. It sells to wholesalers, who in turn sell to resellers or end-user customers. Final products are consolidated on standard shipping pallets of uniform dimensions and weight. Because of this, the cost to ship a pallet to a single destination is the same regardless of the type of box loaded on the pallet. The standard unit for sales and operations planning at IPS is a pallet load.

After recently opening a new factory to satisfy growing demand for its products, IPS is concerned about allocating demand from its customers to the facilities in its production network. It wants to do so in a way that minimizes the total cost of shipping final products to the wholesalers.

It currently has three factories that service a network of eight major wholesalers. Relevant data for the next year are shown in the following tables.

Excel

Excel icons point out concepts where Excel templates are available on the text website.

Walkthrough

Photos and Exhibits

Over 60 photos and 200 exhibits are included in the text to enhance the visual appeal and clarify text discussions. Many of the photos illustrate additional examples of companies that utilize the operations and supply chain concepts in their business.

Water skis and snow skis are examples of complementary products.

© Ingram Publishing/SuperStock RF © Pixtal/AGE fotostock RF

Exhibit 19.2

Required Inputs to the Production Planning System

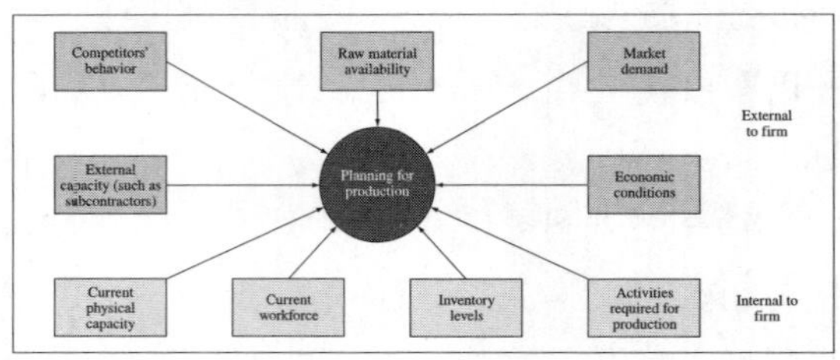

Key Ideas

Important points in the text are called out and summarized in the margins.

ssic accommodation, which entails, for example, o compensate for variations among customers; oor, outsourcing, and self-service to cut the cost ires, for example, customers to engage in more expectations; and *uncompromised reduction,* which res that enable good service, while minimizing the ibit 9.4 illustrates the tactics that are useful in each

gement of variability generally requires a company example of what can be done to reduce variability. e DVDs. Thus, a customer has a strong incentive ot returned, the company still has a revenue stream being held by the customer. In contrast, the Netflix D for as long as they want. A customer's incentive his or her request list. The Netflix approach might Redbox approach assures revenues on DVDs being

Key Ideas

Variability is the major problem with services that require direct customer contact. Innovative approaches are needed to manage this variability.

Encounters

that managers understand customer perceptions as Chase and Dasu, professors at Southern California enhance customer perceptions of three aspects of at's happening), *the flow of time* (how long it seems t you thought about it later). Looking at the service wing six behaviorally based principles for service

Key Ideas

The customer's perception related to a poor encounter may be changed if the problem is addressed quickly.

unter are not created equal. It is widely believed o-called service bookends, are equally weighted in arch indicates this is not the case, however. While

Walkthrough

Solved Problems

Representative problems are placed at the end of appropriate chapters. Each includes a worked-out solution, giving students a review before solving problems on their own.

SOLVED PROBLEMS

LO 15–1 SOLVED PROBLEM 1

Green Energy Technologies (GET) is planning to locate a new solar panel manufacturing plant in the southeastern United States to meet strongly growing demand in that market. It is considering three cities for this new plant: Montgomery, Alabama; Atlanta, Georgia; and Charleston, North Carolina. It has developed a list of important factors to consider in making its decision. After making site visits to each of the three cities, the facility location team has rated each of the cities as shown in the following table.

		City Ratings		
Factor	Max Points	Montgomery	Atlanta	Charleston
Availability of labor	60	55	52	48
Availability of technical skills	50	37	46	41
Transportation infrastructure	40	34	37	32
Warehousing availability/costs	40	30	33	28
Proximity to customers	35	22	27	25
Proximity to suppliers	25	25	22	20
Taxation structure	15	12	10	14
Quality of life	10	7	8	9
Climate	5	3	3	4

Based on this factor-rating system and the points assigned by the facility location team, which location appears to be the best choice?

Solution
The difficulty in applying a factor-rating system lies in the design of the system and the evaluation of each potential site on every factor. Once this is accomplished, evaluating the results is a simple matter of adding up the total points for each candidate location. Based on the ratings shown, the point totals are as follows.

Montgomery	225
Atlanta	238
Charleston	221

Based on the results of the rating system, Atlanta would appear to be the best choice.

CONCEPT CONNECTIONS

LO 16–1 Explain what strategic sourcing is

Summary

- Sourcing is a term that captures the strategic nature of purchasing in today's global and Internet-connected marketplace.
- The sourcing/purchasing design matrix captures the scope of the topic that ranges from one-time spot purchases, to a complex strategic alliance arrangement with another firm.
- A phenomenon known as the bullwhip effect has been observed in many industries. This is when changes in demand are magnified as they move from the customer to the manufacturer. The phenomenon is caused by long lead times and the fact that there are often multiple stages in a supply chain.
- Supply chains can be categorized based on demand and supply uncertainty characteristics. Four types of supply chains are identified: (1) efficient, (2) risk-hedging, (3) responsive, and (4) agile.

Key Terms

Strategic sourcing The development and management of supplier relationships to acquire goods and services in a way that aids in achieving the needs of a business.

Concept Connections

The Concept Connections grid appears at the end of every chapter. This tool draws students' attention to the main points, key terms, and formulas for each learning objective. The organization of the Concept Connections gives students a quick and effective reference when applying the chapter content.

Walkthrough

PRACTICE EXAM

In each of the following, name the term defined or answer the question. Answers are listed at the bottom.

1. Term used for a computer system that integrates application programs for the different functions in a firm.
2. Logic used to calculate the needed parts, components, and other materials needed to produce an end item.
3. This drives the MRP calculations and is a detailed plan for how we expect to meet demand.
4. Period of time during which a customer has a specified level of opportunity to make changes.
5. This identifies the specific materials used to make each item and the correct quantities of each.
6. If an item is used in two places in a bill-of-materials, say level 3 and level 4, what low-level code would be assigned to the item?
7. One unit of part C is used in item A and in item B. Currently, we have 10 As, 20 Bs, and 100 Cs in inventory. We want to ship 60 As and 70 Bs. How many additional Cs do we need to purchase?
8. These are orders that have already been released and are to arrive in the future.
9. This is the total amount required for a particular item.
10. This is the amount needed after considering what we currently have in inventory and what we expect to arrive in the future.
11. The planned-order receipt and planned-order release are offset by this amount of time.
12. These are the part quantities issued in the planned-order release section of an MRP report.
13. The term for ordering exactly what is needed each period without regard to economic considerations.
14. None of the techniques for determining order quantity consider this important noneconomic factor that could make the order quantity infeasible.

Answers to Practice Exam 1. Enterprise resource planning (ERP) 2. Material requirements planning (MRP) 3. Master production schedule 4. Time fence 5. Bill-of-materials 6. Level 4 7. Zero 8. Scheduled receipts 9. Gross requirements 10. Net requirements 11. Lead time 12. Lot sizes 13. Lot-for-lot ordering 14. Capacity

Practice Exams

The Practice Exams are designed to allow students to see how well they understand the material using a format that is similar to what they might see in an exam. This feature includes many straightforward review questions, but also has a selection that tests for mastery and integration/application level understanding, i.e., the kind of questions that make an exam challenging. The practice exams include short answers at the bottom so students can see how well they have answered the questions.

Brief Contents

Contents

Section Two

Manufacturing and Service Processes

Section Three
Supply Chain Processes

Section Four
Supply and Demand Planning and Control

Section Five

Special Topics

SECTION **ONE**

Strategy, Products, and Capacity

1. Introduction
2. Strategy
3. Design of Products and Services
4. Project Management
5. Strategic Capacity Management
6. Learning Curves

Twenty-First-Century Operations and Supply Chain Management

Managing a modern supply chain involves specialists in manufacturing, purchasing, and distribution, of course. However, today it is also vital to the work of chief financial officers, chief information officers, operations and customer service executives, and chief executives. Changes in operations and supply management have been truly revolutionary, and the pace of progress shows no sign of slowing.

In the first section of *Operations and Supply Chain Management,* we lay a foundation for understanding the dynamic field of operations and supply management. This book is about designing and operating processes that deliver a firm's goods and services in a manner that matches customers' expectations.

Chapter 1

Introduction

LEARNING OBJECTIVES

LO 1-1 Identify the elements of operations and supply chain management (OSCM)

LO 1-2 Know the potential career opportunities in operations and supply chain management

LO 1-3 Recognize the major concepts that define the operations and supply chain management field

LO 1-4 Evaluate the efficiency of a firm

EFFICIENCY AT SOUTHWEST AIRLINES

Getting passengers on a plane quickly can greatly affect an airline's cost. Southwest, considered the fastest at turning a plane around, does not assign seats. For Southwest, the goal is to have its airplanes in the air as much as possible. This is difficult, given the multiple short flights that a Southwest jet flies each day.

On average, Southwest's 550 jets fly about 3,400 flights a day. Without adjusting for jets that are not flying for maintenance, this averages out to over 6 flights a day per jet. Turning a jet around—from landing to takeoff—is critical to this type of airline, and it has been estimated that Southwest can do this in 30 to 55 minutes, depending on the airport and plane. Think about this: Even at 45 minutes per turn, a Southwest jet still spends about 4.5 hours on the ground each day. Those precious minutes Southwest can save in loading passengers result in more flights for the airline.

Boarding a Southwest Airlines flight: Quick boarding with no preassigned seats is a key part of the 45-minute turnaround process.

© F. Robert Jacobs

LO 1-1

Identify the elements of operations and supply chain management (OSCM)

INTRODUCTION—THE ELEMENTS OF OSCM

Really successful firms have a clear and focused idea of how they intend to make money. Whether it be high-end products and services custom-tailored to the needs of a single customer or generic and inexpensive commodities bought largely on the basis of cost, competitively producing and distributing these products is a major challenge.

The chapter opening describes the importance of turning planes around quickly at Southwest Airlines. Keeping planes in the air each day is a key factor in the profitability of the company. The process Southwest uses when their planes are on the ground was carefully studied by OSCM (operations and supply chain management) specialists to make it as efficient as possible.

In the context of major business functions, operations and supply chain management involves specialists in product design, purchasing, manufacturing, service operations, logistics, and distribution. These specialists are mixed and matched in many different ways depending on the product or service. For a firm that sells televisions, like Sony, these are the functions responsible for designing televisions, acquiring materials, coordinating equipment resources to convert material to products, moving the product, and exchanging the final product with the customer. Some firms are focused on services, such as a hospital. Here the context involves managing resources, including the operating rooms, labs, and hospital beds used to nurse patients back to health. In this context, acquiring materials, moving patients, and coordinating resource use are keys to success. Other firms are more specialized, such as Amazon. Here purchasing, website services, logistics, and distribution need to be carefully coordinated for success. In our increasingly interconnected and interdependent global economy, the process of delivering finished goods, services, and supplies from one place to another is accomplished by means of mind-boggling technological innovation, clever new applications of old ideas, seemingly magical mathematics, powerful software, and old-fashioned concrete, steel, and muscle.

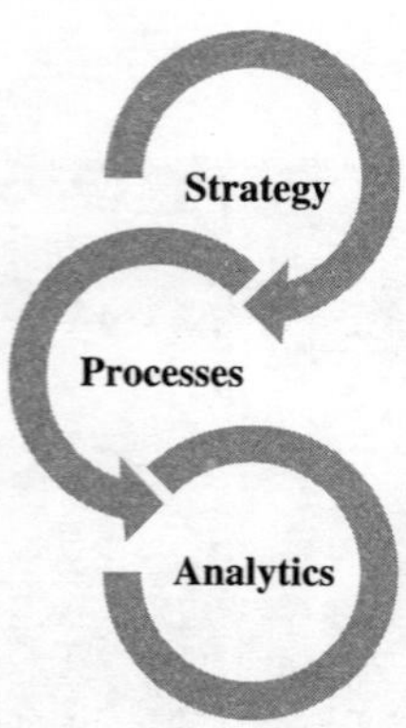

This book is about doing this at low cost while meeting the requirements of demanding customers. Success involves the clever integration of a great operations-related *strategy, processes* that can deliver the products and services, and *analytics* that support the ongoing decisions needed to manage the firm. Our goal in this book is to introduce students to basic operations and supply chain concepts so they understand how things should be done and the importance of these functions to the success of the firm.

No matter what your major is in business, understanding OSCM is critical to your success. If you are interested in the study of finance, you will find that all of the concepts are directly applicable. Just convert all of those widgets to their value in the currency of your choice and you will realize it is all about dollars and cents moving, being stored, and appreciating in value due to exchanges. What you study in finance class is exactly the same, but we look at things in very different ways due to the physical nature of goods and the intangible features of services. The topics presented here are critical to a successful study of marketing, too. If the product or service can't be delivered to the customer at an acceptable cost, then no matter how good your marketing, no one may buy it. Lastly, for those accountants keeping score, operations and supply chain processes generate most of the transactions used to track the financial health of the firm. Understanding why these processes operate the way they do is important to understanding the financial statements of the firm.

What Is Operations and Supply Chain Management?

Operations and supply chain management (OSCM)

The design, operation, and improvement of the systems that create and deliver the firm's primary products and services.

Operations and supply chain management (OSCM) is defined as the design, operation, and improvement of the systems that create and deliver the firm's primary products and services. Like marketing and finance, OSCM is a functional field of business with clear line management responsibilities. OSCM is concerned with the management of the entire system that produces a product or delivers a service. Producing an item such as the Men's Nylon Supplex Parka, or providing a service such as a cell phone account, involves a complex series of transformation processes.

Exhibit 1.1 shows a supply network for a Men's Nylon Supplex Parka sold on websites such as L.L.Bean or Lands' End. We can understand the network by looking at the four color-coded paths. The blue path traces the activities needed to produce the Polartec insulation material used in the parkas. Polartec insulation is purchased in bulk, processed to get the proper finish, and then dyed prior to being

Exhibit 1.1

Process Steps for Men's Nylon Supplex Parkas

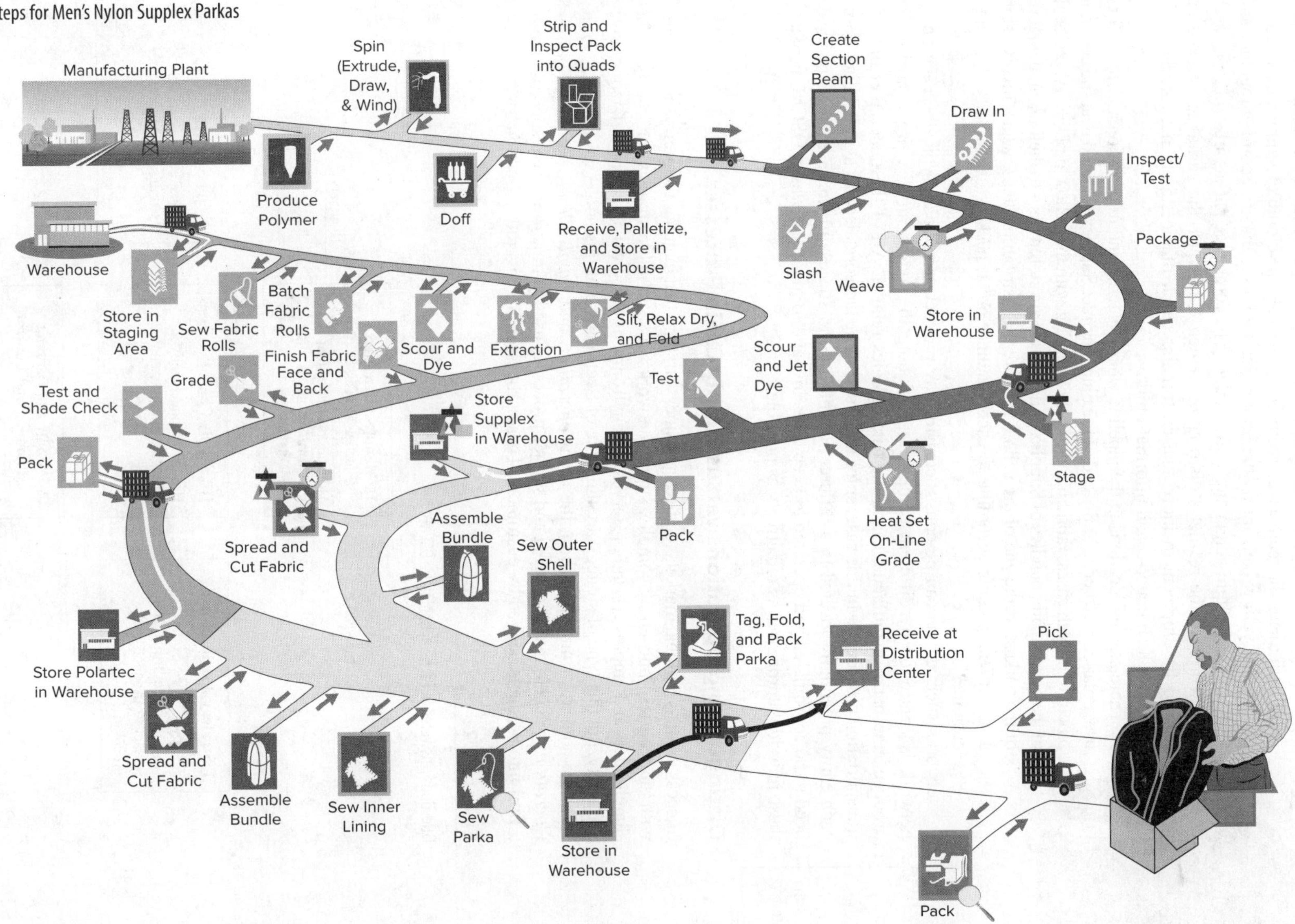

One path traces the production of the nylon, a raw material for the clothlike Supplex material. This is followed by another path, where the nylon is made into Supplex. A separate path includes the steps needed to make Polartec, the insulating material in the parkas. Supplex and Polartec come together and the parkas are assembled. Completed parkas are then distributed to retailers that sell the product.

Courtesy of L.L.Bean, Inc.

checked for consistency—or grading—and color. It is then stored in a warehouse. The red path traces the production of the nylon, Supplex, used in the parkas. Using a petroleum-based polymer, the nylon is extruded and drawn into a yarnlike material. From here, the green path traces the many steps required to fabricate the clothlike Supplex used to make the parkas. The yellow path shows the Supplex and Polartec material coming together and used to assemble the lightweight and warm parkas. The completed parkas are sent to a warehouse, and then on to the retailer's distribution center. Afterward, the parkas are picked out and packed for shipment to individual customers. Think of the supply network as a pipeline through which material and information flow.

There are key locations in the pipeline where material and information are stored for future use: Polartec is stored near the end of the blue pipeline; Supplex is stored near the end of the red pipeline. In both cases, fabric is cut prior to merging with the yellow pipeline. At the beginning of the yellow path, bundles of Supplex and Polartec are stored prior to their use in the fabrication of the parkas. At the end of the yellow path are the distribution steps, which involve storing to await orders, picking according to each customer order, packing, and finally shipping to the customer.

Key Idea

A good starting point for understanding a supply chain is to sketch out the network from start to finish.

Networks such as this can be constructed for any product or service. Typically, each part of the network is controlled by different companies, including the nylon Supplex producer, the Polartec producer, the parka manufacturer, and the catalog sales retailer. All of the material is moved using transportation providers—in this case, ships and trucks. The network also has a global dimension, with each entity potentially located in a different country. For a successful transaction, all of these steps need to be coordinated and operated to keep costs low and to minimize waste. OSCM manages all of these individual processes as effectively as possible.

Distinguishing Operations versus Supply Chain Processes

Success in today's global markets requires a business strategy that matches the preferences of customers with the realities imposed by complex supply networks. A sustainable strategy that meets the needs of shareholders and employees and preserves the environment is critical. Concepts related to developing and analyzing this type of strategy are the topic of Section One of this book (see Exhibit 1.2).

In the context of our discussion, the terms *operations* and *supply chain* take on special meaning. *Operations* refers to manufacturing and service processes used to transform the resources employed by a firm into products desired by customers. These processes are covered in Section Two. For example,

Exhibit 1.2

Questions Answered in Each Section of the OSCM

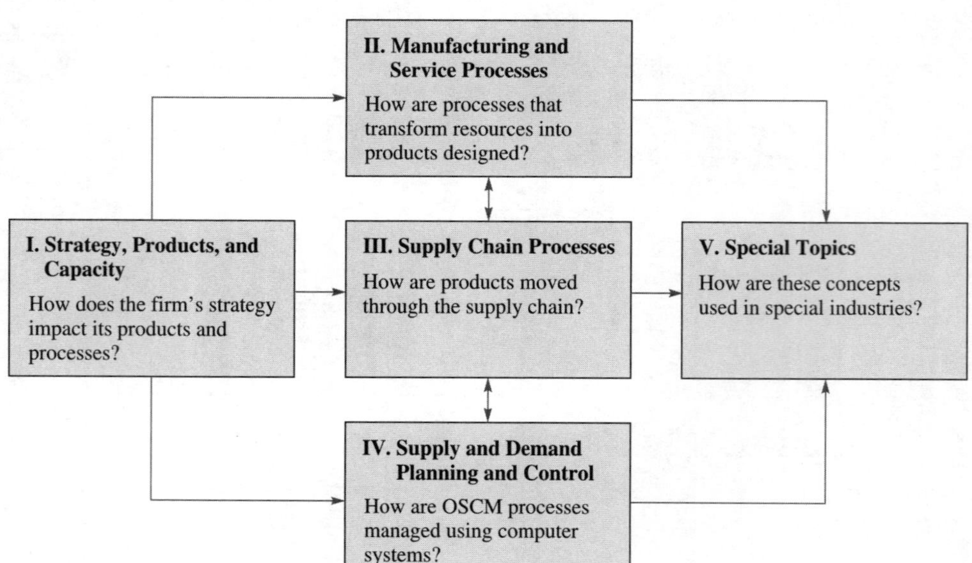

a manufacturing process would produce some type of physical product, such as an automobile or a computer. A service process would produce an intangible product, such as a call center that provides information to customers stranded on the highway or a hospital that treats accident victims in an emergency room. Planning the use of these processes involves analyzing capacity, labor, and material needs over time. Ensuring quality and making ongoing improvements to these processes are needed to manage these processes. Concepts related to this are included in Section Two of this book as well.

Supply chain refers to processes that move information and material to and from the manufacturing and service process of the firm. These include the logistics processes that physically move product and the warehousing and storage processes that position products for quick delivery to the customer. Supply chain in this context refers to providing products and service to plants and warehouses at the input end and also the supply of products and service to the customer on the output end of the supply chain. Details concerning how these supply chain processes work and are analyzed are covered in Section Three.

Section Four of the book is about planning the use of operations and supply chain resources. Starting with a forecast of demand, resources are planned in increasingly shorter increments of time to match supply inputs with the demand-driven outputs of the firm. These planning activities are completed using integrated computer systems that capture the activities and current status of a firm's resources.

The final section of the book shows how these concepts are applied in more specialized types of businesses such as health care and consulting. Part of understanding this material is seeing how the concepts can be directly applied to business processes that are not specifically covered. In this book, in a relatively generic way, manufacturing, service, sourcing, and logistics processes are studied. How these ideas are applied in the context of a few specific businesses is the motivation of this section.

All managers should understand the basic principles that guide the design of transformation processes. This includes understanding how different types of processes are organized, how to determine the capacity of a process, how long it should take a process to make a unit, how the quality of a process is monitored, and how information is used to make decisions related to the design and operation of these processes.

The field of operations and supply chain management is ever changing due to the dynamic nature of competing in global business and the constant evolution of information technology. So while many of the basic concepts have been around for years, their application in new and innovative ways is exciting. Internet technology has made the sharing of reliable real-time information inexpensive. Capturing information directly from the source through such systems as point-of-sale, radio-frequency identification tags, bar-code scanners, and automatic recognition has shifted the focus to understanding both what all the information is saying and also how good the decisions that can be made using it are.

Categorizing Operations and Supply Chain Processes

Operations and supply chain **processes** can be conveniently categorized, particularly from the view of a producer of consumer products and services, as planning, sourcing, making, delivering, and returning. Exhibit 1.3 depicts where the processes are used in different parts of a supply chain. The following describes the work involved in each type of process.

Process
One or more activities that transform inputs into outputs.

1. **Planning** consists of the processes needed to operate an existing supply chain strategically. Here a firm must determine how anticipated demand will be met with available resources. A major aspect of planning is developing a set of metrics to monitor the supply chain so that it is efficient and delivers high quality and value to customers.
2. **Sourcing** involves the selection of suppliers that will deliver the goods and services needed to create the firm's product. A set of pricing, delivery, and payment processes are needed, along with metrics for monitoring and improving the relationships between partners of the firm. These processes include receiving shipment, verifying them, transferring them to manufacturing facilities, and authorizing supplier payments.
3. **Making** is where the major product is produced or the service provided. The step requires scheduling processes for workers and the coordination of material and other critical resources

Exhibit 1.3

Supply Chain Process

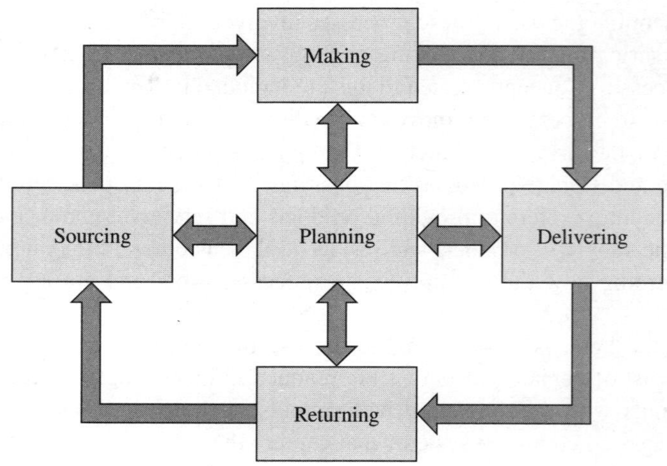

such as equipment to support producing or providing the service. Metrics that measure speed, quality, and worker productivity are used to monitor these processes.

4. **Delivering** is also referred to as logistics processes. Carriers are picked to move products to warehouses and customers, coordinate and schedule the movement of goods and information through the supply network, develop and operate a network of warehouses, and run the information systems that manage the receipt of orders from customers and the invoicing systems that collect payments from customers.
5. **Returning** involves processes for receiving worn-out, defective, and excess products back from customers and support for customers who have problems with delivered products. In the case of services, this may involve all types of follow-up activities required for after-sales support.

Key Idea

Companies are positioned in different places in the supply chain. Within the context of their position, they all require planning, sourcing, making, delivering, and returning processes.

To understand the topic, it is important to consider the many different players that need to coordinate work in a typical supply chain. The aforementioned steps of planning, sourcing, making, delivering, and returning are fine for manufacturing and can also be used for the many processes that do not involve the discrete movement and production of parts. In the case of a service firm such as a hospital, for example, supplies are typically delivered on a daily basis from drug and health care suppliers and require coordination between drug companies, local warehouse operations, local delivery services, and hospital receiving. Patients need to be scheduled into the services provided by the hospital, such as operations and blood tests. Other areas, such as the emergency room, need to be staffed to provide service on demand. The orchestration of all of these activities is critical to providing quality service at a reasonable cost.

Differences Between Services and Goods

Key Idea

The things produced by a service are intangible. Service processes tend to be highly variable and time dependent compared to goods-producing processes.

There are five essential differences between services and goods. The first is that a service is an *intangible* process that cannot be weighed or measured, whereas a good is a tangible output of a process that has physical dimensions. This distinction has important business implications, because a service innovation, unlike a product innovation, cannot be patented. Thus, a company with a new concept must expand rapidly before competitors copy its procedures. Service intangibility also presents a problem for customers because, unlike with a physical product, customers cannot try it out and test it before purchase.

The second is that a service requires some degree of *interaction with the customer* for it to be a service. The interaction may be brief, but it must exist for the service to be complete. Where face-to-face service is required, the service facility must be designed to handle the customer's presence. Goods, on the other hand, are generally produced in a facility separate from the customer. They can be made according to a production schedule that is efficient for the company.

The third difference is that services, with the big exception of hard technologies (such as ATMs) and information technologies (such as answering machines and automated Internet exchanges) are inherently *heterogeneous*—they vary from day to day and even hour to hour as a function of the attitudes of the customers and the servers. Thus, even highly scripted work, such as found in call centers, can produce unpredictable outcomes. Goods, in contrast, can be produced to meet very tight specifications day-in and day-out with essentially zero variability. In those cases where a defective good is produced, it can be reworked or scrapped.

The fourth difference is that services as a process are *perishable and time dependent,* and unlike goods, they can't be stored. You cannot "come back last week" for an air flight or a day on campus.

And fifth, the specifications of a service are defined and evaluated as a *package of features* that affect the five senses. These four features are:

- Supporting facility (location, decoration, layout, architectural appropriateness, supporting equipment)
- Facilitating goods (variety, consistency, quantity of the physical goods that go with the service; for example, the food items that accompany a meal service)
- Explicit services (training of service personnel, consistency of service performance, availability and access to the service, and comprehensiveness of the service)
- Implicit services (attitude of the servers, atmosphere, waiting time, status, privacy and security, and convenience)

The Goods–Services Continuum

Almost any product offering is a combination of goods and services. In Exhibit 1.4, we show this arrayed along a continuum of "pure goods" to "pure services." The continuum captures the main focus of the business and spans from firms that just produce products to those that only provide services. Pure goods industries have become low-margin commodity businesses, and in order to differentiate, they are often adding some services. Some examples are providing help with logistical aspects of stocking items, maintaining extensive information databases, and providing consulting advice.

EXHIBIT 1.4

The Goods–Services Continuum

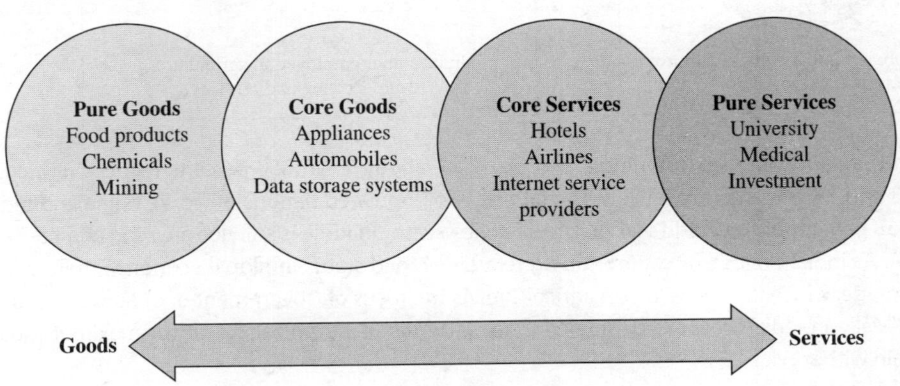

Core goods providers already provide a significant service component as part of their businesses. For example, automobile manufacturers provide extensive spare parts distribution services to support repair centers at dealers.

Core service providers must integrate tangible goods. For example, your cable television company must provide cable hookup and repair services and also high-definition cable boxes. Pure services, such as those offered by a financial consulting firm, may need little in the way of facilitating goods, but what they do use—such as textbooks, professional references, and spreadsheets—are critical to their performance.

Product–Service Bundling

Product–service bundling
When a firm builds service activities into its product offerings to create additional value for the customer.

Product–service bundling refers to a company building service activities into its product offerings for its customers. Such services include maintenance, spare part provisioning, training, and, in some cases, total systems design and R&D. A well-known pioneer in this area is IBM, which treats its business as a service business and views physical goods as a small part of the "business solutions" it provides its customers. Companies that are most successful in implementing this strategy start by drawing together the service aspects of the business under one roof in order to create a consolidated service organization. The service evolves from a focus on enhancing the product's performance to developing systems and product modifications that support the company's move up the "value stream" into new markets. This type of strategy might not be the best approach for all product companies, however. A recent study found that while firms that offer product–service bundles generate higher revenues, they tend to generate lower profits as a percent of revenues when compared to focused firms. This is because they are often unable to generate revenues or margins high enough to cover the additional investment needed for service-related costs.

Growth of Services*

During the past two centuries, the United States of America has witnessed a significant improvement in the productivity of its agriculture sector. Despite this, the percentage of labor force depending on this sector, which was 90 percent in 1800, has now come down to about 3 percent. Major shift has taken place to services, which now absorbs about 70 percent of the labor force.

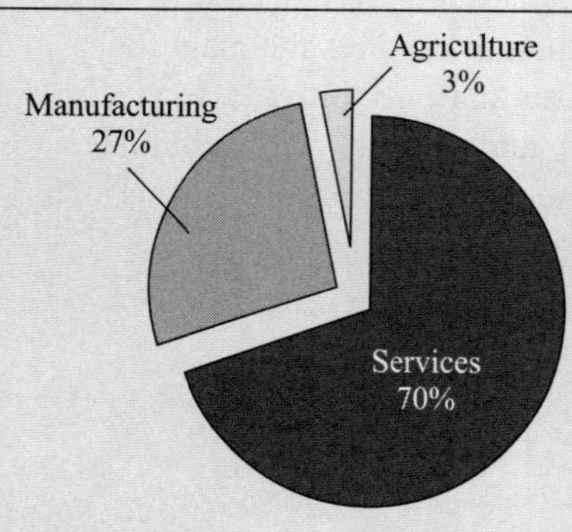

United States–Labor employed in agriculture, manufacturing and services

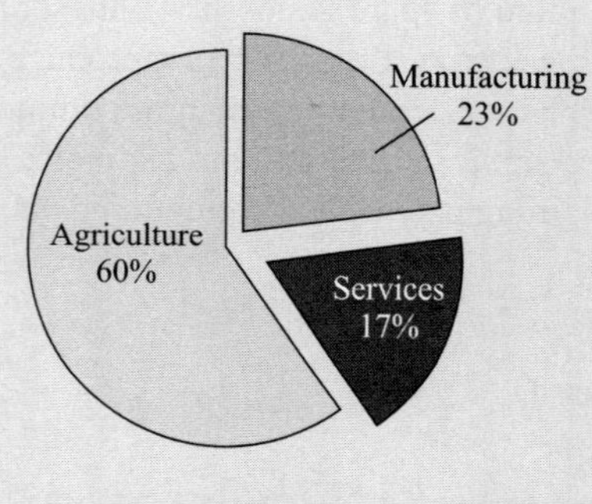

India-Labor employed in agriculture, manufacturing and services

The labor force percentages in the agriculture sector of India and China are about 60 and 50 percent, respectively, and in the services sector, these are about 23 and 35 percent, respectively. The largest two populated nations of world, China and India, have to provide employment to about 38 percent of the world's labor force. Service sector in India is still not growing at a pace that can bring it anywhere near to the USA. As India moves from a developing to a developed status in global economy, there would be a likely reduction in the labor percentage, which is depending on agriculture. As the focus of Government of India is shifting towards manufacturing with initiatives like 'Make-in-India', there can be small shift towards manufacturing also. Still, the maximum absorption capacity of labor force would remain with services.

Another noteworthy difference between India and other countries would be in the absolute number of labor force. As India's population growth is among the fastest in the world, India would need more opportunities in the service sector due to the fact that agricultural land is non-expandable and therefore, cannot absorb more people.

*Richard B. Chase, Ravi Shankar, F. Robert Jacobs and Nichilas J Acquilano, 2012, Operations & Supply Management, 12th Edition, Tata McGraw Hill Education Pvt. Ltd. New Delhi

CAREERS IN OSCM

LO 1-2

Know the potential career opportunities in operations and supply chain management

So what do people who pursue careers in OSCM do? Quite simply, they specialize in managing the planning, production, and distribution of goods and services. Jobs abound for people who can do this well since every organization is dependent on effective performance of this fundamental activity for its long-term success.

It is interesting to contrast entry-level jobs in OSCM to marketing and finance jobs. Many marketing entry-level jobs focus on actually selling products or managing the sales of products. These individuals are out on the front line trying to push product to potential customers. Often, a significant part of their income will depend on commissions from these sales. Entry-level finance (and accounting) jobs are frequently in large public accounting firms. These jobs involve working at a desk auditing transactions to ensure the accuracy of financial statements. Other assignments involve the analysis of transactions to better understand the costs associated with the business.

Contrast the marketing and finance jobs to OSCM jobs. The operations and supply chain manager is out working with people to figure out the best way to deliver the goods and services of the firm. Sure, they work with the marketing folks, but rather than being on the selling side, they are on the buying side: trying to select the best materials and hiring the greatest talent. They will use the data generated by the finance people and analyze processes to figure out how to deliver that good or service. OSCM jobs are hands-on, working with people and figuring out the best way to do things.

Key Idea

OSCM jobs focus on delivering the goods on-time and at low cost. They are interesting, people-oriented jobs.

The following are some typical jobs in OSCM:

- Plant manager—Oversees the workforce and physical resources (inventory, equipment, and information technology) required to produce the organization's product.
- Hospital administrator—Oversees human resource management, staffing, supplies, and finances at a health care facility.
- Branch manager (bank)—Oversees all aspects of financial transactions at a branch.
- Department store manager—Oversees all aspects of staffing and customer service at a store.
- Call center manager—Oversees staffing and customer service activities at a call center.
- Supply chain manager—Negotiates contracts with vendors and coordinates the flow of material inputs to the production process and the shipping of finished products to customers.
- Purchasing manager—Manages the day-to-day aspects of purchasing, such as invoicing and follow-up.
- Logistics manager—Oversees the movement of goods throughout the supply chain.
- Warehouse/distribution manager—Oversees all aspects of running a warehouse, including replenishment, customer order fulfillment, and staffing.
- Business process improvement analyst—Applies the tools of lean production to reduce cycle time and eliminate waste in a process.
- Quality control manager—Applies techniques of statistical quality control, such as acceptance sampling and control charts, to the firm's products.
- Lean improvement manager—Trains organizational members in lean production and continuous improvement methods.
- Project manager—Plans and coordinates staff activities, such as new-product development, new-technology deployment, and new-facility location.
- Production control analyst—Plans and schedules day-to-day production.
- Facilities manager—Ensures that the building facility design, layout, furniture, and other equipment are operating at peak efficiency.

Chief Operating Officer

So how far can you go in a career in OSCM? One goal would be to become the chief operating officer of a company. The chief operating officer (COO) works with the CEO and company president to determine the company's competitive strategy. The COO's ideas are filtered down through the rest

OSCM AT WORK

Operations and Supply Chain Management Professional Societies

If you are interested in career opportunities in operations and supply chain management, you can learn more about the field through the following professional societies. These groups provide industry-recognized certification programs and ongoing training for those seeking to work in the field.

APICS, the Association for Operations Management, www.apics.org.

Council of Supply Chain Management Professionals (CSCMP), www.cscmp.org.

Institute for Supply Management (ISM), www.ism.ws.

The Project Management Institute (PMI), www.pmi.org.

of the company. COOs determine an organization's location, its facilities, which vendors to use, and the implementation of the hiring policy. Once the key decisions are made, lower-level operations personnel carry them out. Operations personnel work to find solutions and then set about fixing the problems. Managing the supply chain, service, and support are particularly challenging aspects of a chief operating officer's job.

Career opportunities in OSCM are plentiful today as companies strive to improve profitability by improving quality and productivity and reducing costs. The hands-on work of managing people is combined with great opportunities to leverage the latest technologies in getting the job done at companies around the world. No matter what you might do for a final career, your knowledge of OSCM will prove to be a great asset.

LO 1-3

Recognize the major concepts that define the operations and supply chain management field

THE MAJOR CONCEPTS THAT DEFINE THE OSCM FIELD

Our purpose in this section is not to go through all the details of the history of OSCM; that would require us to recount the entire Industrial Revolution. Rather, the focus is on the major operations-related concepts that have been popular since the 1980s. Exhibit 1.5 will help clarify the dates as you read about the concepts. Where appropriate, how a supposedly new idea relates to an older idea is discussed. (We seem to keep rediscovering the past.)

Manufacturing strategy
Emphasizes how a factory's capabilities could be used strategically to gain advantage over a competing company.

Strategy

Manufacturing Strategy Paradigm The late 1970s and early 1980s saw the development of the **manufacturing strategy** paradigm, which emphasized how manufacturing executives could use their factories' capabilities as strategic competitive weapons. Central to this thinking was the notion of manufacturing trade-offs among such performance measures as low cost, high quality, and high flexibility.

Source: Library of Congress/ [LC-DIG-det-4a27966]

Just-in-time (JIT)
An integrated set of activities designed to achieve high-volume production using minimal inventories of parts that arrive exactly when they are needed.

Process

Lean Manufacturing, JIT, and TQC The 1980s saw a revolution in the management philosophies and technologies by which production is carried out. **Just-in-time (JIT)** production was the major breakthrough in manufacturing philosophy. Pioneered by the Japanese, JIT is an integrated set of activities designed to achieve high-volume production using minimal inventories of parts that arrive exactly when they are

EXHIBIT 1.5

Time Line Depicting When Major OSCM Concepts Became Popular

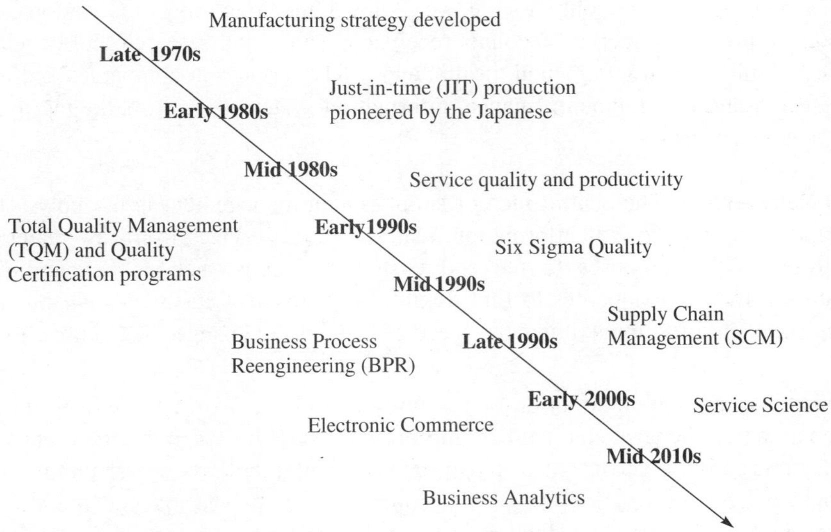

Source: F. Robert Jacobs

needed. The philosophy—coupled with **total quality control (TQC)**, which aggressively seeks to eliminate causes of production defects—is now a cornerstone in many manufacturers' production practices, and the term **lean manufacturing** is used to refer to the set of concepts.

Total quality control (TQC)
Aggressively seeks to eliminate causes of production defects.

Of course, the Japanese were not the first to create a highly integrated, efficient production system. In 1913, Henry Ford developed an assembly line to make the Model-T automobile. Ford developed a system for making the Model-T that was constrained only by the capabilities of the workforce and existing technology. Quality was a critical prerequisite for Ford: The line could not run steadily at speed without consistently good components. On-time delivery was also critical for Ford; the desire to keep workers and machines busy with materials flowing constantly made scheduling critical. Product, processes, materials, logistics, and people were well integrated and balanced in the design and operation of the plant.

Lean manufacturing
To achieve high customer service with minimum levels of inventory investment.

Service Quality and Productivity The unique approach to quality and productivity pioneered by McDonald's has been so successful that it stands as a reference point in thinking about how to deliver high-volume standardized services.

Total Quality Management and Quality Certification Another major development was the focus on **total quality management (TQM)** in the late 1980s and 1990s. Helping the quality movement along was the Baldrige National Quality Award, started in 1987 under the direction of the National Institute of Standards and Technology. The Baldrige Award recognizes companies each year for outstanding quality management systems.

Process

Total quality management (TQM)
Managing the entire organization so it excels in all dimensions of products and services important to the customer.

The ISO 9000 certification standards, created by the International Organization for Standardization, now play a major role in setting quality standards for global manufacturers. Many companies require that their vendors meet these standards as a condition for obtaining contracts.

Business Process Reengineering The need to become lean to remain competitive in the global economic recession in the 1990s pushed companies to seek innovations in the processes by which they run their operations. The **business process reengineering (BPR)** approach seeks to make revolutionary changes as opposed to evolutionary changes (which are commonly advocated in TQM). It does this by taking a fresh look at what the organization is trying to do in all its business processes, and then eliminating non-value-added steps and computerizing the remaining ones to achieve the desired outcome.

Business process reengineering (BPR)
An approach to improving business processes that seeks to make revolutionary changes as opposed to evolutionary (small) changes.

Process

Six Sigma
A statistical term to describe the quality goal of no more than 3.4 defects out of every million units. Also refers to a quality improvement philosophy and program.

Mass customization
The ability to produce a unique product exactly to a particular customer's requirements.

Electronic commerce
The use of the Internet as an essential element of business activity.

Sustainability
The ability to meet current resource needs without compromising the ability of future generations to meet their needs.

Triple bottom line
A business strategy that includes social, economic, and environmental criteria.

Business analytics
The use of current business data to solve business problems using mathematical analysis.

Six Sigma Quality Originally developed in the 1980s as part of total quality management, **Six Sigma** in the 1990s saw a dramatic expansion as an extensive set of diagnostic tools was developed. These tools have been taught to managers as part of "Green and Black Belt Programs" at many corporations. The tools are now applied not only to the well-known manufacturing applications, but also to nonmanufacturing processes such as accounts receivable, sales, and research and development. Six Sigma has been applied to environmental, health, and safety services at companies and is now being utilized in research and development, finance, information systems, legal, marketing, public affairs, and human resource processes.

Supply Chain Management The central idea of supply chain management is to apply a total system approach to managing the flow of information, materials, and services from raw material suppliers through factories and warehouses to the end customer. Trends such as outsourcing and **mass customization** are forcing companies to find flexible ways to meet customer demand. The focus is on optimizing core activities to maximize the speed of response to changes in customer expectations.

Electronic Commerce The quick adoption of the Internet and the World Wide Web during the late 1990s was remarkable. The term **electronic commerce** refers to the use of the Internet as an essential element of business activity. The use of Web pages, forms, and interactive search engines has changed the way people collect information, shop, and communicate. It has changed the way operations managers coordinate and execute production and distribution functions.

Sustainability and the Triple Bottom Line **Sustainability** is the ability to maintain balance in a system. Management must now consider the mandates related to the ongoing economic, employee, and environmental viability of the firm (the **triple bottom line**). Economically, the firm must be profitable. Employee job security, positive working conditions, and development opportunities are essential. The need for nonpolluting and non-resource-depleting products and processes presents new challenges to operations and supply managers.

Business Analytics **Business analytics** involves the analysis of data to better solve business problems. Not that this is something new: Data has always been used to solve business problems. What is new is the reality that so much more data is now captured and available for decision-making analysis than was available in the past. In addition, mathematical tools are now readily available that can be used to support the decision-making process.

In the past, most analysis involved the generation of standard and ad hoc reports that summarized the current state of the firm. Software allowed querying and "drill down" analysis to the level of the individual transaction, useful features for understanding what happened in the past. Decision making was typically left to the decision maker based on judgment or simple alerting rules. The new "analytics" movement takes this to a new level using statistical analysis, forecasting to extrapolate what to expect in the future, and even optimization, possibly in real time, to support decisions. These mathematical results can be used either to support the decision maker or to automate decision making.

Take, for example, an airline manager presented with the task of setting price points for tickets on a flight. Real-time demand data, historic demand patterns, and powerful mathematical models can now be applied to setting price points for different classes of tickets. As it is closer to the time of departure for a particular flight, these price points can be adjusted based on how sales are going. These decisions have a major impact on the utilization of aircraft capacity, which impacts both revenue and costs for the airlines. These decisions can even be made using criteria related to weather conditions, fuel prices, crew schedules, and other flights to maximize the profit of the firm.

Current Issues in Operations and Supply Chain Management

OSCM is a dynamic field, and issues arising in global enterprise present exciting new challenges for operations managers. Looking forward to the future, we believe the major challenges in the field will be as follows:

1. **Coordinating the relationships between mutually supportive but separate organizations.** Recently, there has been a dramatic surge in the outsourcing of parts and services as companies seek to minimize costs. Many companies now even outsource major corporate functions, such as information systems, product development and design, engineering services, and distribution. The ability to coordinate these activities is a significant challenge for today's operations and supply chain manager.

Strategy

2. **Optimizing global supplier, production, and distribution networks.** The implementation of global enterprise resource planning systems, now common in large companies, has challenged managers to use all of this information. Operations and supply chain *analytics* involves leveraging this information for making decisions related to resources such as inventory, transportation, and production.

Process

3. **Managing customer touch points.** As companies strive to cut costs, they often scrimp on the customer support personnel (and training) required to effectively staff service departments, help lines, and checkout counters. This leads to the frustrations we have all experienced, such as being placed in call center limbo seemingly for hours, getting bad advice when finally interacting with a company rep, and so on. The issue here is to recognize that making resource utilization decisions must capture the implicit costs of lost customers as well as the direct costs of staffing.
4. **Raising senior management awareness of OSCM as a significant competitive weapon.** Many senior executives entered the organization through finance, strategy, or marketing, built their reputations on work in these areas, and as a result often take OSCM for granted. As we will demonstrate in this book, this can be a critical mistake when we realize how profitable companies such as Amazon, Apple, Taco Bell, and Southwest Airlines are. These are companies where executives have creatively used OSCM for competitive advantage.

EFFICIENCY, EFFECTIVENESS, AND VALUE

LO 1-4

Evaluate the efficiency of a firm

Compared with most of the other ways managers try to stimulate growth—technology investments, acquisitions, and major market campaigns, for example—innovations in operations are relatively reliable and low cost. As a business student, you are perfectly positioned to come up with innovative operations-related ideas. You understand the big picture of all the processes that generate the costs and support the cash flow essential to the firm's long-term viability.

Through this book, you will become aware of the concepts and tools now being employed by companies around the world as they craft efficient and effective operations. **Efficiency** means doing something at the lowest possible cost. Later in the book, we define this more thoroughly, but roughly speaking, the goal of an efficient process is to produce a good or provide a service by using the smallest input of resources. In general, these resources are the material, labor, equipment, and facilities used in the OSCM processes.

Efficiency

A ratio of the actual output of a process relative to some standard. Also, being "efficient" means doing something at the lowest possible cost.

Effectiveness means doing the right things to create the most value for the company. For example, to be effective at a grocery store it is important to have plenty of operating check-out lines even though they may often stand idle. This is a recognition that the customer's time is valuable and that they do not like waiting to be served in the check-out line. Often, maximizing effectiveness and efficiency at the same time creates conflict between the two goals. We see this trade-off every day in our lives. At

Effectiveness

Doing the things that will create the most value for the customer.

the check-out lines, being efficient means using the fewest people possible to ring up customers. Being effective, though, means minimizing the amount of time customers need to wait in line.

Value
The attractiveness of a product relative to its price.

Related to efficiency and effectiveness is the concept of **value**, which can be abstractly defined as quality divided by price. Here, quality is the attractiveness of the product, considering its features and durability. If you can provide the customer with a better car without changing price, value has gone up. If you can give the customer a better car at a *lower* price, value goes way up. A major objective of this book is to show how smart management can achieve high levels of value.

How Does Wall Street Evaluate Efficiency?

Comparing firms from an operations and supply chain view is important to investors because the relative cost of providing a good or service is essential to high earnings growth. When you think about it, earnings growth is largely a function of the firm's profitability, and profit can be increased through higher sales and/or reduced cost. Highly efficient firms usually shine when demand drops during recession periods because they often can continue to make a profit due to their low-cost structure. These operations-savvy firms may even see a recession as an opportunity to gain market share as their less-efficient competitors struggle to remain in business.

An interesting relationship between the costs related to OSCM functions and profit is the direct impact of a reduction of cost in one of these functions on the profit margin of the firm. In Exhibit 1.6, we show data from a company's balance sheet. The balance sheet on the left shows the return on investment (ROI) for the company prior to a reduction in raw material cost. The balance sheet on the right shows the same data, but with a reduction of 5 percent in the cost of raw materials. The cost of raw materials affects the values throughout the supply chain, including the cost of goods sold, inventory value, and total value of assets; therefore, reducing raw material costs by 5 percent leads to nearly a 29 percent increase in profit margins and a 30 percent increase in the company's ROI. Thus, there is an almost 6:1 leverage on every rupee saved by reducing raw materials costs.

EXHIBIT 1.6

The Impact of Reducing Raw Material Cost

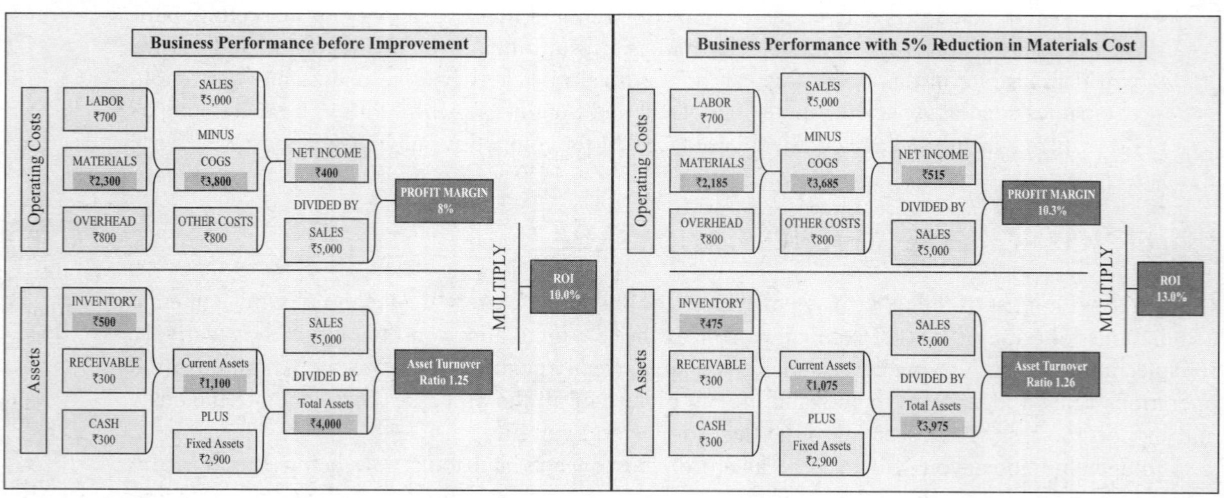

Benchmarking
When one company studies the processes of another company to identify best practices.

A common set of financial indicators that Wall Street tracks to benchmark companies are called management efficiency ratios. **Benchmarking** is a process in which one company studies the processes of another company (or industry) to identify best practices. You probably discussed these measures in one of your accounting classes. It is not our purpose to do an in-depth review of this material, but it is important to recognize the significant impact the operations and supply chain processes have on these ratios. A comparison of a few automobile companies using the ratios is shown in Exhibit 1.7.

The following is a brief review of these ratios. Starting from basic financial data for the firm, the simplest efficiency-related measures relate to the productivity of labor employed by the firm. There are two of these ratios:

EXHIBIT 1.7

A Comparison of Automobile Companies

Efficiency Measure	Toyota (TM)	General Motors (GM)	Ford (F)	Industry
Income per employee	$60,266	$50,255	$17,037	$39,170
Revenue (or sales) per employee	$738,754	$1,949,113	$770,465	$799,932
Receivables turnover	3.3	6.4	1.6	3.2
Inventory turnover	10.5	9.7	15.3	9.5
Asset turnover	0.6	0.9	0.7	0.7

- Net income per employee
- Revenue (or sales) per employee

These labor productivity measures are fairly crude since many employees are not directly employed in operations and supply chain–related functions. Also, it is important to recognize that the concepts described in this book are certainly applicable to the other functions in the firm.

A third efficiency ratio measures the number of times receivables are collected, on average, during the fiscal year. This ratio is called the receivables turnover ratio, and it is calculated as follows:

$$\textit{Receivable Turnover} = \frac{\textit{Annual Credit Sales}}{\textit{Average Account Receivable}} \quad [1.1]$$

The receivables turnover ratio measures a company's efficiency in collecting its sales on credit. Accounts receivable represent the indirect interest-free loans that the company is providing to its clients. A higher receivables ratio implies either that the company operates on a cash basis or that its extension of credit and collection methods are efficient. Also, a high ratio reflects a short lapse of time between sales and the collection of cash, while a low number means collection takes longer. The lower the ratio, the longer receivables are being held and the higher the risk of them not being collected.

A ratio that is low by industry standards will generally indicate that the business needs to improve its credit policies and collection procedures. If the ratio is going up, either collection efforts are improving, sales are rising, or receivables are being reduced. From an operations and supply chain perspective, the firm may be able to impact this ratio by such things as the speed of delivery of products, accuracy in filling orders, and amount of inspection the customer needs to do. Factors such as the outgoing quality of the product and how customer orders are taken, together with other order-processing activities, may have a huge impact on the receivables turnover ratio. This is particularly true when Internet catalogs are the main interface between the customer and the firm.

Another efficiency ratio is inventory turnover. It measures the average number of times inventory is sold and replaced during the fiscal year. The inventory turnover ratio formula is:

$$\textit{Inventory Turnover} = \frac{\textit{Cost of Goods Sold}}{\textit{Average Inventory Value}} \quad [1.2]$$

This ratio measures the company's efficiency in turning its inventory into sales. Its purpose is to measure the liquidity or speed of inventory usage. This ratio is generally compared against industry averages. A low inventory turnover ratio is a signal of inefficiency, because inventory ties up capital that could be used for other purposes. It might imply either poor sales or excess inventory relative to sales. A low turnover ratio can indicate poor liquidity, possible overstocking, and obsolescence, but it may also reflect a planned inventory buildup in the case of material shortages or in anticipation of rapidly rising prices. A high inventory turnover ratio implies either strong sales or ineffective buying (the firm may be buying too often and in small quantities, driving up the buying price). A high inventory turnover ratio can indicate better liquidity, but it can also indicate shortages or inadequate inventory levels, which may lead to a loss in business. Generally, a high inventory turnover ratio when compared to competitors' is good. This ratio is controlled to a great extent by operations and supply chain processes. Factors such as order lead times, purchasing practices, the number of items being stocked, and production and order quantities have a direct impact on the ratio.

The final efficiency ratio considered here is asset turnover. This is the amount of sales generated for every dollar's worth of assets. The formula for the ratio is:

$$Asset\ Turnover = \frac{Revenue\ (or\ Sales)}{Total\ Assets} \qquad [1.3]$$

Asset turnover measures a firm's efficiency at using its assets in generating sales revenue—the higher the number, the better. It also indicates pricing strategy: Companies with low profit margins tend to have high asset turnover, while those with high profit margins have low asset turnover. This ratio varies significantly by industry, so comparisons between unrelated businesses are not useful. To a great extent, the asset turnover ratio is similar to the receivables turnover and the inventory turnover ratio since all three involve the investment in assets. Asset turnover is more general and includes the plants, warehouses, equipment, and other assets owned by the firm. Since many of these facilities are needed to support the operations and supply chain activities, the ratio can be significantly impacted by investments in technology and outsourcing, for example.

These ratios can be calculated from data in a firm's annual financial statements and are readily available on the Internet from websites such as AOL Finance (http://www.aol.com/stock-quotes/).

EXAMPLE 1.1 **Comparing the Management Efficiency of Companies in the Same Industry Using Wall Street Measures**

Building on the data in Exhibit 1.7, compare the Japanese automobile manufacturer Honda to Toyota, General Motors, and Ford. Specifically address the following questions:

1. How does Honda (stock symbol HMC) differ relative to income per employee, revenue per employee, receivables turnover, inventory turnover, and asset turnover?
2. Speculate on why Honda's Wall Street efficiency measures are different from the other automobile companies'. Be sure to consider the fact that Honda is a smaller company compared to the others.

SOLUTION

The first step is to get comparable data on Honda. One Website that has these data is, again, www.aol.com/stock-quotes/. Hyperlink to this site using your browser and then enter HMC in the "Get Quote" block. Then, from the menu find Key Ratios, select Efficiency Ratios. Check to see that you have the correct data.

Example data for Honda on the date this chapter was written were as follows:

Income per employee	30,203
Revenue per employee	585,647
Receivables turnover	4.9
Inventory turnover	6.3
Asset turnover	0.8

Next, we need to try to understand the data. It is probably good to start with asset turnover, because this is the most comprehensive measure. Notice that GM is the highest in the group. Recall that GM recently went bankrupt and was recapitalized, which could explain the higher asset turnover. Honda, though, is fine compared to the industry average on this measure.

On net income per employee, revenue per employee and inventory turn, we see that Honda appears, for the most part, to be stronger than Ford, but weaker than Toyota and General Motors. Ford is strongest in inventory turn. This is surprising because we might expect Toyota to be strong here, given its reputation in managing inventory. It is interesting to see how Ford is weakest in receivables turnover, which may relate to the amount of credit it is giving customers in order to sell vehicles.

CONCEPT CONNECTIONS

LO 1–1 Identify the elements of operations and supply chain management (OSCM)

Summary

- Processes are used to implement the strategy of the firm.
- Analytics are used to support the ongoing decisions needed to manage the firm.

Key Terms

Operations and supply chain management (OSCM) The design, operation, and improvement of the systems that create and deliver the firm's primary products and services.

Process One or more activities that transform inputs into outputs.

Product -service bundling When a firm builds service activities into its product offerings to create additional value for the customer.

LO 1–2 Know the potential career opportunities in operations and supply chain management

Summary

- OSCM people specialize in managing the production of goods and services.
- OSCM jobs are hands-on and require working with others and figuring out the best way to do things.
- The chief operating officer (COO) works with the CEO and company president to determine the company's competitive strategy.
- COOs determine an organization's location, its facilities, which vendors to use, and how the hiring policy will be implemented.

LO 1–3 Recognize the major concepts that define the operations and supply chain management field

Summary

Many of the concepts that form the OSCM field have their origins in the Industrial Revolution in the 1800s. The focus of this book is on popular concepts developed since the 1980s.
These concepts include:

Key Terms

Manufacturing strategy Emphasizes how a factory's capabilities could be used strategically to gain advantage over a competing company.

Just-in-time (JIT) An integrated set of activities designed to achieve high-volume production using minimal inventories of parts that arrive exactly when they are needed.

Total quality control (TQC) Aggressively seeks to eliminate causes of production defects.

Lean manufacturing To achieve high customer service with minimum levels of inventory investment.

Total quality management (TQM) Managing the entire organization so it excels in all dimensions of products and services important to the customer.

Business process reengineering (BPR) An approach to improving business processes that seeks to make revolutionary changes as opposed to evolutionary (small) changes.

Six Sigma A statistical term to describe the quality goal of no more than 3.4 defects out of every million units. Also refers to a quality improvement philosophy and program.

Mass customization The ability to produce a unique product exactly to a particular customer's requirements.

Electronic commerce The use of the Internet as an essential element of business activity.

Sustainability The ability to meet current resource needs without compromising the ability of future generations to meet their needs.

Triple bottom line A business strategy that includes social, economic, and environmental criteria.

Business analytics The use of current business data to solve business problems using mathematical analysis.

LO 1–4 Evaluate the efficiency of a firm

Summary

Criteria that relate to how well the firm is doing include:

- Efficiency
- Effectiveness
- Value created in its products and services

Key Terms

Efficiency A ratio of the actual output of a process relative to some standard. Also, being "efficient" means doing something at the lowest possible cost.

Effectiveness Doing the things that will create the most value for the customer.

Value The attractiveness of a product relative to its price.

Benchmarking When one company studies the processes of another company to identify best practices.

Efficiency Measures:

Income per employee

Revenue (or sales) per employee

[1.1] $$\textit{Receivables turnover} = \frac{\textit{Annual credit sales}}{\textit{Average accounts receivable}}$$

[1.2] $$\textit{Inventory turnover} = \frac{\textit{Cost of goods sold}}{\textit{Average inventory value}}$$

[1.3] $$\textit{Asset turnover} = \frac{\textit{Revenue (or sales)}}{\textit{Total assets}}$$

DISCUSSION QUESTIONS

LO1–1 1. Using Exhibit 1.3 as a model, describe the source-make-deliver-return relationships in the following systems:

a. An airline

b. An automobile manufacturer

c. A hospital

d. An insurance company

2. Define the service package of your college or university. What is its strongest element? Its weakest one?
3. What service industry has impressed you the most with its innovativeness?
4. What is product-service bundling, and what are the benefits to customers?
5. What is the difference between a service and a good?
6. Look at the job postings at www.apics.org and evaluate the opportunities for an OSCM major with several years of experience. LO1–2
7. Recent outsourcing of parts and services that had previously been produced internally is addressed by which current issue facing operation management today? LO1–3
8. What factors account for the resurgence of interest in OSCM today?
9. As the field of OSCM has advanced, new concepts have been applied to help companies compete in a number of ways, including the advertisement of the firm's products or services. One recent concept to gain the attention of companies is promoting *sustainability.* Discuss how you have seen the idea of sustainability used by companies to advertise their goods or services.
10. Some people tend to use the terms *effectiveness* and *efficiency* interchangeably, though we've seen they are different concepts. But is there any relationship at all between them? Can a firm be effective but inefficient? Very efficient but essentially ineffective? Both? Neither? LO1–4
11. Two of the efficiency ratios mentioned in the chapter are the *receivable turnover ratio* and the *inventory turnover ratio.* While they are two completely separate measures, they are very similar in one way. What is the common thread between these two?

OBJECTIVE QUESTIONS

1. What are the three elements that require integration to be successful in operations and supply chain management? (Answer in Appendix D) LO1–1
2. Operations and supply chain management is concerned with the design and management of the entire system that has what function?
3. Match the following OSCM job titles with the appropriate duties and responsibilities. LO1–2

_____ Plant manager	A. Plans and coordinates staff activities such as new product development and new facility location.
_____ Supply chain manager	B. Oversees the movement of goods throughout the supply chain.
_____ Project manager	C. Oversees the workforce and resources required to produce the firm's products.
_____ Business process improvement analyst	D. Negotiates contracts with vendors and coordinates the flow of material inputs to the production process.
_____ Logistics manager	E. Applies the tools of lean production to reduce cycle time and eliminate waste in a process.

4. What high-level position manager is responsible for working with the CEO and company president to determine the company's competitive strategy?
5. Order the following major concepts that have helped define the OSCM field on a time line. Use 1 for the earliest concept to be introduced, and 5 for the most recent. LO1–3

_____ Supply chain management
_____ Manufacturing strategy
_____ Business analytics
_____ Total quality management
_____ Electronic commerce

6. Which major OSCM concept can be described as an integrated set of activities designed to achieve high-volume production using minimal inventories of parts that arrive at workstations exactly when they are needed?
7. Operations and supply chain _____________ leverages the vast amount of data in enterprise resource planning systems to make decisions related to managing resources.
8. Which current issue in OSCM relates to the ability of a firm to maintain balance in a system, considering the ongoing economic, employee, and environmental viability of the firm?

LO1–4

9. Consider the following financial data from the past year for Midwest Outdoor Equipment Corporation. (Answers in Appendix D)

Gross income	\$25,240,000
Total sales	24,324,000
Total credit sales	18,785,000
Net income	2,975,000
Cost of goods sold	12,600,000
Total assets	10,550,000
Average inventory	2,875,000
Average receivables	3,445,000

a. Compute the *receivable turnover ratio.*
b. Compute the *inventory turnover ratio.*
c. Compute the *asset turnover ratio.*

10. A manufacturing company has entered into a new contract with a major supplier of raw materials used in the manufacturing process. Under the new arrangement, called *vendor managed inventory,* the supplier manages its raw material inventory inside the manufacturer's plant, and only bills the manufacturer when the manufacturer consumes the raw material. How is this likely to affect the manufacturer's inventory turnover ratio?
11. What is the name of the process in which one company studies the processes of another firm in order to identify best practices?
12. A company has recently implemented an automated online billing and payment processing system for orders it ships to customers. As a result, it has reduced the average number of days between billing a customer and receiving payment by 10 days. How will this affect the receivables turnover ratio?

ANALYTICS EXERCISE: COMPARING COMPANIES USING WALL STREET EFFICIENCY MEASURES (LO 1–4)

The idea behind this exercise is for the class to generate data comparing companies in many different industries. These data will be used to compare these industries from an operations and supply chain view to better understand differences. Be prepared for a lively class discussion for this session.

Step 1: Pick an industry you find interesting. This may be driven by a company by which you would like to be employed or by some other factor. Within the industry, identify three companies that compete with one another. To find the data for this exercise two sites are suggested http://www.aol.com/stock-quotes/ and http://www.msn.com/money/. These sites are updated frequently, and the data needed should be available for most companies listed on the United States stock exchanges.

Step 2: Collect data related to each company. At a minimum, try to find the income per employee, revenue per employee, receivables turnover, inventory turnover, and asset turnover for each company. It may be necessary to calculate the income per employee and revenue per employee ratios by taking the financial data and dividing by the number of company employees. For the other data, look for "efficiency ratios" on the Website.

Step 3: Compare the companies based on what you have found. Which company appears to have the most productive employees? Which company has the best operations and supply chain processes? Which company is most efficient in its use of credit? Which company makes the best use of its facility and equipment assets?

Step 4: What insights can you draw from your analysis? What could your companies learn from benchmarking each other?

PRACTICE EXAM

Name the term defined in each of the following statements.

1. The pipelinelike movement of the materials and information needed to produce a good or service.
2. A strategy that meets the needs of shareholders and employees and that preserves the environment.
3. The processes needed to determine the set of future actions required to operate an existing supply chain.
4. The selection of suppliers.
5. A type of process where a major product is produced or a service provided.
6. A type of process that moves products to warehouses or customers.
7. Processes that involve the receiving of worn-out, defective, and excess products back from customers and support for customers who have problems.
8. A type of business where the major product is intangible, meaning it cannot be weighed or measured.
9. Refers to when a company builds service activities into its product offerings.
10. Means doing something at the lowest possible cost.
11. Means doing the right things to create the most value for the company.
12. Abstractly defined as quality divided by price.
13. A philosophy that aggressively seeks to eliminate causes of production defects.
14. An approach that seeks to make revolutionary changes as opposed to evolutionary changes (which is advocated by total quality management).
15. An approach that combines TQM and JIT.
16. Tools that are taught to managers in "Green and Black Belt Programs."
17. A program to apply the latest concepts in information technology to improve service productivity.

Answers to Practice Exam 1. Supply (chain) network 2. Triple bottom line strategy 3. Planning 4. Sourcing 5. Making 6. Delivery 7. Returning 8. Service 9. Product-service bundling 10. Efficiency 11. Effectiveness 12. Value 13. Total quality management 14. Business process reengineering 15. Lean manufacturing 16. Six Sigma quality 17. Service science management and engineering

For PowerPoint lecture slides, Solutions Manual, Test Bank, Data files for solved examples, Excel Templates, Step-by-Step Solved Examples in video format, Tutorial Videos and many more, scan the adjacent **QR code**, or **visit http://www.mhhe.com/sie-chase15e**

Chapter 2

Strategy

LEARNING OBJECTIVES

LO 2-1 Know what a sustainable business strategy is and how it relates to operations and supply chain management

LO 2-2 Define operations and supply chain strategy.

LO 2-3 Explain how operations and supply chain strategies are implemented

LO 2-4 Understand why strategies have implications relative to business risk

LO 2-5 Evaluate productivity in operations and supply chain management

TESLA MOTORS

Started by Elon Musk, Tesla Motors is radically changing the way we think about personal travel. The all-electric Model S has features like an autopilot with advanced cruise control and automatic passing. Parking features, where the car can park itself and even be retrieved automatically, are safety and convenience abilities that will be commonly available soon.

The company has needed to address major obstacles for the mass-market acceptance of a battery-powered car. These relate to the limited range of batteries and the time it takes to charge the battery packs.

Consider the strategic initiatives that Tesla has implemented to address these issues:

- They have built thousands of "supercharging" stations around the world that can charge the car in just 30 minutes.
- To drive the cost of the batteries down, they are building a giant battery plant in Reno, Nevada. Tesla refers to this as their "gigafactory," and the intent is to produce a low-cost industry standard around its interchangeable battery pack form-factor and power. Elon Musk turned over the patents associated with the new battery to the public so that the standards can be easily adopted by others.
- Finally, Tesla has introduced a "battery swap" technology that can be easily adopted by gas stations around the world. The automated stations quickly swap the battery and install a freshly charged one. This technology positions Musk where he may well own the energy franchise for electric automobile power for the future.

Courtesy of Michael Gabriel, Vero Beach FL

The innovations, introduced by Tesla in their cars, span many areas, including the design and manufacture of their cars, software technology for safe operation, procurement and development of a new battery, and the infrastructure for use of the car. Taken together, Tesla Motors may well mark the start of a new era in highway transportation.

A SUSTAINABLE OPERATIONS AND SUPPLY CHAIN STRATEGY

LO 2-1

Know what a sustainable business strategy is and how it relates to operations and supply chain management

Strategy should describe how a firm intends to create and sustain value for its current shareholders. By adding **sustainability** to the concept, we add the requirement to meet these current needs without compromising the ability of future generations to meet their own needs. *Shareholders* are those individuals or companies that legally own one or more shares of stock in the company. Many companies today have expanded the scope of their strategy to include stakeholders. *Stakeholders* are those individuals or organizations that are influenced, either directly or indirectly, by the actions of the firm. This expanded view means that the scope of the firm's strategy must not only focus on the economic viability of its shareholders, but should also consider the environmental and social impact on key stakeholders.

To capture this expanded view, the phrase **triple bottom line** has been coined. The triple bottom line, Exhibit 2.1, considers evaluating the firm against social, economic, and environmental criteria. Many companies have developed this expanded view through goals that relate to sustainability along each of these dimensions. Some alternative phrases for the same concept are "People, Planet, and Profit" used by Shell Oil Company, and "Folk, Work, and Place" which originated with twentieth-century writer Patrick Geddes. The following expands on the meaning of each dimension of the triple bottom line framework.

Sustainability
The ability to meet current resource needs without compromising the ability of future generations to meet their needs.

Triple bottom line
A business strategy that includes social, economic, and environmental criteria.

Strategy

- **Social Responsibility.** This pertains to fair and beneficial business practices toward labor, the community, and the region in which a firm conducts its business. A triple bottom line company seeks to benefit its employees, the community, and other social entities that are impacted by the firm's existence. A company should not use child labor, and should pay fair salaries to its workers, maintain a safe work environment with tolerable working hours, and not otherwise exploit a community or its labor force. A business can also give back by contributing to the strength and growth of its community through health care, education, and other special programs.
- **Economic Prosperity.** The firm is obligated to compensate shareholders who provide capital through stock purchases and other financial instruments via a competitive return on investments. Company strategies should promote growth and grow long-term value to this group in the

EXHIBIT 2.1

The Triple Bottom Line

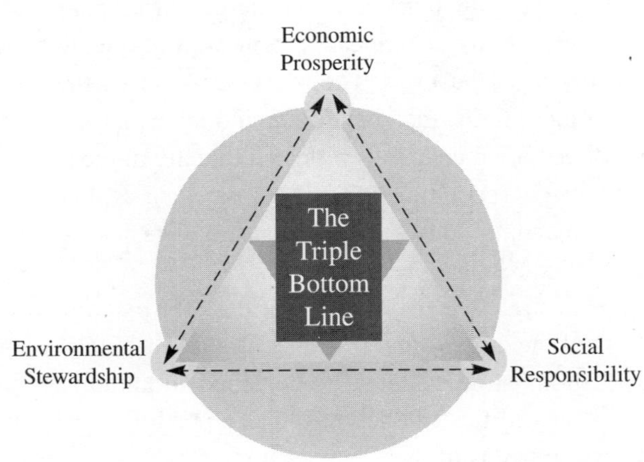

Lights are turned off in an office as employees work on desks equipped with LED bulbs in an energy-saving measure.

form of profit. Within a sustainability framework, this dimension goes beyond just profit for the firm; it also provides lasting economic benefit to society.

- **Environmental Stewardship.** This refers to the firm's impact on the environment. The company should protect the environment as much as possible—or at least cause no harm. Managers should move to reduce a company's ecological footprint by carefully managing its consumption of natural resources and by reducing waste. Many businesses now conduct "cradle-to-grave" assessments of products to determine what the true environmental costs are—from processing the raw material to manufacture to distribution to eventual disposal by the final customer.

Conventional strategy focuses on the economic part of this framework. Because many of the processes that fall under the domain of operations and supply chain management have a social and environment impact, it is important these criteria be considered as well. Some proponents argue that, in many ways, European Union countries are more advanced due to the standardized reporting of ecological and social losses that came with the adoption of the euro.

Although many company planners agree with the goals of improving society and preserving the environment, many others disagree. Dissenting arguments relate to the potential loss of efficiency due to the focus on conflicting criteria. Others argue that these goals may be appropriate for rich societies that can afford to contribute to society and the environment. A company in a poor or developing society/nation must focus on survival. The economic benefit derived from the use of abundant local resources may be viewed as worth their destruction.

In this chapter, we take a customer-centered approach; issues associated with people and the environment are left to an individual case approach. Depending on the country, industry, and scope of the firm, these other issues vary widely, and it would be difficult to provide a general approach for analysis. The issues and their relationship to operations and supply chain management are very real, however, and we anticipate they will become even more relevant in the future.

LO 2-2

Define operations and supply chain strategy

WHAT IS OPERATIONS AND SUPPLY CHAIN STRATEGY?

Operations and supply chain strategy The setting of broad policies and plans that will guide the use of the resources needed by the firm to implement its corporate strategy.

Operations effectiveness Performing activities in a manner that best implements strategic priorities at minimum cost.

Operations and supply chain strategy is concerned with setting broad policies and plans for using the resources of a firm and must be integrated with corporate strategy. So, for example, if the high-level corporate strategy includes goals related to the environment and social responsibility, then the operations and supply chain strategy must consider these goals. A major focus to the operations and supply chain strategy is operations effectiveness. **Operations effectiveness** relates to the core business processes needed to run the business. The processes span all the business functions, from taking customer orders, handling returns, manufacturing, and managing the updating of the Website, to shipping products. Operational effectiveness is reflected directly in the costs associated with doing business. Strategies associated with operational effectiveness, such as quality assurance and control initiatives, process redesign, planning and control systems, and technology investments, can show quick near-term (12 to 24 months) results.

Operations and supply chain strategy can be viewed as part of a planning process that coordinates operational goals with those of the larger organization. Because the goals of the larger organization change over time, the operations strategy must be designed to anticipate future needs. A firm's operations and supply chain capabilities can be viewed as a portfolio best suited to adapting to the changing product and/or service needs of the firm's customers.

Planning strategy is a process just like making a product or delivering a service. The process involves a set of activities that are repeated at different intervals over time. Just as products are made over and over, the strategy planning activities are repeated. A big difference is that these activities are done by executives in the boardroom!

Exhibit 2.2 shows the major activities of a typical strategic planning process. Strategic analysis is performed at least yearly and is where the overall strategy is developed. This step involves looking out and forecasting how business conditions that impact the firm's strategy are going to change in the future. Here, such things as changes in customer preferences, the impact of new technologies, changes in population demographics, and the anticipation of new competitors are considered. As part of the overall strategy, the firm needs to define a clear set of priorities to help guide the implementation of a plan. When possible, it is useful to define specific measures that relate to the objectives of the firm. A successful strategy will anticipate change and formulate new initiatives in response.

EXHIBIT 2.2

Formulating an Operations and Supply Chain Strategy

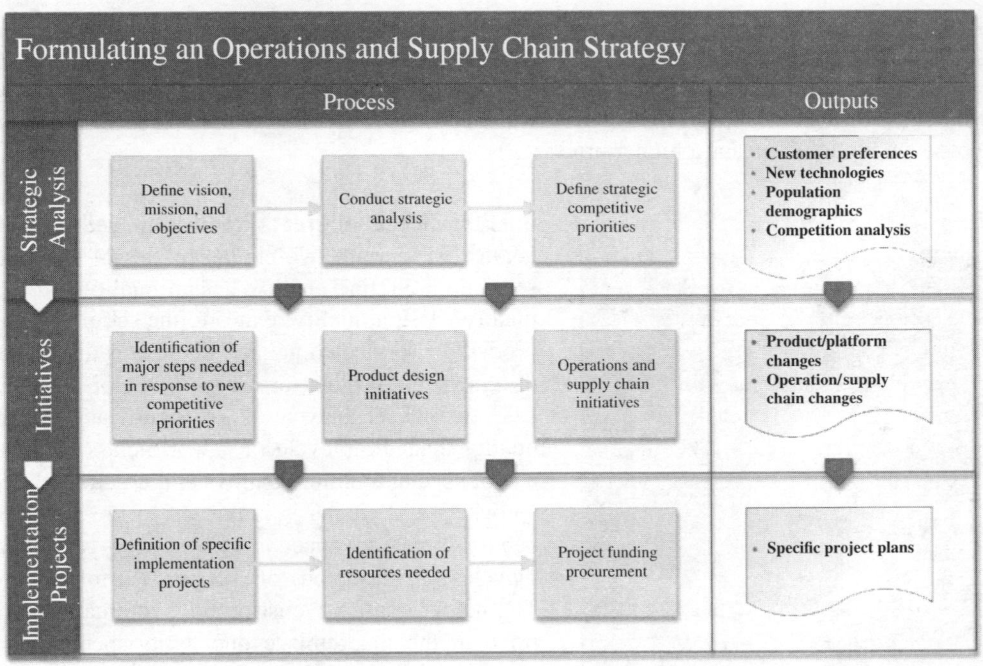

The corporate strategy is operationalized through a set of operations and supply chain initiatives. *Initiatives* are the major steps that need to be taken to drive success in the firm. Many of these initiatives are repeated from year to year, such as the updating of existing product designs and the operation of manufacturing plants in different regions of the world. New initiatives that innovatively respond to market dynamics are extremely important to company success. Initiatives that develop innovative products or open new markets, for example, drive future revenue growth. Other initiatives that reduce costs directly impact the profitability of the firm. Companies with triple bottom line strategies may have initiatives that reduce waste or enhance the welfare of the local communities.

Process

These activities are refined and updated as often as four times a year. Here, each initiative is evaluated and appropriate budget estimates for the next year or more are developed. Measures that relate to the performance of each initiative are needed so that success or failure can be gauged in an unbiased and objective way. Because of the quickly changing nature of global business, many businesses must revise plans several times per year.

Carefully designed projects are used to implement change. The planning of these projects requires the identification of the resources needed, such as the expertise of the project members, special equipment, and other resources. Specific timing of the activities of the project are analyzed as part of each project implementation plan.

Competitive Dimensions

Given the choices customers face today, how do they decide which product or service to buy? Different customers are attracted by different attributes. Some customers are interested primarily in the cost of a product or service and, correspondingly, some companies attempt to position themselves to offer the lowest prices. The major competitive dimensions that form the competitive position of a firm are discussed next.

Key Idea

Competing based on cost can be difficult unless the firm has some unique advantage over the competition. For example, an inexpensive source of raw material or access to low-cost labor may create the necessary advantage.

Cost or Price: "Make the Product or Deliver the Service Inexpensively" Within every industry, there is usually a segment of the market that buys solely on the basis of low cost. To successfully compete in this niche, a firm must be the low-cost producer. However, even this does not always guarantee profitability and success. Products and services sold strictly on the basis of cost are typically commodity-like; in other words, customers cannot distinguish the product or service of one firm from that of another. This segment of the market is frequently very large, and many companies are lured by the potential for significant profits, which they associate with the large unit volumes. As a consequence, however, competition in this segment is fierce—and so is the failure rate. After all, there can be only one low-cost producer, who usually establishes the selling price in the market.

Price, however, is not the only basis on which a firm can compete (although many economists appear to assume it is!). Other companies, such as BMW, seek to attract people who want *higher quality*—in terms of performance, appearance, or features—than what is available in competing products and services, even though it means a higher price.

An aerodynamics expert logs results from a wind tunnel test for cycling clothing and racing bicycle design.

Quality: "Make a Great Product or Deliver a Great Service" There are two characteristics of a product or service that define quality: design quality and process quality. Design quality relates to the set of features the product or service contains. This relates directly to the design of the product or service. Obviously, a child's first two-wheel bicycle is of significantly different quality than the bicycle of a world-class cyclist. The use of special aluminum alloys and unique lightweight sprockets and chains is important to the performance needs of the advanced cyclist. These two types of bicycles are designed for different customers' needs. The higher-quality cyclist product commands a higher price in the marketplace due to its special features. The goal in establishing the proper level of design quality is to focus on the requirements of the customer. Overdesigned products and services with too many or inappropriate features will be viewed as prohibitively expensive. In comparison, underdesigned products and services will lose customers to products that cost a little more but are perceived by customers as offering greater value.

Key Idea

Same-day delivery of items ordered from the Internet is now an important competitive feature for some companies. Keep in mind that competitive priorities may change over time.

Process quality, the second characteristic of quality, is critical because it relates directly to the reliability of the product or service. Regardless of whether the product is a child's first two-wheeler or a bicycle for an international cyclist, customers want products without defects. Thus, the goal of process quality is to produce defect-free products and services. Product and service specifications, given in dimensional tolerances and/or service error rates, define how the product or service is to be made. Adherence to these specifications is critical to ensure the reliability of the product or service as defined by its intended use.

Delivery Speed: "Make the Product or Deliver the Service Quickly" In some markets, a firm's ability to deliver more quickly than its competitors is critical. A company that can offer an onsite repair service in only 1 or 2 hours has a significant advantage over a competing firm that guarantees service only within 24 hours.

Delivery Reliability: "Deliver It When Promised" This dimension relates to the firm's ability to supply the product or service on or before a promised delivery due date. For an automobile manufacturer, it is very important that its supplier of tires provide the needed quantity and types for each day's car production. If the tires needed for a particular car are not available when the car reaches the point on the assembly line where the tires are installed, the whole assembly line may have to be shut down until they arrive. For a service firm such as Federal Express, delivery reliability is the cornerstone of its strategy.

Coping with Changes in Demand: "Change Its Volume" In many markets, a company's ability to respond to increases and decreases in demand is important to its ability to compete. It is well known that a company with increasing demand can do little wrong. When demand is strong and increasing, costs are continuously reduced due to economies of scale, and investments in new technologies can be easily justified. But scaling back when demand decreases may require many difficult decisions about laying off employees and related reductions in assets. The ability to effectively deal with dynamic market demand over the long term is an essential element of operations strategy.

Flexibility and New-Product Introduction Speed: "Change It" Flexibility, from a strategic perspective, refers to the ability of a company to offer a wide variety of products to its customers. An important element of this ability to offer different products is the time required for a company to develop a new product and to convert its processes to offer the new product.

Other Product-Specific Criteria: "Support It" The competitive dimensions just described are certainly the most common. However, other dimensions often relate to specific products or situations. Notice that most of the dimensions listed next are primarily service in nature. Often, special services are provided to augment the sales of manufactured products.

1. **Technical liaison and support.** A supplier may be expected to provide technical assistance for product development, particularly during the early stages of design and manufacturing.
2. **Meeting a launch date.** A firm may be required to coordinate with other firms on a complex project. In such cases, manufacturing may take place while development work is still being completed. Coordinating work between firms and working simultaneously on a project will reduce the total time required to complete the project.
3. **Supplier after-sale support.** An important competitive dimension may be the ability of a firm to support its product after the sale. This involves availability of replacement parts and, possibly, modification of older, existing products to new performance levels. Speed of response to these after-sale needs is often important as well.
4. **Environmental impact.** This dimension is related to criteria such as carbon dioxide emissions, use of nonrenewable resources, or other factors that relate to sustainability.
5. **Other dimensions.** These typically include such factors as colors available, size, weight, location of the fabrication site, customization available, and product mix options.

Key Idea

Often, the services that are included with a product are key differentiators in the marketplace.

The Notion of Trade-Offs

Central to the concept of operations and supply chain strategy is the notion of operations focus and trade-offs. The underlying logic is that an operation cannot excel simultaneously on all competitive dimensions. Consequently, management has to decide which parameters of performance are critical to the firm's success and then concentrate the resources of the firm on these particular characteristics.

For example, if a company wants to focus on speed of delivery, it cannot be very flexible in its ability to offer a wide range of products. Similarly, a low-cost strategy is not compatible with either speed of delivery or flexibility. High quality also is viewed as a trade-off to low cost.

A strategic position is not sustainable unless there are compromises with other positions. Trade-offs occur when activities are incompatible so that more of one thing necessitates less of another. An airline can choose to serve meals—adding cost and slowing turnaround time at the gate—or it can choose not to, but it cannot do both without bearing major inefficiencies.

Straddling
When a firm seeks to match what a competitor is doing by adding new features, services, or technologies to existing activities. This often creates problems if trade-offs need to be made.

Straddling occurs when a company seeks to match the benefits of a successful position while maintaining its existing position. It adds new features, services, or technologies onto the activities it already performs. The risky nature of this strategy is shown by Continental Airlines' ill-fated attempt to compete with Southwest Airlines. While maintaining its position as a full-service airline, Continental set out to match Southwest on a number of point-to-point routes. The airline dubbed the new service Continental Lite. It eliminated meals and first-class service, increased departure frequency, lowered fares, and shortened gate turnaround time. Because Continental remained a full-service airline on other routes, it continued to use travel agents and its mixed fleet of planes and also provide baggage checking and seat assignments.

Trade-offs ultimately grounded Continental Lite. The airline lost hundreds of millions of dollars, and the chief executive officer lost his job. Its planes were delayed, leaving hub cities congested, slowed at the gate by baggage transfers. Late flights and cancellations generated a thousand complaints a day. Continental Lite could not afford to compete on price and still pay standard travel agent commissions, but neither could it do without agents for its full-service business. The airline compromised by cutting commissions for all Continental flights. Similarly, it could not afford to offer the same frequent-flier benefits to travelers paying the much lower ticket prices for Lite service. It compromised again by lowering the rewards of Continental's entire frequent-flier program. The results: angry travel agents and full-service customers. Continental tried to compete in two ways at once and paid an enormous straddling penalty.

Order Winners and Order Qualifiers: The Marketing–Operations Link

Order winners
One or more specific marketing-oriented dimensions that clearly differentiate a product from competing products.

Order qualifiers
Dimensions used to screen a product or service as a candidate for purchase.

A well-designed interface between marketing and operations is necessary to provide a business with an understanding of its markets from both perspectives. The terms *order winner* and *order qualifier* describe marketing-oriented dimensions that are key to competitive success. An **order winner** is a criterion, or possibly a set of criteria, that differentiates the products or services of one firm from those of another. Depending on the situation, the order-winning criteria may be the cost of the product (price), product quality and reliability, or any of the other dimensions developed earlier. An **order qualifier** is a screening criterion that permits a firm's products to even be considered as possible candidates for purchase. Oxford Professor Terry Hill states that a firm must "requalify the order qualifiers" every day it is in business.

For example, consider your purchase of a notebook computer. You might think that such features as screen size, weight, operating system version, and cost are important *qualifying* dimensions. The order-winning feature that actually *differentiates* those candidate notebook computers that qualify is battery life. In doing your search, you develop a list of computers that all have 14-inch screens, weigh less than three pounds, run the latest Microsoft Windows operating system, and cost less than $1,000. From this list of acceptable computers, you select the one that has the longest battery life.

In an industrial setting where a firm is deciding on a supplier, the decision can be quite different. Consider a firm that is deciding on a supplier for its office supplies. Companies such as Office Depot, OfficeMax, Quill, or Staples might be candidates. Here, the qualifying dimensions are: Can the company supply the items needed, can the supplier deliver orders within 24 hours, are the items guaranteed, and is a private Web-based catalog available? Companies that have these capabilities would *qualify* for consideration as possible suppliers. The order winner might be the discount schedule that the company offers on the price of the items purchased.

LO 2-3
Explain how operations and supply chain strategies are implemented

STRATEGIES ARE IMPLEMENTED USING OPERATIONS AND SUPPLY CHAIN ACTIVITIES—IKEA'S STRATEGY

All the activities that make up a firm's operation relate to one another. To make these activities efficient, the firm must minimize its total cost without compromising customers' needs.

To demonstrate how this works, consider how IKEA, the Swedish retailer of home products, implements its strategy using a set of unique activities. IKEA targets young furniture buyers who want style at a low cost. IKEA has chosen to perform activities differently from its rivals.

Consider the typical furniture store, where showrooms display samples of the merchandise. One area may contain many sofas, another area displays dining tables, and there are many other areas focused on particular types of furniture. Dozens of books displaying fabric swatches or wood samples or alternative styles offer customers thousands of product varieties from which to choose. Salespeople escort customers through the store, answering questions and helping them navigate through the maze of choices. Once a customer decides what he or she wants, the order is relayed to a third-party manufacturer. With a lot of luck, the furniture will be delivered to the customer's home within six to eight weeks. This is a supply chain that maximizes customization and service, but does so at a high cost.

Used with the permission of Inter IKEA Systems B.V.

In contrast, IKEA serves customers who are happy to trade service for cost. In addition to using sales associates, IKEA

EXHIBIT 2.3

IKEA—Stylish Low-Cost Furniture

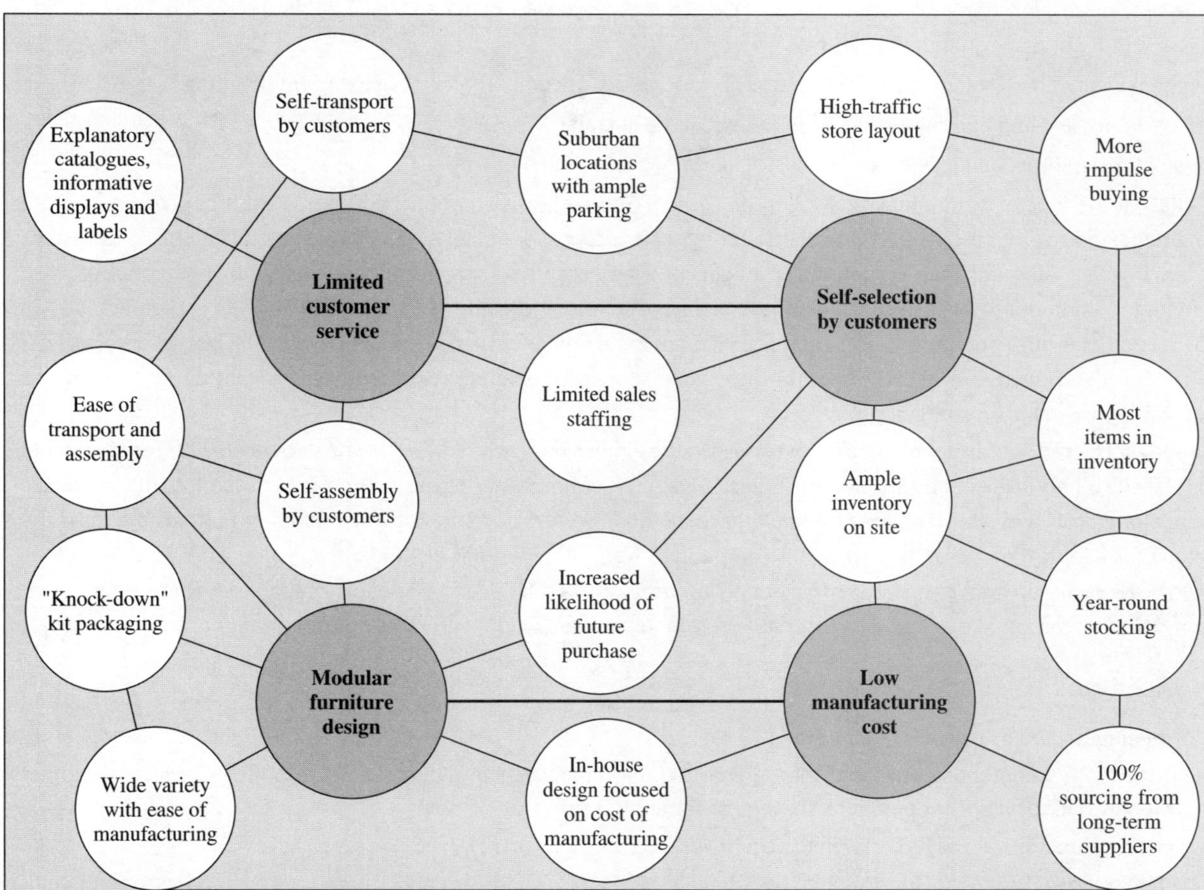

Activity-system maps, such as this one for IKEA, show how a company's strategic position is contained in a set of tailored activities designed to deliver it. In companies with a clear strategic position, a number of higher-order strategic themes (in darker green circles) can be identified and implemented through clusters of tightly linked activities (in lighter circles). The themes here all relate to reducing operations and supply chain–related costs, which are important for the firm's success.

Based on Harvard Business School Press, from *On Competition* by Michael E. Porter, Boston, MA, 1998, p. 50.

Demise of Air Deccan (Kingfisher Red)

Air Deccan was founded by Captain G R Gopinath on 25 August 2003 as the cheapest airlines of Indian aviation history. It revolutionized the aviation industry in India, as it was aiming to come within the reach of a common man. Starting with flights between Bangalore to Mangalore and Hubli, it soon expanded to the other parts of India. After being acquired by Kingfisher Airlines, it was renamed and rebranded as Kingfisher Red. It holds the distinction of being India's first low-cost airline. The airline was passenger friendly with features like frequent flyer miles, low-cost operations, etc.

According to Captain Gopinath, "...it hit me like a ton of bricks. This country has a population of a billion, but only 15 million air passengers. May be the time is right. If one billion people can fly, and we get a miniscule percent of the market, imagine how big that will be? It's not an impossible dream."[1] Air Deccan adopted several operation-strategies to keep the passenger fare low. The following measures were taken to do so[2, 3]:

- Use of smaller aircrafts on the routes where traffic was less and airports were smaller. It resulted in cost savings through lower sales tax on fuel, lower navigation fees, less landing fees and fewer cabin crew members
- Use of dynamic pricing model, which helped the airline to maximize its revenues from ticket sales as well as maintain high seat occupancy
- Reduction in aircraft's turnaround time at the airports
- Exploitation of point-to-point routes so as to eliminate waiting time between flights
- Exploitation of other revenue generation modes, such as sale of food and beverages on flights; sale of advertising space on many possible places, for example seats, storage bins, headrests, tray table, baggage tags, boarding passes, body of aircraft, websites and in-flight magazines
- Improvement in aircraft utilization figure, which was up to 10 hours, as compared to industry norms of around 7 to 8 hours
- Concept of single class and narrow seating arrangement in the aircraft
- Restriction of expenditure on fancy offices, exclusive lounges, size of staff and crew

In August 2008, at the time of its merger with Kingfisher, Captain Gopinath was emotional and said, "...it's like giving away your daughter in marriage and she is going with her husband's surname. This consolidation was done to protect the interest of investors, vendors and employees".[4] Although, the operations strategies of Air Deccan had significant similarity with those of Southwest Airlines, still, mere imitation does not help much if situations, users, culture and country change. Even, partial implementation of these operations strategies does not bring success in the similar environment, as it is evident from Continental Lite, another airlines competing with Southwest Airlines. In this context, the short-time success of operations strategy deployment by Air Deccan was indeed a novel experience in Indian context.

After acquiring Air Deccan, Kingfisher too could not survive in the airlines business. It faced a huge debt of ₹8,000 crore and other huge losses.[5] It failed to find investors for its bail-out. The survival plan of Kingfisher never took off due to the fact that its future operations were strategically unviable. The airlines would have needed heavy traffic and for this, it could not afford to bypass the low-fares strategy for a long time. Also, there was stiff competition from other airlines like Indigo, SpiceJet, GoAir, etc. Therefore, Kingfisher could never come-up from its miseries of mounting interest, unpaid salaries and bills of oil companies. The important point to ponder is why the competitors like Indigo did reasonable well in the market yet the demise of Kingfisher Airlines was inevitable.

Discussion Questions

1. What do you understand by operations strategy?
2. Why Indigo and other competitors of Kingfisher Airlines did reasonably well in the market yet Kingfisher Airlines could not survive? Is it only due to failure of operations strategy or something else?
3. Did Kingfisher commit mistake in its decision to acquire Air Deccan? Why?
4. Do a SWOT (Strength-Weakness-Opportunity-Threat) analysis of airlines industry and suggest ways to an existing airlines company for its expansion plan.

References

1. *The Hindu*, Sunday, August 15, 2004.
2. D.V.R. Seshadri, and Jane Henry, (2005), Air Deccan: Revolutionizing the Indian Skies, *South Asian Journal of Management*, Oct-Dec 2005.
3. G R Gopinath, *Simply Fly: A Deccan Odyssey*, Collins Business, 2010.
4. Air Deccan is now Kingfisher Red: *Times of India*, http://timesofindia.indiatimes.com/Business/India_Business/Air_deccan_us_now_Kingfisher_Red/articleshow/3423550.cms (accessed on 21 April 2010).

uses a self-service model with roomlike displays where furniture is shown in familiar settings. Rather than relying on third-party manufacturers, IKEA designs its own low-cost, ready-to-assemble furniture. In the store there is a self-serve warehouse, where customers can pick up products themselves and take them home the same day. Much of its low-cost operation comes from having customers service themselves, but IKEA offers extra services, such as home delivery, assembly, kitchen planning, and in-store, by-appointment interior design consultation. Those services align well with the needs of its customers, who are young, not wealthy, and likely to have children.

Exhibit 2.3 shows how IKEA's strategy is implemented through a set of activities designed to deliver it. **Activity-system maps** such as the one for IKEA show how a company's strategy is delivered through a set of tailored activities. In companies with a clear strategy, a number of higher-order strategic themes (in darker green) can be identified and implemented through clusters of tightly linked activities. This type of map can be useful in understanding how good the fit is between the system of activities and the company's strategy. Competitive advantage comes from the way a firm's activities fit with and reinforce one another.

Activity-system maps
Diagrams that show how a company's strategy is delivered through a set of supporting activities.

ASSESSING THE RISK ASSOCIATED WITH OPERATIONS AND SUPPLY CHAIN STRATEGIES

LO 2-4
Understand why strategies have implications relative to business risk

The devastating earthquake and tsunami that hit Japan in March 2011 were a grim reminder that managing risk is a critical part of developing an effective operations and supply chain strategy.

The uncertainty in the global environment where most supply chains operate requires strategic planners to evaluate the relative riskiness of their operations and supply chain strategies. **Supply chain risk** is defined as the likelihood of a disruption that would impact the ability of the company to continuously supply products or services. Supply chain disruptions are unplanned and unanticipated events that disrupt the normal flow of goods and materials within a supply chain, and which expose

Supply chain risk
The likelihood of a disruption that would impact the ability of a company to continuously supply products or services.

A factory building collapsed in Sukagawa city, Fukushima prefecture, in northern Japan in 2011. A massive 8.9-magnitude earthquake shook Japan, unleashing a powerful tsunami that sent ships crashing into the shore and carried cars through the streets of coastal towns.

firms within the supply chain to operational and financial risks. Operations and supply chain strategies must consider the risk in their supply chains and develop initiatives to cope with these disruptions and mitigate their impact on the business.

We can categorize risks by viewing the inherent uncertainties related to operations and supply chain management along two dimensions: (1) supply chain coordination risks that are associated with the day-to-day management of the supply chain, which are normally dealt with using safety stock, safety lead time, overtime, and so on; and (2) disruption risks, which are caused by natural or manmade disasters, such as earthquakes, hurricanes, and terrorism.

In this section, our focus is on the concepts and tools that are useful for managing the problems related to disruption risks. The events related to these risks are highly random and virtually impossible to predict with any precision.

Other than the Japan earthquake and tsunami mentioned, the following are examples of the types of events this section relates to:

- In 1996, General Motors experienced an 18-day labor strike at a brake supplier factory. This strike idled workers at 26 assembly plants and led to an estimated $900 million reduction in earnings.
- In 1997, a Boeing supplier's failure to deliver two critical parts led to a loss of $2.6 billion.
- In 2000, a 10-minute fire at a Phillips plant that supplied integrated circuits led to a $400 million loss to the firm.
- There are many other examples, including the 2010 Toyota recalls and the British Petroleum oil rig fire in the Gulf of Mexico.

Risk Management Framework

The nature of these types of risks lends them to a three-step risk management process that can be applied to situations where disruptions are possible. The three steps are as follows:

Process

1. Identify the sources of potential disruptions. Assessing a type of vulnerability is the first step in the risk management framework. These are highly situation dependent, but the focus should be on highly unlikely events that would cause a significant disruption to normal operations. Such types of events include: natural disasters, capacity failures, infrastructure failures (air traffic system), terrorists, supplier failure, labor actions, equipment failure, commodity price volatility, and military/civil conflict.
2. Assess the potential impact of the risk. Here the goal is to quantify the probability and the potential impact of the risk. Depending on the specific incident, this assessment could be based on financial impact, environmental impact, ongoing business viability, brand image/reputation, potential human lives, and so on.
3. Develop plans to mitigate the risk. A detailed strategy for minimizing the impact of the risk could take many different forms, depending on the nature of the problem.

Risk mapping involves assessment of the probability or relative frequency of an event against the aggregate severity of the loss. Depending on the evaluation, some risks might be deemed acceptable and the related costs considered a normal cost of doing business. In some cases, the firm may find it is possible to insure against the loss. There may be other cases where the potential loss is so great that the risk would need to be avoided altogether.

A matrix (see Exhibit 2.4) that maps risks against specific operations and supply chain strategies. The matrix helps to understand the impact of different types of supply chain disruptions when using specific operations and supply chain strategies. For example, the first column evaluates the impact of natural hazards. Here we see that sole sourcing, lean practices, and the use of distribution hubs can have a major impact on the firm.

Exhibit 2.4

Risk Mitigation Strategies

Analytics

Risks	Risk Mitigation Strategy
Natural disaster (e.g., climate change, weather)	Contingency planning (alternate sites, etc.), insurance
Country risks	Hedge currency, produce/source locally
Supplier failures	Use multiple suppliers
Network provider failure	Support redundant digital networks
Regulatory risk (e.g., licensing and regulation issues)	Up-front and continuing research; good legal advice, compliance
Commodity price risks	Multisource, commodity hedging
Logistics failure	Safety stock, detailed tracking and alternate suppliers
Inventory risks	Pool inventory, safety stock
Major quality failure	Carefully select and monitor suppliers
Loss of customers	Service/product innovation
Theft and vandalism	Insurance, security precautions, knowledge of likely risks, patent protection, etc.

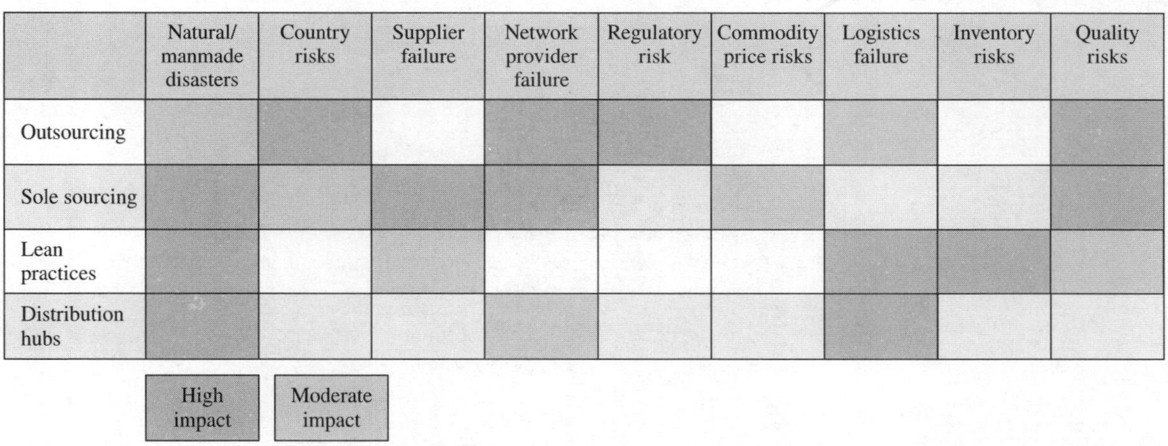

Unfortunately, some of the most cost-effective strategies are also the most risky. It is important to keep this in mind as you consider each concept. Thus far in the book, we have not discussed specific operations and supply chain strategies, such as outsourcing and sole sourcing. You will learn about these as we progress through the book.

LO 2-5

Evaluate productivity in operations and supply chain management

PRODUCTIVITY MEASUREMENT

Productivity is a common measure of how well a country, industry, or business unit is using its resources (or factors of production). Since operations and supply chain management focuses on making the best use of the resources available to a firm, productivity measurement is fundamental to understanding operations-related performance. In this section, we define various measures of productivity. Throughout the rest of the book, many other performance measures will be defined as they relate to the material.

Productivity

A measure of how well resources are used. According to Goldratt's definition (see Chapter 23), all the actions that bring a company closer to its goals.

In its broadest sense, productivity is defined as

$$\text{Productivity} = \frac{\text{Outputs}}{\text{inputs}} \quad [2.1]$$

To increase productivity, we want to make this ratio of outputs to inputs as large as practical.

Productivity is what we call a *relative measure.* In other words, to be meaningful, it needs to be compared with something else. For example, what can we learn from the fact that we operate a restaurant and that its productivity last week was 8.4 customers per labor hour? Nothing!

Analytics

Productivity comparisons can be made in two ways. First, a company can compare itself to similar operations within its industry, or it can use industry data when such data are available (e.g., comparing productivity among the different stores in a franchise). Another approach is to measure productivity over time within the same operation. Here we would compare our productivity in one time period with that in the next.

As Exhibit 2.5 shows, productivity may be expressed as partial measures, multifactor measures, or total measures. If we are concerned with the ratio of some output to a single input, we have a *partial productivity measure.* If we want to look at the ratio of some output to a group of inputs (but not all inputs), we have a *multifactor productivity measure.* If we want to express the ratio of all outputs to all inputs, we can use a *total factor measure of productivity* to describe the productivity of an entire organization or even a nation.

EXHIBIT 2.5

Examples of Productivity Measures

Partial measure	$\frac{\text{Output}}{\text{Labor}}$ or $\frac{\text{Output}}{\text{Capital}}$ or $\frac{\text{Output}}{\text{Material}}$ or $\frac{\text{Output}}{\text{Energy}}$
Multifactor measure	$\frac{\text{Output}}{\text{Labor + Capital + Energy}}$ or $\frac{\text{Output}}{\text{Labor + Capital + Materials}}$
Total measure	$\frac{\text{Output}}{\text{Input}}$ or $\frac{\text{Goods and services produced}}{\text{All resources used}}$

Input and Output Production Data ($1,000)		Productivity Measure Examples
Output		Total measure
1. Finished units	$ 10,000	$\frac{\text{Total output}}{\text{Total input}} = \frac{13,500}{15,193} = 0.89$
2. Work in process	2,500	
3. Dividends	1,000	Multifactor measures:
Total output	$ 13,500	$\frac{\text{Total output}}{\text{Labor + Material}} = \frac{13,500}{3,153} = 4.28$
		$\frac{\text{Finished units}}{\text{Labor + Material}} = \frac{10,000}{3,153} = 3.17$
Input		
1. Labor	$ 3,000	Partial measures:
2. Material	153	$\frac{\text{Total output}}{\text{Energy}} = \frac{13,500}{540} = 25$
3. Capital	10,000	
4. Energy	540	$\frac{\text{Total output}}{\text{Energy}} = \frac{13,500}{540} = 25$
5. Other expenses	1,500	
Total input	$ 15,193	

Partial Measures of Productivity

Business	Productivity Measure
Restaurant	Customers (meals) per labor hour
Retail store	Sales per square foot
Chicken farm	Lb. of meat per lb. of feed
Utility plant	Kilowatt hours per ton of coal
Paper mill	Tons of paper per cord of wood

A numerical example of productivity appears in Exhibit 2.5. The data reflect quantitative measures of input and output associated with the production of a certain product. Notice that for the multifactor and partial measures, it is not necessary to use total output as the numerator. Often, it is desirable to create measures that represent productivity as it relates to some particular output of interest. Using Exhibit 2.5 as an example, total units might be the output of interest to a production control manager, whereas total output may be of key interest to the plant manager. This process of aggregation and disaggregation of productivity measures provides a means of shifting the level of the analysis to suit a variety of productivity measurement and improvement needs.

Exhibit 2.5 shows all units in dollars. Often, however, management can better understand how the company is performing when units other than dollars are used. In these cases, only partial measures of productivity can be used, because we cannot combine dissimilar units such as labor hours and pounds of material. Examples of some commonly used partial measures of productivity are presented in Exhibit 2.5. Such partial measures of productivity give managers information in familiar units, allowing them to easily relate these measures to the actual operations.

Each summer, *USA Today* publishes annual reports of productivity gains by the largest U.S. firms. Productivity has been on the rise for many years now, which is very good for the economy. Productivity often increases in times of recession; as workers are fired, those remaining are expected to do more. Increases also come from technological advances. Think of what the tractor did for farm productivity.

CONCEPT CONNECTIONS

LO 2–1 Know what a sustainable business strategy is and how it relates to operations and supply chain management

Summary

- A strategy that is sustainable needs to create value for the firm's shareholders and stakeholders.
- The shareholders are equity owners in the company.
- The stakeholders are those individuals and organizations that are influenced by the actions of the firm.
- This view means that a firm's strategy must focus not only on economic viability, but also on the environmental and social impact of its actions.

Key Terms

Sustainability The ability to meet current resource needs without compromising the ability of future generations to meet their needs.

Triple bottom line A business strategy that includes social, economic, and environmental criteria.

LO 2–2 Define operations and supply chain strategy

Summary

- This involves setting the broad policies of a firm and creating a plan for using that firm's resources.
- The operations and supply chain strategy coordinates operational goals with those of the larger organization.
- A firm's operational capabilities should match the changing product or service needs of the firm's customers.

Major competitive dimensions that form the competitive position of a firm include:

- Cost
- Quality
- Delivery speed and reliability
- Changes in volume
- Flexibility and new-product introduction speed
- Other product-specific criteria

Usually there are trade-offs that occur relative to these competitive dimensions.

Key Terms

Operations and supply chain strategy The setting of broad policies and plans that will guide the use of the resources needed by the firm to implement its corporate strategy.

Operations effectiveness Performing activities in a manner that best implements strategic priorities at minimum cost.

Straddling When a firm seeks to match what a competitor is doing by adding new features, services, or technologies to existing activities. This often creates problems if trade-offs need to be made.

Order winners One or more specific marketing-oriented dimensions that clearly differentiate a product from competing products.

Order qualifiers Dimensions used to screen a product or service as a candidate for purchase.

LO 2–3 Explain how operations and supply chain strategies are implemented

Summary

- Strategies are implemented through a set of activities designed to deliver products and services in a manner consistent with the firm's overall business strategy.

Key Terms

Activity-system maps Diagrams that show how a company's strategy is delivered through a set of supporting activities.

LO 2–4 Understand why strategies have implications relative to business risk

Summary

- Operations and supply chain strategies need to be evaluated relative to their riskiness.
- Supply chain disruptions are unplanned and unanticipated events that disrupt the normal flow of goods and materials.
- Risks can be categorized along two dimensions: supply chain coordination risks and disruption risks.
- A three-step risk management framework involves identifying the potential disruptions, assessing the potential impact of the risk, and developing plans to mitigate the risk.

Key Terms

Supply chain risk The likelihood of a disruption that would impact the ability of a company to continuously supply products or services.

LO 2–5 Evaluate productivity in operations and supply chain management

Summary

- Productivity measures are used to ensure that the firm makes the best use of its resources.
- Since these are relative measures, they are meaningful only if they are compared to something else. Often, the comparison is to another company.

Key Terms

Productivity A measure of how well resources are used. According to Goldratt's definition (see Chapter 23), all the actions that bring a company closer to its goals.

[2.1] $$\text{Productivity} = \frac{\text{Outputs}}{\text{Inputs}}$$

SOLVED PROBLEM

LO2–5

A furniture manufacturing company has provided the following data (units are $1,000). Compare the labor, raw materials and supplies, and total productivity for the past two years.

		Last Year	This Year
Output:	Sales value of production	$22,000	$35,000
Input:	Labor	10,000	15,000
	Raw materials and supplies	8,000	12,500
	Capital equipment depreciation	700	1,200
	Other	2,200	4,800

Solution

	Last Year	This Year
Partial productivities		
Labor	2.20	2.33
Raw materials and supplies	2.75	2.80
Total productivity	1.05	1.04

DISCUSSION QUESTIONS

1. What is meant by a triple bottom line strategy? Give an example of a company that has adopted this type of strategy. **LO2–1**
2. Find examples where companies have used features related to environmental sustainability to win new customers.
3. What are the major priorities associated with operations and supply chain strategy? For each major priority, describe the unique characteristics of the market niche with which it is most compatible. **LO2–2**
4. Why does the proper operations and supply chain strategy keep changing for companies that are world-class competitors?
5. What do the expressions *order winner* and *order qualifiers* mean? What was the order winner for your last major purchase of a product or service?
6. Pick a company that you are familiar with and describe its operations strategy and how it relates to winning customers. Describe specific activities used by the company that support the strategy (see Exhibit 2.3 for an example). **LO2–3**
7. At times in the past, the dollar showed relative weakness with respect to foreign currencies such as the yen, euro, and pound. This stimulates exports. Why would long-term reliance on a lower-valued dollar be at best a short-term solution to the competitiveness problem? **LO2–4**
8. Identify an operations and supply chain–related disruption that recently impacted a company. What could the company have done to minimize the impact of this type of disruption prior to it occurring?
9. What do we mean when we say productivity is a relative measure? **LO2–5**

OBJECTIVE QUESTIONS*

LO2-1 1. Shell Oil Company's motto "People, Planet and Profit" is a real-world implementation of what OSCM concept? (Answer in Appendix D)

2. A firm's *strategy* should describe how it intends to create and sustain value for what entities?

3. What is the term used to describe individuals or organizations that are influenced by the actions of a firm?

LO2-2 4. How often should a company develop and refine the operations and supply chain strategy?

5. What is the term used to describe product attributes that attract certain customers and can be used to form the competitive position of a firm?

6. What are the two main competitive dimensions related to product delivery?

7. What are the two characteristics of a product or service that define quality?

LO2-3 8. What is the diagram that shows how a company's strategy is delivered by a set of supporting activities?

9. In implementing supply chain strategy, a firm must minimize its total cost without compromising the needs of what group of people?

LO2-4 10. What is defined as the likelihood of disruption that would impact the ability of a company to continuously supply products or services?

11. What are risks caused by natural or manmade disasters, which are impossible to reliably predict, called?

12. Match the following common risks with the appropriate mitigation strategy:

_____ Country risks	A. Detailed tracking, alternate suppliers
_____ Regulatory risk	B. Careful selection and monitoring of suppliers
_____ Logistics failure	C. Contingency planning, insurance
_____ Natural disaster	D. Good legal advice, compliance
_____ Major quality failure	E. Currency hedging, local sourcing

13. What is the term used to describe the assessment of the probability of a negative event against the aggregate severity of the related loss?

LO2-5 14. As operations manager, you are concerned about being able to meet sales requirements in the coming months. You have just been given the following production report:

	Jan	Feb	Mar	Apr
Units produced	2,300	1,800	2,800	3,000
Hours per machine	325	200	400	320
Number of machines	3	5	4	4

Find the average of the monthly productivity figures (units per machine hour).

*Special thanks to Bill Ruck of Arizona State University for the problems in this section.

15. Sailmaster makes high-performance sails for competitive windsurfers. The following is information about the inputs and outputs for one model, the Windy 2000. Calculate the productivity in sales revenue/labor expense.

Units sold	1,217
Sale price each	$1,700
Total labor hours	46,672
Wage rate	$12/hour
Total materials	$60,000
Total energy	$4,000

16. *Live Trap Corporation* received the following data for its rodent cage production unit. Find the total productivity.

Output	Input	
50,000 cages	Production time	620 labor hours
Sales price: $3.50 per unit	Wages	$7.50 per hour
	Raw materials (total cost)	$30,000
	Component parts (total cost)	$15,350

17. Two types of cars (Deluxe and Limited) were produced by a car manufacturer last year. Quantities sold, price per unit, and labor hours follow. What is the labor productivity for each car? Explain the problem(s) associated with the labor productivity. (Answer in Appendix D)

	Quantity	$/Unit
Deluxe car	4,000 units sold	$8,000/car
Limited car	6,000 units sold	$9,500/car
Labor, Deluxe	20,000 hours	$12/hour
Labor, Limited	30,000 hours	$14/hour

18. A U.S. manufacturing company operating a subsidiary in an LDC (less-developed country) shows the following results:

	U.S.	LDC
Sales (units)	100,000	20,000
Labor (hours)	20,000	15,000
Raw materials (currency)	$20,000 (US)	20,000 (FC)
Capital equipment (hours)	60,000	5,000

a. Calculate partial labor and capital productivity figures for the parent and subsidiary. Do the results seem confusing?

b. Compute the multifactor productivity figures for labor and capital together. Do the results make more sense?

c. Calculate raw material productivity figures (units/$ where $1 = 10 units of the foreign currency). Explain why these figures might be greater in the subsidiary.

19. Various financial data for the past two years follow. Calculate the total productivity measure and the partial measures for labor, capital, and raw materials for this company for both years. What do these measures tell you about this company?

		Last Year	This Year
Output:	Sales	$200,000	$220,000
Input:	Labor	30,000	40,000
	Raw materials	35,000	45,000
	Energy	5,000	6,000
	Capital	50,000	50,000
	Other	2,000	3,000

20. An electronics company makes communications devices for military contracts. The company just completed two contracts. The navy contract was for 2,300 devices and took 25 workers two weeks (40 hours per week) to complete. The army contract was for 5,500 devices that were produced by 35 workers in three weeks. On which contract were the workers more productive?

21. A retail store had sales of $45,000 in April and $56,000 in May. The store employs eight full-time workers who work a 40-hour week. In April, the store also had seven part-time workers at 10 hours per week, and in May the store had nine part-timers at 15 hours per week (assume four weeks in each month). Using sales dollars as the measure of output, what is the percentage change in productivity from April to May?

22. A parcel delivery company delivered 103,000 packages last year, when its average employment was 84 drivers. This year, the firm handled 112,000 deliveries with 96 drivers. What was the percentage change in productivity over the past two years?

23. A fast-food restaurant serves hamburgers, cheeseburgers, and chicken sandwiches. The restaurant counts a cheeseburger as equivalent to 1.25 hamburgers and chicken sandwiches as 0.8 hamburger. Current employment is five full-time employees who each work a 40-hour week. If the restaurant sold 700 hamburgers, 900 cheeseburgers, and 500 chicken sandwiches in one week, what is its productivity? What would its productivity have been if it had sold the same number of sandwiches (2,100), but the mix was 700 of each type?

CASE: Narayana Health—An Innovative Healthcare System in India

Dr Devi Shetty is an icon of modern entrepreneurship in healthcare of millions of poor Indians. He pioneered and championed an absolutely unheard model for treating India's poorest people, for whom money was always a constraining factor in healthcare. For example, an open heart surgery, which normally costs ₹2.50 lakhs with over ₹2,500 per month in post-operative care and medicines, common man lacks resources to manage this. Most of the similar heart speciality hospitals in India are beyond the reach of common people as they function in a corporate-style. This does not allow a poor patient to enter into their system. Dr Shetty's *Narayana Health* offers a welcome-note to these poor and yet it is a sustainable and an effective business model. Till 2013, Narayana Health (NH) was known as Narayana Hrudayalaya.

Narayana Health or Narayana Hrudayalaya (NH) is now one of the largest private hospitals in India. It performs more heart surgeries per year than the leading hospitals in the U.S., with matching quality and effectiveness. Dr Shetty has developed a scalable, low-cost model, in which those who can pay are paying for themselves but the hospital is able to treat patients who otherwise cannot afford such healthcare. Majority of other Indian corporate-type modern hospitals just do a lip service to these poor. NH group currently has about 5900 operational beds. It is spread across 23 hospitals, 7 heart-centres and a network of primary care facilities across India. It provides advanced healthcare in over 30 specialities, including cardiology and cardia surgery, cancer care, neurology and neuro-surgery, orthopaedics, etc. On an average, 343 daily surgeries or procedures are done. It has an ambitious plan to expand in the coming seven to ten years so as to become the largest healthcare player in the country.

Strategy of NH to Drive Development and Growth

NH has developed a four pronged strategy for development and growth. It is as follows:

1. *All Healthcare Needs Under One Roof:* NH has branded itself as a recognized and proven centre of excellence in cardiac and renal sciences. Despite the fact that only six core specialities contribute to about 89 percent to group's revenues, NH is committed to provide entire healthcare system under one roof. Its main revenue generating specializations are: Cardiac and Renal Sciences, Oncology, Neuro Sciences, Gastro and Intestinal Sciences, and Orthopaedics.
2. *Adopting Technology, Improving Lives:* NH is always keen to adapt disruptive technology for having excellence in the profession. Through technologies like satellite-based communication systems and many others, it has focused on becoming a true Pan-India healthcare provider.
3. *Leverage upon Operational Synergies:* Providing affordable healthcare is a key to all the planning within the NH system. NH has focused on its supply chain to manage cost. Economy of scale has worked in favor of its profitability.
4. *Tailor-made Engagement Framework*: NH maintains a healthcare ecosystem that is very inclusive in nature. It also ensures optimal utilization of resources.

Strategy of NH to become Cost Effective

Dr Shetty dreams to make cardiac surgery affordable to the poor and the children by creating a chain of heart hospitals in every state of India. The root of this dream lies in an initial generous funding by his father-in-law, who put just one condition to Dr Shetty. No poor and children would be turned away for the lack of money in NH. Developing NH as one of the best equipped hospitals of world was not very difficult for Dr Shetty. He got the best collaborators. Indian Space Research Organisation (ISRO) provided satellite services to link small local hospitals in the country with NH so that immediate advises for a heart attack patient may be sought by local hospitals from NH. During operation of an infant, anaesthetics in the U.S. can support the surgeons in operation theatre of NH. Telemedicine is now possible for people located in remote places too. Biocon has supported NH in offering new drugs, which are considerably cheaper than conventional ones. The attrition of doctors is almost zero. They work at a salary, which is almost half of what they could get elsewhere.

NH is not like a typical government hospital which lacks doctors and equipment. It now symbolizes the best-in-class healthcare delivery system. Therefore, when the rich people come here, they pay the normal charges as NH provides the best care. On the other hand, NH does not turn away the poor for the lack of money. NH Business model has some similarity with that of Wal-Mart. It takes advantage of volume in its favor. It conducts an average of 150 surgeries every day and treats an average of around 80,000 outpatients every month. It is much higher than other Indian hospitals of similar size. Dr Shetty himself provides consultation to almost two patients per five minutes. But, all of them are well examined and diagnosed by an expert support team before they meet Dr Shetty. A large number of pathological tests per day per machine brings down per unit cost due to economy of scale. Some of the expensive machines are on rent from the suppliers so as to save the immediate capital expenditure. However, these suppliers earn regularly by supplying reagents, needed to run the same machine, on use basis. Again, high volume helps in bringing down the rental cost. Lean staff further helps in bringing down cost and reducing corruption.

The initial investment, or capital cost, in a healthcare industry is quite high. It is up to ₹ one crore per bed for a high-end hospital. On the other hand, a typical 200 bed NH hospital has been built at a cost of ₹350 million with pre-fabricated materials, which means only ₹17.5 lakh per bed. To save cost, many non-value added costs have been cut. For example, in place of centralized air-conditioning (AC) for the entire hospital, AC is used at critical places like operation theatres, Intensive Care Units (ICUs), and a few patient recovery rooms[1,2].

Many State governments have understood and supported Dr Shetty's dream for heart care for the poor and the needy. For example, Karnataka State Government supports India's largest Micro Health Insurance Programme called Yeshaswini at a monthly premium of ₹10, to over three million farmers.

Dr Shetty feels lucky to have treated Mother Teresa. As narrated in an interview, Dr Shetty recalls that one day, Mother, who at that point of time was recovering in the intensive care unit of the hospital, saw Dr Shetty examining a blue baby. She told Shetty, "Now I know why you are here. To relieve the agony of children with heart disease, God sent you to this world to fix it". Of course, this must have been the touching moment for this paediatric cardiac surgeon and perhaps the best compliment any professional has ever received for the purpose of his being in the profession. No wonder, he keeps a wall-hanging of Mother Teresa in his office with the following word written below: "*Hands which help are better than the lips that pray*". He says, "When you do your work without expecting anything in return, just for the joy of bringing happiness to others, that's when you'll realize it is not your hands, which do the job, it is the hands of God".

Questions

1. Discuss the need and approaches towards low-cost health delivery in India.
2. How can we implement lean system in services like healthcare?
3. Discuss critical success factors for NH in India. Can these be replicated in other services?

References

1. http://www.daijiworld.com/chan/interviews_view.asp?i_id=34 (accessed on 21 April 2010)
2. http://www.businessworld.in/news/business/pharma/pulse-on-the-future/387829/page-1.html (accessed on 21 March 2014)
3. https://www.narayanahealth.org/about-us/ (accessed on 19 January 2018)
4. https://www.narayanahealth.org/stakeholder-relations/quaterly-report/Investor-Presentation-May-2017.pdf (accessed on 19 January 2018)
5. http://www.narayanahospitals.com/ (accessed on 21 April 2010)

PRACTICE EXAM

In each of the following statements, name the term defined or the items requested. Answers are listed at the bottom.

1. A strategy that is designed to meet current needs without compromising the ability of future generations to meet their needs.
2. The three criteria included in a triple bottom line.
3. The seven operations and supply chain competitive dimensions.
4. It is probably most difficult to compete on this major competitive dimension.
5. This occurs when a company seeks to match what a competitor is doing while maintaining its existing competitve position.

6. A criterion that differentiates the products or services of one firm from those of another.
7. A screening criterion that permits a firm's products to be considered as possible candidates for purchase.
8. A diagram showing the activities that support a company's strategy.
9. A measure calculated by taking the ratio of output to input.

Answers to Practice Exam 1. Sustainable 2. Social, economic, environmental 3. Cost, quality, delivery speed, delivery reliability, coping with changes in demand, flexibility and speed of new product introduction, other product-specific criteria 4. Cost 5. Straddling 6. Order winner 7. Order qualifier 8. Activity-system map 9. Productivity

For PowerPoint lecture slides, Solutions Manual, Test Bank, Data files for solved examples, Excel Templates, Step-by-Step Solved Examples in video format, Tutorial Videos and many more, scan the adjacent **QR code**, or **visit http://www.mhhe.com/sie-chase15e**

Chapter 3

Design of Products and Services

LEARNING OBJECTIVES

LO3-1 Know the issues associated with product design and the typical processes used by companies

LO3-2 Illustrate how different criteria can impact the design of a product

LO3-3 Contrast how service products can have different design criteria compared to manufactured products

LO3-4 Evaluate the economic impact of a new product on a company

LO3-5 Illustrate how product development is measured in a company

IDEO, A DESIGN AND INNOVATION FIRM

IDEO (pronounced "eye-dee-oh") is the world's most celebrated design and innovation consultancy. Its ultimate creation is the process of creativity itself. For co-founder David M. Kelley and his colleagues, work is play, brainstorming is a science, and the most important rule is to break the rules (www.ideo.com). The focus of the company is purely on the design of new products, services, and other interactive experiences desired by customers.

One of many collaborative design sessions in IDEO's Munich office.

Courtesy of IDEO

The scope of work done by the company ranges from projects related to Smart Mobility with Ford Motor Company to the development of digital healthcare apps that give people the ability to track their mood, sleep, and breathlessness. Rather than thinking of design as a linear process requiring a set of steps, IDEO sees the process as overlapping thought spaces. These spaces are referred to as follows:

- Inspiration—the problem or opportunity that motivates the need for a new design;
- Ideation—where model prototypes, visual pictures, or quantitative analysis is done to test ideas;
- Implementation—where ideas are made into new products and services.

Human desirability, business viability, and technical feasibility are the basic tenets of the IDEO design thinking process, and innovation requires the integration of these tenets. One of IDEO's early design projects was Apple Computer's first mouse, a striking and beautiful design that has endured the test of time.

Designing new products and getting them to market quickly is the challenge facing manufacturers in industries as diverse as computer chips and potato chips. Customers of computer chip manufacturers, such as computer companies, need ever-more-powerful semiconductors for their evolving product lines. Food producers need to provide their grocery store customers with new taste sensations to sustain or enlarge their retail market share. How manufactured products are designed and how the process to produce them is selected are the topics of this chapter.

PRODUCT DESIGN

LO 3-1

Know the issues associated with product design and typical processes used by companies

Companies continuously bring new products to market as customer needs and wants change. Product design is integral to the success of many companies and differs significantly depending on the industry. For consumer products, understanding consumer preferences and market testing prospective products are very important activities. For pharmaceuticals, extensive clinical tests are often required that involve carefully controlled experiments to test both the safety and the effectiveness of a potential product. Companies that specialize in the design of products have highly developed processes to support the activities needed for an industry.

In today's world, companies often outsource major functions (such as product design) rather than support these functions in-house. Companies that specialize in designing and manufacturing products for other companies have become very successful. The producing companies are called **contract manufacturers**, and they have become successful in industries such as electronic products, clothing, drugs, plastics, and custom manufacturing. A simple definition of a contract manufacturer is an organization that performs manufacturing and/or purchasing needed to produce a product or device not for itself, but as a service to another firm.

Contract manufacturer
An organization that performs manufacturing and/or purchasing needed to produce a product or device not for itself, but as a service to another firm.

The use of contract manufacturers has dramatically changed the way traditional manufacturing companies now operate. Depending on the situation, contract manufacturers will take various roles for a company. For example, in the automobile industry, contract manufacturers produce many of the parts and subassemblies, such as the seats and other interior parts, the headlight and taillight assemblies, and the electronic equipment such as radio/CD and GPS navigation systems. The actual automobiles are often built regionally in the countries where the products will be sold to reduce transportation cost and manage currency exchange risk. Close coordination is required to manage the network of assembly plants and contract manufacturing partners for success.

Given the potential advantages of using contract manufacturers for producing products and employing specialized design firms for designing their products, a firm must decide what its core competency should be. A company's **core competency** is the one thing that it can do better than its competitors. A core competency can be anything from product design to sustained dedication of a firm's employees. The goal is to have a core competency that yields a long-term competitive advantage to the company.

Core competency
The one thing that a firm can do better than its competitors. The goal is to have a core competency that yields a long-term competitive advantage to the company.

As an example, consider Honda's expertise in engines. Honda has been able to exploit this core competency to develop a variety of quality products, from lawn mowers and snow blowers to trucks and automobiles. To take another example from the automotive industry, it has been claimed that Volvo's core competency is safety.

A core competency has three characteristics:

1. It provides potential access to a wide variety of markets.
2. It increases perceived customer benefits.
3. It is hard for competitors to imitate.

A good example is Black & Decker, the U.S. manufacturer of tools. Black & Decker's core technological competency is in 200- to 600-watt electric motors. All of its products are modifications of this basic technology (with the exception of workbenches, flashlights, battery-charging systems, toaster ovens, and coffee percolators). The company produces products for three markets:

1. **The home workshop market.** In the home workshop market, small electric motors are used to produce drills, circular saws, sanders, routers, rotary tools, polishers, and drivers.

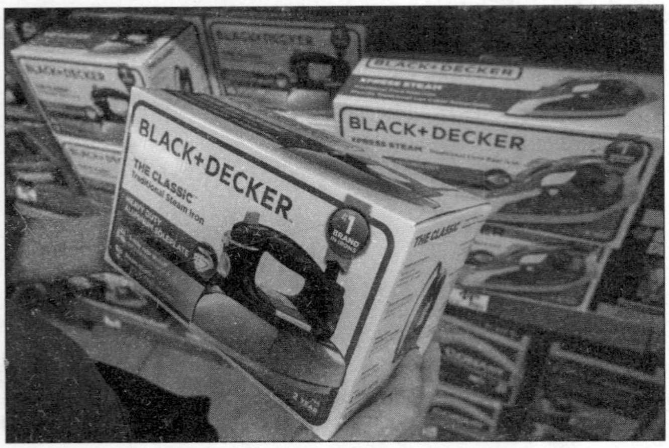

2. **The home cleaning and maintenance market.** In the home cleaning and maintenance market, small electric motors are used to produce handheld and full-size vacuum cleaners, hedge trimmers, edge trimmers, lawn mowers, leaf blowers, and pressure sprayers.
3. **The kitchen appliance market.** In the kitchen appliance market, small electric motors are used to produce can openers, food processors, blenders, breadmakers, and fans.

The real challenge for a firm is to decide exactly how the various functions critical to success will be handled. At one extreme is the fully vertically integrated firm where all activities from the design to the fabrication of the individual parts are handled in-house. At the other extreme is a company that only sells products and outsources all the design and manufacturing functions.

The following are a few examples of what some highly successful companies are doing:

Strategy

- Apple Computer designs the iPhone but subcontracts the fabrication of these devices (while maintaining ownership of the intellectual property).
- Tesla Motors has developed an all electric car that has a range of 265 miles, the range of a typical gasoline powered car. In the past, electric cars were considered a big fire risk due to their large batteries. So Tesla developed small cylindrical batteries that are distributed to reduce the risk of fire. In addition, the new Tesla's supercharging technology reduces the time required to recharge the battery to the point where soon it may take no longer to recharge a Tesla that it takes to fill the gasoline tank in a regular car. Tesla's network of charging stations along major highways makes their cars practical for longer road trips. The company's new innovations related to self-driving technology may totally change the way we think about automobile transportation in the future.
- A pharmaceutical company may purchase information on genetic targets from a genomics company, contract with a specialist in combinatorial chemistry for rapid synthesis and screening of candidate compounds, and even utilize a contract research organization to conduct clinical trials but retain ownership of the intellectual property (patents, experimental data, trademarks, etc.) of the drug that eventually comes to market.

Product Development Process

Process

We begin by defining a generic product development process that describes the basic steps needed to design a product. This process represents the basic sequence of steps or activities that a firm employs to conceive, design, and bring a product to market. Many of these tasks involve intellectual rather than physical activities. Some firms define and follow a precise and detailed development process, while others may not even be able to describe their processes. Every organization employs a process that is different from that of every other organization; in fact, the same organization may follow different processes for different product groups.

Our generic product development process consists of six phases, as illustrated in Exhibit 3.1. The process begins with a planning phase, which is the link to advanced research and technology development activities. The output of the planning phase is the project's mission statement, which is the input required to begin the concept development phase and serves as a guide to the development team. The conclusion of the product development process is the product launch, at which time the product becomes available for purchase in the marketplace. Exhibit 3.1 identifies the key activities and responsibilities of the different functions of the firm during each development phase. Because of their continuous involvement in the process, we articulate the roles of marketing, design, and manufacturing. Representatives from other functions, such as research, finance, field service, and sales, also play key roles at points in the process.

Exhibit 3.1

The Generic Product Development Process. Six phases are shown, including the tasks and responsibilities of the key functions of the organization for each phase.

Phase 0: Planning	Phase 1: Concept Development	Phase 2: System-Level Design	Phase 3: Detail Design	Phase 4: Testing and Refinement	Phase 5: Production Ramp-Up
Marketing					
• Articulate market opportunity. • Define market segments.	• Collect customer needs. • Identify lead users. • Identify competitive products.	• Develop plan for product options and extended product family. • Set target sales price point(s).	• Develop marketing plan.	• Develop promotion and launch materials. • Facilitate field testing.	• Place early production with key customers.
Design					
• Consider product platform and architecture. • Assess new technologies.	• Investigate feasibility of product concepts. • Develop industrial design concepts. • Build and test experimental prototypes.	• Generate alternative product architectures. • Define major subsystems and interfaces. • Refine industrial design.	• Define part geometry. • Choose materials. • Assign tolerances. • Complete industrial design control documentation.	• Test performance, life, and reliability. • Obtain regulatory approvals. • Implement design changes.	• Evaluate early production output.
Manufacturing					
• Identify production constraints. • Set supply chain strategy.	• Estimate manufacturing cost. • Assess production feasibility.	• Identify suppliers for key components. • Perform make–buy analysis. • Define final assembly scheme. • Set target costs.	• Define piece-part production processes. • Design tooling. • Define quality assurance processes. • Begin procurement of long-lead tooling.	• Facilitate supplier ramp-up. • Refine fabrication and assembly processes. • Train workforce. • Refine quality assurance processes.	• Begin operation of entire production system.
Other Functions					
• Research: Demonstrate available technologies. • Finance: Provide planning goals. • General Management: Allocate project resources.	• Finance: Facilitate economic analysis. • Legal: Investigate patent issues.	• Finance: Facilitate make–buy analysis. • Service: Identify service issues.		• Sales: Develop sales plan.	

The six phases of the generic development process are the following:

Process

Phase 0: Planning. The planning activity is often referred to as "phase zero" because it precedes the project approval and launch of the actual product development process. This phase begins with corporate strategy and includes assessment of technology developments and market objectives. The output of the planning phase is the project mission statement, which specifies the target market for the product, business goals, key assumptions, and constraints.

Phase 1: Concept development. In this phase, the needs of the target market are identified, alternative product concepts are generated and evaluated, and one or more concepts are selected for further development and testing. A concept is a description of the form, function, and features of a product and is usually accompanied by a set of specifications, an analysis of competitive products, and an economic justification of the project.

Phase 2: System-level design. The system-level design phase includes the definition of the product architecture and the decomposition of the product into subsystems and components. The final assembly scheme (which we discuss later in the chapter) for the production system is usually defined during this phase as well. The output of this phase usually includes a geometric layout of the product, a functional specification of each of the product's subsystems, and a preliminary process flow diagram for the final assembly process.

Phase 3: Detail design. This phase includes the complete specification of the geometry, materials, and tolerances of all the unique parts in the product and the identification of all the standard parts to be purchased from suppliers. A process plan is established, and tooling is designed for each part to be fabricated within the production system. The output of this phase is the drawings or computer files describing the geometry of each part and its production tooling, the specifications of purchased parts, and the process plans for the fabrication and assembly of the product.

Key Idea

Executing this development process within a firm is often organized using project management techniques. These techniques are described in the next chapter.

Phase 4: Testing and refinement. The testing and refinement phase involves the construction and evaluation of multiple preproduction versions of the product. Early prototypes are usually built with parts with the same geometry and material properties as the production version of the product but not necessarily fabricated with the actual processes to be used in production. Prototypes are tested to determine whether the product will work as designed and whether the product satisfies customer needs.

Phase 5: Production ramp-up. In the production ramp-up phase, the product is made using the intended production system. The purpose of the ramp-up is to train the workforce and to work out any remaining problems in the production processes. Products produced during production ramp-up are sometimes supplied to preferred customers and are carefully evaluated to identify any remaining flaws. The transition from production ramp-up to ongoing production is usually gradual. At some point in the transition, the product is *launched* and becomes available for widespread distribution.

The development process described in Exhibit 3.1 is generic, and particular processes will differ in accordance with a firm's unique context. The generic process is most like the process used in a *market-pull* situation. This is when a firm begins product development with a market opportunity and then uses whatever available technologies are required to satisfy the market need (i.e., the market "pulls" the development decisions). In addition to the generic market-pull processes, several variants are common and correspond to the following: *technology-push* products, *platform* products, *process-intensive* products, *customized* products, *high-risk* products, *quick-build* products, and *complex systems.* Each of these situations is described below. The characteristics of these situations and the resulting deviations from the generic process are summarized in Exhibit 3.2.

Technology-Push Products In developing technology-push products, a firm begins with a new proprietary technology and looks for an appropriate market in which to apply this technology (that is, the technology "pushes" development). Gore-Tex, an expanded Teflon sheet manufactured by W. L. Gore & Associates, is a good example of technology push. The company has developed dozens of products incorporating Gore-Tex, including artificial veins for vascular surgery, insulation for high-performance electric cables, fabric for outerwear, dental floss, and liners for bagpipe bags.

Platform Products A platform product is built around a preexisting technological subsystem (a technology *platform*). Examples include the hybrid motor used in the Toyota Prius (as shown in the photo to the right), the Apple iOS operating system, and the video imaging system used in Canon cameras. Huge investments were made in developing these platforms, and therefore every attempt is made to incorporate them into several different products. In some sense, platform products are very similar to technology-push products in that the team begins the development effort with an assumption that the product concept will embody a particular technology. The primary difference is that a technology platform has already demonstrated its usefulness in the marketplace in meeting customer needs. The firm, in many cases, can assume that the technology also will be useful in related markets. Products built on technology platforms are much simpler to develop than if the technology

EXHIBIT 3.2

Summary of Variants of Generic Product Development Process

Process Type	Description	Distinct Features	Examples
Generic (market-pull products)	The team begins with a market opportunity and selects appropriate technologies to meet customer needs	Process generally includes distinct planning, concept development, system-level design, detail design, testing and refinement, and production ramp-up phases	Sporting goods, furniture, tools
Technology-push products	The team begins with a new technology, then finds an appropriate market	Planning phase involves matching technology and market; concept development assumes a given technology	Gore-Tex rainwear, Tyvek envelopes
Platform products	The team assumes that the new product will be built around an established technological subsystem	Concept development assumes a proven technology platform	Consumer electronics, computers, printers
Process-intensive products	Characteristics of the product are highly constrained by the production process	Either an existing production process must be specified from the start or both product and process must be developed together from the start	Snack foods, breakfast cereals, chemicals, semiconductors
Customized products	New products are slight variations of existing configurations	Similarity of projects allows for a streamlined and highly structured development process	Motors, switches, batteries, containers
High-risk products	Technical or market uncertainties create high risks of failure	Risks are identified early and tracked throughout the process; analysis and testing activities take place as early as possible	Pharmaceuticals, space systems
Quick-build products	Rapid modeling and prototyping enables many design-build-test cycles	Detail design and testing phases are repeated a number of times until the product is completed or time/budget runs out	Software, cellular phones
Complex systems	System must be decomposed into several subsystems and many components	Subsystems and components are developed by many teams working in parallel, followed by system integration and validation	Airplanes, jet engines, automobiles

were developed from scratch. For this reason, and because of the possible sharing of costs across several products, a firm may be able to offer a platform product in markets that could not justify the development of a unique technology.

Key Idea

The product development process needs to be adapted depending on market and product characteristics.

Process-Intensive Products Examples of process-intensive products include semiconductors, foods, chemicals, and paper. For these products, the production process has an impact on properties of the product so that product design cannot be separated from the production process design. In many cases, process-intensive products are produced at very high volumes and are bulk, rather than discrete, goods. Often, the new product and new process are developed simultaneously. For example, creating a new shape of breakfast cereal or snack food requires both product and process development activities. In other cases, the existing process will constrain the product design by the capabilities of the process. This

might be true of a new paper product to be made in a particular paper mill or a new semiconductor device to be made in an existing wafer fabrication facility, for example.

Customized Products Customized products are slight variations of standard configurations and are typically developed in response to a specific order by a customer. Examples include switches, motors, batteries, and containers. Developing these products consists primarily of setting values of design variables such as physical dimensions and materials. Companies can become very good at quickly producing these custom products using a highly structured design and development process structured around the capabilities of the process to be used.

High-Risk Products High-risk products are those that entail unusually large uncertainties related to the technology or market so that there is substantial technical or market risk. The generic product development process is modified to face high-risk situations by taking steps to address the largest risks in the early stages of product development. This usually requires completing some design and test activities earlier in the process. For example, if there is high uncertainty related to the technical performance of the product, it makes sense to build working models of the key features and to test these earlier in the process. Multiple solution paths may be explored in parallel to ensure that one of the solutions succeeds. Design reviews must assess levels of risk on a regular basis, with the expectation that risk is being reduced over time and not postponed.

Quick-Build Products For the development of some products, such as software and many electronic products, building and testing prototype models has become such a rapid process that the design-build-test cycle can be repeated many times. Following concept development in this process, the system-level design phase entails decomposition of the product into high-, medium-, and low-priority features. This is followed by several cycles of design, build, integrate, and test activities, beginning with the highest-priority items. This process takes advantage of the fast prototyping cycle by using the result of each cycle to learn how to modify the priorities for the next cycle. Customers may even be involved in the testing process. When time or budget runs out, usually all of the high- and medium-priority features have been incorporated into the evolving product, and the low-priority features may be omitted until the next product generation.

Complex Systems Larger-scale products such as automobiles and airplanes are complex systems composed of many interacting subsystems and components. When developing complex systems, modifications to the generic product development process address a number of system-level issues. The concept development phase considers the architecture of the entire system, and multiple architectures may be considered as competing concepts for the overall system. The system-level design becomes critical. During this phase, the system is decomposed into subsystems, and these are decomposed further into many components. Teams are assigned to develop each component. Additional teams are assigned

OSCM AT WORK

Google Virtual Reality Cardboard

The Google Cardboard is a simple cardboard viewer that is used with your smartphone so you can experience virtual reality. The simple $20 product was bought by over 5 million people in less than a year. You can virtually travel to locations all over the world, even totally imaginary places. Special Cardboard apps like *Chair In A Room, Vrse, Lamper VR: Firefly Rescue, Caaaaardboard!,* and *Proton Pulse* allow you to better understand science and nature by putting you in the center of the action. The gadget is the winner of many design innovation awards.

the special challenge of integrating components into the subsystems, and then integrating these into the overall system. Detail design of the components is a highly parallel process, often referred to as **concurrent engineering**, with many separate development teams working at once. System engineering specialists manage the interactions across the components and subsystems. The testing and refinement phase includes not only system integration but extensive testing and validation of the product.

Concurrent engineering
Emphasizes cross-functional integration and concurrent development of a product and its associated processes.

PRODUCT DESIGN CRITERIA

LO 3-2

Illustrate how different criteria can impact the design of a product

In this section, we illustrate how different criteria can impact the design of a product. The most fundamental criteria are those that relate directly to what the customer wants. Matching a product's design with the desire of the target customer group is essential from a marketing view. Value is another criterion that we address in this section. This criterion involves designing the product so that it can be produced at a low cost while maintaining those features desired by the customer. Next, criteria related to the manufacturability of the product are essential to having a low-cost manufacturing process. Finally, we address the environmental impact of a product and how this relates to product design.

Designing for the Customer

Before we detail the hows and whys of designing and producing products, it is useful to reflect (or, perhaps more accurately, to editorialize) on the issue of product design from the user's standpoint. In recent years, companies have been so caught up with technological efforts and advances—especially in the field of electronics—that somewhere along the line, consumers were forgotten. Designing for aesthetics and for the user is generally termed *industrial design.* IDEO is one of the most successful industrial design firms in the world. The unique concepts used at the company are described in the chapter's opening vignette titled "IDEO, A Design and Innovation Firm."

Quality Function Deployment One approach to getting the voice of the customer into the design specification of a product is **quality function deployment (QFD)**. This approach, which uses interfunctional teams from marketing, design engineering, and manufacturing, has been credited by Toyota Motor Corporation for reducing costs on its cars by more than 60 percent by significantly shortening design times.

Quality function deployment (QFD)
A process that helps a company determine the product characteristics important to the consumer and to evaluate its own product in relation to others.

The QFD process begins with studying and listening to customers to determine the characteristics of a superior product. Through market research, the consumers' product needs and preferences are defined and broken down into categories called *customer requirements*. One example is an auto

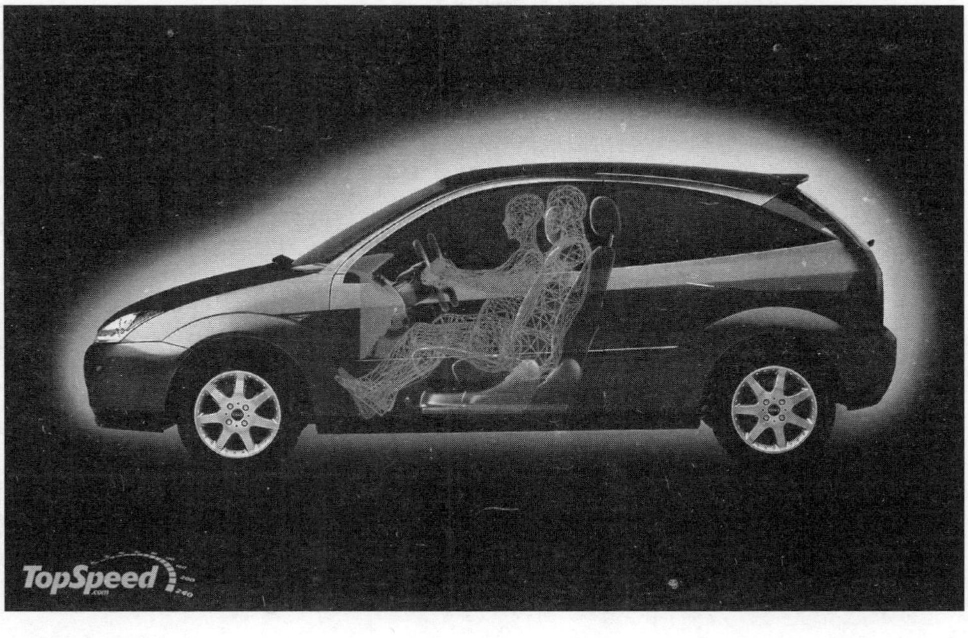

QFD involves converting the expectations and demands of customers into clear objectives, which are then translated into vehicle specifications. For example, TopSpeed found that passengers became uncomfortable if the car rolled more than two degrees and side acceleration exceeded 13.2 feet per second squared. These data were used to help define design criteria for the chassis engineers.

Courtesy of Topspeed.com/ Ford Images

manufacturer that would like to improve the design of a car door. Through customer surveys and interviews, it determines that two important customer requirements in a car door are that it "stays open on a hill" and is "easy to close from the outside." After the customer requirements are defined, they are weighted based on their relative importance to the customer. Next, the consumer is asked to compare and rate the company's products with the products of competitors. This process helps the company determine the product characteristics that are important to the consumer and to evaluate its product in relation to others. The end result is a better understanding and focus on product characteristics that require improvement.

House of quality
A matrix that helps a product design team translate customer requirements into operating and engineering goals.

Customer requirement information forms the basis for a matrix called the **house of quality** (see Exhibit 3.3). By building a house of quality matrix, the cross-functional QFD team can use customer feedback to make engineering, marketing, and design decisions. The matrix helps the team translate customer requirements into concrete operating or engineering goals. The important product characteristics and goals for improvement are jointly agreed on and detailed in the house. This process encourages the different departments to work closely together, and it results in a better understanding of one another's goals and issues. However, the most important benefit of the house of quality is that it helps the team focus on building a product that satisfies customers.

EXHIBIT 3.3

Completed House of Quality Matrix for a Car Door

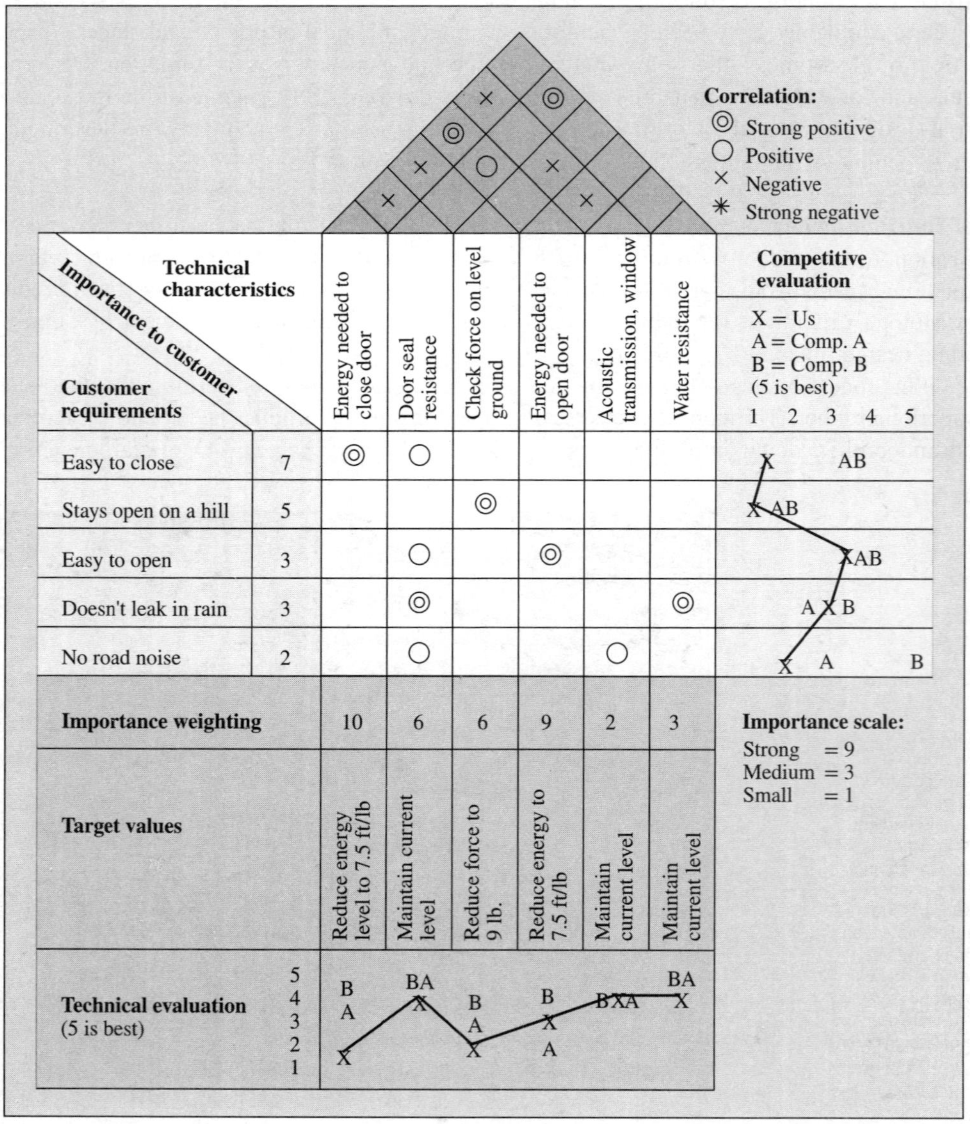

The first step in building the house of quality is to develop a list of customer requirements for the product. These requirements should be ranked in order of importance. Customers are then asked to compare the company's product to the competition. Next, a set of technical characteristics of the product is developed. These technical characteristics should relate directly to customer requirements. An evaluation of these characteristics should support or refute customer perception of the product. These data are then used to evaluate the strengths and weaknesses of the product in terms of technical characteristics.

Value Analysis/Value Engineering

Another way to consider customers in designing products is by analyzing the "value" they see in the end product. Because it is so important that value be designed into products, we briefly describe value analysis and value engineering. The purpose of **value analysis/value engineering (VA/VE)** is to simplify products and processes. Its objective is to achieve equivalent or better performance at a lower cost while maintaining all functional requirements defined by the customer. VA/VE does this by identifying and eliminating unnecessary cost. Technically, VA deals with products already in production and is used to analyze product specifications and requirements as shown in production documents and purchase requests. Typically, purchasing departments use VA as a cost reduction technique. Performed before the production stage, value engineering is considered a cost-avoidance method. In practice, however, there is a looping back and forth between the two for a given product. This occurs because new materials, processes, and so forth require the application of VA techniques to products that have previously undergone VE. The VA/VE analysis approach involves brainstorming such questions as:

Value analysis/ value engineering (VA/VE)
Analysis with the purpose of simplifying products and processes by achieving equivalent or better performance at a lower cost.

- Does the item have any design features that are not necessary?
- Can two or more parts be combined into one?
- How can we cut down the weight?
- Can any nonstandard parts be eliminated?

Majority of auto manufacturing companies in India have used VA/VE approach and got significant support from their vendors. For example, Minda is a supplier of lighting, horns, etc. to many OEMs like Maruti. It has used VA/VE approach to reduce cost and improve functionality of its products, which in turn has improved the bottom line of both the supply chain partners.

In the following section, we describe a more formal approach that is often used to guide the process of designing and improving the design of products.

Key Idea
QFD and VA/VE are intended to ensure that what the customer wants is considered in the design of a product.

Designing Products for Manufacture and Assembly

The word *design* has many different meanings. To some, it means the aesthetic design of a product, such as the external shape of a car or the color, texture, and shape of the casing of a can opener. In another sense, design can mean establishing the basic parameters of a system. For example, before considering any details, the design of a power plant might mean establishing the characteristics of the various units such as generators, pumps, boilers, connecting pipes, and so forth.

Yet another interpretation of the word *design* is the detailing of the materials, shapes, and tolerance of the individual parts of a product. This is the concern of this section. It is an activity that starts with sketches of parts and assemblies and then progresses to the computer-aided design (CAD) workstation (described in Appendix B on Operations Technology), where assembly drawings and detailed part drawings are produced. Traditionally, these drawings are then passed to the manufacturing and assembly engineers, whose job it is to optimize the processes used to produce the final product. Frequently, at this stage manufacturing and assembly problems are encountered and requests are made for design changes. Often, these design changes are major and result in considerable additional expense and delays in the final product release.

Traditionally, the attitude of designers has been "We design it; you build it." This has now been termed the "over-the-wall approach," where the designer is sitting on one side of the wall and throwing the design over the wall to the manufacturing engineers. These manufacturing engineers then have

CAD designer working at computer monitors in office.

to deal with the problems that arise because they were not involved in the design effort. One way to overcome this problem is to consult the manufacturing engineers during the design stage. The resulting teamwork avoids many of the problems that will arise. These concurrent engineering teams require analysis tools to help them study proposed designs and evaluate them from the point of view of manufacturing difficulty and cost.

How Does Design for Manufacturing and Assembly (DFMA) Work? Let's follow an example from the conceptual design stage. Exhibit 3.4 represents a motor drive assembly that is required to sense and control its position on two steel guide rails. This might be the motor that controls a power window in a drive-through window at McDonald's, for example. The motor must be fully enclosed and have a removable cover for access to adjust the position sensor. A major requirement is a rigid base designed to slide up and down the guide rails, which will both support the motor and locate the sensor. The motor and sensor have wires connecting to a power supply and control unit.

Key Idea

DFMA is oriented toward the engineering of the product with an emphasis on reducing production cost.

Exhibit 3.4

Configuration of Required Motor Drive Assembly

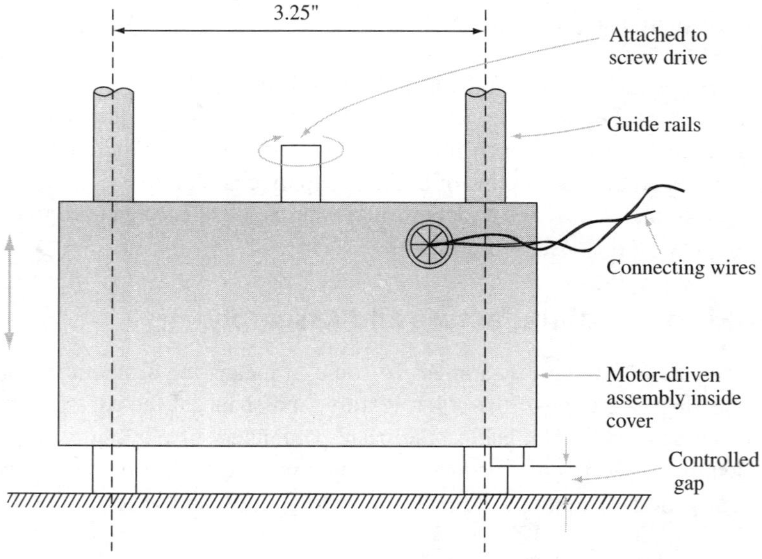

A proposed solution is shown in Exhibit 3.5. The base has two bushing inserts so that the holes will not wear out. The motor is secured to the base with two screws, and a hole accepts the cylindrical sensor, which is held in place with a set screw. To provide the required covers, an end plate is screwed to two stand-offs, which are screwed into the base. To keep the wires from shorting out on the metal cover, should they become worn, a plastic bushing is fitted to the end plate, through which the wires pass. Finally, a box-shaped cover slides over the whole assembly from below the base and is held in place by four screws, two passing into the base and two passing into the end cover.

The current design has 19 parts that must be assembled to make the motor drive. These parts consist of the two subassemblies—the motor and the sensor—an additional eight main parts (cover, base, two bushings, two stand-offs, a plastic bushing, and the end plate), and nine screws.

EXHIBIT 3.5

Proposed Motor Drive Design

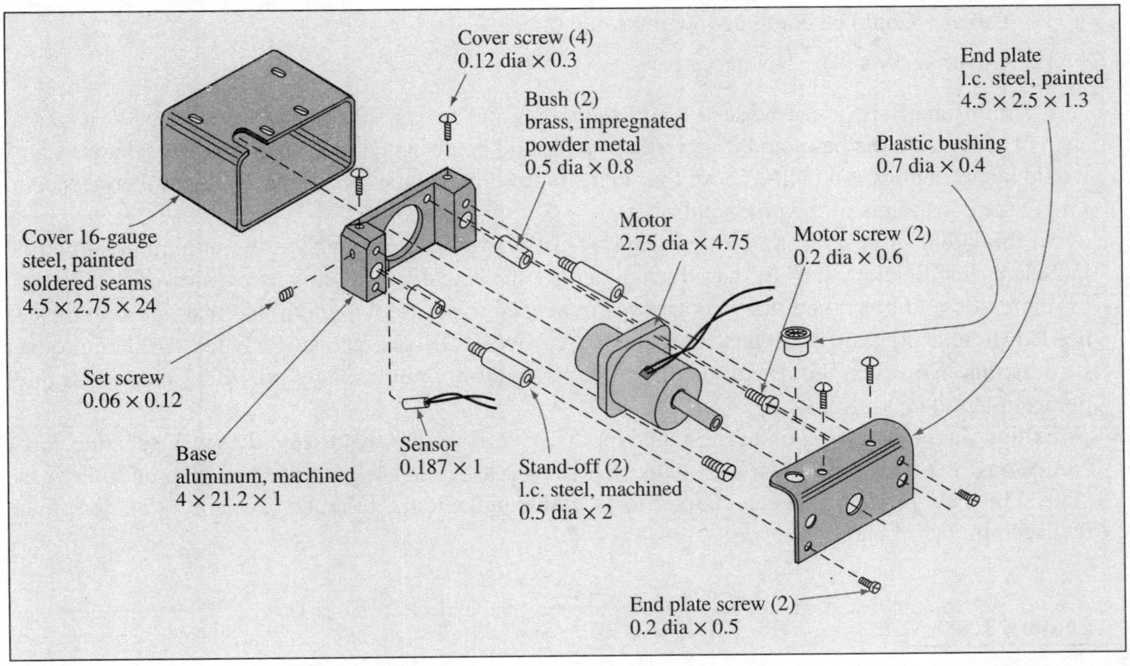

The greatest improvements related to DFMA arise from simplification of the product by reducing the number of separate parts. In order to guide the designer in reducing the part count, the methodology provides three criteria against which each part must be examined as it is added to the product during assembly:

1. During the operation of the product, does the part move relative to all other parts already assembled?
2. Must the part be of a different material than, or be isolated from, other parts already assembled?
3. Must the part be separate from all other parts to allow the disassembly of the product for adjustment or maintenance?

Application of these criteria to the proposed design would proceed as follows:

1. **Base.** Because this is the first part to be assembled, there are no other parts with which to combine, so it is theoretically a necessary part.
2. **Bushings (2).** These do not satisfy the second criterion. Theoretically, the base and bushings could be of the same material.
3. **Motor.** The motor is a subassembly purchased from a supplier. The criteria do not apply.
4. **Motor screws (2).** In most cases, separate fasteners are not needed, because a fastening arrangement integral to the design (for example, snapping the part into place) is usually possible.
5. **Sensor.** This is another standard subassembly.
6. **Set screw.** Similar to 4, this should not be necessary.
7. **Standoffs (2).** These do not meet the second criterion; they could be incorporated into the base.

8. **End plate.** This must be separate to allow disassembly (apply criterion three).
9. **End plate screws (2).** These should not be necessary.
10. **Plastic bushing.** Could be of the same material as, and therefore combined with, the end plate.
11. **Cover.** Could be combined with the end plate.
12. **Cover screws (4).** Not necessary.

From this analysis, it can be seen that if the motor and sensor subassemblies could be arranged to snap or screw into the base, and if a plastic cover could be designed to snap on, only 4 separate items would be needed instead of 19. These four items represent the theoretical minimum number needed to satisfy the constraints of the product design.

At this point, it is up to the design team to justify why the parts above the minimum should be included. Justification may be based on practical, technical, or economic considerations. In this example, it could be argued that two screws are needed to secure the motor and that one set screw is needed to hold the sensor, because any alternatives would be impractical for a low-volume product such as this. However, the design of these screws could be improved by providing them with pilot points to facilitate assembly.

Exhibit 3.6 is a drawing of a redesigned motor drive assembly that uses only seven separate parts. Notice how the parts have been eliminated. The new plastic cover is designed to snap on to the base plate. This new product is much simpler to assemble and should be much less expensive due to the reduced number of parts.

EXHIBIT 3.6

Redesign of Motor Drive Assembly Following Design for Assembly (DFA) Analysis

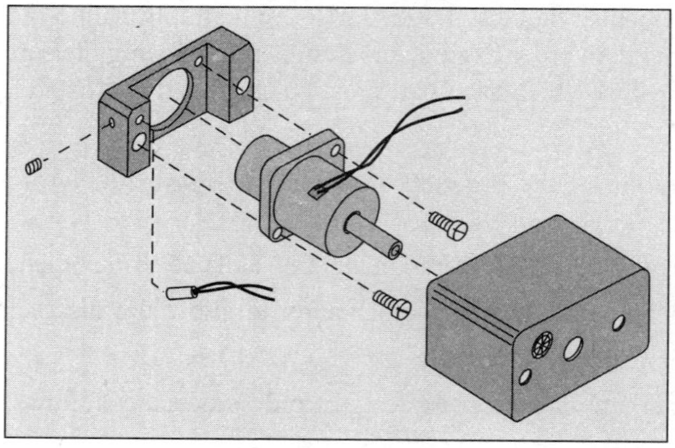

Ecodesign
The incorporation of environmental considerations into the design and development of products or services. These concerns relate to the entire life cycle, including materials, manufacturing, distribution, and the eventual disposal of waste.

Ecodesign **Ecodesign** is the incorporation of environmental considerations in the design and development of products or services. Ecodesign is an extension of the other important requirements considered in the design process such as quality, costs, manufacturability, functionality, durability, ergonomics, and aesthetics. As a result, ecodesigned products are innovative, have better environmental performance, and are of a quality at least equal to the market standard. This makes the use of ecodesign increasingly important for business and leads to clear advantages for those companies incorporating ecodesign. Ecodesign adopts an integrated approach to the relationship between products and services and the environment on three levels:

- The whole life cycle of the product or service is considered. The environmental impacts of a product arise not only during its manufacturing and use or when it has become waste, but throughout its entire life cycle. It includes the extraction and transport of resources needed to manufacture the product, the manufacturing processes, distribution, use and maintenance, reuse, and the treatment of its waste.

- The product is considered as a system. All the elements needed to develop the product's function (consumables, packaging, energy networks) must also be taken into account.
- A multicriteria approach is considered. All different environmental impacts that can be generated by a product system along its life cycle are assessed in order to avoid trade-offs between different impact categories (for example, resource depletion, greenhouse effect, and toxicity).

BioBag biodegradable and compostable plastic bags on a roll are used for carrying produce at Garment District. Text on the bag says "This Bag Is Certified Compostable. Use, Reuse, Then Compost."

The application of ecodesign can benefit business, users, and society at the same time because it responds to the common interest of obtaining more efficient products in an economic as well as environmental dimension. The producer manufactures a product using fewer materials; using less water, energy, and so on; and generating less waste to be managed. Consequently, the manufacturing costs are reduced. The user buys a more reliable and durable product that will need less energy or consumables to function and can be easily repaired when necessary. Society will benefit by increasing the future availability of resources for other products or services and by preventing possible environmental damage, thereby saving any corresponding treatment or remediation costs.

In addition, European regulations recognize and emphasize producers' responsibility in minimizing the environmental impacts of their products and services. Ecodesign can help producers to manage that responsibility and comply with product-related legislation.

DESIGNING SERVICE PRODUCTS

LO 3-3

Contrast how service products can have different design criteria compared to manufactured products

As we saw in the last section, the detailed design of manufactured products is focused on reducing the number of parts in the item and designing the item in such a way that it can be efficiently produced. Service products are very different because direct customer involvement in the process introduces significant variability in the process in terms of both the time that it takes to serve a customer and the level of knowledge required of the firm's employees. Questions that should be addressed in the design of a service include: How will this variability be addressed? *and* What are the implications for operational cost and the customer service experience?

Guests have their pictures taken with Mickey Mouse

An important issue when developing a new service or changing an existing one is the question of how different the new service is compared to the current services offered by the firm. Here are three general factors to consider when determining this:

Process

1. **Similarity to current services.** This means that the new service should fit into the current service experience for the customer. For example, Disneyland has started positioning employees with cameras around the park at memorable locations offering to take pictures of visitors that can be viewed online later. As a part of the greater service experience of making dreams come true and recording them, this has a good service experience fit. However, some services, like a car wash with a restaurant in the waiting area, are less complementary.

2. **Similarity to current processes.** Even the greatest service ideas require operational support to execute. One example of this is when grocery stores decided to offer home delivery. Even though this seemed like a logical extension of the service experience, it required completely new operational skills, such as selecting perishables for customers and delivering frozen foods.
3. **Financial justification.** Designing and implementing a new service is costly and should be financially justified. Although this is often thought of in a positive sense of making a profit, it can just as well be introducing a new service in order to keep from losing valued customers.

Complexity and Divergence A useful way of analyzing the process similarity for new service development is by specifying the *complexity* and *divergence* of the proposed service process relative to the basic service process. Complexity is the number of steps involved in a service and the possible actions that can be taken at each step. Divergence is the number of ways a customer/service provider interaction can vary at each step according to the needs and abilities of each. The result may be a combination of higher complexity/divergence on some steps and lower complexity/divergence on others. This can be used to determine different resource requirements such as worker skills, layout, and process controls. For example, the hypothetical family restaurant considered in Exhibit 3.7 is considering whether to change the service to create a new process format. Relative to the current process, a minimum service format would have lower complexity/divergence, while an upscale format would have higher complexity/divergence.

EXHIBIT 3.7

Process Alternatives for a Family Restaurant

Process Name	Lower Complexity / Divergence	Current Process	Higher Complexity / Divergence
Reservations	No reservations	Take reservation	Specific table selection
Seating	Guests seat themselves	Host shows guests the table	Maitre d escorts guests to seats, pulls out chairs, and places napkins in their laps
Menus	No menu	Menus on the table	Recite menu; describe entrees and specials
Bread	No bread offered at the table	Serve bread and butter	Assortment of hot breads and hors d'oeuvres
Ordering	Guests select their food from buffet line	Take orders	At table; taken personally by maitre d
Salads	Salad bar	Prepare orders	Individually prepared at table
Entrees	Entrees offered on the buffet	Entree (15 choices)	Expand to 20 choices; add flaming or sizzling dishes, deboning fish at the table
Desserts	Dessert bar	Dessert (6 choices)	Expand to 12 choices
Beverages	Guests get their drinks from the drink station	Beverage (6 choices)	Add exotic coffees, wine list, liqueurs
Service during the meal	No service	Serve orders	Separate-course service; hand-grind pepper
Payment	Paid at entry to buffet	Collect payment	Choice of payment, including house accounts
Table clearing	Guests are asked to clear the table themselves	Table attendant clears table at the end	Table attendant clears table throughout the meal

LO 3-4

Evaluate the economic impact of a new product on a company

ECONOMIC ANALYSIS OF PRODUCT DEVELOPMENT PROJECTS

Consider the case of a product development team in the midst of developing a new photograph printer, the CI-700. The CI-700 would produce large-scale, full-color pictures from digital images. The primary markets for the product are the graphic arts, insurance, and real estate industries. During the CI-700's development, the team faces several decisions that it knows could have a significant impact on the product's profitability:

- Should the team take more time for development in order to make the product available on multiple computer "platforms," or would a delay in bringing the CI-700 to market be too costly?
- Should the product use proprietary print media or commonly available premium-quality print media?
- Should the team increase development spending in order to increase the reliability of the CI-700?

Analytics

It is important to remember that economic analysis can capture only those factors that are measurable and that projects often have both positive and negative implications that are difficult to quantify. Also, it is difficult for an economic analysis to capture the characteristics of a dynamic and competitive environment. Economic analysis is useful in at least two different circumstances:

1. Go/no-go milestones. For example: Should we try to develop a product to address a new market opportunity? Should we proceed with the implementation of a selected concept? Should we launch the product we have developed? These decisions typically arise at the end of each phase of development.
2. Operational design and development decisions. Operational decisions involve questions such as: Should we spend $100,000 to hire an outside firm to develop this component in order to save two months of development time? Should we launch the product in four months at a unit cost of $450 or wait six months, when we can reduce the cost to $400?

We recommend that a base-case financial model be initially built to understand the financial implications of a product development project. In the following, we describe how to construct this model.

Key Idea

In developing these models, it is best to start with a simple model and then expand the analysis if needed.

Build a Base-Case Financial Model

Constructing the base-case model consists of estimating the timing and magnitude of future cash flows and then computing the net present value (NPV) of those cash flows. The timing and magnitude of the cash flows are estimated by merging the project schedule with the project budget, sales volume forecasts, and estimated production costs. The level of detail of cash flows should be coarse enough to be convenient to work with, yet contain enough detail to facilitate effective decision making. The most basic categories of cash flow for a typical new product development project are:

- Development cost (all remaining design, testing, and refinement costs up to production ramp-up)
- Ramp-up cost
- Marketing and support cost
- Production cost
- Sales revenue

The financial model we use is simplified to include only the major cash flows that are typically used in practice, but conceptually it is identical to more complex models. The numerical values of the cash flows come from budgets and other estimates obtained from the development team, the manufacturing organization, and the marketing organization. We will illustrate the approach by using data similar to what might have been used by the Canon team developing the CI-700.

The following are cost estimates that we will use for our sample model:

Development cost	$5 million
Ramp-up cost	$2 million
Marketing and support cost	$1 million/year
Unit production cost	$400/unit
Sales and production volume	20,000 units/year
Unit price	$800/unit

For our model, we assume that all revenue and expenses that have occurred prior to today are sunk costs and are irrelevant to NPV calculations. For those of you not familiar with NPV calculations, see Appendix C at the end of the book.

Key Idea

In this section, we assume you have done this type of analysis before. If you are not familiar with this analysis process, you should study Appendix C to learn how it works.

To complete the model, the financial estimates must be merged with timing information. This can be done by considering the project schedule and sales plan. Exhibit 3.8 shows the project timing information in Gantt chart form for the CI-700. For most projects, a time increment of months or quarters is most appropriate. The remaining time to market is estimated to be 5 quarters, and the product sales are anticipated to last 11 quarters.

EXHIBIT 3.8

CI-700 Project Schedule from Inception through Market Withdrawal

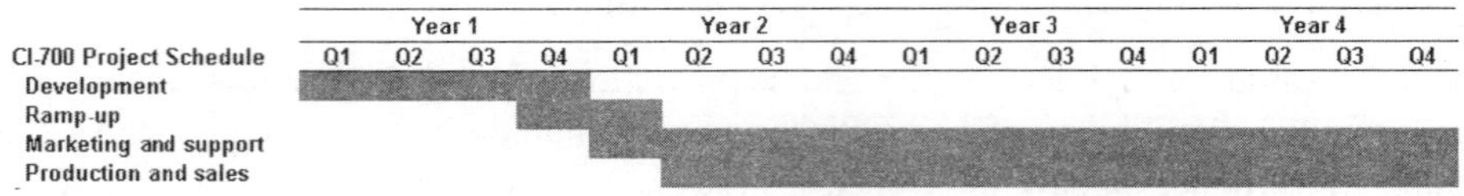

A simple method of organizing project cash flow is with a spreadsheet. The rows of the spreadsheet are the different cash flow categories, while the columns represent successive time periods. To keep things simple, we assume that the rate of cash flow for any category is constant across any time period. For example, total development spending of $5 million over one year is allocated equally to each of the four quarters. In practice, of course, the values can be arranged in any way that best represents the team's forecast of the cash flows. We multiply the unit sales quantity by the unit price to find the total product revenues in each period. We also multiply the unit production quantity by the unit production cost to find the total production cost in each period. Exhibit 3.9 illustrates the resulting spreadsheet.

EXHIBIT 3.9

Merging the Project Financials and Schedule into a Cash Flow Report

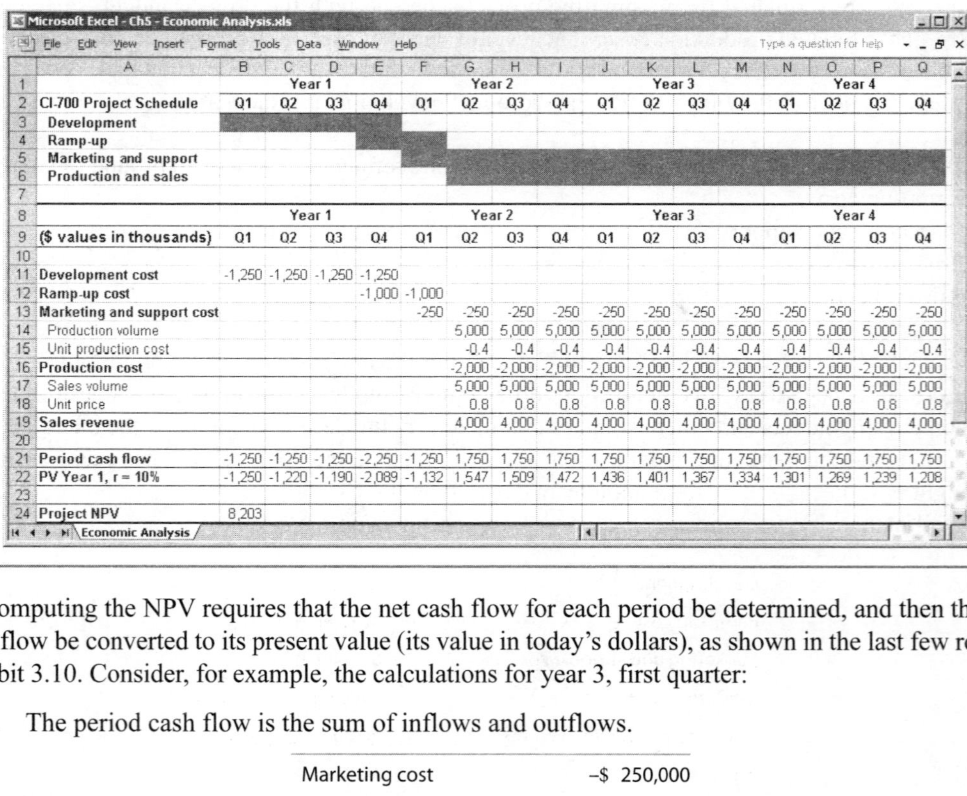

Microsoft Excel - Ch5 - Economic Analysis.xls

($ values in thousands)	Year 1 Q1	Q2	Q3	Q4	Year 2 Q1	Q2	Q3	Q4	Year 3 Q1	Q2	Q3	Q4	Year 4 Q1	Q2	Q3	Q4
Development cost	-1,250	-1,250	-1,250	-1,250												
Ramp-up cost				-1,000	-1,000											
Marketing and support cost					-250	-250	-250	-250	-250	-250	-250	-250	-250	-250	-250	-250
Production volume						5,000	5,000	5,000	5,000	5,000	5,000	5,000	5,000	5,000	5,000	5,000
Unit production cost						-0.4	-0.4	-0.4	-0.4	-0.4	-0.4	-0.4	-0.4	-0.4	-0.4	-0.4
Production cost						-2,000	-2,000	-2,000	-2,000	-2,000	-2,000	-2,000	-2,000	-2,000	-2,000	-2,000
Sales volume						5,000	5,000	5,000	5,000	5,000	5,000	5,000	5,000	5,000	5,000	5,000
Unit price						0.8	0.8	0.8	0.8	0.8	0.8	0.8	0.8	0.8	0.8	0.8
Sales revenue						4,000	4,000	4,000	4,000	4,000	4,000	4,000	4,000	4,000	4,000	4,000
Period cash flow	-1,250	-1,250	-1,250	-2,250	-1,250	1,750	1,750	1,750	1,750	1,750	1,750	1,750	1,750	1,750	1,750	1,750
PV Year 1, r = 10%	-1,250	-1,220	-1,190	-2,089	-1,132	1,547	1,509	1,472	1,436	1,401	1,367	1,334	1,301	1,269	1,239	1,208
Project NPV	8,203															

Economic Analysis

Computing the NPV requires that the net cash flow for each period be determined, and then that this cash flow be converted to its present value (its value in today's dollars), as shown in the last few rows of Exhibit 3.10. Consider, for example, the calculations for year 3, first quarter:

Analytics

1. The period cash flow is the sum of inflows and outflows.

Marketing cost	–$ 250,000
Product revenues	4,000,000
Production cost	– 2,000,000
Period cash flow	$ 1,750,000

2. The present value of this period cash flow discounted at 10 percent per year (2.5 percent per quarter) back to the first quarter of year 1 (a total of nine quarters) is \$1,401,275. (The concepts and spreadsheet functions for calculating present value, net present value, and discount rate are reviewed in Appendix C.)

$$\frac{\$1,750,000}{1.025^9} = \$1,401,275$$

3. The project NPV is the sum of the discounted cash flows for each of the periods, or \$8,002,819. (Note that in the spreadsheet we have rounded the numbers to the nearest \$1,000.)

The NPV of this project, according to the base-case model, is positive, so the model supports and is consistent with the decision to proceed with development. Such modeling also can be used to support major investment decisions. Say, for example, the development team was deciding between two different production facilities with different ramp-up, production, and support costs. The team could develop a model for each of the two scenarios and then compare the NPVs. The scenario with the higher NPV would better support the investment decision. We now consider sensitivity analysis as a technique for studying multiple scenarios for ongoing product development decisions.

Sensitivity Analysis to Understand Project Trade-Offs

Analytics

Sensitivity analysis uses the financial model to answer "what if" questions by calculating the change in NPV corresponding to a change in the factors included in the model. As an example, consider the sensitivity of NPV to changes in development cost. By making incremental changes to development cost while holding other factors constant, we can see the incremental impact on project NPV. For example, what will be the change in NPV if the development cost is decreased by 20 percent? A 20 percent decrease would lower the total development spending from \$5 million to \$4 million. If development time remains one year, then the spending per quarter would decrease from \$1.25 million to \$1 million. This change is simply entered in the model, and the resulting NPV is calculated.

A 20 percent decrease in development cost will increase NPV to \$9,167,000. This represents a dollar increase of \$964,000 and a percentage increase of 11.8 in NPV. This is an extremely simple case: We assume we can achieve the same project goals by spending \$1 million less on development, and we therefore have increased the project value by the present value of \$1 million in savings accrued over a one-year period of time. The CI-700 development cost sensitivity analysis for a range of changes is shown in Exhibit 3.10.

Key Idea

Some companies call this "what if" analysis. Answering these "what if" questions can be useful for understanding how sensitive an analysis is to cost and profit assumptions.

Many other scenarios can be developed for the project, including the following:

1. **Project development time.** Consider the impact of a 25 percent increase in the project development time. This would raise the development time from four to five quarters and delay the start of the production ramp-up, marketing efforts, and product sales.

EXHIBIT 3.10

CI-700 Development Cost Sensitivity

Change in Development Cost (%)	Development Cost (\$ thousands)	Change in Development Cost (\$ thousands)	Change in NPV (%)	NPV (\$ thousands)	Change in NPV (\$ thousands)
50	7,500	2,500	−29.4	5,793	−2,410
20	6,000	1,000	−11.8	7,239	−964
10	5,500	500	−5.9	7,721	−482
Base case	5,000	Base case	0.0	8,203	0
−10	4,500	−500	5.9	8,685	482
−20	4,000	−1,000	11.8	9,167	964
−30	2,500	−2,500	29.4	10,613	2,410

2. **Sales volume.** Increasing sales is a powerful way to increase profit. Of course, a decrease in sales can result in significant loss. Consider, for example, the impact of a 25 percent increase and a 25 percent decrease on the profitability of the new product.
3. **Product cost or sales price.** Consider that a $1 increase in price or a $1 decrease in cost results in a $1 increase in profit. Of course, the $1 increase in price may have a significant impact on demand. Scenarios relating to these parameters are often useful to study.
4. **Development cost.** A dollar spent or saved on development cost is worth the present value of that dollar to the value of the project.

Time-to-market

A measure of product development success. There are two measures here: the frequency of new product introductions, and the time from initial concept to market introduction.

Productivity

A measure of how well resources are used. According to Goldratt's definition (see Chapter 23), all the actions that bring a company closer to its goals.

Financial modeling and sensitivity analysis are powerful tools for supporting product development decisions, but these techniques have important limitations. Many argue that rigorous financial analyses are required to bring discipline and control to the product development process. Others argue that financial analysis only focuses on measurable quantities and that it is often extremely difficult to predict these values accurately. The analysis is only as good as the assumptions built into the model, so these limitations must be considered. Then there are those that argue, perhaps more significantly, that activities associated with economic modeling can be very expensive and may significantly reduce the productivity associated with the real product development activities. Their point is that potentially productive development time is devoted to preparation of analyses and meetings and the cumulative effect of this planning and review time can significantly increase development costs.

Development teams must understand the strengths and limitations of the techniques and refrain from developing a stifling bureaucracy around the development of new products. New-product development should be a process that nurtures innovation and creativity. The purpose of economic modeling is simply to ensure that the team is making decisions that are economically sound.

LO 3-5

Illustrate how product development is measured in a company

MEASURING PRODUCT DEVELOPMENT PERFORMANCE

Quality

Measures that relate to the reliability of the product in use (referred to as **conformance quality**), the product's performance features compared to customer expectations (referred to as **design quality**), and the ability of a factory or service process to produce the product (**defects per million opportunities** or delivery speed, for example).

There is strong evidence that generating a steady stream of new products to market is extremely important to competitiveness. To succeed, firms must respond to changing customer needs and the moves of their competitors. The ability to identify opportunities, mount the development effort, and bring to market new products and processes quickly is critical. Firms also must bring new products and processes to market efficiently. Because the number of new products and new process technologies has increased while model lives and life cycles have shrunk, firms must mount more development projects than previously, and these projects must use substantially fewer resources per project.

In the U.S. automobile market, for example, the growth of models and market segments over the last 25 years has meant that an auto firm must initiate close to four times as many development projects simply to maintain its market share position. But smaller volumes per model and shorter design lives mean resource requirements must drop dramatically. Remaining competitive requires efficient engineering, design, and development activities.

Measures of product development success can be categorized into those that relate to the speed and frequency of bringing new products online, to the productivity of the actual development process, and to the quality of the actual products introduced. The following are generic descriptions of typical measures:

Conformance quality

The degree to which the product or service design specifications are met.

Design quality

The inherent value of the product in the marketplace.

Defects per million opportunities (DPMO)

A metric used to describe the variability of a process.

- **Time to market**—There are two aspects to this, the frequency of new product introductions and the time from initial concept to market introduction.
- **Productivity**—Such measures as the number of engineering hours, the cost of materials, and tooling costs are used in these measures. Often, comparison of actual versus planned costs are used.
- **Quality**—Measures that relate to the reliability of the product in use (referred to as **conformance quality)**, the product's performance features compared to customer expectations (referred to as **design quality)**, and the ability of a factory or service process to produce the product (**defects per million opportunities** or time-to-market, for example).

Taken together, time, productivity, and quality define the performance of development, and in combination with other activities—sales, manufacturing, advertising, and customer service—determine the market impact of the project and its profitability.

CONCEPT CONNECTIONS

LO 3–1 Know the issues associated with product design and the typical processes used by companies

Summary

- Product development is a major challenge that directly impacts the long-range success of a firm.
- Effectively managing the process requires an integrated effort involving all the functional areas of the firm.
- Many companies today outsource product design to companies that specialize in different industries. The use of contract manufacturers has changed the way many companies now operate.
- An issue is often deciding what a firm's core competency should be to yield a long-term competitive advantage to the company.
- Product development is a multistep process that is unique to each organization. Typical steps in the process are planning, concepts development, system-level design, design detail, testing and refinement, and production ramp-up.

Key Terms

Contract manufacturer An organization that performs manufacturing and/or purchasing needed to produce a product or device not for itself, but as a service to another firm.

Core competency The one thing that a firm can do better than its competitors. The goal is to have a core competency that yields a long-term competitive advantage to the company.

Concurrent engineering Emphasizes cross-functional integration and concurrent development of a product and its associated processes.

LO 3–2 Illustrate how different criteria can impact the design of a product

Summary

- Different sets of criteria drive the design of a product. Criteria that relate to customer wants are fundamental, while other criteria related to the cost of the product, its manufacturability, and the impact on the environment are also important.

Key Terms

Quality function deployment (QFD) A process that helps a company determine the product characteristics important to the consumer and to evaluate its own product in relation to others.

House of quality A matrix that helps a product design team translate customer requirements into operating and engineering goals.

Value analysis / value engineering (VA/VE) Analysis with the purpose of simplifying products and processes by achieving equivalent or better performance at a lower cost.

Ecodesign The incorporation of environmental considerations into the design and development of products or services. These concerns relate to the entire life cycle, including materials, manufacturing, distribution, and the eventual disposal of waste.

LO 3–3 Contrast how service products can have different design criteria compared to manufactured products

Summary

- Service products are different because direct customer involvement in the process introduces variability in terms of both the time it takes to serve a customer and the level of knowledge required of the firm's employees.
- Fitting the service experience to the expectations of the customer will drive what needs to be done operationally to provide the service.
- Financial justification of service features must be done to ensure that customers can be retained while the company is making a profit from expected activities.

LO 3–4 Evaluate the economic impact of a new product on a company

Summary

- Economic analysis that consists of estimating the timing and magnitude of future cash flows is used to understand the financial implications of a product development project. Typical flows include development cost, ramp-up cost, marketing and support cost, production cost, and sales revenue.
- Sensitivity analysis can be used to answer "what if" questions that relate to project timing and costs.

LO 3–5 Illustrate how product development is measured in a company

Summary

- Generating a steady stream of new products to market is important to the competitiveness of the firm.
- Measures that relate to the time it takes to bring a product to market, costs related to engineering and production, and the quality of the product can be used to evaluate product development success.

Key Terms

time-to-market A measure of product development success. There are two measures here: the frequency of new product introductions, and the time from initial concept to market introduction.

Productivity A measure of how well resources are used. According to Goldratt's definition (see Chapter 23), all the actions that bring a company closer to its goals.

quality Measures that relate to the reliability of the product in use (referred to as **conformance quality**), the product's performance features compared to customer expectations (referred to as **design quality**), and the ability of a factory or service process to produce the product (**defects per million opportunities** or delivery speed, for example).

Conformance quality The degree to which the product or service design specifications are met.

Design quality The inherent value of the product in the marketplace.

Defects per million opportunities (DPMO) A metric used to describe the variability of a process.

SOLVED PROBLEM

LO3–4

VidMark, a manufacturer of cell phones, is currently developing a new model (VidPhone X70) that will be released on the market when development is complete. This phone will will allow the user to place ultra high definition video phone calls. VidMark is concerned about the development cost and time. It is also worried about market estimates of the sales of the new VidPhone X70. The cost estimates and forecast are given in the following table.

Development Cost	$2,000,000
Development Time	2 years
Ramp-up Cost	$750,000
Marketing and Support Cost	$500,000/year
Unit Production Cost	$75
Unit Price	$135
Sales and Production Volume	
Year 3	40,000
Year 4	50,000
Year 5	40,000

Use the given data to develop a base-case analysis. The project schedule is shown as follows with timings of the cash flows.

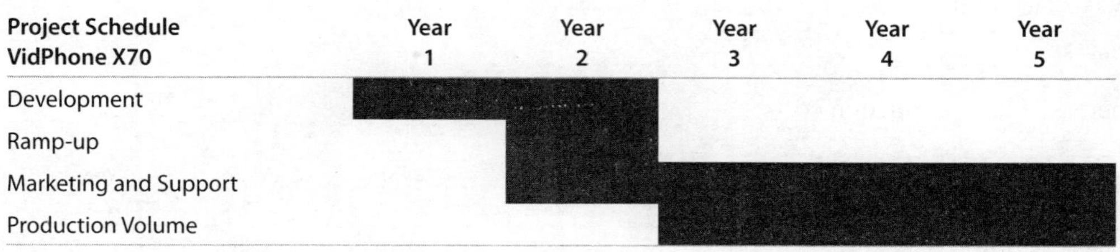

Several questions need to be answered for VidMark about this project:

a. What are the yearly cash flows and their present value (discounted at 12 percent) of this project? What is the net present value?
b. What is the impact on VidMark if sales estimates are off by 20 percent? (Assume that VidMark reduces production volume to correspond to the new sales numbers.)
c. What is the impact on VidMark if unit production cost is $85? (Assume sales estimates are accurate.)
d. VidMark thinks it can cut the development time in half by spending an extra $1,500,000 on development for this project. If the product is launched a year earlier, then the product will still have a 3-year life but the forecasts starting in year 2 will be 48,000, 60,000, and 50,000. Is it worth it to VidMark to spend the extra money on development? (Assume the ramp-up, marketing and support costs will start in year 1.)

Solution

a. Start by building the base-case scenario (analysis is in 000s).

Project Schedule VidPhone X70	Year 1	Year 2	Year 3	Year 4	Year 5
Development	–$1,000	–$1,000			
Ramp-up		–$750			
Marketing and Support		–$500	–$500	–$500	–$500
Production Volume			40	50	40
Unit Production Cost (dollars)			–$75	–$75	–$75
Production Costs			–$3,000	–$3,750	–$3,000
Sales Volume			40	50	40
Unit Price (dollars)			$135	$135	$135
Sales Revenue			$5,400	$6,750	$5,400
Period Cash Flow	–$1,000	–$2,250	$1,900	$2,500	$1,900
PV Year 1 (r = 12%)	–$893	–$1,794	$1,352	$1,589	$1,078
Project NPV	$1,333				

The cash flows and present value of the cash flows are shown. The project NPV under the base case is $1.333 million.

b. If sales are reduced by 20 percent, then project NPV drops to $337,000.

Project Schedule VidPhone X70	Year 1	Year 2	Year 3	Year 4	Year 5
Period Cash Flow	–$1,000	–$2,250	$1,420	$1,900	$1,420
PV Year 1 (r = 12%)	–$893	–$1,794	$1,011	$1,207	$806
Project NPV	$337				

If sales are increased by 20 percent, then project NPV goes up to $2.328 million. A change of 20 percent either way has a large impact on the NPV.

Project Schedule VidPhone X70	Year 1	Year 2	Year 3	Year 4	Year 5
Period Cash Flow	–$1,000	–$2,250	$2,380	$3,100	$2,380
PV Year 1 (r = 12%)	–$893	–$1,794	$1,694	$1,970	$1,350
Project NPV	$2,328				

c. Increased unit production costs:

Project Schedule VidPhone X70	Year 1	Year 2	Year 3	Year 4	Year 5
Period Cash Flow	–$1,000	–$2,250	$1,500	$2,000	$1,500
PV Year 1 (r = 12%)	–$893	–$1,794	$1,068	$1,271	$851
Project NPV	$503				

The cash flows are severely affected by the increased unit production cost. Increased future cash outflow of $1.3 million (130,000 units * $10 increase) causes a decrease in net present value of $830,000 ($1.333 million – $0.503 million). However, it still appears to be worth developing the new phone.

d. Here are the changes proposed by VidMark:

Development Cost	$3,500,000
Development Time	1 year
Ramp-up Cost	$750,000
Marketing and Support Cost	$500,000/year
Unit Production Cost	$75
Unit Price	$135
Sales and Production Volume	
Year 2	48,000
Year 3	60,000
Year 4	50,000

Use this data to develop a base-case analysis. The project schedule is shown as follows with timings of cash flows.

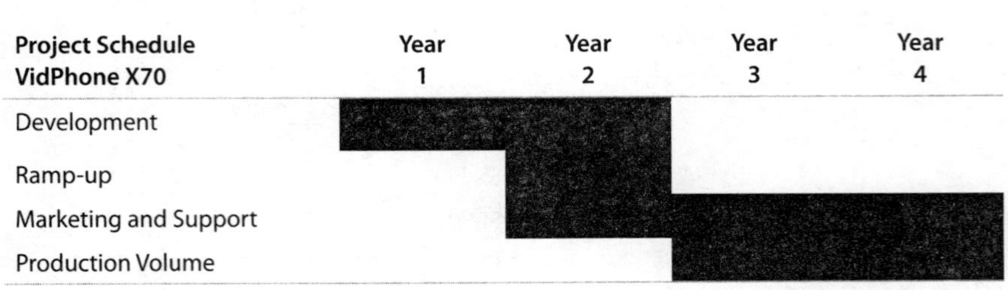

It appears that VidMark is better off to take a fast approach to develop its new VidPhone X70 because the NPV of the base case is $1.333 million versus the fast development NPV of $1.452 million (see the following table).

Project Schedule VidPhone X70	Year 1	Year 2	Year 3	Year 4
Development	–$3,500			
Ramp-up	–$750			
Marketing and Support	–$500	–$500	–$500	–$500
Production Volume		48	60	50
Unit Production Cost (dollars)		–$75	–$75	–$75
Production Costs		–$3,600	–$4,500	–$3,750
Sales Volume		48	60	50
Unit Price (dollars)		$135	$135	$135
Sales Revenue		$6,480	$8,100	$6,750
Period Cash Flow	–$4,750	$2,380	$3,100	$2,500
PV Year 1 (r = 12%)	–$4,241	$1,897	$2,207	$1,589
Project NPV	$1,452			

DISCUSSION QUESTIONS

1. Describe the generic product development process described in the chapter. How does the process change for technology-push products? **LO3–1**
2. How does the QFD approach help? What are some limitations of this approach? **LO3–2**
3. Discuss the product design philosophy behind industrial design and design for manufacture and assembly. Which one do you think is more important in a customer-focused product development?
4. Discuss design-based incrementalism, which is frequent product redesign throughout the product's life. What are the pros and cons of this idea?
5. Do the concepts of complexity and divergence apply to an online sales company such as Dell Computer? **LO3–3**
6. What factors must be traded off in the product development process before introducing a new product? **LO3–4**
7. Coca-Cola is a well-established consumer products company with a strong position in the global market. The sales of its core soda products have remained relatively stable for decades, yet the company has continued to grow and has remained extremely profitable. Discuss Coca-Cola's history in light of the statement that "generating a steady stream of new products to market is extremely important to competitiveness." Does Coca-Cola's success disprove that statement? Is the company an exception to the rule or an example of its application? **LO3–5**

OBJECTIVE QUESTIONS

1. Which phase of the *generic development process* involves construction and evaluation of multiple preproduction versions of the product? (Answer in Appendix D) **LO3–1**
2. A process that emphasizes cross-functional integration and concurrent development of a product and its associated processes is known as _____.
3. Match the following product types to the appropriate product development description.

______	Technology-push products	A. Entail unusually large uncertainties about the technology or market. The development process takes steps to address those uncertainties.
______	Platform products	B. A firm with a new proprietary technology seeks out a market where that technology can be applied.
______	Process-intensive products	C. Uses a repeated prototyping cycle. Results from one cycle are used to modify priorities in the ensuing cycle.
______	High-risk products	D. The production process has an impact on the product properties. Therefore, product design and process design cannot be separated.
______	Quick-build products	E. Products are designed and built around a preexisting technological subsystem.

LO3–2

4. Designing products for aesthetics and with the user in mind is generally called what?
5. The first step in developing a *house of quality* is to develop a list of _____.
6. The purpose of *value analysis/value engineering* is to _____.

LO3–3

7. What is it about service processes that makes their design and operation so different from manufacturing processes?
8. What are the three general factors that determine the *fit* of a new or revised service process?

LO3–5

9. Measures of product development success can be organized into what three categories? (Answer in Appendix D)
10. Tuff Wheels was getting ready to start its development project for a new product to be added to its small motorized vehicle line for children. The new product is called the Kiddy Dozer. It will look like a miniature bulldozer, complete with caterpillar tracks and a blade. Tuff Wheels has forecasted the demand and the cost to develop and produce the new Kiddy Dozer. The following table contains the relevant information for this project.

Development Cost	$1,000,000
Estimated Development Time	9 months
Pilot Testing	$200,000
Ramp-up Cost	$400,000
Marketing and Support Cost	$150,000 per year
Sales and Production Volume	60,000 per year
Unit Production Cost	$100
Unit Price	$170
Interest Rate	8%

Tuff Wheels also has provided the project plan shown as follows. As can be seen in the project plan, the company thinks that the product life will be three years until a new product must be created.

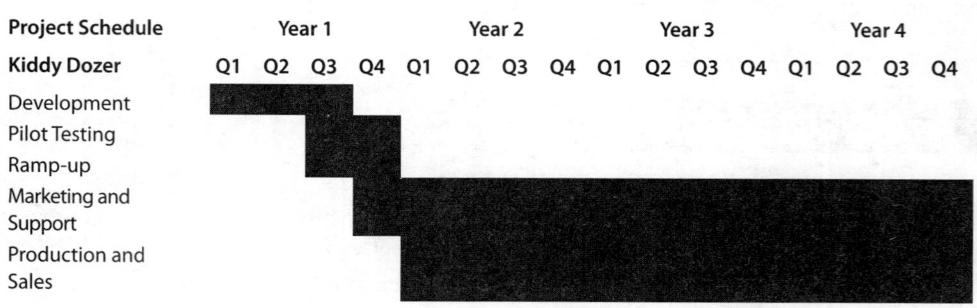

a. What are the yearly cash flows and their present value (discounted at 8 percent) of this project? What is the net present value?
b. What is the impact on NPV for the Kiddy Dozer if the actual unit sales are 50,000 per year or 70,000 per year?
c. What is the effect caused by changing the discount rate to 9, 10, or 11 percent?

11. Perot Corporation is developing a new CPU chip based on a new type of technology. Its new chip, the Patay2 chip, will take two years to develop. However, because other chip manufacturers will be able to copy the technology, it will have a market life of two years after it is introduced. Perot expects to be able to price the chip higher in the first year, and it anticipates a significant production cost reduction after the first year as well. The relevant information for developing and selling the Patay2 is given as follows.

Patay2 Chip Product Estimates

Development Cost	$20,000,000
Pilot Testing	$5,000,000
Debug	$3,000,000
Ramp-up Cost	$3,000,000
Advance Marketing	$5,000,000
Marketing and Support Cost	$1,000,000 per year
Unit Production Cost Year 1	$655.00
Unit Production Cost Year 2	$545.00
Unit Price Year 1	$820.00
Unit Price Year 2	$650.00
Sales and Production Volume Year 1	250,000
Sales and Production Volume Year 2	150,000
Interest Rate	10%

Patay2 Chip Project Timing

Project Schedule	**Year 1**		**Year 2**		**Year 3**		**Year 4**	
Patay2 Chip	**1st half**	**2nd half**	**1st half**	**2nd half**	**1st half**	**2nd half**	**1st half**	**2nd half**
Development	■	■	■	■				
Pilot Testing			■	■				
Debug			■	■				
Ramp-up				■				
Advance Marketing				■				
Marketing and Support					■	■	■	■
Production and Sales					■	■	■	■

a. What are the yearly cash flows and their present value (discounted at 10 percent) of this project? What is the net present value?
b. Perot's engineers have determined that spending $10 million more on development will allow them to add even more advanced features. Having a more advanced chip will allow them to price the chip $50 higher in both years ($870 for year 1 and $700 for year 2). Is it worth the additional investment?
c. If sales are only 200,000 the first year and 100,000 the second year, would Perot still do the project?

12. Pick a product and list issues that need to be considered in its design and manufacture. The product can be something like a stereo, cell phone, desk, or kitchen appliance. Consider the functional and aesthetic aspects of design as well as the important concerns for manufacturing.
13. The following chart is a partial house of quality for a golf country club. Provide an importance weighting from your perspective (or that of a golfing friend) in the unshaded areas. If you can, using the QFD approach, compare it to a club where you or your friends play.

WHATs versus HOWs Strong Relationship: ● Medium Relationship: ○ Weak Relationship: △	Physical Aspects	Course location	Grounds maintenance	Landscaping	Pin placement	Course tuning	Tee placement	Service Facilities	Customer-trained attendants	Top-quality food	Highly rated chefs	Attractive restaurant	Tournament Activities	Calloway handicapping	Exciting door prizes	Perception Issues	Invitation only	Types of guests	Income level	Celebrity
Physical Aspects																				
Manicured grounds																				
Easy access																				
Challenging																				
Service Facilities																				
Restaurant facilities																				
Good food																				
Good service																				
Good layout																				
Plush locker room																				
Helpful service attendants																				
Tournament Facilities																				
Good tournament prize																				
Types of players																				
Fair handicapping system																				
Perception Issues																				
Prestigious																				

CASE: Tata Swach—An Innovation for Need is an Innovation Indeed

The Government of India has an ambitious plan for rural drinking water as clean drinking water is a basic necessity of life. Supply of clean drinking water in the rural areas is always a top priority for the government [1]. There are many road blocks to this national priority. Corporates too are agog with this problem. Tata Group sensed this opportunity and took advantage of synergy within its group companies like TCS, Tata Chemicals, Titan, etc. It came up with a collaborative innovation product named Tata Swach. It is a low-cost water purifier, which requires no running water, no electricity, and no boiling. It is a replaceable filter-based product, which is entirely portable. This innovation is the culmination of a philanthropic dream project of Mr. Ratan Tata, who was then the Chairman of Tata Group.

"Safe drinking water is the most basic of human needs. The social cost of water contamination is already enormous and increases every year. Although, today's announcement is about giving million more people affordable access to safe water, it is an important step in the long term strategy to find a solution to provide affordable access to safe water for all".
Ratan Tata, Chairman, Tata Sons
On Launch of 'Tata Swach', on 7th Dec 2009,
(Source: LiveMint)

How was the Product Developed?

This innovative concept was developed by the TCS Innovation Labs – TRDDC. It developed a highly efficient product working on a technology, which combined low-cost ingredients such as rice husk ash with superior nano-material. A leading nano-scientist and Chief Scientific Officer at the Innovation Center, Mr. Murali Sastry, said, "It is an enormous privilege to be a part of the development team on a project, which has the potential of positively impacting the lives of millions of people globally".[2] The key to design was the concept that a natural and cheap material like rice husk can be processed to significantly reduce water borne germs and odors when impure water is passed through it. The cartridge bulb is packed with a purification medium, which has the capability to kill bacteria and disease causing organisms without boiling or requiring electricity.

The Managing Director of Tata Chemicals and a partner in the innovation and design, Mr. R Makundan, said, "With the launch of Tata Swach, we are taking a small step towards fulfilling our Chairman's vision of marking safe drinking water available for all at an affordable cost. Just as Tata Chemicals dedicated itself to the eradication of goitre with Tata Salt, so with the launch of this product, we are committing ourselves to work towards wiping out the curse of water-borne diseases". [2] At its launch on 7 December 2009, one of the basic models of Swach was priced at INR 999, which was capable of providing safe drinking water at a new marked benchmark cost of 30 per month for a family of five.[3]

As mentioned on the website of Tata Swach, it can purify up to 3000 liter of water after which the cartridge stops the flow before giving the user enough lead time for cartridge replacement. The product has very low maintenance requirement and no wonder, this innovation has helped filing fourteen patents.[4]

Questions

1. Discuss any other product innovation that has helped to tackle the need of rural India.
2. Tata Swach requires aggressive marketing in rural India. What are the barriers and enablers to this effort?
3. Search Internet for few technology diffusion frameworks. Can these frameworks be used to improve the acceptability of this product?
4. What, if any, could be the reason for a failure of such type of innovation? Discuss.

References

[1] Govt. of India, Rural Water Supply Programme, http://india.gov.in/sectors/rural_water.php (Accessed on 21 March 2014)

[2] http://www.tata.com/media/releases/inside.aspx?artid=TtOdcdNuSRk= (Accessed on 21 April 2010)

[3] http://www.deccanherald.com/content/40000/tata-launches-swach-water-filters.html (Accessedd on 21 April 2010)

[4] Tata Swach Corporate Website www.tataswach.com (Accessed on 21 April 2010)

CASE: IKEA—Design and Pricing

The Swedish retailer dominates markets in 32 countries, and now it's poised to conquer North America. Its battle plan: Keep making its offerings less expensive, without making them cheap.

Above all else, one factor accounts for IKEA's success: good quality at a low price. IKEA sells household items that are cheap but not cheapo, at prices that typically run 30 to 50 percent below the competition's. While the price of other companies' products tends to rise over time, IKEA says it has reduced its retail prices by a total of about 20 percent during the past four years. At IKEA, the process of driving down costs starts the moment a new item is conceived and continues relentlessly throughout its production run. The price of a basic Pöang chair, for example, has fallen from $149 in 2000 to $99 in 2001 to $79 today. IKEA expects the most recent price cut to increase Pöang sales by 30 to 50 percent.

IKEA's corporate mantra is "Low price with meaning." The goal is to make things less expensive without ever making customers feel cheap. Striking that balance demands a special kind of design, manufacturing, and distribution expertise. But IKEA pulls it off in its own distinctive way: tastefully, methodically, even cheerfully, and yet somehow differently than any other company anywhere. Here's a step-by-step guide to how IKEA designs, builds, and distributes the items that the entire world wants to buy.

The Trofé mug is one of the most popular IKEA products. The story of the mug is an example of how IKEA works, from a co-worker's bright idea through to production and sales. It is also a story about all the demands that customers place on IKEA. A low price tag is the obvious one, but other requirements include function, modern design, environmental considerations, and making sure products have been manufactured under acceptable working conditions. Both customers and co-workers must be able to rely on IKEA.

Step 1. Pick a Price

Product Development—A sketch for a new product? Yes, but it's also a calculation of what that product will cost. The low price begins at the drawing board.

The team behind each product consists of designers, product developers, and purchasers who get together to discuss design, materials, and suitable suppliers. Everyone contributes with their specialist knowledge. Purchasers, for example, use their contacts with suppliers all over the world via IKEA Trading Service Offices. Who can make this at the best quality for the right price at the right time?

When product developers were given the task of creating a new mug over five years ago, they were told how much it should cost in the stores. In the case of Trofé, the price had to be incredibly low—five Swedish kronor! This mug had to have a real knockout price.

To produce the right mug at the right price, the developers had to take into account materials, colors, and design. For example, the mug is made in green, blue, yellow, or white because these pigments cost less than other shades, such as red.

Step 2. Choose a Manufacturer

Suppliers and Purchasing—The task of developing products never ends. Working with suppliers, the mug was shortened and the handle changed so it stacks more efficiently, saving space for transport, warehousing, and store display—and, not least, in the customers' cupboards at home. IKEA is always keen to banish as much air as possible from its packaging. Packages should preferably be flat for efficient transport and storage.

One supplier, a factory in Romania, has worked with IKEA for 15 years. Long-term relationships help both parties to build up a huge fund of knowledge about demands and expectations. That is why products are often developed in close cooperation with suppliers. In the case of Trofé, for example, the new size has rationalized production by making better use of the space in the kiln during the firing process. That's cost-effective and saves time.

IKEA has introduced a code of conduct governing working conditions and environmental awareness among suppliers. This deals with matters such as health and safety in the workplace and forbids the use of child labor. The practical work of implementing this code of conduct is carried out by co-workers in IKEA Trading Service Offices worldwide. Many suppliers already meet the demands; others are working together with IKEA to carry out the necessary improvements. IKEA also works closely with external quality control and audit companies that check that IKEA and its suppliers live up to the requirements of the code of conduct.

The low price tag is crucial to the vision IKEA has of creating a better everyday life for many people. That is why IKEA works nonstop to reduce costs. But it's also a question of saving raw materials and, ultimately, the environment. The low-cost mug is one example of how environmental considerations can influence the development of products. For example, the new mug is lighter in color—a move that cuts costs and is more environmentally friendly. The less pigment that is used, the better. The mug is also lead- and cadmium-free.

Step 3. Design the Product

With a price point and a manufacturer in place, IKEA once again uses internal competition to find a designer and select a design for production. The designer begins the design process by writing a brief that explains the product's price, its function, the materials to be used, and the fabricator's capabilities. The designer then sends the brief to IKEA's staff designers and freelancers, and refines promising designs until settling on the one to produce. The designer wants products to be like Swiss Army knives—to get maximum functionality at minimum cost.

Step 4. Ship It

Distribution and logistics are the lifeblood of IKEA and important pieces of the puzzle on the road to a low price. IKEA strives to deliver the right number of goods to the right stores at the right time. It calculates the goods requirements and makes sure that deliveries are efficient.

Each pallet holds 2,024 mugs, which are transported from Romania by rail, road, and sea to IKEA distribution centers around the world. Transportation does, of course, have an effect on the environment, but IKEA is working toward reducing environmental impact.

Many of IKEA's products are bulky—for example, tables and chairs. IKEA pioneered the concept of flat. The company's eureka moment occurred in 1956, when one of IKEA's first designers watched a customer trying to fit a table into his car. There was only one way to do it: Remove the legs. From that day forward, most IKEA products have been designed to ship disassembled, flat enough to be slipped into the cargo hatch of a station wagon or safely tied down on an auto's roof rack.

In IKEA's innately frugal corporate culture, where waste has been declared a "deadly sin," the flat package is also an excellent way to lower shipping costs by maximizing the use of space inside shipping containers. The company estimates transport volume would be six times greater if its items were shipped assembled. From the design studio to the warehouse floor, IKEA employees' mantra is always the same: "We don't want to pay to ship air."

Making things flat is an IKEA obsession. How many times can you redesign a simple fired-clay coffee mug? IKEA's mug was redesigned three times—simply to maximize the number of them that could be stored on a pallet. Originally, only 864 mugs would fit. A redesign added a rim such as you'd find on a flowerpot, so that each pallet could hold 1,280 mugs. Yet another redesign created a shorter mug with a new handle, allowing 2,024 to squeeze onto a pallet. While the mug's sales price has remained at 50 cents, shipping costs have been reduced by 60 percent, which is a significant savings, given that IKEA sells about 25 million of the mugs each year. Even better, the cost of production at IKEA's Romanian factory also has fallen because the more compact mugs require less space in the kiln.

When you ship 25 million cubic meters of goods all over the globe, flat-pack frugality adds up. IKEA now uses a 65 percent average fill-rate target for all the containers it ships, and it hopes to increase that to 75 percent. Meeting that goal will require further design changes and sometimes even sucking the air out of items (like IKEA's shrink-wrapped pillows, which look like giant crackers on store shelves). And, of course, flat packing shifts the cost of product assembly to the customer, saving even more.

As IKEA has shifted more of its buying from Europe to the Far East, shipping time and costs have become an even more critical concern. Last year, China tied Sweden atop IKEA's list of supplier countries. The company has responded by creating a global network of distribution centers, most of which are near container ports and major truck and rail routes. There are 18 IKEA distribution centers worldwide—which handle about 70 percent of IKEA's total product line—and 4 more are under construction. The other 30 percent of IKEA's products travel directly from supplier to store.

Sometimes, however, product components actually come together for the first time in the store. In the case of the Pöang chair, the cushion comes from Poland and the frame from China. The two pieces are united only when the customer pulls each one off the shelf.

Step 5. Sell It

IKEA sells a lot of expensive furniture, and in a traditional store this is relatively easy: Put a piece in a lush setting, let the customer fall prey to visions of wealth and comfort, then offer plenty of easy credit. But to keep prices low, IKEA needs to sell furniture and other products such as the mug without salespeople or conspicuous price reductions. The company asks customers to assemble their furniture themselves. And IKEA doesn't want to ship it to you either. By any conventional measure, these are formidable hurdles to overcome. Yet they also explain why IKEA has worked so hard to create a separate world inside its stores—a kind of theme park masquerading as a furniture outlet—where normal rules and expectations don't apply.

The Trofé mugs arrive at IKEA stores packed on pallets. Any transportation packaging is collected for recycling. Price tags have already been placed on the mugs at the suppliers. In-store display is important. It's not just a question of displaying mugs and other products. It's also about providing inspiration for smart interior solutions. Customers contribute to the low prices at IKEA by selecting and collecting the products from the self-serve area, taking them home, and using the instructions enclosed to assemble them. Many will have already chosen the products from the IKEA catalog, of which 110 million copies are printed in 34 different language versions.

When you walk through the door of an IKEA store, you enter a meticulously constructed virtual Sweden. The first thing you encounter is a company-sponsored child-care facility. Hungry? Have some of those Swedish meatballs and lingonberries. The layout of an IKEA store guides shoppers in a predetermined path past several realistic model homes, which convey an eerily lived-in impression but are open for customers to sit in. Information kiosks provide advice on home decor. Color-coordinated cards offer plenty of suggestions on offbeat uses for products.

But the emphasis is always on price. Low-priced products that IKEA calls BTIs ("breathtaking items") are often perched on risers, framed by a huge yellow price tag. Nearby, shoppers will find other products—pricier, more design-oriented—as substitutes for the BTI.

The model homes suggest cheerful young people throwing dinner parties in hallways, using mismatched office chairs and narrow side tables. These aren't the aspirational images you'll find at Pottery Barn or Crate & Barrel. These are people who are living well in modest circumstances—frugal folks who know the value of a comfortable place to sit.

IKEA says its biggest selling point is the price tag, but it can't hurt that getting through one of IKEA's huge stores takes a lot of time. The layout is blatantly manipulative—though in a friendly, knowing way, not unlike at Disneyland—but when customers finally arrive at the checkout counter, they've had plenty of time to fully consider their purchases.

IKEA products broadcast an ethos for living in the modern world: Don't buy an ugly pitcher if you can get a stylish one for the same price. If you organize your plastic bags, you'll feel more in control of your life. It's left-brain logic applied to the right-brain art of living well. And if happiness involves dragging a cumbersome flat package off the shelf, standing in line at the checkout, hauling the box home, and spending hours assembling a kitchen cabinet, well, 260 million customers a year are willing to make that trade-off.

And, of course, next year it will be even cheaper.

Questions

1. What are IKEA's competitive priorities?
2. Describe IKEA's process for developing a new product.
3. What are additional features of the IKEA concept (beyond its design process) that contribute to creating exceptional value for the customer?
4. What would be important criteria for selecting a site for an IKEA store?

Source: Information about the Trofé coffee mug was obtained from www.ikea.com.

CASE: Dental Spa

Would a warm paraffin hand treatment during your dental cleaning or dental treatment put you at ease and make the process more bearable? That is the idea behind the new "dental spa" services opening in major cities throughout the United States. Beyond calming music and comfortable chairs and flat-screen TVs mounted on the ceiling with sound from the noise-canceling headphones that block unpleasant dental noises, at the same time foot scrubs, pedicures, or other spa services are sometimes possible. Two major trends have helped fuel the growth of dental spas: lessening of the painful associations of dentistry and the increased cosmetic focus of dentistry that goes along with other spa treatments.

Questions

1. Which one of the three new service requirements would a dental spa least likely pass: service experience fit, operational fit, or financial impact? Why?
2. What are some of the main areas of complexity and divergence in this kind of operation relative to the standard dental clinic?

PRACTICE EXAM

In each of the following statements, name the term defined or the items requested. Answers are listed at the bottom.

1. An organization capable of manufacturing or purchasing all the components needed to produce a finished product or device.
2. The one thing that a company can do better than its competitors.
3. The six phases of the product development process.
4. A useful tool for the economic analysis of a product development project.
5. An approach that uses interfunctional teams to get input from the customer in design specification.
6. A matrix of information that helps a team translate customer requirements into operating or engineering goals.
7. The greatest improvements from this arise from simplification of the product by reducing the number of separate parts.
8. The incorporation of environmental considerations into the design and development of products or services.

Answers to Practice Exam 1. Contract manufacturer 2. Core competency 3. Planning, concept development, system-level design, detail design, testing, production ramp-up 4. Net present value 5. Quality function development 6. House of quality 7. Design for manufacturing and assembly 8. Ecodesign

For PowerPoint lecture slides, Solutions Manual, Test Bank, Data files for solved examples, Excel Templates, Step-by-Step Solved Examples in video format, Tutorial Videos and many more, scan the adjacent **QR code**, or **visit http://www.mhhe.com/sie-chase15e**

Chapter 4

Project Management

LEARNING OBJECTIVES

LO 4-1 Explain what projects are and how projects are organized

LO 4-2 Analyze projects using network-planning models

LO 4-3 Evaluate projects using earned value management

LO 4-4 Exemplify how network-planning models and earned value management are implemented in commercial software packages

CAN A 15-STORY HOTEL BE BUILT IN LESS THAN A WEEK?

A Chinese construction company recently built a 15-story hotel in just six days. To show this was not a fluke, it then built a 30-story hotel in only 15 days! The company believes it can construct buildings that are 150 stories tall using the same high-speed techniques. Using these techniques, construction takes less than one-third the time it would take on a normal schedule.

The company uses many workers during the short construction period, and detailed schedules coordinate the many teams working simultaneously and around the clock on the building. Materials are prefabricated ahead of time in a factory. Premade modules are carried to the construction site on large trucks where they are placed in the steel structure with cranes. Special inspection and review processes are used to eliminate these delays in the construction process.

LO 4-1

Explain what projects are and how projects are organized

WHAT IS PROJECT MANAGEMENT?

Although most of the material in this chapter focuses on the technical aspects of project management (structuring project networks and calculating the critical path), the management aspects are certainly equally important. Success in project management is very much an activity that requires careful control of critical resources. We spend much of the time in this book focused on the management of nonhuman resources such as machines and material; for projects, however, the key resource is often our employees' time. Human resources are frequently the most expensive, and those people involved in the projects critical to the success of the firm are often the most valuable managers, consultants, and engineers.

At the highest levels in an organization, management often involves juggling a portfolio of projects. There are many different types of projects, ranging from the development of totally new products, to revisions of old products, to new marketing plans, as well as a vast array of projects for better serving customers and reducing costs.

Most companies deal with projects individually—pushing each through the pipeline as quickly and cost-effectively as possible. Many of these same companies are very good at applying the techniques described in this chapter in a manner where myriad tasks are executed flawlessly, but the projects just do not deliver the expected results. Worse, what often happens is that the projects consuming the most resources have the least connection to the firm's strategy.

Projects can be categorized based on the *type of change* being planned. For example, a development project might be looking at ways to change the *product* in response to market feedback, or it might be looking at ways to change the *process* in order to improve efficiency or quality. The four major types of change are product change, process change, research and development, and alliance and partnership. Projects can also be categorized based on the *amount of change* that is planned. In the case of a project that will make changes to the product itself, it might involve just some minor tweaks to the product—as often happens from year to year with automobiles—or it could be a complete redesign of the product that might happen once or twice a decade, as in the case of a new automobile model. The three categories based on the amount of change are derivative (incremental changes such as new packaging or no-frills versions), platform (fundamental improvements to existing products), and breakthrough (major changes that create entirely new markets). Exhibit 4.1 relates these two dimensions of projects with some examples.

In this chapter, we only scratch the surface in our introduction to the topic of project management. Professional project managers are individuals skilled at not only the technical aspects of calculating such things as early start and early finish time but, just as important, the people skills related to motivation. In addition, the ability to resolve conflicts as key decision points occur in the project is a

EXHIBIT 4.1

Types of Development Projects

More ← Amount of Change → Less

Types of Change	Breakthrough Projects	Platform Projects	Derivative Projects
Product Change	New core product	Addition to product family	Product enhancement
Process Change	New core process	Process upgrade	Incremental change
Research & Development	New core technology	Technology upgrade	Incremental change
Alliance & Partnership	Outsource of major activity	Selection of new partner	Incremental change

critical skill. Without a doubt, leading successful projects is the best way to prove your promotability to the people who make promotion decisions. Virtually all project work is teamwork, and leading a project involves leading a team. Your success at leading a project will spread quickly through the individuals in the team. As organizations flatten (through reengineering, downsizing, outsourcing), more will depend on projects and project leaders to get work done, work that previously was handled within departments.

A **project** may be defined as a series of related jobs usually directed toward some major output and requiring a significant period of time to perform. **Project management** can be defined as planning, directing, and controlling resources (people, equipment, material) to meet the technical, cost, and time constraints of the project.

Project
A series of related jobs usually directed toward some major output and requiring a significant period of time to perform.

Project management
Planning, directing, and controlling resources (people, equipment, material) to meet the technical, cost, and time constraints of a project.

Although projects are often thought to be one-time occurrences, the fact is that many projects can be repeated or transferred to other settings or products. The result will be another project output. A contractor building houses or a firm producing low-volume products such as supercomputers, locomotives, or jet airliners can effectively consider these as projects.

DMRC: Marvel of Project Management

Since November 1997, as the first Managing Director of one of the most talked-about complex projects of independent India, Delhi Metro Rail Corporation (DMRC), Dr. E. Sreedharan faced a series of challenges. Those who did not know his sound engineering background and many successful projects under his belt, including that of Konkan Railways, always doubted whether the DMRC project would ever be completed. DMRC project challenges were many times complex than building a house or building a stadium. The meticulousness in project planning and execution has made DMRC as one of the finest engineering marvels of India in recent times.

At the outset, the biggest challenge for DMRC was relocation of a large number of people, business establishments, water pipes, sewerage lines, telephone lines, electric cables, and that too without disrupting the normal life of Delhi, the capital city of India. World class quality with scope, schedule and cost management is a day-to-day concern in this project. Cost and time overruns are very common in such projects. For example, Kolkata Metro took about 22 years to complete with expenditure, which was 14 times more than what was originally planned.

According to Dr. Sreedharan, "It (DMRC) will be much more than a cheap and safer means of transport. It will reduce congestion on roads making movement easier. It will also reduce atmospheric pollution to a great level making the environment healthy. The Metro will totally transform our social culture giving us a sense of discipline, cleanliness and enhance multifold development of this cosmopolitan city [1]."

Thanks to the world-class leadership and project management techniques, the first phase of Delhi Metro, covering about 65 km, of which about 12 km was underground and the remaining on elevated corridors, got completed not only before schedule but also within the budgetary allocations of ₹10,570 crore (₹105.7 billion). Without any major disruption to the political nerve-centre of India, DMRC is like a dream come true for Delhi.

Reference

1. Joshi, S. (2001) Delhi Metro is quake proof. *The Hindu Online Edition*, 4 February. http://www.hinduonnet.com/2001/02/04/stories/14042184.htm [Accessed on 16 January 2018]
2. http://www.delhimetrorail.com/ [Accessed on 16 January 2018]

Organizing the Project Team

Before the project starts, senior management must decide which of three organizational structures will be used to tie the project to the parent firm: pure project, functional project, or matrix project. We next discuss the strengths and weaknesses of the three main forms.

Strategy

Pure Project

Pure project
A structure for organizing a project where a self-contained team works full time on the project.

Tom Peters predicts that most of the world's work will be "brainwork," done in semipermanent networks of small project-oriented teams, each one an autonomous, entrepreneurial center of opportunity, where the necessity for speed and flexibility dooms the hierarchical management structures we and our ancestors grew up with. Thus, out of the three basic project organizational structures, Peters favors the **pure project** (nicknamed *skunkworks*), where a self-contained team works full time on the project.

Advantages

- The project manager has full authority over the project.
- Team members report to one boss. They do not have to worry about dividing loyalty with a functional-area manager.
- Lines of communication are shortened. Decisions are made quickly.
- Team pride, motivation, and commitment are high.

Disadvantages

- Duplication of resources. Equipment and people are not shared across projects.
- Organizational goals and policies are ignored, as team members are often both physically and psychologically removed from headquarters.
- The organization falls behind in its knowledge of new technology due to weakened functional divisions.
- Because team members have no functional area home, they worry about life-after-project, and project termination is delayed.

Functional Project

Functional project
In this structure, team members are assigned from the functional units of the organization. The team members remain a part of their functional units and typically are not dedicated to the project.

At the other end of the project organization spectrum is the **functional project**, housing the project within a functional division.

Advantages

- A team member can work on several projects.
- Technical expertise is maintained within the functional area even if individuals leave the project or organization.
- The functional area is a home after the project is completed. Functional specialists can advance vertically.
- A critical mass of specialized functional-area experts creates synergistic solutions to a project's technical problems.

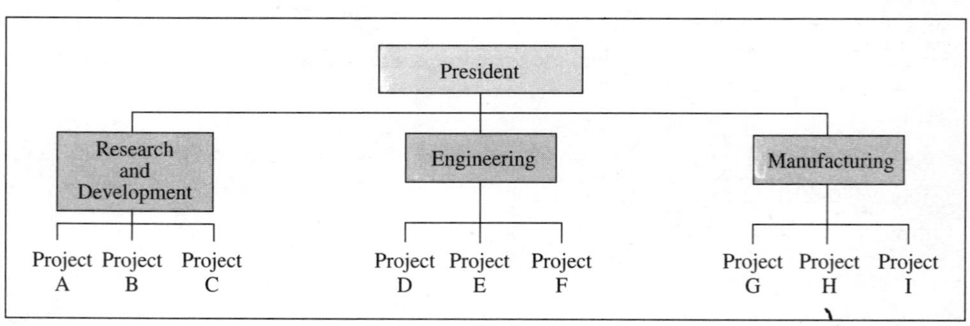

Disadvantages

- Aspects of the project that are not directly related to the functional area get shortchanged.
- Motivation of team members is often weak.
- Needs of the client are secondary and are responded to slowly.

Matrix Project

The classic specialized organizational form, the **matrix project**, attempts to blend properties of functional and pure project structures. Each project utilizes people from different functional areas. The project manager (PM) decides what tasks will be performed and when, but the functional managers control which people and technologies are used. If the matrix form is chosen, different projects (rows of the matrix) borrow resources from functional areas (columns). Senior management must then decide whether a weak, balanced, or strong form of a matrix is to be used. This establishes whether project managers have little, equal, or more authority than the functional managers with whom they negotiate for resources.

Matrix project
A structure that blends the functional and pure project structures. Each project uses people from different functional areas. A dedicated project manager decides what tasks need to be performed and when, but the functional managers control which people to use.

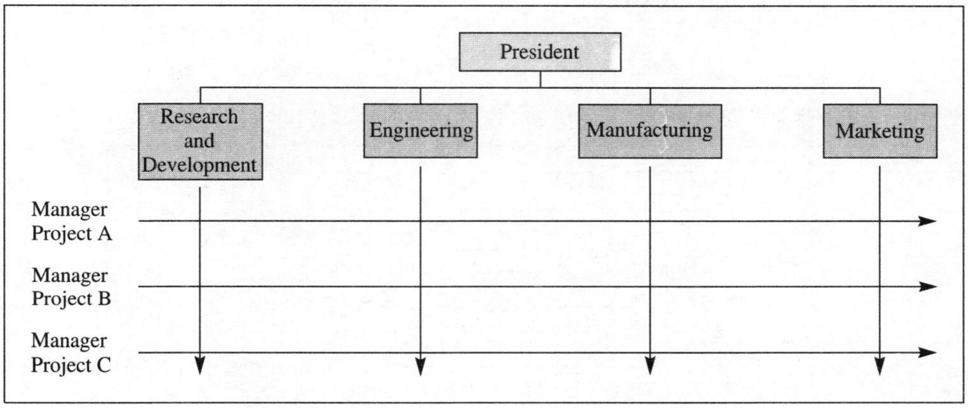

Advantages

- Communication between functional divisions is enhanced.
- A project manager is held responsible for successful completion of the project.
- Duplication of resources is minimized.
- Team members have a functional "home" after project completion, so they are less worried about life-after-project than if they were a pure project organization.
- Policies of the parent organization are followed. This increases support for the project.

Disadvantages

- There are two bosses. Often the functional manager will be listened to before the project manager. After all, who can promote you or give you a raise?
- It is doomed to failure unless the PM has strong negotiating skills.
- Suboptimization is a danger, because PMs hoard resources for their own project, thus harming other projects.

Note that regardless of which of the three major organizational forms is used, the project manager is the primary contact point with the customer. Communication and flexibility are greatly enhanced because one person is responsible for successful completion of the project.

Organizing Project Tasks

A project starts out as a *statement of work* (*SOW*). The SOW may be a written description of the objectives to be achieved, with a brief statement of the work to be done and a proposed schedule specifying the start and completion dates. It also could contain performance measures in terms of budget and completion steps (milestones) and the written reports to be supplied.

Process

A *task* is a further subdivision of a project. It is usually not longer than several months in duration and is performed by one group or organization. A *subtask* may be used if needed to further subdivide the project into more meaningful pieces.

Project milestone
A specific event in a project.

A *work package* is a group of activities combined to be assignable to a single organizational unit. It still falls into the format of all project management; the package provides a description of what is to be done, when it is to be started and completed, the budget, measures of performance, and specific events to be reached at points in time. These specific events are called **project milestones**. Typical milestones might be the completion of the design, the production of a prototype, the completed testing of the prototype, and the approval of a pilot run.

Work breakdown structure (WBS)
The hierarchy of project tasks, subtasks, and work packages.

The **work breakdown structure (WBS)** defines the hierarchy of project tasks, subtasks, and work packages. Completion of one or more work packages results in the completion of a subtask; completion of one or more subtasks results in the completion of a task; and, finally, the completion of all tasks is required to complete the project. A representation of this structure is shown in Exhibit 4.2.

Exhibit 4.3 shows the WBS for an optical scanner project. The WBS is important in organizing a project because it breaks the project down into manageable pieces. The number of levels will vary depending on the project. How much detail or how many levels to use depends on the following:

Exhibit 4.2

An Example of a Work Breakdown Structure

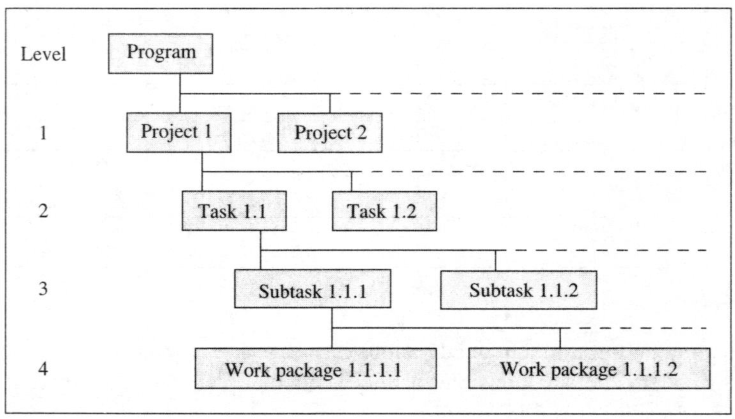

Exhibit 4.3

Work Breakdown Structure, Large Optical Scanner Design

Level 1	2	3	4		
x				1	Optical simulator design
	x			1.1	Optical design
		x		1.1.1	Telescope design/fab
		x		1.1.2	Telescope/simulator optical interface
		x		1.1.3	Simulator zoom system design
		x		1.1.4	Ancillary simulator optical component specification
	x			1.2	System performance analysis
		x		1.2.1	Overall system firmware and software control
			x	1.2.1.1	Logic flow diagram generation and analysis
			x	1.2.1.2	Basic control algorithm design
		x		1.2.2	Far beam analyzer
		x		1.2.3	System inter- and intra-alignment method design
		x		1.2.4	Data recording and reduction requirements
	x			1.3	System integration
	x			1.4	Cost analysis
		x		1.4.1	Cost/system schedule analysis
		x		1.4.2	Cost/system performance analysis
	x			1.5	Management
		x		1.5.1	System design/engineering management
		x		1.5.2	Program management
	x			1.6	Long lead item procurement
		x		1.6.1	Large optics
		x		1.6.2	Target components
		x		1.6.3	Detectors

- The level at which a single individual or organization can be assigned responsibility and accountability for accomplishing the work package.
- The level at which budget and cost data will be collected during the project.

There is not a single correct WBS for any project, and two different project teams might develop different WBSs for the same project. Some experts have referred to project management as an art rather than a science, because there are so many different ways that a project can be approached. Finding the correct way to organize a project depends on experience with the particular task.

Activities are defined within the context of the work breakdown structure and are pieces of work that consume time. Activities do not necessarily require the expenditure of effort by people, although they often do. For example, waiting for paint to dry may be an activity in a project. Activities are identified as part of the WBS. From our sample project in Exhibit 4.3, activities would include telescope design and fabrication (1.1.1), telescope/simulator optical interface (1.1.2), and data recording (1.2.4). Activities need to be defined in such a way that when they are all completed, the project is done.

Activities
Pieces of work within a project that consume time. The completion of all the activities of a project marks the end of the project.

NETWORK-PLANNING MODELS

LO 4-2
Analyze projects using network-planning models

Analytics

The two best-known network-planning models were developed in the 1950s. The Critical Path Method (CPM) was developed for scheduling maintenance shutdowns at chemical processing plants owned by DuPont. Since maintenance projects are often performed in this industry, reasonably accurate time estimates for activities are available. CPM is based on the assumptions that project activity times can be estimated accurately and that they do not vary. The Program Evaluation and Review Technique (PERT) was developed for the U.S. Navy's Polaris missile project. This was a massive project involving over 3,000 contractors. Because most of the activities had never been done before, PERT was developed to handle uncertain time estimates. As years passed, features that distinguished CPM from PERT have diminished, so in our treatment here we just use the term CPM.

In a sense, the CPM techniques illustrated here owe their development to their widely used predecessor, the Gantt chart. Although the Gantt chart is able to relate activities to time in a usable fashion for small projects, the interrelationship of activities, when displayed in this form, becomes extremely difficult to visualize and to work with for projects that include more than about 25 activities.

The **critical path** of activities in a project is the sequence of activities that form the longest chain in terms of their time to complete. If any one of the activities in the critical path is delayed, then the entire project is delayed. It is possible and it often happens that there are multiple paths of the same length through the network so there are multiple critical paths. Determining scheduling information about each activity in the project is the major goal of CPM techniques. The techniques calculate when an activity must start and end, together with whether the activity is part of the critical path.

Critical path
The sequence(s) of activities in a project that form the longest chain in terms of their time to complete. This path contains zero slack time. It is possible for there to be multiple critical paths in a project. Techniques used to find the critical path are called CPM, or critical path method, techniques.

Critical Path Method (CPM)

Here is a procedure for scheduling a project. In this case, a single time estimate is used because we are assuming that the activity times are known. A very simple project will be scheduled to demonstrate the basic approach.

Consider that you have a group assignment that requires a decision on whether you should invest in a company. Your instructor has suggested that you perform the analysis in the following four steps:

A. Select a company.
B. Obtain the company's annual report and perform a ratio analysis.
C. Collect technical stock price data and construct charts.
D. Individually review the data and make a team decision on whether to buy the stock.

Your group of four people decides that the project can be divided into four activities as suggested by the instructor. You decide that all the team members should be involved in selecting the company and that it should take one week to complete this activity. You will meet at the end of the week to decide what company the group will consider. During this meeting, you will divide up your group: Two people will be responsible for the annual report and ratio analysis, and the other two will collect the technical data and construct the charts. Your group expects it to take two weeks to get the annual report and perform the ratio analysis, and a week to collect the stock price data and generate the charts. You agree that the two groups can work independently. Finally, you agree to meet as a team to make the purchase decision. Before you meet, you want to allow one week for each team member to review all the data.

This is a simple project, but it will serve to demonstrate the approach. The following are the appropriate steps.

1. **Identify each activity to be done in the project and estimate how long it will take to complete each activity.** This is simple, given the information from your instructor. We identify the activities as follows: A(1), B(2), C(1), D(1). The number is the expected duration of the activity.

Immediate predecessor
Activities that need to be completed immediately before another activity.

2. **Determine the required sequence of activities and construct a network reflecting the precedence relationships.** An easy way to do this is to first identify the **immediate predecessors** associated with an activity. The immediate predecessors are the activities that need to be completed immediately before an activity. Activity A needs to be completed before activities B and C can start. B and C need to be completed before D can start. The following table reflects what we know so far:

Activity	Designation	Immediate Predecessors	Time (Weeks)
Select company	A	None	1
Obtain annual report and perform ratio analysis	B	A	2
Collect stock price data and perform technical analysis	C	A	1
Review data and make a decision	D	B and C	1

Here is a diagram that depicts these precedence relationships:

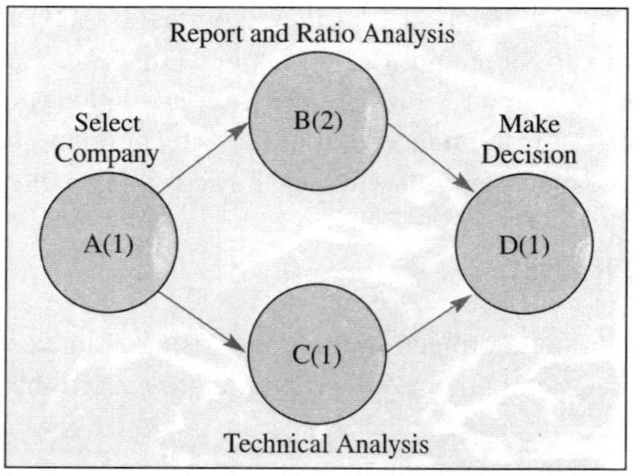

3. **Determine the critical path.** Consider each sequence of activities that runs from the beginning to the end of the project. For our simple project, there are two paths: A–B–D and A–C–D. The critical path is the path where the sum of the activity times is the longest. A–B–D has a duration of four weeks and A–C–D has a duration of three weeks. The critical path, therefore, is A–B–D. If any activity along the critical path is delayed, then the entire project will be delayed.

4. **Determine the early start/finish and late start/finish schedule.** To schedule the project, find when each activity needs to start and when it needs to finish. For some activities in a project there may be some leeway in when an activity can start and finish. This is called the **slack time** in an activity. For each activity in the project, we calculate four points in time: the early start, early finish, late start, and late finish times. The early start and early finish are the earliest times that the activity can start and be finished. Similarly, the late start and late finish are the latest times the activities can start and finish without delaying the project. The difference between the late start time and early start time is the slack time. To help keep all of this straight, we place these numbers in special places around the nodes that represent each activity in our network diagram, as shown here.

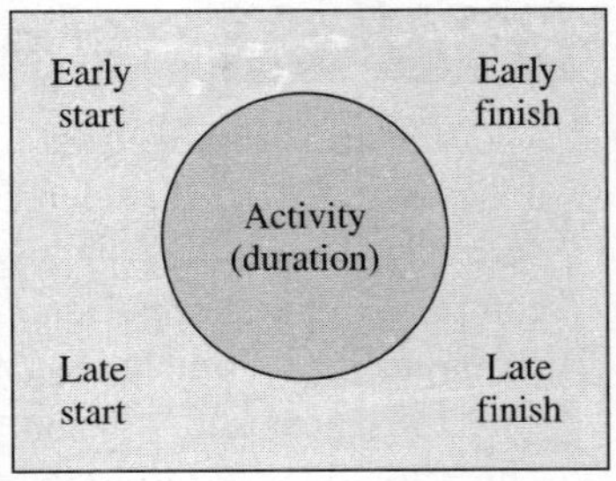

Slack time
The time that an activity can be delayed without delaying the entire project; the difference between the late and early start times of an activity.

To calculate numbers, start from the beginning of the network and work to the end, calculating the early start and early finish numbers. Start counting with the current period, designated as period 0. Activity A has an early start of 0 and an early finish of 1. Activity B's early start is A's early finish or 1. Similarly, C's early start is 1. The early finish for B is 3, and the early finish for C is 2. Now consider activity D. D cannot start until both B and C are done. Because B cannot be done until 3, D cannot start until that time. The early start for D, therefore, is 3, and the early finish is 4. Our diagram now looks like this.

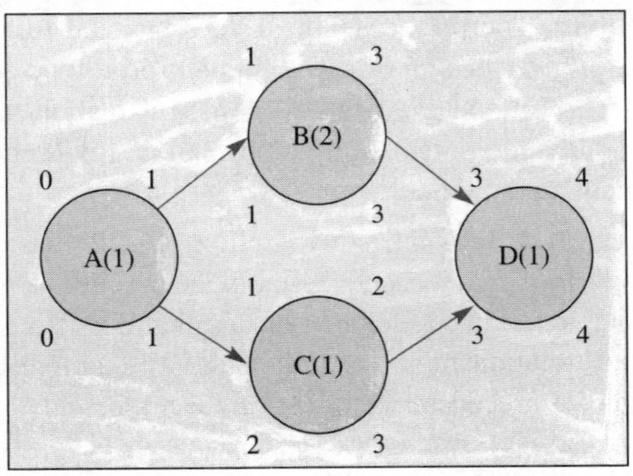

To calculate the late finish and late start times, start from the end of the network and work toward the front. Consider activity D. The earliest it can be done is at time 4; and if we do not want to delay the completion of the project, the late finish needs to be set to 4. With a duration of 1, the latest that D can start is 3. Now consider activity C. C must be done by time 3 so that D can start, so C's late finish time is 3 and its late start time is 2. Notice the difference between the early and late start and finish times: This activity has one week of slack time. Activity B must be done by time 3 so that D can start, so its late finish time is 3 and late start time is 1. There is no slack in B. Finally, activity A must be done so that B and C can start. Because B must start earlier than C, and A must get done in time for B to start, the late finish time for A is 1. Finally, the late start time for A is 0. Notice there is no slack in activities A, B, and D. The final network looks like this. (Hopefully the stock your investment team has chosen is a winner!)

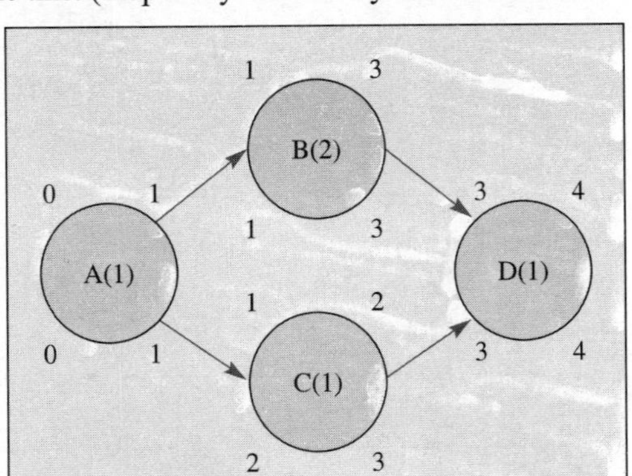

EXAMPLE 4.1 Critical Path Method

Many firms that have tried to enter the notebook computer market have failed. Suppose your firm believes there is a big demand in this market because existing products have not been designed correctly. They are too heavy, too large, or too small to have standard-size keyboards. Your intended computer will be small enough to carry inside a jacket pocket if need be. The ideal size will be no larger than 5 inches × 9½ inches × 1 inch with a folding keyboard. It should weigh no more than 15 ounces and have an LCD display, a solid state drive, and a wireless bluetooth connection. This should appeal to traveling businesspeople, but it could have a much wider market, including students. It should be priced in the $175 to $200 range.

The project, then, is to design, develop, and produce a prototype of this small computer. In the rapidly changing computer industry, it is crucial to hit the market with a product of this sort in less than a year. Therefore, the project team has been allowed approximately eight months (35 weeks) to produce the prototype.

SOLUTION

The first charge of the project team is to develop a project network chart and determine if the prototype computer can be completed within the 35-week target. Let's follow the steps in the development of the network.

1. **Activity identification.** The project team decides that the following activities are the major components of the project: design of the computer, prototype construction, prototype testing, methods specification (summarized in a report), evaluation studies of automatic assembly equipment, an assembly equipment study report, and a final report summarizing all aspects of the design, equipment, and methods.
2. **Activity sequencing and network construction.** On the basis of discussion with staff, the project manager develops the precedence table and sequence network shown in Exhibit 4.4. When constructing a network, take care to ensure that the activities are in the proper order and that the logic of their relationships is maintained. For example, it would be illogical to have a situation where Event A precedes Event B, B precedes C, and C precedes A.

EXHIBIT 4.4

CPM Network for Computer Design Project

CPM Activity Designations And Time Estimates

Activity	Designation	Immediate Predecessors	Time (Weeks)
Design	A	–	21
Build prototype	B	A	5
Evaluate equipment	C	A	7
Test prototype	D	B	2
Write equipment report	E	C, D	5
Write methods report	F	C, D	8
Write final report	G	E, F	2

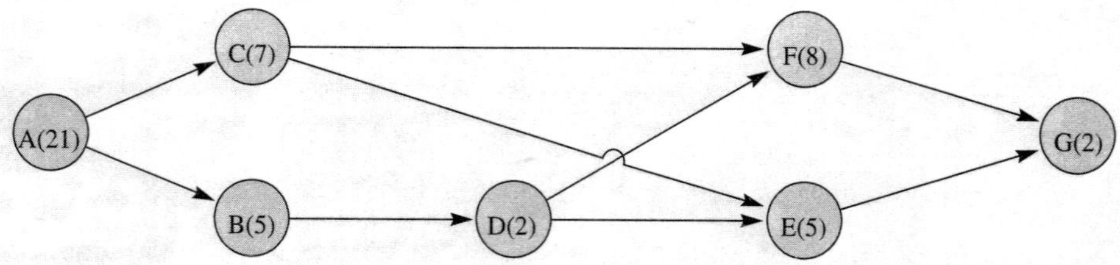

3. **Determine the critical path.** The critical path is the longest sequence of connected activities through the network and is defined as the path with zero slack time. This network has four different paths: A–C–F–G, A–C–E–G, A–B–D–F–G, and A–B–D–E–G. The lengths of these paths are 38, 35, 38, and 35 weeks. Note that this project has two different critical paths; this might indicate that this would be a fairly difficult project to manage. Calculating the early start and late start schedules gives additional insight into how difficult this project might be to complete on time.

Early Start and Late Start Schedules An **early start schedule** is one that lists all of the activities by their early start times. For activities not on the critical path, there is slack time between the completion of each activity and the start of the next activity. The early start schedule completes the project and all its activities as soon as possible.

Early start schedule
A project schedule that lists all activities by their early start times.

A **late start schedule** lists the activities to start as late as possible without delaying the completion date of the project. One motivation for using a late start schedule is that savings are realized by postponing purchases of materials, the use of labor, and other costs until necessary. These calculations are shown in Exhibit 4.5. From this, we see that the only activity that has slack is activity E. This certainly would be a fairly difficult project to complete on time.

Late start schedule
A project schedule that lists all activities by their late start times. This schedule may create savings by postponing purchases of material and other costs associated with the project.

Exhibit 4.5

CPM Network for Computer Design Project with Slack Calculations

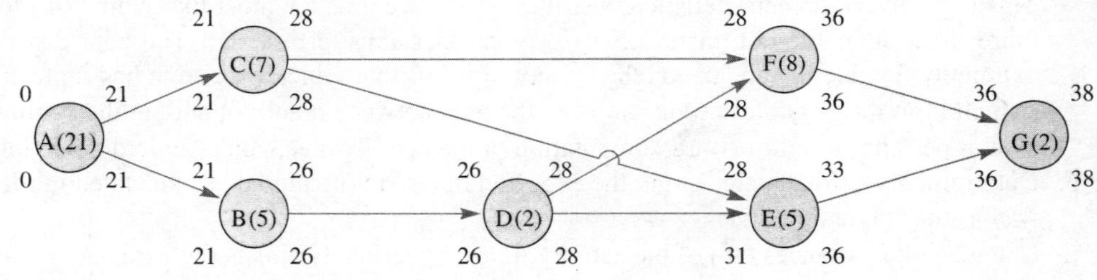

Slack Calculations and Critical Path Determinations

Activity	LS–Es	Slack	On Critical Path
A	0–0	0	✓
B	21–21	0	✓
C	21–21	0	✓
D	26–26	0	✓
E	31–28	3	
F	28–28	0	✓
G	36–36	0	✓

CPM with Three Activity Time Estimates

If a single estimate of the time required to complete an activity is not reliable, the best procedure is to use three time estimates. These three times not only allow us to estimate the activity time but also let us obtain a probability estimate for completion time for the entire network. Briefly, the procedure is as follows: The estimated activity time is calculated using a weighted average of a minimum, maximum, and most likely time estimate. The expected completion time of the network is computed using the procedure described previously. Using estimates of variability for the activities on the critical path, the probability of completing the project by particular times can be estimated. (Note that the probability calculations are a distinguishing feature of the classic PERT approach.)

EXAMPLE 4.2 Three Time Estimates

We use the same information as in Example 4.1 with the exception that activities have three time estimates.

SOLUTION

1. Identify each activity to be done in the project.
2. Determine the sequence of activities and construct a network reflecting the precedence relationships.
3. The three estimates for an activity time are

   a = Optimistic time: The minimum reasonable period of time in which the activity can be completed. (There is only a small probability, typically assumed to be 1 percent, that the activity can be completed in less time.)

   m = Most likely time: The best guess of the time required. Since m would be the time thought most likely to appear, it is also the mode of the beta distribution discussed in step 4.

   b = Pessimistic time: The maximum reasonable period of time the activity would take to be completed. (There is only a small probability, typically assumed to be 1 percent, that it would take longer.)

   Typically, this information is gathered from those people who are to perform the activity.
4. Calculate the expected time (ET) for each activity. The formula for this calculation is

$$\text{ET} = \frac{a + 4m + b}{6} \qquad [4.1]$$

   This is based on the beta statistical distribution and weights the most likely time (m) four times more than either the optimistic time (a) or the pessimistic time (b). The beta distribution is extremely flexible. It can take on the variety of forms that typically arise; it has finite end points (which limit the possible activity times to the area between a and b); and, in the simplified version, it permits straightforward computation of the activity mean and standard deviation.
5. Determine the critical path. Using the expected times, a critical path is calculated in the same way as the single time case.
6. Calculate the variances (σ^2) of the activity times. Specifically, this is the variance, σ^2, associated with each ET and is computed as follows:

$$\sigma^2 = \left(\frac{b - a}{6}\right)^2 \qquad [4.2]$$

   As you can see, the variance is the square of one-sixth the difference between the two extreme time estimates. Of course, the greater this difference, the larger the variance.
7. Determine the probability of completing the project on a given date, based on the application of the standard normal distribution. A valuable feature of using three time estimates is that it enables the analyst to assess the effect of uncertainty on project completion time. (If you are not familiar with this type of analysis, see the box titled Probability Analysis.) The mechanics of deriving this probability are as follows:

   a. Sum the variance values associated with each activity on the critical path.

   b. Substitute this figure, along with the project due date and the project expected completion time, into the Z transformation formula. This formula is

$$Z = \frac{D - T_E}{\sqrt{\Sigma \sigma^2_{cp}}} \qquad [4.3]$$

   where

   D = Desired completion date for the project

   T_E = Expected completion time for the project

   $\Sigma\sigma^2_{cp}$ = Sum of the variances along the critical path *c.* Calculate the value of Z, which is the number of standard deviations (of a standard normal distribution) that the project due date is from the expected completion time.

d. Using the value of Z, find the probability of meeting the project due date (using a table of normal probabilities such as Appendix G). The *expected completion time* is the starting time plus the sum of the activity times on the critical path.

Following the steps just outlined, we developed Exhibit 4.6 showing expected times and variances. The project network was created the same way we did previously. The only difference is that the activity times are weighted averages. We determine the critical path as before, using these values as if they were single numbers. The difference between the single time estimate and the three times (optimistic, most likely, and pessimistic) is in computing probabilities of completion. Exhibit 4.7 shows the network and critical path.

EXHIBIT 4.6

Activity Expected Times and Variances

Activity	Activity Designation	Time Estimates a	m	b	Expected Times (ET) $\frac{a+4m+b}{6}$	Activity Variance (σ^2) $\left(\frac{b-a}{6}\right)^2$
Design	A	10	22	28	21	9
Build prototype	B	4	4	10	5	1
Evaluate equipment	C	4	6	14	7	2.7778
Test prototype	D	1	2	3	2	0.1111
Write report	E	1	5	9	5	1.7778
Write methods report	F	7	8	9	8	0.1111
Write final report	G	2	2	2	2	0

EXHIBIT 4.7

Computer Design Project with Three Time Estimates

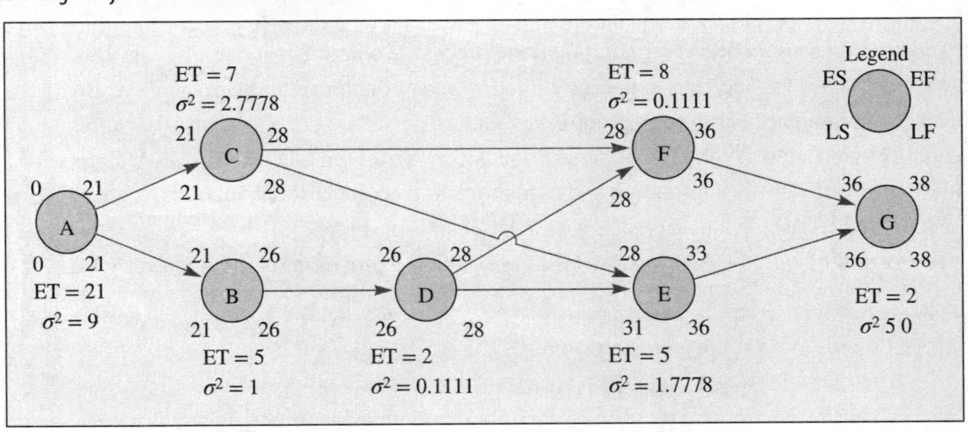

Because there are two critical paths in the network, we must decide which variances to use in arriving at the probability of meeting the project due date. A conservative approach dictates using the critical path with the largest total variance to focus management's attention on the activities most likely to exhibit broad variations. On this basis, the variances associated with activities A, C, F, and G would be used to find the probability of completion. Thus $\Sigma\sigma^2_{cp} = 9 + 2.7778 + 0.1111 + 0 = 11.8889$.

Suppose management asks for the probability of completing the project in 35 weeks. *D*, then, is 35. The expected completion time was found to be 38. Substituting into the *Z* equation and solving, we obtain

$$Z = \frac{D - T_E}{\sqrt{\Sigma\sigma_{cp}^2}} = \frac{35 - 38}{\sqrt{11.8889}} = -0.87$$

Looking at Appendix G, we see that a *Z* value of -0.87 yields a probability of 0.1922, which means that the project manager has only about a 19 percent chance of completing the project in 35 weeks. Note that this probability is really the probability of completing the critical path A–C–F–G. Because there is another critical path and other paths that might become critical, the probability of completing the project in 35 weeks is actually less than 0.19.

Aadhaar: An Ambitious Mega Project of Government of India

Aadhaar is one of the most ambitious mega projects of India, which has multi-faceted uses, like providing an identity to a common man so that he/she is empowered to take direct benefits from the government without any middleman. It can be valid anywhere in India through online verification with features like countrywide portability. It helps to remove mounting corruption in the implementation of welfare schemes of the government. There are many other reasons due to which Aadhaar is important to the nation.

In the local language, Hindi, Aadhaar means foundation. **UIDAI** was formed as a statutory authority recognized under the provisions of the Aadhaar (Targeted Delivery of Financial and Other Subsidies, Benefits and Services) Act, 2016 (Aadhaar Act 2016) on 12th July 2016, by the Government of India. UIDAI aimed to issue **U**nique **ID**entification (UID) numbers, named as "Aadhaar", to all citizens of India. Aadhaar is a 12-digit number pertaining to the resident's demographic information. The vision and mission of UIDAI are as follows[1]:

Vision of UIDAI

To empower residents of India with a unique identity and a digital platform to authenticate anytime, anywhere.

Mission of UIDAI

- To provide for good governance, efficient, transparent and targeted delivery of subsidies, benefits and services, the expenditure for which is incurred from the Consolidated Fund of India, to individuals residing in India through assigning of unique identity numbers
- To develop policy, procedure and system for issuing Aadhaar number to individuals, who request for same by submitting their demographic information and biometric information by undergoing the process of enrolment
- To develop policy, procedure and systems for Aadhaar holders for updating and authenticating their digital identity
- To ensure availability, scalability and resilience of the technology infrastructure
- To build a long term sustainable organization to carry forward the vision and values of the UIDAI
- To ensure security and confidentiality of identity information and authentication records of individuals
- To ensure compliance of Aadhaar Act by all individual and agencies in letter and spirit
- To make regulations and rules consistent with the Aadhaar Act, for carrying out the provisions of the Aadhaar Act

Project Timeline

A complete timeline of Aadhaar project is presented in the following table.

Table: Aadhaar Timeline[2, 3]

1999	2000	2001	2003
The Kargil review committee (KRC) was formed under the supervision of Mr. K. Subrahmanyam to examine the status of national security.	A KRC submitted its report to then Prime Minister Atal Bihari Vajpayee in January 2000. It recommended that identity cards should be issued to the citizens of India who are living in villages near border region.	In May 2001, another committee under Mr. L. K. Advani recommended that a project on multipurpose national identity card be initiated at the earliest.	The Citizenship (Amendment) Bill was announced, which confirmed that the central government may mandate to register every citizen of India and provide them a national identity card.

2009		2010	
In accordance with the recommendation of Planning Commission of India (Now called as NITI Aayog, with a changed mandate), the UIDAI was formed in January 2009. In June, the same year, Mr. Nandan Nilekani, a technocrat and co-founder of Infosys, was asked to be the Chairman of UIDAI.		UIDAI Chairman launched the logo and the brand name 'Aadhaar' for this project in April 2010. UIDAI approved 15 agencies to provide training to the personnel involved in the enrolment process in July 2010. The first UID number was delivered on 29 September 2010 to a resident of Nandurbar, Maharashtra.	
2012	**2013**	**2014**	**2015**
The year saw the launch of an online system for Aadhaar verification by UIDAI in February. Direct benefits transfer (DBT) scheme was launched in November 2012. It aimed at plugging the leakages of benefit transferred to beneficiaries by eliminating middlemen and direct transfer to the bank account of beneficiaries.	A setback came in September 2013 when the Supreme Court of India ordered that government cannot refuse any service to a citizen, as Aadhaar is voluntary.	In July 2014, Prime Minister Narendra Modi announced linking of Aadhaar project with passports.	In March 2015, the DigiLocker service was launched to facilitate Aadhaar-holders to save and scan their documents on cloud.
2016	**2017**		
In March 2016, the Aadhaar (Targeted Delivery of Financial and Other Subsidies, Benefits and Services) Bill, 2016, was approved in the Lok Sabha as a Money Bill.	The government made Aadhaar compulsory to avail benefits for about three dozen central schemes.		

Success of a nationwide multi-purpose project like Aadhaar requires open source technologies. Dependency on specific operating system or computer hardware or storage devise or database vendor or other vendor-based technologies is counter-productive in speedy and cost-effective diffusion of benefits of such projects. Aadhaar project had to handle this along with another challenge of data security.

Benefits of Aadhar Project

This 12-digit unique identity number contains personal and biometric information about the citizen that is very helpful in verification of identity. In the lack of this, corruption in public welfare schemes was at its nadir (rock bottom). Some of the benefits of Aadhaar are as follows:

1. Aadhaar card is now used to transfer LPG subsidy money directly to the bank account of beneficiary. This DBTL (Direct Benefit Transfer of LPG) pattern is named as PAHAL. Earlier, the middlemen used to grab this.
2. Pradhan Mantri Jan Dhan Yojana (PMJDY) allows Aadhaar document as sufficient to open the bank account. This helps poors to have their own accounts through which loan can be taken, be genuine farmers and businessmen, thus eliminating the involvement of middlemen.
3. Aadhaar linked Digital Locker service is available that can scan and save important documents on the cloud and may be shared with a third party including government.
4. To manage fake voter list, Aadhaar card can be linked with voter ID.
5. Pensioners can now link their pension account with Aadhaar, which eliminates fake withdrawal of pension by unauthorized persons.
6. Similar to pension, provident fund accounts are also linked to Aadhaar.
7. All bank accounts are now getting linked to Aadhaar. This helps the tracing of illegal transfer and deposit or withdrawal of money. Even tax collection would also improve.

It is expected that many government schemes, bank transactions, property transfer, tax recovery, etc. would have better operational efficiency with Aadhaar linked processes and procedures.

Discussion Questions

1. Why is Aadhaar project so important in India? Is the investment in this project justified with reference to tangible and intangible benefits to the nation and its citizens?
2. Why did certain people object to data security in Aadhaar system? What are the measures UIDAI had taken to prevent the security breach in the Aadhaar database?
3. How would you rate Aadhaar as a project in terms of cost, time and scope over-run?

References

1. https://uidai.gov.in/about-uidai/about-uidai.html#main-content [Accessed on 18 January 2018]
2. https://aadharcard.in/aadhar-histroy [Accessed on 18 January 2018]
3. http://www.thehindubusinessline.com/blink/cover/the-aadhaar-of-all things/article9609603.ece [Accessed on 18 January 2018]
4. https://en.wikipedia.org/wiki/Aadhaar#Data_Leaks [Accessed on 18 January 2018]
5. http://www.allonmoney.com/information/benefits-of-aadhar-card [Accessed on 18 January 2018]

PROBABILITY ANALYSIS

The three-time-estimate approach introduces the ability to consider the probability that a project will be completed within a particular amount of time. The assumption needed to make this probability estimate is that the activity duration times are independent random variables. If this is true, the central limit theorem can be used to find the mean and the variance of the sequence of activities that form the critical path. The central limit theorem says that the sum of a group of independent, identically distributed random variables approaches a normal distribution as the number of random variables increases. In the case of project management problems, the random variables are the actual times for the activities in the project. (Recall that the time for each activity is assumed to be independent of other activities and to follow a beta statistical distribution.) For this, the expected time to complete the critical path activities is the sum of the activity times.

Likewise, because of the assumption of activity time independence, the sum of the variances of the activities along the critical path is the variance of the expected time to complete the path. Recall that the standard deviation is equal to the square root of the variance.

To determine the actual probability of completing the critical path activities within a certain amount of time, we need to find where on our probability distribution the time falls. Appendix G shows the areas of the cumulative standard normal distribution for different values of Z. Z measures the number of standard deviations either to the right or to the left of zero in the distribution. The values correspond to the cumulative probability associated with each value of Z. For example, the first value in the table, −4.00, has a $G(z)$ equal to .00003. This means that the probability associated with a Z value of −4.0 is only .003 percent. Similarly, a Z value of 1.50 has a $G(z)$ equal to .93319 or 93.319 percent. The Z values are calculated using Equation (4.3) given in Step 7b of the "Three Time Estimates" example solution. These cumulative probabilities also can be obtained by using the NORMSDIST (Z) function built into Microsoft Excel.

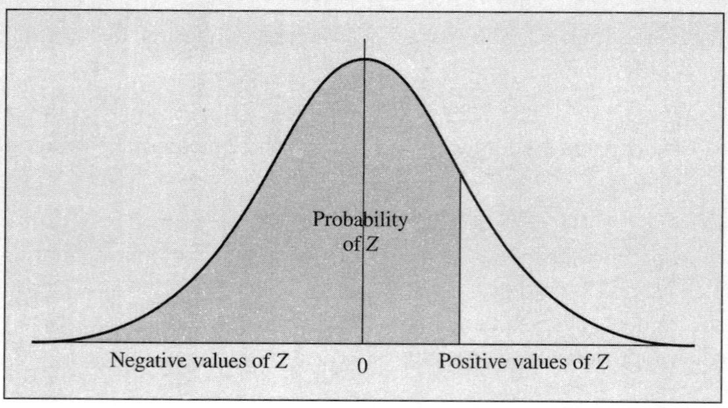

Time–Cost Models and Project Crashing

In practice, project managers are as much concerned with the cost to complete a project as with the time to complete the project. For this reason, **time–cost models** have been devised. These models—extensions of the basic critical path method—attempt to develop a minimum-cost schedule for an entire project and to control expenditures during the project.

Time–cost models
Extension of the critical path models that considers the trade-off between the time required to complete an activity and the cost. This is often referred to as "crashing" the project.

Minimum-Cost Scheduling (Time–Cost Trade-Off) The basic assumption in minimum-cost scheduling, also known as "crashing," is that there is a relationship between activity completion time and the cost of a project. *Crashing* refers to the compression or shortening of the time to complete the project. On one hand, it costs money to expedite an activity; on the other, it costs money to sustain (or lengthen) the project. The costs associated with expediting activities are termed *activity direct costs* and add to the project direct cost. Some may be worker-related, such as requiring overtime work, hiring more workers, and transferring workers from other jobs; others are resource-related, such as buying or leasing additional or more efficient equipment and drawing on additional support facilities.

Analytics

The costs associated with sustaining the project are termed *project indirect costs:* overhead, facilities, and resource opportunity costs, and, under certain contractual situations, penalty costs or lost incentive payments. Because activity direct costs and project indirect costs are opposing costs dependent on time, the scheduling problem is essentially one of finding the project duration that minimizes their sum or, in other words, finding the optimum point in a time–cost trade-off.

EXAMPLE 4.3 Time–Cost Trade-off Procedure

The procedure for project crashing consists of the following five steps. It is explained by using the simple four-activity network shown in Exhibit 4.8. Assume that indirect costs are $10 per day for the first eight days of the project. If the project takes longer than eight days, indirect costs increase at the rate of $5 per day.

SOLUTION

1. **Prepare a CPM-type network diagram.** For each activity, this diagram should list:
   a. Normal cost (NC): the lowest expected activity costs. (These are the lesser of the cost figures shown under each node in Exhibit 4.8.)
   b. Normal time (NT): the time associated with each normal cost.
   c. Crash time (CT): the shortest possible activity time.
   d. Crash cost (CC): the cost associated with each crash time.
2. **Determine the cost per unit of time (assume days) to expedite each activity.** The relationship between activity time and cost may be shown graphically by plotting CC and CT coordinates and connecting them to the NC and NT coordinates by a concave, convex, or straight line—or some other form, depending on the actual cost structure of activity performance, as in Exhibit 4.8. For activity A, we assume a linear relationship between time and cost. This assumption is common in practice and helps us derive the cost per day to expedite because this value may be found directly by taking the slope of the line using the formula Slope = (CC − NC) ÷ (NT − CT). (When the assumption of linearity cannot be made, the cost of expediting must be determined graphically for each day the activity may be shortened.)

   The calculations needed to obtain the cost of expediting the remaining activities are shown in Exhibit 4.9A.
3. **Compute the critical path.** For the simple network we have been using, this schedule would take 10 days. The critical path is A–B–D.

EXHIBIT 4.8

Example of Time–Cost Trade-Off Procedure

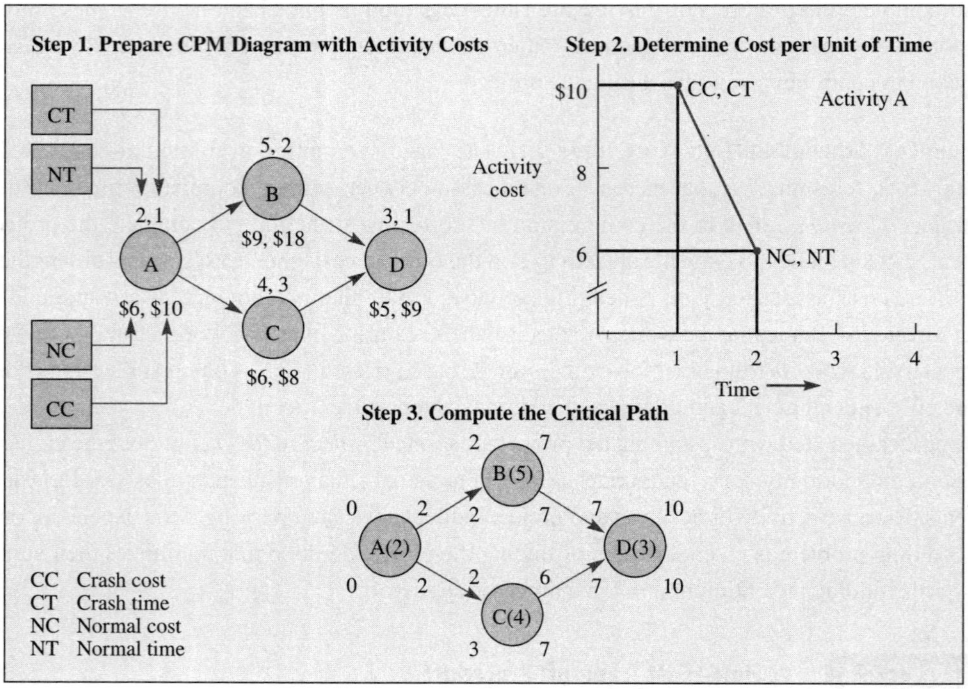

4. **Shorten the critical path at the least cost.** The easiest way to proceed is to start with the normal schedule, find the critical path, and reduce the path time by one day using the lowest-cost activity. Then, recompute and find the new critical path and reduce it by one day also. Repeat this procedure until the time of completion is satisfactory, or until there can be no further reduction in the project completion time. Exhibit 4.9B shows the reduction of the network one day at a time.

Working through Exhibit 4.9B might initially seem difficult. In the first line, all activities are at their normal time, and costs are at their lowest value. The critical path is A–B–D, cost for completing the project is $26, and the project completion time is 10 days.

The goal in line two is to reduce the project completion time by one day. We know it is necessary to reduce the time for one or more of the activities on the critical path. In the second column, we note that activity A can be reduced one day (from two days to on), activity B can be reduced three days (from five to two days), and activity D can be reduced two days (from three days to one). The next column tracks the cost to reduce each of the activities by a single day. For example, for activity A, it normally costs $6 to complete in two days. It could be completed in one day at a cost of $10, a $4 increase. So we indicate the cost to expedite activity A by one day is $4. For activity B, it normally costs $9 to complete in five days. It could be completed in two days at a cost of $18. Our cost to reduce B by three days is $9, or $3 per day. For C, it normally costs $5 to complete in three days. It could be completed in one day at a cost of $9; a two-day reduction would cost $4 ($2 per day). The least expensive alternative for a one-day reduction in time is to expedite activity D at a cost of $2. Total cost for the network goes up to $28 and the project completion time is reduced to nine days.

Our next iteration starts in line three, where the goal is to reduce the project completion time to eight days. The nine-day critical path is A–B–D. We could shorten activity A by one day, B by three days, and D by one day (note D has already been reduced from three to two days). Cost to

EXHIBIT 4.9

A. Calculation of Cost per Day to Expedite Each Activity

Activity	CC − NC	NT − CT	$\frac{CC - NC}{NT - CT}$	Cost per Day To Expedite	Maximum Number of Days Activity May Be Shortened
A	\$10 − \$6	2 − 1	$\frac{\$10 - \$6}{2 - 1}$	\$4	1
B	\$18 − \$9	5 − 2	$\frac{\$18 - \$9}{5 - 2}$	\$3	3
C	\$8 − \$6	4 − 3	$\frac{\$8 - \$6}{4 - 3}$	\$2	1
D	\$9 − \$5	3 − 1	$\frac{\$9 - \$5}{3 - 1}$	\$2	2

B. Reducing the Project Completion Time One Day at a Time

Current Critical Path(s)	Remaining Number of Days Activity May Be Shortened	Cost per Day to Expedite Each Activity	Least-Cost Activity to Expedite	Total Cost of All Activities in Network	Project Completion Time
ABD	All activity times and costs are normal.			\$26	10
ABD	A–1, B–3, D–2	A–4, B–3, D–2	D	28	9
ABD	A–1, B–3, D–1	A–4, B–3, D–2	D	30	8
ABD	A–1, B–3	A–4, B–3	B	33	7
ABD ACD	A–1, B–2, C–1	A–4, B–3, C–2	A*	37	6
ABD ACD	B–2, C–1	B–3, C–2	B&C†	42	5
ABD ACD	B–1	B–3	B‡	45	5

*To reduce the critical path by one day, reduce either A alone or B and C together at the same time (either B or C by itself just modifies the critical path without shortening it).
†B and C must be crashed together to reduce the path by one day.
‡Crashing activity B does not reduce the length of the project, so this additional cost would not be incurred.

reduce each activity by one day is the same as in line two. Again, the least expensive activity to reduce is D. Reducing activity D from two days to one results in the total cost for all activities in the network going up to \$30 and the project completion time being reduced to eight days.

Line four is similar to line three, but now only A and B are on the critical path and can be reduced. B is reduced, which takes our cost up \$3 to \$33 and reduces the project completion time to seven days.

In line five (actually our fourth iteration in solving the problem), activities A, B, C, and D are all critical. D cannot be reduced, so our only options are activities A, B, and C. Note that B and C are in parallel, so it does not help to reduce B without reducing C. Our options are to reduce A alone at a cost of \$4 or B and C together at a cost of \$5 (\$3 for B and \$2 for C), so we reduce A in this iteration.

In line six, we take the B and C option that was considered in line five. Finally, in line seven, our only option is to reduce activity B. Since B and C are in parallel and we cannot reduce C, there is no value in reducing B alone. We can reduce the project completion time no further.

5. **Plot project direct, indirect, and total-cost curves and find the minimum-cost schedule.** Exhibit 4.10 shows the indirect cost plotted as a constant \$10 per day for up to eight days and increasing \$5 per day thereafter (as stated in the problem). The direct costs are plotted from Exhibit 4.9B, and the total project cost is shown as the total of the two costs.

EXHIBIT 4.10

Plot of Costs and Minimum-Cost Schedule

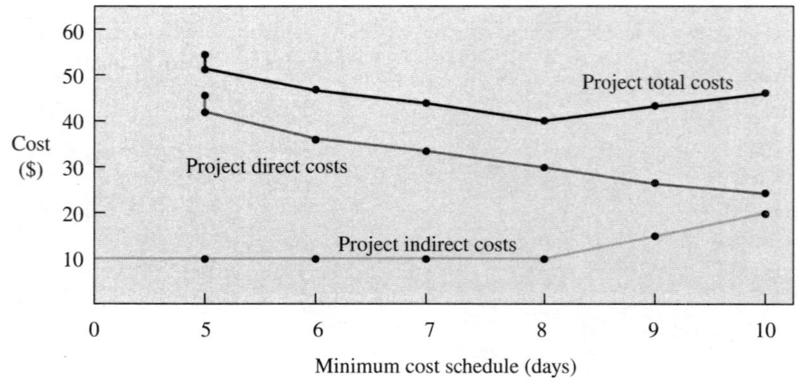

Summing the values for direct and indirect costs for each day yields the project total cost curve. As you can see, this curve is at its minimum with an eight-day schedule, which costs $40 ($30 direct + $10 indirect).

LO 4-3

Evaluate projects using earned value management

MANAGING PROJECTS

After seeing the arithmetic used when projects are being planned, we now look at how projects are actually managed while they are being completed. Charts and various types of standard forms are useful because their visual presentations are easily understood. Computer programs are available to quickly generate the charts, and we discuss these later in the chapter.

Gantt chart

Shows in a graphic manner the amount of time involved and the sequence in which activities can be performed. Often referred to as a **bar chart.**

Exhibit 4.11 is a sample **Gantt chart**, sometimes referred to as a *bar chart,* showing both the amount of time involved and the sequence in which activities can be performed. The chart is named after Henry L. Gantt, who won a presidential citation for his application of this type of chart to shipbuilding during World War I. In the example in Exhibit 4.11A, "long lead procurement" and "manufacturing schedules" are independent activities and can occur simultaneously. All other activities must be done in the sequence from top to bottom. Exhibit 4.11B graphs the amounts of money spent on labor, material, and overhead. Its value is its clarity in identifying sources and amounts of cost.

Exhibit 4.11C shows the percentage of the project's labor hours that come from the various areas of manufacturing, finance, and so on. These labor hours are related to the proportion of the project's total labor cost. For example, manufacturing is responsible for 50 percent of the project's labor hours, but this 50 percent has been allocated just 40 percent of the total labor dollars charged.

The top half of Exhibit 4.11D shows the degree of completion of these projects. The dotted vertical line signifies today. Project 1, therefore, is already late because it still has work to be done. Project 2 is not being worked on temporarily, so there is a space before the projected work. Project 3 continues to be worked on without interruption. The bottom of Exhibit 4.11D compares actual total costs and projected costs. As we see, two cost overruns occurred, and the current cumulative costs are over the projected cumulative costs.

Exhibit 4.11E is a milestone chart. The three milestones mark specific points in the project where checks can be made to see if the project is on time and where it should be. The best place to locate milestones is at the completion of a major activity. In this exhibit, the major activities completed were "purchase order release," "invoices received," and "material received."

Other standard reports can be used for a more detailed presentation comparing cost to progress (such as cost schedule status report—CSSR) or reports providing the basis for partial payment (such as the earned value report, which we discuss next).

Exhibit 4.11

Sample of Graphic Project Reports

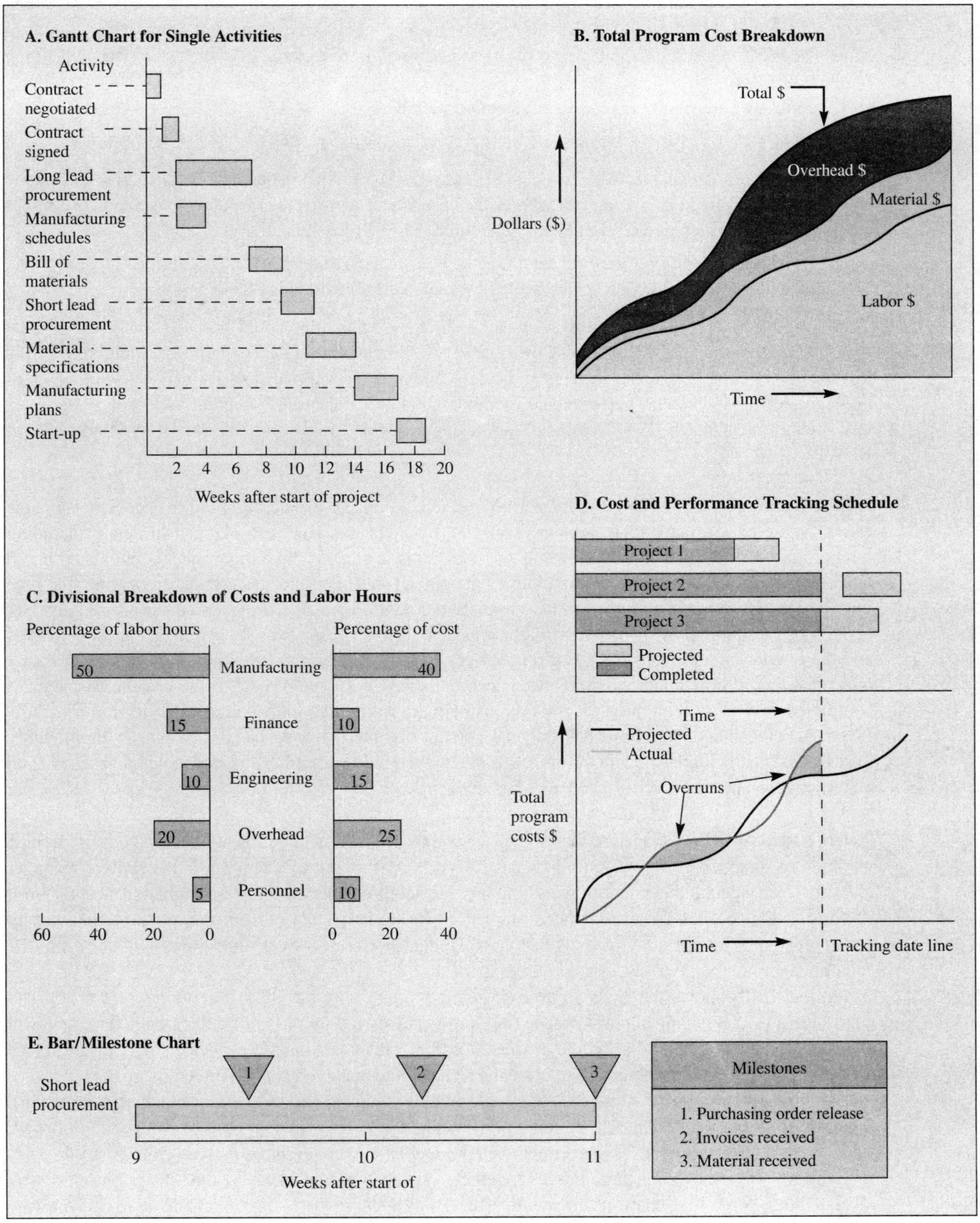

Earned Value Management (EVM)

Earned value management (EVM)
Technique that combines measures of scope, schedule, and cost for evaluating project progress.

Earned value management (EVM) is a technique for measuring project progress in an objective manner. EVM has the ability to combine measurements of scope, schedule, and cost in a project. When properly applied, EVM provides a method for evaluating the relative success of a project at a point in time. The measures can be applied to projects focused on either *revenue generation* or *cost,* depending on the type of project.

Essential features of any EVM implementation include:

1. A project plan that identifies the activities to be accomplished.
2. A valuation of each activity work. In the case of a project that generates revenue, this is called the Planned Value (PV) of the activity. In the case where a project is evaluated based on cost, this is called the Budgeted Cost of Work Scheduled (BCWS) for the activity.
3. Predefined *earning or costing rules* (also called *metrics*) to quantify the accomplishment of work, called Earned Value (EV) or Budgeted Cost of Work Performed (BCWP).

The terminology used in the features is general since the valuations could be based on either a value measure (revenue or profit) or a cost measure. EVM implementations for large or complex projects include many more features, such as indicators and forecasts of cost performance (overbudget or underbudget) and schedule performance (behind schedule or ahead of schedule). However, the most basic requirement of an EVM system is that it quantifies progress using PV (or BCWS) and EV (or BCWP).

Key Ideas
Comparing the work that has been completed in a project to the work that should have been completed according to the project plan is the key idea behind EVM analysis.

Project Tracking without EVM It is helpful to see an example of project tracking that does not include earned value performance management. Consider a project that has been planned in detail, including a time-phased spend plan for all elements of work. This is a case where the project is evaluated based on cost. Exhibit 4.12A shows the cumulative cost budget for this project as a function of time (the blue line, labeled BCWS). It also shows the cumulative actual cost of the project (red line) through week 8. To those unfamiliar with EVM, it might appear that this project was over budget through week 4 and then under budget from week 6 through week 8. However, what is missing from this chart is any understanding of how much work has been accomplished during the project. If the project was actually completed at week 8, then the project would actually be well under budget and well ahead of schedule. If, on the other hand, the project is only 10 percent complete at week 8, the project is significantly over budget and behind schedule. A method is needed to measure technical performance objectively and quantitatively, and that is what EVM accomplishes.

Project Tracking with EVM Consider the same project, except this time the project plan includes predefined methods of quantifying the accomplishment of work. At the end of each week, the project manager identifies every detailed element of work that has been completed, and sums the Budgeted Cost of Work Performed for each of these completed elements by estimating the percent complete of the activity and multiplying by the activity budgeted cost. Budgeted Cost of Work Performed (BCWP) may be accumulated monthly, weekly, or as progress is made.

Exhibit 4.12B shows the BCWS curve (in orange) along with the BCWP curve from Chart C. The chart indicates that technical performance (i.e., progress) started more rapidly than planned, but slowed significantly and fell behind schedule at week 7 and 8. This chart illustrates the schedule performance aspect of EVM. It is complementary to critical path schedule management (described in the next section).

Exhibit 4.12C shows the same BCWP curve (blue) with the actual cost data from Chart A (in green). It can be seen that the project was actually under budget, relative to the amount of work accomplished, since the start of the project. This is a much better conclusion than might be derived from Chart A.

Exhibit 4.12D shows all three curves together—which is a typical EVM line chart. The best way to read these three-line charts is to identify the BCWS curve first, then compare it to BCWP (for schedule performance) and AC (for cost performance). It can be seen from this illustration that a true understanding of cost performance and schedule performance *relies first on measuring technical performance objectively.* This is the *foundational principle* of EVM.

EXHIBIT 4.12

Earned Value Management Charts

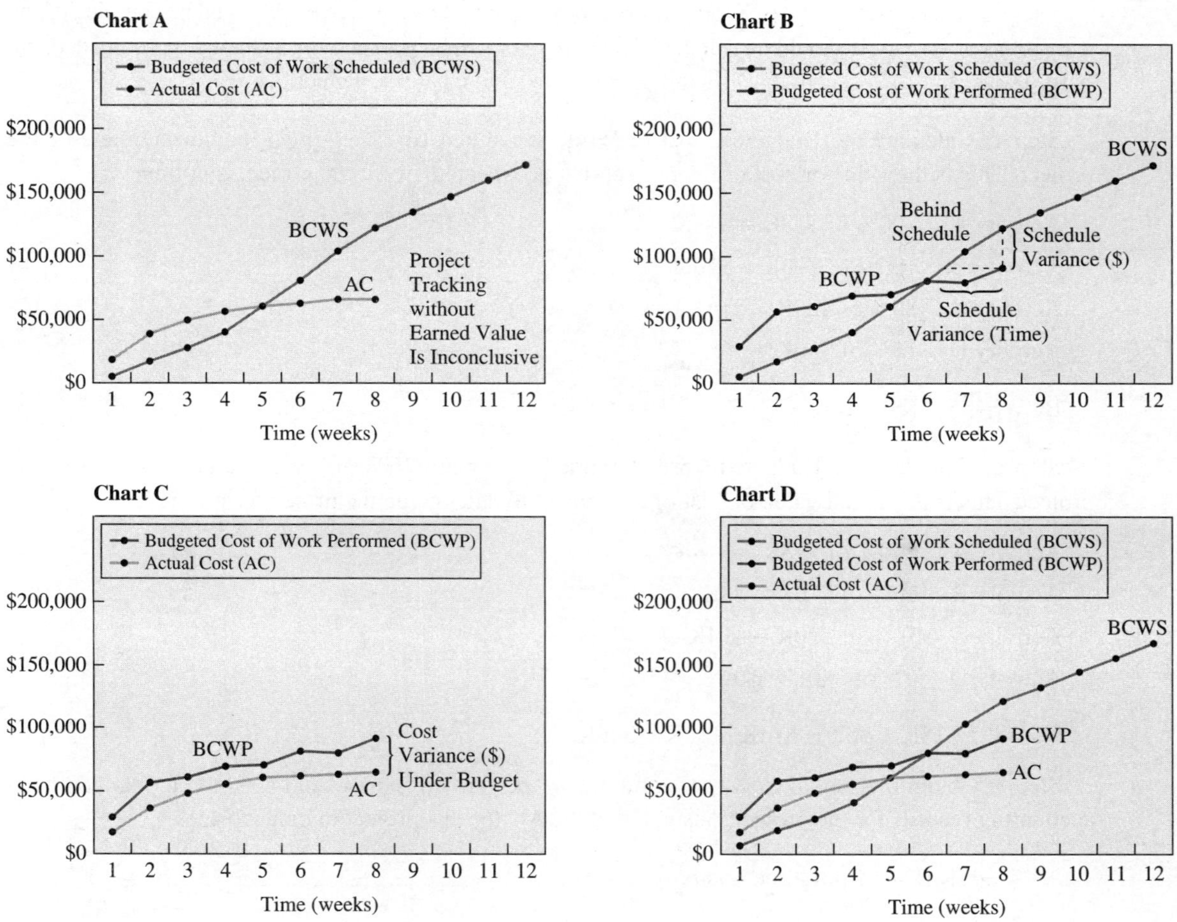

EXAMPLE 4.4 **Earned Value Management**

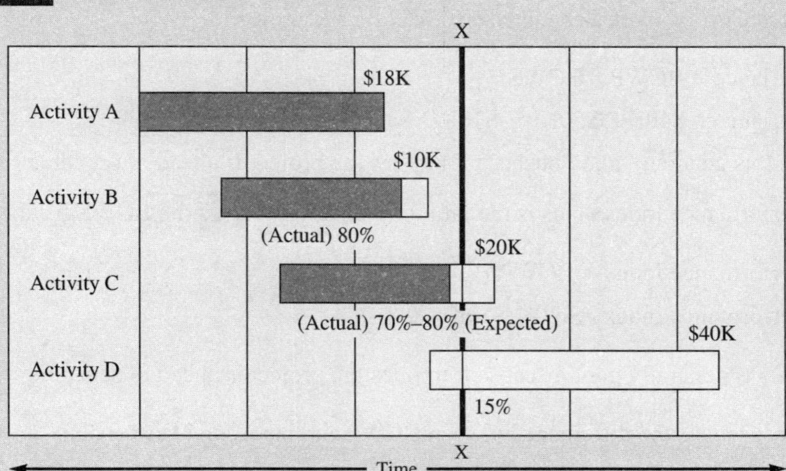

The figure illustrates how to determine the Budgeted Cost of Work Scheduled by summing the dollar values (in $1,000s) of the work scheduled for accomplishment at the end of period X. The Budgeted Cost of Work Performed is determined by summing the earned value for the work actually accomplished, shown in red shading.

SOLUTION

From the diagram, the budgeted cost of all the project work is the following: Activity A = \$18K, B = \$10K, C = \$20K, D = \$40K. This is the cost of each activity when they are 100% completed.

The project is currently at day X, and so from the diagram, 100% of activity A should be completed, and it is; 100% of activity B should be completed, but only 80% is; 80% of activity C should be completed, but only 70% is; and 15% of activity D should be completed, but it has not started.

Analytics

Step 1: Calculate the Budgeted Cost of Work Scheduled (BCWS) given the current state of the project. This is the value or cost of the project that is expected, given the project is at time X:

Activity A 100% of \$18K = \$18K

Activity B 100% of \$10K = \$10K

Activity C 80% of \$20K = \$16K

Activity D 15% of \$40K = \$6K

BCWS = \$18K + \$10K + \$16K + \$6K = \$50K

Step 2: Calculate the Budgeted Cost of Work Performed (BCWP) given the current state of the project. This is the actual value or cost of the project to date, given the project is at time X:

Activity A 100% of \$18K = \$18K

Activity B 80% of \$10K = \$8K

Activity C 70% of \$20K = \$14K

Activity D 0% of \$40K = \$0

BCWP = \$18K + \$8K + \$14K + \$0K = \$40K

Step 3: Obtain the Actual Cost (AC) of the work performed. This would need to be obtained from accounting records for the project. Assume that the AC for this project to date is \$45K.

AC = \$45K (Data from Acct. System)

Step 4: Calculate key performance measures for the project:

Schedule Variance: This is the difference between the Budgeted Cost of Work Performed (BCWP) and the Budgeted Cost of Work Scheduled (BCWS) for the project:

Schedule Variance = BCWP – BCWS

Schedule Variance = \$40K – \$50K = –\$10K

Greater than 0 is generally good because it implies the project is ahead of schedule.

Schedule Performance Index: This is the ratio of the BCWP versus the BCWS for the project:

Schedule Performance Index = BCWP/BCWS

Schedule Performance Index = \$40K/\$50K = 0.8

Greater than 1 is generally good because it implies the project is ahead of schedule.

Cost Variance: This is the difference between BCWP and the Actual Cost (AC):

Cost Variance = BCWP – AC

Cost Variance = \$40K – \$45K = –\$5K

Greater than 0 is generally good because it implies under budget.

Cost Performance Index: This is the ratio of the BCWP versus the AC for the project to date:

Cost Performance Index = BCWP/AC

Cost Performance Index = \$40K/\$45K = 0.89

< 1 means the cost of completing the work is higher than planned, which is bad.

= 1 means the cost of completing the work is right on plan, which is good.

> 1 means the cost of completing the work is lower than planned, which is usually good.

That CPI means the project is spending about \$1.13 for every \$1.00 of budgeted work accomplished. This is not very good because the project is overbudget and tasks are not being completed on time or on budget. A Schedule Performance Index and a Cost Performance Index greater than 1 are desirable.

PROJECT MANAGEMENT INFORMATION SYSTEMS

LO 4-4 Exemplify how network-planning models and earned value management are implemented in commercial software packages

Interest in the techniques and concepts of project management has exploded in the past 10 years. This has resulted in a parallel increase in project management software offerings. Now there are over 100 companies offering project management software. For the most up-to-date information about software available, check out the website of the Project Management Institute (www.pmi.org). Two of the leading companies are Microsoft, with Microsoft Project, and Primavera, with Primavera Project Planner.

The Microsoft Project program comes with an excellent online tutorial, which is one reason for its overwhelming popularity with project managers tracking midsized projects. This package is compatible with the Microsoft Office Suite, which opens all the communications and Internet integration capability that Microsoft offers. The program includes features for scheduling, allocating, and leveling resources, as well as controlling costs and producing presentation-quality graphics and reports.

For managing very large projects or programs having several projects, Primavera Project Planner is often the choice. Primavera was the first major vendor of this type of software and has possibly the most sophisticated capability.

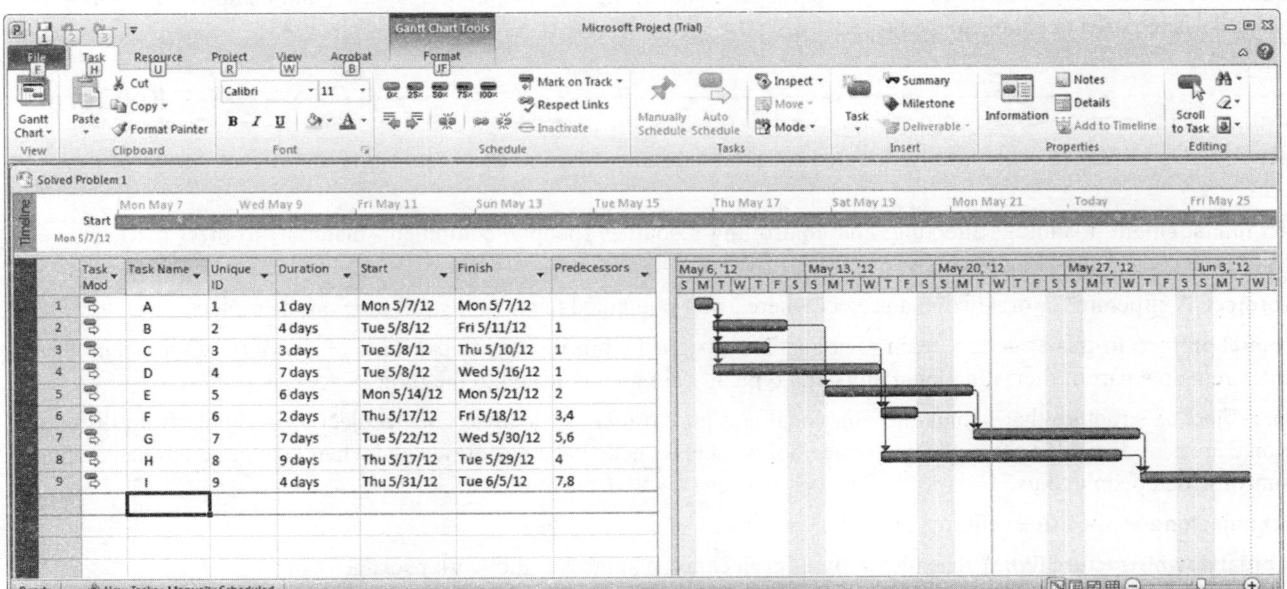

In addition to scheduling tasks, a major capability of all these software packages is assigning resources to competing tasks and projects. For example, the systems can schedule back labor and equipment for a project. Mid- to high-level project management information systems (PMIS) software can also resolve overallocations through a "leveling" feature. Several rules of thumb can be used. You can specify that low-priority tasks should be delayed until higher-priority ones are complete, or that the project should end before or after the original deadline.

The real action starts after the project gets under way. Actual progress will differ from your original, or baseline, planned progress. Software can hold several different baseline plans, so you can compare monthly snapshots.

A *tracking Gantt chart* superimposes the current schedule onto a baseline plan so deviations are easily noticed. If you prefer, a spreadsheet view of the same information could be output. Deviations between planned start/finish and newly scheduled start/finish also appear, and a "slipping filter" can be applied to highlight or output only those tasks that are scheduled to finish at a later date than the planned baseline. Management by exception also can be applied to find deviations between budgeted costs and actual costs.

CONCEPT CONNECTIONS

LO 4–1 Explain what projects are and how projects are organized

Summary

- Projects can be categorized into four major types: product change, process change, research and development, and alliance and partnerships.
- Even though some projects are often thought to be one-time occurrences, they are sometimes repeated.
- The project team can be organized in different ways. The most common are pure project, where the team works full time on the project; functional project, where team members stay in their functional group and work on many different projects at the same time; and matrix project, which blends the pure project and functional project structures.
- The activities of the projects are organized according to the work breakdown structure, which groups them into subtasks and work packages. Completion of a work package results in the completion of a subtask, and completion of all of the subtasks is required to complete the project.

Key Terms

Project A series of related jobs usually directed toward some major output and requiring a significant period of time to perform.

Project management Planning, directing, and controlling resources (people, equipment, material) to meet the technical, cost, and time constraints of a project.

Pure project A structure for organizing a project where a self-contained team works full time on the project.

Functional project In this structure, team members are assigned from the functional units of the organization. The team members remain a part of their functional units and typically are not dedicated to the project.

Matrix project A structure that blends the functional and pure project structures. Each project uses people from different functional areas. A dedicated project manager decides what tasks need to be performed and when, but the functional managers control which people to use.

Project milestone A specific event in a project.

Work breakdown structure (WBS) The hierarchy of project tasks, subtasks, and work packages.

Activities Pieces of work within a project that consume time. The completion of all the activities of a project marks the end of the project.

LO 4–2 Analyze projects using network-planning models

Summary

- The critical path method (CPM) is the most widely used approach to scheduling projects. There are a number of variations on the basic approach.
- The goal is to find the earliest time that the entire project can be completed.
- The techniques also identify what activities are critical, meaning that there cannot be delays without delaying the earliest time that the project can be completed.
- The three techniques studied in the chapter are the following: CPM with a single activity time, CPM with three activity time estimates, and time–cost models with project crashing.

Key Terms

Critical path The sequence(s) of activities in a project that form the longest chain in terms of their time to complete. This path contains zero slack time. It is possible for there to be multiple critical paths in a project. Techniques used to find the critical path are called CPM, or critical path method, techniques.

Immediate predecessor Activities that need to be completed immediately before another activity.

Slack time The time that an activity can be delayed without delaying the entire project; the difference between the late and early start times of an activity.

Early start schedule A project schedule that lists all activities by their early start times.

Late start schedule A project schedule that lists all activities by their late start times. This schedule may create savings by postponing purchases of material and other costs associated with the project.

Time–cost models Extension of the critical path models that considers the trade-off between the time required to complete an activity and the cost. This is often referred to as "crashing" the project.

$$\mathrm{ET} = \frac{a + 4m + b}{6} \quad [4.1]$$

$$\sigma^2 = \left(\frac{b - a}{6}\right)^2 \quad [4.2]$$

$$Z = \frac{D - T}{\sqrt{\Sigma \sigma_{cp}^2}} \quad [4.3]$$

LO 4–3 Evaluate projects using earned value management

Summary

- A key aspect to managing a project is understanding the current status of its activities.
- Simple graphical techniques are often augmented with standard reports that give a detailed analysis of the work completed together with what is left to be done.
- Earned value management (EVM) is a technique commonly used for measuring project progress.

Key Terms

Gantt chart Shows in a graphic manner the amount of time involved and the sequence in which activities can be performed. Often referred to as a bar chart.

Earned value management (EVM) Technique that combines measures of scope, schedule, and cost for evaluating project progress.

LO 4–4 **Exemplify how network-planning models and earned value management are implemented in commercial software packages**

Summary

- The techniques and concepts described in this chapter are implemented in commercially available software packages.
- Two of the most common packages are Microsoft Project and Primavera Project Planner.
- These packages are capable of managing multiple projects at the same time and can help resolve resource usage conflicts of competing projects.

SOLVED PROBLEMS

LO4–2 SOLVED PROBLEM 1

A project has been defined to contain the following list of activities, along with their required times for completion:

Activity	Time (days)	Immediate Predecessors
A	1	—
B	4	A
C	3	A
D	7	A
E	6	B
F	2	C, D
G	7	E, F
H	9	D
I	4	G, H

a. Draw the critical path diagram.
b. Show the early start, early finish, late start, and late finish times.
c. Show the critical path.
d. What would happen if activity F was revised to take four days instead of two?

Solution

The answers to *a, b,* and *c* are shown in the following diagram.

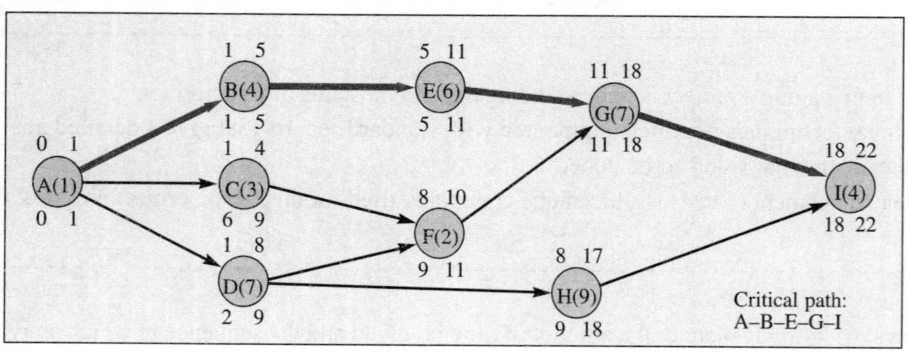

Path	Length (days)
A-B-E-G-I	**22 (critical path)**
A-C-F-G-I	17
A-D-F-G-I	21
A-D-H-I	21

d. New critical path: A–D–F–G–I. Time of completion is 23 days.

LO4–3 SOLVED PROBLEM 2

A project has been defined to contain the following activities, along with their time estimates for completion:

	Time Estimates (weeks)			
Activity	*a*	*m*	*b*	**Immediate Predecessor**
A	1	4	7	—
B	2	6	7	A
C	3	4	6	D
D	6	12	14	A
E	3	6	12	D
F	6	8	16	B, C
G	1	5	6	E, F

a. Calculate the expected time and the variance for each activity.
b. Draw the critical path diagram.
c. Show the early start, early finish times, and late start, late finish times.
d. Show the critical path.
e. What is the probability that the project can be completed in 34 weeks?

Solution

a.

Activity	Expected Time $\frac{a+4m+b}{6}$	Activity Variance $\left(\frac{b-a}{6}\right)^2$
A	4.00	1
B	5.50	0.6944
C	4.17	0.2500
D	11.33	1.7778
E	6.50	2.2500
F	9.00	2.7778
G	4.50	0.6944

b.

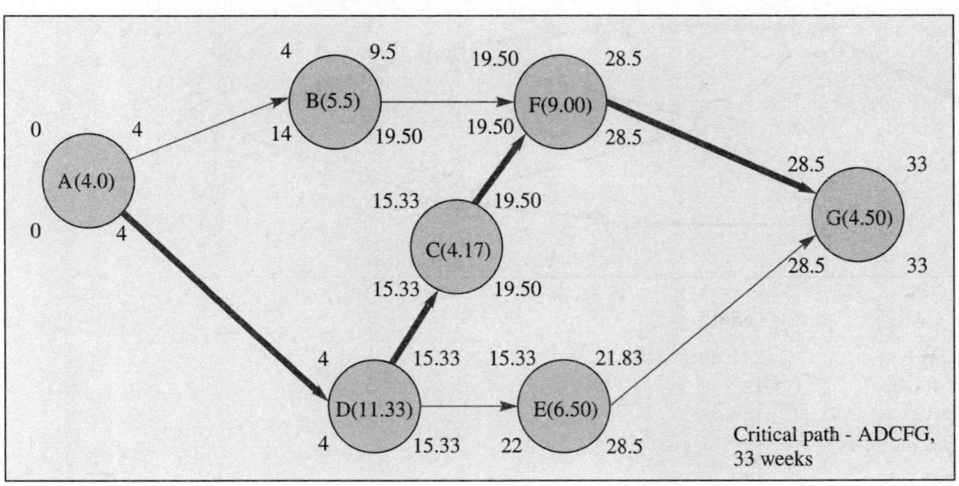

c. Shown on diagram.
d. Shown on diagram.

Path	Length (weeks)
A-B-F-G	23
A-D-C-F-G	**33 (critical path)**
A-D-E-G	26.33

e. $$Z = \frac{D - T_E}{\sqrt{\Sigma \sigma^2_{cp}}} = \frac{34 - 33}{\sqrt{1 + 1.7778 + .25 + 2.7778 + .6944}} = \frac{1}{2.5495} = .3922$$

Look up that value in Appendix E and we see that there is about a 65 percent chance of completing the project by that date.

LO 4-2 SOLVED PROBLEM 3

Here are the precedence requirements, normal and crash activity times, and normal and crash costs for a construction project:

Activity	Preceding Activities	Required Time (weeks)		Cost	
		Normal	Crash	Normal	Crash
A	—	4	2	$10,000	$11,000
B	A	3	2	6,000	9,000
C	A	2	1	4,000	6,000
D	B	5	3	14,000	18,000
E	B, C	1	1	9,000	9,000
F	C	3	2	7,000	8,000
G	E, F	4	2	13,000	25,000
H	D, E	4	1	11,000	18,000
I	H, G	6	5	20,000	29,000

a. What are the critical path and the estimated completion time?
b. To shorten the project by three weeks, which tasks would be shortened and what would the final total project cost be?

Solution

The construction project network is shown as follows:

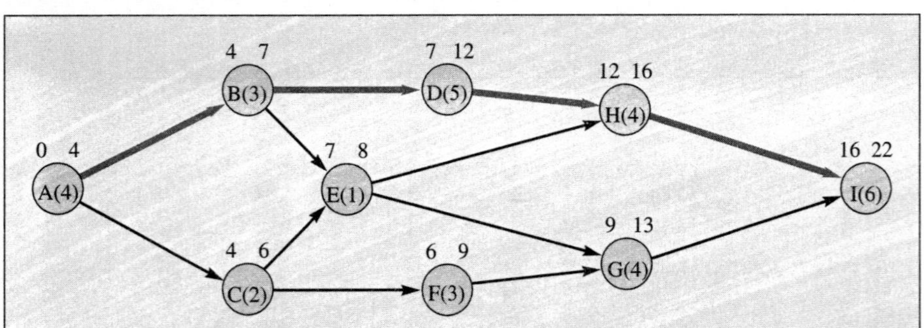

a.

Path	Length
A-B-D-H-I	22 (critical path)
A-B-E-H-I	18
A-B-E-G-I	18
A-C-E-H-I	17
A-C-E-G-I	17
A-C-F-G-I	19

Normal completion time is 22 weeks.

b. Activity	Crash Cost	Normal Cost	Normal Time	Crash Time	Cost per Week	Weeks
A	$11,000	$10,000	4	2	$ 500	2
B	9,000	6,000	3	2	3,000	1
C	6,000	4,000	2	1	2,000	1
D	18,000	14,000	5	3	2,000	2
E	9,000	9,000	1	1		0
F	8,000	7,000	3	2	1,000	1
G	25,000	13,000	4	2	6,000	2
H	18,000	11,000	4	1	2,333	3
I	29,000	20,000	6	5	9,000	1

(1) 1st week: CP = A–B–D–H–I. A is least expensive at $500. Critical path stays the same.
(2) 2nd week: A is still the least expensive at $500. Critical path stays the same.
(3) 3rd week: Because A is no longer available, the choices are B (at $3,000), D (at $2,000), H (at $2,333), or I (at $9,000). Therefore, choose D at $2,000.

The total project cost if shortened by three weeks is

A	$11,000
B	6,000
C	4,000
D	16,000
E	9,000
F	7,000
G	13,000
H	11,000
I	20,000
	$97,000

LO4–3 SOLVED PROBLEM 4

You have been asked to calculate the Cost Performance Index for a project using earned value management techniques. It is currently day 20 of the project and the following summarizes the current status of the project:

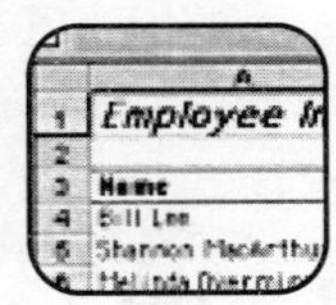

Activity	Expected Cost	Activity Duration	Expected Start Date	Expected Completion Date	Expected % Complete	Actual % Complete	Actual Cost to Date
Startup	$100,000	10 days	0	10	100%	100%	$105,000
Construction	325,000	14 days	8	22	12/14 = 85.714%	90%	280,000
Finishing	50,000	12 days	18	30	2/12 = 16.667%	25%	2,500

Calculate the Schedule Variance, Schedule Performance Index, and Cost Performance Index for the project.

Solution

Step 1: Calculate Budgeted Cost of the Work Scheduled (BCWS) to date:

Startup is 100 percent complete and we are beyond the expected completion date, so budgeted cost is $100,000 for this activity.

Would expect Construction to be 85.714 percent complete and cost $278,571 to date.
Would expect Finishing to be 16.667 percent complete at a cost of $8,333 to date.

$$\text{Budgeted Cost of Work Scheduled} = \$100{,}000 + \$278{,}571 + \$8{,}333 = \$386{,}904$$

Step 2: Calculate the Budgeted Cost of the Work Performed (BCWP) to date:

Startup is 100 percent complete, so budgeted cost is $100,000.
Construction is actually only 90 percent complete, so budgeted cost for this much of the activity is (325,000 × .9) = $292,500.

Finishing is now 25 percent complete, so budgeted cost is ($50,000 × .25) = $12,500.

$$\text{Budgeted Cost of Work Performed} = \$100{,}000 + \$292{,}500 + \$12{,}500 = \$405{,}000$$

Step 3: Actual Cost (AC) of the project to date is $105,000 + $280,000 + $2,500 = $387,500.

Step 4: Calculate performance measures:

$$\text{Schedule Variance} = \$405{,}000 - \$386{,}904 = \$18{,}096$$
$$\text{Schedule Performance Index} = \$405{,}000/\$386{,}904 = 1.05$$
$$\text{Cost Performance Index} = \$405{,}000/\$387{,}500 = 1.05$$

The project looks good because it is both ahead of schedule and below the budgeted cost.

DISCUSSION QUESTIONS

LO4–1
1. What was the most complex project you have been involved in? Give examples of the following as they pertain to the project: the work breakdown structure, tasks, subtasks, and work package. Were you on the critical path? Did it have a good project manager?

LO4–2
2. What are some reasons project scheduling is not done well?
3. Which characteristics must a project have for critical path scheduling to be applicable? What types of projects have been subjected to critical path analysis?
4. What are the underlying assumptions of minimum-cost scheduling? Are they equally realistic?
5. "Project control should always focus on the critical path." Comment.

LO4–3
6. Why would subcontractors for a government project want their activities on the critical path? Under what conditions would they try to avoid being on the critical path?
7. Discuss the graphic presentations in Exhibit 4.11. Are there any other graphic outputs you would like to see if you were project manager?
8. Why is it important to use *earned value management (EVM)* in the overall management of projects? Compare this to the use of baseline and current schedules only.
9. Consider the EVM charts in Exhibit 4.12. Are there any other measures you might want to use in the management of a project? What are some controllable variables that may affect the costs being tracked?

LO4–4
10. What do you think might be some barriers to the successful, effective use of the project management software packages discussed in the chapter?

OBJECTIVE QUESTIONS

LO4–1
1. What are the three types of projects based on the amount of change involved?
2. What are the four major categories of projects based on the type of change involved?

b.

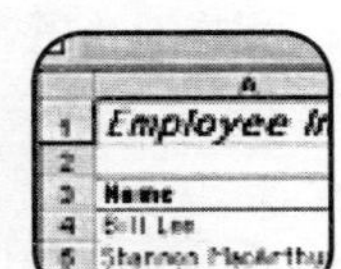

3. Match the following characteristics with their relevant project team organizational structures:

____	The project is housed within a functional division of the firm.	A. Pure project
____	A project manager leads personnel from different functional areas.	B. Functional project
____	Personnel work on a dedicated project team.	C. Matrix project
____	A team member reports to two bosses.	
____	Team pride, motivation, and commitment are high.	
____	Team members can work on several projects.	
____	Duplication of resources is minimized.	

4. What is the term for a group of project activities that are assigned to a single organizational unit?

5. The following activities are part of a project to be scheduled using CPM: **LO4–2**

Activity	Immediate Predecessor	Time (weeks)
A	—	6
B	A	3
C	A	7
D	C	2
E	B, D	4
F	D	3
G	E, F	7

a. Draw the network.
b. What is the critical path?
c. How many weeks will it take to complete the project?
d. How much slack does activity B have?

6. Schedule the following activities using CPM:

Activity	Immediate Predecessor	Time (weeks)
A	—	1
B	A	4
C	A	3
D	B	2
E	C, D	5
F	D	2
G	F	2
H	E, G	3

a. Draw the network.
b. What is the critical path?
c. How many weeks will it take to complete the project?
d. Which activities have slack, and how much?

7. The R&D department is planning to bid on a large project for the development of a new communication system for commercial planes. The accompanying table shows the activities, times, and sequences required (answers in Appendix D).

Activity	Immediate Predecessor	Time (weeks)
A	—	3
B	A	2
C	A	4
D	A	4
E	B	6
F	C, D	6
G	D, F	2
H	D	3
I	E, G, H	3

a. Draw the network diagram.
b. What is the critical path?
c. Suppose you want to shorten the completion time as much as possible, and you have the option of shortening any or all of B, C, D, and G each one week. Which would you shorten?
d. What is the new critical path and earliest completion time?

8. The following represents a project that should be scheduled using CPM:

		Times (days)		
Activity	Immediate Predecessors	*a*	*m*	*b*
A	—	1	3	5
B	—	1	2	3
C	A	1	2	3
D	A	2	3	4
E	B	3	4	11
F	C, D	3	4	5
G	D, E	1	4	6
H	F, G	2	4	5

a. Draw the network.
b. What is the critical path?
c. What is the expected project completion time?
d. What is the probability of completing this project within 16 days?

9. There is an 82 percent chance the following project can be completed in *X* weeks or less. What is *X*?

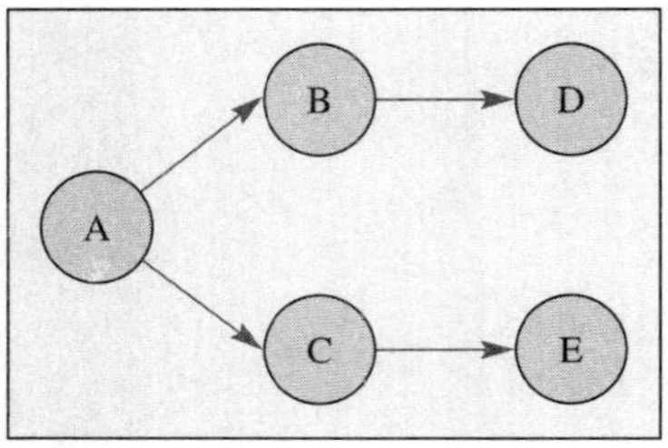

Activity	Most Optimistic	Most Likely	Most Pessimistic
A	2	5	11
B	3	3	3
C	1	3	5
D	6	8	10
E	4	7	10

10. The following table represents a plan for a project:

		Times (days)		
Job No.	Predecessor Job(s)	*a*	*m*	*b*
1	—	2	3	4
2	1	1	2	3
3	1	4	5	12
4	1	3	4	11
5	2	1	3	5
6	3	1	2	3
7	4	1	8	9
8	5, 6	2	4	6
9	8	2	4	12
10	7	3	4	5
11	9, 10	5	7	8

a. Construct the appropriate network diagram.
b. Indicate the critical path.
c. What is the expected completion time for the project?
d. You can accomplish any one of the following at an additional cost of \$1,500:

(1) Reduce job 5 by two days.
(2) Reduce job 3 by two days.
(3) Reduce job 7 by two days.

If you will save \$1,000 for each day that the earliest completion time is reduced, which action, if any, would you choose?

e. What is the probability that the project will take more than 30 days to complete?

11. A construction project is broken down into the following 10 activities:

Activity	Immediate Predecessor	Time (weeks)
1	—	4
2	1	2
3	1	4
4	1	3
5	2, 3	5
6	3	6
7	4	2
8	5	3
9	6, 7	5
10	8, 9	7

a. Draw the network diagram.
b. Find the critical path.
c. If activities 1 and 10 cannot be shortened, but activities 2 through 9 can be shortened to a minimum of one week each at a cost of \$10,000 per week, which activities would you shorten to cut the project by four weeks?

12. Here is a CPM network with activity times in weeks (answers in Appendix D):

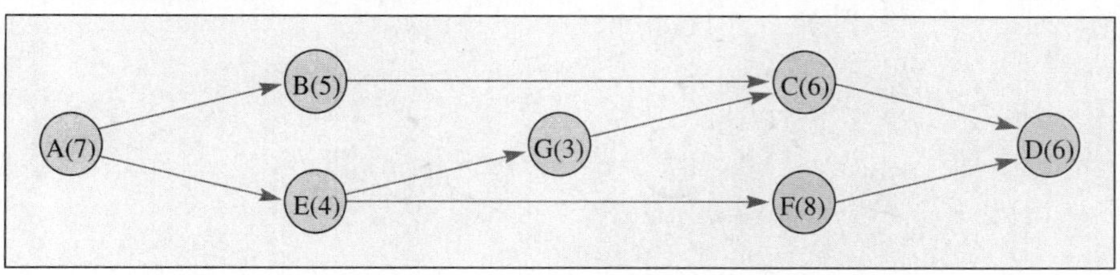

a. Determine the critical path.
b. How many weeks will the project take to complete?
c. Suppose F could be shortened by two weeks and B by one week. How would this affect the completion date?

13. Here is a network with the activity times shown in days:

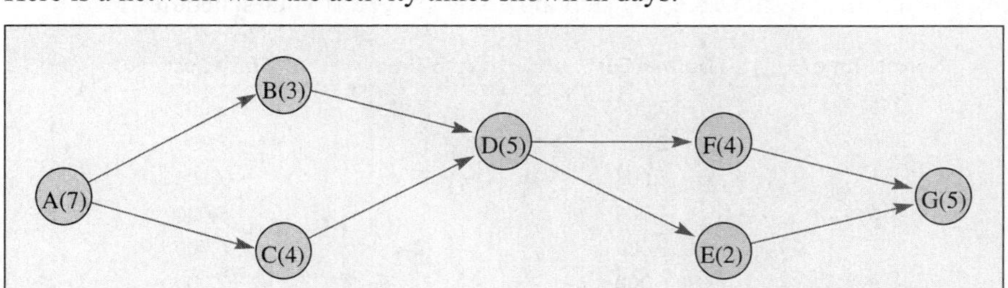

a. Find the critical path.
b. The following table shows the normal times and the crash times, along with the associated costs for each activity.

Activity	Normal Time	Crash Time	Normal Cost	Crash Cost
A	7	6	$7,000	$ 8,000
B	2	1	5,000	7,000
C	4	3	9,000	10,200
D	5	4	3,000	4,500
E	2	1	2,000	3,000
F	4	2	4,000	7,000
G	5	4	5,000	8,000

If the project is to be shortened by four days, show which activities, in order of reduction, would be shortened and the resulting cost.

14. The home office billing department of a chain of department stores prepares monthly inventory reports for use by the stores' purchasing agents. Given the following information, use the critical path method to determine:
    a. How long the total process will take.
    b. Which jobs can be delayed without delaying the early start of any subsequent activity.

	Job and Description	Immediate Predecessors	Time (hours)
A	Start	—	0
B	Get computer printouts of customer purchases	A	10
C	Get stock records for the month	A	20
D	Reconcile purchase printouts and stock records	B, C	30
E	Total stock records by department	B, C	20
F	Determine reorder quantities for coming period	E	40
G	Prepare stock reports for purchasing agents	D, F	20
H	Finish	G	0

15. For the network shown:

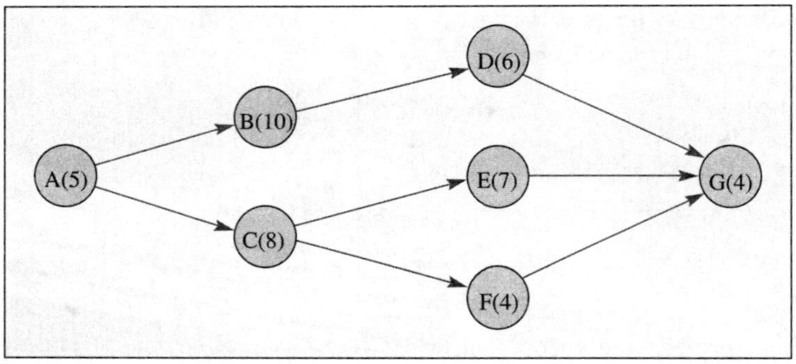

    a. Determine the critical path and the early completion time in weeks for the project.
    b. For the data shown, reduce the project completion time by three weeks. Assume a linear cost per week shortened, and show, step by step, how you arrived at your schedule.

Activity	Normal Time	Normal Cost	Crash Time	Crash Cost
A	5	$ 7,000	3	$13,000
B	10	12,000	7	18,000
C	8	5,000	7	7,000
D	6	4,000	5	5,000
E	7	3,000	6	6,000
F	4	6,000	3	7,000
G	4	7,000	3	9,000

16. The following CPM network has estimates of the normal time in weeks listed for the activities:

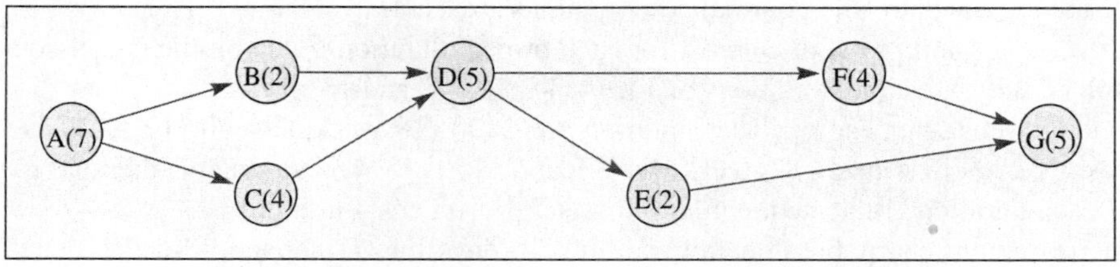

a. Identify the critical path.
b. What is the length of time to complete the project?
c. Which activities have slack, and how much?
d. Here is a table of normal and crash times and costs. Which activities would you shorten to cut two weeks from the schedule in a rational fashion? What would be the incremental cost? Is the critical path changed?

Activity	Normal Time	Crash Time	Normal Cost	Crash Cost
A	7	6	$7,000	$8,000
B	3	2	5,000	7,000
C	4	3	9,000	10,200
D	5	4	3,000	4,500
E	2	1	2,000	3,000
F	4	2	4,000	7,000
G	5	4	5,000	8,000

17. Bragg's Bakery is building a new automated bakery in downtown Sandusky. Here are the activities that need to be completed to get the new bakery built and the equipment installed.

Activity	Predecessor	Normal Time (weeks)	Crash Time (weeks)	Expediting Cost/Week
A	—	9	6	$3,000
B	A	8	5	3,500
C	A	15	10	4,000
D	B, C	5	3	2,000
E	C	10	6	2,500
F	D, E	2	1	5,000

a. Draw the project diagram.
b. What is the normal project length?
c. What is the project length if all activities are crashed to their minimum?
d. Bragg's loses $3,500 in profit per week for every week the bakery is not completed. How many weeks will the project take if we are willing to pay crashing cost as long as it is less than $3,500?

18. Assume the network and data that follow:

Activity	Normal Time (weeks)	Normal Cost	Crash Time (weeks)	Crash Cost	Immediate Predecessors
A	2	$ 50	1	$70	—
B	4	80	2	160	A
C	8	70	4	110	A
D	6	60	5	80	A
E	7	100	6	130	B
F	4	40	3	100	D
G	5	100	4	150	C, E, F

a. Construct the network diagram.
b. Indicate the critical path when normal activity times are used.
c. Compute the minimum total direct cost for each project duration based on the cost associated with each activity. Consider durations of 13, 14, 15, 16, 17, and 18 weeks.
d. If the indirect costs for each project duration are $400 (18 weeks), $350 (17 weeks), $300 (16 weeks), $250 (15 weeks), $200 (14 weeks), and $150 (13 weeks), what is the total project cost for each duration? Indicate the minimum total project cost duration.

LO4–3 19. Your project to obtain charitable donations is now 30 days into a planned 40-day project. The project is divided into three activities. The first activity is designed to solicit individual donations. It is scheduled to run the first 25 days of the project and to bring in $25,000. Even though we are 30 days into the project, we still see that we have only 90 percent of this activity complete. The second activity relates to company donations and is scheduled to run for 30 days starting on day 5 and extending through day 35. We estimate that, even though we should have 83 percent (25/30) of this activity complete, it is actually only 50 percent complete. This part of the project was scheduled to bring in $150,000 in donations. The final activity is for matching funds. This activity is scheduled to run the last 10 days of the project and has not started. It is scheduled to bring in an additional $50,000. So far, $175,000 has actually been brought in on the project.

Calculate the Schedule Variance, Schedule Performance Index, and Cost (actually value in this case) Performance Index. How is the project going? (*Hint:* Note that this problem is different since revenue rather than cost is the relevant measure. Use care in how the measures are interpreted.)

20. A project to build a new bridge seems to be going very well because the project is well ahead of schedule and costs seem to be running very low. A major milestone has been reached where the first two activities have been totally completed and the third activity is 60 percent complete. The planners were expecting to be only 50 percent through the third activity at this time. The first activity involves prepping the site for the bridge. It was expected that this would cost $1,420,000 and it was done for only $1,300,000. The second activity was the pouring of concrete for the bridge. This was expected to cost $10,500,000 but was actually done for $9,000,000. The third and final activity is the actual construction of the bridge superstructure. This was expected to cost a total of $8,500,000. To date, they have spent $5,000,000 on the superstructure.

Calculate the Schedule Variance, Schedule Performance Index, and Cost Performance Index for the project to date. How is the project going?

LO4–3 21. What feature in project management information systems can be used to resolve over-allocation of project resources?

22. What was the first major project management information system that is now commonly used for managing very large projects?

23. What type of chart compares the current project schedule with the original baseline schedule so that deviations from the original plan can be easily noticed?

CASE: Cost Management in Phase I of Delhi Metro Project

Delhi Metro project involved four phases covering around 414 km across Delhi and its suburbs. The work started in 1997 and as per the original plan, it is expected to be completed by 2021. The cost management had been a major concern since the beginning of this project. Baring Kolkata Metro, which is running at a loss, fare of Delhi Metro is one of the lowest among the metro fares anywhere in the world. The first phase of Delhi Metro covering about 65 km, of which about 12 kilometres are underground and the remaining on elevated corridors, was completed not only before schedule but also within the budgetary allocations of ₹10,570 crore (₹105.7 billion). The project work started in October 1998; the first section became operational in December 2002, followed by the second section in September 2003. The remaining five sections were completed by September 2005.

Table Phase-I Network of DMRC (DMRC Sources)

Line No.	Route	Length (Kms)	Number Of Stations
1	Shahdara–Tri Nagar–Rithala	22.06	18
2	Vishwavidyalaya–Central Secretariat	10.84	10
3	Indraprastha–Barakhamba Road–Dwarka Sub City	32.10	31

About 60 percent of the cost of first phase was financed via loan by Japan International Cooperation Agency (JICA), 28 percent came through equity contribution by the Central and State Governments, they additionally contributed nearly 5 percent through subordinate loan to cover land acquisition, and remaining 7 percent was generated internally through property development. The cost of the first phase got recovered in around two years earlier than estimated by Central Road Research Institute (CRRI). With an initial expected economic rate of return (ERR) of 16.90 percent, the break-even period for the first phase comes out as the year 2013. DAMR scaled up the ERR to 19.98 percent during the same period, which squeezed the break-even period to December 2011.

Other than revenue from 900,000 commuters per day in 2009, advertisements rentals, etc. there are intangible economic and social benefits, which have been quantified. For an average travel distance per passenger of 20 km, at least one hour of travel time is saved. This, according to DMRC sources, is equivalent to an opportunity cost of ₹725 crore per annum. Around 40,000 vehicles would be out-of-road due to these commuters using first phase of Metro. This would result into a reduction of 57,800 tonnes of fuel per year. According to Dr. Sreedharan, then Managing Director of DMRC, monthly revenue inflows are mainly in the form of total fare revenue of about ₹45 crore and through advertisement and rentals of ₹12 crore. On the expenditure side, ₹30 crore per month goes to meet the expenditure and rest is used to pay back loans, for which the annual interest is about ₹250 crore.

The second phase was planned for another 130 km costing ₹20,000 crores. DMRC is successful in completing all the major segments of its project with cost efficiency and excellent time management.

Questions

1. Explain the concept of break-even time of a project financing.
2. Explore the funding pattern of DMRC's other phases of this project and comment on it. Compare this with first phase of DMRC.

References

1. http://www.delhimetrorail.com/ [Accessed on 18 January 2018]
2. http://www.delhimetrorail.com/funding.aspx [Accessed on 18 January 2018]
3. Bhatnagar, V. (2002) Metro shows the way – all the way. The Hindu, 11 October. http://www.the-hindu.com/2002/10/12/stories/.
4. Sreedharan, E. (2002) Delhi MRTS Project. Indian Railways April, 81-7.
5. DMRC (2003) Driving Delhi forward. Delhi Metro railways Corporation, Delhi.
6. DMRC (20040 Need for mass rapid transit system. http://www.delhimetrorail.com/corporate/need-for_mrts.html [Accessed 30 May 2006].
7. Matti Siemiatychi, 2006, Message in a Metro: Building urban rail Infrastructure and Image in Delhi, India, International Journal of Urban and Regional Research, Volume 30(2), pp. 277-292.
8. Joshi, S. (2001) Delhi Metro is quake proof. The Hindu Online Edition, 4 February. http://www.thehindu.com/2001/02/04/stories/14042184.htm [Accessed on 19 January 2018]

ANALYTICS EXERCISE: PRODUCT DESIGN PROJECT

You work for Nokia in its global cell phone group. You have been made project manager for the design of a new cell phone. Your supervisors have already scoped the project, so you have a list showing the work breakdown structure, and this includes major project activities. You must plan the project schedule and calculate project duration. Your boss wants the schedule on his desk tomorrow morning!

Exhibit 4.13

Work Breakdown Structure and Activities for the Cell Phone Design Project

Major Subprojects/Activities	Activity Identification	Dependency	Duration (weeks)
Product specifications (P)			
Market research	P1	—	2
Overall product specifications	P2	P1	4
Hardware	P3	P2	5
Software	P4	P3	5
Supplier specifications (S)			
Hardware	S1	P4	5
Software	S2	P4	6
Product design (D)			
Battery	D1	S1	1
Display	D2	S1	2
Camera	D3	S1	1
Outer cover	D4	D1, D2, D3	4
Product integration (I)			
Hardware	I1	D4	3
User interface	I2	D2	4
Software coding	I3	I2	4
Prototype testing	I4	I1, I3	4
Subcontracting (V)			
Suppliers selection	V1	S1, S2	10
Contract negotiation	V2	I4, V1	2

You have been given the information in Exhibit 4.13. It includes all the activities required in the project and the duration of each activity. Also, dependencies between the activities have been identified. Remember that the preceding activity must be fully completed before work on the following activity can be started.

Your project is divided into five major subprojects. Subproject "P" involves developing specifications for the new cell phone. Here, decisions related to such things as battery life, size of the phone, and features need to be made. These details are based on how a customer uses the cell phone. These user specifications are redefined in terms that have meaning to the subcontractors that will actually make the new cell phone in subproject "S" supplier specifications. These involve engineering details for how the product will perform.

The individual components that make up the product are the focus of subproject "D." Subproject "I" brings all the components together, and a working prototype is built and tested.

Finally, in subproject "V," suppliers are selected and contracts are negotiated.

1. Draw a project network that includes all the activities.
2. Calculate the start and finish times for each activity and determine the minimum number of weeks for completing the project. Find the activities that are on the critical path for completing the project in the shortest time.
3. Identify slack in the activities not on the project critical path.
4. Your boss would like you to study the impact of making two changes to how the project is organized. The first change involves using dedicated teams that would work strictly in parallel on the activities in each subproject. For example, in subproject P (product specifications) the team would work on P1, P2, P3, and P4 all in parallel. In other words, there would be no precedence relationships within a subproject—all tasks within a subproject would be worked on at the same time and each would take the same amount of time as originally specified. With this new design, all the subprojects would be done sequentially with P done first, then S, D, I, and finally V. What would be the expected impact on how long it would take to complete the project if this change were made?

5. The second change your boss would like you to consider would be to select the suppliers during subproject P and have them work directly with the dedicated teams as described in step 4. This would involve adding an additional activity to subproject P called supplier selection and contract negotiation (P5) with a duration of 12 weeks. This new activity would be done in parallel with P1, P2, P3, and P4. Subprojects S and V would be eliminated from the project. What would be the expected impact on how long it would take to complete the project if this additional change were made?
6. Evaluate the impact of making these changes using criteria other than just the time to complete the project. Do you think it would be in Nokia's best interest to try to make these changes in how it runs this and future cell phone design projects?

PRACTICE EXAM

Name the term defined in each of the following statements. Answers are listed at the bottom.

1. A project structured where a self-contained team works full time on the project.
2. Specific events that upon completion mark important progress toward completing a project.
3. This defines the hierarchy of project tasks, subtasks, and work packages.
4. Pieces of work in a project that consume time to complete.
5. A chart that shows both the time and sequence for completing the activities in a project.
6. Activities that in sequence form the longest chain in a project.
7. The difference between the late and early start time for an activity.
8. When activities are scheduled with probabilistic task times.
9. The procedure used to reduce project completion time by trading off time versus cost.
10. A key assumption related to the resources needed to complete activities when using the critical path method.

Answers to Practice Exam 1. Pure project or skunkworks 2. Milestones 3. Work breakdown structure 4. Activities 5. Gantt chart 6. Critical path(s) 7. Slack 8. The Program Evaluation and Review Technique (PERT) 9. Crashing 10. Resources are always available.

For PowerPoint lecture slides, Solutions Manual, Test Bank, Data files for solved examples, Excel Templates, Step-by-Step Solved Examples in video format, Tutorial Videos and many more, scan the adjacent **QR code**, or **visit http://www.mhhe.com/sie-chase15e**

Chapter 5

Strategic Capacity Management

LEARNING OBJECTIVES

LO 5-1 Explain what capacity management is and why it is strategically important

LO 5-2 Exemplify how to plan capacity

LO 5-3 Evaluate capacity alternatives using decision trees

LO 5-4 Compare capacity planning in services to capacity planning in manufacturing

ECONOMIES OF SCALE MADE OF STEEL

The *Eleonora Maersk,* almost 400m long is one of the E Series container ships operated by the Danish A. P. Moller-Maersk Group. These ships can carry 7,500 40-foot shipping containers. Given that each of these containers can hold 70,000 T-shirts allowing a T-shirt made in China to be sent to the Netherlands for just 2.5 cents.

These large ships and the even larger ones currently being launched, allow goods to be shipped around the world at very low cost. Of course, the only downside is the time that it takes these ships to make the long journeys as they move the goods from the factories in countries such as China, India and Indonesia to the large consumer markets in the United States, Canada, Australia, and Western Europe.

CAPACITY MANAGEMENT IN OPERATIONS AND SUPPLY CHAIN MANAGEMENT

LO 5-1

Explain what capacity management is and why it is strategically important

A dictionary definition of capacity is "the ability to hold, receive, store, or accommodate." In a general business sense, it is most frequently viewed as the amount of output that a system is capable of achieving over a specific period of time. In a service setting, this might be the number of customers that can be handled between noon and 1:00 P.M. In manufacturing, this might be the number of automobiles that can be produced in a single shift.

When looking at capacity, operations managers need to look at both resource inputs *and* product outputs. For planning purposes, real (or effective) capacity depends on what is to be produced. For example, a firm that makes multiple products inevitably can produce more of one kind than of another with a given level of resource inputs. Thus, while the managers of an automobile factory may state that their facility has 6,000 production hours available per year, they are also thinking that these hours can be used to make either 150,000 two-door models or 120,000 four-door models (or some mix of the two- and four-door models). This reflects their knowledge of what their current technology and labor force inputs can produce and the product mix that is to be demanded from these resources.

While many industries measure and report their capacity in terms of outputs, those whose product mix is very uncertain often express capacity in terms of inputs. For example, hospital capacity is expressed as the number of beds because the number of patients served and the types of services provided will depend on patient needs.

Strategy

An operations and supply chain management view also emphasizes the time dimension of capacity. That is, capacity must also be stated relative to some period of time. This is evidenced in the common distinction drawn between long-range, intermediate-range, and short-range capacity planning.

Capacity planning is generally viewed in three time durations:

Long range—greater than one year. Where productive resources (such as buildings, equipment, or facilities) take a long time to acquire or dispose of, long-range capacity planning requires top management participation and approval.

Intermediate range—monthly or quarterly plans for the next 6 to 18 months. Here, capacity may be varied by such alternatives as hiring, layoffs, new tools, minor equipment purchases, and subcontracting.

Short range—less than one month. This is tied into the daily or weekly scheduling process and involves making adjustments to eliminate the variance between planned and actual output. This includes alternatives such as overtime, personnel transfers, and alternative production routings.

In this chapter, our focus is on capacity planning related to the long-term decisions. These involve the purchase of highly capital-intensive items, such as buildings, equipment, and other assets. The medium-term capacity-related decisions are considered as part of the aggregate operations planning decisions, which are the topic of Chapter 19. Short-term capacity planning is discussed in the context of the different types of processes discussed in the book: manufacturing in Chapter 7, service in Chapter 9, and material requirements planning in Chapter 21.

Although there is no one person with the job title "capacity manager," there are several managerial positions charged with the effective use of capacity. *Capacity* is a relative term; in an operations management context, it may be defined as *the amount of resource inputs available relative to output requirements over a particular period of time.*

The objective of **strategic capacity planning** is to provide an approach for determining the overall capacity level of capital-intensive resources—facilities, equipment, and overall labor force size—that best supports the company's long-term competitive strategy. The capacity level selected has a critical impact on the firm's response rate, its cost structure, its inventory policies, and its management and staff support requirements. If capacity is inadequate, a company may lose customers through slow service or by allowing competitors to enter the market. If capacity is excessive, a company may have to reduce prices to stimulate demand; underutilize its workforce; carry excess inventory; or seek additional, less profitable products to stay in business.

Strategic capacity planning

Finding the overall capacity level of capital-intensive resources to best support the firm's long-term strategy.

Capacity Planning Concepts

Capacity
The output that a system is capable of achieving over a period of time.

Best operating level
The level of capacity for which the process was designed and the volume of output at which average unit cost is minimized.

Capacity utilization rate
Measure of how close the firm's current output rate is to its best operating level (percent).

The term **capacity** implies an attainable rate of output, for example, 480 cars per day, but says nothing about how long that rate can be sustained. Thus, we do not know if this 480 cars per day is a one-day peak or a six-month average. To avoid this problem, the concept of **best operating level** is used. This is the level of capacity for which the process was designed and thus is the volume of output at which average unit cost is minimized. Determining this minimum is difficult because it involves a complex trade-off between the allocation of fixed overhead costs and the cost of overtime, equipment wear, defect rates, and other costs.

An important measure is the **capacity utilization rate**, which reveals how close a firm is to its best operating level:

$$\textit{Capacity utilization rate} = \frac{\textit{Capacity used}}{\textit{Best operating level}} \tag{5.1}$$

$$\textit{Capacity utilization rate} = \frac{480}{500} = .96 \text{ or } 96\%$$

The capacity utilization rate is expressed as a percentage and requires that the numerator and denominator be measured in the same units and time periods (such as machine hours/day, barrels of oil/day, or dollars of output/day).

Economies and Diseconomies of Scale

Economies of scale
Idea that as the plant gets larger and volume increases, the average cost per unit drops. At some point, the plant gets too large and cost per unit increases.

The basic notion of **economies of scale** is that as a plant gets larger and volume increases, the average cost per unit of output drops. This is partially due to lower operating and capital cost, because a piece of equipment with twice the capacity of another piece typically does not cost twice as much to purchase or operate. Plants also gain efficiencies when they become large enough to fully utilize dedicated resources (people and equipment) for information technology, material handling, and administrative support.

At some point, the size of a plant becomes too large and diseconomies of scale become a problem. These diseconomies may surface in many different ways. For example, maintaining the demand required to keep the large facility busy may require significant discounting of the product. The U.S. automobile manufacturers continually face this problem. Another typical example involves using a few large-capacity pieces of equipment. Minimizing equipment downtime is essential in this type of operation. M&M Mars, for example, has highly automated, high-volume equipment to make M&Ms. A single packaging line moves 2.6 million M&Ms each hour. Even though direct labor to operate the equipment is very low, the labor required to maintain the equipment is high.

In many cases, the size of a plant may be influenced by factors other than the internal equipment, labor, and other capital expenditures. A major factor may be the cost to transport raw materials and finished product to and from the plant. A cement factory, for example, would have a difficult time serving customers more than a few hours from its plant. Similarly, automobile companies such as Ford, Honda, Nissan, and Toyota have found it advantageous to locate plants within specific international markets. The anticipated size of these intended markets will largely dictate the size and capacity of the plants.

Jaguar, the luxury automobile producer, recently found it had too many plants. Jaguar was employing 8,560 workers in three plants that produced 126,122 cars, about 15 cars per employee. In comparison, Volvo's plant in Torslanda, Sweden, was nearly twice as productive, building 158,466 cars with 5,472 workers, or 29 cars per employee. By contrast, BMW AG's Mini unit made 174,000 vehicles at a single British plant with just 4,500 workers, or 39 cars per employee.

Capacity Focus

The concept of a **focused factory** holds that a production facility works best when it focuses on a fairly limited set of production objectives. This means, for example, that a firm should not expect to excel in every aspect of manufacturing performance: cost, quality, delivery speed and reliability, changes in demand, and flexibility to adapt to new products. Rather, it should select a limited set of tasks that contribute the most to corporate objectives. Typically, the focused factory would produce a specific product or related group of products. A focused factory allows capacity to be focused on producing those specific items.

Focused factory
A facility designed around a limited set of production objectives. Typically, the focus would relate to a specific product or product group.

The capacity focus concept can be operationalized through the mechanism of **plant within a plant**—or **PWP**. A focused factory (Exhibit 5.1) may have several PWPs, each of which may have separate suborganizations, equipment and process policies, workforce management policies, production control methods, and so forth, for different products—even if they are made under the same roof. This, in effect, permits finding the best operating level for each department of the organization and thereby carries the focus concept down to the operating level.

Plant within a plant (PWP)
An area in a larger facility that is dedicated to a specific production objective (for example, product group). This can be used to operationalize the focused factory concept.

EXHIBIT 5.1

Focused Factories—Plant within a Plant

This company needs to produce two different products. Product A is high volume and standard (there is no variation in how it is made). Product B is low volume and needs to be customized to each order. This plant is divided into three distinct areas that operate independently. The Product Line A area is a high-volume assembly line designed to produce A. B Machine Shop is an area where custom parts are made for product B. Assembly B is where product B is assembled based on each customer order. This factory, with its plants within a plant, can operate more efficiently than if both products were made with a single common production process.

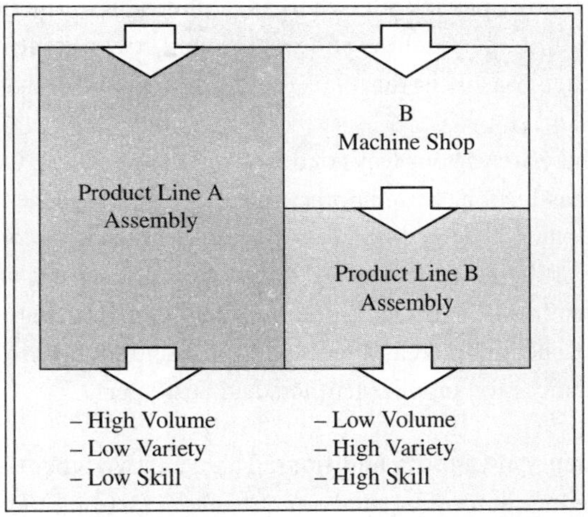

Capacity Flexibility

Capacity flexibility means having the ability to rapidly increase or decrease production levels, or to shift production capacity quickly from one product or service to another. Such flexibility is achieved through flexible plants, processes, and workers, as well as through strategies that use the capacity of other organizations. Increasingly, companies are taking the idea of flexibility into account as they design their supply chains. Working with suppliers, they can build capacity into their whole systems.

Flexible Plants Perhaps the ultimate in plant flexibility is the *zero-changeover-time* plant. Using movable equipment, knockdown walls, and easily accessible and reroutable utilities, such a plant can quickly adapt to change. An analogy to a familiar service business captures the flavor well: a plant with equipment that is easy to install and easy to tear down and move—like the Ringling Bros. and Barnum & Bailey Circus in the old tent-circus days.

Flexible Processes Flexible processes are epitomized by flexible manufacturing systems on the one hand and simple, easily set up equipment on the other. Both of these technological approaches permit rapid low-cost switching from one product to another, enabling what are sometimes referred to as **economies of scope**. (By definition, economies of scope exist when multiple products can be combined and produced at one facility at a lower cost than they can be produced separately.)

Economies of scope
When multiple products can be produced at lower cost in combination than they can be separately.

Flexible Workers Flexible workers have multiple skills and the ability to switch easily from one kind of task to another. They require broader training than specialized workers and need managers and staff support to facilitate quick changes in their work assignments.

LO 5-2

Exemplify how to plan capacity

CAPACITY PLANNING

Considerations in Changing Capacity

Many issues must be considered when adding or decreasing capacity. Three important ones are maintaining system balance, frequency of capacity additions or reductions, and use of external capacity.

Strategy

Maintaining System Balance In a perfectly balanced plant with three production stages, the output of stage 1 provides the exact input requirement for stage 2. Stage 2's output provides the exact input requirement for stage 3, and so on. In practice, however, achieving such a "perfect" design is usually both impossible and undesirable. One reason is that the best operating levels for each stage generally differ. For instance, department 1 may operate most efficiently over a range of 90 to 110 units per month, whereas department 2, the next stage in the process, is most efficient at 75 to 85 units per month, and department 3 works best over a range of 150 to 200 units per month. Another reason is that variability in product demand and the processes themselves may lead to imbalance.

There are various ways of dealing with imbalance. One is to add capacity to stages that are bottlenecks. This can be done by temporary measures, such as scheduling overtime, leasing equipment, or purchasing additional capacity through subcontracting. A second way is through the use of buffer inventories in front of the bottleneck stage to ensure it always has something to work on. A third approach involves duplicating or increasing the facilities of one department on which another is dependent. All these approaches are increasingly being applied to supply chain design. This supply planning also helps reduce imbalances for supplier partners and customers.

Frequency of Capacity Additions There are two types of costs to consider when adding capacity: the cost of upgrading too frequently and that of upgrading too infrequently. Upgrading capacity too frequently is expensive. Direct costs include removing and replacing old equipment and training employees on the new equipment. In addition, the new equipment must be purchased, often for considerably more than the selling price of the old. Finally, there is the opportunity cost of idling the plant or service site during the changeover period.

Conversely, upgrading capacity too infrequently is also expensive. Infrequent expansion means that capacity is purchased in larger chunks. Any excess capacity that is purchased must be carried as overhead until it is utilized. (Exhibit 5.2 illustrates frequent versus infrequent capacity expansion.)

External Sources of Operations and Supply Capacity In some cases, it may be cheaper not to add capacity at all, but rather to use some existing external source of capacity. Two common strategies used by organizations are outsourcing and sharing capacity. An example of outsourcing is Dell Computer using a Chinese company to assemble its notebook computers. An example of sharing capacity is two domestic airlines flying different routes with different seasonal demands exchanging aircraft (suitably repainted) when one's routes are heavily used and the other's are not. A new twist is airlines sharing routes—using the same flight number even though the airline company may change through the route. Outsourcing is covered in more depth in Chapter 16.

EXHIBIT 5.2

Frequent versus Infrequent Capacity Expansion

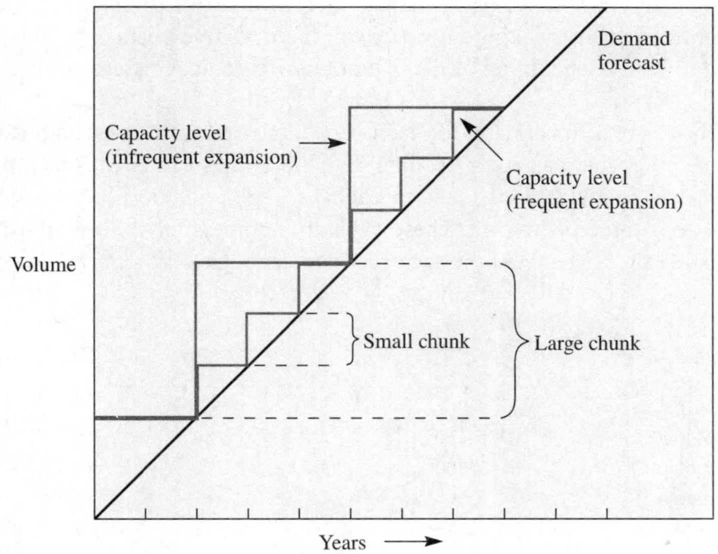

Decreasing Capacity Although we normally think in terms of expansions, shedding capacity in response to decreased demand can create significant problems for a firm. Temporary strategies such as scheduling fewer hours or scheduling an extended shutdown period are often used. More permanent reductions in capacity would typically require the sale of equipment or possibly even the liquidation of entire facilities.

Determining Capacity Requirements

In determining capacity requirements, we must address the demands for individual product lines, individual plant capabilities, and allocation of production throughout the plant network. Typically, this is done according to the following steps:

1. Use forecasting techniques (see Chapter 18) to predict sales for individual products within each product line.
2. Calculate equipment and labor requirements to meet product line forecasts.
3. Project labor and equipment availabilities over the planning horizon.

Capacity cushion
Capacity in excess of expected demand.

Often, the firm then decides on some **capacity cushion** that will be maintained between the projected requirements and the actual capacity measured as a percentage in excess of the expected demand. A capacity cushion is an amount of capacity in excess of expected demand. For example, if the expected annual demand on a facility is \$10 million in products per year and the design capacity is \$12 million per year, it has a 20 percent capacity cushion. A 20 percent capacity cushion equates to an 83 percent utilization rate (100 percent/120 percent).

When a firm's design capacity is less than the capacity required to meet its demand, it is said to have a negative capacity cushion. If, for example, a firm has a demand of \$12 million in products per year but can produce only \$10 million per year, it has a negative capacity cushion of 16.7 percent.

We now apply these three steps to an example.

EXAMPLE 5.1 Determining Capacity Requirements

Stewart Company produces two brands of salad dressings: Paul's and Newman's. Each is available in bottles and single-serving plastic bags. Management would like to determine yearly equipment and labor requirements for its packing operation for the next five years. The details related to the exact weekly and monthly scheduling of the operations are done at different levels in the planning process.

The demand for the two flavors and for each packaging option is given in this table. The company has three machines that can each package 150,000 bottles each year (each machine has two operators). It also has five machines that can each package 250,000 plastic bags per year (each of these machines has three operators). These capacity numbers have been adjusted for expected downtime and quality problems. Will the company have enough yearly packaging capacity to meet future demand?

	Year				
	1	2	3	4	5
Paul's					
Bottles (000s)	60	100	150	200	250
Plastic bags (000s)	100	200	300	400	500
Newman's					
Bottles (000s)	75	85	95	97	98
Plastic bags (000s)	200	400	600	650	680

SOLUTION

Step 1. Use forecasting techniques to predict sales for individual products within each product line. The marketing department, which is now running a promotional campaign for Newman's dressing, provided the forecast demand values given in the previous table (in thousands) for the next five years. The campaign is expected to continue for the next two years.

Step 2. Calculate equipment and labor requirements to meet product line forecasts. Currently, three machines that can package up to 150,000 bottles each per year are available. Each machine requires two operators and can produce bottles of both Newman's and Paul's dressings. Six bottle machine operators are available. Also, five machines that can package up to 250,000 plastic bags each per year are available. Three operators are required for each machine, which can produce plastic bags of both Newman's and Paul's dressings. Currently, 15 plastic bag machine operators are available.

Total product line forecasts can be calculated from the preceding table by adding the yearly demand for bottles and plastic bags as follows.

	Year				
	1	2	3	4	5
Bottles (000s)	135	185	245	297	348
Plastic bags (000s)	300	600	900	1,050	1,180

We can now calculate equipment and labor requirements for the current year (year 1). Because the total available capacity for packaging bottles is 450,000/year (3 machines × 150,000 each), we will be using 135,000/450,000 = 0.3 or 30 percent of the available capacity for the current year, or 135,000/150,000 = 0.9 machine. Similarly, we will need 300,000/1,250,000 = 0.24 or 24 percent of the available capacity for plastic bags for the current year, or 300,000/250,000 = 1.2 machines. The total number of crew required to support our forecast demand for the first year will equal the crew required for the bottle machine plus the crew required for the plastic bag machine.

The labor requirement for year 1 is

$$0.9 \text{ bottle machine} \times 2 \text{ operators} = 1.8 \text{ operators}$$

$$1.2 \text{ bag machines} \times 3 \text{ operators} = 3.6 \text{ operators}$$

Step 3. Project labor and equipment availabilities over the planning horizon. We repeat the preceding calculations for the remaining years.

	Year				
	1	2	3	4	5
Bottle Operation					
Percentage machine capacity utilized	30%	41%	54.4%	66%	77.3%
Machine requirement	0.9	1.23	1.63	1.98	2.32
Labor requirement	1.8	2.46	3.26	3.96	4.64
Plastic Bag Operation					
Percentage machine capacity utilized	24%	48%	72%	84%	94%
Machine requirement	1.2	2.4	3.6	4.2	4.7
Labor requirement	3.6	7.2	10.8	12.6	14.1

A positive capacity cushion exists for all five years relative to the availability of machines because the available capacity for both operations always exceeds the expected demand. Stewart Company can now begin to develop the intermediate-range sales and operations plan for the two production lines. This operations plan would need to address the issue of how these machines might actually be scheduled relative to the use of overtime and/or multiple shifts over weekly and monthly time intervals.

USING DECISION TREES TO EVALUATE CAPACITY ALTERNATIVES

LO 5-3 Evaluate capacity alternatives using decision trees

A convenient way to lay out the steps of a capacity problem is through the use of decision trees. The tree format helps not only in understanding the problem but also in finding a solution. A *decision tree* is a schematic model of the sequence of steps in a problem and the conditions and consequences of each step. In recent years, a few commercial software packages have been developed to assist in the construction and analysis of decision trees. These packages make the process quick and easy.

Decision trees are composed of decision nodes with branches extending to and from them. Usually squares represent decision points and circles represent chance events. Branches from decision points show the choices available to the decision maker; branches from chance events show the probabilities for their occurrence.

In solving decision tree problems, we work from the end of the tree backward to the start of the tree. As we work back, we calculate the expected values at each step. In calculating the expected value, the time value of money is important if the planning horizon is long.

Analytics

Once the calculations are made, we prune the tree by eliminating from each decision point all branches except the one with the highest payoff. This process continues to the first decision point, and the decision problem is thereby solved.

We now demonstrate an application of capacity planning for Hackers Computer Store.

EXAMPLE 5.2 Decision Trees

The owner of Hackers Computer Store is considering what to do with his business over the next five years. Sales growth over the past couple of years has been good, but sales could grow substantially if a major proposed electronics firm is built in his area. Hackers' owner sees three options. The first is to enlarge his current store, the second is to locate at a new site, and the third is to simply wait and do nothing. The process of expanding or moving would take little time, and, therefore, the store would not lose revenue. If nothing were done the first year and strong growth occurred, then the decision to expand could be reconsidered. Waiting longer than one year would allow competition to move in and would make expansion no longer feasible.

The assumptions and conditions are as follows:

1. Strong growth as a result of the increased population of computer fanatics from the new electronics firm has a 55 percent probability.
2. Strong growth with a new site would give annual returns of $195,000 per year. Weak growth with a new site would mean annual returns of $115,000.

3. Strong growth with an expansion would give annual returns of $190,000 per year. Weak growth with an expansion would mean annual returns of $100,000.
4. At the existing store with no changes, there would be returns of $170,000 per year if there is strong growth and $105,000 per year if growth is weak.
5. Expansion at the current site would cost $87,000.
6. The move to the new site would cost $210,000.
7. If growth is strong and the existing site is enlarged during the second year, the cost would still be $87,000.
8. Operating costs for all options are equal.

SOLUTION

We construct a decision tree to advise Hackers' owner on the best action. Exhibit 5.3 shows the decision tree for this problem. There are two decision points (shown with the square nodes) and three chance occurrences (round nodes).

EXHIBIT 5.3

Decision Tree for Hackers Computer Store Problem

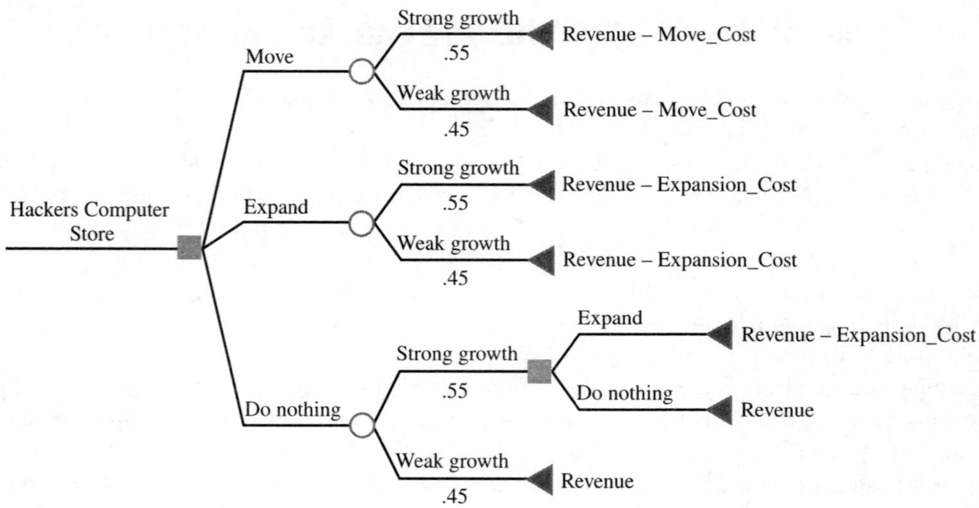

The values of each alternative outcome shown on the right of the diagram in Exhibit 5.4 are calculated as follows.

Alternative	Revenue	Cost	Value
Move to new location, strong growth	$195,000 × 5 yrs	$210,000	$765,000
Move to new location, weak growth	$115,000 × 5 yrs	$210,000	$365,000
Expand store, strong growth	$190,000 × 5 yrs	$87,000	$863,000
Expand store, weak growth	$100,000 × 5 yrs	$87,000	$413,000
Do nothing now, strong growth, expand next year	$170,000 × 1 yr + $190,000 × 4 yrs	$87,000	$843,000
Do nothing now, strong growth, do not expand next year	$170,000 × 5 yrs	$0	$850,000
Do nothing now, weak growth	$105,000 × 5 yrs	$0	$525,000

Working from the rightmost alternatives, which are associated with the decision of whether to expand, we see that the alternative of doing nothing has a higher value than the expansion alternative. We therefore eliminate the expansion in the second year alternatives. What this means is that if we do nothing in the first year and we experience strong growth, then in the second year it makes no sense to expand.

EXHIBIT 5.4

Decision Tree Analysis

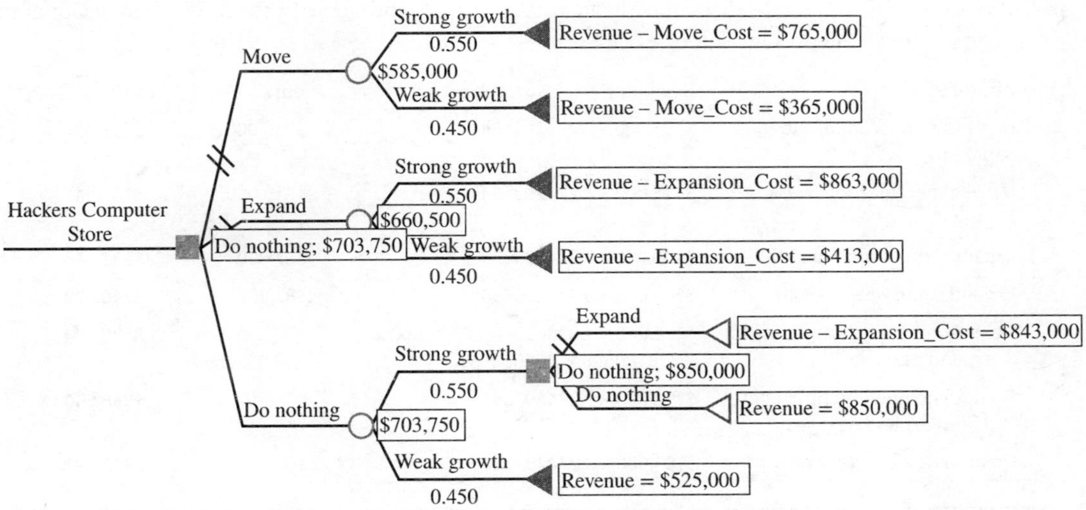

Now we can calculate the expected values associated with our current decision alternatives. We simply multiply the value of the alternative by its probability and sum the values. The expected value for the alternative of moving now is $585,000. The expansion alternative has an expected value of $660,500, and doing nothing now has an expected value of $703,750. Our analysis indicates that our best decision is to do nothing (both now and next year)!

Due to the five-year time horizon, it may be useful to consider the time value of the revenue and cost streams when solving this problem. If we assume a 16 percent interest rate, the first alternative outcome (move now, strong growth) has a discounted revenue valued at $428,487 (195,000 × 3.274293654) minus the $210,000 cost to move immediately. Exhibit 5.5 shows the analysis considering the discounted flows. Details of the calculations are given as follows. The present value table in Appendix E can be used to look up the discount factors. In order to make our calculations agree with those completed by Excel—in Excel, calculate the discount factor = $(1 + \text{interest rate})^{(-\text{years})}$—we have used discount factors that are calculated to 10 digits of precision. The only calculation that is a little

EXHIBIT 5.5

Decision Tree Analysis Using Net Present Value Calculations

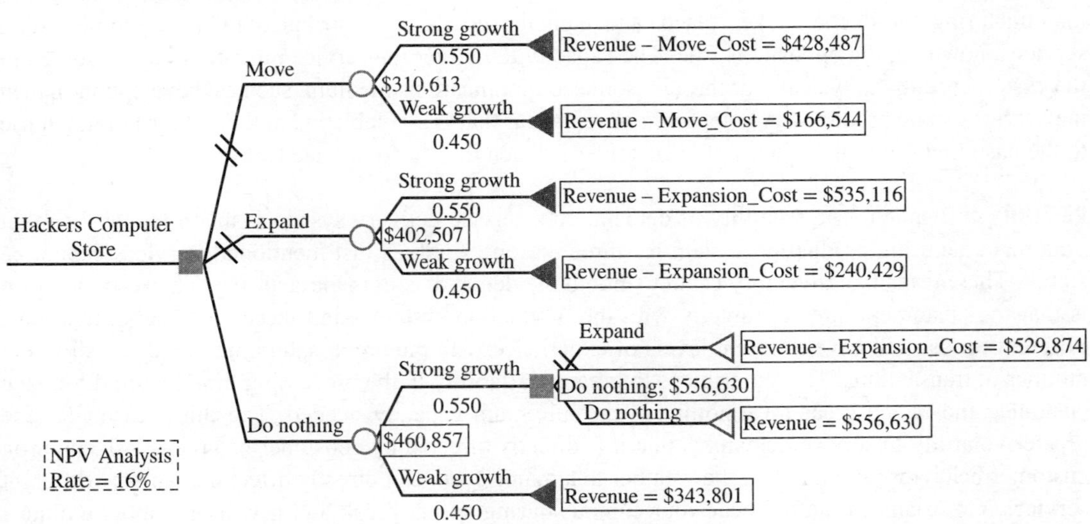

tricky is the one for revenue when we do nothing now and expand at the beginning of next year. In this case, we have a revenue stream of $170,000 the first year, followed by four years at $190,000. The first part of the calculation (170,000 × .862068966) discounts the first-year revenue to the present. The next part (190,000 × 2.798180638) discounts the next four years to the start of year 2. We then discount this four-year stream to the present value.

Alternative	Revenue	Cost	Value
Move to new location, strong growth	$195,000 × 3.274293654	$210,000	$428,487
Move to new location, weak growth	$115,000 × 3.274293654	$210,000	$166,544
Expand store, strong growth	$190,000 × 3.274293654	$87,000	$535,116
Expand store, weak growth	$100,000 × 3.274293654	$87,000	$240,429
Do nothing now, strong growth, expand next year	$170,000 × .862068966 + $190,000 × 2.798180638 × .862068966	$87,000 × .862068966	$529,874
Do nothing now, strong growth, do not expand next year	$170,000 × 3.274293654	$0	$556,630
Do nothing now, weak growth	$105,000 × 3.274293654	$0	$343,801

LO 5-4

Compare capacity planning in services to capacity planning in manufacturing

PLANNING SERVICE CAPACITY

Capacity Planning in Services versus Manufacturing

Although capacity planning in services is subject to many of the same issues as manufacturing capacity planning, and facility sizing can be done in much the same way, there are several important differences. Service capacity is more time- and location-dependent, it is subject to more volatile demand fluctuations, and utilization directly impacts service quality.

Time Unlike goods, services cannot be stored for later use. As such, in services, managers must consider time as one of their supplies. The capacity must be available to produce a service when it is needed. For example, a customer cannot be given a seat that went unoccupied on a previous airline flight if the current flight is full. Nor can the customer purchase a seat on a particular day's flight and take it home to be used at some later date.

Strategy

Location In face-to-face settings, the service capacity must be located near the customer. In manufacturing, production takes place, and then the goods are distributed to the customer. With services, however, the opposite is true. The capacity to deliver the service must first be distributed to the customer (either physically or through some communications medium, such as the telephone), then the service can be produced. A hotel room or rental car that is available in another city is not much use to the customer—it must be where the customer is when that customer needs it.

Key Idea

Typically, a firm can run a factory at a much higher capacity utilization rate than a service facility such as a call center. Less predictable demand requires a lower capacity operating point for good service.

Volatility of Demand The volatility of demand on a service delivery system is much higher than that on a manufacturing production system for three reasons. First, as just mentioned, services cannot be stored. This means that inventory cannot smooth the demand as in manufacturing. The second reason is that the customers interact directly with the production system—and these customers often have different needs, will have different levels of experience with the process, and may require a different number of transactions. This contributes to greater variability in the processing time required for each customer and hence greater variability in the minimum capacity needed. The third reason for the greater volatility in service demand is that it is directly affected by consumer behavior. Influences on customer behavior ranging from the weather to a major event can directly affect demand for different services. Go to any restaurant near your campus during spring break and it will probably be almost empty. This behavioral effect can be seen over even shorter time frames, such as the lunch-hour rush at a fast-food restaurant's drive-through window. Because of this volatility, service capacity is often planned in increments as small as 10 to 30 minutes, as opposed to the one-week increments more common in manufacturing.

Capacity Utilization and Service Quality

Planning capacity levels for services must consider the day-to-day relationship between service utilization and service quality. Exhibit 5.6 shows a service situation using waiting line terms (arrival rates and service rates). The term *arrival rate* refers to the average number of customers that come to a facility during a specific period of time. The *service rate* is the average number of customers that can be processed over the same period of time when the facility is operating at maximum capacity. The best operating point is near 70 percent of the maximum capacity. This is enough to keep servers busy but allows enough time to serve customers individually and keep enough capacity in reserve so as not to create too many managerial headaches. In the critical zone, customers are processed through the system, but service quality declines. Above the critical zone, where customers arrive at a rate faster than they can be served, the line builds up and it is likely that many customers may never be served. (Details related to how waiting lines operate relative to capacity are presented in Chapter 10, "Waiting Line Analysis and Simulation.")

EXHIBIT 5.6

Relationship between the Rate of Service Utilization (ρ) and Service Quality

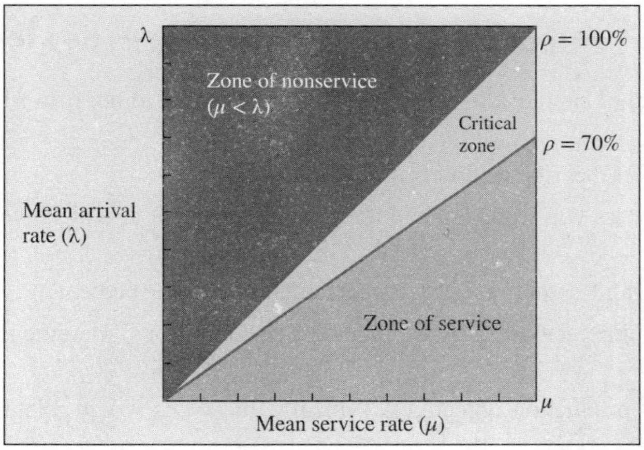

J. Haywood–Farmer and J. Nollet, *Services Plus: Effective Service Managment* (Boucherville, Quebec, Canada: G. Morin Publisher Ltd., 1991), p. 59.

The optimal utilization rate is very context specific. Low rates are appropriate when both the degree of uncertainty and the stakes are high. For example, hospital emergency rooms and fire departments should aim for low utilization because of the high level of uncertainty and the life-or-death nature of their activities. Relatively predictable services such as commuter trains or service facilities without customer contact (for example, postal sorting operations) can plan to operate much nearer to 100 percent utilization. Interestingly, there is a third group for which high utilization is desirable. All sports teams like sellouts, not only because of the virtually 100 percent contribution margin of each customer, but because a full house creates an atmosphere that pleases customers, motivates the home team to perform better, and boosts future ticket sales. Stage performances and bars share this phenomenon.

Packed stadium with fans

CONCEPT CONNECTIONS

LO 5–1 Explain what capacity management is and why it is strategically important

Summary

- An operations and supply chain management view of capacity emphasizes the time dimension of capacity.
- Three time horizons are generally used: long range (greater than a year), intermediate range (next 6 to 18 months), and short range (less than a month).
- To distinguish between the absolute maximum capacity of the system (the highest output rate attainable) and the rate that is sustainable by the system (that it can be run at efficiently and for a long period of time), the term *best operating level* is used. The utilization of the system is a measure of how close the system is operating relative to the best level.
- When a producing resource, such as a manufacturing plant, gets larger and volume increases while the average cost per unit of output simultaneously drops, then the resource is exhibiting economies of scale.
- At some point, the resource may be too large and the average cost will start to rise. This is when diseconomies of scale are a problem.
- Focused manufacturing plants are designed to produce multiple products using a concept called plant within a plant to improve economies of scale even though multiple products are produced in the same facility. This type of facility demonstrates the concept of economies of scope.
- Having capacity flexibility is often important to meeting the needs of a firm's customers.

Key Terms

Strategic capacity planning Finding the overall capacity level of capital-intensive resources to best support the firm's long-term strategy.

Capacity The output that a system is capable of achieving over a period of time.

Best operating level The level of capacity for which the process was designed and the volume of output at which average unit cost is minimized.

Capacity utilization rate Measure of how close the firm's current output rate is to its best operating level (percent).

Economies of scale Idea that as the plant gets larger and volume increases, the average cost per unit drops. At some point, the plant gets too large and cost per unit increases.

Focused factory A facility designed around a limited set of production objectives. Typically, the focus would relate to a specific product or product group.

Plant within a plant (PWP) An area in a larger facility that is dedicated to a specific production objective (for example, product group). This can be used to operationalize the focused factory concept.

Economies of scope When multiple products can be produced at lower cost in combination than they can be separately.

$$\textit{Capacity utilization rate} = \frac{\textit{Capacity used}}{\textit{Best operating level}} \qquad [5.1]$$

LO 5–2 Exemplify how to plan capacity

Summary

- From a strategic, long-term view, capacity additions or reductions come in chunks (fixed amounts). For example, an additional machine of a certain type is added to the existing pool of machines. Issues involve how frequently and how much capacity is added or removed over time.

Key Terms

Capacity cushion Capacity in excess of expected demand.

LO 5–3 Evaluate capacity alternatives using decision trees

Summary

- A useful technique for analyzing capacity problems is the decision tree.
- With this format, the sequences of decisions are organized like branches in a tree.
- The potential consequences of the decisions are enumerated and evaluated based on their probability of occurrence and corresponding expected value.

LO 5–4 Compare capacity planning in services to capacity planning in manufacturing

Summary

- Often, services require that capacity be available immediately and that it be near where the customer resides. For example, a bank needs automated teller machines (ATMs) close to where customers want immediate cash, and enough of them so customers will not have to wait in long lines.
- Also, firms that offer services often need to deal with dramatic changes in customer demand over time (for example, the lunch-hour rush at a bank's drive-through window).

SOLVED PROBLEM

LO 5–3

E-Education is a new startup that develops and markets MBA courses offered over the Internet. The company is currently located in Chicago and employs 150 people. Due to strong growth, the company needs additional office space. The company has the option of leasing additional space at its current location in Chicago for the next two years, but after that will need to move to a new building. Another option the company is considering is moving the entire operation to a small Midwest town immediately. A third option is for the company to lease a new building in Chicago immediately. If the company chooses the first option and leases new space at its current location, it can, at the end of two years, either lease a new building in Chicago or move to the small Midwest town.

The following are some additional facts about the alternatives and current situation:

1. The company has a 75 percent chance of surviving the next two years.
2. Leasing the new space for two years at the current location in Chicago would cost $750,000 per year.
3. Moving the entire operation to a Midwest town would cost $1 million. Leasing space would run only $500,000 per year.
4. Moving to a new building in Chicago would cost $200,000, and leasing the new building's space would cost $650,000 per year.
5. The company can cancel the lease at any time.
6. The company will build its own building in five years, if it survives.
7. Assume all other costs and revenues are the same no matter where the company is located.

What should E-Education do?

Solution

Step 1: Construct a decision tree that considers all of E-Education's alternatives. The following shows the tree that has decision points (with the square nodes) followed by chance occurrences (round nodes). In the case of the first decision point, if the company survives, two additional decision points need consideration.

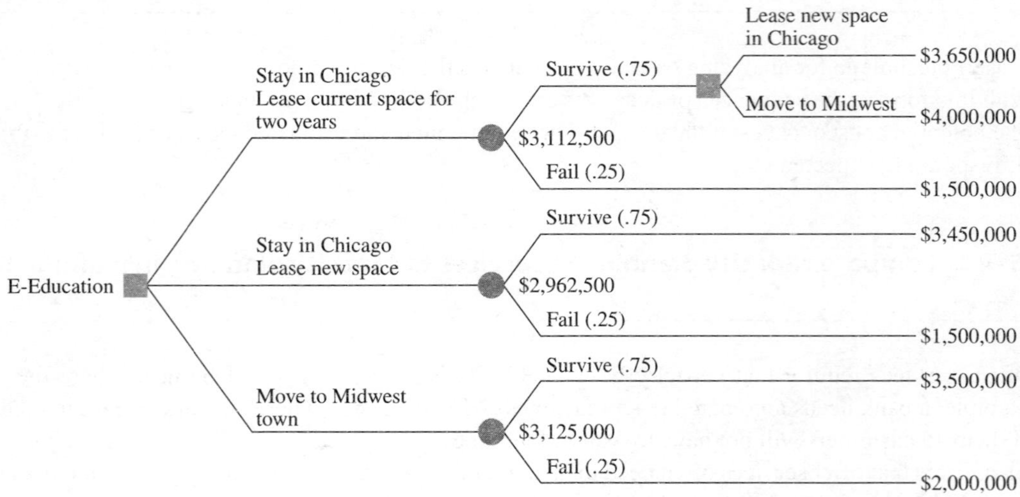

Step 2: Calculate the values of each alternative as follows.

Alternative	Calculation	Value
Stay in Chicago, lease current space for two years, survive, lease new building in Chicago	(750,000) × 2 + 200,000 + (650,000) × 3 =	$3,650,000
Stay in Chicago, lease current space for two years, survive, move to Midwest	(750,000) × 2 + 1,000,000 + (500,000) × 3 =	$4,000,000
Stay in Chicago, lease current space for two years, fail	(750,000) × 2 =	$1,500,000
Stay in Chicago, lease new building in Chicago, survive	200,000 + (650,000) × 5 =	$3,450,000
Stay in Chicago, lease new building in Chicago, fail	200,000 + (650,000) × 2 =	$1,500,000
Move to Midwest, survive	1,000,000 + (500,000) × 5 =	$3,500,000
Move to Midwest, fail	1,000,000 + (500,000) × 2 =	$2,000,000

Working from our rightmost alternatives, the first two alternatives end in decision nodes. If we fail after the first two years, represented by the third alternative, the cost is only $1,500,000. The expected value of the first option of staying in Chicago and leasing space for the first two years is .75 × 3,650,000 + .25 × 1,500,000 = $3,112,500.

The second option, staying in Chicago and leasing a new building now, has an expected value of .75 × 3,450,000 + .25 × 1,500,000 = $2,962,500.

Finally, the third option of moving to the Midwest immediately has an expected value of .75 × 3,500,000 + .25 × 2,000,000 = $3,125,000.

From this, it looks like the best alternative is to stay in Chicago and lease a new building immediately.

DISCUSSION QUESTIONS

LO5–1

1. What capacity problems are encountered when a new drug is introduced to the market?
2. List some practical limits to economies of scale. In other words, when should a plant stop growing?
3. What are some capacity balance problems faced by the following organizations or facilities?
   a. An airline terminal
   b. A university computing lab
   c. A clothing manufacturer

4. At first glance, the concepts of the focused factory and capacity flexibility may seem to contradict each other. Do they really?
5. Management may choose to build up capacity in anticipation of demand or in response to developing demand. Cite the advantages and disadvantages of both approaches. **LO5–2**
6. What is capacity balance? Why is it hard to achieve? What methods are used to deal with capacity imbalances?
7. What are some reasons for a plant to maintain a capacity cushion? How about a negative capacity cushion?
8. Will the use of decision tree analysis guarantee the best decision for a firm? Why or why not? If not, why bother using it? **LO5–3**
9. Consider the example in Exhibit 5.5. Can you think of anything else you might do with that example that would be helpful to the ultimate decision maker?
10. What are some major capacity considerations in a hospital? How do they differ from those of a factory? **LO5–4**
11. Refer to Exhibit 5.6. Why is it that the critical zone begins at a utilization rate of about 70 percent in a typical service operation? Draw upon your own experiences as either a customer or a server in common service establishments.

OBJECTIVE QUESTIONS

1. A manufacturing shop is designed to operate most efficiently at an output of 550 units per day. In the past month, the plant averaged 490 units per day. What was its capacity utilization rate last month? (Answer in Appendix D) **LO5–1**
2. A company has a factory that is designed so that it is *most efficient* (average unit cost is minimized) when producing 15,000 units of output each month. However, it has an absolute maximum output capability of 17,250 units per month, and can produce as little as 7,000 units per month without corporate headquarters shifting production to another plant. If the factory produces 10,925 units in October, what is the *capacity utilization rate* in October for this factory?
3. Hoosier Manufacturing operates a production shop that is designed to have the lowest unit production cost at an output rate of 100 units per hour. In the month of July, the company operated the production line for a total of 175 hours and produced 16,900 units of output. What was its capacity utilization rate for the month?
4. AlwaysRain Irrigation, Inc. would like to determine capacity requirements for the next four years. Currently, two production lines are in place for making bronze and plastic sprinklers. Three types of sprinklers are available in both bronze and plastic: 90-degree nozzle sprinklers, 180-degree nozzle sprinklers, and 360-degree nozzle sprinklers. Management has forecast demand for the next four years as follows. **LO5–2**

	Yearly Demand			
	1 (in 000s)	2 (in 000s)	3 (in 000s)	4 (in 000s)
Plastic 90	32	44	55	56
Plastic 180	15	16	17	18
Plastic 360	50	55	64	67
Bronze 90	7	8	9	10
Bronze 180	3	4	5	6
Bronze 360	11	12	15	18

Both production lines can produce all the different types of nozzles. The bronze machines needed for the bronze sprinklers require two operators and can produce up to 12,000 sprinklers. The plastic injection molding machine needed for the plastic sprinklers requires four operators and can produce up to 200,000 sprinklers. Three bronze machines and only one injection molding machine are available. What are the capacity requirements for the next four years? (Assume that there is no learning.)

5. Suppose that AlwaysRain Irrigation's marketing department will undertake an intense ad campaign for the bronze sprinklers, which are more expensive but also more durable than the plastic ones. Forecast demand for the next four years is as follows.

	Yearly Demand			
	1 (in 000s)	2 (in 000s)	3 (in 000s)	4 (in 000s)
Plastic 90	32	44	55	56
Plastic 180	15	16	17	18
Plastic 360	50	55	64	67
Bronze 90	11	15	18	23
Bronze 180	6	5	6	9
Bronze 360	15	16	17	20

What are the capacity implications of the marketing campaign (assume no learning)?

6. In anticipation of the ad campaign, AlwaysRain bought an additional bronze machine. Will this be enough to ensure that adequate capacity is available?
7. Suppose that operators have enough training to operate both the bronze machines and the injection molding machine for the plastic sprinklers. Currently, AlwaysRain has 10 such employees. In anticipation of the ad campaign described in problem 5, management approved the purchase of two additional bronze machines. What are the labor requirement implications?

LO5–3

8. Expando, Inc. is considering the possibility of building an additional factory that would produce a new addition to its product line. The company is currently considering two options. The first is a small facility that it could build at a cost of \$6 million. If demand for new products is low, the company expects to receive \$10 million in discounted revenues (present value of future revenues) with the small facility. On the other hand, if demand is high, it expects \$12 million in discounted revenues using the small facility. The second option is to build a large factory at a cost of \$9 million. Were demand to be low, the company would expect \$10 million in discounted revenues with the large plant. If demand is high, the company estimates that the discounted revenues would be \$14 million. In either case, the probability of demand being high is .40, and the probability of it being low is .60. Not constructing a new factory would result in no additional revenue being generated because the current factories cannot produce these new products. Construct a decision tree to help Expando make the best decision. (Answer in Appendix D)
9. A builder has located a piece of property that she would like to buy and eventually build on. The land is currently zoned for four homes per acre, but she is planning to request new zoning. What she builds depends on approval of zoning requests and your analysis of this problem to advise her. With her input and your help, the decision process has been reduced to the following costs, alternatives, and probabilities:

   Cost of land: \$2 million

   Probability of rezoning: .60

   If the land is rezoned, there will be additional costs for new roads, lighting, and so on, of \$1 million.

   If the land is rezoned, the contractor must decide whether to build a shopping center or 1,500 apartments that the tentative plan shows would be possible. If she builds a shopping center, there is a 70 percent chance that she can sell the shopping center to a large department store chain for \$4 million over her construction cost, which excludes the land; and there is a 30 percent chance that she can sell it to an insurance company for \$5 million over her construction cost (also excluding the land). If, instead of the shopping center, she decides to build the 1,500 apartments, she places probabilities on the profits as follows: There is a 60 percent chance that she can sell the apartments to a real estate investment corporation for $3,000 each over her construction cost; there is a 40 percent chance that she can get only $2,000 each over her construction cost. (Both exclude the land cost.)

If the land is not rezoned, she will comply with the existing zoning restrictions and simply build 600 homes, on which she expects to make $4,000 over the construction cost on each one (excluding the cost of land).

Draw a decision tree of the problem and determine the best solution and the expected net profit.

10. Owners of a local restaurant are concerned about their ability to provide quality service as they continue to grow and attract more customers. They have collected data from Friday and Saturday nights, their busiest times of the week. During these time periods, about 75 customers arrive per hour for service. Given the number of tables and chairs, and the typical time it takes to serve a customer, the owners estimate they can serve, on average, about 100 customers per hour. During these nights, are they in the *zone of service,* the *critical zone,* or the *zone of nonservice*? (Answer in Appendix D) **LO5–4**
11. Owners of the restaurant in the prior problem anticipate that in one year their demand will double as long as they can provide good service to their customers. How much will they have to increase their service capacity to stay out of the critical zone?

CASE: Strategic Capacity Management in Indian Railways

Indian Railways (IR) plays an important role in supporting the economic activities of India. It operates on the largest rail networks of the world. It achieved an amazing double digit growth in freight revenue after 2004. One of the major contributors to the so called turnaround of IR is increase in the freight revenue. During financial year 2016–17, it carried 1107 million tons of goods and earned a record level of INR 1.67 lakh crore from freight transportation[1]. Capacity management, modernization and professional management practices were at the core of this achievement. Increased axle loading, reduced wagon turnaround, and market-oriented tariffs were three important pillars of IR's operating practices to achieve this. The first two helped to achieve a jump in IR's capacity for next loading. Through enhanced capacity to handle substantially higher volume of loaded freight on the wheel at a shorter time for each turnaround time of wagons by 14 percent, the IR increased the available wagon capacity per day by 36 percent[2].

Increased Axle Load Capacity

Enhanced axle load increases the capacity on the same wagon. IR relaxed its four decade old wagon loading norm of 20.3 tonnes per wagon and scaled it up by increasing the loading limit by another eight tonnes. This immediately created an extra 64 million tonnes of freight capacity per year.

There were few criticisms due to the apprehensions on safety compromises. However, technocrats in IR believed that due to a switchover from locomotive engine to electric and diesel engines, an additional 25–30 percent track load was created. This was due to "hammer blow" phenomenon of locomotive engines, which no longer exists now. Moreover, now IR is using superior 60-kg rails, which is placed on concrete as compared to earlier 45-kg rails on wooden-sleepers.

According to the then Railway Minister, freight earnings were increased through carrying increased tonnage which was by enhancement of loading limits[3]. About 170 million tonnes increase in loading capacity was achieved in three years starting from the year 2004. This resulted in an increase in about 170 million tonnes of capacity, which exceeded the total incremental loading in the 1990's by 120 percent.

Increased Turnaround Time

To increase the turnaround time, following operational measures were taken: (i) faster train movement on the track, (ii) high speed of loading/unloading, (iii) increase in the working hours of loading/unloading, (iv) mechanization of track modernization,

(v) reduced number of level-crossing, (vi) dedicated freight corridors to decrease the turnaround time and thus increase in on-the-move time available for the rakes. Round the clock, loading and unloading was facilitated, which was earlier possible during the day time only. Freight Operations Information System (FOIS) helped strict control of the idle wagon capacity. With these efforts, average wagon turnaround time very easily decreased from seven days to five days. Theoretically, it is equivalent to creating an extra 30 percent capacity ((100*(7-5)/7) = 30).

Dedicated Freight Corridors

IR is already working on its busiest route to create additional capacity by developing Dedicated Freight Corridors (DFCs)[4]. Around 1,504 kilometres of Western DFC is planned from Jawaharlal Nehru Port (JNPT) in Mumbai to Tughlakabad and Dadri near Delhi. It would support the transportation requirements of containers between the existing and emerging ports in Maharashtra and Gujrat, and the northern part of India. Similarly, around 1,856 kilometres of Eastern DFC is planned from Ludhiana in Punjab to Dankuni near Kolkata. DFCs will help IR to substantially increase its capacity as DFCs can handle double stack containers of 25 tonnes axle load, resulting in an additional 25 percent cargo handling capacity. It can support a 1.5 kilometres long train as compared to a conventional goods train of 650 meter long. The speed of these high capacity goods train can be fast as 100 kilometres per hours as compared to current maximum of 75 kilometres per hours.

The learning of IR's freight capacity management is simple, yet useful. Extra capacity can be created by removing inefficiencies, in-built redundancies and over-precautions in the existing systems. Faster speed in operation and delivery can result into extra capacity of system without adding extra resources like, machines, manpower, wagon, etc.

Questions

1. Critically examine the IR turnaround story. What are the criticisms related to its capacity expansion plans?
2. Explain different approaches towards capacity expansion of IR. Is there any learning lesson for Indian manufacturing and service industry?

References

1. https://www.indiatoday.in/india/story/railways-freight-passenger-revenue-increase-record-suresh-prabhu-969486-2017-04-04 (Accessed on 15 January 2018)
2. KPMG: *Indian Railways*: *The turnaround*, International Railway Conference, New Delhi (Background note). Available at http://www.in.kpmg.com/pdf/Railway_Conf.pdf (Accessed on 15 January 2018)
3. Yadav. L. P. 2007. Speech of Shri Lalu Prasad Yadav: Railway Budget 2007-08 (Part I), February 26.
4. Yadav, L.P. 2007. Speech of Shri Lalu Prasad Yadav: Railway Budget 2007-08 (Part I), February 26, [http://www.rediff.com/money/2007/feb/26bud28.htm] (Accessed on 15 January 2018)
5. Corporate website of Dedicated Freight Corridor Corporation of India (DFCCIL) http://dfccil.gov.in/dfccil_app/Home (Accessed on 15 January 2018)

CASE: Shouldice Hospital—A Cut Above

"Shouldice Hospital, the house that hernias built, is a converted country estate which gives the hospital 'a country club' appeal."

A quote from *American Medical News*

Shouldice Hospital in Canada is widely known for one thing—hernia repair! In fact, that is the only operation it performs, and it performs a great many of them. Over the past two decades this small 90-bed hospital has averaged 7,000 operations annually. Last year, it had a record year and performed nearly 7,500 operations. Patients' ties to Shouldice do not end when they leave the hospital. Every year, the gala Hernia Reunion dinner (with complimentary hernia inspection) draws in over 1,000 former patients, some of whom have been attending the event for over 30 years.

A number of notable features in Shouldice's service delivery system contribute to its success: (1) Shouldice accepts only patients with uncomplicated external hernias, and uses a superior technique developed for this type of hernia by Dr. Shouldice during World War II. (2) Patients are subject to early ambulation, which promotes healing. (Patients literally walk off the operating table and engage in light exercise throughout their stay, which lasts only three days.) (3) Its country club atmosphere, gregarious nursing staff, and built-in socializing make a surprisingly pleasant experience out of an inherently unpleasant medical problem. Regular times are set aside for tea, cookies, and socializing. All patients are paired up with a roommate with a similar background and interests.

The Production System

The medical facilities at Shouldice consist of five operating rooms, a patient recovery room, a laboratory, and six examination rooms. Shouldice performs, on average, 150 operations per week, with patients generally staying at the hospital for three days. Although operations are performed only five days a week, the remainder of the hospital is in operation continuously to attend to recovering patients.

An operation at Shouldice Hospital is performed by one of the 12 full-time surgeons, and assisted by one of seven part-time assistant surgeons. Surgeons generally take about one hour to prepare for and perform each hernia operation, and they operate on four patients per day. The surgeons' day ends at 4 P.M., although they can expect to be on call every 14th night and every 10th weekend.

The Shouldice Experience

Each patient undergoes a screening exam prior to setting a date for his or her operation. Patients in the Toronto area are encouraged to walk in for the diagnosis. Examinations are done between 9 A.M. and 3:30 P.M. Monday through Friday, and between 10 A.M. and 2 P.M. on Saturday. Out-of-town patients are mailed a medical information questionnaire (also available over the Internet), which is used for the diagnosis. A small percentage of the patients who are overweight or otherwise represent an undue medical risk are refused treatment. The remaining patients receive confirmation cards with the scheduled dates for their operations. A patient's folder is transferred to the reception desk once an arrival date is confirmed.

Patients arrive at the clinic between 1 and 3 P.M. the day before their surgery. After a short wait, they receive a brief preoperative examination. They are then sent to an admissions clerk to complete any necessary paperwork. Patients are next directed to one of the two nurses' stations for blood and urine tests and then are shown to their rooms. They spend the remaining time before orientation getting settled and acquainting themselves with their roommates.

Orientation begins at 5 P.M., followed by dinner in the common dining room. Later in the evening, at 9 P.M., patients gather in the lounge area for tea and cookies. Here, new patients can talk with patients who have already had their surgery. Bedtime is between 9:30 and 10 P.M.

On the day of the operation, patients with early operations are awakened at 5:30 A.M. for preoperative sedation. The first operations begin at 7:30 A.M. Shortly before an operation starts, the patient is administered a local anesthetic, leaving him or her alert and fully aware of the proceedings. At the conclusion of the operation, the patient is invited to walk from the operating table to a nearby wheelchair, which is waiting to return the patient to his or her room. After a brief period of rest, the patient is encouraged to get up and start exercising. By 9 P.M. that day, he or she is in the lounge having cookies and tea and talking with new, incoming patients.

The skin clips holding the incision together are loosened, and some even removed, the next day. The remainder are removed the following morning just before the patient is discharged.

When Shouldice Hospital started, the average hospital stay for hernia surgery was three weeks. Today, many institutions push "same day surgery" for a variety of reasons. Shouldice Hospital firmly believes that this is not in the best interests of patients and is committed to its three-day process. Shouldice's postoperative rehabilitation program is designed to enable the patient to resume normal activities with minimal interruption and discomfort. Shouldice patients frequently return to work in a few days; the average total time off is eight days.

"It is interesting to note that approximately 1 out of every 100 Shouldice patients is a medical doctor."

Future Plans

The management of Shouldice is thinking of expanding the hospital's capacity to serve considerable unsatisfied demand. To this effect, the vice president is seriously considering two options. The first involves adding one more day of operations (Saturday) to the existing five-day schedule, which would increase capacity by 20 percent. The second option is to add another floor of rooms to the hospital, increasing the number of beds by 50 percent. This would require more aggressive scheduling of the operating rooms.

The administrator of the hospital, however, is concerned about maintaining control over the quality of the service delivered. He thinks the facility is already getting very good utilization. The doctors and the staff are happy with their jobs, and the patients are satisfied with the service. According to him, further expansion of capacity might make it hard to maintain the same kind of working relationships and attitudes.

Questions

Exhibit 5.7 is a room-occupancy table for the existing system. Each row in the table follows the patients who checked in on a given day. The columns indicate the number of patients in the hospital on a given day. For example, the first row of the table shows that 30 people checked in on Monday and were in the hospital for Monday, Tuesday, and Wednesday. By summing the columns of the table for Wednesday, we see that there are 90 patients staying in the hospital that day.

EXHIBIT 5.7

Operations with 90 Beds (30 patients per day)

	Beds Required						
Check-in Day	Monday	Tuesday	Wednesday	Thursday	Friday	Saturday	Sunday
Monday	30	30	30				
Tuesday		30	30	30			
Wednesday			30	30	30		
Thursday				30	30	30	
Friday							
Saturday							
Sunday	30	30					30
Total	60	90	90	90	60	30	30

1. How well is the hospital currently utilizing its beds?
2. Develop a similar table to show the effects of adding operations on Saturday. (Assume that 30 operations would still be performed each day.) How would this affect the utilization of the bed capacity? Is this capacity sufficient for the additional patients?
3. Now look at the effect of increasing the number of beds by 50 percent. How many operations could the hospital perform per day before running out of bed capacity? (Assume operations are performed five days per week, with the same number performed on each day.) How well would the new resources be utilized relative to the current operation? Could the hospital really perform this many operations? Why? (*Hint:* Look at the capacity of the 12 surgeons and the five operating rooms.)
4. Although financial data are sketchy, an estimate from a construction company indicates that adding bed capacity would cost about $100,000 per bed. In addition, the rate charged for the hernia surgery varies between about $900 and $2,000 (U.S. dollars), with an average rate of $1,300 per operation. The surgeons are paid a flat $600 per operation. Due to all the uncertainties in government health care legislation, Shouldice would like to justify any expansion within a five-year time period.

PRACTICE EXAM

In each of the following, name the term defined or answer the question. Answers are listed at the bottom.

1. The level of capacity for which a process was designed and at which it operates at minimum cost.
2. A facility has a maximum capacity of 4,000 units per day using overtime and skipping the daily maintenance routine. At 3,500 units per day, the facility operates at a level where average cost per unit is minimized. Currently, the process is scheduled to operate at a level of 3,000 units per day. What is the capacity utilization rate?
3. The concept that relates to gaining efficiency through the full utilization of dedicated resources, such as people and equipment.
4. A facility that limits its production to a single product or a set of very similar products.
5. When multiple (usually similar) products can be produced in a facility less expensively than a single product.

6. The ability to serve more customers than expected.
7. In considering a capacity expansion, we have two alternatives. The first alternative is expected to cost $1,000,000 and has an expected profit of $500,000 over the next three years. The second alternative has an expected cost of $800,000 and an expected profit of $450,000 over the next three years. Which alternative should we select, and what is the expected value of the expansion? Assume a 10 percent interest rate.
8. In a service process such as the checkout counter in a discount store, what is a good target percent for capacity utilization?

Answers to Practice Exam 1. Best operating level 2. 85.7 percent 3. Economies of scale 4. Focused factory 5. Economies of scope 6. Capacity cushion 7. Alternative 1: Present value = 500,000 × (.909 + .826 + .751) − 1,000,000 = $243,000; Alternative 2: Present value = 450,000 × (.909 + .826 + .751) − 800,000 = $318,700; Alternative 2 is best. 8. 70 percent.

For PowerPoint lecture slides, Solutions Manual, Test Bank, Data files for solved examples, Excel Templates, Step-by-Step Solved Examples in video format, Tutorial Videos and many more, scan the adjacent **QR code**, or **visit http://www.mhhe.com/sie-chase15e**

Chapter 6

Learning Curves

LEARNING OBJECTIVES

LO 6–1 Understand what a learning curve is and where learning curves are applicable

LO 6–2 Plot and analyze learning curves

LO 6–3 Compare the impact of learning on different industries

BOEING SPEEDS UP 737 OUTPUT

Boeing 737 jet inside the Alaskan Airlines maintenance hanger at Seattle Tacoma international airport.

To boost production of its best-selling 737 jetliner to meet surging airline demand, Boeing Co. plans to increase production at its Renton, Washington, plant from 42 per month now, to 47 in 2017, and then up to 57 airplanes in 2019. To achieve this, Boeing will rely on its engineers to streamline work and make jets more efficiently. Expanding the factory is not an option due to the limited space at the plant.

Executives say they are studying ways to eventually reach quantities in the low 60s each month as they plan a retooled version of the plane called the 737 Max, a jet that Boeing expects to begin delivering in 2017. The company is trying to address an order backlog of some 4,300 jetliners, including about 3,000 of its best-selling 737s.

Boeing has reported that it currently takes about 11 days for the final assembly of a 737 at the Renton, Washington, plant. That's down from 22 days about a decade ago. The company's near-term goal is to reduce that number to nine days. Clearly, learning curves (the topic of this chapter) are important to the success of Boeing.

Source: Boeing earnings call on January 27, 2016.

WHAT ARE LEARNING CURVES?

LO 6-1

Understand what a learning curve is and where learning curves are applicable

A **learning curve** is a line displaying the relationship between unit production time and the cumulative number of units produced. Learning (or experience) curve theory has a wide range of applications in the business world. In manufacturing, it can be used to estimate the time for product design and production, as well as costs. Learning curves are also an integral part in planning corporate strategy, such as decisions concerning pricing, capital investment, and operating costs based on experience curves.

Learning curve
A line displaying the relationship between unit production time and the cumulative number of units produced.

Learning curves can be applied to individuals or organizations. **Individual learning** is improvement that results when people repeat a process and gain skill or efficiency from their own experience. That is, "practice makes perfect." **Organizational learning** results from practice as well, but it also comes from changes in administration, equipment, and product design. In organizational settings, we expect to see both kinds of learning occurring simultaneously and often describe the combined effect with a single learning curve.

Learning curve theory is based on three assumptions:

1. The amount of time required to complete a given task or unit of a product will be less each time the task is undertaken.
2. The unit time will decrease at a decreasing rate.
3. The reduction in time will follow a predictable pattern.

Individual learning
Improvement that results when people repeat a process and gain skill or efficiency from their own experience.

Each of these assumptions was found to hold true in the airplane industry, where learning curves were first applied. In this application, it was observed that, as output doubled, there was a 20 percent reduction in direct production worker-hours per unit between doubled units. Thus, if it took 100,000 hours for Plane 1, it would take 80,000 hours for Plane 2, 64,000 hours for Plane 4, and so forth. Because the 20 percent reduction meant that, say, Unit 4 took only 80 percent of the production time required for Unit 2, the line connecting the coordinates of output and time was referred to as an "80 percent learning curve." (By convention, the percentage learning rate is used to denote any given exponential learning curve.)

Organizational learning
Improvement that comes both from experience and from changes in administration, equipment, and product design.

A learning curve may be developed from an arithmetic tabulation, by logarithms, or by some other curve-fitting method, depending on the amount and form of the available data.

There are two ways to think about the improved performance that comes with learning curves: time per unit (as in Exhibit 6.1A) or units of output per time period (as in Exhibit 6.1B). *Time per unit* shows the decrease in time required for each successive unit. *Cumulative average time* shows the cumulative average performance times as the total number of units increases. Time per unit and cumulative average times are also called *progress curves* or *product learning* and are useful for complex products or products with a longer cycle time. *Units of output per time period* is also called *industry learning* and is generally applied to high-volume production (short cycle time).

Exhibit 6.1

Learning Curves Plotted as Times and Numbers of Units

A.

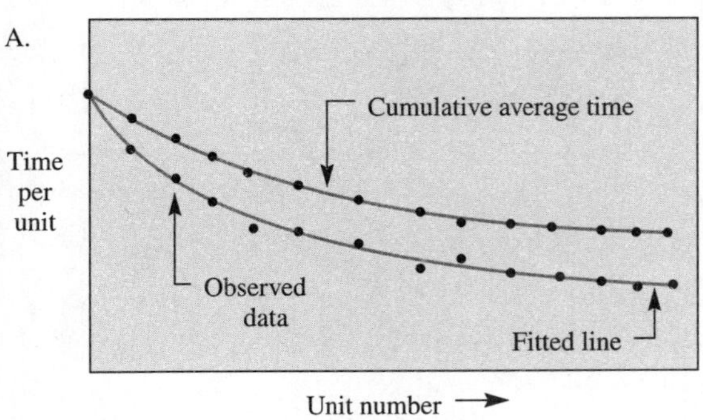

A Progress Curve

B.

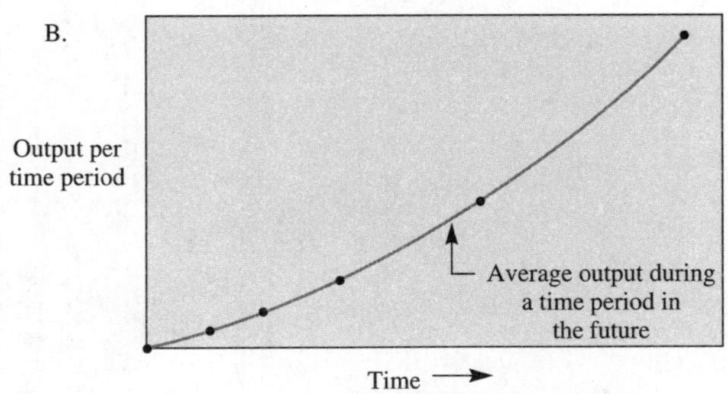

Industrial Learning

Note in Exhibit 6.1A that the cumulative average curve does not decrease as fast as the time per unit because the time is being averaged. For example, if the time for Units 1, 2, 3, and 4 were 100, 80, 70, and 64, they would be plotted that way on the time per unit graph, but would be plotted as 100, 90, 83.3, and 78.5 on the cumulative average time graph.

LO 6-2

Plot and analyze learning curves

HOW ARE LEARNING CURVES MODELED?

There are many ways to analyze past data to fit a useful trend line. We will use the simple exponential curve first as an arithmetic procedure and then by a logarithmic analysis. In an arithmetical tabulation approach, a column for units is created by doubling, row by row, as 1, 2, 4, 8, 16 . . . The time for the first unit is multiplied by the learning percentage to obtain the time for the second unit. The second unit is multiplied by the learning percentage for the fourth unit, and so on. Thus, if we are developing an 80 percent learning curve, we would arrive at the figures listed in column 2 of Exhibit 6.2. Because it is often desirable for planning purposes to know the cumulative direct labor hours, column 3, which lists this information, is also provided. Column 4, the cumulative average direct labor hours, is found by dividing the entry in column 3 by the column 1 entry. (See the next section for the exploration of how to do these calculations for each individual unit.)

Analytics

Exhibit 6.3A shows three curves with different learning rates: 90 percent, 80 percent, and 70 percent. Note that if the cost of the first unit was \$100, the 30th unit would cost \$59.63 at the 90 percent rate and \$17.37 at the 70 percent rate. Differences in learning rates can have dramatic effects.

In practice, learning curves are plotted using a graph with logarithmic scales. The unit curves become linear throughout their entire range, and the cumulative curve becomes linear after the first few units. The property of linearity is desirable because it facilitates extrapolation and permits a more accurate reading of the cumulative curve. This type of scale is an option in Microsoft Excel. Simply generate a regular scatter plot in your spreadsheet and then select each axis and format the axis with the logarithmic option. Exhibit 6.3B shows the 80 percent unit cost curve and average cost curve on a logarithmic scale. Note that the cumulative average cost is essentially linear after the eighth unit.

Although the arithmetic tabulation approach is useful, direct logarithmic analysis of learning curve problems is generally more efficient because it does not require a complete enumeration of successive time–output combinations. Moreover, where such data are not available, an analytical model that uses logarithms may be the most convenient way of obtaining output estimates.

EXHIBIT 6.2

Unit, Cumulative, and Cumulative Average Direct Labor Worker-Hours Required for an 80 Percent Learning Curve

(1) Unit Number	(2) Unit Direct Labor Hours	(3) Cumulative Direct Labor Hours	(4) Cumulative Average Direct Labor Hours
1	100,000	100,000	100,000
2	80,000	180,000	90,000
4	64,000	314,210	78,553
8	51,200	534,591	66,824
16	40,960	892,014	55,751
32	32,768	1,467,862	45,871
64	26,214	2,392,447	37,382
128	20,972	3,874,384	30,269
256	16,777	6,247,572	24,405

EXHIBIT 6.3

Learning Curve Plots

A. Arithmetic Plot of 70, 80, and 90 Percent Learning Curves

B. Logarithmic Plot of an 80 Percent Learning Curve

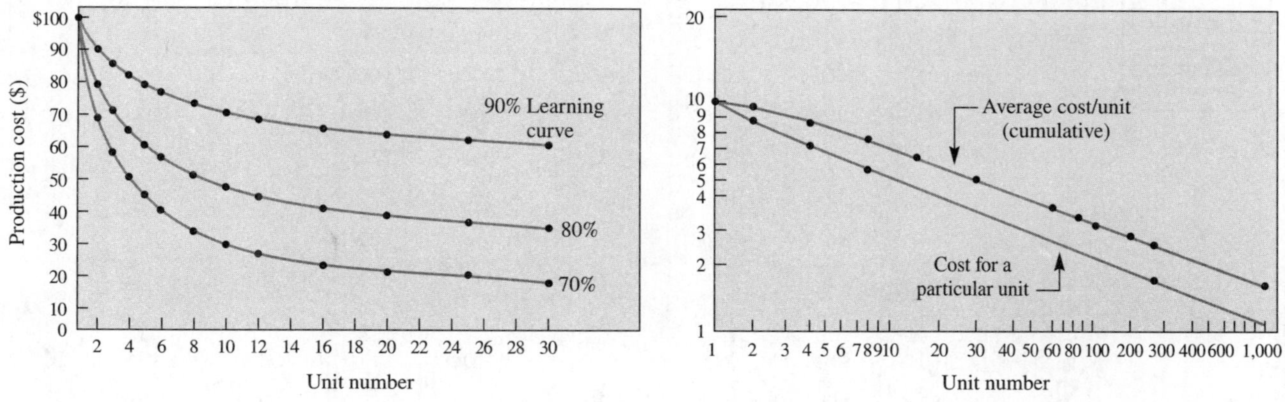

Logarithmic Analysis

The normal form of the learning curve equation is

$$Y_x = Kx^n \qquad [6.1]$$

where

x = Unit number

Y_x = Number of direct labor hours required to produce the xth unit

K = Number of direct labor hours required to produce the first unit

n = log b/log 2, where b = Learning decimal percentage (i.e. .8 for 80%)

We can solve this mathematically or by using a table, as shown in the next section. Mathematically, to find the labor-hour requirement for the eighth unit in our example (Exhibit 6.2) where the 1st unit took 100,000 hours to produce and there is 80 percent learning, we would substitute as follows:

$$Y_8 = (100{,}000)(8)^n$$

Using logarithms:

$$\begin{aligned} Y_8 &= 100{,}000\,(8)^{\log 0.8/\log 2} \\ &= 100{,}000\,(8)^{-0.322} = \frac{100{,}000}{(8)^{0.322}} \\ &= \frac{100{,}000}{1.9534} = 51{,}193 \end{aligned}$$

Therefore, it would take 51,193 hours to make the eighth unit. Your answer may vary slightly due to rounding. To get the exact answer, use the Excel formula = 100000 × 8 (Log (0.8)/Log (2)), for example. (See Exhibit 6.2 in spreadsheet).

Learning Curve Tables

When the learning percentage is known, Exhibits 6.4 and 6.5 can be used to easily calculate estimated labor hours for a specific unit or for cumulative groups of units. We need only multiply the initial unit labor hour figure by the appropriate tabled value. An alternative way to obtain the unit and cumulative improvement factors is from the OSCM Tools application available at http://oscm-pro.com/tools/.

EXHIBIT 6.4

Improvement Curves: Table of Unit Values

	Unit Improvement Factor							
Unit	**60%**	**65%**	**70%**	**75%**	**80%**	**85%**	**90%**	**95%**
1	1.0000	1.0000	1.0000	1.0000	1.0000	1.0000	1.0000	1.0000
2	.6000	.6500	.7000	.7500	.8000	.8500	.9000	.9500
3	.4450	.5052	.5682	.6338	.7021	.7729	.8462	.9219
4	.3600	.4225	.4900	.5625	.6400	.7225	.8100	.9025
5	.3054	.3678	.4368	.5127	.5956	.6857	.7830	.8877
6	.2670	.3284	.3977	.4754	.5617	.6570	.7616	.8758
7	.2383	.2984	.3674	.4459	.5345	.6337	.7439	.8659
8	.2160	.2746	.3430	.4219	.5120	.6141	.7290	.8574
9	.1980	.2552	.3228	.4017	.4930	.5974	.7161	.8499
10	.1832	.2391	.3058	.3846	.4765	.5828	.7047	.8433
12	.1602	.2135	.2784	.3565	.4493	.5584	.6854	.8320
14	.1430	.1940	.2572	.3344	.4276	.5386	.6696	.8226
16	.1290	.1785	.2401	.3164	.4096	.5220	.6561	.8145
18	.1188	.1659	.2260	.3013	.3944	.5078	.6445	.8074
20	.1099	.1554	.2141	.2884	.3812	.4954	.6342	.8012
22	.1025	.1465	.2038	.2772	.3697	.4844	.6251	.7955
24	.0961	.1387	.1949	.2674	.3595	.4747	.6169	.7904
25	.0933	.1353	.1908	.2629	.3548	.4701	.6131	.7880
30	.0815	.1208	.1737	.2437	.3346	.4505	.5963	.7775
35	.0728	.1097	.1605	.2286	.3184	.4345	.5825	.7687
40	.0660	.1010	.1498	.2163	.3050	.4211	.5708	.7611
45	.0605	.0939	.1410	.2060	.2936	.4096	.5607	.7545
50	.0560	.0879	.1336	.1972	.2838	.3996	.5518	.7486
60	.0489	.0785	.1216	.1828	.2676	.3829	.5367	.7386
70	.0437	.0713	.1123	.1715	.2547	.3693	.5243	.7302
80	.0396	.0657	.1049	.1622	.2440	.3579	.5137	.7231
90	.0363	.0610	.0987	.1545	.2349	.3482	.5046	.7168
100	.0336	.0572	.0935	.1479	.2271	.3397	.4966	.7112
120	.0294	.0510	.0851	.1371	.2141	.3255	.4830	.7017
140	.0262	.0464	.0786	.1287	.2038	.3139	.4718	.6937
160	.0237	.0427	.0734	.1217	.1952	.3042	.4623	.6869
180	.0218	.0397	.0691	.1159	.1879	.2959	.4541	.6809
200	.0201	.0371	.0655	.1109	.1816	.2887	.4469	.6757
250	.0171	.0323	.0584	.1011	.1691	.2740	.4320	.6646
300	.0149	.0289	.0531	.0937	.1594	.2625	.4202	.6557
350	.0133	.0262	.0491	.0879	.1517	.2532	.4105	.6482
400	.0121	.0241	.0458	.0832	.1453	.2454	.4022	.6419

(Contd.)

(Contd.)

	Unit Improvement Factor							
Unit	**60%**	**65%**	**70%**	**75%**	**80%**	**85%**	**90%**	**95%**
450	.0111	.0224	.0431	.0792	.1399	.2387	.3951	.6363
500	.0103	.0210	.0408	.0758	.1352	.2329	.3888	.6314
600	.0090	.0188	.0372	.0703	.1275	.2232	.3782	.6229
700	.0080	.0171	.0344	.0659	.1214	.2152	.3694	.6158
800	.0073	.0157	.0321	.0624	.1163	.2086	.3620	.6098
900	.0067	.0146	.0302	.0594	.1119	.2029	.3556	.6045
1,000	.0062	.0137	.0286	.0569	.1082	.1980	.3499	.5998
1,200	.0054	.0122	.0260	.0527	.1020	.1897	.3404	.5918
1,400	.0048	.0111	.0240	.0495	.0971	.1830	.3325	.5850
1,600	.0044	.0102	.0225	.0468	.0930	.1773	.3258	.5793
1,800	.0040	.0095	.0211	.0446	.0895	.1725	.3200	.5743
2,000	.0037	.0089	.0200	.0427	.0866	.1683	.3149	.5698
2,500	.0031	.0077	.0178	.0389	.0806	.1597	.3044	.5605
3,000	.0027	.0069	.0162	.0360	.0760	.1530	.2961	.5530

EXHIBIT 6.5

Improvement Curves: Table of Cumulative Values

	Cumulative Improvement Factor							
Unit	**60%**	**65%**	**70%**	**75%**	**80%**	**85%**	**90%**	**95%**
1	1.000	1.000	1.000	1.000	1.000	1.000	1.000	1.000
2	1.600	1.650	1.700	1.750	1.800	1.850	1.900	1.950
3	2.045	2.155	2.268	2.384	2.502	2.623	2.746	2.872
4	2.405	2.578	2.758	2.946	3.142	3.345	3.556	3.774
5	2.710	2.946	3.195	3.459	3.738	4.031	4.339	4.662
6	2.977	3.274	3.593	3.934	4.299	4.688	5.101	5.538
7	3.216	3.572	3.960	4.380	4.834	5.322	5.845	6.404
8	3.432	3.847	4.303	4.802	5.346	5.936	6.574	7.261
9	3.630	4.102	4.626	5.204	5.839	6.533	7.290	8.111
10	3.813	4.341	4.931	5.589	6.315	7.116	7.994	8.955
12	4.144	4.780	5.501	6.315	7.227	8.244	9.374	10.62
14	4.438	5.177	6.026	6.994	8.092	9.331	10.72	12.27
16	4.704	5.541	6.514	7.635	8.920	10.38	12.04	13.91
18	4.946	5.879	6.972	8.245	9.716	11.41	13.33	15.52
20	5.171	6.195	7.407	8.828	10.48	12.40	14.61	17.13
22	5.379	6.492	7.819	9.388	11.23	13.38	15.86	18.72
24	5.574	6.773	8.213	9.928	11.95	14.33	17.10	20.31
25	5.668	6.909	8.404	10.19	12.31	14.80	17.71	21.10

(Contd.)

(Contd.)

	Cumulative Improvement Factor							
Unit	**60%**	**65%**	**70%**	**75%**	**80%**	**85%**	**90%**	**95%**
30	6.097	7.540	9.305	11.45	14.02	17.09	20.73	25.00
35	6.478	8.109	10.13	12.72	15.64	19.29	23.67	28.86
40	6.821	8.631	10.90	13.72	17.19	21.43	26.54	32.68
45	7.134	9.114	11.62	14.77	18.68	23.50	29.37	36.47
50	7.422	9.565	12.31	15.78	20.12	25.51	32.14	40.22
60	7.941	10.39	13.57	17.67	22.87	29.41	37.57	47.65
70	8.401	11.13	14.74	19.43	25.47	33.17	42.87	54.99
80	8.814	11.82	15.82	21.09	27.96	36.80	48.05	62.25
90	9.191	12.45	16.83	22.67	30.35	40.32	53.14	69.45
100	9.539	13.03	17.79	24.18	32.65	43.75	58.14	76.59
120	10.16	14.11	19.57	27.02	37.05	50.39	67.93	90.71
140	10.72	15.08	21.20	29.67	41.22	56.78	77.46	104.7
160	11.21	15.97	22.72	32.17	45.20	62.95	86.80	118.5
180	11.67	16.79	24.14	34.54	49.03	68.95	95.96	132.1
200	12.09	17.55	25.48	36.80	52.72	74.79	105.0	145.7
250	13.01	19.28	28.56	42.05	61.47	88.83	126.9	179.2
300	13.81	20.81	31.34	46.94	69.66	102.2	148.2	212.2
350	14.51	22.18	33.89	51.48	77.43	115.1	169.0	244.8
400	15.14	23.44	36.26	55.75	84.85	127.6	189.3	277.0
450	15.72	24.60	38.48	59.80	91.97	139.7	209.2	309.0
500	16.26	25.68	40.58	63.68	98.85	151.5	228.8	340.6
600	17.21	27.67	44.47	70.97	112.0	174.2	267.1	403.3
700	18.06	29.45	48.04	77.77	124.4	196.1	304.5	465.3
800	18.82	31.09	51.36	84.18	136.3	217.3	341.0	526.5
900	19.51	32.60	54.46	90.26	147.7	237.9	376.9	587.2
1,000	20.15	31.01	57.40	96.07	158.7	257.9	412.2	647.4
1,200	21.30	36.59	62.85	107.0	179.7	296.6	481.2	766.6
1,400	22.32	38.92	67.85	117.2	199.6	333.9	548.4	884.2
1,600	23.23	41.04	72.49	126.8	218.6	369.9	614.2	1001
1,800	24.06	43.00	76.85	135.9	236.8	404.9	678.8	1116
2,000	24.83	44.84	80.96	144.7	254.4	438.9	742.3	1230
2,500	26.53	48.97	90.39	165.0	296.1	520.8	897.0	1513
3,000	27.99	52.62	98.90	183.7	335.2	598.9	1047	1791

To illustrate, suppose we want to double-check the figures in Exhibit 6.2 for unit and cumulative labor hours for Unit 16. From Exhibit 6.4, the unit improvement factor for Unit 16 at 80 percent is .4096. This multiplied by 100,000 (the hours for Unit 1) gives 40,960, the same as in Exhibit 6.2. From Exhibit 6.5, the cumulative improvement factor for cumulative hours for the first 16 units is 8.920. When multiplied by 100,000, this gives 892,000, which is reasonably close to the exact value of 892,014 shown in Exhibit 6.2.

The following is a more involved example of the application of a learning curve to a production problem.

EXAMPLE 6.1 Sample Learning Curve Problem

Captain Nemo, owner of Suboptimum Underwater Boat Company (SUB), is puzzled. He has a contract for 12 boats and has completed 4 of them. He has observed that his production manager, young Mr. Overick, has been reassigning more and more people to torpedo assembly after the construction of the first four boats. The first boat, for example, required 225 workers, each working a 40-hour week, while 45 fewer workers were required for the second boat. Overick has told them that "this is just the beginning" and that he will complete the last boat in the current contract with only 100 workers!

Overick is banking on the learning curve, but has he gone overboard?

SOLUTION

Because the second boat required 180 workers, a simple exponential curve shows that the learning percentage is 80 percent (180 ÷ 225). To find out how many workers are required for the 12th boat, we look up Unit 12 for an 80 percent improvement ratio in Exhibit 6.4 and multiply this value by the number required for the first boat. The improvement ratio is equal to .4493. This yields 101.0925 workers (.4493 × 225). (Note, the spreadsheet can be used to find values that are not included in the tables, they can be calculated directly from Equation 6.1.) Thus, Overick's estimate missed the boat by only one person.

EXAMPLE 6.2 Estimating Cost Using Learning Curves

SUB has produced the first unit of a new line of minisubs at a cost of $500,000: $200,000 for materials and $300,000 for labor. It has agreed to accept a 10 percent profit, based on cost, and it is willing to contract on the basis of a 70 percent learning curve. What will be the contract price for three minisubs? (Assume that the cost of materials does not change.)

SOLUTION

Cost of first sub		$ 500,000
Cost of second sub		
Materials	$200,000	
Labor: $300,000 × .70	210,000	410,000
Cost of third sub		
Materials	200,000	
Labor: $300,000 × .5682	170,460	370,460
Total cost		1,280,460
Markup: $1,280,460 × .10		128,046
Selling price		$1,408,506

If the operation is interrupted, then some relearning must occur. How far to go back up the learning curve can be estimated in some cases.

Estimating the Learning Percentage

If production has been underway for some time, the learning percentage is easily obtained from production records. Generally speaking, the longer the production history, the more accurate the estimate. Because a variety of other problems can occur during the early stages of production, most companies do not begin to collect data for learning curve analysis until some units have been completed.

If production has not started, estimating the learning percentage becomes enlightened guesswork. In such cases, the analyst has these options:

1. Assume that the learning percentage will be the same as it has been for previous applications within the same industry.
2. Assume that it will be the same as it has been for the same or similar products.
3. Analyze the similarities and differences between the proposed startup and previous startups and develop a revised learning percentage that appears to best fit the situation.

How Long Does Learning Go On?

Does output stabilize, or is there continual improvement? Some areas can be shown to improve continually even over decades (radios, computers, and other electronic devices; and, if we allow for the effects of inflation, also automobiles, washing machines, refrigerators, and most other manufactured goods). If the learning curve has been valid for several hundreds or thousands of units, it will probably be valid for several hundreds or thousands more. On the other hand, highly automated systems may have a near-zero learning curve because, after installation, they quickly reach a constant volume.

LO 6-3

Compare the impact of learning on different industries

IN PRACTICE, HOW MUCH LEARNING OCCURS?

Here we offer guidelines for two categories of "learners": individuals and organizations.

Individual Learning

Key Idea

Individual learning can vary greatly across different employees. This can create challenges when estimating expected production rates.

A number of factors affect an individual's performance and rate of learning. Remember that two elements are involved: the rate of learning and the initial starting level. To explain this more clearly, compare the two learning curves in Exhibit 6.6. Suppose these were the times for two individuals who performed a simple mechanical test administered by the personnel department as part of their application for employment in the assembly area of manufacturing.

Which applicant would you hire? Applicant A had a much lower starting point but a slower learning rate. Applicant B, although starting at a much higher point, is clearly the better choice. This points out that performance times are important—not just the learning rate by itself.

Some general guidelines to improve individual performance based on learning curves include the following:

Strategy

1. **Proper selection of workers.** A test should be administered to help choose the workers. These tests should be representative of the planned work: a dexterity test for assembly work, a mental ability test for mental work, tests for interaction with customers for front office work, and so on.
2. **Proper training.** The more effective the training, the faster the learning rate.
3. **Motivation.** Productivity gains based on learning curves are not achieved unless there is a reward. Rewards can be money (individual or group incentive plans) or nonmonetary (employee of the month awards, etc.).
4. **Work specialization.** As a general rule, the simpler the task, the faster the learning. Be careful that boredom doesn't interfere; if it does, redesign the task.

EXHIBIT 6.6

Test Results of Two Job Applicants

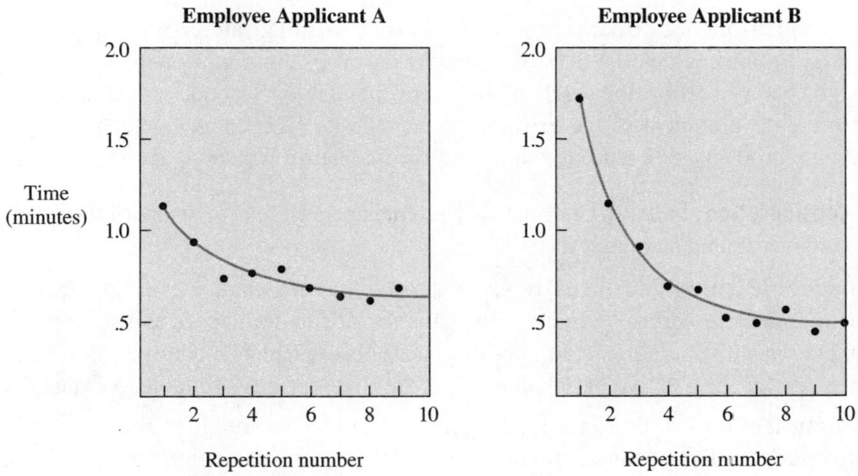

5. **Do one or very few jobs at a time.** Learning is faster on each job if completed one at a time, rather than working on all jobs simultaneously.
6. **Use tools or equipment that assists or supports performance.**
7. **Provide quick and easy access for help.** The benefits from training are realized and continue when assistance is available.
8. **Allow workers to help redesign their tasks.** Taking more performance factors into the scope of the learning curve can, in effect, shift the curve downward.

The following guidelines are useful for estimating the impact of learning on manufacturing tasks. These guidelines use estimates of the percentage of time spent on manual work (i.e., hand assembly) versus the time spent on machine-controlled work (i.e., machining).

- 75 percent hand assembly/25 percent machining = 80 percent learning
- 50 percent hand assembly/50 percent machining = 85 percent
- 25 percent hand assembly/75 percent machining = 90 percent

Organizational Learning

Organizations learn as well. It has been argued that organizational learning is critical to sustaining a competitive advantage. For the individual, it is easy to conceptualize how knowledge is acquired and retained and how this results in an individual learning effect. Certainly, a main source of organizational learning is the individual learning of the employees. An organization also acquires knowledge in its technology, its structure, documents that it retains, and standard operating procedures. For example, as a manufacturing unit becomes experienced, knowledge is embedded in software and in tooling used for production. Knowledge also can be embedded in the organization's structure. For example, when an organization shifts its industrial engineering group from a functional organization centralized in one area to a decentralized organization where individuals are deployed to particular parts of the plant floor, knowledge about how to become more productive is embedded in the organization's structure.

A set of guidelines based on what is seen in specific industries is the following:

- Aerospace, 85 percent
- Shipbuilding, 80 to 85 percent
- Complex machine tools for new models, 75 to 85 percent
- Repetitive electronics manufacturing, 90 to 95 percent
- Repetitive machining or punch-press operations, 90 to 95 percent
- Repetitive electrical operations (wiring and circuit board fabrication), 75 to 85 percent

- Repetitive welding operations, 90 percent
- Raw materials manufacturing, 93 to 96 percent
- Purchased parts fabrication, 85 to 88 percent

There are two reasons for disparities between a firm's learning rate and that of its industry. First, differences in operating characteristics between any two firms, stemming from the equipment, methods, product design, plant organization, and so forth, are inevitable. Second, procedural differences are manifested in the development of the learning percentage itself, such as whether the industry rate is based on a single product or on a product line, and the manner in which the data were aggregated.

Managerial Considerations in Using Learning Curves Managers should be aware of the following factors when using and interpreting learning curves.

1. **Individual learning and incentives.** Extensive research indicates a rather obvious fact: In order to enhance worker learning, there must be adequate incentives for the worker and the organization. (It should be noted, however, that the concept of incentives may be broadened to include any of the positive or negative administrative options available to managers.)
2. **Learning on new jobs versus old jobs.** The newer the job, the greater will be the improvement in labor hours and cost. Conversely, when production has been underway for a long time, improvement will be less discernible. For example, for an 80 percent learning curve situation, the improvement between the first and second units will be 20 percent. However, if the product has been manufactured for 50 years, it will take another 50 years to reduce labor hours by 20 percent, assuming that yearly production volume remains the same.
3. **Improvement comes from working smarter, not harder.** While incentives must be included to motivate the individual worker, most improvement in output comes from better methods and effective support systems rather than simply increased worker effort.

Key Idea

Learning curves are most valuable to companies that produce complex products at low volume levels, and when there are major changes to a product or the product is new.

4. **Built-in production bias through suggesting any learning rate.** If a manager expects an 80 percent improvement factor, he or she may treat this percentage as a goal rather than as an unbiased measure of actual learning. In short, it may be a "self-fulfilling prophecy." This, however, is not necessarily undesirable. What is wrong with setting a target improvement factor and then attempting to control production to achieve it?
5. **Preproduction versus postproduction adjustments.** The amount of learning shown by the learning curve depends both on the initial unit(s) of output and on the learning percentage. If there is much preproduction planning, experimentation, and adjustment, the early units will be produced more rapidly than if improvements are made after the first few units—other things being equal. In the first case, therefore, the apparent learning will be less than in the second case, even though subsequent "actual" learning may be the same in each instance.
6. **Changes in indirect labor and supervision.** Learning curves represent direct labor output, but if the mix of indirect labor and supervision changes, it is likely that the productivity of direct labor will be altered. We expect, for example, that more supervisors, repairpersons, and material handlers would speed up production, whereas a reduction in their numbers would slow it down.
7. **Changes in purchasing practices, methods, and organization structure.** Obviously, significant adjustments in any of these factors will affect the production rate and, hence, the learning curve. Likewise, the institution of preventive maintenance programs, zero-defect programs, and other schemes designed to improve efficiency or product quality generally would have some impact on the learning phenomenon.
8. **Contract phase-out.** Though not relevant to all contract situations, the point should be made that the learning curve may begin to turn upward as a contract nears completion. This may result from transferring trained workers to other projects, nonreplacement of worn tooling, and reduced attention to efficiency on the part of management.

CONCEPT CONNECTIONS

LO 6–1 Understand what a learning curve is and where learning curves are applicable

Summary

- A learning curve maps the relationship between unit production time and the cumulative number of units produced.
- These curves are useful for estimating the time required to produce a product and to estimate cost.
- It is particularly useful for large-scale, capital- and labor-intensive products, such as airplanes.
- The fundamental idea is that as output doubles, there is a fixed percentage reduction in the time needed to produce each unit.
- Learning can be due to improvements as people repeat a process and gain skill. Learning can also come from bigger picture improvements in a firm's administration, equipment and technology, and product design.

Key Terms

Learning curve A line displaying the relationship between unit production time and the cumulative number of units produced.

Individual learning Improvement that results when people repeat a process and gain skill or efficiency from their own experience.

Organizational learning Improvement that comes both from experience and from changes in administration, equipment, and product design.

LO 6–2 Plot and analyze learning curves

Summary

- Learning curves can be analyzed using graphs or by mathematically using the learning curve equations.
- When a spreadsheet is not available, learning curve tables are used to simplify the calculations so they can be done with a calculator.
- The most common calculations are made to estimate the time to make a particular unit in the future, and also the cumulative time to make a number of units in the future.

Key Formula

Logarithmic curve:

[6.1] $$Y_x = Kx^n$$

LO 6–3 Compare the impact of learning on different industries

- In practice, individual learning can be estimated by administering simple tests to job applicants. Different types of manual tasks typically have different expected learning rates.
- Expected organizational learning rates differ depending on the industry. If a firm can sustain a higher learning rate than other firms in the industry, they may have a significant competitive advantage.

SOLVED PROBLEMS

LO 6–2 SOLVED PROBLEM 1

A job applicant is being tested for an assembly-line position. Management feels that steady-state times have been approximately reached after 1,000 performances. Regular assembly-line workers are expected to perform the task within four minutes.

a. If the job applicant performed the first test operation in 10 minutes and the second one in 9 minutes, should this applicant be hired?
b. What is the expected time that the job applicant would take to finish the 10th unit?
c. What is a significant limitation of this analysis?

Solution

a. Learning rate = 9 minutes/10 minutes = 90%

   From Exhibit 6.4, the time for the 1,000th unit is .3499 × 10 minutes = 3.499 minutes. Yes, hire the person.
b. From Exhibit 6.4, unit 10 at 90% is .7047. Therefore, the time for the 10th unit = .7047 × 10 = 7.047 minutes.
c. More data should be collected on the job applicant's performance.

SOLVED PROBLEM 2

Boeing Aircraft collected the following cost data on the first 8 units of its new business jet.

Unit Number	Cost ($ millions)	Unit Number	Cost ($ millions)
1	$100	5	60
2	83	6	57
3	73	7	53
4	62	8	51

a. Estimate the learning curve for the new business jet.
b. Estimate the average cost for the first 1,000 units of the jet.
c. Estimate the cost to produce the 1,000th jet.

Solution

a. First, estimate the learning curve rate by calculating the average learning rate with each doubling of production.

$$\begin{aligned} \text{Units 1 to 2} &= 83/100 = 83\% \\ \text{Units 2 to 4} &= 62/83 = 74.7\% \\ \text{Units 4 to 8} &= 51/62 = 82.26\% \\ \text{Average} &= (83 + 74.7 + 82.26)/3 = 80\% \end{aligned}$$

b. The average cost of the first 1,000 units can be estimated using Exhibit 6.5. The cumulative improvement factor for the 1,000th unit at 80% learning is 158.7. The cost to produce the first 1,000 units is

$$\$100M \times 158.7 = \$15{,}870M$$

   The average cost for each of the first 1,000 units is

$$\$15{,}870M/1{,}000 = \$15.9M$$

c. To estimate the cost to produce the 1,000th unit, use Exhibit 6.4.
   The unit improvement factor for the 1,000th unit at 80% is .1082.
   The cost to produce the 1,000th unit is

$$\$100M \times .1082 = \$10.82M$$

DISCUSSION QUESTIONS

1. How might the following business specialists use learning curves: accountants, marketers, financial analysts, personnel managers, and computer programmers? **LO6-1**
2. What relationship is there between learning curves and productivity measurement?
3. What relationship is there between learning curves and capacity analysis?
4. Do you think learning curve analysis has an application in a service business like a restaurant? Why or why not?
5. As shown in the chapter, the effect of learning in a *given* system eventually flattens out over time. At that point in the life of a system, learning still exists, though its effect continues to diminish. Beyond that point, is it impossible to significantly reduce the time to produce a unit? What would it take to do that? **LO6-2**
6. The learning curve phenomenon has been shown in practice to be widely applicable. Once a company has established a learning rate for a process, they can use it to predict future system performance. Would there be any reason to reevaluate the process's learning rate once it has been initially established?
7. As a manager, which learning percentage would you prefer (other things being equal), 110 percent or 60 percent? Explain.
8. Will the Human Resource Management (HRM) policies of a firm have much of an effect on the learning rates the firm may be able to achieve? **LO6-3**
9. One manufacturer has seen a typical learning percentage of 90 percent in the firm. It has recently found out that a competitor has a percentage of 85 percent. What do you think about this?
10. What difference does it make if a customer wants a 10,000-unit order produced and delivered all at one time or in 2,500-unit batches?

OBJECTIVE QUESTIONS

1. Firm A typically sees a learning percentage of 85 percent in its processes. Firm B has a learning percentage of 80 percent. Which firm has the faster learning rate? **LO 6–1**
2. Company Z is just starting to make a brand new product it has never made before. It has completed two units so far. The first unit took 12 hours to complete and the next unit took 11 hours. Based only on this information, what would be the estimate of the learning percentage in this process?
3. Omega Technology is starting production of a new supercomputer for use in large research universities. It has just completed the first unit, which took 120 labor hours to produce. Based on its experience, it estimates its learning percentage to be 80 percent. How many labor hours should it expect in manufacturing the second unit?
4. You've just completed a pilot run of 10 units of a major product and found the processing time for each unit was as follows: **LO 6–2**

Unit Number	Time (hours)
1	970
2	640
3	420
4	380
5	320
6	250
7	220
8	207
9	190
10	190

a. According to the pilot run, what would you estimate the learning rate to be?
b. Based on (*a*), how much time would it take for the next 190 units, assuming no loss of learning?
c. How much time would it take to make the 1,000th unit?

5. Jack Simpson, contract negotiator for Nebula Airframe Company, is currently involved in bidding on a follow-up government contract. In gathering cost data from the first three units, which Nebula produced under a research and development contract, he found that the first unit took 2,000 labor hours, the second took 1,800 labor hours, and the third took 1,692 hours.

   In a contract for three more units, how many labor hours should Simpson plan for? (Answer in Appendix D)

6. Lazer Technologies Inc. (LTI) has produced a total of 20 high-power laser systems that could be used to destroy any approaching enemy missiles or aircraft. The 20 units have been produced, funded in part as private research within the research and development arm of LTI, but the bulk of the funding came from a contract with the U.S. Department of Defense (DoD).

   Testing of the laser units has shown that they are effective defense weapons, and if redesigned to add portability and easier field maintenance, the units could be truck-mounted.

   The DoD has asked LTI to submit a bid for 100 units.

   The 20 units that LTI has built so far cost the following amounts and are listed in the order in which they were produced.

Unit Number	Cost ($ millions)	Unit Number	Cost ($ millions)
1	$12	11	3.9
2	10	12	3.5
3	6	13	3.0
4	6.5	14	2.8
5	5.8	15	2.7
6	6	16	2.7
7	5	17	2.3
8	3.6	18	3.0
9	3.6	19	2.9
10	4.1	20	2.6

a. Based on past experience, what is the learning rate?
b. What bid should LTI submit for the total order of 100 units, assuming that learning continues?
c. What is the cost expected to be for the last unit under the learning rate you estimated?

7. Johnson Industries received a contract to develop and produce four high-intensity long-distance receiver/transmitters for cellular telephones. The first took 2,000 labor hours and $39,000 worth of purchased and manufactured parts; the second took 1,500 labor hours and $37,050 in parts; the third took 1,450 labor hours and $31,000 in parts; and the fourth took 1,275 labor hours and $31,492 in parts.

   Johnson was asked to bid on a follow-on contract for another dozen receiver/transmitter units. Ignoring any forgetting factor effects, what should Johnson estimate time and parts costs to be for the dozen units? (*Hint:* There are two learning curves—one for labor and one for parts.) (Answer in Appendix D)

8. Lambda Computer Products competed for and won a contract to produce two prototype units of a new type of computer that is based on laser optics rather than on electronic binary bits.

   The first unit produced by Lambda took 5,000 hours to produce and required $250,000 worth of material, equipment usage, and supplies. The second unit took 3,500 hours and used $200,000 worth of materials, equipment usage, and supplies. Labor is $30 per hour.

   a. Lambda was asked to present a bid for 10 additional units as soon as the second unit was completed. Production would start immediately. What would this bid be?
   b. Suppose there was a significant delay between the contracts. During this time, personnel and equipment were reassigned to other projects. Explain how this would affect the subsequent bid.

9. Honda Motor Company has discovered a problem in the exhaust system of one of its automobile lines and has voluntarily agreed to make the necessary modifications to conform with government safety requirements. Standard procedure is for the firm to pay a flat fee to dealers for each modification completed.

   Honda is trying to establish a fair amount of compensation to pay dealers and has decided to choose a number of randomly selected mechanics and observe their performance and learning rate. Analysis demonstrated that the average learning rate was 90 percent, and Honda then decided to pay a \$60 fee for each repair (3 hours × \$20 per flat-rate hour).

   Southwest Honda, Inc., has complained to Honda Motor Company about the fee. Six mechanics, working independently, have completed two modifications each. All took 9 hours, on average, to do the first unit and 6.3 hours to do the second. Southwest refuses to do any more unless Honda allows at least 4.5 hours. The dealership expects to perform the modification to approximately 300 vehicles.

   What is your opinion of Honda's allowed rate and the mechanics' performance?

10. United Research Associates (URA) had received a contract to produce two units of a new cruise missile guidance control. The first unit took 4,000 hours to complete and cost \$30,000 in materials and equipment usage. The second took 3,200 hours and cost \$21,000 in materials and equipment usage. Labor cost is charged at \$18 per hour.

    The prime contractor has now approached URA and asked to submit a bid for the cost of producing another 20 guidance controls.

    a. What will the last unit cost to build?
    b. What will be the average time for the 20 missile guidance controls?
    c. What will the average cost be for guidance control for the 20 in the contract?

11. Which type of system is likely to have a faster learning rate—one with primarily highly automated equipment or one that is very labor intensive? **LO 6–3**

12. Which industry will typically have a faster learning rate: a repetitive electronics manufacturer or a manufacturer of large complex products such as a shipbuilder?

13. True or False: The only learning for an organization comes from the individual learning of its employees.

14. A company has just tested the skills of two applicants for the same job. They found that applicant A had a higher learning rate than applicant B. Should they definitely hire applicant A?

PRACTICE EXAM

In each of the following, name the term defined or answer the question. Answers are listed at the bottom.

1. The line that shows the relationship between the time to produce a unit and the cumulative number of units produced.
2. Improvement that derives from people repeating a process and gaining skill or efficiency.
3. Improvement that comes from changes in administration, equipment, and product design.
4. Assuming an 80 percent learning rate, if the 4th unit takes 100 hours to produce, the 16th unit should take how long to produce?
5. The resulting plot of a learning curve when logarithmic scales are used.
6. Systems that have this characteristic usually have near-zero learning.

Answers to Practice Exam 1. Learning curve 2. Individual learning 3. Organizational learning 4. 64 hours 5. A straight line 6. Highly automated systems

For PowerPoint lecture slides, Solutions Manual, Test Bank, Data files for solved examples, Excel Templates, Step-by-Step Solved Examples in video format, Tutorial Videos and many more, scan the adjacent **QR code**, or **visit http://www.mhhe.com/sie-chase15e**

SECTION
TWO

Manufacturing and Service Processes

Manufacturing and Service Processes

The second section of *Operations and Supply Chain Management* is centered on the design and analysis of business processes. Have you ever wondered why you always have to wait in line at one store but another one seems to be on top of the crowds? The key to serving customers well, whether with products or with services, is having a great process.

Companies also need to develop a quality philosophy and integrate it into their processes. Actually, quality and process efficiency are closely related. Have you ever done something but then had to do it again because it was not done properly the first time? This section considers these subjects in manufacturing and service businesses.

Chapter 7

Manufacturing Processes

LEARNING OBJECTIVES

LO 7-1 Understand what a manufacturing process is

LO 7-2 Explain how manufacturing processes are organized

LO 7-3 Analyze simple manufacturing processes

THREE-DIMENSIONAL PRINTING—THE TECHNOLOGY COULD BE USED TO MAKE PARTS THAT PERFORM BETTER AND COST LESS

The technology for printing three-dimensional objects has existed for decades, but its application has been largely limited to novelty items and specialized custom fabrication, such as making personalized prosthetics. The technology has now improved to the point where these printers can make intricate objects out of durable materials, including ceramics and metals (such as titanium and aluminum), with a resolution on the scale of tens of micrometers.

The impact of advanced manufacturing technology on productivity is dramatic. Every year, U.S. manufacturing firms invest millions of dollars to convert manufacturing plants into computerized environments in an effort to improve the firm's competitive position. Companies in other major manufacturing countries such as Germany, Japan, and South Korea are making similar investments. Chinese companies, though, are the productivity leaders, with the country's combination of advanced technology and low labor costs.

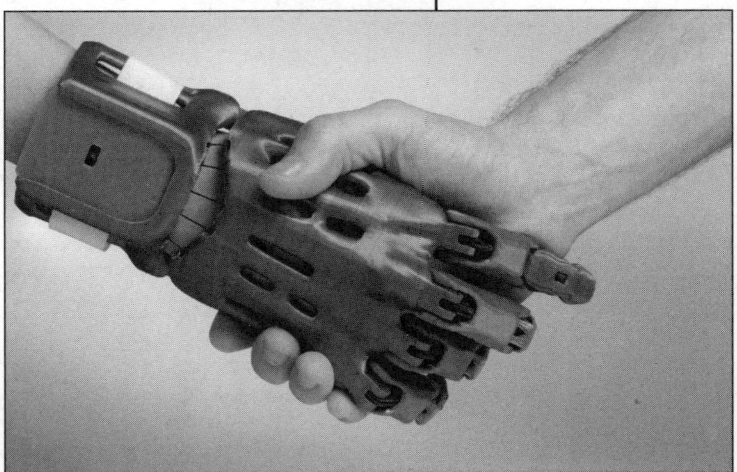

Hand with prosthesis printed on FDM 3D printer

LO 7-1

Understand what a manufacturing process is

Strategy

WHAT ARE MANUFACTURING PROCESSES?

In this chapter, we consider processes used to make tangible goods. Manufacturing processes are used to make everything that we buy ranging from the apartment building in which we live to the ink pens with which we write. The high-level view of what is required to make something can be divided into three simple steps. The first step is sourcing the parts we need, followed by actually making the item, and then sending the item to the customer. As discussed in Chapter 1, a supply chain view of this may involve a complex series of players where subcontractors feed suppliers, suppliers feed manufacturing plants, manufacturing plants feed warehouses, and finally warehouses feed retailers. Depending on the item being produced, the supply chain can be very long with subcontractors and manufacturing plants spread out over the globe (such as an automobile or computer manufacturer) or short where parts are sourced and the product is made locally (such as a house builder).

Consider Exhibit 7.1, which illustrates the Source step where parts are procured from one or more suppliers, the Make step where manufacturing takes place, and the Deliver step where the product is shipped to the customer. Depending on the strategy of the firm, the capabilities of manufacturing, and the needs of customers, these activities are organized to minimize cost while meeting the competitive priorities necessary to attract customer orders. For example, in the case of consumer products such as televisions or clothes, customers normally want these products "on-demand" for quick delivery from a local department store. As a manufacturer of these products, we build them ahead of time in anticipation of demand and ship them to the retail stores where they are carried in inventory until they are sold. At the other end of the spectrum are custom products, such as military airplanes, that are ordered with very specific uses in mind and that need to be designed and then built to the design. In the case of an airplane, the time needed to respond to a customer order, called the **lead time**, could easily be years compared to only a few minutes for the television.

Lead time
The time needed to respond to a customer order.

A key concept in manufacturing processes is the **customer order decoupling point** which determines where inventory is positioned to allow processes or entities in the supply chain to operate independently. For example, if a product is stocked at a retailer, the customer pulls the item from the shelf and the manufacturer never sees a customer order. Inventory acts as a buffer to separate the customer from the manufacturing process. Selection of decoupling points is a strategic decision that

Customer order decoupling point
Where inventory is positioned in the supply chain.

EXHIBIT 7.1

Positioning Inventory in the Supply Chain

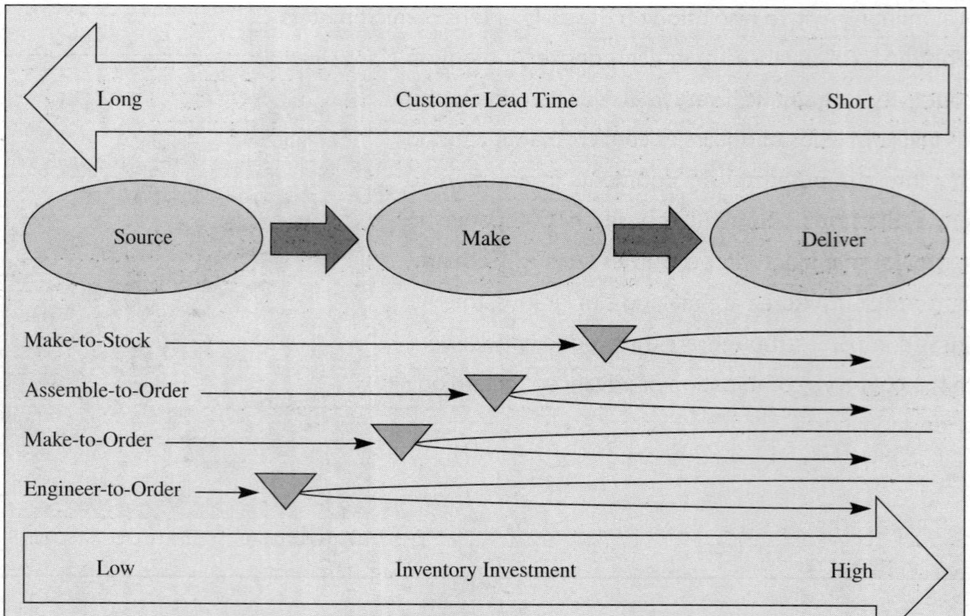

The inverted triangles represent customer order decoupling points.

determines customer lead times and can greatly impact inventory investment. The closer this point is to the customer, the quicker the customer can be served. Typically, there is a trade-off where quicker response to customer demand comes at the expense of greater inventory investment because finished goods inventory is more expensive than raw material inventory. An item in finished goods inventory typically contains all the raw materials needed to produce the item. So, from a cost view it includes the cost of the material, plus the cost to fabricate the finished item.

Positioning of the customer order decoupling point is important to understanding manufacturing environments. Firms that serve customers from finished goods inventory are known as **make-to-stock** firms. Those that combine a number of preassembled modules to meet a customer's specifications are called **assemble-to-order** firms. Those that make the customer's product from raw materials, parts, and components are **make-to-order** firms. An **engineer-to-order** firm will work with the customer to design the product, and then make it from purchased materials, parts, and components. Of course, many firms serve a combination of these environments and a few will have all simultaneously. Depending on the environment and the location of the customer order decoupling point, one would expect inventory concentrated in finished goods, work-in-process (this is inventory in the manufacturing process), manufacturing raw material, or at the supplier as shown in Exhibit 7.1.

Make-to-stock
A production environment where the customer is served "on-demand" from finished goods inventory.

Assemble-to-order
A production environment where pre-assembled components, subassemblies, and modules are put together in response to a specific customer order.

Make-to-order
A production environment where the product is built directly from raw materials and components in response to a specific customer order.

Engineer-to-order
Here the firm works with the customer to design the product, which is then made from purchased material, parts, and components.

The essential issue in satisfying customers in the make-to-stock environment is to balance the level of finished inventory against the level of service to the customer. Examples of products produced by these firms include televisions, clothing, and packaged food products. If unlimited inventory were possible and free, the task would be trivial. Unfortunately, that is not the case. Providing more inventory increases costs, so a trade-off between the costs of the inventory and the level of customer service must be made. The trade-off can be improved by better estimates (or knowledge) of customer demand, by more rapid transportation alternatives, by speedier production, and by more flexible manufacturing. Many make-to-stock firms invest in **lean manufacturing** programs in order to achieve higher service levels for a given inventory investment. Regardless of the trade-offs involved, the focus in the make-to-stock environment is on providing finished goods where and when the customers want them.

Lean manufacturing
To achieve high customer service with minimum levels of inventory investment.

In the assemble-to-order environment, a primary task is to define a customer's order in terms of alternative components and options since it is these components that are carried in inventory. A good example is the way Dell Computer makes desktop computers. The number of combinations that can be made may be nearly infinite (although some might not be feasible). One of the capabilities required for success in the assemble-to-order environment is an engineering design that enables as much flexibility as possible in combining components, options, and modules into finished products. Similar to make-to-stock, many assemble-to-order companies have applied lean manufacturing principles to dramatically decrease the time required to assemble finished goods. By doing so, they are delivering customers' orders so quickly that they appear to be make-to-stock firms from the perspective of the customer.

When assembling-to-order, there are significant advantages from moving the customer order decoupling point from finished goods to components. The number of finished products is usually substantially greater than the number of components combined to produce the finished product. Consider, for example, a computer for which there are four processor alternatives, three hard disk drive choices, four DVD alternatives, two speaker systems, and four monitors available. If all combinations of these 17 components are valid, they can be combined into a total of 384 different final configurations. This can be calculated as follows.

Delayed Product Differntiation: Strategy Towards Inventory Reduction and Service-Level Improvement

An interesting supply chain strategy is delayed product differentiation or postponement strategy. Many supply chains have tried to position the decoupling point towards customer end of supply chain. For example, many years back, a leading Indian paint making company used to produce different shades of paints in their factory. Demand for different shades is highly uncertain. Paint demand is also highly seasonal in nature. Paints have relatively short shelf-life and if not consumed within a few months, these may lose the value for the customers. Distribution lead time is long enough to have a good forecast for knowing the demand for each shade and determining a right production plan that should match with actual demand that is known only at the time when customer places the order at the point of sale (PoS). Therefore, produced quantity of each shade used to differ significantly with the actual demand. This supply chain was facing severe problem of stock-out and inventory at the same point of time.

While there were many shades of paints which used to be in stock with dealers, at the same time, many other shades used to be stock-out. The situation was highly perplexing for the managers as the paint company was bleeding financially either way.

The paint company introduced a new concept and designed a new coloring machine called Dealer Tinting Machine (DTM), which was placed at the dealers' shop. Once a small DTM set up was installed with dealers, the factory started making only one base paint, i.e. white color paint. At the dealers' shop, when customers come, they look at the computerized catalogue and select the shade and quantity that they want to buy. Based on this order, an automatic program in DTM releases a few coloring ingredients in required quantity for getting mixed in the base color. After proper mixing, the required paint is produced in the quantity and shade as demanded by the customers. The entire phenomenon is termed as 'delayed product differentiation' or 'postponement strategy' in a supply chain.

Through this postponement strategy, stock-out of paints is now ruled out till the time base paint is available. In place of keeping sufficient quantity of each shade, now the dealer keeps much lesser quantity of only base paint. So, the total money blocked in inventory is much less. This strategy helped in controlling both stock-out and inventory. Cost reduction with lesser inventory along with higher service level is a 'dream come true' situation in a supply chain.

Takeaway (or Guru-mantra) of this illustrative case study is as follows: Try to have a generic product (like base paint) as late as possible in a supply chain; differentiate the generic product into a customized one (like different shades of paints), preferably when demand enters the supply chain (at the retailer point) or as close to that.

There are many such examples to substantiate this takeaway. Male trousers are sold in limited number waist sizes and many a times the trousers are of free-length. Free-length trousers become a generic product for a given waist size. When a customer buys a trouser, he gets the altering option from the same retailer, who is ready to provide facility to get the trouser-length adjusted within a couple of hours. As compared to the situation when the trouser company makes many combinations of trouser lengths and waist sizes, postponement strategy is very promising as it reduces both inventory and stock-out problem.

Discussion Questions

1. Explain the postponement strategy in supply chain. How does this strategy resolve both inventory and stock-out problem simultaneously?
2. Give a few examples to illustrate the application of postponement strategy in a supply chain.

If N_i is the number of alternatives for component i, the total number of combinations of n components (given all are viable) is:

$$\text{Total number of combinations} = N_1 \times N_2 \times \ldots \times N_n \qquad [7.1]$$
$$\text{Or } 384 = 4 \times 3 \times 4 \times 2 \times 4 \text{ for this example.}$$

It is much easier to manage and forecast the demand for 17 components than for 384 computers.

In the make-to-order and engineer-to-order environments, the customer order decoupling point could be in either raw materials at the manufacturing site or possibly even with the supplier inventory. Boeing's process for making commercial aircraft is an example of make-to-order. The need for engineering resources in the engineer-to-order case is somewhat different than make-to-order because engineering determines what materials will be required and what steps will be required in manufacturing. Depending on how similar the products are, it might not even be possible to pre-order parts. Rather than inventory, the emphasis in these environments may be more toward managing capacity of critical resources such as engineering and construction crews. Lockheed Martin's Satellite division uses an engineer-to-order strategy.

HOW MANUFACTURING PROCESSES ARE ORGANIZED

LO 7-2

Explain how manufacturing processes are organized

Process selection refers to the strategic decision of selecting which kind of production processes to use to produce a product or provide a service. For example, in the case of Toshiba notebook computers, if the volume is very low, we may just have a worker manually assemble each computer by hand. In contrast, if the volume is higher, setting up an assembly line is appropriate.

The format by which a facility is arranged is defined by the general pattern of workflow; there are five basic structures (project, workcenter, manufacturing cell, assembly line, and continuous process).

Project layout
A setup in which the product remains at one location, and equipment is moved to the product.

In a **project layout**, the product (by virtue of its bulk or weight) remains in a fixed location. Manufacturing equipment is moved to the product rather than vice versa. Construction sites (houses and bridges) and movie shooting lots are examples of this format. Items produced with this type of layout are typically managed using the project management techniques described in Chapter 4. Areas on the site will be designated for various purposes, such as material staging, subassembly construction, site access for heavy equipment, and a management area.

In developing a project layout, visualize the product as the hub of a wheel, with materials and equipment arranged concentrically around the production point in the order of use and movement difficulty. Thus, in building commercial aircraft, for example, rivets that are used throughout construction would be placed close to or in the fuselage; heavy engine parts, which must travel to the fuselage only once, would be placed at a more distant location; and cranes would be set up close to the fuselage because of their constant use.

Workcenter
Often referred to as a job shop, a process structure suited for low-volume production of a great variety of nonstandard products. Workcenters sometimes are referred to as departments and are focused on a particular type of operation.

In a project layout, a high degree of task ordering is common. To the extent that this task ordering, or precedence, determines production stages, a project layout may be developed by arranging materials according to their assembly priority. This procedure would be expected in making a layout for a large machine tool, such as a stamping machine, where manufacturing follows a rigid sequence; assembly is performed from the ground up, with parts being added to the base in almost a building-block fashion.

A **workcenter** layout, sometimes referred to as a job shop, is where similar equipment or functions are grouped together, such as all drilling machines in one area and all stamping machines in another. A part being worked on travels, according to the established sequence of operations, from workcenter to workcenter, where the proper machines are located for each operation.

Project Layout
© *Ingram Publishing RF*

The most common approach to developing this type of layout is to arrange workcenters in a way that optimizes the movement of material. A workcenter sometimes is referred to as a department and is focused on a particular type of operation. Examples include a workcenter for drilling holes, one for performing grinding operations, and a painting area. The workcenters in a low-volume toy factory might consist of shipping and receiving, plastic molding and stamping, metal forming, sewing, and painting. Parts for the toys are fabricated in these workcenters and then sent to the assembly workcenter, where they are put together. In many installations, optimal placement often means placing workcenters with large amounts of interdepartmental traffic adjacent to each other.

Manufacturing cell
Dedicated area where a group of similar products are produced.

A **manufacturing cell** layout is a dedicated area where products that are similar in processing requirements are produced. These cells are designed to perform a specific set of processes, and the cells are dedicated to a limited range of products. A firm may have many different cells in a production area, each set up to produce a single product or a similar group of products efficiently, but typically at lower volume levels. These cells typically are scheduled to produce "as needed" in response to current customer demand.

Workcenter

Manufacturing cells are formed by allocating dissimilar machines to cells that are designed to work on products that have similar shapes and processing requirements. Manufacturing cells are widely used in metal fabricating, computer chip manufacture, and assembly work.

An **assembly line** is where work processes are arranged according to the progressive steps by which the product is made. These steps are defined so that a specific production rate can be achieved. The path for each part is, in effect, a straight line. Discrete products are made by moving from workstation to workstation at a controlled rate, following the sequence needed to build the product. Examples include the assembly of toys, appliances, and automobiles. These are typically used in high-volume items where the specialized process can be justified.

Assembly line
A setup in which an item is produced through a fixed sequence of workstations, designed to achieve a specific production rate.

Manufacturing Cell
Source: Official US Navy photo

The assembly line steps are done in areas referred to as "stations," and typically the stations are linked by some form of material handling device. In addition, usually there is some form of pacing by which the amount of time allowed at each station is managed. Rather than develop the process for designing assembly at this time, we will devote the entire next section of this chapter to the topic of assembly line design because these designs are used so often by manufacturing firms around the world. A continuous or flow process is similar to an assembly line except that the product continuously moves through the process. Often, the item being produced by the continuous process is a liquid or chemical that actually "flows" through the system; this is the origin of the term. A gasoline refinery is a good example of a flow process.

A **continuous process** is similar to an assembly line in that production follows a predetermined sequence of steps, but the flow is continuous (such as with liquids) rather than discrete. Such structures are usually highly automated and, in effect, constitute one integrated "machine" that may operate 24 hours a day to avoid expensive shutdowns and startups. Conversion and processing of undifferentiated materials such as petroleum, chemicals, and drugs are good examples.

Continuous process
A process that converts raw materials into finished product in one contiguous process.

Assembly Line

The relationship between layout structures is often depicted on a **product–process matrix** similar to the one shown in Exhibit 7.2. Two dimensions are shown. The horizontal dimension relates to the volume of a particular product or

Product–process matrix
A framework depicting when the different production process types are typically used, depending on product volume and how standardized the product is.

Make In India: The Transformation is on the Anvil

In the recent past, India has demonstrated its consistent prowess in global software industries. In most of the successful multinational software companies, Indian software personnel have been contributing for many years now. The same is not true for manufacturing industries. 'Make in India', which was launched by Indian Prime Minister Mr. Narendra Modi in September 2014, brought a new focus towards moving faster on growth trajectory in the manufacturing sector.

Traditionally, Indian manufacturing sector was plagued with severe license regime till 1991, when liberalization, privatization and globalization (LPG) got an initial thrust. The approach gave some results yet it was far from satisfactory looking at other developing economies of that time. It fell short of bringing Indian manufacturing sector at global reckoning. This is reflected in the fact that World Bank survey ranked India's global position in 'ease of doing business' as 130 in 2017. As a result of changed focus on developing an ecosystem for doing business, India is ranked 100 out of 190 countries in World Bank report (2018) of 'Ease of Doing Business'. One of the aims is to bring India in the top three manufacturing destinations within a few years.

Everything encapsulated in 'Make in India' programme is designed to revive the growth of manufacturing sector in India. First major departure from earlier approach is a change in Government mind-set—'Minimum Government, Maximum Governance'. This approach has helped in developing right ecosystem in which businesses operate. For example, focus is on developing a conducive environment for investment, starting new sectors for foreign investments, infrastructure development, local sourcing of parts and components, indigenous defense production system, and building a partnership between industry and government.

FOUR PILLARS OF MAKE IN INDIA

The changed approach in 'Make in India' is based on the following four pillars to give a new thrust on entrepreneurship both in manufacturing and services.

1. **New Procedures**: Old and typical bureaucratic style of governance, which was plagued with licensing raj, will give way to more transparent business ecosystem, driven by 'Ease of doing Business' framework. Simplified rules and business-friendly transparent governance structure would prevail to facilitate influx of local and foreign investments in business.
2. **New Infrastructure**: Smart cities, industrial corridors, single window clearance of application for starting business, high speed communication network, dedicated freight corridors, innovation and R&D hubs, etc. are some of the measures to ensure changes in providing conducive infrastructure to ensure the success of Make in India.
3. **New Sectors**: Focus attention is being provided to 25 sectors in manufacturing, services and infrastructure. These sectors include: (i) automobiles, (ii) aviation, (iii) chemicals, (iv) information technology, (v) pharmaceuticals, (vi) construction, (vii) defense (viii) manufacturing, (ix) electrical machinery, (x) food processing, (xi) textiles and garments, (xii) ports, (xiii) leather, (xiv) media and entertainment, (xv) wellness, (xvi) mining, (xvii) tourism and hospitality, (xviii) railways, (xix) automobile components, (xx) renewable energy, (xxi) biotechnology, (xxii) space, (xxiii) thermal power, (xxiv) roads and highways, and (xxv) electronics systems. These are treated as high growth sectors in this initiative.
4. **New Mindset**: Government role as envisaged in the Make in India approach is more of a facilitator rather than a regulator.

Global competiveness of Indian manufacturing sector is always a matter of concern. This has led to reform in the National Manufacturing Policy. This aims at increasing the share of manufacturing in India's GDP from 16% to 25% by year 2022 and creating around 100 million additional jobs by 2022 in manufacturing sector. It also aims for sustainable growth of manufacturing with concern toward protecting environment.

Defense Production: An Untapped Potential till Now

Despite India being the third largest military in the world, local defense production is minuscule. About 60% of defense requirements are presently met through imports. A great opportunity that lies ahead in 'Make in India' is to focus on developing indigenous and self-reliant defense production. Defense Procurement Procedure (DPP) got reformed in April 2016 to facilitate indigenous R&D, development and production of local defense equipment.

Automotive Sector: One of the Most Vibrant Sectors in Manufacturing

Indian automotive sector has an average production of around 24 million vehicles annually and employer of over 29 million people. It contributes 7.1 percent to the overall GDP and almost 49 percent to the nation's manufacturing GDP (FY 2015–16). In very near future, one can see an eminent change in operations and supply chain of auto manufacturing firm due to changed priority towards more production of electric vehicles (EVs). 'Make in India' initiative would help in running the show for automotive sector.

Operational Part of Make in India

To operationalize the good intents of Make in India, an action plan is also needed. Out of many such initiatives, following steps can be highlighted.

1. **Invest India Cell**: This is the first reference point for providing guidance and support to all foreign investors on all aspects of legal and regulatory issues right from entry point of being into business in India.
2. **Consolidated Services and Faster Clearances**: Single online portal would help clearance of all requirements to start businesses that may need involvement of many government departments. Security clearance of investment proposals within three months, acceptance of self-certification to reduce the non-value added operations in clearance of files, etc. are some of the many steps towards nurturing 'Make in India' initiatives.
3. **Industry-friendly Policies and Laws**: Many laws and rigid governance frameworks have given way to new orders in this initiative. Defense production is much more open to private sectors; 'Skill India' focusses on providing trained manpower to support 'Make in India', while many other initiatives focus on developing and supporting entrepreneurial temperament through 'Startup India' (https://www.startupindia.gov.in/), Standup India' (https://www.standupmitra.in/), etc.
4. **Dedicated Portal for Business Queries**: An effective portal (www.makeinindia.com) is available to handle all queries of investors and entrepreneurs for new proposals.
5. **Incentives to Local Production**: Government has clearly indicated its preference towards locally made goods and services in all government procurements. Locally made goods and services mean that at least 50 percent value addition is made in India.

Make in India, as strong government intent, has the potential to boost Indian manufacturing (and also service) sector. Its four pillars can unlock the hidden potential of manufacturing sector. The success lies in effective implementation of its operational part and trust building measures with potential investors and entrepreneurs.

Discussion Questions

1. Discuss the various initiatives at policy and regulatory level to facilitate growth of local manufacturing. What role has 'Make in India' played towards global competiveness of Indian manufacturing sector?
2. Discuss how well many other initiatives like 'Startup India', 'Standup India', etc. are interwoven and integrated with 'Make in India' initiative.
3. Rate the success of 'Make in India' through support from different statistical indicators like contribution of manufacturing on GDP, employment generation, inflow of Foreign Direct Investment (FDI), etc.
4. Discuss the critical success factors (CSFs) of Make in India.
5. Discuss the impediments to the success of Make in India.
6. Globally benchmark the progress of Indian manufacturing sector and discuss the role of 'Make in India' initiative.

group of standardized products. Standardization is shown on the vertical axis and refers to variations in the product that is produced. These variations are measured in terms of geometric differences, material differences, and so on. Standardized products are highly similar from a manufacturing processing point of view, whereas low standardized products require different processes.

Exhibit 7.2 shows the processes approximately on a diagonal. In general, it can be argued that it is desirable to design processes along the diagonal. For example, if we produce nonstandard products at relatively low volumes, workcenters should be used. A highly standardized product (commodity) produced at high volumes should be produced using an assembly line or a continuous process, if possible. As a result of the advanced manufacturing technology available today, we see that some of the layout structures span relatively large areas of the product–process matrix. For example, manufacturing cells can be used for a very wide range of applications, and this has become a popular layout structure that often is employed by manufacturing engineers.

Break-Even Analysis

Analytics

The choice of which specific equipment to use in a process often can be based on an analysis of cost trade-offs. There is often a trade-off between more and less specialized equipment. Less specialized equipment is referred to as "general-purpose," meaning it can be used easily in many different ways if it is set up in the proper manner. More specialized equipment, referred to as "special-purpose," is often available as an alternative to a general-purpose machine. For example, if we need to drill holes in a piece of metal, the general-purpose option may be to use a simple hand drill. An alternative special-purpose drill is a drill press. Given the proper setup, the drill press can drill holes much quicker than the hand drill can. The trade-offs involve the cost of the equipment (the manual drill is inexpensive, and the drill press expensive), the setup time (the manual drill is quick, while the drill press takes some time), and the time per unit (the manual drill is slow, and the drill press quick).

EXHIBIT 7.2

Product–Process Matrix: Framework Describing Layout Strategies

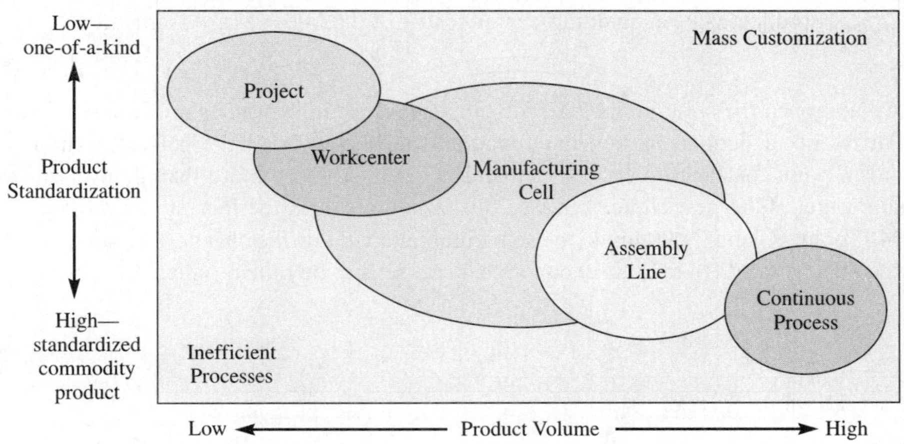

An Example of a Continuous Process

Analytics

A standard approach to choosing among alternative processes or equipment is *break-even analysis.* A break-even chart visually presents alternative profits and losses due to the number of units produced or sold. The choice obviously depends on anticipated demand. The method is most suitable when processes and equipment entail a large initial investment and fixed cost, and when variable costs are reasonably proportional to the number of units produced.

EXAMPLE 7.1 Break-Even Analysis

Suppose a manufacturer has identified the following options for obtaining a machined part: It can buy the part at \$200 per unit (including materials); it can make the part on a numerically controlled semiautomatic lathe at \$75 per unit (including materials); or it can make the part on a machining center at \$15 per unit (including materials). There is negligible fixed cost if the item is purchased; a semiautomatic lathe costs \$80,000; and a machining center costs \$200,000.

The total cost for each option is

$$\begin{aligned}\text{Purchase cost} &= \$200 \times \text{Demand}\\ \text{Produce-using-lathe cost} &= \$80{,}000 + \$75 \times \text{Demand}\\ \text{Produce-using-machining-center cost} &= \$200{,}000 + \$15 \times \text{Demand}\end{aligned}$$

SOLUTION

Whether we approach the solution to this problem as cost minimization or profit maximization really makes no difference as long as the revenue function is the same for all alternatives. Exhibit 7.3 shows the break-even point for each process. If demand is expected to be more than 2,000 units (point A), the machine center is the best choice because this would result in the lowest total cost. If demand is between 640 (point B) and 2,000 units, the semiautomatic lathe is the cheapest. If demand is less than 640 (between 0 and point B), the most economical course is to buy the product.

EXHIBIT 7.3

Break-Even Chart of Alternative Processes

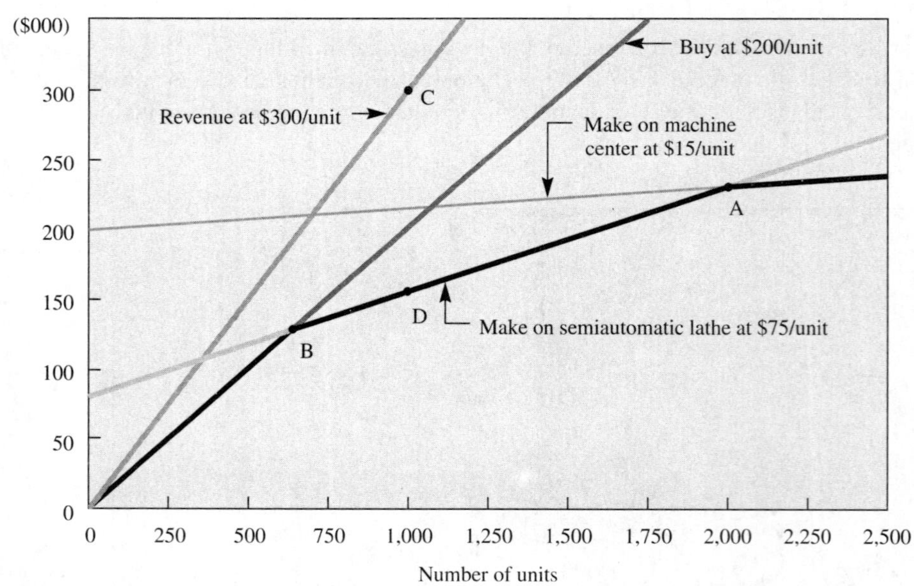

The break-even point A calculation is

$$\$80{,}000 + \$75 \times \text{Demand} = \$200{,}000 + \$15 \times \text{Demand}$$
$$\text{Demand (point A)} = 120{,}000/60 = 2{,}000 \text{ units}$$

The break-even point B calculation is

$$\begin{aligned} \$200 \times \text{Demand} &= \$80{,}000 + \$75 \times \text{Demand} \\ \text{Demand (point B)} &= 80{,}000/125 = 640 \text{ units} \end{aligned}$$

Consider the effect of revenue, assuming the part sells for $300 each. As Exhibit 7.3 shows, profit (or loss) is the vertical distance between the revenue line and the alternative process cost at a given number of units. At 1,000 units, for example, maximum profit is the difference between the $300,000 revenue (point C) and the semiautomatic lathe cost of $155,000 (point D). For this quantity, the semiautomatic lathe is the cheapest alternative available. The optimal choices for both minimizing cost and maximizing profit are the lowest segments of the lines: origin to B, to A, and to the right side of Exhibit 7.3 as shown in green.

MANUFACTURING PROCESS FLOW DESIGN

LO 7-3

Analyze simple manufacturing processes

Manufacturing process flow design is a method to evaluate the specific processes that raw materials, parts, and subassemblies follow as they move through the plant. The most common production management tools used in planning and designing the process flow are assembly drawings, assembly charts, route sheets, and flow process charts. Each of these charts is a useful diagnostic tool and can be used to improve operations during the steady state of the production system. Indeed, the standard first step in analyzing any production system is to map the flows and operations using one or more of these techniques. These are the "organization charts" of the manufacturing system.

An *assembly drawing* (Exhibit 7.4) is simply an exploded view of the product showing its component parts. An *assembly chart* (Exhibit 7.5) uses the information presented in the assembly drawing and defines (among other things) how parts go together, their order of assembly, and often the overall material flow pattern. An *operation and route sheet* (Exhibit 7.6), as its name implies, specifies operations and process routing for a particular part. It conveys such information as the type of equipment, tooling, and operations required to complete the part.

Process

A *process flowchart* such as that shown in Exhibit 7.7 denotes what happens to the product as it progresses through the productive facility. Process flowcharting is covered in Chapter 11. The focus in analyzing a manufacturing operation should be the identification of activities that can be minimized or eliminated, such as movement and storage within the process. As a rule, the fewer the moves, delays, and storages in the process, the better the flow.

EXHIBIT 7.4

Plug Assembly Drawing

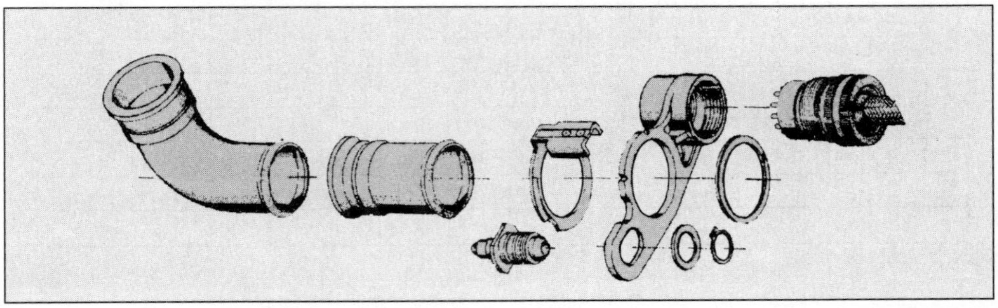

EXHIBIT 7.5

Assembly (or Gozinto) Chart for Plug Assembly

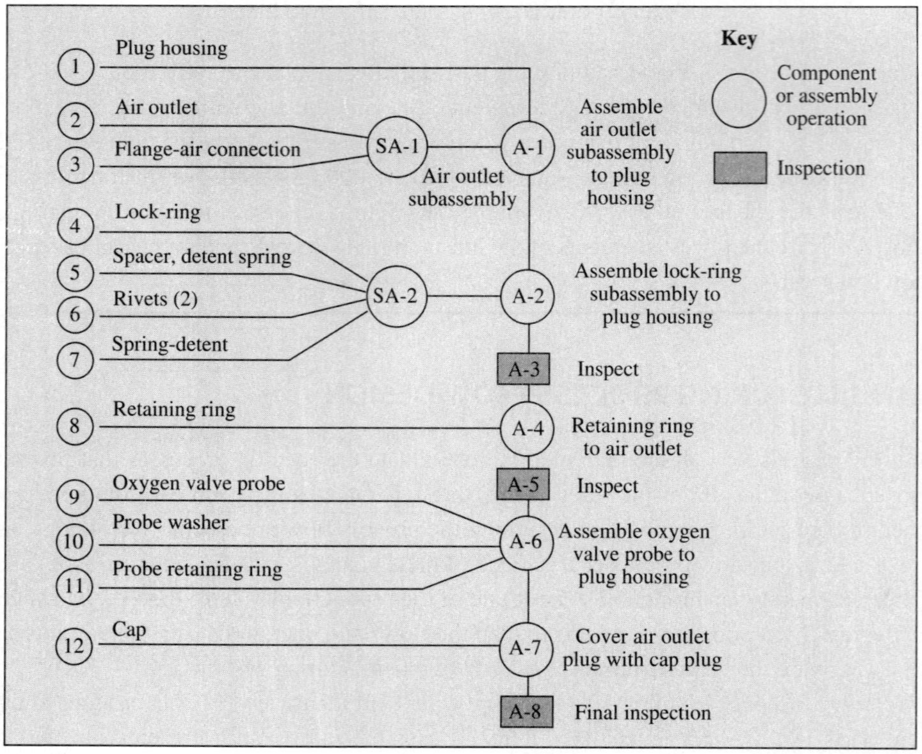

EXHIBIT 7.6

Operation and Route Sheet for Plug Assembly

Material Specs		Part Name	Plug Housing
Purchased Stock Size		Usage	Plug Assembly
Pcs. Per Pur Size		Assy. No.	TA 1279
Weight		Sub.Assy. No.	
Part No.	TA 1274		
Date Issued			
Date Supplied			
Issued By			

Oper. No.	Operation Description	Dept.	Machine	Setup Hr.	Rate Pc. Hr.	Tools
20	Drill hole .32 $^{+.015}_{-.005}$	Drill	Mach. 513 Drill	1.5	254	Drill fixture L-76 Jig # 10393
30	Deburr .312 $^{+.015}_{-.005}$ dia. hole	Drill	Mach. 510 Drill	.1	424	Multitooth burring tool
40	Chamfer .009/875. bore .878/.875 dia (2 passes). bore .7600/7625 (1 pass)	Lathe	Mach. D 109 lathe	1.0	44	Ramet-1, TPG 221, chamfer tool
50	Tap hole as designated 1/4 min. full thread	Tap	Mach. 517 drill tap	2.0	180	Fixture #CR-353 tap. 4 Flute sp.
60	Bore hole 1.33 to 1.138 dia.	Lathe	H&H E107	3.0	158	L44 turret fixture Hartford
						Superspacer, pl. #45 holder #L46
						FDTW-100, insert #21 chk. fixture
70	Deburr .005 to.010 both sides, hand feed to hard stop	Lathe	E162 lathe	.3	175	Collect CR #179 1327 RPM
80	Broach keyway to remove thread burrs	Drill	Mach. 507 drill	.4	91	B87 fixture, L59 broach tap. .875120 G-H6
90	Hone thread I.D. .822/ .828	Grind	Grinder	1.5	120	
95	Hone .7600/ .7625	Grind	Grinder	1.5	120	

EXHIBIT 7.7

Process Flowchart for the Plug Housing (partial)

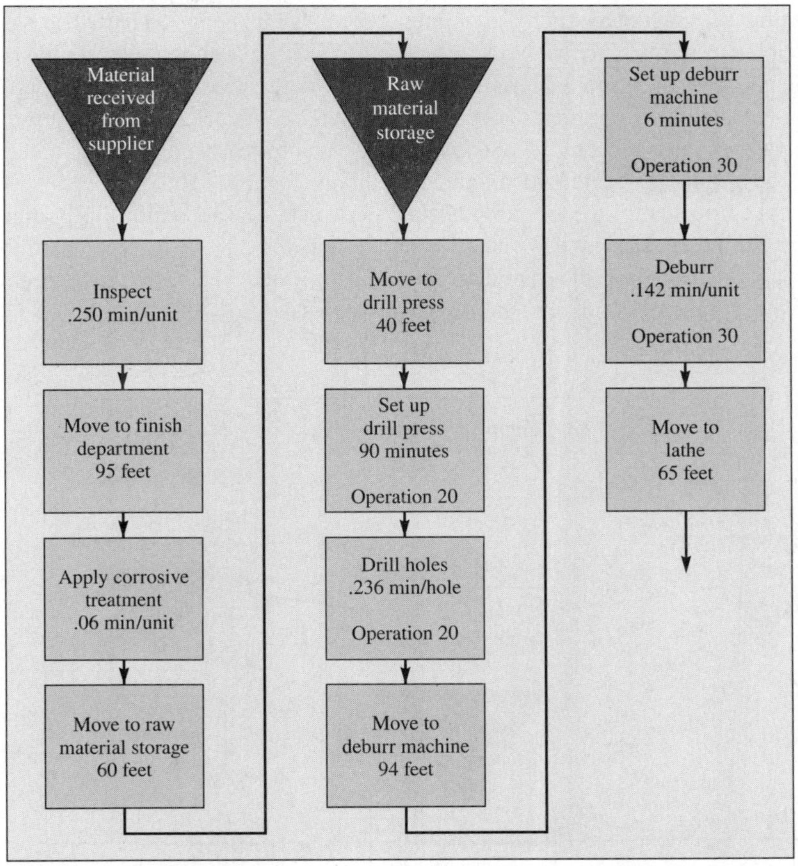

EXAMPLE 7.2 Manufacturing Process Analysis

A process usually consists of (1) a set of *tasks,* (2) a *flow* of material and information that connects the set of tasks, and (3) *storage* of material and information.

1. Each task in a process accomplishes, to a certain degree, the transformation of input into the desired output.
2. The flow in a process consists of material flow, as well as flow of information. The flow of material transfers a product from one task to the next task. The flow of information helps in determining how much of the transformation has been done in the previous task and what exactly remains to be completed in the present task.
3. When neither a task is being performed nor a part is being transferred, the part has to be stored. Goods in storage, waiting to be processed by the next task, are often called *work-in-process inventory.*

Process analysis involves adjusting the capacities and balance among different parts of the process to maximize output or minimize the costs with available resources. Our company supplies a component from our emerging plant to several large auto manufacturers. This component is assembled in a shop by 15 workers working an eight-hour shift on an assembly line that moves at the rate of 150 components per hour. The workers receive their pay in the form of a group incentive amounting to 30 cents per completed good part. This wage is distributed equally among the workers. Management believes that it can hire 15 more workers for a second shift if necessary.

Parts for the final assembly come from two sources. The molding department makes one very critical part, and the rest come from outside suppliers. There are 11 machines capable of molding the one part done in-house; however, historically, one machine is being overhauled or repaired at any given time. Each machine requires a full-time operator. The machines could each produce 25 parts per hour, and the workers are paid on an individual piece rate of 20 cents per good part. The workers will work overtime at a 50 percent increase in rate, or for 30 cents per good part. The workforce for molding is flexible; currently, only six workers are on this job. Four more are available from a labor pool within the company. The raw materials for each part molded cost 10 cents per part; a detailed analysis by the accounting department has concluded that 2 cents of electricity is used in making each part. The parts purchased from the outside cost 30 cents for each final component produced.

This entire operation is located in a rented building costing $100 per week. Supervision, maintenance, and clerical employees receive $1,000 per week. The accounting department charges depreciation for equipment against this operation at $50 per week.

The following process flow diagram describes the process. The tasks have been shown as rectangles and the storage of goods (inventories) as triangles.

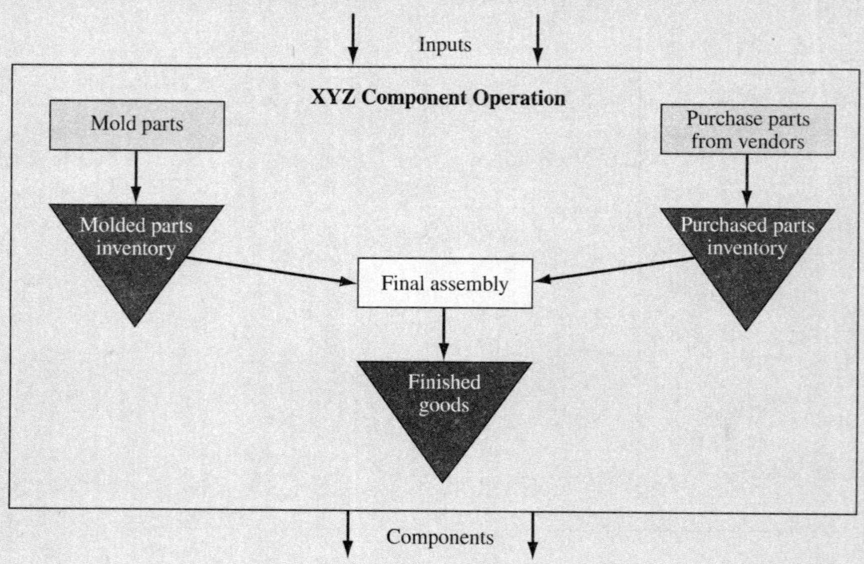

SOLUTION

a. ***Determine the capacity (number of components produced per week) of the entire process. Are the capacities of all the processes balanced?***

Capacity of the molding process:

Only six workers are employed for the molding process, each working as a full-time operator for one machine. Thus, only 6 of the 11 machines are operational at present.

Molding capacity = 6 machines × 25 parts per hour per machine × 8 hours per day × 5 days per week
= 6,000 parts per week

Capacity of the assembly process:

Assembly capacity = 150 components per hour × 8 hours per day × 5 days per week
= 6,000 components per week

Because capacity of both the tasks is 6,000 units per week, they are balanced.

b. ***If the molding process were to use 10 machines instead of 6, and no changes were to be made in the final assembly task, what would be the capacity of the entire process?***

Molding capacity with 10 machines:

Molding capacity = 10 machines × 25 parts per hour per machine × 8 hours per day × 5 days per week
= 10,000 parts per week

Because no change has been made in the final assembly task, the capacity of the assembly process remains 6,000 components per week. Thus, even though the molding capacity is 10,000 per week, the capacity of the entire process is only 6,000 per week because in the long run the overall capacity cannot exceed the slowest task.

c. ***If our company went to a second shift of eight more hours on the assembly task, what would be the new capacity?***

A second shift on the assembly task:

As calculated in the previous section, the molding capacity is 10,000.

Assembly capacity = 150 components per hour × 16 hours per day × 5 days per week
= 12,000 components per week

Here, even though the assembly capacity is 12,000 per week, the capacity of the entire process remains at 10,000 per week because now the slowest task is the molding process, which has a capacity of 10,000 per week. Thus, we can note here that capacity of a process is not a constant factor; it depends on the availability of inputs and the sequence of tasks. In fact, it depends on several other factors not covered here.

d. ***Determine the cost per unit output when the capacity is (1) 6,000 per week or (2) 10,000 per week.***

1. *Cost per unit when output per week = 6,000*

First, we calculate the cost of producing all the 6,000 parts per week:

Item	Calculation	Cost
Raw material for molding	\$0.10 per part × 6,000 =	\$ 600
Parts purchased from outside	\$0.30 per component × 6,000 =	1,800
Electricity	\$0.02 per part × 6,000 =	120
Molding labor	\$0.20 per part × 6,000 =	1,200
Assembly labor	\$0.30 per part × 6,000 =	1,800
Rent	\$100 per week	100
Supervision	\$1,000 per week	1,000
Depreciation	\$50 per week	50
Total cost		\$6,670

$$\text{Cost per unit} = \frac{\text{Total cost per week}}{\text{Number of units produced per week}} = \frac{\$6{,}670}{6{,}000} = \$1.11$$

2. *Cost per unit when output per week = 10,000*

Next, we calculate the cost of producing all the 10,000 parts per week:

Item	Calculation	Cost
Raw material for molding	\$0.10 per part × 10,000 =	\$ 1,000
Parts purchased from outside	\$0.30 per component × 10,000 =	3,000
Electricity	\$0.02 per part × 10,000 =	200
Molding labor	\$0.20 per part × 10,000 =	2,000
Assembly labor	\$0.30 per part × 10,000 =	3,000
Rent	\$100 per week	100
Supervision	\$1,000 per week	1,000
Depreciation	\$50 per week	50
Total cost		\$10,350

$$\text{Cost per unit} = \frac{\text{Total cost per week}}{\text{Number of units produced per week}} = \frac{\$10{,}350}{10{,}000} = \$1.04$$

As you can see, our cost per unit has been reduced by spreading the fixed cost over a greater number of units.

Such process analysis calculations are required for many production decisions discussed throughout this book.

CONCEPT CONNECTIONS

Summary

LO 7–1 Understand what a manufacturing process is

- Manufacturing processes are used to make tangible items.
- At a high level, these processes can be divided into three steps: (1) sourcing the parts needed, (2) making the item, and (3) sending the item to the customer.
- In order to allow parts of the process to operate independently, inventory is strategically positioned in the process. These places in the process are called decoupling points.
- Positioning the decoupling points has an impact on how fast a customer can be served, the flexibility the firm has in responding to specific customer requests, and many other trade-offs.

Key Terms

Lead time The time needed to respond to a customer order.

Customer order decoupling point Where inventory is positioned in the supply chain.

Make-to-stock A production environment where the customer is served "on-demand" from finished goods inventory.

Assemble-to-order A production environment where pre-assembled components, subassemblies, and modules are put together in response to a specific customer order.

Make-to-order A production environment where the product is built directly from raw materials and components in response to a specific customer order.

Engineer-to-order Here the firm works with the customer to design the product, which is then made from purchased material, parts, and components.

Lean manufacturing To achieve high customer service with minimum levels of inventory investment.

Key Formulas

[7.1] Total number of combinations $= N_1 \times N_2 \times \cdots \times N_n$
Or $384 = 4 \times 3 \times 4 \times 2 \times 4$ for this example.

LO 7–2 Explain how manufacturing processes are organized

Summary

- Manufacturing layouts are designed based on the nature of the product, the volume needed to meet demand, and the cost of equipment.
- The trade-offs are depicted in the product–process matrix, which shows the type of layout relative to product volume and the relative standardization of the product.
- Break-even analysis is useful for understanding the cost trade-offs between alternative equipment choices.

Key Terms

Project layout A setup in which the product remains at one location, and equipment is moved to the product.

Workcenter Often referred to as a job shop, a process structure suited for low-volume production of a great variety of nonstandard products. Workcenters sometimes are referred to as departments and are focused on a particular type of operation.

Manufacturing cell Dedicated area where a group of similar products are produced.

Assembly line A setup in which an item is produced through a fixed sequence of workstations, designed to achieve a specific production rate.

Continuous process A process that converts raw materials into finished product in one contiguous process.

Product–process matrix A framework depicting when the different production process types are typically used, depending on product volume and how standardized the product is.

LO 7–3 Analyze simple manufacturing processes

Summary

- Visual charts can be used to document manufacturing process flows. Some common charts are assembly drawings, assembly charts, route sheets, and flowcharts.
- Flowcharts are often very informative in business endeavors. They provide a simple but insightful analysis of the capacity of a process and the variable cost to produce each unit of product.

SOLVED PROBLEMS

LO 7–1 SOLVED PROBLEM 1

An automobile manufacturer is considering a change in an assembly line that should save money by reducing labor and material cost. The change involves the installation of four new robots that will automatically install windshields. The cost of the four robots, including installation and initial programming, is \$400,000. Current practice is to amortize the initial cost of robots over two years on a straight-line basis. The process engineer estimates that one full-time technician will be needed to monitor, maintain, and reprogram the robots on an ongoing basis. This person will be paid approximately \$60,000 per year. Currently, the company uses four full-time employees on this job and each makes about \$52,000 per year. One of these employees is a material handler, and this person will still be needed with the new process. To complicate matters, the process engineer estimates that the robots will apply the windshield sealing material in a manner that will result in a savings of \$0.25 per windshield installed. How many automobiles need to be produced over the next two years to make the new robots an attractive investment? Due to the relatively short time horizon, do not consider the time value of money.

Solution

The cost of the current process over the next two years is just the cost of the four full-time employees.

$$\$52{,}000/\text{employee} \times 4 \text{ employees} \times 2 \text{ years} = \$416{,}000$$

The cost of the new process over the next two years, assuming the robot is completely costed over that time, is the following:

$$(\$52{,}000/\text{material handler} + \$60{,}000/\text{technician}) \times 2 + \$400{,}000/\text{robots} - \$0.25 \times \text{autos}$$

Equating the two alternatives:

$$\$416{,}000 = \$624{,}000 - \$0.25 \times \text{autos}$$

Solving for the break-even point:

$$-\$208{,}000/-\$0.25 = 832{,}000 \text{ autos}$$

This indicates that, to break even, 832,000 autos would need to be produced with the robots over the next two years.

LO 7–3 SOLVED PROBLEM 2

A contract manufacturer makes a product for a customer that consists of two items, a cable with standard RCA connectors and a cable with a mini-plug, which are then packaged together as the final product (each product sold contains one RCA and one mini-plug cable). The manufacturer makes both cables on the same assembly line and can only make one type at a time: either it can make RCA cables or it can make mini-plug cables. There is a setup time when switching from one cable to the other. The assembly line costs \$500/hour to operate, and this rate is charged whether it is being set up or actually making cables.

Current plans are to make 100 units of the RCA cable, then 100 units of the mini-plug cable, then 100 units of the RCA cable, then 100 units of the mini-plug cable, and so on, where the setup and run times for each cable are given as follows.

Component	Setup/Changeover Time	Run Time/Unit
RCA cable	5 minutes	0.2 minute
Mini-plug cable	10 minutes	0.1 minute

Assume the packaging of the two cables is totally automated and takes only two seconds per unit of the final product and is done as a separate step from the assembly line. Since the packaging step is quick and the time required does not depend on the assembly-line batch size, its cost does not vary and need not be considered in the analysis.

What is the average hourly output in terms of the number of units of packaged product (which includes one RCA cable and one mini-plug cable)? What is the average cost per unit for assembling the product? If the batch size were changed from 100 to 200 units, what would be the impact on the assembly cost per unit?

Solution

The average hourly output rate when the batch size is 100 units is calculated by first calculating the total time to produce a batch of cable. The time consists of the setup + the run time for a batch:

$$5 + 10 + 0.2(100) + 0.1(100) = 15 + 30 = 45 \text{ minutes/100 units}$$

So if we can produce 100 units in 45 minutes, we need to calculate how many units can be produced in 60 minutes; we can find this with the following ratio:

$$45/100 = 60/X$$

Solving for X:

$$X = 133.3 \text{ units/hour}$$

The cost per unit is then

$$\$500/133.3 = \$3.75/\text{unit}$$

If the batch size were increased to 200 units:

$$5 + 10 + 0.2(200) + 0.1(200) = 15 + 60 = 75 \text{ minutes/200 units}$$
$$75/200 = 60/X$$
$$X = 160/\text{hour}$$
$$\$500/160 = \$3.125/\text{unit}$$

DISCUSSION QUESTIONS

LO 7–1

1. What is meant by a process? Describe its important features.
2. What is a *customer order decoupling point*? Why is it important?
3. What's the relationship between the design of a manufacturing process and the firm's strategic competitive dimensions (Chapter 2)?

LO 7–2

4. What does the product–process matrix tell us? How should the kitchen of a Chinese restaurant be structured?
5. It has been noted that, during World War II, Germany made a critical mistake by having its formidable Tiger tanks produced by locomotive manufacturers, while the less formidable U.S. Sherman tank was produced by American car manufacturers. Use the product–process matrix to explain that mistake and its likely result.

6. How does the production volume affect break-even analysis?
7. What is meant by *manufacturing process flow*? LO 7–3
8. Why is it that reducing the number of moves, delays, and storages in a manufacturing process is a good thing? Can they be completely eliminated?

OBJECTIVE QUESTIONS

1. What is the first of the three simple steps in the high-level view of manufacturing? LO 7–1
2. The customer order decoupling point determines the position of what in the supply chain?
3. Dell Computer's primary consumer business takes orders from customers for specific configurations of desktop and laptop computers. Customers must select from a certain model line of computer and choose from available parts, but within those constraints they may customize the computer as they desire. Once the order is received, Dell assembles the computer as ordered and delivers it to the customer. What type of manufacturing process is described here?
4. What term is used to mean manufacturing designed to achieve high customer satisfaction with minimum levels of inventory investment?
5. How would you characterize the most important difference for the following issues when comparing a workcenter (job shop) and an assembly line? LO 7–2

Issue	Workcenter (Job Shop)	Assembly Line
Number of setups/job changeovers		
Labor content of product		
Flexibility		

6. The product–process matrix is a convenient way of characterizing the relationship between product volumes (one-of-a-kind to continuous) and the processing system employed by a firm at a particular location. Characterize the nature of the intersection between the type of shop (column) and process dimension (row) in the following table.

	Workcenter	Assembly Line
Engineering emphasis		
General workforce skill		
Facility layout		
WIP inventory level		

7. For each of the following variables, explain the differences (in general) as one moves from a workcenter to an assembly line environment.
   a. Throughput time (time to convert raw material into product)
   b. Capital/labor intensity
   c. Bottlenecks
8. A book publisher has fixed costs of \$300,000 and variable costs per book of \$8.00. The book sells for \$23.00 per copy.
   a. How many books must be sold to break even?
   b. If the fixed cost increased, would the new break-even point be higher or lower?
   c. If the variable cost per unit decreased, would the new break-even point be higher or lower?
9. A manufacturing process has a fixed cost of \$150,000 per month. Each unit of product being produced contains \$25 worth of material and takes \$45 of labor. How many units are needed to break even if each completed unit has a value of \$90? (Answer in Appendix D)
10. Assume a fixed cost of \$900, a variable cost of \$4.50, and a selling price of \$5.50.
    a. What is the break-even point?
    b. How many units must be sold to make a profit of \$500.00?
    c. How many units must be sold to average \$0.25 profit per unit? \$0.50 profit per unit? \$1.50 profit per unit?

11. Aldo Redondo drives his own car on company business. His employer reimburses him for such travel at the rate of 36 cents per mile. Aldo estimates that his fixed costs per year—such as taxes, insurance, and depreciation—are $2,052. The direct or variable costs—such as gas, oil, and maintenance—average about 14.4 cents per mile. How many miles must he drive to break even?
12. A firm is selling two products—chairs and bar stools—each at $50 per unit. Chairs have a variable cost of $25, and bar stools $20. The fixed cost for the firm is $20,000.
    a. If the sales mix is 1:1 (one chair sold for every bar stool sold), what is the break-even point in dollars of sales? In units of chairs and bar stools?
    b. If the sales mix changes to 1:4 (one chair sold for every four bar stools sold), what is the break-even point in dollars of sales? In units of chairs and bar stools?

LO 7–3

13. Owen Conner works part-time packaging software for a local distribution company in Indiana. The annual fixed cost is $10,000 for this process, direct labor is $3.50 per package, and material is $4.50 per package. The selling price will be $12.50 per package. How much revenue do we need to take in before breaking even? What is the break-even point in units?
14. AudioCables, Inc., is currently manufacturing an adapter that has a variable cost of $.50 per unit and a selling price of $1.00 per unit. Fixed costs are $14,000. Current sales volume is 30,000 units. The firm can substantially improve the product quality by adding a new piece of equipment at an additional fixed cost of $6,000. Variable costs would increase to $.60, but sales volume should jump to 50,000 units due to a higher-quality product. Should AudioCables buy the new equipment?
15. The Goodparts Company produces a component that is subsequently used in the aerospace industry. The component consists of three parts (A, B, and C) that are purchased from outside and cost 40, 35, and 15 cents per piece, respectively. Parts A and B are assembled first on assembly line 1, which produces 140 components per hour. Part C undergoes a drilling operation before being finally assembled with the output from assembly line 1. There are, in total, six drilling machines, but at present only three of them are operational. Each drilling machine drills part C at a rate of 50 parts per hour. In the final assembly, the output from assembly line 1 is assembled with the drilled part C. The final assembly line produces at a rate of 160 components per hour. At present, components are produced eight hours a day and five days a week. Management believes that if the need arises, it can add a second shift of eight hours for the assembly lines.

    The cost of assembly labor is 30 cents per part for each assembly line; the cost of drilling labor is 15 cents per part. For drilling, the cost of electricity is one cent per part. The total overhead cost has been calculated as $1,200 per week. The depreciation cost for equipment has been calculated as $30 per week.

    a. Draw a process flow diagram and determine the process capacity (number of components produced per week) of the entire process.
    b. Suppose a second shift of eight hours is run for assembly line 1 and the same is done for the final assembly line. In addition, four of the six drilling machines are made operational. The drilling machines, however, operate for just eight hours a day. What is the new process capacity (number of components produced per week)? Which of the three operations limits the capacity?
    c. Management decides to run a second shift of eight hours for assembly line 1, plus a second shift of only four hours for the final assembly line. Five of the six drilling machines operate for eight hours a day. What is the new capacity? Which of the three operations limits the capacity?
    d. Determine the cost per unit output for questions (*b*) and (*c*).
    e. The product is sold at $4.00 per unit. Assume that the cost of a drilling machine (fixed cost) is $30,000 and the company produces 8,000 units per week. Assume that four drilling machines are used for production. If the company had an option to buy the same part at $3.00 per unit, what would be the break-even number of units?
16. The following diagram represents a process where two components are made at stations A1 and A2 (one component is made at A1 and the other at A2). These components are then assembled at station B and moved through the rest of the process, where some additional work is completed at stations C, D, and E.

Assume that one and only one person is allowed at each station. Assume that the times given for each station represent the amount of work that needs to be done at that station by that person, with no processing time variation. Assume that inventory is not allowed to build in the system.

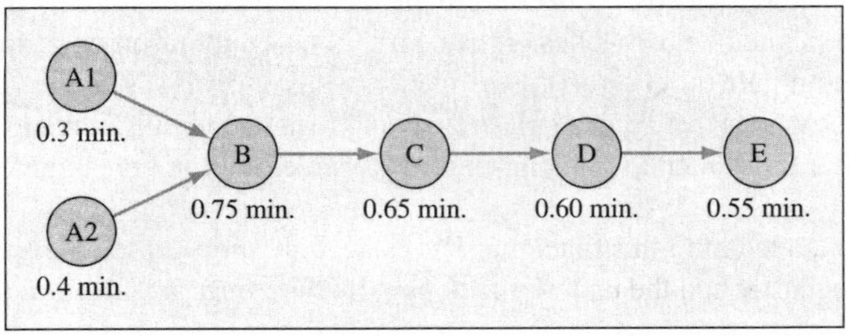

What is the average hourly output of the process when it is in normal operation? (Answer in Appendix D)

17. A certain custom engraving shop has traditionally had orders for between 1 and 50 units of whatever a customer orders. A large company has contacted this shop about engraving "reward" plaques (which are essentially identical to each other). It wants the shop to place a bid for this order. The volume is expected to be 12,000 units per year and will most likely last four years. To successfully bid (low enough price) for such an order, what will the shop likely have to do?

CASE: Circuit Board Fabricators, Inc.

Circuit Board Fabricators, Inc. (CBF), is a small manufacturer of circuit boards located in California near San Jose. Companies such as Apple Computer and Hewlett-Packard use the company to make boards for prototypes of new products. It is important that CBF give quick and very high-quality service. The engineers working on the new products are on a tight schedule and have little patience with sloppy work or missed delivery dates.

Circuit boards are a rigid flat surface where electronic components are mounted. Electronic components such as integrated circuits, resistors, capacitors, and diodes are soldered to the boards. Lines called "traces" are etched on the board and electronically connect the components. Since the electronic traces cannot cross, holes through the circuit board are used to connect traces on both sides of the boards, thus allowing complex circuits to be implemented. These boards often are designed with 40 to 50 components that are connected through hundreds of traces on a small four-by six-inch board.

CBF has developed a good business plan. It has four standard-size board configurations and has automated much of its process for making these standard boards. Fabricating the boards requires CBF's numerically controlled (NC) equipment to be programmed. This is largely an automated process that works directly from engineering drawings that are formatted using industry standard codes.

Currently, the typical order is for 60 boards. Engineers at customer companies prepare a computer-aided design (CAD) drawing of the board. This CAD drawing precisely specifies each circuit trace, circuit pass-through holes, and component mounting points on the board. An electronic version of the drawing is used by a CBF process engineer to program the NC machines used to fabricate the boards.

Due to losses in the system, CBF has a policy of increasing the size of an order by 25 percent. For example, for a typical order consisting of 60 boards, 75 boards would be started through the process. Fifteen percent of the boards are typically rejected during an inspection that occurs early in the manufacturing process and another 5 percent of the remaining boards are rejected in the final test.

Board Fabrication Process

CBF purchases circuit board blanks from a vendor. These boards are made from woven fiberglass cloth that is impregnated with epoxy. A layer of copper is laminated onto each side to form a blank board. The blank board comes from the vendor trimmed to the standard sizes that CBF's numerically controlled equipment can handle.

The following is a description of the steps involved in processing an order at CBF:

1. **Order acceptance.** Check to verify that the order fits within the specification of boards that can be produced with CBF equipment. The process engineer at CBF works with the customer engineer to resolve any problems with the order.

2. **NC machine programming.** CAD information is used to program the machines to produce the order.
3. **Board fabrication.**
   a. **Clean.** Each board is manually loaded into this machine by an operator. The machine then cleans the boards with a special chemical. Each board is then automatically transferred to the coating machine.
   b. **Coat.** A liquid plastic coating is deposited on both sides of the board. Following this process, an operator places the boards on a cart. Each cart, with a complete order of boards, is then moved immediately to the "clean room."
   c. **Expose.** This photographic process makes the exposed plastic coating resistant to dissolving in the areas where the copper traces are needed. An operator must attend to this machine 100 percent of the time, and load and unload each individual board.
   d. **Develop.** Each board is manually loaded onto this machine. The boards are dipped by the machine, one-at-a-time, in a chemical bath that dissolves the plastic and the underlying copper in the proper areas. After dipping, the machine places each board on a conveyor.
   e. **Inspect.** Each board is picked from the conveyor as it comes from the developer. The board is optically checked for defects using a machine similar to a scanner. Approximately 15 percent of the boards are rejected at this point. Boards that pass inspection are placed back on the conveyor that feeds the bake oven. Two inspectors are used at this station.
   f. **Bake.** Boards travel through a bake oven that hardens the plastic coating, thus protecting the traces. Boards are then manually unloaded and placed on a cart. When all the boards for an order are on the cart, it is moved to the drilling machines.
   g. **Drilling.** Holes are drilled using an NC machine to connect circuits on both sides of the board. The boards are manually loaded and unloaded. The machines are arranged so that one person can keep two machines going simultaneously. The cart is used to move the boards to the copper plate bath.
   h. **Copper plate.** Copper is deposited inside the holes by running the boards through a special copper plating bath. This copper connects the traces on both sides of the board. Each board is manually loaded on a conveyor that passes through the plating bath. Two people are needed for this process, one loading and a second unloading the conveyor. On completion of plating, boards are moved on the cart to the final test machines.

EXHIBIT 7.8

Circuit Board Fabricators—Process Data

Required output per shift	1,000
Average job size (boards)	60
Production hours per day	7.5
Working days per week	5

Process/Machine	Number of Machines	Number of Employees	Setup (minutes per job)	Run (minutes per part)
Load	1	1	5	0.33
Clean	1			0.5
Coat	1			0.5
Unload	1	1		0.33
Expose	5	5	15	1.72
Load	1	1	5	0.33
Develop	1			0.33
Inspect	2	2		0.5
Bake	1			0.33
Unload	1	1		0.33
Drilling	6	3	15	1.5
Copper plate	1	2	5	0.2
Final test	6	6	15	2.69

i. **Final test.** Using a special NC machine, a final electrical test of each board is performed to check the integrity of the circuits. On average, approximately 5 percent of the boards fail this test. The boards are manually loaded and unloaded. One person is needed to operate each machine and sort the good and bad boards. The cart is used to move the good boards to the shipping area. The bad boards are scrapped.

4. **Shipping.** The completed order is packed and shipped to the customer.

The plant was designed to run 1,000 boards per day when running five days a week and one eight-hour shift per day. Unfortunately, to date, it has not come near that capacity, and on a good day it is able to produce only about 700 boards. Data concerning the standard setup and run times for the fabrication process are given in Exhibit 7.8. These times include allowances for morning and afternoon breaks, but do not include time for the half-hour lunch period. In addition, data on current staffing levels also are provided. The CBF process engineer insists that the capacity at each process is sufficient to run 1,000 boards per day.

In order to help understand the problem, CBF hired a consulting company to help solve the problem.

Questions

CBF hired you to help determine why it is not able to produce the 1,000 boards per day.

1. What type of process flow structure is CBF using?
2. Diagram the process in a manner similar to Exhibit 7.7.
3. Analyze the capacity of the process.
4. What is the impact of losses in the process in the inspection and final test?
5. What recommendations would you make for a short-term solution to CBF's problems?
6. What long-term recommendations would you make?

PRACTICE EXAM

In each of the following, name the term defined or answer the question. Answers are listed at the bottom.

1. A firm that makes predesigned products directly to fill customer orders has this type of production environment.
2. A point where inventory is positioned to allow the production process to operate independently of the customer order delivery process.
3. A firm that designs and builds products from scratch according to customer specifications would have this type of production environment.
4. If a production process makes a unit every two hours and it takes 42 hours for the unit to go through the entire process, what is the expected work-in-process equal to?
5. A finished goods inventory, on average, contains 10,000 units. Demand averages 1,500 units per week. Given that the process runs 50 weeks a year, what is the expected inventory turn for the inventory? Assume that each item held in inventory is valued at about the same amount.
6. This is a production layout where similar products are made. Typically, it is scheduled on an as-needed basis in response to current customer demand.
7. The relationship between how different layout structures are best suited depending on volume and product variety characteristics is depicted on this type of graph.

Answers to Practice Exam 1. Make-to-order. 2. Customer order decoupling point. 3. Engineer-to-order. 4. 21 units = 42/2. 5. 7.5 turns = (1,500 × 50)/10,000. 6. Manufacturing cell. 7. Product–process matrix.

For PowerPoint lecture slides, Solutions Manual, Test Bank, Data files for solved examples, Excel Templates, Step-by-Step Solved Examples in video format, Tutorial Videos and many more, scan the adjacent **QR code**, or **visit http://www.mhhe.com/sie-chase15e**

Chapter 8

Facility Layout

LEARNING OBJECTIVES

LO 8-1 Analyze the common types of manufacturing layouts

LO 8-2 Illustrate the layouts used in nonmanufacturing settings

Toshiba: Producer of the First Notebook Computer

Tokyo Shibaura Denki (Tokyo Shibaura Electric Co. Ltd.) was formed in 1939 by a merger of two highly innovative Japanese companies: Shibaura Seisaku-sho (Shibaura Engineering Works), which manufactured transformers, electrical motors, hydroelectric generators, and X-ray tubes, and Tokyo Electric Company, which produced light bulbs, radio receivers, and cathode-ray tubes. The company was soon after known as "Toshiba," which became its official name in 1978. Toshiba became the first company in Japan to make fluorescent lamps (1940), radar (1942), broadcasting equipment (1952), and digital computers (1954). Toshiba also became the first in the world to produce the powerful 1-megabit DRAM chip and the first laptop computer, the T3100, both in 1985.

Toshiba has built its strength in the notebook PC market by beating its competitors to the market with aggressively priced, technologically innovative products. Competition in the notebook PC market is fierce, and Toshiba can retain its position as a market leader only by relentlessly improving its manufacturing processes and lowering its costs.

Dell Computer is a formidable competitor and seeks to minimize its costs by assembling to order and selling directly to customers. Toshiba has some significant advantages over Dell that stem largely from huge investments in technologies, such as thin-film transistor (TFT) color displays, hard disk drives, lithium-ion batteries, and DVD drives. In addition, by forming partnerships and joint ventures with other industry giants, Toshiba can share the risk of developing expensive new technologies.

Put yourself in the position of Toshihiro Nakamura, the production supervisor at Toshiba's Ome Works plant. Production of Toshiba's latest subnotebook computer is scheduled to begin in only 10 days. As he wends his way through a maze of desks, heading to the factory floor, he wonders if it is really feasible to get the line designed in time.

Read the details related to designing the new assembly line in the Analytics Exercise at the end of this chapter titled "Designing a Manufacturing Process."

LO 8-1

Analyze the common types of manufacturing layouts

Layout decisions entail determining the placement of departments, work groups within the departments, workstations, machines, and stock-holding points within a production facility. The objective is to arrange these elements in a way that ensures a smooth work flow (in a factory) or a particular traffic pattern (in a service organization). In general, the inputs to the layout decision are as follows:

1. Specification of the objectives and corresponding criteria to be used to evaluate the design. The amount of space required and the distance that must be traveled between elements in the layout are common basic criteria.
2. Estimates of product or service demand on the system.
3. Processing requirements in terms of number of operations and amount of flow between the elements in the layout.
4. Space requirements for the elements in the layout.
5. Space availability within the facility itself or, if this is a new facility, possible building configurations.

In our treatment of layout, we examine how layouts are developed under various formats (or workflow structures). Our emphasis is on quantitative techniques, but we also show examples of how qualitative factors are important in the design of the layout. Both manufacturing and service facilities are covered in this chapter.

Overview of an engineering factory floor workcenter.

ANALYZING THE FOUR MOST COMMON LAYOUT FORMATS

The formats by which departments are arranged in a facility are defined by the general pattern of workflow. There are three basic types (workcenter, assembly line, and project layout) and one hybrid type (manufacturing cell).

A **workcenter** (also called a *job-shop* or *functional layout*) is a format in which similar equipment or functions are grouped together, such as all lathes in one area and all stamping machines in another. A part being worked on then travels, according to the established sequence of operations, from area to area, where the proper machines are located for each operation. This type of layout is typical in hospitals, for example, where areas are dedicated to particular types of medical care, such as maternity wards and intensive care units.

Workcenter
Often referred to as a job shop, a process structure suited for low-volume production of a great variety of nonstandard products. Workcenters sometimes are referred to as departments and are focused on a particular type of operation.

An **assembly line** (also called a *flow-shop layout*) is one in which equipment or work processes are arranged according to the progressive steps by which the product is made. The path for each part is, in effect, a straight line. Assembly lines for shoes, chemical plants, and car washes are all product layouts.

Assembly line
A setup in which an item is produced through a fixed sequence of workstations, designed to achieve a specific production rate.

Manufacturing cell
Groups dissimilar machines to work on products that have similar shapes and processing requirements.

A **manufacturing cell** groups dissimilar machines to work on products that have similar shapes and processing requirements. A manufacturing cell is similar to a workcenter in that cells are designed to perform a specific set of processes, and it is similar to an assembly line in that the cells are dedicated to a limited range of products. (*Group technology* refers to the parts classification and coding system used to specify machine types that go into a cell.)

Project layout
A setup in which the product remains at one location, and equipment is moved to the product.

In a **project layout**, the product (by virtue of its bulk or weight) remains at one location. Manufacturing equipment is moved to the product rather than vice versa. Construction sites and movie lots are examples of this format.

Many manufacturing facilities present a combination of two layout types. For example, a given production area may be organized as a workcenter, while another area may be an assembly line. It is also common to find an entire plant arranged according to product flow—for example, a parts fabrication area followed by a subassembly area, with a final assembly area at the end of the process. Different types of layouts may be used in each area, with workcenters used in fabrication, manufacturing cells in subassembly, and an assembly line used in final assembly.

Workcenters (Job Shops)

The most common approach to developing a workcenter layout is to arrange workcenters consisting of like processes in a way that optimizes their relative placement. For example, the workcenters in a low-volume toy factory might consist of the shipping and receiving workcenter, the plastic molding and stamping workcenter, the metal forming workcenter, the sewing workcenter, and the painting workcenter. Parts for the toys are fabricated in these workcenters and then sent to assembly workcenters where they are put together. In many installations, optimal placement often means placing workcenters with large amounts of interdepartment traffic adjacent to one another.

EXAMPLE 8.1 Workcenter Layout Design

Suppose we want to arrange the eight workcenters of a toy factory to minimize the interdepartmental material handling cost. Initially, let us make the simplifying assumption that all workcenters have the same amount of space (say, 40 feet by 40 feet) and that the building is 80 feet wide and 160 feet long (and thus compatible with the workcenter dimensions). The first things we would want

Lotus Evora manufacturing facility in Hethel, United Kingdom. Top row; assembly line, paint shop. Bottom row; assembly line, test track.
Courtesy of Group Lotus Plc.

to know are the nature of the flow between workcenters and how the material is transported. If the company has another factory that makes similar products, information about flow patterns might be abstracted from the records. On the other hand, if this is a new-product line, such information would have to come from routing sheets or from estimates by knowledgeable personnel such as process or industrial engineers. Of course, these data, regardless of their source, will have to be modified to reflect the nature of future orders over the projected life of the proposed layout.

Analytics

Let us assume that this information is available. We find that all material is transported in a standard-size crate by forklift truck, one crate to a truck (which constitutes one "load"). Now suppose that transportation costs are \$1 to move a load between adjacent workcenters and \$1 extra for each workcenter in between. The expected loads between workcenters for the first year of operation are tabulated in Exhibit 8.1; available plant space is depicted in Exhibit 8.2. Note that, in our example, diagonal moves are permitted so that workcenters 2 and 3, and 3 and 6, are considered adjacent.

EXHIBIT 8.1

Interworkcenter Flow

	Flow between Workcenters (Number of Moves)								Workcenter	Activity
	1	2	3	4	5	6	7	8		
1		175	50	0	30	200	20	25	1	Shipping and receiving
2			0	100	75	90	80	90	2	Plastic molding and stamping
3				17	88	125	99	180	3	Metal forming
4					20	5	0	25	4	Sewing
5						0	180	187	5	Small toy assembly
6							374	103	6	Large toy assembly
7								7	7	Painting
8									8	Mechanism assembly

EXHIBIT 8.2

Building Dimensions and Workcenters

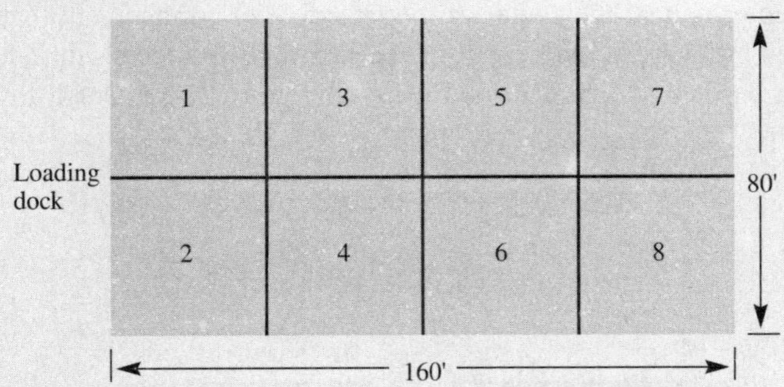

SOLUTION

Given this information, our first step is to illustrate the interworkcenter flow by a model, such as Exhibit 8.3. This provides the basic layout pattern, which we will try to improve.

The second step is to determine the cost of this layout by multiplying the material handling cost by the number of loads moved between each pair of workcenters. Exhibit 8.4 presents this information, which is derived as follows: The annual material handling cost between Workcenters 1 and 2 is \$175 (\$1 × 175 moves), \$60 between Workcenters 1 and 5 (\$2 × 30 moves), \$60 between Workcenters 1

EXHIBIT 8.3

Interworkcenter Flow Graph with Number of Annual Movements

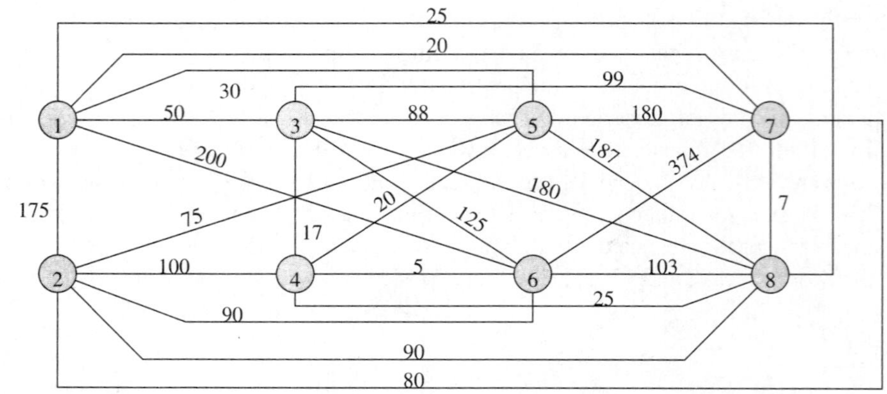

and 7 ($3 × 20 moves), $240 between diagonal Workcenters 2 and 7 ($3 × 80), and so forth. (The "distances" are taken from Exhibit 8.2 or 8.3, not Exhibit 8.4.)

The third step is a search for workcenter location changes that will reduce costs. On the basis of the graph and the cost matrix, it seems desirable to place Workcenters 1 and 6 closer together to reduce their high move-distance costs. However, this requires shifting several other workcenters, thereby affecting their move-distance costs and the total cost of the second solution. Exhibit 8.5 shows the revised layout resulting from relocating Workcenter 6 and an adjacent workcenter. (Workcenter 4 is arbitrarily selected for this purpose.) The revised cost matrix for the exchange, showing the cost changes, is given in Exhibit 8.6. Note the total cost is $262 *greater* than in the initial solution. Clearly, doubling the distance between Workcenters 6 and 7 accounted for the major part of the cost increase. This points out the fact that, even in a small problem, it is rarely easy to decide the correct "obvious move" on the basis of casual inspection.

Thus far, we have shown only one exchange among a large number of potential exchanges; in fact, for an eight-workcenter problem, there are 8! (or 40,320) possible arrangements. Therefore, the procedure we have employed would have only a remote possibility of achieving an optimal combination in a reasonable number of tries. Nor does our problem stop here.

Suppose that we *do* arrive at a good solution solely on the basis of material handling cost, such as that shown in Exhibit 8.7 (whose total cost is $3,550). We would note, first of all, that our shipping and receiving workcenter is near the center of the factory—an arrangement that probably would not be acceptable. The sewing workcenter is next to the painting workcenter, introducing the hazard that lint, thread, and cloth particles might drift onto painted items. Further, small toy assembly and large

EXHIBIT 8.4

Cost Matrix—First Solution

$	1	2	3	4	5	6	7	8
1		175	50	0	60	400	60	75
2			0	100	150	180	240	270
3				17	88	125	198	360
4					20	5	0	50
5						0	180	187
6							374	103
7								7
8								

Total cost: $3,474

EXHIBIT 8.5

Revised Interworkcenter Flowchart (Only interworkcenter flow with effect on cost is depicted.)

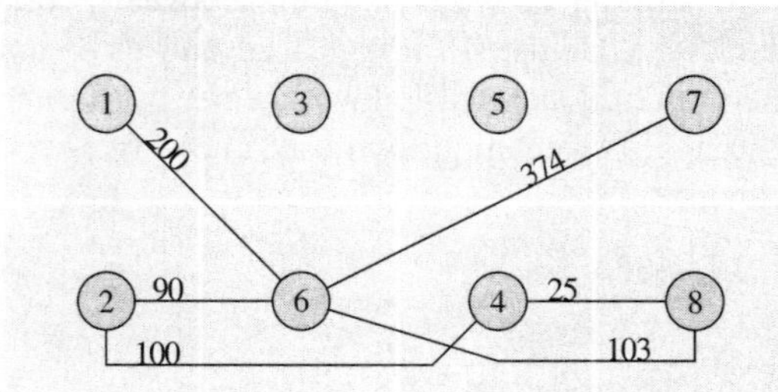

EXHIBIT 8.6

Cost Matrix—First Solution

	1	2	3	4	5	6	7	8	Net cost change
1		175	50	0	60	200	60	75	–$200
2			0	200	150	90	240	270	+ 10
3				17	88	125	198	360	
4					20	5	0	25	– 25
5						0	180	187	
6							748	206	+ $374, + $103
7								7	
8									
									+ $262 Total cost: $3,736

EXHIBIT 8.7

A Feasible Layout

Small toy assembly 5	Mechanism assembly 8	Shipping and receiving 1	Large toy assembly 6
Metal forming 3	Plastic molding and stamping 2	Sewing 4	Painting 7

toy assembly are located at opposite ends of the plant, which would increase travel time for assemblers (who very likely would be needed in both workcenters at various times of the day) and for supervisors (who might otherwise supervise both workcenters simultaneously). Often, factors other than material handling cost need to be considered in finalizing a layout.

Systematic Layout Planning

In certain types of layout problems, numerical flow of items between workcenters either is impractical to obtain or does not reveal the qualitative factors that may be crucial to the placement decision. In

Systematic layout planning (SLP)
A technique for solving process layout problems when the use of numerical flow data between departments is not practical. The technique uses an activity relationship diagram that is adjusted by trial and error until a satisfactory adjacency pattern is obtained.

these situations, the venerable technique known as **systematic layout planning (SLP)** can be used. It involves developing a relationship chart showing the degree of importance of having each workcenter located adjacent to every other workcenter. From this chart, an activity relationship diagram, similar to the flow graph used for illustrating material handling between workcenters, is developed. The activity relationship diagram is then adjusted through trial and error until a satisfactory adjacency pattern is obtained. This pattern, in turn, is modified workcenter by workcenter to meet building space limitations. Exhibit 8.8 illustrates the technique with a simple five-workcenter problem involving laying out a floor of a department store.

Exhibit 8.8

Systematic Layout Planning for a Floor of a Department Store

A. Relationship Chart (based on Tables B and C)

From	To 2	3	4	5	Area (sq. ft.)
1. Credit department	I 6	U —	E 4	U —	100
2. Toy department		U —	I 1	A 1,6	400
3. Wine department			U —	X 1	300
4. Camera department				X 1	100
5. Candy department					100

Letter	Closeness rating
Number	Reason for rating

B.

Code	Reason*
1	Type of customer
2	Ease of supervision
3	Common personnel
4	Contact necessary
5	Share same space
6	Psychology

*Others may be used.

C.

Value	Closeness	Line Code*	Numerical Weights
A	Absolutely necessary	≣	16
E	Especially important	≡	8
I	Important	=	4
O	Ordinary closeness OK	—	2
U	Unimportant		0
X	Undesirable	⋀⋀⋀	−80

*Used for example purposes only.

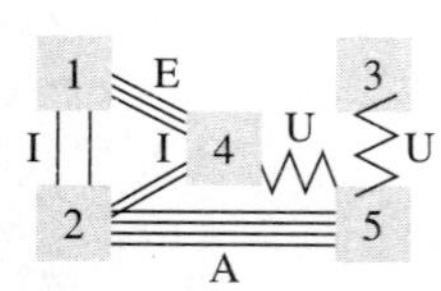

Initial relationship diagram (based on Tables A and C)

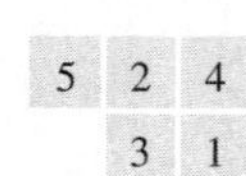

Initial layout based on relationship diagram (ignoring space and building constraints)

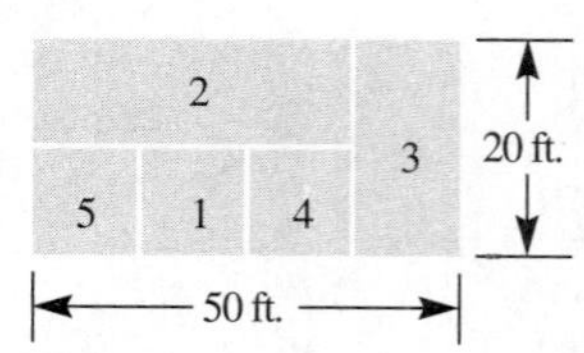

Final layout adjusted by square footage and building size

Assembly Lines

The term *assembly line* refers to progressive assembly linked by some material handling device. The usual assumption is that some form of pacing is present and the allowable processing time is equivalent for all workstations. Within this broad definition, there are important differences among line types. A few of these are material handling devices (belt or roller conveyor, overhead crane); line configuration (U-shape, straight, branching); pacing (mechanical, human); product mix (one product or multiple products); workstation characteristics (workers may sit, stand, walk with the line, or ride the line); and length of the line (few or many workers).

The range of products partially or completely assembled on lines includes toys, appliances, autos, planes, guns, garden equipment, clothing, and a wide variety of electronic components. In fact, it is probably safe to say that virtually any product that has multiple parts and is produced in large volume uses assembly lines to some degree. Clearly, lines are an important technology. To really understand their managerial requirements, we should have some familiarity with how a line is balanced.

Assembly-Line Design

The most common assembly line is a moving conveyor that passes a series of workstations in a uniform time interval called the **workstation cycle time** (which is also the time between successive units coming off the end of the line). At each workstation, work is performed on a product either by adding parts or by completing assembly operations. The work performed at each station is made up of many bits of work, termed *tasks*. Normally, the concern is for the work that is performed by people, and the task times would reflect this work.

Workstation cycle time
The time between successive units coming off the end of an assembly line.

The total work to be performed at a workstation is equal to the sum of the tasks assigned to that workstation. The **assembly-line balancing** problem is one of assigning all tasks to a series of workstations so that each workstation has no more than can be done in the workstation cycle time and so that the unassigned (that is, idle) time across all workstations is minimized.

Assembly-line balancing
The problem of assigning tasks to a series of workstations so that the required cycle time is met and idle time is minimized.

The problem is complicated by the relationships among tasks imposed by product design and process technologies. This is called the **precedence relationship**, which specifies the order in which tasks must be performed in the assembly process.

Precedence relationship
The required order in which tasks must be performed in an assembly process.

The steps in balancing an assembly line are straightforward:

1. Specify the sequential relationships among tasks using a precedence diagram. The diagram consists of circles and arrows. Circles represent individual tasks; arrows indicate the order of task performance. This is similar to the project network diagram in Chapter 5.
2. Determine the required workstation cycle time (C), using the formula

$$C = \frac{\text{Production time per day}}{\text{Required output per day (in units)}} \qquad [8.1]$$

3. Determine the theoretical minimum number of workstations (Nt) required to satisfy the workstation cycle time constraint using the formula (note that this must be rounded up to the next highest integer)

$$N_t = \frac{\text{Sum of task times } (T)}{\text{Cycle time } (C)} \qquad [8.2]$$

Analytics

4. Select a primary rule by which tasks are to be assigned to workstations and a secondary rule to break ties. For example, the primary rule might be the longest task time, and the secondary rule, the task with the longest number of following tasks. In this case, for the tasks that can be assigned, pick the one with the longest task time. If there is a tie, pick the one that has the greatest number of following tasks.
5. Assign tasks, one at a time, to the first workstation until the sum of the task times is equal to the workstation cycle time or no other tasks are feasible because of time or sequence restrictions. Every time a task is assigned, re-create the list of tasks that are feasible to assign and then pick one based on the rule defined in 4. Repeat the process for workstation 2, workstation 3, and so on, until all tasks are assigned.
6. Evaluate the efficiency of the balance derived using the formula

$$\text{Efficiency} = \frac{\text{Sum of task times } (T)}{\text{Actual number of workstations } (N_a) \times \text{Workstation cycle time } (C)} \qquad [8.3]$$

Here we assume there is one worker per workstation. When, for some reason, the number of workstations does not equal the number of workers, we would usually substitute the number of workers for number of workstations since the concern is normally related to the use of labor. Often, it is the case that the line is run at a cycle time different than the time calculated in equation 8.1. In this case, the actual cycle time used by the assembly line should be used in the efficiency calculation.

7. If efficiency is unsatisfactory, re-balance using a different decision rule. Keep in mind that the efficiency cannot be improved if the current solution uses the theoretical number of workstations calculated in step 3.

EXAMPLE 8.2 Assembly-Line Balancing

The Model J Wagon is to be assembled on a conveyor belt. Five hundred wagons are required per day. Production time per day is 420 minutes, and the assembly steps and times for the wagon are given in Exhibit 8.9A. *Assignment:* Find the balance that minimizes the number of workstations, subject to cycle time and precedence constraints.

SOLUTION

1. Draw a precedence diagram. Exhibit 8.9B illustrates the sequential relationships identified in Exhibit 8.9A. (The length of the arrows has no meaning.)
2. Determine workstation cycle time. Here we have to convert to seconds because our task times are in seconds.

$$C = \frac{\text{Production time per day}}{\text{Output per day}} = \frac{60\text{ sec.} \times 420\text{ min.}}{500\text{ wagons}} = \frac{25,200}{500} = 50.4$$

3. Determine the theoretical minimum number of workstations required (the actual number may be greater):

$$N\,t = \frac{T}{C} = \frac{195\text{ seconds}}{50.4\text{ seconds}} = 3.87 = 4\text{ (rounded up)}$$

4. Select assignment rules. In general, the strategy is to use a rule assigning tasks that either have many followers or are of long duration because they effectively limit the balance achievable. In this case, we use the following as our primary rule.
   a. Prioritize tasks in order of the largest number of following tasks.

Task	Number of Following Tasks
A	6
B or D	5
C or E	4
F, G, H, or I	2
J	1
K	0

   Our secondary rule, to be invoked where ties exist from our primary rule, is:
   b. Prioritize tasks in order of longest task time (shown in Exhibit 8.10). Note that D should be assigned before B, and E assigned before C due to this tiebreaking rule.
5. Make task assignments to form Workstation 1, Workstation 2, and so forth, until all tasks are assigned. The actual assignment is given in Exhibit 8.10A and is shown graphically in Exhibit 8.10B. To understand this, it is best to trace through the task assignments in sequence in Exhibit 8.10A. See that when an assignment is made, the feasible remaining assignments are updated along with the priority rules. It is important to meet precedence and cycle time requirements as the assignments are made.
6. Calculate the efficiency. This is shown in Exhibit 8.10C.
7. Evaluate the solution. An efficiency of 77 percent indicates an imbalance or idle time of 23 percent (1.0–.77) across the entire line. From Exhibit 8.10A we can see that there are 57 total seconds of idle time, and the “choice” job is at Workstation 5.

Exhibit 8.9

A. Assembly Steps and Times for Model J Wagon

Task	Task Time (in seconds)	Description	Tasks That Must Precede
A	45	Position rear axle support and hand fasten four screws to nuts.	—
B	11	Insert rear axle.	A
C	9	Tighten rear axle support screws to nuts.	B
D	50	Position front axle assembly and hand fasten with four screws to nuts.	—
E	15	Tighten front axle assembly screws.	D
F	12	Position rear wheel #1 and fasten hubcap.	C
G	12	Position rear wheel #2 and fasten hubcap.	C
H	12	Position front wheel #1 and fasten hubcap.	E
I	12	Position front wheel #2 and fasten hubcap.	E
J	8	Position wagon handle shaft on front axle assembly and hand fasten bolt and nut.	F, G, H, I
K	9 195	Tighten bolt and nut.	J

B. Assembly Steps and Times for Model J Wagon

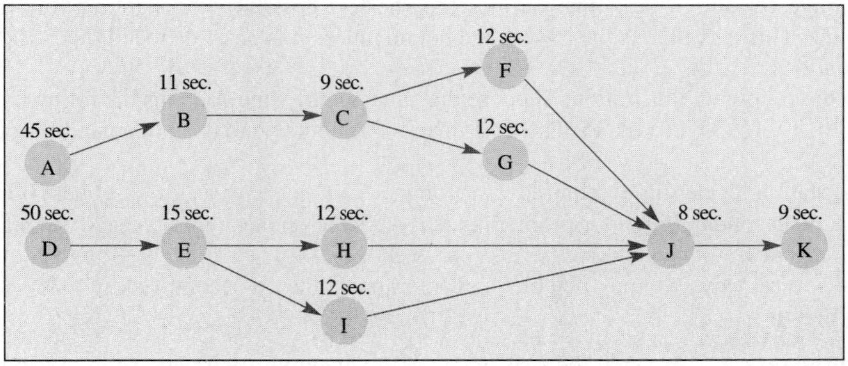

Exhibit 8.10

A. Balance Made According to Largest-Number-of-Following-Tasks Rule

	Task	Task Time (in seconds)	Remaining Unassigned Time (in seconds)	Feasible Remaining Tasks	Task with Most Followers	Task with Longest Operation Time
Station 1	A	45	5.4 idle	None		
Station 2	D	50	0.4 idle	None		
Station 3	B	11	39.4	C, E	C, E	E
	E	15	24.4	C, H, I	C	
	C	9	15.4	F, G, H, I	F, G, H, I	F, G, H, I
	F*	12	3.4 idle	None		
Station 4	G	12	38.4	H, I	H, I	H, I
	H*	12	26.4	I		
	I	12	14.4	J		
	J	8	6.4 idle	None		
Station 5	K	9	41.4 idle	None		

*Denotes task arbitrarily selected where there is a tie between longest operation times.

Is a better balance possible? In this case, yes. Try balancing the line with rule (*b*) and breaking ties with rule (*a*). (This will give you a feasible four-station balance.)

B. Precedence Graph for Model J Wagon

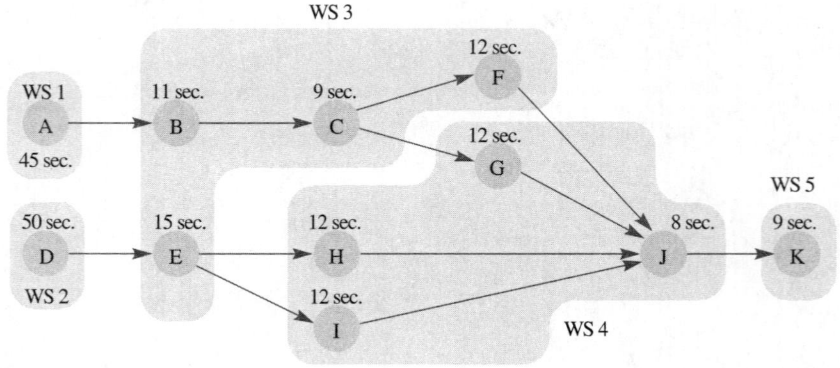

C. Efficiency Calculation

$$\text{Efficiency} = \frac{T}{N_a C} = \frac{195}{(5)(50.4)} = .77, \text{or } 77\%$$

Splitting Tasks

Often, the longest required task time defines the shortest possible workstation cycle time for the production line. This task time is the lower time bound unless it is possible to split the task into two or more workstations.

Consider the following illustration: Suppose that an assembly line contains the following task times in seconds: 40, 30, 15, 25, 20, 18, 15. The line runs for 7½ hours per day and demand for output is 750 per day.

The workstation cycle time required to produce 750 per day is 36 seconds ([7½ hours × 60 minutes × 60 seconds]/750). Our problem is that we have one task that takes 40 seconds. How do we deal with this task?

There are several ways we may be able to accommodate the 40-second task in a 36-second cycle. Possibilities are

1. **Split the task.** Can we split the task so that complete units are processed in two workstations?
2. **Share the task.** Can the task somehow be shared so an adjacent workstation does part of the work? This differs from the split task in the first option because the adjacent station acts to assist, not to do some units containing the entire task.
3. **Use parallel workstations.** It may be necessary to assign the task to two workstations that would operate in parallel.
4. **Use a more skilled worker.** Because this task exceeds the workstation cycle time by just 11 percent, a faster worker may be able to meet the 36-second time.
5. **Work overtime.** Producing at a rate of one every 40 seconds would create 675 per day, 75 short of the needed 750. The amount of overtime required to produce the additional 75 is 50 minutes (75 × 40 seconds/60 seconds).
6. **Redesign.** It may be possible to redesign the product to reduce the task time slightly.

Other possibilities to reduce the task time include an equipment upgrade, a roaming helper to support the line, a change of materials, and multiskilled workers to operate the line as a team rather than as independent workers.

Flexible and U-Shaped Line Layouts

As we saw in the preceding example, assembly-line balances frequently result in unequal workstation times. Flexible line layouts, such as those shown in Exhibit 8.11, are a common way of dealing with

EXHIBIT 8.11

Flexible Line Layouts

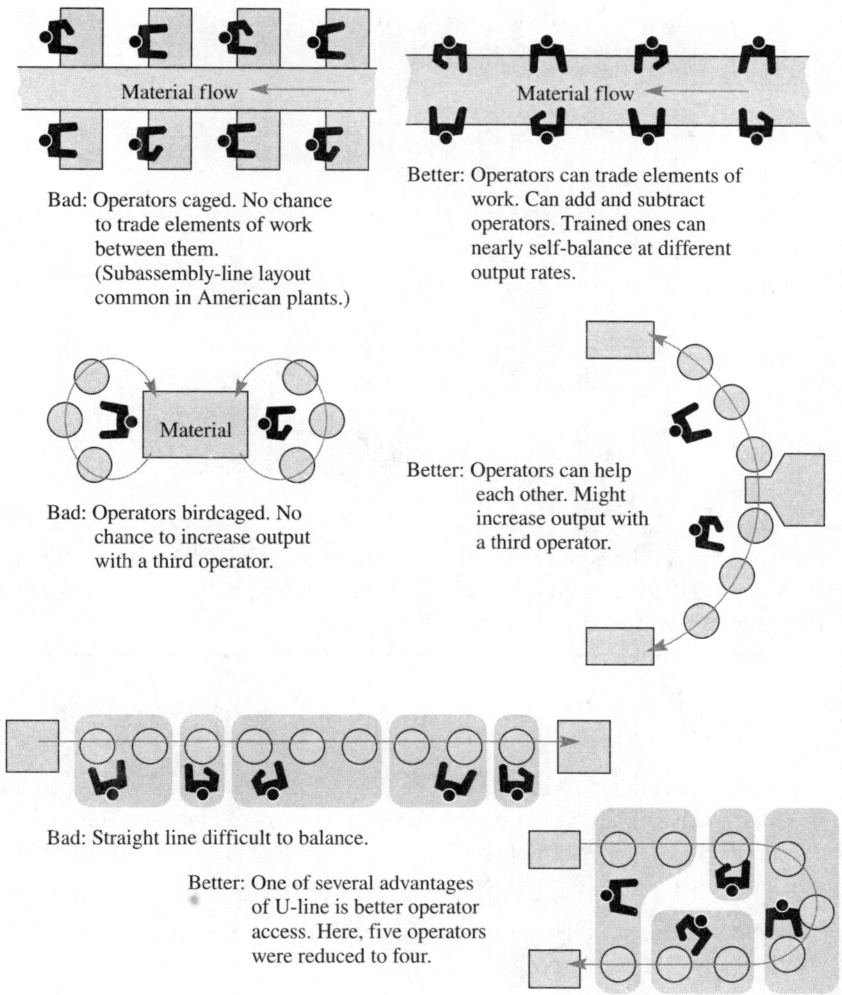

this problem. In our toy company example, the U-shaped line with work-sharing at the bottom of the figure could help resolve the imbalance.

Mixed-Model Line Balancing

Mixed-model line balancing involves scheduling several different models to be produced over a given day or week on the same line in a cyclical fashion. This approach is used by JIT manufacturers such as Toyota. Its objective is to meet the demand for a variety of products and to avoid building high inventories.

EXAMPLE 8.3 Mixed-Model Line Balancing

To illustrate how this is done, suppose our toy company has a fabrication line to bore holes in its Model J wagon frame and its Model K wagon frame. The time required to bore the holes is different for each wagon type.

Assume that the final assembly line downstream requires equal numbers of Model J and Model K wagon frames. Assume also that we want to develop a cycle time for the fabrication line that is balanced for the production of equal numbers of J and K frames. Of course, we could produce Model J frames for several days and then produce Model K frames until an equal number of frames have been produced. However, this would build up unnecessary work-in-process inventory.

Analytics

If we want to reduce the amount of in-process inventory, we could develop a cycle mix that greatly reduces inventory buildup while keeping within the restrictions of equal numbers of J and K wagon frames.

Process times: 6 minutes per J and 4 minutes per K.

The day consists of 480 minutes (8 hours × 60 minutes).

SOLUTION

$$6J + 4K = 480$$

Because equal numbers of J and K are to be produced (or J = K), produce 48J and 48K per day, or 6J and 6K per hour.

The following shows one balance of J and K frames.

Balanced Mixed-Model Sequence

Model sequence	JJ	KKK	JJ	JJ	KKK	
Operation time	6 6	4 4 4	6 6	6 6	4 4 4	Repeats 8 times per day
Minicycle time	12	12	12	12	12	
Total cycle time			60			

This line is balanced at 6 frames of each type per hour with a minicycle time of 12 minutes.

Another balance is J K K J K J, with times of 6, 4, 4, 6, 4, 6. This balance produces 3J and 3K every 30 minutes with a minicycle time of 10 minutes (JK, KJ, KJ).

Cells

Cellular layouts allocate dissimilar machines into cells to work on products that have similar shapes and processing requirements. Manufacturing cell layouts are now widely used in metal fabricating, computer chip manufacture, and assembly work. The overall objective is to gain the benefits of assembly lines in workcenter kinds of production. These benefits include

1. **Better human relations.** Cells consist of a few workers who form a small work team; a team turns out complete units of work.
2. **Improved operator expertise.** Workers see only a limited number of different parts in a finite production cycle, so repetition means quick learning.
3. **Less in-process inventory and material handling.** A cell combines several production stages, so fewer parts travel through the shop.
4. **Faster production setup.** Fewer jobs mean reduced tooling and hence faster tooling changes.

Developing a Manufacturing Cell Shifting from a workcenter layout to a cellular layout entails three steps:

1. Grouping parts into families that follow a common sequence of steps. This step requires developing and maintaining a computerized parts classification and coding system. This is often a major expense with such systems, although many companies have developed shortcut procedures for identifying parts families.
2. Identifying dominant flow patterns of parts families as a basis for location or relocation of processes.
3. Physically grouping machines and processes into cells. Often, there will be parts that cannot be associated with a family, and specialized machinery that cannot be placed in any one cell because of its general use. These unattached parts and machinery are placed in a "remainder cell."

Exhibit 8.12 illustrates the cell development process for four part families. Part A shows the original workcenter layout. Part B shows a routing matrix based on flow of parts. Part C illustrates the final organization of cells, with equipment organized in the traditional U shape. The example assumes that there are multiple lathes, mills, and so forth, so that each cell will have the requisite number of each type physically located within it.

EXHIBIT 8.12

Development of Manufacturing Cell

A. Original workcenter layout

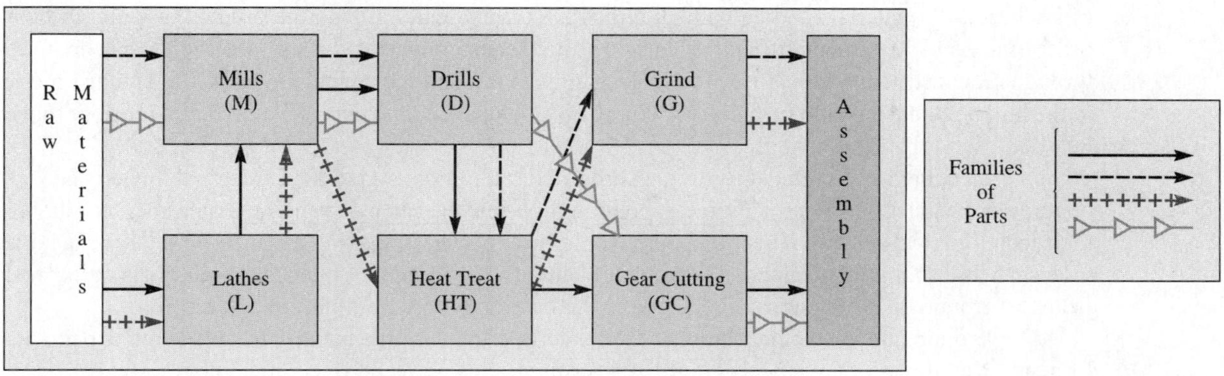

B. Routing matrix based upon flow of parts

Raw Materials	Part Family	Lathes	Mills	Drills	Heat Treating	Grinders	Gear Cutting	To	Assembly
	--->		X	X	X	X		--->	
	▷–▷–		X	X			X	▷–▷–	
	——>	X	X	X	X		X	——>	
	+++>	X	X		X	X		+++>	

C. Reallocating machines to form cells according to part family processing requirements.

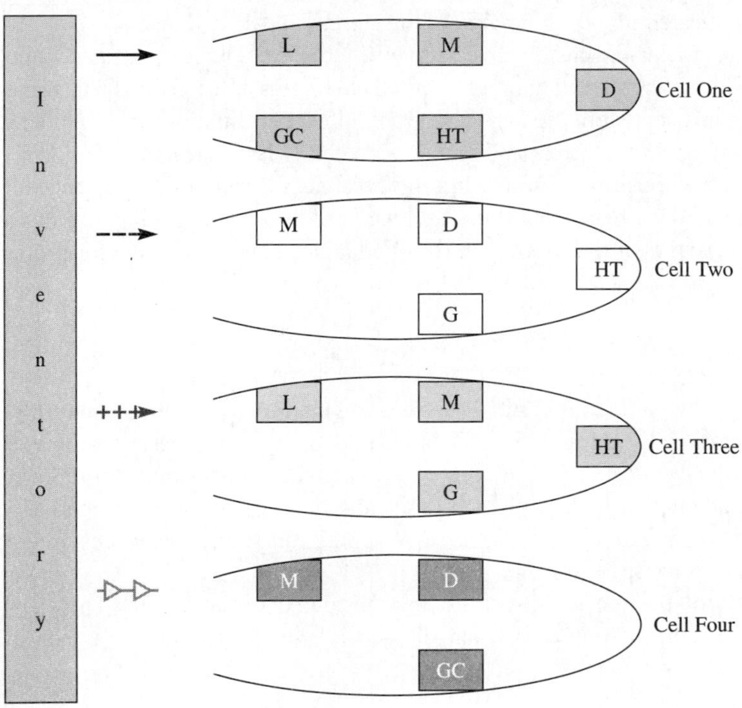

Virtual Manufacturing Cells When equipment is not easily movable, many companies dedicate a given machine out of a set of identical machines in a workcenter layout. A virtual manufacturing cell for, say, a two-month production run for the job might consist of Drill 1 in the drills area, Mill 3 in the mill area, and Assembly Area 1 in the machine assembly area. To approximate cell flow, all work on the particular part family would be done only on these specific machines.

Project Layouts

Project layouts are characterized by a relatively low number of production units in comparison with workcenter and assembly-line formats. In developing a project layout, visualize the product as the hub of a wheel with materials and equipment arranged concentrically around the production point in their order of use and movement difficulty. Thus, in building custom yachts, for example, rivets that are used throughout construction would be placed close to or in the hull; heavy engine parts, which must travel to the hull only once, would be placed at a more distant location; and cranes would be set up close to the hull because of their constant use.

In a project layout, a high degree of task ordering is common, and to the extent that this precedence determines production stages, a project layout might be developed by arranging materials according to their technological priority. This procedure would be expected in making a layout for a large machine tool, such as a stamping machine, where manufacture follows a rigid sequence. Assembly is performed from the ground up, with parts being added to the base in almost a building-block fashion.

As far as quantitative layout techniques are concerned, there is little in the literature devoted to project formats, even though they have been utilized for thousands of years. In certain situations, however, it may be possible to specify objective criteria and develop a project layout through quantitative means. For instance, if the material handling cost is significant and the construction site permits more or less straight-line material movement, the workcenter layout technique might be advantageously employed.

LO 8-2

Illustrate the layouts used in nonmanufacturing settings

RETAIL SERVICE LAYOUT

The objective of a *retail service layout* (as is found in stores, banks, and restaurants) is to maximize net profit per square foot of store space. A company that has been very successful leveraging every inch of its layout space to achieve this objective is Apple Computer. Exhibit 8.13 illustrates an Apple retail store layout. Customers enter and exit the store from the "cashwrap" area. The entry-level products (Macs and iPods) are located in the first section on the left and right in counter and wall displays. Accessories for these products are located in the center area of the store.

All Apple stores feature a Genius bar, where customers can receive technical advice or set up service and repair for their products. To address increasing numbers of iPod customers at the Genius bar, some new stores also feature an iPod bar. Most stores feature a station called The Studio, a Genius bar–like setting where customers can meet with a "Creative" and receive help with projects ranging from organizing a photo album to music composition to film editing. The areas for trying out the products and "experimenting" are located toward the rear of the store. Software and books also are located in the rear of the store. A special area for kids, with low seating and a round table, provides an area for trying out popular products.

Servicescapes

As previously noted, the broad objective of layout in retail services is generally to maximize net profit per square foot of floor space. Operationally, this goal is often translated into such criteria as "minimize handling cost" or "maximize product exposure." However, employing these and similar criteria in service layout planning results in stores that look like warehouses and requires shoppers to approach the task like order pickers or display case stockers. Of course, Walmart and Home Depot customers gladly accept such arrangements for price savings.

Other, more humanistic aspects of the service also must be considered in the layout. The term *servicescape* refers to the physical surroundings in which the service takes place and how these

EXHIBIT 8.13

Apple Retail Store Layout

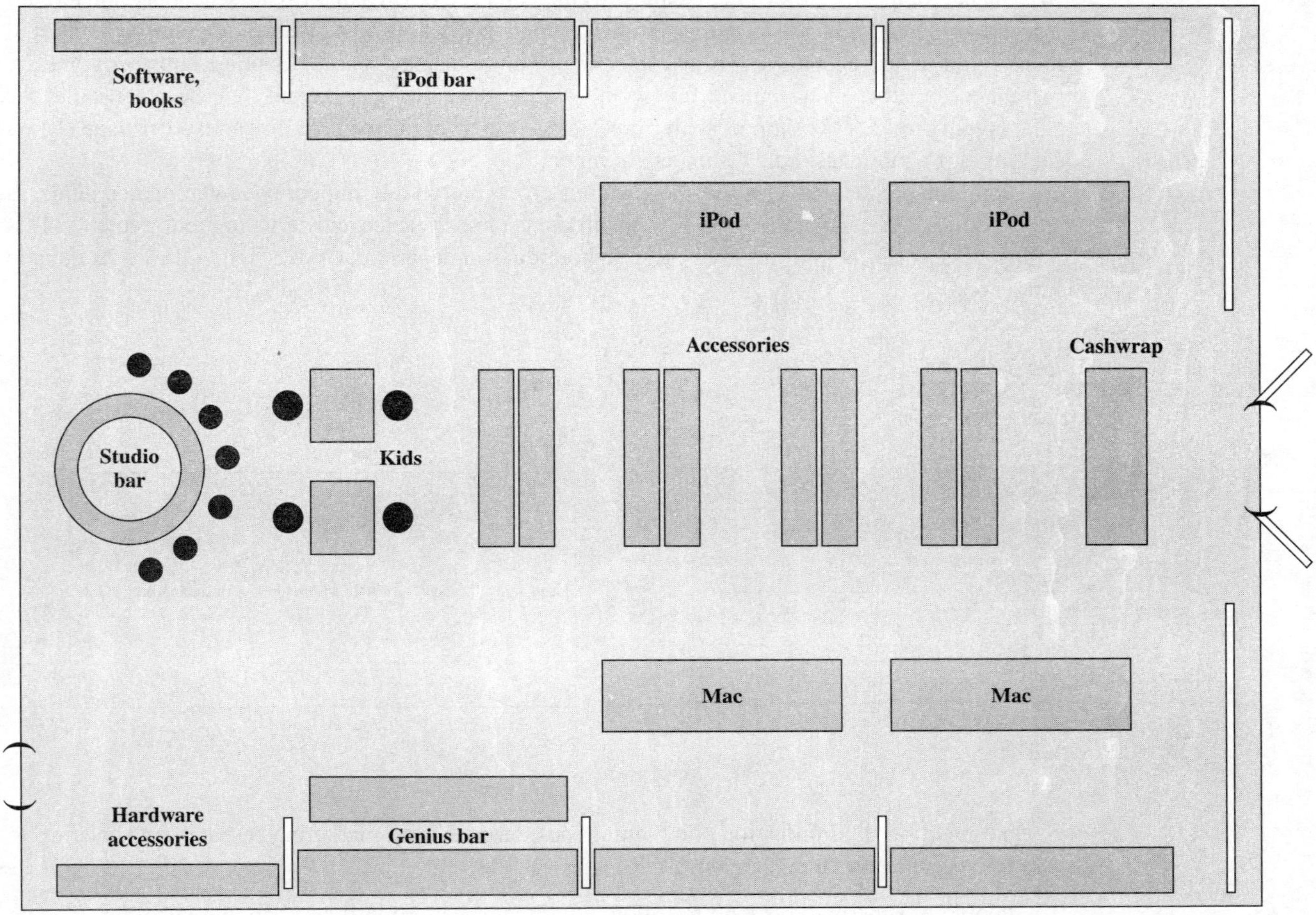

surroundings affect customers and employees. An understanding of the service-scape is necessary to create a good layout for the service firm (or the service-related portions of the manufacturing firm). The servicescape has three elements that must be considered: the ambient conditions; the spatial layout and functionality; and the signs, symbols, and artifacts.

> **Key Idea**
> In a retail setting, the layout is designed to increase sales rather than minimize cost, as done in a manufacturing layout.

The term *ambient conditions* refers to background characteristics such as the noise level, music, lighting, temperature, and scent that can affect employee performance and morale as well as customers' perceptions of the service, how long they stay, and how much money they spend. Although many of these characteristics are influenced primarily by the design of the building (such as the placement of light fixtures, acoustic tiles, and exhaust fans), the layout within a building also can have an effect. Areas near food preparation will smell like food, lighting in a hallway outside a theater must be dim, tables near a stage will be noisy, and locations near an entrance will be drafty.

Two aspects of the *spatial layout and functionality* are especially important: planning the circulation path of the customers and grouping the merchandise. The goal of circulation planning is to provide a path for the customers that exposes them to as much of the merchandise as possible while placing any needed services along this path in the sequence they will be needed. For example, IKEA furniture stores are designed to ensure that customers pass every product before they pay and leave. They also place snack bars along the way so that shoppers can grab a bite to eat without getting off the path. Aisle characteristics are of particular importance. Aside from determining the number of aisles to be provided, decisions must be made as to the width of the aisles because this is a direct function of expected or desired traffic. Aisle width also can affect the direction of flow through the service. Some retail stores are designed so that turning around a shopping cart once you have entered the shopping flow path is virtually impossible. Focal points that catch the customers' attention in the layout also can be used to draw the customers in the desired direction. The famous blue light at Kmart is an example.

To enhance shoppers' view of merchandise as they proceed down a main aisle, secondary and tertiary aisles may be set at an angle. Consider the two layouts in Exhibit 8.14. The rectangular layout would probably require less expensive fixtures and contain more display space. If storage considerations are important to the store management, this would be the more desirable layout. On the other hand, the angular layout provides the shopper with a much clearer view of the merchandise and, other things being equal, presents a more desirable selling environment.

It is common practice now to base merchandise groupings on the shopper's view of related items, as opposed to the physical characteristics of the products or shelf space and servicing requirements. This grouping-by-association philosophy is seen in boutiques in department stores and gourmet sections in supermarkets.

EXHIBIT 8.14

Alternative Store Layouts

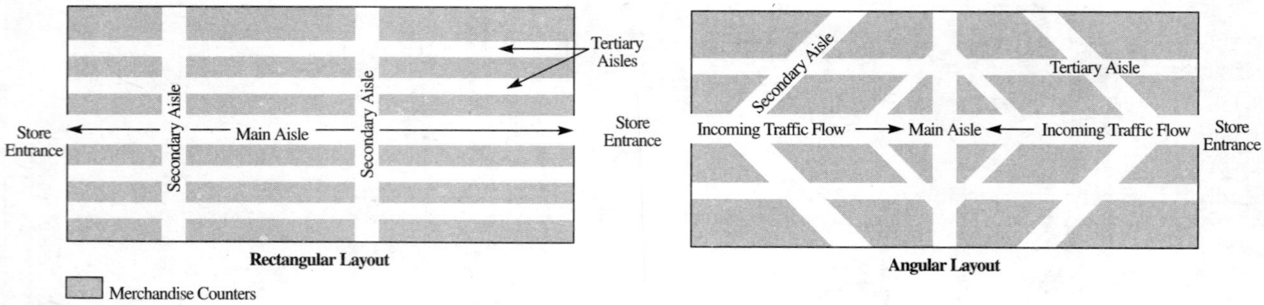

Special mention is in order for a few guidelines derived from marketing research and relating to circulation planning and merchandise grouping:

1. People in supermarkets tend to follow a perimeter pattern in their shopping behavior. Placing high-profit items along the walls of a store will enhance their probability of purchase.
2. Sale merchandise placed at the end of an aisle in supermarkets almost always sells better than the same sale items placed in the interior portion of an aisle.
3. Credit and other nonselling departments that require customers to wait for the completion of their services should be placed either on upper floors or in "dead" areas.
4. In department stores, locations nearest the store entrances and adjacent to front-window displays are most valuable in terms of sales potential.

Signs, Symbols, and Artifacts

Signs, symbols, and artifacts refer to the parts of the service that have social significance. As with the ambiance, these are often a characteristic of the design of the building, although the orientation, location, and size of many objects and areas can carry special meaning. As examples,

- Bank loan officers are easily identified because their desks are typically located in glass-walled offices in the bank.
- A person seated at the standup desk closest to the entrance is usually in charge of greeting customers and directing them to their destination.
- In a workcenter store, the tiled areas may indicate the aisles for travel, while carpeted areas indicate departments for browsing.

As you might have gathered from these examples, the influence of behavioral factors makes the development of hard-and-fast rules for servicescape layout rather difficult. Suffice it to say that determining the layout choice is not simply a matter of choosing between the amount of display space given for a product and the flow of customers through the space. It is a much more complex design issue due to these behavioral factors.

Office Layout

The trend in *office layout* is toward more open offices, with personal work spaces separated only by low divider walls. Companies have removed fixed walls to foster greater communication and teamwork. Signs, symbols, and artifacts, as discussed in the section on service layout, are possibly even more important in office layout than in retailing. For instance, the size and orientation of desks can indicate the importance or professionalism of the people behind them.

Central administration offices are often designed and laid out to convey the desired image of the company. For example, Scandinavian Airlines System's (SAS) administrative office complex outside Stockholm is a two-story collection of glass-walled pods that provide the feeling of the open communication and flat hierarchy (few levels of organization) that characterize the company's management philosophy.

Apple's new headquarters in Cupertino, California, is often referred to as the "spaceship" due to its flying saucer–like design. The environmentally conscious design and methods of construction include the use of recycled water to flush toilets, and gigantic arrays of solar panels to meet much of the building's energy needs. Much of the material from the old building on the site was recycled into new material used to make the new building. All of this reflects Apple's core focus on environmentally friendly products and trend-setting innovation.

CONCEPT CONNECTIONS

LO 8–1 Analyze the common types of manufacturing layouts

Summary

- The focus is on understanding the quantitative techniques used to design manufacturing layouts. The four most common types of layouts employed for manufacturing are the workcenter, assembly line, manufacturing cell, and project layouts.
- Workcenter layouts (often referred to as job shops) involve arranging functional workcenters (areas where a specific type of work is done) to optimize the flow between these areas.
- The assembly-line design is centered on defining the work content of workstations that are typically spaced along the line. This technique is called assembly-line balancing. The workstations need to be defined so that efficiency is maximized while meeting maximum cycle times and precedence constraints. In many settings, it is desirable to make similar items on the same assembly line. This is called mixed-model line balancing.
- Manufacturing cells are used for lower volume settings (compared to assembly lines). The idea is to allocate dissimilar general-purpose machines (like those used in a workcenter) to an area that is designed to produce similar items. Typically, a team of workers perform the work in a cell.

Key Terms

Workcenter Often referred to as a job shop, a process structure suited for low-volume production of a great variety of nonstandard products. Workcenters sometimes are referred to as departments and are focused on a particular type of operation.

Assembly line A setup in which an item is produced through a fixed sequence of workstations, designed to achieve a specific production rate.

Manufacturing cell Groups dissimilar machines to work on products that have similar shapes and processing requirements.

Project layout A setup in which the product remains at one location, and equipment is moved to the product.

Systematic layout planning (SLP) A technique for solving process layout problems when the use of numerical flow data between departments is not practical. The technique uses an activity relationship diagram that is adjusted by trial and error until a satisfactory adjacency pattern is obtained.

Workstation cycle time The time between successive units coming off the end of an assembly line.

Assembly-line balancing The problem of assigning tasks to a series of workstations so that the required cycle time is met and idle time is minimized.

Precedence relationship The required order in which tasks must be performed in an assembly process.

Key Formulas

Workstation cycle time

[8.1] $$C = \frac{\text{Production time per day}}{\text{Required output per day (in units)}}$$

Minimum number of workstations required to satisfy the workstation cycle time constraint

[8.2] $$N_t = \frac{\text{Sum of task times } (T)}{\text{Cycle time } (C)}$$

Effieicncy

[8.2] $$\text{Efficiency} = \frac{\text{Sum of task times } (T)}{\text{Actual number of workstations } (N_a) \times \text{Workstation cycle time } (C)}$$

LO 8–2 Illustrate the layouts used in nonmanufacturing settings

Summary

- Other types of layouts include those used in retail stores and offices.
- In the case of a retail store, the objective is often based on maximizing the net profit per square foot of floor space.

SOLVED PROBLEMS

LO 8–1 SOLVED PROBLEM 1

A university advising office has four rooms, each dedicated to specific problems: petitions (Room A), schedule advising (Room B), grade complaints (Room C), and student counseling (Room D). The office is 80 feet long and 20 feet wide. Each room is 20 feet by 20 feet. The present location of rooms is A, B, C, D—that is, a straight line. The load summary shows the number of contacts that each adviser in a room has with other advisers in the other rooms. Assume that all advisers are equal in this value.

Load summary: $AB = 10, AC = 20, AD = 30, \quad BC = 15, BD = 10, CD = 20.$

a. Evaluate this layout according to the material handling cost method.

b. Improve the layout by exchanging functions within rooms. Show your amount of improvement using the same method as in *a*.

Solution

a.

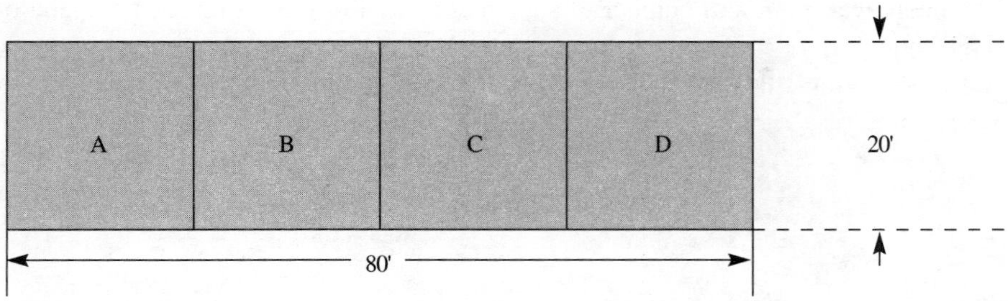

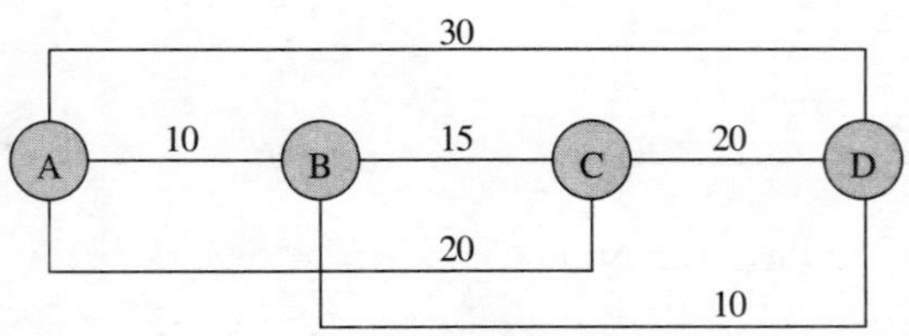

Using the material handling cost method shown in the toy company example (see Exhibits 8.1 through 8.7), we obtain the following costs, assuming that every nonadjacency doubles the initial cost/unit distance:

$AB = 10 \times 1 = 10$
$AC = 20 \times 2 = 40$
$AD = 30 \times 3 = 90$
$BC = 15 \times 1 = 15$
$BD = 10 \times 2 = 20$
$CD = 20 \times 1 = 20$
Current cost = 195

b. A better layout would be *BCDA*.

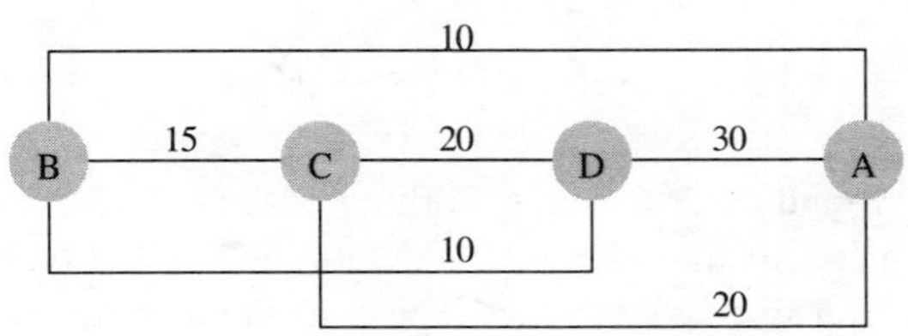

$AB = 10 \times 3 = 30$
$AC = 20 \times 2 = 40$
$AD = 30 \times 1 = 30$
$BC = 15 \times 1 = 15$
$BD = 10 \times 2 = 20$
$CD = 20 \times 1 = 20$
Improved cost = 155

SOLVED PROBLEM 2

The following tasks must be performed on an assembly line in the sequence and times specified.

a. Draw the schematic diagram.

Task	Task Time (Seconds)	Tasks That Must Precede Other Tasks
A	50	–
B	40	–
C	20	A
D	45	C
E	20	C
F	25	D
G	10	E
H	35	B, F, G

a. Draw the schematic diagram.

b. What is the theoretical minimum number of stations required to meet a forecast demand of 400 units per eight-hour day?

c. Use the longest-task-time rule and balance the line in the minimum number of stations to produce 400 units per day.

Solution

a.

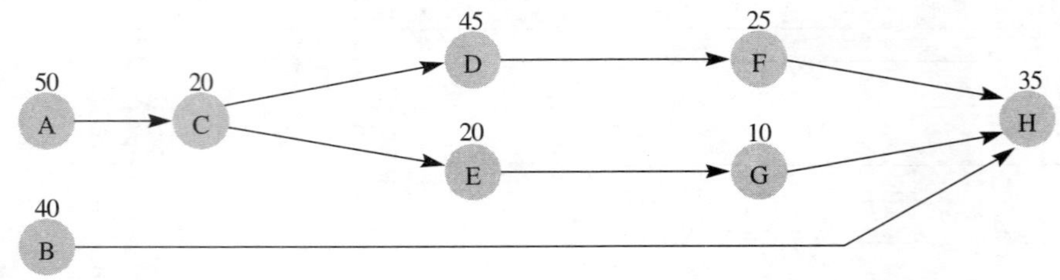

b. The theoretical minimum number of stations to meet $D = 400$ is

$$N_t = \frac{T}{C} = \frac{245 \text{ seconds}}{\left(\frac{60 \text{ seconds} \times 480 \text{ minutes}}{400 \text{ units}}\right)} = \frac{245}{72} = 3.4 \text{ stations}$$

c.

	Task	Task Time (Seconds)	Remaining Unassigned Time	Feasible Remaining Task
Station 1	A	50	22	C
	C	20	2	None
Station 2	D	45	27	E, F
	F	25	2	None
Station 3	B	40	32	E
	E	20	12	G
	G	10	2	None
Station 4	H	35	37	None

SOLVED PROBLEM 3

The manufacturing engineers at Suny Manufacturing were working on a new remote-controlled toy monster truck. They hired a production consultant to help them determine the best type of production process to meet the forecasted demand for this new product. The consultant recommended that they use an assembly line. He told the manufacturing engineers that the line must be able to produce 600 monster trucks per day to meet the demand forecast. The workers in the plant work eight hours per day. The task information for the new monster truck is given as follows.

Task	Task Time (Seconds)	Tasks That Must Precede Other Tasks
A	28	–
B	13	–
C	35	B
D	11	A
E	20	C
F	6	D, E
G	23	F
H	25	F
I	37	G
J	11	G, H
K	27	I, J
Total	236	

a. Draw the schematic diagram.
b. What is the required cycle time to meet the forecasted demand of 600 trucks per day based on an eight-hour workday?
c. What is the theoretical minimum number of workstations given the answer in part (*b*)?
d. Use longest task time, with alphabetical order as the tie breaker, and balance the line in the minimum number of stations to produce 600 trucks per day.
e. Use shortest task time, with largest number of following tasks as the tie breaker, and balance the line in the minimum number of stations to produce 600 trucks per day.

Solution

a.

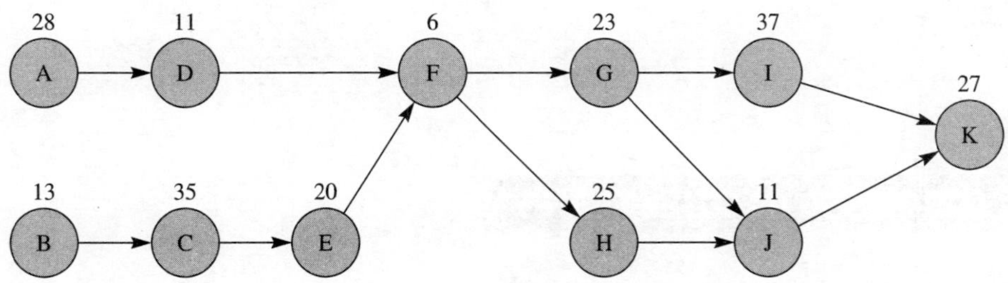

b. $C = \dfrac{\text{Production time per day}}{\text{Output per day}} = \dfrac{60 \text{ seconds} \times 480 \text{ minutes}}{600 \text{ trucks}} = \dfrac{28,800}{600} = 48 \text{ seconds}$

c. $N t = \dfrac{T}{C} = \dfrac{236 \text{ seconds}}{48 \text{ seconds}} = 4.92 = 5(\text{rounded up})$

d.

	Feasible Tasks	Task	Task Time (Seconds)	Remaining Unassigned Time
Station 1	A, B	A	28	20
	B, D	B	13	7
Station 2	C, D	C	35	13
	D	D	11	2
Station 3	E	E	20	28
	F	F	6	22
Station 4	G, H	H	25	23
	G	G	23	0
Station 5	I, J	I	37	11
	J	J	11	0
Station 6	K	K	27	21

e.

Task	Number of Following Tasks
A	7
B	8
C	7
D	6
E	6
F	5
G	3
H	2
I	1
J	1
K	0

	Feasible Tasks	Task	Task Time (Seconds)	Remaining Unassigned Time
Station 1	A, B	B	13	35
	A, C	A	28	7
Station 2	C, D	D	11	37
	C	C	35	2
Station 3	E	E	20	28
	F	F	6	22
Station 4	G, H	G	23	25
	H, I	H	25	0
Station 5	I, J	J	11	37
	I	I	37	0
Station 6	K	K	27	21

DISCUSSION QUESTIONS

LO8-1 1. What kind of layout is used in a physical fitness center?
2. What is the objective of assembly-line balancing? How would you deal with the situation where one worker, although trying hard, is 20 percent slower than the other 10 people on a line?
3. How do you determine the idle time percentage from a given assembly-line balance?
4. What is the essential requirement for mixed-model lines to be practical?
5. Why might it be difficult to develop a manufacturing cell?

LO8-2 6. In what respects is facility layout a marketing problem in services? Give an example of a service system layout designed to maximize the amount of time the customer is in the system.
7. Consider a department store. Which departments probably should not be located near each other? Would any departments benefit from close proximity?
8. How would a flowchart help in planning the servicescape layout? What sorts of features would act as focal points or otherwise draw customers along certain paths through the service? In a supermarket, what departments should be located first along the customers' path? Which should be located last?

OBJECTIVE QUESTIONS

LO8-1 1. Cyprus Citrus Cooperative ships a high volume of individual orders for oranges to northern Europe. The paperwork for the shipping notices is done in the accompanying layout. Revise the layout to improve the flow and conserve space if possible.

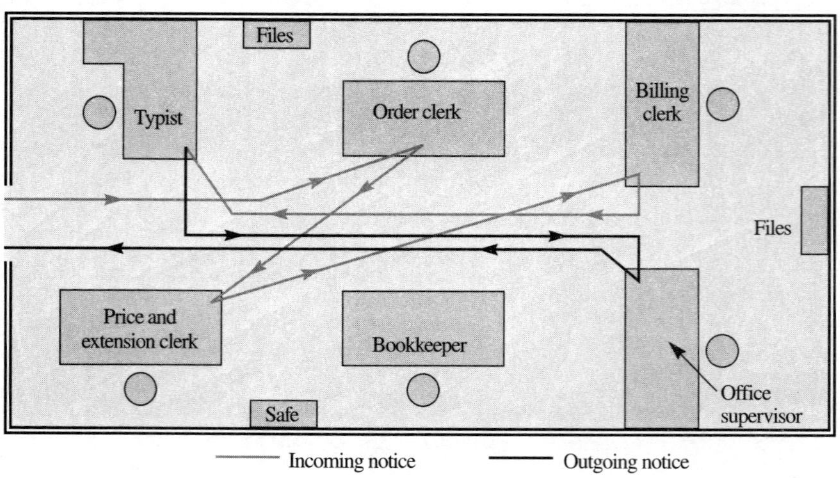

2. S. L. P. Craft would like your help in developing a layout for a new outpatient clinic to be built in California. From analysis of another recently built clinic, she obtains the data shown in the following diagram. This includes the number of trips made by patients between departments on a typical day (shown above the diagonal line) and the lettered weights (defined in Exhibit 8.8C) between departments, as specified by the new clinic's physicians (below the diagonal). The new building will be 60 feet by 20 feet. (Assume distances are measured from the center of the departments and "straight line" to the other department centers.)
   a. Develop an interdepartmental flow graph that considers patient travel trips.
   b. Develop a "good" relationship diagram using systematic layout planning.
   c. Choose either of the layouts obtained in (*a*) or (*b*) and sketch the departments to scale within the building.
   d. Will this layout be satisfactory to the nursing staff? Explain.

Departments	2	3	4	5	6	Area Requirement (Sq. Ft.)
1 Reception	2 / A	5 / O	200 / E	0 / U	10 / O	100
2 X-ray		10 / E	300 / I	0 / U	8 / O	100
3 Surgery			100 / I	0 / U	4 / A	200
4 Examining rooms (5)				0 / U	15 / I	500
5 Lab					3 / O	100
6 Nurses' station						100

3. The Dorton University president has asked the OSCM department to assign eight biology professors (A, B, C, D, E, F, G, and H) to eight offices (numbered 1 to 8 in the diagram) in the new biology building.

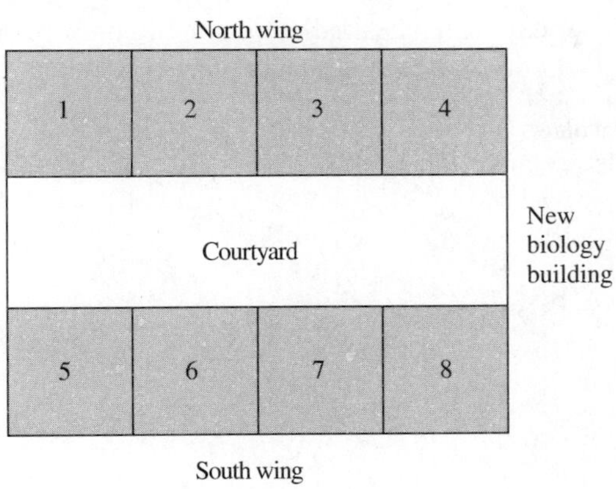

The following distances and two-way flows are given:

Distances between Offices (Feet)

	1	2	3	4	5	6	7	8
1	—	10	20	30	15	18	25	34
2		—	10	20	18	15	18	25
3			—	10	25	18	15	18
4				—	34	25	18	15
5					—	10	20	30
6						—	10	20
7							—	10
8								—

Two-Way Flows (Units per Period)

	A	B	C	D	E	F	G	H
A	—	2	0	0	5	0	0	0
B		—	0	0	0	3	0	2
C			—	0	0	0	0	3
D				—	4	0	0	0
E					—	1	0	0
F						—	1	0
G							—	4
H								—

a. If there are no restrictions (constraints) on the assignment of professors to offices, how many alternative assignments are there to evaluate?

b. The biology department has sent the following information and requests to the OSCM department:

Offices 1, 4, 5, and 8 are the only offices with windows.

A must be assigned Office 1.

D and E, the biology department co-chairpeople, must have windows.

H must be directly across the courtyard from D.

A, G, and H must be in the same wing.

F must *not* be next to D or G or directly across from G.

Find the optimal assignment of professors to offices that meets all the requests of the biology department and minimizes total material handling cost. You may use the path flow list as a computational aid.

Path	Flow	Path	Flow	Path	Flow	Path	Flow	Path	Flow
A–B	2	B–C	0	C–D	0	D–E	4	E–F	1
A–C	0	B–D	0	C–E	0	D–F	0	E–G	0
A–D	0	B–E	0	C–F	0	D–G	0	E–H	0
A–E	5	B–F	3	C–G	0	D–H	0	F–G	1
A–F	0	B–G	0	C–H	3			F–H	0
A–G	0	B–H	2					G–H	4
A–H	0								

4. An assembly line makes two models of trucks: a Buster and a Duster. Busters take 12 minutes each and Dusters take 8 minutes each. The daily output requirement is 24 of each per day. Develop a perfectly balanced mixed-model sequence to satisfy demand.
5. An assembly line is to operate eight hours per day with a desired output of 240 units per day. The following table contains information on this product's task times and precedence relationships.

Task	Task Time (Seconds)	Immediate Predecessor
A	60	–
B	80	A
C	20	A
D	50	A
E	90	B, C
F	30	C, D
G	30	E, F
H	60	G

a. Draw the precedence diagram. (Answers in Appendix D)

b. What is the workstation cycle time required to produce 240 units per day?

c. Balance this line using the longest task time.

d. What is the efficiency of your line balance, assuming it is running at the cycle time from part (*b*)?

6. The desired daily output for an assembly line is 360 units. This assembly line will operate 450 minutes per day. The following table contains information on this product's task times and precedence relationships.

a. Draw the precedence diagram.

b. What is the workstation cycle time required to produce 360 units per day?

Task	Task Time (Seconds)	Immediate Predecessor
A	30	–
B	35	A
C	30	A
D	35	B
E	15	C
F	65	C
G	40	E, F
H	25	D, G

c. Balance this line using the largest number of following tasks. Use the longest task time as a secondary criterion.

d. What is the efficiency of your line balance, assuming it is running at the cycle time from part (*b*)?

7. Some tasks and the order in which they must be performed according to their assembly requirements are shown in the following table. These are to be combined into workstations to create an assembly line. The assembly line operates 7½ hours per day. The output requirement is 1,000 units per day.

Task	Preceding Tasks	Time (Seconds)
A	–	15
B	A	24
C	A	6
D	B	12
E	B	18
F	C	7
G	C	11
H	D	9
I	E	14
J	F, G	7
K	H, I	15
L	J, K	10

a. What is the workstation cycle time required to produce 1,000 units per day?

b. Balance the line using the longest task time based on the 1,000-unit forecast, stating which tasks would be done in each workstation.

c. For (*b*), what is the efficiency of your line balance, assuming it is running at the cycle time from part (*a*)?

d. After production was started, Marketing realized that it understated demand and must increase output to 1,100 units. What action would you take? Be specific and quantitative in your answer.

8. An initial solution has been given to the following workcenter layout problem. Given the flows described and a cost of $2.00 per unit per foot, compute the total cost for the layout. Each location is 100 feet long and 50 feet wide as shown in the following figure. Use the centers of departments for distances and measure distance using metropolitan-rectilinear distance.

Department		A	B	C	D
	A	0	10	25	55
Department	B		0	10	5
	C			0	15
	D				0

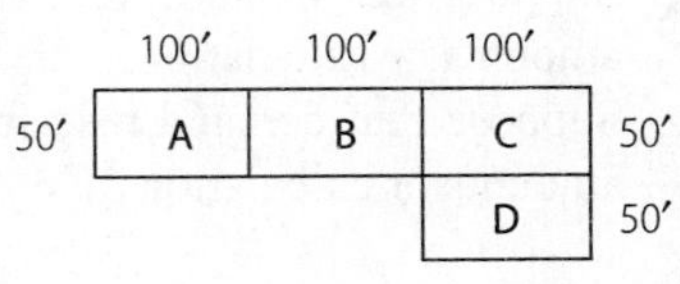

9. An assembly line is to be designed to operate 7½ hours per day and supply a steady demand of 300 units per day. Here are the tasks and their performance times:

Task	Preceding Tasks	Performance Time (Seconds)
a	–	70
b	–	40
c	–	45
d	a	10
e	b	30
f	c	20
g	d	60
h	e	50
i	f	15
j	g	25
k	h, i	20
l	j, k	25

a. Draw the precedence diagram.
b. What is the workstation cycle time required to produce 300 units per day?
c. What is the theoretical minimum number of workstations?
d. Assign tasks to workstations using the longest operating time.
e. What is the efficiency of your line balance, assuming it is running at the cycle time from part (*b*)?
f. Suppose demand increases by 10 percent. How would you react to this? Assume you can operate only 7½ hours per day.

10. The following tasks are to be performed on an assembly line.

Task	Seconds	Tasks That Must Precede It
A	20	–
B	7	A
C	20	B
D	22	B
E	15	C
F	10	D
G	16	E, F
H	8	G

The workday is seven hours long. The demand for the completed product is 750 per day. (Answers in Appendix D)

a. Find the cycle time required to produce 750 units per day.
b. What is the theoretical number of workstations?
c. Draw the precedence diagram.
d. Balance the line using sequential restrictions and the longest-operating-time rule.
e. What is the efficiency of the line balanced as in part (*d*), assuming it is running at the cycle time from part (*a*)?
f. Suppose that demand rose from 750 to 800 units per day. What would you do? Show any amounts or calculations.
g. Suppose that demand rose from 750 to 1,000 units per day. What would you do? Show any amounts or calculations.

11. The flow of materials through eight departments is shown as follows. Even though the table shows flows into and out of the different departments, assume that the direction of flow is not important. In addition, assume that the cost of moving material depends only on the distance moved.

	Departments							
	1	2	3	4	5	6	7	8
1	–	20						
2	15	–	25				4	
3		5	–	40	5			
4			5	–	10			
5	1			20	–	30		
6						–	20	
7				3			–	10
8							5	–

a. Construct a schematic layout where the departments are arranged on a 2 × 4 grid with each cell representing a 10-by-10-meter square area.

b. Evaluate your layout using a distance-times-flow measure. Assume that distance is measured rectilinearly (in this case, departments that are directly adjacent are 10 meters apart and those that are diagonal to one another are 20 meters apart).

12. A firm uses a serial assembly system and needs answers to the following:

a. An output of 900 units per shift (7.5 hours) is desired for a new processing system. The system requires product to pass through four stations where the work content at each station is 30 seconds. What is the required cycle time for such a system?

b. How efficient is your system with the cycle time you calculated?

c. Station 3 changes and now requires 45 seconds to complete. What will need to be done to meet demand (assume only 7.5 hours are available)? What is the efficiency of the new system?

13. The Sun River beverage company is a regional producer of teas, exotic juices, and energy drinks. With an interest in healthier lifestyles, there has been an increase in demand for its sugar-free formulation.

The final packing operation requires 13 tasks. Sun River bottles its sugar-free product 5 hours a day, 5 days a week. Each week, there is a demand for 3,000 bottles of this product. Using the following data, solve the assembly-line balancing problem and calculate the efficiency of your solution, assuming the line runs at the cycle time required to meet demand. Use the longest task time for your decision criteria. Use the largest number of following tasks as a secondary criterion.

Task	Performance Time (Minutes)	Tasks That Must Follow
1	0.1	–
2	0.1	1
3	0.1	2
4	0.2	2
5	0.1	2
6	0.2	3, 4, 5
7	0.1	1
8	0.15	7
9	0.3	8
10	0.5	9
11	0.2	6
12	0.2	10, 11
13	0.1	12

14. Consider the following tasks, times, and predecessors for an assembly of set-top cable converter boxes.

Task Element	Time (Minutes)	Element Predecessor
A	1	–
B	1	A
C	2	B
D	1	B
E	3	C, D
F	1	A
G	1	F
H	2	G
I	1	E, H

Given a cycle time of four minutes, develop two alternative layouts. Use the longest task time rule and the largest number of following tasks as a secondary criterion.
What is the efficiency of your layouts, assuming the 4-minute cycle time?

ADVANCED PROBLEMS

15. Francis Johnson's plant needs to design an efficient assembly line to make a new product. The assembly line needs to produce 15 units per hour, and there is room for only four workstations. The tasks and the order in which they must be performed are shown in the following table. Tasks cannot be split, and it would be too expensive to duplicate any task.

Task	Task Time (Minutes)	Immediate Predecessor
A	1	–
B	2	–
C	3	–
D	1	A, B, C
E	3	C
F	2	E
G	3	E

a. Draw the precedence diagram.
b. What is the workstation cycle time required to produce 15 units per hour?
c. Balance the line so that only four workstations are required. Use whatever method you feel is appropriate.
d. What is the efficiency of your line balance, assuming the cycle time from part (*b*)?

LO8-2 16. In manufacturing layout design, the key concern is the resulting efficiency of the operation. In retail service operations, what is the primary concern or objective?
17. What is the term used to refer to the physical surroundings in which service operations occur and how these surroundings affect customers and employees?
18. What are the three terms used to describe the parts of a service operation that have *social significance*?

ANALYTICS EXERCISE: DESIGNING A MANUFACTURING PROCESS

Toshiba's Notebook Computer Assembly Line

Toshihiro Nakamura, manufacturing engineering section manager, is examining the prototype assembly process sheet (shown in Exhibit 8.15) for the newest subnotebook computer model. With every new model introduced, management felt that the assembly line had to increase productivity and lower costs, usually resulting in changes to the assembly process. When a new model is designed, considerable attention is directed toward reducing the number of components and simplifying parts production and assembly requirements. This new computer was a marvel of high-tech, low-cost innovation and should give Toshiba an advantage during the upcoming fall/winter selling season.

Production of the subnotebook is scheduled to begin in 10 days. Initial production for the new model is to be 150 units per day, increasing to 250 units per day the following week (management thought that eventually production would reach 300 units per day). Assembly lines at the plant normally are staffed by 10 operators who work at a 14.4-meter-long assembly line. The line is organized in a straight line with workers shoulder to shoulder on one side. The line can accommodate up to 12 operators if there is a need. The line normally operates for 7.5 hours a day (employees work from 8:15 A.M. to 5:00 P.M. and regular hours includes one hour of unpaid lunch and 15 minutes of scheduled breaks). It is possible to run one, two, or three hours of overtime, but employees need at least three days' notice for planning purposes.

EXHIBIT 8.15

Notebook Computer Assembly Process Sheet

Task	Task Time (Seconds)	Tasks That Must Precede This Task
1. Assemble Cover	75	None
2. Install LCD in Cover	61	Task 1
3. Prepare Base Assembly	24	None
4. Install M-PCB in Base	36	Task 3
5. Install CPU	22	Task 4
6. Install Backup Batteries and Test	39	Task 4
7. Install Accupoint Pointing Device and Wrist Rest	32	Task 4
8. Install Speaker and Microphone	44	Task 4
9. Install Auxiliary Printed Circuit Board (A-PCB) on M-PCB	29	Task 4
10. Prepare and Install Keyboard	26	Task 9
11. Prepare and Install Digital Video Drive (DVD) and Hard Disk Drive (HDD)	52	Task 10
12. Install Battery Pack	7	Task 11
13. Insert Memory Card	5	Task 12
14. Start Software Load	11	Tasks 2, 5, 6, 7, 8, 13
15. Software Load (labor not required)	310	Task 14
16. Test Video Display	60	Task 15
17. Test Keyboard	60	Task 16

The Assembly Line

At the head of the assembly line, a computer displays the daily production schedule, consisting of a list of model types and corresponding lot sizes scheduled to be assembled on the line. The models are simple variations of hard disk size, memory, and battery power. A typical production schedule includes seven or eight model types in lot sizes varying from 10 to 100 units. The models are assembled sequentially: All the units of the first model are assembled, followed by all the units of the second, and so on. This computer screen also indicates how far along the assembly line is in completing its daily schedule, which serves as a guide for the material handlers who supply parts to the assembly lines.

The daily schedules are shared with the nearby Fujihashi Parts Collection and Distribution Center. Parts are brought from Fujihashi to the plant within two hours of when they are needed. The material supply system is very tightly coordinated and works well.

The assembly line consists of a 14.4-meter conveyor belt that carries the computers, separated at 1.2-meter intervals by white stripes on the belt. Workers stand shoulder to shoulder on one side of the conveyor and work on the units as they move by. In addition to the assembly workers, a highly skilled worker, called a "supporter," is assigned to each line. The supporter moves along the line, assisting workers who are falling behind and replacing workers who need to take a break. Supporters also make decisions about what to do when problems are encountered during the assembly process (such as a defective part). The line speed and the number of workers vary from day to day, depending on production demand and the workers' skills and availability. Although the assembly line has 12 positions, often they are not all used.

Exhibit 8.16 provides details of how the engineers who designed the new subnotebook computer felt that the new line should be organized. These engineers designed the line assuming that one notebook would be assembled every two minutes by six line workers.

The following is a brief description of what is done at each workstation:

Workstation 1: The first operator lays out the major components of a computer between two white lines on the conveyor. The operator then prepares the cover for accepting the LCD screen by installing fasteners and securing a cable.

Workstation 2: The second operator performs two different tasks. First, the LCD screen is installed in the cover. This task needs to be done after the cover is assembled (task 1). A second independent task done by the operator is the preparation of the base so that the main printed circuit board (M-PCB) can be installed.

Workstation 3: Here the M-PCB is installed in the base. After this is done, the central processing unit (CPU) and backup batteries are installed and tested.

Workstation 4: The Accupoint Pointing Device (touch pad) and wrist rest are installed, the speaker and microphone installed, and the auxiliary printed circuit board (A-PCB) installed. These are all independent tasks that can be done after the M-PCB is installed.

Exhibit 8.16

Engineers' Initial Design of the Assembly Line

Assembly-Line Position	Tasks	Workstation Number	Labor Time (seconds)
1	1. Assemble Cover (75)	1	75
2	2. Install LCD in Cover (61) 3. Prepare Base Assembly (24)	2	61 + 24 = 85
3	4. Install Main Printed Circuit Board (M-PCB) in Base (36) 5. Install CPU (22) 6. Install Backup Batteries and Test (39)	3	36 + 22 + 39 = 97
4	7. Install Accupoint Pointing Device and Wrist Rest (32) 8. Install Speaker and Microphone (44) 9. Install Auxiliary Printed Circuit Board (A-PCB) on M-PCB (29)	4	32 + 44 + 29 = 105
5	10. Prepare and Install Keyboard (26) 11. Prepare and Install Digital Video Drive (DVD) and Hard Disk Drive (HDD) (52) 12. Install Battery Pack (7) 13. Insert Memory Card (5) 14. Start Software Load (11) 15. Software Load (19)	5	26 + 52 + 7 + 5 + 11 = 101
6	Software Load (120)		
7	Software Load (120)		
8	Software Load (51)		
9	16. Test Video Display (60) 17. Test Keyboard (60)	6	60 + 60 = 120
10	Empty		
11	Empty		
12	Empty		

Workstation 5: Here tasks are performed in a sequence. First, the keyboard is installed, followed by the DVD and hard disk drive (HDD). The battery pack is then installed, followed by the memory card. The computer is then powered up and a program started that loads software that can be used to test the computer. Actually loading the software takes 310 seconds, and this is done while the computer travels through positions 6, 7, and 8 on the assembly line. Computers that do not work are sent to a rework area where they are fixed. Only about 1 percent of the computers fail to start, and these are usually quickly repaired by the supporter.

Workstation 6: The video display and keyboard are tested in this workstation.

After assembly, the computers are moved to a separate burn-in area that is separate from the assembly line. Here, computers are put in racks for a 24-hour, 25°C "burn-in" of the circuit components. After burn-in, the computer is tested again, software is installed, and the finished notebook computer is packaged and placed on pallets for shipment to Toshiba distribution centers around the world.

Tweaking the Initial Assembly-Line Design

From past experience, Toshihiro has found that the initial assembly-line design supplied by the engineers often needs to be tweaked. Consider the following questions that Toshihiro is considering:

1. What is the daily capacity of the assembly-line designed by the engineers? Assume that the assembly line has a computer at every position when it is started at the beginning of the day.
2. The line designed by the engineers is running at maximum capacity. What is the efficiency of the line relative to its use of labor? Assume that the supporter is not included in efficiency calculations.
3. How should the line be redesigned to operate at the initial 250 units per day target, assuming that no overtime will be used? What is the efficiency of your new design relative to its use of labor?
4. What about running the line at 300 units per day? If overtime were used with the engineers' initial design, how much time would the line need to be run each day?
5. Design an assembly line that can produce 300 units per day without using overtime (specify the tasks at each position in the line as done in Exhibit 8.16)?
6. What other issues might Toshihiro consider when bringing the new assembly line up to speed?

PRACTICE EXAM

In each of the following, name the term defined or answer the question. Answers are listed at the bottom.

1. Three terms commonly used to refer to a layout where similar equipment or functions are grouped together.
2. A layout where the work to make an item is arranged in progressive steps and work is moved between the steps at fixed intervals of time.
3. A measure used to evaluate a workcenter layout.
4. This is a way to shorten the cycle time for an assembly line that has a task time that is longer than the desired cycle time. Assume that it is not possible to speed up the task, split the task, use overtime, or redesign the task.
5. This involves scheduling several different models of a product to be produced over a given day or week on the same line in a cyclical fashion.
6. If you wanted to produce 20 percent of one product (A), 50 percent of another (B), and 30 percent of a third product (C) in a cyclic fashion, what schedule would you suggest?
7. A term used to refer to the physical surroundings in which a service takes place and how these surroundings affect customers and employees.
8. A firm is using an assembly line and needs to produce 500 units during an eight-hour day. What is the required cycle time in seconds?
9. What is the efficiency of an assembly line that has 25 workers and a cycle time of 45 seconds? Each unit produced on the line has 16 minutes of work that needs to be completed based on a time study completed by engineers at the factory.

Answers to Practice Exam 1. Workcenter, job-shop, or functional 2. Assembly line 3. Number of annual movements multiplied by the distance of each movement, and then multiplied by the cost 4. Use parallel workstations 5. Mixed-model line balancing 6. AABBBBBCCC (then repeat) 7. Servicescape 8. 57.6 seconds = (8 × 60 × 60)/500 9. 85% = (16 × 60)/(25 × 45)

For PowerPoint lecture slides, Solutions Manual, Test Bank, Data files for solved examples, Excel Templates, Step-by-Step Solved Examples in video format, Tutorial Videos and many more, scan the adjacent **QR code**, or visit **http://www.mhhe.com/sie-chase15e**

Chapter 9

Service Processes

LEARNING OBJECTIVES

- LO 9–1 Understand the characteristics of service processes
- LO 9–2 Explain how service systems are organized
- LO 9–3 Analyze simple service systems
- LO 9–4 Contrast different service designs

Paying with A Wave of Your Phone

Futurists have long predicted that shoppers at retail stores would soon pay with the waving of a cellphone instead of credit cards. Starbucks, in its stores in the United States, has done this for many years using a special Starbucks card app where customers hold their smartphone in front of a scanner at the cash register. The money is then deducted from their Starbucks account, which they load with credit cards or PayPal funds.

A much more convenient approach from Apple Computer called Apple Pay now allows this to be done at virtually any store. All users have to do is position their iPhone near a reader at the store and hold their finger on the touch ID. A special "near field" antenna, built into the iPhone, connects and completes the transaction. A quick vibration and beep lets the user know the checkout is complete.

Paying with these quick cellphone apps simplifies and quickens the transaction and could reduce waiting in line for everyone.

THE NATURE OF SERVICES

LO 9-1

Understand the characteristics of service processes

Strategy

A glance at the management book section in your local bookstore gives ample evidence of the concern for service among practitioners. The way we now view service parallels the way we view quality: The *customer* is (or should be) the focal point of all decisions and actions of the service organization. This philosophy is captured nicely in the service triangle in Exhibit 9.1. Here, the customer is the center of things—the service strategy, the systems, and the employees who serve him or her. From this view, the organization exists to serve the customer, and the systems and the employees exist to facilitate the process of service. Some suggest that the service organization also exists to serve the workforce because they generally determine how the service is perceived by the customers. Relative to the latter point, the customer gets the kind of service that management deserves; in other words, how management treats the worker is how the worker will treat the public. If the workforce is well trained and well motivated by management, they will do good jobs for their customers.

EXHIBIT 9.1

The Service Triangle

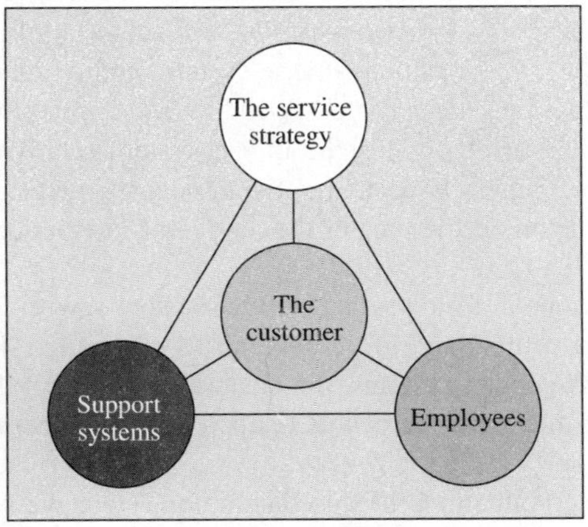

The role of operations in the triangle is a major one. Operations is responsible for service systems (procedures, equipment, and facilities) and is responsible for managing the work of the service workforce, who typically make up the majority of employees in large service organizations. But before we discuss this role in depth, it is useful to classify services to show how the customer affects the operations function.

Every service has a **service package**, which is defined as a bundle of goods and services that is provided in some environment. This bundle consists of five features:

Service package
A bundle of goods and services that is provided in some environment.

1. *Supporting facility:* The physical resources that must be in place before a service can be offered. Examples are an Internet website, a golf course, a ski lift, an airline, and an auto repair facility.
2. *Facilitating goods:* The material purchased or consumed by the buyer or the items provided to the customer. Examples are golf clubs, skis, beverages, auto parts, and services sold by the firm.
3. *Information:* Operations data or information that is provided to the customer, to enable efficient and customized services. Examples include detailed descriptions of the items offered, tee-off times, weather reports, medical records, seat preferences, and item availability.
4. *Explicit services:* The benefits that are readily observable by the senses and that consist of the essential or intrinsic features of the service. Examples are the response time of an ambulance, air conditioning in a hotel room, and a smooth-running car after a tune-up.
5. *Implicit services:* Psychological benefits that the customer may sense only vaguely, or the extrinsic features of the service. Examples are the status of a degree from an Ivy League school, the privacy of a loan office, and worry-free auto repair.

An Operational Classification of Services

Waitress serving a pizza to teenagers in a restaurant.

© Anderson Ross/Blend Images LLC RF

Service organizations are generally classified according to who the customer is, for example, individuals or other businesses, and to the service they provide (financial services, health services, transportation services, and so on). These groupings, though useful in presenting aggregate economic data, are not particularly appropriate for OSCM purposes because they tell us little about the process. Manufacturing, by contrast, has fairly evocative terms to classify production activities (such as intermittent and continuous production). When applied to a manufacturing setting, they readily convey the essence of the process. Although it is possible to describe services in these same terms, we need one additional item of information to reflect the fact that the customer is involved in the production system. That item, which we believe operationally distinguishes one service system from another in its production function, is the extent of customer contact in the creation of the service.

Customer contact refers to the physical presence of the customer in the system, and *creation of the service* refers to the work process involved in providing the service itself. *Extent of contact* here may be roughly defined as the percentage of time the customer must be in the system relative to the total time needed to perform the customer service. Generally speaking, the greater the percentage of contact time between the service system and the customer, the greater the degree of interaction between the two during the production process.

High and low degrees of customer contact
The physical presence of the customer in the system and the percentage of time the customer must be in the system relative to the total time it takes to perform the service.

From this conceptualization, it follows that service systems with a **high degree of customer contact** are more difficult to control and more difficult to rationalize than those with a **low degree of customer contact**. In high-contact systems, the customer can affect the time of demand, the exact nature of the service, and the quality, or perceived quality, of service because the customer is involved in the process.

Exhibit 9.2 describes the implications of this distinction. Here we see that each design decision is impacted by whether the customer is present during service delivery. We also see that when work is done behind the scenes (in this case, in a bank's processing center), it is performed on customer surrogates—reports, databases, and invoices. We can thus design it according to the same principles we would use in designing a factory—to maximize the amount of items processed during the production day.

There can be tremendous diversity of customer influence and, hence, system variability within high-contact service systems. For example, a bank branch offers both simple services such as cash withdrawals that take just a minute or so and complicated services such as loan application preparation that can take in excess of an hour. Moreover, these activities may range from being self-service through an ATM, to coproduction where bank personnel and the customer work as a team to develop the loan application.

LO 9-2 Explain how service systems are organized

DESIGNING SERVICE ORGANIZATIONS

In designing service organizations we must remember one distinctive characteristic of services: We cannot inventory services. Unlike manufacturing, where we can build up inventory during slack periods for peak demand and thus maintain a relatively stable level of employment and production planning, in services we must (with a few exceptions) meet demand as it arises. Consequently, in services, capacity becomes a dominant issue. Think about the many service situations you find yourself in—for example, eating in a restaurant or going to a Saturday night movie. Generally speaking, if the restaurant or the theater is full, you will decide to go someplace else. So, an important design parameter in services is "What capacity should we aim for?" Too much capacity generates excessive costs. Insufficient

EXHIBIT 9.2

Major Differences between High- and Low-Contact Systems in a Bank

Design Decision	High-Contact System (A Branch Office)	Low-Contact System (A Check Processing Center)
Facility location	Operations must be near the customer.	Operations may be placed near supply, transport, or labor.
Facility layout	The facility should accommodate the customer's physical and psychological needs and expectations.	The facility should focus on production efficiency.
Product design	The environment, as well as the physical product, define the nature of the service.	The customer is not in the service environment, so the product can be defined by fewer attributes.
Process design	Stages of production process have a direct, immediate effect on the customer.	The customer is not involved in the majority of processing steps.
Scheduling	The customer is in the production schedule and must be accommodated.	The customer is concerned mainly with completion dates.
Production planning	Orders cannot be stored, so smoothing production flow will result in loss of business.	Both backlogging and production smoothing are possible.
Worker skills	The direct workforce constitutes a major part of the service product and so must be able to interact well with the public.	The direct workforce need only have technical skills.
Quality control	Quality standards are often in the eye of the beholder and, thus, are variable.	Quality standards are generally measurable and, thus, fixed.
Time standards	Service time depends on customer needs, so time standards are inherently loose.	Work is performed on customer surrogates (such as forms), so time standards can be tight.
Wage payment	Variable output requires time-based wage systems.	"Fixable" output permits output-based wage systems.
Capacity planning	To avoid lost sales, capacity must be set to match peak demand.	

capacity leads to lost customers. In these situations, of course, we seek the assistance of marketing to influence demand. This is one reason we have discount airfares, hotel specials on weekends, and so on. This is also a good illustration of why it is difficult to separate the operations management functions from marketing in services.

Waiting line models, which are discussed in Chapter 10, provide a powerful mathematical tool for analyzing many common service situations. Questions such as how many tellers we should have in a bank or how many telephone lines we need in an Internet service operation can be analyzed with these models, and they can easily be implemented using spreadsheets.

Process

Several major factors distinguish service design and development from typical manufactured product development. First, the process and the product must be developed simultaneously; indeed, in services, the process is the product. (We say this with the general recognition that many manufacturers are using such concepts as concurrent engineering and DFM [design for manufacture] as approaches to more closely link product design and process design.)

Second, although equipment and software that support a service can be protected by patents and copyrights, a service operation itself lacks the legal protection commonly available to goods production. Third, the service package, rather than a definable good, constitutes the major output of the development process. Fourth, many parts of the service package are often defined by the training individuals receive before they become part of the service organization. In particular, in professional service organizations (PSOs) such as law firms and hospitals, prior certification is necessary for hiring. Fifth, many service organizations can change their service offerings virtually overnight. Routine service organizations (RSOs) such as barbershops, retail stores, and restaurants have this flexibility.

Key Ideas

When reflecting on the effectiveness of service encounters, consider your experiences with servers who try to sell you something in addition to what you are already purchasing. Additionally, consider "self-service" where the customer does the work. How does this fit into the matrix? This is discussed later in the chapter.

Strategy

Structuring the Service Encounter: The Service-System Design Matrix

Service encounters can be configured in a number of different ways. The service-system design matrix in Exhibit 9.3 identifies six common alternatives.

The top of the matrix shows the degree of customer/server contact: the *buffered core,* which is physically separated from the customer; the *permeable system,* which is penetrable by the customer via phone or face-to-face contact; and the *reactive system,* which is both penetrable and reactive to the customer's requirements. The left side of the matrix shows what we believe to be a logical marketing proposition—namely, that the greater the amount of contact, the greater the sales opportunity; the right side shows the impact on production efficiency as the customer exerts more influence on the operation.

The entries within the matrix list the ways in which service can be delivered. At one extreme, service contact is by mail; customers have little interaction with the system. At the other extreme, customers "have it their way" through face-to-face contact. The remaining four entries in the matrix contain varying degrees of interaction.

As one would guess, process efficiency decreases as the customer has more contact (and therefore more influence) on the system. To offset this, the face-to-face contact provides a high sales opportunity to sell additional products. Conversely, low contact, such as mail, allows the system to work more efficiently because the customer is unable to significantly affect (or disrupt) the system. However, there is relatively little opportunity for additional product sales.

EXHIBIT 9.3

Service-System Design Matrix

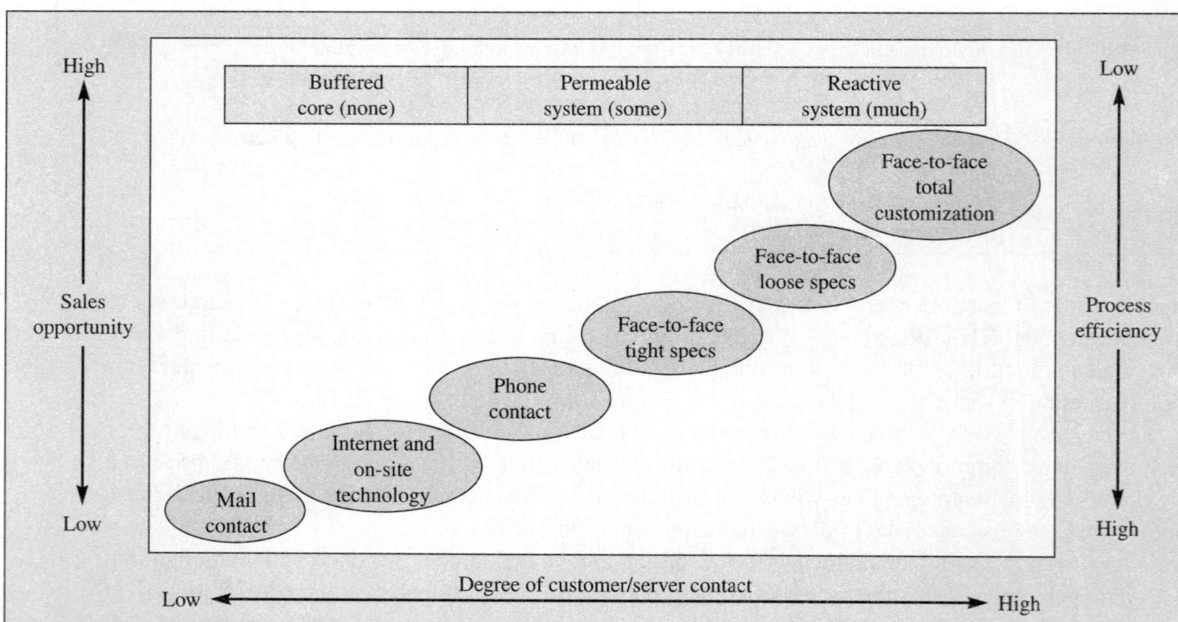

Characteristics of Workers, Operations, and Innovations Relative to the Degree of Customer/Service Contact

Degree of customer/server contact: Low → High

Worker requirements	Clerical skills	Helping skills	Verbal skills	Procedural skills	Trade skills	Diagnostic skills
Focus of operations	Paper handling	Demand management	Scripting calls	Flow control	Capacity management	Client mix
Technological innovations	Office automation	Routing methods	Computer databases	Electronic aids	Self-serve	Client/worker teams

There can be some shifting in the positioning of each entry. For our first example, consider the "Internet and on-site technology" entry in the matrix. The Internet clearly buffers the company from the customer, but interesting opportunities are available to provide relevant information and services to the customer. Because the website can be programmed to intelligently react to the inputs of the customer, significant opportunities for new sales may be possible. In addition, the system can be made to interface with real employees when the customer needs assistance that goes beyond the programming of the website. The Internet is truly a revolutionary technology when applied to the services that need to be provided by a company.

Another example of shifting in the positioning of an entry can be shown with the "face-to-face tight specs" entry in the matrix. This entry refers to those situations where there is little variation in the service process—neither customer nor server has much discretion in creating the service. Fast-food restaurants and Disneyland come to mind. Face-to-face loose specs refer to situations where the service process is generally understood but there are options in how it will be performed or in the physical goods that are part of it. A full-service restaurant and a car sales agency are examples. Face-to-face total customization refers to service encounters whose specifications must be developed through some interaction between the customer and server. Legal and medical services are of this type, and the degree to which the resources of the system are mustered for the service determines whether the system is reactive, possibly to the point of even being proactive, or merely permeable. Examples would be the mobilization of an advertising firm's resources in preparation for an office visit by a major client or an operating team scrambling to prepare for emergency surgery.

The changes in workers, operations, and types of technical innovations as the degree of customer/service system contact changes are described in the bottom of Exhibit 9.3. For worker requirements, the relationships between mail contact and clerical skills, Internet technology and helping skills, and phone contact and verbal skills are self-evident. Face-to-face tight specs require procedural skills in particular, because the worker must follow the routine in conducting a generally standardized, high-volume process. Face-to-face loose specs frequently call for trade skills (bank teller, draftsperson, maitre d', dental hygienist) to finalize the design for the service. Face-to-face total customization tends to call for diagnostic skills of the professional to ascertain the needs or desires of the client.

Strategic Uses of the Matrix The matrix in Exhibit 9.3 has both operational and strategic uses. The operational uses are reflected in their identification of worker requirements, focus of operations, and innovations previously discussed. The strategic uses include

1. Enabling systematic integration of operations and marketing strategy. Trade-offs become more clear-cut, and, more important, at least some of the major design variables are crystallized for analysis purposes. For example, the matrix indicates that it would make little sense relative to sales for a service firm to invest in high-skilled workers if it plans to operate using tight specs.
2. Clarifying exactly which combination of service delivery the firm is in fact providing. As the company incorporates the delivery options listed on the diagonal, it is becoming diversified in its production process.
3. Permitting comparison with how other firms deliver specific services. This helps to pinpoint a firm's competitive advantage.
4. Indicating evolutionary or life cycle changes that might be in order as the firm grows. Unlike the product–process matrix for manufacturing, however, where natural growth moves in one direction (from workcenter to assembly line as volume increases), evolution of service delivery can move in either direction along the diagonal as a function of a sales–efficiency trade-off.

Virtual Service: The New Role of the Customer The service–system design matrix was developed from the perspective of the production system's utilization of company resources. With the advent of virtual services through the Internet, we need to account not just for a customer's interactions with a business, but for his or her interaction with other customers as well. As suggested by Brigham Young University professor Scott Sampson, we have two categories of contact: *pure virtual customer contact* where companies such as eBay and Second Life enable customers to interact with one another in an open

Ease of Doing Business: Opportunities Ahead

The growth and development agenda of India had many roadblocks in the past. One of the major problems that nation faced was lack of attention towards support to businesses and corruption riddled in different approvals, tax liabilities, procurement of government orders, etc. Normal day-to-day business operations were inflicted with many hassles. Things have changed significantly and Government of India has taken major steps to bring back the investors' confidence in governance. 'Ease of Doing Business' is a recent initiative in this direction. It has also presented opportunities to redesign new services and simplify business processes.

Every year, World Bank comes up with ranking on Ease of Doing Business in different countries. In 2018, on different indicators of Ease of Doing Business, 190 countries were assessed. These indicators are listed in Table 1. It is evident that there are many opportunities for improvement. For example, dealing with construction permit and enforcing contract are the two opportune areas for improvement. According to the Doing Business (DB) report published in 2018, India is ranked 100 among 190 countries, which is 30 places up as compared to its 2017 ranking. This is possibly for the first time that any developing economy has improved so much in such a short span of time. The way these improvements are visible, it requires commitment and involvement of not only the government but also the private sector. For example, time to get electricity connection for a business has come down from 138 days to 45 days in the past four years. Just for comparison, it is around 20 days lesser than average time taken in OECD high-income economies. The 29th global ranking on 'getting electricity' in India speaks volumes about the role of private electricity distribution companies as well.

Table 1 India's Global Ranking on Different Indicators of 'Ease of Doing Business'

S. No.	Indicator (Ranking)	2017	2018	Remark
1	Starting a business	155	156	High opportune area for improvement due to the need for local entrepreneurs to go through 12 procedures to start a business, as opposed to five in high-income countries
2	Dealing with construction permits	185	181	Very high opportune area for improvement
3	Getting credit	44	29	Reasonably good
4	Protecting minority investors	13	4	World benchmark status due to the fact that India's corporate law and securities regulations are recognized as highly advanced
5	Paying taxes	172	119	Showed significant improvement in 2017–18
6	Trading across borders	143	146	High opportune area for improvement
7	Enforcing contracts	172	164	High opportune area for improvement as it takes longer to enforce a contract today
8	Getting electricity	26	29	Reasonably good
9	Registering property	138	154	Slipped due to increase in time taken, cost, and number of procedures for registration.

Implementation of Goods and Service Tax (GST) on 01 July 2017 is another step in Ease of Doing Business. GST subsumes many taxes with which businesses used to comply earlier. Some of these taxes that do not exist now are central excise duty, service tax, state VAT, central sales tax, luxury tax, entry tax in states, tax on advertisement, purchase tax, etc. The GST is basically a consumption-based tax structure on goods and services. The nation-wide common tax structure has made the taxation process simpler for businesses. The logistics sector can harvest many benefits as the need for multiple sales depots for FMCG products would no longer be needed. Similarly, once fully implemented and absorbed, GST will help warehouse consolidation and many other benefits to supply chains.

Discussion Questions

1 How does Ease of Doing Business help in startups and day-to-day operations?

2 Make an assessment of the success/failure of initiatives like 'Ease of Doing Business' and 'Make in India'. Are these related?

3 What are the barriers and enablers of Ease of Doing Businesses? How can government or businesses overcome these barriers?

environment; and *mixed virtual and actual customer contact* where customers interact with one another in a server-moderated environment such as product discussion groups, YouTube, and Wikipedia. In these environments, the operations management challenge is to keep the technology functioning and up to date and to provide a policing function through monitoring the encounters that take place.

Managing Customer-Introduced Variability

Process

Among the decisions that service managers must make is how much they should accommodate the variation introduced by the customer into a process. The standard approach is to treat this decision as a trade-off between cost and quality. More accommodation implies more cost; less accommodation implies less-satisfied customers. This narrow type of analysis overlooks ways that companies can accommodate the customer while at the same time control cost. To develop these, a company must first determine which of five types of variability is causing operational difficulties and then select which of four types of accommodation would be most effective.

The five basic types of variability, along with examples, are *arrival variability*—the arrival time of customers at a restaurant may be inconsistent with average demand, leading to times when servers are overloaded or underutilized (this is the type of variability that is dealt with in the waiting line analysis in Chapter 10); *request variability*—travelers requesting a room with a view at a crowded hotel; *capability variability*—a patient being unable to explain his or her symptoms to a doctor; *effort variability*—shoppers not bothering to put their shopping carts in a designated area in a supermarket parking lot; and *subjective preference variability*—one bank customer interpreting a teller addressing him by his first name as a sign of warmth, while another customer feels that such informality is unbusinesslike.

The four basic accommodation strategies are *classic accommodation,* which entails, for example, extra employees or additional employee skills to compensate for variations among customers; *low-cost accommodation,* which uses low-cost labor, outsourcing, and self-service to cut the cost of accommodation; *classic reduction,* which requires, for example, customers to engage in more self-service, use reservation systems, or adjust their expectations; and *uncompromised reduction,* which uses knowledge of the customer to develop procedures that enable good service, while minimizing the variation impact on the service delivery system. Exhibit 9.4 illustrates the tactics that are useful in each of the four accommodation categories.

Key Ideas

Variability is the major problem with services that require direct customer contact. Innovative approaches are needed to manage this variability.

As we can see from Exhibit 9.4, effective management of variability generally requires a company to influence customer behavior. Redbox provides an example of what can be done to reduce variability. It charges on a per-day basis for the rental of movie DVDs. Thus, a customer has a strong incentive to return the rented DVD in 24 hours, and if it is not returned, the company still has a revenue stream from the DVDs that are not available for rental and being held by the customer. In contrast, the Netflix subscription model allows customers to keep the DVD for as long as they want. A customer's incentive to return them is being able to get the next movie on his or her request list. The Netflix approach might better accommodate the customer's behavior, but the Redbox approach assures revenues on DVDs being held by customers.

Applying Behavioral Science to Service Encounters

Effective management of service encounters requires that managers understand customer perceptions as well as the technical features of service processes. Chase and Dasu, professors at Southern California University, suggest applying behavioral concepts to enhance customer perceptions of three aspects of the encounter: *the flow of the service experience* (what's happening), *the flow of time* (how long it seems to take), and *judging of encounter performance* (what you thought about it later). Looking at the service encounter from this perspective has led to the following six behaviorally based principles for service encounter design and management.

Key Ideas

The customer's perception related to a poor encounter may be changed if the problem is addressed quickly.

1. **The front end and the back end of the encounter are not created equal.** It is widely believed that the start and finish of a service, or the so-called service bookends, are equally weighted in the eyes of the customer. A good deal of research indicates this is not the case, however. While

EXHIBIT 9.4

Strategies for Managing Customer-Introduced Variability

	Classic Accommodation	Low-Cost Accommodation	Classic Reduction	Uncompromised Reduction
Arrival rate variability	• Make sure plenty of employees are on hand	• Hire lower-cost labor • Automate tasks • Outsource customer contact • Create self-service options	• Require reservations • Provide off-peak pricing • Limit service availability	• Create complementary demand to smooth arrivals without requiring customers to change their behavior
Variability in the services requested by the customers	• Make sure many employees with specialized skills are on hand • Train employees to handle many kinds of requests	• Hire lower-cost specialized labor • Automate tasks • Create self-service options	• Require customers to make reservations for specific types of service • Persuade customers to compromise their requests • Limit service breadth	• Limit service breadth • Target customers on the basis of their requests
Variability in customer capability	• Make sure employees are on hand who can adapt to customers' varied skill levels • Do work for customers	• Hire lower-cost labor • Create self-service options that require no special skills	• Require customers to increase their level of capability before they use the service	• Target customers on the basis of their capability
Variability in the effort customers are willing to expend	• Make sure employees are on hand who can compensate for customers' lack of effort • Do work for customers	• Hire lower-cost labor • Create self-service options with extensive automation	• Use rewards and penalties to get customers to increase their effort	• Target customers on the basis of motivation • Use a normative approach to get customers to increase their effort
Variability in customer preferences and expectations	• Make sure employees are on hand who can diagnose differences in expectations and adapt accordingly	• Create self-service options that permit customization	• Persuade customers to adjust their expectations to match the value proposition	• Target customers on the basis of their subjective preferences

it is essential to achieve a base level of satisfactory performance at the beginning so that the customer remains throughout the service, a company is likely to be better off with a relatively weak start and a modest upswing on the end than having a great start and a so-so ending. This ties in with two important findings from behavioral decision theory: the preference for improvement and the dominant effect of the ending in our recollections. The disproportionate influence of the ending gives rise to a corollary principle—that is, end on an up note. The following are examples of companies that "finish strong": Malaysian Airlines, which lavishes attention on baggage collection and ground transportation in order to leave the customer with a good feeling; a kitchen cabinet company that ties bright bows on all the installed work and leaves behind a vase of flowers; cruise lines that end each day with raffles, contests, and shows end the cruise with the captain's dinner, and pass out keepsakes or bottles of wine upon reaching the home port. All of these strategies are designed to make the final interaction a good one. In a similar vein, relative to unpleasant experiences, researchers have found that prolonging a colonoscopy by painlessly leaving the colon scope in place for about a minute after the procedure was completed produced significant improvements in how patients perceived the procedure. (Note here that we are actually extending the duration of discomfort, yet the overall perception is superior to immediate cessation of the procedure!)

2. **Segment the pleasure; combine the pain.** Breaking up may be hard to do, but depending upon the type of encounter, it might be the best thing to do. Events seem longer when they are segmented. This suggests that we want to break pleasant experiences into multiple stages and combine

unpleasant ones into a single stage. Thus, it makes sense to, say, reduce the number of stages in a visit to a clinic, even if it extends the time of the visit somewhat, and to provide two 90-second rides at Disneyland rather than one three-minute ride.

3. **Let the customer control the process.** Giving people control over how a process is to be conducted enhances their satisfaction with it. In the medical area, allowing people to choose which arm a blood sample is drawn from reduces the perceived pain of the procedure. For certain repair jobs, allowing people to select a future date they want it to be scheduled may be preferred to doing it right away.

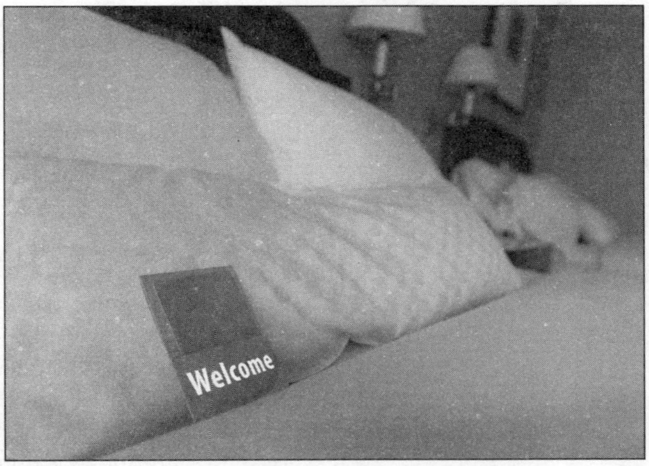

A welcome note in a Hotel Room

4. **Pay attention to norms and rituals.** Deviations from norms are likely to be overly blamed for failures. This is particularly true for professional services whose processes and outcomes are not clearly ascertainable by the client, and hence adherence to norms is the central basis for evaluation. Consulting firms are expected to make presentations to the boss, even if he or she has little or nothing to do with the problem being studied. At such presentations, all members of the client team are to be lauded for their assistance even if they were less than helpful in accomplishing the work.

5. **People are easier to blame than systems.** When things go wrong, people's gut reaction is to blame the server rather than the system. We want to put a human face on the problem. This is seen especially in complex services where what goes on behind the scenes or in the system is difficult for the customer to untangle. The gate agent is frequently blamed for not allowing a late arrival to get on the plane, even though it is a rule of the airline association that no one can board 15 minutes before departure. (A corollary to this principle is that "a miss is worse than a mile." That is, if someone arrives late for a service, it's better not to say, "too bad, you just missed it.")

6. **Let the punishment fit the crime in service recovery.** How do you make up for an encounter error? Research suggests that the most appropriate recovery action depends upon whether it is a task (outcome) error or a treatment (interpersonal process) error. A botched task calls for material compensation, while poor treatment from a server calls for an apology. Reversing these recovery actions is unlikely to be effective. For example, having a copying job done poorly at a copy store, of course, calls for a quick apology, but more importantly, it calls for quick rework and perhaps some compensation for the customer's inconvenience. On the other hand, if the copying job is done correctly but the clerk is rude, a sincere apology from the store manager and the clerk is far more likely to result in a satisfied customer than giving the customer a free coupon or some other minor tangible form of compensation.

Service Guarantees as Design Drivers The phrase "Positively, absolutely, overnight" is an example of a service guarantee most of us know by heart. Hiding behind such marketing promises of service satisfaction is a set of actions that must be taken by the operations organization to fulfill these promises.

Thousands of companies have launched **service guarantees** as a marketing tool designed to provide peace of mind for customers unsure about trying their service. From an operations perspective, a service guarantee can be used not only as an improvement tool but also at the design stage to focus the firm's delivery system squarely on the things it must do well to satisfy the customer.

Service guarantees
A promise of service satisfaction backed up by a set of actions that must be taken to fulfill the promise.

Even professional service firms such as Rath and Strong Consulting have service guarantees. (Theirs allows the client to choose from a menu of payouts if they do not, for example, cut lead time by x percent. Menu options include refunds and no charge for overtime work to get the job done.)

The elements of a good service guarantee are that it is unconditional (no small print); meaningful to the customer (the payoff fully covers the customer's dissatisfaction); easy to understand and communicate (for employees as well as customers); and painless to invoke (given proactively).

Some guidelines for using service guarantees are the following:

1. Any guarantee is better than no guarantee. The most effective guarantees are big deals. They put the company at risk in the eyes of the customer.
2. Involve the customer as well as employees in the design.
3. Avoid complexity or legalistic language. Use big print, not small print.
4. Do not quibble or wriggle when a customer invokes the guarantee.
5. Make it clear that you are happy for customers to invoke the guarantee.

An issue of growing importance in service relates to the ethical and possibly legal responsibility of a company to actually provide the service that is promised. For example, is an airline responsible for transporting a passenger with a guaranteed reservation, even though the flight has been overbooked? These are difficult issues because having excess capacity is expensive. Demand can be nearly impossible to predict with great accuracy, thus making the estimates of needed capacity difficult.

A very powerful tool—waiting line analysis—is available to help better understand the relationships between the factors that drive a service system. These factors include the average number of customers that arrive over a period of time, the average time that it takes to serve each customer, the number of servers, and information about the size of the customer population. Waiting line models have been developed that allow the estimation of expected waiting time and expected resource utilization. This is the topic of Chapter 10.

EXHIBIT 9.5

Fail-Safing an Automotive Service Operation

Failure: Customer forgets the need for service.
Poka-yoke: Send automatic reminders with a 5 percent discount.

Failure: Customer cannot find service area, or does not follow proper flow.
Poka-yoke: Clear and informative signage directing customers.

Failure: Customer has difficulty communicating problem.
Poka-yoke: Joint inspection—service adviser repeats his/her understanding of the problem for confirmation or elaboration by the customer.

Failure: Customer does not understand the necessary service.
Poka-yoke: Preprinted material for most services, detailing work, reasons, and possibly a graphic representation.

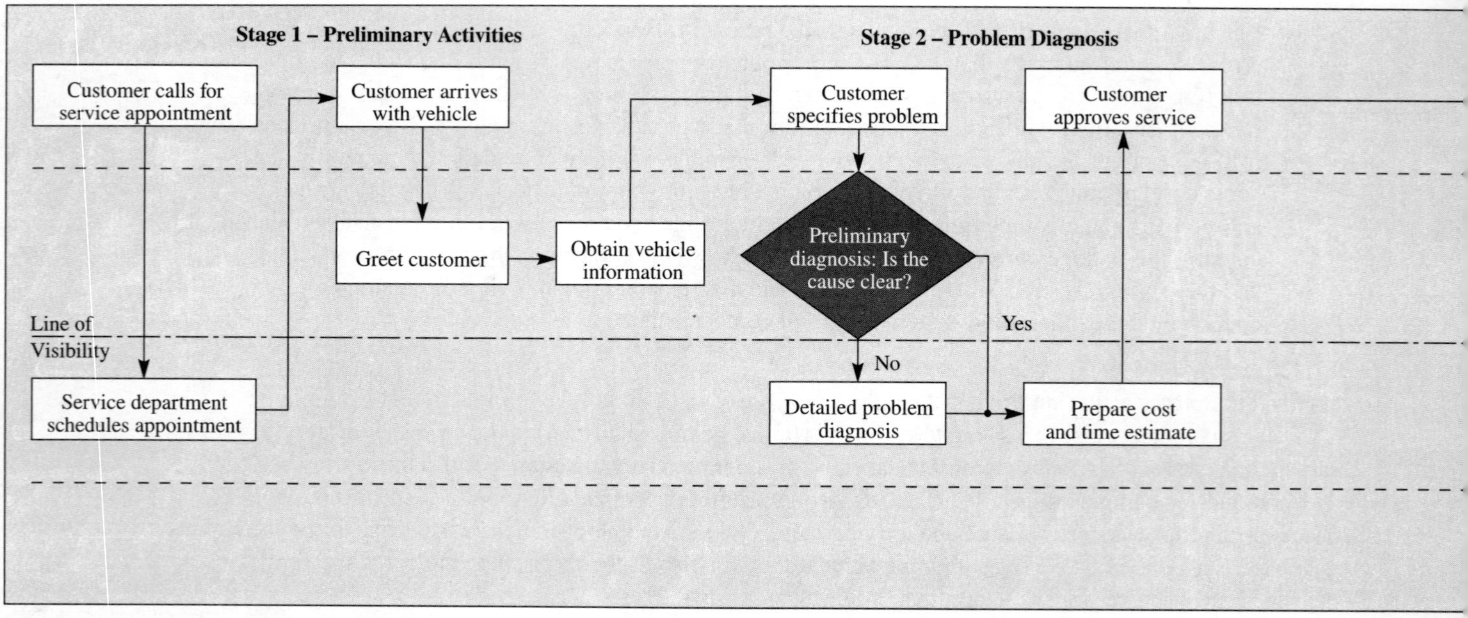

Failure: Customer arrival unnoticed.
Poka-yoke: Use a bell chain to signal arrivals.

Failure: Customers not served in order of arrival.
Poka-yoke: Place numbered markers on cars as they arrive.
Failure: Vehicle information incorrect and process is time-consuming.
Poka-yoke: Maintain customer database and print forms with historical information.

Failure: Incorrect diagnosis of the problem.
Poka-yoke: High-tech checklists, such as expert systems and diagnostic equipment.

Failure: Incorrect estimate.
Poka-yoke: Checklists itemizing costs by common repair types.

SERVICE BLUEPRINTING AND FAIL-SAFING

LO 9-3

Analyze simple service systems

Service blueprint

The flowchart of a service process, emphasizing what is visible and what is not visible to the customer.

Poka-yokes

Procedures that prevent mistakes from becoming defects. They are commonly found in manufacturing but also can be used in service processes.

Process

Just as is the case with manufacturing process design, the standard tool for service process design is the flowchart. Recently, the service gurus have begun calling the flowchart a **service blueprint** to emphasize the importance of process design. A unique feature of the service blueprint is the distinction made between the high customer contact aspects of the service (the parts of the process that the customer sees) and those activities that the customer does not see. This distinction is made with a "line of visibility" on the flowchart.

Exhibit 9.5 is a blueprint of a typical automobile service operation. Each activity that makes up a typical service encounter is mapped into the flowchart. To better show the entity that controls the activities, levels are shown in the flowchart. The top level consists of activities that are under the control of the customer. Next are those activities performed by the service manager in handling the customer. The third level is the repair activities performed in the garage; the lowest level is the internal accounting activity.

Basic blueprinting describes the features of the service design but does not provide any direct guidance for how to make the process conform to that design. An approach to this problem is the application of **poka-yokes**—procedures that block the inevitable mistake from becoming a service defect. Poka-yokes (roughly translated from the Japanese as "avoid mistakes") are common in factories (see Chapter 12, "Six Sigma Quality," for examples) and consist of such things as fixtures to ensure

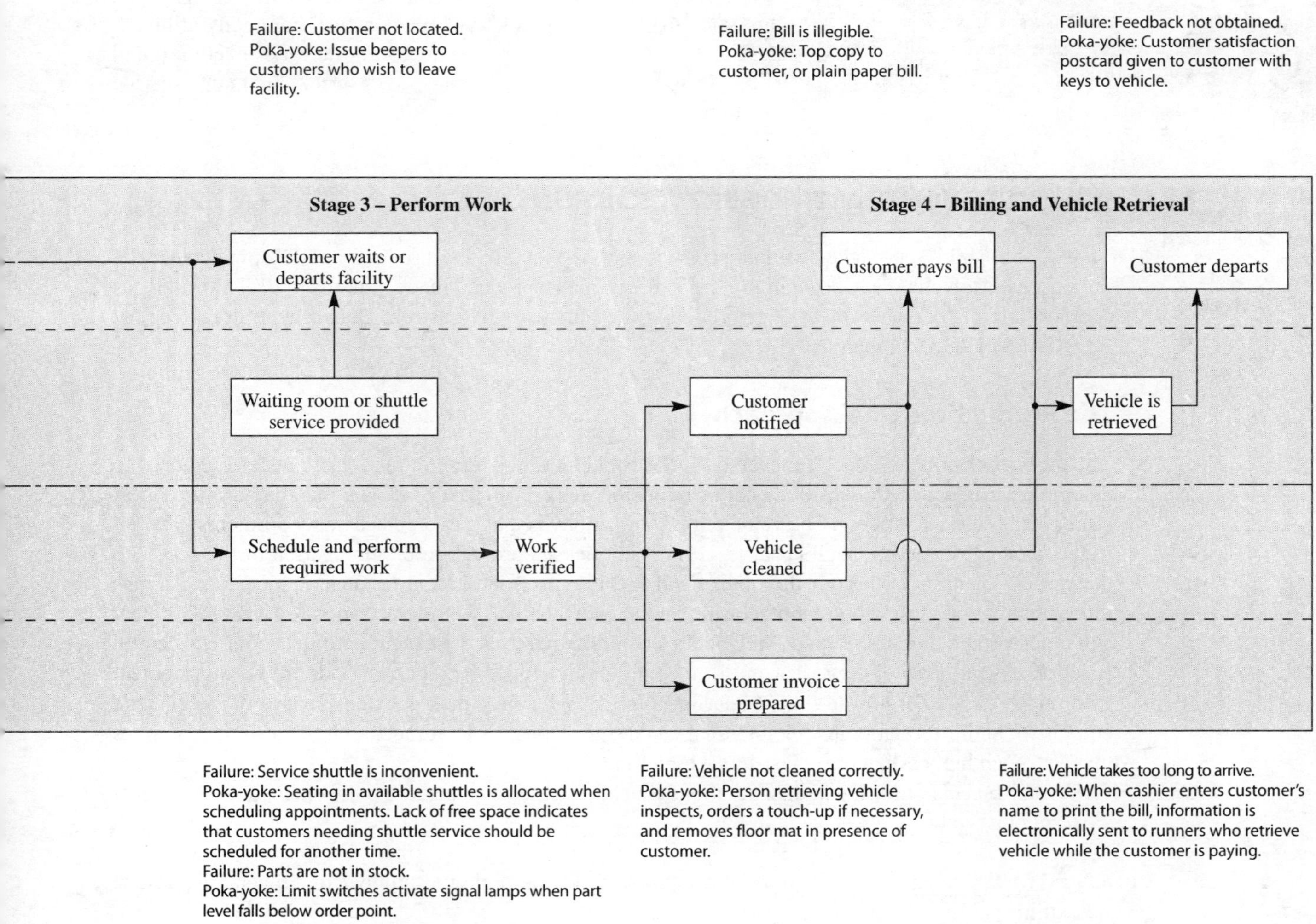

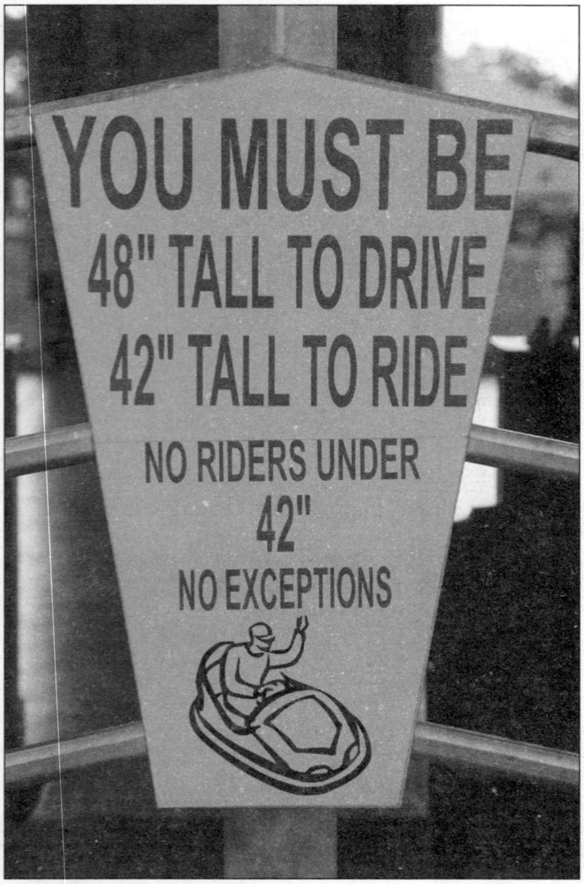

Height-requirement sign outside carnival ride

that parts can be attached only in the right way, electronic switches that automatically shut off equipment if a mistake is made, kitting of parts prior to assembly to make sure the right quantities are used, and checklists to ensure that the right sequence of steps is followed.

There are many applications of poka-yokes to services as well. These can be classified into warning methods, physical or visual contact methods, and what we call the *Three Ts*—the Task to be done (Was the car fixed right?), the Treatment accorded to the customer (Was the service manager courteous?), and the Tangible or environmental features of the service facility (Was the waiting area clean and comfortable?). Finally (unlike in manufacturing), service poka-yokes often must be applied to fail-safing the actions of the customer as well as the service worker.

Poka-yoke examples include height bars at amusement parks; indented trays used by surgeons to ensure that no instruments are left in the patient; chains to configure waiting lines; take-a-number systems; turnstiles; alarms on ATMs to warn people to take their cards out of the machine; beepers at restaurants to make sure customers do not miss their table calls; mirrors on telephones to ensure a "smiling voice"; reminder calls for appointments; locks on airline lavatory doors that activate lights inside; small gifts in comment card envelopes to encourage customers to provide feedback about a service; and pictures of what "a clean room" looks like for kindergarten children.

Exhibit 9.5 illustrates how a typical automobile service operation might be fail-safed using poka-yokes. As a final comment, although these procedures cannot guarantee the level of error protection found in the factory, they still can reduce such errors in many service situations.

LO 9-4

Contrast different service designs

THREE CONTRASTING SERVICE DESIGNS

Three contrasting approaches to delivering on-site service are the production-line approach, made famous by McDonald's Corporation; the self-service approach, made famous by ATMs and gas stations; and the personal-attention approach, made famous by Nordstrom Department Stores and the Ritz-Carlton Hotel Company.

The Production-Line Approach

The production-line approach pioneered by McDonald's refers to more than just the steps required to assemble a Big Mac. Rather, McDonald's treats the delivery of fast food as a manufacturing process rather than a service process. The value of this philosophy is that it overcomes many problems inherent in the concept of service itself. That is, service implies subordination or subjugation of the server to the served; manufacturing, on the other hand, avoids this connotation because it focuses on things rather than people. Thus, in manufacturing and at McDonald's, the orientation is toward the efficient and quick production of the food. McDonald's carefully controls the execution of each outlet's central function—the rapid delivery of a uniform, high-quality mix of prepared foods in an environment of obvious cleanliness, order, and cheerful courtesy. The firm makes extensive use of specialized equipment and information technology that enables McDonald's to attract and hold customers at rates that are much higher than other fast-food restaurants.

Several aspects of McDonald's operations illustrate these concepts. Note the extensive use of what we term poka-yokes.

- The McDonald's French fryer allows cooking of the optimum number of French fries at one time.

- A wide-mouthed scoop is used to pick up the precise amount of French fries for each order size. (The employee never touches the product.)
- Storage space is expressly designed for a predetermined mix of prepackaged and premeasured products.
- Cleanliness is pursued by providing ample trash cans in and outside each facility. (Larger outlets have motorized sweepers for the parking area.)
- Hamburgers are wrapped in color-coded paper.
- Through painstaking attention to total design and facilities planning, everything is built integrally into the (McDonald's) machine itself—into the technology of the system. The only choice available to the attendant is to operate it exactly as the designers intended. Using our service-system design matrix (Exhibit 9.3), we would categorize this as a face-to-face tight spec service.

The Self-Service Approach

In contrast to the production-line approach, the service process can be enhanced by having the customer take a greater role in the production of the service. Company websites, automatic teller machines, self-service gas stations, salad bars, and e-tickets are approaches that shift the service burden to the consumer. Based on our service-system design matrix, these are great examples of the use of Internet and on-site technology. Many customers like self-service because it puts them in control. For others, this philosophy might not be attractive and require some incentive to make the approach attractive. Incentives such as the benefit of reduced cost, quicker speed, and convenience can be used. Also, following up to make sure that the procedures are being effectively used is important. In essence, this turns customers into "partial employees" who must be trained in what to do and, as noted earlier, must be "fail-safed" in case of a mistake.

The Personal-Attention Approach

An interesting contrast in the way personal attention is provided can be seen in Nordstrom Department Stores and the Ritz-Carlton Hotel Company.

At Nordstrom, a rather loose, unstructured process relies on developing a relationship between the individual salesperson and the customer (this is a face-to-face with total customization service). At the Ritz-Carlton, the process is virtually scripted, and the information system rather than the employee keeps track of the guest's (customer's) personal preferences (this is a face-to-face loose spec example).

The Ritz-Carlton approach is best captured in the company's Gold Standards, which cover the values and philosophy by which the company operates. Exhibit 9.6 shows the formalized service procedure (the Three Steps of Service).

The frontline providers of this good service are well paid. Nordstrom's salespersons earn a couple of bucks an hour more than competitors, plus a significant commission. Its top

Shoppers enter the Nordstrom store on Eaton Centre, Toronto

Exhibit 9.6

The Ritz-Carlton Hotel Company (Three Steps of Service)

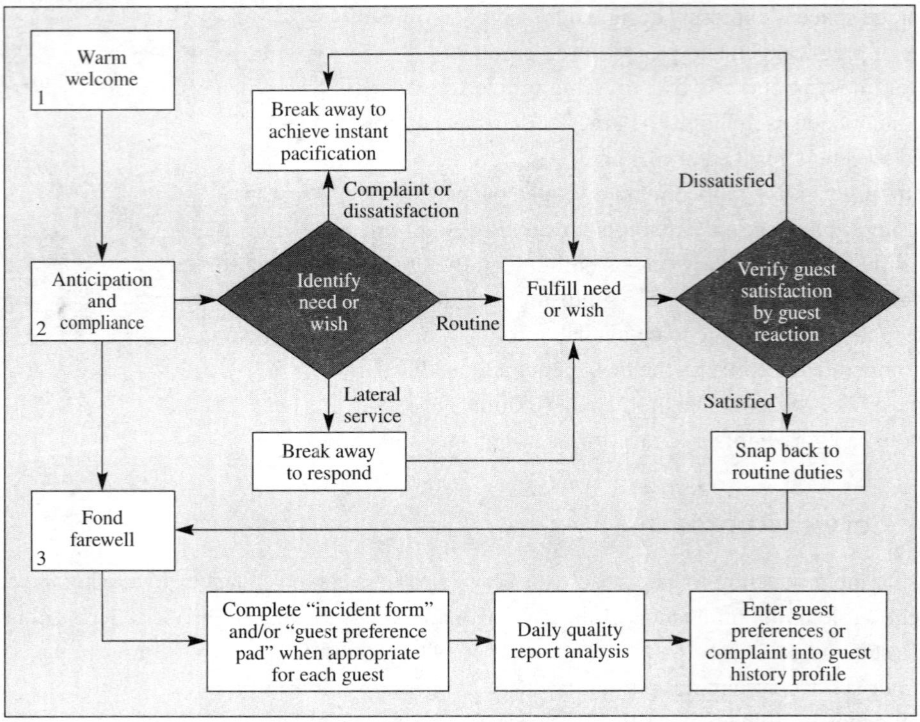

Process

salesperson moves over $2 million a year in merchandise. Nordstrom lives for its customers and salespeople. Its only official organization chart puts the customer at the top, followed by sales and sales support people. Next come department managers, then store managers, and the board of directors at the very bottom.

Salespersons religiously carry a "personal book," where they record information about each of their customers. The system helps in the goal of getting one new personal customer a day. Each salesperson has a budget to send cards, flowers, and thank-you notes to customers. They are also encouraged to shepherd his or her customer to any department in the store to assist in a successful shopping trip.

Key Ideas

Good employee training, information systems and processes, and a supportive reward structure are essential to exemplary service.

Exhibit 9.7 displays the information system used to capture data about guests ("The Ritz-Carlton Repeat Guest History Program"). Note that the three steps of service are integrated into the guest history information system.

He also is abetted by what may be the most liberal returns policy in this or any other business: Return *anything,* no questions asked. No bureaucracy gets in the way of serving the customer. Employees are encouraged to use their own judgment at all times.

Seven Characteristics of a Well-Designed Service System

No matter what approach is taken to design a service, the following are typical characteristics of a well-designed system.

1. **Each element of the service system is consistent with the operating focus of the firm.** For example, when the focus is on speed of delivery, each step in the process should help foster speed.
2. **It is user-friendly.** This means that the customer can interact with it easily—that is, it has good signage, understandable forms, logical steps in the process, and service workers available to answer questions.
3. **It is robust.** That is, it can cope effectively with variations in demand and resource availability. For example, if the computer goes down, effective backup systems are in place to permit service to continue.

EXHIBIT 9.7

The Ritz-Carlton Repeat Guest History Program (An Aid to Highly Personalized Service Delivery)

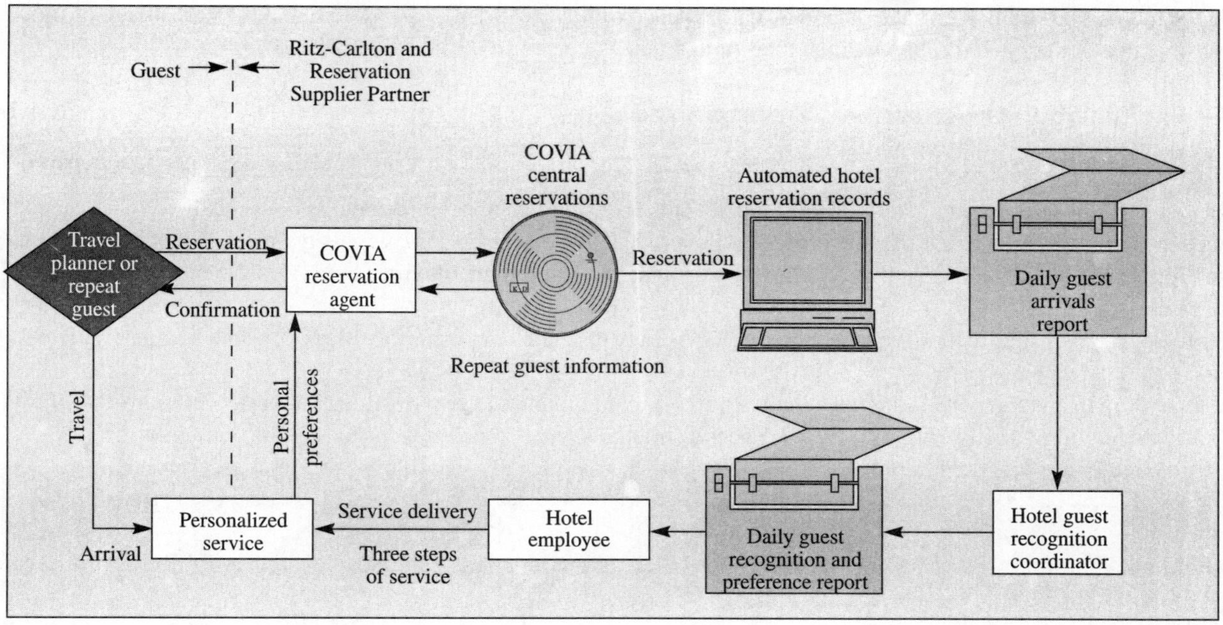

4. **It is structured so that consistent performance by its people and systems is easily maintained.** This means the tasks required of the workers are doable, and the supporting technologies are truly supportive and reliable.
5. **It provides effective links between the back office and the front office so that nothing falls between the cracks.** In football parlance, there should be "no fumbled handoffs."
6. **It manages the evidence of service quality in such a way that customers see the value of the service provided.** Many services do a great job behind the scenes but fail to make this visible to the customer. This is particularly true where a service improvement is made. Unless customers are made aware of the improvement through explicit communication about it, the improved performance is unlikely to gain maximum impact.
7. **It is cost-effective.** There is minimum waste of time and resources in delivering the service. Even if the service outcome is satisfactory, customers are often put off by a service company that appears inefficient.

CONCEPT CONNECTIONS

LO 9–1 Understand the characteristics of service processes

Summary

- A service package is the bundle of goods and services that is provided to the customer in some environment.
- Services can be conveniently classified according to the degree of "contact" or physical presence of the customer in the system.
- In some cases, the customer need not be present at all—for example, when a customer order is processed from an online transaction. In other cases, the customer is directly involved—for instance, when a tooth is removed at a dentist's office.

Key Terms

Service package A bundle of goods and services that is provided in some environment.

High and low degrees of customer contact The physical presence of the customer in the system and the percentage of time the customer must be in the system relative to the total time it takes to perform the service.

LO 9–2 Explain how service systems are organized

Summary

- Service systems differ from manufacturing systems in a number of significant ways, including: (1) typically services cannot be placed in inventory for later use, (2) the process is the product, (3) patents and copyrights typically cannot be obtained, (4) a service is not a tangible item, and (5) specific training and certifications are often required (for example, for law offices and hospitals).
- The service-system design matrix explores the trade-offs between sales opportunity, efficiency, and characteristics of workers.
- A challenge in managing service systems, which is not as great in manufacturing, is the great variability introduced by a customer interacting directly with the system. Special strategies are available for managing this variability.
- Service guarantees are designed to provide a customer with a clear idea of what to expect from a service.

Key Terms

Service guarantees A promise of service satisfaction backed up by a set of actions that must be taken to fulfill the promise.

LO 9–3 Analyze simple service systems

Summary

- Service blueprints are a unique type of flowchart tool that places special emphasis on identifying the high customer contact and low customer contact aspects of a service.
- The distinction is made with a "line of visibility" on the flowchart.

Key Terms

Service blueprint The flowchart of a service process, emphasizing what is visible and what is not visible to the customer.

Poka-yokes Procedures that prevent mistakes from becoming defects. They are commonly found in manufacturing but also can be used in service processes.

LO 9–4 Contrast different service designs

Summary

- Contrasting service designs include: (1) the production-line approach used by McDonald's, (2) the self-service approach used by gas stations, and (3) the personal-attention approach used by Nordstrom's Department Stores and the Ritz-Carlton Hotel Company.
- Well-designed service systems have the following characteristics: They have consistent elements, are user-friendly, are robust, are consistent, have integrated front- and back-office operations, generate value for the customer, and are cost-effective.

DISCUSSION QUESTIONS

LO9–1

1. What is the service package of your college or university?
2. Relative to the behavioral science discussion, what practical advice do you have for a hotel manager to enhance the ending of a guest's stay in the hotel?

3. List some occupations or sporting events where the ending is a dominant element in evaluating success.
4. Behavioral scientists suggest that we remember events as snapshots, not movies. How would you apply this to designing a service? **LO9–2**
5. Some suggest that customer expectation is the key to service success. Give an example from your own experience to support or refute this assertion.
6. Where would you place a drive-in church, a campus food vending machine, and a bar's automatic mixed drink machine on the service-system design matrix?
7. Can a manufacturer have a service guarantee in addition to a product guarantee?
8. Suppose you were the manager of a restaurant and you were told honestly that a couple eating dinner had just seen a mouse. What would you say to them? How would you recover from this service crisis?
9. What strategy do the following organizations seem to use to manage customer-introduced variability?
   a. eBay
   b. Ritz-Carlton Hotels
   c. New airline check-in procedures
10. How have price and variety competition changed McDonald's basic formula for success?
11. Could a service firm use a production-line approach or self-service design and still keep a high customer focus (personal attention)? Explain and support your answer with examples.
12. Why should a manager of a bank home office be evaluated differently from a manager of a bank branch? **LO9–3**
13. Identify the high-contact and low-contact operations of the following services:
    a. A dental office
    b. An airline
    c. An accounting office
    d. An automobile agency
    e. Amazon.com
14. At first glance, asking customers to provide their own service in the self-service approach may not seem very consumer friendly. What are some of the characteristics of self-service operations that have led to their acceptance and significant popularity? **LO9–4**
15. Do you think a service operation can be successful by developing a system that combines characteristics from the three contrasting service designs presented in the chapter? Why or why not? Please provide examples.

OBJECTIVE QUESTIONS

1. What is the term used for the bundle of goods and services that are provided in some environment by every service operation? (Answer in Appendix D) **LO9–1**
2. Are service operations with a high degree of customer contact more or less difficult to control than those with a low degree of customer contact?
3. List at least three significant ways in which service systems differ from manufacturing systems. **LO9–2**
4. A ride at an amusement park is an example of a service operation where there is direct contact between the customer and server, but little variation in the service process—neither the customer nor server has much discretion in how the service will be provided. As shown on the service-system design matrix, which type of service is being delivered? (Answer in Appendix D)
5. As the degree of customer contact increases in a service operation, what generally happens to the efficiency of the operation?

6. As the degree of customer contact increases in a service system, what worker skills would be more important, clerical skills or diagnostic skills?
7. An important difference between service and manufacturing operations is that customers introduce far more variability into the operations in a service system. Name at least three of the basic types of variation that customers bring to a service system.

LO9–3

8. Flowcharts are a common process design and analysis tool used in both manufacturing and services. What is a key feature on flowcharts used in service operations that differentiates between the front-office and back-office aspects of the system?
9. What are the Three Ts relevant to poka-yokes in service systems?

LO9–4

10. List at least four characteristics of a well-designed service system.
11. A psychological therapist treats patients according to their individual needs. Patients are all treated in the same office on a scheduled basis. Each patient's treatment is developed and customized for the individual according to the therapist's professional training. Which of the contrasting service designs in the chapter would best describe the therapist's service operation?

CASE: Pizza USA—An Exercise in Translating Customer Requirements into Process Design Requirements

A central theme of contemporary operations management is *focus on the customer.* This is commonly understood to mean that if a company does focus on its customers and if it is able to consistently deliver what the customer wants in a cost-effective manner, then the company should be successful. The hard part is to be able to truly understand what the customer wants. Translating what the customer wants into a deliverable product (meaning some combination of goods and services) and designing a set of processes that will consistently deliver the product in a cost-effective manner are every bit as difficult. Finally, connecting the management of these products and processes to obtain desired business outcomes of the organization is a further challenge.

The following exercise will try to illustrate how difficult all of this can be.

The Setting

Pizza USA is a chain of pizza restaurants that currently offers sit-down and take-out service. Many customers have said they would buy more pizzas from Pizza USA if it offered a delivery service. This exercise is in two parts. In Part I, you play the customer. In Part II, you play the manager at Pizza USA who is responsible for developing the pizza delivery process design requirements.

Part I

To start with, you have to think *like* a customer. This should be easy since you probably have experience with *ordering pizza to be delivered.* Put that experience to work! Make a list of the attributes of *pizza delivery* that are important to you *AS A CUSTOMER!*

As we said, this should be easy. Right? Or is it? In devising your list, consider the following:

> What must a pizza delivery service accomplish so that you are reasonably satisfied? Beyond your being reasonably satisfied, what could a pizza delivery service do that would make it really unique and create a differential advantage? In other words, what could a pizza delivery service do that might cause you to ALWAYS order from one particular service (and, perhaps, to pay more for the privilege)?

As you develop your list, remember that you are considering *only the delivery service* and NOT the pizza itself. Assume that this pizza restaurant can make whatever kind of pizza (and side items) that you want.

Part II

Now, put on your "*Pizza USA manager's hat.*" For this part of the exercise, you will be teamed with some other students. First, using the lists of all of your team members, create a master list. Next, try to group the items on your list under a series of major headings; for example, "condition of the delivered pizza" or "quick, on-time delivery" or "order accuracy," and so on. Finally, make a list of the "pizza delivery process design requirements" that your pizza delivery process will have

© Steve Mason/Getty Images RF

to meet. As you do this, think about measurable standards. In other words, what would you measure in order to ensure that your process is operating effectively and efficiently? Why do you think that these measures will be useful?

Here's an example of how a part of this analysis could go. One customer requirement may be that *the pizza should be hot when it is delivered.* The fact is that as soon as the pizza comes out of the oven, it starts to cool. So, how could you keep the pizza from dropping below some minimum temperature before you hand it to your customer?

Questions

1. Make a list of pizza delivery attributes that are important to you as a customer.
2. Combine your list with the lists of a few other class members and categorize the items under a series of major headings.
3. Make a list of pizza delivery process design requirements. Associate with each requirement a measure that would ensure that the process meets the requirement.
4. Design a process that meets your requirements. Describe it by using a flowchart similar to that shown in Exhibit 9.5.

PRACTICE EXAM

In each of the following, name the term defined. Answers are listed at the bottom.

1. Service systems can generally be categorized according to this characteristic that relates to the customer.
2. A service triangle consists of these four features.
3. This framework relates to the customer service system encounter.
4. This is the key feature that distinguishes a service blueprint from a normal flowchart.
5. Having your luggage arrive on time when you land at an airport is what type of service in the service package?
6. SecondLife would be this type of virtual service.
7. These procedures are done to make a system mistake-proof.
8. These are the three steps of service at Nordstrom.
9. What are the four strategies for managing customer-induced variability?
10. The front end and the back end of a service encounter are referred to as what?

Answers to Practice Exam 1. Customer contact 2. Service strategy, support systems, employees, customer 3. Service-system design matrix 4. Line of visibility 5. Implicit service 6. Pure virtual customer contact 7. Poka-yokes 8. Warm Welcome, Anticipation and Compliance, Fond Farewell 9. Classic accommodation, low-cost accommodation, classic reduction, uncompromised reduction 10. Service bookends

For PowerPoint lecture slides, Solutions Manual, Test Bank, Data files for solved examples, Excel Templates, Step-by-Step Solved Examples in video format, Tutorial Videos and many more, scan the adjacent **QR code**, or **visit http://www.mhhe.com/sie-chase15e**

Chapter 10

Waiting Line Analysis and Simulation

LEARNING OBJECTIVES

LO 10-1 Understand what a waiting line problem is

LO 10-2 Analyze waiting line problems

LO 10-3 Analyze complex waiting lines using simulation

DOES WAITING IN LINE DRIVE YOU CRAZY?

Most of us are very impatient, and standing in line can be one of the most frustrating things we must deal with. At times, its seems we are confronted with waiting in lines nearly everywhere we go. In the grocery store, at the restaurant, and at the doctor's office, we usually need to wait in line.

Have you ever noticed that when you have nothing to do, that time seems to pass less quickly? So if you are waiting in line, try to think about something. Review the menu at a restaurant or read a book at the doctor's office. Do anything to keep your mind from thinking about waiting.

It is natural that people want to get started. Waiting can often create anxiety when having such thoughts as: Why did I get into the slowest line? Will there still be a ticket left when I get to the teller? Will I have everything I need when it is my turn to be served?

We can easily spend two to three years of our life waiting in lines. Given this, it probably makes sense to spend a little time learning how waiting lines work and what can be done to manage them. Some quick math can go a long way toward understanding the problem.

The technology deployed at order stations and pick-up windows at a high volume restaurant like McDonald's or Taco Bell is amazing. Every step is measured, every movement calculated, every word scripted. Taco Bell, with more than 6,500 locations in the United States, currently operates some of the fastest and most accurate drive-thru windows in the industry. We analyze how the service delivery process works at Taco Bell in our Analytics Exercise at the end of the chapter.

© Rubberball/Getty Images RF

THE WAITING LINE PROBLEM

LO 10-1

Understand what a waiting line problem is

Process

A central problem in many service settings is the management of waiting time. The manager must weigh the added cost of providing more rapid service (more traffic lanes, additional landing strips, more checkout stands) against the inherent cost of waiting.

Frequently, the cost trade-off decision is straightforward. For example, if we find that the total time our employees spend in line waiting to use a copying machine would otherwise be spent in productive activities, we could compare the cost of installing one additional machine to the value of employee time saved. The decision could then be reduced to dollar terms and the choice easily made.

On the other hand, suppose that our waiting line problem centers on demand for beds in a hospital. We can compute the cost of additional beds by summing the costs for building construction, additional equipment required, and increased maintenance. But what is on the other side of the scale? Here, we are confronted with the problem of trying to place a dollar figure on a patient's need for a hospital bed that is unavailable. While we can estimate lost hospital income, what about the human cost arising from this lack of adequate hospital care?

The Practical View of Waiting Lines

Before we proceed with a technical presentation of waiting line theory, it is useful to look at the intuitive side of the issue to see what it means. Exhibit 10.1 shows arrivals at a service facility (such as a bank) and service requirements at that facility (such as tellers and loan officers). One important variable is the number of arrivals over the hours that the service system is open. From the service delivery viewpoint, customers demand varying amounts of service, often exceeding normal capacity. We can control arrivals in a variety of ways. For example, we can have a short line (such as a drive-in at a fast-food restaurant with only several spaces), we can establish specific hours for specific customers, or we can run specials. For the server, we can affect service time by using faster or slower servers, faster or slower machines, different tooling, different material, different layout, faster setup time, and so on.

The essential point is waiting lines are *not* a fixed condition of a productive system but are to a very large extent within the control of the system management and design. Useful suggestions for managing queues based on research in the banking industry are the following.

EXHIBIT 10.1

Arrival and Service Profiles

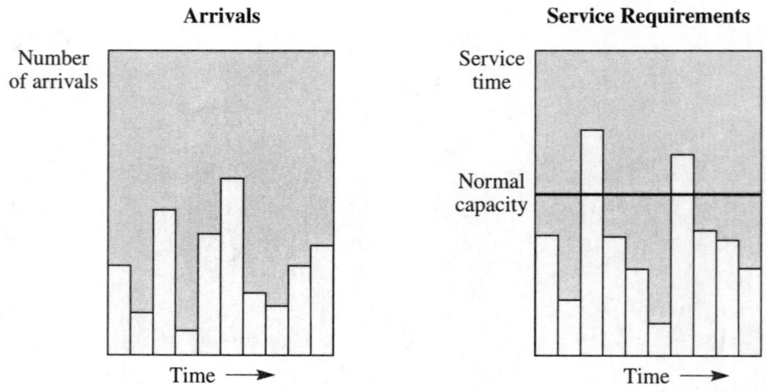

- **Segment the customers.** If a group of customers need something that can be done very quickly, give them a special line so they do not have to wait for the slower customers. This is commonly done at grocery stores where checkout lines are designated for "12 items or less."
- **Train your servers to be friendly.** Greeting the customer by name or providing another form of special attention can go a long way toward overcoming the negative feeling of a long wait. Psychologists suggest that servers be told when to invoke specific friendly actions such as smiling when greeting customers, taking orders, and giving change (for example, in a convenience store). Tests using such specific behavioral actions have shown significant increases in the perceived friendliness of the servers in the eyes of the customer.
- **Inform your customers of what to expect.** This is especially important when the waiting time will be longer than normal. Tell them why the waiting time is longer than usual and what you are doing to alleviate the wait.
- **Try to divert the customer's attention when waiting.** Providing music, a video, or some other form of entertainment may help distract the customers from the fact that they are waiting.
- **Encourage customers to come during slack periods.** Inform customers of times when they usually would not have to wait; also tell them when the peak periods are—this may help smooth the load.

The Queuing System

Queuing system
A process where customers wait in line for service.

The **queuing system** consists essentially of three major components: (1) the source population and the way customers arrive at the system, (2) the servicing system, and (3) the condition of the customers exiting the system (back to source population or not?), as seen in Exhibit 10.2. The following sections discuss each of these areas.

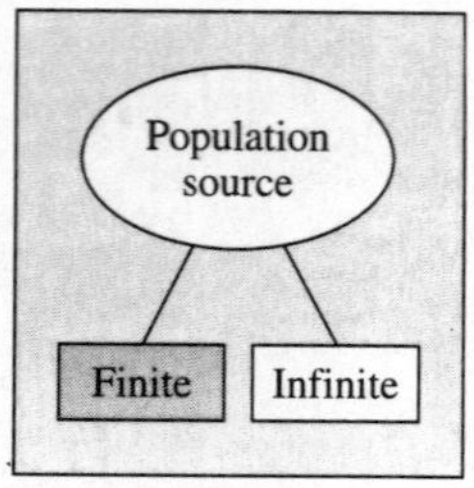

Customer Arrivals Arrivals at a service system may be drawn from a *finite* or an *infinite* population. The distinction is important because the analyses are based on different premises and require different equations for their solution.

Finite Population A *finite population* refers to the limited-size customer pool that will use the service and, at times, form a line. The reason this finite classification is important is that when a customer leaves their position as a member of the population (due to a machine breaking down and requiring service, for example), the size of the user group is reduced by one, which reduces the probability of the next occurrence. Conversely, when a customer is serviced and returns to the user group, the population increases and the probability of a user requiring service also increases. This finite class of problems requires a separate set of formulas from that of the infinite population case.

As an example, consider a group of six machines maintained by one repairperson. In this case, the machines are the customers of the repairperson. When one machine breaks down, the source

Exhibit 10.2

Components of a Queuing System

population is reduced to five, and the chance of one of the remaining five breaking down and needing repair is certainly less than when six machines were operating. If two machines are down with only four operating, the probability of another breakdown is again changed. Conversely, when a machine is repaired and returned to service, the machine population increases, thus raising the probability of the next breakdown.

Infinite Population An *infinite population* is large enough in relation to the service system so that the population size caused by subtractions or additions to the population (a customer needing service or a serviced customer returning to the population) does not significantly affect the system probabilities. If, in the preceding finite explanation, there were 100 customer machines instead of 6, then if 1 or 2 machines broke down, the probabilities for the next breakdowns would not be very different and the assumption could be made without a great deal of error that the population (for all practical purposes) was infinite. Nor would the formulas for "infinite" queuing problems cause much error if applied to a physician with 1,000 patients or a department store with 10,000 customers.

Distribution of Arrivals When describing a waiting system, we need to define the manner in which customers or the waiting units are arranged for service.

Waiting line formulas generally require an **arrival rate**, or the number of units per period (such as an average of one every six minutes). A *constant* arrival distribution is periodic, with exactly the same time between successive arrivals. In productive systems, the only arrivals that truly approach a constant interval period are those subject to machine control. Much more common are *variable* (random) arrival distributions.

Arrival rate
The expected number of customers that arrive each period.

In observing arrivals at a service facility, we can look at them from two viewpoints: First, we can analyze the time between successive arrivals to see if the times follow some statistical distribution. Usually, we assume that the time between arrivals is exponentially distributed. Second, we can set some time length (T) and try to determine how many arrivals might enter the system within T. We typically assume that the number of arrivals per time unit is Poisson distributed.

Analytics

Exponential Distribution

In the first case, when arrivals at a service facility occur in a purely random fashion, a plot of the interarrival times yields an **exponential distribution** such as that shown in Exhibit 10.3. The probability function is

$$f(t) = \lambda e^{-\lambda t} \qquad [10.1]$$

where λ is the mean number of arrivals per time period.

Exponential distribution
A probability distribution associated with the time between arrivals.

Exhibit 10.3

Exponential Distribution

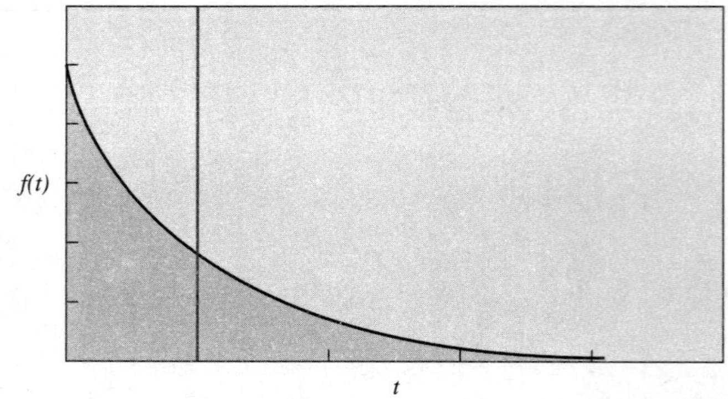

The cumulative area beneath the curve in Exhibit 10.3 is the summation of Equation 10.1 over its positive range, which is $e^{-\lambda t}$. This integral allows us to compute the probabilities of arrivals within a specified time. For example, for the case of one arrival per minute to a waiting line ($\lambda = 1$), the following table can be derived either by solving $e^{-\lambda t}$ or by using Appendix D. Column 2 shows the probability that it will be more than t minutes until the next arrival, while column 3 shows the probability of the next arrival within t minutes (computed as 1 minus column 2).

(1) *t* (Minutes)	(2) Probability that the Next Arrival Will Occur in *t* Minutes or More (from Appendix D or Solving e^{-t})	(3) Probability that the Next Arrival Will Occur in *t* Minutes or Less [1 − Column (2)]
0	100%	0%
0.5	61%	39%
1.0	37%	63%
1.5	22%	78%
2.0	14%	86%

Poisson distribution
Probability distribution for the number of arrivals during each time period.

Poisson Distribution In the second case, where one is interested in the number of arrivals during some time period T, the distribution appears as in Exhibit 10.4 and is obtained by finding the probability of

Exhibit 10.4

Poisson Distribution for $\lambda T = 3$

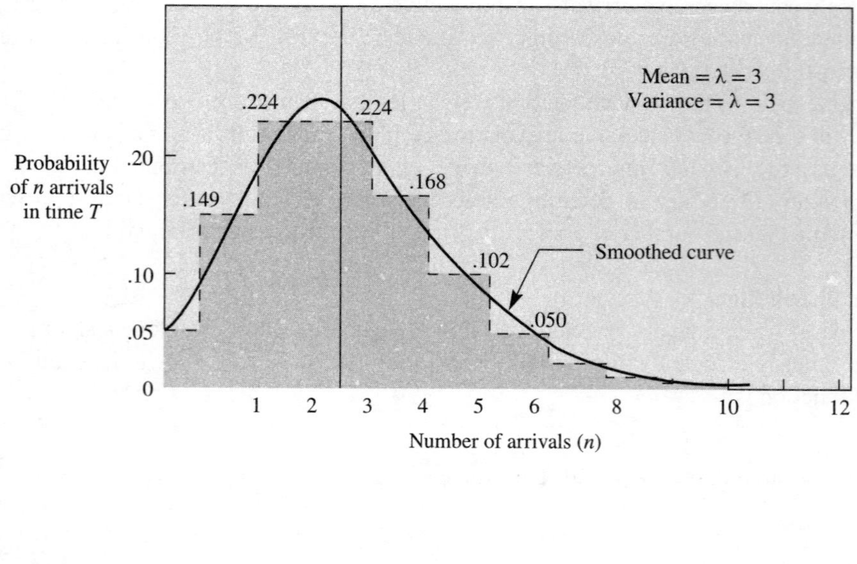

exactly n arrivals during T. If the arrival process is random, the distribution is the **Poisson**, and the formula is

$$P_T(n) = \frac{(\lambda T)^n e^{-\lambda T}}{n!} \qquad [10.2]$$

Equation 10.2 shows the probability of exactly n arrivals in time T. (Note that $n!$ is defined as $n(n-1)(n-2)\ldots(2)(1)$.) For example, if the mean arrival rate of units into a system is three per minute ($\lambda = 3$) and we want to find the probability that exactly five units will arrive within a one-minute period ($n = 5$, $T = 1$), we have

$$P_1(5) = \frac{(3 \times 1)^5 e^{-3\times 1}}{5!} = \frac{3^5 e^{-3}}{120} = 2.025\,e^{-3} = 0.101$$

That is, there is a 10.1 percent chance that there will be five arrivals in any one-minute interval.

Although often shown as a smoothed curve, as in Exhibit 10.4, the Poisson is a discrete distribution. (The curve becomes smoother as n becomes large.) The distribution is discrete because, in our example, n refers to the number of arrivals in a system, and this must be an integer. (For example, there cannot be 1.5 arrivals.)

Also note that the exponential and Poisson distributions can be derived from one another. The mean and variance of the Poisson are equal and denoted by λ. The mean of the exponential is $1/\lambda$ and its variance is $1/\lambda^2$. (Remember that the time between arrivals is exponentially distributed and the number of arrivals per unit of time is Poisson distributed.)

Other arrival characteristics include arrival patterns, size of arrival units, and degree of patience. (See Exhibit 10.5.)

- **Arrival patterns.** The arrivals at a system are far more controllable than is generally recognized. Barbers may decrease their Saturday arrival rate (and supposedly shift it to other days of the week) by charging an extra $1 for adult haircuts or charging adult prices for children's haircuts. Department stores run sales during the off-season or hold one-day-only sales in part for purposes of control. Airlines offer excursion and off-season rates for similar reasons. The simplest of all arrival-control devices is the posting of business hours.

EXHIBIT 10.5

Customer Arrivals in Queues

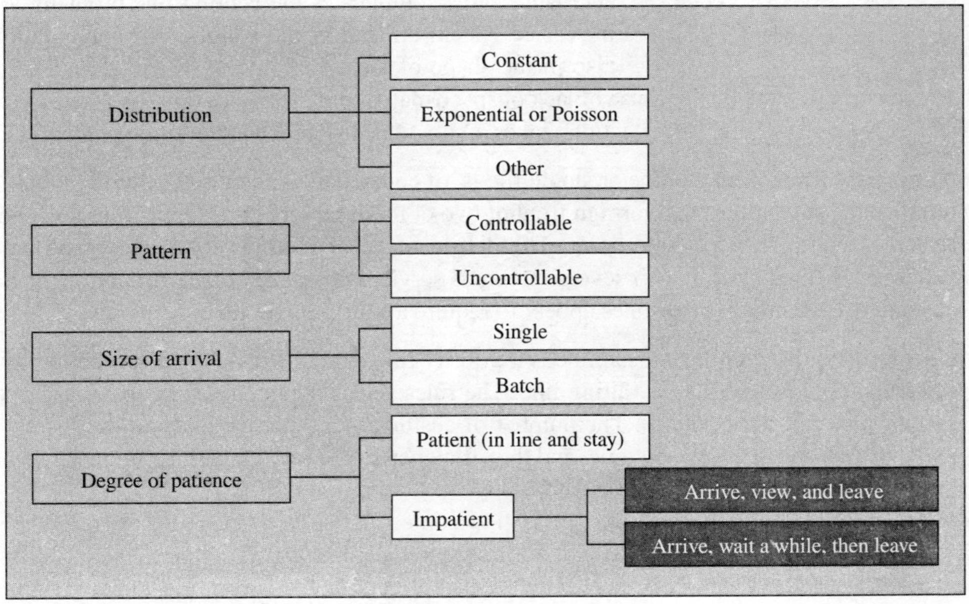

Some service demands are clearly uncontrollable, such as emergency medical demands on a city's hospital facilities. But even in these situations, arrivals at emergency rooms in specific hospitals are controllable to some extent by, say, keeping ambulance drivers in the service region informed of the status of their respective host hospitals.

- **Size of arrival units.** A *single arrival* may be thought of as one unit. (A unit is the smallest number handled.) A single arrival on the floor of the New York Stock Exchange (NYSE) is 100 shares of stock; a single arrival at an egg-processing plant might be a dozen eggs or a flat of 2½ dozen; a single arrival at a restaurant is a single person.

  A *batch arrival* is some multiple of the unit, such as a block of 1,000 shares on the NYSE, a case of eggs at the processing plant, or a party of five at a restaurant.

- **Degree of patience.** A *patient* arrival is one who waits as long as necessary until the service facility is ready to serve him or her. (Even if arrivals grumble and behave impatiently, the fact that they wait is sufficient to label them as patient arrivals for purposes of waiting line theory.)

  There are two classes of *impatient* arrivals. Members of the first class arrive, survey both the service facility and the length of the line, and then decide to leave. Those in the second class arrive, view the situation, join the waiting line, and then, after some period of time, depart. The behavior of the first type is termed *balking,* while the second is termed *reneging.* To avoid balking and reneging, companies that provide high service levels typically try to target server utilization levels (the percentage of time busy) at no more than 70 to 80 percent.

A busy toll-plaza needs many queues (lanes) to reduce waiting time

Waiting Lines and Servers The queuing system consists primarily of the waiting line(s) and the available number of servers. Here, we discuss issues pertaining to waiting line characteristics and management, line structure, and service rate. Factors to consider with waiting lines include the line length, number of lines, and queue discipline.

Length. In a practical sense, an infinite line is simply one that is very long in terms of the capacity of the service system. Examples of *infinite potential length* are a line of vehicles backed up for miles at a bridge crossing and customers who must form a line around the block as they wait to purchase tickets at a theater.

Gas stations, loading docks, and parking lots have *limited line capacity* caused by legal restrictions or physical space characteristics. This complicates the waiting line problem not only in service system utilization and waiting line computations but also in the shape of the actual arrival distribution. The arrival denied entry into the line because of lack of space may rejoin the population for a later try or may seek service elsewhere. Either action makes an obvious difference in the finite population case.

- **Number of lines.** A single line or single file is, of course, one line only. The term *multiple lines* refers to the single lines that form in front of two or more servers or to single lines that converge at some central redistribution point. The disadvantage of multiple lines in a busy facility is that arrivals often shift lines if several previous services have been of short duration or if those customers currently in other lines appear to require a short service time.

- **Queue discipline.** A queue discipline is a priority rule or set of rules for determining the order of service to customers in a waiting line. The rules selected can have a dramatic effect on the system's overall performance. The number of customers in line, the average waiting time, the range of variability in waiting time, and the efficiency of the service facility are just a few of the factors affected by the choice of priority rules.

Probably the most common priority rule is first come, first served (FCFS). This rule states that customers in line are served on the basis of their chronological arrival; no other characteristics have any bearing on the selection process. This is popularly accepted as the fairest rule, although in practice it discriminates against the arrival requiring a short service time.

Reservations first, emergencies first, highest-profit customer first, largest orders first, best customers first, longest waiting time in line, and soonest promised date are other examples of priority rules. There are two major practical problems in using any rule: One is ensuring that customers know and follow the rule. The other is ensuring that a system exists to enable employees to manage the line (such as take-a-number systems).

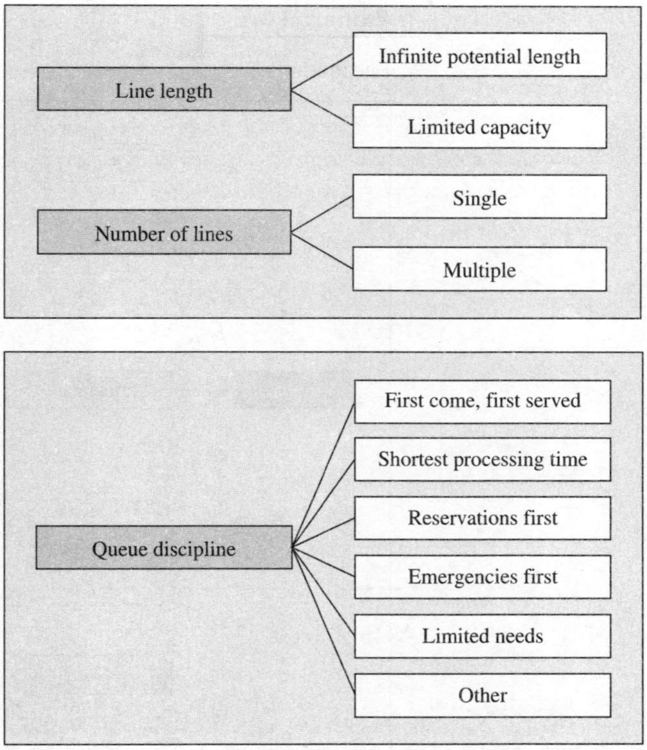

Service Time Distribution Another important feature of the waiting structure is the time the customer or unit spends with the server once the service has started. Waiting line formulas generally specify **service rate** as the capacity of the server in number of units per time period (such as 12 completions per hour) and *not* as service time, which might average five minutes each. A constant service time rule states that each service takes exactly the same time. As in constant arrivals, this characteristic is generally limited to machine-controlled operations.

When service times are random, they can be approximated by the exponential distribution. When using the exponential distribution as an approximation of the service times, we will refer to μ as the average number of units or customers that can be served per time period.

Line Structures As Exhibit 10.6 shows, the flow of items to be serviced may go through a single line, multiple lines, or some mixture of the two. The choice of format depends partly on the volume of customers served and partly on the restrictions imposed by sequential requirements governing the order in which service must be performed.

Service rate
The number of customers a server can handle during a given time period.

1. **Single channel, single phase.** This is the simplest type of waiting line structure, and straightforward formulas are available to solve the problem for standard distribution patterns of arrival and service. When the distributions are nonstandard, the problem is easily solved by computer simulation. A typical example of a single-channel, single-phase situation is the one-person barbershop.
2. **Single channel, multiphase.** A car wash is an illustration because a series of services (vacuuming, wetting, washing, rinsing, drying, window cleaning, and parking) is performed in a fairly uniform sequence. A critical factor in the single-channel case with service in series is the amount of buildup of items allowed in front of each service, which in turn constitutes separate waiting lines.
3. **Multichannel, single phase.** Tellers' windows in a bank and checkout counters in high-volume department stores exemplify this type of structure. The difficulty with this format is that the uneven service time given each customer results in unequal speed or flow among the lines. This results in some customers being served before others who arrived earlier, as well as in some degree of line shifting. Varying this structure to ensure the servicing of arrivals in chronological order would require forming a single line, from which, as a server becomes available, the next customer in the queue is assigned.

   The major problem of this structure is that it requires rigid control of the line to maintain order and to direct customers to available servers. In some instances, assigning numbers to customers in the order of their arrival helps alleviate this problem.
4. **Multichannel, multiphase.** This case is similar to the preceding one except that two or more services are performed in sequence. The admission of patients in a hospital uses this pattern because a specific sequence of steps is usually followed: initial contact at the admissions desk, filling out forms, making identification tags, obtaining a room assignment, escorting the patient to the room, and so forth. Because several servers are usually available for this procedure, more than one patient at a time may be processed.

EXHIBIT 10.6

Line Structures

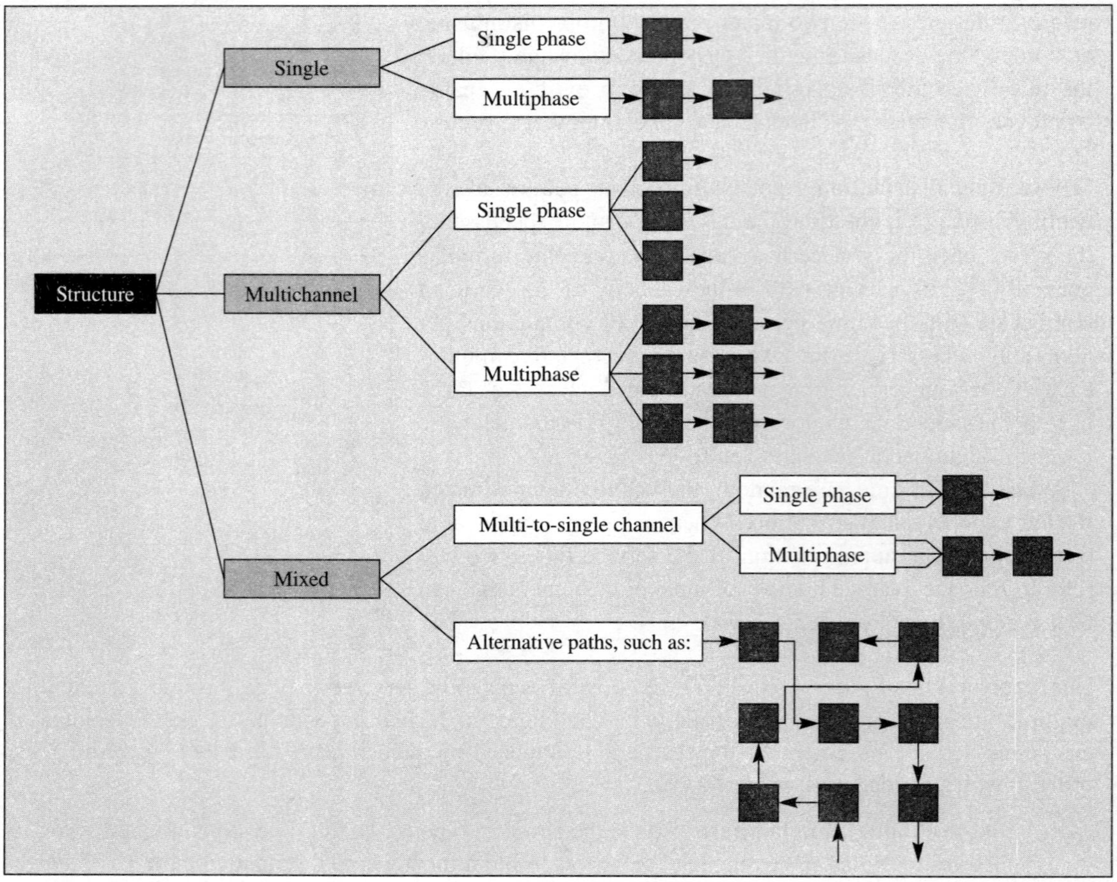

5. **Mixed.** Under this general heading, we consider two subcategories: (1) multiple-to-single channel structures and (2) alternative path structures. Under (1), we find either lines that merge into one for single-phase service, as at a bridge crossing where two lanes merge into one, or lines that merge into one for multiphase service, such as subassembly lines feeding into a main line. Under (2), we encounter two structures that differ in directional flow requirements. The first is similar to the multichannel–multiphase case, except that (a) there may be switching from one channel to the next after the first service has been rendered and (b) the number of channels and phases may vary—again—after performance of the first service.

Exiting the Queuing System Once a customer is served, two exit fates are possible: (1) The customer may return to the source population and immediately become a competing candidate for service again or (2) there may be a low probability of reservice. The first case can be illustrated by a customer machine that has been routinely repaired and returned to duty but may break down again; the second can be illustrated by a customer machine that has been overhauled or modified and has a low probability of reservice over the near future. In a lighter vein, we might refer to the first as the "recurring-common-cold case" and to the second as the "appendectomy-only-once case."

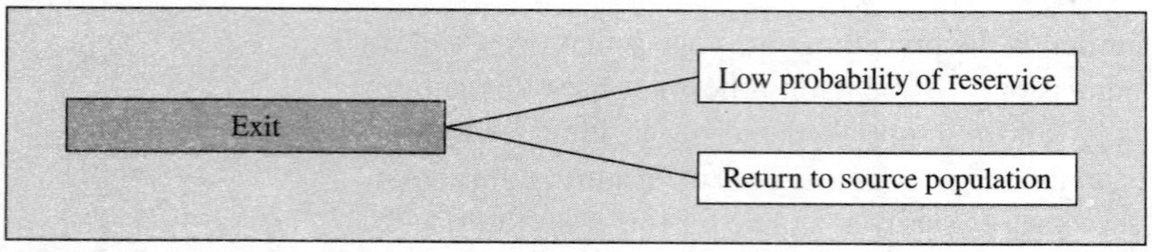

It should be apparent that when the population source is finite, any change in the service performed on customers who return to the population modifies the arrival rate at the service facility. This, of course, alters the characteristics of the waiting line under study and necessitates reanalysis of the problem.

WAITING LINE MODELS

LO 10-2

Analyze waiting line problems

In this section, we present four sample waiting line problems followed by their solutions. Each has a slightly different structure (see Exhibit 10.7) and solution equation (see Exhibit 10.8). There are more types of models than these four, but the formulas and solutions become quite complicated, and those problems are generally solved using computer simulation. Also, in using these formulas, keep in mind they are steady-state formulas derived on the assumption that the process under study is ongoing. Thus, they may provide inaccurate results when applied to processes where the arrival rates and/or service rates change over time. A handy app available at that can be used to solve these problems. In addition, a spreadsheet "10 Waiting Line Analysis.xls" is available.

Analytics

EXHIBIT 10.7

Properties of Some Specific Waiting Line Models

Model	Layout	Service Phase	Source Population	Arrival Pattern	Queue Discipline	Service Pattern	Permissible Queue Length	Typical Example
1	Single channel	Single	Infinite	Poisson	FCFS	Exponential	Unlimited	Drive-in teller at bank; one-lane toll bridge
2	Single channel	Single	Infinite	Poisson	FCFS	Constant	Unlimited	Roller coaster rides in amusement park
3	Multichannel	Single	Infinite	Poisson	FCFS	Exponential	Unlimited	Parts counter in auto agency
4	Single channel	Single	Finite	Poisson	FCFS	Exponential	Unlimited	Machine breakdown and repair in a factory

EXHIBIT 10.8

Notations for Equations

Infinite Queuing Notation: Models 1–3	Finite Queuing Notation: Model 4
λ = Arrival rate μ = Service rate $\frac{1}{\mu}$ = Average service time $\frac{1}{\lambda}$ = Average time between arrivals ρ = Ratio of total arrival rate to service rate for a single server $\left(\frac{\lambda}{\mu}\right)^*$ L_q = Average number waiting in line L_s = Average number in system (including any being served) W_q = Average time waiting in line W_s = Average total time in system (including any being served) n = Number of units in the system S = Number of identical service channels P_n = Probability of exactly n units in system P_w = Probability of waiting in line	D = Probability that an arrival must wait in line F = Efficiency factor, a measure of the effect of having to wait in line H = Average number of units being serviced J = Population source less those in queuing system $(N - n)$ L = Average number of units in line S = Number of service channels n = Average number of units in queuing system (including the one being served) N = Number of units in population source P_n = Probability of exactly n units in queuing system T = Average time to perform the service U = Average time between customer service requirements W = Average waiting time in line X = Service factor, or proportion of service time required

*For single-server queues, this is equivalent to utilization.

Here is a quick preview of our four problems to illustrate each of the four waiting line models in Exhibits 10.7 and 10.8.

Problem 1: Customers in line. A bank wants to know how many customers are waiting for a drive-in teller, how long they have to wait, the utilization of the teller, and what the service rate would have to be so that 95 percent of the time there would not be more than three cars in the system at any time.

Problem 2: Equipment selection. A franchise for Robot Car Wash must decide which equipment to purchase out of a choice of three. Larger units cost more but wash cars faster. To make the decision, costs are related to revenue.

Problem 3: Determining the number of servers. An auto agency parts department must decide how many clerks to employ at the counter. More clerks cost more money, but there is a savings because mechanics wait less time.

Equations for Solving Four Model Problems

Simple system

Model 1

$$\begin{cases} L_q = \dfrac{\lambda^2}{\mu(\mu-\lambda)} \quad W_q = \dfrac{L_q}{\lambda} \quad P_n = \left(1-\dfrac{\lambda}{\mu}\right)\left(\dfrac{\lambda}{\mu}\right)^n \quad P_0 = \left(1-\dfrac{\lambda}{\mu}\right) \\ L_s = \dfrac{\lambda}{\mu-\lambda} \quad W_s = \dfrac{L_s}{\lambda} \quad \rho = \dfrac{\lambda}{\mu} \end{cases} \qquad [10.3]$$

Constant service time system

Model 2

$$\begin{cases} L_q = \dfrac{\lambda^2}{2\mu(\mu-\lambda)} \quad W_q = \dfrac{L_q}{\lambda} \\ L_s = L_q + \dfrac{\lambda}{\mu} \quad W_s = \dfrac{L_s}{\lambda} \end{cases} \qquad [10.4]$$

Multichannel system

Model 3

$$\begin{cases} L_s = L_q + \lambda/\mu \quad W_s = L_s/\lambda \\ W_q = L_q/\lambda \quad P_w = L_q\left(\dfrac{S\mu}{\lambda} - 1\right) \end{cases} \qquad [10.5]$$

(Exhibit 10.9 provides the value of L_q given λ/μ and the number of servers S.)

Finite customer system

Model 4

$$\begin{cases} X = \dfrac{T}{T+U} \quad H = FNX \quad L = N(1-F) \quad n = L + H \\ P_n = \dfrac{N!}{(N-n)!}X^n P_0 \quad J = NF(1-X) \\ W = \dfrac{L(T+U)}{N-L} = \dfrac{LT}{H} \quad F = \dfrac{T+U}{T+U+W} \end{cases} \qquad [10.6]$$

Exhibit 10.10 provides values for S, D, and F given X.

Problem 4: Finite population source. Whereas the previous models assume a large population, finite queuing employs a separate set of equations for those cases where the calling customer population is small. In this last problem, mechanics must service four weaving machines to keep them operating. Based on the costs associated with machines being idle and the costs of mechanics to service them, the problem is to decide how many mechanics to use.

EXAMPLE 10.1 Customers in Line

Western National Bank is considering opening a drive-thru window for customer service. Management estimates that customers will arrive at the rate of 15 per hour. The teller who will staff the window can service customers at the rate of one every three minutes.

Analytics

Part 1 Assuming Poisson arrivals and exponential service, find

1. Utilization of the teller.
2. Average number in the waiting line.
3. Average number in the system.

4. Average waiting time in line.
5. Average waiting time in the system, including service.

SOLUTION—PART 1

1. The average utilization of the teller is (using Model 1)

$$\rho = \frac{\lambda}{\mu} = \frac{15}{20} = 75 \text{ percent}$$

2. The average number in the waiting line is

$$L_q = \frac{\lambda^2}{\mu(\mu-\lambda)} = \frac{(15)^2}{20(20-15)} = 2.25 \text{ customers}$$

3. The average number in the system is

$$L_s = \frac{\lambda}{\mu-\lambda} = \frac{15}{20-15} = 3 \text{ customers}$$

4. Average waiting time in line is

$$W_q = \frac{L_q}{\lambda} = \frac{2.25}{15} = 0.15 \text{ hour, or 9 minutes}$$

5. Average waiting time in the system is

$$W_s = \frac{L_s}{\lambda} = \frac{3}{15} = 0.2 \text{ hour, or 12 minutes}$$

Part 2 Because of limited space availability and a desire to provide an acceptable level of service, the bank manager would like to ensure, with 95 percent confidence, that no more than three cars will be in the system at any time. What is the present level of service for the three-car limit? What level of teller use must be attained and what must be the service rate of the teller to ensure the 95 percent level of service?

SOLUTION—PART 2

The present level of service for three or fewer cars is the probability that there are 0, 1, 2, or 3 cars in the system. From Model 1, Exhibit 10.8,

$$P_n = \left(1-\frac{\lambda}{\mu}\right)\left(\frac{\lambda}{\mu}\right)^n$$

at $n = 0$, $P_0 = (1 - 15/20)$	$(1 - 15/20)(15/20)^0 = 0.250$		
at $n = 1$, $P_1 = (1/4)$	$(1 - 15/20)(15/20)^1 = 0.188$		
at $n = 2$, $P_2 = (1/4)$	$(1 - 15/20)(15/20)^2 = 0.141$		
at $n = 3$, $P_3 = (1/4)$	$(1 - 15/20)(15/20)^3 = 0.105$		
	0.684	or	68.4 percent

The probability of having more than three cars in the system is 1.0 minus the probability of three or fewer cars (1.0 – 0.684 = 31.6 percent).

For a 95 percent service level of three or fewer cars, this states that $P_0 + P_1 + P_2 + P_3 = 95$ percent.

$$0.95 = \left(1-\frac{\lambda}{\mu}\right)\left(\frac{\lambda}{\mu}\right)^0 + \left(1-\frac{\lambda}{\mu}\right)\left(\frac{\lambda}{\mu}\right)^1 + \left(1-\frac{\lambda}{\mu}\right)\left(\frac{\lambda}{\mu}\right)^2 + \left(1-\frac{\lambda}{\mu}\right)\left(\frac{\lambda}{\mu}\right)^3$$

$$0.95 = \left(1-\frac{\lambda}{\mu}\right)\left[1 + \frac{\lambda}{\mu} + \left(\frac{\lambda}{\mu}\right)^2 + \left(\frac{\lambda}{\mu}\right)^3\right]$$

We can solve this by trial and error for values of λ/μ. If $\lambda/\mu = 0.50$,

$$0.95 \stackrel{?}{=} 0.5(1 + 0.5 + 0.25 + 0.125)$$
$$0.95 \neq 0.9375$$

With $\lambda/\mu = 0.45$,

$$0.95 \stackrel{?}{=} (1 - 0.45)(1 + 0.45 + 0.203 + 0.091)$$
$$0.95 \neq 0.96$$

With $\lambda/\mu = 0.47$,

$$0.95 \stackrel{?}{=} (1 - 0.47)(1 + 0.47 + 0.221 + 0.104) = 0.95135$$
$$0.95 \approx 0.95135$$

Therefore, with the utilization $\rho = \lambda/\mu$ of 47 percent, the probability of three or fewer cars in the system is 95 percent.

To find the rate of service required to attain this 95 percent service level, we simply solve the equation $\lambda/\mu = 0.47$, where λ = number of arrivals per hour. This gives $\mu = 32$ per hour. That is, the teller must serve approximately 32 people per hour (a 60 percent increase over the original 20-per-hour capability) for 95 percent confidence that not more than three cars will be in the system. Perhaps service may be sped up by modifying the method of service, adding another teller, or limiting the types of transactions available at the drive-thru window. Note that, with the condition of 95 percent confidence, three or fewer cars will be in the system, and the teller will be idle 53 percent of the time.

EXAMPLE 10.2 Equipment Selection

Robot Company franchises combination gas and car wash stations throughout the United States. Robot gives a free car wash for a gasoline fill-up or, for a wash alone, charges \$0.50. Past experience shows that the number of customers that have car washes following fill-ups is about the same as for a wash alone. The average profit on a gasoline fill-up is about \$0.70, and the cost of the car wash to Robot is \$0.10. Robot stays open 14 hours per day.

Robot has three power units and drive assemblies, and a franchisee must select the unit preferred. Unit I can wash cars at the rate of one every five minutes and is leased for \$12 per day. Unit II, a larger unit, can wash cars at the rate of one every four minutes but costs \$16 per day. Unit III, the largest, costs \$22 per day and can wash a car in three minutes.

The franchisee estimates that customers will not wait in line more than five minutes for a car wash. A longer time will cause Robot to lose the gasoline sales as well as the car wash sale.

If the estimate of customer arrivals resulting in washes is 10 per hour, which wash unit should be selected?

SOLUTION

Using unit I, calculate the average waiting time of customers in the wash line (μ for unit I = 12 per hour). From the Model 2 equations (Exhibit 10.8),

$$L_q = \frac{\lambda^2}{2\mu(\mu - \lambda)} = \frac{10^2}{2(12)(12 - 10)} = 2.08333$$

$$W_q = \frac{L_q}{\lambda} = \frac{2.08333}{10} = 0.208 \text{ hour, or } 12\frac{1}{2} \text{ minutes}$$

For unit II at 15 per hour,

$$L_q = \frac{10^2}{2(15)(15-10)} = 0.667$$

$$W_q = \frac{0.667}{10} = 0.0667 \text{ hour, or 4 minutes}$$

If waiting time is the only criterion, unit II should be purchased. But before we make the final decision, we must look at the profit differential between both units.

With unit I, some customers would balk and renege because of the 12½-minute wait. And, although this greatly complicates the mathematical analysis, we can gain some estimate of lost sales with unit I by increasing W_q = 5 minutes or ½ hour (the average length of time customers will wait) and solving for λ. This would be the effective arrival rate of customers:

$$W_q = \frac{L_q}{\lambda} = \left(\frac{\lambda^2/2\mu(\mu-\lambda)}{\lambda}\right)$$

$$W_q = \frac{\lambda}{2\mu(\mu-\lambda)}$$

$$\lambda = \frac{2W_q\mu^2}{1+2W_q\mu} = \frac{2\left(\frac{1}{12}\right)(12)^2}{1+2\left(\frac{1}{12}\right)(12)} = 8 \text{ per hour}$$

Therefore, because the original estimate of λ was 10 per hour, an estimated 2 customers per hour will be lost. Lost profit of 2 customers per hour × 14 hours × $\frac{1}{2}$ (\$0.70 fill-up profit + \$0.40 wash profit) = \$15.40 per day.

Because the additional cost of unit II over unit I is only \$4 per day, the loss of \$15.40 profit obviously warrants installing unit II.

The original five-minute maximum wait constraint is satisfied by unit II. Therefore, unit III is not considered unless the arrival rate is expected to increase.

EXAMPLE 10.3 Determining the Number of Servers

In the service department of the Glenn-Mark Auto Agency, mechanics requiring parts for auto repair or service present their request forms at the parts department counter. The parts clerk fills a request while the mechanic waits. Mechanics arrive in a random (Poisson) fashion at the rate of 40 per hour, and a clerk can fill requests at the rate of 20 per hour (exponential). If the cost for a parts clerk is \$30 per hour and the cost for a mechanic is \$60 per hour, determine the optimum number of clerks to staff the counter. (Because of the high arrival rate, an infinite source may be assumed.)

Analytics

SOLUTION

First, assume that three clerks will be used because having only one or two clerks would create infinitely long lines (since $\lambda = 40$ and $\mu = 20$). The equations for Model 3 from Exhibit 10.8 will be used here. But first we need to obtain the average number in line using the table in Exhibit 10.9. (Note the table is located at the end of the chapter.) Using the table and values $\lambda/\mu = 2$ and $S = 3$, we obtain $L_q = 0.8889$ mechanic.

Expected Number of People Waiting in Line (L_q) for Various Values of S and λ/μ

At this point, we see that we have an average of 0.8889 mechanic waiting all day. For an eight-hour day at \$60 per hour, there is a loss of mechanic's time worth 0.8889 mechanic × \$60 per hour × 8 hours = \$426.67.

Our next step is to reobtain the waiting time if we add another parts clerk. We then compare the added cost of the additional employee with the time saved by the mechanics. Again, using the table in Exhibit 10.9 at the end of the chapter but with $S = 4$, we obtain

$L_q = 0.1739$ mechanic in line	
$0.1739 \times \$60 \times 8$ hours = \$83.47 cost of a mechanic waiting in line	
Value of mechanic's time saved is \$426.67 – \$83.47	= \$342.20
Cost of an additional parts clerk is 8 hours × \$30/hour	= 240.00
Cost of reduction by adding fourth clerk	= \$102.20

This problem could be expanded to consider the addition of runners to deliver parts to mechanics; the problem then would be to determine the optimal number of runners. This, however, would have to include the added cost of lost time caused by errors in parts receipts. For example, a mechanic would recognize a wrong part at the counter and obtain immediate correction, whereas the parts runner might not.

Analytics

EXAMPLE 10.4 Finite Population Source

Studies of a bank of four weaving machines at the Loose Knit textile mill have shown that, on average, each machine needs adjusting every hour and that the current repair person averages 7½ minutes per adjustment. Assuming Poisson arrivals, exponential service, and a machine idle time cost of \$80 per hour, determine if a second servicer (who also averages 7½ minutes per adjustment) should be hired at a rate of \$14 per hour.

SOLUTION

This is a finite queuing problem that can be solved by using finite queuing tables. (See Exhibit 10.10 that is located at the end of the chapter.) The approach in this problem is to compare the cost of machine downtime (either waiting in line or being serviced) and of one repairer to the cost of machine downtime and two repairers. We do this by finding the average number of machines that are in the service system and multiplying this number by the downtime cost per hour. To this we add the repairers' cost.

Before we proceed, we first define some terms:

N = Number of machines in the population
S = Number of repairers
T = Time required to service a machine
U = Average time a machine runs before requiring service
X = Service factor , or proportion of service time required for each machine ($X = T/(T + U)$)
L = Average number of machines waiting in line to be serviced
H = Average number of machines being serviced

The values to be determined from the finite tables are

D = Probability that a machine needing service will have to wait
F = Efficiency factor, which measures the effect of having to wait in line to be serviced

The tables are arranged according to three variables: N, population size; X, service factor; and S, the number of service channels (repairers in this problem). To look up a value, first find the table for the correct N size, then search the first column for the appropriate X, and finally find the line for S. Then, read off D and F. (In addition to these values, other characteristics about a finite queuing system can be found by using the finite formulas.)

Exhibit 10.11

A Comparison of Downtime Costs for Service and Repair of Four Machines

Number of Repairers	Number of Machines Down ($H + L$)	Cost per Hour for Machines Down [($H + L$) × \$80/Hour]	Cost of Repairers (\$14/Hour Each)	Total Cost per Hour
1	0.597	\$47.76	\$ 14.00	\$61.76
2	0.451	36.08	28.00	64.08

$N = 4$

$S = 1$

$T = 7\frac{1}{2}$ minutes

$U = 60$ minutes

$$X = \frac{T}{T + U} = \frac{7.5}{7.5 + 60} = 0.111$$

From Exhibit 10.10, which displays the table for $N = 4$, F is interpolated as being approximately 0.957 at $X = 0.111$ and $S = 1$.

The number of machines waiting in line to be serviced is L, where

$$L = N(1 - F) = 4(1 - 0.957) = 0.172 \text{ machine}$$

The number of machines being serviced is H, where

$$H = FNX = 0.957(4)(0.111) = 0.425 \text{ machine}$$

Exhibit 10.11 shows the cost resulting from unproductive machine time and the cost of the repairer.

Case II: Two repairers. From Exhibit 10.10, at $X = 0.111$ and $S = 2$, $F = 0.998$.

The number of machines waiting in line, L, is

$$L = N(1 - F) = 4(1 - 0.998) = 0.008 \text{ machine}$$

The number of machines being serviced, H, is

$$H = FNX = 0.998(4)(0.111) = 0.443 \text{ machine}$$

The costs for the machines being idle and for the two repairers are shown in Exhibit 10.11. The final column of that exhibit shows that retaining just one repairer is the better choice.

Approximating Customer Waiting Time

Good news for managers. All you need is the mean and standard deviation to compute average waiting time! Some good research has led to a "quick and dirty" mathematical approximation to the queuing models illustrated earlier in the chapter. What's nice about the approximation is that it does not assume a particular arrival rate or service distribution. All that is needed is the mean and standard deviation of the interarrival time and the service time. We will not burden you with all the details of how the approximations were derived, just how to use the formulas.

First, you will need to collect some data on your service time. The service time is the amount of time it takes to serve each customer. Keep in mind that you want to collect your data during a period of time that fairly represents what you expect to happen during the period you are concerned about. For example, if you want to know how many bank tellers you should have to service customers on Friday around the lunch period, collect your data during that period. This will ensure the transactions being performed are similar to those you expect in the future. You can use a stopwatch to time how long it takes to serve each customer. Using these data, calculate the mean and standard deviation of the service time.

Recall from your statistics that the mean is

Analytics

$$\overline{X} = \sum_{i=1}^{N} x_i / N \qquad [10.7]$$

where x_i = observed value and N = total number of observed values.

The standard deviation is

$$s = \sqrt{\frac{\sum_{i=1}^{N} (x_i - \overline{X})^2}{N - 1}} \qquad [10.8]$$

Next, capture data on the amount of time between the arrivals of each new customer during the period of time you are studying. This is called the interarrival time. From the data, calculate the mean and standard deviation of the interarrival time. From these calculations, we have

$\overline{X}_s$ = Mean service time

$\overline{X}_a$ = Mean interarrival time

S_s = Standard deviation of the service time sample

S_a = Standard deviation of the interarrival time sample

Next, define the following:

$$C_s = \text{Coefficient of variation of service time} = \frac{S_s}{\overline{X}_s}$$

$$C_a = \text{Coefficient of variation of interarrival time} = \frac{S_a}{\overline{X}_a} \qquad [10.9]$$

$$\lambda = \text{Customer arrival rate} = \frac{1}{\overline{X}_a}$$

$$\mu = \text{Customer service rate} = \frac{1}{\overline{X}_s}$$

Now, we can calculate some statistics about our system. First, define S as the number of servers that we intend to use. Then,

$$\rho = \text{Utilization of the servers} = \frac{\lambda}{S\mu}$$

$$L_q = \text{Expected length of the waiting line} = \frac{\rho^{\sqrt{2(s+1)}}}{1-\rho} \times \frac{C_a^2 + C_s^2}{2} \qquad [10.10]$$

$$L_s = \text{Expected number of people in the system} = \mathrm{L}_q + S\rho$$

$$W_q = \text{Expected time waiting in line} = \frac{L_q}{\lambda}$$

$$W_s = \text{Expected time in the system} = \frac{L_s}{\lambda}$$

The utilization (ρ) is the percentage of time that the servers are expected to be busy. Often, companies that provide high service target this number at between 70 and 80 percent depending on the amount of variance there is in the customer arrival and service rates. L_q is how long the queue is expected to be, and W_q is how long a customer is expected to have to wait in the queue. L_s and W_s are the expected number of customers in the system and the expected time that a customer is in the system. These statistics consider that the total number of customers and the total waiting time must include those that are actually being served.

EXAMPLE 10.5 Waiting Line Approximation

Let's consider an example of a call center that takes orders for a mail order business. During the peak period, the average time between call arrivals ($\overline{X}_a$) is 0.5 minute with a standard deviation (S_a) of 0.203 minute. The average time to service a call ($\overline{X}_s$) is 4 minutes and the standard deviation of the service time (S_s) is 2.5 minutes. If the call center is using nine operators to service calls, how long would you expect customers to wait before being serviced? What would be the impact of adding an additional operator?

SOLUTION

W_q is the time we expect a customer to wait before being served. The best way to do these calculations is with a spreadsheet. The spreadsheet "Queue_Models.xls" can be easily used. The following steps are needed for the calculation of the customer wait time.

Step 1. Calculate expected customer arrival rate (λ), service rate per server (μ), and coefficient of variation for the interarrival time (C_a) and service time (C_s).

$$\lambda = \frac{1}{\overline{X}_a} = \frac{1}{0.5} = 2 \text{ customers per minute}$$

$$\mu = \frac{1}{\overline{X}_s} = \frac{1}{4} = 0.25 \text{ customer per minute}$$

$$C_a = \frac{S_a}{\overline{X}_a} = \frac{0.203}{0.5} = 0.406$$

$$C_s = \frac{S_s}{\overline{X}_s} = \frac{2.5}{4} = 0.625$$

Step 2. Calculate the expected server utilization (ρ).

$$\rho = \frac{\lambda}{S\mu} = \frac{2}{9 \times 0.25} = 0.888889 \quad \text{(Operators are expected to be busy 89 percent of the time.)}$$

Step 3. Calculate the expected number of people waiting (L_q) and the length of the wait (W_q).

$$L_q = \frac{\rho^{\sqrt{2(s+1)}}}{1-\rho} \times \frac{C_a^2 + C_s^2}{2} = \frac{0.888889^{\sqrt{2(9+1)}}}{1-0.888889} \times \frac{0.406^2 + 0.625^2}{2} = 1.476064 \text{ customers}$$

(This is the number of customers that we expect to be waiting on hold.)

$$W_q = \frac{L_q}{\lambda} = \frac{1.476064}{2} = 0.738032 \text{ minute}$$

On average, we expect customers to wait 44 seconds (0.738032×60) before talking to an operator. For 10 operators, the calculations are as follows:

$$\rho = \frac{\lambda}{S\mu} = \frac{2}{10 \times 0.25} = 0.8 \quad \text{(Operators are expected to be busy 80 percent of the time.)}$$

$$L_q = \frac{\rho^{\sqrt{2(s+1)}}}{1-\rho} \times \frac{C_a^2 + C_s^2}{2} = \frac{0.8^{\sqrt{2(10+1)}}}{1-0.8} \times \frac{0.406^2 + 0.625^2}{2} = 0.487579 \text{ customer}$$

$$W_q = \frac{L_q}{\lambda} = \frac{0.487579}{2} + 0.24379 \text{ minute}$$

With 10 operators, the waiting time is cut about 66 percent to 14.6 seconds. If you add two operators (bringing the total to 11), the waiting time in queue is 6.4 seconds. Adding the first additional operator has a significant impact on customer wait time.

This approximation is useful for many typical queuing situations. It is easy to implement using a spreadsheet such as the "10 Waiting Line Analysis.xls" spreadsheet. Keep in mind that the approximation assumes that the population to be served is large and customers arrive one at a time. The approximation can be useful for a quick analysis of a queuing situation.

LO 10-3

Analyze complex waiting lines using simulation

SIMULATING WAITING LINES

Some waiting line problems that seem simple on first impression turn out to be extremely difficult or impossible to solve. Throughout this chapter, we have been treating waiting line situations that are independent; that is, either the entire system consists of a single phase or else each service that is performed in a series is independent. (This could happen if the output of one service location is allowed to build up in front of the next one so that, in essence, it becomes a calling population for the next service.) When a series of services is performed in sequence where the output rate of one becomes the input rate of the next, we can no longer use the simple formulas. This is also true for any problem where conditions do not meet the requirements of the equations, as specified in Exhibit 10.8. The technique best suited to solving this type of problem is computer simulation.

Analytics

Waiting lines that occur in series and parallel (such as in assembly lines and workcenters) usually cannot be solved mathematically. Often, they can be easily simulated using a spreadsheet.

Example: A Two-Stage Assembly Line

Consider an assembly line that makes a product of significant physical size, such as a refrigerator, stove, car, boat, TV, or furniture. Exhibit 10.12 shows two workstations on such a line.

EXHIBIT 10.12

Two Workstations on an Assembly Line

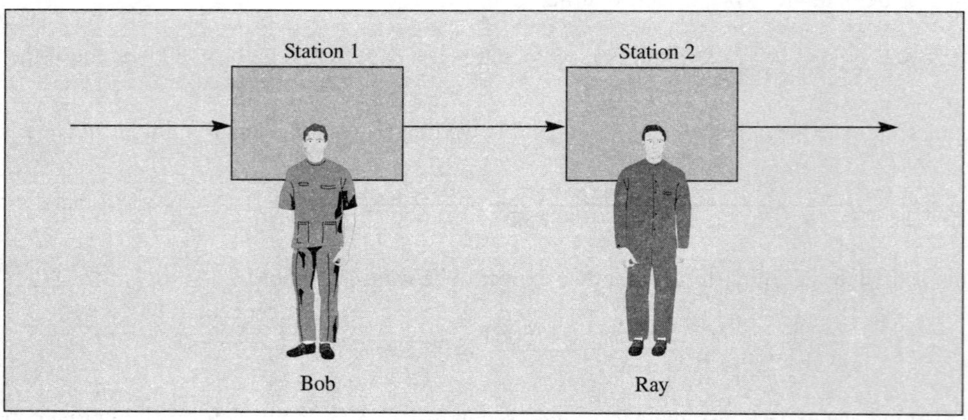

The size of the product is an important consideration in assembly-line analysis and design because the number of products that can exist at each workstation affects worker performance. If the product is large, then the workstations are dependent on each other. Exhibit 10.12, for example, shows Bob and Ray working on a two-stage line where Bob's output in Station 1 is fed to Ray in Station 2. If the workstations are adjacent, leaving no room for items between them, then Bob, by working slowly, would cause Ray to wait. Conversely, if Bob completes a product quickly (or if Ray takes longer to finish the task), then Bob must wait for Ray.

In this simulation, assume that Bob, the first worker on the line, can pull over a new item to work on whenever needed. We concentrate our analysis on the interactions between Bob and Ray.

Objective of the Study We would like to answer a number of questions about the assembly line from this study. A partial list would be

- What is the average performance time of each worker?
- What is the output rate of product through this line?
- How much time does Bob wait for Ray?
- How much time does Ray wait for Bob?
- If the space between the two stations were increased so that items could be stored there and give workers some independence, how would this affect output rates, wait times, and so on?

Data Collection To simulate this system, we need the performance times of Bob and Ray. One way to collect these data is to divide the range of performance times into segments and then observe each worker. A simple check or tally mark in each of these segments results in a useful histogram of data.

Exhibit 10.13 shows the data collection form used to observe the performances of Bob and Ray. To simplify the procedure, performance time was divided into 10-second intervals. Bob was observed for 100 repetitions of the work task and Ray was observed just 50 times. The number of observations does not have to be the same, but the more there are and the smaller the size of the time segments, the more accurate the study will be. The trade-off is that more observations and smaller segments take more time and more people (as well as more time to program and run a simulation).

EXHIBIT 10.13

Data Collection Form for Worker Observation

Seconds to Complete Task	Bob	Totals	Ray	Totals
5–14.99	||||	4	||||	4
15–24.99	卌 |	6	卌	5
25–34.99	卌 卌	10	卌 |	6
35–44.99	卌卌卌卌	20	卌 ||	7
45–54.99	卌卌卌卌卌卌卌卌	40	卌卌	10
55–64.99	卌卌 |	11	卌 |||	8
65–74.99	卌	5	卌 |	6
75–84.99	||||	4	||||	4
		100		50

Collecting data in this way defines an empirical frequency distribution that can be used for the simulation. As shown with our example, an empirical distribution is derived from observing the relative frequency of some event. In this case, the time to complete a task was observed. Other examples that could be observed are the number of arrivals of customers in a line over some interval of time, demand for a product, and the time needed to serve a customer.

For a simulation, random numbers are matched to the frequency of a particular event. A random number is one that is totally uncorrelated to other numbers in a sequence. Appendix H contains a table of totally random digits. If we wanted to have random numbers that were between 00 and 99, numbers would be drawn from the table in the exact order they appear in the table. For example, 56, 97, 08, 31, and 25 would be the first five two-digit random numbers in the table. The spreadsheet function RAND() returns a number between zero and one, and the function RANDBETWEEN (minimum, maximum) returns numbers between the minimum and maximum values).

For this example, random numbers between 00 and 99 are used. If an event occurs 10 percent of the time, 10 numbers would be assigned; if an event occurs 32 percent of the time, 32 numbers would be assigned; and so forth. In this way, the random numbers are matched to the empirical frequency distribution obtained from our observations.

Exhibit 10.14 contains the random number intervals assigned that correspond to the same ratio as the actual observed data. For example, Bob had 4 out of 100 times at 10 seconds. Therefore, if we used 100 numbers, we would assign 4 of those numbers as corresponding to 10 seconds. We could have assigned any four numbers, for example, 42, 18, 12, and 93. However, these would be a nuisance to search for, so we assign consecutive numbers, such as 00, 01, 02, and 03.

Exhibit 10.14

Random Number Intervals for Bob and Ray

Seconds	Time Frequencies for Bob (Operation 1)	RN Intervals	Time Frequencies for Ray (Operation 2)	RN Intervals
10	4	00–03	4	00–07
20	6	04–09	5	08–17
30	10	10–19	6	18–29
40	20	20–39	7	30–43
50	40	40–79	10	44–63
60	11	80–90	8	64–79
70	5	91–95	6	80–91
80	4	96–99	4	92–99
	100		50	

There were 50 observations of Ray, and there are two ways we could assign random numbers. First, we could use just 50 numbers (say, 00 to 49) and ignore any numbers over that. However, this is wasteful because we would discard 50 percent of all the numbers from the list. Another choice would be to double the frequency number. For example, rather than assign, say, numbers 00 to 03 to account for the 4 observations out of 50 that took 10 seconds, we could assign numbers 00 to 07 to represent 8 observations out of 100, which is double the observed number but the same frequency. Actually, for this example and the speed of computers, the savings of time by doubling is insignificant.

Exhibit 10.15 shows a hand simulation of 10 items processed by Bob and Ray. The random numbers used were from Appendix H, starting at the first column of two numbers and working downward.

Exhibit 10.15

Simulation of Bob and Ray—Two-Stage Assembly Line

	Bob						Ray				
Item Number	Random Number	Start Time	Performance Time	Finish Time	Wait Time	Storage Space	Random Time	Start Time	Performance Time	Finish Time	Wait Time
1	56	00	50	50		0	83	50	70	120	50
2	55	50	50	100	20	0	47	120	50	170	
3	84	120	60	180		0	08	180	20	200	10
4	36	180	40	220		0	05	220	10	230	20
5	26	220	40	260		0	42	260	40	300	30
6	95	260	70	330		0	95	330	80	410	30
7	66	330	50	380	30	0	17	410	20	430	
8	03	410	10	420	10	0	21	430	30	460	
9	57	430	50	480		0	31	480	40	520	20
10	69	480	50	530		0	90	530	70	600	10
			470		60				430		170

Assume that we start out at time 00 and run it in continuous seconds (not bothering to convert this to hours and minutes). The first random number is 56 and corresponds to Bob's performance at 50 seconds on the first item. The item is passed to Ray, who starts at 50 seconds. Relating the next random number, 83, to Exhibit 10.14, we find that Ray takes 70 seconds to complete the item. In the meantime, Bob starts on the next item at time 50 and takes 50 seconds (random number 55), finishing at time 100. However, Bob cannot start on the third item until Ray gets through with the first item at time 120. Bob, therefore, has a wait time of 20 seconds. (If there was storage space between Bob and Ray, this item could have been moved out of Bob's workstation, and Bob could have started the next item at time 100.) The remainder of the exhibit was calculated following the same pattern: obtaining a random number, finding the corresponding processing time, noting the wait time (if any), and computing the finish time. Note that, with no storage space between Bob and Ray, there was considerable waiting time for both workers.

We can now answer some questions and make some statements about the system. For example,

- The output time averages 60 seconds per unit (the complete time 600 for Ray divided by 10 units).
- Utilization of Bob is $\frac{470}{530} = 88.7$ percent.
- Utilization of Ray is $\frac{430}{550} = 78.2$ percent (disregarding the initial startup wait for the first item of 50 seconds).
- The average performance time for Bob is $\frac{470}{10} = 47$ seconds.
- The average performance time for Ray is $\frac{430}{10} = 43$ seconds.

We have demonstrated how this problem would be solved in a simple manual simulation. A sample of 10 is really too small to place much confidence in, so this problem should be run on a computer for several thousand iterations. (We extend this same problem further in the next section of this chapter.)

It is also vital to study the effect of item storage space between workers. The problem would be run to see what the throughput time and worker utilization times are with no storage space between workers. A second run should increase this storage space to one unit, with the corresponding changes noted. Repeating the runs for two, three, four, and so on, offers management a chance to compute the additional cost of space compared with the increased use. Such increased space between workers may require a larger building, more materials and parts in the system, material handling equipment, and a transfer machine, plus added heat, light, building maintenance, and so on.

These also would be useful data for management to see what changes in the system would occur if one worker position was automated. The assembly line could be simulated using data from the automated process to see if such a change would be cost justified.

Spreadsheet Simulation

As we have stated throughout this book, spreadsheets are very useful for a variety of problems. Exhibit 10.16 shows Bob and Ray's two-stage assembly line on an Excel spreadsheet. The procedure follows the same pattern as our manual display in Exhibit 10.15.

The total simulation on Excel passed through 1,200 iterations (shown in Exhibit 10.17); that is, 1,200 parts were finished by Ray. Simulation, as an analytic tool, has an advantage over quantitative methods in that it is dynamic, whereas analytic methods show long-run average performance. As you can see in Exhibit 10.17A, there is an unmistakable startup (or transient) phase. We could even raise some questions about the long-term operation of the line because it does not seem to have settled to a constant (steady state) value, even after the 1,200 items. Exhibit 10.17A shows 100 items that pass through the Bob and Ray two-stage system. Notice the wide variation in time for the first units completed. These figures are the average time that units take. It is a cumulative number; that is, the first unit takes the time generated by the random numbers. The average time for two units is the average time of the sum of the first and second units. The average time for three units is the average time for the sum of the first three units, and so on. This display could have almost any starting shape, not necessarily what we have shown. It all depends on the stream of random numbers. What we can be sure of is that the times do oscillate for a while until they settle down as units are finished and smooth the average.

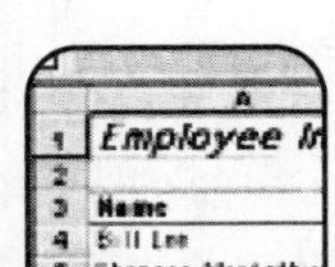

Exhibit 10.17B shows the average time that parts spend in the system. At the start, the display shows an increasing amount of time in the system. This can be expected because the system started empty and there are no interruptions for parts passing from Bob to Ray. Often, parts enter the system and may have to wait between stages as work-in-process; this causes delays for subsequent parts and adds to the waiting time. As time goes on, however, stability should occur unless the capacity of the

EXHIBIT 10.16

Bob and Ray Two-Stage Assembly Line on Microsoft Excel

	Bob					Ray							
Item	RN	Start Time	Perf. Time	Finish Time	Wait Time	RN	Start Time	Perf. time	Finish Time	Wait Time	Average Time/Unit	Total Time	Average Time in System
1	93	0	70	70	0	0	70	10	80	70	80.0	80	80.0
2	52	70	50	120	0	44	120	50	170	40	85.0	100	90.0
3	15	120	30	150	20	72	170	60	230	0	76.7	110	96.7
4	64	170	50	220	10	35	230	40	270	0	67.5	100	97.5
5	86	230	60	290	0	2	290	10	300	20	60.0	70	92.0
6	20	290	40	330	0	82	330	70	400	30	66.7	110	95.0
7	83	330	60	390	10	31	400	40	440	0	62.9	110	97.1
8	89	400	60	460	0	13	460	20	480	20	60.0	80	95.0
9	69	460	50	510	0	53	510	50	560	30	62.2	100	95.6
10	41	510	50	560	0	48	560	50	610	0	61.0	100	96.0
11	32	560	40	600	10	13	610	20	630	0	57.3	70	93.6
12	1	610	10	620	10	67	630	60	690	0	57.5	80	92.5
13	11	630	30	660	30	91	690	70	760	0	58.5	130	95.4
14	2	690	10	700	60	76	760	60	820	0	58.6	130	97.9
15	11	760	30	790	30	41	820	40	860	0	57.3	100	98.0
16	55	820	50	870	0	34	870	40	910	10	56.9	90	97.5
17	18	870	30	900	10	28	910	30	940	0	55.3	70	95.9
18	39	910	40	950	0	53	950	50	1000	10	55.6	90	95.6
19	13	950	30	980	20	41	1000	40	1040	0	54.7	90	95.3
20	7	1000	20	1020	20	21	1040	30	1070	0	53.5	70	94.0
21	29	1040	40	1080	0	54	1080	50	1130	10	53.8	90	93.8
22	58	1080	50	1130	0	39	1130	40	1170	0	53.2	90	93.6
23	95	1130	70	1200	0	70	1200	60	1260	30	54.8	130	95.2
24	27	1200	40	1240	20	60	1260	50	1310	0	54.6	110	95.8
25	59	1260	50	1310	0	93	1310	80	1390	0	55.6	130	97.2
26	85	1310	60	1370	20	51	1390	50	1440	0	55.4	130	98.5
27	12	1390	30	1420	20	35	1440	40	1480	0	54.8	90	98.1
28	34	1440	40	1480	0	51	1480	50	1530	0	54.6	90	97.9
29	60	1480	50	1530	0	87	1530	70	1600	0	55.2	120	98.6
30	97	1530	80	1610	0	29	1610	30	1640	10	54.7	110	99.0

second stage is less than the first stage's. In our present case, we did not allow space between them. Therefore, if Bob finished first, he had to wait for Ray. If Ray finished first, he had to wait for Bob.

Exhibit 10.17C shows the results of simulating Bob and Ray completing 1,200 units of product. Compare these figures to those we obtained simulating 10 items by hand. Not too bad, is it? The average performance time for Bob is shown as 46.48 seconds. This is close to the weighted average of what you would expect in the long run. For Bob, it is $(10 \times 4 + 20 \times 6 + 30 \times 10$, etc.$)\ 100 = 45.9$ seconds. Ray's expected time is $(10 \times 4 + 20 \times 5 + 30 \times 6$, etc.$)\ 50 = 46.4$ seconds.

The two-stage assembly line simulation is a good example of a specially designed spreadsheet for analyzing this problem. More general simulation programs built within Excel are available. John McClain, professor of operations management at Cornell University, has developed two simulation

EXHIBIT 10.17

A. Average Time per Unit of Output (Finish Time/Number of Units)

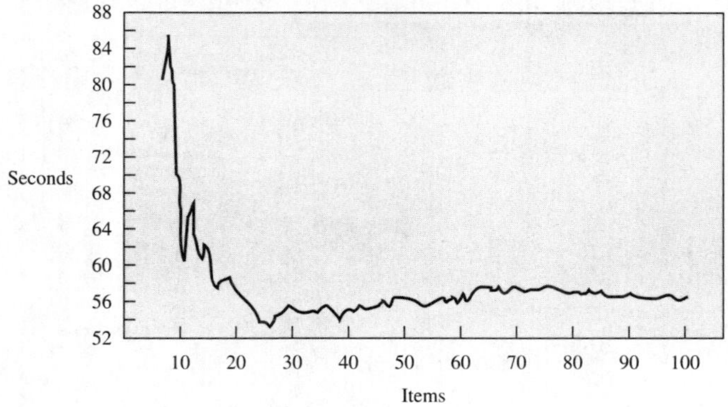

B. Average Time the Product Spends in the System

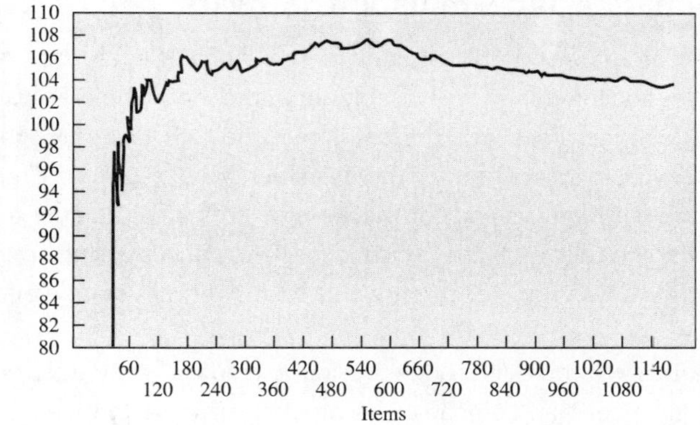

C. Results of Simulating 1,200 Units Processed by Bob and Ray

	Bob	Ray	Unit
Utilization	0.81	0.85	
Average wait time	10.02	9.63	
Average performance time	46.48	46.88	
Average time per unit			57.65
Average time in system			103.38

spreadsheets that can be used to demonstrate a variety of common systems. These spreadsheets have been included on this book's website.

The first spreadsheet, titled "LineSim," is designed to analyze a simple serial production line. This is a system with a series of machines; the output of one machine goes to a storage area, which is the input to the next machine. The spreadsheet can be easily configured for different numbers of machines, different buffer sizes, and numerous processing time distributions. In addition, machine breakdowns and repairs can be modeled. The second spreadsheet, "CellSim," is similar but allows machines to be arranged more generally. We thank Professor McClain for making these spreadsheets available.

Simulation Programs and Languages

Simulation models can be classified as *continuous* or *discrete.* Continuous models are based on mathematical equations and therefore are continuous, with values for all points in time. In contrast, discrete simulation occurs only at specific points. For example, customers arriving at a bank teller's window would be discrete simulation. The simulation jumps from point to point: the arrival of a customer, the start of service, the ending of service, the arrival of the next customer, and so on. Discrete simulation also can be triggered to run by units of time (daily, hourly, minute by minute). This is called *event simulation;* points in between either have no value to our simulation or cannot be computed because of the lack of some sort of mathematical relationship to link the succeeding events. Operations and supply management applications almost exclusively use discrete (event) simulation.

Simulation programs also can be categorized as general purpose and special purpose. General-purpose software allows programmers to build their own models. Special-purpose software simulation programs are specially built to simulate specific applications. In a specialized simulation for manufacturing, for example, provisions in the model allow for specifying the number of workcenters, their description, arrival rates, processing time, batch sizes, quantities of work in process, and available resources including labor, sequences, and so on. Additionally, the program may allow the observer to watch the animated operation and see the quantities and flows throughout the system as

OSCM AT WORK

Animation and Simulation Software

Call centers are a good application for simulation. They are easy to model, and information is available about the service time, arrival rates, renege times, and the paths that the calls take through the center. In this call center, there are four types of calls arriving at random intervals and four types of agents who are able to answer the calls. Each agent type is specialized in a particular call type. However, some agents are able to answer calls of different types.

This was quickly modeled using ExtendSim, a product of the Imagine That! company. The product makes extensive use of animation so that the user can actually watch the call center operate. You can learn more about this product at www.extendsim.com.

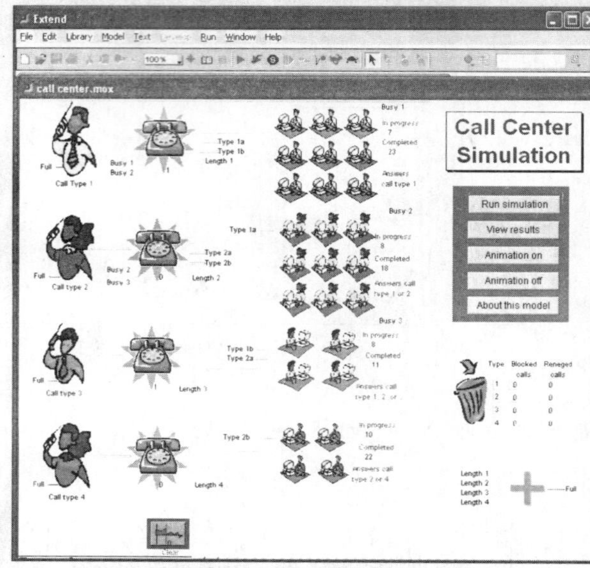

the simulation is running. Data are collected, analyzed, and presented in a form most suitable for that type of application. The software package called ExtendSim is featured in the Breakthrough box titled "Animation and Simulation Software."

As a last comment on simulation programs, do not rule out spreadsheets for simulation. As you noticed, we simulated Bob and Ray on a spreadsheet in the preceding section. The simplicity in using a spreadsheet for simulation may well compensate for any needed reduction in the complexity of the problem in order to use the spreadsheet.

@RISK is an add-in program that works with Microsoft Excel. The program adds many useful simulation-related functions to the spreadsheet. Using @RISK automates the process of taking random values from a specified distribution function, automates the recalculation of the spreadsheet with the new random values, and captures output values and statistics. @RISK simplifies the process of building and running spreadsheet simulations.

CONCEPT CONNECTIONS

LO 10–1 Understand what a waiting line problem is

Summary

- The study of waiting in line is the essence of this problem. Queuing theory is the mathematical analysis of the waiting line.
- A queuing (or waiting line) system is composed of three major parts: (1) the customers arriving to the system, (2) the servicing of the customers, and (3) how customers exit the system.
- Queuing theory assumes that customers arrive according to a Poisson arrival distribution and are served according to an exponential service time distribution. These are specific probability distributions that often match well with actual situations.

Key Terms

Queues A line of waiting persons, jobs, things, or the like.

Queuing system A process where customers wait in line for service.

Arrival rate The expected number of customers that arrive each period.

Exponential distribution A probability distribution associated with the time between arrivals.

Poisson distribution Probability distribution for the number of arrivals during each time period.

Service rate The number of customers a server can handle during a given time period.

Key Formulas

Exponential distribution

[10.1] $$f(t) = \lambda e^{-\lambda t}$$

Poisson distribution

[10.2] $$P_T(n) = \frac{(\lambda T)^n e^{-\lambda T}}{n!}$$

LO 10–2 Analyze waiting line problems

Summary

- There are many different waiting line models, and in this chapter, four of the most common ones are covered.
- Model 1 is useful for a simple situation where there is a single line of customers who arrive according to a Poisson distribution, and who are processed by a single server that serves each customer in the order they came according to an exponential distribution (for example, an automatic teller machine).
- Model 2 is similar to Model 1 with the difference being that it takes exactly the same time to serve each customer (i.e., there is no service time variability) (for example, a robot making the same part over and over again).
- Model 3 is like Model 1 but two or more servers are available (for example, a bank lobby with multiple tellers).
- Model 4 differs in that only a small number of customers exist (for example, a mechanic that services four specific printing presses when they break down).
- In addition to the four models, a simpler model that approximates waiting times is also covered.

Key Formulas

Model 1 (See Exhibit 10.8.)

[10.3] $$L_q = \frac{\lambda^2}{\mu(\mu - \lambda)} \qquad W_q = \frac{L_q}{\lambda} \qquad P_n = \left(1 - \frac{\lambda}{\mu}\right)\left(\frac{\lambda}{\mu}\right)^n \qquad P_0 = \left(1 - \frac{\lambda}{\mu}\right)$$

$$L_s = \frac{\lambda}{\mu - \lambda} \qquad W_s = \frac{L_s}{\lambda} \rho = \frac{\lambda}{\mu}$$

Model 2

[10.4] $$L_q = \frac{\lambda^2}{2\mu(\mu - \lambda)} \qquad W_q = \frac{L_q}{\lambda}$$

$$L_s = L_q + \frac{\lambda}{\mu} \qquad W_s = \frac{L_s}{\lambda}$$

Model 3

[10.5]
$$L_s = L_q + \lambda/\mu \qquad W_s = L_s/\lambda$$

$$W_q = L_q/\lambda \qquad P_w = L_q\left(\frac{S\mu}{\lambda} - 1\right)$$

Model 4

$$X = \frac{T}{T+U} \qquad H = FNX \qquad L = N(1-F) \qquad n = L + H$$

[10.6]
$$P_n = \frac{N!}{(N-n)!}X^n P_0 \qquad J = NF(1-X)$$

$$W = \frac{L(T+U)}{N-L} = \frac{LT}{H} \qquad F = \frac{T+U}{T+U+W}$$

Waiting time approximation

[10.7]
$$X = \sum_{i=1}^{N} x_i/N \qquad \text{(mean)}$$

[10.8]
$$s = \sqrt{\frac{\sum_{i=1}^{N}(x_i - \overline{X})^2}{N-1}} \qquad \text{(standard deviation)}$$

[10.9]
$$C_s = \frac{S_s}{\overline{X}_s} \qquad C_a = \frac{S_a}{\overline{X}_a} \qquad \lambda = \frac{1}{\overline{X}_a} \qquad \mu = \frac{1}{\overline{X}_s}$$

[10.10]
$$\rho = \frac{\lambda}{S\mu} \qquad L_q = \frac{\rho^{\sqrt{2(S+1)}}}{1-\rho} \times \frac{C_a^2 + C_s^2}{2} \qquad L_s = L_q + S\rho$$

$$W_q = \frac{L_q}{\lambda} \qquad W_s = \frac{L_s}{\lambda}$$

LO 10–3 Analyze complex waiting lines using simulation

Summary

- A more general way to analyze waiting lines is simulation. The advantage of using simulation over the queuing models is that fewer assumptions need to be made. Also, much more complex situations can be analyzed using simulation.
- A simple two-stage assembly line is analyzed to show an example of using simulation. The simulation is performed manually and also with a spreadsheet.

SOLVED PROBLEMS

LO10–2 SOLVED PROBLEM 1

Quick Lube Inc. operates a fast lube and oil change garage. On a typical day, customers arrive at the rate of three per hour and lube jobs are performed at an average rate of one every 15 minutes. The mechanics operate as a team on one car at a time.

Assuming Poisson arrivals and exponential service, find

a. Utilization of the lube team.
b. The average number of cars in line.
c. The average time a car waits before it is lubed.
d. The total time it takes to go through the system (that is, waiting in line plus lube time).

Solution

$\lambda = 3, \mu = 4$

a. Utilization $\rho = \frac{\lambda}{\mu} = \frac{3}{4} = 75\%$.

b. $L_q = \frac{\lambda^2}{\mu(\mu - \lambda)} = \frac{3^2}{4(4-3)} = \frac{9}{4} = 2.25$ cars in line.

c. $W_q = \frac{L_q}{\lambda} = \frac{2.25}{3} = 0.75$ hour, or 45 minutes.

d. $W_s = \frac{L_s}{\lambda} = \frac{\lambda}{\mu - \lambda} / \lambda = \frac{3}{4-3} / 3 = 1$ hour (waiting + lube).

SOLVED PROBLEM 2

American Vending Inc. (AVI) supplies vended food to a large university. Because students often kick the machines out of anger and frustration, management has a constant repair problem. The machines break down on an average of three per hour, and the breakdowns are distributed in a Poisson manner. Downtime costs the company \$25 per hour per machine, and each maintenance worker gets \$16 per hour. One worker can service machines at an average rate of five per hour, distributed exponentially; two workers working together can service seven per hour, distributed exponentially; and a team of three workers can do eight per hour, distributed exponentially.

What is the optimal maintenance crew size for servicing the machines?

Solution

Case I—One worker:

$\lambda = 3$/hour Poisson, $\mu = 5$/hour exponential

The average number of machines in the system is

$$L_s = \frac{\lambda}{\mu - \lambda} = \frac{3}{5-3} = \frac{3}{2} = 1\tfrac{1}{2} \text{ machines}$$

Downtime cost is \$25 × 1.5 = \$37.50 per hour; repair cost is \$16.00 per hour; and total cost per hour for 1 worker is \$37.50 + \$16.00 = \$53.50.

Downtime cost is 1.5 × \$25	=	\$37.50
Labor (1 worker × \$16)	=	16.00
		\$53.50

Case II—Two workers:

$\lambda = 3, \mu = 7$

$$L_s = \frac{\lambda}{\mu - \lambda} = \frac{3}{7-3} = 0.75 \text{ machine}$$

Downtime (0.75 × $25) =	$18.75
Labor (2 workers × $16) =	32.00
	$50.75

Case III—Three workers:

$\lambda = 3, \mu = 8$

$$L_s = \frac{\lambda}{\mu - \lambda} = \frac{3}{8-3} = \frac{3}{5} = 0.60 \text{ machine}$$

Downtime (0.60 × $25) =	$15.00
Labor (3 workers × $16) =	48.00
	$63.00

Comparing the costs for one, two, or three workers, we see that Case II with two workers is the optimal decision.

SOLVED PROBLEM 3

American Bank has a single automated teller machine (ATM) located in a shopping center. Data were collected during a period of peak usage on Saturday afternoon, and it was found that the average time between customer arrivals is 2.1 minutes with a standard deviation of 0.8 minute. It also was found it takes an average of 1.9 minutes (with a standard deviation of 2 minutes) for a customer to complete a transaction. Approximately how long will customers need to wait in line during the peak usage period?

Solution

Step 1. Calculate expected customer arrival rate (λ), service rate per server (μ), and coefficient of variation for the arrival distribution (C_a) and service distribution (C_s).

$$\lambda = \frac{1}{\overline{X}_a} = \frac{1}{2.1} = 0.47619 \text{ customer per minute}$$

$$\mu = \frac{1}{\overline{X}_s} = \frac{1}{1.9} = 0.526316 \text{ customer per minute}$$

$$C_a = \frac{S_a}{\overline{X}_a} = \frac{0.8}{2.1} = 0.380952$$

$$C_s = \frac{S_s}{\overline{X}_s} = \frac{2}{1.9} = 1.052632$$

Step 2. Calculate the expected server utilization (ρ).

$$\rho = \frac{\lambda}{S\mu} = \frac{0.47619}{1 \times 0.526316} = 0.904762$$

(Operators are expected to be busy 90.5 percent of the time.)

Step 3. Calculate the expected number of people waiting (L_q) and the length of the wait (W_q).

$$L_q = \frac{\rho^{\sqrt{2(S+1)}}}{1-\rho} \times \frac{C_a^2 + C_s^2}{2} = \frac{0.904762^{\sqrt{2(1+1)}}}{1 - 0.904762} \times \frac{0.380952^2 + 1.052632^2}{2}$$

$= 5.355596$ customer (This is the number of customers we expect to be waiting on hold.)

$$W_q = \frac{L_q}{\lambda} = \frac{5.385596}{0.47619} = 11.30975 \text{ minutes}$$

On average, we expect customers to wait 11 minutes and 19 seconds (11 minutes plus 0.30975 minutes × 60 seconds/minute) before having access to the ATM.

SOLVED PROBLEM 4

A rural clinic receives a delivery of fresh plasma once each week from a central blood bank. The supply varies according to demand from other clinics and hospitals in the region but ranges between four and nine pints of the most widely used blood type, type O. The number of patients per week requiring this blood varies from zero to four, and each patient may need from one to four pints. Given the following delivery quantities, patient distribution, and demand per patient, what would be the number of pints in excess or lacking for a six-week period? Use simulation to derive your answer. Consider that plasma is storable and there is currently none on hand.

Delivery Quantities		Patient Distribution		Demand per Patient	
Pints per Week	Probability	Patients per Week Requiring Blood	Probability	Pints	Probability
4	0.15	0	0.25	1	0.40
5	0.20	1	0.25	2	0.30
6	0.25	2	0.30	3	0.20
7	0.15	3	0.15	4	0.10
8	0.15	4	0.05		
9	0.10				

Solution

First, develop a random number sequence, and then simulate.

Delivery			Number of Patients			Patient Demand		
Pints	Probability	Random Number	Blood	Probability	Random Number	Pints	Random Probability	Number
4	.15	00–14	0	.25	00–24	1	.40	00–39
5	.20	15–34	1	.25	25–49	2	.30	40–69
6	.25	35–59	2	.30	50–79	3	.20	70–89
7	.15	60–74	3	.15	80–94	4	.10	90–99
8	.15	75–89	4	.05	95–99			
9	.10	90–99						

Week No.	Beginning Inventory	Quantity Delivered		Total Blood on Hand	Patients Needing Blood			Quantity Needed		Number of Pints Remaining
		RN	Pints		RN	Patients	Patient	RN	Pints	
1	0	74	7	7	85	3	First	21	1	6
							Second	06	1	5
							Third	71	3	2
2	2	31	5	7	28	1		96	4	3
3	3	02	4	7	72	2	First	12	1	6
							Second	67	2	4
4	4	53	6	10	44	1		23	1	9
5	9	16	5	14	16	0				14
6	14	40	6	20	83	3	First	65	2	18
							Second	34	1	17
							Third	82	3	14
7	14									

At the end of six weeks, there were 14 pints on hand.

DISCUSSION QUESTIONS

LO 10–1

1. Distinguish between a *channel* and a *phase.*
2. In what way might the first-come, first-served rule be unfair to the customer waiting for service in a bank or hospital?
3. Define, in a practical sense, what is meant by an *exponential service time.*
4. Would you expect the exponential distribution to be a good approximation of service times for
   a. Buying an airline ticket at the airport?
   b. Riding a merry-go-round at a carnival?
   c. Checking out of a hotel?
   d. Completing a midterm exam in your OSCM class?
5. Would you expect the Poisson distribution to be a good approximation of
   a. Runners crossing the finish line in the Boston Marathon?
   b. Arrival times of the students in your OSCM class?
   c. Arrival times of the bus to your stop at school?

LO 10–2

6. What major cost trade-off must be made in managing waiting line situations?
7. Which assumptions are necessary to employ the formulas given for Model 1?

LO 10–3

8. Why is simulation often called a technique of last resort?
9. Must you use a computer to get good information from a simulation? Explain.
10. What methods are used to analyze time in a simulation model? How do they work?
11. What are the pros and cons of starting a simulation with the system empty? With the system in equilibrium?
12. Distinguish between known mathematical distributions and empirical distributions. What information is needed to simulate using a known mathematical distribution?

OBJECTIVE QUESTIONS

LO 10–1

1. The *exponential distribution* is often used to model what in a queuing system?
2. If the average time between customer arrivals is eight minutes, what is the hourly arrival rate?
3. How much time, on average, would a server need to spend on a customer to achieve a service rate of 20 customers per hour?
4. What is the term used for the situation where a potential customer arrives at a service operation and decides to leave upon seeing a long line?
5. What is the most commonly used priority rule for setting queue discipline, likely because it is seen as most fair?

LO 10–2

6. Students arrive at the Administrative Services Office at an average of one every 15 minutes, and their requests take, on average, 10 minutes to be processed. The service counter is staffed by only one clerk, Judy Gumshoes, who works eight hours per day. Assume Poisson arrivals and exponential service times. (Answers in Appendix D)
   a. What percentage of time is Judy idle?
   b. How much time, on average, does a student spend waiting in line?
   c. How long is the (waiting) line, on average?
   d. What is the probability that an arriving student (just before entering the Administrative Services Office) will find at least one other student waiting in line?
7. Burrito King (a new fast-food franchise opening up nationwide) has successfully automated burrito production for its drive-up fast-food establishments. The Burro-Master 9000 requires a constant 45 seconds to produce a batch of burritos. It has been estimated that customers will arrive at the drive-up window according to a Poisson distribution at an average of one every 50 seconds.

To help determine the amount of space needed for the line at the drive-up window, Burrito King would like to know the expected average time in the system, the average line length (in cars), and the average number of cars in the system (both in line and at the window).

8. The Bijou Theater shows vintage movies. Customers arrive at the theater line at the rate of 100 per hour. The ticket seller averages 30 seconds per customer, which includes placing validation stamps on customers' parking lot receipts and punching their frequent watcher cards. (Because of these added services, many customers don't get in until after the feature has started.)
   a. What is the average customer time in the system?
   b. What would be the effect on customer time in the system of having a second ticket taker doing nothing but validations and card punching, thereby cutting the average service time to 20 seconds?
   c. Would system waiting time be less than you found in (*b*) if a second window was opened with each server doing all three tasks?
9. To support National Heart Week, the Heart Association plans to install a free blood pressure testing booth in El Con Mall for the week. Previous experience indicates that, on average, 10 persons per hour request a test. Assume arrivals are Poisson distributed from an infinite population. Blood pressure measurements can be made at a constant time of five minutes each. Assume the queue length can be infinite with FCFS discipline.
   a. What average number in line can be expected?
   b. What average number of persons can be expected to be in the system?
   c. What is the average amount of time a person can expect to spend in line?
   d. On average, how much time will it take to measure a person's blood pressure, including waiting time?
   e. On weekends, the arrival rate can be expected to increase to over 12 per hour. What effect will this have on the number in the waiting line?
10. A cafeteria serving line has a coffee urn from which customers serve themselves. Arrivals at the urn follow a Poisson distribution at the rate of three per minute. In serving themselves, customers take about 15 seconds, exponentially distributed.
   a. How many customers would you expect to see, on average, at the coffee urn?
   b. How long would you expect it to take to get a cup of coffee?
   c. What percentage of time is the urn being used?
   d. What is the probability that three or more people are in the cafeteria?
   e. If the cafeteria installs an automatic vendor that dispenses a cup of coffee at a constant time of 15 seconds, how does this change your answers to (*a*) and (*b*)?
11. An engineering firm retains a technical specialist to assist four design engineers working on a project. The help that the specialist gives engineers ranges widely in time consumption. The specialist has some answers available in memory, others require computation, and still others require significant search time. On average, each request for assistance takes the specialist one hour.

    The engineers require help from the specialist on the average of once each day. Because each assistance takes about an hour, each engineer can work for seven hours, on average, without assistance. One further point: Engineers needing help do not interrupt if the specialist is already involved with another problem.

    Treat this as a finite queuing problem and answer the following questions:
   a. How many engineers, on average, are waiting for the technical specialist for help?
   b. What is the average time an engineer has to wait for the specialist?
   c. What is the probability an engineer will have to wait in line for the specialist?
12. L. Winston Martin (an allergist) has an excellent system for handling his regular patients who come in just for allergy injections. Patients arrive for an injection and fill out a name slip, which is then placed in an open slot that passes into another room staffed by one or two nurses. The specific injections for a patient are prepared, and the patient is called through a speaker system into the room to receive the injection. At certain times during the day, patient load drops and only one nurse is needed to administer the injections.

    Let's focus on the simpler case of the two—namely, when there is one nurse. Also, assume that patients arrive in a Poisson fashion and the service rate of the nurse is exponentially distributed.

During this slower period, patients arrive with an interarrival time of approximately three minutes. It takes the nurse an average of two minutes to prepare the patients' serum and administer the injection.

a. What is the average number you would expect to see in Dr. Martin's facilities?
b. How long would it take for a patient to arrive, get an injection, and leave?
c. What is the probability that there will be three or more patients on the premises?
d. What is the utilization of the nurse?
e. Assume three nurses are available. Each takes an average of two minutes to prepare the patients' serum and administer the injection. What is the average total time of a patient in the system?

13. A graphics reproduction firm has four units of equipment that are automatic but occasionally become inoperative because of the need for supplies, maintenance, or repair. Each unit requires service roughly twice each hour, or, more precisely, each unit of equipment runs an average of 30 minutes before needing service. Service times vary widely, ranging from a simple service (such as pressing a restart switch or repositioning paper) to more involved equipment disassembly. The average service time, however, is five minutes.

    Equipment downtime results in a loss of $60 per hour. The one equipment attendant is paid $18 per hour.

    Using finite queuing analysis, answer the following questions:

    a. What is the average number of units in line?
    b. What is the average number of units still in operation?
    c. What is the average number of units being serviced?
    d. The firm is considering adding another attendant at the same $18 rate. Should the firm do it?

14. Benny the Barber owns a one-chair shop. At barber college, they told Benny that his customers would exhibit a Poisson arrival distribution and that he would provide an exponential service distribution. His market survey data indicate that customers arrive at a rate of two per hour. It will take Benny an average of 20 minutes to give a haircut. Based on these figures, find the following:

    a. The average number of customers waiting.
    b. The average time a customer waits.
    c. The average time a customer is in the shop.
    d. The average utilization of Benny's time.

15. Bobby, another enterprising barber, is thinking about advertising in the local newspaper because he is idle 45 percent of the time. Currently, customers arrive, on average, every 40 minutes. What does the arrival rate need to be for Bobby to be busy 85 percent of the time?

16. Customers enter the camera department of a store at the average rate of six per hour. The department is staffed by one employee, who takes an average of six minutes to serve each arrival. Assume this is a simple Poisson arrival, exponentially distributed service time situation.

    a. As a casual observer, how many people would you expect to see in the camera department (excluding the clerk)? How long would a customer expect to spend in the camera department (total time)?
    b. What is the utilization of the clerk?
    c. What is the probability that there are more than two people in the camera department (excluding the clerk)?
    d. Another clerk has been hired for the camera department who also takes an average of six minutes to serve each arrival. How long would a customer expect to spend in the department now?

17. An office employs several clerks who create documents and has one operator who enters the document information in a computer system. The group creates documents at a rate of 25 per hour. The operator can enter the information with an average exponentially distributed time of two minutes. Assume the population is infinite, arrivals are Poisson, and queue length is infinite with FCFS discipline.

    a. Calculate the percentage utilization of the operator.
    b. Calculate the average number of documents in the system.
    c. Calculate the average time in the system.
    d. Calculate the probability of four or more documents being in the system.
    e. If another clerk were added, the document origination rate would increase to 30 per hour. What would the expected average number of documents in the system become? Show why.

18. A study-aid desk staffed by a graduate student has been established to answer students' questions and help in working problems in your OSCM course. The desk is staffed eight hours per day. The dean wants to know how the facility is working. Statistics show that students arrive at a rate of four per hour and the distribution is approximately Poisson. Assistance time averages 10 minutes, distributed exponentially. Assume population and line length can be infinite and queue discipline is FCFS.
    a. Calculate the percentage utilization of the graduate student.
    b. Calculate the average number of students in the system, excluding the graduate student service.
    c. Calculate the average time in the system.
    d. Calculate the probability of four or more students being in line or being served.
    e. Before a test, the arrival of students increases to six per hour, on average. What will the new average line length be?
19. At a border inspection station, vehicles arrive at the rate of 10 per hour in a Poisson distribution. For simplicity in this problem, assume there is only one lane and one inspector, who can inspect vehicles at the rate of 12 per hour in an exponentially distributed fashion.
    a. What is the average length of the waiting line?
    b. What is the average time that a vehicle must wait to get through the system?
    c. What is the utilization of the inspector?
    d. What is the probability that when you arrive there will be three or more vehicles ahead of you?
20. During the campus Spring Fling, the bumper car amusement attraction has a problem of cars becoming disabled and in need of repair. Repair personnel can be hired at the rate of $20 per hour, but they only work as one team. Thus, if one person is hired, he or she works alone; two or three people work together on the same repair.

    One repairer can fix cars in an average time of 30 minutes. Two repairers take 20 minutes, and three take 15 minutes. While these cars are down, lost income is $40 per hour. Cars tend to break down at the rate of two per hour.

    How many repairers should be hired?
21. A toll tunnel has decided to experiment with the use of a debit card for the collection of tolls. Initially, only one lane will be used. Cars are estimated to arrive at this experimental lane at the rate of 750 per hour. It will take exactly four seconds to verify the debit card. (Answers in Appendix D)
    a. In how much time would you expect the customer to wait in line, pay with the debit card, and leave?
    b. How many cars would you expect to see in the system?
22. You are planning employees for a bank. You plan for six tellers. Tellers take 15 minutes per customer, with a standard deviation of seven minutes. Customers will arrive one every three minutes according to an exponential distribution (recall that the standard deviation is equal to the mean). Every customer who arrives eventually gets serviced.
    a. On average, how many customers would be waiting in line?
    b. On average, how long would a customer spend in the bank?
    c. If a customer arrived, saw the line, and decided not to get in line, that customer has ________.
    d. A customer who enters the line but decides to leave the line before getting service is said to have ________.
23. You are planning the new layout for the local branch of the Sixth Ninth Bank. You are considering separate cashier windows for the three different classes of service. Each class of service would be separate, with its own cashiers and customers. Oddly enough, each class of service, while different, has exactly the same demand and service times. People for one class of service arrive every four minutes and arrival times are exponentially distributed (the standard deviation is equal to the mean). It takes seven minutes to service each customer, and the standard deviation of the service times is three minutes. You assign two cashiers to each type of service.
    a. On average, how long will each line be at each of the cashier windows?
    b. On average, how long will a customer spend in the bank (assume they enter, go directly to one line, and leave as soon as service is complete)?

You decide to consolidate all the cashiers so they can handle all types of customers without increasing the service times.

c. What will happen to the amount of time each cashier spends idle? (increase, decrease, stay the same, depend on ________)

d. What will happen to the average amount of time a customer spends in the bank? (increase, decrease, stay the same, depend on ________)

24. A local fast-food restaurant wants to analyze its drive-thru window. At this time, the only information known is the average number of customers in the system (4.00) and the average time a customer spends at the restaurant (1.176 minutes). What are the arrival rate and the service rate?

LO 10-3 25. The manager of a small post office is concerned that the growing township is overloading the one-window service being offered. Sample data are collected on 100 individuals who arrive for service.

Time between Arrivals (Minutes)	Frequency	Service Time (Minutes)	Frequency
1	8	1.0	12
2	35	1.5	21
3	34	2.0	36
4	17	2.5	19
5	6	3.0	7
	100	3.5	5
			100

Using the following random number sequence, simulate six arrivals; estimate the average customer waiting time and the average idle time for clerks.

RN: 08, 74, 24, 34, 45, 86, 31, 32, 45, 21, 10, 67, 60, 17, 60, 87, 74, 96

26. A bank of machines in a manufacturing shop breaks down according to the following interarrival time distribution. The time it takes one repairperson to complete the repair of a machine is given in the service time distribution.

Interarrival Time (Hours)	*P(X)*	RN	Service Time (Hours)	*P(X)*	RN
.5	.30	0–29	.5	.25	0–24
1.0	.22	30–51	1.0	.20	25–44
1.5	.16	52–67	2.0	.25	45–69
2.0	.10	68–77	3.0	.15	70–84
3.0	.14	78–91	4.0	.10	85–94
4.0	.08	92–99	5.0	.05	95–99
	1.00			1.00	

Simulate the breakdown of five machines. Calculate the average machine downtime using two repairpersons and the following random number sequence. (Both repairpersons cannot work on the same machine.)

RN: 30, 81, 02, 91, 51, 08, 28, 44, 86, 84, 29, 08, 37, 34, 99

CASE: Community Hospital Evening Operating Room

The American College of Surgeons has developed criteria for determining operating room standards in the United States. Level I and II trauma centers are required to have in-house operating room (OR) staff 24 hours per day. So a base level of a single OR team available 24 hours a day is mandatory. During normal business hours, a hospital will typically have additional OR teams available because surgery is scheduled during these times and these additional teams can be used in an emergency. An important decision, though, must be made concerning the availability of a backup team during the evening hours.

A backup team is needed during the evening hours if the probability of having two or more cases simultaneously is significant. "Significant" is difficult to judge, but for the purposes of this case assume that a backup OR team should be employed if the expected probability of two or more cases occurring simultaneously is greater than 1 percent.

A real application was studied by doctors at a hospital in Stamford, Connecticut. The doctors studied emergency OR patients that arrived after 11 P.M. and before 7 A.M. during a one-year period. During this time period, there were 62 patients that required OR treatment. The average service time was 80.79 minutes.

In analyzing the problem, think about this as a single-channel, single-phase system with Poisson arrivals and exponential service times.

Questions

1. Calculate the average customer arrival rate and service rate per hour.
2. Calculate the probability of zero patients in the system (*P*0), probability of one patient (*P*1), and the probability of two or more patients simultaneously arriving during the night shift.
3. Using a criterion that if the probability is greater than 1 percent, a backup OR team should be employed, make a recommendation to hospital administration.

ANALYTICS EXERCISE: PROCESSING CUSTOMER ORDERS

Analyzing a Taco Bell Restaurant

The scenario was written by a reporter who became a Taco Bell worker for a few hours to experience what it's like to work at one of the most high-tech quick-serve restaurant chains in the world. In the scenario, you could analyze how a Taco Bell using the queuing models we discussed in this chapter. At the end of this, we will give you some hints related to how you can model the Quick Service (QS) restaurant and then ask a series of questions related to your model.

Modeling the Restaurant

In the scenario, they indicate that it takes about 164 seconds, on average, to serve a customer during the busy lunch-hour period. Put yourself in the seat of your car getting food at the QS restaurant. Let's assume you are using the drive-thru window and that you will pick up the food and take it home to eat with some friends.

You drive into the restaurant lot and notice a line of cars has formed at the order kiosk. You wait for your turn to talk to the Customer Service Champion so you can place your order. The menu is clearly in view, so you can see exactly what you want. Soon it is your turn and you quickly place your order, learn what the bill will be, and move your car to the line at the drive-thru window. While waiting, you get your money out and count out the exact change you will need. After a short time, it's your turn at the window and you give the Service Champion your money, take your drink and food, and carefully drive out of the parking lot.

Think about what happened at the restaurant. First, you waited in two lines. The first was at the order kiosk and the second at the drive-thru window. Next, consider the work the restaurant needed to complete to process your order. The Service Champion took your order and entered it in the POS system, prepared your drink, and then, when the food was ready, collected your money, and delivered your drink and food. One of the Food Champions prepared your food using information from a screen that shows orders as they are entered by the Service Champion.

The total time it takes between when you arrive at the restaurant until you leave is made up of the following elements:

1. The service time for the Service Champion to process your order.
2. The service time for the Food Champion to prepare your order.
3. The waiting while the Service Champion and Food Champion serve other customers.

To model this using the queuing models in the chapter, assume you have two totally independent service processes. The first process is the Service Champion and the second is the Food Champion. Each process has potentially a different mean service time per customer. The Service Champion must serve each customer, and they arrive at a particular rate. The Food Champion prepares the individual items on the order such as a burrito, taco, chalupa, or gorditas taco. As the orders are taken, each individual item appears on a monitor telling the Food Champion what should be made next. The average time for a customer to run through the system is the sum of the average service times (time to take the order by the Service Champion and time to make the order by the Food Champion) plus the sum of the expected waiting times for the two processes. This assumes these processes operate totally independent of each other, which might not be exactly true. But we leave that to a later discussion.

Assume that the queues in front of each process are large, meaning there is plenty of room for cars in the line before and after the order kiosk. Also, assume there are a single Service Champion and two Food Champions each operating independently and working just on the drive-thru orders. Also, assume that the arrival pattern is Poisson, customers are handled first come, first served, and the service pattern is exponential.

Given this, answer the following questions:

1. Draw a diagram of the process using the format in Exhibit 9.5.
2. Consider a base case where a customer arrives every 40 seconds and the Customer Service Champion can handle 120 customers per hour. There are two Food Champions, each capable of handling 100 orders per hour. How long should it take to be served by the restaurant (from the time a customer enters the kiosk queue until her food is delivered)? Use queuing models to estimate this.
3. On average, how busy are the Customer Service Champions and the two Food Champions?
4. On average, how many cars do you expect to have in the drive-thru line? (Include those waiting to place orders and those waiting for food.)
5. If the restaurant runs a sale and the customer arrival rate increases by 20 percent, how would this change the total time expected to serve a customer? How would this change the average number of cars in the drive-thru line?
6. Currently, relatively few customers (less than ½ percent) order the Crunchwrap Supreme. What would happen if the restaurant ran the sale, demand jumped on the Crunchwrap Supreme, and 30 percent of the orders were for this item? Take a quantitative approach to answering this question. Assume that the Customer Service Champion never helps the Food Champions and that these two processes remain independent.
7. For the type of analysis done in this case, what are the key assumptions? What would be the impact on our analysis if these assumptions were not true?
8. Could this type of analysis be used for other service-type businesses? Give examples to support your answer.

PRACTICE EXAM

Answer the following questions. Answers are listed at the end of this section.

1. The queuing models assume that customers are served in what order?
2. Consider two identical queuing systems except for the service time distribution. In the first system, the service time is random and Poisson distributed. The service time is constant in the second system. How would the waiting time differ in the two systems?
3. What is the average utilization of the servers in a system that has three servers? On average, 15 customers arrive every 15 minutes. It takes a server exactly three minutes to wait on each customer.
4. What is the expected waiting time for the system described in question 3?
5. Firms that desire high service levels where customers have short wait times should target server utilization levels at no more than this percentage.

6. In most cases, if a firm increases its service capacity by 10 percent, it would expect waiting times to be reduced by what percentage? Assume customer arrivals and service times are random.
7. An ice cream stand has a single window and one employee to serve customers. During their busy season, 30 customers arrive each hour, on average. It takes 1.5 minutes, on average, to serve a customer. What is the utilization of the employee?
8. How long would customers have to wait in line, on average, at the ice cream shop discussed in question 7?
9. Random service times can be modeled by this.
10. A bank teller takes 2.4 minutes, on average, to serve a customer. What would be the hourly service rate used in the queuing formulas?
11. There are three teller windows in the bank described in the prior question. On average, 60 customers per hour arrive at the bank. What will be the average number of customers in line at the bank?

Answers to Practice Exam 1. First come, first served 2. Waiting time in the first system is two times the second. 3. 100% 4. Infinite 5. 70–80% 6. Greater than 10% 7. 75% 8. .075 hours, or 4.5 minutes 9. Exponential distribution 10. 25 customers per hour 11. 2.5888 (from Exhibit 10.9)

EXHIBIT 10.9

Excel: Expected Length

λ/μ	M	L_q	P_0
0.15	1	0.026	0.850
	2	0.001	0.860
0.20	1	0.050	0.800
	2	0.002	0.818
0.25	1	0.083	0.750
	2	0.004	0.778
0.30	1	0.129	0.700
	2	0.007	0.739
0.35	1	0.188	0.650
	2	0.011	0.702
0.40	1	0.267	0.600
	2	0.017	0.667
0.45	1	0.368	0.550
	2	0.024	0.633
	3	0.002	0.637
0.50	1	0.500	0.500
	2	0.033	0.600
	3	0.003	0.606
0.55	1	0.672	0.450
	2	0.045	0.569
	3	0.004	0.576
0.60	1	0.900	0.400
	2	0.059	0.538
	3	0.006	0.548

λ/μ	M	L_q	P_0
0.65	1	1.207	0.350
	2	0.077	0.509
	3	0.008	0.521
0.70	1	1.633	0.300
	2	0.098	0.481
	3	0.011	0.495
0.75	1	2.250	0.250
	2	0.123	0.455
	3	0.015	0.471
0.80	1	3.200	0.200
	2	0.152	0.429
	3	0.019	0.447
0.85	1	4.817	0.150
	2	0.187	0.404
	3	0.024	0.425
	4	0.003	0.427
0.90	1	8.100	0.100
	2	0.229	0.379
	3	0.030	0.403
	4	0.004	0.406
0.95	1	18.050	0.050
	2	0.277	0.356
	3	0.037	0.383
	4	0.005	0.386

λ/μ	M	L_q	P_0
1.00	2	0.333	0.333
	3	0.045	0.364
	4	0.007	0.367
1.10	2	0.477	0.290
	3	0.066	0.327
	4	0.011	0.332
1.20	2	0.675	0.250
	3	0.094	0.294
	4	0.016	0.300
	5	0.003	0.301
1.30	2	0.951	0.212
	3	0.130	0.264
	4	0.023	0.271
	5	0.004	0.272
1.40	2	1.345	0.176
	3	0.177	0.236
	4	0.032	0.245
	5	0.006	0.246
1.50	2	1.929	0.143
	3	0.237	0.211
	4	0.045	0.221
	5	0.009	0.223
1.60	2	2.844	0.111
	3	0.313	0.187

(Contd.)

(Contd.)

λ/μ	M	L_q	P_0
	4	0.060	0.199
	5	0.012	0.201
1.70	2	4.426	0.081
	3	0.409	0.166
	4	0.080	0.180
	5	0.017	0.182
1.80	2	7.674	0.053
	3	0.532	0.146
	4	0.105	0.162
	5	0.023	0.165
1.90	2	17.587	0.026
	3	0.688	0.128
	4	0.136	0.145
	5	0.030	0.149
	6	0.007	0.149
2.00	3	0.889	0.111
	4	0.174	0.130
	5	0.040	0.134
	6	0.009	0.135
2.10	3	1.149	0.096
	4	0.220	0.117
	5	0.052	0.121
	6	0.012	0.122
2.20	3	1.491	0.081
	4	0.277	0.105
	5	0.066	0.109
	6	0.016	0.111
2.30	3	1.951	0.068
	4	0.346	0.093
	5	0.084	0.099
	6	0.021	0.100
2.40	3	2.589	0.056
	4	0.431	0.083
	5	0.105	0.089
	6	0.027	0.090
	7	0.007	0.091
2.50	3	3.511	0.045
	4	0.533	0.074
	5	0.130	0.080
	6	0.034	0.082
	7	0.009	0.082
2.60	3	4.933	0.035
	4	0.658	0.065
	5	0.161	0.072
	6	0.043	0.074
	7	0.011	0.074
2.70	3	7.354	0.025
	4	0.811	0.057
	5	0.198	0.065
	6	0.053	0.067
	7	0.014	0.067
2.80	3	12.273	0.016
	4	1.000	0.050
	5	0.241	0.058
	6	0.066	0.060
	7	0.018	0.061
2.90	3	27.193	0.008
	4	1.234	0.044
	5	0.293	0.052
	6	0.081	0.054
	7	0.023	0.055
3.00	4	1.528	0.038
	5	0.354	0.047
	6	0.099	0.049
	7	0.028	0.050
	8	0.008	0.050
3.10	4	1.902	0.032
	5	0.427	0.042
	6	0.120	0.044
	7	0.035	0.045
	8	0.010	0.045
3.20	4	2.386	0.027
	5	0.513	0.037
	6	0.145	0.040
	7	0.043	0.040
	8	0.012	0.041
3.30	4	3.027	0.023
	5	0.615	0.033
	6	0.174	0.036
	7	0.052	0.037
	8	0.015	0.037
3.40	4	3.906	0.019
	5	0.737	0.029
	6	0.209	0.032
	7	0.063	0.033
	8	0.019	0.033
3.50	4	5.165	0.015
	5	0.882	0.026
	6	0.248	0.029
	7	0.076	0.030
	8	0.023	0.030
	9	0.007	0.030
3.60	4	7.090	0.011
	5	1.055	0.023
	6	0.295	0.026
	7	0.019	0.027
	8	0.028	0.027
	9	0.008	0.027
3.70	4	10.347	0.008
	5	1.265	0.020
	6	0.349	0.023
	7	0.109	0.024
	8	0.034	0.025
	9	0.010	0.025
3.80	4	16.937	0.005
	5	1.519	0.017
	6	0.412	0.021
	7	0.129	0.022

(Contd.)

(Contd.)

λ/μ	M	L_q	P_0
	8	0.041	0.022
	9	0.013	0.022
3.90	4	36.859	0.002
	5	1.830	0.015
	6	0.485	0.019
	7	0.153	0.020
	8	0.050	0.020
	9	0.016	0.020
4.00	5	2.216	0.013
	6	0.570	0.017
	7	0.180	0.018
	8	0.059	0.018
	9	0.019	0.018
4.10	5	2.703	0.011
	6	0.668	0.015
	7	0.212	0.016
	8	0.070	0.016
	9	0.023	0.017
4.20	5	3.327	0.009
	6	0.784	0.013
	7	0.248	0.014
	8	0.083	0.015
	9	0.027	0.015
	10	0.009	0.015
4.30	5	4.149	0.008
	6	0.919	0.012
	7	0.289	0.130
	8	0.097	0.013
	9	0.033	0.014
	10	0.011	0.014
4.40	5	5.268	0.006
	6	1.078	0.010
	7	0.337	0.012
	8	0.114	0.012
	9	0.039	0.012
	10	0.013	0.012

λ/μ	M	L_q	P_0
4.50	5	6.862	0.005
	6	1.265	0.009
	7	0.391	0.010
	8	0.134	0.011
	9	0.046	0.011
	10	0.015	0.011
4.60	5	9.289	0.004
	6	1.487	0.008
	7	0.453	0.009
	8	0.156	0.010
	9	0.054	0.010
	10	0.018	0.010
4.70	5	13.382	0.003
	6	1.752	0.007
	7	0.525	0.008
	8	0.181	0.009
	9	0.064	0.009
	10	0.022	0.009
4.80	5	21.641	0.002
	6	2.071	0.006
	7	0.607	0.008
	8	0.209	0.008
	9	0.074	0.008
	10	0.026	0.008
4.90	5	46.566	0.001
	6	2.459	0.005
	7	0.702	0.007
	8	0.242	0.007
	9	0.087	0.007
	10	0.031	0.007
	11	0.011	0.007
5.00	6	2.938	0.005
	7	0.810	0.006
	8	0.279	0.006
	9	0.101	0.007
	10	0.036	0.007

λ/μ	M	L_q	P_0
	11	0.013	0.007
5.10	6	3.536	0.004
	7	0.936	0.005
	8	0.321	0.006
	9	0.117	0.006
	10	0.042	0.006
	11	0.015	0.006
5.20	6	4.301	0.003
	7	1.081	0.005
	8	0.368	0.005
	9	0.135	0.005
	10	0.049	0.005
	11	0.018	0.006
5.30	6	5.303	0.003
	7	1.249	0.004
	8	0.422	0.005
	9	0.155	0.005
	10	0.057	0.005
	11	0.021	0.005
	12	0.007	0.005
5.40	6	6.661	0.002
	7	1.444	0.004
	8	0.483	0.004
	9	0.178	0.004
	10	0.066	0.004
	11	0.024	0.005
	12	0.009	0.005
5.50	6	8.590	0.002
	7	1.674	0.003
	8	0.553	0.004
	9	0.204	0.004
	10	0.077	0.004
	11	0.028	0.004
	12	0.010	0.004
5.60	6	11.519	0.001
	7	1.944	0.003

(Contd.)

(Contd.)

λ/μ	M	L_q	P_0
	8	0.631	0.003
	9	0.233	0.004
	10	0.088	0.004
	11	0.033	0.004
	12	0.012	0.004
5.70	6	16.446	0.001
	7	2.264	0.002
	8	0.721	0.003
	9	0.266	0.003

λ/μ	M	L_q	P_0
	10	0.102	0.003
	11	0.038	0.003
	12	0.014	0.003
5.80	6	26.373	0.001
	7	2.648	0.002
	8	0.823	0.003
	9	0.303	0.003
	10	0.116	0.003
	11	0.044	0.003

λ/μ	M	L_q	P_0
	12	0.017	0.003
5.90	6	56.300	0.000
	7	3.113	0.002
	8	0.939	0.002
	9	0.345	0.003
	10	0.133	0.003
	11	0.051	0.003
	12	0.019	0.003

Exhibit 10.10

Finite Queuing Tables

Population 4			
X	S	D	F
.015	1	.045	.999
.022	1	.066	.998
.030	1	.090	.997
.034	1	.102	.996
.038	1	.114	.995
.042	1	.126	.994
.046	1	.137	.993
.048	1	.143	.992
.052	1	.155	.991
.054	1	.161	.990
.058	1	.173	.989
.060	1	.179	.988
.062	1	.184	.987
.064	1	.190	.986
.066	1	.196	.985
.070	2	.014	.999
	1	.208	.984
.075	2	.016	.999
	1	.222	.981
.080	2	.018	.999
	1	.237	.978

Population 4			
X	S	D	F
.085	2	.021	.999
	1	.251	.975
.090	2	.023	.999
	1	.265	.972
.095	2	.026	.999
	1	.280	.969
.100	2	.028	.999
	1	.294	.965
.105	2	.031	.998
	1	.308	.962
.110	2	.034	.998
	1	.321	.958
.115	2	.037	.998
	1	.335	.954
.120	2	.041	.997
	1	.349	.950
.125	2	.044	.997
	1	.362	.945
.130	2	.047	.997
	1	.376	.941
.135	2	.051	.996

(Contd.)

(Contd.)

Population 4			
X	S	D	F
	1	.389	.936
.140	2	.055	.996
	1	.402	.931
.145	2	.058	.995
	1	.415	.926
.150	2	.062	.995
	1	.428	.921
.155	2	.066	.994
	1	.441	.916
.160	2	.071	.994
	1	.454	.910
.165	2	.075	.993
	1	.466	.904
.170	2	.079	.993
	1	.479	.899
.180	2	.088	.991
	1	.503	.887
.190	2	.098	.990
	1	.526	.874
.200	3	.008	.999
	2	.108	.988
.200	1	.549	.862
.210	3	.009	.999
	2	.118	.986
	1	.572	.849
.220	3	.011	.999
	2	.129	.984
	1	.593	.835
.230	3	.012	.999
	2	.140	.982
	1	.614	.822
.240	3	.014	.999
	2	.151	.980
	1	.634	.808

Population 4			
X	S	D	F
.250	3	.016	.999
	2	.163	.977
	1	.654	.794
.260	3	.018	.998
	2	.175	.975
	1	.673	.780
.270	3	.020	.998
	2	.187	.972
	1	.691	.766
.280	3	.022	.998
	2	.200	.968
	1	.708	.752
.290	3	.024	.998
	2	.213	.965
	1	.725	.738
.300	3	.027	.997
	2	.226	.962
	1	.741	.724
.310	3	.030	.997
	2	.240	.958
	1	.756	.710
.320	3	.033	.997
	2	.254	.954
	1	.771	.696
.330	3	.036	.996
	2	.268	.950
	1	.785	.683
.340	3	.039	.996
	2	.282	.945
	1	.798	.670
.360	3	.047	.994
	2	.312	.936
	1	.823	.644
.380	3	.055	.993

(Contd.)

Population 4			
X	*S*	*D*	*F*
	2	.342	.926
	1	.846	.619
.400	3	.064	.992
	2	.372	.915
	1	.866	.595
.420	3	.074	.990
	2	.403	.903
	1	.884	.572
.440	3	.085	.986
	2	.435	.891
	1	.900	.551
.460	3	.097	.985
	2	.466	.878
	1	.914	.530
.480	3	.111	.983
	2	.498	.864
	1	.926	.511
.500	3	.125	.980
	2	.529	.850
	1	.937	.492
.520	3	.141	.976
	2	.561	.835
	1	.947	.475
.540	3	.157	.972
	2	.592	.820
	1	.956	.459
.560	3	.176	.968

Population 4			
X	*S*	*D*	*F*
	2	.623	.805
	1	.963	.443
.580	3	.195	.964
	2	.653	.789
	1	.969	.429
.600	3	.216	.959
	2	.682	.774
	1	.975	.415
.650	3	.275	.944
	2	.752	.734
	1	.985	.384
.700	3	.343	.926
	2	.816	.695
	1	.991	.357
.750	3	.422	.905
	2	.871	.657
	1	.996	.333
.800	3	.512	.880
	2	.917	.621
	1	.998	.312
.850	3	.614	.852
	2	.954	.587
	1	.999	.294
.900	3	.729	.821
	2	.979	.555
.950	3	.857	.786
	2	.995	.526

For PowerPoint lecture slides, Solutions Manual, Test Bank, Data files for solved examples, Excel Templates, Step-by-Step Solved Examples in video format, Tutorial Videos and many more, scan the adjacent **QR code**, or
visit http://www.mhhe.com/sie-chase15e

Chapter 11

Process Design and Analysis

LEARNING OBJECTIVES

- LO 11-1 Exemplify a typical business process and how it can be analyzed
- LO 11-2 Compare different types of processes
- LO 11-3 Explain how jobs are designed
- LO 11-4 Analyze manufacturing, service, and logistics processes to ensure the competitiveness of a firm

AMAZON—THE MASTER OF EFFICIENCY AND LOGISTICS

How does the world's largest online retailer run the fulfillment centers that process the thousands of orders received by the company each hour? They employ more than 120,000 full-time and part-time workers around the world and use an optimized combination of humans and machines to efficiently process each order.

The fulfillment centers use conveyor belts to transport items and employ machines to print and stick mailing labels on them. The company's computers track every item using bar codes. All of this happens with the assistance of workers who are as efficient as the machines.

The company's amazingly efficient process allows them to offer free two-day delivery for it's Prime membership customers. In major cities, Amazon even offers same day delivery to some areas.

Amazon is experimenting with the use of drones that may someday deliver packages within 30 minutes. Amazon calls the service Prime Air. With no human intervention, a small plastic package containing your items are loaded under the drone, which then automatically flies to your home. It may be a few years before the Prime Air is operational, but it offers an intriguing opportunity for Amazon.

This wildly efficient infrastructure is what sets Amazon apart and ahead of competitors such as Walmart, Target, and the Chinese Alibaba.com.

LO 11-1

Exemplify a typical business process and how it can be analyzed

PROCESS ANALYSIS

Understanding how processes work is essential to ensuring the competitiveness of a company. A process that does not match the needs of the firm will punish the firm every minute that the firm operates. Take, for example, two fast-food restaurants. If one restaurant can deliver a quarter-pound hamburger to the customer for $0.50 in direct costs and a second restaurant costs $0.75, no matter what the second restaurant does, it will lose $0.25 in profit for every hamburger it sells compared to the first restaurant. Many factors need to be considered when one sets up the process to make those hamburgers. These factors include the cost of the raw materials, the costs associated with how the hamburger is prepared, and the cost of taking the order and delivering it to the customer.

Process
Any set of activities performed by an organization that takes inputs and transforms them into outputs ideally of greater value to the organization than the original inputs.

What is a process? A **process** is any part of an organization that takes inputs and transforms them into outputs that, it is hoped, are of greater value to the organization than the original inputs. Consider some examples of processes. Honda Motors assembles the Accord in a plant in Marysville, Ohio. The assembly plant takes in parts and components that have been fabricated for the plant. Using labor, equipment along an assembly line, and energy, these parts and components are transformed into automobiles. McDonald's, at each of its restaurants, uses inputs such as hamburger meat, lettuce, tomatoes, and potatoes. To these inputs, trained labor is added in the form of cooks and order takers, and capital equipment is used to transform the inputs into hamburgers, french fries, and other foods.

In both of these examples, the process makes products as output. However, the outputs of many processes are services. In a hospital, for example, specialized equipment and highly trained doctors, nurses, and technicians are combined with another input, the patient. The patient is transformed through proper treatment and care into a healthy patient. An airline is another example of a service organization. The airline uses airplanes, ground equipment, flight crews, ground crews, reservation personnel, and fuel to transport customers between locations all over the world.

Process

This chapter describes how to analyze a process. Analyzing a process allows some important questions to be answered, such as these: How many customers can the process handle per hour? How long will it take to serve a customer? What change is needed in the process to expand capacity? How much does the process cost? A difficult but important first step in process analysis is to clearly define the purpose of the analysis. Is the purpose to solve a problem? Is it to better understand the impact of a change in how business will be done in the future?

Clearly understanding the purpose of the analysis is critical to setting the level of detail in modeling the process. The analysis must be kept as simple as possible. The following sections of this chapter discuss the details of constructing flowcharts and measures that are appropriate for different types of processes. But first, consider a simple example.

Example—Analyzing a Las Vegas Slot Machine

The slot machine is common in casinos around the world. Let's use this machine to illustrate how a simple process is analyzed.

Assume that we work for a casino where management is considering a new type of electronic slot machine that is much faster than the current mechanical machine. Management has asked how much we can expect to make from the new electronic machine over a 24-hour period compared to the old mechanical machine.

Step 1. Analyzing the Mechanical Slot Machine Begin by analyzing a mechanical slot machine. The slot machine is activated when the customer puts one or more coins in the machine and then pulls the arm on the machine (slot machines are often called "one-armed bandits"). Three wheels spin, and after a time each wheel stops and displays a particular symbol. The machine pays money when certain combinations of symbols simultaneously appear.

Slot machines are designed to pay back a certain percentage of what they take in. Typical paybacks would be 90 to 95 percent of what is taken in; the casino keeps 5 to 10 percent. These payback percentages are a function of the number of different symbols on each wheel. Each symbol is repeated on each wheel a certain number of times. For example, if a wheel has 10 symbols, one might be a single bar, one a double bar, and one a lemon; two might be cherries, three lucky sevens, and two liberty bells. Because the wheels stop on a random symbol, the probability of lucky sevens coming up on all three wheels is $\frac{3}{10} \times \frac{3}{10} \times \frac{3}{10} = 0.027$, or 2.7 percent of the time. The probability of certain combinations of symbols coming up, combined with the payout for each combination, sets the average percentage that the machine is expected to pay out. Consider a mechanical slot machine that pays out 95 percent of the coins played. With this machine, assume the average player feeds coins into the machine at a pace of one coin each 15 seconds. This 15-second interval is called the *cycle time* of the process. The **cycle time** of a repetitive process is the average time between completions of successive units. In the case of the slot machine, the unit is a silver dollar. With a 15-second cycle time, our mechanical slot machine can process \$4 (60 seconds/15 seconds) per minute, or \$240 (\$4/minute × 60 minutes) per hour. Because our slot machine has a payout of 95 percent, we would expect the machine to give the customer 228 (240 × 0.95) of the silver dollars that it took in and keep \$12 for the casino for each hour that it is in operation. If we started with \$100, we could expect to play for about 8.3 hours (\$100/\$12 per hour) before we would run out of silver dollars. We might be lucky and win the jackpot, or we might be unlucky and lose it all in the first hour. However, on average, we would expect to lose the entire \$100 in 8.3 hours.

Cycle time
The average time between completions of successive units in a process (this is the definition used in this book).

Step 2. Analyzing the New Electronic Slot Machine Now consider the new electronic slot machine. It operates in exactly the same manner; the only difference is that it uses "electronic" coins and it takes only 10 seconds to process each bet. With a 10-second cycle time, the machine processes \$6 (60 seconds/10 seconds) per minute, or \$360 (\$6/minute × 60 minutes) per hour. With a 95 percent payout, the machine would give the customer back 342 (360 × 0.95) silver dollars and keep \$18 for the casino each hour. This machine would take our \$100 in only 5.6 hours (\$100/\$18 per hour).

Step 3. Comparison So how much does the electronic slot machine make for the casino in 24 hours compared to the mechanical slot machine? One more critical piece of information is needed to answer this question: How long will the slot machine operate over the 24 hours? The casino feels that the machine will be used 12 out of the 24 hours; this 12 out of 24 hours is the expected utilization of the machine. **Utilization** is the ratio of the time a resource is actually activated relative to the time it is available for use. Adjusting for utilization, the expected revenue from the mechanical machine is \$144/day (\$12/hour × 24 hours × 0.5) compared to revenue of \$216/day (\$18/hour × 24 hours × 0.5) for the electronic machine. When an analysis is performed, it is important to qualify the analysis with the assumptions made. In this comparison, we assumed that the operator only bets one silver dollar at a time and that the utilization would be the same for the mechanical and electronic slot machines.

Utilization
The ratio of the time that a resource is actually activated relative to the time that it is available for use.

Step 4. The Slot Machine Is One of Many Casino Processes The speed of the slot machine can have a major impact on the casino's revenue. The single slot machine is only a small part of the casino. To really understand how much revenue the casino can generate, we need to consider all of the other revenue-generating processes, such as the blackjack and poker tables, keno games, craps, and the other games in the casino. Many times, analyzing an enterprise involves evaluating a number of independent activities, like our slot machine. The aggregate performance of each individual activity may be all that is needed to understand the overall process. On the other hand, there is often significant interaction between individual activities or processes that must be considered.

Think about our gambling casino. Many casinos offer great deals on food, which is served right in the casino. What do you think would be the main priority of the food operations manager in one of these casinos? Would great-tasting food be important? How important is the cost of the food? Is speed of service important? Good food certainly is important. If the food is unpleasant, the customer will not even consider eating at the casino. This is bad for the casino because if the customers leave, they take their money with them. Remember, the casino makes money based on how long the customers gamble. The more time spent gambling, the more money the casino makes. What about cost? If the customers think the meals are too expensive, they might leave. So it is important to keep the cost of the meals down so they can be priced inexpensively. Many casinos even give meals away. How important is it to serve the customer quickly? Think about it this way: Every minute that the customers are sitting in the restaurant, they are not feeding silver dollars into a slot machine. So speed is important because it impacts the revenue generated at the games in the casino.

Process Flowcharting

Key Idea

Drawing a picture is always the first step in analyzing a process. Keep the drawing simple to start with.

Activities associated with a process often affect one another, so it is important to consider the simultaneous performance of a number of activities, all operating at the same time. A good way to start analyzing a process is with a diagram showing the basic elements of a process—typically tasks, flows, and storage areas. Tasks are shown as rectangles, flows as arrows, and the storage of goods or other items as inverted triangles. Sometimes flows through a process can be diverted in multiple directions depending on some condition. Decision points are depicted as a diamond, with the different flows running from the points on the diamond. Exhibit 11.1 displays examples of these symbols. Separating a diagram into different horizontal or vertical bands sometimes is useful because it allows the separation of tasks that are part of the process. For example, with the slot machine, the tasks performed by the customer can be separated from the tasks performed by the slot machine.

EXHIBIT 11.1

Process Flowchart Example

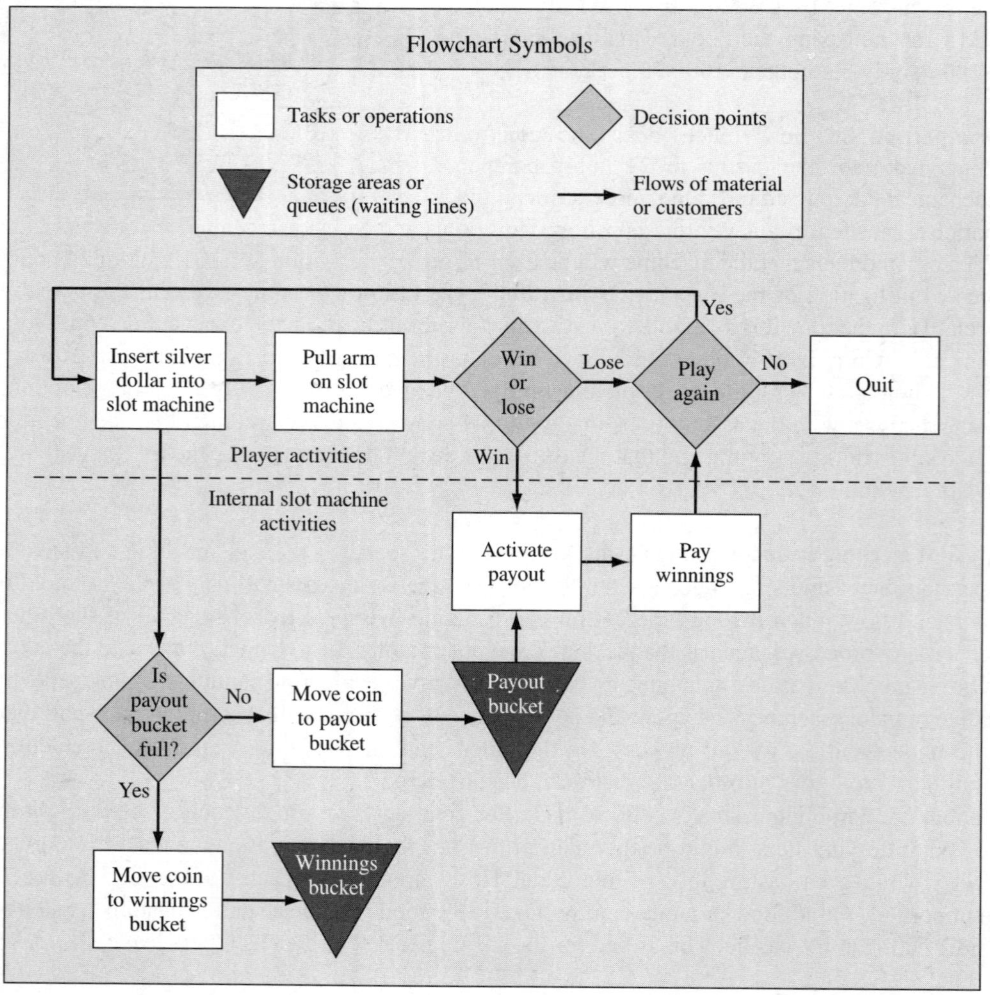

In the slot machine example, the level of abstraction considers the slot machine as a simple black box that takes in silver dollars and either keeps them or returns some of them during each cycle. Viewing the slot machine as a black box might be fine if the purpose is just to analyze how much the machine is expected to make for the casino each hour. In reality, more activities are required to support the slot machine. Inside an old-style mechanical slot machine are two buckets of silver dollars. One bucket stores coins needed for internal use by the slot machine. When a customer wins, the payout comes from this payout bucket. The slot machine is designed to automatically keep this payout bucket filled during play. When the payout bucket is full, the silver dollars are deposited in a second winnings bucket. The winnings bucket must be periodically emptied to claim the winnings for the casino. The flowchart in Exhibit 11.1 depicts the external activities of the player and the internal movement of the coins within the machine.

Probably the most interesting thing about the payout bucket is how big it should be. The slot machine is programmed so that if the payout bucket empties, the machine stops and lights on the top of the machine flash, thus notifying casino personnel that a lucky customer has emptied the machine. The payout bucket would be sized to keep this a rare occurrence. Think of the payout bucket as a buffer or intermediate storage area for silver dollars that allows the slot machine to operate on its own. The smaller the payout bucket, the more the casino personnel need to attend to the machine, and the more time the machine is idle for lack of silver dollars. On the other hand, with a larger bucket more money is tied up.

The situation with the winnings bucket in the machine is similar. A small winnings bucket will need to be emptied more often. On the other hand, a large winnings bucket means that the casino does not deposit the money into its bank account as quickly. The advantage of buffering operations with the slot machine is easily seen. Large buffers allow the process to operate independently, whereas small buffers require more attention. In the case of the slot machine, the buffer is composed of the silver dollars. In other situations, where the buffer is other items such as a raw material, these items have a value, so they also represent money.

Consider a slot machine that we expect to deposit $12 into the winnings bucket every hour. If our winnings bucket can hold 1,000 silver dollars, then we expect to need to empty the winnings bucket every 83.3 hours ($1,000/$12 per hour) if the slot machine is used 100 percent of the time. What happens when the winnings bucket fills up? If the slot machine is smart enough to know that the winnings bucket is full, it might be programmed to just stop working with its lights flashing, as they do when the payout bucket empties. This would cause downtime on the machine and might upset a customer using the machine because the customer would have to move to another slot machine. If the slot machine were not programmed to stop working, the silver dollars would fill the cavity where the bucket is located in the base of the machine. Imagine the mess when the casino worker opens that overflowed machine and all those silver dollars come pouring out. How often would you plan on emptying the winnings bucket?

An easy way to draw flowcharts is to use the Shapes gallery available in the Microsoft Office programs (i.e., Word, Excel, and PowerPoint). To access this gallery, go to the Insert tab and then select "Shapes." This will display a number of flowchart symbols to use in creating your flowchart. Text can be added by selecting a symbol and then clicking the right mouse button. Select "Add text" to insert text in the symbol. The symbols can be connected by using "Connectors" available from the Shapes gallery. Nice flowcharts can be made using these tools.

UNDERSTANDING PROCESSES

LO 11-2

Compare different types of processes

It is useful to categorize processes to describe how a process is designed. By being able to quickly categorize a process, we can show the similarities and differences between processes.

The first way to categorize a process is to determine whether it is a *single-stage* or a *multiple-stage* process. If the slot machine were viewed as a simple black box, it would be categorized as a single-stage process. In this case, all of the activities involved in the operation of the slot machine would be collapsed and analyzed using a single cycle time to represent the speed of the

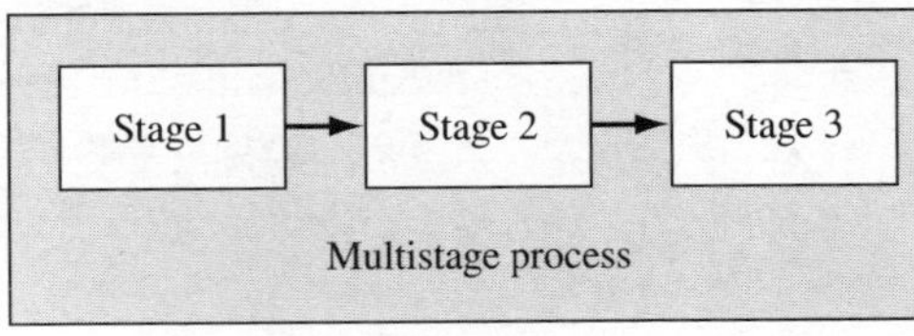

Multistage process

slot machine. A multiple-stage process has multiple groups of activities that are linked through flows. The term *stage* is used to indicate that multiple activities have been pulled together for analysis purposes.

Process

Buffering, Blocking, and Starving

A multiple-stage process may be buffered internally. A **buffer** refers to a storage area between stages where the output of a stage is placed prior to being used in a downstream stage. Buffering allows the stages to operate independently. If one stage feeds a second stage with no intermediate buffer, then the assumption is that the two stages are directly linked. When a process is designed this way, the most common problems that can happen are blocking and starving. **Blocking** occurs when the activities in the stage must stop because there is no place to deposit the item just completed. **Starving** occurs when the activities in a stage must stop because there is no work.

Buffer
A storage area between stages where the output of a stage is placed prior to being used in a downstream stage.

Blocking
The activities in the stage must stop because there is no place to deposit the item just completed.

Starving
The activities in a stage must stop because there is no work.

Bottleneck
A resource that limits the capacity or maximum output of the process.

Consider a two-stage process where the first stage has a cycle time of 30 seconds and the second a cycle time of 45 seconds. If this process needs to produce 100 units, then for each unit produced, the first stage would be blocked for 15 seconds.

What would happen if an inventory buffer were placed between the two stages? In this case, the first stage would complete the 100 units in 3,000 seconds (30 seconds/unit × 100 units). During these 3,000 seconds, the second stage would complete only 66 units ((3,000 – 30) seconds/45 seconds/unit). The 30 seconds are subtracted from the 3,000 seconds because the second stage is starved for the first 30 seconds. This would mean that the inventory would build to 34 units (100 units – 66 units) over that first 3,000 seconds. All of the units would be produced in 4,530 seconds. The second stage in this case is called a **bottleneck** because it limits the capacity of the process.

What would happen if the first stage required 45 seconds and the second stage had the 30-second cycle time? In this case, the first stage would be the bottleneck, and each unit would go directly from the first stage to the second. The second stage would be starved for 15 seconds waiting for each unit to arrive; however, it would still take 4,530 seconds to complete all 100 units. All of this assumes that there is no variability in the cycle time. With the relatively low 67 percent utilization on the second stage, variability would have little impact on the performance of this system, but if the cycle times were closer, some inventory might collect in the buffer.

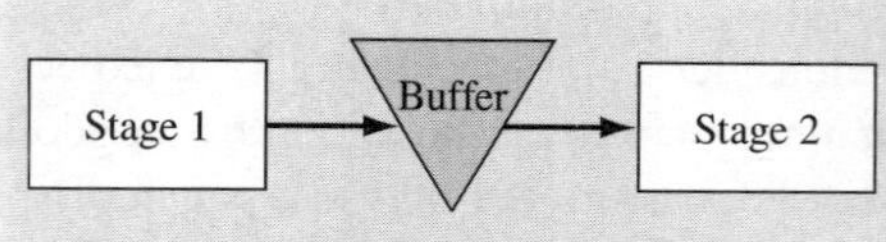

Multistage process with buffer

Often, activities, stages, and even entire processes are operated in parallel. For example, operating two identical activities in parallel would theoretically double capacity. Or perhaps two different sets of activities can be done at the same time on the unit being produced. In analyzing a system with parallel activities or stages, it is important to understand the context. In the case where parallel processes represent alternatives, for example, a diamond should show that flows divert and what percentage of the flow moves in each direction. Sometimes two or more processes terminate in a common inventory buffer. This normally indicates that the two processes make identical items that are going into this inventory. Separate inventories should be used in the diagram if the outputs of the parallel processes are different.

Make-to-Stock vs. Make-to-Order

Another useful way to characterize a process is whether the process *makes to stock* or *makes to order.* To illustrate these concepts, consider the processes used to make hamburgers at the three major fast-food restaurant chains in the United States: McDonald's, Burger King, and Wendy's. In the case of McDonald's, in 1999 the company converted to a new make-to-order process, but the company has now revised that into a "hybrid" system. We begin our tour of the approaches used by the top fast-food restaurants by first reviewing the traditional approach.

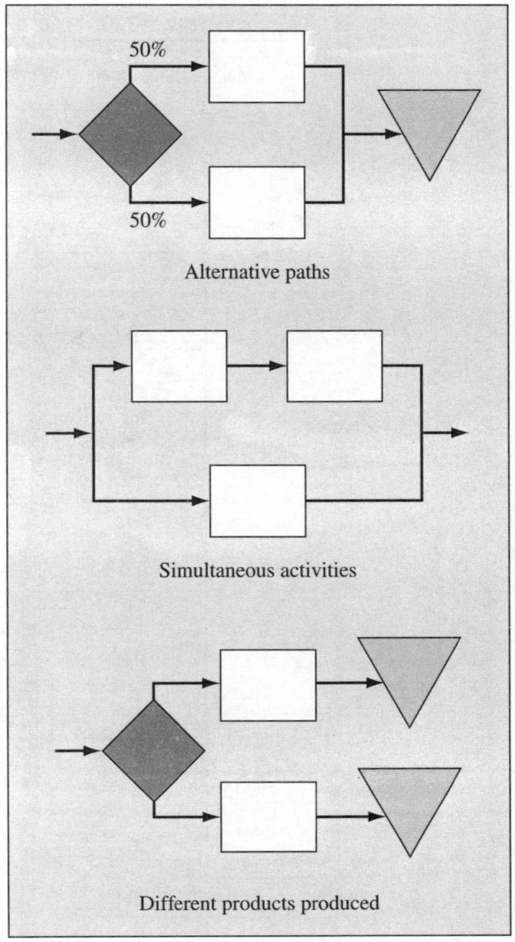

Consider a traditional restaurant making hamburgers. Before the era of fast food, hamburgers were always made to order. In the traditional process, the customer places an order specifying the degree of doneness (medium or well done) and requests specific condiments (pickles, cheese, mustard, onions, catsup). Using this specification, the cook takes raw hamburger meat from inventory (typically this inventory is refrigerated and the patties have already been made), cooks the hamburger, and warms the bun. The hamburger is then assembled and delivered to the customer. The quality of the hamburger is highly dependent on the skill of the cook.

This **make-to-order** process is activated only in response to an actual order. Inventory (both work-in-process and finished goods) is kept to a minimum. Theoretically, one would expect that response time would be slow because all the activities need to be completed before the product is delivered to the customer. Services by their very nature often use make-to-order processes.

McDonald's revolutionized the hamburger-making process by developing a high-volume approach. A diagram of McDonald's traditional process is shown in Exhibit 11.2A. With the old process, hamburgers were grilled in batches. Standard hamburgers (for example, the "Big Mac" consists of two beef patties, sauce, lettuce, cheese, pickles, and onion on a sesame seed bun) were then prepared and stored in a holding bin for immediate delivery to the customer. A person that judged current demand and placed orders to keep inventory in the bin at an appropriate level controlled the whole process. This is a highly efficient **make-to-stock** process that produces standard products that can be delivered quickly to the customer. This quick process appeals to families with small children, for whom speed of delivery is important.

In general, a make-to-stock process ends with finished goods inventory; customer orders are then served from this inventory. A make-to-stock process can be controlled based on the actual or anticipated amount of finished goods inventory. A target stocking level, for example, might be set, and the process would be periodically activated to maintain that target stocking level. Make-to-stock processes are also used when demand is seasonal. In this case, inventory can be built during the slow season and used during the peak season, thus allowing the process to run at a constant rate throughout the year.

Strategy

The unique feature of the Burger King process, shown in Exhibit 11.2B, is a highly specialized conveyor–broiler. Raw hamburger patties are placed on a moving conveyor that runs through a flaming broiler. In exactly 90 seconds, the patties are cooked on both sides with a unique broiler taste. To move a patty through the conveyor–broiler in a fixed time, the thickness of the patties must be the same for all the hamburger products. The buns are also warmed on a conveyor. This system results in a unique, highly consistent product. The cooked patties are stored in a warmed storage container. During periods of high demand, some standard hamburgers are prepared and inventoried for immediate delivery. Custom hamburgers with unique combinations of condiments are prepared to order. This *hybrid* process provides flexibility to respond to customer preferences through the assemble-to-order backend process—thus, the Burger King "have it your way" slogan. In general, **hybrid** processes combine the features of both make-to-order and make-to-stock. Here, two types of process are parallel alternatives at the end of the Burger King process. In the most common hybrid form, a generic product is made and stocked at some point in the process. These generic units are then finished in a final process based on actual orders.

Continuing with our tour, Wendy's uses a make-to-order process (as shown in Exhibit 11.2C) that is in full view of the customer. Hamburger patties are cooked on a grill. During high-volume times, the cook tries to get a little ahead and anticipates the arrival of customers. Patties that are on the grill too long are used in the chili soup. On arrival of a customer order, a patty is taken from the grill and the hamburger is assembled to the exact specifications of the customer. Because the process starts with the cooking of the patty, it is a little slower. The customer can see what is going on, and the perception is of a high-quality custom product.

Make-to-order
A production environment where the product is built directly from raw materials and components in response to a specific customer order.

Make-to-stock
A production environment where the customer is served "on-demand" from finished goods inventory.

Hybrid
Combines the features of both make-to-order and make-to-stock.

Exhibit 11.2

Making Hamburgers at McDonald's, Burger King, and Wendy's

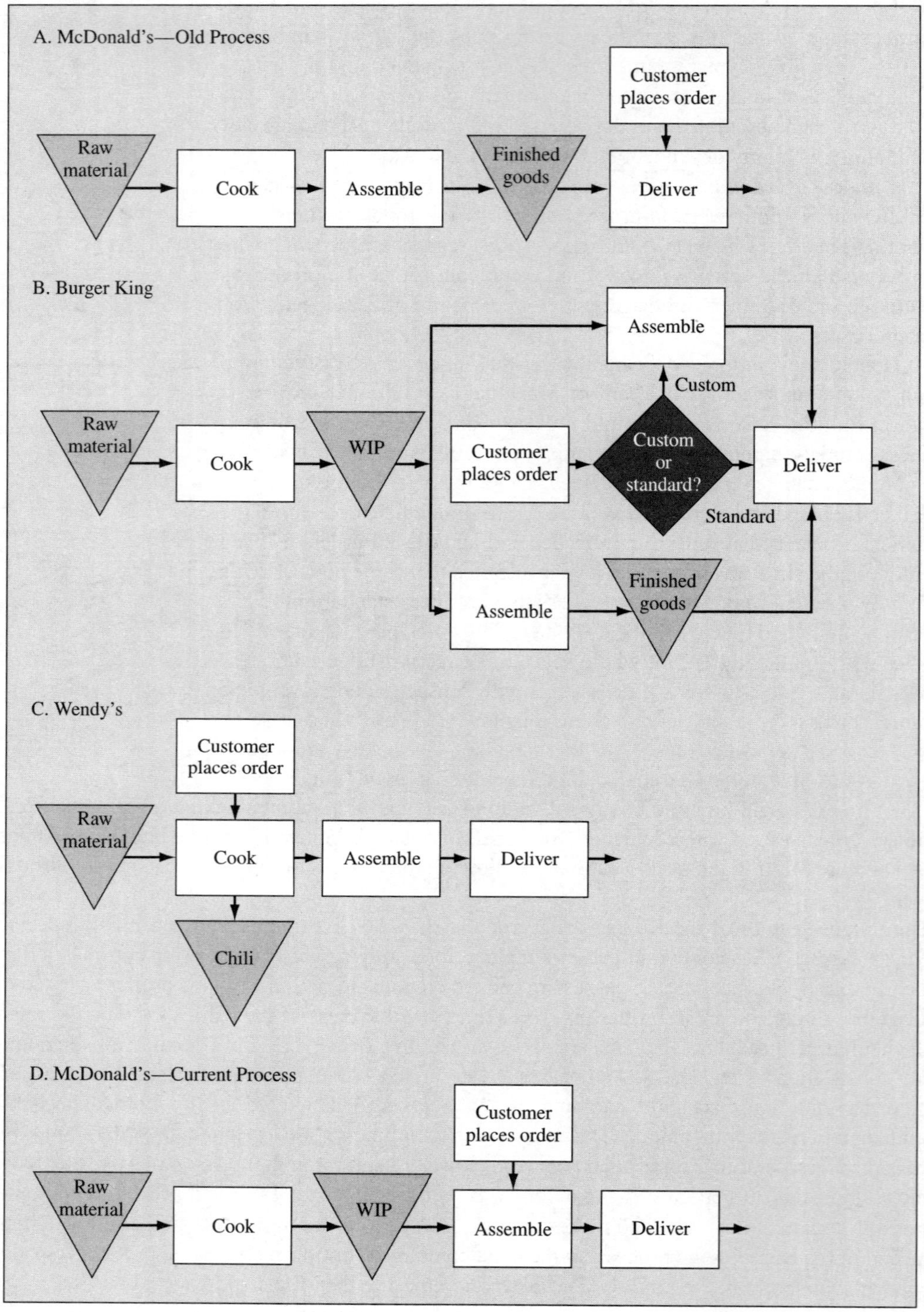

Finally, the current McDonald's process introduced in 1999 (Exhibit 11.2D) is a hybrid process. Cooked hamburger patties are inventoried in a special storage device that maintains the moistness of the cooked patties for up to 30 minutes. The process makes extensive use of the latest cooking technologies. Hamburger patties are cooked in less than 45 seconds. Buns are toasted in only 11 seconds. Individual items on each customer order are transmitted immediately to the area where the hamburgers are assembled using a specially designed computer system. The assembly process that includes toasting

the buns is designed to respond to a customer order in only 15 seconds. By combining the latest technology and clever process engineering, McDonald's has developed a very quick response process. The product is fresh, delivered quickly, and made to the exact specifications of the customer.

Each of the processes used by these companies has its strengths and weaknesses. McDonald's is the high-volume leader, catering to families with young children. Burger King has its unique taste. Wendy's appeals to those who want their hamburgers prepared the old-fashioned way. Each company focuses advertising and promotional efforts toward attracting the segment of the market its process characteristics best support.

One final method for categorizing a process is by whether it is paced or nonpaced. Recall that Burger King uses the conveyor–broiler to cook hamburgers in exactly 90 seconds. **Pacing** refers to the fixed timing of the movement of items through the process. In a serial process, the movement of items through each activity (or stage) is often paced in some mechanical way in order to coordinate the line. An assembly line may, for example, move every 45 seconds. Another mechanism used is a clock that counts down the amount of time left in each cycle. When the clock reaches zero, the parts are manually moved to the next activity. Dividing the time available to produce a certain product by customer demand for the product calculates the required cycle time for a process. For example, if an automobile manufacturer needs to produce 1,000 automobiles during a shift where the assembly line operates 420 minutes, the cycle time is 25.2 seconds (420 minutes/1,000 automobiles × 60 seconds/minute = 25.2 seconds/automobile).

Measuring Process Performance

There is much variation in the way performance metrics are calculated in practice. This section defines metrics in a manner consistent with the most common use in practice. It is vital, though, to understand exactly how a metric coming from a particular company or industry is calculated prior to making any decisions. This would be easier if metrics were calculated more consistently, but this just is not the case. So if a manager says that his utilization is 90 percent or her efficiency is 115 percent, a standard follow-up question is "How did you calculate that?" Metrics often are calculated in the context of a particular process. Metrics used in cases that you are studying may be defined slightly differently from what is given here. It is important to understand, within the context of the case, how a term is being used.

Comparing the metrics of one company to another, often referred to as *benchmarking,* is an important activity. Metrics tell a firm if progress is being made toward improvement. Similar to the value of financial measures to accountants, process performance metrics give the operations manager a gauge on how productively a process currently is operating and how productivity is changing over time. Often, operations managers need to improve the performance of a process or project the impact of a proposed change. The metrics described in this section are important for answering these questions. To help in understanding these calculations, Exhibit 11.3 shows how these metrics relate to one another.

Analytics

Possibly the most common process metric is utilization. As discussed earlier in the chapter, utilization is the ratio of the time that a resource is actually being used relative to the time it is available for use. Utilization is always measured in reference to some resource—for example, the utilization

Pacing
Movement of items through a process is coordinated through a timing mechanism.

Exhibit 11.3

Process Performance Metrics

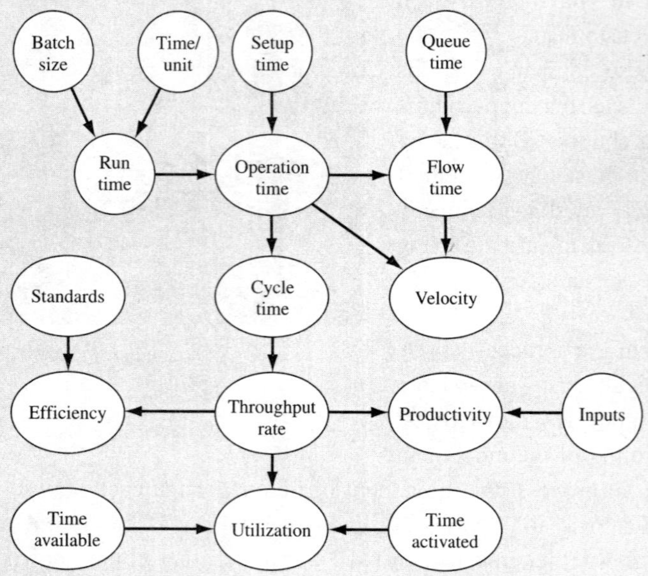

Operation time = Setup time + Run time

Flow time = Average time for a unit to move through the system

$$\textit{Velocity} = \frac{\textit{Value-added time}}{\textit{Flow time}}$$

Cycle time = Average time between completion of units

$$\textit{Throughput rate} = \frac{1}{\textit{Cycle time}}$$

$$\textit{Efficiency} = \frac{\textit{Actual output}}{\textit{Standard output}}$$

$$\textit{Productivity} = \frac{\textit{Output}}{\textit{Input}}$$

$$\textit{Utilization} = \frac{\textit{Time activated}}{\textit{Time available}}$$

Productivity
A measure of how well resources are used. According to Goldratt's definition (see Chapter 23), all the actions that bring a company closer to its goals.

Efficiency
A ratio of the actual output of a process relative to some standard. Also, being "efficient" means doing something at the lowest possible cost.

Run time
The time required to produce a batch of parts.

Setup time
The time required to prepare a machine to make a particular item.

Operation time
The sum of the setup time and run time for a batch of parts that are run on a machine.

of direct labor or the utilization of a machine resource. The distinction between productivity and utilization is important. **Productivity** is the ratio of output to input. Total factor productivity is usually measured in monetary units—dollars, for example—by taking the dollar value of the output (such as goods and services sold) and dividing by the cost of all the inputs (that is, material, labor, and capital investment). Alternatively, *partial factor productivity* is measured based on an individual input, labor being the most common. Partial factor productivity answers the question of how much output we can get from a given level of input; for example, how many computers are made per employee working in the computer manufacturing plant? (See Chapter 2 for additional information about productivity.) Utilization measures the actual activation of the resource. For example, what is the percentage of time that an expensive machine is actually operating?

Efficiency is a ratio of the actual output of a process relative to some standard. For example, consider a machine designed to package cereal at a rate of 30 boxes per minute. If during a shift the operators actually produce at a rate of 36 boxes per minute, then the efficiency of the machine is 120 percent (36/30). An alternative way that the term *efficiency* is used is to measure the loss or gain in a process. For example, if 1,000 units of energy are put into a process designed to convert that energy to some alternative form, and the process produces only 800 units of energy in the new form, then the process is 80 percent efficient.

Run time is the time required to produce a batch of parts. This is calculated by multiplying the time required to produce each unit by the batch size. The **Setup time** is the time required to prepare a machine to make a particular item. Machines that have significant setup time will typically run parts in batches. The **operation time** is the sum of the setup time and run time for a batch of parts that are run on a machine. Consider the cereal-boxing machine that is designed to produce at a rate of 30 boxes per minute. The run time for each box is 2 seconds. To switch the machine from 16-ounce boxes to 12-ounce boxes requires a setup time of 30 minutes. The operation time to make a batch of 10,000 12-ounce boxes is 21,800 seconds (30 minutes' setup × 60 seconds/minute + 2 seconds/box × 10,000 boxes), or 363.33 minutes.

In practice, setup time is often not included in the utilization of the process. In essence, setup time is categorized like the downtime caused by repair or some other disruption to the process. This assumption can vary from company to company, so it is important when comparing the utilization of a machine or other resource to understand exactly how the company categorizes setup time.

The cycle time (also defined earlier in this chapter) is the elapsed time between starting and completing a job. Another related term is **flow time**. Flow time includes the time the unit spends actually being worked on, together with the time spent waiting in a queue. In practice, the term *cycle time* is often used to mean *flow time*. It is important to carefully determine how the term is being used in the context of the process being studied.

Flow time
The average time it takes a unit to move through an entire process.

As a simple example, consider a paced assembly line that has six stations and runs with a cycle time of 30 seconds. If the stations are located one right after another, and every 30 seconds parts move from one station to the next, then the flow time is three minutes (30 seconds × 6 stations/60 seconds per minute).

The **throughput rate** is the output rate that the process is expected to produce over a period of time. The throughput rate of the assembly line is 120 units per hour (60 minutes/hour × 60 seconds/minute + 30 seconds/unit). In this case, the throughput rate is the mathematical inverse of the cycle time.

Often units are not worked on 100 percent of the time as they move through a process. Because there often is some variability in the cycle time of a process, buffers are incorporated in the process to allow individual activities to operate independently, at least to some extent. In the six-station assembly line just described, consider the impact of having 10 additional buffer positions along the line. Assume that two of these positions are between the first and second workstations, two are between stations 2 and 3, and so forth. If these positions are always occupied, then the flow time would be eight minutes (assuming a total of 16 positions along the assembly line and an average cycle time of 30 seconds).

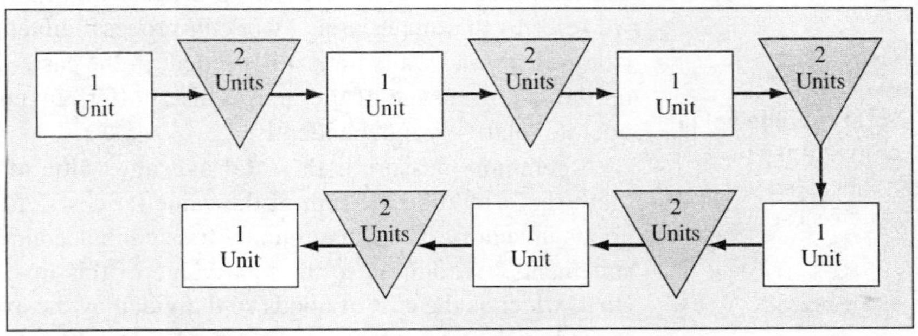

Process velocity (also known as **throughput ratio**) is the ratio of the value-added time to the flow time. **Value-added time** is the time in which useful work is actually being done on the unit. Assuming that all of the activities included in the process are value-added activities, value-added time should be the sum of the activity operation times in the process. The process velocity (or throughput ratio) for our assembly line with the 10 additional buffer positions, assuming the positions are used 100 percent of the time, is 0.375 (3 minutes/8 minutes).

Throughput rate
The output rate that the process is expected to produce over a period of time.

Process velocity (throughput ratio)
The ratio of the value-added time to the flow time.

Value-added time
The time in which useful work is actually being done on the unit.

Production Process Mapping and Little's Law

Next, we look at how to quickly develop a high-level map of a process, which can be useful to understand how material flows and where inventory is held. The approach used here should be the first step in analyzing the flow of material through a production process. This idea will be further developed in "Value Stream Mapping" in Chapter 12.

Consider a simple system that might be typical of many make-to-stock companies. As shown in Exhibit 11.4, material is purchased from a set of suppliers and initially staged in raw material inventory. The material is used in a manufacturing process where the product is fabricated. After fabrication, the product is put into finished goods inventory and from here it is shipped according to orders received from customers.

Focusing on the Make part of the process, it is useful to analyze how this step operates using performance measures that relate to the inventory investment and also how quickly material flows through the process. A simplified way of thinking about material in a process is that it is in one of two states. The first state is where material is moving or "in transit." The second state is material that is sitting in inventory and acting as a "buffer" waiting to be used.

Exhibit 11.4

Make-to-Stock Process Map

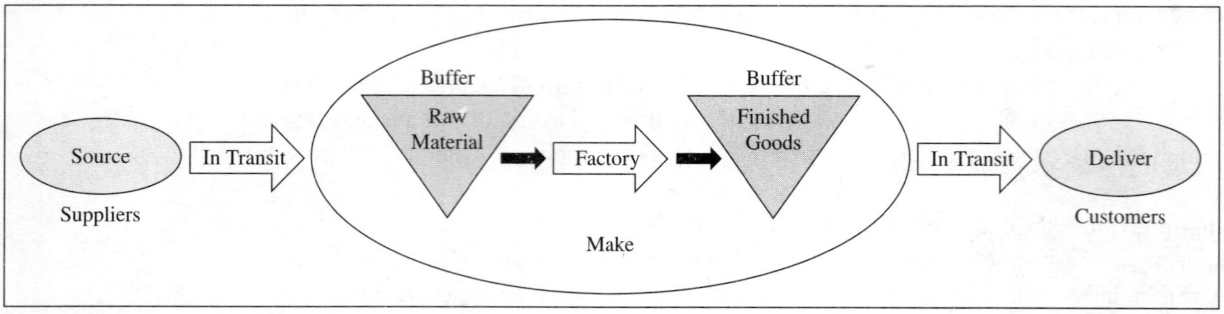

In the first state, material is moving in the process. This is material that is in transit between entities in the process—for example, between the vendor and the raw material inventory at the manufacturer. Material that is in a manufacturing process in a factory can also be considered in transit. Actually, we refer to this material as "work-in-process" inventory. In the second state, material is held in a storage area and waits until it is needed. In the case of raw material inventory, the need is dependent on the factory usage of the item. This "buffer" inventory allows different entities in the process to operate relatively independently.

Total average value of inventory
The total average investment in raw material, work-in-process, and finished goods inventory.

A common measure is the **total average value of inventory** in the process. From an accounting view, this would be the sum of the value (at cost) of the raw material, work-in-process, and finished goods inventory. This is commonly tracked in accounting systems and reported in the firm's financial statements. In addition to the total value of this inventory, another measure is the firm's **inventory turn**, which is the cost of goods sold divided by the average inventory value.

Inventory turn
A measure of the expected number of times inventory is replaced over a year.

Although useful for accounting purposes, the total average value of inventory might not be particularly useful for evaluating the performance of a process within a firm. What is better, a firm that has $2 million worth of inventory, on average, or one that has $4 million? This depends greatly on the size of the firm, the type of strategy being used (make-to-order or make-to-stock, for example), and the relative cost of the product being produced.

Days-of-supply
The number of days of inventory of an item.

A better measure than the total value of inventory is inventory turn. Since inventory turn scales the amount of inventory relative to the cost of goods sold, this provides a measure that has some comparability, at least across similar firms. For two similar consumer products manufacturers, an inventory turn of six times per year is certainly much better than a firm turning inventory two times per year. A measure directly related is **days-of-supply**, which is the inverse of inventory turn scaled to days. For example, if a firm turns inventory six times per year, the days of supply is equal to one-sixth times per year or approximately every 61 days (this is calculated as 1/6 year × 365 days/year = 60.8 days).

Little's law
States a mathematical relationship between throughput rate, flow time, and the amount of work-in-process inventory

Simple systems can be analyzed quickly using a principle known as **Little's law**. Little's law says there is a long-term relationship between the inventory, throughput, and flow time of a production system in steady state. The relationship is:

$$\textit{Inventory} = \textit{Throughput rate} \times \textit{Flow time} \qquad [11.1]$$

As noted earlier, throughput rate is the long-term average rate that items are flowing through the process, and flow time is the time it takes a unit to flow through the process from beginning to end. Consider the factory process in Exhibit 11.4. Raw material is brought into the factory and is transformed and then stored in finished goods inventory. The analysis assumes that the process is operating in "steady state," meaning that over a long enough period of time the amount that is produced by the factory is equal to the amount shipped to customers. The throughput rate of the process is equal to average demand, and the process is not producing any excess or shortage. If this was not true and the amount produced by the manufacturing process was greater than demand, for example, the finished goods inventory would build over time. So if demand averages 1,000 units per day and 20 days are needed for a unit to flow through the factory, then the expected work-in-process in the factory would be 20,000 units.

We can think of Little's law as a relationship between units and time. Inventory is measured in pieces, flow time in days, and throughput in pieces per day. Therefore, if we divide inventory by throughput, we get flow time. For example, 20,000 units divided by 1,000 units per day is 20 days. We can also take inventory and divide by flow time and get throughput rate. Here 20,000 units divided by 20 days is equal to 1,000 units a day. This conversion is useful when diagnosing a plant's performance.

Workers scanning inventory in a warehouse.
© DreamPictures/Shannon Faulk/Getty Images RF

To appreciate a major limitation, suppose a process has just started with no inventory on hand. Some of the initial production will be used to fill the system, thus limiting initial throughput. In this case, Little's law will not hold, but after the process has been operating for a while, and there is inventory at every step, the process stabilizes, and then the relationship holds.

Little's law is actually much more general than a simple way to convert between units. It can be applied to single work stations, multistep production lines, factories, or even entire supply chains. Further, it applies to processes with variability in the arrival rate (or demand rate) and processing time. It can be applied to single or multiple product systems. It even applies to nonproduction systems where inventory represents people, financial orders, or other entities.

For our factory, it is common for accounting systems to capture average work-in-process in terms of the value (at cost) of the inventory that is being worked on in the factory. For our example, say that work-in-process averages \$200,000 and that each unit is valued at cost at \$10.00. This would imply that there are 20,000 units in the factory (calculated \$200,000 ÷ \$10.00 per unit = 20,000 units).

Analytics

The following example shows how these concepts can be applied to quickly analyze simple processes.

EXAMPLE 11.1

An automobile company assembles cars in a plant and purchases batteries from a vendor in China. The average cost of each battery is \$45. The automobile company takes ownership of the batteries when they arrive at the plant. It takes exactly 12 hours to make a car in the plant and the plant assembles 200 cars per 8-hour shift (currently the plant operates one shift per day). Each car uses one battery. The company holds, on average, 8,000 batteries in raw material inventory at the plant as a buffer.

Assignment: Find the total number of batteries in the plant, on average (in work-in-process at the plant and in raw material inventory). How much are these batteries worth? How many days of supply are held in raw material inventory, on average?

SOLUTION

We can split this into two inventories, work-in-process and raw material. For the work-in-process, Little's law can be directly applied to find the amount of work-in-process inventory:

$$\textit{Inventory} = \textit{Throughput} \times \textit{Flow time}$$

Throughput is the production rate of the plant: 200 cars per 8-hour shift, or 25 cars per hour. Since we use one battery per car, our throughput rate for the batteries is 25 per hour. Flow time is 12 hours, so the work-in-process is:

$$\text{Work-in-process inventory} = 25 \text{ batteries/hour} \times 12 \text{ hours} = 300 \text{ batteries}$$

We know from the problem that there are 8,000 batteries in raw material inventory, so the total number of batteries in the pipeline, on average, is:

$$\text{Total inventory} = 8{,}000 + 300 = 8{,}300 \text{ batteries}$$

These batteries are worth 8,300 × \$45 = \$373,500.

The days of supply in raw material inventory is the "flow time" for a battery in raw material inventory (or the average amount of time a battery spends in raw material inventory). Here, we need to assume they are used in the same order they arrive. Rearranging our Little's law formula:

Flow time = Inventory/Throughput

So, flow time = 8,000 batteries/(200 batteries/day) = 40 days, which represents a 40-day supply of inventory.

LO 11-3

Explain how jobs are designed

JOB DESIGN DECISIONS

Thus far in the chapter, we have assumed that we know how long it takes to perform a task. Actually determining this time is a significant task in itself. In this section, concepts that relate to designing meaningful jobs are discussed together with the problem of estimating how long it should take to do the jobs. **Job design** may be defined as the function of specifying the work activities of an individual or group in an organizational setting. Its objective is to develop job structures that meet the requirements of the organization and its technology and that satisfy the jobholders' personal and individual requirements.

Job design
Specification of the work activities of an individual or group.

The diversity of the workforce's cultural and educational background, coupled with frequent organization restructuring, calls for a high level of people management skills. The operations and supply chain manager uses job design techniques to structure the work so it will meet both the physical and psychological needs of the worker. Work measurement methods are used to determine the most efficient means of performing a given task, as well as to set reasonable standards for performing it.

Strategy

Behavioral Considerations in Job Design

Specialization of labor is the double-edged sword of job design. On one hand, specialization has made possible high-speed, low-cost production, and from a materialistic standpoint, it has greatly enhanced our standard of living. On the other hand, extreme specialization (as we see in mass-production industries) often has serious adverse effects on workers, which in turn are passed on to management. In essence, the problem is to determine how much specialization is enough.

Specialization of labor
Simple, repetitive jobs are assigned to each worker.

Job enrichment generally entails adjusting a specialized job to make it more interesting to the job holder. A job is said to be enlarged *horizontally* if the worker performs a greater number or variety of tasks, and it is said to be enlarged *vertically* if the worker is involved in planning, organizing, and inspecting his or her own work. Horizontal job enrichment is intended to counteract oversimplification and to permit the worker to perform a "whole unit of work." Vertical enrichment attempts to broaden workers' influence in the transformation process by giving them certain managerial powers over their own activities.

Job enrichment
Specialized work is made more interesting by giving the worker a greater variety of tasks.

The organizational benefits of job enrichment occur in both quality and productivity. Quality in particular improves dramatically because when individuals are responsible for their work output, they take ownership of it and simply do a better job. Also, because they have a broader understanding of the work process, they are more likely to catch errors and make corrections than if the job is narrowly focused. Productivity improvements also occur from job enrichment, but they are not as predictable or as large as the improvements in quality. The reason is that enriched work invariably contains a mix of tasks that (for manual labor) causes interruptions in rhythm and different motions when switching from one task to the next. This is not the case for specialized jobs.

Work Measurement and Standards

Work measurement
Setting time standards for a job.

The fundamental purpose of **work measurement** is to set time standards for a job. Such standards are necessary for four reasons:

1. **To schedule work and allocate capacity.** All scheduling approaches require some estimate of how much time it takes to do the work being scheduled.
2. **To provide an objective basis for motivating the workforce and measuring workers' performance.** Measured standards are particularly critical where output-based incentive plans are employed.
3. **To bid for new contracts and to evaluate performance on existing ones.** Questions such as "Can we do it?" and "How are we doing?" presume the existence of standards.
4. **To provide benchmarks for improvement.** In addition to internal evaluation, benchmarking teams regularly compare work standards in their company with those of similar jobs in other organizations.

Work measurement and its resulting work standards have been controversial. Much of this criticism has come from unions, which argue that management often sets standards that cannot be regularly achieved. (To counter this, in some contracts, the industrial engineer who sets the standard must demonstrate that he or she can do the job over a representative period of time at the rate that was set.) There is also the argument that workers who find a better way of doing the job get penalized by having a revised rate set. (This is commonly called *rate cutting.*)

Despite these criticisms, work measurement and standards have proved effective. Much depends on sociotechnical aspects of the work. Where the job requires work groups to function as teams and create improvements, worker-set standards often make sense. On the other hand, where the job really boils down to doing the work quickly, with little need for creativity (such as delivering packages for UPS), tightly engineered, professionally set standards are appropriate.

There are four basic techniques for measuring work and setting standards. These consist of two direct observational methods and two indirect methods: The direct methods are time study, which uses a stopwatch to time the work, and work sampling, which entails recording random observations of a person or teams at work. The two indirect methods are predetermined motion-time data systems (PMTS), which sum data from tables of generic movement times developed in the laboratory to arrive at a time for the job, and elemental data, which sums times from a database of similar combinations of movements to arrive at job time. The choice of techniques depends on the level of detail desired and the nature of the work itself. Highly detailed, repetitive work usually calls for time study and predetermined motion-time data analysis. When work is done in conjunction with fixed-processing-time equipment, elemental data are often used to reduce the need for direct observation. When work is infrequent or entails a long cycle time, work sampling is the tool of choice.

PROCESS ANALYSIS EXAMPLES

LO 11-4

Analyze manufacturing, service, and logistics processes to ensure the competitiveness of a firm

In this section, the concepts described thus far in the chapter are illustrated with three examples. These examples are typical of the types of analysis performed in manufacturing, services, and logistics businesses. Keep in mind that the analysis used in each example can be applied to many different contexts. Be creative in applying something you have seen in another context to the problem at hand. The first example analyzes a bread-making process. Following this, a restaurant operation is evaluated. Finally, a typical logistics operation is appraised.

A Bread-Making Operation

EXAMPLE 11.2 Bread Making

Analytics

For the manager of a bakery, a first priority is to understand the products made and the process steps required. Exhibit 11.5A is a simplified diagram of the bread-making process. Two steps are required to prepare the bread. The first is preparing the dough and baking the loaves, here referred to as bread making. The second is packaging the loaves. Due to the size of the mixers in the bakery, bread is made in batches of 100 loaves. Bread making completes a batch of 100 loaves every hour, which is the cycle time for the activity. Packaging needs only 0.75 hour to place the 100 loaves in bags. We can assume that packaging starts up an hour after bread making, otherwise it would be idle for a full hour before getting any work at the start of the day.

From this, we see that bread making is the bottleneck in the process. A bottleneck is the activity in a process that limits the overall capacity of the process. So if we assume that the bread making and packaging activities both operate the same amount of time each day, then the bakery has a capacity of 100 loaves per hour. Notice that over the course of the day the packaging operation will be idle for quarter-hour periods in which the next batch of bread is still being made, but packaging has already completed bagging the previous batch. One would expect that the packaging operation would be utilized only 75 percent of the time under this scenario.

Suppose that instead of having only one bread making operation we now have two, as shown in Exhibit 11.5B. The cycle time for each individual bread-making operation is still one hour per 100 loaves. The cycle time for the two bread-making lines operating together is half an hour. Because the packaging operation takes 0.75 hour to bag 100 loaves, the packaging operation now is the bottleneck. If both bread making and packaging were operated the same number of hours each day, it would be necessary to limit how much bread was made because we do not have the capacity to package it. However, if we operated the packaging operation for three eight-hour shifts and bread making for two shifts each day, then the daily capacity of each would be identical at 3,200 loaves a day (this assumes that the packaging operation starts up one hour after the bread-making operation). Doing this requires building up inventory each day as work-in-process. Packaging would bag this during the third shift. So what is the flow time of our bakery?

EXHIBIT 11.5

Bread-Making Processes

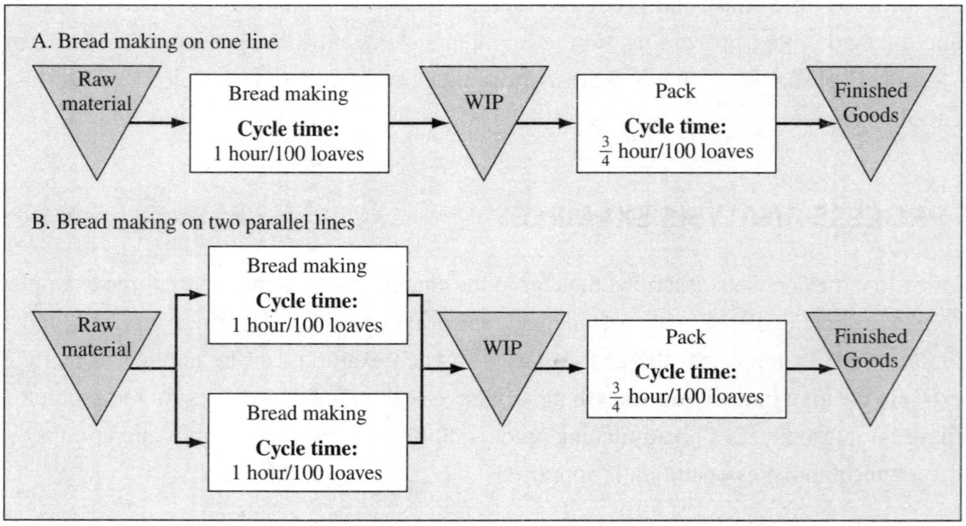

SOLUTION

In the original operation with just the single bread-making process, this is easy to calculate because inventory would not build between the bread-making and packaging processes. In this case, the flow time would be 1.75 hours.

In the case where we delay the start of the packing operation for one hour, and then operate it for three shifts, the average wait in work-in-process inventory needs to be considered. If both bread-making operations start at the same time, then at the end of the first hour the first 100 loaves move immediately into packaging while the second 100 loaves wait. The waiting time for each 100-loaf batch increases until the baking is done at the end of the second shift.

This is a case where Little's law can estimate the time that the bread is sitting in work-in-process. To apply Little's law, we need to estimate the average work-in-process between bread making and packaging. During the first two shifts, inventory builds from 0 to 1,200 loaves. We can estimate the average work-in-process over this 16-hour period to be 600 loaves (half the maximum). Over the last hour of the packaging operation's second shift, and the final eight-hour shift, inventory drops from the 1,200-loaf maximum down to 0. Again, the average work-in-process is 600 loaves. Given this, the overall average over the 24-hour period is simply 600 loaves of bread. The packing process limits the cycle time for the process to 0.75 hour per 100 loaves (assume that the loaves are packaged in a batch), and this is equivalent to a throughput rate of 133.3 loaves/hour (100/0.75 = 133.3). Little's law calculates that the average time that loaves are in work-in-process is 4.5 hours (600 loaves/133.3 loaves/hour).

The total flow time is the time that the loaves are in work-in-process, plus the operations time for the bread-making and packaging processes. The total flow time then is 6.25 hours (1 hour for bread making + 4.5 hours in inventory + 0.75 hour packaging).

A Restaurant Operation

EXAMPLE 11.3 A Restaurant

Analytics

Our bakery operates in what is referred to as *steady state,* meaning that the operation is started up and runs at a steady rate during the entire time it is in operation. The output of this steady state process is adjusted by setting the amount of time that the operation is run. In the case of the bakery, we assumed that bread making worked for two shifts and packaging for three shifts.

A restaurant cannot run in this manner. The restaurant must respond to varying customer demand throughout the day. During some peak times, it may be impossible to serve all customers immediately, and some customers may have to wait to be seated. The restaurant, because of this varying demand, is a *non–steady state* process. Keep in mind that many of the menu items in a restaurant can be preprepared. The preprepared items—salads and desserts, for example—help speed the processes that must be performed when customers are at the restaurant being served.

Consider the restaurant in the casino that we discussed earlier. Because it is important that customers be served quickly, the managers have set up a buffet arrangement where customers serve themselves. The buffet is continually replenished to keep items fresh. To further speed service, a fixed amount is charged for the meal, no matter what the customer eats. Assume that we have designed our buffet so customers take an average of 30 minutes to get their food and eat. Further, assume that they typically eat in groups (or customer parties) of two or three to a table. The restaurant has 40 tables. Each table can accommodate four people. What is the maximum capacity of this restaurant?

SOLUTION

It is easy to see that the restaurant can accommodate 160 people seated at tables at a time. Actually, in this situation, it might be more convenient to measure the capacity in terms of customer parties because this is how the capacity will be used. If the average customer party is 2.5 individuals, then the average seat utilization is 62.5 percent (2.5 seats/party ÷ 4 seats/table) when the restaurant is operating at capacity. The cycle time for the restaurant, when operating at capacity, is 0.75 minute (30 minutes/

table ÷ 40 tables). So, on average, a table would become available every 45 seconds. The restaurant could handle 80 customer parties per hour (60 minutes ÷ 0.75 minute/party).

The problem with this restaurant is that everyone wants to eat at the same time. Management has collected data and expects the following profile for customer parties arriving during lunch, which runs from 11:30 A.M. until 1:30 P.M. Customers are seated only until 1:00 P.M.

Time	Parties Arriving
11:30–11:45	15
11:45–12:00	35
12:00–12:15	30
12:15–12:30	15
12:30–12:45	10
12:45–1:00	5
Total parties	110

Because the restaurant operates for two hours for lunch and the capacity is 80 customer parties per hour, the restaurant does not appear to have a problem. In reality, though, the uneven flow of customers into the restaurant is a problem. A simple way to analyze the situation is to calculate how we expect the system to look in terms of number of customers being served and number waiting in line at the end of each 15-minute interval. Think of this as taking a snapshot of the restaurant every 15 minutes.

Time Period	Parties Arriving during Period (Cumulative)	Parties Departing during Period (Cumulative)	Parties Either at Table or Waiting to Be Served (at End of Period)	Tables Used (at End of Period)	Customer Parties Waiting (at End of Period)	Expected Waiting Time (at End of Period)
11:30–11:45	15	0	15	15		
11:45–12:00	35 (50)	0	50	40	10	7.5 minutes
12:00–12:15	30 (80)	15	65	40	25	18.75 minutes
12:15–12:30	15 (95)	20 (35)	60	40	20	15 minutes
12:30–12:45	10 (105)	20 (55)	50	40	10	7.5 minutes
12:45–1:00	5 (110)	20 (75)	35	35		
1:00–1:30	0 (110)	35 (110)				

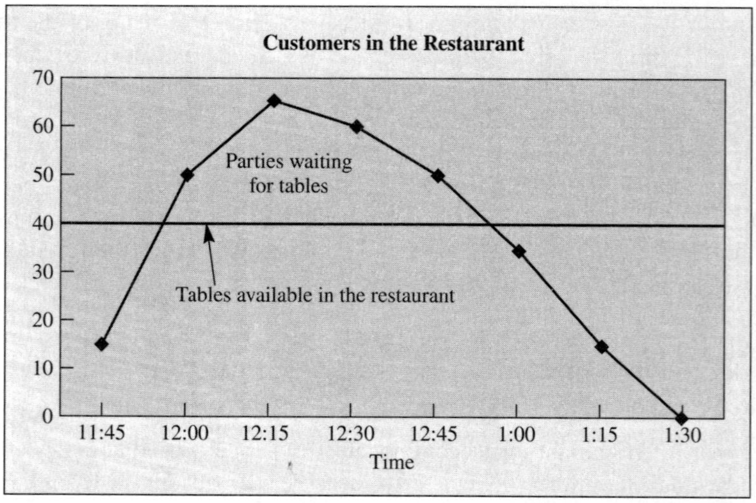

The key to understanding the analysis is to look at the cumulative numbers. The difference between cumulative arrivals and cumulative departures gives the number of customer parties in the restaurant (those seated at tables and those waiting). Because there are only 40 tables, when the cumulative difference through a time interval is greater than 40, a waiting line forms. When all 40 tables are busy, the system is operating at capacity; and, from the previous calculation, we know the cycle time for the entire restaurant is 45 seconds per customer party at this time (this means that, on average, a table empties every 45 seconds or 20 tables empty during each 15-minute interval). The last party will need to wait for all of the earlier parties to get a table, so the expected waiting time is the number of parties in line multiplied by the cycle time.

The analysis shows that by 12 noon, 10 customer parties are waiting in line. This line builds to 25 parties by 12:15. The waiting line shortens to only 10 parties by 12:45.

So what can we do to solve our waiting line problem? One idea might be to shorten the cycle time for a single table, but customers are unlikely to be rushed through their lunch in less than 30 minutes. Another idea would be to add tables. If the restaurant could add 25 tables, then a wait would not be expected. Of course, this would eat into the space used for slot machines, so this alternative might not be attractive to casino management. A final idea might be to double up parties at the tables, thus getting a higher seat utilization. Doubling up might be the easiest thing to try. If 25 out of the 40 tables were doubled up, our problem would be solved.

Planning a Transit Bus Operation

EXAMPLE 11.4 Transit Bus Operation

Analytics

The final example involves a *logistics* system. The term *logistics* refers to the movement of things such as materials, people, or finished goods. Our example involves a bus route that would be typical of one used on campus or in a metropolitan area. A similar analysis could be used for analyzing plane routes, truck routes, or ships. Similar to the restaurant, a bus transit route does not operate in steady state. There are definite peaks in demand during the day and evening. A good approach to take, the same as was done with the restaurant, is to analyze distinct periods of time that represent the different types of demand patterns placed on the service. These distinct analyses can be referred to as *scenarios.* Depending on the situation, it might be reasonable to develop either a single solution that covers all the relevant scenarios or a set of solutions for the different scenarios.

A great bus route is the Balabus, or "tourist bus," in Paris. This route loops past all the major attractions in Paris. Some of the sights along the route include Notre-Dame, the Louvre, Concorde, Champs-Elysées, the Arc de Triomphe, the Eiffel Tower, and others.

Consider the problem of planning the number of buses needed to service this route. A number of factors need to be considered. Let's assume that a single bus takes exactly two hours to traverse the route during peak traffic. The bus company has designed delays in the route so that even though traffic is busy, the bus can keep on schedule. The route has 60 stops, although the bus stops only when passengers on the bus request a stop or when the driver sees customers waiting to board at a stop. Each bus has seating capacity of about 50 passengers, and another 30 passengers can stand. This route is busy much of the day because visitors to the city tend to start visiting the sites early and continue until dark. Finally, the transit authority wants to give good service and have enough capacity to handle peak customer loads. The following is an analysis of the situation.

SOLUTION

A key measure of service is how long a customer must wait prior to the arrival of a bus. Consider initially the case of only a single bus serving the route. If a person comes to a bus stop at a random time, we know that the maximum time that the customer needs to wait is two hours. Here we assume that the bus is able to cover the route in exactly two hours. If this cycle time varies significantly, the waiting time goes up. We discussed the impact of variability in Chapter 10. This would be the case when the unlucky customer just missed the bus. If the bus was halfway through the route (relative to where the customer is waiting), then the customer needs to wait one hour. Continuing with this logic, we can estimate the average wait time for the customer to be one hour. In general, we can say that the average wait time would be half the cycle time of the process. If two buses are used, the cycle time is one hour and the average wait is 30 minutes. If we want the average wait to be two minutes, then the required cycle time is four minutes, and 30 buses are needed (120 minutes ÷ 4 minutes/bus = 30 buses).

The next issue relates to the capacity of the system. If we have 30 buses on the route and each bus seats 50 passengers with another 30 standing, we know we can accommodate 1,500 seated or 2,400 passengers in total at one point in time.

Assume that the following table is an estimate of the number of passengers that travel the route during a typical tourist season day. The table shows calculations of the amount of bus capacity required during each hour. If a customer rides the bus for 45 minutes, then one seat is needed for 45 minutes, or 0.75 hour, to handle that passenger. Of course, 60 minutes, or a full hour's worth of capacity, is available for each seat we have. At maximum utilization including standing, each bus can handle 80 passenger-hours' worth of load. Dividing the expected passenger load during the hour by the maximum load for a single bus calculates the minimum number of buses needed. Similarly, dividing the expected passenger load by the number of seats on each bus calculates the number of buses needed so that all passengers can be seated.

From the analysis, if the Paris transit authority uses only 30 buses throughout the day, many people will need to stand. Further, during the morning rush between 10 and 11 A.M. and the evening rush between 5 and 6 P.M., not all of the customers can be accommodated. It would seem reasonable that at least 40 buses should be used between 9 A.M. and 7 P.M. Even with this number of buses, one would expect passengers to be standing most of the time.

If the transit authority decided to use 40 buses between the extended hours of 8 A.M. through 8 P.M., what would be the average utilization of the buses in terms of seats occupied? Over this 12-hour period, 24,000 seat-hours of capacity would be available (40 buses × 12 hours × 50 seats/bus). The table indicates that 25,875 seat-hours are needed. The utilization would be 107.8 percent (25,875/24,000 × 100). What this means is that, on average, 7.8 percent of the customers must stand. Of course, this average value significantly understates the severe capacity problem that occurs during the peak times of the day.

Time	Number of Customers	Average Time on Bus	Load (Passenger Hours)	Minimum Number of Buses Needed	Buses Needed for All Passengers to Be Seated
8:00–9:00 A.M.	2,000	45 minutes	1,500	18.75	30
9:00–10:00 A.M.	4,000	30 minutes	2,000	25	40
10:00–11:00 A.M.	6,000	30 minutes	3,000	37.5	60
11:00 A.M.–12:00 noon	5,000	30 minutes	2,500	31.25	50
12:00–1:00 P.M.	4,000	30 minutes	2,000	25	40
1:00–2:00 P.M.	3,500	30 minutes	1,750	21.875	35
2:00–3:00 P.M.	3,000	45 minutes	2,250	28.125	45
3:00–4:00 P.M.	3,000	45 minutes	2,250	28.125	45
4:00–5:00 P.M.	3,000	45 minutes	2,250	28.125	45
5:00–6:00 P.M.	4,000	45 minutes	3,000	37.5	60
6:00–7:00 P.M.	3,000	45 minutes	2,250	28.125	45
7:00–8:00 P.M.	1,500	45 minutes	1,125	14.0625	22.5
TOTALS	42,000		25,875		

Consider in the preceding example how useful this type of analysis is to the Paris transit authority. Data can be collected for each day of the week, and the analysis performed. Interesting questions concerning the design of the route or the capacity of the buses can be evaluated. For example, what would happen if the route were split into two parts. What if larger buses that could carry 120 passengers were put into service? The analysis can be extended to include the cost of providing the service by considering the wages paid to the operators, the cost to maintain and operate the vehicles, and depreciation of the buses. As seen from the given example, designing a transit system involves a trade-off between the convenience of the service, or how frequently buses arrive at each stop, and the capacity utilization of the buses.

Process Flow Time Reduction

Critical processes are subject to the well-known rule that time is money. For example, the longer a customer waits, the more likely the customer is to switch to a different vendor. The longer material is kept in inventory, the higher the investment cost. There are exceptions in services, where more time in process can lead to more money. See the OSCM at Work box, "Efficiency Meets Corporate Goals: A Love Story" later in this section.

Unfortunately, critical processes often depend on specific limited resources, resulting in bottlenecks. Flow time can sometimes be reduced without purchasing additional equipment. The following are some suggestions for reducing the flow time of a process that do not require the purchase of new equipment. Often, a combination of ideas is appropriate.

Process

1. **Perform activities in parallel.** Most of the steps in an operations process are performed in sequence. A serial approach results in the flow time for the entire process being the sum of the individual steps plus transport and waiting time between steps. Using a parallel approach can reduce flow time by as much as 80 percent and produces a better result.

   A classic example is product development, where the current trend is toward concurrent engineering. Instead of forming a concept, making drawings, creating a bill of materials, and mapping processes, all activities are performed in parallel by integrated teams. Development time is reduced dramatically, and the needs of all those involved are addressed during the development process.

2. **Change the sequence of activities.** Documents and products are often transported back and forth between machines, departments, buildings, and so forth. For instance, an item might be

Based on "Efficiency Meets Corporate Goals: A Love Story," Anonymous, posted July 21, 2006, on www.pavilion.com.

OSCM AT WORK

Efficiency versus Corporate Goals

Consider the following process improvement idea at a local coffee shop.

The process improvement idea is to improve the efficiency with which the coffee shop provides value to their customers by reducing the wait time, reducing the length of the line, and delivering coffee faster.

The Problem: Why is it that regular coffee drinkers wait in the same line as drinkers of a double latte cinnamon frappuccino, which takes much longer to prepare?

Idea: Give the regular coffee drinkers their own line. Simple, yet brilliant.

So, armed with good intentions, the consultant approached the coffee shop owner, and explained the idea of having two lines, one for regular coffee drinkers and the other for the exotic drinks.

The coffee shop owner agreed that it was indeed his goal to make more money at the shop. Further, he explained that the consultant needs to understand that it is during this pause provided while waiting in line and prior to pouring coffee that patrons peer into the pastry case, and decide they want a coffee *and* a pastry! The consultant was amazed at the coffee shop owners perfect logic and very effective process. It was, in fact, a beautiful thing. The consultant learned that always being fast did not always maximize profit.

The most efficient process does not always attain your business goals. It is imperative that the process and goal be aligned. Also, learn to appreciate the process that is in place and the businesspeople that designed it. The people that designed the current problem may have known what they were doing. It is essential for you study all aspects of the process before proposing changes that may make no sense.

© Plush Studios/Bill Reitzel/Getty Images RF

transferred between two machines a number of times for fabrication and inspection. If the process can be streamlined, it may be possible to perform all of the fabrication before the inspection, thus eliminating the waiting associated with the back and forth transfer.

3. **Reduce interruptions.** Many processes are performed with relatively large time intervals between the activities. For example, purchase orders may be issued only every other day. Individuals preparing reports that result in purchase orders should be aware of deadlines to avoid missing them, because improved timing in these processes can save many days of flow time.

To illustrate these ideas, consider an electronics manufacturer that has been receiving customer complaints about a long order lead time of 29 days. An assessment of the order-processing system revealed 12 instances where managers had to approve employees' work. It was determined that the first 10 approvals were not needed. This saved an average of seven to eight days in the order processing.

Many subsystems—each performing the same or similar tasks—had interfered with the process. The logical step was to eliminate redundancy, and a detailed flowchart of the process was created. At close inspection, 16 steps proved very similar to one another. Changing the sequence of activities and creating one company-wide order document removed 13 of these steps.

Over four months, the order system was totally redesigned to allow information to be entered once and become available to the entire organization. Due to this adjustment, activities could be handled in a parallel manner. After a value-added analysis (focused on eliminating the non–value-adding activities), the manufacturer was able to reduce the customer order lead time from 29 days to 9 days, save cost and employee time per order, and increase customer satisfaction.

Process analysis is a basic skill needed to understand how a business operates. Great insight is obtained by drawing a simple flowchart showing the flow of materials or information through an enterprise. The diagram should include all the operating elements and show how they fit together. Be sure to indicate where material is stored or where orders are queued. Often, 90 percent or more of the time that is required to serve a customer is spent just waiting. Hence, merely eliminating the waiting time can dramatically improve the performance of the process.

Remember this fundamental concept when analyzing a process: What goes into the process must come out of the process. A process taken as a whole is like the funnel shown in Exhibit 11.6. The outlet of the funnel restricts the amount that can flow through. In a real business process, certain resources limit output. If liquid is poured into the funnel at a rate greater than it can exit, the level in the funnel

EXHIBIT 11.6

What Goes into a Process Must Come Out of the Process. Input Rate Must Be Less Than or Equal to the Output Rate; Otherwise, the System Will Overflow.

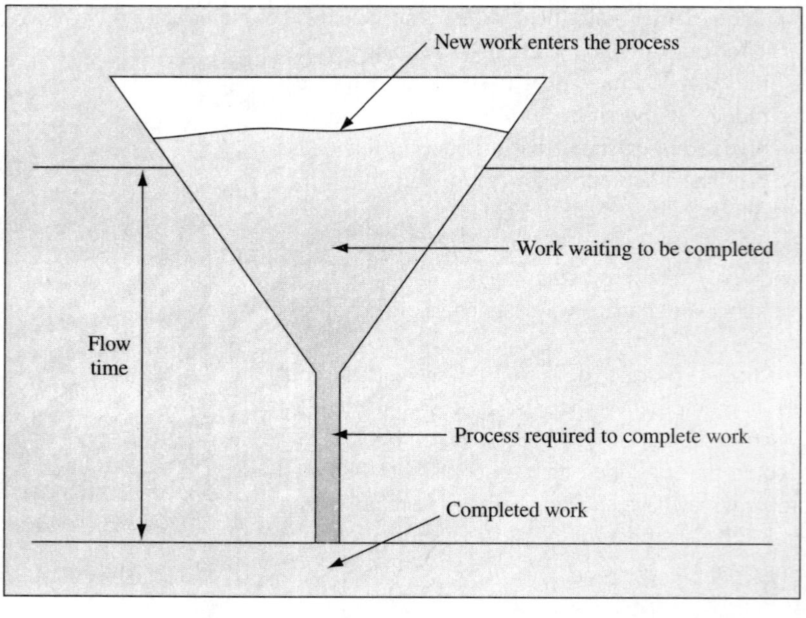

will continue to grow. As the level of liquid in the funnel grows, the time needed for the liquid to flow through the funnel increases. If too much liquid is poured into the funnel, it just spills over the top and never flows through.

The same is true of a real process. If too many jobs are pumped into the process, the time it takes to complete a job will increase because the waiting time will increase. At some point, customers will go somewhere else and the business will be lost. When a process is operating at capacity, the only way to take on more work without increasing the waiting time is to add more capacity. This requires finding what activity is limiting the output of the process and increasing the capacity of that activity. In essence, the tube leading out of the funnel needs to be made larger.

CONCEPT CONNECTIONS

LO 11–1 Exemplify a typical business process and how it can be analyzed

Summary

- Companies get things done with processes. A process takes inputs and transforms them into outputs that create value for the organization.
- Everything from ordering material from vendors on the supply side and fabricating a product in a factory to shipping goods to customers on the demand side is done with processes. A company may have literally thousands of different processes.
- Designing processes is the focus of this chapter.
- Understanding a process usually starts with the preparation of a flowchart that depicts tasks, flows, and storage areas.

Key Terms

Process Any set of activities performed by an organization that takes inputs and transforms them into outputs ideally of greater value to the organization than the original inputs.

Cycle time The average time between completions of successive units in a process (this is the definition used in this book).

Utilization The ratio of the time that a resource is actually activated relative to the time that it is available for use.

LO 11–2 Compare different types of processes

Summary

- In the case of a multistage process that has a sequence of activities that must be done in a specific order, it is often useful to buffer the activities by placing inventory between the activities. This allows the activities to operate relatively independently and helps prevent starving and blocking.
- The bottleneck is the activity or stage in the process that limits output the most and limits the capacity of the entire process.
- A process that is only activated after an actual order arrives is called make-to-order.
- Make-to-stock processes supply inventory from which actual customer orders are filled.
- There are many variations related to how the work in a process is coordinated to meet demand.
- Basic process performance is measured by its speed and capacity.
- Measures that drive cost include the efficiency, productivity, and utilization of resources used in the process.
- Little's law is a mathematical formula that captures the relationship between the amount of inventory of all types in the process, the time required to produce a unit by the process, and the production rate or capacity of the process.
- These concepts are important in analyzing how a process operates and how quick and costly the process is.

Key Terms

Buffer A storage area between stages where the output of a stage is placed prior to being used in a downstream stage.

Blocking The activities in the stage must stop because there is no place to deposit the item just completed.

Starving The activities in a stage must stop because there is no work.

Bottleneck A resource that limits the capacity or maximum output of the process.

Make-to-order A production environment where the product is built directly from raw materials and components in response to a specific customer order.

Make-to-stock A production environment where the customer is served "on-demand" from finished goods inventory.

Hybrid Combines the features of both make-to-order and make-to-stock.

Pacing Movement of items through a process is coordinated through a timing mechanism.

Productivity A measure of how well resources are used. According to Goldratt's definition (see Chapter 23), all the actions that bring a company closer to its goals.

Efficiency A ratio of the actual output of a process relative to some standard. Also, being "efficient" means doing something at the lowest possible cost.

Run time The time required to produce a batch of parts.

Setup time The time required to prepare a machine to make a particular item.

Operation time The sum of the setup time and run time for a batch of parts that are run on a machine.

Flow time The average time it takes a unit to move through an entire process.

Throughput rate The output rate that the process is expected to produce over a period of time.

Process velocity The ratio of the value-added time to the flow time.

Value-added time The time in which useful work is actually being done on the unit.

Total average value of inventory The total average investment in raw material, work-in-process, and finished goods inventory.

Inventory turn A measure of the expected number of times inventory is replaced over a year.

Days-of-supply The number of days of inventory of an item.

Little's law States a mathematical relationship between throughput rate, flow time, and the amount of work-in-process inventory

Key Formulas

[11.1] Little's law

$$\textit{Inventory} = \textit{Throughput rate} \times \textit{Flow time}$$

LO 11–3 Explain how jobs are designed

Summary

- Designing each task that must be performed in a process is important. Each task takes time and must be performed by either a person or a machine.
- Job design is the study of how work activities are designed for individuals or groups of workers.
- A key design decision is the amount of specialization that a job entails.
- Jobs that are too specialized may be boring and create health problems for workers.
- Trade-offs exist between the quality and relative productivity of a process and depend on how the jobs are designed.

Key Terms

Job design Specification of the work activities of an individual or group.

Specialization of labor Simple, repetitive jobs are assigned to each worker.

Job enrichment Specialized work is made more interesting by giving the worker a greater variety of tasks.

Work measurement Setting time standards for a job.

LO 11–4 **Analyze manufacturing, service, and logistics processes to ensure the competitiveness of a firm**

Summary

- There are many different types of processes. This chapter provided examples of a bread-making operation, a restaurant, and a transit bus operation.
- There are many "tricks" for speeding up a process.
- A fundamental concept is that what goes into a process must come out of the process in some form. If inputs such as materials are going into the process faster than they are being consumed, then these inputs will build up within the process. This can create serious problems for the firm.
- Coordinating the inputs and outputs is important to having a good process.

SOLVED PROBLEMS

LO11–2 SOLVED PROBLEM 1

Suppose we schedule shipments to our customers so that we expect each shipment to wait for two days in finished goods inventory (in essence we add two days to when we expect to be able to ship). We do this as protection against system variability to ensure a high on-time delivery service. If we ship approximately 2,000 units each day, how many units do we expect to have in finished goods inventory after allowing this extra time? If the items are valued at $4.50 each, what is the expected value of this inventory?

Solution

Using Little's law, the expected finished goods inventory is:

Inventory = 2,000 units per day × 2 days = 4,000 units

This would be valued at 4,000 units × $4.50 per unit = $18,000

LO11–4 SOLVED PROBLEM 2

Daffy Dave's Sub Shop makes custom submarine sandwiches to order. It is analyzing the processes at its shop. The general flow of the process is shown as follows. A different person is working at each of the steps in the process.

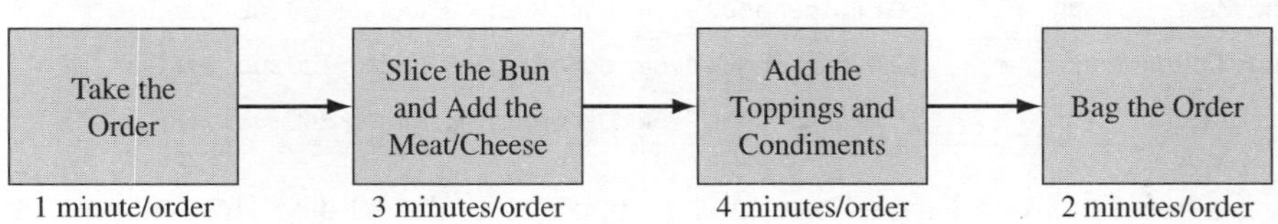

Daffy Dave wants to figure out the following for a typical eight-hour work day.

a. What is the current maximum output of the process?

b. If we add another person, where would we add him or her and what is the benefit?

c. Is there a benefit if we can shift one minute from Bun and Meat to Order Taking? Assume we do not make the change in part (*b*).

d. Is there a benefit if we shift one minute of work from Condiments to Bagging? Assume we do not make the changes in parts (*b*) and (*c*).

Solution

a. Maximum output is 120 subs per day.

Operation	Output
Take Orders	(60 min. per hour/1 min. per order) × 8 hours = 480 subs per day
Bun and Meat	(60 min. per hour/3 min. per order) × 8 hours = 160 subs per day
Toppings/Condiments	(60 min. per hour/3 min. per order) × 8 hours = 160 subs per day
Bag the Order	(60 min. per hour/3 min. per order) × 8 hours = 160 subs per day

Output per day is determined by the slowest station; therefore, we can only produce 120 per day because that is the limit of the Toppings/Condiments station.

b. Dave should add the person to the slowest station (Condiments/Toppings) since it is the bottleneck.

Operation	Output
Take Orders	480 subs per day
Bun and Meat	160 subs per day
Toppings/Condiments	120 × 2 = 240 subs per day
Bag the Order	240 subs per day

The impact is not a very big one. Even though the Toppings/Condiments station now can do 240 subs per day, the Bun and Meat station can only do 160, so that is the maximum output.

c. Order Taking station will go from 1 minute to 2 minutes, and Bun and Meat goes from 3 minutes to 2 minutes.

Operation	Output
Take Orders	(60 min. per hour/2 min. per order) × 8 hours = 240 subs per day
Bun and Meat	(60 min. per hour/2 min. per order) × 8 hours = 240 subs per day
Toppings/Condiments	(60 min. per hour/4 min. per order) × 8 hours = 120 subs per day
Bag the Order	(60 min. per hour/2 min. per order) × 8 hours = 240 subs per day

There is no benefit to this change. Dave can still only make 120 subs per day since we can only produce 120 per day because that is the limit of the Toppings/Condiments station.

d. Toppings/Condiments station will go from 4 minutes to 3 minutes, and Bagging goes from 2 minutes to 3 minutes.

Operation	Output
Take Orders	(60 min. per hour/1 min. per order) × 8 hours = 480 subs per day
Bun and Meat	(60 min. per hour/3 min. per order) × 8 hours = 160 subs per day
Toppings/Condiments	(60 min. per hour/4 min. per order) × 8 hours = 120 subs per day
Bag the Order	(60 min. per hour/2 min. per order) × 8 hours = 240 subs per day

There is a benefit to this change. Dave can now make 160 subs per day. This will provide the same benefit as hiring another worker. However, if Dave wants to increase output further, he will have to hire some additional staff.

DISCUSSION QUESTIONS

LO 11–1

1. Define a process in general. Apply this definition in detail to a university, a grocery store, and a beer brewing company.
2. Consider your favorite fast-food restaurant. The next time you are there, pay special attention to how the food preparation and delivery process works. Develop a flowchart of the process like that

in Exhibit 11.1. Try to include as much detail as is needed to explain the process, remembering to differentiate between your activities as a customer and those of the service process.
3. Describe *cycle time* as it relates to business processes. Why is it important to the management of business processes? How does it relate to concepts like productivity and capacity utilization?
4. Compare McDonald's old and current processes for making hamburgers. How valid is McDonald's claim that the new process will produce fresher hamburgers for the customer? Comparing McDonald's current process to the processes used by Burger King and Wendy's, which process would appear to produce the freshest hamburgers? **LO 11-2**
5. State in your own words what Little's law means. Describe an example that you have observed where Little's law applies.
6. Explain how having more work-in-process inventory can improve the efficiency of a process. How can this be bad?
7. Recently, some operations management experts have begun insisting that simply maximizing process velocity, which actually means minimizing the time it takes to process something through the system, is the single most important measure for improving a process. Can you think of a situation in which this might not be true?
8. What is job enrichment and what has led to its importance in job design? **LO 11-3**
9. Why are work measurements and time standards important for a firm? Are there any negatives to the implementation of these standards? Are there ways to achieve the same objectives without setting firm standards?
10. From your own experiences, compare the processes of your favorite brick-and-mortar department store and a comparable online retailer. What advantages does each have over the other? What advantages does each offer you, the customer? **LO 11-4**
11. What is the effect of waiting time on a manufacturing process? Why is it good to reduce waiting time? Can it be eliminated altogether?
12. How does seasonal variability in demand affect the flow and waiting time through a process? How might a company respond to reduce the effect of this variability?

OBJECTIVE QUESTIONS

1. A manufacturing company has a small production line dedicated to making a particular product. The line has four stations in serial. Inputs arrive at station 1 and the output from station 1 becomes the input to station 2. The output from station 2 is the input to station 3 and so on. The output from station 4 is the finished product. Station 1 can process 2,700 units per month, station 2 can process 2,500/month, station 3 can process 2,300/month, and station 4 can process 2,100/month. What station sets the maximum possible output from this system? What is that maximum output number? **LO 11-1**
2. In a flowchart, what is used to represent a storage activity in a process?
3. A process is part of an organization that takes _____, turns them into _____, and adds _____ while doing so.
4. You are in a line at the bank drive-through and 10 cars are in front of you. You estimate that the clerk is taking about five minutes per car to serve. How long do you expect to wait in line? **LO 11-2**
5. A firm has redesigned its production process so that it now takes 10 hours for a unit to be made. Using the old process, it took 15 hours to make a unit. If the process makes one unit each hour, on average, and each unit is worth $1,500, what is the reduction in work-in-process value?
6. Avis Company is a car rental company that is located three miles from the Los Angeles airport (LAX). Avis is dispatching a bus from its offices to the airport every 2 minutes. The average traveling time (round-trip) is 20 minutes.
   a. How many Avis buses are traveling to and from the airport?

b. The branch manager wants to improve the service and suggests dispatching buses every 0.5 minutes. She argues that this will reduce the average traveling time from the airport to the Avis offices to 2.5 minutes. Is she correct? If your answer is negative, what will the average traveling time be?

7. At the Children's Hospital in Seattle there are, on average, 60 births per week. Mother and child stay, on average, two days before they leave the hospital. At the Swedish Hospital (also in Seattle), the average number of births per week is 210. Mothers and children stay in the hospital two days, on average.
   a. How many new mothers, on average, are staying at the Children's Hospital?
   b. How many new mothers, on average, are staying at the Swedish Hospital?
   c. The directors of the two hospitals are negotiating unifying the maternity wards of the two hospitals. They believe this will help reduce the number of new mothers staying in the unified ward. Are they correct? How many new mothers will stay, on average, in the unified ward? You may assume that the average number of births and the length of stay of the new mothers will not change.

LO 11-3

8. What are the four basic techniques for measuring work and setting time standards?
9. Which work measurement technique is most appropriate for tasks that are infrequent or have a long cycle time?

LO 11-4

10. An enterprising student has set up an internship clearinghouse for business students. Each student who uses the service fills out a form and lists up to 10 companies that he or she would like to have contacted. The clearinghouse has a choice of two methods to use for processing the forms. The traditional method requires about 20 minutes to review the form and arrange the information in the proper order for processing. Once this setup is done, it takes only two minutes per company requested to complete the processing. The other alternative uses an optical scan/retrieve system, which takes only a minute to prepare but requires five minutes per company for completing the processing. If it costs about the same amount per minute for processing with either of the two methods, when should each be used? (Answer in Appendix D)
11. Rockness Recycling refurbishes rundown business students. The process uses a moving belt, which carries each student through the five steps of the process in sequence. The five steps are as follows.

Step	Description	Time Required per Student
1	Unpack and place on belt	1.0 minute
2	Strip off bad habits	1.5 minutes
3	Scrub and clean mind	0.8 minute
4	Insert modern methods	1.0 minute
5	Polish and pack	1.2 minutes

One faculty member is assigned to each of these steps. Faculty members work a 40-hour week and rotate jobs each week. Mr. Rockness has been working on a contract from General Eclectic, which requires delivery of 2,000 refurbished students per week. A representative of the human resources department has just called complaining that the company hasn't been receiving the agreed-upon number of students. A check of finished goods inventory by Mr. Rockness reveals that there is no stock left. What is going on?

12. The bathtub theory of operations management is being promoted as the next breakthrough for global competitiveness. The factory is a bathtub with 50 gallons of capacity. The drain is the outlet to the market and can output three gallons per hour when wide open. The faucet is the raw material input and can let material in at a rate of four gallons per hour. Now, to test your comprehension of the intricacies of operations (assume the bathtub is empty to begin with): (Answers in Appendix D)
    a. Draw a diagram of the factory and determine the maximum rate at which the market can be served if all valves are set to maximum. What happens to the system over time?

b. Suppose that, instead of a faucet, a five-gallon container is used for filling the bathtub (assume a full container is next to the tub to begin with); it takes two hours to refill the container and return it to the bathtub. What happens to the system over time?

13. A local market research firm has just won a contract for several thousand small projects involving data gathering and statistical analysis. In the past, the firm has assigned each project to a single member of its highly trained professional staff. This person would both gather and analyze the data. Using this approach, an experienced person can complete an average of 10 such projects in an eight-hour day.

    The firm's management is thinking of assigning two people to each project in order to allow them to specialize and become more efficient. The process would require the data gatherer to fill out a matrix on the computer, check it, and transmit it to the statistical analysis program for the analyst to complete. Data can be gathered on one project while the analysis is being completed on another, but the analysis must be complete before the statistical analysis program can accept the new data. After some practice, the new process can be completed with a standard time of 20 minutes for the data gathering and 30 minutes for the analysis.

    a. What is the production (output per hour) for each alternative? What is the productivity (output per labor hour)?

    b. How long would it take to complete 1,000 projects with each alternative? What would be the labor content (total number of labor hours) for 1,000 projects for each alternative?

14. A processor makes two components, A and B, which are then packaged together as the final product (each product sold contains one A and one B). The processor can do only one component at a time: Either it can make As or it can make Bs. There is a setup time when switching from A to B.

    Current plans are to make 100 units of component A, then 100 units of component B, then 100 units of component A, then 100 units of component B, and so forth, where the setup and run times for each component are given as follows.

Component	Setup/Changeover Time	Run Time/Unit
A	5 minutes	0.2 minute
B	10 minutes	0.1 minute

    Assume the packaging of the two components is totally automated and takes only two seconds per unit of the final product. This packaging time is small enough that you can ignore it. What is the average hourly output, in terms of the number of units of packaged product (which includes one component A and one component B)?

15. The following represents a process used to assemble a chair with an upholstered seat. Stations A, B, and C make the seat; stations J, K, and L assemble the chair frame; station X is where the two subassemblies are brought together; and some final tasks are completed in stations Y and Z. One worker is assigned to each of the stations. The line is paced using a countdown clock to synchronize production at each station. Generally, there is no inventory kept anywhere in the system, although there is room for one unit between each of the stations that might be used for a brief amount of time.

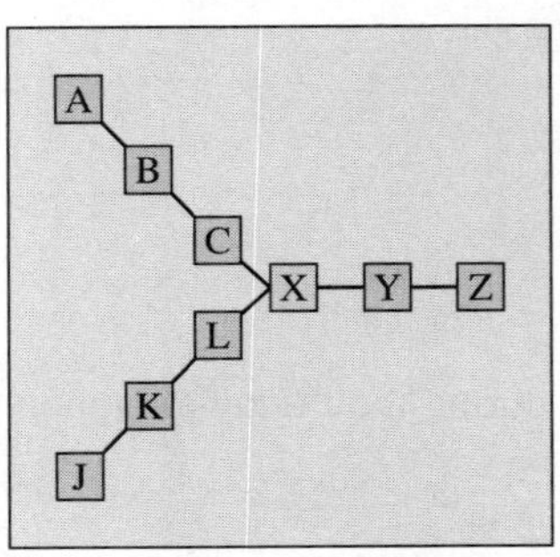

    Given the following amount of work in seconds required at each station:

A	38	J	32	X	22
B	34	K	30	Y	18
C	35	L	34	Z	20

a. What is the possible daily output of this "process" if eight hours of processing time is available each day?

b. Given your output rate in part (*a*), what is the efficiency of the process?

c. What is the flow time of the process?

16. Wally's Widget Warehouse takes orders from 7 A.M. to 7 P.M. The manager wants to analyze the process and has provided the following process flow diagram. There are three steps required to ship a customer order. The first step is to take the order from a customer. The second step is to pick the order for the customer, and then they have to pack the order to ready it for shipping. Wally promises that every order placed today gets shipped tomorrow. That means the picking and packing operations must finish all orders before they go home.

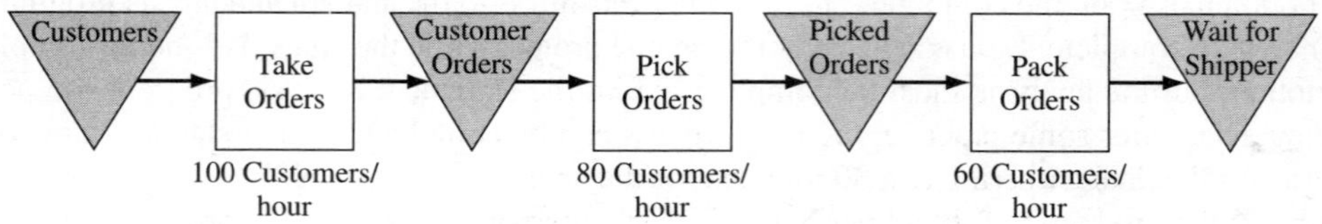

Wally wants to figure out the following:

a. What is the current maximum output of the process assuming that no one works overtime?

b. How long will the picking and packing operations have to work if we have a day where the order taker works at his maximum capacity?

c. Given *b*, what is the maximum number of orders waiting to be picked?

d. Given *b*, what is the maximum number of orders waiting to be packed?

e. If we double the packing capacity (from 60 to 120 orders per hour), what impact does this have on your answers in parts (*b*), (*c*), and (*d*)?

17. The National State Bank is trying to make sure it has enough tellers to handle the Friday afternoon rush of workers wanting to cash their paychecks. It is only concerned with the last hour of the day from 4:00 to 5:00 P.M. It takes 5 minutes per customer to be processed by the tellers. The average customer arrivals are shown in the following table.

Time	Customers Arriving
4:00–4:05	2
4:05–4:10	5
4:10–4:15	6
4:15–4:20	8
4:20–4:25	10
4:25–4:30	12
4:30–4:35	16
4:35–4:40	12
4:40–4:45	10
4:45–4:50	6
4:50–4:55	4
4:55–5:00	2
5:00–5:05	0
Total	93

The bank currently has eight teller stations, and all are staffed during the Friday afternoon rush hour.

a. What is the current maximum output at the bank during rush hour?

b. Can the bank process all the customers by 5:00 p.m.?

c. What is the maximum waiting time for customers, and what time period does it occur in?

18. I-mart is a discount optical shop that can fill most prescription orders in around 1 hour. The management is analyzing the processes at the store. There currently is one person assigned to each task. The optometrist assigned to task B takes an hour off for lunch and the other employees work the entire day.

Task	Time
A. Greet/register the patient	2 minutes/patient
B. Optometrist conducts eye exam	25 minutes/patient
C. Frame/lenses selection	20 minutes/patient
D. Glasses made (process can run 6 pairs of glasses at the same time)	60 minutes/patient
E. Final fitting	5 minutes/patient

For a typical 10-hour retail day (10 A.M. to 8 P.M.), the manager would like to calculate the following:

a. What is the current maximum output of the process per day (assuming every patient requires glasses)?

b. If another person were added, where would be the logical place?

c. What effect would a mail order lab (where the glasses are made off-site and returned in five to seven days) have on the process?

19. A quoting department for a custom publishing house can complete 4 quotes per day, and there are 20 quotes in various stages in the department. Applying Little's law, the current lead time for a quote is how many days?
20. A small barber shop has a single chair and an area for waiting, where only one person can be in the chair at a time, and no one leaves without getting their hair cut. So the system is roughly:

$$Entrance \rightarrow Wait \rightarrow Haircut \rightarrow Exit$$

Assume customers arrive at the rate of 10 per hour and stay an average of 0.5 hour.
What is the average number of customers in the barber shop?

Advanced Problem

21. Remember Mr. Rockness in Question 11? He now retrains college professors. It is a much more challenging task but still involves five steps. He has worked hard to balance the line; however, there is a lot of variability. Each stage in the process now handles between one and six faculty members per hour depending on how bad the case is. If there is some inventory available for every position (do not worry about the startup), what is the expected output per hour? Assume that each stage is independent and that it is equally likely that one, two, three, four, five, or six faculty members get processed each hour at each stage.

CASE: Service Design for Mobile Banking

Anjali joined ABC Bank Limited, immediately after finishing her MBA from a leading technical Institute in India, which also offers a flagship MBA with specialization in "Telecommunication Technology & Management." During her MBA, she also completed a minor area specialization in Finance and has been with this Bank through the last seven years. She was recently posted at the Bank's head office at Bangalore, in southern part of India, after a short international assignment in Africa. She was made in-charge of the Special Projects Cell (SPC) directly reporting to the Managing Director.

The ABC Bank is a pioneer in automation and is widely appreciated for its technology initiatives. It also enjoyed an edge over other mid-cap banks by way of effective deployment of Information Technology (IT) and networking for managing its costs of service delivery and efficiency in operations. Keeping in line with this technology-savvy image, bank's management had been closely tracking the world-wide developments related to use of mobile phones for banking and payment applications, over the past few years.

As on December 2013, India had over 915 million mobile subscriber base, which is growing at a pace, being the fastest in the world. Mobile banking provides one of the most exciting opportunities in a developing economy like India, where a large percentage of population do not have accessibility to organized banking. Mobile money transfer has potential to become one of the most exciting service designs of this decade.

Directors of the ABC Bank are well aware of the successful m-banking implementations in developing countries like Philippines (Smart Communications, Globe Telecom), South Africa (MTN, Wizzit) and Kenya (M-Pesa). They have been following the local developments and have studied the RBI (Reserve Bank of India) directives and guidelines on the subject.

Reserve Bank of India (RBI) has issued guidelines for banks to provide mobile banking among different accounts of banks. Currently (year 2013), banks in India are permitted to offer m-banking services subject to a daily cap of ₹50,000 with a calendar month limit of ₹2,50,000 per customer for both funds transfer and transactions involving purchase of goods and services. In a few countries, non-banking transactions are also allowed; for example, M-Pesa model in Kenya allows mobile service provider (MPS) to collect pre-paid amount and facilitate person to person transaction. In India, the mobile banking is going through a growing trend with more than 100% increase in the volume per year (53.3 million in 2012-13 to 25.56 million in 2011-12) and more than 200% increase in value per year (₹59.9 billion in 2012-13 against ₹18.21 billion in 2011-12) [5]. ABC Bank is absolutely sure that if some of the risks areas are well addressed; mobile banking can be the most value-added services for rural India. There is still room for a more standardised and simplified procedure for registration and authentication of customers for mobile banking services.

Mobile Banking Guidelines in India—Operative Guidelines for Banks 2016–17

- Allowed only for banks, which are licensed, supervised and having physical presence in India and have implemented core banking. Coverage to be limited to customers holding accounts or debit/credit cards of banks.
- Only domestic rupee transactions are permitted subject without any daily cap for transactions involving purchase of goods/services. In case of cash-out, the maximum value of such transfers shall be Rs 10,000 per transaction. However, banks are allowed to place a suitable cap on velocity of such transactions, subject to a maximum of Rs 25,000 per month per beneficiary.
- Mobile banking to be also governed by KYC (know Your Customer), AML (Anti Money Laundering) and CFT (Combating the Financing of Terrorism) and any other guidelines issued by the RBI from time to time.
- Banks must ensure that customers having mobile phones of any telco are in a position to avail the service. Technology used must be secure and should ensure confidentiality, integrity, authenticity and non-repudiability.

Reference

https://www.rbi.org.in/SCRIPTs/BS_ViewMasterCirculars.aspx?Id=10509&Mode=0

The management of ABC Bank (in 2013) expects their services to move in this area and play a significant role. It wants to quickly launch its m-banking services in India. Therefore, keeping in view Anjali's performance and her international exposure in Africa, management decided to assign m-banking launch as her first special project. Anjali did a quick survey of risk factors in m-banking, and listed these as follows.

Risk Factors in Mobile Banking[1]

Risk Factors	Remarks
Anonymity	Due to not knowing the actual identity of one or more stakeholder in transaction.
Elusiveness	Due to possibility to hide transaction details like destination, origin, amount, etc.
Rapidity	Due to fast speed with which illegal transaction can take place.
Poor oversight	Due to low level of regulations of service providers.

Based on her interaction with colleagues, Anjali is convinced that after successful deployment of **U**nique **ID**entification (UID) project in India[2], the risk related to anonymity and elusiveness can be managed better. According to her perception on current scenario, following efforts would be needed in India for a highly functional mobile banking.

- Scaling up of infrastructure of MSPs
- Improving security in transaction
- Putting transparency in pricing model for these transactions
- Reaching to the rural population which is deprived of conventional banking network
- Having fully functional UID for citizen

- Adhering to strict norms to avoid money laundering
- Defining role of banking system regulators, MSPs and other channel partner
- Developing effective business model to fit into the mobile banking now.

There are interesting inputs in RBI Monetary Policy Statement for 2010–11, "Given the penetration levels of mobile telephony in India, this could become an important medium for achieving financial inclusion in the country," According to the recommendations, such services will also enable transfer of funds of various government schemes like *National Rural Employment Guarantee Scheme* (NERGS), which is a historic employment scheme for providing one hundred days guaranteed wage employment for all employment seekers above 18 years of age and willing to do work.[3]

Anjali is thrilled at the confidence that management has reposed trust in her by assigning this important task to her. She quickly takes stock of the mobile banking implementation in other countries, studies the RBI guidelines and m-banking readiness of all the banks operating in India and concludes that attractive design of service would be the key to successful launch of ABC Bank's m-banking.

Anjali, being professionally trained in her MBA Programme, refers to the literature on service quality and decides on using the 22-item SERVQUAL tool to determine the gaps in customer expectations and their perceptions of ABC Bank's regular banking services. She then intends to get the responses of urban and rural customer compiled and analyzed for various attributes under five broad categories viz. Reliability, Assurance, Tangibles, Empathy and Responsiveness. Once she is ready with the gap analysis of customer requirements (CRs), Anjali plans to set up a cross-functional team involving members from Marketing, Operations, Regulatory, Customer service and Accounting, to identify the m-banking design characteristics to address each of those CRs.

Anjali expects the team to thoroughly discuss the SERVQUAL findings and then do a cost-benefit analysis for each of the CRs to freeze the design characteristics for m-banking services in such a way that ABC Banks's services have a competitive edge in the market and its customers also perceive the new service as 'useful' and 'easy-to-use'. Knowing that service design exercise would delay the launch by about six months, Anjali has already prepared a presentation for the top management to convey that customer acceptance of a 'reliable and responsive service' would work in ABC's favor and the Bank would be able to achieve a much faster penetration to overtake the competition within six months of service launch. Anjali recalls that her Professor of Operations Management in her MBA programme taught her "Quality Function Deployment" (QFD), which can translate CR into product or services specifications. She thought of using this approach. *First mover advantage* is a key to capture a substantial market share in the value-added-services (VAS) in the mobile business.

Thus, by scientifically translating the CRs into design characteristics of the new m-banking services, Anjali expects to address the gaps in bank's existing services. She wants to ensure that new service is quickly accepted by its existing customers and also wants to build an m-banking USP to attract some of the high-value customers from competition as well as new customers in rural areas, where presence of traditional banking systems is not sufficient.

Questions

1. Explore the latest provisions of RBI for mobile banking. Based on these, what should be Anjali's approach – thorough analysis and professional service design or quick solution? Why?
2. Explain, how can QFD help in service design?
3. Give illustrative examples to explain how SERVEQUAL framework would help in designing m-banking services?
4. Explain the recent status of m-Banking in India?
5. What are the possible business applications of m-Banking?
6. What are the possible applications of m-Banking for rural development, agriculture, daily wage earners in cities, students residing in hostels, micro-financing, government schemes for poor and farmers, and NGOs in India?

Reference

1. K. C. Chakraborty: Potential of mobile banking, *The Hindu Business Line*, December 19, 2009.
2. http://uidai.gov.in/ (Accessed on 12 April 2014)
3. http://beta.thehindu.com/business/Economy/article406132.ece (Accessed on 22 April 2014)
4. http://coai.in/ (Accessed on 12 April 2014)
5. http://articles.economictimes.indiatimes.com/2014-02-07/news/47126512_1_mobile-banking-rbi-governor-raghuram-rajan-mobile-number (Accessed on 12 April 2014)

Case: Analyzing Casino Money-Handling Processes

Retrieving money from a mechanical slot machine is referred to as the *drop process.* The drop process begins with a security officer and the slot drop team leader obtaining the slot cabinet keys from the casino cashier's cage. Getting the keys takes about 15 minutes. The slot drop team consists of employees from the hard count coin room, security, and accounting. The slot drop leader, under the observation of a security officer and a person from accounting, actually removes the drop bucket from the slot machine cabinet. When the drop bucket is pulled from the slot cabinet, a tag with the proper slot machine number is placed on top of the coins to identify where that bucket came from when the weigh process begins. Retrieving the drop bucket takes about 10 minutes per slot machine. Once a cart is filled with buckets from 20 different slot machines, the drop team leader and security and accounting people deliver the buckets to the hard count room. The buckets are securely locked in the hard count room to await the start of the hard count process. Delivering and securing the buckets takes about 30 minutes per cart.

The hard count process is performed at a designated time known to gaming regulatory authorities. The hard count team first tests the weigh scale, which takes 10 minutes. The scale determines the dollar value, by denomination, for set weights of 10 and 25 pounds. These results are compared to calibration results, calculated when the scale was last serviced, to determine if a significant variance exists. If one does exist, the hard count supervisor must contact the contractor responsible for maintaining the scale and the controller's office. If no significant variance is found, the weigh process can continue.

Following the scale check, each drop bucket is emptied into the weigh scale holding hopper. Using information from the identification tag, the specific slot machine number from which the bucket originated is entered into the weigh scale computer. The weigh scale computer is programmed to convert the weight of coins, by denomination, into specific dollar values, which are recorded in the weigh journal along with the slot machine number. This weighing and recording process takes seven minutes per bucket. Once the scale has weighed the contents of the drop bucket, the coins automatically drop onto a conveyor belt, which transports them to wrapping machines. As the coins are wrapped, the rolls of coins drop onto another conveyor belt, which takes them to a canning station. Twenty-five silver dollars are wrapped in each roll at a rate of 10 rolls per minute.

At the canning station, the coin rolls are placed in metal or plastic cans that hold specific dollar amounts based on coin denomination. The cans are stacked to facilitate counting the wrapped coins. Silver dollar cans hold \$1,000, or 40 rolls, and take five minutes to fill and stack. When the weigh process is completed, the weigh scale computer runs a summary report totaling the weight by denomination. These totals are recorded on the weigh/wrap verification report, which takes five minutes to produce.

When the wrap portion of the count is completed and all of the rolled coins have been canned and stacked, they are manually counted by denomination. These totals are also recorded on the weigh/wrap verification report. The variance in both dollar amounts and percentages, for each denomination, is calculated. Variances that exceed 2 percent of the total or \$1,000 (whichever is less) must be investigated by the hard count supervisor, who writes an explanatory report. If no significant variances exist, all members of the hard count team sign the weigh/wrap verification report. To complete the hard count process, the casino cashier's cage is then notified that the slot drop is ready to be transferred into cage accountability. Manually counting and verifying the counts take, on average, two minutes per can.

In a process separate from the hard count, a cage cashier performs an independent count and verification, by denomination, of the wrap. If everything balances, the main bank cashier signs the weigh/wrap verification report, accepting the slot drop into cage accountability. It is at this point that the actual slot gross gaming revenue is recognized.

Questions

1. Draw a diagram of the drop process. How long should it take to empty 300 silver dollar slot machines?
2. Draw a diagram of the hard count process. How long should this process take to complete for 300 silver dollar slot machines? Assume that each slot machine has an average of 750 silver dollars when it is emptied.

3. The casino is considering the purchase of a second coin-wrapping machine. What impact would this have on the hard count process? Is this the most desirable machine to purchase?
4. What would be the impact of purchasing "electronic" slot machines that do not use coins?

PRACTICE EXAM

In each of the following, name the term defined or answer the question. Answers are listed at the bottom.

1. This is a part of an organization that takes inputs and transforms them into outputs.
2. This is the ratio of the time that a resource is activated relative to the time it is available for use.
3. This is when one or more activities stop because of a lack of work.
4. This is when an activity stops because there is no place to put the work that was just completed.
5. This is a step in a process that is the slowest compared to the other steps. This step limits the capacity of the process.
6. What is the difference between McDonald's old and current processes?
7. This refers to the fixed timing of the movement of items through a process.
8. This is when one company compares itself to another relative to operations performance.
9. This is the time it takes a unit to travel through the process from beginning to end. It includes time waiting in queues and buffers.
10. The relationship between time and units in a process is called this.
11. What is the mathematical relationship between time and units in a process?
12. What is the major assumption about how a process is operating for Little's law to be valid?
13. What is the double-edged sword of job design?
14. This is when a job is increased vertically or horizontally.
15. What are the four basic work measurement techniques?

Answers to Practice Exam 1. A process 2. Utilization 3. Starving 4. Blocking 5. Bottleneck 6. Make-to-stock versus make-to-order 7. Pacing 8. Benchmarking 9. Flow time 10. Little's law 11. Inventory = Throughput rate × Flow time 12. Process is operating in steady state 13. Specialization 14. Job enrichment and enlargement 15. Time study, work sampling, predetermined motion-time data systems, elemental data

For PowerPoint lecture slides, Solutions Manual, Test Bank, Data files for solved examples, Excel Templates, Step-by-Step Solved Examples in video format, Tutorial Videos and many more, scan the adjacent **QR code**, or **visit http://www.mhhe.com/sie-chase15e**

Chapter 12

Six Sigma Quality

LEARNING OBJECTIVES

LO 12-1 Explain the scope of total quality management in a firm

LO 12-2 Understand the Six Sigma approach to improving quality and productivity

LO 12-3 Illustrate globally recognized quality benchmarks

GE Six Sigma Supply Chain Processes

General Electric (GE) has been a major advocate of Six Sigma for over 15 years. Jack Welch, the legendary and now retired CEO, declared, "The big myth is that Six Sigma is about quality control and statistics. It *is* that—but it's much more. Ultimately, it drives leadership to be better by providing tools to think through tough issues. At Six Sigma's core is an idea that can turn a company inside out, focusing the organization outward on the customer." GE's commitment to quality centers on Six Sigma.

So, what is Six Sigma? It's best to first explain what it is not. It is not a secret society, a slogan, or a cliché. Six Sigma is a highly disciplined process that helps us focus on developing and delivering near-perfect products and services. Why "Sigma"? The word is a statistical term that measures how far a given process deviates from perfection. The central idea behind Six Sigma is that if you can measure how many "defects" you have in a process, you can systematically figure out how to eliminate them and get as close to "zero defects" as possible. To achieve Six Sigma Quality, a process must produce no more than 3.4 defects per million opportunities. An "opportunity" is defined as a chance for nonconformance, or not meeting the required specifications. This means we need to be nearly flawless in executing our key processes.

TOTAL QUALITY MANAGEMENT

LO 12-1

Explain the scope of total quality management in a firm

Total quality management (TQM) may be defined as managing the entire organization so it excels in all dimensions of products and services important to the customer. It has two fundamental operational goals, namely

1. Careful design of the product or service.
2. Ensuring that the organization's systems can consistently produce the design.

Total quality management (TQM)
Managing the entire organization so it excels in all dimensions of products and services important to the customer.

These two goals can only be achieved if the entire organization is oriented toward them—hence, the term *total* quality management. TQM became a national concern in the United States in the 1980s, primarily as a response to Japanese quality superiority in manufacturing automobiles and other durable goods, such as room air conditioners. So severe was the quality shortfall in the United States that improving it throughout industry became a national priority, with the Department of Commerce establishing the **Malcolm Baldrige National Quality Award** in 1987 to help companies review and structure their quality programs. Also gaining major attention at this time was the requirement that suppliers demonstrate they were measuring and documenting their quality practices according to specified criteria, called ISO standards, if they wished to compete for international contracts. We will discuss this more later.

Malcolm Baldrige National Quality Award
An award established by the U.S. Department of Commerce given annually to companies that excel in quality.

The philosophical leaders of the quality movement, notably Philip Crosby, W. Edwards Deming, and Joseph M. Juran—the so-called Quality Gurus—had slightly different definitions of what quality is and how to achieve it (see Exhibit 12.1), but they all had the same general message: To achieve outstanding quality requires quality leadership from senior management, a customer focus,

EXHIBIT 12.1

The Quality Gurus Compared

	Crosby	Deming	Juran
Definition of quality	Conformance to requirements	A predictable degree of uniformity and dependability at low cost and suited to the market	Fitness for use (satisfies customer's needs)
Degree of senior management responsibility	Responsible for quality	Responsible for 94% of quality problems	Less than 20% of quality problems are due to workers
Performance standard/motivation	Zero defects	Quality has many "scales"; use statistics to measure performance in all areas; critical of zero defects	Avoid campaigns to do perfect work
General approach	Prevention, not inspection	Reduce variability by continuous improvement; cease mass inspection	General management approach to quality, especially human elements
Structure	14 steps to quality improvement	14 points for management	10 steps to quality improvement
Statistical process control (SPC)	Rejects statistically acceptable levels of quality [wants 100% perfect quality]	Statistical methods of quality control must be used	Recommends SPC but warns that it can lead to tool-driver approach
Improvement basis	A process, not a program; improvement goals	Continuous to reduce variation; eliminate goals without methods	Project-by-project team approach; set goals
Teamwork	Quality improvement teams; quality councils	Employee participation in decision making; break down barriers between departments	Team and quality circle approach
Costs of quality	Cost of nonconformance; quality is free	No optimum; continuous improvement	Quality is not free; there is not an optimum
Purchasing and goods received	State requirements; supplier is extension of business; most faults due to purchasers themselves	Inspection too late; sampling allows defects to enter system; statistical evidence and control charts required	Problems are complex; carry out formal surveys
Vendor rating	Yes, quality audits useless	No, critical of most systems	Yes, but help supplier improve

OSCM AT WORK

Malcolm Baldrige National Quality Award

The Malcolm Baldrige National Quality Award is given to organizations that have demonstrated outstanding quality in their products and processes. The award program is administered by the National Institute of Standards and Technology, an agency of the U.S. Department of Commerce. A total of up to 18 awards may be given annually in these categories: manufacturing, service, small business, education, health care, and not-for-profit.

Candidates for the award must submit an application of up to 50 pages that details the approach, deployment, and results of their quality activities under seven major categories: Leadership, Strategic Planning, Customer and Market Focus, Information and Analysis, Human Resource Focus, Process Management, and Business Results. These applications are scored on total points out of 1,000 by examiners and judges. Those who score above roughly 650 are selected for site visits. Winners selected from this group are then honored at an annual meeting in Washington, D.C. A major benefit to all applicants is feedback from the examiners, which is essentially an audit of their practices. Many states have used the Baldrige Criteria as the basis of their own quality award programs. A report, *Building on Baldrige: American Quality for the 21st Century,* by the private Council on Competitiveness, said, "More than any other program, the Baldrige Quality Award is responsible for making quality a national priority and disseminating best practices across the United States."

total involvement of the workforce, and continuous improvement based upon rigorous analysis of processes. Later in the chapter, we will discuss how these precepts are applied in the latest approach to TQM—Six Sigma. We will now turn to some fundamental concepts that underlie any quality effort: quality specifications and quality costs.

Quality Specifications and Quality Costs

Fundamental to any quality program is the determination of quality specifications and the costs of achieving (or *not* achieving) those specifications.

Developing Quality Specifications

The quality specifications of a product or service derive from decisions and actions made relative to the quality of its design and the quality of its conformance to that design.

Design quality refers to the inherent value of the product in the marketplace and is thus a strategic decision for the firm. The dimensions of quality are listed in Exhibit 12.2. These dimensions refer to features of the product or service that relate directly to design issues.

Design quality
The inherent value of the product in the marketplace.

A firm designs a product or service with certain performance characteristics and features based on what an intended market expects. Materials and manufacturing process attributes can greatly impact the reliability and durability of a product. Here the company attempts to design a product or service that can be produced or delivered at reasonable cost. The serviceability of the product may have a great impact on the cost of the product or service to the customer after the initial purchase is made. It also

EXHIBIT 12.2

The Dimensions of Design Quality

Dimension	Meaning
Performance	Primary product or service characteristics
Features	Added touches, bells and whistles, secondary characteristics
Reliability/durability	Consistency of performance over time, probability of failing, useful life
Serviceability	Ease of repair
Aesthetics	Sensory characteristics (sound, feel, look, and so on)
Perceived quality	Past performance and reputation

OSCM AT WORK

J.D. Power Initial Quality Study

J.D. Power uses concepts similar to those discussed in this section to measure the quality of new automobiles during the first 90 days of ownership. The study is conducted each year and includes vehicles produced by manufacturers from around the world. Each year, results from the study are published at www.jdpower.com. The study captures problems experienced by owners in two distinct categories—design-related problems and defects and malfunctions. The following is a list of its measures:

Powertrain Quality: This score is based on problems with the engine or transmission, as well as problems that affect the driving experience. Some of the items checked are ride smoothness, responsiveness of the steering system and brakes, and handling/stability.

Body and Interior Quality: This score is based on problems with the design of the basic car. Some of the items checked are wind noise, water leaks, poor interior fit/finish, paint imperfection, and squeaks/rattles.

Features, Controls, and Display Quality: This score is based on problems with special items such as the seats, windshield wipers, navigation system, rear-seat entertainment system, heater, air conditioner, stereo system, sunroof, and trip computer.

Source: www.jdpower.com.

may impact the warranty and repair cost to the firm. Aesthetics may greatly impact the desirability of the product or service, in particular consumer products. Especially when a brand name is involved, the design often represents the next generation of an ongoing stream of products or services. Consistency in the relative performance of the product compared to the state of the art, for example, may have a great impact on how the quality of the product is perceived. This may be very important to the long-run success of the product or service.

Conformance quality
The degree to which the product or service design specifications are met.

Conformance quality refers to the degree to which the product or service design specifications are met. The activities involved in achieving conformance are of a tactical, day-to-day nature. It should be evident that a product or service can have high design quality but low conformance quality, and vice versa.

Quality at the source
The philosophy of making workers personally responsible for the quality of their output. Workers are expected to make the part correctly the first time and to stop the process immediately if there is a problem.

Quality at the source is frequently discussed in the context of conformance quality. This means that the person who does the work takes responsibility for making sure that his or her output meets specifications. Where a product is involved, achieving the quality specifications is typically the responsibility of manufacturing management; in a service firm, it is usually the responsibility of the location operations manager. Exhibit 12.3 shows two examples of the **dimensions of quality**. One is a laser printer that meets the pages-per-minute and print density standards; the second is a checking account transaction in a bank.

Dimensions of quality
Criteria by which quality is measured.

Both quality of design and quality of conformance should provide products that meet the customer's objectives for those products. This is often termed the product's *fitness for use,* and it entails identifying the dimensions of the product (or service) that the customer wants (that is, the voice of the customer) and developing a quality control program to ensure that these dimensions are met.

Cost of Quality

Cost of quality (COQ)
Expenditures related to achieving product or service quality, such as the costs of prevention, appraisal, internal failure, and external failure.

Although few can quarrel with the notion of prevention, management often needs hard numbers to determine how much prevention activities will cost. This issue was recognized by Joseph Juran, who wrote about it in 1951 in his *Quality Control Handbook.* Today, **cost of quality (COQ)** analyses are common in industry and constitute one of the primary functions of QC departments.

There are a number of definitions and interpretations of the term *cost of quality.* From the purist's point of view, it means all of the costs attributable to the production of quality that is not 100 percent perfect. A less stringent definition considers only those costs that are the difference between what can be expected from excellent performance and the current costs that exist.

How significant is the cost of quality? It has been estimated at between 15 and 20 percent of every sales dollar—the cost of reworking, scrapping, repeated service, inspections, tests, warranties,

Taj Mahal: A Perfect Example of "Quality at Its Best"

Taj Mahal, located in Agra in Northern India, is one of the Seven Wonders of the World. It is a perfect example of excellent quality, architectural marvel and tourists' delight. It look around 22 years of time to complete. It involved over 20,000 workforce and costed over $200,000,000 in today's currency. Since 1631, this white marble mausoleum, built by the Mughal Emperor Shah Jahan in memory of his wife Mumtaz, has stood the test of time. Due to its symmetry, majesty and architectural beauty, it is rated as one of the most perfect buildings existing on the earth. Designed by artists from Persia, Italy and France, and built mainly with marbles, which were gifted by The Maharaja of Jaipur, it is an unmatched example of perfection and architectural beauty.

Exhibit 12.3

Examples of Dimensions of Quality

	Measures	
Dimension	**Product Example: Laser Printer**	**Service Example: Checking Account at a Bank**
Performance	Pages per minute Print density	Time to process customer requests
Features	Multiple paper trays Color capability	Automatic bill paying
Reliability/ durability	Mean time between failures Estimated time to obsolescence Expected life of major components	Variability of time to process requests Keeping pace with industry trends
Serviceability	Availability of authorized repair centers Number of copies per print cartridge Modular design	Online reports Ease of getting updated information
Aesthetics	Control button layout Case style Courtesy of dealer	Appearance of bank lobby Courtesy of teller
Perceived quality	Brand name recognition Rating in *Consumer Reports*	Endorsed by community leaders

and other quality-related items. It is generally believed that the correct cost for a well-run quality management program should be under 2.5 percent.

Three basic assumptions justify an analysis of the costs of quality: (1) Failures occur, (2) prevention is cheaper, and (3) performance can be measured.

The costs of quality are generally classified into four types:

1. **Appraisal costs.** Costs of the inspection, testing, and other tasks to ensure that the product or process is acceptable.
2. **Prevention costs.** The sum of all the costs to prevent defects, such as the costs to identify the cause of the defect, to implement corrective action to eliminate the cause, to train personnel, to redesign the product or system, and to purchase new equipment or make modifications.

3. **Internal failure costs.** Costs for defects incurred within the system: scrap, rework, repair.
4. **External failure costs.** Costs for defects that pass through the system: customer warranty replacements, loss of customers or goodwill, handling complaints, and product repair.

Exhibit 12.4 illustrates the type of report that might be submitted to show the various costs by categories. Prevention is the most important influence. A rule of thumb says that for every dollar you spend in prevention, you can save $10 in failure and appraisal costs.

Often, increases in productivity occur as a by-product of efforts to reduce the cost of quality. A bank, for example, set out to improve quality and reduce the cost of quality and found that it had also boosted productivity. The bank developed this productivity measure for the loan processing area: the number of tickets processed divided by the resources required (labor cost, computer time, ticket forms). Before the quality improvement program, the productivity index was 0.2661 [2,080/($11.23 × 640 hours + $0.05 × 2,600 forms + $500 for systems costs)]. After the quality improvement project was completed, labor time fell to 546 hours

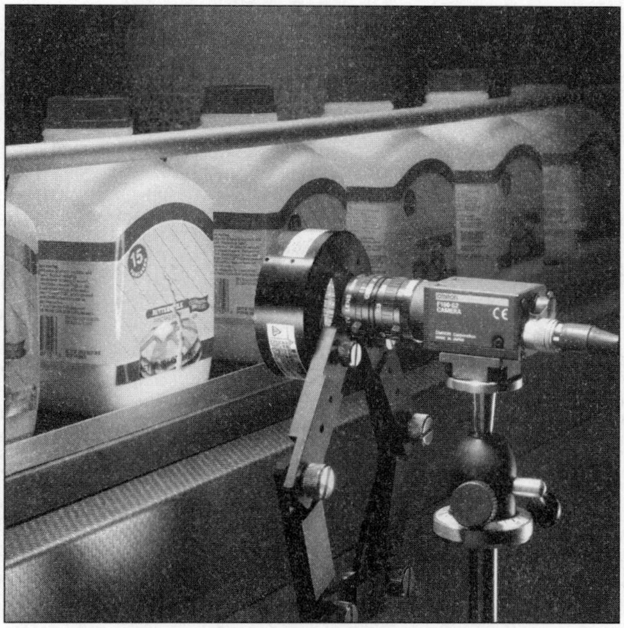

Products with torn or improperly positioned labels reflect poorly on the brand and bring into question the quality of the contents. A vision sensor is used to check the labels before the bottles are placed in cartons for shipment.

© Omron Electronics LLC

EXHIBIT 12.4

Quality Cost Report

	Current Month's Cost	Percentage of Total
Prevention costs		
Quality training	$ 2,000	1.3%
Reliability consulting	10,000	6.5
Pilot production runs	5,000	3.3
Systems development	8,000	5.2
Total prevention	25,000	16.3
Appraisal costs		
Materials inspection	6,000	3.9
Supplies inspection	5,000	3.3
Reliability testing	3,000	2.0
Laboratory testing	25,000	16.3
Total appraisal	39,000	25.5
Internal failure costs		
Scrap	15,000	9.8
Repair	18,000	11.8
Rework	12,000	7.8
Downtime	6,000	3.9
Total internal failure	51,000	33.3
External failure costs		
Warranty costs	14,000	9.2
Out-of-warranty repairs and replacement	6,000	3.9
Customer complaints	3,000	2.0
Product liability	10,000	6.5
Transportation losses	5,000	3.3
Total external failure	38,000	24.8
Total quality costs	$153,000	100.0%

Mahatma Gandhi on Customer

Quality is what a customer wants. Majority of six-sigma projects are based on the criteria, which are "critical-to-quality" (CTQ) for a customer. Although, during 1980s, the corporate world observed the TQM and Six Sigma as a formal strategy to meet customer requirement, visionary like Mr Mohan Das Karamchand Gandhi, popularly known as Mahatma Gandhi, had a far-sighted view on these even as early as in 1940s. The father of the nation, as people call him in India, Mahatma Gandhi, who played an important role in Indian freedom struggle, once said, "A customer is the most important visitor on our premises. He is not dependent on us. We are dependent on him. He is not an interruption in our work. He is the purpose of it. He is not an outsider in our business. He is a part of it. We are not doing him a favor by serving him. He is doing us a favor by giving us an opportunity to do so." Such a powerful statement on customer is generally rare in the literature of quality management.

and the number of forms rose to 2,100, for a change in the index to 0.3106 [2,100/(11.23 × 546 + 2,600 + 500)], an increase in productivity of over 16 percent.

LO 12-2

Understand the Six Sigma approach to improving quality and productivity

SIX SIGMA QUALITY

Six Sigma

A statistical term to describe the quality goal of no more than 3.4 defects out of every million units. Also refers to a quality improvement philosophy and program.

Defects per million opportunities (DPMO)

A metric used to describe the variability of a process.

Six Sigma refers to the philosophy and methods companies such as General Electric and Motorola use to eliminate defects in their products and processes. A defect is simply any component that does not fall within the customer's specification limits. Each step or activity in a company represents an opportunity for defects to occur, and Six Sigma programs seek to reduce the variation in the processes that lead to these defects. Indeed, Six Sigma advocates see variation as the enemy of quality, and much of the theory underlying Six Sigma is devoted to dealing with this problem. A process that is in Six Sigma control will produce no more than two defects out of every billion units. Often, this is stated as 3.4 defects per million units, which is true if the process is only running somewhere within 1.5 sigma of the target specification.

One of the benefits of Six Sigma thinking is that it allows managers to readily describe the performance of a process in terms of its variability and to compare different processes using a common metric. This metric is **defects per million opportunities (DPMO)**. This calculation requires three pieces of data:

1. **Unit.** The item produced or being serviced.
2. **Defect.** Any item or event that does not meet the customer's requirements.
3. **Opportunity.** A chance for a defect to occur.

A straightforward calculation is made using the following formula:

$$\text{DPMO} = \frac{\text{Number of defects}}{\text{Number of opportunities for error per unit} \times \text{Number of units}} \times 1{,}000{,}000$$

OSCM AT WORK

Mumbai Dabbawallah

Six-sigma level of accuracy in any distribution network of our corporate world is unheard of. Even the well-managed, technology-enabled supply chains lack this distinction. *Mumbai Dabbawallahs,* who collect, transport and distribute home-cooked food in tiffin boxes from home to workplace and bring-back the empty tiffin-boxes in the afternoon, have achieved a unique level of perfection and customer satisfaction. In 1998, Forbes Global Magazine ranked its operational excellence at a six-sigma level with an accuracy rating of 99.999999. Any six-sigma company would defect lesser than 3.6 per million opportunities.

Followings are the five main characteristics of Mumbai *Dabbawallahs'* operations, which have created a lethal combination to deliver six-sigma quality.

(i) Error-free distribution of lunch-boxes
(ii) Highest level of customer satisfaction
(iii) Highly motivated workforce
(iv) Minimum use of modern technology
(v) Low cost of operations

One of the most important aspects in six-sigma quality is identification and management of issues, which are 'critical-to-quality' (CTQ) for a customer. It is well recognised that quality is what customer wants. For the customers of Mumbai *Dabbawallahs*, there are three CTQs: (i) there should never be a mix-up of lunch-boxes, (ii) delivery is neither too early nor too late, and (iii) cost of services is affordable. To ensure these, Mumbai *Dabbawallahs* have devised a unique coding system for the tiffin-boxes, so that there is no mix-up during identification of these boxes in the distribution network. They maintain a strictly well-defined schedule, which is linked to the timing of local trains, running between originating and culminating local stations of Mumbai. Monthly charge for a customer is around ₹300 per lunch box and an annual bonus during festival season. They use low-cost local-trains for a long-distance tiffin-box movement within Mumbai. Otherwise, for short distances, they use carts to carry these tiffin boxes.

Traditionally, they do not use modern technology in their operations. More recently, they are using mobile phone for SMS and internet for online booking. Yet, the cost of operation is very low. Mumbai *Dabbawallahs* have demonstrated an exemplary commitment to work, which is the main reason why their distribution system has shown an unprecedented growth and customer loyalty.

Discussion Questions

1 What are the possible reasons due to which Mumbai *Dabbawallahs* are called as six-sigma organisation?
2 How would you relate CTQs with six-sigma quality?
3 While everybody talks of six-sigma quality, the term five-sigma and seven-sigma are not very common. Why?

EXAMPLE 12.1

Analytics

The customers of a mortgage bank expect to have their mortgage applications processed within 10 days of filing. This would be called a *critical customer requirement,* or *CCR,* in Six Sigma terms. Suppose all defects are counted (loans in a monthly sample taking more than 10 days to process), and it is determined that there are 150 loans in the 1,000 applications processed last month that don't meet this customer requirement. Thus, the DPMO = 150/1,000 × 1,000,000, or 150,000 loans out of every million processed that fail to meet a CCR. Put differently, it means that only 850,000 loans out of a million are approved within time expectations. Statistically, 15 percent of the loans are defective and 85 percent are correct. This is a case where all the loans processed in less than 10 days meet our criteria. Often, there are upper and lower customer requirements rather than just a single upper requirement as we have here.

In the following section, we describe the Six Sigma process cycle and tools commonly used in Six Sigma projects.

Six Sigma Methodology

While Six Sigma's methods include many of the statistical tools that were employed in other quality movements, here they are used in a systematic project-oriented fashion through the define, measure, analyze, improve, and control (**DMAIC**) cycles. The overarching focus of the methodology is understanding and achieving what the customer wants, because that is seen as key to profitability of a production process. In fact, to get across this point, some use the DMAIC as an acronym for "Dumb Managers Always Ignore Customers."

DMAIC
An acronym for the *define, measure, analyze, improve, and control* improvement methodology followed by companies engaging in Six Sigma programs.

Process

A standard approach to Six Sigma projects is the following DMAIC methodology:

1. Define (D)
   - Identify customers and their priorities.
   - Identify a project suitable for Six Sigma efforts based on business objectives as well as customer needs and feedback.
   - Identify CTQs (critical-to-quality characteristics) that the customer believes have the most impact on quality.
2. Measure (M)
   - Determine how to measure the process and how it is performing.
   - Identify the key internal processes that influence CTQs and measure the defects currently generated relative to those processes.
3. Analyze (A)
   - Determine the most likely causes of defects.
   - Understand why defects are generated by identifying the key variables most likely to create process variation.
4. Improve (I)
   - Identify means to remove the causes of defects.
   - Confirm the key variables and quantify their effects on the CTQs.
   - Identify the maximum acceptance ranges of the key variables and a system for measuring deviations of the variables.
   - Modify the process to stay within an acceptable range.
5. Control (C)
   - Determine how to maintain the improvements.
   - Put tools in place to ensure that the key variables remain within the maximum acceptance ranges under the modified process.

Analytical Tools for Six Sigma

The analytical tools of Six Sigma have been used for many years in traditional quality improvement programs. What makes their application to Six Sigma unique is the integration of these tools in a corporatewide management system. The tools common to all quality efforts are flowcharts, run charts, Pareto charts, histograms, checksheets, cause-and-effect diagrams, and control charts. Examples of these, along with an opportunity flow diagram, are shown in Exhibit 12.5, arranged according to DMAIC categories where they commonly appear.

Flowcharts. There are many types of flowcharts. The one shown in Exhibit 12.5 depicts the process steps as part of a SIPOC (supplier, input, process, output, customer) analysis. SIPOC is essentially a formalized input-output model, used in the define stage of a project.

Run charts. They depict trends in data over time, and thereby help in understanding the magnitude of a problem at the define stage.

Pareto charts. These charts help to break down a problem into the relative contributions of its components. They are based on the common empirical finding that a large percentage of problems are due to a small percentage of causes. In the example, 80 percent of customer complaints are due to late deliveries, which are 20 percent of the causes listed.

Checksheets. These are basic forms that help standardize data collection. They are used to create histograms such as shown on a Pareto chart.

EXHIBIT 12.5

Analytical Tools for Six Sigma and Continuous Improvement

Define

Flowcharts of Major Steps in a Process*

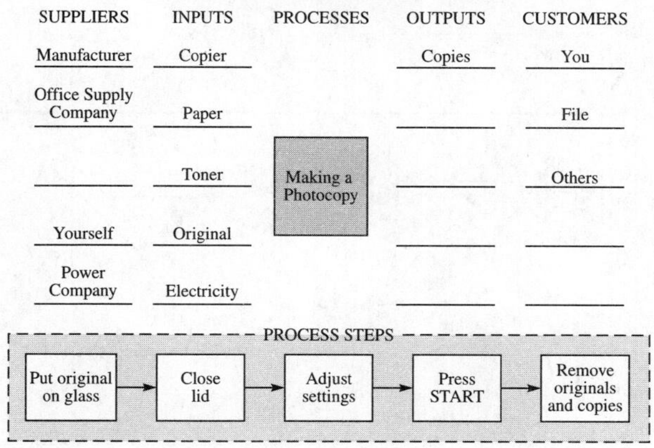

Measure

Run Chart**

Average monthly volume of deliveries (per shop)

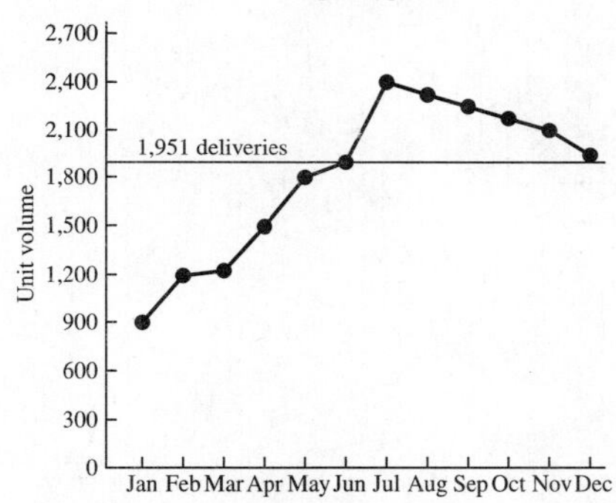

Data Collection Forms*

Checksheets are basic forms that help standardize data collection by providing specific spaces where people should record data.

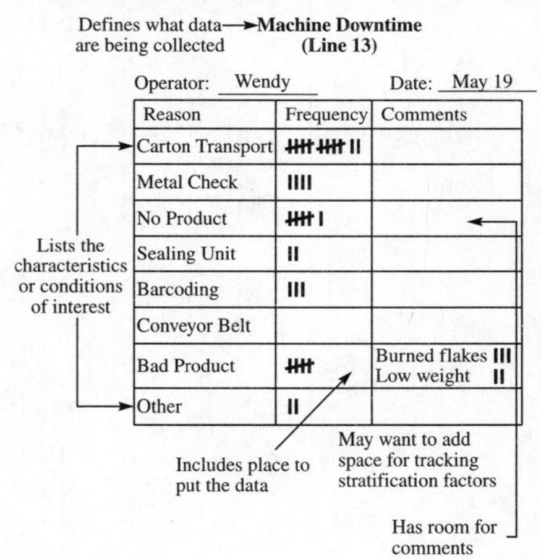

Pareto Chart**

Types of customer complaints
Total = 2,520 October–December
(across 6 shops)

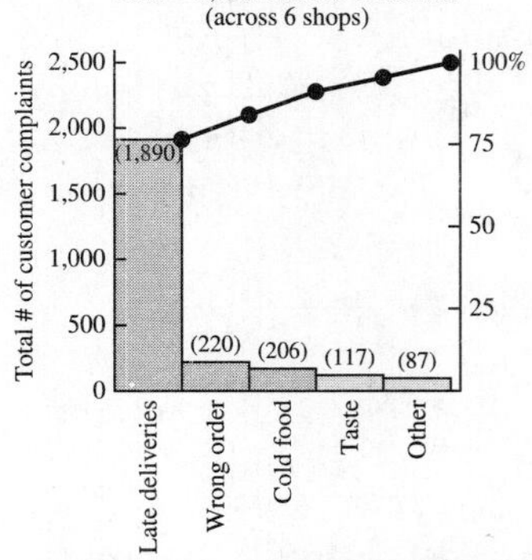

Illustration note: Delivery time was defined by the total time from when the order was placed to when the customer received it.

C & E/Fishbone Diagram**

Reasons for late pizza deliveries

Analyze

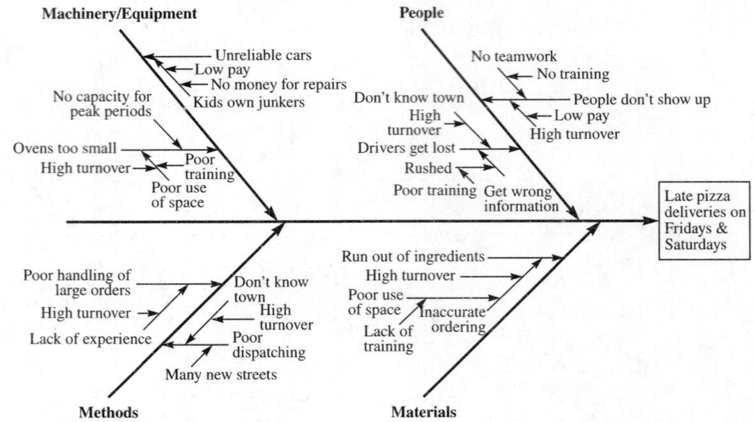

Opportunity Flow Diagram*

Organized to separate value-added steps from non–value-added steps.

Improve

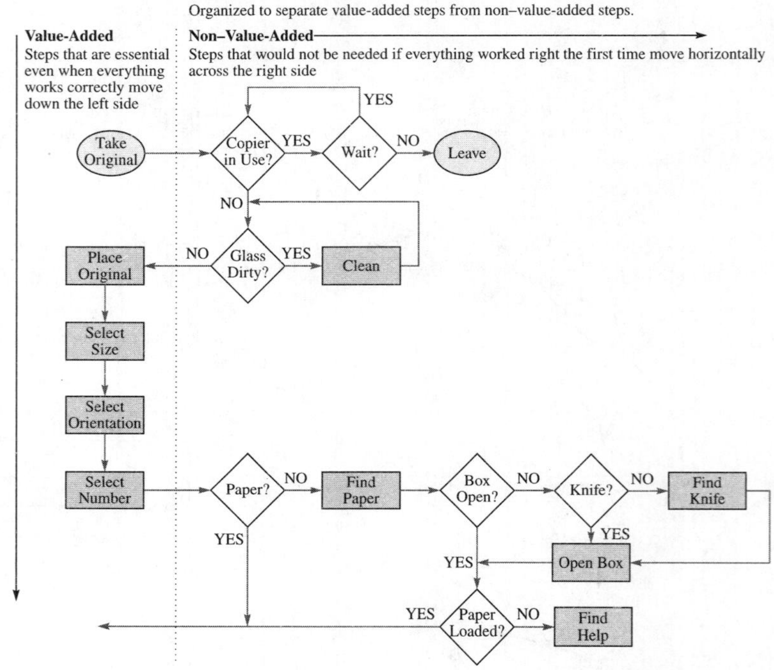

Process Control Chart Features*

Control

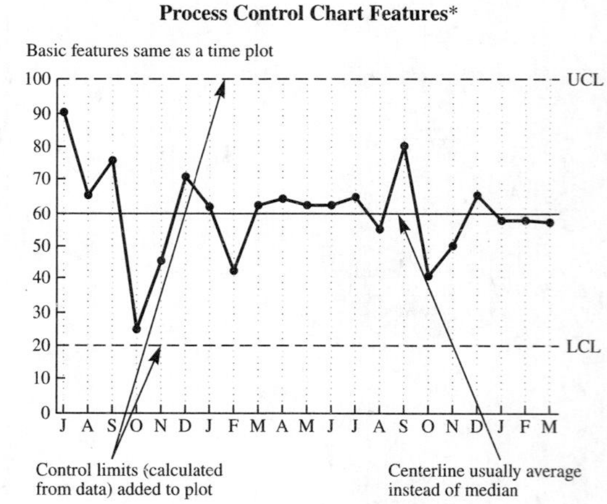

Cause-and-effect diagrams. Also called *fishbone diagrams,* they show hypothesized relationships between potential causes and the problem under study. Once the C&E diagram is constructed, the analysis would proceed to find out which of the potential causes were in fact contributing to the problem.

Opportunity flow diagram. This is used to separate value-added from non–value-added steps in a process.

Process control charts. These are time-sequenced charts showing plotted values of a statistic, including a centerline average and one or more control limits. It is used to assure that processes are in statistical control.

Other tools that have seen extensive use in Six Sigma projects are failure mode and effect analysis (FMEA) and design of experiments (DOE).

Failure mode and effect analysis. This is a structured approach to identify, estimate, prioritize, and evaluate risk of possible failures at each stage of a process. It begins with identifying each element, assembly, or part of the process and listing the potential failure modes, potential causes, and effects of each failure. A risk priority number (RPN) is calculated for each failure mode. It is an index used to measure the rank importance of the items listed in the FMEA chart (see Exhibit 12.6). These conditions include the probability that the failure takes place (occurrence), the damage resulting from the failure (severity), and the probability of detecting the failure in-house (detection). High RPN items should be targeted for improvement first. The FMEA suggests a recommended action to eliminate the failure condition by assigning a responsible person or department to resolve the failure by redesigning the system, design, or process and recalculating the RPN.

Design of experiments (DOE). DOE, sometimes referred to as *multivariate testing,* is a statistical methodology used for determining the cause-and-effect relationship between process variables (X's) and the output variable (Y). In contrast to standard statistical tests, which require changing each individual variable to determine the most influential one, DOE permits experimentation with many variables simultaneously by carefully selecting a subset of them.

Lean Six Sigma combines the implementation and quality control tools of Six Sigma and the inventory management concept of *lean manufacturing.* Lean manufacturing (discussed in detail in Chapter 14) achieves high-volume production and minimal waste through the use of just-in-time

Lean Six Sigma
Combines the implementation and quality control tools of Six Sigma and the inventory management concept of lean manufacturing.

EXHIBIT 12.6

FMEA Form

FMEA Analysis

Project: ________________ Date: ________(original)

Team: ________________ ________(revised)

Item or Process Step	Potential Failure Mode	Potential Effects of Failure	Severity	Potential Cause(s)	Occurrence	Current Controls	Detection	RPN	Recommended Action	Responsibility and Target Date	"After" → Action Taken	Severity	Occurrence	Detection	RPN
Total Risk Priority Number:									"After" Risk Priority Number:						

Rath and Strong, *Rath & Strong's Six Sigma Pocket Guide,* 2001, p. 31

inventory methods. The term *lean* in this context is a focus on reducing cost by lowering raw material, work-in-process, and finished goods inventory to an absolute minimum. Lowering inventory requires a high level of quality because processes need to be predictable since extra inventory is not available. Reducing variability is a key driver in successful lean Six Sigma programs.

Six Sigma Roles and Responsibilities

Successful implementation of Six Sigma is based on using sound personnel practices, as well as technical methodologies. The following is a brief summary of the personnel practices commonly employed in Six Sigma implementation.

Black belts
Individuals with sufficient Six Sigma training to lead improvement teams.

Master black belts
Individuals with in-depth training on statistical tools and process improvement.

Green belts
Employees who have enough Six Sigma training to participate in improvement teams.

1. ***Executive leaders,* who are truly committed to Six Sigma and who promote it throughout the organization, and *champions,* who take ownership of the processes to be improved.** Champions are drawn from the ranks of the executives, and managers are expected to identify appropriate metrics early in the project and make certain that the improvement efforts focus on business results. (See the "What Makes a Good Champion?")
2. **Corporatewide training in Six Sigma concepts and tools.** To convey the need to vigorously attack problems, professionals in Six Sigma firms are given martial arts titles reflecting their skills and roles: **black belts**, who coach or actually lead a Six Sigma improvement team; **master black belts**, who receive in-depth training on statistical tools and process improvement (they perform many of the same functions as black belts but for a larger number of teams); and **green belts**, who are employees who have received enough Six Sigma training to participate in a team or, in some companies, to work individually on a small-scale project directly related to their own job. Different companies use these "belts" in different combinations with sponsors and champions to guide teams.
3. **Setting of stretch objectives for improvement.**
4. **Continuous reinforcement and rewards.** Before savings from a project are declared, the black belt in charge must provide proof that the problems are fixed permanently.

The Shingo System: Fail-Safe Design

The Shingo system developed in parallel and in many ways in conflict with the statistically based approach to quality control. This system—or, to be more precise, philosophy of production management—is named after the co-developer of the Toyota just-in-time system, Shigeo Shingo. Two aspects of the Shingo system in particular have received great attention. One is how to accomplish drastic cuts in equipment setup times by *single-minute exchange of die* (SMED) procedures. The other, the focus of this section, is the use of source inspection and the poka-yoke system to achieve zero defects.

OSCM AT WORK

What Makes a Good Champion?

At a manufacturing company implementing Six Sigma, a designated champion regularly met with his black belts. At one report-out meeting, a black belt informed him that she needed to purchase and install a table for sorting defects offline. It would cost about $17,000, but it would provide an alternative to shutting down the entire line, which would cost far more. The controller told her to go through the normal requisition process and she'd have her table in about four months. That delay would have killed the project right then and there: To submit the project to "business as usual" would have shown little real commitment to supporting Six Sigma. So the champion asked for the data that backed up her request, analyzed it, agreed with it, and then got immediate executive sign-off on securing a table the following week.

This is the stuff of a good champion: removing barriers and sending a clear signal that he or she and upper management are aligned and committed to Six Sigma. The champion does whatever it takes to support the black belts.

Source: Greg Brue, *Six Sigma for Managers* (New York: McGraw-Hill, 2002), p. 84

Shingo argued that SQC methods do not prevent defects. Although they provide information to tell us probabilistically when a defect will occur, they are after the fact. The way to prevent defects from coming out at the end of a process is to introduce controls within the process. Central to Shingo's approach is the difference between errors and defects. Defects arise because people make errors. Even though errors are inevitable, defects can be prevented if feedback leading to corrective action takes place immediately after the errors are made. Such feedback and action require inspection, which should be done on 100 percent of the items produced. This inspection can be one of three types: successive check, self-check, and source inspection. *Successive check* inspection is performed by the next person in the process or by an objective evaluator such as a group leader. Information on defects is immediate feedback for the worker who produced the product, who then makes the repair. *Self-check* is done by the individual worker and is appropriate by itself on all but items that require sensory judgment (such as existence or severity of scratches, or correct matching of shades of paint). These require successive checks. *Source inspection* is also performed by the individual worker, except instead of checking for defects, the worker checks for the errors that will cause defects. This prevents the defects from ever occurring and, hence, requiring rework. All three types of inspection rely on controls consisting of **fail-safe procedures** or devices called **poka-yokes**. Poka-yokes includes such things as checklists or special tooling that (1) prevents the worker from making an error that leads to a defect before starting a process or (2) gives rapid feedback of abnormalities in the process to the worker in time to correct them.

Process

Fail-safe procedures
Simple practices that help prevent errors.

Poka-yokes
Procedures that prevent mistakes from becoming defects. They are commonly found in manufacturing but also can be used in service processes.

There are a wide variety of poka-yokes, ranging from kitting parts from a bin (to ensure that the right number of parts are used in assembly) to sophisticated detection and electronic signaling devices. An example taken from the writings of Shingo is shown in Exhibit 12.7.

EXHIBIT 12.7

Poka-Yoke Example (placing labels on parts coming down a conveyor)

Before Improvement

The operation depended on the worker's vigilance.

After Improvement

Device to ensure attachment of labels

The tape fed out by the labeler turns sharply so that the labels detach and project out from the tape. This is detected by a photoelectric tube and, if the label is not removed and applied to the product with 20 seconds, a buzzer sounds and the conveyor stops.

Effect: Label application failures were eliminated.
Cost: ¥ 15,000 ($145)

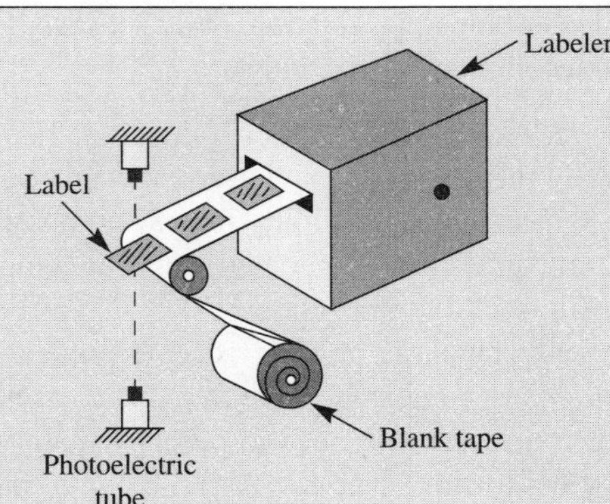

ISO 9000 AND ISO 14000

LO 12-3
Illustrate globally recognized quality benchmarks

ISO 9000 and ISO 14000 are international standards for quality management and assurance. The standards are designed to help companies document that they are maintaining an efficient quality system. The standards were originally published in 1987 by the International Organization for Standardization (ISO), a specialized international agency recognized by affiliates in more than 160 countries. **ISO 9000** has become an international reference for quality management requirements in business-to-business dealing, and ISO 14000 is primarily concerned with environmental management.

ISO 9000
Formal standards for quality certification developed by the International Organization for Standardization.

The idea behind the standards is that defects can be prevented through the planning and application of *best practices* at every stage of business—from design through manufacturing and then installation and servicing. These standards focus on identifying criteria by which any organization, regardless of whether it is manufacturing or service-oriented, can ensure that products leaving its facility meet the requirements of its customers. These standards ask a company first to document and implement its systems for quality management and then to verify, by means of an audit conducted by an independent accredited third party, the compliance of those systems with the requirements of the standards.

The ISO 9000 standards are based on seven quality management principles. These principles focus on business processes related to the following areas in the firm: (1) customer focus, (2) leadership, (3) involvement of people, (4) process approach, (5) continual improvement, (6) factual approach to decision making, and (7) mutually beneficial supplier relationships. The ISO documents provide detailed requirements for meeting the standards and describe standard tools used for improving quality in the firm. These documents are intended to be generic and applicable to any organization producing products or services.

The ISO 14000 family of standards on environmental management addresses the need to be environmentally responsible. The standards define a three-pronged approach for dealing with environmental challenges. The first is the definition of more than 350 international standards for monitoring the quality of air, water, and soil. For many countries, these standards serve as the technical basis for environmental regulation. The second part of ISO 14000 is a strategic approach defining the requirements of an environmental management system that can be implemented using the monitoring tools. Finally, the environmental standard encourages the inclusion of environment aspects in product design and encourages the development of profitable environment-friendly products and services.

In addition to the generic ISO 9000 and ISO 14000 standards, many other specific standards have been defined. The following are some examples:

- QS-9000 is a quality management system developed by Chrysler, Ford, and General Motors for suppliers of production parts, materials, and services to the automotive industry.
- ISO/TS 16949, developed by the International Automotive Task Force, aligns existing American, German, French, and Italian automotive quality standards within the global automotive industry.
- ISO 14001 environmental standards are applied by automobile suppliers as a requirement from Ford and General Motors.
- ANSI/ASQ Z1.4-2003 provides methods for collecting, analyzing, and interpreting data for inspection by attributes, while Z1.9-2003 relates to inspection by variables.
- TL 9000 defines the telecommunications quality system requirements for the design, development, production, delivery, installation, and maintenance of products and services in the telecommunications industry.

New ISO documents are being developed on an ongoing basis. ISO 26000, which offers guidance on socially responsible behavior, has recently been adopted. The standard encourages organizations to discuss the social responsibility issues and possible actions with relevant stakeholders. Although not a strict "standard," the document argues that being socially responsible is a requirement for both public- and private-sector organizations.

The ISO standards provide accepted global guidelines for quality. Although certification is not required, many companies have found it is essential to be competitive in the global markets. Consider the situation where you need to purchase parts for your firm and there are several suppliers offering similar parts at similar prices. Assume one of these firms has been ISO 9000–certified and the others have not. From whom would you purchase the parts? There is no doubt that the ISO 9000–certified company would have the inside track in your decision making. Why? Because ISO 9000 specifies the way the supplier firm operates, as well as its quality standards, delivery times, service levels, and so on.

There are three forms of certification:

1. First party: A firm audits itself against ISO 9000 standards.
2. Second party: A customer audits its supplier.
3. Third party: A "qualified" national or international standards or certifying agency serves as an auditor.

The best certification of a firm is through a third party. Once passed by the third-party audit, a firm is certified and may be registered and recorded as having achieved ISO 9000 status; thus, it becomes a part of a registry of certified companies. This third-party certification also has legal advantages in the European Community. For example, a manufacturer is liable for injury to a user of the product.

The firm, however, can free itself from any liability by showing that it has used the appropriate standards in its production process and carefully selected its suppliers as part of its purchasing requirements. For this reason, there is strong motivation to choose ISO 9000–certified suppliers.

External Benchmarking for Quality Improvement

The quality improvement approaches described so far are more or less inward looking. They seek to make improvements by analyzing in detail the current practices of the company itself. **External benchmarking**, however, goes outside the organization to examine what industry competitors and excellent performers outside the industry are doing. Benchmarking typically involves the following steps:

External benchmarking Looking outside the company to examine what excellent performers inside and outside the company's industry are doing in the way of quality.

Identify processes needing improvement. Identify a firm that is the world leader in performing the process. For many processes, this may be a company that is not in the same industry. Examples would be Procter & Gamble using Amazon as the benchmark in evaluating its order entry system, or Ford Motor Company benchmarking Walmart to improve its distribution system. Many companies select a team of workers from the process needing improvement as part of the team of visitors sent to the company being benchmarked.

Analyze data. This entails looking at gaps between what your company is doing and what the benchmarking company is doing. There are two aspects of the study: One is comparing the actual processes; the other is comparing the performance of these processes according to a set of measures. The processes are often described using flowcharts and subjective evaluations of how workers relate to the process. In some cases, companies even permit video recording.

Reliability and Maintainability

Reliability is an important concept, as we are always interested in knowing how well a system would perform the intended function when operating under stable condition for a given period. Similarly, *maintainability* is another concept that refers to the probability that a failed system would be restored within a given period. The mean value for the duration between two consecutive failures is called as '*Mean Time Between Failure*' (MTBF). Efforts are needed and strategies need to be designed to improve system reliability. For example, to improve the system reliability, parallel redundant system(s), like extra engine in an aircraft, can be connected that can perform similar task when the main component fails.

The failure rate of a typical mechanical component follows the shape of a bath-tub over a period of time. When the component is new, during first few hours of operation, there is a high chance that it can fail due to manufacturing defects, incorrect assembly, etc. Then after, the failure rate remains constant and very low for a long period. For the aged components, due to wear-out, the failure rate once again picks up. Thus, the failure rate curve looks like a typical bath-tub during the life time of the product.

Reliability study is also helpful in designing parts and components that can survive for a long period leading to better customer satisfaction. Generally, a product or service involves many components or service dimensions. If one of these fails, in a majority of the cases, the whole system suffers a down-time. Such situations can be managed using reliability study.

CONCEPT CONNECTIONS

LO 12–1 Explain the scope of total quality management in a firm

Summary

- Total quality management is a comprehensive approach to quality, with a focus on what is important to the customer.
- The concept centers on two major operational goals: (1) The design of the product or service, and (2) ensuring that the firm's processes can consistently produce or deliver the design.
- Quality specifications are fundamental to a sound quality program. These start with making sure that features of the design relate to what the intended market for the product expects and its inherent value.

- Processes are designed so that particular design specifications such as size, surface, finish, or delivery speed are consistently met when the product is produced or the service delivered.
- Costs related to quality include the expenses related to inspection, rework, and repair or warranty; some of these costs may be difficult to measure.

Key Terms

Total quality management Managing the entire organization so it excels in all dimensions of products and services important to the customer.

Malcolm Baldrige National Quality Award An award established by the U.S. Department of Commerce given annually to companies that excel in quality.

Design quality The inherent value of the product in the marketplace.

Conformance quality The degree to which the product or service design specifications are met.

Quality at the source The philosophy of making workers personally responsible for the quality of their output. Workers are expected to make the part correctly the first time and to stop the process immediately if there is a problem.

Dimensions of quality Criteria by which quality is measured.

Cost of quality Expenditures related to achieving product or service quality, such as the costs of prevention, appraisal, internal failure, and external failure.

LO 12–2 Understand the Six Sigma approach to improving quality and productivity

Summary

- This is a philosophy and set of tools developed to measure and reduce defects.
- Six Sigma projects follow five steps: (1) define, (2) measure, (3) analyze, (4) improve, and (5) control.
- A comprehensive set of analysis tools can be used in Six Sigma projects. Many of these tools use statistics to analyze performance data.
- Training in Six Sigma is recognized using martial arts titles that reflect skill levels such as black belts and green belts.
- Often, procedures can be included in a process that guarantees a very high level of quality. These are called fail-safe procedures.

Key Terms

Six Sigma A statistical term to describe the quality goal of no more than 3.4 defects out of every million units. Also refers to a quality improvement philosophy and program.

Defects per million opportunities (DPMO) A metric used to describe the variability of a process.

DMAIC (define, measure, analyze, improve, and control) An acronym for the *define, measure, analyze, improve, and control* improvement methodology followed by companies engaging in Six Sigma programs.

Lean Six Sigma Combines the implementation and quality control tools of Six Sigma and the inventory management concept of lean manufacturing.

Black belts, master black belts, *and* green belts Terms used to describe different levels of personal skills and responsibilities in Six Sigma programs. Black belts have sufficient training to lead teams. Master black belts have additional in-depth training on statistical tools and process improvement, and support the teams with these skills. Green belts are employees who have enough training to participate in the improvement teams.

Fail-safe procedures Simple practices that help prevent errors.

Poka-yokes Procedures that prevent mistakes from becoming defects. They are commonly found in manufacturing but also can be used in service processes.

LO 12–3 Illustrate globally recognized quality benchmarks

Summary

- The International Organization for Standardization (ISO) has developed specifications that define best-quality practices that are accepted internationally.

- The two most accepted specifications are ISO 9000, which relate to manufacturing and business-to-business processes, and ISO 14000, which are concerned with environmental management.

Key Terms

ISO 9000 Formal standards for quality certification developed by the International Organization for Standardization.

External benchmarking Looking outside the company to examine what excellent performers inside and outside the company's industry are doing in the way of quality.

DISCUSSION QUESTIONS

1. Is the goal of Six Sigma realistic for services such as Blockbuster Video stores or Redbox DVD kiosks? **LO 12–1**
2. "If line employees are required to work on quality improvement activities, their productivity will suffer." Discuss.
3. "You don't inspect quality into a product; you have to build it in." Discuss the implications of this statement.
4. "Before you build quality in, you must think it in." How do the implications of this statement differ from those in question 3?
5. Business writer Tom Peters has suggested that in making process changes, we should "Try it, test it, and get on with it." How does this square with the DMAIC/continuous improvement philosophy? **LO 12–2**
6. Develop a cause-and-effect (fishbone) diagram to address everything that impacts your grade in this course. How much is under your control?
7. Shingo told a story of a poka-yoke he developed to make sure that the operators avoided the mistake of putting fewer than the required four springs in a push-button device. The existing method involved assemblers taking individual springs from a box containing several hundred and then placing two of them behind an *on* button and two more behind an *off* button. What was the poka-yoke that Shingo created? **LO 12–3**
8. A typical word processing package is loaded with poka-yokes. List three. Are there any others you wish the packages had?
9. Is certification under the ISO standards in this chapter necessary for competing in the modern market? What should companies consider when deciding whether or not to become certified?
10. Do you see any relationship between the ISO standards mentioned in this chapter and the competitive strategy concepts mentioned earlier in the text?

OBJECTIVE QUESTIONS

1. What is the name of the national quality award given by the government of the United States? **LO 12–1**
2. Match the quality "guru" with the specific aspects of their teachings. Use C for Crosby, D for Deming, and J for Juran.

___________ Defined quality as "fitness for use."

___________ Defined quality as "conformance to requirements."

___________ Set the performance standard as "zero defects."

___________ Defined 14 points for management to follow.

___________ Emphasized a general management approach to quality, especially the human elements.

___________ Rejected the concept of statistically acceptable levels of quality.

___________ Stated that less than 20 percent of quality problems are due to workers.

___________ Recommended continuous improvement to reduce variations.

3. What is the term that means making the person who does the work responsible for ensuring that specifications are met?
4. What are the four general categories of quality costs?
5. What term means managing the entire organization so that it excels on all dimensions of products and services that are important to customers?

LO 12-2

6. A manager states that her process is really working well. Out of 1,500 parts, 1,477 were produced free of a particular defect and passed inspection. Based upon Six Sigma theory, how would you rate this performance, other things being equal? (Answer in Appendix D)
7. The following table lists all costs of quality incurred by Sam's Surf Shop last year. What was Sam's appraisal cost for quality last year?

Annual inspection costs	$ 155,000
Annual cost of scrap materials	286,000
Annual rework cost	34,679
Annual cost of quality training	456,000
Annual warranty cost	1,546,000
Annual testing cost	543,000

8. The following is a table of data collected over a six-month period in a local grocery store. Construct a Pareto analysis of the data and determine the percentage of total complaints represented by the two most common categories.

All Other	71	Price Marking	45
Checker	59	Product Quality	87
General	58	Product Request	105
Service Level	55	Checkout Queue	33
Policy/Procedures	40	Stock Condition	170

9. A common problem that many drivers encounter is a car that will not start. Create a fishbone diagram to assist in the diagnosis of the potential causes of this problem.
10. A manufacturing company has been inspecting units of output from a process. Each product inspected is evaluated on five criteria. If the unit does not meet standards for the criteria, it counts as a defect for the unit. Each unit could have as few as zero defects, and as many as five. After inspecting 2,000 units, they discovered 33 defects. What is the DPMO measure for this process?
11. What is the term for a flowchart that is used to separate value-added from non–value-added steps in a process? (Answer in Appendix D)
12. What does the acronym DMAIC stand for?
13. A customer call center is evaluating customer satisfaction surveys to identify the most prevalent quality problems in their process. Specific customer complaints have been analyzed and grouped into eight different categories. Every instance of a complaint adds to the count in its category. Which Six Sigma analytical tool would be most helpful to management here?

LO 12-3

14. Which international standard has recently been developed to address and encourage socially responsible behavior in firms?
15. Which industry-specific standard has been developed by the big three automakers for suppliers of parts, materials, and services to the automotive industry?
16. What is it called when a firm examines other companies for examples of best practices?

CASE: Quality Managemet In Agri-Business

News about food scandals and incidents of contamination in food products are quite common. Consumers all over the world are expecting safe and quality food. This has built up additional pressure on food industries to become more resilient and quick in dealing with various food quality issues. The performance of the food-based companies is now-a-days evaluated at both national and international levels on the basis of their capability to ensure safety and hygiene of food products. Failure to perform may not only result in the economic loss but also long-term loss of reputation and brand of a company. In the year 2015, India's Food Safety administration ordered Nestle to recall its product (Maggi) after being reported presence of high levels of lead and MSG in the noodles. Due to this, Nestle India lost a good amount of money and also suffered a dent in its reputation. To eliminate the possibility of occurrence of such incidents, companies are supposed to adopt multiple changes in their production and preparation processes in order to make their supply chain more competitive and resilient. As customers are very sensitive towards food quality and safety, a number of food quality standards and programs have emerged. These include good agricultural practices (GAP), good manufacturing practices (GMP), good production practices (GPP), hazard analysis critical control point (HACCP), quality and safety management standards such as ISO 9001 and ISO 22000, etc. In agri-business, the quality attributes can be classified in two categories: intrinsic and extrinsic (Figure 1). Management of these quality attributes is important.

FIGURE 1

Food quality attributes

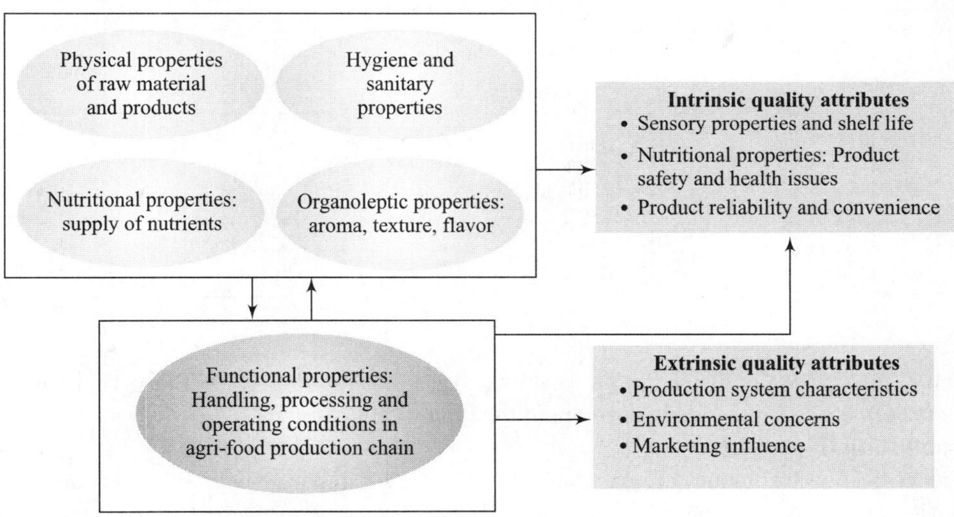

In India, it is a big challenge to cater to the needs of the growing population, which is expected to touch 1.7 billion by 2050. Maintaining the availability and quality of food is a major concern for the food industries of any nation. A huge quantity of food produce gets wasted every day due to many inefficiencies in the existing food supply chain. The reasons for unhealthy and poor quality food involve infrastructural issues during each stage of the supply chain, lack of clearly defined practices, lack of storage space, improper post-harvest management practices, poor transportation facilities, lack of awareness, inadequate packaging, inefficiencies in stock management and distribution, fraudulent activities performed by various actors, natural calamities, etc.

Food Safety Management System

Millions of consumers get affected due to consumption of unsafe and poor quality food, which is the result of food contamination. Foodborne illness has now become very common globally. Therefore, there is a great need to have an effective food safety management system. A food safety management system is referred to as a group of practices and procedures that are adopted in order to deal with various risks and hazards, affecting safety and quality of food, throughout the food supply chain. One such system to ensure quality of food is HACCP, which follows operations as per ISO standards. HACCP system helps in preventing food contamination by identifying unsafe links in the food processing chain.

Another concept, which has gained high popularity in recent times to ensure safety and quality of food products is 'traceability'. It works like a monitoring system, which can continuously track the movement of food product, starting from farm till it reaches the end-consumer. An effective and efficient food traceability system may help in tracing the source of contamination, if any, as well as ensures the correct and on-time delivery of food products at the right place. This would further contribute in reducing food wastages and product recalls. The design and implementation of a whole chain traceability starting from farm-to-fork help in gaining consumer's confidence through the supply of safe, nutritious and quality food. Traceability is mainly comprised of three major components: (i) tracking (to track the physical movement of product flow from upstream to downstream of a supply chain), (ii) tracing (to trace backwards from downstream to upstream in a supply chain for identifying the source of contamination), and (iii) maintaining history of the product (such as, its origin, fertilizers used, internal components, place to be delivered, etc.). Integration of a food traceability system with various practices adopted at each stage of a food supply chain, such as good production practices (GPP), good manufacturing practices (GMP), good handling practices (GHP), good distribution practices (GDP), good retailing practices (GRP), good consumption practices (GCP) along with HACCP, can help in ensuring safety and quality of food products (Figure 2).

FIGURE 2

Food traceability information system for improving food quality

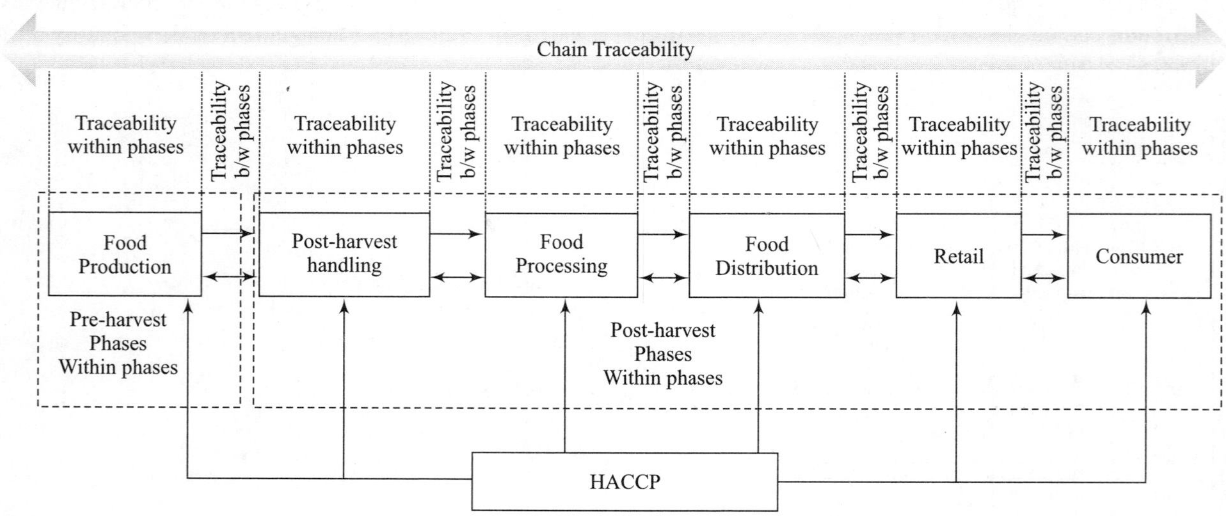

India should work more on regulation for implementing traceability. Agencies like FSSAI, APEDA, GS1 India, ITC's eChaupal, Fruit Products Order (FPO), etc. are involved in developing food traceability system.

Traceability Techniques and Initiatives in India

Currently, many product identification techniques are existing. These include barcode, hologram, alphanumeric codes, radio frequency identification (RFID) tags, geographical indication (GI) tags, etc. There are few other food traceability techniques, which can be utilized in an integrated way. These include bio-tracing, nano sensor, global positioning system (GPS) and geographical information system (GIS). Many organizations are taking necessary steps to implement end-to-end food traceability system. For example, Cargill, a major player in food and agriculture business has announced to formulate a sustainable and fully traceable supply chain of the palm oil in India. APEDA is implementing an end-to-end traceability system for most of the farm products like grape, mango, onion, banana, soybean and poultry. Tea board of India has introduced Trustea and Rain Forest Alliance (RFA) certifications for all tea manufacturers to certificate reliable tea suppliers.

Despite many traceability initiatives by various organizations, India is considered to be at an early stage of implementation of traceability system. It is due to inconsistency in the Indian food market, cost involved in the implementation of devices like RFID tags and lack of awareness towards food safety.

Questions

1 Prepare a report on different quality standards and framework used in India for food safety.
2 Define and explain food traceability system. Why are such systems important?
3 List and explain how technology can support food traceability systems.
4 What role do you see for block-chain technology in food traceability systems?

CASE: Quality Journey of Sundaram Clayton

"Quality is the way of life" and this is reflected in the practices at Sundaram Clayton Limited (SCL), which is a leading supplier of aluminium die castings to automotive and non-automotive sector. SCL is a part of the $5 billion TVS group, one of the largest auto components manufacturing and distribution group in India. Its product range includes, air brake actuation system used for medium and heavy commercial vehicles, compressors for generation of air, air-dryers and reservoirs for processing and storage of air, valves for control and regulation of the system, actuators for actuating the brakes, electronic control system for air brakes [anti-lock braking system (ABS) and anti-spin regulation (ASR)] vacuum brake products for light commercial vehicles, etc. It has 3 Manufacturing Plants, 3 Regional offices in USA, Sweden & Germany and 17 Third Party Logistics' (3PL) locations [1]. The journey of SCL is a true example of commitment to quality and growth through business excellence in all walks of corporate endeavor. It started as a joint venture with Clayton Dewandre Holdings Plc, UK (now part of WABCO Automotive Group) in Chennai in 1962, established its die-casting facility in 1968, established another plant at Hosur in 1998, and established a plant at Mahindra World City, Chennai in 2009.

Sundaram's quality achievements within the plant and to its customers all over the world were immediately noticed by everyone else when its brakes division was conferred the prestigious Deming Prize in 1996. It was the Asia's first-ever winner of the Deming Prize for Overseas Companies. Soon, in 1998, it was awarded Japanese Quality Medal–the first in India and the second company outside Japan to win this honour [2]. This is a clear recognition of sustained quality journey of SCL as Japan Quality Medal is an annual award presented to a Deming Prize winner, who have demonstrated sustained effort since then by continuously applying TQM to priority issues and have been achieving objectives steadily and effectively in a changing business environment. In 2009, it was awarded for TPM Excellence in Category A.

Deming Prize is conferred either to a company or stand alone division, which manages its business in an autonomous mode like the brakes division of SCL. It looks for exemplary improvement in performance through the practices of TQM, establishment and achievement of challenging and customer-oriented business objectives and outstanding results. SCL integrated Deming's 10 parameters into the 4 streams of its quality practices, namely policies, people, processes, and products, respectively. Its TQM model ensures Total Employee Involvement, Policy Deployment, Standardization, Kaizen, and Training, besides promoting employer-employee relations.

The secret of SCL achievements in quality management lies in its total commitment to quality and involvement from early design stage to development and supply of finished products, which is dovetailed in the strategic intent to build strategic partnership with global customers as well as tier one supply chain partners. Another important focus is the development of a robust manufacturing system, which is inter-woven with the continuous improvement practices of TQM and TPM, lean practices and investments in the state of the art technologies[1].

The beginning of Sundaram's journey to TQM path was on a tough terrain, when in late 1980s it was struggling to overcome the after-effect of recessionary trend in auto-sector and fast emerging stiff completion in this sector. For the company, Japanese style of quality management suited better as according to Mr. C. Narasimhan, President, Sundaram-Clayton Ltd., it was congruent with Indian culture, like Guru-Student relationship[2].

Four important phases can be noticed in the SCL journey to TQM: (i) introduction phase (1987 to 1990), (ii) promotion phase (1990 to 1994), (iii) methodology deployment phase (1994 to 1998), and (iv) consolidation and growth phase (1998 onwards). In the first phase, two important steps were taken. First step was "training and involvement of all concerned" and the second was "change management." Every possible platform of communication was exploited to stress upon the importance of change to all the employees and clear messages were given about top-management commitment to quality. Top management focused on removing all possible barriers to employees' participation and team working. Uniform dress, common canteen, and open office for managers were clearly aimed at breaking the wall between departments and between managers and workers [3]. The company realised well that the only way to succeed in the TQM journey is through employees' involvement, team-work and continuous improvement. This required use of well-designed trainings in problem solving and statistical tools, participation in quality control circles, suggestion scheme, cross functional teams (CFT), supervisory improvement teams (SIT) and task forces. Factory layout was changed from functional to product-layout. This streamlined production, improved capacity utilization, and helped workers to acquire multi-skills.

Focus of the second phase was mainly on alignment of each department towards the common objective of the company. The company's annual goals were deployed to each department/divisions. Third phase involved daily work management in the form of defining and monitoring key processes, ensuring that they met set targets, detecting abnormalities and preventing their recurrence [3]. Amazing results started coming in second and third phases when employees started participating in problem solving and continuous improvement activity through statistical tool rather than intuition. Simple quality control (QC) tools worked wonder in these activities. "Daily activities were streamlined through standard operating procedures (SOP) and 'Genba' management. The daily management targets were deployed up to the supervisor level in the company through 'managing points and checking points' (MPCP). Specific objectives for obtaining breakthrough results are established, deployed and reviewed company-wide through policy management process"[2]. New tools, such as quality function deployment (QFD), benchmarking and structured design reviews were institutionalised. The culture of "quality by inspection" started giving way to "quality at source," quality control and quality assurance (QA).

Sundarm noticed many tangible and intangible benefits in this journey of TQM. There were all-round improvements in customer satisfaction, new product development, supplier satisfaction, employees and their family fulfilment, industrial relations, ownership among employees for improving organizational performance, breakthrough achievements in business results, local society satisfaction.

Status after Deming Prize

SCL believes that Deming Prize is not its destination, but only a ticket for TQM journey towards organizational excellence. Quality goals are moving targets. It knows that its future lies in further improving the product quality and productivity along with reducing cost and implementing lean manufacturing systems and Total Productive Maintenance (TPM).

Questions

1. Based on the case study, define a road-map for pursuing quality management in a manufacturing company.
2. Discuss the purpose of award models in a quality journey.
3. What are the lessons for service industries from this case study?

References

1. http://www.sundaram-clayton.com/Profile.htm (Accessed on 12 April 2014)
2. http://www.sundaram-clayton.com/Milestones.htm (Accessed on 12 April 2014)
3. http://www.juse.or.jp/e/deming/ (Accessed on 12 April 2014)
4. http://ibef.org/attachment/Sundaramclaytonlimited.pdf (Accessed on 12 April 2014)

CASE: Tesla's Quality Challenge

On March 31, 2016, Tesla Motors announced the release of its new Model 3 electric car. Over 276,000 people from around the world put down $1,000 reservations for the car within three days. First deliveries of the car are expected in late 2017. The innovative new car is a follow-up to the much more expensive Model S and Model X cars. Tesla delivered about 110,000 of these cars prior to the Model 3 announcement. Elon Musk, the brilliant CEO of the company, has said that he has confidence that the company can sell 500,000 cars a year by 2020. Given the interest shown at the Model 3 announcement, some experts think this might be possible.

The fledging Palo Alto, California, automaker has struggled with ramping up manufacturing, particularly with the Model X sport utility vehicle introduced in 2015. The company reported that there were many sourcing changes made late in the process of planning production. Tesla tends to make items, such as the middle seats in the Model X, in-house rather than outsourcing them, which is done by many car manufacturers.

The issues associated with the production of the cars are a complex combination of mechanical and computer software problems. Popular features of the cars include driving-assist autopilot functions, auto-parallel parking, and auto-braking. The cars even have an auto-summons feature that lets a driver park and retrieve their car with no one inside. Many post-production issues have been addressed through software updates downloaded to customers over wireless connections. Other mechanical problems are more difficult to resolve.

Owners have complained that the Model X falcon-wing doors will not open. When owners have problems like this, Tesla typically schedules a time to pick up the car for repair and leaves a loaner for use by the customer.

Another recent issue was a latch on the third-row seat that could come undone during a collision. Tesla decided to recall 2,700 Model X cars to replace the latches with a new design. This recall totally overloaded Tesla's service outlets with waits of more than two weeks to make the repair. Some customers were offered rental cars due to the long wait.

So far, customers expect the "white-glove" treatment that Tesla currently offers, but a big concern is what Tesla will do when there are hundreds of thousands of vehicles on the road. Mr. Musk's Tesla cars have many loyal customers, even though problems have been encountered. But moving from tens of thousands of vehicles to hundreds of thousands may be difficult, unless some major service improvements are made.

Put yourself in the position of a manager at Tesla responsible for quality and customer satisfaction. What would you suggest relative to the following questions?

Questions

1. *Consumer Reports,* the service that reports unbiased testing and ratings on cars (together with about everything else we buy), recommends avoiding new cars in their first year of production, especially those loaded with new technology. What can Tesla do to refute this recommendation?
2. How should Tesla "manage" the delivery of the new Model 3 during the initial production ramp-up? Think about this relative to where cars should be delivered geographically and how the service process should be designed.
3. Should Tesla deliver cars to customers on a first-come-first-served basis (i.e., in the order of when deposits were placed)?
4. What other suggestions would you have for Tesla relative to ensuring the quality of their new Model 3 car?

PRACTICE EXAM

In each of the following, name the term defined or answer the question. Answers are listed at the bottom.

1. This refers to the inherent value of the product in the marketplace and is a strategic decision for the firm.
2. Relates to how well a product or service meets design specifications.
3. Relates to how the customer views the ability of the product to meet his or her objectives.
4. The series of international quality standards.
5. What is the enemy of good quality?
6. A Six Sigma process that is running at the center of its control limits would expect this defect rate.
7. The standard quality improvement methodology developed by General Electric.

Answers to Practice Exam 1. Design quality 2. Conformance quality 3. Fitness for use 4. ISO 9000 5. Variation 6. 2 parts per billion units 7. DMAIC cycle

For PowerPoint lecture slides, Solutions Manual, Test Bank, Data files for solved examples, Excel Templates, Step-by-Step Solved Examples in video format, Tutorial Videos and many more, scan the adjacent **QR code**, or **visit http://www.mhhe.com/sie-chase15e**

Chapter 13

Statistical Quality Control

LEARNING OBJECTIVES

LO 13-1 Illustrate process variation and explain how to measure it

LO 13-2 Analyze process quality using statistics

LO 13-3 Analyze the quality of batches of items using statistics

CONTROL CHARTS HELP IN PROCESS MANAGEMENT DURING A QUALITY JOURNEY

Quality is what customer wants. Customer is always conscious for getting the best product and services. An important way to look at the quality is defining it as something that helps in meeting the specifications. However, when the product or services are delivered to a customer, it is quite improbable that these are delivered with a hundred percent exact specification on each and every occasion. For example, in a mechanical workshop, a lathe machine is used for turning operation. Turning is used to machine the diameter of a cylindrical work-piece, so that the diameter of the work-piece is reduced to a size that the specification demands. One can produce an iron shaft through this simple process. Is it possible to produce one thousand shafts, whose diameter is exactly a single value and always the same? Not only this, can this single value of shafts' diameter be the same as the one mentioned in the specification? It is quite intuitive that the answer is no. Little bit of variation is always there due to many reasons.

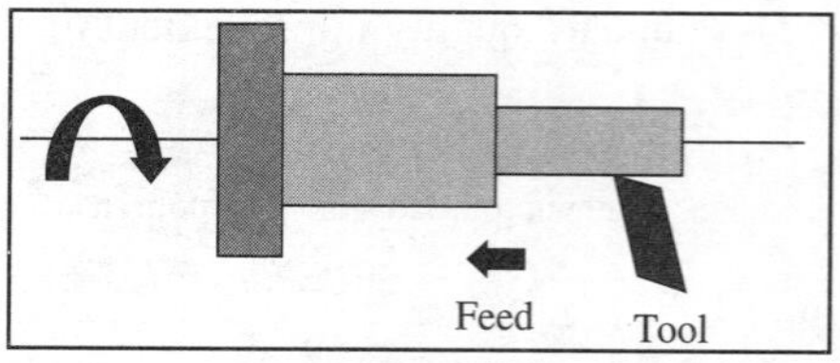

Then, how should an operations and supply chain manager deal with variability in the outcomes of a process? The variations in the process outcomes of the delivered products or services are due to natural causes and/or assignable causes. Natural causes are due to system variability for which there are statistical control limits, which one can always set. However, there can be assignable causes too. For the selected example of turning operation on the lathe machine, the assignable causes may be machine tools getting worn-out, power fluctuations affecting the surface finish, vibration and chatter of the lathe machine, non-trained worker in a particular shift who are not able to manage good surface-finish and other specifications, improper loading of work-piece on the lathe machine, etc.

Here, statistical process control (SPC) comes to the rescue of operations and supply chain managers. Control charts, which are a very commonly used tool in SPC, can clearly indicate the occasions when the variations in the process outcomes are due to assignable causes. Once, these occasions are spotted, the job of a manager would be to look back into the process and trace out the reasons for these. Since control charts clearly indicate the time or samples for which there existed an assignable cause for poor process outcome, pin-pointing the assignable cause for that sample and its corresponding production lot is relatively an easy task. Once assignable causes are identified, the most important task would be to improve the process so that such quality problems do not recur in future.

Not only this, sometimes indications start coming through a sequence of past observations, which though appear as under control on a control chart, yet they sufficiently indicate a poor quality and problematic process outcome in a near future. Such likely forthcoming out-of-control situations can be red-flagged before they actually occur. Therefore, corrective actions could be taken proactively. In the above example of the turning operation on a lathe, suppose that there are 5 continuous observations (called as run-of-five) above the central line of a control chart, then there is a likelihood that this phenomenon might have taken place due to an assignable cause. Therefore, an investigation is warranted to identify and correct the assignable cause, if it had ever existed. If such situations are ignored by operations & supply chain managers, then there is a strong possibility that a subsequent process-outcome (such as diameter of a shaft in the turning operation) may go out-of-control.

It is well accepted now that tools and techniques of SPC are scientifically designed. These are generally easy to use. Therefore, SPC tools and techniques are playing a very important role in improving the overall productivity of a firm through delivery of better quality product and/or services.

STATISTICAL QUALITY CONTROL

LO 13-1

Illustrate process variation and explain how to measure it

This chapter on **statistical quality control (SQC)** covers the quantitative aspects of quality management. In general, SQC is a number of different techniques designed to evaluate quality from a conformance view; that is, how well are we doing at meeting the specifications that have been set during the design of the parts or services we are providing? Managing quality performance using SQC techniques usually involves periodic sampling of a process and analysis of these data using statistically derived performance criteria.

Statistical quality control (SQC)
A number of different techniques designed to evaluate quality from a conformance view.

As you will see, SQC can be applied to logistics, manufacturing, and service processes. Here are some examples of situations where SQC can be applied:

- How many paint defects are there in the finish of a car? Have we improved our painting process by installing a new sprayer?
- How long does it take to execute market orders in our Web-based trading system? Has the installation of a new server improved the service? Does the performance of the system vary over the trading day?
- How well are we able to maintain the dimensional tolerance on our three-inch ball bearing assembly? Given the variability of our process for making this ball bearing, how many defects would we expect to produce per million bearings that we make?
- How long does it take for customers to be served from our drive-thru window during the busy lunch period?

Processes that provide goods and services usually exhibit some variation in their output. This variation can be caused by many factors, some of which we can control and others that are inherent in the process. Variation that is caused by factors that can be clearly identified and possibly even managed is called **assignable variation**. For example, variation caused by workers not being equally trained or by improper machine adjustment is assignable variation. Variation that is inherent in the process itself is called **common variation**. Common variation is often referred to as *random variation* and may be the result of the type of equipment used to complete a process, for example.

Assignable variation
Deviation in the output of a process that can be clearly identified and managed.

As the title of this section implies, this material requires an understanding of very basic statistics. Recall the definition of the mean and standard deviation from your study of statistics involving numbers that are normally distributed. The mean ($\overline{X}$) is just the average value of a set of numbers. Mathematically, this is

Common variation
Deviation in the output of a process that is random and inherent in the process itself.

$$\overline{X} = \frac{\sum_{i=1}^{n} x_i}{n} \qquad [13.1]$$

The Elmo Chicken Dance toy gets a sound check at a Mattel lab in Shenzhen, China. Mattel lobbied to let its labs certify toy safety. The California company has 10 labs in 6 countries.

© Chang W. Lee/The New York Times/Redux

where

x_i = Observed value

n = Total number of observed values

Analytics

The standard deviation is

$$\sigma = \frac{\sqrt{\sum_{i=1}^{n}(x_i - \overline{X})^2}}{n} \qquad [13.2]$$

In monitoring a process using SQC, samples of the process output would be taken and sample statistics calculated. The distribution associated with the samples should exhibit the same kind of variability as the actual distribution of the process, although the actual variance of the sampling distribution would be less. This is good because it allows the quick detection of changes in the actual distribution of the process. The purpose of sampling is to find when the process has changed in some nonrandom way, so that the reason for the change can be quickly determined.

In SQC terminology, *sigma* (σ) is often used to refer to the sample standard deviation. As you will see in the examples, sigma is calculated in a few different ways, depending on the underlying theoretical distribution (i.e., a normal distribution or a Poisson distribution).

Understanding and Measuring Process Variation

It is generally accepted that as variation is reduced, quality is improved. Sometimes that knowledge is intuitive. If a commuter train is always on time, schedules can be planned more precisely. If clothing sizes are consistent, time can be saved by ordering from a catalog. But rarely are such things thought about in terms of the value of low variability. When engineering a mechanical device such as an automobile, the knowledge is better defined. Pistons must fit cylinders, doors must fit openings, electrical components must be compatible, and tires must be able to handle the required load—otherwise, quality will be unacceptable and customers will be dissatisfied.

Upper and lower specification limits
The range of values in a measure associated with a process that is allowable given the intended use of the product or service.

However, engineers also know that it is impossible to have zero variability. For this reason, designers establish specifications that define not only the target value of something but also acceptable limits about the target. For example, if the target value of a dimension is 10 inches, the design specifications might then be 10.00 inches $\pm$ 0.02 inch. This would tell the manufacturing department that, while it should aim for exactly 10 inches, anything between 9.98 and 10.02 inches is OK. These design limits are often referred to as the **upper and lower specification limits**.

A traditional way of interpreting such a specification is that any part that falls within the allowed range is equally good, whereas any part falling outside the range is totally bad. This is illustrated in

EXHIBIT 13.1

A Traditional View of the Cost of Variability

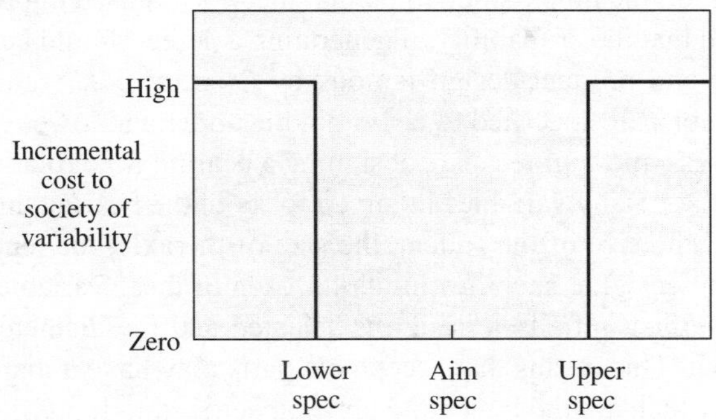

Exhibit 13.1. (Note that the cost is zero over the entire specification range, and then there is a quantum leap in cost once the limit is violated.)

Genichi Taguchi, a noted quality expert from Japan, has pointed out that the traditional view illustrated in Exhibit 13.1 is nonsense for two reasons:

1. From the customer's view, there is often practically no difference between a product just inside specifications and a product just outside. Conversely, there is a far greater difference in the quality of a product that is at the target and the quality of one that is near a limit.
2. As customers get more demanding, there is pressure to reduce variability. However, Exhibit 13.1 does not reflect this logic.

Taguchi suggests that a more correct picture of the loss is shown in Exhibit 13.2. Notice that in this graph the cost is represented by a smooth curve. There are dozens of illustrations of this notion: the meshing of gears in a transmission, the speed of photographic film, the temperature in a workplace or department store. In nearly anything that can be measured, the customer sees not a sharp line, but a gradation of acceptability away from the "Aim" specification. Customers see the loss function as Exhibit 13.2 rather than Exhibit 13.1.

EXHIBIT 13.2

Taguchi's View of the Cost of Variability

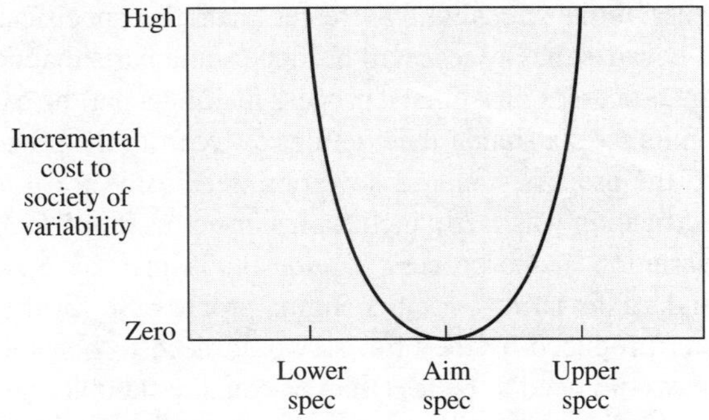

Of course, if products are consistently scrapped when they are outside specifications, the loss curve flattens out in most cases at a value equivalent to scrap cost in the ranges outside specifications. This is because such products, theoretically at least, will never be sold so there is no external cost to society. However, in many practical situations, either the process is capable of producing a very high percentage of product within specifications and 100 percent checking is not done, or if the process is not capable of producing within specifications, 100 percent checking is done and out-of-spec products can be reworked to bring them within specs. In any of these situations, the parabolic loss function is usually a reasonable assumption.

Measuring Process Capability

Taguchi argues that being within specification is not a yes/no decision, but rather a continuous function. Motorola quality experts, on the other hand, argue that the process used to produce a good or deliver a service should be so good that the probability of generating a defect should be very, very low. Motorola made process capability and product design famous by adopting Six Sigma limits. When a part is designed, certain dimensions are specified to be within the upper and lower specification limits.

As a simple example, assume engineers are designing a bearing for a rotating shaft—say, an axle for the wheel of a car. There are many variables involved for both the bearing and the axle—for example, the width of the bearing, the size of the rollers, the size of the axle, the length of the axle, how it is supported, and so on. The designer specifies limits for each of these variables to ensure that the parts will fit properly. Suppose that initially a design is selected and the diameter of the bearing is set at 1.250 inches ± 0.005 inch. This means that acceptable parts may have a diameter that varies between 1.245 and 1.255 inches (which are the lower and upper specification limits).

Next, consider the process in which the bearing will be made. Consider that many different processes for making the bearing are available. Usually, there are trade-offs that need to be considered when designing a process for making a part. The process, for example, might be fast but not consistent, or alternatively it might be slow but consistent. The consistency of a process for making the bearing can be measured by the standard deviation of the diameter measurement. A test can be run by making, say, 100 bearings and measuring the diameter of each bearing in the sample.

After running the test, the average or mean diameter is found to be 1.250 inches. Another way to say this is that the process is "centered" right in the middle of the upper and lower specification limits. In reality, it may be difficult to have a perfectly centered process like this example. Consider that the diameter values have a standard deviation or sigma equal to 0.002 inch. What this means is that the process does not make each bearing exactly the same size.

Key Idea

The main point of this is that the process should be able to make a part well within design specifications. Here, we show how statistics are used to evaluate how good a process is.

As is discussed later in this chapter, normally a process is monitored using control charts such that if the process starts making bearings that are more than three standard deviations (± 0.006 inch) above or below 1.250 inches, the process is stopped. This means that the process will produce parts that vary between 1.244 (this is 1.250 – 3 × .002) and 1.256 (this is 1.250 + 3 × .002) inches. The 1.244 and 1.256 are referred to as the upper and lower process limits. Be careful and do not get confused with the terminology here. The *process* limits relate to how consistent the process is for making the bearing. The goal in managing the process is to keep it within plus or minus three standard deviations of the process mean. The *specification* limits are related to the design of the part. Recall that, from a design view, acceptable parts have a diameter between 1.245 and 1.255 inches (which are the lower and upper specification limits).

As can be seen, process limits are slightly greater than the specification limits given by the designer. This is not good because the process will produce some parts that do not meet specifications. Companies with Six Sigma processes insist that a process making a part be capable of operating so that the design specification limits are six standard deviations away from the process mean. For the bearing process, how small would the process standard deviation need to be for it to be Six Sigma capable? Recall that the design specification was 1.250 inches plus or minus 0.005 inch. Consider that the 0.005 inch must relate to the variation in the process. Divide 0.005 inch by 6, which equals 0.00083, to determine the process standard deviation for a Six Sigma process. So for the process to be Six Sigma capable, the mean diameter produced by the process would need to be exactly 1.250 inches and the process standard deviation would need to be less than or equal to 0.00083 inch.

We can imagine that some of you are really confused at this point with the whole idea of Six Sigma. Why doesn't the company, for example, just check the diameter of each bearing and throw out the ones with a diameter less than 1.245 or greater than 1.255? This could certainly be done and for many, many parts 100 percent testing is done. The problem is for a company that is making thousands of parts each hour, testing each critical dimension of each part made can be very expensive. For the bearing, there could easily be 10 or more additional critical dimensions in addition to the diameter. These would all need to be checked. Using a 100 percent testing approach, the company would spend more time testing than it takes to actually make the part! This is why a company uses small samples to periodically check that the process is in statistical control. We discuss exactly how this statistical sampling works later in the chapter.

EXHIBIT 13.3

Process Capability

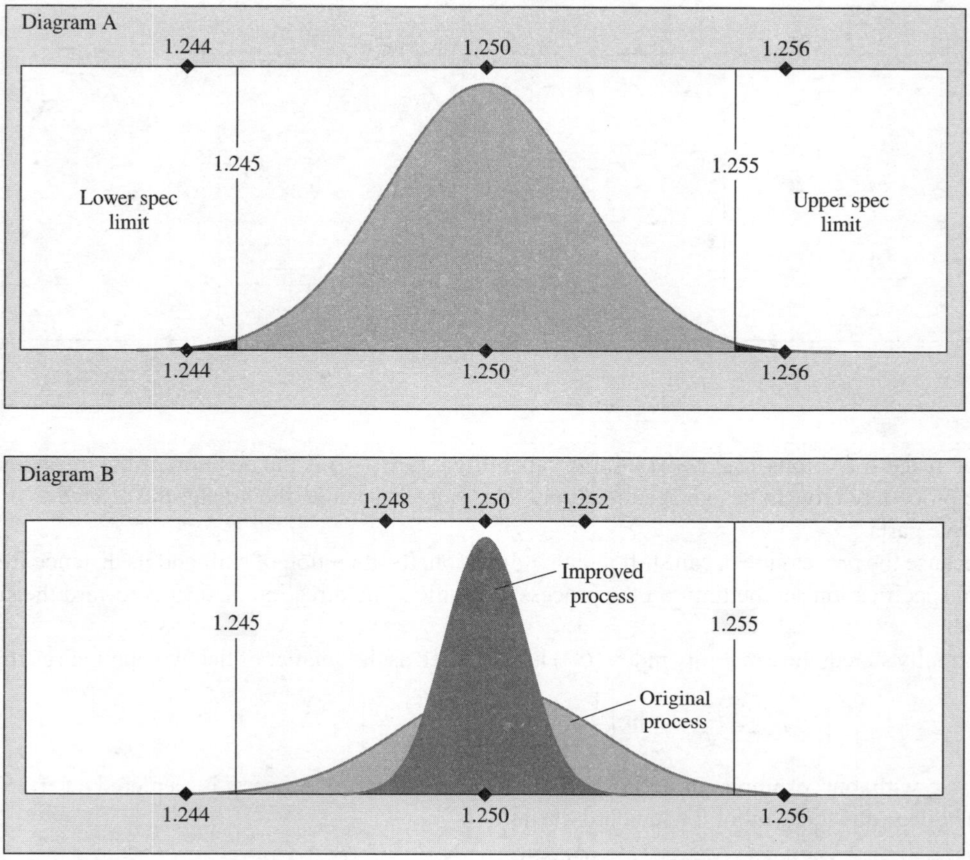

We say that a process is *capable* when the mean and standard deviation of the process are operating such that the upper and lower control limits are acceptable relative to the upper and lower specification limits. Consider diagram A in Exhibit 13.3. This represents the distribution of the bearing diameter dimension in our original process. The average or mean value is 1.250 and the lower and upper design specifications are 1.245 and 1.255, respectively. Process control limits are plus and minus three standard deviations (1.244 and 1.256). Notice that there is a probability (the red areas) of producing defective parts.

If the process can be improved by reducing the standard deviation associated with the bearing diameter, the probability of producing defective parts can be reduced. Diagram B in Exhibit 13.3 shows a new process where the standard deviation has been reduced to 0.00083 (the area outlined in yellow). Even though we cannot see it in the diagram, there is some probability that a defect could be produced by this new process, but that probability is very, very small.

Suppose that the central value or mean of the process shifts away from the mean. Exhibit 13.4 shows the mean shifted one standard deviation closer to the upper specification limit. This, of course, causes a slightly higher number of expected defects, but we can see that this is still very, very good. The *capability index* is used to measure how well our process is capable of producing relative to the design specifications. A description of how to calculate this index is in the next section.

Capability index
The ratio of the range of values allowed by the design specifications divided by the range of values produced by a process.

Capability Index (C_{pk}) The **capability index (C_{pk})** shows how well the parts being produced fit into the range specified by the design specification limits. If the specification limits are larger than the three sigma allowed in the process, then the mean of the process can be allowed to drift off-center before readjustment, and a high percentage of good parts will still be produced.

Exhibit 13.4

Process Capability with a Shift in the Process Mean

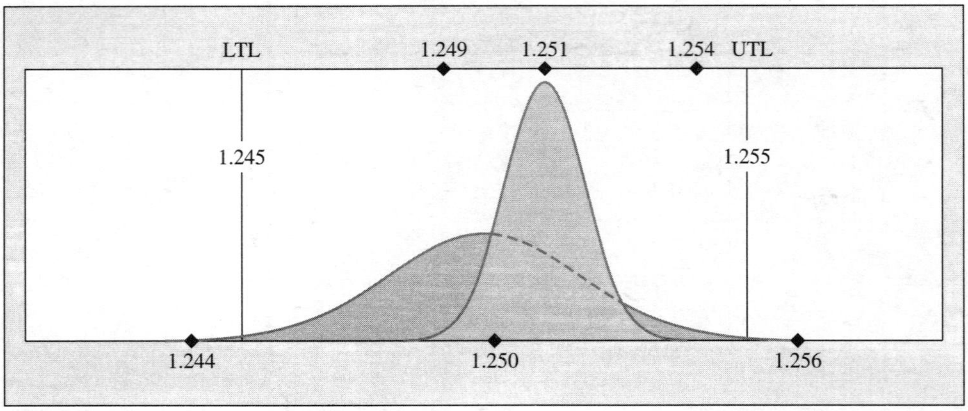

Referring to Exhibits 13.3 and 13.4, the capability index (C_{pk}) is the position of the mean and tails of the process relative to design specifications. The more off-center, the greater the chance to produce defective parts.

Because the process mean can shift in either direction, the direction of shift and its distance from the design specification set the limit on the process capability. The direction of shift is toward the smaller number.

Formally stated, the capability index (C_{pk}) is calculated as the smaller of the two numbers as follows:

Analytics

$$C_{pk} = \min\left[\frac{\bar{\bar{X}} - \text{LSL}}{3\sigma} \text{ or } \frac{\text{USL} - \bar{\bar{X}}}{3\sigma}\right] \quad [13.3]$$

Working with our example in Exhibit 13.4, let's assume our process is centered at 1.251 and $\sigma = 0.00083$ (σ is the symbol for standard deviation).

$$C_{pk} = \min\left[\frac{1.251 - 1.245}{3(.00083)} \text{ or } \frac{1.255 - 1.251}{3(.00083)}\right]$$

$$= \min\left[\frac{.006}{.00249} \text{ or } \frac{.004}{.00249}\right]$$

$$C_{pk} = \min[2.4 \text{ or } 1.6]$$

$C_{pk} = 1.6$, which is the smaller number. This is a pretty good capability index because few defects will be produced by this process.

This tells us that the process mean has shifted to the right, similar to that shown in Exhibit 13.4, but parts are still well within design specification limits.

At times, it is useful to calculate the actual probability of producing a defect. Assuming that the process is producing with a consistent standard deviation, this is a fairly straightforward calculation, particularly when we have access to a spreadsheet. The approach to use is to calculate the probability of producing a part outside the lower and upper design specification limits given the mean and standard deviation of the process.

Working with our example, where the process is not centered, with a mean of 1.251 inches, $\sigma = .00083$, LSL = 1.245, and USL = 1.255, we first need to calculate the Z score associated with the upper and lower specification limits. Recall from your study of statistics that the Z score is the standard deviation either to the right or to the left of zero in a probability distribution.

$$Z_{\text{LSL}} = \frac{\text{LSL} - \bar{\bar{X}}}{\sigma} \qquad Z_{\text{USL}} = \frac{\text{USL} - \bar{\bar{X}}}{\sigma}$$

For our example,

$$Z_{\text{LSL}} = \frac{1.245 - 1.251}{.00083} = -7.2289 \qquad Z_{\text{USL}} = \frac{1.255 - 1.251}{.00083} = 4.8193$$

An easy way to get the probabilities associated with these Z values is to use the NORMSDIST function built into Excel (you also can use the table in Appendix G). The format for this function is NORMSDIST(Z), where Z is the Z value calculated previously. Excel returns the following values. (We have found that you might get slightly different results from those given here, depending on the version of Excel you are using.)

$$\text{NORMSDIST}(-7.2289) = 2.43461\text{E-}13 \quad \text{and} \quad \text{NORMSDIST}(4.8193) = .99999928$$

Interpreting this information requires understanding exactly what the NORMSDIST function is providing. NORMSDIST is giving the cumulative probability to the left of the given Z value. Since $Z = -7.2289$ is the number of standard deviations associated with the lower specification limit, the fraction of parts that will be produced lower than this is 2.43461E-13. This number is in scientific notation and that E-13 at the end means we need to move the decimal over 13 places to get the real fraction defective. So the fraction defective is .00000000000024361, which is a very small number! Similarly, we see that approximately .99999928 of our parts will be below our upper specification limit. What we are really interested in is the fraction that will be above this limit because these are the defective parts. This fraction defective above the upper spec is 1 – .99999928 = .00000072 of our parts.

Adding these two fraction defective numbers together we get .00000072000024361. We can interpret this to mean that we expect only about .72 parts per million to be defective. Clearly, this is a great process. You will discover as you work the problems at the end of the chapter that this is not always the case.

EXAMPLE 13.1

The quality assurance manager is assessing the capability of a process that puts pressurized grease in an aerosol can. The design specifications call for an average of 60 pounds per square inch (psi) of pressure in each can with an upper specification limit of 65 psi and a lower specification limit of 55 psi. A sample is taken from production and it is found that the cans average 61 psi with a standard deviation of 2 psi. What is the capability of the process? What is the probability of producing a defect?

SOLUTION

Step 1—Interpret the data from the problem.

$$\text{LSL} = 55 \quad \text{USL} = 65 \quad \overline{\overline{X}} = 61 \quad \sigma = 2$$

Step 2—Calculate the C_{pk}.

$$C_{pk} = \min\left[\frac{\overline{\overline{X}} - \text{LSL}}{3\sigma}, \frac{\text{USL} - \overline{\overline{X}}}{3\sigma}\right]$$

$$C_{pk} = \min\left[\frac{61 - 55}{3(2)}, \frac{65 - 61}{3(2)}\right]$$

$$C_{pk} = \min[1, .6667] = .6667$$

This is not a very good capability index. We see why this is true in Step 3.

Step 3—Calculate the probability of producing a defective can:
Probability of a can with less than 55 psi

$$Z = \frac{X - \overline{\overline{X}}}{\sigma} = \frac{55 - 61}{2} = -3$$

$$\text{NORMSDIST}(-3) = 0.001349898$$

Probability of a can with more than 65 psi

$$Z = \frac{X - \bar{\bar{X}}}{\sigma} = \frac{65 - 61}{2} = 2$$

$$1 - \text{NORMSDIST}(2) = 1 - 0.977249868 = 0.022750132$$

Probability of a can less than 55 psi or more than 65 psi

$$\text{Probability} = 0.001349898 + 0.022750132 = .024100030$$

Or approximately 2.4 percent of the cans will be defective.

The following table is a quick reference for the fraction of defective units for various design specification limits (expressed in standard deviations). This table assumes that the standard deviation is constant and that the process is centered exactly between the design specification limits.

Design Limits	C_{pk}	Defective Parts	Fraction Defective
$\pm 1\sigma$	.333	317 per thousand	.3173
$\pm 2\sigma$	.667	45 per thousand	.0455
$\pm 3\sigma$	1.0	2.7 per thousand	.0027
$\pm 4\sigma$	1.333	63 per million	.000063
$\pm 5\sigma$	1.667	574 per billion	.000000574
$\pm 6\sigma$	2.0	2 per billion	.000000002

Motorola's design specification limit of Six Sigma with a shift of the process off the mean by 1.5σ ($C_{pk} = 1.5$) gives 3.4 defects per million. If the mean is exactly in the center ($C_{pk} = 2$), then 2 defects per *billion* are expected, as the table shows.

LO 13-2

Analyze process quality using statistics

STATISTICAL PROCESS CONTROL PROCEDURES

Statistical process control (SPC)
Techniques for testing a random sample of output from a process to determine whether the process is producing items within a prescribed range.

Attributes
Quality characteristics that are classified as either conforming or not conforming to specification.

Process control is concerned with monitoring quality *while the product or service is being produced.* Typical objectives of process control plans are to provide timely information about whether currently produced items are meeting design specifications and to detect shifts in the process that signal that future products may not meet specifications. **Statistical process control (SPC)** involves testing a random sample of output from a process to determine whether the process is producing items within a preselected range.

The examples given so far have all been based on quality characteristics (or *variables*) that are measurable, such as the diameter or weight of a part. **Attributes** are quality characteristics that are classified as either conforming or not conforming to specification. Goods or services may be observed to be either good or bad, or functioning or malfunctioning. For example, a lawnmower either runs or it doesn't; it attains a certain level of torque and horsepower or it doesn't. This type of measurement is known as sampling by attributes. Alternatively, a lawnmower's torque and horsepower can be measured as an amount of deviation from a set standard. This type of measurement is known as sampling by variables. The following section describes some standard approaches to controlling processes: first an approach useful for attribute measures and then an approach for variable measures. Both of these techniques result in the construction of control charts. Exhibit 13.5 shows some examples for how control charts can be analyzed to understand how a process is operating.

Process Control with Attribute Measurements: Using *p*-Charts

Measurement by attributes means taking samples and using a single decision—the item is good or it is bad. Because it is a yes or no decision, we can use simple statistics to create a *p*-chart with an upper process control limit (UCL) and a lower process control limit (LCL). We can draw these control limits on a graph and then plot the fraction defective of each individual sample tested. The process

EXHIBIT 13.5

Process Control Chart Evidence for Investigation

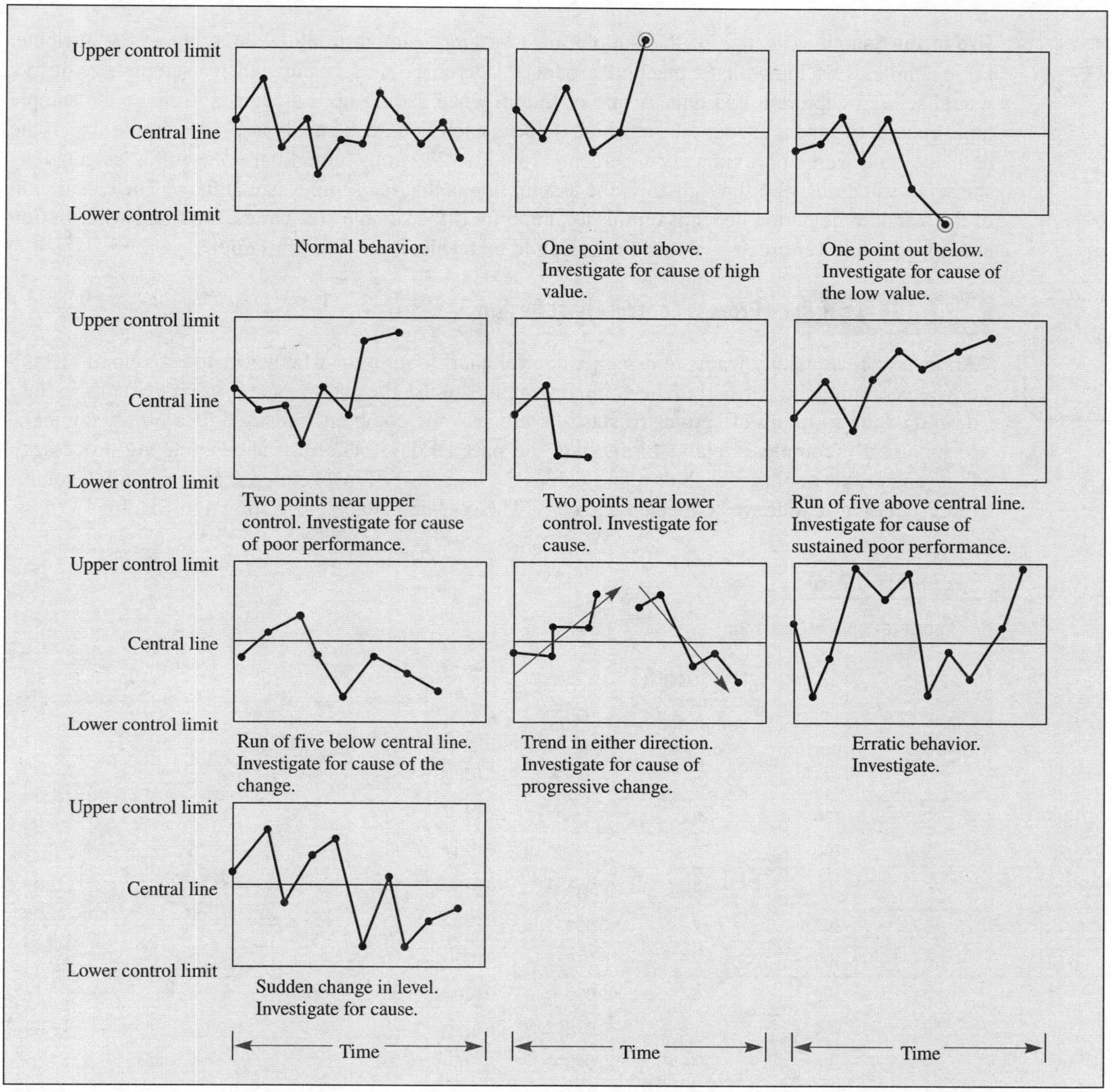

is assumed to be working correctly when the samples, which are taken periodically during the day, continue to stay between the control limits.

$$\bar{p} = \frac{\text{Total number of defective units from all samples}}{\text{Number of samples} \times \text{Sample size}} \qquad [13.4]$$

$$S_p = \frac{\sqrt{\bar{p}(1-\bar{p})}}{n} \qquad [13.5]$$

$$\text{UCL} = \bar{p} + zs_p \qquad [13.6]$$

$$\text{LCL} = \bar{p} - zs_p \text{ or 0 if less than 0} \qquad [13.7]$$

where $\bar{p}$ is the fraction defective, s_p is the standard deviation, n is the sample size, and z is the number of standard deviations for a specific confidence. Typically, $z = 3$ (99.7 percent confidence) or $z = 2.58$ (99 percent confidence) is used.

Size of the Sample The size of the sample must be large enough to allow counting of the attribute. For example, if we know that a machine produces 1 percent defective units, then a sample size of five would seldom capture a bad unit. A rule of thumb when setting up a p-chart is to make the sample large enough to expect to count the attribute twice in each sample. So an appropriate sample size, if the defective rate were approximately 1 percent, would be 200 units. One final note: In the calculations shown in equations 13.4 through 13.7, the assumption is that the sample size is fixed. The calculation of the standard deviation depends on this assumption. If the sample size varies, the standard deviation and upper and lower process control limits should be recalculated for each sample.

EXAMPLE 13.2 Process Control Chart Design

An insurance company wants to design a control chart to monitor whether insurance claim forms are being completed correctly. The company intends to use the chart to see if improvements in the design of the form are effective. To start the process, the company collected data on the number of incorrectly completed claim forms over the past 10 days. The insurance company processes thousands of these forms each day, and due to the high cost of inspecting each form, only a small representative sample was collected each day. The data and analysis are shown in Exhibit 13.6.

Exhibit 13.6

Insurance Company Claim Form

Sample	Number Inspected	Number of Forms Completed Incorrectly	Fraction Defective
1	300	10	0.03333
2	300	8	0.02667
3	300	9	0.03000
4	300	13	0.04333
5	300	7	0.02333
6	300	7	0.02333
7	300	6	0.02000
8	300	11	0.03667
9	300	12	0.04000
10	300	8	0.02667
Totals	3,000	91	0.03033
Sample standard deviation			0.00990

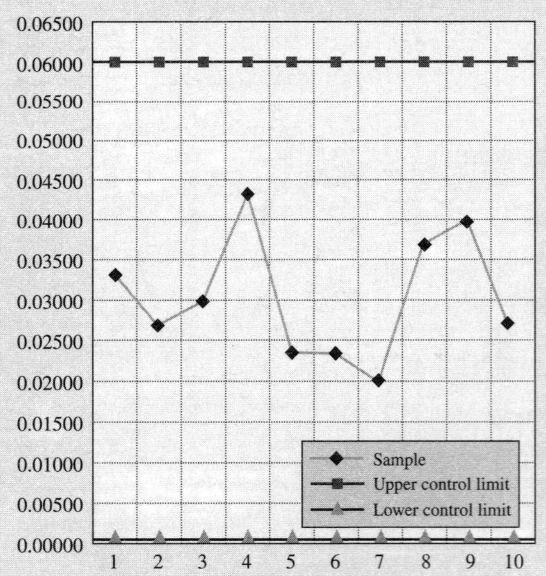

SOLUTION

To construct the control chart, first calculate the overall fraction defective from all samples. This sets the centerline for the control chart.

$$\bar{p} = \frac{\text{Total number of defective units from all samples}}{\text{Number of samples} \times \text{Sample size}} = \frac{91}{3,000} = .03033$$

Next, calculate the sample standard deviation:

$$s_p = \sqrt{\frac{\bar{p}(1-\bar{p})}{n}} = \sqrt{\frac{.03033(1-.03033)}{300}} = .00990$$

Finally, calculate the upper and lower process control limits. A *z*-value of 3 gives 99.7 percent confidence that the process is within these limits.

$$\text{UCL} = \bar{p} + 3s_p = .03033 + 3(.00990) = .06003$$
$$\text{LCL} = \bar{p} - 3s_p = .03033 - 3(.00990) = .00063$$

The calculations in Exhibit 13.6, including the control chart, are contained in the spreadsheet "SPC.xls."

Process Control with Attribute Measurements: Using *c*-Charts

In the case of the *p*-chart, the item was either good or bad. There are times when the product or service can have more than one defect. For example, a board sold at a lumberyard may have multiple knotholes and, depending on the quality grade, may or may not be defective. When it is desired to monitor the number of defects per unit, the *c*-chart is appropriate.

The underlying distribution for the *c*-chart is the Poisson, which is based on the assumption that defects occur randomly on each unit. If c is the number of defects for a particular unit, then $\bar{c}$ is the average number of defects per unit, and the standard deviation is $\sqrt{\bar{c}}$. For the purposes of our control chart, we use the normal approximation to the Poisson distribution and construct the chart using the following control limits.

$$\bar{c} = \text{Average number of defects per unit} \qquad [13.8]$$

$$s_c = \sqrt{\bar{c}} \qquad [13.9]$$

$$\text{UCL} = \bar{c} + z\sqrt{\bar{c}} \qquad [13.10]$$

$$\text{LCL} = \bar{c} - z\sqrt{\bar{c}} \text{ or 0 if less than 0} \qquad [13.11]$$

Just as with the *p*-chart, typically $z = 3$ (99.7 percent confidence) or $z = 2.58$ (99 percent confidence) is used.

EXAMPLE 13.3

The owners of a lumberyard want to design a control chart to monitor the quality of 2 × 4 boards that come from their supplier. For their medium-quality boards, they expect an average of four knotholes per 8-foot board. Design a control chart for use by the person receiving the boards using three-sigma (standard deviation) limits.

SOLUTION

For this problem, $\bar{c} = 4, s_c = \sqrt{\bar{c}} = 2$

$$\text{UCL} = \bar{c} + z\sqrt{\bar{c}} = 4 + 3(2) = 10$$

$$\text{LCL} = \bar{c} - z\sqrt{\bar{c}} = 4 - 3(2) = -2 \rightarrow 0$$ (Zero is used since it is not possible to have a negative number of defects.)

Process Control with Variable Measurements: Using $\overline{X}$- and R-Charts

$\overline{X}$- and R- (range) charts are widely used in statistical process control.

In attribute sampling, we determine whether something is good or bad, fits or doesn't fit—it is a go/no-go situation. In **variables** sampling, however, we measure the actual weight, volume, number of inches, or other variable measurements, and we develop control charts to determine the acceptability or rejection of the process based on those measurements. For example, in attribute sampling, we might decide that if something is over 10 pounds, we will reject it, and under 10 pounds, we will accept it. In variables sampling, we measure a sample and may record weights of 9.8 pounds or 10.2 pounds. These values are used to create or modify control charts and to see whether they fall within the acceptable limits.

Variables
Quality characteristics that are measured in actual weight, volume, inches, centimeters, or other measure.

Control check of production of liquid dosage form ampules

There are four main issues to address in creating a control chart: the size of the samples, number of samples, frequency of samples, and control limits.

Size of Samples For industrial applications in process control involving the measurement of variables, it is preferable to keep the sample size small. There are two main reasons. First, the sample needs to be taken within a reasonable length of time; otherwise, the process might change while the samples are taken. Second, the larger the sample, the more it costs to take.

Sample sizes of four or five units seem to be the preferred numbers. The *means* of samples of this size have an approximately normal distribution, no matter what the distribution of the parent population looks like. Sample sizes greater than five give narrower process control limits and thus more sensitivity. For detecting finer variations of a process, it may be necessary, in fact, to use larger sample sizes. However, when sample sizes exceed 15 or so, it would be better to use $\overline{X}$-charts with standard deviation σ rather than $\overline{X}$-charts with the range R, as we use in Example 13.3.

Number of Samples Once the chart has been set up, each sample taken can be compared to the chart and a decision can be made about whether the process is acceptable. To set up the charts, however, prudence and statistics suggest that 25 or so sample sets be analyzed.

Frequency of Samples How often to take a sample is a trade-off between the cost of sampling (along with the cost of the unit if it is destroyed as part of the test) and the benefit of adjusting the system. Usually, it is best to start off with frequent sampling of a process and taper off as confidence in the process builds. For example, one might start with a sample of five units every half hour and end up feeling that one sample per day is adequate.

Control Limits Standard practice in statistical process control for variables is to set control limits three standard deviations above the mean and three standard deviations below. This means that 99.7 percent of the sample means are expected to fall within these process control limits (that is, within a 99.7 percent confidence interval). Thus, if one sample mean falls outside this obviously wide band, we have strong evidence that the process is out of control.

How to Construct $\overline{X}$- and R-Charts

Analytics

If the standard deviation of the process distribution is known, the $\overline{X}$-chart may be defined:

$$\mathrm{UCL}_{\overline{X}} = \overline{\overline{X}} + zS_{\overline{X}} \quad \text{and} \quad \mathrm{LCL}_{\overline{X}} = \overline{\overline{X}} - zS_{\overline{X}} \tag{13.12}$$

where

$S_{\overline{X}} = s/\sqrt{n}$ = Standard deviation of sample means

s = Standard deviation of the process distribution

n = Sample size

$\overline{\overline{X}}$ = Average of sample means or a target value set for the process

z = Number of standard deviations for a specific confidence level (typically, $z = 3$)

An $\overline{X}$-chart is simply a plot of the means of the samples that were taken from a process. $\overline{\overline{X}}$ is the average of the means.

In practice, the actual standard deviation of the process is not known. For this reason, an approach that uses a substitute measure called the range is used. This practical approach is described in the following paragraphs.

An R-chart is a plot of the average of the range within each sample. The range is the difference between the highest and the lowest numbers in that sample. R values provide an easily calculated measure of variation used, like a standard deviation. $\overline{R}$ is the average of the range of each sample. More specifically defined, these are

$$\overline{X} = \frac{\sum_{i=1}^{n} x_i}{n} \qquad \text{[Same as 13.1]}$$

where

$\overline{X}$ = Mean of the sample

i = Item number

n = Total number of items in the sample

$$\overline{\overline{X}} = \frac{\sum_{j=1}^{m} \overline{X}_j}{m} \qquad [13.13]$$

where

$\overline{\overline{X}}$ = The average of the means of the samples

j = Sample number

m = Total number of samples

$$\overline{R} = \frac{\sum_{j=1}^{m} R_j}{m} \qquad [13.14]$$

where

R_j = Difference between the highest and lowest measurement in the sample

$\overline{R}$ = Average of the measurement differences R for all samples

The table in Exhibit 13.7 allows us to easily compute the upper and lower control limits for both the $\overline{X}$-chart and the R-chart. These are defined as

$$\text{Upper control limit for } \overline{X} = \overline{\overline{X}} + A_2\overline{R} \qquad [13.15]$$

$$\text{Lower control limit for } \overline{X} = \overline{\overline{X}} - A_2\overline{R} \qquad [13.16]$$

$$\text{Upper control limit for } R = D_4\overline{R} \qquad [13.17]$$

$$\text{Lower control limit for } R = D_3\overline{R} \qquad [13.18]$$

EXHIBIT 13.7

Factor for Determining from $\overline{R}$ the Three-Sigma Control Limits for $\overline{X}$- and R-Charts

Number of Observations in each sample n	Factor for $\overline{X}$-Chart A_2	Factors for R-Chart: Lower Control Limit D_3	Factors for R-Chart: Upper Control Limit D_4
2	1.88	0	3.27
3	1.02	0	2.57
4	0.73	0	2.28
5	0.58	0	2.11
6	0.48	0	2.00
7	0.42	0.08	1.92
8	0.37	0.14	1.86
9	0.34	0.18	1.82
10	0.31	0.22	1.78
11	0.29	0.26	1.74
12	0.27	0.28	1.72
13	0.25	0.31	1.69
14	0.24	0.33	1.67
15	0.22	0.35	1.65
16	0.21	0.36	1.64
17	0.20	0.38	1.62
18	0.19	0.39	1.61
19	0.19	0.40	1.60
20	0.18	0.41	1.59

Upper control limit for $\overline{X} = UCL_{\overline{X}} = \overline{\overline{X}} + A_2\overline{R}$

Lower control limit for $\overline{X} = LCL_{\overline{X}} = \overline{\overline{X}} - A_2\overline{R}$

Upper control limit for $R = UCL_R = D_4\overline{R}$

Lower control limit for $R = LCL_R = D_3\overline{R}$

Note: All factors are based on the normal distribution.

EXAMPLE 13.4 $\overline{X}$- and R-Charts

We would like to create $\overline{X}$- and R-charts for a process. Exhibit 13.8 shows measurements for all 25 samples. The last two columns show the average of the sample $\overline{X}$, and the range, R.

Values for A_2, D_3, and D_4 were obtained from Exhibit 13.7.

$$\text{Upper control limit for } \overline{X} = \overline{\overline{X}} + A_2\overline{R} = 10.21 + .58(.60) = 10.56$$

$$\text{Lower control limit for } \overline{X} = \overline{\overline{X}} - A_2\overline{R} = 10.21 - .58(.60) = 9.86$$

$$\text{Upper control limit for } R = D_4\overline{R} = 2.11(.60) = 1.27$$

$$\text{Lower control limit for } R = D_3\overline{R} = 0(.60) = 0$$

SOLUTION

Exhibit 13.9 shows the $\overline{X}$-chart and R-chart with a plot of all the sample means and ranges of the samples. All the points are well within the control limits, although sample 23 is close to the $\overline{X}$ lower control limit and samples 13 through 17 are above the target.

Analytics

EXHIBIT 13.8

Measurements in Samples of Five from a Process

Sample Number	Each Unit in Sample					Average $\overline{X}$	Range R
1	10.60	10.40	10.30	9.90	10.20	10.28	.70
2	9.98	10.25	10.05	10.23	10.33	10.17	.35
3	9.85	9.90	10.20	10.25	10.15	10.07	.40
4	10.20	10.10	10.30	9.90	9.95	10.09	.40
5	10.30	10.20	10.24	10.50	10.30	10.31	.30
6	10.10	10.30	10.20	10.30	9.90	10.16	.40
7	9.98	9.90	10.20	10.40	10.10	10.12	.50
8	10.10	10.30	10.40	10.24	10.30	10.27	.30
9	10.30	10.20	10.60	10.50	10.10	10.34	.50
10	10.30	10.40	10.50	10.10	10.20	10.30	.40
11	9.90	9.50	10.20	10.30	10.35	10.05	.85
12	10.10	10.36	10.50	9.80	9.95	10.14	.70
13	10.20	10.50	10.70	10.10	9.90	10.28	.80
14	10.20	10.60	10.50	10.30	10.40	10.40	.40
15	10.54	10.30	10.40	10.55	10.00	10.36	.55
16	10.20	10.60	10.15	10.00	10.50	10.29	.60
17	10.20	10.40	10.60	10.80	10.10	10.42	.70
18	9.90	9.50	9.90	10.50	10.00	9.96	1.00
19	10.60	10.30	10.50	9.90	9.80	10.22	.80
20	10.60	10.40	10.30	10.40	10.20	10.38	.40
21	9.90	9.60	10.50	10.10	10.60	10.14	1.00
22	9.95	10.20	10.50	10.30	10.20	10.23	.55
23	10.20	9.50	9.60	9.80	10.30	9.88	.80
24	10.30	10.60	10.30	9.90	9.80	10.18	.80
25	9.90	10.30	10.60	9.90	10.10	10.16	.70
						$\overline{\overline{X}}=10.21$	$\overline{R}=.60$

EXHIBIT 13.9

$\overline{X}$-Chart and R-Chart

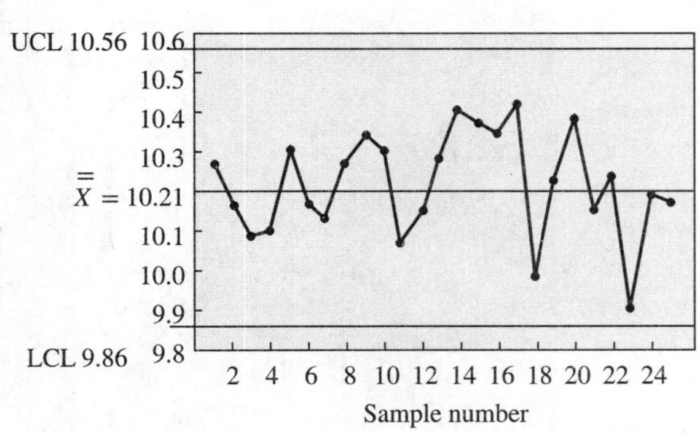

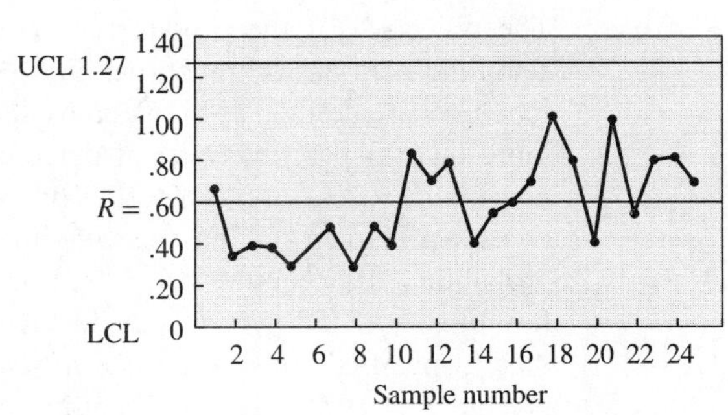

LO 13-3

Analyze the quality of batches of items using statistics

ACCEPTANCE SAMPLING

Design of a Single Sampling Plan for Attributes

Acceptance sampling is performed on goods that already exist to determine what percentage of products conform to specifications. These products may be items received from another company and evaluated by the receiving department, or they may be components that have passed through a processing step and are evaluated by company personnel either in production or later in the warehousing function. Whether inspection should be done at all is addressed in the following example.

Acceptance sampling is executed through a sampling plan. In this section, we illustrate the planning procedures for a single sampling plan—that is, a plan in which the quality is determined from the evaluation of one sample. (Other plans may be developed using two or more samples. See comprehensive books focused on Quality Control for a discussion of these plans.)

EXAMPLE 13.5 Costs to Justify Inspection

Total (100 percent) inspection is justified when the cost of a loss incurred by not inspecting is greater than the cost of inspection. For example, suppose a faulty item results in a $10 loss and the average percentage of defective items in the lot is 3 percent.

SOLUTION

If the average percentage of defective items in a lot is 3 percent, the expected cost of faulty items is $0.03 \times \$10$, or $0.30 each. Therefore, if the cost of inspecting each item is less than $0.30, the economic decision is to perform 100 percent inspection. Not all defective items will be removed, however, because inspectors will pass some bad items and reject some good ones.

Analytics

The purpose of a sampling plan is to test the lot to either (1) find its quality or (2) ensure that the quality is what it is supposed to be. Thus, if a quality control supervisor already knows the quality (such as the 0.03 given in the example), he or she does not sample for defects. Either all of them must be inspected to remove the defects or none of them should be inspected, and the rejects pass into the process. The choice simply depends on the cost to inspect and the cost incurred by passing a reject.

A single sampling plan is defined by n and c, where n is the number of units in the sample and c is the acceptance number. The size of n may vary from one up to all the items in the lot (usually denoted as N) from which it is drawn. The acceptance number c denotes the maximum number of defective items that can be found in the sample before the lot is rejected. Values for n and c are determined by the interaction of four factors (AQL, α, LTPD, and β) that quantify the objectives of the product's producer and its consumer. The objective of the producer is to ensure that the sampling plan has a low probability of rejecting good lots. Lots are defined as high quality if they contain no more than a specified level of defectives, termed the *acceptable quality level (AQL)*.The objective of the consumer is to ensure that the sampling plan has a low probability of accepting bad lots. Lots are defined as low quality if the percentage of defectives is greater than a specified amount, termed *lot tolerance percent defective (LTPD)*. The probability associated with rejecting a high-quality lot is denoted by the Greek letter alpha (α) and is termed the *producer's risk*. The

© Thinkstock/Corbis RF

probability associated with accepting a low-quality lot is denoted by the letter beta (β) and is termed the *consumer's risk.* The selection of particular values for AQL, α, LTPD, and β is an economic decision based on a cost trade-off or, more typically, on company policy or contractual requirements.

There is a humorous story supposedly about Hewlett-Packard during its first dealings with Japanese vendors, who place great emphasis on high-quality production. HP had insisted on 2 percent AQL in a purchase of 100 cables. During the purchase negotiations, some heated discussion took place wherein the Japanese vendor did not want this AQL specification; HP insisted that it would not budge from the 2 percent AQL. The Japanese vendor finally agreed. Later, when the box arrived, there were two packages inside. One contained 100 good cables. The other package had 2 cables with a note stating: "We have sent you 100 good cables. Since you insisted on 2 percent AQL, we have enclosed 2 defective cables in this package, though we do not understand why you want them."

The following example, using an excerpt from a standard acceptance sampling table, illustrates how the four parameters—AQL, α, LTPD, and β—are used in developing a sampling plan.

EXAMPLE 13.6 Values of *n* and *c*

Hi-Tech Industries manufactures Z-Band radar scanners used to detect speed traps. The printed circuit boards in the scanners are purchased from an outside vendor. The vendor produces the boards to an AQL of 2 percent defectives and is willing to run a 5 percent risk (α) of having lots of this level or fewer defectives rejected. Hi-Tech considers lots of 8 percent or more defectives (LTPD) unacceptable and wants to ensure that it will accept such poor quality lots no more than 10 percent of the time (β). A large shipment has just been delivered. What values of n and c should be selected to determine the quality of this lot?

SOLUTION

The parameters of the problem are AQL = 0.02, α = 0.05, LTPD = 0.08, and β = 0.10. We can use Exhibit 13.10 to find c and n. First, divide LTPD by AQL (0.08/0.02 = 4). Then, find the ratio in column 2 that is equal to or just greater than that amount (4). This value is 4.057, which is associated with $c = 4$. Finally, find the value in column 3 that is in the same row as $c = 4$, and divide that quantity by AQL to obtain n (1.970/0.02 = 98.5). The appropriate sampling plan is $c = 4$, $n = 99$. Ninety-nine scanners will be inspected and if more than four defective units are found, the lot will be rejected.

Analytics

EXHIBIT 13.10

Excerpt from a Sampling Plan Table for $\alpha = 0.05, \beta = 0.10$

c	LTPD/AQL	$n \times$ AQL
0	44.890	0.052
1	10.946	0.355
2	6.509	0.818
3	4.890	1.366
4	4.057	1.970
5	3.549	2.613
6	3.206	3.286
7	2.957	3.981
8	2.768	4.695
9	2.618	5.426

Operating Characteristic Curves

While a sampling plan such as the one just described meets our requirements for the extreme values of good and bad quality, we cannot readily determine how well the plan discriminates between good and bad lots at intermediate values. For this reason, sampling plans are generally displayed graphically through the use of operating characteristic (OC) curves. These curves, which are unique for each combination of n and c, simply illustrate the probability of accepting lots with varying percentages of defectives. The procedure we have followed in developing the plan, in fact, specifies two points on an OC curve: one point defined by AQL and $1 - \alpha$ and the other point defined by LTPD and β. Curves for common values of n and c can be computed or obtained from tables available in more advanced Quality Control books.

Shaping the OC Curve A sampling plan discriminating perfectly between good and bad lots has an infinite slope (vertical) at the selected value of AQL. In Exhibit 13.11, any percentage defective to the left of 2 percent would always be accepted, and those to the right, always rejected. However, such a curve is possible only with complete inspections of all units, and thus is not a possibility with a true sampling plan.

Exhibit 13.11

Operating Characteristic Curve for AQL = 0.02, $\alpha = 0.05$, LTPD = 0.08, $\beta = 0.10$

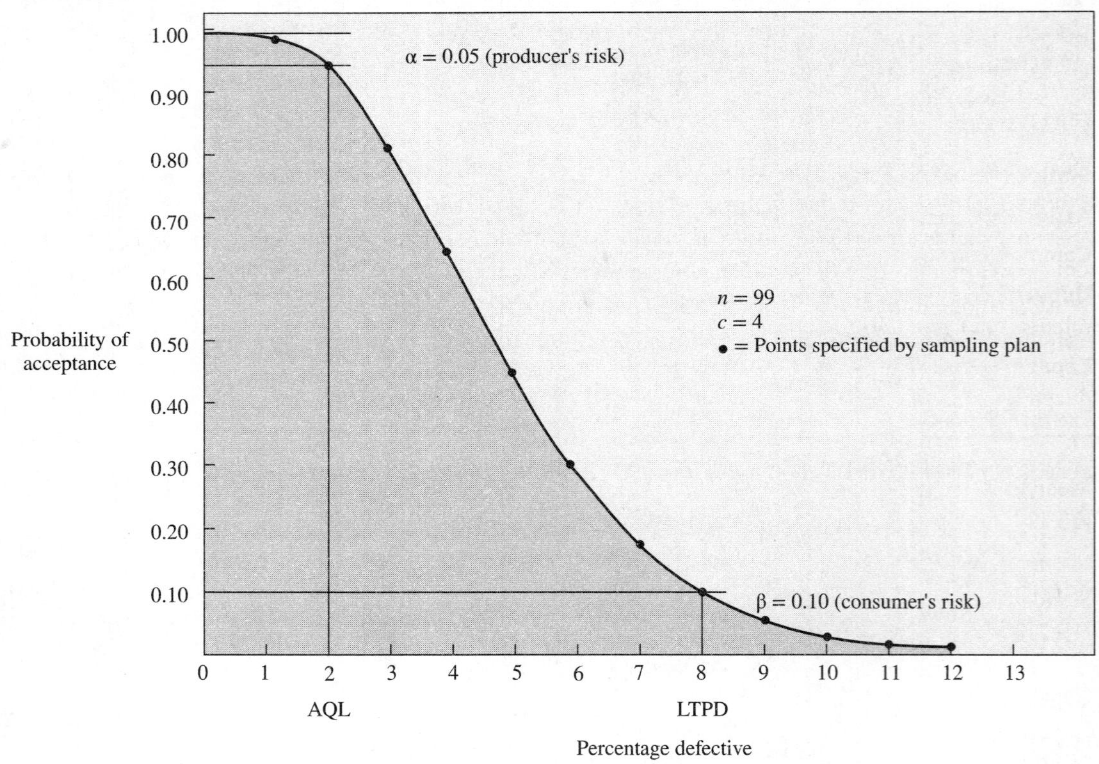

An OC curve should be steep in the region of most interest (between the AQL and the LTPD), which is accomplished by varying n and c. If c remains constant, increasing the sample size n causes the OC curve to be more vertical. While holding n constant, decreasing c (the maximum number of defective units) also makes the slope more vertical, moving closer to the origin.

The Effects of Lot Size The size of the lot that the sample is taken from has relatively little effect on the quality of protection. Consider, for example, that samples—all of the same size of 20 units—are taken from different lots ranging from a lot size of 200 units to a lot size of infinity. If each lot is known to have 5 percent defectives, the probability of accepting the lot based on the sample of 20 units ranges from about 0.34 to about 0.36. This means that as long as the lot size is several times the sample size, it makes little difference how large the lot is. It seems a bit difficult to accept, but statistically (on the average in the long run) whether we have a carload or box full, we'll get about the same answer. It just seems that a carload should have a larger sample size. Of course, this assumes that the lot is randomly chosen and that defects are randomly spread through the lot.

CONCEPT CONNECTIONS

LO 13–1 Illustrate process variation and explain how to measure it

Summary

- This chapter covers the quantitative aspect of quality management.
- Variation is inherent in all processes and can be caused by many factors. Variation caused by identifiable factors is called assignable variation and can possibly be managed. Variation inherent in a process is called common or random variation.
- Statistical quality control (SQC) involves sampling output from a process and using statistics to find when the process has changed in a nonrandom way.
- When a product or service is designed, specification limits are assigned relative to critical parameters. The process is designed to work so that the probability of output being outside these limits is relatively low.
- The capability index of a process measures its ability to consistently produce within the specification limits.

Key Terms

Statistical quality control (SQC) A number of different techniques designed to evaluate quality from a conformance view.

Assignable variation Deviation in the output of a process that can be clearly identified and managed.

Common variation Deviation in the output of a process that is random and inherent in the process itself.

Upper and lower specification limits The range of values in a measure associated with a process that is allowable given the intended use of the product or service.

Capability index The ratio of the range of values allowed by the design specifications divided by the range of values produced by a process.

Key Formulas

Mean or average
[13.1]
$$\overline{X} = \frac{\sum_{i=1}^{n} x_i}{n}$$

Standard deviation
[13.2]
$$\sigma = \frac{\sqrt{\sum_{i=1}^{n}(x_i - \overline{X})^2}}{n}$$

Capability index
[13.3]
$$C_{pk} = \min\left[\frac{\overline{\overline{X}} - \text{LSL}}{3\sigma}, \frac{\text{USL} - \overline{\overline{X}}}{3\sigma}\right]$$

LO 13–2 Analyze process quality using statistics

Summary

- Statistical process control involves monitoring the quality of a process as it is operating.
- Control charts are used to visually monitor the status of a process over time.
- Attributes are characteristics that can be evaluated as either conforming or not conforming to the design specifications. Control charts useful for attribute characteristics are the *p*-chart and the *c*-chart.
- When the characteristic is measured as a variable measure—for example, weight or diameter—$\overline{X}$ and *R*-charts are used.

Key Terms

Statistical process control (SPC) Techniques for testing a random sample of output from a process to determine whether the process is producing items within a prescribed range.

Attributes Quality characteristics that are classified as either conforming or not conforming to specification.

Variables Quality characteristics that are measured in actual weight, volume, inches, centimeters, or other measure.

Key Formulae

Process control charts using attribute measurements

[13.4] $$\bar{p} = \frac{\text{Total number of defective units from all samples}}{\text{Number of samples} \times \text{Sample size}}$$

[13.5] $$s_p = \sqrt{\frac{\bar{p}(1-\bar{p})}{n}}$$

[13.6] $$\text{UCL} = \bar{p} + zs_p$$

[13.7] $$\text{LCL} = \bar{p} + zs_p \text{ or 0 if less than 0}$$

[13.8] $$\bar{c} = \text{Average number of defects per unit}$$

[13.9] $$s_c = \sqrt{\bar{c}}$$

[13.10] $$\text{UCL} = \bar{c} + z\sqrt{\bar{c}}$$

[13.11] $$\text{LCL} = \bar{c} - z\sqrt{\bar{c}} \text{ or 0 if less than 0}$$

Process control $\bar{X}$ and R-charts

[13.12] $$\text{UCL}_{\bar{X}} = \bar{\bar{X}} + zS_{\bar{X}} \quad \text{and} \quad \text{LCL}_{\bar{X}} = \bar{\bar{X}} - zS_{\bar{X}}$$

[13.13] $$\bar{\bar{X}} = \frac{\sum_{j=1}^{m} \bar{X}_j}{m}$$

[13.14] $$\bar{R} = \frac{\sum_{j=1}^{m} R_j}{m}$$

[13.15] Upper control limit for $\bar{X} = \bar{\bar{X}} + A_2\bar{R}$

[13.16] Lower control limit for $\bar{X} = \bar{\bar{X}} - A_2\bar{R}$

[13.17] Upper control limit for $R = D_4\bar{R}$

[13.18] Lower control limit for $R = D_3\bar{R}$

LO 13–3 Analyze the quality of batches of items using statistics

Summary

- Acceptance sampling is used to evaluate if a batch of parts—as received in an order, for example—conforms to specification limits. This is useful in the area where material is received from suppliers.
- An acceptance sampling plan is defined by a sample size and the number of acceptable defects in the sample.
- Since the sampling plan is defined using statistics, there is the possibility that a bad lot will be accepted, which is the consumer's risk, and that a good lot will be rejected, which is the producer's risk.

SOLVED PROBLEMS

LO 13-1 SOLVED PROBLEM 1

HVAC Manufacturing produces parts and materials for the heating, ventilation, and air conditioning industry. One of its facilities produces metal ductwork in various sizes for the home construction market. One particular product is 6-inch diameter round metal ducting. It is a simple product, but the diameter of the finished ducting is critical. If it is too small or large, contractors will have difficulty fitting the ducting into other parts of the system. The target diameter is 6 inches exactly, with an acceptable tolerance of $\pm.03$ inches. Anything produced outside of specifications is considered defective. The line supervisor for this product has data showing that the actual diameter of finished product is 5.99 inches with a standard deviation of .01 inches.

a. What is the current capability index of this process? What is the probability of producing a defective unit in this process?

b. The line supervisor thinks he will be able to adjust the process so that the mean diameter of output is the same as the target diameter, without any change in the process variation. What would the capability index be if he is successful? What would be the probability of producing a defective unit in this adjusted process?

c. Through better training of employees and investment in equipment upgrades, the company could produce output with a mean diameter equal to the target and a standard deviation of .005 inches. What would the capability index be if this were to happen? What would be the probability of producing a defective unit in this case?

SOLUTION

a. $\overline{\overline{X}} = 5.99 \quad \text{LSL} = 6.00 - .03 = 5.97 \quad \text{USL} = 6.00 + .03 = 6.03 \quad \sigma = .01$

$$C_{pk} = \min\left[\frac{5.99-5.97}{.03} \quad or \quad \frac{6.03-5.99}{.03}\right] = \min[.667 \ or \ 1.333] = 0.667$$

This process is not what would be considered capable. The capability index is based on the LSL, showing that the process mean is lower than the target.

To find the probability of a defective unit, we need to find the *Z*-scores of the LCL and USL with respect to the current process:

$$Z_{\text{LSL}} = \frac{\text{LSL}-\overline{\overline{X}}}{\sigma} = \frac{5.97-5.99}{.01} = -2.00 \quad \text{NORMSDIST}(-2.00) = .02275$$

2.275 percent of output will be too small.

$$Z_{\text{USL}} = \frac{\text{USL}-\overline{\overline{X}}}{\sigma} = \frac{6.03-5.99}{.01} = 4.00 \quad \text{NORMSDIST}(4.00) = .999968$$

The probability of too large a unit is 1 – .999968 = .000032, so .0032 percent of output will be too small.

The probability of producing a defective unit is .02275 + .000032 = .022782, so 2.2782 percent of output will be defective. As a numerical example, 22,782 out of every million units will be defective.

b. $\overline{\overline{X}} = 6.00 \quad \text{LSL} = 6.00 - .03 = 5.97 \quad \text{USL} = 6.00 + .03 = 6.03 \quad \sigma = .01$

$$C_{pk} = \min\left[\frac{6.00-5.97}{.03} \quad or \quad \frac{6.03-6.00}{.03}\right] = \min[1.00 \ or \ 1.00] = 1.00$$

$$Z_{\text{LSL}} = \frac{\text{LSL}-\overline{\overline{X}}}{\sigma} = \frac{5.97-6.00}{.01} = -3.00 \quad \text{NORMSDIST}(-3.00) = .00135$$

Only 0.135 percent of output will be too small.

$$Z_{\text{USL}} = \frac{\text{USL} - \overline{\overline{X}}}{\sigma} = \frac{6.03 - 6.00}{.01} = 3.00 \quad \text{NORMSDIST}(3.00) = .99865$$

The probability of too large a unit is 1 – .99865 = .00135, so 0.135 percent of output will be too large.

The probability of producing a defective unit is .00135 + .00135 = .0027, so 0.27 percent of output will be defective. As a numerical example, 2,700 out of every million units will be defective. That's about a 90 percent reduction in defective output just from adjusting the process mean!

Because the process is exactly centered on the target and the specification limits are three standard deviations away from the process mean, this adjusted process has a C_{pk} = 1.00. In order to do any better than that, we would need to reduce the variation in the process, as shown in part (*c*).

c. $\overline{\overline{X}} = 6.00 \quad \text{LSL} = 6.00 - .03 = 5.97 \quad \text{USL} = 6.00 + .03 = 6.03 \quad \sigma = .005$

$$C_{pk} = \min\left[\frac{6.00 - 5.97}{.015} \quad or \quad \frac{6.03 - 6.00}{.015}\right] = \min\,[2.00 \ or \ 2.00] = 2.00$$

We have doubled the process capability index by cutting the standard deviation of the process in half. What will be the effect on the probability of defective output?

$$Z_{\text{LSL}} = \frac{\text{LSL} - \overline{\overline{X}}}{\sigma} = \frac{5.97 - 6.00}{.005} = -6.00 \quad \text{NORMSDIST}(-6.00) = 0.0000000009866$$

$$Z_{\text{USL}} = \frac{\text{USL} - \overline{\overline{X}}}{\sigma} = \frac{6.03 - 6.00}{.005} = 6.00 \quad \text{NORMSDIST}(6.00) = 0.9999999990134$$

Following earlier logic, the probability of producing a defective unit in this case is just 0.000000001973, a very small probability indeed! Using the earlier numerical example, this would result in only .001973 defective units out of every million. By cutting the process standard deviation in half, we could gain far more than a 50 percent reduction in defective output—in this case, essentially eliminating defective units due to the diameter of the ducting. This example demonstrates the power and importance of Six Sigma quality concepts.

LO 13-2 SOLVED PROBLEM 2

Completed forms from a particular department of an insurance company were sampled daily to check the performance quality of that department. To establish a tentative norm for the department, one sample of 100 units was collected each day for 15 days, with these results:

Sample	Sample Size	Number of Forms with Errors	Sample	Sample Size	Number of Forms with Errors
1	100	4	9	100	4
2	100	3	10	100	2
3	100	5	11	100	7
4	100	0	12	100	2
5	100	2	13	100	1
6	100	8	14	100	3
7	100	1	15	100	1
8	100	3			

a. Develop a *p*-chart using a 95 percent confidence interval (z = 1.96).
b. Plot the 15 samples collected.
c. What comments can you make about the process?

Solution

a. $\bar{p} = \dfrac{46}{15(100)} = .0307$

$$s_p = \sqrt{\frac{\bar{p}(1-\bar{p})}{n}} = \sqrt{\frac{.0307(1-.0307)}{100}} = \sqrt{.0003} = .017$$

$$\text{UCL} = \bar{p} + 1.96s_p = .031 + 1.96(.017) = .064$$

$$\text{LCL} = \bar{p} - 1.96s_p = .031 - 1.96(.017) = -.00232 \text{ or zero}$$

b. The defectives are plotted as follows.

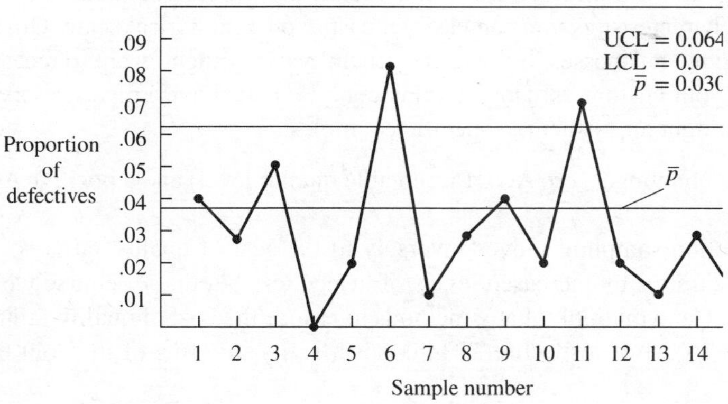

c. Of the 15 samples, 2 were out of the control limits. Because the control limits were established as 95 percent, or 1 out of 20, we would say that the process is out of control. It needs to be examined to find the cause of such widespread variation.

LO 13–3 SOLVED PROBLEM 3

Management is trying to decide whether Part A, which is produced with a consistent 3 percent defective rate, should be inspected. If it is not inspected, the 3 percent defectives will go through a product assembly phase and have to be replaced later. If all Part A's are inspected, one-third of the defectives will be found, thus raising the quality to 2 percent defectives.

a. Should the inspection be done if the cost of inspecting is \$0.01 per unit and the cost of replacing a defective in the final assembly is \$4.00?

b. Suppose the cost of inspecting is \$0.05 per unit rather than \$0.01. Would this change your answer in (*a*)?

Solution

Should Part A be inspected?

.03 defective with no inspection.

.02 defective with inspection.

a. This problem can be solved simply by looking at the opportunity for 1 percent improvement.
Benefit = .01(\$4.00) = \$0.04
Cost of inspection = \$0.01
Therefore, inspect and save \$0.03 per unit.

b. A cost of \$0.05 per unit to inspect would be \$0.01 greater than the savings, so inspection should not be performed.

DISCUSSION QUESTIONS

LO 13–1

1. The capability index allows for some drifting of the process mean. Discuss what this means in terms of product quality output.
2. In an agreement between a supplier and a customer, the supplier must ensure that all parts are within specification before shipment to the customer. What is the effect on the cost of quality to the customer?
3. In the situation described in question 2, what would be the effect on the cost of quality to the supplier?

LO 13–2

4. Discuss the purposes of and differences between *p*-charts and $\overline{X}$ and *R*-charts.
5. The application of control charts is straightforward in manufacturing processes when you have tangible goods with physical characteristics you can easily measure on a numerical scale. Quality control is also important in service businesses, but you are generally not going to want to measure the physical characteristics of your customers! Do you think control charts have a place in service businesses? Discuss how you might apply them to specific examples.

LO 13–3

6. Discuss the trade-off between achieving a zero AQL (acceptable quality level) and a positive AQL (such as an AQL of 2 percent).
7. The cost of performing inspection sampling moves inversely to the cost of quality failures. We can reduce the cost of quality failures by increased levels of inspection, but that of course would increase the cost of inspection. Can you think of any methods to reduce the cost of quality failures without increasing a company's cost of inspection? Think specifically in terms of material purchased from vendors.

OBJECTIVE QUESTIONS

LO 13–1

1. A company currently using an inspection process in its material receiving department is trying to install an overall cost reduction program. One possible reduction is the elimination of one inspection position. This position tests material that has a defective content on the average of 0.04. By inspecting all items, the inspector is able to remove all defects. The inspector can inspect 50 units per hour. The hourly rate including fringe benefits for this position is $9. If the inspection position is eliminated, defects will go into product assembly and will have to be replaced later at a cost of $10 each when they are detected in final product testing. (Answer in Appendix D)
   a. Should this inspection position be eliminated?
   b. What is the cost to inspect each unit?
   c. Is there benefit (or loss) from the current inspection process? How much?
2. A metal fabricator produces connecting rods with an outer diameter that has a $1 \pm .01$–inch specification. A machine operator takes several sample measurements over time and determines the sample mean outer diameter to be 1.002 inches with a standard deviation of .003 inch.
   a. Calculate the process capability index for this example.
   b. What does this figure tell you about the process?
3. Output from a process contains 0.02 defective unit. Defective units that go undetected into final assemblies cost $25 each to replace. An inspection process, which would detect and remove all defectives, can be established to test these units. However, the inspector, who can test 20 units per hour, is paid $8 per hour, including fringe benefits. Should an inspection station be established to test all units?
   a. What is the cost to inspect each unit?
   b. What is the benefit (or loss) from the inspection process?

4. There is a 3 percent error rate at a specific point in a production process. If an inspector is placed at this point, all the errors can be detected and eliminated. However, the inspector is paid \$8 per hour and can inspect units in the process at the rate of 30 per hour.

   If no inspector is used and defects are allowed to pass this point, there is a cost of \$10 per unit to correct the defect later on.

   Should an inspector be hired?
5. Design specifications require that a key dimension on a product measure 100 ± 10 units. A process being considered for producing this product has a standard deviation of four units.
   a. What can you say (quantitatively) regarding the process capability?
   b. Suppose the process average shifts to 92. Calculate the new process capability.
   c. What can you say about the process after the shift? Approximately what percentage of the items produced will be defective?
6. C-Spec, Inc., is attempting to determine whether an existing machine is capable of milling an engine part that has a key specification of $4 \pm .003$ inches. After a trial run on this machine, C-Spec has determined that the machine has a sample mean of 4.001 inches with a standard deviation of .002 inch. (Answer in Appendix D)
   a. Calculate the C_{pk} for this machine.
   b. Should C-Spec use this machine to produce this part? Why?
7. Ten samples of 15 parts each were taken from an ongoing process to establish a *p*-chart for control. The samples and the number of defectives in each are shown in the following table. **LO 13–2**

Sample	*n*	Number of Defective Items in the Sample
1	15	3
2	15	1
3	15	0
4	15	0
5	15	0
6	15	2
7	15	0
8	15	3
9	15	1
10	15	0

   a. Develop a *p*-chart for 95 percent confidence (1.96 standard deviation).
   b. Based on the plotted data points, what comments can you make?
8. A shirt manufacturer buys cloth by the 100-yard roll from a supplier. For setting up a control chart to manage the irregularities (e.g., loose threads and tears), the following data were collected from a sample provided by the supplier.

Sample	1	2	3	4	5	6	7	8	9	10
Irregularities	3	5	2	6	5	4	6	3	4	5

   a. Using these data, set up a *c*-chart with $z = 2$.
   b. Suppose the next five rolls from the supplier had three, two, five, three, and seven irregularities. Is the supplier process under control?
9. Resistors for electronic circuits are manufactured on a high-speed automated machine. The machine is set up to produce a large run of resistors of 1,000 ohms each.

   To set up the machine and to create a control chart to be used throughout the run, 15 samples were taken with four resistors in each sample. The complete list of samples and their measured values are as follows.

Sample Number	Readings (in ohms)			
1	1010	991	985	986
2	995	996	1009	994
3	990	1003	1015	1008
4	1015	1020	1009	998
5	1013	1019	1005	993
6	994	1001	994	1005
7	989	992	982	1020
8	1001	986	996	996
9	1006	989	1005	1007
10	992	1007	1006	979
11	996	1006	997	989
12	1019	996	991	1011
13	981	991	989	1003
14	999	993	988	984
15	1013	1002	1005	992

Develop an $\overline{X}$chart and an *R*-chart and plot the values. From the charts, what comments can you make about the process? (Use three-sigma control limits as in Exhibit 13.7.) (Answer in Appendix D)

10. You are the newly appointed assistant administrator at a local hospital, and your first project is to investigate the quality of the patient meals put out by the food-service department. You conducted a 10-day survey by submitting a simple questionnaire to the 400 patients with each meal, asking that they simply check off that the meal was either satisfactory or unsatisfactory. For simplicity in this problem, assume that the response was 1,000 returned questionnaires from the 1,200 meals each day. The results are as follows.

	Number of Unsatisfactory Meals	Sample Size
December 1	74	1,000
December 2	42	1,000
December 3	64	1,000
December 4	80	1,000
December 5	40	1,000
December 6	50	1,000
December 7	65	1,000
December 8	70	1,000
December 9	40	1,000
December 10	75	1,000
	600	10,000

a. Construct a *p*-chart based on the questionnaire results, using a confidence interval of 95.5 percent, which is two standard deviations.

b. What comments can you make about the results of the survey?

11. The state and local police departments are trying to analyze crime rates so they can shift their patrols from decreasing-rate areas to areas where rates are increasing. The city and county have been geographically segmented into areas containing 5,000 residences. The police recognize that not all crimes and offenses are reported: People do not want to become involved, consider the offenses too small to report, are too embarrassed to make a police report, or do not take the time, among other reasons. Every month, because of this, the police are contacting by phone a random sample of 1,000 of the 5,000 residences for data on crime. (Respondents are guaranteed anonymity.) Here are the data collected for the past 12 months for one area.

Month	Crime Incidence	Sample Size	Crime Rate
January	7	1,000	0.007
February	9	1,000	0.009
March	7	1,000	0.007
April	7	1,000	0.007
May	7	1,000	0.007
June	9	1,000	0.009
July	7	1,000	0.007
August	10	1,000	0.010
September	8	1,000	0.008
October	11	1,000	0.011
November	10	1,000	0.010
December	8	1,000	0.008

Construct a *p*-chart for 95 percent confidence (1.96) and plot each of the months. If the next three months show crime incidences in this area as

January = 10 (out of 1,000 sampled)
February = 12 (out of 1,000 sampled)
March = 11 (out of 1,000 sampled)

what comments can you make regarding the crime rate?

12. Some citizens complained to city council members that there should be equal protection under the law against the occurrence of crimes. The citizens argued that this equal protection should be interpreted as indicating that high-crime areas should have more police protection than low-crime areas. Therefore, police patrols and other methods for preventing crime (such as street lighting or cleaning up abandoned areas and buildings) should be used proportionately to crime occurrence.

    In a fashion similar to problem 11, the city has been broken down into 20 geographic areas, each containing 5,000 residences. The 1,000 sampled from each area showed the following incidence of crime during the past month.

Area	Number of Crimes	Sample Size	Crime Rate
1	14	1,000	0.014
2	3	1,000	0.003
3	19	1,000	0.019
4	18	1,000	0.018
5	14	1,000	0.014
6	28	1,000	0.028
7	10	1,000	0.010
8	18	1,000	0.018
9	12	1,000	0.012
10	3	1,000	0.003
11	20	1,000	0.020
12	15	1,000	0.015
13	12	1,000	0.012
14	14	1,000	0.014
15	10	1,000	0.010
16	30	1,000	0.030
17	4	1,000	0.004
18	20	1,000	0.020
19	6	1,000	0.006
20	30	1,000	0.030
	300		

Suggest a reallocation of crime protection effort, if indicated, based on a *p*-chart analysis. To be reasonably certain in your recommendation, select a 95 percent confidence level (that is, $Z = 1.96$).

13. The following table contains the measurements of the key length dimension from a fuel injector. These samples of size five were taken at one-hour intervals.

	Observations				
Sample Number	**1**	**2**	**3**	**4**	**5**
1	.486	.499	.493	.511	.481
2	.499	.506	.516	.494	.529
3	.496	.500	.515	.488	.521
4	.495	.506	.483	.487	.489
5	.472	.502	.526	.469	.481
6	.473	.495	.507	.493	.506
7	.495	.512	.490	.471	.504
8	.525	.501	.498	.474	.485
9	.497	.501	.517	.506	.516
10	.495	.505	.516	.511	.497
11	.495	.482	.468	.492	.492
12	.483	.459	.526	.506	.522
13	.521	.512	.493	.525	.510
14	.487	.521	.507	.501	.500
15	.493	.516	.499	.511	.513
16	.473	.506	.479	.480	.523
17	.477	.485	.513	.484	.496
18	.515	.493	.493	.485	.475
19	.511	.536	.486	.497	.491
20	.509	.490	.470	.504	.512

Construct a three-sigma $\overline{X}$ chart and R-chart (use Exhibit 13.7) for the length of the fuel injector. What can you say about this process?

LO 13–3 14. In the past, Alpha Corporation has not performed incoming quality control inspections but has taken the word of its vendors. However, Alpha has been having some unsatisfactory experience recently with the quality of purchased items and wants to set up sampling plans for the receiving department to use.

For a particular component, X, Alpha has a lot tolerance percentage defective of 10 percent. Zenon Corporation, from which Alpha purchases this component, has an acceptable quality level in its production facility of 3 percent for component X. Alpha has a consumer's risk of 10 percent and Zenon has a producer's risk of 5 percent.

a. When a shipment of product X is received from Zenon Corporation, what sample size should the receiving department test?

b. What is the allowable number of defects in order to accept the shipment?

15. Large-scale integrated (LSI) circuit chips are made in one department of an electronics firm. These chips are incorporated into analog devices that are then encased in epoxy. The yield is not particularly good for LSI manufacture, so the AQL specified by that department is 0.15, while the LTPD acceptable by the assembly department is 0.40.

a. Develop a sampling plan.

b. Explain what the sampling plan means; that is, how would you tell someone to do the test?

ANALYTICS EXERCISE: Hot Shot Plastics Company

Plastic keychains are being produced in a company named Hot Shot Plastics. The plastic material is first molded and then trimmed to the required shape. The curetimes (which is the time for the plastic to cool) during the molding process affect the edge quality of the keychains produced. The aim is to achieve statistical control of the curetimes using $\overline{X}$ and R-charts.

Curetime data of 25 samples, each of size four, have been taken when the process is assumed to be in control. These are shown as follows. (*Note:* The spreadsheet "13 Statistical Process Control" has these data.)

Sample No.	Observations				Mean	Range
1	27.34667	27.50085	29.94412	28.21249	28.25103	2.59745
2	27.79695	26.15006	31.21295	31.33272	29.12317	5.18266
3	33.53255	29.32971	29.70460	31.05300	30.90497	4.20284
4	37.98409	32.26942	31.91741	29.44279	32.90343	8.54130
5	33.82722	30.32543	28.38117	33.70124	31.55877	5.44605
6	29.68356	29.56677	27.23077	34.00417	30.12132	6.77340
7	32.62640	26.32030	32.07892	36.17198	31.79940	9.85168
8	30.29575	30.52868	24.43315	26.85241	28.02750	6.09553
9	28.43856	30.48251	32.43083	30.76162	30.52838	3.99227
10	28.27790	33.94916	30.47406	28.87447	30.39390	5.67126
11	26.91885	27.66133	31.46936	29.66928	28.92971	4.55051
12	28.46547	28.29937	28.99441	31.14511	29.22609	2.84574
13	32.42677	26.10410	29.47718	37.20079	31.30221	11.09669
14	28.84273	30.51801	32.23614	30.47104	30.51698	3.39341
15	30.75136	32.99922	28.08452	26.19981	29.50873	6.79941
16	31.25754	24.29473	35.46477	28.41126	29.85708	11.17004
17	31.24921	28.57954	35.00865	31.23591	31.51833	6.42911
18	31.41554	35.80049	33.60909	27.82131	32.16161	7.97918
19	32.20230	32.02005	32.71018	29.37620	31.57718	3.33398
20	26.91603	29.77775	33.92696	33.78366	31.10110	7.01093
21	35.05322	32.93284	31.51641	27.73615	31.80966	7.31707
22	32.12483	29.32853	30.99709	31.39641	30.96172	2.79630
23	30.09172	32.43938	27.84725	30.70726	30.27140	4.59213
24	30.04835	27.23709	22.01801	28.69624	26.99992	8.03034
25	29.30273	30.83735	30.82735	31.90733	30.71869	2.60460
				Means	30.40289	5.932155

Questions

1. Prepare $\overline{X}$ and R-charts using these data with the method described in the chapter.
2. Analyze the charts and comment on whether the process appears to be in control and stable.
3. Twelve additional samples of curetime data from the molding process were collected from an actual production run. The data from these new samples are shown as follows. Update your control charts and compare the results with the previous data. The $\overline{X}$ and R-charts are drawn with the new data using the same control limits established before. Comment on what the new charts show.

Sample No.	Observations				Mean	Range
1	31.65830	29.78330	31.87910	33.91250	31.80830	4.12920
2	34.46430	25.18480	37.76689	39.21143	34.15686	14.02663
3	41.34268	39.54590	29.55710	32.57350	35.75480	11.78558
4	29.47310	25.37840	25.04380	24.00350	25.97470	5.46960
5	25.46710	34.85160	30.19150	31.62220	30.53310	9.38450
6	46.25184	34.71356	41.41277	44.63319	41.75284	11.53828
7	35.44750	38.83289	33.08860	31.63490	34.75097	7.19799
8	34.55143	33.86330	35.18869	42.31515	36.47964	8.45185
9	43.43549	37.36371	38.85718	39.25132	39.72693	6.07178
10	37.05298	42.47056	35.90282	38.21905	38.41135	6.56774
11	38.57292	39.06772	32.22090	33.20200	35.76589	6.84682
12	27.03050	33.63970	26.63060	42.79176	32.52314	16.16116

ANALYTICS EXERCISE: QUALITY MANAGEMENT—TOYOTA

Quality Control Analytics at Toyota

As part of the process for improving the quality of their cars, Toyota engineers have identified a potential improvement to the process that makes a washer that is used in the accelerator assembly. The tolerances on the thickness of the washer are fairly large since the fit can be loose, but if it does happen to get too large, it can cause the accelerator to bind and create a potential problem for the driver. (*Note:* This case has been fabricated for teaching purposes, and none of these data were obtained from Toyota.)

Let's assume that, as a first step to improving the process, a sample of 40 washers coming from the machine that produces the washers was taken and the thickness measured in millimeters. The following table has the measurements from the sample:

1.9	2.0	1.9	1.8	2.2	1.7	2.0	1.9	1.7	1.8
1.8	2.2	2.1	2.2	1.9	1.8	2.1	1.6	1.8	1.6
2.1	2.4	2.2	2.1	2.1	2.0	1.8	1.7	1.9	1.9
2.1	2.0	2.4	1.7	2.2	2.0	1.6	2.0	2.1	2.2

Questions

1. If the specification is such that no washer should be greater than 2.4 millimeters, assuming that the thicknesses are distributed normally, what fraction of the output is expected to be greater than this thickness?
2. If there are upper and lower specifications, where the upper thickness limit is 2.4 and the lower thickness limit is 1.4, what fraction of the output is expected to be out of tolerance?
3. What is the C_{pk} for the process?
4. What would be the C_{pk} for the process if it were centered between the specification limits (assume the process standard deviation is the same)?
5. What percentage of output would be expected to be out of tolerance if the process were centered?
6. Set up $\overline{X}$ and range control charts for the current process. Assume the operators will take samples of 10 washers at a time.
7. Plot the data on your control charts. Does the current process appear to be in control?
8. If the process could be improved so that the standard deviation were only about .10 millimeter, what would be the best that could be expected with the processes relative to fraction defective?

PRACTICE EXAM

In each of the following, name the term defined or answer the question. Answers are listed at the bottom.

1. A Six Sigma process that is running at the center of its control limits would expect this defect rate.
2. Variation that can be clearly identified and possibly managed.
3. Variation inherent in the process itself.
4. If a process has a capability index of 1 and is running normally (centered on the mean), what percentage of the units would one expect to be defective?
5. An alternative to viewing an item as simply good or bad due to it falling in or out of the tolerance range.
6. Quality characteristics that are classified as either conforming or not conforming to specification.
7. A quality characteristic that is actually measured, such as the weight of an item.
8. A quality chart suitable for when an item is either good or bad.
9. A quality chart suitable for when a number of blemishes are expected on each unit, such as a spool of yarn.
10. Useful for checking quality when we periodically purchase large quantities of an item and it would be very costly to check each unit individually.
11. A chart that depicts the manufacturer's and consumer's risks associated with a sampling plan.

Answers to Practice Exam 1. Two parts per billion units 2. Assignable variation 3. Common variation 4. Design limits are at $\pm 3\sigma$ or 2.7 defects per thousand 5. Taguchi loss function 6. Attributes 7. Variable 8. *p*-chart 9. *c*-chart 10. Acceptance sampling 11. Operating characteristic curve

For PowerPoint lecture slides, Solutions Manual, Test Bank, Data files for solved examples, Excel Templates, Step-by-Step Solved Examples in video format, Tutorial Videos and many more, scan the adjacent **QR code**, or **visit http://www.mhhe.com/sie-chase15e**

SECTION THREE

Supply Chain Processes

The Green Supply Chain

An important part of sustainability initiatives at global organizations is the close examination of their supply chain environmental footprint. The term *environmental footprint* relates to the impact that running the supply chain has on the environment. It is essential that companies orchestrate greening efforts across all supply chain processes, starting with product development, sourcing, manufacturing, packaging, transportation, demand fulfillment, and end-of-life management.

Managing logistics, which are transportation-related processes, is probably one of the more discussed greening efforts in supply chain management. There is a direct relationship between transportation efficiency and transportation costs. Minimizing miles traveled, using more efficient means for moving goods, and improving capacity utilization through consolidation of shipments reduces energy consumption and transportation costs, while at the same time reducing carbon emissions.

Chapter 14

Lean Supply Chains

LEARNING OBJECTIVES

LO 14-1 Explain what lean production is

LO 14-2 Illustrate how lean concepts can be applied to supply chain processes

LO 14-3 Analyze supply chain processes using value stream mapping

LO 14-4 Apply lean concepts to service processes

FROM LEAN SUPPLY CHAIN TO LEAN DESIGN

As seen in the diagram, the just-in-time approach to manufacturing has resulted in major reductions in inventory in U.S. companies over the past two decades. As we can see in the more recent data, some companies think it has gone too far and that having a little extra inventory might be a healthier option.

Although being lean helps companies hold down costs by keeping stockpiles of components and finished goods low, it can leave them high and dry if there is some disruption in the supply chain, such as an earthquake or some other natural disaster. Just-in-time makes sense, but it makes supply chains vulnerable to disruptions, so what we are seeing now is how these concepts are being adapted to meet the practical world.

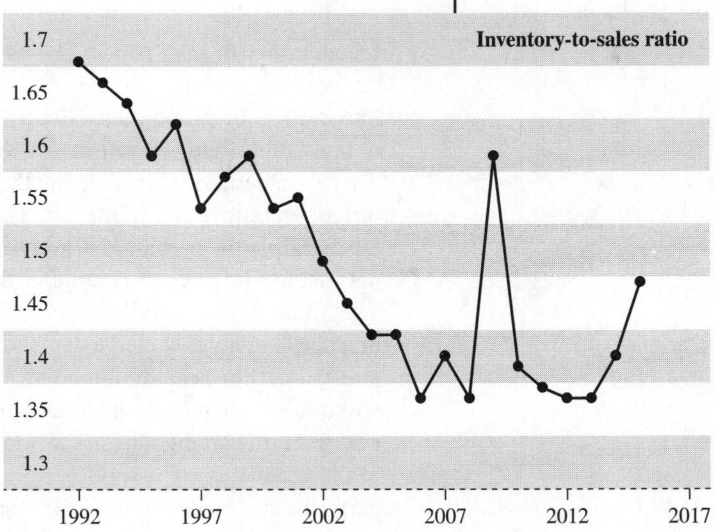

Toyota Motors, the just-in-time pioneer, is adapting as well and has recently announced a new process called the Toyota New Global Architecture. In an effort to lower costs, Toyota is implementing a new global modular assembly program that extends back to the design of the vehicles. The new process takes advantage of greatly increased component sharing across the product line. Toyota will be able to order parts in bulk and save costs through greater economies of scale.

LO 14-1

Explain what lean production is

Lean production
Integrated activities designed to achieve high-volume, high-quality production using minimal inventories of raw materials, work-in-process, and finished goods.

Customer value
In the context of lean production, something for which the customer is willing to pay.

Waste
Anything that does not add value from the customer's perspective.

LEAN PRODUCTION

The most significant operations and supply management approach of the past 50 years is **lean production**. In the context of supply chains, lean production refers to a focus on eliminating as much waste as possible. Moves that are not needed, unnecessary processing steps, and excess inventory in the supply chain are targets for improvement during the *leaning* process. Some consultants in industry have coined the phrase *value chain* to refer to the concept that each step in the supply chain processes that deliver products and services to customers should create value. If a step does not create value, it should be removed from the process. Lean production may be one of the best tools for implementing green strategies in manufacturing and service processes.

The basis of lean thinking came from the just-in-time (JIT) production concepts pioneered in Japan at Toyota. Even though JIT gained worldwide prominence in the 1970s, some of its philosophy can be traced to the early 1900s in the United States. Henry Ford used JIT concepts as he streamlined his moving assembly lines to make automobiles. For example, to eliminate waste, he used the bottom of the packing crates for car seats as the floor board of the car. Although elements of JIT were being used by Japanese industry as early as the 1930s, it was not fully refined until the 1970s when Tai-ichi Ohno of Toyota Motors used JIT to take Toyota's cars to the forefront of delivery time and quality.

Customer value, in the context of lean production, is defined as something for which the customer is willing to pay. Value-adding activities transform materials and information into something the customer wants. Non–value-adding activities consume resources and do not directly contribute to the end result desired by the customer. **Waste**, therefore, is defined as anything that does not add value from the customer's perspective. Examples of process wastes are defective products, overproduction, inventories, excess motion, processing steps, transportation, and waiting.

Waste elimination is a reasonable goal in service operations, just as it is in manufacturing operations, but there is a difference in the sources of variation that cause the waste. Manufacturing operations, compared to service operations, are far more controllable. Uncertainty does result from material and labor inputs, but those can be anticipated and controlled to a great extent. The workers, the design of the product, and the production tools are all under the control of operations to a very large extent. If sales and marketing are part of the process, the demand uncertainty also can be reduced.

In contrast, services operate in a sea of uncertainty and variability that are much harder to control. Let's look at these sources.

- **Uncertainty in task times.** The nature of service products is that the execution of each service delivery has some uniqueness. This variability typically leads to a negative exponential distribution of task times. Simply put, this means that while most task executions will fall within some tight range, some executions will take a long time. Consider airplane boarding. There's uncertainty here, yet Southwest found a way to reduce the uncertainty and achieve faster turnaround times at airports, increasing effective capacity.
- **Uncertainty in demand.** While service demand can be forecasted, no forecast is 100 percent perfect. Manufacturers can buffer this forecast uncertainty with some finished goods inventory. The simultaneous production and consumption in services precludes this tactic. The capacity must be available when the demand arises. Think about the number of available tables needed in a restaurant for peak dining hours.
- **Customers' production roles.** Both of the previous uncertainties have much to do with customer involvement in service operations. Because customers typically have some role to play in the production of a service, variability is introduced based on how well the service provider performs his or her role. Customers usually have to provide information to service agents to initiate service, and they typically have tangible tasks to perform.

Lean production and Six Sigma work best in repeatable, standardized operations. While many services are repeatable, given the aforementioned, how well can they be truly standardized? Let's look at the recent experience of the airline industry.

Airline companies such as Southwest have very efficient operations, and they achieve high ratings in customer satisfaction—until a major storm causes a disruption. Consider the horrible storms that often strike the eastern third of the United States in the spring. Weather is one of those uncertainties that the airlines simply cannot control. Flights will be canceled, and passengers will need to be rebooked. This is an extreme example of demand uncertainty that leads to huge demand spikes.

At the same time, to eliminate waste and become more efficient, airlines have tended to cut capacity and fill flights. Today, you seldom fly on a plane that is not 90 to 100 percent booked. With few available seats, it can take days to rebook all passengers from flights canceled due to weather. Our point is that there is often a price to pay for being lean, and that price often is at the expense of customer service when unlikely events occur. Whether in a service or manufacturing business, potential trade-offs exist with lean production and must be dealt with.

This chapter starts by reviewing the evolution of lean concepts from Japan and Toyota. We then expand this view to encompass a complete supply chain. The remainder of the chapter is devoted to value stream mapping, a tool that can be used to drive out waste and improve the efficiency of the supply chain.

Strategy

Lean production is an integrated set of activities designed to achieve production using minimal inventories of raw materials, work-in-process, and finished goods. Parts arrive at the next workstation "just-in-time" and are completed and move through the process quickly. Lean is also based on the logic that nothing will be produced until it is needed. Exhibit 14.1 illustrates the process. Production need is created by actual demand for the product. When an item is sold, in theory the market pulls a replacement from the last position in the system—final assembly in this case. This triggers an order to the factory production line, where a worker then pulls another unit from an upstream station in the flow to replace the unit taken. This upstream station then pulls from the next station further upstream and so on back to the release of raw materials. To enable this pull process to work smoothly, lean production demands high levels of quality at each stage of the process, strong vendor relations, and a fairly predictable demand for the end product.

Exhibit 14.1

Lean Production Pull System

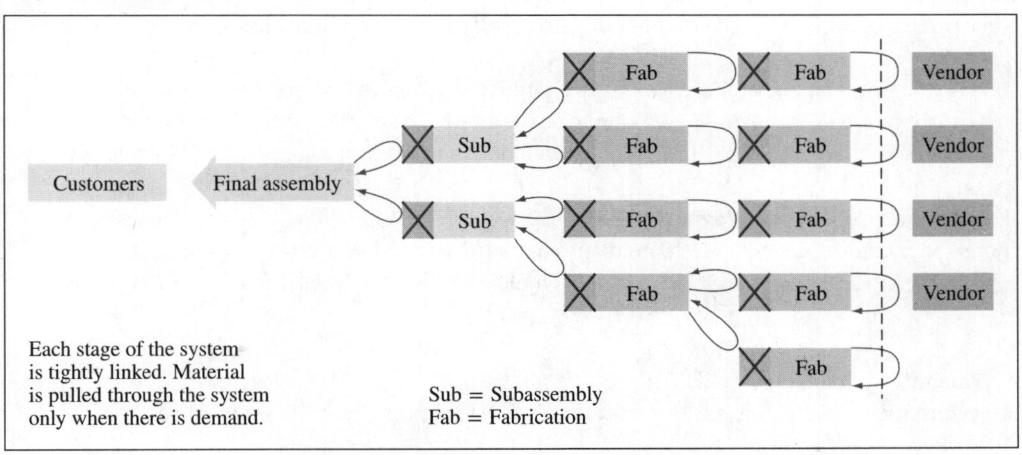

The Toyota Production System

In this section, we develop the philosophy and elements of lean production developed in Japan and embodied in the Toyota Production System—the benchmark for lean manufacturing. The Toyota Production System was developed to improve quality and productivity and is predicated upon two philosophies central to the Japanese culture: elimination of waste and respect for people.

Elimination of Waste Waste is anything that is not absolutely essential to production. An expanded lean definition identifies seven prominent types of waste to be eliminated from the supply chain: (1) waste from overproduction, (2) waste of waiting time, (3) transportation waste, (4) inventory waste, (5) processing waste, (6) waste of motion, and (7) waste from product defects.

OSCM AT WORK

Best Practices at LG Electronics India Ltd.

Best operations management practices of global leaders like typical Korean company LG Electronics, typical Japanese company Suzuki and many others are well reflected in their Indian counterpart. These companies have adapted to the concept of open, responsive and flexible approach towards developing operations and supply chain strategies. For example, in 1998, with an investment of around ₹500 crore, LG Electronics India Ltd. (LGEIL) has set up a world-class manufacturing facility for color televisions, washing machines, air-conditioners and microwave ovens at Greater Noida, very near to the capital city of India—Delhi. Production of eco-friendly refrigerators and PC monitor started here in the year 2001 [1].

LGEIL has developed many good practices to improve its operational strategies. For example, the Production, Sales and Inventory (PSI) plan and Rolling Sales Plan-review (RSP) are conducted daily, followed by on weekly and monthly basis, with an aim to increase the accuracy in planning activities of sales and production. To maintain a high quality six-sigma level and 100 PPM, it aims to reduce defects through modification in process using S.M.A.R.T. targets. Vendor performance-linked rating system, called as ABC system in LGEIL, identifies A-class as excellent vendors, B-class as Ok and C-class as "should-improve vendors." Open communication systems, such as pizza-lunch with MD helps LGEIL employees to share work-related issues with MD. Dosti tour is another concept used to improve team work in continuous improvement process. It provides a forum where an operator shows to his supervisor the job or process-related improvements to get acknowledgement and reward. [2] Like LG Electronics Korea, LGEIL has also launched its own codes of conduct by nurturing a "green partnership" with the first-tier suppliers in order to maintain high standards of environmentally-sound practice and product quality [3].

The goal of innovation is to introduce a positive change, to make someone or something better. LGEIL believes in open innovation culture, where employees at all levels are encouraged to create, implement and share their innovative ideas. It encourages various approaches to innovate the products, processes & systems, e.g. Six Sigma & TDR (Tear Down Re-engineering). Six-sigma, a statistical approach for product quality improvement, is used to optimize the existing processes by reducing the overall variation in the process. Through this, the root cause of the problem are identified and eliminated by means of statistical tools and techniques. The quality issues are identified at different stages like (i) incoming part issues from suppliers, (ii) assembly processes during manufacturing, (iii) product issues while actual usage by consumer. These issues are resolved by quality experts known as Six Sigma Black Belts certified by Korea HQ. These black belts follow DMAIC (Define, Measure, Analyse, Improve & Control) approach to eliminate the root causes of quality issues.

In order to focus on waste elimination, Lean Six Sigma drive has been initiated across the whole organisation of LGEIL. In the process, employees use value-stream-mapping to identify and eliminate the non-value-added activities to improve the level of prevailing processes through different statistical approaches. The idea behind using Six Sigma approach is to create value and eliminate waste.

In his foreword to a book authored by Dr. Yasho V. Verma – the then COO of LGEIL, Mr. Y.K. Kim, LG Electronics at Seoul writes, "LGEIL has often been benchmarked by other LG Electronics subsidiaries and also credited as a successful localization case... From planning and administration, to marketing and sales, to R&D, local Indian employees are actively engaged in all areas of business." [4]

Question

(1) What are the reasons of competitive advantages of LGEIL?

(2) Map the growth of LGEIL in consumer durables and electronics-goods in India in terms of product, brand, best practices in manufacturing and HR.

References:

1. http://www.zoominfo.com/people/PersonDetailLimited.aspx?PersonID=60359777&lastName=Verma&id=60359777&firstName=Y.V.&searchSource=page&page=1
2 Ki-Hoon Lee and Ji-Whan Kim, Current status of CSR in the realm of supply management: the case of the Korean electronics industry, Supply Chain Management: An International Journal, 14(2), 2009, pp. 138-148.
3 http://www.in.lge.com/AboutUs/aboutus-companyProfile-overview.aspx
4 Y. V. Verma (2000) LG Electronics: Towards Openness, Global Journal of Flexible Systems Management, 1(1), 81-83.

Respect for People Respect for people is key to the Toyota Production System. They have traditionally striven to ensure lifetime employment for permanent positions and to maintain level payrolls even when business conditions deteriorate. Permanent workers (about one-third of the total workforce of Japan) have job security and tend to be more flexible, remain with a company, and do all they can to help a firm achieve its goals. (Global recessions have caused many Japanese companies to move away from this ideal.)

Company unions at Toyota, as well as elsewhere in Japan, exist to foster a cooperative relationship with management. All employees receive two bonuses a year in good times. Employees know that if the company performs well, they will get a bonus. This encourages workers to improve productivity. Management views workers as assets, not as human machines. Automation and robotics are used extensively to perform dull or routine jobs so employees are free to focus on important improvement tasks.

Toyota relies heavily on subcontractor networks. Indeed, more than 90 percent of all Japanese companies are part of this supplier network of small firms. Some suppliers are specialists in a narrow field, usually serving multiple customers. Firms have long-term partnerships with their suppliers and customers. Suppliers consider themselves part of a customer's family.

LEAN SUPPLY CHAINS

LO 14-2

Illustrate how lean concepts can be applied to supply chain processes

The focus of the Toyota Production System is on elimination of waste and respect for people. As the concepts have evolved and become applied to the supply chain, the goal of maximizing customer value has been added. Customer value when considered from the entire supply chain should center on the perspective of the end customer with the goal being to maximize what the customer is willing to pay for a firm's goods or services. The **value stream** consists of the value-adding and non–value-adding activities required to design, order, and provide a product or service from concept to launch, order to delivery, and raw materials to customers. This all-inclusive view of the system is a significant expansion of the scope of application of the lean concepts pioneered by Toyota. When applied to supply chains, **waste reduction** relates to the optimization of the value-adding activities and the elimination of non–value-adding activities that are part of the value stream. In the next section, the value stream analysis tool is discussed.

Value stream
These are the value-adding and non–value-adding activities required to design, order, and provide a product from concept to launch, order to delivery, and raw materials to customers.

Waste reduction
The optimization of value-adding activities and elimination of non–value-adding activities that are part of the value stream.

In the following paragraphs, we discuss the different components of a supply chain and what would be expected using a lean focus.

- **Lean Suppliers** Lean suppliers are able to respond to changes. Their prices are generally lower due to the efficiency of lean processes, and their quality has improved to the point that incoming inspection at the next link is not needed. Lean suppliers deliver on time and their culture is one of continuous improvement. To develop lean suppliers, organizations should include them in their value stream planning. This will help them fix problems and share savings.
- **Lean Procurement** A key to lean procurement is automation. The term *e-procurement* relates to automatic transaction, sourcing, bidding and auctions using Web-based applications, and the use of software that removes human interaction and integrates with the financial reporting of the firm. The key to lean procurement is visibility. Suppliers must be able to "see" into the customers' operations, and customers must be able to "see" into their suppliers' operations. The overlap of these processes needs to be optimized to maximize value from the end-customer perspective.
- **Lean Manufacturing** Lean manufacturing systems produce what the customers want, in the quantity they want, when they want it, and with minimum resources. Applying lean concepts in manufacturing typically presents the greatest opportunities for cost reduction and quality improvement.
- **Lean Warehousing** This relates to eliminating non–value-added steps and waste in product storage processes. Typical functions include the following: receiving material; putting-away/storing; replenishing inventory; picking inventory; packing for shipment; and shipping. Waste can be found in many warehousing processes including shipping defects, which creates returns; overproduction or overshipment of products; excess inventory, which requires extra space and reduces warehouse efficiency; excess motion and handling; waiting for parts; and inadequate information systems.

© wavebreakmedia/Shutterstock.com

Here, a worker visually checks production of pralines as they move on conveyor. This process could probably be made more efficient.

- **Lean Logistics** Lean concepts can be applied to the functions associated with the movement of material through the system. Some of the key areas include optimized mode selection and pooling orders; combined multistop truckloads; optimized routing; cross docking; import/export transportation processes; and backhaul minimization. Just as with the other areas, these logistics functions need to be optimized by eliminating non–value-adding activities while improving the value-adding activities.
- **Lean Customers** Lean customers have a great understanding of their business needs and specify meaningful requirements. They value speed and flexibility and expect high levels of delivery performance. Lean customers are interested in establishing effective partnerships with their suppliers. Lean customers expect value from the products they purchase and provide value to their customers.

The benefits of a lean supply chain primarily are in the improved responsiveness to the customer. As business conditions change, the supply chain adapts to dynamic needs. The ideal is a culture of rapid change with a bias for change when it is needed. The reduced inventory inherent in a lean supply chain reduces obsolescence and reduces flow time through the value-added processes. The reduced cost along with improved customer service allows the firms using a lean supply chain a significant competitive advantage when competing in the global marketplace.

LO 14-3

Analyze supply chain processes using value stream mapping

VALUE STREAM MAPPING

Value stream mapping

A graphical way to analyze where value is or is not being added as material flows through a process.

Value stream mapping (VSM) is a special type of flowcharting tool that is valuable for the development of lean processes. The technique is used to visualize product flows through various processing steps. The tool also illustrates information flows that result from the process, as well as information used to control flow through the process. The aim of this section is to provide a brief introduction to VSM and to illustrate its use with an example.

To create a lean process, one needs to have a full understanding of the business, including production processes, material flows, and information flows. In this section, we discuss this in the context of a production process where a product is being made. VSM is not limited to this context and can be readily applied to service, logistics, distribution, or virtually any type of process.

EXHIBIT 14.2

Manufacturing Process Map

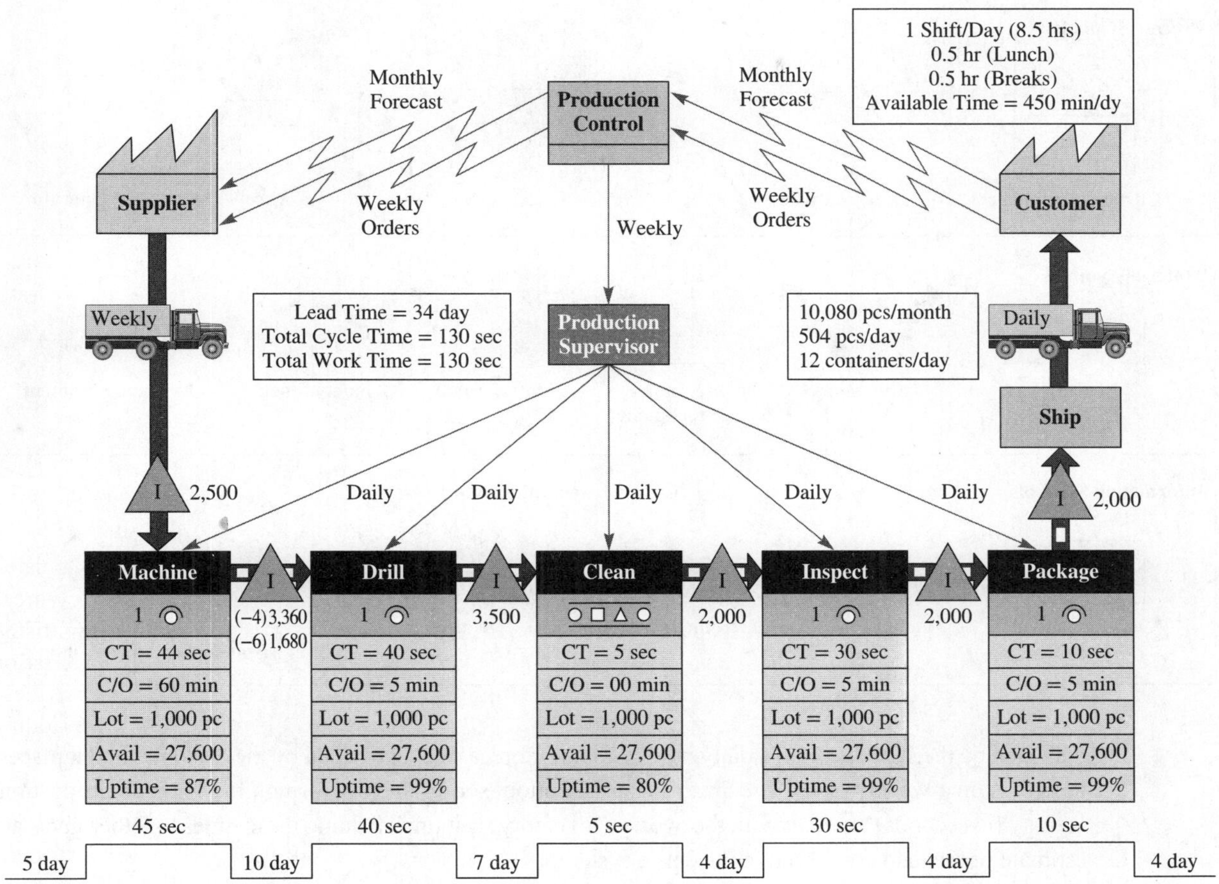

In the context of a production process such as a manufacturing plant, the technique is used to identify all of the value-adding, as well as non–value-adding, processes that materials are subjected to within a plant, from raw material coming into the plant through delivery to the customer. Exhibit 14.2 is a sample map that depicts a production process. With this map, identification of wasteful processes and flows can be made so they can be modified or eliminated, and the manufacturing system made more productive.

Details explaining the symbols will be discussed later in the section, but here it is useful to discuss what the information in the map depicted in Exhibit 14.2 actually means. Starting from the left, we see that material is supplied on a weekly basis and deposited in a raw material inventory indicated by the triangle. The average level for this inventory is 2,500 units. This material is run through a five-step process consisting of machining, drilling, cleaning, inspection, and packaging. The machining, drilling, inspection, and packaging processes all use a single operator. Under each of these process symbols is the activity cycle time (CT), changeover time (C/O time to switch from one type of item to another), lot size, available number of seconds per day, and percentage of uptime. The cleaning activity is a multistep process where items are handled on a first-come-first-served basis. In between each process are inventory buffers, with the average inventory in these buffers depicted in the exhibit. Material flows through the process at an average rated 504 pieces per day over 20 days of operations each month.

Information flows are shown on the map. In Exhibit 14.2, we see that production control issues monthly demand forecasts, weekly orders to the supplier, and a weekly production schedule that is

EXHIBIT 14.3

Value Stream Mapping Symbols

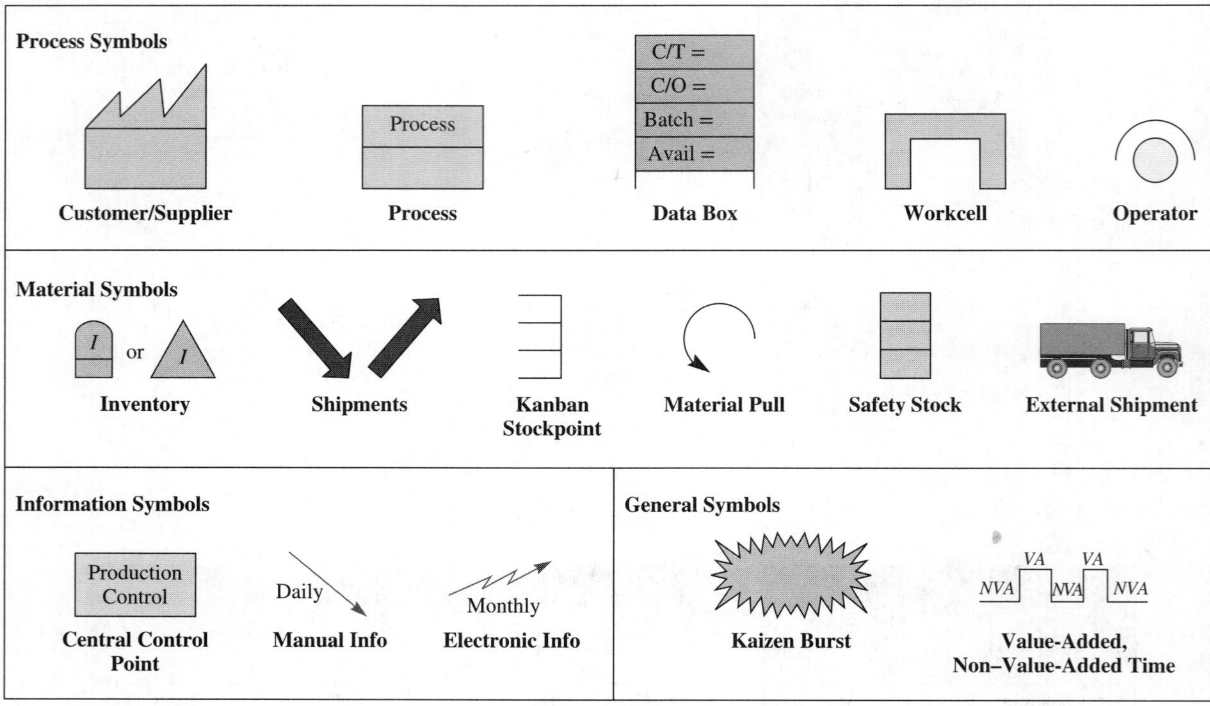

managed by the supervisor on a daily basis. Monthly forecasts are provided by the customer and it places its orders on a weekly basis. The time line at the bottom shows the processing time for each production activity (in seconds) together with the average inventory wait time. Adding these times together gives an estimate of the lead time through the entire system.

VSM symbols are somewhat standardized but there are many variations. Several common symbols are depicted in Exhibit 14.3. These are categorized as Process, Material, Information, and General symbols.

Value stream mapping is a two-part process—first depicting the "current state" of the process and second a possible "future state." Exhibit 14.4 depicts another map of the same process with suggested improvements. The map has been annotated using Kaizen bursts that suggest the areas for improvement. **Kaizen** is the Japanese philosophy that focuses on continuous improvement. The Kaizen bursts identify specific short-term projects (often referred to as "Kaizen events") that teams work on to implement changes to the process. In this exhibit, we see a totally redesigned process where the individual production operations have been combined into a workcell operated by three employees. In addition, rather than "pushing" material through the system based on weekly schedules generated by production control, the entire process is converted to a pull system that is operated directly in response to customer demand. Note that the lead time in the new system is only 5 days, compared to the 34-day lead time with the old system.

Kaizen
Japanese philosophy that focuses on continuous improvement.

To study another example using value stream mapping (VSM), consider the Solved Problem 2 at the end of the chapter. VSM is a great visual way to analyze an existing system and to find areas where waste can be eliminated. Value stream maps are simple to draw and it is possible to construct the maps totally with paper and pencil. These maps can, however, be more easily constructed using standard office software or graphics packages. Additionally, dedicated VSM software is available from Strategos (www.strategosinc.com) and Systems2win (www.Systems2win.com).

EXHIBIT 14.4

Analysis Showing Potential Areas for Improving a Process

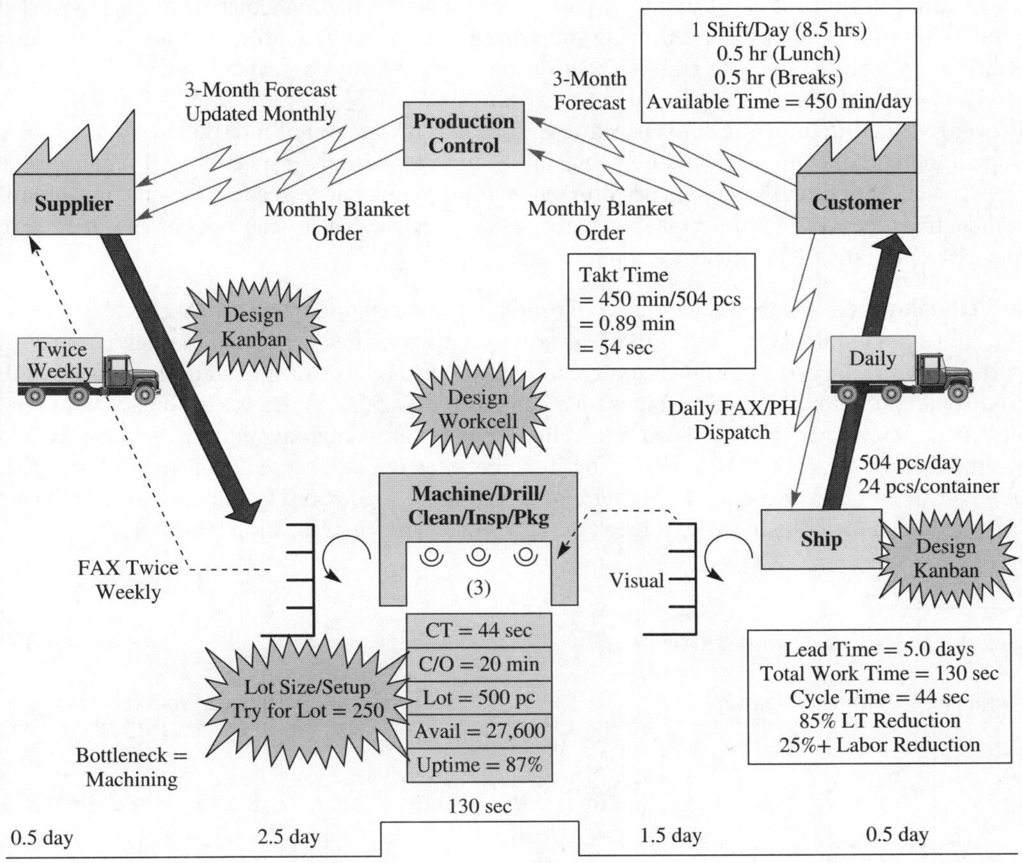

LEAN SUPPLY CHAIN DESIGN PRINCIPLES

Looking for ways to improve supply chain processes should be based on ideas that have been proven over time. In the following, we review a set of key principles that can guide the design of lean supply chains. We divide our design principles into three major categories. The first two sets of principles relate to internal production processes. These are the processes that actually create the goods and services within a firm. The third category applies lean concepts to the entire supply chain. These principles include

1. Lean Layouts
    a. Group technology
    b. Quality at the source
    c. JIT production
2. Lean Production Schedules
    a. Uniform plant loading
    b. Kanban production control system
    c. Determination of number of Kanbans needed
    d. Minimized setup times
3. Lean Supply Chains
    a. Specialized plants
    b. Collaboration with suppliers
    c. Building a lean supply chain

Process

Lean Concepts

Lean requires the plant layout to be designed to ensure balanced workflow with a minimum of work-in-process inventory. Each workstation is part of a production line, whether or not a physical line actually exists. Capacity is balanced using the same logic for an assembly line, and operations are linked through a pull system. In addition, the system designer must visualize how all aspects of the internal and external logistics system tie to the layout.

Preventive maintenance
Periodic inspection and repair designed to keep equipment reliable.

Preventive maintenance is emphasized to ensure that flows are not interrupted by downtime or malfunctioning equipment. Preventive maintenance involves periodic inspection and repair designed to keep a machine reliable. Operators perform much of the maintenance because they are most familiar with their machines and because machines are easier to repair, since lean operations favor several simple machines rather than one large complex one.

Group technology
A philosophy in which similar parts are grouped into families, and the processes required to make the parts are arranged in a specialized workcell.

Group Technology **Group technology** is a philosophy in which similar parts are grouped into families, and the processes required to make the parts are arranged in a manufacturing cell. Instead of transferring jobs from one specialized department to another, group technology considers all operations required to make a part and groups those machines together. Exhibit 14.5 illustrates the difference between the clusters of different machines grouped into cells versus departmental layouts. The group technology cells eliminate movement and queue (waiting) time between operations, reduce inventory, and reduce the number of employees required. Workers, however, must be flexible to run several machines and processes. Due to their advanced skill level, these workers have increased job security.

EXHIBIT 14.5

Group Technology versus Departmental Specialty

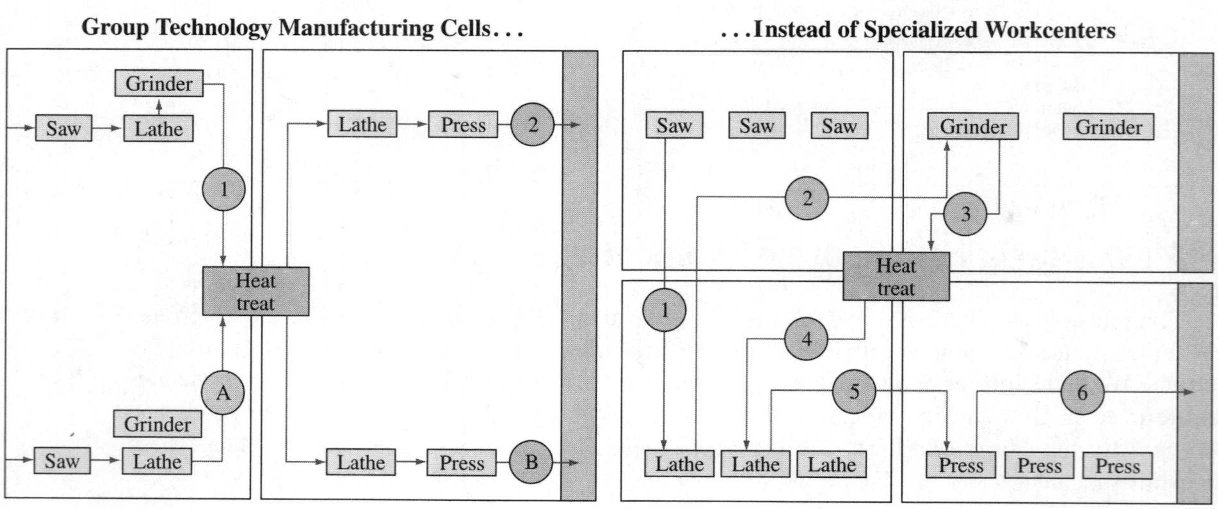

Quality at the source
The philosophy of making workers personally responsible for the quality of their output. Workers are expected to make the part correctly the first time and to stop the process immediately if there is a problem.

Quality at the Source **Quality at the source** means do it right the first time, and when something goes wrong, stop the process or assembly line immediately. Factory workers become their own inspectors, personally responsible for the quality of their output. Workers concentrate on one part of the job at a time so quality problems are uncovered. If the pace is too fast, if the worker finds a quality problem, or if a safety issue is discovered, the worker is obligated to push a button to stop the line and turn on a visual signal. People from other areas respond to the alarm and the problem. Workers are empowered to do their own maintenance and housekeeping until the problem is fixed.

JIT Production JIT (just-in-time) means producing what is needed when needed and no more. Anything over the minimum amount necessary is viewed as waste because effort and material expended for something not needed now cannot be utilized now. This is in contrast to relying on extra material just in case something goes wrong.

JIT is typically applied to repetitive manufacturing, which is when the same or similar items are made one after another. JIT does not require large volumes and can be applied to any repetitive segments of a business regardless of where they appear. Under JIT, the ideal lot size or production batch is one. Although workstations may be geographically dispersed, it is important to minimize transit time and keep transfer quantities small—typically one-tenth of a day's production. Vendors even ship several times a day to their customers to keep lot sizes small and inventory low. The goal is to drive all inventory queues to zero, thus minimizing inventory investment and shortening lead times.

When inventory levels are low, quality problems become very visible. Exhibit 14.6 illustrates this idea. If the water in a pond represents inventory, the rocks represent problems that could occur in a firm. A high level of water hides the problems (rocks). Management assumes everything is fine, but as the water level drops in an economic downturn, problems are presented. If you deliberately force the water level down (particularly in good economic times), you can expose and correct problems before they cause worse problems. JIT manufacturing exposes problems otherwise hidden by excess inventories and staff.

EXHIBIT 14.6

Inventory Hides Problems

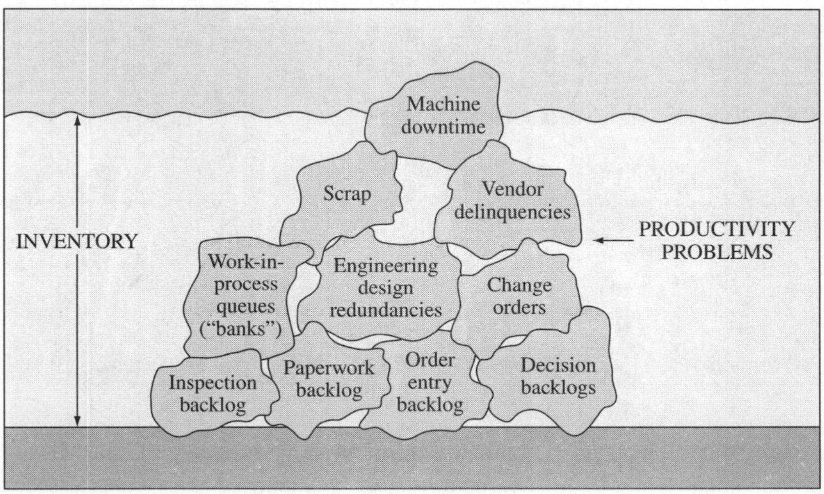

Lean Production Schedules

As noted earlier, lean production requires a stable schedule over a lengthy time horizon. This is accomplished by level scheduling, freeze windows, and underutilization of capacity. A **level schedule** is one that requires material to be pulled into final assembly in a pattern uniform enough to allow the various elements of production to respond to pull signals. It does not necessarily mean that the usage of every part on an assembly line is identified hour by hour for days on end; it does mean that a given production system equipped with flexible setups and a fixed amount of material in the pipelines can respond to the dynamic needs of the assembly line.

The term **freeze window** refers to that period of time during which the schedule is fixed and no further changes are possible. An added benefit of the stable schedule is seen in how parts and components are accounted for in a pull system. Here, the concept of **backflush** is used where the parts that go into each unit of the product are periodically removed from inventory and accounted for based on the number of units produced. For example, if 1,000 road bicycles are made, 1,000 of the appropriate handlebars, 2,000 tires, one seat, and so on are automatically removed from on-hand inventory. This eliminates much of the shop-floor data collection activity, which is required if each part must be tracked and accounted for during production.

Underutilization and overutilization of capacity are controversial features of lean production. Conventional approaches use safety stocks and early deliveries as a hedge against production problems like poor quality, machine failures, and unanticipated bottlenecks in traditional manufacturing. Under lean production, excess labor, machines, and overtime provide the hedge. The excess capacity in labor and equipment that results is much cheaper than carrying excess inventory. When demand is greater

Level schedule
A schedule that pulls material into final assembly at a constant rate.

Freeze window
The period of time during which the schedule is fixed and no further changes are possible.

Backflush
Calculating how many of each part were used in production and using these calculations to adjust actual on-hand inventory balances. This eliminates the need to actually track each part used in production.

than expected, overtime must be used. Often, part-time labor is used when additional capacity is needed. During idle periods, personnel can be put to work on other activities such as special projects, work group activities, and workstation housekeeping.

Uniform plant loading
Smoothing the production flow to dampen schedule variation.

Uniform Plant Loading Smoothing the production flow to dampen the reaction waves that normally occur in response to schedule variations is called **uniform plant loading**. When a change is made in a final assembly, the changes are magnified throughout the line and the supply chain. The only way to eliminate the problem is to make adjustments as small as possible by setting a firm monthly production plan for which the output rate is frozen.

Toyota found it could do this by building the same mix of products every day in small quantities. Thus, it always has a total mix available to respond to variations in demand. A Toyota example is shown in Exhibit 14.7. Monthly car style quantities are reduced to daily quantities (assuming a 20-day month) in order to compute a model *cycle time* (defined here as the time between two identical units being completed on the line). The cycle time figure is used to adjust resources to produce the precise quantity needed. The speed of equipment or of the production line is adjusted so only the needed quantity is produced each day. JIT strives to produce on schedule, on cost, and on quality.

EXHIBIT 14.7

Toyota Example of Mixed-Model Production Cycle in a Japanese Assembly Plant

Model	Monthly Quantity	Daily Quantity	Model Cycle Time (Minutes)
Sedan	5,000	250	2
Hardtop	2,500	125	4
Wagon	2,500	125	4
Sequence: Sedan, hardtop, sedan, wagon, sedan, hardtop, sedan, wagon, and so on (one minute apart)			

Kanban
A signaling device used to control production.

Kanban pull system
An inventory or production control system that uses a signaling device to regulate flows.

Kanban Production Control Systems A kanban control system uses a signaling device to regulate JIT flows. **Kanban** means "sign" or "instruction card" in Japanese. In a paperless control system, containers can be used instead of cards. The cards or containers make up the **kanban pull system**. The authority to produce or supply additional parts comes from downstream operations. Consider Exhibit 14.8, where we show an assembly line that is supplied with parts by a machine center. The machine center makes two parts, A and B. These two parts are stored in containers that are located next to the assembly line and next to the machine center. Each container next to the assembly line has a withdrawal kanban, and each container next to the machine center has a production kanban. This is often referred to as a two-card kanban system.

When the assembly line takes the first part A from a full container, a worker takes the withdrawal kanban from the container, and takes the card to the machine center storage area. In the machine center area, the worker finds a container of part A, removes the production kanban, and replaces it with the

Process

EXHIBIT 14.8

Flow of Two Kanbans

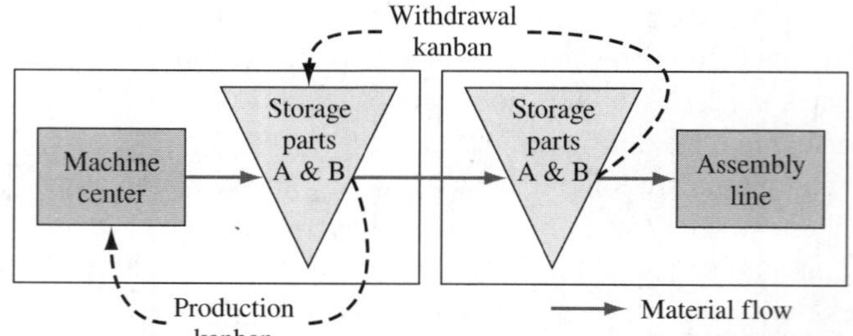

withdrawal kanban. Placement of this card on the container authorizes the movement of the container to the assembly line. The freed production kanban is placed on a rack by the machine center, which authorizes the production of another lot of material. A similar process is followed for part B. The cards on the rack visually show upcoming work for the machine center. Cards are not the only way to signal the need for production of a part; other visual methods are possible, as shown in Exhibit 14.9.

EXHIBIT 14.9

Diagram of Outbound Stockpoint with Warning Signal Marker

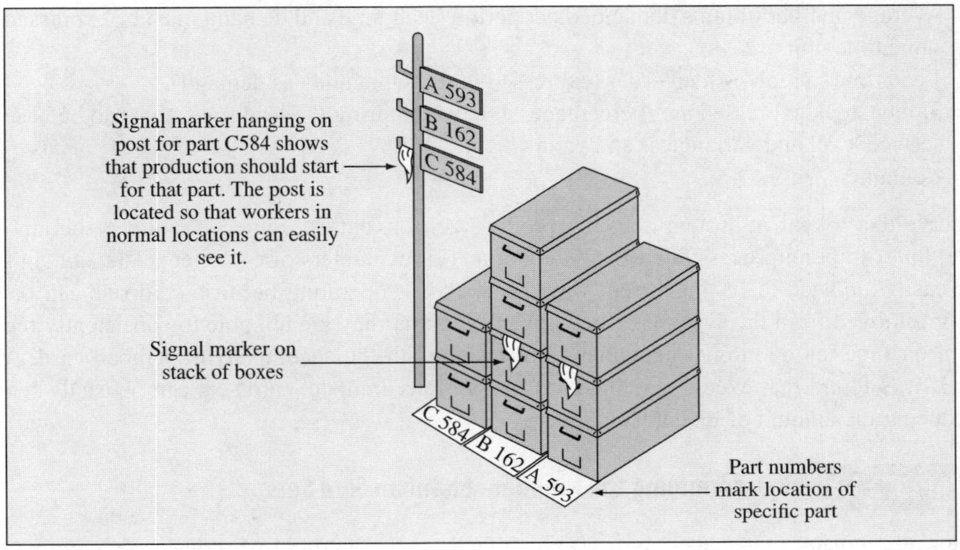

The following are some other possible approaches:

- **Kanban squares.** Some companies use marked spaces on the floor or on a table to identify where material should be stored. When the square is empty, the supplying operations are authorized to produce; when the square is full, no parts are needed.
- **Container system.** Sometimes the container itself can be used as a signal device. In this case, an empty container on the factory floor visually signals the need to fill it. The amount of inventory is adjusted by simply adding or removing containers.
- **Colored golf balls.** At a Kawasaki engine plant, when a part used in a subassembly is down to its queue limit, the assembler rolls a colored golf ball down a pipe to the replenishment machine center. This tells the operator which part to make next. Many variations have been developed on this approach.

The kanban pull approach can be used not only within a manufacturing facility but also between manufacturing facilities (pulling engines and transmissions into an automobile assembly operation, for example) and between manufacturers and external suppliers.

Determining the Number of Kanbans Needed Setting up a kanban control system requires determination of the number of kanban cards (or containers) needed. In a two-card system, we are finding the number of sets of withdrawal and production cards. The kanban cards represent the number of containers of material that flow back and forth between the supplier and the user areas. Each container represents the minimum production lot size to be supplied. The number of containers, therefore, directly controls the amount of work-in-process inventory in the system.

Accurately estimating the lead time needed to produce a container of parts is the key to determining the number of containers. This lead time is a function of the processing time for the container, any waiting time during the production process, and the time required to transport the material to the user.

Enough kanbans are needed to cover the expected demand during this lead time plus some additional amount for safety stock. The number of kanban card sets is

Analytics

$$k = \frac{\text{Expected demand during lead time} + \text{Safety stock}}{\text{Size of the container}}$$

$$= \frac{DL(1+S)}{C} \qquad [14.1]$$

where

k = Number of kanban card sets
D = Average number of units demanded per period (lead time and demand must be expressed in the same time units)
L = Lead time to replenish an order (expressed in the same units as demand)
S = Safety stock expressed as a percentage of demand during the lead time (this can be based on a service level and variance as shown in Chapter 20).
C = Container size

Observe that a kanban system does not produce zero inventory; rather, it controls the amount of material that can be in process at a time—the number of containers of each item. The kanban system can be easily adjusted to fit the current way the system is operating because card sets can be easily added or removed from the system. If the workers find that they are not able to consistently replenish the item on time, an additional container of material, with the accompanying kanban cards, can be added. If it is found that excess containers of material accumulate, card sets can be easily removed, thus reducing the amount of inventory.

EXAMPLE 14.1 Determining the Number of Kanban Card Sets

Meritor, a company that makes muffler assemblies for the automotive industry, is committed to the use of kanban to pull material through its manufacturing cells. Meritor has designed each cell to fabricate a specific family of muffler products. Fabricating a muffler assembly involves cutting and bending pieces of pipe that are welded to a muffler and a catalytic converter. The mufflers and catalytic converters are pulled into the cell based on current demand. The catalytic converters are made in a specialized cell.

Catalytic converters are made in batches of 10 units and are moved in special hand carts to the fabrication cells. The catalytic converter cell is designed so that different types of catalytic converters can be made with virtually no setup loss. The cell can respond to an order for a batch of catalytic converters in approximately four hours. Because the catalytic converter cell is right next to the muffler assembly fabrication cell, transportation time is virtually zero.

The muffler assembly fabrication cell averages approximately eight assemblies per hour. Each assembly uses the same catalytic converter. Due to some variability in the process, management has decided to have safety stock equivalent to 10 percent of the needed inventory.

How many kanban sets are needed to manage the replenishment of the catalytic converters?

SOLUTION

In this case, the lead time for replenishment of the converters (L) is four hours. The demand (D) for the catalytic converters is eight per hour. Safety stock (S) is 10 percent of the expected demand, and the container size (C) is 10 units.

$$k = \frac{8 \times 4(1 + .1)}{10} = \frac{35.2}{10} = 3.52 \text{ or } 4 \text{ sets}$$

In this case, we would need four kanban card sets, and we would have four containers of converters in the system. In all cases, when we calculate k, we will round the number up because we always need to work with full containers of parts. When the first unit of a batch of 10 catalytic converters is used in the muffler fabrication cell, a "signal" card is sent to the catalytic converter cell to trigger the production of another batch.

EXHIBIT 14.10

Relationship between Lot Size and Setup Cost

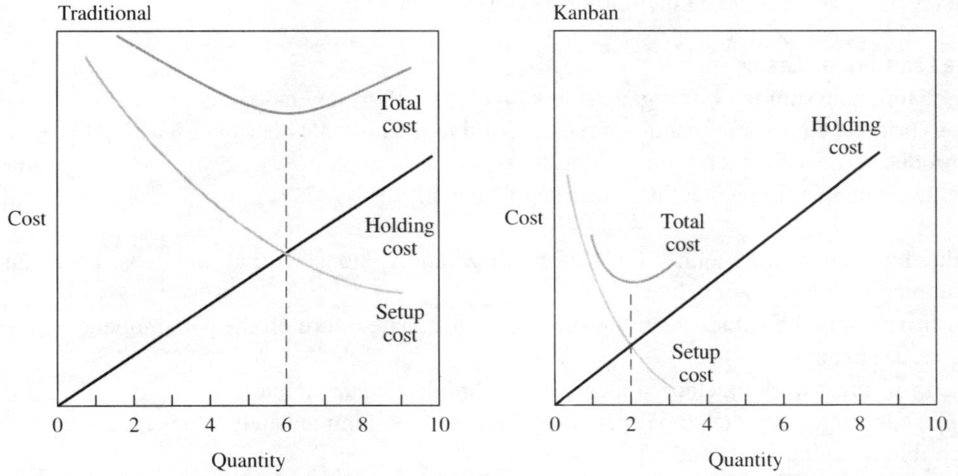

Definitions: *Holding* cost includes the costs of storing inventory and the cost of money tied up in inventory. *Setup* cost includes the wage costs attributable to workers making the setup, and various administrative and supplies costs. (These are defined in total in Chapter 20, "Inventory Management.")

Minimized Setup Times The reductions in setup and changeover times are necessary to achieve a smooth flow. Exhibit 14.10 shows the relationship between lot size and setup costs. Under a traditional approach, setup cost is treated as a constant, and the optimal order quantity is shown as six. Under the kanban approach, setup cost is significantly reduced and the corresponding optimal order quantity is reduced. In the exhibit, the order quantity has been reduced from six to two under lean methods by employing setup-time-saving procedures. This organization will ultimately strive for a lot size of one.

A simple idea used to achieve such setup time reductions involves dividing the setup time into internal and external activities. Internal activities must be done while a machine is stopped. External activities can be done while the machine is running. The setup process is then changed so that external activities are done while the machine is running in anticipation of the next setup. Other time-saving devices such as duplicate tool holders also are used to speed setups.

Lean Supply Chains

Building a lean supply chain involves taking a systems approach to integrating the partners. Supply must be coordinated with the need of the production facilities, and production must be tied directly to the demand of the customers for products. The importance of speed and steady consistent flow that is responsive to actual customer demand cannot be overemphasized. Concepts that relate to lean network design are discussed next.

Strategy

Specialized Plants Small specialized plants rather than large vertically integrated manufacturing facilities are important. Large operations and their inherent bureaucracies are difficult to manage and are not in line with the lean philosophy. Plants designed for one purpose can be constructed and operated more economically. These plants need to be linked together so they can be synchronized to one another and to the actual need of the market. Speed and quick response to changes are keys to the success of a lean supply chain.

Collaboration with Suppliers Just as customers and employees are key components of lean systems, suppliers are also important to the process. If a firm shares its projected usage requirements with its vendors, they have a long-term picture of the demands that will be placed on their production and distribution systems. Some vendors are linked online with a customer to share production scheduling and input needs data. This permits them to develop level production systems. Confidence in the supplier or vendor's delivery commitment allows reductions of buffer inventories. Maintaining stock at a lean level requires frequent deliveries during the day. Some suppliers even deliver directly to a location on the production line and not to a receiving dock. When vendors adopt quality practices, incoming receiving inspections of their products can be bypassed.

Building a Lean Supply Chain

A supply chain is the sum total of organizations involved—from raw materials firms through tiers of suppliers to original equipment manufacturers, onward to the ultimate distribution and delivery of the finished product to the customer. Womack and Jones, in their seminal work *Lean Thinking,* provide the following guidelines for implementing a lean supply chain:

- Value must be defined jointly for each product family, along with a target cost based on the customer's perception of value.
- All firms along the value stream must make an adequate return on their investments related to the value stream.
- The firms must work together to identify and eliminate *muda* (waste).
- When cost targets are met, the firms along the stream will immediately conduct new analyses to identify remaining *muda* and set new targets.
- Every participating firm has the right to examine every activity in every firm relevant to the value stream as part of the joint search for waste.

In summary, to be lean, everyone's got to be on the same page!

LO 14-4

Apply lean concepts to service processes

LEAN SERVICES

Many lean techniques have been successfully applied by service firms. Just as in manufacturing, the suitability of each technique and the corresponding work steps depend on the characteristics of the firm's markets, production and equipment technology, skill sets, and corporate culture. Service firms are no different in this respect. Here are 10 of the more successful techniques applied to service companies:

Process

1. **Organize Problem-Solving Groups** Honeywell is extending its use of quality teams from manufacturing into its service operations. Other corporations as diverse as First Bank/Dallas, Standard Meat Company, and Miller Brewing Company are using similar approaches to improve service. British Airways used quality teams as a fundamental part of its strategy to implement new service practices.
2. **Upgrade Housekeeping** Good housekeeping means more than winning the clean broom award. It means that only the necessary items are kept in a work area, that there is a place for everything, and that everything is clean and in a constant state of readiness. The employees clean their own areas.

   Service organizations such as McDonald's, Disneyland, and Speedi-Lube have recognized the critical nature of housekeeping. Their dedication to housekeeping has meant that service processes work better, the attitude of continuous improvement is easier to develop, and customers perceive that they are receiving better service.
3. **Upgrade Quality** The only cost-effective way to improve quality is to develop reliable process capabilities. Process quality is quality at the source—it guarantees first-time production of consistent and uniform products and services.

   McDonald's is famous for building quality into its service delivery process. It literally "industrialized" the service delivery system so that part-time, casual workers could provide the same eating experience anywhere in the world. Quality doesn't mean producing the best; it means consistently producing products and services that give the customers their money's worth.
4. **Clarify Process Flows** Clarification of flows, based on JIT themes, can dramatically improve the process performance. The following are three examples.

First, Federal Express Corporation changed air flight patterns from origin-to-destination to origin-to-hub, where the freight is transferred to an outbound plane heading for the destination. This revolutionized the air transport industry. Second, the order-entry department of a manufacturing firm converted from functional subdepartments to customer-centered work groups and reduced the order processing lead time from eight to two days. Finally, Supermaids sends in a team of house cleaners, each with a specific responsibility, to clean a part of each house quickly with parallel processes. Changes in process flows can literally revolutionize service industries.

5. **Revise Equipment and Process Technologies** Revising technologies involves evaluation of the equipment and processes for their ability to meet the process requirements, to process consistently within tolerance, and to fit the scale and capacity of the work group.

Speedi-Lube converted the standard service station concept to a specialized lubrication and inspection center by changing the service bays from drive-in to drive-through and by eliminating the hoists and instead building pits under the cars where employees have full access to the lubrication areas on the vehicle.

A hospital reduced operating room setup time so it had the flexibility to perform a wider range of operations without reducing the operating room availability.

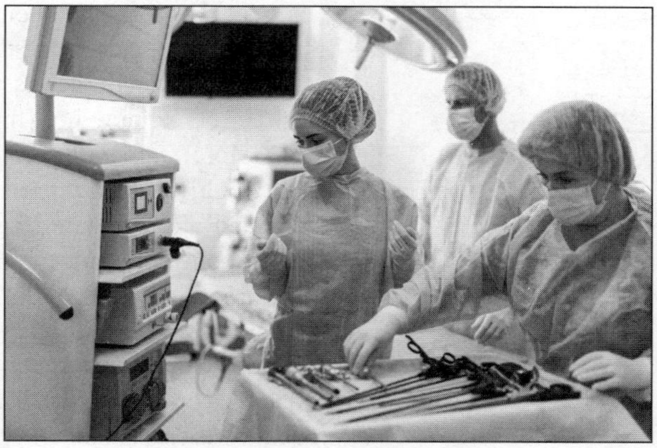

Prior to an operation, nurses in protective masks and sterile gloves checking laparoscopic instruments and medical equipment

6. **Level the Facility Load** Service firms synchronize production with demand. They have developed unique approaches to leveling demand so they can avoid making customers wait for service. McDonald's offers a special breakfast menu in the morning. Retail stores use take-a-number systems. The post office charges more for next-day delivery. These are all examples of the service approach for creating uniform facility loads.
7. **Eliminate Unnecessary Activities** A step that does not add value is a candidate for elimination. A step that does add value may be a candidate for reengineering to improve the process consistency or to reduce the time to perform the tasks.

A hospital discovered that significant time was spent during an operation waiting for an instrument that was not available when the operation began. It developed a checklist of instruments required for each category of operation. Speedi-Lube eliminated steps, but also added steps that did not improve the lubrication process but did make customers feel more assured about the work being performed.

8. **Reorganize Physical Configuration** Work area configurations frequently require reorganization during a lean implementation. Often, manufacturers accomplish this by setting up manufacturing cells to produce items in small lots, synchronous to demand. These cells amount to microfactories inside the plant.

Most service firms are far behind manufacturers in this area. However, a few interesting examples do come out of the service sector. Some hospitals—instead of routing patients all over the building for tests, exams, X-rays, and injections—are reorganizing their services into work groups based on the type of problem. Teams that treat only trauma are common, but other work groups have been formed to treat less immediate conditions like hernias. These amount to microclinics within the hospital facility.

9. **Introduce Demand-Pull Scheduling** Due to the nature of service production and consumption, demand-pull (customer-driven) scheduling is necessary for operating a service business. Moreover, many service firms are separating their operations into "back room" and "customer contact" facilities. This approach creates new problems in coordinating schedules between the facilities. The original Wendy's restaurants were set up so cooks could see cars enter the parking lot. They put a pre-established number of hamburger patties on the grill for each car. This pull system was designed to have a fresh patty on the grill before the customer even placed an order.

10. **Develop Supplier Networks** The term *supplier networks* in the lean context refers to the cooperative association of suppliers and customers working over the long term for mutual benefit. Service firms have not emphasized supplier networks for materials because the service costs are often predominantly labor. Notable exceptions include service organizations like McDonald's, one of the biggest food products purchasers in the world, which has been developing lean practices. Manpower and other employment agencies have established lean-type relationships with a temporary employment service and a trade school to develop a reliable source of trained assemblers.

Sustainable Supply Chain Management

Businesses all across the globe are talking about sustainable supply chain management. Although name or practices may differ but the aim is to reduce the pressure on environment in an economical way, which is operationally viable and useful for the society. Green supply chain, closed-loop supply chains, circular economy, extended producer responsibility, low-carbon supply chain are just a few names that are being used now to aim at environment-friendly businesses.

It is a common knowledge that use of conventional sources of energy like petroleum products etc. release CO_2 and many other gases that goes into the environment. These greenhouse gases (GHGs) are responsible for trapping heat into the earth's atmosphere leading to a phenomenal rise in temperature on earth. More temperature rise may lead to more energy consumptions. For example, refrigerated logistics would consume more energy in a cold chains. To break this vicious cycle, there is a need for concerted effort from all industries and people together to lower energy consumption leading to reduced carbon-foot print.

There are many ways to define and explain Sustainable Supply Chain Management (SSCM). The most common way is to look at all supply chain partners, all processes and all customers so that three sustainability dimensions (economic, environmental and social) are achieved in the best possible way. In Chapter 2, through Exhibit 2.1, we have already explained it through Triple Bottom Line (TBL) approach towards sustainability.

Literature and practicing world have reported positive impact of sustainable practices on financial performance of firms. Use of renewable sources of energy like solar and wind, if economically viable should be a strong option to reduce the carbon-footprint of a supply chain. This would lead to an environment-friendly or green supply chain. Social dimension of triple-bottom-line framework is also very important. Just for example purpose, if we assume that a supply chain replaces a battery operated material transportation device with child-labor, though the economic and environmental goals are achieved, yet social dimension of sustainability is defeated.

There are various practices adopted by organizations to make their supply chain sustainable. These involves, green sourcing (Ref. Chapter 16), green transportation process, sustainable warehousing process and use of Information Technology.

Transportation companies are looking at reduction in the carbon-footprint in their operations. Use of full-truck load (FTL) helps in reduction in CO_2 emission per unit transported as compared to less-than- truck-load (LTL). Route optimization also helps in minimization of distances travelled resulting in less energy consumption in transportation.

CONCEPT CONNECTIONS

LO 14–1 Explain what lean production is

Summary

- Lean production involves improving processes by eliminating waste and excess inventory.
- The just-in-time philosophy, pioneered by Toyota, is the basis for the concept.
- The concept includes the entire supply chain with the goal of creating value for the customer by eliminating all non–value-adding activities.

Key Terms

Lean production Integrated activities designed to achieve high-volume, high-quality production using minimal inventories of raw materials, work-in-process, and finished goods.

Customer value In the context of lean production, something for which the customer is willing to pay.

Waste Anything that does not add value from the customer's perspective.

LO 14–2 Illustrate how lean concepts can be applied to supply chain processes

Summary

- Lean concepts can be applied to virtually all the processes in the supply chain.
- Key areas include production layout, the scheduling of production, and the design of the supply chain.
- Flow throughout the supply chain can be managed using just-in-time systems that pull material based on need.
- The kanban card is an example of this type of system.

Key Terms

Value stream These are the value-adding and non–value-adding activities required to design, order, and provide a product from concept to launch, order to delivery, and raw materials to customers.

Waste reduction The optimization of value-adding activities and elimination of non–value-adding activities that are part of the value stream.

LO 14–3 Analyze supply chain processes using value stream mapping

Summary

- Value stream mapping is a flowcharting tool used to visualize flows through a process.
- Features of the tool are the identification of value adding and non–value-adding activities, together with a time line for each activity and the process as a whole.
- The tool can be applied to production, logistics, and distribution processes.
- The goal in using the tool is to identify ways to "lean" a process by eliminating waste and creating value for the customer.
- A Kaizen event is a short-term project designed to quickly improve a process.

Key Terms

Value stream mapping A graphical way to analyze where value is or is not being added as material flows through a process.

Kaizen Japanese philosophy that focuses on continuous improvement.

Preventive maintenance Periodic inspection and repair designed to keep equipment reliable.

Group technology A philosophy in which similar parts are grouped into families, and the processes required to make the parts are arranged in a specialized workcell.

Quality at the source The philosophy of making workers personally responsible for the quality of their output. Workers are expected to make the part correctly the first time and to stop the process immediately if there is a problem.

Level schedule A schedule that pulls material into final assembly at a constant rate.

Freeze window The period of time during which the schedule is fixed and no further changes are possible.

Backflush Calculating how many of each part were used in production and using these calculations to adjust actual on-hand inventory balances. This eliminates the need to actually track each part used in production.

Uniform plant loading Smoothing the production flow to dampen schedule variation.

Kanban A signaling device used to control production.

Kanban pull system An inventory or production control system that uses a signaling device to regulate flows.

[14.1]
$$k = \frac{DL(1+S)}{C}$$

LO 14–4 Apply lean concepts to service processes

Summary

- Lean concepts can be successfully applied by service firms.
- Just as with production processes, waste elimination and customer value creation are also goals of service processes.
- Often, services operate in an environment with more uncertainty, making them more difficult to control.

SOLVED PROBLEMS

LO 14–2 SOLVED PROBLEM 1

A local hospital wants to set up a kanban system to manage its supply of blood with the regional blood bank. The regional blood bank delivers blood to the hospital each day with a one-day order lead time (an order placed by 6 P.M. today will be delivered tomorrow afternoon). Internally, the hospital purchasing group places orders for blood each day at 5 P.M. Blood is measured by the pint and is shipped in containers that contain six pints. For a particular blood type, the hospital uses an average of 12 pints per day. Due to the critical nature of a blood shortage, the hospital wants to carry a safety stock of two days' expected supply. How many kanban card sets should the hospital prepare?

Solution

This problem is typical of how a real application might look. Using the data given, the variables for this problem are as follows:

$D = 12$ pints per day (average demand)
$L = 1$ day (lead time)
$S = 200$ percent (safety stock, as a fraction this is 2.0)
$C = 6$ pints (container size)

$$k = \frac{DL(1+S)}{C} = \frac{12(1+2)}{6} = 6$$

This indicates that we need to prepare six kanban card sets. Each time a new container of blood (containing six pints) is opened, the card will be sent to purchasing and another six pints of blood will be ordered. When the blood is received, the card will be attached to the new container and moved to the blood storage area.

LO 14–3 SOLVED PROBLEM 2

Value Stream Mapping Example: Bolt Manufacturing

A simple example will illustrate the use of value stream mapping. Exhibit 14.11 depicts a bolt manufacturing operation that ships 7,500 bolts per week. The current state map provides cycle time and setup time information for each of the 15 processes used, and it provides inventory levels at each location. The map also depicts information flow between the steel supplier, the bolt customer, and management via production scheduling. The total value-added time, denoted as processing time, is obtained by summing all of the individual value-added contributions at each processing step on the time line. For the example, it equals 28.88 seconds. At each inventory location, lead time is calculated by dividing inventory level by daily production demand, which is 1,500 bolts. Summing all of the lead time produces an overall production lead time of 66.1 days, which is the entire time it takes an individual bolt to make its way through the plant.

There are several possibilities to optimize the current production scenario. Exhibit 14.12 provides a few of these, shown as Kaizen bursts, including eliminating several processing steps, modifying some of the existing processes, and reducing travel distances between processes. Exhibit 14.13, the future state map, illustrates the incorporation of these modifications. As shown, the changes reduce production lead time to 50.89 days, which is a 23 percent reduction. The production scenario could be enhanced even more if pull systems were incorporated at various locations.

Exhibit 14.11

Current State Map for Bolt Manufacturing Example

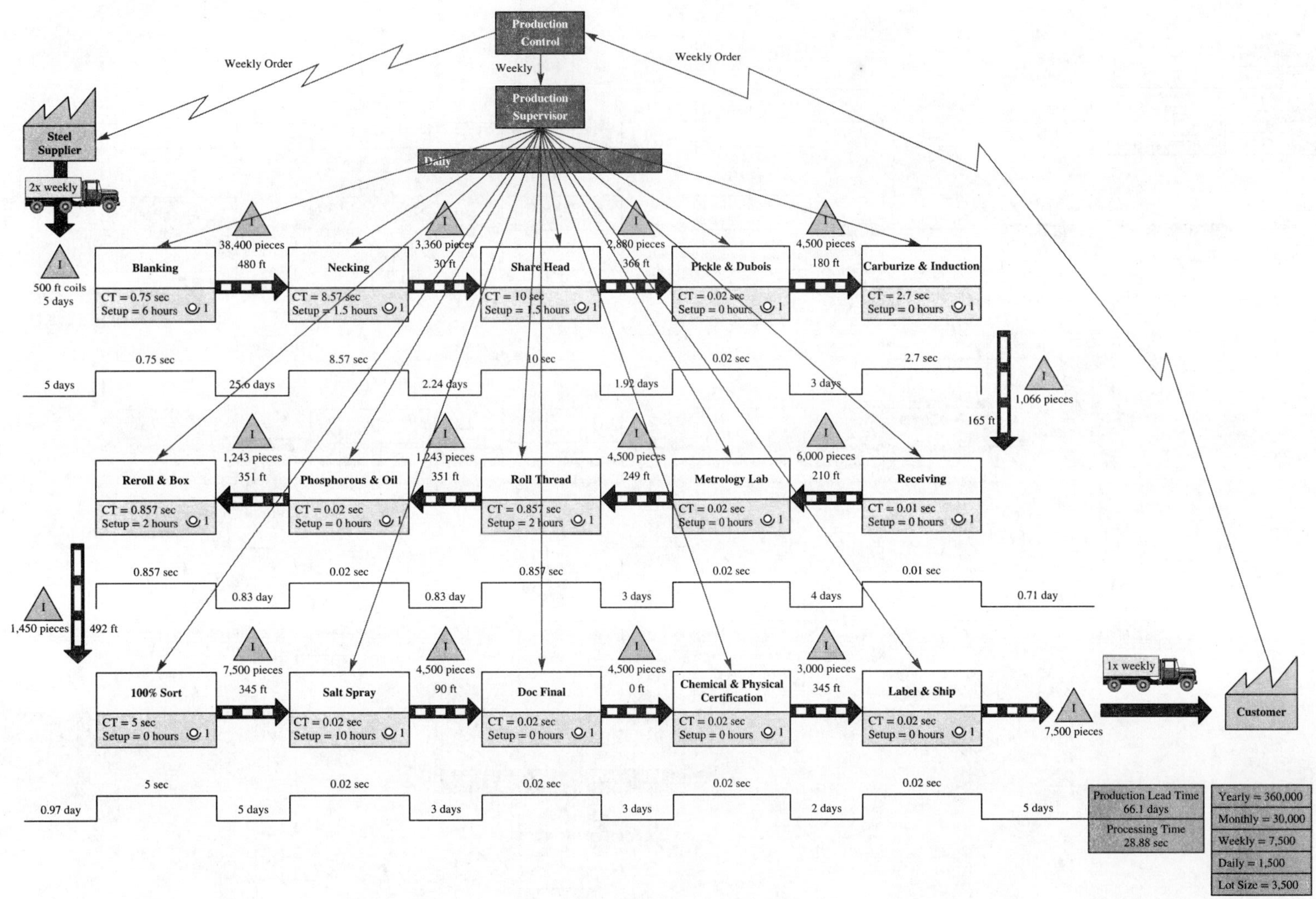

Exhibit 14.12

Potential Process Changes for Bolt Manufacturing Example

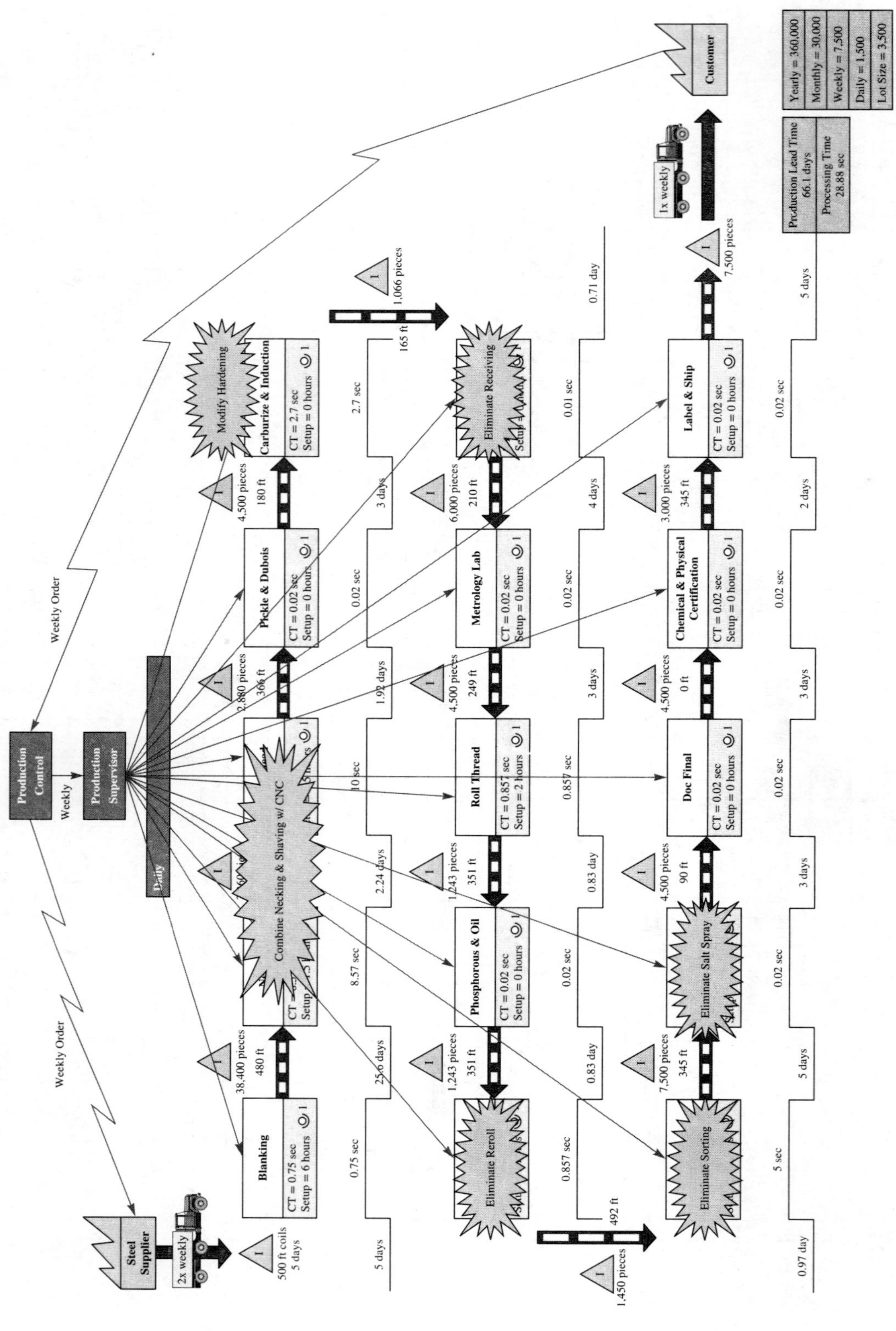

EXHIBIT 14.13

Future State Map for Bolt Manufacturing Example

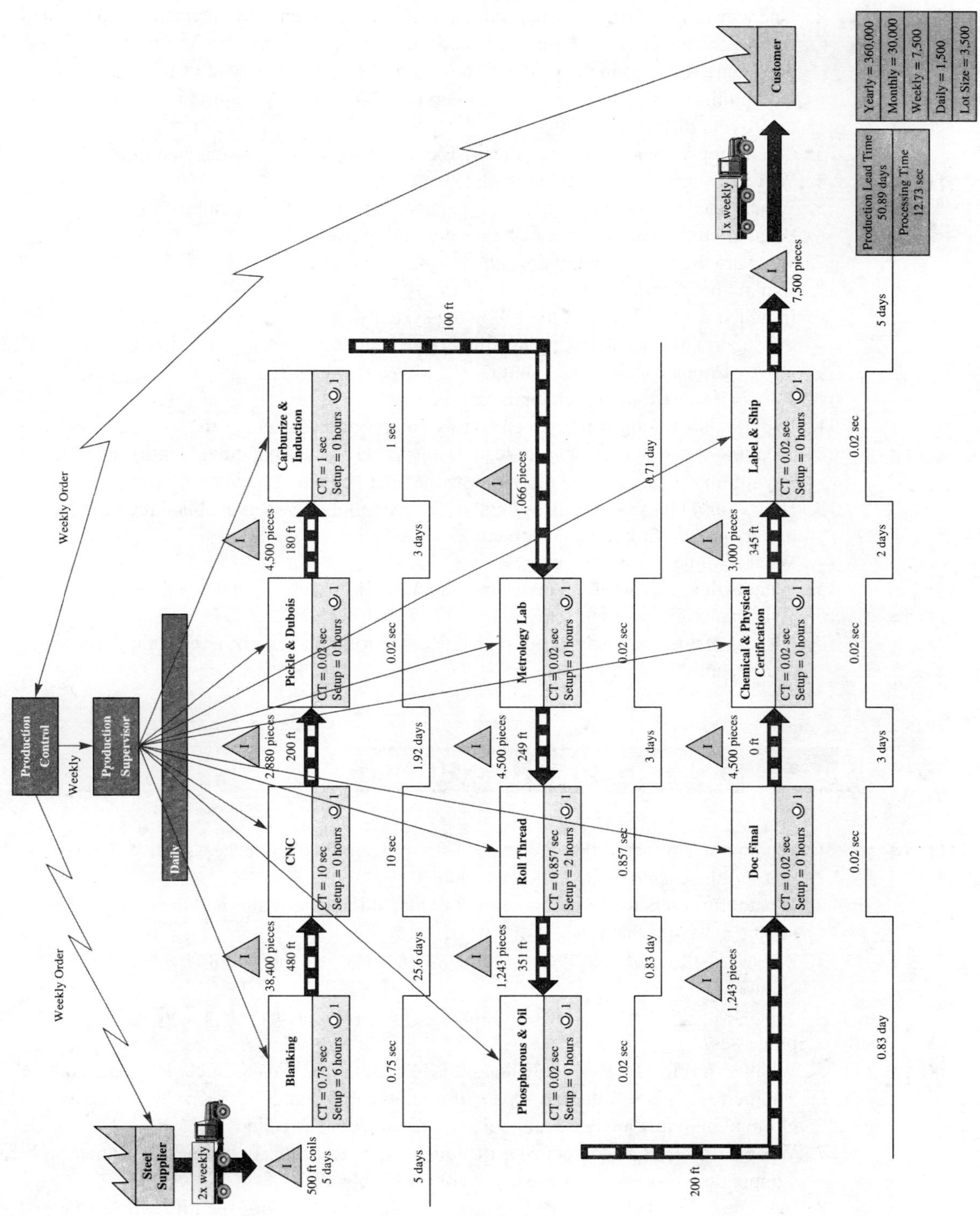

DISCUSSION QUESTIONS

LO 14–1

1. Is it possible to achieve zero inventories? Why or why not?
2. One way to help achieve lean production systems is to employ flexible automated manufacturing equipment and automated material handling systems. A natural result of such a move is that fewer people are required in the process, an issue addressed regularly in negotiations with labor unions. Do you think there is a conflict between such a move and the principle of *Respect for People* in the Toyota Production System?
3. Can a supply chain become too lean? Explain your answer—using examples if possible.

LO 14–2

4. Why must lean have a stable schedule?
5. What objections might a marketing manager have to uniform plant loading?
6. What are the implications for cost accounting of lean production?
7. What are the roles of suppliers and customers in a lean system?
8. Explain how cards are used in a kanban system.
9. In which ways, if any, are the following systems analogous to kanban: returning empty bottles to the supermarket and picking up filled ones; running a hot dog stand at lunchtime; withdrawing money from a checking account; raking leaves into bags?
10. Why is lean hard to implement in practice?
11. Explain the relationship between quality and productivity under the lean philosophy.

LO 14–3

12. Stopping waste is a vital part of lean. Using value stream mapping, identify some sources of waste in your home or dorm and discuss how they may be eliminated.
13. How would you show a pull system in VSM symbols between the blanking and CNC stages of the bolt manufacturing Solved Problem 2?
14. What is value stream mapping?
15. What is the purpose of value stream mapping? How can it be achieved?

LO 14–4

16. Will lean work in service environments? Why or why not?
17. Discuss ways to use lean to improve one of the following: a pizza restaurant, a hospital, or an auto dealership.

OBJECTIVE QUESTIONS

LO 14–1

1. What phrase refers to the idea that all steps in supply chain processes that deliver goods and services to the customer should create value?
2. What term refers to the optimization of value-adding activities and the elimination of non–value-adding activities that are part of a value stream?
3. List at least four of the seven prominent types of waste that should be eliminated from the supply chain.
4. What lean concept relates to eliminating non–value-added steps and waste in product storage processes?

LO 14–2

5. What term refers to a schedule that pulls material into final assembly at a constant rate?
6. The periodic inspection and repair of equipment designed to keep the equipment reliable, thus eliminating unplanned downtime due to malfunctions is called _____.
7. What term refers to the concept of doing things right the first time and, when problems occur, stopping the process to fix the source of the problem?
8. In some JIT systems, marked spaces on a table or the floor identify where material should be stored. Supplying operations are signaled to produce more when the space is empty. What are these spaces called?
9. Under a kanban approach to lean manufacturing, order quantities should be as small as possible. For a part that is manufactured in-house, what part of its manufacturing process needs to be reduced to reduce the optimal order quantity for an item?

10. A supplier of instrument gauge clusters uses a kanban system to control material flow. The gauge cluster housings are transported five at a time. A fabrication center produces approximately 10 gauges per hour. It takes approximately two hours for the housing to be replenished. Due to variations in processing times, management has decided to keep 20 percent of the needed inventory as safety stock. How many kanban card sets are needed? (Answer in Appendix D)
11. Transmissions are delivered to the fabrication line four at a time. It takes one hour for transmissions to be delivered. Approximately four vehicles are produced each hour, and management has decided that 50 percent of expected demand should be maintained as safety stock. How many kanban card sets are needed?
12. A bottling plant fills 2,400 bottles every two hours. The lead time is 40 minutes and a container accommodates 120 bottles. The safety stock is 10 percent of expected demand. How many kanban cards are needed?
13. Refer to Example 14.1 as the basis for this problem. Meritor hires a team of consultants. The consultants suggest a partial robotic automation, as well as an increase in safety stock to 12.5 percent. Meritor implements these suggestions. The result is an increase in efficiency in both the fabrication of muffler assembly and the making of catalytic converters. The muffler assembly fabrication cell now averages 16 assemblies per hour and the lead time has been decreased to two hours' response time for a batch of 10 catalytic converters. How many kanban cards are now needed?
14. Meritor is so pleased with the outcome from previous suggestions that the consultants are invited back for more work. The consultants now suggest a more complete robotic automation of the making of muffler assemblies and also a reduction in container size to eight per container. Meritor implements these suggestions and the result is that the muffler assembly fabrication cell now averages approximately 32 assemblies per hour, and the catalytic converter assembly cell can now respond to an order for a batch of catalytic converters in one hour. The safety stock remains at 12.5 percent. How many kanban cards are needed? (Answer in Appendix D)
15. In value stream mapping, what does an arrow in the shape of a lightning bolt mean? **LO 14-3**
16. What does an inverted triangle represent in a value stream map?
17. In a data box on a value stream map, what do the abbreviations CT and C/O mean?
18. What is used to indicate suggested changes in a process that may lead to improvements in a value stream?
19. Compared to manufacturing systems, what is it about the environment of service operations that make them much harder to control? **LO 14-4**
20. The chapter presents multiple techniques that service firms can use to make their processes leaner. Which technique is demonstrated by a restaurant that offers special discounts midweek to attract more demand during a traditionally slow period?

CASE: Quality Parts Company

Quality Parts Company supplies gizmos for a computer manufacturer located a few miles away. The company produces two different models of gizmos in production runs ranging from 100 to 300 units.

The production flow of models X and Y is shown in Exhibit 14.14. Model Z requires milling as its first step, but otherwise follows the same flow pattern as X and Y. Skids can hold up to 20 gizmos at a time. Approximate times per unit by operation number and equipment setup times are shown in Exhibit 14.15.

Demand for gizmos from the computer company ranges between 125 and 175 per month, equally divided among X, Y, and Z. Subassembly builds up inventory early in the month to make certain that a buffer stock is always available. Raw materials and purchased parts for subassemblies each constitute 40 percent of the manufacturing cost of a gizmo. Both categories of parts are multiple-sourced from about 80 vendors and are delivered at random times. (Gizmos have 40 different part numbers.)

Scrap rates are about 10 percent at each operation, inventory turns twice yearly, employees are paid on a day rate, employee turnover is 25 percent per year, and net profit from operations is steady at 5 percent per year. Maintenance is performed as needed.

EXHIBIT 14.14

Gizmo Production Flow

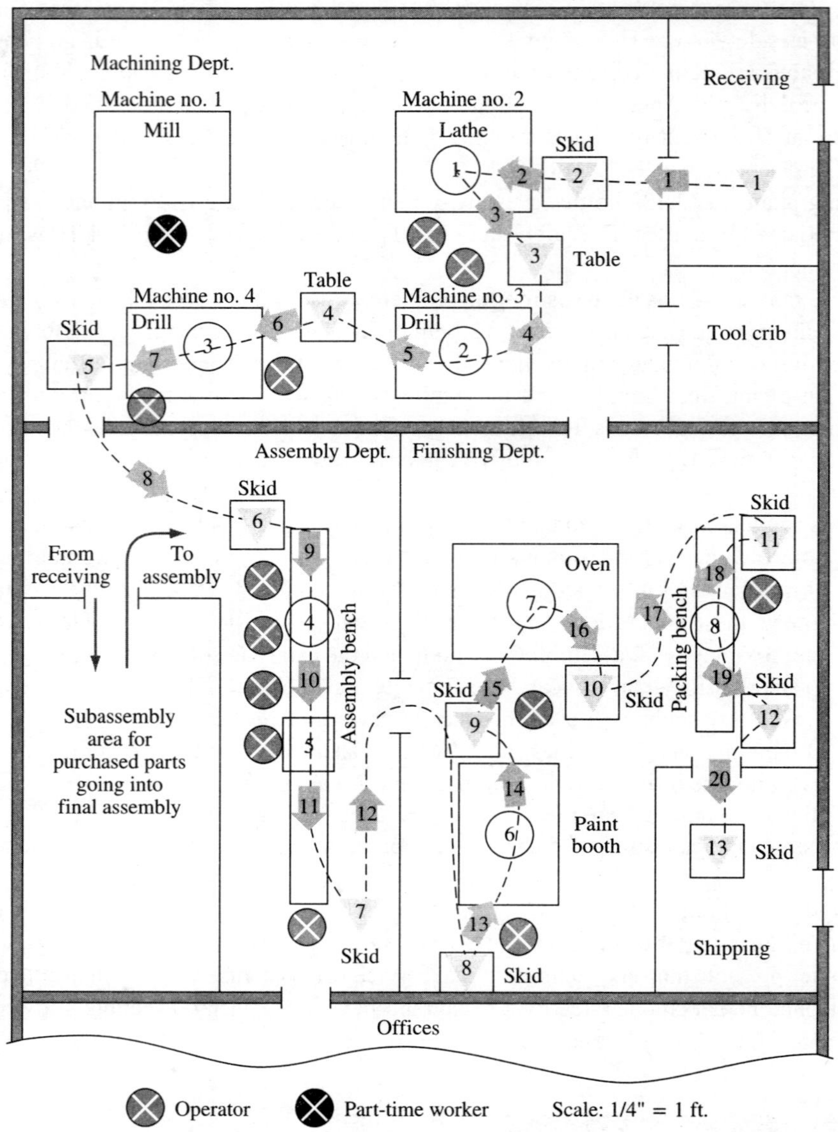

EXHIBIT 14.15

Operations and Setup Time

Operation Number and Name	Operation Time (Minutes)	Setup Time (Minutes)
Milling for Model Z	20	60
1 Lathe	50	30
2 Mod. 14 drill	15	5
3 Mod. 14 drill	40	5
4 Assembly step 1	50	
Assembly step 2	45	
Assembly step 3	50	
5 Inspection	30	
6 Paint	30	
7 Oven	50	20
8 Packing	5	

The manager of Quality Parts Company has been contemplating installing an automated ordering system to help control inventories and to "keep the skids filled." (She feels that two days of work in front of a workstation motivates the worker to produce at top speed.) She is also planning to add three inspectors to clean up the quality problem. Further, she is thinking about setting up a rework line to speed repairs. Although she is pleased with the high utilization of most of her equipment and labor, she is concerned about the idle time of the milling machine. Finally, she has asked the industrial engineering department to look into high-rise shelving to store parts coming off machine 4.

Questions

1. Which of the changes being considered by the manager of Quality Parts Company are counter to the lean philosophy?
2. Make recommendations for lean improvements in such areas as scheduling, layout, kanban, task groupings, and inventory. Use quantitative data as much as possible; state necessary assumptions.
3. Sketch the operation of a pull system for running Quality Parts Company's current system.
4. Outline a plan for introducing lean at Quality Parts Company.

CASE: Value Stream Mapping

Value stream mapping involves first developing a baseline map of the current situation of a company's external and/or internal operations, and then applying lean concepts, developing a future state map that shows improved operations. Exhibit 14.16, for example, shows the current state with a production lead time of 4.5 days. This system is a batch/push system (indicated by striped arrows), resulting in long delays and inventory buildups. Exhibit 14.17 shows the future state map with a production lead time of 0.25 day. This was accomplished by moving to a continuous-flow pull system and attacking the seven wastes. Value stream mapping uses a number of special icons and a display format of boxes and flows.

EXHIBIT 14.16

Map of the Current State

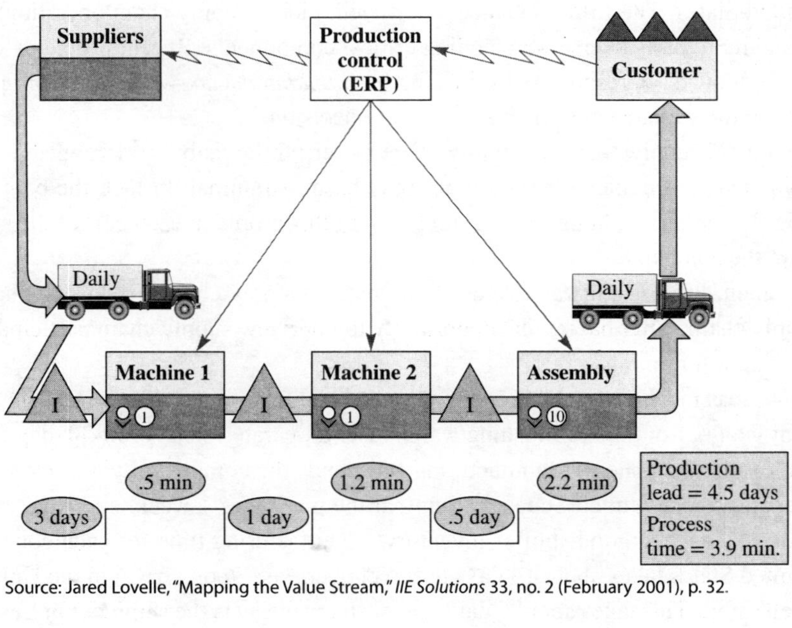

Source: Jared Lovelle, "Mapping the Value Stream," *IIE Solutions* 33, no. 2 (February 2001), p. 32.

Questions

1. Eliminating the queue of work dramatically quickens the time it takes a part to flow through the system. What are the disadvantages of removing those queues?
2. How do you think the machine operators would react to the change?
3. What would you do to ensure that the operators were kept busy?

EXHIBIT 14.17

Map of the Future State

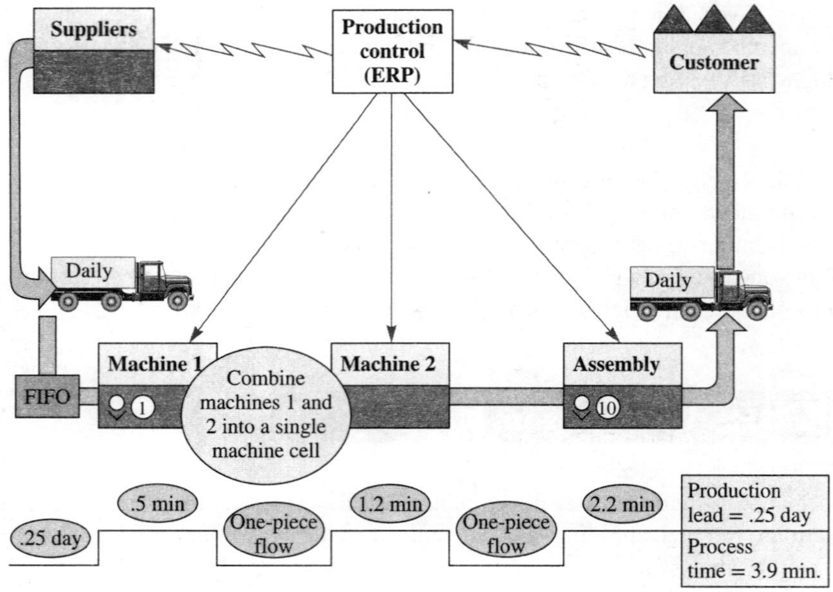

Source: Jared Lovelle, "Mapping the Value Stream," *IIE Solutions* 33, no. 2 (February 2001), p. 32.

CASE: Pro Fishing Boats—A Value Stream Mapping Exercise

A fishing boat manufacturer, Pro Fishing Boats, is having many problems with critical globally sourced parts. Pro Fishing has two manufacturing facilities in the United States. The firm's reliance on efficient global supply chain operations is increasing as the manufacturer is sourcing more and more parts overseas, including critical components. Recent problems with a number of these critical parts have caused line shutdowns. In response, Pro Fishing has *mandated* a six-week inventory on all globally sourced parts. Management has asked you to evaluate whether this is the right decision.

First, you must understand Pro Fishing's supply chain. Currently, there is very little visibility (knowledge of the current status) of inventory in the supply chain, and communication with the supply base is minimal. In fact, the boat manufacturer does not have *any* visibility past the Tier I suppliers. Adding to the complexity of this problem, each part of the supply chain is handled by different departments within the company.

In order to understand the supply chain, Pro Fishing has asked you to map its supply chain. To do so, it has identified a critical component to follow in the supply chain. After having the opportunity to interview supply chain participants, including suppliers, you have collected the following information.

The component is manufactured overseas in China by the Tier I supplier, Manufacturing Inc. The Manufacturing Inc. production schedule is based on orders sent via fax from the Pro Fishing warehouse. It operates on a 90-60-30–day forecast, along with a weekly order. Upon completion of the component, Manufacturing Inc. sends the component via truck to the Shanghai Port, where it is loaded onto a ship heading to the United States. Loading at the port takes 1 week, and truck transport takes 3 days. Manufacturing Inc. holds a 9-week finished goods buffer inventory. Manufacturing time for each component is only about 3 days. The ship bound to the United States takes about 14 days to travel overseas. Upon arrival in the United States, the component is unloaded at the Los Angeles port. This takes about 5 days and customs inspects the shipment in Los Angeles. The goods travel by train to Chicago, which takes about 7 days. Goods are held in Chicago for about half a week. From there, the component is trucked to a Pro Fishing warehouse where the 6-week inventory buffer has been mandated. Shipment to the Pro Fishing warehouse takes 2 days. From the warehouse, the components are trucked to plants in the United States triggered by electronic orders from each of the Pro Fishing plants.

In talking to Manufacturing Inc., Pro Fishing has learned that the component is made up of two main raw materials: one from China and the other from the United States. Due to the risk of running out of these raw materials, Manufacturing Inc.

maintains a 4-week buffer of the China-based raw materials and a 12-week buffer of the U.S.-based raw materials. These Tier II supplier orders are by formal purchase order only. It is interesting to note that Manufacturing Inc. uses these suppliers due to Pro Fishing's strict supplier qualification requirements.

Questions

1. Create a value stream map (VSM) of this supply chain. What other information is needed?
2. Where is there risk for supply chain disruptions or stoppages to the flow of materials?
3. Where do opportunities reside in improving supply chain operations and how has VSM helped reveal these?

PRACTICE EXAM

In each of the following, name the term defined or answer the question. Answers are listed at the bottom.

1. Anything that does not add value from the customer's perspective.
2. An integrated set of activities designed to achieve production using minimal inventories of raw materials, work-in-process, and finished goods.
3. The Toyota Production System is founded on these two philosophies.
4. The set of value- and non–value-adding activities required to design, order, and provide a product from concept to launch, order to delivery, and raw materials to customers.
5. The Japanese philosophy that focuses on continuous improvement.
6. A philosophy in which similar parts are brought together in families for production purposes.
7. Means producing only what is needed when needed and no more.
8. A period of time during which the production schedule cannot be changed.
9. Producing a mix of products that matches demand as closely as possible.
10. A production control system that uses a signaling device to regulate the flow of material.
11. If the lead time for an item is exactly five days, the demand is a constant four units per day, and the shipment container contains two units, how many kanban card sets would be needed? (Assume 0 percent safety stock.)
12. A firm wants to justify smaller lot sizes economically. Management knows that it cannot change the cost to carry one unit in inventory because this is largely based on the value of the item. To justify a smaller lot size, what must it do?

Answers to Practice Exam 1. Waste 2. Lean production 3. Elimination of waste and respect for people 4. Value stream 5. Kaizen 6. Group technology 7. JIT (just-in-time) production 8. Freeze window 9. Uniform plant loading 10. Kanban 11. 10 card sets 12. Reduce setup cost

For PowerPoint lecture slides, Solutions Manual, Test Bank, Data files for solved examples, Excel Templates, Step-by-Step Solved Examples in video format, Tutorial Videos and many more, scan the adjacent **QR code**, or **visit http://www.mhhe.com/sie-chase15e**

Chapter 15

Logistics, Distribution, and Transportation

LEARNING OBJECTIVES

LO15-1 Explain what logistics is

LO15-2 Contrast logistics and warehouse design alternatives

LO15-3 Analyze logistics-driven location decisions

NEW WIDE LANE IN THE PANAMA CANAL

Much of the U.S. imports from Asia arrive by ship on the West Coast, and then get transferred to rail lines for transit to the rest of the country. On July 26, 2016, Panama rocked the world of logistics. That's when it opened a fat new lane of its canal for big ships that can carry three times as much as vessels sailing the old channel. Larger vessels should make it cheaper to send cargo through the canal to ports in the East and on the Gulf Coast of the United States. Several logistics experts are calling the expansion a game changer and a threat to the western ports and railroads.

© EvrenKalinbacak/Getty Images RF

It takes about 18 days total to make the ship and train journey from Asia to the West Coast, and then across the country to East Coast businesses. When conditions are good, the all-water route through the Panama Canal takes about 22 days, roughly the same as via the Suez Canal—a competing route from Asia to the East Coast. At times, the sea voyages can take substantially longer, depending on ship speed and route congestion.

The ship-to-rail route costs 10 percent to 25 percent more than the pure all-water route, but it is faster and usually more reliable. The economies of the expanded canal makes the pure all-water route even more attractive from a cost view. Shippers like alternatives and now there are actually three alternatives for moving goods from Asia to the eastern U.S., the enlarged Panama Canal, the Suez Canal, and the mixed-mode ship and train journey.

LOGISTICS

LO 15-1

Explain what logistics is

A major issue in designing a great supply chain for manufactured goods is determining the way those items are moved from the manufacturing plant to the customer. For consumer products, this often involves moving product from the manufacturing plant to a warehouse and then to a retail store. You probably do not think about this often, but consider all those items with "Made in China" on the label. That sweatshirt probably has made a trip longer than you may ever make. If you live in Chicago in the United States and the sweatshirt is made in the Fujian region of China, that sweatshirt traveled over 6,600 miles, or 10,600 kilometers, nearly halfway around the world, to get to the retail store where you bought it. To keep the price of the sweatshirt down, that trip must be made as efficiently as possible. There is no telling how that sweatshirt made the trip. It might have been flown in an airplane or might have traveled in a combination of vehicles, possibly going by truck part of the way and by boat or plane the rest. Logistics is about this movement of goods through the supply chain.

APICS, the supply chain and operations professional organization, defines **logistics** as "the art and science of obtaining, producing, and distributing material and product in the proper place and in proper quantities." This is a fairly broad definition, and this chapter will focus on how to analyze where we locate warehouses and plants and how to evaluate the movement of materials to and from those locations. The term **international logistics** refers to managing these functions when the movement is on a global scale. Clearly, if the China-made sweatshirt is sold in the United States or Europe, this involves international logistics.

logistics
The art and science of obtaining, producing, and distributing material and product in the proper place and in the proper quantities.

There are companies that specialize in logistics, such as United Parcel Service (UPS), FedEx, and DHL. These global companies are in the business of moving everything from flowers to industrial equipment. Today, a manufacturing company most often will contract with one of those companies to handle many of its logistics functions. In this case, those transportation companies often are called a **third-party logistics company**. The most basic function would be simply moving the goods from one place to another. The logistics company also may provide additional services such as warehouse management, inventory control, and other customer service functions.

International logistics
All functions concerned with the movement of materials and finished goods on a global scale.

Logistics is big business, accounting for 8 to 9 percent of the U.S. gross domestic product, and growing. Today's modern, efficient warehouse and distribution centers are the heart of logistics. These centers are carefully managed and efficiently operated to ensure the secure storage and quick flow of goods, services, and related information from the point of origin to the point of consumption.

Third-party logistics company
A company that manages all or part of another company's product delivery operations.

EACH BUSINESS DAY, FEDEX EXPRESS MOVES MORE THAN 3.5 MILLION PACKAGES THROUGH 10 AIR EXPRESS HUBS AROUND THE GLOBE.

LO 15-2

Contrast logistics and warehouse design alternatives

DECISIONS RELATED TO LOGISTICS

The problem of deciding how best to transport goods from plants to customers is a complex one that affects the cost of a product. Major trade-offs related to the cost of transporting the product, speed of delivery, and flexibility to react to changes are involved. Information systems play a major role in coordinating activities and include activities such as allocating resources, managing inventory levels, scheduling, and order tracking. A full discussion of these systems is beyond the scope of this book, but we cover basic inventory control in other chapters.

Transportation Modes

A key decision area is deciding how material will be transported. The Logistics-System Design Matrix shown in Exhibit 15.1 depicts the basic alternatives. There are six widely recognized modes of transportation: highway (trucks), water (ships), air (aircraft), rail (trains), pipelines, and hand delivery. Each mode is uniquely suited to handle certain types of products, as described next.

Strategy

- **Highway (truck)** Actually, few products are moved without some highway transportation. The highway offers great flexibility for moving goods to virtually any location not separated by water. Size of the product, weight, and liquid or bulk can all be accommodated with this mode.
- **Water (ship)** Very high capacity and very low cost, but transit times are slow, and large areas of the world are not directly accessible to water carriers. This mode is especially useful for bulk items such as oil, coal, and chemical products.
- **Air** Fast but expensive. Small, light, expensive items are most appropriate for this mode of transportation.
- **Rail (trains)** This is a fairly low-cost alternative, but transit times can be long and may be subject to variability. The suitability of rail can vary depending on the rail infrastructure. The European infrastructure is highly developed, making this an attractive alternative compared to trucks, while in the United States, the railroad infrastructure has declined over the last 50 years, making it less attractive.
- **Pipelines** This is highly specialized and limited to liquids, gases, and solids in slurry forms. No packaging is needed and the costs per mile are low. The initial cost to build a pipeline is very high.
- **Hand Delivery** This is the last step in many supply chains. Getting the product in the customer's hand is often a slow and costly activity due to the high labor content.

EXHIBIT 15.1

Logistics-System Design Matrix: Framework Describing Logistics Processes

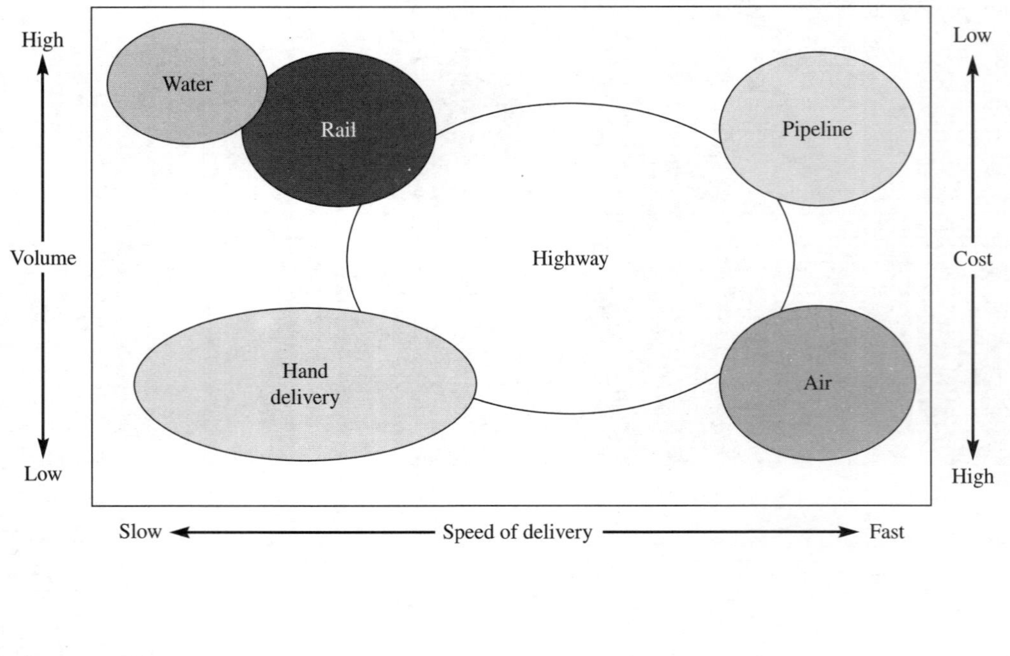

Few companies use a single mode of transportation. Multimodal solutions are the norm, and finding the correct multimode strategies can be a significant problem. The problem of coordination and scheduling the carriers requires comprehensive information systems capable of tracking goods through the system. Standardized containers often are used so that a product can be transferred efficiently from a truck to an airplane or ship.

Warehouse Design

Special consolidation warehouses are used when shipments from various sources are pulled together and combined into larger shipments with a common destination. This improves the efficiency of the entire system. **Cross-docking** is an approach used in these consolidation warehouses, where, rather than making larger shipments, large shipments are broken down into small shipments for local delivery in an area. This often can be done in a coordinated manner so the goods are never stored in inventory.

Cross-docking
An approach used in consolidation warehouses where, rather than making larger shipments, large shipments are broken down into small shipments for local delivery in an area.

Retailers receive shipments from many suppliers in their regional warehouses and immediately sort those shipments for delivery to individual stores by using cross-docking systems coordinated by computerized control systems. This results in a minimal amount of inventory being carried in the warehouses.

Hub-and-spoke systems combine the idea of consolidation and that of cross-docking. Here, the warehouse is referred to as a "hub" and its sole purpose is sorting goods. Incoming goods are sorted immediately to consolidation areas, where each area is designated for shipment to a specific location. Hubs are located in strategic locations near the geographic center of the region they are to serve to minimize the distance a good must travel.

Hub-and-spoke systems
Systems that combine the idea of consolidation and that of cross-docking.

Designing a system is an interesting and complex task. The following section focuses on the plant and warehouse location problem as representative of the types of logistics decisions that need to be made. Logistics is a broad topic, and its elements evolve as the value-added services provided by major logistics vendors expand. Having the proper network design is fundamental to efficiency in the industry.

LOCATING LOGISTICS FACILITIES

LO 15-3
Analyze logistics-driven location decisions

The problem of facility location is faced by both new and existing businesses, and its solution is critical to a company's eventual success. An important element in designing a company's supply chain is the location of its facilities. For instance, 3M has moved a significant part of its corporate activity, including R&D, to the more temperate climate of Austin, Texas. Toys "R" Us has opened locations in Japan as part of its global strategy. Disney chose Shanghai for its Chinese theme park, and Boeing assembles the 787 Dreamliner in South Carolina. Manufacturing and service companies' location decisions are guided by a variety of criteria defined by competitive imperatives. Criteria that influence manufacturing plant and warehouse location planning are discussed next.

Strategy

Proximity to Customers: For example, Japan's NTN Driveshafts built a major plant in Columbus, Indiana, to be closer to major automobile manufacturing plants in the United States, whose buyers want their goods delivered yesterday. Such proximity also helps ensure that customer needs are incorporated into products being developed and built.

Business Climate: A favorable business climate can include the presence of similar-sized businesses, the presence of companies in the same industry and, in the case of international locations, the presence of other foreign companies. Probusiness government legislation and local government intervention to facilitate businesses locating in an area via subsidies, tax abatements, and other support are also factors.

Total Costs: The objective is to select a site with the lowest total cost. This includes regional costs, inbound distribution costs, and outbound distribution costs. Land, construction, labor, taxes, and energy costs make up the regional costs. In addition, there are hidden costs that are difficult to measure. These involve (1) excessive moving of preproduction material between locations before final delivery to the customers and (2) loss of customer responsiveness arising from locating away from the main customer base.

OSCM AT WORK

Relocation of 'Tata Nano ' Manufacturing Plant

Site selection in India is often dominated by tax incentives provided by different state governments. More often than not political reasons dominate the location decision of government projects, for example, many Indian Railways projects are decided based on political proximity of dominating political party in the Central Government. One of the most talked about plant re-location problem of recent past is that of shifting of Tata Nano plant from 'Singur' in West Bengal, to Sanand in Gujarat, India.

Tata Nano, an ambitious family-car project from Tata Group, is aimed at providing world's cheapest car to the consumers. Its manufacturing facilities were finally set up in Sanand to avail the financial subsidies, tax holidays, etc. Land availability and its low cost, cheap labor, raw material availability, etc. were other governing factors in site selection for the low cost manufacturing.

Singur, a small village in the state of West Bengal, was originally selected as the plant site, which required over 1000 acres of land. However, political disagreements started growing up soon from opposition political party and the hostility from local communities became unmanageable for Tata Group. In October 2008, Tata Motors eventually had to pull out its ₹2,000-crore project from Singur despite the fact that it had already suffered a loss to the tune of about ₹500 crore.

Many other state governments came up with lucrative proposals to attract Tata Nano project after its re-location problem. State of Kerala, Jharkhand, Orissa, Andhra Pradesh, Gujarat, and even countries like Sri Lanka came forward with their attractive proposals. However, Sanand in Gujarat could make it because of various factors such as political stability, availability of economical land and labor, proximity to ports (benefits for both exports and imports), financial incentives like tax holiday for first 10 years, etc. According to Mr. Ratan Tata, "the group had opted for Gujarat because it had "already lost a lot of time (in the Singur controversy) and urgency was the need of the day...We had an urgency to move to a new location...the 'reputation of Gujarat' and the 'speed' at which provisions were made, forced us to opt for Gujarat [1]." Sanand is located at a distance of 40 kms from Ahmedabad. It is very close to ports like Rajkot as well as Mundra, which is an advantage for export [2]. Sanand plant of Tata Nano is spread over an area of about 1,100 acres, with an estimated cost of about ₹2,000 crore.

There is no doubt that West Bengal's loss is Gujarat's gain. Tata's decision of plant relocation was based on the strategy to minimization of the future losses and salvation of the existing situations in the best possible manner. Captains of Indian corporate world have learnt their lesson that without socio-political stability, industrial growth is a distant dream.

References

1. "India: Modi Wins as Gujarat Gets Tata's Nano Plant", *Business Week*, available on http://www.businessweek.com/globalbiz/content/oct2008/gb2008108_390634.htm (accessed on 24 April 2014).
2. 'Tata Nano's Plant in Sanand' available on Corporate Website of Tata Nano http://www.tatanano.in/tata-nano-plant-in-sanand.html (accessed on 24 April 2014).

Infrastructure: Adequate road, rail, air, and sea transportation is vital. Energy and telecommunications requirements also must be met. In addition, the local government's willingness to invest in upgrading infrastructure to the levels required may be an incentive to select a specific location.

Quality of Labor: The educational and skill levels of the labor pool must match the company's needs. Even more important are their willingness and ability to learn.

Suppliers: A high-quality and competitive supplier base makes a given location suitable. The proximity of important suppliers' plants also supports lean production methods.

Free trade zone
A closed facility (under the supervision of government customs officials) into which foreign goods can be brought without being subject to the payment of normal import duties.

Other Facilities: The location of other plants or distribution centers of the same company may influence a new facility's location in the network. Issues of product mix and capacity are strongly interconnected to the location decision in this context.

Free Trade Zones: A foreign trade zone or a **free trade zone** is typically a closed facility (under the supervision of the customs department) into which foreign goods can be brought without being subject to the normal customs requirements. There are about 260 such free trade zones in the

United States today. Such specialized locations also exist in other countries. Manufacturers in free trade zones can utilize imported components used in the production of the final product and delay payment of customs duties until the product is shipped into the host country.

Political Risk: The fast-changing geopolitical scenes in numerous nations present exciting and challenging opportunities. But the extended phase of transformation that many countries are undergoing makes the decision to locate in those areas extremely difficult. Political risks in both the country of location and the host country influence location decisions.

Government Barriers: Barriers to enter and locate in many countries are being removed today through legislation. Yet many nonlegislative and cultural barriers should be considered in location planning.

Trading Blocs: The Central America Free Trade Agreement (CAFTA) is one of the new **trading blocs** in our hemisphere. Such agreements influence location decisions, both within and outside

Trading blocs
A group of countries that agree on a set of special arrangements governing the trading of goods between member countries. Companies may locate in places affected by the agreement to take advantage of new market opportunities.

OSCM AT WORK

787 Dreamliner Assembled in South Carolina from Components Sourced from around the World

Boeing has always assembled its large jets in Seattle, Washington, but that recently changed. Boeing rolled out the first jetliner made in the American South on April 27, 2012, amid fireworks and the cheers of thousands of workers. By 2016, the plant was producing 12 of the revolutionary aircraft per month and that is expected to increase to 14 per month by 2020.

Other than the new assembly location, the 787 uses global subcontractors who deliver completed sub-assemblies to the South Carolina plant. Wings, for example, are manufactured in Japan, horizontal stabilizers in Italy and South Korea, passenger doors in France, and cargo and access doors in Sweden. In order to move all these parts, Boeing modified four used 747-400 into 747 Dreamlifters, gigantic planes capable of carrying completed wings and large fuselage sections.

This radically different approach to building planes is designed to save cost and speed production.

trading bloc countries. Firms typically locate, or relocate, within a bloc to take advantage of new market opportunities or lower total costs afforded by the trading agreement. Other companies (those outside the trading bloc countries) decide on locations within the bloc so as not to be disqualified from competing in the new market. Examples include the location of various Japanese auto manufacturing plants in Europe before 1992, as well as recent moves by many communications and financial services companies into Mexico in a post-NAFTA environment.

Environmental Regulation: The environmental regulations that impact a certain industry in a given location should be included in the location decision. Besides measurable cost implications, these regulations influence the relationship with the local community.

Host Community: The host community's interest in having the plant in its midst is a necessary part of the evaluation process. Local educational facilities and the broader issue of quality of life are also important.

Competitive Advantage: An important decision for multinational companies is the nation in which to locate the home base for each distinct business. A company can have different home bases for distinct businesses or segments. Competitive advantage is created at a home base where strategy is set, the core product and process technology are created, and a critical mass of production takes place. So a company should move its home base to a country that stimulates innovation and provides the best environment for global competitiveness. This concept can also be applied to domestic companies seeking to gain sustainable competitive advantage. It partly explains the southeastern states' recent emergence as the preferred corporate destination within the United States (that is, their business climate fosters innovation and low-cost production).

Plant Location Methods

Analytics

As we will see, there are many techniques available for identifying potential sites for plants or other types of facilities. The process required to narrow the decision down to a particular area can vary significantly depending on the type of business and the competitive pressures that must be considered. As we have discussed, there are often many different criteria that need to be considered when selecting from the set of feasible sites.

In this section, we sample three different types of techniques that have proven to be very useful to many companies. The first is the *factor-rating system* that allows us to consider many different types of criteria using simple point-rating scales. Next, we consider the *transportation method of linear programming,* a powerful technique for estimating the cost of using a network of plants and warehouses. Following this, we consider the *centroid method,* a technique often used by communications companies (cell phone providers) to locate their transmission towers. Finally, later in the chapter we consider how service firms such as McDonald's and State Farm Insurance use statistical techniques to find desirable locations for their facilities.

Keep in mind that each of the techniques described here would be used within the context of a more comprehensive strategy for locating a facility. Typically, the strategy would employ some type of search where major regions are first considered; it is narrowed down to areas, then to potential sites, and finally a choice is made between a few alternatives. Think of these techniques as simple tools that are used in different ways to zero in on a site. The factor-rating system is useful when nonquantitative factors are important. The linear programming and centroid methods are quantitative and may be tied to cost and service-related criteria. The statistical techniques are good when there is significant variability in criteria measures. The techniques are often used in combination to solve a real problem.

Factor-rating systems
An approach for selecting a facility location by combining a diverse set of factors. Point scales are developed for each criterion. Each potential site is then evaluated on each criterion and the points are combined to calculate a rating for the site.

Factor-Rating Systems **Factor-rating systems** are perhaps the most widely used of the general location techniques because they provide a mechanism to combine diverse factors in an easy-to-understand format.

By way of example, a refinery was assigned the following range of point values to major factors affecting a set of possible sites.

	Range
Fuels in region	0 to 330
Power availability and reliability	0 to 200
Labor climate	0 to 100
Living conditions	0 to 100
Transportation	0 to 50
Water supply	0 to 10
Climate	0 to 50
Supplies	0 to 60
Tax policies and laws	0 to 20

Each site was then rated against each factor, and a point value was selected from its assigned range. The sums of assigned points for each site were then compared. The site with the most points was selected.

A major problem with simple point-rating schemes is that they do not account for the wide range of costs that may occur within each factor. For example, there may be only a few hundred dollars' difference between the best and worst locations on one factor and several thousands of dollars' difference between the best and the worst on another. The first factor may have the most points available to it but provide little help in making the location decision; the second may have few points available but potentially show a real difference in the value of locations. To deal with this problem, it has been suggested that points possible for each factor be derived using a weighting scale based on standard deviations of costs rather than simply total cost amounts. In this way, relative costs can be considered.

Transportation Method of Linear Programming The **transportation method** is a special linear programming method. (Note that linear programming is developed in detail in Appendix A.) It gets its name from its application to problems involving transporting products from several sources to several destinations. The two common objectives of such problems are to either (1) minimize the cost of shipping *n* units to *m* destinations or (2) maximize the profit of shipping *n* units to *m* destinations.

Transportation method
A special linear programming method that is useful for solving problems involving transporting products from several sources to several destinations.

EXAMPLE 15.1 U.S. Pharmaceutical Company

Suppose the U.S. Pharmaceutical Company has four factories supplying the warehouses of four major customers and its management wants to determine the minimum-cost shipping schedule for its monthly output to these customers. Factory supply, warehouse demands, and shipping costs per case for these drugs are shown in Exhibit 15.2A.

The transportation matrix for this example appears in Exhibit 15.2B, where supply availability at each factory is shown in the far right column and the warehouse demands are shown in the bottom row. The shipping costs are shown in the small boxes within the cells. For example, the cost to ship one unit from the Indianapolis factory to the customer warehouse in Columbus is $25. The actual flows would be shown in the cells intersecting the factory rows and warehouse columns.

SOLUTION

This problem can be solved by using Microsoft Excel's Solver function. If you are not familiar with the Solver, you should study Appendix A, "Linear Programming Using the Excel Solver." Exhibit 15.3 shows how the problem can be set up in the spreadsheet. Cells B6 through E6 contain the requirement for each customer warehouse. Cells F2 through F5 contain the amount that can be supplied from each plant. Cells B2 through E5 are the cost of shipping one unit for each potential plant and warehouse combination.

Cells for the solution of the problem are B9 through E12. These cells can initially be left blank when setting up the spreadsheet. Column cells F9 through F12 are the sum of each row, indicating how much is actually being shipped from each factory in the candidate solution. Similarly, row cells B13 through E13 are sums of the amount being shipped to each customer in the candidate solution. The Excel Sum function can be used to calculate these values.

Exhibit 15.2

A. Data for U.S. Pharmaceutical Transportation Problem

					Shipping Costs per Case (in Dollars)			
Factory	Supply	Warehouse	Demand	From	To Columbus	To St. Louis	To Denver	To Los Angeles
Indianapolis	15	Columbus	10	Indianapolis	$25	$35	$36	$60
Phoenix	6	St. Louis	12	Phoenix	55	30	25	25
New York	14	Denver	15	New York	40	50	80	90
Atlanta	11	Los Angeles	9	Atlanta	30	40	66	75

B. Transportation Matrix for U.S. Pharmaceutical Problem

From \ To	Columbus	St. Louis	Denver	Los Angeles	Factory supply
Indianapolis	25	35	36	60	15
Phoenix	55	30	25	25	6
New York	40	50	80	90	14
Atlanta	30	40	66	75	11
Destination requirements	10	12	15	9	46 / 46

Exhibit 15.3

Excel Screen Showing the U.S. Pharmaceutical Problem

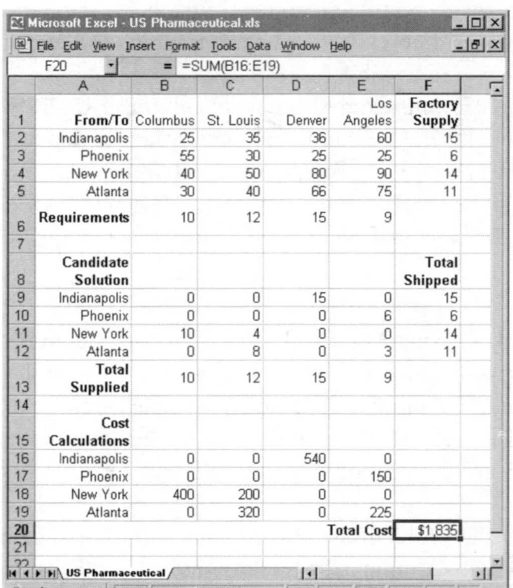

	A	B	C	D	E	F
1	From/To	Columbus	St. Louis	Denver	Los Angeles	Factory Supply
2	Indianapolis	25	35	36	60	15
3	Phoenix	55	30	25	25	6
4	New York	40	50	80	90	14
5	Atlanta	30	40	66	75	11
6	Requirements	10	12	15	9	
7						
8	Candidate Solution					Total Shipped
9	Indianapolis	0	0	15	0	15
10	Phoenix	0	0	0	6	6
11	New York	10	4	0	0	14
12	Atlanta	0	8	0	3	11
13	Total Supplied	10	12	15	9	
14						
15	Cost Calculations					
16	Indianapolis	0	0	540	0	
17	Phoenix	0	0	0	150	
18	New York	400	200	0	0	
19	Atlanta	0	320	0	225	
20					Total Cost	$1,835

The cost of the candidate solution is calculated in cells B16 through E19. Multiplying the amount shipped in the candidate solution by the cost per unit of shipping over that particular route makes this calculation. For example, multiplying B2 by B9 in cell B16 gives the cost of shipping between Indianapolis and Columbus for the candidate solution. The total cost shown in cell F20 is the sum of all these individual costs.

To solve the problem, the Excel Solver application needs to be accessed. The Solver is found by selecting Data and then Solver from the Excel menu. A screen similar to what is shown here should appear. If you cannot find Solver at that location, the required add-in might not have been activated when Excel was initially installed on your computer.

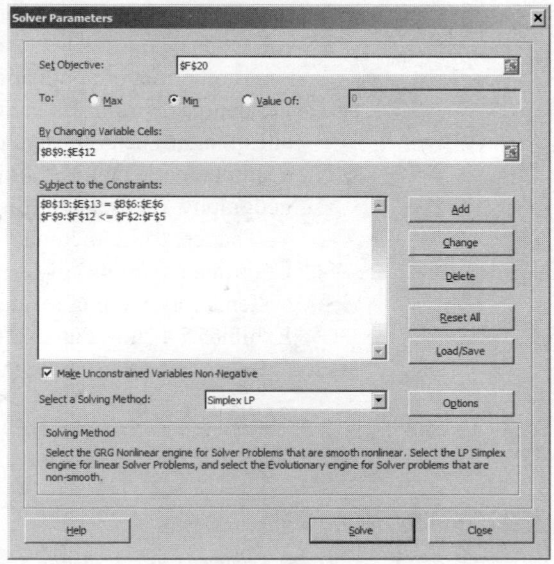

Excel screen shots from Microsoft Excel. © 2010 Microsoft Corporation

Solver parameters now need to be set. First, set the target cell. This is the cell where the total cost associated with the solution is calculated. In our sample problem, this is cell F20, which sums the values in cells B16 through E19. Next, we need to indicate that we are minimizing this cell. Selecting the "Min" button does this. The location of our solution is indicated in the "By Changing Variable Cells." These cells are B9 through E12 in our example.

Next, we need to indicate the constraints for our problem. For our transportation problem, we must be sure customer demand is met and we do not exceed the capacity of our manufacturing plants. To ensure that demand is met, click on "Add" and highlight the range of cells where we have calculated the total amount being shipped to each customer. This range is B13 to E13 in our example. Next select "=" indicating that we want the amount shipped to equal demand. Finally, on the right side enter the range of cells where the actual customer demand is stated in our spreadsheet. This range is B6 to E6 in our example.

The second set of constraints that ensures that the capacity of our manufacturing plants is not exceeded is entered similarly. The range of cells that indicate how much is being shipped from each factory is F9 to F12. These values need to be less than or equal to (< =) the capacity of each factory, which is in cells F2 to F5.

Two options need to be set for solving transportation problems. First, set the solving method to "Simplex LP." This tells the Solver that there are no nonlinear calculations in our spreadsheet. This is important because the Solver can use a very efficient algorithm to calculate the optimal solution to this problem if this condition exists. Next, check the "Make Unconstrained Variables Non-Negative" box. This tells Solver that the values in our solution need to be greater than or equal to zero. In transportation problems, shipping negative quantities does not make any sense. Click "Solve" to actually solve the problem. Solver will notify you that it found a solution. Indicate that you want that solution saved. Finally, click OK to go back to the main spreadsheet. The solution should be in cells B9 to E12.

The transportation method can be used to solve many different types of problems if it is applied innovatively. For example, it can be used to test the cost impact of different candidate locations on the entire production–distribution network. To do this, we might add a new row that contains the unit shipping cost from a factory in a new location, say, Dallas, to the existing set of customer warehouses, along with the total amount it could supply. We could then solve this particular matrix for minimum total cost. Next we would replace the factory located in Dallas in the same row of the matrix with a factory at a different location, Houston, and again solve for minimum total cost. Assuming the factories in Dallas and Houston would be identical in other important respects, the location resulting in the lower total cost for the network would be selected.

For additional information about using the Solver, see Appendix A, "Linear Programming Using the Excel Solver."

Centroid Method

Centroid method
A technique for locating single facilities that considers the existing facilities, the distances between them, and the volumes of goods to be shipped.

The **centroid method** is a technique for locating single facilities that considers the existing facilities, the distances between them, and the volumes of goods to be shipped. The technique is often used to locate intermediate or distribution warehouses. In its simplest form, this method assumes that inbound and outbound transportation costs are equal, and it does not include special shipping costs for less than full loads.

Another major application of the centroid method today is the location of communication towers in urban areas. Examples include radio, TV, and cell phone towers. In this application, the goal is to find sites that are near clusters of customers, thus ensuring clear radio signals. The centroid method finds a simple mathematical point. Once it is found, the problem should consider qualitative factors such as geography, roads, and utilities to find an exact location.

The centroid method begins by placing the existing locations on a coordinate grid system. Coordinates are usually based on longitude and latitude measures due to the rapid adoption of GPS systems for mapping locations. To keep it simple for our examples, we use arbitrary *X, Y* coordinates. Exhibit 15.4 shows an example of a grid layout.

Exhibit 15.4

Grid Map for Centroid Example

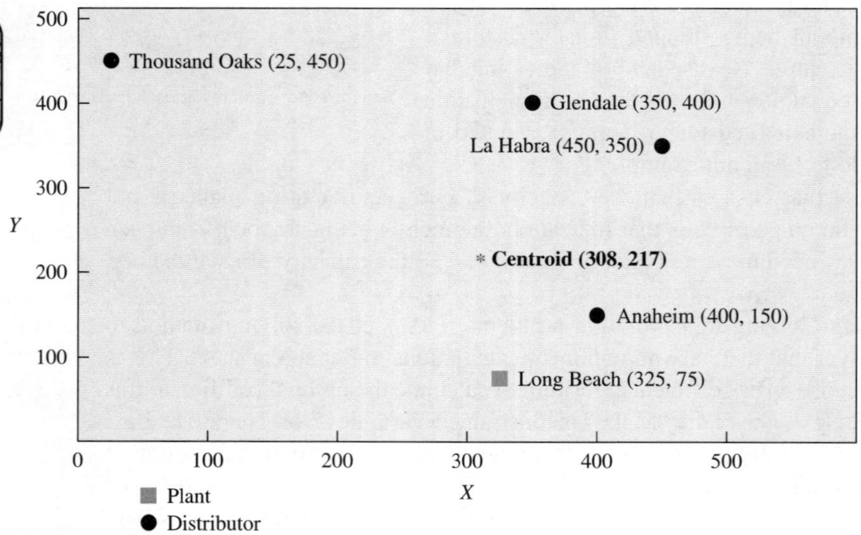

Locations	Gallons of Gasoline per Month (000,000)
Long Beach	1,500
Anaheim	250
La Habra	450
Glendale	350
Thousand Oaks	450

The centroid is found by calculating the *X* and *Y* coordinates that result in the minimal transportation cost. We use the formulas

$$C_x = \frac{\sum d_{ix} V_i}{\sum V_i} \qquad C_y = \frac{\sum d_{iy} V_i}{\sum V_i} \tag{15.1}$$

where

C_x = *X* coordinate of the centroid

C_y = *Y* coordinate of the centroid

d_{ix} = *X* coordinate of the *i*th location

d_{iy} = *Y* coordinate of the *i*th location

V_i = Volume of goods moved to or from the *i*th location

EXAMPLE 15.2 **HiOctane Refining Company**

HiOctane Refining Company needs to locate an intermediate holding facility between its refining plant in Long Beach and its major distributors. Exhibit 15.4 shows the coordinate map and the amount of gasoline shipped to or from the plant and distributors.

In this example, for the Long Beach location (the first location), $d_{ix} = 325$, $d_{iy} = 75$, and $V_i = 1{,}500$.

SOLUTION

Using the information in Exhibit 15.4, we can calculate the coordinates of the centroid:

$$C_x = \frac{(325 \times 1{,}500) + (400 \times 250) + (450 \times 450) + (350 \times 350) + (25 \times 450)}{1{,}500 + 250 + 450 + 350 + 450}$$

$$= \frac{923{,}750}{3{,}000} = 307.9$$

$$C_y = \frac{(75 \times 1{,}500) + (150 \times 250) + (350 \times 450) + (400 \times 350) + (450 \times 450)}{1{,}500 + 250 + 450 + 350 + 450}$$

$$= \frac{650{,}000}{3{,}000} = 216.7$$

This gives management the X and Y coordinates of approximately 308 and 217, respectively, and provides an initial starting point to search for a new site. By examining the location of the calculated centroid on the grid map, we can see that it might be more cost-efficient to ship directly between the Long Beach plant and the Anaheim distributor than to ship via a warehouse near the centroid. Before a location decision is made, management would probably recalculate the centroid, changing the data to reflect this (that is, decrease the gallons shipped from Long Beach by the amount Anaheim needs and remove Anaheim from the formula).

Locating Service Facilities

Because of the variety of service firms and the relatively low cost of establishing a service facility compared to one for manufacturing, new service facilities are far more common than new factories and warehouses. Indeed, there are few communities in which rapid population growth has not been paralleled by concurrent rapid growth in retail outlets, restaurants, municipal services, and entertainment facilities.

Services typically have multiple sites to maintain close contact with customers. The location decision is closely tied to the market selection decision. If the target market is college-age groups, locations in retirement communities—despite desirability in terms of cost, resource availability, and so forth—are not viable alternatives. Market needs also affect the number of sites to be built and the size and characteristics of the sites. Whereas manufacturing location decisions are often made by minimizing costs, many service location decision techniques maximize the profit potential of various sites. Next, we present a multiple regression model that can be used to help select good sites.

EXAMPLE 15.3 **Screening Hotel Location Sites**

Selecting good sites is crucial to a hotel chain's success. Of the four major marketing considerations (price, product, promotion, and location), location and product have been shown to be most important for multisite firms. As a result, hotel chain owners who can pick good sites quickly have a distinct competitive advantage.

Exhibit 15.5 shows the initial list of variables included in a study to help a hotel chain screen potential locations for its new hotels. Data were collected on 57 existing sites. Analysis of the data identified the variables that correlated with operating profit in two years. (See Exhibit 15.6.)

Exhibit 15.5

Independent Variables Collected for the Initial Model-Building Stage

Category	Name	Description
Competitive	INNRATE	Inn price
	PRICE	Room rate for the inn
	RATE	Average competitive room rate
	RMS 1	Hotel rooms within 1 mile
	RMSTOTAL	Hotel rooms within 3 miles
	ROOMSINN	Inn rooms
Demand generators	CIVILIAN	Civilian personnel on base
	COLLEGE	College enrollment within 4 miles
	HOSP1	Hospital beds within 1 mile
	HOSPTOTL	Hospital beds within 4 miles
	HVYIND	Heavy industrial employment
	LGTIND	Light industrial acreage
	MALLS	Shopping mall square footage
	MILBLKD	Military base blocked
	MILITARY	Military personnel
	MILTOT	MILITARY+CIVLIAN
	OFC1	Office space within 1 mile
	OFCTOTAL	Office space within 4 miles
	OFCCBD	Office space in Central Business District
	PASSENGR	Airport passengers enplaned
	RETAIL	Scale ranking of retail activity
	TOURISTS	Annual tourists
	TRAFFIC	Traffic count
	VAN	Airport van
Demographic	EMPLYPCT	Unemployment percentage
	INCOME	Average family income
	POPULACE	Residential population
Market awareness	AGE	Years inn has been open
	NEAREST	Distance to nearest inn
	STATE	State population per inn
	URBAN	Urban population per inn
Physical	ACCESS	Accessibility
	ARTERY	Major traffic artery
	DISTCBD	Distance to downtown
	SIGNVIS	Sign visibility

Exhibit 15.6

A Summary of the Variables that Correlated with Operating Margin

Variable	Year 1	Year 2
ACCESS	.20	
AGE	.29	.49
COLLEGE		.25
DISTCBD		–.22
EMPLYPCT	–.22	–.22
INCOME		–.23
MILTOT		.22
NEAREST	–.51	
OFCCBD	.30	
POPULACE	.30	.35
PRICE	.38	.58
RATE		.27
SIGNVIS	.25	
STATE	–.32	–.33
TRAFFIC	.32	
URBAN	–.22	–.26

SOLUTION

An introduction into how *regression* models are constructed is included in Chapter 18. The details of how variables are selected for inclusion in the model are beyond the scope of this book. Basically the variables that are the most strongly correlated (as shown in Exhibit 15.6) are used in a linear mathematical model to maximize the fit between the profitability and characteristics of each potential site. The correlations are a relative measure of the amount of statistical variation explained by each variable. Variables with values closer to 1 or –1 explain more variation than those closer to zero.

The analysis done by the hotel chain indicated that the best variables to include in the model were the following:

- State population per inn (STATE)
- Room rate for the inn (PRICE)
- Square root of the income of the area (INCOME)
- College enrollment within four miles (COLLEGE)

The final form for this model is as follows:

$$\begin{aligned}\text{Profitability} = \ & 39.05 - 5.41 \times \text{State population per inn (1,000)}\\ & + 5.86 \times \text{Room rate for the inn}\\ & - 3.91 \times \text{Square root of the income of the area (1,000)}\\ & + 1.75 \times \text{College enrollment within 4 miles}\end{aligned}$$

The model shows that profitability is negatively affected by the state population per inn, positively affected by room rate, negatively affected by area income (the inns do better in lower-income areas), and positively affected by colleges nearby.

The hotel chain implemented the model on a spreadsheet and routinely uses the spreadsheet to screen potential real estate acquisitions. The founder and president of the hotel chain has accepted the model's validity and no longer feels obligated to personally select the sites.

This example shows that a specific model can be obtained from the requirements of service organizations and used to identify the most important features in site selection.

CONCEPT CONNECTIONS

LO 15–1 Explain what logistics is

Summary

- Logistics covers the entire scope of obtaining, producing, and distributing material and product to the proper place and in the correct quantities.
- The focus here is on the movement of material and the location of warehouses and manufacturing plants with consideration of the cost of material movement.
- Third-party logistics companies, such as FedEx and DHL, provide services to many companies.

Key Terms

Logistics Management functions that support the complete cycle of material flow: from the purchase and internal control of production materials; to the planning and control of work-in-process; to the purchasing, shipping, and distribution of the finished product.

International logistics All functions concerned with the movement of materials and finished goods on a global scale.

Third-party logistics company A company that manages all or part of another company's product delivery operations.

LO 15–2 Contrast logistics and warehouse design alternatives

Summary

- Decision related to how material will be transported and where plants and warehouses are located have an impact on the cost of the product.
- Trade-offs relate to the cost of transporting the product, delivery speed, and the ability to efficiently react to changes in plans.
- Transportation alternatives, called "modes" of transportation, include water, rail, highways, air, pipelines, and hand delivery. Often, multiple modes are used as a product moves through the supply chain.
- Warehouses and distribution centers are used to consolidate shipments from various sources to improve the efficiency of the supply chain.
- Finding the optimal logistics-system design—consisting of manufacturing plants, distribution centers and warehouses, and, ultimately, delivery to the final customer—is a complex task.

Key Terms

Cross-docking An approach used in consolidation warehouses where, rather than making larger shipments, large shipments are broken down into small shipments for local delivery in an area.

Hub-and-spoke systems Systems that combine the idea of consolidation and that of cross-docking.

LO 15–3 Analyze logistics-driven location decisions

Summary

- There are a variety of criteria that go beyond cost for determining the location of the facilities that form a company's supply chain.
- The factor-rating system is an analytical tool that allows consideration of many different types of criteria using point-rating scales for each criterion.
- Linear programming, in particular the transportation method, is useful when transportation cost is the major criterion in the decision.
- A third technique is the centroid method, which is useful for finding desirable geographic coordinates for a facility such as a cellphone tower.
- Locating service type businesses is often very dependent on how close the contact needs to be to customers. For example, an automatic teller machine for a bank needs to be in close proximity to existing and potential customers.

Key Terms

Free trade zone A closed facility (under the supervision of government customs officials) into which foreign goods can be brought without being subject to the payment of normal import duties.

Trading blocs A group of countries that agree on a set of special arrangements governing the trading of goods between member countries. Companies may locate in places affected by the agreement to take advantage of new market opportunities.

Factor-rating system An approach for selecting a facility location by combining a diverse set of factors. Point scales are developed for each criterion. Each potential site is then evaluated on each criterion and the points are combined to calculate a rating for the site.

Transportation method A special linear programming method that is useful for solving problems involving transporting products from several sources to several destinations.

Centroid method A technique for locating single facilities that considers the existing facilities, the distances between them, and the volumes of goods to be shipped.

Key Formulas

Centroid

[15.1] $$C_x = \frac{\sum d_{ix} V_i}{\sum V_i} \qquad C_y = \frac{\sum d_{iy} V_i}{\sum V_i}$$

SOLVED PROBLEMS

LO 15-1 SOLVED PROBLEM 1

Green Energy Technologies (GET) is planning to locate a new solar panel manufacturing plant in the southeastern United States to meet strongly growing demand in that market. It is considering three cities for this new plant: Montgomery, Alabama; Atlanta, Georgia; and Charleston, North Carolina. It has developed a list of important factors to consider in making its decision. After making site visits to each of the three cities, the facility location team has rated each of the cities as shown in the following table.

Factor	Max Points	City Ratings		
		Montgomery	Atlanta	Charleston
Availability of labor	60	55	52	48
Availability of technical skills	50	37	46	41
Transportation infrastructure	40	34	37	32
Warehousing availability/costs	40	30	33	28
Proximity to customers	35	22	27	25
Proximity to suppliers	25	25	22	20
Taxation structure	15	12	10	14
Quality of life	10	7	8	9
Climate	5	3	3	4

Based on this factor-rating system and the points assigned by the facility location team, which location appears to be the best choice?

Solution

The difficulty in applying a factor-rating system lies in the design of the system and the evaluation of each potential site on every factor. Once this is accomplished, evaluating the results is a simple matter of adding up the total points for each candidate location. Based on the ratings shown, the point totals are as follows.

Montgomery	225
Atlanta	238
Charleston	221

Based on the results of the rating system, Atlanta would appear to be the best choice.

LO 15-2 SOLVED PROBLEM 2

Industrial Packaging Solutions (IPS) is a manufacturer of corrugated fiberboard shipping boxes used by companies across the United States. It sells to wholesalers, who in turn sell to resellers or end-user customers. Final products are consolidated on standard shipping pallets of uniform dimensions and weight. Because of this, the cost to ship a pallet to a single destination is the same regardless of the type of box loaded on the pallet. The standard unit for sales and operations planning at IPS is a pallet load.

After recently opening a new factory to satisfy growing demand for its products, IPS is concerned about allocating demand from its customers to the facilities in its production network. It wants to do so in a way that minimizes the total cost of shipping final products to the wholesalers.

It currently has three factories that service a network of eight major wholesalers. Relevant data for the next year are shown in the following tables.

Factory Location	Production Capacity (pallets × 1,000)
Denver, CO	25
Chicago, IL	50
Baltimore, MD	35

Wholesaler Location	Demand (pallets × 1,000)
Spokane, WA	8.5
Los Angeles, CA	19.6
Kansas City, MO	9.3
Minneapolis, MN	8.8
Indianapolis, IN	11.8
Atlanta, GA	13.6
New York, NY	17.2
Orlando, FL	8.4

Based on contracts with its transportation suppliers, IPS is confident that the following transportation rates will be valid over the next year. Rates provided are to transport one pallet of product. There is no quantity discount given for volume shipments.

	Destination City and Transportation Rates							
Factory Location	Spokane	L.A.	K.C.	Minn.	Indy	Atlanta	N.Y.	Orlando
Denver, CO	$42	$49	$45	$54	$56	$65	$70	$72
Chicago, IL	65	69	49	38	32	45	50	55
Baltimore, MD	75	77	68	62	43	44	35	38

Use the transportation method of linear programming to develop a low-cost transportation plan for IPS for the upcoming year.

Solution

The first step is to consolidate the capacity, demand, and cost data in a single table. This table is shown as follows. Note that the capacity and demand numbers have been converted to single pallets to match the transportation cost units. You could instead convert the transportation cost data into 1,000 pallet units. Either way is fine, as long as you have consistent units for all data.

	Destination City and Transportation Rates								
Factory Location	Spokane	L.A.	K.C.	Minn.	Indy	Atlanta	N.Y.	Orlando	Capacity
Denver, CO	$42	$49	$45	$54	$56	$465	$70	$72	25,000
Chicago, IL	$65	$69	$49	$38	$32	$45	$50	$55	50,000
Baltimore, MD	$75	$77	$68	$62	$43	$44	$35	$38	35,000
Demand:	8,500	19,600	9,300	8,800	11,800	13,600	17,200	8,400	

The next step is to insert this table in Excel, along with a copy of the table to indicate the candidate solution and a smaller table to calculate the costs based on the candidate solution. The following screen capture from Excel shows how this would be set up.

The blank cells in the candidate solution table represent the amount to ship from each factory to each destination—they will be set up as changing cells in Solver. The Demand Met row in that table sums up each column in the table, telling us how much demand is being met in each city by our solution. For example, the formula in cell B14 is SUM(B11:B13). Similarly, the Capacity Used column sums up each row in the table, telling us how much product is shipped from each plant in our solution. For example, the formula in cell J11 is SUM(Bl1:I11). The cells in the Cost Calculations table each multiply the relevant cells from the candidate solution and the cost data tables, telling us how much our candidate solution costs for each factory–customer combination. For example, the formula in B18 is B11*B4. The Total cell simply sums up all the costs in the table.

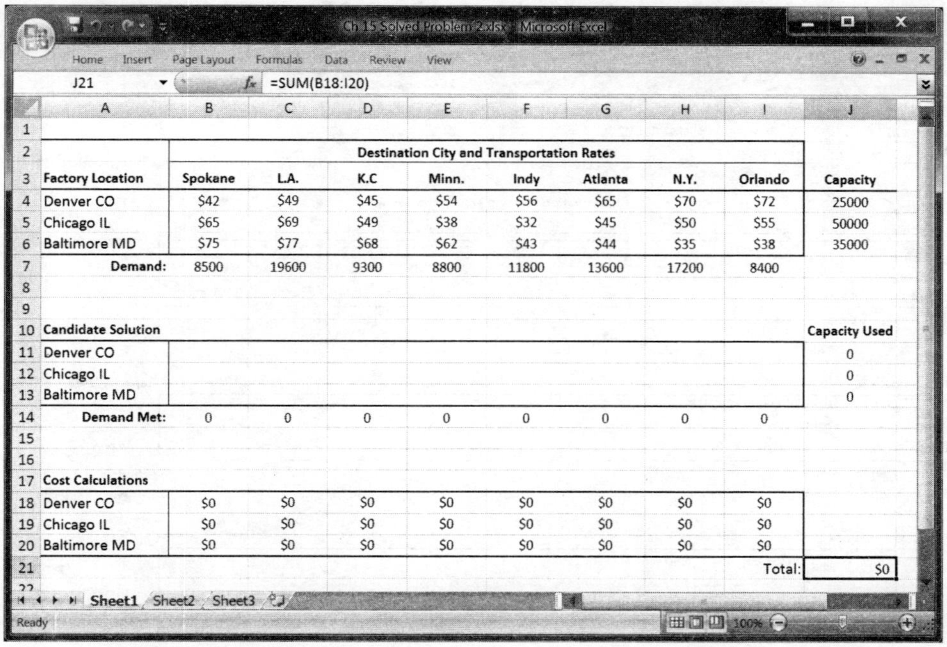

Next, we need to set up Solver to let it solve the problem for us. This is fairly easy given the structure of the tables. We need to tell Solver the following things:

- We want to minimize the total cost.
- It can change the values of the empty cells in the Candidate Solution table.
- The amount shipped to each customer must match the amount demanded.
- The amount shipped from each factory must not exceed the capacity of that factory.

After starting Solver, we would set up the parameters as shown. Be sure to set the options to "Assume Linear Model" and "Assume Non-Negative." (The latter could also be accomplished by adding a constraint that all changing cells be greater than or equal to zero.)

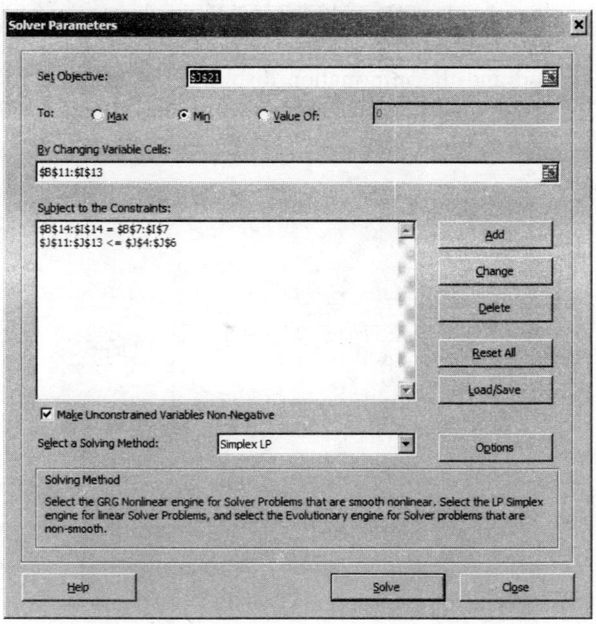

After running Solver, we get the following solution:

	A	B	C	D	E	F	G	H	I	J
1										
2		Destination City and Transportation Rates								
3	Factory Location	Spokane	L.A.	K.C	Minn.	Indy	Atlanta	N.Y.	Orlando	Capacity
4	Denver CO	$42	$49	$45	$54	$56	$65	$70	$72	25000
5	Chicago IL	$65	$69	$49	$38	$32	$45	$50	$55	50000
6	Baltimore MD	$75	$77	$68	$62	$43	$44	$35	$38	35000
7	Demand:	8500	19600	9300	8800	11800	13600	17200	8400	
8										
9										
10	Candidate Solution									Capacity Used
11	Denver CO	8500	16500	0	0	0	0	0	0	25000
12	Chicago IL	0	3100	9300	8800	11800	4200	0	0	37200
13	Baltimore MD	0	0	0	0	0	9400	17200	8400	35000
14	Demand Met:	8500	19600	9300	8800	11800	13600	17200	8400	
15										
16										
17	Cost Calculations									
18	Denver CO	$357,000	$808,500	$0	$0	$0	$0	$0	$0	
19	Chicago IL	$0	$213,900	$455,700	$334,400	$377,600	$189,000	$0	$0	
20	Baltimore MD	$0	$0	$0	$0	$0	$413,600	$602,000	$319,200	
21									Total:	$4,070,900

If IPS follows the plan presented by Solver, it will spend a little over $4 million to ship its products to its customers next year. The recommended plan should not be too surprising—Denver primarily satisfies the West Cost demand, Chicago serves the middle of the country, and Baltimore serves the East. This makes sense given the reality that transportation costs increase as distance traveled increases. Further, we can see that both Denver and Baltimore will max out their capacity in this plan, with Chicago using only about 75 percent of capacity.

LO 15-3 SOLVED PROBLEM 3

Cool Air, a manufacturer of automotive air conditioners, currently produces its XB-300 line at three different locations: plant A, plant B, and plant C. Recently, management decided to build all compressors, a major product component, in a separate dedicated facility, plant D.

Using the centroid method and the information displayed in Exhibit 15.7, determine a location for plant D. Assume a linear relationship between volumes shipped and shipping costs (no premium charges).

Exhibit 15.7

Plant Location Matrix

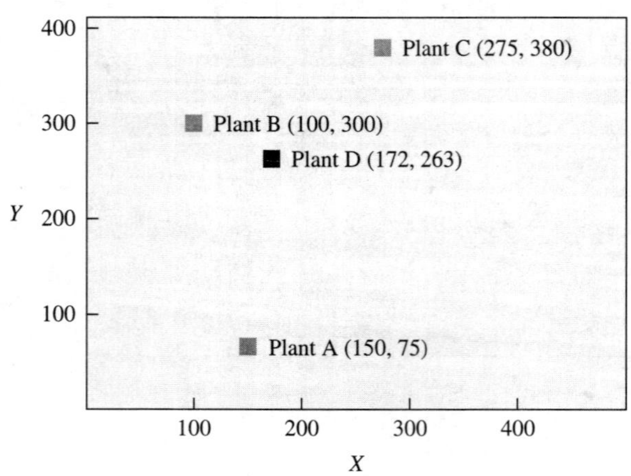

Plant	Compressors Required per Year
A	6,000
B	8,200
C	7,000

Solution

$d_{1x} = 150 \quad d_{1y} = 75 \quad V_1 = 6{,}000$

$d_{2x} = 100 \quad d_{2y} = 300 \quad V_2 = 8{,}200$

$d_{3x} = 275 \quad d_{3y} = 380 \quad V_3 = 7{,}000$

$$C_x = \frac{\sum d_{ix} V_i}{\sum V_i} = \frac{(150 \times 6{,}000) + (100 \times 8{,}200) + (275 \times 7{,}000)}{6{,}000 + 8{,}200 + 7{,}000} = 171.9$$

$$C_y = \frac{\sum d_{iy} V_i}{\sum V_i} = \frac{(75 \times 6{,}000) + (300 \times 8{,}200) + (380 \times 7{,}000)}{21{,}200} = 262.7$$

Plant $D[C_x, C_y] = D[172{,}263]$

DISCUSSION QUESTIONS

1. What motivations typically cause firms to initiate a facilities location or relocation project? **LO15-1**
2. List five major reasons why a new electronic components manufacturing firm should move into your city or town.
3. Recent figures show that almost 60 percent of the volume of freight movements in the United States ship by truck. Railroads are far more fuel efficient on a ton-mile basis—CSX advertises it can move a ton of freight 468 miles on a gallon of fuel. Why is it that rail does not have a greater share of the freight market in the United States? **LO15-2**
4. What is required to make cross-docking a viable solution for a logistics provider?
5. What are the pros and cons of relocating a small or mid-sized manufacturing firm (that makes mature products) from the United States to China? **LO15-3**
6. How do facility location decisions differ for service facilities and manufacturing plants?
7. If you could locate your new software development company anywhere in the world, which place would you choose, and why?

OBJECTIVE QUESTIONS

1. Some manufacturing firms contract with an outside company to manage the firm's logistics functions. What is the general term for a firm that provides such services? **LO15-1**
2. Logistics accounts for about what percent of the U.S. gross domestic product?
3. What mode of transportation is involved in the movement of the greatest number of products? **LO15-2**
4. What mode of transportation is limited to specialized products such as liquids and gases?
5. A manufacturer has decided to locate a new factory in the northwestern United States to serve the growing demand in that market. It has narrowed the potential sites down to two finalists: city A and city B. It has developed a list of important factors to consider in selecting a site, and rated each as shown in the following table. **LO15-3**

Factor	City A	City B
Utility rates	100	115
Availability of skilled labor	78	75
Tax rates	40	35
Transportation	46	38
Proximity to suppliers	35	34
Quality of life	19	16

Based on these data, which city appears to be the better choice?

6. Logistics Consultants Inc. (LCI) provides various logistics analysis services to other firms, including facility location decisions. It has just completed a project for a major customer, but on the eve of its presentation it discovered a computer malfunction had partially deleted some of its data. One file that was impacted contains the final factor rating results. Following are the partial results it was able to recover. As you'll notice, some ratings are missing.

		Ratings	
Factor	**Max Points**	**City X**	**City Y**
Availability of labor	150	130	123
Availability of utilities	130	122	110
Transportation infrastructure	80	73	
Warehousing availability/costs	75	70	63
Proximity to customers	65	59	
Business climate	40	30	24
Taxation structure	30	15	
Quality of life	25	22	17

If you were the project manager for LCI, what would you do given that you are missing some crucial data?

7. Bindley Corporation has a one-year contract to supply motors for all washing machines produced by Rinso Ltd. Rinso manufactures the washers at four locations around the country: New York, Fort Worth, San Diego, and Minneapolis. Plans call for the following numbers of washing machines to be produced at each location.

New York	50,000
Fort Worth	70,000
San Diego	60,000
Minneapolis	80,000

Bindley has three plants that can produce the motors. The plants and production capacities are

Boulder	100,000
Macon	100,000
Gary	150,000

Due to varying production and transportation costs, the profit Bindley earns on each 1,000 units depends on where they were produced and where they were shipped. The following table gives the accounting department estimates of the dollar profit per unit. (Shipment will be made in lots of 1,000.)

	Shipped to			
Produced at	**New York**	**Fort Worth**	**San Diego**	**Minneapolis**
Boulder	7	11	8	13
Macon	20	17	12	10
Gary	8	18	13	16

Given profit maximization as a criterion, Bindley would like to determine how many motors should be produced at each plant and how many motors should be shipped from each plant to each destination.

a. Develop a transportation grid for this problem.

b. Find the optimal solution using Microsoft Excel.

8. Rent'R Cars is a multisite car rental company in the city. It is trying out a new "return the car to the location most convenient for you" policy to improve customer service. But this means that the company has to constantly move cars around the city to maintain required levels of vehicle

availability. The supply and demand for economy cars, and the total cost of moving these vehicles between sites, are shown as follows.

From \ To	*D*	*E*	*F*	*G*	Supply
A	$9	$8	$6	$5	50
B	9	8	8	0	40
C	5	3	3	10	75
Demand	50	60	25	30	165 \ 165

a. Find the solution that minimizes moving costs using Microsoft Excel.

b What would you have to do to the costs to assure that *A* always sends a car to *D* as part of the optimal solution?

9. Sycamore Plastics (SP) is a manufacturer of polyethylene plastic pellets used as a raw material by manufacturers of plastic goods around the U.S. SP currently operates four manufacturing centers in Philadelphia, PA; Atlanta, GA; St. Louis, MO; and Salt Lake City, UT. The plants have different capacities and production costs, as indicated in the following table.

Plant	Maximum Capacity (× 100,000 lbs.)	Prod. Costs (per 1,000 lbs.)
Philadelphia	7.5	$325.00
Atlanta	9.0	$275.00
St. Louis	12.0	$305.00
Salt Lake City	10.3	$250.00

SP currently has six contract customers located in New York City; Birmingham, AL; Terre Haute, IN; Dallas, TX; Spokane, WA; and San Diego, CA. Transportation costs between the plants and various customers, as well as contracted demand from each customer, are shown in the following table. (Answers in Appendix D)

Transport Costs per 1,000 lbs.

From/To	NYC	Birmingham	Terre Haute	Dallas	Spokane	San Diego
Philadelphia	$45	$52	$56	$62	$78	$85
Atlanta	$55	$42	$58	$59	$80	$82
St. Louis	$57	$60	$50	$54	$65	$70
Salt Lake City	$72	$71	$67	$57	$52	$60
Total Demand (× 1,000 lbs.)	525	415	925	600	325	400

a. Create a solver model and find the optimal solution to help SP develop a distribution plan that will minimize costs to supply the customers' demand.

b Comment briefly on your solution. Beyond the obvious, does your proposed solution have any other implications for SP?

10. A small manufacturing facility is being planned that will feed parts to three heavy manufacturing facilities. The locations of the current plants with their coordinates and volume requirements are given in the following table.

Plant Location	Coordinates (*x*, *y*)	Volume (Parts per Year)
Peoria	300, 320	4,000
Decatur	375, 470	6,000
Joliet	470, 180	3,000

Use the centroid method to determine a location for this new facility. (Answer in Appendix D)

11. DM Office Products (DMOP) is a wholesale supplier of office products with one facility in Pennsylvania. It has decided to build a new distribution warehouse in the state of New York to help serve the growing demand in that market. It has four major customers located in Buffalo, Syracuse, Albany, and New York City. Though New York City is the largest market, it also has the greatest competition, and DMOP is not a major player there. When DMOP ships an order to a customer, it uses its own small fleet of two trucks to deliver, so the cost of delivery is essentially the same for a full or partially full truck. The expected number of annual shipments to each city and their coordinates on an *x, y* grid is shown in the following table.

City	*x*-coordinates	*y*-coordinates	Number of shipments
Buffalo	325	850	78
Syracuse	1,420	900	82
Albany	2,300	630	122
New York	2,275	25	62

Use the centroid method to recommend a location for the new warehouse for DMOP. Round your coordinates to one decimal place.

12. Santa Cruz Bottling is a manufacturer of organic soft drinks on the coast of central California. Its products are enjoying a growing reputation and increased demand throughout the American Southwest. Because of the high cost of transporting soft drinks, it is considering a new plant to serve the states of New Mexico and Arizona. A key concern in its search for a new location is the resultant transportation costs to serve its key markets. Following is a list of cities where its main wholesale customers are located, along with estimated annual demand in cases of product for each.

City	*x*-coordinate	*y*-coordinate	Number of cases
Phoenix	250	250	25,000
Tucson	350	125	20,000
Albuquerque	800	450	28,000
Santa Fe	850	520	17,000

a. Use the centroid method to recommend a location for the new bottling plant. Round your coordinates to one decimal place.

b. Do you have any concerns about the result? How would you deal with them?

ANALYTICS EXERCISE: DISTRIBUTION CENTER LOCATION

Grainger: Reengineering the China/U.S. Supply Chain

W. W. Grainger, Inc., is a leading supplier of maintenance, repair, and operating (MRO) products to businesses and institutions in the United States, Canada, and Mexico, with an expanding presence in Japan, India, China, and Panama. The company works with more than 3,000 suppliers and runs an extensive Website (www.grainger.com) where Grainger offers nearly 900,000 products. The products range from industrial adhesives used in manufacturing, to hand tools, janitorial supplies, lighting equipment, and power tools. When something is needed by one of its 1.8 million customers, it is often needed quickly, so quick service and product availability are key drivers to Grainger's success.

Your assignment involves studying U.S. distribution in Grainger's supply chain. Grainger works with over 250 suppliers in the China and Taiwan region. These suppliers produce products to Grainger's specifications and ship to the United States using ocean freight carriers from four major ports in China and Taiwan. From these ports, product is shipped to U.S. entry ports in either Seattle, Washington, or Los Angeles, California. After passing through customs, the 20- and 40-foot containers are shipped by rail to Grainger's central distribution center in Kansas City, Kansas. The containers are unloaded and quality is checked in Kansas City. From there, individual items are sent to regional warehouses in nine U.S. locations, a Canadian site, and Mexico.

Grainger: U.S. Distribution

In the United States, approximately 40 percent of the containers enter in Seattle, Washington, and 60 percent at the Los Angeles, California, port. Containers on arrival at the port cities are inspected by federal agents and then loaded onto rail cars for movement to the Kansas City distribution center. Variable costs for processing at the port are $5.00 per cubic meter (CBM) in both Los Angeles and Seattle. The rate for shipping the containers to Kansas City is $0.0018 per CBM per mile.

In Kansas City, the containers are unloaded and processed through a quality assurance check. This costs $3.00 per CMB processed. A very small percentage of the material is actually sent back to the supplier, but errors in quantity and package size are often found that require accounting adjustments.

Items are stored in the Kansas City distribution center, which serves nine warehouses in the United States. Items are also sent to warehouses in Canada and Mexico, but for the purposes of this study we focus on the United States. The nine warehouses each place orders at the distribution center that contains all the items to be replenished. Kansas City picks each item on the order, consolidates the items onto pallets, and ships the items on 53-foot trucks destined to each warehouse. Truck freight costs $0.0220 per CBM per mile. The demand forecasts for the items purchased from China/Taiwan for next year in cubic meters, as well as the shipping distances, are given in the following table.

	Demand (CBM)		Distances		
Warehouse	Average	% of Demand	Miles from Kansas City	Miles from Los Angeles	Miles from Seattle
Kansas City	20,900	11%	0	1,620	1,870
Cleveland	17,100	9%	800	2,350	2,410
New Jersey	24,700	13%	1,200	2,780	2,890
Jacksonville	15,200	8%	1,150	2,420	2,990
Chicago	22,800	12%	520	2,020	2,060
Greenville	15,200	8%	940	2,320	2,950
Memphis	17,100	9%	510	1,790	2,330
Dallas	22,800	12%	500	1,430	2,130
Los Angeles	34,200	18%	1,620	0	1,140
Total	190,000				

Although a high percentage of demand was from warehouses either south or east of Kansas City, the question has surfaced concerning the 18 percent that will be shipped to Kansas City and then shipped back to the Los Angeles warehouse. This double-transportation could potentially be eliminated if a new distribution center were built in Los Angeles. The idea might be to ship material arriving at the Seattle port by rail to a new Los Angeles distribution center, which would be located at the current location of the Los Angeles warehouse.

It is estimated that the Los Angeles facility could be upgraded at a one-time cost of $1,500,000 and then operated for $350,000 per year. In the new Los Angeles distribution center, containers would be unloaded and processed through a quality assurance check, just as is now done in Kansas City. The variable cost for doing this would be $5.00 per CBM processed, which includes the cost to move the containers from the Los Angeles port to the distribution center.

After the material is processed in Los Angeles, the amount needed to replenish the Los Angeles warehouse (approximately 18 percent) would be kept and the rest sent by rail to Kansas City. It would then be directly stocked in the Kansas City distribution center and used to replenish the warehouses. Grainger expects that very little would need to be shipped back to the Los Angeles warehouse after the new system has been operating for six months.

Grainger management feels that it may be possible to make this change, but it is not sure if it would actually save any money and whether it would be a good strategic change.

Specific questions to address in your analysis:

1. Relative to the U.S. distribution network, calculate the cost associated with running the existing system. Assume that 40 percent of the volume arrives in Seattle and 60 percent in Los Angeles

and that the port processing fee for federal processing at both locations is $5.00 per CBM. Assume that everything is transferred to the Kansas City distribution center by rail, where it is unloaded and quality-checked. Assume that all volume is then transferred by truck to the nine existing warehouses in the United States.

2. Consider the idea of upgrading the Los Angeles warehouse to include a distribution center capable of processing all the volume coming into the United States. Assume that containers coming into Seattle would be inspected by federal officials (this needs to be done at all port locations) and then immediately shipped by rail in their original containers to Los Angeles. All volume would be unloaded and quality-checked in Los Angeles (the quality check cost $5.00 per CBM when done in Los Angeles). Eighteen percent of the volume would then be kept in Los Angeles for distribution through that warehouse and the rest transshipped by rail to the Kansas City warehouse. Assume the cost to transship by rail is $0.0018 per CBM per mile. The material sent to Kansas City would not need to go through the "unload and quality check process," and would be stored directly in the Kansas City distribution center. Assume that the remaining volume would be transferred by truck to the eight remaining warehouses in the United States at a cost of $0.0220 per CBM per mile.
3. What should be done based on your analytics analysis of the U.S. distribution system? Should the new Los Angeles distribution center be added? Is there any obvious change that Grainger might make to have this option be more attractive?
4. Is this strategically something that Grainger should do? What has the company not considered that may be important?

Many thanks to Gary Scalzitti of Grainger for help with developing this case.

PRACTICE EXAM

In each of the following, name the term defined. Answers are listed at the bottom.

1. This is the art and science of obtaining, producing, and distributing material and product in the proper place and in the proper quantities.
2. A company that is hired to handle logistics functions.
3. A mode of transportation that is the most flexible relative to cost, volume, and speed of delivery.
4. When large shipments are broken down directly into smaller shipments for local delivery.
5. Sorting goods is the main purpose of this type of warehouse.
6. A place where foreign goods can be brought into the United States without being subject to normal customs requirements.
7. The main cost criterion employed when a transportation model is used for analyzing a logistics network.
8. The Microsoft Excel function used to solve the transportation model.
9. For the transportation model to be able to find a feasible solution, this must always be greater than or equal to total demand.
10. The "changing cells" in a transportation model represent this.
11. This is a method that locates facilities relative to an *X*, *Y* grid.
12. A technique that is useful for screening potential locations for services.

Answers to Practice Exam 1. Logistics 2. Third-party logistics company 3. Highway 4. Cross-docking 5. Hub 6. Free trade zone 7. Cost of shipping 8. Solver 9. Total capacity 10. Allocation of demand to a plant or warehouse 11. Centroid method 12. Regression analysis

For PowerPoint lecture slides, Solutions Manual, Test Bank, Data files for solved examples, Excel Templates, Step-by-Step Solved Examples in video format, Tutorial Videos and many more, scan the adjacent **QR code**, or **visit http://www.mhhe.com/sie-chase15e**

Chapter 16

Global Sourcing and Procurement

LEARNING OBJECTIVES

LO 16-1 Explain what strategic sourcing is

LO 16-2 Explain why companies outsource processes

LO 16-3 Analyze the total cost of ownership

LO 16-4 Evaluate sourcing performance

The Factoryless Goods Producers

Consider a company like Apple Inc. and its iPhone and iPad. Apple handles every part of making its products except the actual fabrication. Currently, Apple outsources the production of many of its products to Taiwan's Hon Hai Precision Industry. Hon Hai, which is better known as Foxconn, draws 40 to 50 percent of its revenue from assembling Apple products.

As many industries have become global suppliers, this type of global outsourcing has become common for clothing, most retail household products, furniture, and computers. These factoryless goods producers do most of the functions of manufacturing, and in many cases, design the product and oversee distribution.

Much of the attraction for this arrangement is the traditionally low labor costs in Chinese factories. Because labor cost has recently surged in China, outsourcing specialists such as Foxconn have diversified their operations to other low-wage countries, including Vietnam, Indonesia, Turkey, Brazil, Mexico, and Hungary.

LO 16-1

Explain what strategic sourcing is

STRATEGIC SOURCING

Strategic sourcing
The development and management of supplier relationships to acquire goods and services in a way that aids in achieving the needs of a business.

Strategic sourcing is the development and management of supplier relationships to acquire goods and services in a way that aids in achieving the immediate needs of the business. In the past, the term *sourcing* was just another term for purchasing, a corporate function that financially was important but strategically was not the center of attention. Today, as a result of globalization and inexpensive communications technology, the basis for competition is changing. A firm is no longer constrained by the capabilities it owns; what matters is its ability to make the most of available capabilities, whether they are owned by the firm or not. Outsourcing is so sophisticated that even core functions such as engineering, research and development, manufacturing, information technology, and marketing can be moved outside the firm.

Sourcing
A process suitable for procuring products that are strategically important to the firm.

Sourcing activities can vary greatly and depend on the item being purchased. Exhibit 16.1 maps different processes for sourcing or purchasing an item. The term **sourcing** implies a more complex process suitable for products that are strategically important. Purchasing processes that span from a simple "spot" or one-time purchase to a long-term strategic alliance are depicted on the diagram. The diagram positions a purchasing process according to the specificity of the item, contract duration, and intensity of transaction costs.

Strategy

Exhibit 16.1

The Sourcing/Purchasing Design Matrix

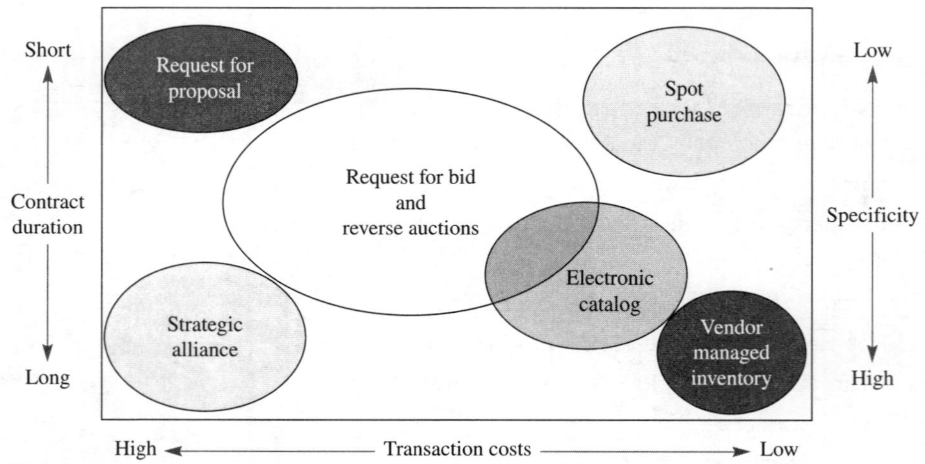

Specificity
Refers to how commonly available the material is and whether substitutes can be used.

Specificity refers to how common the item is and, in a relative sense, how many substitutes might be available. For example, blank DVD disks are commonly available from many different vendors and would have low specificity. A custom-made envelope that is padded and specially shaped to contain a specific item that is to be shipped would be an example of a high-specificity item.

Commonly available products can be purchased using a relatively simple process. For low-volume and inexpensive items purchased during the regular routine of work, a firm may order from an online catalog. Often, these online catalogs are customized for a customer. Special user identifications can be set up to authorize a customer's employees to purchase certain groups of items, with limits on how much they can spend. Other items require a more complex process.

Request for proposal
A solicitation that asks for a detailed proposal from a vendor interested in supplying an item.

A **request for proposal (RFP)** is commonly used for purchasing items that are more complex or expensive and where there may be a number of potential vendors. A detailed information packet describing what is to be purchased is prepared and distributed to potential vendors. The vendor then responds with a detailed proposal of how the company intends to meet the terms of the RFP. A request for bid or reverse auction is similar in terms of the information packet needed. A major difference is how the bid price is negotiated. In the RFP, the bid is included in the proposal, whereas in a request for bid or reverse auction, vendors actually bid on the item in real time and often using Internet software.

Vendor-managed inventory is when a customer actually allows the supplier to manage the inventory policy of an item or group of items for them. In this case, the supplier is given the freedom to replenish the item as they see fit. Typically, there are some constraints related to the maximum that the customer is willing to carry, the required service levels, and other billing transaction processes. Selecting the proper process depends on minimizing the balance between the supplier's delivered costs of the item over a period of time, say a year, and the customer's costs of managing the inventory. This is discussed later in the chapter in the context of the "total cost of ownership" for a purchased item.

Instead of sending purchase orders, customers electronically send daily demand information to the supplier. The supplier generates replenishment orders for the customer based on this demand information.

The Bullwhip Effect

In many cases, there are adversarial relations between supply chain partners, as well as dysfunctional industry practices such as a reliance on price promotions. Consider the common food industry practice of offering price promotions every January on a product. Retailers respond to the price cut by stocking up, in some cases buying a year's supply—a practice the industry calls **forward buying**. Nobody wins in the deal. Retailers have to pay to carry the year's supply, and the shipment bulge adds cost throughout the supplier's system. For example, the supplier plants must go on overtime starting in October to meet the bulge. Even the vendors that supply the manufacturing plants are affected because they must quickly react to the large surge in raw material requirements.

The impact of these types of practices has been studied at companies such as Procter & Gamble. Exhibit 16.2 shows typical order patterns faced by each node in a supply chain that consists of a manufacturer, a distributor, a wholesaler, and a retailer. In this case, the demand is for disposable baby diapers. The retailer's orders to the wholesaler display greater variability than the end-consumer sales; the wholesaler's orders to the manufacturer show even more oscillations; and, finally, the manufacturer's orders to its suppliers are the most volatile. This phenomenon of variability magnification as we move from the customer to the producer in the supply chain is often referred to as the **bullwhip effect**. The effect indicates a lack of synchronization among supply chain members. Even a slight change in consumer sales ripples backward in the form of magnified oscillations upstream, resembling the result of a flick of a bullwhip handle. Because the supply patterns do not match the demand patterns, inventory accumulates at various stages, and shortages and delays occur at others. This bullwhip effect has been observed by many firms in numerous industries, including Campbell Soup and Procter & Gamble in consumer products; Hewlett-Packard, IBM, and Motorola in electronics; General Motors in automobiles; and Eli Lilly in pharmaceuticals.

Campbell Soup pioneered a program called **continuous replenishment** that typifies what many manufacturers are doing to smooth the flow of materials through their supply chain. Here is how the program works. Campbell establishes electronic data interchange (EDI) links with retailers and offers an "everyday low price" that eliminates discounts. Every morning, retailers electronically inform the company of their demand for all Campbell products and of the level of inventories in their distribution centers. Campbell uses that information to forecast future demand and to determine which products require replenishment based on upper and lower inventory limits previously established with each supplier. Trucks leave the Campbell shipping plant that afternoon and arrive at the retailers' distribution centers with the required replenishments the same day. Using this system, Campbell can cut the retailers' inventories, which under the old system averaged four weeks of supply, to about two weeks of supply.

Vendor-managed inventory
When a customer allows the supplier to manage the inventory policy of an item or group of

Forward buying
A term that refers to when a customer, responding to a promotion, buys far in advance of when an item will be used.

Bullwhip effect
The variability in demand is magnified as we move from the customer to the producer in the supply chain.

Continuous replenishment
A program for automatically supplying groups of items to a customer on a regular basis.

EXHIBIT 16.2

Increasing Variability of Orders Up the Supply Chain

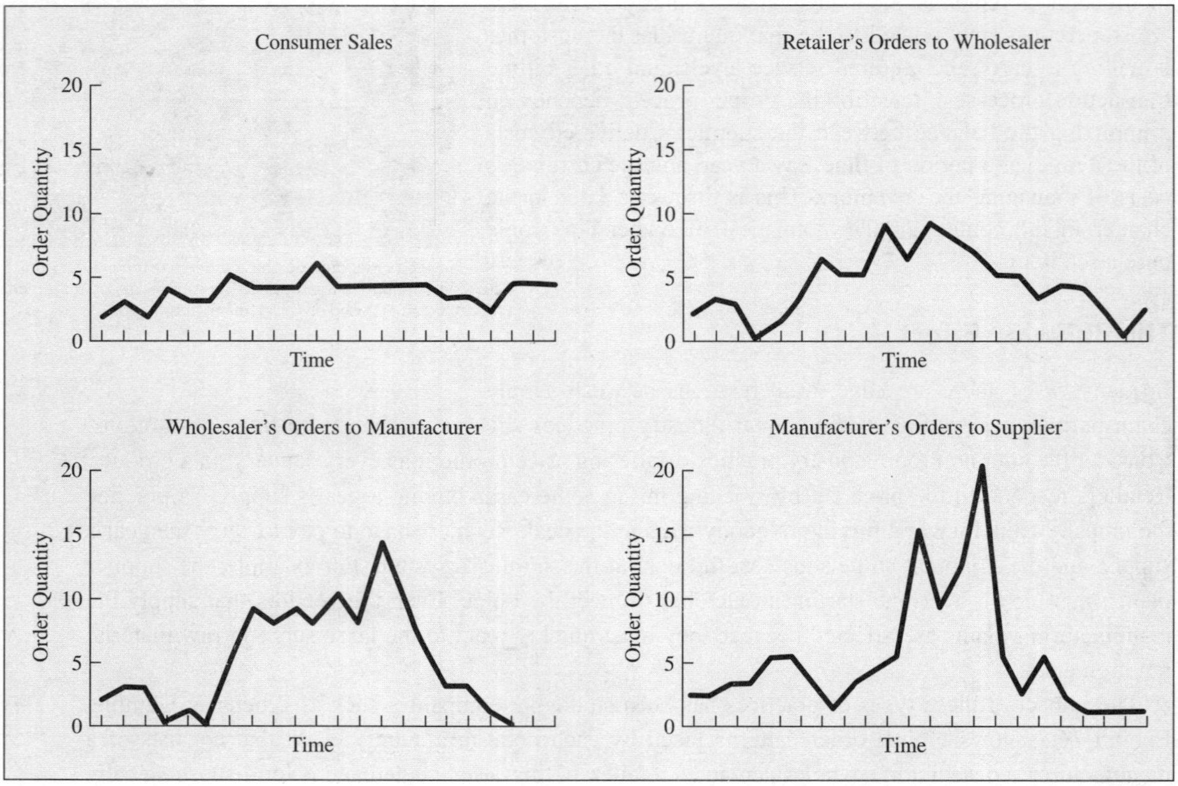

This solves some problems for Campbell Soup, but what are the advantages for the retailer? Most retailers figure that the cost to carry the inventory of a given product for a year equals at least 25 percent of what they paid for the product. A two-week inventory reduction represents a cost savings equal to nearly 1 percent of sales. The average retailer's profits equal about 2 percent of sales, so this saving is enough to increase profits by 50 percent. Because the retailer makes more money on Campbell products delivered through continuous replenishment, it has an incentive to carry a broader line of them and to give them more shelf space. Campbell Soup found that after it introduced the program, sales of its products grew twice as fast through participating retailers as they did through other retailers.

Supply Chain Uncertainty Framework

Strategy

The supply chain uncertainty framework (Exhibit 16.3) is designed to help managers understand the nature of demand for their products and then devise the supply chain that can best satisfy that demand. Many aspects of a product's demand are important—for example, product life cycle, demand predictability, product variety, and market standards for lead times and service. Products can be categorized as either primarily functional or primarily innovative. Because each category requires a distinctly different kind of supply chain, the root cause of supply chain problems is a mismatch between the type of product and type of supply chain.

Functional products
Staples that people buy in a wide range of retail outlets, such as grocery stores and gas stations.

Functional products include the staples that people buy in a wide range of retail outlets, such as grocery stores and gas stations. Because such products satisfy basic needs, which do not change much over time, they have stable, predictable demand and long life cycles. But their stability invites competition, which often leads to low profit margins. Specific criteria for identifying functional products include the following: product life cycle of more than two years, contribution margin of 5 to 20 percent, only 10 to 20 product variations, an average forecast error at time of production of only 10 percent, and a lead time for make-to-order products of from six months to one year.

OSCM AT WORK

E-Choupal: Transforming the Rural India

The ITC group is one of India's foremost private sector companies, with a diversified presence in tobacco, hotels, paperboards, specialty papers, packaging, agri-business, branded apparel, packaged foods and other FMCG products. Its International Business Division (IBD) was created in 1990 as an agro-trading company, which is now a USD 150 million company that trades in commodities such as feed ingredients, food-grains, coffee, black pepper, edible nuts, marine products, and processed fruits.

Traditionally, farmers sell their farm produce through middlemen or mandi systems, which are highly inefficient and loaded with a lot of margin for intermediaries in the supply chain. Farmers have no information on the price trends and during harvesting season, the sales prices are exceptionally low due to sudden jump in supply of produce. ITC provides a unique solution to this problem through e-Choupal, which is an internet-based network connecting rural India.

Supply Chain of E-Choupal

The supply chain of e-Choupal has transformed the life of involved farmers by creating a community of e-Farmers with an access to daily prices of a variety of crops in India and abroad, thus helping the farmers to get the best price, who were earlier dependent on local middlemen. In addition, e-Choupal now supports information on weather forecasts, the latest farming techniques, crop insurance, etc. A local farmer acting as a *sanchalak* (coordinator) runs the village e-Choupal with a computer, usually located in his home. ITC also involves a local commission agent, known as the *samyojak* (collaborator) who acts as the provider of logistical support and gets 0.5% commission. Typically, e-Choupal serves about 10 villages within five-kilometer radius. As of early 2010, about 6500 e-Choupal covers more than four million farmers in nearly 40,000 villages in 10 states of India [1]. The computer in the house of *sanchalak* is connected to the Internet via phone lines or by a VSAT connection.

ITC channels all its communication through the local *sanchalaks*. They are trained at the nearest ITC plant and after training, receive a commission for every transaction processed through the e-Choupal. *Samyojaks* earn income from ITC by providing logistical services that substitute for the lack of rural infrastructure, by providing information and market signals to the e-Choupal system. Their support as information provider helps ITC know which farmers grow soya, what is their financial situation, etc. They are the strongest link in the supply chain as they help in procurement hub logistics, labour management at the hub, cash disbursement, bagging, storage management, transportation from the hub to processing factories, etc.

e-Choupal works as follows. The farmer brings samples of his agro-produce to the e-Choupal, where the sample is inspected by the *sanchalak* for its quality. Farmer then receives a conditional price-quote and in case this farmer chooses to sell his produce to ITC, the *sanchalak* gives him a note containing farmer's name, village, detail of the quality tests such as foreign matter and moisture content, quantity and conditional price. With this note, the farmer goes to the nearest ITC procurement hub. Here, a sample of the farmer's produce is taken for laboratory tests for verifying the assessment of the *sanchalak*. After the inspection and weighing, payment is made to the farmer for his produce and transportation to the procurement hub.

In addition to the above, e-Choupal has the following features.

- It provides a gateway of an expanding spectrum of commodities leaving farms – wheat, rice, pulses, soya, maize, spices, coffee, and aqua-products [1].
- Supply chain is scalable and over the time it has demonstrated sustainability.
- Direct participation of stakeholders has helped in building trust.
- It can be customized, validated and expanded to fulfil the local needs.

e-Choupal has demonstrated the power of IT-enablement of an agro-based supply chain, which is the prime-mover of rural economy.

References

1. http://www.itcportal.com/businesses/agri-business/e-choupal.aspx [Acccessed on 14 April 2014]
2. Surjeet Das Gupta, The choupal as a meta market, Business standard, Strategist, 5 March 2002.
3. http://www.itcportal.com/businesses/agri-business/ycd-speech.aspx. [Accessed on 14 April 2014]

EXHIBIT 16.3

Product and Process Uncertainty Characteristics

	Product (Demand) Characteristics			Manufacturing (Supply) Process Characteristics	
	Functional	**Innovative**		**Stable**	**Evolving**
Demand	Predictable	Unpredictable	Breakdowns	Few	Higher
Product Life	Long	Short	Process Yield	High	Lower
Inventory Value	Low	High	Quality Problems	Few	More
Product Variety	Low	High	Supply Sources	Many	Few
Volume	High	Low	Process Changes	Few	Many
Stock-out Cost	Low	High	Lead Time	Dependable	Difficult to predict

Based on research conducted by Marshall Fisher (Wharton School of Business, University of Pennsylvania).

Innovative products
Products such as fashionable clothes and personal computers that typically have a life cycle of just a few months.

Stable supply process
A process where the underlying technology is stable.

Evolving supply process
A process where the underlying technology changes rapidly.

To avoid low margins, many companies introduce innovations in fashion or technology to give customers an additional reason to buy their products. Fashionable clothes and personal computers are good examples. Although innovation can enable a company to achieve higher profit margins, the very newness of the innovative products makes demand for them unpredictable. These **innovative products** typically have a life cycle of just a few months. Imitators quickly erode the competitive advantage that innovative products enjoy, and companies are forced to introduce a steady stream of newer innovations. The short life cycles and the great variety typical of these products further increase unpredictability. Exhibit 16.3 summarizes the differences between functional and innovative products.

We expand on this idea by focusing on the "supply" side of the supply chain. While the Supply Chain uncertainty framework captures important demand characteristics, there are uncertainties revolving around the supply side that are equally important drivers for the right supply chain strategy.

A **stable supply process** is where the manufacturing process and the underlying technology are mature and the supply base is well established. In contrast, an **evolving supply process** is where the manufacturing process and the underlying technology are still under early development and are rapidly changing. As a result, the supply base may be limited in both size and experience. In a stable supply process, manufacturing complexity tends to be low or manageable. Stable manufacturing processes tend to be highly automated, and long-term supply contracts are prevalent. In an evolving supply process, the manufacturing process requires a lot of fine-tuning and is often subject to breakdowns and uncertain yields. The supply base may not be reliable, because the suppliers themselves are going through process innovations. Exhibit 16.3 summarizes some of the differences between stable and evolving supply processes.

While functional products tend to have a more mature and stable supply process, that is not always the case. For example, the annual demand for electricity and other utility products in a locality tends to be stable and predictable, but the supply of hydroelectric power, which relies on rainfall in a region, can be erratic year by year. Some food products also have a very stable demand, but the supply (both quantity and quality) of the products depends on yearly weather conditions. Similarly, there are also innovative products with a stable supply process. Fashion apparel products have a short selling season and their demand is highly unpredictable. However, the supply process is very stable, with a reliable supply base and a mature manufacturing process technology. Exhibit 16.4 gives some examples of products that have different demand and supply uncertainties.

In most cases, it is more challenging to operate a supply chain that is in the right column of Exhibit 16.4 than in the left column, and similarly it is more challenging to operate a supply chain that is in the lower row of Exhibit 16.4 than in the upper row. Before setting up a supply chain strategy, it is necessary to understand the sources of the underlying uncertainties and explore ways to reduce these uncertainties. If it is possible to move the uncertainty characteristics of the product from the right column to the left or from the lower row to the upper, then the supply chain performance will improve.

Exhibit 16.4

Supply Chain Uncertainty Framework

		Product (Demand) Characteristics	
		Functional	**Innovative**
Manufacturing (Supply) Process Characteristics	**Stable**	**Efficient Supply Chain** Grocery, basic apparel, food, oil and gas	**Responsive Supply Chain** Fashion apparel, low-end computers, seasonal products
	Evolving	**Risk-Hedging Supply Chain** Hydroelectric power, food dependent on weather	**Agile Supply Chain** Cellphones, high-end computers, semiconductors

Based on research conducted by Hau Lee (Stanford University).

Using the supply and demand characteristics discussed so far, four types of supply chain strategies, as shown in Exhibit 16.4, are possible. Information technologies play an important role in shaping such strategies.

- **Efficient supply chains** These are supply chains that utilize strategies aimed at creating the highest levels of cost efficiency. For such efficiencies to be achieved, non–value-added activities should be eliminated, scale economies should be pursued, optimization techniques should be deployed to get the best capacity utilization in production and distribution, and information linkages should be established to ensure the most efficient, accurate, and cost-effective transmission of information across the supply chain.
- **Risk-hedging supply chains** These are supply chains that utilize strategies aimed at pooling and sharing resources in a supply chain so that the risks in supply disruption can be shared. A single entity in a supply chain can be vulnerable to supply disruptions, but if there is more than one supply source or if alternative supply resources are available, then the risk of disruption is reduced. A company may, for example, increase the safety stock of its key component to hedge against the risk of supply disruption, and by sharing the safety stock with other locations that also need this key component, the cost of maintaining this safety stock can be shared. This type of strategy is common in retailing, where different retail stores or dealerships share inventory. Information technology is important for the success of these strategies because real-time information on inventory and demand allows the most cost-effective management and transshipment of goods between partners sharing the inventory.
- **Responsive supply chains** These are supply chains that utilize strategies aimed at being responsive and flexible to the changing and diverse needs of the customers. To be responsive, companies use build-to-order and mass customization processes as a means to meet the specific requirements of customers.
- **Agile supply chains** These are supply chains that utilize strategies aimed at being responsive and flexible to customer needs, while the risks of supply shortages or disruptions are hedged by pooling inventory and other capacity resources. These supply chains essentially have strategies in place that combine the strengths of "hedged" and "responsive" supply chains. They are agile because they have the ability to be responsive to the changing, diverse, and unpredictable demands of customers on the front end, while minimizing the back-end risks of supply disruptions.

Demand and supply uncertainty is a good framework for understanding supply chain strategy. Innovative products with unpredictable demand and an evolving supply process face a major challenge. Because of shorter and shorter product life cycles, the pressure for dynamically adjusting and adopting a company's supply chain strategy is great. In the following section, we explore the concepts of outsourcing, green sourcing, and total cost of ownership. These are important tools for coping with demand and supply uncertainty.

OSCM AT WORK

Complexity of Global Supply Chains

Tipco Foods (Thailand) Public Company Limited is a Thailand-based producer and exporter of canned pineapple, pineapple juice concentrates and canned mixed fruits. Thailand has the largest global market share of around 45% in processed pineapple. Tipco Food's supply chain has a strong global presence as its exports represent about 50 per cent of its total revenue. Its total revenue in 2009 was Baht 4.68 billion (over ₹6 billion) as compared with Baht 5.36 billion (over ₹7 billion) in the previous year. Its present decline in revenue is due to global economic crisis.

In the year 2006-07, due to weakening of US dollar (USD) against most of the global currencies, including Baht, the local currency of Thailand, Tipco's global supply chain faced a very peculiar situation. For illustration, the dollar weakened against Baht as follows:

- Late 2006–Baht 41 per USD
- Early 2007–Baht 37 per USD
- July 2007–Baht 33 per USD

Therefore, compared with late 2006, USD depreciated by around 20 percent by July 2007. Due to this, the revenue inflow in the global supply chain, when converted in local currency, declined by 20 percent. Majority of expenses, including raw material cost, wages, etc. are in local currency. This phenomenon had badly affected the bottom-line of Tipco Foods.

Prof. Surendra S. Yadav, Professor of Finance and International Business, at I.I.T. Delhi believes that this situation is due to an inherent risk of any global supply chain. Managers must learn ways to handle the risks in their global supply chain, which may be due to exchange rate fluctuations and also due to other risks arising out of political, cultural, legal and environmental changes. To the extent possible, hedging against risk must be a norm. Had Tipco focused on its share in Asian market, which is currently less than 5 percent, the negative impact of fluctuation in exchange rate of dollar might have got offset due to relatively lesser exchange rate fluctuations among other global currencies. Besides, financial instruments such as forwards, futures and options could have been appropriately used to hedge against exchange rate fluctuations.

Prof Yadav further adds that the India-ASEAN Free Trade Agreement (FTA) has already been signed on 13 August 2009. Benefits of the Asean Free-trade Agreement may now facilitate a diversification of risk in Indian supply chains. Secondly, as a protective measure, export-oriented firms may explore ways to distribute the risk by focusing on local markets as well.

Reference

1. Bangkok Post: 4 August 2007, p. B4.
2. http://www.nationmultimedia.com/home/2010/04/13/business/Tipco-to-push-sales-to-Asean-market-30127110.html (Accessed on 15 May 2014).
3. David Simchi-Levi, Philip Kaminsky, Edith Simchi-Levi and Ravi Shankar, Designing and Managing the Supply Chain: Concepts, Strategies, and Case studies (Third Edition: *Special Indian Edition*), Tata McGraw-Hill Publishing Company Ltd, New Delhi (2008).

LO 16-2

Explain why companies outsource processes

OUTSOURCING

Outsourcing
Moving some of a firm's internal activities and decision responsibility to outside providers.

Outsourcing is the act of moving some of a firm's internal activities and decision responsibility to outside providers. The terms of the agreement are established in a contract. Outsourcing goes beyond the more common purchasing and consulting contracts because not only are the activities transferred, but also resources that make the activities occur, including people, facilities, equipment, technology, and other assets, are transferred. The responsibilities for making decisions over certain elements of the activities are transferred as well. Taking complete responsibility for this is a specialty of contract manufacturers such as Flextronics.

The reasons why a company decides to outsource can vary greatly. Exhibit 16.5 lists examples of reasons to outsource and the accompanying benefits. Outsourcing allows a firm to focus on activities that represent its core competencies. Thus, the company can create a competitive advantage while reducing cost. An entire function may be outsourced, or some elements of an activity may be outsourced, with the rest kept in-house. For example, some of the elements of information technology may be strategic,

EXHIBIT 16.5

Reasons to Outsource and the Resulting Benefits

Financially Driven Reasons
Improve return on assets by reducing inventory and selling unnecessary assets. Generate cash by selling low-return entities. Gain access to new markets, particularly in developing countries. Reduce costs through a lower cost structure. Turn fixed costs into variable costs.
Improvement-Driven Reasons
Improve quality and productivity. Shorten cycle time. Obtain expertise, skills, and technologies that are not otherwise available. Improve risk management. Improve credibility and image by associating with superior providers.
Organizationally Driven Reasons
Improve effectiveness by focusing on what the firm does best. Increase flexibility to meet changing demand for products and services. Increase product and service value by improving response to customer needs.

Strategy

some may be critical, and some may be performed less expensively by a third party. Identifying a function as a potential outsourcing target, and then breaking that function into its components, allows decision makers to determine which activities are strategic or critical and should remain in-house and which can be outsourced like commodities. As an example, outsourcing the logistics function will be discussed.

Logistics Outsourcing

There has been dramatic growth in outsourcing in the logistics area. **Logistics** is a term that refers to the management functions that support the complete cycle of material flow: from the purchase and internal control of production materials; to the planning and control of work-in-process; to the purchasing, shipping, and distribution of the finished product. The emphasis on lean inventory means there is less room for error in deliveries. Trucking companies such as Ryder have started adding the logistics aspect to their businesses—changing from merely moving goods from point A to point B, to managing all or part of all shipments over a longer period, typically three years, and replacing the shipper's employees with their own. Logistics companies now have complex computer tracking technology that reduces the risk in transportation and allows the logistics company to add more value to the firm than it could if the function were performed in-house. Third-party logistics providers track freight using electronic data interchange technology and a satellite system to tell customers exactly where its drivers are and when deliveries will be made. Such technology is critical in some environments where the delivery window may be only 30 minutes long.

Logistics
Management functions that support the complete cycle of material flow: from the purchase and internal control of production materials; to the planning and control of work-in-process; to the purchasing, shipping, and distribution of the finished product.

FedEx has one of the most advanced systems available for tracking items being sent through its services. The system is available to all customers over the Internet. It tells the exact status of each item currently being carried by the company. Information on the exact time a package is picked up, when it is transferred between hubs in the company's network, and when it is delivered is available on the system. You can access this system at the FedEx website (www.fedex.com). Select your country on the initial screen and then select "Track Shipments" in the Track box in the lower part of the page. Of course, you will need the actual tracking number for an item currently in the system to get information. FedEx has integrated its tracking system with many of its customers' in-house information systems.

Another example of innovative outsourcing in logistics involves Hewlett-Packard. Hewlett-Packard turned over its inbound raw materials warehousing in Vancouver, British Columbia, to Roadway Logistics. Roadway's 140 employees operate the warehouse 24 hours a day, seven days a week,

Azim Premji: The Man Who Brought WIPRO to Great Heights

The person, who has contributed most to the rise of Indian software industry is the iconic visionary of recent times and Chairman of WIPRO, Mr. Azim H. Premji. Under his leadership, WIPRO had a series of achievements in delivering quality IT products and services to its world-wide clients, a majority of whom trusted WIPRO for outsourcing their critical jobs—spanning the entire IT lifecycle. WIPRO domain of expertise includes consulting, business solutions, enterprise applications, testing, product engineering, BPO, system integration, infrastructure and application management and total outsourcing services where WIPRO services all IT needs of a customer [1]. For example, Wipro Total Outsourcing Services (TOS) are targeted at achieving maximum value by providing end-to-end best of breed IT practices. From technology optimization to mitigating risks, WIPRO expertises to fulfil the clients' constant IT infrastructure and application demands while evaluating, deploying and managing flexible, responsive and economical solutions [2]. Wlipro delivers its services through about 145,000 employees, who are serving to over 900 clients in 60 countries [1].

WIPRO, under the leadership of Premji, became the first CMMi Level 5 quality-certified software services company and the first outside USA to receive the IEEE Software Process Award. Through its over fifty five "Centre of Excellence,' WIPRO provides customized solutions to clients all over the world. Since past many years, it is among the top three companies of India, which has successfully delivered quality IT-solutions to the outsourced jobs that India received from other parts of the world [3].

Business Week has recognized Mr. Azim H. Premji as one of the all-time top thirty entrepreneurs of the world in the year 2007 for his visionary leadership, which has helped Wipro to emerge as one of the world`s fastest growing companies. He is the second richest Indian with a wealth of USD 17 billion in 2010 [3] and he also figures in the club of top richest persons of the world. His father expired in 1966 and he had to take over WIPRO, then a small company dealing in cooking oil product. By sheer determination and guts, he transformed it into a diversified, integrated corporation in services, medical systems, technology products and consumer items. It is now ranked among the top 100 technology companies of the world [4].

For his numerous contributions, Azim Premji was awarded Padma Bhushan in 2005 [5] and **Economic Times Life Time Achievement Award** in 2013 [1]. He is a source of inspiration to a number of budding entrepreneurs.

Reference

1. http://www.wipro.com/corporate/aboutus/index.htm (Accessed on 14 April 2014).
2. http://www.wipro.com/services/index.htm (Accessed on 14 April 2014).
3. http://www.spiritus-temporis.com/azim-premji/(Accessed on 14 April 2014).
4. "The World's Billionaires". *Forbes*. March 3, 2009.
5. http://connect.in.com/azim-premji/biography-392.html (Accessed on 14 April 2010).

coordinating the delivery of parts to the warehouse and managing storage. Hewlett-Packard's 250 employees were transferred to other company activities. Hewlett-Packard reports savings of 10 percent in warehousing operating costs.

One of the drawbacks to outsourcing is the layoffs that often result. Even in cases where the outsourcing partner hires former employees, they are often hired back at lower wages with fewer benefits. Outsourcing is perceived by many unions as an effort to circumvent union contracts.

Framework for Supplier Relationships

Strategy

In theory, outsourcing is a no-brainer. Companies can unload noncore activities, shed balance sheet assets, and boost their return on capital by using third-party service providers. But in reality, things are more complicated. It is often difficult to determine what is core and noncore today, because situations change so quickly today.

Exhibit 16.6 is a useful framework to help managers make appropriate choices for the structure of supplier relationships. The decision goes beyond the notion that "core competencies" should be maintained under the direct control of management of the firm and that other activities should be outsourced. In this framework, a continuum that ranges from vertical integration to arm's-length relationships forms the basis for the decision.

EXHIBIT 16.6

A Framework for Structuring Supplier Relationships

	Do not outsource	Outsource
Coordination characteristics	Coordination and interfaces are not well defined. The information and coordination is specific to each job. Technology is immature and there is a need for "expert" knowledge obtained by experience.	Standardized interfaces, required information is highly codified and standardized (prices, quantities, delivery schedules, etc.).
Investment is strategic assets characteristics	Significant investments in highly specialized assets are needed. The investments cannot be easily recovered if the relationship terminates. Long-term investments in specialized R&D, and lengthy learning curves.	Assets are commonly available from a large number of potential customers or suppliers.
Intellectual property characteristics	Weak intellectual property protection. Easy-to-imitate technology when access is given.	Strong intellectual property protection Difficult-to-imitate technology

Key Idea

Companies usually outsource standard activities when they are not part of the "core competency" of the firm.

An activity can be evaluated using the following characteristics: required coordination, strategic control, and intellectual property. Required coordination refers to how difficult it is to ensure that the activity will integrate well with the overall process. Uncertain activities that require much back-and-forth exchange of information should not be outsourced, whereas activities that are well understood and highly standardized can easily move to business partners who specialize in the activity. Strategic control refers to the degree of loss that would be incurred if the relationship with the partner were severed. There could be many types of losses that would be important to consider, including specialized facilities, knowledge of major customer relationships, and investment in research and development. A final consideration is the potential loss of intellectual property through the partnership.

Intel is an excellent example of a company that recognized the importance of this type of decision framework in the mid-1980s. During the early 1980s, Intel found itself being squeezed out of the market for memory chips (the type it had invented) by Japanese competitors such as Hitachi, Fujitsu, and NEC. These companies had developed stronger capabilities to develop and rapidly scale up complex semiconductor manufacturing processes. It was clear by 1985 that a major Intel competency was its ability to design complex integrated circuits—something it did much better than manufacturing or developing processes for more standardized chips. As a result, faced with growing financial losses, Intel was forced to exit the memory chip market.

Learning a lesson from the memory market, Intel shifted its focus to the market for microprocessors, which it had invented in the late 1960s. To keep from repeating the mistake with memory chips, Intel felt it was essential to develop strong capabilities in process development and manufacturing. A pure "core competency" strategy would have suggested that Intel focus on the design of microprocessors and use outside partners to manufacture them. Given the close connection between semiconductor product development and process development, however, relying on outside parties for manufacturing would likely have created costs in terms of longer development lead times. Over the late-1980s, Intel invested heavily in building world-class capabilities in process development and manufacturing. These capabilities are one of the chief reasons it has been able to maintain approximately 90 percent of the

OSCM AT WORK

Capability Sourcing at 7-Eleven

The term *capability sourcing* was coined to refer to the way companies focus on the things they do best and outsource other functions to key partners. The idea is that owning capabilities may not be as important as having control of those capabilities. This allows many additional capabilities to be outsourced. Companies are under intense pressure to improve revenue and margins because of increased competition. An area where this has been particularly intense is the convenience store industry, where 7-Eleven is a major player.

Before 1991, 7-Eleven was one of the most vertically integrated convenience store chains. When it is vertically integrated, a firm controls most of the activities in its supply chain. In the case of 7-Eleven, the firm owned its own distribution network, which delivered gasoline to each store, made its own candy and ice, and required the managers to handle store maintenance, credit card processing, store payroll, and even the in-store information technology (IT) system. For a while, 7-Eleven even owned the cows that produced the milk sold in the stores. But it was difficult for 7-Eleven to manage costs in this diverse set of functions.

At that time, 7-Eleven had a Japanese branch that was very successful but was based on a totally different integration model. Rather than using a company-owned and vertically integrated model, the Japanese stores had partnerships with suppliers that carried out many of the day-to-day functions. Those suppliers specialized in each area, enhancing quality and improving service while reducing cost. The Japanese model involved outsourcing everything possible without jeopardizing the business by giving competitors critical information. A simple rule said that if a partner could provide a capability more effectively than 7-Eleven could itself, that capability should be outsourced. In the United States, the company eventually outsourced activities such as human resources, finance, information technology, logistics, distribution, product development, and packaging. 7-Eleven still maintains control of all vital information and handles all merchandising, pricing, positioning, promotion of gasoline, and ready-to-eat food.

The following chart shows how 7-Eleven has structured key partnerships.

Activity	Outsourcing Strategy
Gasoline	Outsourced distribution to Citgo. Maintains control over pricing and promotion. These are activities that can differentiate its stores.
Snack foods	Frito-Lay distributes its products directly to the stores. 7-Eleven makes critical decisions about order quantities and shelf placement. 7-Eleven mines extensive data on local customer purchase patterns to make these decisions at each store.
Prepared foods	Joint venture with E. A. Sween: Combined Distribution Centers (CDCs), a direct-store delivery operation that supplies 7-Eleven stores with sandwiches and other fresh goods two times a day
Specialty products	Many are developed specially for 7-Eleven customers. For example, 7-Eleven worked with Hershey to develop an edible straw used with the popular Twizzler treat. Worked with Anheuser-Busch on special NASCAR and Major League Baseball promotions.
Data analysis	7-Eleven relies on an outside vendor, IRI, to maintain and format purchasing data while keeping the data proprietary. Only 7-Eleven can see the actual mix of products its customers purchase at each location.
New capabilities	American Express supplies automated teller machines. Western Union handles money wire transfers. CashWorks furnishes check-cashing capabilities. Electronic Data Systems (EDS) maintains network functions.

personal computer microprocessor market, despite the ability of competitors like AMD to "clone" Intel designs relatively quickly. Expanding its capabilities beyond its original core capability of product design has been a critical ingredient in Intel's sustained success.

Good advice is to keep control of—or acquire—activities that are true competitive differentiators or have the potential to yield a competitive advantage, and to outsource the rest. It is important to make a distinction between "core" and "strategic" activities. Core activities are key to the business, but do not confer a competitive advantage, such as a bank's information technology operations. Strategic activities are a key source of competitive advantage. Because the competitive environment can change rapidly, companies need to monitor the situation constantly, and adjust accordingly. As an example, Coca-Cola, which decided to stay out of the bottling business in the early 1900s, partnered instead with independent bottlers and quickly built market share. The company reversed itself in the 1980s when bottling became a key competitive element in the industry.

Green Sourcing

Being environmentally responsible has become a business imperative, and many firms are looking to their supply chains to deliver "green" results. A significant area of focus relates to how a firm works with suppliers where the opportunity to save money and benefit the environment might not be a strict trade-off proposition. Financial results can often be improved through both cost reductions and boosting revenues.

Green sourcing is not just about finding new environmentally friendly technologies or increasing the use of recyclable materials. It can also help drive cost reductions in a variety of ways, including product content substitution, waste reduction, and lower usage.

A comprehensive green sourcing effort should assess how a company uses items that are purchased internally, in its own operations, or in its products and services. As costs of commodity items like steel, electricity, and fossil fuels continue to increase, properly designed green sourcing efforts should find ways to significantly reduce and possibly eliminate the need for these types of commodities. As an example, consider retrofitting internal lighting in a large office building to a modern energy-efficient technology. Electricity cost savings of 10 to 12 percent per square foot can easily translate into millions of dollars in associated electricity cost savings.

Another important cost area in green sourcing is waste reduction opportunities. This includes everything from energy and water to packaging and transportation. A great example of this is the redesigned milk jug introduced recently by leading grocery retailers. Using the new jug, with more rectangular dimensions and a square base, cuts the associated water consumption of the jugs by 60 to 70 percent compared to earlier jug designs because the new design does not require the use of milk crates. Milk crates typically become filthy during use due to spillage and other natural factors; thus, they are usually hosed down before reuse, consuming thousands of gallons of water. The new design also reduces fuel costs. Since crates are no longer used, they also do not have to be transported back to the dairy plant or farm distribution point for future shipments. Furthermore, the new jugs have the unexpected benefit of fitting better in modern home refrigerator doors and allow retailers to fit more of them in their in-store coolers. Breakthrough results like the new milk jug can result from comprehensive partnerships between users and their suppliers working to find innovative solutions.

Many companies have found that working with suppliers can result in opportunities that improve revenue. The opportunity to turn waste products into sources of revenue might be significant. For example, a leading beverage manufacturer operates a recycling subsidiary that sources used aluminum cans from a large number of suppliers. The subsidiary actually processes more aluminum cans than are used in the company's own products, consequently developing a strong secondary revenue stream for the company.

In other cases, green sourcing can help establish entirely new lines of business to serve environmentally conscious customers. In the cleaning products aisle of a supermarket, shoppers will find numerous options of "green" cleaning products from a variety of consumer products companies. These products typically use natural ingredients in lieu of chemicals, and many are in concentrated amounts to reduce overall packaging costs.

Logistics suppliers could find business opportunities coming directly to them as a result of the green trend. A large automobile manufacturer completed a project to "green" its logistics/distribution network. The automaker analyzed the shipping carriers, locations, and overall efficiency of its distribution network for both parts and finished automobiles. By increasing the use of rail transportation for parts, consolidating shipments in fewer ports, and partnering with its logistics providers to increase fuel efficiency for both marine and road transportation, the company reduced its overall distribution-related carbon dioxide emissions by several thousand tons per year.

Exhibit 16.7

Six-Step Process for Green Sourcing

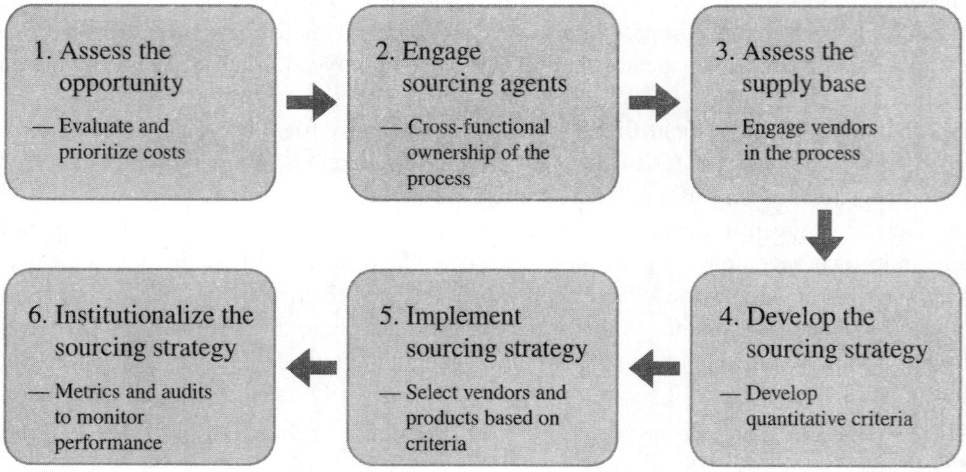

The following is an outline of a six-step process (see Exhibit 16.7) designed to transform a traditional process to a green sourcing process.

Process

1. **Assess the opportunity.** For a given category of expense, all relevant costs need to be taken into account. The five most common areas include electricity and other energy costs; disposal and recycling; packaging; commodity substitution (alternative materials to replace materials such as steel or plastic); and water (or other related resources). These costs are identified and incorporated into an analysis of total cost (sometimes referred to as "spend" cost analysis) at this step. From this analysis, it is possible to prioritize the different costs based on the highest potential savings and criticality to the organization. This is important in directing effort to where it will likely have the most impact on the firm's financial position and cost reduction goals.

Fly ash is generally stored at coal power plants or placed in landfills as shown here. About 43 percent is recycled, reducing the harmful impact on the environment from landfills.

2. **Engage internal supply chain sourcing agents.** Internal sourcing agents are those within the firm that purchase items and have direct knowledge of business requirements, product specifications, and other internal perspectives inherent in the supply chain. These individuals and groups need to be "on-board" and be partners in the improvement process to help set realistic green goals. The goal of generating no waste, for example, becomes a cross-functional supply chain effort that relies heavily on finding and developing the right suppliers. These internal managers need to identify the most significant opportunities. They can develop a robust baseline model of what should be possible for reducing current and ongoing costs. In the case of procuring new equipment, for example, the baseline model would include not just the initial price of the equipment as in traditional sourcing, but also energy, disposal, recycling, and maintenance costs.
3. **Assess the supply base.** A sustainable sourcing process requires engaging new and existing vendors. As in traditional sourcing, the firm needs to understand vendor capabilities, constraints, and product offering. The green process needs to be augmented with formal requirements that relate to green opportunities, including possible commodity substitutions and new manufacturing processes. These requirements need to be incorporated in vendor bid documents or the request for proposals (RFPs).

A good example is concrete that uses fly ash, a by-product from coal-fired power plants. Fly ash can be substituted for Portland cement in ready-mix concrete or in concrete blocks to produce a stronger and lighter product with reduced water consumption. Fly ash substitution helped a company reduce its exposure to volatile and rapidly increasing prices for cement. At the same time, the reduced weight of the block lowered transportation costs to the company's new facilities. The company was also able to establish a specification incorporating fly ash for all new construction sites to follow. Finally, the substitution also helped the power plant by providing a new market for the fly ash, which previously had to be discarded.

4. **Develop the sourcing strategy.** The main goal with this step is to develop quantitative and qualitative criteria that will be used to evaluate the sourcing process. These are needed to properly analyze associated costs and benefits. These criteria need to be clearly articulated in bid documents and RFPs when working with potential suppliers so that their proposals will address relevant goals related to sustainability.
5. **Implement the sourcing strategy.** The evaluation criteria developed in step 4 should help in the selection of vendors and products for each business requirement. The evaluation process should consider initial cost and the total cost of ownership for the items in the bid. So, for example, energy-efficient equipment that is proposed with a higher initial cost may, over its productive life, actually result in a lower total cost due to energy savings and a related lower carbon footprint. Relevant green opportunities such as energy efficiency and waste reduction need to be modeled and then incorporated into the sourcing analysis to make it as comprehensive as possible and to facilitate an effective vendor selection process that supports the firm's needs.
6. **Institutionalize the sourcing strategy.** Once the vendor is selected and contracts finalized, the procurement process begins. Here, the sourcing and procurement department needs to define a set of metrics against which the supplier will be measured for the contract's duration. These metrics should be based on performance, delivery, compliance with pricing guidelines, and similar factors. It is vital that metrics that relate to the company's sustainability goals are considered as well. Periodic audits may also need to be incorporated in the process to directly observe practices that relate to these metrics to ensure honest reporting of data.

A key aspect of green sourcing, compared to a traditional process, is the expanded view of the sourcing decision. This expanded view requires the incorporation of new criteria for evaluating alternatives. Further, it requires a wider range of internal integration such as designers, engineers, and marketers. Finally, visualizing and capturing the green sourcing savings often involve greater complexity and longer payback periods compared to a traditional process.

TOTAL COST OF OWNERSHIP

LO 16-3

Analyze the total cost of ownership

Total cost of ownership

Estimate of the cost of an item that includes all the costs related to the procurement and use of the item, including disposing of the item after its useful life.

The **total cost of ownership** (TCO) is an estimate of the cost of an item that includes all the costs related to its procurement and use, including any related costs in disposing of the item after it is no longer useful. The concept can be applied to a company's internal costs or it can be viewed more broadly to consider costs throughout the supply chain. To fully appreciate the cost of purchasing an item from a particular vendor, an approach that captures the costs of the activities associated with purchasing and actually using the item should be considered. Depending on the complexity of the purchasing process, activities such as prebid conferences, visits by potential suppliers, and even visits to potential suppliers can significantly impact the total cost of the item.

A TCO analysis is highly dependent on the actual situation; in general, though, the costs outlined in Exhibit 16.8 should be considered. The costs can be categorized into three broad areas: acquisition costs, ownership costs, and post-ownership costs. Acquisition costs are the initial costs associated with the purchase of materials, products, and services. They are not long-term costs of ownership but represent an immediate cash outflow. Acquisition costs include the prepurchase costs associated with preparing documents to distribute to potential suppliers, identifying suppliers and evaluating suppliers, and other costs associated with actually procuring the item. The actual purchase prices, including taxes, tariffs, and transportation costs, are also included.

EXHIBIT 16.8

Total Cost of Ownership

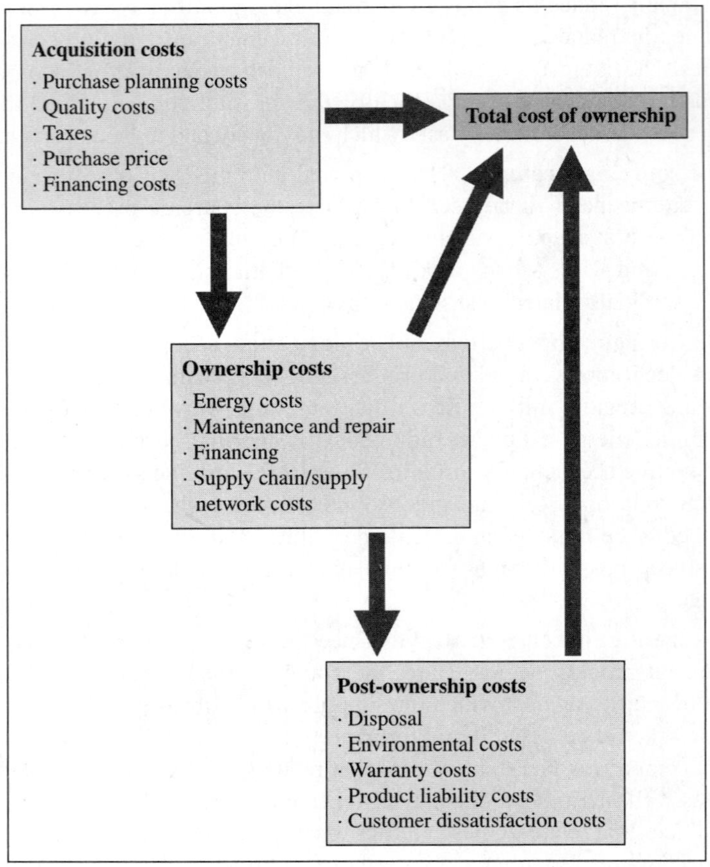

Ownership costs are incurred after the initial purchase and are associated with the ongoing use of the product or material. Examples of costs that are quantifiable include energy usage, scheduled maintenance, repair, and financing (leasing situation). There can also be qualitative costs such as aesthetic factors (e.g., the item is pleasing to the eye), and ergonomic factors (e.g., productivity improvement or reducing fatigue). These ownership costs can often exceed the initial purchase price and have an impact on cash flow, profitability, and even employee morale and productivity.

Major costs associated with post-ownership include salvage value and disposal costs. For many purchases, there are established markets that provide data to help estimate reasonable future values, such as the *Kelley Blue Book* for used automobiles. Other areas that can be included are the long-term environmental impact (particularly when the firm has sustainability goals), warranty and product liabilities, and the negative marketing impact of low customer satisfaction with the item.

Overemphasis on acquisition cost or purchase price frequently results in a failure to address other significant ownership and post-ownership costs. TCO is a philosophy for understanding all relevant costs of doing business with a particular supplier for a good or service. It is not only relevant for a business that wants to reduce its cost of doing business but also for a firm that aims to design products or services that provide the lowest total cost of ownership to customers. For example, some automobile manufacturers have extended the tune-up interval on many models to 100,000 miles, thereby reducing vehicle operating cost for car owners. Viewing TCO in this way can lead to an increased value of the product to existing and potential customers.

Analytics

These costs can be estimated as cash inflows (the sale of used equipment, etc.) or outflows (such as purchase prices, demolition of an obsolete facility, etc.). The following example shows how this analysis can be organized using a spreadsheet. Keep in mind that the costs considered need to be adapted to the decision being made. Costs that do not vary based on the decision need not be considered, but relevant costs that vary depending on the decision should be included in the analysis.

TCO actually draws on many areas for a thorough analysis. These include finance (net present value), accounting (product pricing and costing), operations management (reliability, quality, need, and inventory planning), marketing (demand), and information technology (systems integration). It is probably best to approach this using a cross-functional team representing the key functional areas.

EXAMPLE 16.1 Total Cost of Ownership Analysis

Consider the analysis of the purchase of a copy machine that might be used in a copy center. The machine has an initial cost of $120,000 and is expected to generate income of $40,000 per year. Supplies are expected to be $7,000 per year and the machine needs to be overhauled during year 3 at a cost of $9,000. It has a salvage value of $7,500 when we plan to sell it at year 6.

SOLUTION

Laying these costs out over time can lead to the use of net present value analysis to evaluate the decision. Consider Exhibit 16.9, where the present values of each yearly stream are discounted to now. (See Appendix E for a present value table.) As we can see, the present value in this analysis shows that the present value cost of the copier is $12,955.

EXHIBIT 16.9

Analysis of the Purchase of an Office Copier

Year	Now	1	2	3	4	5	6
Initial Investment	−$120,000						
Manufacturer required overhaul				−$9,000			
Cash inflows from using the machine		$ 40,000	$ 40,000	$ 40,000	$ 40,000	$ 40,000	$ 40,000
Supplies needed to use the machine		−$7,000	−$7,000	−$7,000	−$7,000	−$7,000	−$7,000
Salvage value							$ 7,500
Total of annual streams	−$120,000	$ 33,000	$ 33,000	$ 24,000	$ 33,000	$ 33,000	$ 40,500
Discount factor from Appendix C $1/(1+.2)^{Year}$	1.000	0.833	0.694	0.579	0.482	0.402	0.335
Present value – yearly	−$120,000	$ 27,500	$ 22,917	$ 13,889	$ 15,914	$ 13,262	$ 13,563
Present value	−$12,955						

Discount factor = 20%.
Note: These calculations were done using the full precision of a spreadsheet.

It is important that any analysis is adapted to the particular scenario. Such factors as exchange rates, the risk of doing business in a particular region of the world, transportation, and other items are often important. Depending on the alternatives, there are a host of factors, often going beyond cost, that need to be considered. Adapting this type of cost analysis and combining it with a more qualitative risk analysis are useful in actual company situations.

MEASURING SOURCING PERFORMANCE

LO 16-4 Evaluate sourcing performance

One view of sourcing is centered on the inventories that are positioned in the system. Exhibit 16.10 shows how hamburger meat and potatoes are stored in various locations in a typical fast-food restaurant chain. Here we see the steps that the beef and potatoes move through on their way to the local retail store and then to the customer. Inventory is carried at each step, and this inventory has a particular cost to the company. Inventory serves as a buffer, thus allowing each stage to operate independently of the others. For example, the distribution center inventory allows the system that supplies the retail stores to operate independently of the meat and potato packing operations.

EXHIBIT 16.10

Inventory in the Supply Chain—Fast-Food Restaurant

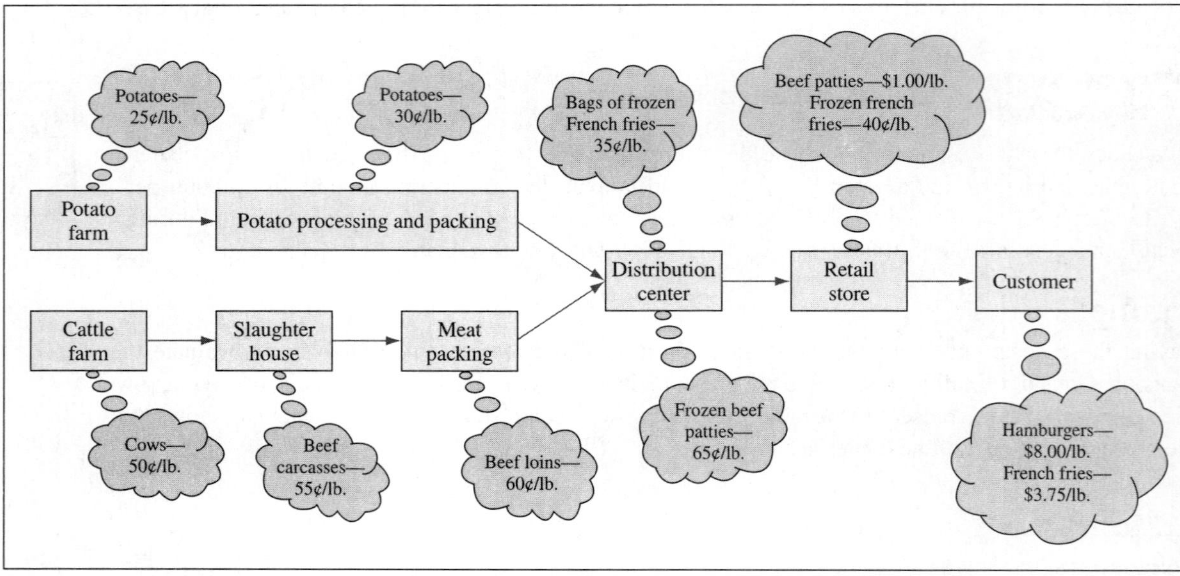

Analytics

Because the inventory at each stage ties up money, it is important that the operations at each stage are synchronized to minimize the size of these buffer inventories. The efficiency of the supply chain can be measured based on the size of the inventory investment in the supply chain. The inventory investment is measured relative to the total cost of the goods that are provided through the supply chain.

Inventory turnover
A measure of supply chain efficiency.

Two common measures to evaluate supply chain efficiency are *inventory turnover* and *weeks of supply*. These essentially measure the same thing. Weeks of supply is the inverse of inventory turnover times 52. **Inventory turnover** is calculated as follows:

$$\text{Inventory turnover} = \frac{\text{Cost of goods sold}}{\text{Average aggregate inventory value}} \quad [16.1]$$

Cost of goods sold
The annual cost for a company to produce the goods or services provided to customers.

Average aggregate inventory value
The average total value of all items held in inventory for the firm, valued at cost.

The **cost of goods sold** is the annual cost for a company to produce the goods or services provided to customers; it is sometimes referred to as the *cost of revenue*. This does not include the selling and administrative expenses of the company. The **average aggregate inventory value** is the average total value of all items held in inventory for the firm valued at cost. It includes the raw material, work-in-process, finished goods, and distribution inventory considered owned by the company.

Good inventory turnover values vary by industry and the type of products being handled. At one extreme, a grocery store chain may turn inventory over 100 times per year. Values of six to seven are typical for manufacturing firms.

In many situations, particularly when distribution inventory is dominant, **weeks of supply** is the preferred measure. This is a measure of how many weeks' worth of inventory is in the system at a particular point in time. The calculation is as follows:

$$\text{Weeks of supply} = \left(\frac{\text{Average aggregate inventory value}}{\text{Cost of goods sold}}\right) \times 52 \text{ weeks} \quad [16.2]$$

Weeks of supply
Preferred measure of supply chain efficiency that is mathematically the inverse of inventory turnover times 52.

When company financial reports cite inventory turnover and weeks of supply, we can assume that the measures are being calculated firmwide. We show an example of this type of calculation in the example that follows using Dell Computer data. These calculations, though, can be done for individual entities within the organization. For example, we might be interested in the production raw materials inventory turnover or the weeks of supply associated with the warehousing operation of a firm. In these cases, the cost would be that associated with the total amount of inventory that runs through the specific inventory. In some very-low-inventory operations, days or even hours are a better unit of time for measuring supply.

A firm considers inventory an investment because the intent is for it to be used in the future. Inventory ties up funds that could be used for other purposes, and a firm may have to borrow money to finance the inventory investment. The objective is to have the proper amount of inventory and to have it in the correct locations in the supply chain. Determining the correct amount of inventory to have in each position requires a thorough analysis of the supply chain coupled with the competitive priorities that define the market for the company's products.

EXAMPLE 16.2 Inventory Turnover Calculation

Dell Computer reported the following information in a recent annual report (all dollar amounts are expressed in millions):

Net revenue	\$49,205
Cost of revenue	\$40,190
Production materials on hand	\$228
Work-in-process and finished goods on hand	\$231
Days of supply in inventory	4 days

The cost of revenue corresponds to what we call cost of goods sold. One might think that U.S. companies, at least, would use a common accounting terminology, but this is not true. The inventory turnover calculation is

$$\text{Inventory turnover} = \frac{40{,}190}{228 + 231} = 87.56 \text{ turns per year}$$

This is amazing performance for a high-tech company, but it explains much of why the company is such a financial success.

The corresponding weeks of supply calculation is

$$\text{Weeks of supply} = \left(\frac{228 + 231}{40{,}190}\right) \times 52 = .59 \text{ week}$$

CONCEPT CONNECTIONS

LO 16–1 Explain what strategic sourcing is

Summary

- Sourcing is a term that captures the strategic nature of purchasing in today's global and Internet-connected marketplace.
- The sourcing/purchasing design matrix captures the scope of the topic that ranges from one-time spot purchases, to a complex strategic alliance arrangement with another firm.
- A phenomenon known as the bullwhip effect has been observed in many industries. This is when changes in demand are magnified as they move from the customer to the manufacturer. The phenomenon is caused by long lead times and the fact that there are often multiple stages in a supply chain.
- Supply chains can be categorized based on demand and supply uncertainty characteristics. Four types of supply chains are identified: (1) efficient, (2) risk-hedging, (3) responsive, and (4) agile.

Key Terms

Strategic sourcing The development and management of supplier relationships to acquire goods and services in a way that aids in achieving the needs of a business.

Sourcing A process suitable for procuring products that are strategically important to the firm.

Specificity Refers to how commonly available the material is and whether substitutes can be used.

Request for proposal (RFP) A solicitation that asks for a detailed proposal from a vendor interested in supplying an item.

Vendor managed inventory When a customer allows the supplier to manage the inventory policy of an item or group of items.

Forward buying A term that refers to when a customer, responding to a promotion, buys far in advance of when an item will be used.

Bullwhip effect The variability in demand is magnified as we move from the customer to the producer in the supply chain.

Continuous replenishment A program for automatically supplying groups of items to a customer on a regular basis.

Functional products Staples that people buy in a wide range of retail outlets, such as grocery stores and gas stations.

Innovative products Products such as fashionable clothes and personal computers that typically have a life cycle of just a few months.

Stable supply process A process where the underlying technology is stable.

Evolving supply process A process where the underlying technology changes rapidly.

LO 16–2 Explain why companies outsource processes

Summary

- Outsourcing is when a firm contracts with an outside provider for activities essential to the firm's success.
- The transportation of a firm's products (referred to as logistics) is often outsourced.
- Whether an activity is outsourced or not often depends on criteria related to (1) coordination requirements, (2) strategic control, and (3) intellectual property issues.
- Green sourcing has become an imperative for many firms and it may create new markets for a firm's products.

Key Terms

Outsourcing Moving some of a firm's internal activities and decision responsibility to outside providers.

Logistics Management functions that support the complete cycle of material flow: from the purchase and internal control of production materials; to the planning and control of work-in-process; to the purchasing, shipping, and distribution of the finished product.

LO 16–3 Analyze the total cost of ownership

Summary

- This is an approach to understanding the total cost of an item.
- Costs can generally be categorized into three areas: (1) acquisition costs, (2) ownership costs, and (3) post-ownership costs.

Key Terms

Total cost of ownership Estimate of the cost of an item that includes all the costs related to the procurement and use of the item, including disposing of the item after its useful life.

LO 16–4 Evaluate sourcing performance

- Inventory turn and weeks of supply are the most common measures to evaluate supply chain efficiency. These measures can vary greatly depending on the industry.

Key Terms

Inventory turnover A measure of supply chain efficiency.

Cost of goods sold The annual cost for a company to produce the goods or services provided to customers.

Average aggregate inventory value The average total value of all items held in inventory for the firm, valued at cost.

Weeks of supply Preferred measure of supply chain efficiency that is mathematically the inverse of inventory turnover times 52.

$$\text{Inventory turnover} = \frac{\text{Cost of goods sold}}{\text{Average aggregate inventory value}} \quad [16.1]$$

$$\text{Weeks of supply} = \left(\frac{\text{Average aggregate inventory value}}{\text{Cost of goods sold}}\right) \times 52 \text{ weeks} \quad [16.2]$$

DISCUSSION QUESTIONS

1. What recent changes have caused supply chain management to gain importance? **LO 16–1**
2. Describe the differences between functional and innovative products.
3. What are characteristics of efficient, responsive, risk-hedging, and agile supply chains? Can a supply chain be both efficient and responsive? Risk-hedging and agile? Why or why not?
4. With so much productive capacity and room for expansion in the United States, why would a company based in the United States choose to purchase items from a foreign firm? Discuss the pros and cons. **LO 16–2**
5. As a supplier, which factors about a buyer (your potential customer) would you consider to be important in setting up a long-term relationship?
6. Describe how outsourcing works. Why would a firm want to outsource?
7. Have you ever purchased a product based on purchase price alone and were surprised by the eventual total cost of ownership (TCO), either in money or in time? Describe the situation. **LO 16–3**
8. Why might managers resist buying a more expensive piece of equipment, known to have a lower TCO, than a less expensive item?
9. Why is it desirable to increase a company's inventory turnover ratio? **LO 16–4**
10. Research and compare the inventory turnover ratios of three large retailers: Walmart, Target, and Nordstrom. Use the same financial Website for all three, and compare numbers from the same time frame. What do these ratios tell you? Are you surprised by what you found?

OBJECTIVE QUESTIONS

1. What term refers to the development and management of supplier relationships in order to acquire goods and services in a way that helps achieve the immediate needs of a business? **LO 16–1**
2. Sometimes a company may need to purchase goods or services that are unique, very complex, and/or extremely expensive. These would not be routine purchases, but there may be a number of vendors that could supply what is needed. What process would be used to transmit the company's needs to the available vendors, asking for a detailed response to the needs?
3. Sony Electronics produces a wide variety of electronic products for the consumer marketplace, such as laptop computers, PlayStation game consoles, and tablet computers. What type of products would these be considered in the Supply Chain Uncertainty Framework?
4. One product that Staples sells a lot of is copy paper. According to the Supply Chain Uncertainty Framework, what supply chain strategy is appropriate for this product?
5. What is the term used for the act of moving some of a company's internal activities and decision-making processes to outside providers? **LO 16–2**

6. What is the term used for a company moving management of the complete cycle of material flow to an outside provider?
7. Many bottled water manufacturers have recently worked with their suppliers to switch over to bottles using much less plastic than before, reducing the amount of plastic that needs to be transported, recycled, and/or disposed of. What sourcing practice is this an example of?
8. What term is used to refer to those activities that are the key source of competitive advantage?

LO 16–3

9. What three main categories of costs are considered in figuring the total cost of ownership?
10. Which category of lifetime product costs are sometimes overemphasized, leading to a failure to fully recognize the total cost of ownership?
11. One of your Taiwanese suppliers has bid on a new line of molded plastic parts that is currently being assembled at your plant. The supplier has bid \$0.10 per part, given a forecast you provided of 200,000 parts in year 1; 300,000 in year 2; and 500,000 in year 3. Shipping and handling of parts from the supplier's factory is estimated at \$0.01 per unit. Additional inventory handling charges should amount to \$0.005 per unit. Finally, administrative costs are estimated at \$20 per month.

    Although your plant is able to continue producing the part, the plant would need to invest in another molding machine, which would cost \$10,000. Direct materials can be purchased for \$0.05 per unit. Direct labor is estimated at \$0.03 per unit plus a 50 percent surcharge for benefits; indirect labor is estimated at \$0.011 per unit plus 50 percent benefits. Up-front engineering and design costs will amount to \$30,000. Finally, management has insisted that overhead be allocated if the parts are made in-house at a rate of 100 percent of direct labor cost. The firm uses a cost of capital of 15 percent per year.

    What should you do, continue to produce in-house or accept the bid from your Taiwanese supplier? (Answer in Appendix D)
12. Your company assembles five different models of a motor scooter that is sold in specialty stores in the United States. The company uses the same engine for all five models. You have been given the assignment of choosing a supplier for these engines for the coming year. Due to the size of your warehouse and other administrative restrictions, you must order the engines in lot sizes of 1,000 each. Because of the unique characteristics of the engine, special tooling is needed during the manufacturing process for which you agree to reimburse the supplier. Your assistant has obtained quotes from two reliable engine suppliers and you need to decide which to use. The following data have been collected.

Requirements (annual forecast)	12,000 units
Weight per engine	22 pounds
Order processing cost	\$125 per order
Inventory carry cost	20 percent of the average value of inventory per year

Note: Assume that half of the lot size is in inventory, on average (1,000/2 = 500 units).

Two qualified suppliers have submitted the following quotations.

Order Quantity	Supplier 1 Unit Price	Supplier 2 Unit Price
1 to 1,499 units/order	\$510.00	\$505.00
1,500 to 2,999 units/order	500.00	\$505.00
3,000+ units/order	490.00	488.00
Tooling costs	\$22,000	\$20,000
Distance	125 miles	100 miles

Your assistant has obtained the following freight rates from your carrier.

Truckload (40,000 lb. each load):	\$0.80 per ton-mile
Less-than-truckload:	\$1.20 per ton-mile

Note: Per ton-mile = 2,000 lb. per mile

a. Perform a total cost of ownership analysis and select a supplier.
b. Would it make economic sense to order in truckload quantities? Would your supplier selection change if you ordered truckload quantities?

13. Which supply chain efficiency measure is more appropriate when the majority of inventory is held in distribution channels? **LO 16–4**
14. What do you call the average total value of all items held in inventory for a firm, at cost?
15. The owner of a large machine shop has just finished its financial analysis from the prior fiscal year. Following is an excerpt from the final report:

Net revenue	$375,000
Cost of goods sold	322,000
Value of production materials on-hand	42,500
Value of work-in-process inventory	37,000
Value of finished goods on-hand	12,500

a. Compute the inventory turnover ratio (ITR).
b. Compute the weeks of supply (WS).

16. The McDonald's fast-food restaurant on campus sells an average of 4,000 quarter-pound hamburgers each week. Hamburger patties are resupplied twice a week, and on average the store has 350 pounds of hamburger in stock. Assume that the hamburger patties cost $1.00 a pound. What is the inventory turnover for the hamburger patties? On average, how many days of supply are on-hand? (Answer in Appendix D)
17. U.S. Airfilter has hired you as a supply chain consultant. The company makes air filters for residential heating and air-conditioning systems. These filters are made in a single plant located in Louisville, Kentucky, in the United States. They are distributed to retailers through wholesale centers in 100 locations in the United States, Canada, and Europe. You have collected the following data relating to the value of inventory in the U.S. Airfilter supply chain.

	Quarter 1 (January through March)	Quarter 2 (April through June)	Quarter 3 (July through September)	Quarter 4 (October through December)
Sales (total quarter):				
United States	300	350	405	375
Canada	75	60	75	70
Europe	30	33	20	15
Cost of goods sold (total quarter)	280	295	340	350
Raw materials at the Louisville plant (end-of-quarter)	50	40	55	60
Work-in-process and finished goods at the Louisville plant (end-of-quarter)	100	105	120	150
Distribution center Inventory (end-of-quarter):				
United States	25	27	23	30
Canada	10	11	15	16
Europe	5	4	5	5

All amounts in millions of U.S. dollars.

a. What is the average inventory turnover for the firm?
b. If you were given the assignment to increase inventory turnover, what would you focus on? Why?
c. The company reported that it used $500M worth of raw material during the year. On average, how many weeks of supply of raw material are on-hand at the factory?

ANALYTICS EXERCISE: GLOBAL SOURCING DECISIONS—GRAINGER: REENGINEERING THE CHINA/U.S. SUPPLY CHAIN

W. W. Grainger, Inc., is a leading supplier of maintenance, repair, and operating (MRO) products to businesses and institutions in the United States, Canada, and Mexico, with an expanding presence in Japan, India, China, and Panama. The company works with more than 3,000 suppliers and runs an extensive Website (www.grainger.com), where it offers nearly 900,000 products. The products range from industrial adhesives used in manufacturing, to hand tools, janitorial supplies, lighting equipment, and power tools. When something is needed by one of its 1.8 million customers, it is often needed quickly, so quick service and product availability are key drivers to Grainger's success.

Your assignment involves studying a specific part of Grainger's supply chain. Grainger works with over 250 suppliers in the China and Taiwan region. These suppliers produce products to Grainger's specifications and ship to the United States using ocean freight carriers from four major ports in China and Taiwan. From these ports, product is shipped to U.S. entry ports in either Seattle, Washington, or Los Angeles, California. After passing through customs, the 20- and 40-foot containers are shipped by rail to Grainger's central distribution center in Kansas City, Kansas. The containers are unloaded and quality is checked in Kansas City. From there, individual items are sent to regional warehouses in nine U.S. locations, a Canadian site, and Mexico.

The Current China/Taiwan Logistics Arrangement

The contracts that Grainger has with Chinese and Taiwanese suppliers currently specify that the supplier owns the product and is responsible for all costs incurred until the product is delivered to the shipping port. These are commonly referred to as free on board (FOB) shipping port contracts. Grainger works with a freight forwarding company that coordinates all shipments from the Asian suppliers.

Currently, suppliers have the option of either shipping product on pallets to consolidation centers at the port locations or packing the product in 20- and 40-foot containers that are loaded directly on the ships bound for the United States. In many cases, the volume from a supplier is relatively small and will not sufficiently fill a container. The consolidation centers are where individual pallets are loaded into the containers that protect the product while being shipped across the Pacific Ocean and then to Grainger's Kansas City distribution center. The freight forwarding company coordinates the efficient shipping of the 20- and 40-foot containers. These are the same containers that are loaded onto rail cars in the United States.

Currently, about 190,000 cubic meters of material are shipped annually from China and Taiwan. This is expected to grow about 15 percent per year over the next five years. About 89 percent of all the volume shipped from China and Taiwan are sent directly from the suppliers in 20- and 40-foot containers that are packed by the supplier at the supplier site. Approximately 21 percent are packed in the 20-foot containers and 79 percent in 40-foot containers. The 20-foot containers can hold 34 cubic meters (CBM) of material, and the 40-foot containers, 67 CBM. The cost to ship a 20-foot container is \$480, and for a 40-foot container, \$600; this is from any port location in China or Taiwan and to either Los Angeles or Seattle. Grainger estimates that these supplier-filled containers average 85 percent full when they are shipped.

The remaining 11 percent shipped from China and Taiwan go through consolidation centers that are located at each port. These consolidation centers are run by the freight forwarding company and cost about \$75,000 per year each to operate. At the volumes that are currently running through these centers, the variable cost is \$4.90 per CBM. The variable cost of running a consolidation center could be reduced to about \$1.40 per CBM using technology if the volume could be increased to at least 50,000 CBM per year. Now there is much variability in the volume run at each center and it only averages about 5,000 CBM per site.

Material at the consolidation centers is accumulated on an ongoing basis, and as containers are filled they are sent to the port. Volume is sufficient enough that at least one 40-foot container is shipped from each consolidation center each week. Grainger has found that the consolidation centers can load all material into 40-foot containers and utilize 96 percent of the capacity of the container.

Grainger ships from four major port locations. Approximately 10 percent of the volume is shipped from the north China port of Qingdao, while 42 percent is shipped from the central China port of Shanghai/Ningbo. Another 10 percent is shipped from Kaohsiung in Taiwan. The final 38 percent is shipped from the southern Yantian/Hong Kong port. Consolidation centers are currently run in each location.

Grainger management feels that it may be possible to make this part of its supply chain more efficient.

Specific questions to address in your analysis:

1. Evaluate the current China/Taiwan logistics costs. Assume a current total volume of 190,000 CBM and that 89 percent is shipped direct from the supplier plants in containers. Use the data from the case and assume that the supplier-loaded containers are 85 percent full. Assume that consolidation centers are run at each of the four port locations. The consolidation centers use only 40-foot containers and fill them to 96 percent capacity. Assume that it costs \$480 to ship a 20-foot container and \$600 to ship a 40-foot container. What is the total cost to get the containers to the United States? Do not include U.S. port costs in this part of the analysis.
2. Evaluate an alternative that involves consolidating all 20-foot container volumes and using only a single consolidation center in Shanghai/Ningbo. Assume that all the existing 20-foot container volumes and the existing consolidation center volumes are sent to this single consolidation center by suppliers. This new consolidation center volume would be packed into 40-foot containers, filled to 96 percent, and shipped to the United States. The existing 40-foot volume would still be shipped direct from the suppliers at 85 percent capacity utilization.
3. What should be done based on your analytics analysis? What have you not considered that may make your analysis invalid or that may strategically limit success? What do you think Grainger management should do?

Many thanks to Gary Scalzitti of Grainger for help with developing this case.

PRACTICE EXAM

In each of the following, name the term defined. Answers are listed at the bottom.

1. Refers to how common an item is or how many substitutes might be available.
2. When a customer allows the supplier to manage inventory policy for an item or group of items.
3. A phenomenon characterized by increased variation in ordering as we move from the customer to the manufacturer in the supply chain.
4. Products that satisfy basic needs and do not change much over time.
5. Products with short life cycles and typically high profit margins.
6. A supply chain that must deal with high levels of both supply and demand uncertainty.
7. In order to cope with high levels of supply uncertainty, a firm would use this strategy to reduce risk.
8. Used to describe functions related to the flow of material in a supply chain.
9. When a firm works with suppliers to look for opportunities to save money and benefit the environment.
10. Refers to an estimate of the cost of an item that includes all costs related to the procurement and use of an item, including the costs of disposing after its useful life.

Answers To Practice Exam 1. Specificity 2. Vendor-managed inventory 3. Bullwhip effect 4. Functional products 5. Innovative products 6. Agile supply chain 7. Multiple sources of supply (pooling) 8. Logistics 9. Green sourcing 10. Total cost of ownership

For PowerPoint lecture slides, Solutions Manual, Test Bank, Data files for solved examples, Excel Templates, Step-by-Step Solved Examples in video format, Tutorial Videos and many more, scan the adjacent **QR code**, or **visit http://www.mhhe.com/sie-chase15e**

SECTION FOUR

Supply and Demand Planning and Control

Information Technology Plays an Important Role in Operations and Supply Chain Management Success

Running a business requires a great planning system. What do we expect to sell in the future? How many people should we hire to handle the Christmas rush? How much inventory do we need? What should we make today? This section discusses various approaches used to answer these questions. The use of comprehensive software packages is common practice, but it is important to understand the basic planning concepts that underlie them so that the right software can be purchased and configured correctly. Moreover, given this basic understanding, a spreadsheet can be created for simple production planning situations.

Chapter 17

Enterprise Resource Planning Systems

LEARNING OBJECTIVES

LO17-1 Understand what an enterprise resource planning (ERP) system is

LO17-2 Explain how ERP integrates business units through information sharing

LO17-3 Illustrate how supply chain planning and control fits within ERP

LO17-4 Evaluate supply chain performance using data from the ERP system

ERP IN THE CLOUD!

Imagine having your PC, your cell phone, and your iPad all being in sync—all the time. Imagine being able to access all of your personal data, your bank accounts, your investments, or the location of your partner at any given moment. Imagine having the ability to organize and retrieve data from any online source. Imagine being able to share that data—photos, movies, contracts, e-mail, documents, and so forth—with your friends, family, and co-workers in an instant. Imagine being able to do this without being tethered to an Ethernet cable. Everything is wireless and security is ensured. This is what personal **cloud computing** promises to deliver.

Cloud computing A term that refers to delivering hosted ERP services over the Internet. This can significantly reduce the cost of ERP.

Now move this into the business realm. Companies can make all of their data available through simple apps. Every employee, no matter where they are located, can set up an instant office with a simple and secure wireless connection. New applications are instantly deployed globally to all employees when they are ready. All employees are looking at the same data, using the same application software, and reacting to the same real-time information. The savings on cabling, on server utilization, training, and support are dramatic. But the real benefits come from optimization and more consistent decisions, sharing customer information, and transparency from knowing the exact current status of the firm. Welcome to the world of ERP and working in "the cloud."

© Ronda Churchill/ Bloomberg via Getty Images

Enterprise resource planning (ERP)
A computer system that integrates application programs in accounting, sales, manufacturing, and the other functions in a firm. This integration is accomplished through a database shared by all the application programs.

This chapter discusses the integrated **enterprise resource planning (ERP)** systems that are now commonly used by large companies to support supply and demand planning and control, the topic of this section of the book. Major software vendors such as JDA Software, Microsoft, Oracle, and SAP (see Exhibit 17.1) offer state-of-the-art systems designed to provide real-time data to support better routine decision making, improve the efficiency of transaction processing, foster cross-functional integration, and provide improved insights into how a business should be run.

In most companies, ERP provides the information backbone needed to manage day-to-day execution. These systems support the standard planning and control functions covered in this section of the book. In particular, standard applications include forecasting covered in Chapter 18, sales and operations planning in Chapter 19, inventory control in Chapter 20, material requirements planning in Chapter 21, and workcenter scheduling in Chapter 22. The standard offering from the major vendors are often extended through more specialized industry-specific applications, or through custom modules built with spreadsheets or other general-purpose software.

LO 17-1
Understand what an enterprise resource planning (ERP) system is

WHAT IS ERP?

The term *enterprise resource planning (ERP)* can mean different things, depending on one's viewpoint. From the view of managers in a company, the emphasis is on the word *planning;* ERP represents a comprehensive software approach to support decisions concurrent with planning and controlling the business. On the other hand, for the information technology community, ERP is a term describing a software system that integrates application programs in finance, manufacturing, logistics, sales and marketing, human resources, and other functions in a firm. This integration is accomplished through a database shared by all the functions and data-processing applications. ERP systems typically are very efficient at handling the many transactions that document the activities of a company. For our purposes, we begin by describing our view of what ERP should accomplish for management, with an emphasis on planning. Following this, we describe how the ERP software programs are designed and then provide points to consider in choosing an ERP system. Our special interest is in how the software supports supply chain planning and control decisions.

ERP systems allow for integrated planning across the functional areas in a firm. Perhaps more importantly, ERP also supports integrated *execution* across functional areas. Today, the focus is moving to coordinated planning and execution across companies. In many cases, this work is supported by ERP systems.

Consistent Numbers

Strategy

ERP requires a company to have consistent definitions across functional areas. Consider the problem of measuring demand. How is demand measured? Is it when manufacturing completes an order? When items are picked from finished goods? When they physically leave the premises? When they

Exhibit 17.1

Major ERP Vendors

Company	Special Features	Website
JDA Software	Recent growth through purchase of software companies including i2 and Manugistics. Specializes in supply chain applications.	www.jda.com
Microsoft	Windows integration and the Office suite (Word, Excel, PowerPoint). The ERP product is Microsoft Dynamics that features customer relationship management.	www.microsoft.com
Oracle	Major database vendor (hardware and software).	www.oracle.com
SAP	Largest ERP vendor. Comprehensive scope of products across many industries.	www.sap.com

are invoiced? When they arrive at the customer sites? What is needed is a set of agreed-on definitions that are used by all functional units when they are processing their transactions. Consistent reporting of such measures as demand, stockouts, raw materials inventory, and finished goods inventory, for example, can then be accomplished. This is a basic building block for ERP systems.

Companies implementing ERP strive to derive benefits through much greater efficiency gained by an integrated supply chain planning and control process. In addition, better responsiveness to the needs of customers is obtained through the real-time information provided by the system. To better understand how this works, we next describe features of ERP software.

Software Imperatives

There are four aspects of ERP software that determine the quality of an ERP system:

1. The software should be multifunctional in scope with the ability to track financial results in monetary terms, procurement activity in units of material, sales in terms of product units and services, and manufacturing or conversion processes in units of resources or people. That is, excellent ERP software produces results closely related to the needs of people for their day-to-day work.
2. The software should be integrated. When a transaction or piece of data representing an activity of the business is entered by one of the functions, data regarding the other related functions are updated as well. This eliminates the need for reposting data to the system. Integration also ensures a common vision—we all sing from the same sheet of music.
3. The software needs to be modular in structure so it can be combined into a single expansive system, narrowly focused on a single function, or connected with software from another source/application.
4. The software must facilitate basic planning and control activities, including forecasting, production planning, and inventory management.

An ERP system is most appropriate for a company seeking the benefits of data and process integration supported by its information system. Benefit is gained from the elimination of redundant processes, increased accuracy in information, superior processes, and improved speed in responding to customer requirements.

An ERP software system can be built with software modules from different vendors, or it can be purchased from a single vendor. A multivendor approach can provide the opportunity to purchase "best in class" of each module. But this is usually at the expense of increased cost and greater resources that may be needed to implement and integrate the functional modules. On the other hand, a single-vendor approach may be easier to implement, but the features and functionality may not be the best available.

Routine Decision Making

It is important to make a distinction between the transaction processing capability and the decision support capability of an ERP system. **Transaction processing** relates to the posting and tracking of the activities that document the business. When an item is purchased from a vendor, for example, a specific sequence of activities occurs. The solicitation of the offer, acceptance of the offer, delivery of goods, storage in inventory, and payment for the purchase are all activities that occur as a result of the purchase. The efficient handling of the transactions as goods move through each step of the process is the primary goal of an ERP system.

Transaction processing
This is the posting and tracking of the detailed activities of a business.

A second objective of an ERP system is decision support. **Decision support** relates to how well the system helps the user make intelligent judgments about how to run the business. A key point here is that *people,* not software, make the decisions. The system *supports* better decision making. In the case of purchasing an item, for example, the amount to purchase, the selection of the vendor, and how it should be delivered will need to be decided. These decisions are made by professionals, while ERP systems are oriented toward transaction processing. However, over time, they evolve using decision logic based on parameters set in the system. For example, for items stored in inventory, the specific reorder points,

Decision support
This is the ability of the system to help a user make intelligent judgments about how to run the business.

order quantities, vendors, transportation vendors, and storage locations can be established when the items are initially entered in the system. At a later point, the decision logic can be revisited to improve the results. A major industry has been built around the development of bolt-on software packages designed to provide more intelligent decision support to ERP systems.

LO 17-2

Explain how ERP integrates business units through information sharing

HOW ERP CONNECTS THE FUNCTIONAL UNITS

A typical ERP system is made up of functionally oriented and tightly integrated modules. All the modules of the system use a common database that is updated in real time. Each module has the same user interface, similar to that of the familiar Microsoft Office products, thus making the use of the different modules much easier for users trained on the system. ERP systems from various vendors are organized in different ways, but typically modules are focused on at least the following four major areas: finance, manufacturing and logistics, sales and marketing, and human resources.

© Jag_cz/Shutterstock.com

ERP systems have evolved in much the same way as car models at automobile manufacturers. Automakers introduce new models every year or two and make many minor refinements. Major (platform) changes are made much less frequently, perhaps every five to eight years. The same is true of ERP software. ERP vendors are constantly looking for ways to improve the functionality of their software, so new features are often added. Many of these minor changes are designed to improve the usability of the software through a better screen interface or added features that correspond to the "hot" idea of the time. Major software revisions that involve changes to the structure of the database, and changes to the network and computer hardware technologies, though, are made only every three to five years. The basic ERP platform cannot be easily changed because of the large number of existing users and support providers. But these changes do occur.

Exhibit 17.2 depicts the scope of ERP applications. The diagram is meant to show how a comprehensive information system uses ERP as its core or backbone. Many other software-based functions may be integrated with the ERP system but are not necessarily included in the ERP system. The use of more specialized software such as decision support systems can often bring significant competitive advantages to a firm. The following brief descriptions of typical module functionality give an indication of how comprehensive the applications can be.

Finance

As a company grows through acquisition, and as business units make more of their own decisions, many companies find themselves with incompatible and sometimes conflicting financial data. An ERP system provides a common platform for financial data capture, a common set of numbers, and processes, facilitating rapid reconciliation of the general ledger. The real value of an ERP system is in the automatic capture of basic accounting transactions from the source of the transactions. The actual order from a customer, for example, is used not only by manufacturing to trigger production requirements, but also becomes the information for updating accounts payable when the order is actually shipped.

Process

Manufacturing and Logistics

This set of applications is the largest and most complex of the module categories. The system components discussed in this section of the book are concentrated in this area. Typical components include:

- **Sales and operations planning** coordinates the various planning efforts, including marketing planning, financial planning, operations planning, and human resource planning.

EXHIBIT 17.2

The Scope of ERP Applications

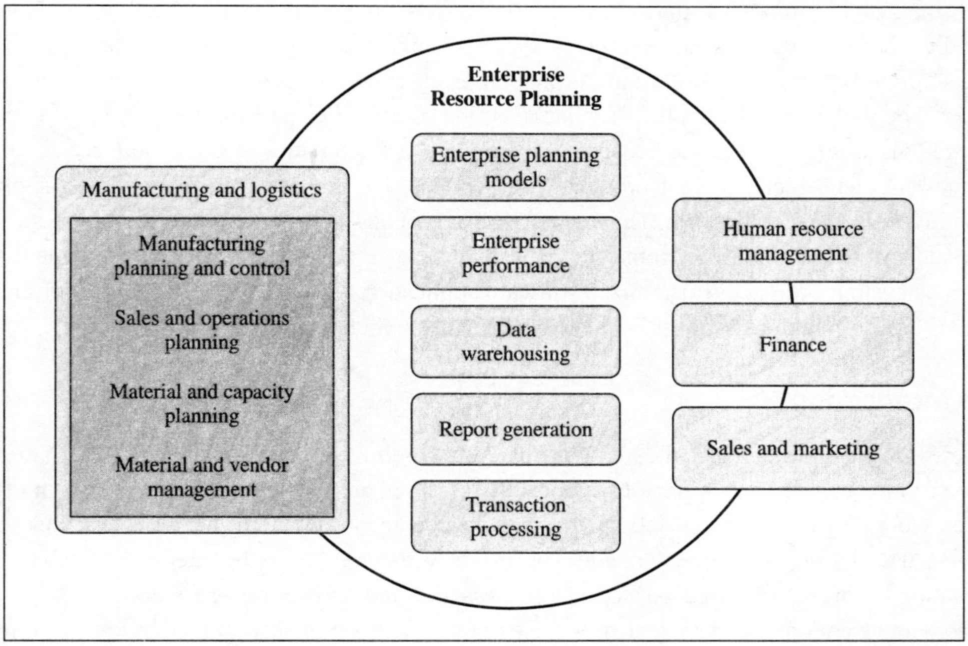

- **Materials management** covers tasks within the supply chain, including purchasing, vendor evaluation, and invoice management. It also includes inventory and warehouse management functions to support the efficient control of materials.
- **Plant maintenance** supports the activities associated with planning and performing repairs and preventative maintenance.
- **Quality management** software implements procedures for quality control and assurance.
- **Production planning and control** supports both discrete and process manufacturing. Repetitive and configure-to-order approaches are typically provided. Most ERP systems address all phases of manufacturing, including capacity leveling, material requirements planning, just-in-time (JIT), product costing, bill of materials processing, and database maintenance. Orders can be generated from sales orders or from links to an Internet site.
- **Project management** systems facilitate the setup, management, and evaluation of large, complex projects.

Sales and Marketing

This group of system components supports activities such as customer management; sales order management; forecasting, order management, credit checking configuration management; distribution, export controls, shipping, transportation management; and billing, invoices, and rebate processing. These modules, like the others, are increasingly implemented globally, allowing firms to manage the sales process worldwide. For example, if an order is received in Hong Kong, but the products are not available locally, they may be internally procured from warehouses in other parts of the world and shipped to arrive together at the Hong Kong customer's site.

Human Resources

This set of applications supports the capabilities needed to manage, schedule, pay, hire, and train the people who make an organization run. Typical functions include payroll, benefits administration, hiring procedures, personnel development planning, workforce planning, schedule and shift planning, time management, and travel expense accounting.

Customized Software

In addition to the standard application modules, many companies utilize special add-on modules that link to the standard modules, thus tailoring applications to specific needs. These modules may be tailored to specific industries such as chemical/petrochemical, oil and gas, hospital, or banking. They may also provide special decision support functions such as optimal scheduling of critical resources.

Even though the scope of applications included in standard ERP packages is very large, additional software will usually be required because of the unique characteristics of each company. A company generates its own unique mix of products and services that are designed to provide a significant competitive advantage to the firm. This unique mix of products and services will need to be supported by unique software capabilities, some of which may be purchased from vendors and some that will need to be custom-designed. Customized software applications are also widely used to coordinate the activities of a firm with its supply chain customers and suppliers.

Data Integration

The software modules, as described earlier, form the core of an ERP system. This core is designed to process the business transactions to support the essential activities of an enterprise in an efficient manner. Working from a single database, transactions document each of the activities that compose the processes used by the enterprise to conduct business. A major value of the integrated database is that information is not reentered at each step of a process, thus reducing errors and work.

Real time
As soon as a transaction is entered, the effect is known by all users of the system.

Transactions are processed in **real time**, meaning that as soon as the transaction is entered into the system, the effect on items such as inventory status, order status, and accounts receivable is known to all users of the system. There is no delay in the processing of a transaction in a real-time system. A customer could, for example, call into an order desk to learn the exact status of an order—or determine the status independently through an Internet connection. From a decision analysis viewpoint, the amount of detail available in the system is extremely rich. If, for example, one wishes to analyze the typical lead time for a make-to-order product, the analyst could process an information request that selects all of the orders for the product over the past three months, calculate the time between order date and delivery date for each order, and finally average the time for the whole set of orders. Analyses, such as this lead time, can be valuable for evaluating improvements designed to make the process more responsive, for example.

Data warehouse
A special program that is designed to automatically capture and process data for uses that are outside the basic ERP system applications.

To facilitate queries not built into the standard ERP system software, a separate **data warehouse** is commonly employed. A data warehouse is a special program (often running on a totally separate computer) that is designed to automatically archive and process data for uses that are outside the basic ERP system applications. For example, the data warehouse could, on an ongoing basis, perform the calculations needed for the average lead time question. The data warehouse software and database is set up so that users may access and analyze data without placing a burden on the operational ERP system. This is a powerful mechanism to support higher-level decision support applications. See the nearby OSCM at Work box titled "Open Information Warehouse."

A good example of a company making use of a data warehouse is Walmart. Walmart is now able to put two full years of retail store sales data online. The data are used by both internal Walmart buyers and outside suppliers—sales and current inventory data on products sold at Walmart and Sam's Club stores. Vendors, who are restricted to viewing products they supply, use a Web-based extranet site to collaborate with Walmart's buyers in managing inventory and making replenishment decisions. A vendor's store-by-store sales results for a given day are available to vendors by 4 A.M. the following day. The database is more than 130 terabytes in size. Each terabyte is the equivalent of 250 million pages of text. At an average of 500 pages per book, a terabyte is a half-million books. For Walmart as a whole, that is about 20 major university libraries.

OSCM AT WORK

Open Information Warehouse

Any modern database will let you easily formulate an SQL query like "What sales did my company have in Italy in 2016?" A report generated in response to such a query could look like this:

Region	Q1	Q2	Q3	Q4	Total
Umbria	1,000	1,200	800	2,000	5,000
Toscana	2,000	2,600	1,600	2,800	9,000
Calabria	400	300	150	450	1,300
Total	3,400	4,100	2,550	5,250	15,300

But things get more complex if, for instance, we then want to use this answer as the basis for *drilling down* to look at the sales for different quarters and sales representatives in the various regions. Drilling down means descending through an existing hierarchy to bring out more and more detail.

In the following example, we drill down through the sales hierarchy (sales representatives in Toscana). Signore Corleone's sales do not appear to have been affected by the holiday season in the third quarter.

Sales	Q1	Q2	Q3	Q4	Total
S. Paolo	500	600	300	500	1,900
S. Vialli	700	600	200	700	2,200
S. Ferrari	600	700	400	700	2,400
S. Corleone	200	700	700	900	2,500
Total	2,000	2,600	1,600	2,800	9,000

At this point, you can switch to another dimension—for instance, from sales representative to product sold. This is often referred to as *slice and dice.*

Product	Q1	Q2	Q3	Q4	Total
X-11	2,000	2,500	1,500	3,550	9,550
Z-12	1,400	1,600	1,050	1,700	5,750
Total	3,400	4,100	2,550	5,250	15,300

From the standpoint of a data analyst, it can now be useful to check sales of particular products in each region. Current software allows the end user to do this easily using the data warehouse approach implemented within the system.

HOW SUPPLY CHAIN PLANNING AND CONTROL FITS WITHIN ERP

LO 17-3

Illustrate how supply chain planning and control fits within ERP

ERP is concerned with all aspects of a supply chain, including managing materials, scheduling machines and people, and coordinating suppliers and key customers. The coordination required for success runs across all functional units in the firm. Consider the following simple example to illustrate the degree of coordination required.

Simplified Example

Ajax Food Services Company has one plant that makes sandwiches. These are sold in vending machines, cafeterias, and small stores. One of the sandwiches is peanut butter and jelly (PBJ). It is made from bread, butter, peanut butter, and grape jelly. When complete, it is wrapped in a standard plastic package used for all Ajax sandwiches. One loaf of bread makes 10 sandwiches, a package of butter makes 50 sandwiches, and containers of peanut butter and jelly each make 20 sandwiches.

Consider the information needed by Ajax for planning and control. First, Ajax needs to know what demand to expect for its PBJ sandwich in the future. This might be forecast by analyzing detailed sales data from each location where the sandwiches are sold. Because sales are all handled by sales representatives who travel between the various sites, data based on the actual orders and sales reports provided by the reps can be used to make this forecast. The same data are used by human resources to calculate commissions owed to the reps for payroll purposes. Marketing uses the same data to analyze each current location and evaluate the attractiveness of new locations.

Freshness is very important to Ajax, so daily demand forecasts are developed to plan sandwich making. Consider, for example, that Ajax sees that it needs to make 300 PBJ sandwiches to be delivered to the sales sites this Friday. Ajax will actually assemble the sandwiches on Thursday. According to the usage data given earlier, this requires 30 loaves of bread, 6 packages of butter, and 15 containers of peanut butter and jelly. Freshness is largely dictated by the age of the bread, so it is important that Ajax works closely with the local baker because the baker delivers bread each morning on the basis of the day's assembly schedule. Similarly, the delivery schedules for the butter, peanut butter, and jelly need to be coordinated with the vendors of these items.

Process

Ajax uses college students who work on a part-time basis to assemble the sandwiches. A student can make 60 sandwiches per hour and sandwiches must be ready for loading into the delivery trucks by 4:00 P.M. on the day prior to delivery. Our 300 sandwiches require five hours of work, so any one student doing this work needs to start at or before 11:00 A.M. on Thursday to make the sandwiches on time.

An ERP system is designed to provide the information and decision support needed to coordinate this type of activity. Of course, with our simplified example, the coordination is trivial, but consider if our company were making hundreds of different types of sandwiches in 1,000 cities around the world, and these sandwiches were sold at hundreds of sites in each of these cities. This is exactly the scale of operations that can be handled by a modern ERP system.

Precisely how all of these calculations are made is, of course, the main focus of this section of the book. All of the details for how material requirements are calculated, capacity is planned, and demand forecasts are made, for example, are explained in great detail.

SAP Supply Chain Management

In this section, we see how SAP, a major ERP vendor, has approached the details of supply chain planning and control. Here, we are using SAP to show how one vendor organizes the functions. Other major vendors like JDA Software, Oracle, and Microsoft each have a unique approach to packaging supply chain software.

SAP divides its supply chain software into four main functions: supply chain planning, supply chain execution, supply chain collaboration, and supply chain coordination. Current information about products is on vendors' Websites, and readers are encouraged to download the white papers that describe a vendor's current thinking. These publications are informative and indicate where a vendor will move in the future. Moreover, comparing/contrasting this information can be very educational—and help in making key choices as to which business processes can be supported by standard (plain vanilla) software.

The *supply chain design module* provides a centralized overview of the entire supply chain and key performance indicators, which helps identify weak links and potential improvements. It supports strategic planning by enabling the testing of various scenarios to determine how changes in the market or customer demand can be addressed by the supply chain. Here, for our simplified example of Ajax food services, we could evaluate the relative profitability of particular market channels and locations such as vending machines versus shops in train stations.

Collaborative demand and supply planning helps match demand to supply. Demand-planning tools take into account historical demand data, causal factors, marketing events, market intelligence, and sales objectives and enable the supply chain network to work on a single forecast. Supply planning tools create an overall supply plan that covers materials management, production, distribution and transportation requirements, and constraints. Here, Ajax would be able to anticipate the demands for each kind of sandwich in each location and plan replenishments accordingly.

SAP Supply Chain Execution

Materials management shares inventory and procurement order information to ensure that the materials required for manufacturing are available in the right place and at the right time. This set of applications supports plan-driven procurement, inventory management, and invoicing, with a feedback loop between demand and supply to increase responsiveness. In this set of applications, Ajax would plan for all the sandwich components to be delivered to the right places at the right times. Inventories might be maintained on some items such as peanut butter, while others such as bread might be planned on a just-in-time basis.

Collaborative manufacturing shares information with partners to coordinate production and enable everyone to work together to increase both visibility and responsiveness. These applications support all types of production processes: engineer-to-order, assemble-to-order, make-to-order, and make-to-stock. They create a continuous information flow across engineering, planning, and execution and can optimize production schedules across the supply chain, taking into account material and capacity constraints. Here, Ajax might do joint planning with key suppliers and perhaps organize the planning of special promotions.

Collaborative fulfillment supports partnerships that can intelligently commit to delivery dates in real time and fulfill orders from all channels on time. This set of applications includes a global available-to-promise (ATP) feature that locates finished products, components, and machine capacities in a matter of seconds. It also manages the flow of products through sales channels, matching supply to market demand, reassigning supply and demand to meet shifts in customer demand, and managing transportation and warehousing. Clearly, all these logistics activities are critical to Ajax in order to deliver fresh sandwiches in the right amounts.

SAP Supply Chain Collaboration

The *inventory collaboration hub* uses the Internet to gain visibility to suppliers and manage the replenishment process. Suppliers can see the status of their parts at all plants, receive automatic alerts when inventory levels get low, and respond quickly via the Web. The hub can also be integrated with back-end transaction and planning systems to update them in real time. Here, Ajax could provide real-time inventory views to its suppliers—not only of material suppliers, but also of downstream inventories (i.e., sandwiches).

Collaborative replenishment planning is particularly useful in the consumer products and retail industries. These applications allow manufacturers to collaborate with their strategic retail customers to increase revenue, improve service, and lower inventory levels and costs. They enable an exception-based collaborative planning, forecasting, and replenishment (CPFR) process that allows the firm to add retail partners without a proportional increase in staff. This set of applications would be particularly useful to Ajax as it grows its global business and adds new channels of distribution.

Vendor managed inventory (*VMI*) is a set of processes to enable vendor-driven replenishment that can be implemented over the Web. Now, Ajax vendors would no longer receive "orders." They would replenish Ajax inventories as they like—but be paid for their materials only when items are consumed by Ajax.

Enterprise portal gives users personalized access to a range of information, applications, and services supported by the system. It uses role-based technology to deliver information to users according to their individual responsibilities within the supply chain network. It can also use Web-based tools to integrate third-party systems in the firm's supply chain network. Here, for example, marketing people at Ajax might like to examine the detailed sales data (and perhaps customer questionnaires) in relation to a new product introduction.

Mobile supply chain management is a set of applications so that people can plan, execute, and monitor activity using mobile and remote devices. Mobile data entry using personal data assistant devices and automated data capture using wireless "smart tags," for example, are supported. Here, Ajax can have marketing and even delivery personnel report on actual store conditions—not just sales but also category management. For example, how well does the actual assortment of sandwiches match the standard?

OSCM AT WORK

Ice Project of ONGC: One of the Finest Examples of ERP Implementation

Amongst the top Indian corporate giants, Oil and Natural Gas Commission (ONGC) is the front leader in effectively using Information and Communication Technology (ICT) tools like Enterprise Resource Planning (ERP). It launched its ambitious dream-project ICE (Information Consolidation for Efficiency) in July 2002 and completed in a record 30 months, i.e., December 2004. ICE project included ₹95 crore implementation of the ERP package on SAP. This is one of the world's biggest ERP projects, across 400 locations and serving to over 10,000 end-users of ONGC. It was the culmination of the dream of Mr. Subir Raha, then Chairman and Managing Director of ONGC, who said, "The differentials in quality of information and speed of access to information make or break your business" [1].

ONGC has served to India's hydrocarbon need by establishing 6.61 billion tonnes of in-place hydrocarbon reserves with more than 300 discoveries of oil and gas. Six out of seven producing basins in India have been discovered by ONGC [2]. The core areas of the ONGC is to plan, promote, organize and implement programs for development of petroleum resources and the production and sale of petroleum and petroleum products produced by it.

Implementation of ICE project was certainly very challenging for ONGC due to high degree of complexity involved in it. For example, Exploration and Production (E&P) business of ONGC is uniquely different from a typical manufacturing, trading or service industry. According to Mr Subir Raha, ``The main objective of the ICE project is to optimize and standardize the business processes for integrated information availability. The ERP package will enable availability of information on real time basis and elimination of duplication of activities across the business process by capturing data at the source point. This will, in turn, facilitate decision support, better operation control and efficient cost management [3]." Today, ICE provides a comprehensive IT solution encompassing end-to-end business process requirements, in which all the previous fragmented IT applications got merged. Therefore, it addresses the expectations of the total business transaction needs of ONGC, enabling tactical and strategic decision-making based on on-line information, which is now accessible from a single platform and a single data-base across the entire enterprise.

Few important modules of ICE Project are as follows:

MM Module: It integrates the Material Requirement Planning, Procurement and Inventory Management, and Services and Contracts.

PS Module: It covers the Engineering Services, Drilling Services, Work Over, Survey, Dry Docking, Consultancy and R&D. It tracks all costs, based on work break down structure activities.

PM Module: It manages all planned and break-down maintenance, and it tracks the audit activities and all associated cost.

PP Module: It covers all production and procession activities and tracks all planned and actual cost.

SD Module: It integrates all sales activities including disposal and services (consultancy).

For the specific requirements of ONGC, SAP was extended to include different activities, such as:

OLM Module: It is used for the offshore logistics management, including helicopter movements

PS (Project System): It covers upstream activities, like Drilling, Survey, Well Services, etc.

After implementing ICE project, ONGC achieved:

- Higher information visibility and self regulation
- More objective decision making at all levels
- Analytical capabilities for better strategic decisions
- Comprehensive business process mapping
- Cleaned material masters files in which over 14.2 lakh material codes were reduced to 2.9 lakh

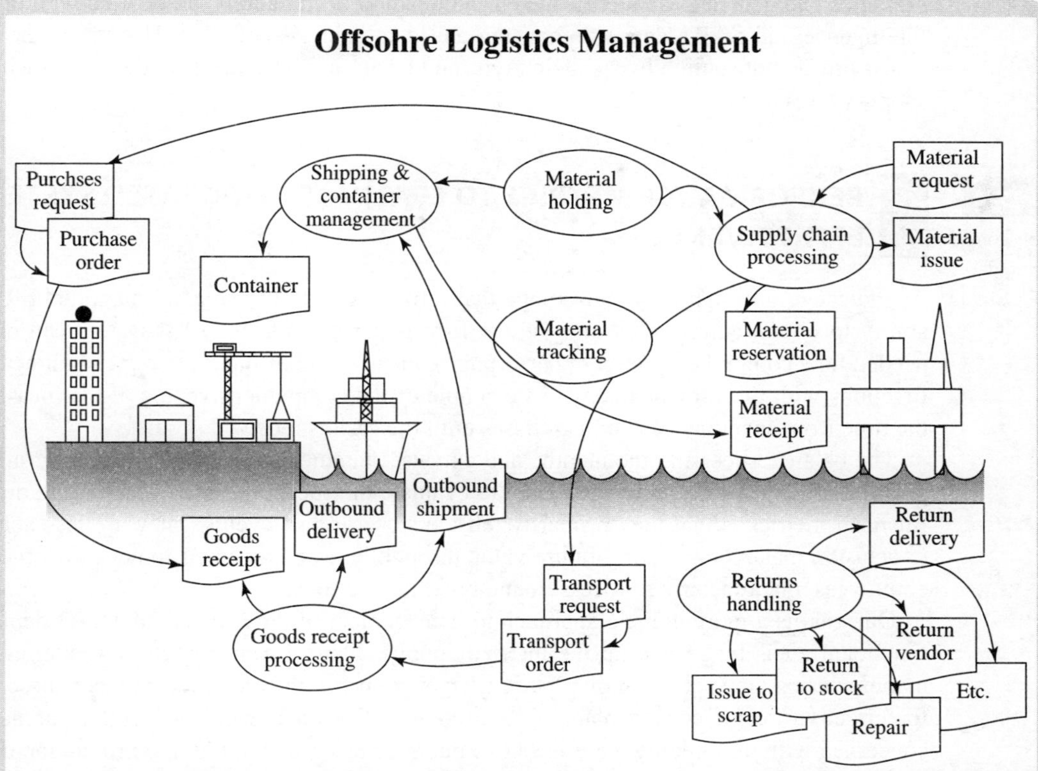

- Site inventory brought to books
- Elimination of repeated entries
- Standardized reports
- Immediate availability of data across the organization
- Data security
- Prevention of unauthorized transactions
- Integrated business plan
- Self auditing
- Upgraded IT Infrastructure, including one of the largest data centers in Asia, etc.

All major business activities of ONGC are now seamlessly integrated on one single platform, and one can see the usefulness of having this system, which helps ONGC objective–one organization-one database.

References

1 *Business Today*, March 28, 2004.
2 http://www.ongcindia.com/ (Accessed on 4 April 2014).
3 *Business Line*, August 22, 2002.

SAP Supply Chain Coordination

Supply chain event management monitors the execution of supply chain events, such as the issue of a pallet or the departure of a truck, and flags any problems that come up. This set of applications is particularly useful for product tracking/traceability. For Ajax, if there is a customer complaint about a sandwich, it is critical to quickly determine if this is an isolated instance or whether there might be a large group of bad quality sandwiches—and how to find them.

Supply chain performance management allows the firm to define, select, and monitor key performance indicators, such as costs and assets, and use them to gain an integrated, comprehensive view of performance across the supply chain. It provides constant surveillance of key performance measures and generates an alert if there is a deviation from plan. It can be used with mySAP Business Intelligence and SAP's data warehousing and data analysis software. Here, Ajax needs to not only assess profit contribution by sandwich type and location, it also needs to determine which are the best supplier and customer partners.

LO 17-4

Evaluate supply chain performance using data from the ERP system

PERFORMANCE METRICS TO EVALUATE INTEGRATED SYSTEM EFFECTIVENESS

As indicated, one significant advantage that a firm gains from using an integrated ERP system is the ability to obtain current data on how the firm is performing. An ERP system can provide the data needed for a comprehensive set of performance measures to evaluate strategic alignment of the various functions with the firm's strategy. An example of the comprehensiveness of the measures is tracking the time from spending cash on purchases until the cash is received in sales.

The balance sheet and the income and expense statements contain financial measures, such as net profit, that traditionally have been used to evaluate the success of the firm. A limitation of traditional financial metrics is that they primarily tell the story of past events. They are less helpful as a guide to decision makers in creating future value through investments in customer infrastructure, suppliers, employees, manufacturing processes, and other innovations.

Our goal is a more holistic approach to management of the firm. Exhibit 17.3 depicts three major functional areas that make up the internal supply chain of a manufacturing enterprise: purchasing, manufacturing, and sales and distribution. Tight cooperation is required between these three functions for effective manufacturing planning and control. Considered independently, purchasing is mainly concerned with minimizing materials cost, manufacturing with minimum production costs, sales with selling the greatest amount, and distribution with minimum distribution and warehousing costs. Let us consider how each independently operating function might seek to optimize its operation.

Exhibit 17.3

Manufacturing Operating Cycle

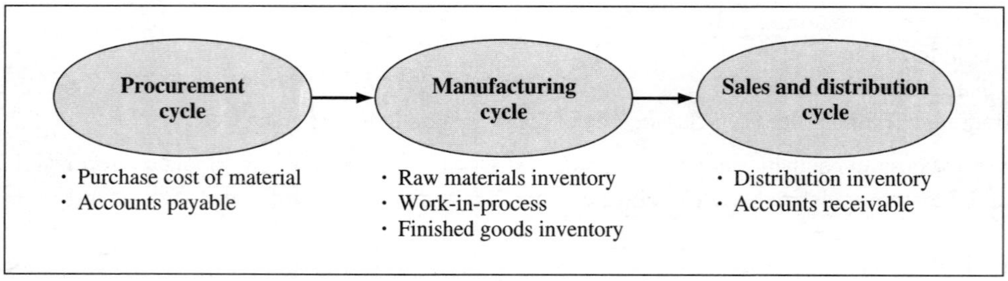

The "Functional Silo" Approach

The purchasing function is responsible for buying all of the material required to support manufacturing operations. When operating independently, this function wishes to know what materials and quantities are going to be needed over the long term. The purchasing group then solicits bids for the best price for each material. The main criterion is simply the cost of the material, and the purchasing function is *evaluated* on this criterion: What is latest actual cost versus standard cost? Of course, quality is always going to be important to the group, so typically some type of quality specification will need to be guaranteed by the supplier. But quality is more of a constraint than a goal; suppliers must achieve some minimal level of specification. Consideration of delivery schedules, quantities, and responsiveness are also important, but again these considerations are often secondary at best in how the purchasing function is evaluated in a traditional firm.

For manufacturing, making the product at the lowest possible cost is the classic metric. To do this requires minimum equipment downtime, with high equipment and labor utilization. Stopping to set up equipment is not the desire of this group. This group is focused on high-volume output, with minimum changeovers. Quality is again "important"—but as in purchasing, it is more of a minimum hurdle.

Long production runs lead to lower unit costs, but they also generate larger inventories. For sales, larger inventories appear at first to be desirable, since these should support customer service. Alas, it is not so; a one-year supply of product A is of no help when we are out of product B.

Distribution can be equally narrow-minded and suboptimal. In the classic case, its job is moving the product from the manufacturing site to the customer at the lowest possible cost. Depending on the product, it may need to be stored in one or more distribution centers and be moved via one or more different modes of transportation (truck, rail, etc.). Evaluation of activities tends to focus on the specific activity involved. For example, many firms focus on the lowest price quotation for moving a product from one stage of the distribution chain to another, rather than on the *total* costs of moving materials *into* and *out of* the overall firm. And even here this cost focus needs to be integrated with other objectives such as lower inventories, faster response times, and customer service.

Consider the implications if all three areas are allowed to work independently. To take advantage of discounts, purchasing will buy the largest quantities possible. This results in large amounts of raw material inventory. The manufacturing group desires to maximize production volumes in order to spread the significant fixed costs of production over as many units as possible. These large lot sizes result in high amounts of work-in-process inventory, with large quantities of goods pushed into finished goods whether they are needed or not. Large lot sizes also mean that the time between batches increases; therefore, response times to unexpected demand increase. Finally, distribution will try to fully load every truck that is used to move material to minimize transportation cost. Of course, this may result in large amounts of inventory in distribution centers (perhaps the wrong ones) and might not match well with what customers really need. Given the opportunity, the sales group might even sell product that cannot possibly be delivered on time. After all, they are evaluated on sales, not deliveries. A more coordinated approach is facilitated by the use of an ERP system. The following is an example of a consistent set of metrics useful for managing supply chain functions effectively.

Integrated Supply Chain Metrics

The APICS Supply Chain Council has developed many metrics to measure the performance of the overall supply chain. It has used these standardized measures to develop benchmarks for comparisons between companies. Exhibit 17.4 contains a list of some of these measures with average and best-in-class benchmarks. The average and best-in-class measures are for typical large industrial products. The APICS Supply Chain Council has developed sets of measures similar to these for many different categories of companies.

A particularly useful approach to measuring performance not only captures the integrated impact that the three classic functions have on the entire business supply chain, it also integrates the finance function. Such a metric, which measures the relative efficiency of a supply chain, is **cash-to-cash cycle time**. Cash-to-cash cycle time integrates the purchasing, manufacturing, and sales/distribution cycles depicted in Exhibit 17.3. But it also relates well to the financial maxim: Cash is king! Calculating the measure requires the use of data related to purchasing, accounting, manufacturing, and sales.

Cash-to-cash cycle time
The average number of days that it takes a business to convert cash spent for raw material and other resources into cash inflows from sales.

Actually, cash-to-cash cycle time is a measure of cash flow. Cash flow indicates where cash comes from (its source), where cash is spent (its use), and the net change in cash for the year. Understanding how cash flows through a business is critical to managing the business effectively. Accountants use the term *operating cycle* to describe the length of time it takes a business to convert cash outflows for raw materials, labor, and so forth into cash inflows. This cycle time determines, to a large extent, the amount of capital needed to start and operate a business. Conceptually, cash-to-cash cycle time is calculated as follows:

$$\text{Cash-to-cash cycle time} = \text{Inventory days of supply} + \text{Days of sales outstanding} - \text{Average payment period for material} \quad [17.1]$$

EXHIBIT 17.4

Supply Chain Metrics

Measure	Description	Best in Class	Average or Median
Delivery performance	What percentage of orders is shipped according to schedule?	93%	69%
Fill rate by line item	Orders often contain multiple line items. This is the percentage of the actual line items filled.	97%	88%
Perfect order fulfillment	This measures how many complete orders were filled and shipped on time.	92.4%	65.7%
Order fulfillment lead time	The time from when an order is placed to when it is received by the customer.	135 days	225 days
Warranty cost of % of revenue	This is the actual warranty expense divided by revenue.	1.2%	2.4%
Inventory days of supply	How long an item spends in inventory before being used.	55 days	84 days
Cash-to-cash cycle time	Considering accounts payable, accounts receivable, and inventory, this is the amount of time it takes to turn cash used to purchase materials into cash from a customer.	35.6 days	99.4 days
Asset turns	This is a measure of how many times the same assets can be used to generate revenue and profit.	4.7 turns	1.7 turns

The overall result is the number of days between paying for raw materials and getting paid for the product. Going through the details of calculating cash-to-cash cycle time demonstrates the power of integrated information. These calculations are straightforward in an ERP system. The calculation can be divided into three parts: the accounts receivable cycle, the inventory cycle, and the accounts payable cycle.

Exhibit 17.5 shows the data that are used for calculating cash-to-cash cycle time. The data are controlled by different functions within the company. The current accounts payable amount, an account that is dependent on the credit terms that purchasing negotiates with suppliers, captures the current money the firm owes its suppliers. As will be seen in the calculation, this is a form of credit to the company.

The inventory account gives the value of the entire inventory within the company. This includes raw materials, work-in-process, finished goods, and distribution inventory. The value of inventory depends on the quantities stored and also the cost of the inventory to the firm. All three major functional areas affect the inventory account. Purchasing has a major influence on raw materials. Manufacturing largely determines work-in-process and finished goods. Sales/distribution influences the location of finished goods—as well as the amounts, through their forecasts and orders.

Just as inventory is affected by all three functions, the cost of sales is dependent on costs that are incurred throughout the firm. For the purposes of the cash-to-cash cycle time calculation, this is expressed as a percentage of total sales. This percentage depends on such items as material cost, labor cost, and all other direct costs associated with the procurement of materials, manufacturing process, and distribution of the product.

Sales are simply the total sales revenue over a given period of time. Finally, accounts receivable is the amount owed the firm by its customers. The accounts receivable amount will depend on the firm's credit policy and its ability to deliver product in a timely manner. Exhibit 17.5 shows how the three major functional areas influence the cash-to-cash cycle calculation.

EXHIBIT 17.5

Integrated ERP Data for Cash-to-Cash Cycle Time Calculation

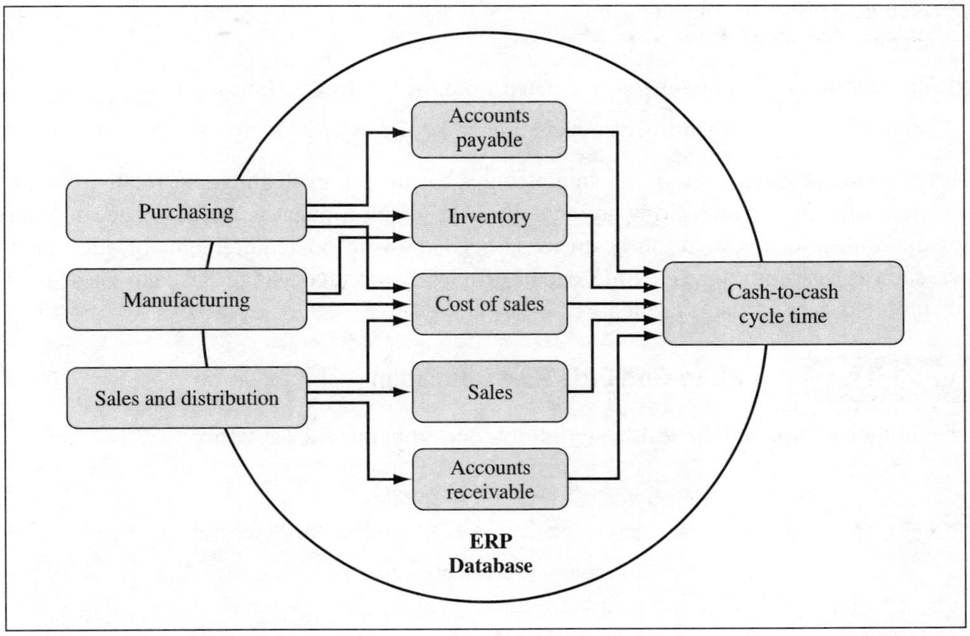

Calculating the Cash-to-Cash Cycle Time

Analytics

As noted, the first task in determining the cash-to-cash cycle time is to calculate accounts receivable cycle time. This measures the length of time it takes a business to convert a sale into cash. In other words, how long does it take a business to collect the money owed for goods already sold? One way is to calculate the number of days of sales invested in accounts receivable:

$$S_d = \frac{S}{d} \quad [17.2]$$

where

S_d = average daily sales
S = sales over d days

$$AR_d = \frac{AR}{S_d} \quad [17.3]$$

where

AR_d = average days of accounts receivable
AR = accounts receivable

The next part of the calculation is the inventory cycle time. This is the number of days of inventory measured relative to the cost of sales:

$$C_d = S_d CS \quad [17.4]$$

where

C_d = average daily cost of sales
CS = cost of sales (percent)

$$I_d = \frac{I}{C_d} \quad [17.5]$$

where

I_d = average days of inventory
I = current value of inventory (total)

Next, the accounts payable cycle time measures the level of accounts payable relative to the cost of sales:

$$AP_d = \frac{AP}{C_d} \quad [17.6]$$

where
AP_d = average days of accounts payable
AP = accounts payable

Finally, the cash-to-cash cycle time is calculated from the three cycle times.

$$\text{Cash-to-cash cycle time} = AR_d + I_d - AP_d \quad [17.7]$$

The cash-to-cash cycle time is an interesting measure for evaluating the relative supply chain effectiveness of a firm. Some firms are actually able to run a negative value for the measure. This implies the ability to invest in the business as needed—with no requirement for additional funds! Metrics, such as cash-to-cash cycle time, can be efficiently reported using ERP data. These metrics can even be reported in real time if needed.

EXAMPLE 17.1 Cash-to-Cash Cycle Time Calculation

Accounting has supplied the following information from our ERP system:

Data:	Sales over last 30 days = \$1,020,000
	Accounts receivable at the end of the month = \$200,000
	Inventory value at the end of the month = \$400,000
	Cost of sales = 60 percent of total sales
	Accounts payable at the end of the month = \$160,000

Calculate our current cash-to-cash cycle time.

SOLUTION

$$S_d = \frac{S}{d} = \frac{1,020,000}{30} = 34,000$$

$$AR_d = \frac{AR}{S_d} = \frac{200,000}{34,000} = 5.88 \text{ days}$$

$$C_d = S_d CS = 34,000(0.6) = 20,400$$

$$I_d = \frac{I}{C_d} = \frac{400,000}{20,400} = 19.6 \text{ days}$$

$$AP_d = \frac{AP}{C_d} = \frac{160,000}{20,400} = 7.84 \text{ days}$$

$$\text{Cash-to-cash cycle time} = AR_d + I_d - AP_d = 5.88 + 19.6 - 7.84 = 17.64 \text{ days}$$

CONCEPT CONNECTIONS

LO 17-1 Understand what an enterprise resource planning (ERP) system is

Summary

- ERP is a comprehensive software system that integrates data from all functional areas of a business. This integration is accomplished through a database that is shared by all the applications.
- Benefits gained are better processes, information accuracy, and responsiveness through the real-time information provided by the system.
- The system is designed to efficiently handle the transactions that document the activities of the firm, and also enables the users to make better business decisions.

Key Terms

Cloud computing A term that refers to delivering hosted ERP services over the Internet. This can significantly reduce the cost of ERP.

Enterprise resource planning (ERP) A computer system that integrates application programs in accounting, sales, manufacturing, and the other functions in a firm. This integration is accomplished through a database shared by all the application programs.

Transaction processing This is the posting and tracking of the detailed activities of a business.

Decision support This is the ability of the system to help a user make intelligent judgments about how to run the business.

LO 17-2 Explain how ERP integrates business units through information sharing

Summary

- Typical ERP systems have application modules in finance, manufacturing and logistics, sales and marketing, and human resources.
- The software modules connect to a common database that is updated in real time. Data is shared across the modules in such a way that a transaction entered in one area is propagated to the others.
- In addition to the standard modules, many companies use specialized modules that tailor the system to their specific needs.

Key Terms

Real time As soon as a transaction is entered, the effect is known by all users of the system.

Data warehouse A special program that is designed to automatically capture and process data for uses that are outside the basic ERP system applications.

LO 17-3 Illustrate how supply chain planning and control fits within ERP

Summary

- Applications for supply chain activities such as managing materials, scheduling machines and people, coordinating suppliers, and processing customer orders are all included within an ERP system.
- The activities commonly supported are: design of the supply chain system, future planning to meet supply and demand objectives, execution of activities to meet these activities, collaboration between suppliers and customers, and coordination to track activities against plans.

LO 17-4 Evaluate supply chain performance using data from the ERP system

Summary

- Performance measures that span functional areas are most useful to ensure that each area is not optimizing their own processes at the expense of the other areas. For example, manufacturing might minimize cost by focusing on high-volume production, with minimum changeovers. This may result in producing too much of one item and not enough of another, thus not allowing sales to fill customer orders.
- The APICS Supply Chain Council is a good source for data relating to the metrics commonly used in different industries. Cash-to-cash cycle time is a useful supply chain metric because it captures how quickly a dollar spent on raw material is converted into income from the firm's customers. It is calculated from accounting data captured by the ERP system.

Key Terms

Cash-to-cash cycle time The average number of days that it takes a business to convert cash spent for raw material and other resources into cash inflows from sales.

Key Formulae

[17.1] Cash-to-cash cycle time = Inventory days of supply + Days of sales outstanding −Average payment period for material

[17.2] $S_d = \frac{S}{d}$

[17.3] $AR_d = \frac{AR}{S_d}$

[17.4] $C_d = S_d CS$

[17.5] $I_d = \frac{I}{C_d}$

[17.6] $AP_d = \frac{AP}{C_d}$

[17.7] Cash-to-cash cycle time $= AR_d + I_d - AP_d$

SOLVED PROBLEMS

LO17-4

Midwest Baking Products manufactures a variety of dry goods used in industrial and consumer baking. As the company has grown, it has found it increasingly difficult to keep accurate tabs on inventory and cash flows. Six months ago, it completed an ERP implementation project, and the ERP system is running smoothly now. The information systems department is training various functional areas about how to retrieve reports from the system, and the result of one report shows the following data from the prior month (May).

Gross sales	$1,440,000
Cost of goods sold	720,000
Accounts receivable (end-of-month)	250,000
Accounts payable (end-of-month)	150,000
Net assets	3,754,000
Inventory value (end-of-month)	470,000

Use this report to calculate the cash-to-cash cycle time. Round interim calculations to two decimal places if needed.

Solution

We calculate the cash-to-cash cycle time by using formulas 17.2 through 17.7, in order. Equation 17.7 will give us the cash-to-cash cycle time.

Average Daily Sales

$$S_d = \frac{S}{d} = \frac{1{,}440{,}000}{31} = 46{,}451.61$$

[Unlike Example 17.1, we use 31 in the denominator of the given equation because May has 31 days.]

Average Days Accounts Receivable

$$AR_d = \frac{AR}{S_d} = \frac{250{,}000}{46{,}451.61} = 5.38$$

Inventory Cycle Time

Equation 17.4 is used here, and it asks for the cost of sales as a percent of total sales. We instead have the cost of goods sold (same as cost of sales) in dollars. We first need to convert this to a percentage to use Equation 17.4.

$$CS = \frac{\text{COGS}}{\text{Total Sales}} = \frac{720{,}000}{1{,}440{,}000} = 0.50$$

Now we can apply Equation 17.4:

$$C_d = S_d * CS = 46,451.61 * 0.50 = 23,225.81$$

Average Days of Inventory

$$I_d = \frac{I}{C_d} = \frac{470,000}{23,225.81} = 20.24$$

Accounts Payable Cycle Time

$$AP_d = \frac{AP}{C_d} = \frac{150,000}{23,225.81} = 6.46$$

Cash-to-Cash Cycle Time

$$AR_d + I_d + AP_d = 5.38 + 20.24 - 6.46 = 19.16 \text{ days}$$

The cash-to-cash cycle time based on this recent report is 19.16 days.

DISCUSSION QUESTIONS

1. Describe the benefits of using an ERP system. **LO17-1**
2. Are the ERP systems discussed in the chapter appropriate for use in all firms? Explain.
3. Describe how an ERP system fits into the overall information system structure in a firm. **LO17-2**
4. ERP systems provide a wealth of information that can be used and analyzed in a wide variety of ways. What is an inherent risk with so much information?
5. Visit the vendors' Websites to read up on both SAP and Microsoft Dynamics ERP systems. Provide a list of four ways in which the two differ in their approach to implementing ERP. **LO17-3**
6. Briefly describe how supply chain planning and control is managed in an ERP system.
7. Explain how an ERP system can improve the evaluation and analysis of performance metrics. **LO17-4**
8. Why is the cash-to-cash cycle time such an important supply chain performance measure?

OBJECTIVE QUESTIONS

1. What company is the largest ERP vendor? **LO17-1**
2. What term relates to the posting and tracking of activities that document a business?
3. Is it true that, for an ERP system to be effective, it must be completely purchased from a single vendor?
4. ERP systems from different vendors vary quite a bit, but typically they will focus on at least which four major areas? **LO17-2**
5. Which common ERP module category is typically the largest and most complex? (Answer in Appendix D)
6. What is the term for a computer program often used to facilitate database queries that are not part of a standard ERP system?
7. What are the four main functions within SAP's supply chain software? **LO17-3**
8. What term refers to the sharing of information with partners to coordinate production, enabling everyone to work together to increase visibility and responsiveness?

9. What part of SAP gives users personalized access to a range of information, applications, and services supported by the system?

LO17-4 10. What supply chain metric measures how many complete orders were filled and shipped on time?

11. During the past month a firm shows the following metrics:

Average days of accounts receivable	6.75 days
Average daily cost of sales	$ 35,000
Current total value of inventory	$300,000
Current value of accounts payable	$200,000

Compute the cash-to-cash cycle time. Round to two decimal places in all of your calculations. (Answer in Appendix D)

PRACTICE EXAM

In each of the following, name the term defined or answer the question. Answers are listed at the bottom.

1. A computer system that links all areas of a company using an integrated set of application programs and a common database.
2. The application programs are designed in accordance with industry norms or _____.
3. True/False: Implementing an ERP system is a simple exercise that involves loading software on a computer.
4. A term used for delivering ERP services on demand over the Internet.
5. The name of Microsoft's ERP offering.
6. Part of an ERP system that manages the activities within a certain functional area.
7. A set of processes to enable vendor-driven replenishment.
8. A metric that measures the percentage of orders shipped according to schedule.

Answers to Practice Exam 1. Enterprise resource planning (ERP) system 2. Best practices 3. False 4. Cloud computing 5. Microsoft Dynamics 6. Module 7. Vendor-managed inventory 8. Delivery performance

For PowerPoint lecture slides, Solutions Manual, Test Bank, Data files for solved examples, Excel Templates, Step-by-Step Solved Examples in video format, Tutorial Videos and many more, scan the adjacent **QR code**, or **visit http://www.mhhe.com/sie-chase15e**

Chapter 18

Forecasting

LEARNING OBJECTIVES

- LO 18-1 Understand how forecasting is essential to supply chain planning
- LO 18-2 Evaluate demand using quantitative forecasting models
- LO 18-3 Apply qualitative techniques to forecast demand
- LO 18-4 Apply collaborative techniques to forecast demand

From Bean to Cup: Starbucks Global Supply Chain Challenge

Starbucks Corporation is the largest coffeehouse company in the world, with over 17,000 stores in more than 50 countries. The company serves some 50 million customers each week.

Forecasting demand for a Starbucks is an amazing challenge. The product line goes well beyond drip-brewed coffee sold on demand in the stores. It includes espresso-based hot drinks, other hot and cold drinks, coffee beans, salads, hot and cold sandwiches and panini, pastries, snacks, and items such as mugs and tumblers. Many of the company's products are seasonal or specific to the locality of the store. Starbucks-branded ice cream and coffee are also offered at grocery stores around the world.

The creation of a single, global logistics system was important for Starbucks because of its far-flung supply chain. The company generally brings coffee beans from Latin America, Africa, and Asia to the United States and Europe in ocean containers. From the port of entry, the "green" (unroasted) beans are trucked to storage sites, either at a roasting plant or nearby. After the beans are roasted and packaged, the finished product is trucked to regional distribution centers, which range from 200,000 to 300,000 square feet in size. Coffee, however, is only one of the many products held at these distribution centers. They also handle other items required by Starbucks retail outlets, everything from furniture to cappuccino mix.

In the Analytics Exercise at the end of the chapter, we consider the challenging demand forecasting problem that Starbucks must solve to be able to successfully run this complex supply chain.

LO 18-1

Understand how forecasting is essential to supply chain planning

FORECASTING IN OPERATIONS AND SUPPLY CHAIN MANAGEMENT

Forecasts are vital to every business organization and for every significant management decision. Forecasting is the basis of corporate planning and control. In the functional areas of finance and accounting, forecasts provide the basis for budgetary planning and cost control. Marketing relies on sales forecasting to plan new products, compensate sales personnel, and make other key decisions. Production and operations personnel use forecasts to make periodic decisions involving supplier selection, process selection, capacity planning, and facility layout, as well as for continual decisions about purchasing, production planning, scheduling, and inventory.

In considering what forecasting approach to use, it is important to consider the purpose of the forecast. Some forecasts are for very high-level demand analysis. What do we expect the demand to be for a group of products over the next year, for example? Some forecasts are used to help set the strategy of how, in an aggregate sense, we will meet demand. We will call these **strategic forecasts**. Relative to the material in the book, strategic forecasts are most appropriate when making decisions related to overall strategy (Chapter 2), capacity (Chapter 5), manufacturing process design (Chapter 7), service process design (Chapter 9), location and distribution design (Chapter 15), sourcing (Chapter 16), and in sales and operations planning (Chapter 19). These all involve medium and long-term decisions that relate to how demand will be met strategically.

Strategic forecasts
Medium and long-term forecasts that are used for decisions related to strategy and aggregate demand.

Forecasts are also needed to determine how a firm operates processes on a day-to-day basis. For example, when should the inventory for an item be replenished, or how much production should we schedule for an item next week? These are **tactical forecasts** where the goal is to estimate demand in the relatively short term, a few weeks or months. These forecasts are important to ensure that in the short term we are able to meet customer lead time expectations and other criteria related to the availability of our products and services.

Tactical forecasts
Short-term forecasts used for making day-to-day decisions related to meeting demand.

In Chapter 7, the concept of decoupling points is discussed. These are points within the supply chain where inventory is positioned to allow processes or entities in the supply chain to operate independently. For example, if a product is stocked at a retailer, the customer pulls the item from the shelf and the manufacturer never sees a customer order. Inventory acts as a buffer to separate the customer from the manufacturing process. Selection of decoupling points is a strategic decision that determines customer lead times and can greatly impact inventory investment. The closer this point is to the customer, the quicker the customer can be served. Typically, a trade-off is involved where quicker response to customer demand comes at the expense of greater inventory investment because finished goods inventory is more expensive than raw material inventory.

Strategy

Forecasting is needed at these decoupling points to set appropriate inventory levels for these buffers. The actual setting of these levels is the topic of Chapter 20, "Inventory Management," but an essential input into those decisions is a forecast of expected demand and the expected error associated with that demand. If, for example, we are able to forecast demand very accurately, then inventory levels can be set precisely to expected customer demand. On the other hand, if predicting short-term demand is difficult, then extra inventory to cover this uncertainty will be needed.

The same is true relative to service settings where inventory is not used to buffer demand. Here, capacity availability relative to expected demand is the issue. If we can predict demand in a service setting very accurately, then tactically all we need to do is ensure that we have the appropriate capacity in the short term. When demand is not predictable, then excess capacity may be needed if servicing customers quickly is important.

Bear in mind that a perfect forecast is virtually impossible. Too many factors in the business environment cannot be predicted with certainty. Therefore, rather than search for the perfect forecast, it is far more important to establish the practice of continual review of forecasts and to learn to live with inaccurate forecasts. This is not to say that we should not try to improve the forecasting model or methodology or even to try to influence demand in a way that reduces demand uncertainty. When forecasting, a good strategy is to use two or three methods and look at them from a common-sense view. Will expected changes in the general economy affect the forecast? Are there changes in our customers' behaviors that will impact demand that are not being captured by our current approaches? In this chapter, we look at *qualitative* techniques that use managerial judgment

Forecasting is critical in determining how much inventory to keep to meet customer needs.

and also at *quantitative* techniques that rely on mathematical models. It is our view that combining these techniques is essential to a good forecasting process that is appropriate to the decisions being made.

QUANTITATIVE FORECASTING MODELS

LO 18-2

Evaluate demand using quantitative forecasting models

Forecasting can be classified into four basic types: *qualitative, time series analysis, causal relationships,* and *simulation.*

Qualitative techniques are covered later in the chapter. **Time series analysis**, the primary focus of this chapter, is based on the idea that data relating to past demand can be used to predict future demand. Past data may include several components, such as trend, seasonal, or cyclical influences, and are described in the following section. Causal forecasting, which we discuss using the linear regression technique, assumes that demand is related to some underlying factor or factors in the environment. Simulation models allow the forecaster to run through a range of assumptions about the condition of the forecast. In this chapter, we focus on qualitative and time series techniques because these are most often used in supply chain planning and control.

Time series analysis

A forecast in which past demand data is used to predict future demand.

Components of Demand

In most cases, demand for products or services can be broken down into six components: average demand for the period, a trend, seasonal element, cyclical elements, random variation, and autocorrelation. Exhibit 18.1 illustrates a demand over a four-year period, showing the average, trend, and seasonal components and randomness around the smoothed demand curve.

Cyclical factors are more difficult to determine because the time span may be unknown or the cause of the cycle may not be considered. Cyclical influence on demand may come from such occurrences as political elections, war, economic conditions, or sociological pressures.

Random variations are caused by chance events. Statistically, when all the known causes for demand (average, trend, seasonal, cyclical, and autocorrelative) are subtracted from total demand, what remains is the unexplained portion of demand. If we cannot identify the cause of this remainder, it is assumed to be purely random chance.

EXHIBIT 18.1

Historical Product Demand Consisting of a Growth Trend and Seasonal Demand

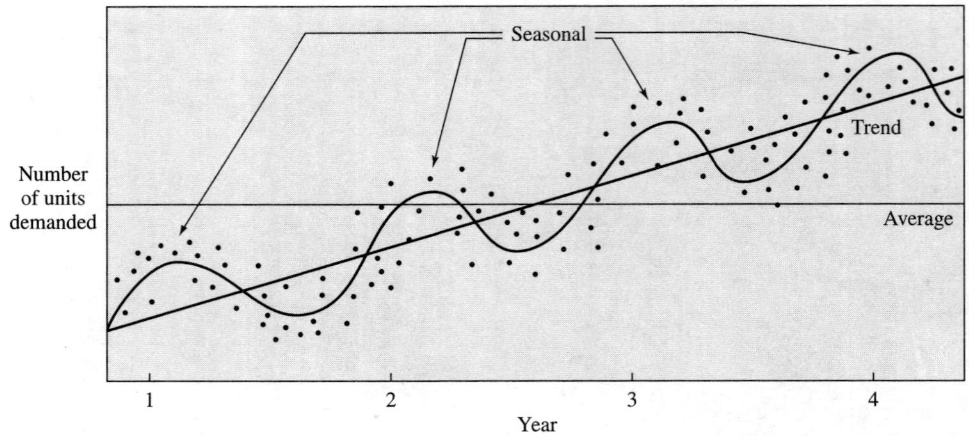

Autocorrelation denotes the persistence of occurrence. More specifically, the value expected at any point is highly correlated with its own past values. In waiting line theory, the length of a waiting line is highly autocorrelated. That is, if a line is relatively long at one time, then shortly after that time we would expect the line still to be long.

When demand is random, it may vary widely from one week to another. Where high autocorrelation exists, the rate of change in demand is not expected to change very much from one week to the next.

Key Idea

Remember that we are illustrating long-term patterns, so these should be considered when making long-term forecasts. When making short-term forecasts, these patterns are often not so strong.

Trend lines are the usual starting point in developing a forecast. These trend lines are then adjusted for seasonal effects, cyclical elements, and any other expected events that may influence the final forecast. Exhibit 18.2 shows four of the most common types of trends. A linear trend is obviously a straight continuous relationship. An S-curve is typical of a product growth and maturity cycle. The most important point in the S-curve is where the trend changes from slow growth to fast growth or from fast to slow. An asymptotic trend starts with the highest demand growth at the beginning but then tapers off. Such a curve could happen when a firm enters an existing market with the objective of saturating and capturing a large share of the market. An exponential curve is common in products with explosive growth. The exponential trend suggests that sales will grow at an ever-increasing rate—an assumption that may not be safe to make.

A widely used forecasting method plots data and then searches for the curve pattern (such as linear, S-curve, asymptotic, or exponential) that fits best. The attractiveness of this method is that because the mathematics for the curve are known, solving for values for future time periods is easy.

Sometimes our data do not seem to fit any standard curve. This may be due to several causes essentially beating the data from several directions at the same time. For these cases, a simplistic but often effective forecast can be obtained by simply plotting data.

Time Series Analysis

Time series forecasting models try to predict the future based on past data. For example, sales figures collected for the past six weeks can be used to forecast sales for the seventh week. Quarterly sales figures collected for the past several years can be used to forecast future quarters. Even though both examples contain sales, different forecasting time series models would likely be used.

Exhibit 18.3 shows the time series models discussed in the chapter and some of their characteristics. Terms such as *short, medium,* and *long* are relative to the context in which they are used. However, in business forecasting *short term* usually refers to under three months; *medium term,* three months to two years; and *long term,* greater than two years. We would generally use short-term forecasts for tactical decisions such as replenishing inventory or scheduling employees in the near term, and medium-term forecasts for planning a strategy for meeting demand over the next six months to a year and a half. In general, the short-term models compensate for random variation and adjust for short-term changes (such as consumers' responses to a new product). They are especially good for measuring the current

EXHIBIT 18.2

Common Types of Trends

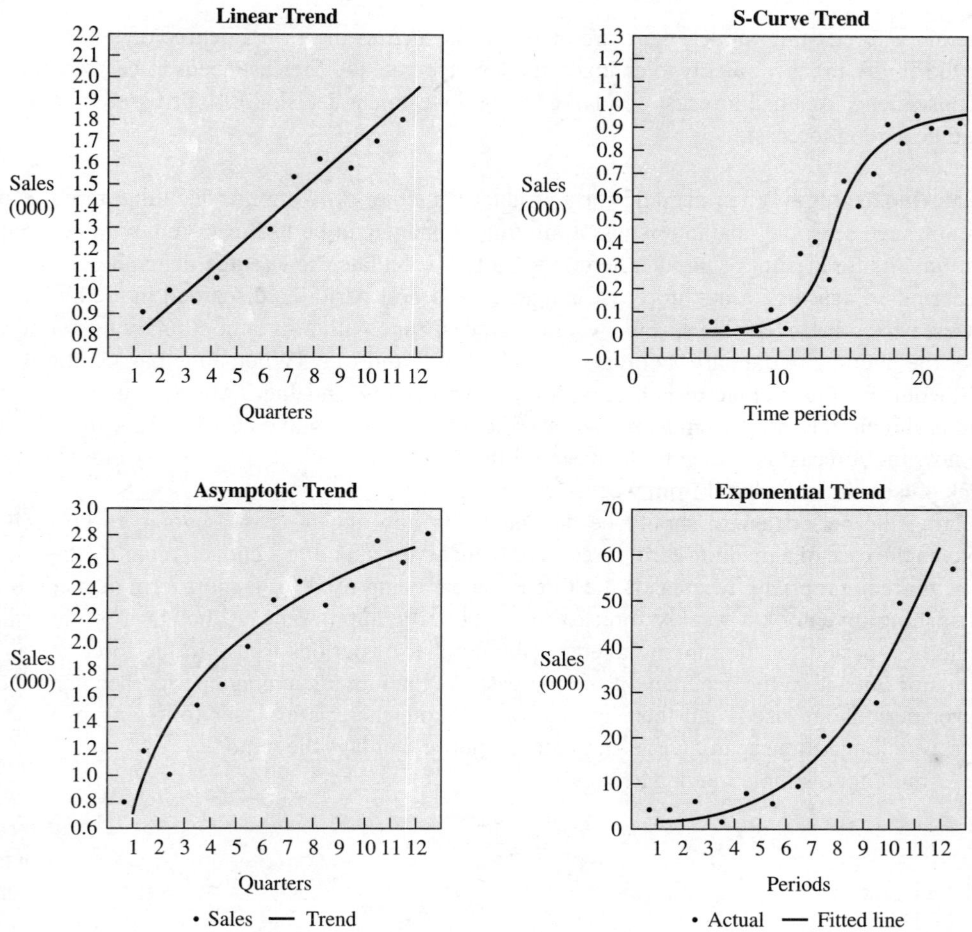

EXHIBIT 18.3

A Guide to Selecting an Appropriate Forecasting Method

Forecasting Method	Amount of Historical Data	Data Pattern	Forecast Horizon
Simple moving average	6 to 12 months; weekly data are often used	Stationary only (i.e., no trend or seasonality)	Short
Weighted moving average and simple exponential smoothing	5 to 10 observations needed to start	Stationary only	Short
Exponential smoothing with trend	5 to 10 observations needed to start	Stationary and trend	Short
Linear regression	10 to 20 observations	Stationary, trend, and seasonality	Short to medium
Trend and seasonal models	2 to 3 observations per season	Stationary, trend, and seasonality	Short to medium

variability in demand, which is useful for setting safety stock levels or estimating peak loads in a service setting. Medium-term forecasts are useful for capturing seasonal effects, and long-term models detect general trends and are especially useful in identifying major turning points.

Which forecasting model a firm should choose depends on:

1. Time horizon to forecast
2. Data availability

3. Accuracy required
4. Size of forecasting budget
5. Availability of qualified personnel

In selecting a forecasting model, there are other issues such as the firm's degree of flexibility. (The greater the ability to react quickly to changes, the less accurate the forecast needs to be.) Another item is the consequence of a bad forecast. If a large capital investment decision is to be based on a forecast, it should be a good forecast.

Moving Average
A forecast based on average past demand.

Simple Moving Average When demand for a product is neither growing nor declining rapidly, and if it does not have seasonal characteristics, a **moving average** can be useful in removing the random fluctuations for forecasting. The idea here is to simply calculate the average demand over the most recent periods. Each time a new forecast is made, the oldest period is discarded in the average and the newest period included. Thus, if we want to forecast June with a five-month moving average, we can take the average of January, February, March, April, and May. When June passes, the forecast for July would be the average of February, March, April, May, and June. An example using weekly demand is shown in Exhibit 18.4. Here, 3-week and 9-week moving average forecasts are calculated. Notice how the forecast is shown in the period following the data used. The 3-week moving average for week 4 uses actual demand from weeks 1, 2, and 3.

Selecting the period length should be dependent on how the forecast is going to be used. For example, in the case of a medium-term forecast of demand for planning a budget, monthly time periods might be more appropriate, whereas if the forecast were being used for a short-term decision related to replenishing inventory, a weekly forecast might be more appropriate. Although it is important to select the best period for the moving average, the number of periods to use in the forecast can also have a major impact on the accuracy of the forecast. As the moving average period becomes shorter, and fewer periods are used, and there is more oscillation, there is a closer following of the trend. Conversely, a longer time span gives a smoother response, but lags the trend.

The formula for a simple moving average is

$$F_t = \frac{A_{t-1} + A_{t-2} + A_{t-3} + \ldots + A_{t-n}}{n} \qquad [18.1]$$

where

F_t = Forecast for the coming period
n = Number of periods to be averaged
A_{t-1} = Actual occurrence in the past period
A_{t-2}, A_{t-3}, and A_{t-n} = Actual occurrences two periods ago, three periods ago, and so on, up to n periods ago

A plot of the data in Exhibit 18.4 shows the effects of using different numbers of periods in the moving average. We see that the growth trend levels off at about the 23rd week. The three-week moving average responds better in following this change than the nine-week average, although overall, the nine-week average is smoother.

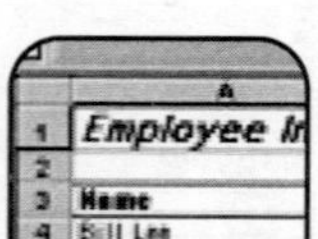

The main disadvantage in calculating a moving average is that all individual elements must be carried as data because a new forecast period involves adding new data and dropping the earliest data. For a three- or six-period moving average, this is not too severe. But plotting a 60-day moving average for the usage of each of 100,000 items in inventory would involve a significant amount of data.

Weighted moving average
A forecast made with past data where more recent data is given more significance than older data.

Weighted Moving Average Whereas the simple moving average assigns equal importance to each component of the moving average database, a **weighted moving average** allows any weights to be placed on each element, provided, of course, that the sum of all weights equals 1. For example, a department store may find that, in a four-month period, the best forecast is derived by using 40 percent of the actual sales for the most recent month, 30 percent of two months ago, 20 percent of three months ago, and 10 percent of four months ago. If actual sales experience was

Exhibit 18.4

Forecast Demand Based on a Three- and a Nine-Week Simple Moving Average

Week	Demand	3 Week	9 Week
1	800		
2	1,400		
3	1,000		
4	1,500	1,067	
5	1,500	1,300	
6	1,300	1,333	
7	1,800	1,433	
8	1,700	1,533	
9	1,300	1,600	
10	1,700	1,600	1,367
11	1,700	1,567	1,467
12	1,500	1,567	1,500
13	2,300	1,633	1,556
14	2,300	1,833	1,644
15	2,000	2,033	1,733
16	1,700	2,200	1,811
17	1,800	2,000	1,800
18	2,200	1,833	1,811
19	1,900	1,900	1,911
20	2,400	1,967	1,933
21	2,400	2,167	2,011
22	2,600	2,233	2,111
23	2,000	2,467	2,144
24	2,500	2,333	2,111
25	2,600	2,367	2,167
26	2,200	2,367	2,267
27	2,200	2,433	2,311
28	2,500	2,333	2,311
29	2,400	2,300	2,378
30	2,100	2,367	2,378

Analytics

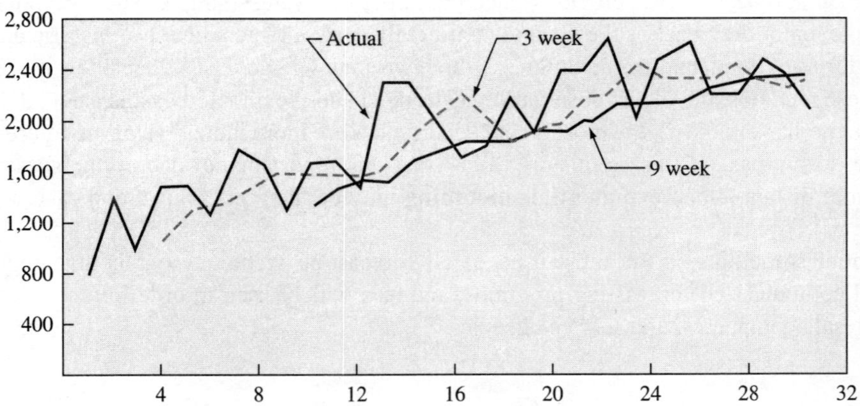

Month 1	Month 2	Month 3	Month 4	Month 5
100	90	105	95	?

the forecast for month 5 would be

$$\begin{aligned} F_5 &= 0.40(95) + 0.30(105) + 0.20(90) + 0.10(100) \\ &= 38 + 31.5 + 18 + 10 \\ &= 97.5 \end{aligned}$$

The formula for a weighted moving average is

$$F_t = w_1 A_{t-1} + w_2 A_{t-2} + \ldots + w_n A_{t-n} \qquad [18.2]$$

where

w_1 = Weight to be given to the actual occurrence for the period $t-1$
w_2 = Weight to be given to the actual occurrence for the period $t-2$
w_n = Weight to be given to the actual occurrence for the period $t-n$
n = Total number of prior periods in the forecast

Although many periods may be ignored (that is, their weights are zero) and the weighting scheme may be in any order (for example, more distant data may have greater weights than more recent data), the sum of all the weights must equal 1.

$$\sum_{i=1}^{n} w_i = 1$$

Suppose sales for month 5 actually turned out to be 110. Then, the forecast for month 6 would be

$$\begin{aligned} F_6 &= 0.40(110) + 0.30(95) + 0.20(105) + 0.10(90) \\ &= 44 + 28.5 + 21 + 9 \\ &= 102.5 \end{aligned}$$

Experience and trial and error are the simplest ways to choose weights. As a general rule, the most recent past is the most important indicator of what to expect in the future, and, therefore, it should get higher weighting. The past month's revenue or plant capacity, for example, would be a better estimate for the coming month than the revenue or plant capacity of several months ago.

However, if the data are seasonal, for example, weights should be established accordingly. Bathing suit sales in July of last year should be weighted more heavily than bathing suit sales in December (in the Northern Hemisphere).

The weighted moving average has a definite advantage over the simple moving average in being able to vary the effects of past data. However, it is more inconvenient and costly to use than the exponential smoothing method, which we examine next.

Exponential Smoothing In the previous methods of forecasting (simple and weighted moving averages), the major drawback is the need to continually carry a large amount of historical data. (This is also true for regression analysis techniques, which we soon will cover.) As each new piece of data is added in these methods, the oldest observation is dropped and the new forecast is calculated. In many applications (perhaps in most), the most recent occurrences are more indicative of the future than those in the more distant past. If this premise is valid—that the importance of data diminishes as the past becomes more distant—then **exponential smoothing** may be the most logical and easiest method to use.

Exponential smoothing
A time series forecasting technique using weights that decrease exponentially $(1 - \alpha)$ for each past period.

Exponential smoothing is the most used of all forecasting techniques. It is an integral part of virtually all computerized forecasting programs, and it is widely used in ordering inventory in retail firms, wholesale companies, and service agencies.

Exponential smoothing techniques have become well accepted for six major reasons:

1. Exponential models are surprisingly accurate.
2. Formulating an exponential model is relatively easy.
3. The user can understand how the model works.
4. Little computation is required to use the model.
5. Computer storage requirements are small because of the limited use of historical data.
6. Tests for accuracy as to how well the model is performing are easy to compute.

In the exponential smoothing method, only three pieces of data are needed to forecast the future: the most recent forecast, the actual demand that occurred for that forecast period, and a **smoothing constant alpha** (**α**). This smoothing constant determines the level of smoothing and the speed of reaction to differences between forecasts and actual occurrences. The value for the constant is determined both by the nature of the product and by the manager's sense of what constitutes a good response rate. For example, if a firm produced a standard item with relatively stable demand, the reaction rate to differences between actual and forecast demand would tend to be small, perhaps just 5 or 10 percentage points. However, if the firm were experiencing growth, it would be desirable to have a higher reaction rate, perhaps 15 to 30 percentage points, to give greater importance to recent growth experience. The more rapid the growth, the higher the reaction rate should be. Sometimes users of the simple moving average switch to exponential smoothing but like to keep the forecasts about the same as the simple moving average. In this case, α is approximated by $2 \div (n + 1)$, where n is the number of time periods in the corresponding simple moving average.

Smoothing constant alpha (α)
The parameter in the exponential smoothing equation that controls the speed of reaction to differences between forecasts and actual demand.

The equation for a single exponential smoothing forecast is simply

$$F_t = F_{t-1} + \alpha(A_{t-1} - F_{t-1}) \qquad [18.3]$$

where

F_t = The exponentially smoothed forecast for period t
F_{t-1} = The exponentially smoothed forecast made for the prior period
A_{t-1} = The actual demand in the prior period
α = The desired response rate, or smoothing constant

This equation states that the new forecast is equal to the old forecast plus a portion of the error (the difference between the previous forecast and what actually occurred).

To demonstrate the method, assume that the long-run demand for the product under study is relatively stable and a smoothing constant (α) of 0.05 is considered appropriate. If the exponential smoothing method were used as a continuing policy, a forecast would have been made for last month. Assume that last month's forecast (F_{t-1}) was 1,050 units. If 1,000 actually were demanded, rather than 1,050, the forecast for this month would be

$$\begin{aligned} F_t &= F_{t-1} + \alpha(A_{t-1} - F_{t-1}) \\ &= 1{,}050 + 0.05(1{,}000 - 1{,}050) \\ &= 1{,}050 + 0.05(-50) \\ &= 1{,}047.5 \text{ units} \end{aligned}$$

Because the smoothing coefficient is small, the reaction of the new forecast to an error of 50 units is to decrease the next month's forecast by only 2½ units.

When exponential smoothing is first used for an item, an initial forecast may be obtained by using a simple estimate, like the first period's demand, or by using an average of preceding periods, such as the average of the first two or three periods.

Single exponential smoothing has the shortcoming of lagging changes in demand. Exhibit 18.5 presents actual data plotted as a smooth curve to show the lagging effects of the exponential forecasts. The forecast lags during an increase or decrease, but overshoots when a change in direction occurs. Note that the higher the value of alpha, the more closely the forecast follows the actual. To more

EXHIBIT 18.5

Exponential Forecasts versus Actual Demand for Units of a Product over Time Showing the Forecast Lag

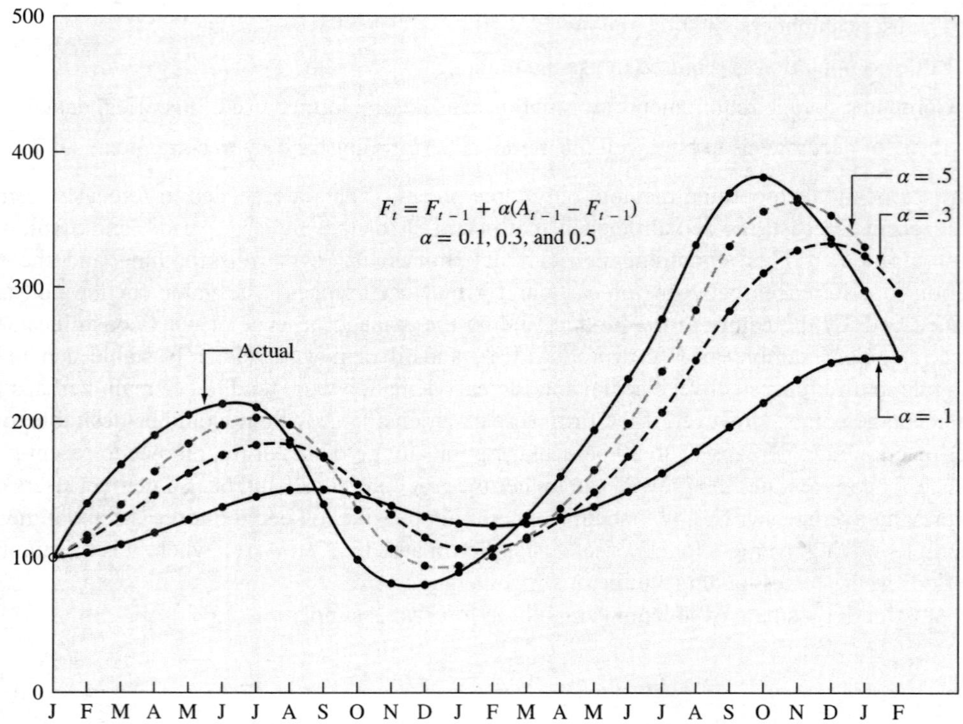

closely track actual demand, a trend factor may be added. Adjusting the value of alpha also helps. This is termed *adaptive forecasting.* Both trend effects and adaptive forecasting are briefly explained in the following sections.

Smoothing constant delta (δ)
An additional parameter used in an exponential smoothing equation that includes an adjustment for trend.

Exponential Smoothing with Trend Remember that an upward or downward trend in data collected over a sequence of time periods causes the exponential forecast to always lag behind (be above or below) the actual occurrence. Exponentially smoothed forecasts can be corrected somewhat by adding in a trend adjustment. To correct the trend, we need two smoothing constants. Besides the smoothing constant α, the trend equation also uses a **smoothing constant delta** (δ). Both alpha and delta reduce the impact of the error that occurs between the actual and the forecast. If both alpha and delta are not included, the trend overreacts to errors.

To get the trend equation going, the first time it is used the trend value must be entered manually. This initial trend value can be an educated guess or a computation based on observed past data.

The equations to compute the forecast including trend (FIT) are

$$F_t = \text{FIT}_{t-1} + \alpha(A_{t-1} - \text{FIT}_{t-1}) \quad [18.4]$$

$$\text{T}_t = \text{T}_{t-1} + \delta(F_t - \text{FIT}_{t-1}) \quad [18.5]$$

$$\text{FIT}_t = F_t + \text{T}_t \quad [18.6]$$

where

F_t = The exponentially smoothed forecast that does not include trend for period t
T_t = The exponentially smoothed trend for period t
FIT_t = The forecast including trend for period t
FIT_{t-1} = The forecast including trend made for the prior period
A_{t-1} = The actual demand for the prior period
α = Smoothing constant (alpha)
δ = Smoothing constant (delta)

To make an exponential forecast that includes trend, step through the equations one at a time.

Step 1: Using Equation 18.4, make a forecast that is not adjusted for trend. This uses the previous forecast and previous actual demand.

Step 2: Using Equation 18.5, update the estimate of trend using the previous trend estimate, the unadjusted forecast just made, and the previous forecast.

Step 3: Make a new forecast that includes trend by using the results from steps 1 and 2.

EXAMPLE 18.1 Forecast Including Trend

Assume a previous forecast, including a trend of 110 units, a previous trend estimate of 10 units, an alpha of .20, and a delta of .30. If actual demand turned out to be 115 rather than the forecast 110, calculate the forecast for the next period.

SOLUTION

The actual A_{t-1} is given as 115. Therefore,

$$\begin{aligned} F_t &= \text{FIT}_{t-1} + \alpha(A_{t-1} - \text{FIT}_{t-1}) \\ &= 110 + .2(115 - 110) = 111.0 \\ T_t &= T_{t-1} + \delta(F_t - \text{FIT}_{t-1}) \\ &= 10 + .3(111 - 110) = 10.3 \\ \text{FIT}_t &= F_t + T_t = 111.0 + 10.3 = 121.3 \end{aligned}$$

If, instead of 121.3, the actual turned out to be 120, the sequence would be repeated and the forecast for the next period would be

$$\begin{aligned} F_{t+1} &= 121.3 + .2(120 - 121.3) = 121.04 \\ T_{t+1} &= 10.3 + .3(121.04 - 121.3) = 10.22 \\ \text{FIT}_{t+1} &= 121.04 + 10.22 = 131.26 \end{aligned}$$

Exponential smoothing requires that the smoothing constants be given a value between 0 and 1. Typically, fairly small values are used for alpha and delta in the range of .1 to .3. The values depend on how much random variation there is in demand and how steady the trend factor is. Later in the chapter, error measures are discussed that can be helpful in picking appropriate values for these parameters.

Linear Regression Analysis *Regression* can be defined as a functional relationship between two or more correlated variables. It is used to predict one variable given the others. The relationship is usually developed from observed data. The data should be plotted first to see if they appear linear or if at least parts of the data are linear. *Linear regression* refers to the special class of regression where the relationship between variables forms a straight line.

The linear regression line is of the form $Y = a + bt$, where Y is the value of the dependent variable that we are solving for, a is the Y intercept, b is the slope, and t is an index for the time period.

Linear regression is useful for long-term forecasting of major occurrences and aggregate planning. For example, linear regression would be very useful to forecast demands for product families. Even though demand for individual products within a family may vary widely during a time period, demand for the total product family is surprisingly smooth.

The major restriction in using **linear regression forecasting** is, as the name implies, that past data and future projections are assumed to fall in about a straight line. Although this does limit its application sometimes, if we use a shorter period of time, linear regression analysis can still be used. For example, there may be short segments of the longer period that are approximately linear.

Linear regression forecasting
A forecasting technique that fits a straight line to past demand data.

Linear regression is used both for time series forecasting and for causal relationship forecasting. When the dependent variable (usually the vertical axis on a graph) changes as a result of time (plotted as the horizontal axis), it is time series analysis. If one variable changes because of the change in another variable, this is a causal relationship (such as the number of deaths from lung cancer increasing with the number of people who smoke).

We use the following example to demonstrate linear least squares regression analysis.

EXAMPLE 18.2 Least Squares Method

A firm's sales for a product line during the 12 quarters of the past three years were as follows:

Quarter	Sales	Quarter	Sales
1	600	7	2,600
2	1,550	8	2,900
3	1,500	9	3,800
4	1,500	10	4,500
5	2,400	11	4,000
6	3,100	12	4,900

The firm wants to forecast each quarter of the fourth year—that is, quarters 13, 14, 15, and 16.

SOLUTION

The least squares equation for linear regression is

$$Y = a + bt \tag{18.7}$$

where

Y = Dependent variable computed by the equation
y = The actual dependent variable data point (used as follows)
a = Y intercept
b = Slope of the line
t = Time period

The least squares method tries to fit the line to the data *that minimizes the sum of the squares of the vertical distance* between each data point and its corresponding point on the line. If a straight line is drawn through the general area of the points, the difference between the point and the line is $y - Y$. Exhibit 18.6 shows these differences. The sum of the squares of the differences between the plotted data points and the line points is

$$(y_1 - Y_1)^2 + (y_2 - Y_2)^2 + \ldots + (y_{12} - Y_{12})^2$$

The best line to use is the one that minimizes this total.

As before, the straight line equation is

$$Y = a + bt$$

In the least squares method, the equations for a and b are

$$b = \frac{\sum ty - n\bar{t}\cdot\bar{y}}{\sum t^2 - n\bar{t}^2} \tag{18.8}$$

$$a = \bar{y} - b\bar{t} \tag{18.9}$$

where

a = Y intercept
b = Slope of the line
$\bar{y}$ = Average of all ys
$\bar{t}$ = Average of all ts
t = t value at each data point

EXHIBIT 18.6

Least Squares Regression Line

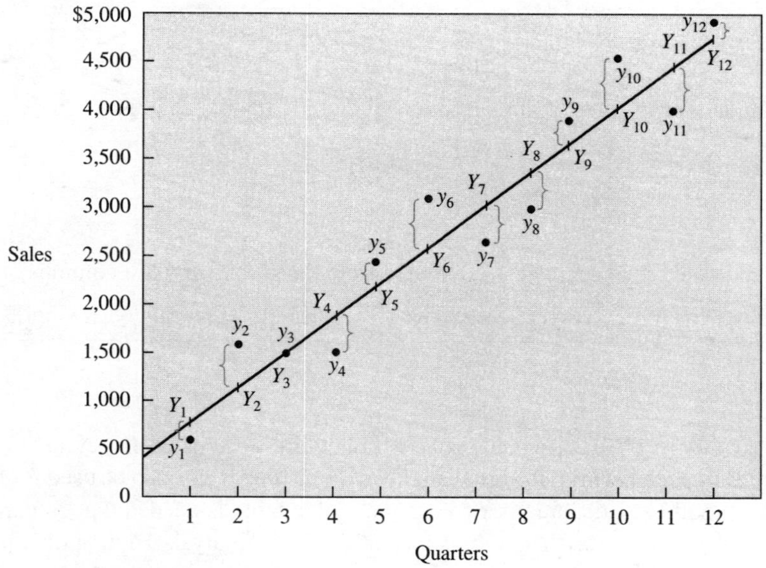

$y = y$ value at each data point
n = Number of data points
Y = Value of the dependent variable computed with the regression equation

Exhibit 18.7 shows these computations carried out for the 12 data points in the problem. Note that the final equation for Y shows an intercept of 441.67 and a slope of 359.6. The slope shows that for every unit change in t, Y changes by 359.6. Note that these calculations can be done with the INTERCEPT and SLOPE functions in Microsoft Excel.

EXHIBIT 18.7

Least Squares Regression Analysis

(1) t	(2) y	(3) $t \times y$	(4) t^2	(5) y^2	(6) y
1	600	600	1	360,000	801.3
2	1,550	3,100	4	2,402,500	1,160.9
3	1,500	4,500	9	2,250,000	1,520.5
4	1,500	6,000	16	2,250,000	1,880.1
5	2,400	12,000	25	5,760,000	2,239.7
6	3,100	18,600	36	9,610,000	2,599.4
7	2,600	18,200	49	6,760,000	2,959.0
8	2,900	23,200	64	8,410,000	3,318.6
9	3,800	34,200	81	14,440,000	3,678.2
10	4,500	45,000	100	20,250,000	4,037.8
11	4,000	44,000	121	16,000,000	4,397.4
12	4,900	58,800	144	24,010,000	4,757.1
78	33,350	268,200	650	112,502,500	

$\bar{t} = 6.5 \quad b = 359.6154$
$\bar{y} = 2{,}779.17 \quad a = 441.6667$
Therefore, $Y = 441.67 + 359.6t$
$S_{yt} = 363.9$

Strictly based on the equation, forecasts for periods 13 through 16 would be

$$Y_{13} = 441.67 + 359.6\,(13) = 5{,}116.5$$
$$Y_{14} = 441.67 + 359.6\,(14) = 5{,}476.1$$
$$Y_{15} = 441.67 + 359.6\,(15) = 5{,}835.7$$
$$Y_{16} = 441.67 + 359.6\,(16) = 6{,}195.3$$

The standard error of estimate, or how well the line fits the data, is

$$S_{yt} = \sqrt{\frac{\sum_{i=1}^{n} (y_i - Y_i)^2}{n-2}} \qquad [18.10]$$

The standard error of estimate is computed from the second and last columns of Exhibit 18.7:

$$S_{yt} = \sqrt{\frac{(600-801.3)^2 + (1{,}550-1{,}160.9)^2 + (1{,}500-1{,}520.5)^2 + \ldots + (4{,}900-4{,}757.1)^2}{10}}$$
$$= 363.9$$

In addition to the INTERCEPT and SLOPE functions, Microsoft Excel has a very powerful regression tool designed to perform these calculations. (Note that it can also be used for moving average and exponential smoothing calculations.) To use the tool, a table is needed that contains data relevant to the problem (see Exhibit 18.8). The tool is part of the Data Analysis ToolPak that is accessed from the Data menu (you may need to add this to your Data options by using the Add-In option under File → Options → Add-Ins).

EXHIBIT 18.8

Excel Regression Tool

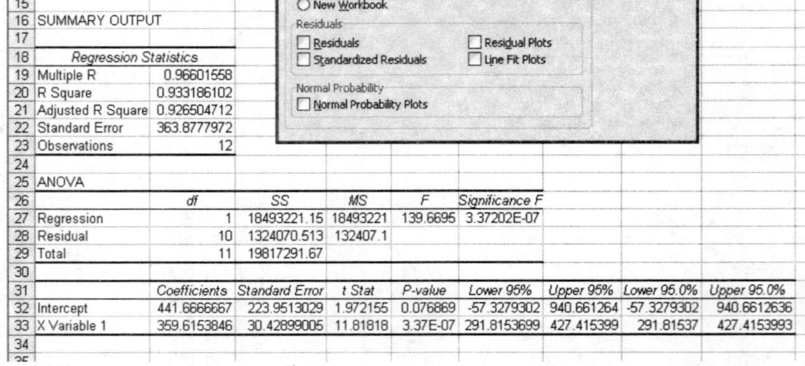

To use the tool, first input the data in two columns in your spreadsheet, then access the Regression option from the → Data menu. Next, specify the Y Range, which is B2:B13, and the time periods in the X Range, which is A2:A13 in our example. Finally, an Output Range is specified. This is where you would like the results of the regression analysis placed in your spreadsheet. In the example, A16 is entered. There is some information provided that goes beyond what we have covered, but what you are looking for is the Intercept and X Variable coefficients that correspond to the intercept and slope values in the linear equation. These are in cells B32 and B33 in Exhibit 18.8.

Decomposition of a Time Series A *time series* can be defined as chronologically ordered data that may contain one or more components of demand: trend, seasonal, cyclical, autocorrelation, and random. **Decomposition** of a time series means identifying and separating the time series data into these components. In practice, it is relatively easy to identify the trend (even without mathematical analysis, it is usually easy to plot and see the direction of movement) and the seasonal component (by comparing the same period year to year). It is considerably more difficult to identify the cycles (these may be many months or years long), the autocorrelation, and the random components. (The forecaster usually calls random anything left over that cannot be identified as another component.)

Decomposition
The process of identifying and separating time series data into fundamental components such as trend and seasonality.

When demand contains both seasonal and trend effects at the same time, the question is how they relate to each other. In this description, we examine two types of seasonal variation: *additive* and *multiplicative.*

Additive seasonal variation simply assumes that the seasonal amount is a constant no matter what the trend or average amount is.

$$\text{Forecast including trend and seasonal} = \text{Trend} + \text{Seasonal}$$

Exhibit 18.9A shows an example of increasing trend with constant seasonal amounts.

In multiplicative seasonal variation, the trend is multiplied by the seasonal factors.

$$\text{Forecast including trend and seasonal} = \text{Trend} \times \text{Seasonal factor}$$

Exhibit 18.9B shows the seasonal variation increasing as the trend increases because its size depends on the trend.

EXHIBIT 18.9

Additive and Multiplicative Seasonal Variation Superimposed on Changing Trend

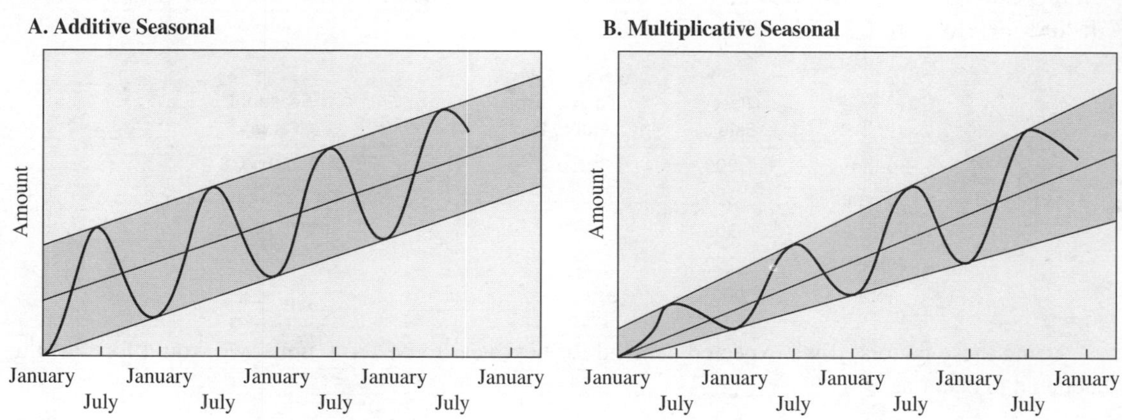

The multiplicative seasonal variation is the usual experience. Essentially, this says that the larger the basic amount projected, the larger the variation around this that we can expect.

A seasonal factor is the amount of correction needed in a time series to adjust for the season of the year.

We usually associate *seasonal* with a period of the year characterized by some particular activity. We use the word *cyclical* to indicate other than annual recurrent periods of repetitive activity.

The following examples show how seasonal indexes are determined and used to forecast (1) a simple calculation based on past seasonal data and (2) the trend and seasonal index from a hand-fit regression line. We follow this with a more formal procedure for the decomposition of data and forecasting using least squares regression.

Companies such as Toro manufacture lawnmowers and snow blowers to match seasonal demand. Using the same equipment and assembly lines provides better capacity utilization, workforce stability, productivity, and revenue.

Courtesy of The Toro Company

EXAMPLE 18.3 Simple Proportion

Assume that in past years, a firm sold an average of 1,000 units of a particular product line each year. On the average, 200 units were sold in the spring, 350 in the summer, 300 in the fall, and 150 in the winter. The seasonal factor (or index) is the ratio of the amount sold during each season divided by the average for all seasons.

SOLUTION

In this example, the yearly amount divided equally over all seasons is 1,000 ÷ 4 = 250. The seasonal factors therefore are

	Past Sales	Average Sales for Each Season (1,000/4)	Seasonal Factor
Spring	200	250	200/250 = 0.8
Summer	350	250	350/250 = 1.4
Fall	300	250	300/250 = 1.2
Winter	150	250	150/250 = 0.6
Total	1,000		

Using these factors, if we expected demand for next year to be 1,100 units, we would forecast the demand to occur as

	Expected Demand for Next Year	Average Sales for Each Season (1,100/4)		Seasonal Factor		Next Year's Seasonal Forecast
Spring		275	×	0.8	=	220
Summer		275	×	1.4	=	385
Fall		275	×	1.2	=	330
Winter		275	×	0.6	=	165
Total	1,100					

The seasonal factor may be periodically updated as new data are available. The following example shows the seasonal factor and multiplicative seasonal variation.

EXAMPLE 18.4 Computing Trend and Seasonal Factor from a Linear Regression Line Obtained with Excel

Forecast the demand for each quarter of the next year using trend and seasonal factors. Demand for the past two years is in the following table:

Quarter	Amount	Quarter	Amount
1	300	5	520
2	200	6	420
3	220	7	400
4	530	8	700

SOLUTION

First, we plot as in Exhibit 18.10 and then calculate the slope and intercept using Excel. For Excel, the quarters are numbered 1 through 8. The "known *ys*" are the amounts (300, 200, 220, etc.), and the "known *xs*" are the quarter numbers (1, 2, 3, etc.). We obtain a slope = 52.3 (rounded), and intercept = 176.1 (rounded). The equation for the line is

$$\text{Forecast Including Trend (FIT)} = 176.1 + 52.3t$$

Next, we can derive a seasonal index by comparing the actual data with the trend line, as in Exhibit 18.10. The seasonal factor was developed by averaging the same quarters in each year.

EXHIBIT 18.10

Computing a Seasonal Factor from the Actual Data and Trend Line

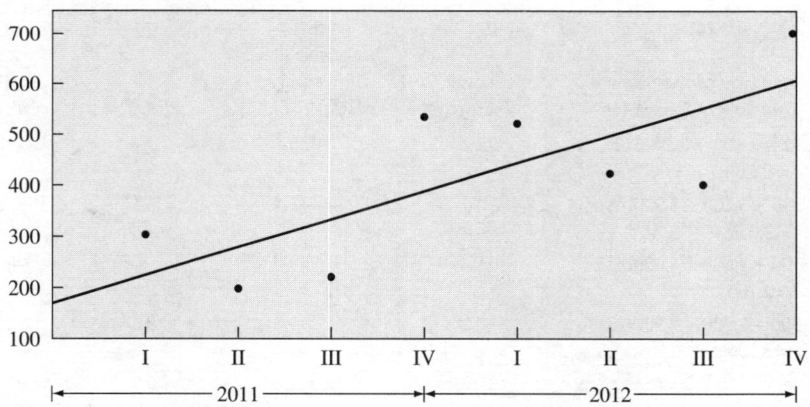

Quarter	Actual amount	From trend equation $FIT_t = 176.1 + 52.3t$	Ratio of actual ÷ trend	Seasonal factor (average of same quarters in both years)
2011				
I	300	228.3	1.31	I 1.25
II	200	280.6	0.71	II 0.79
III	220	332.9	0.66	III 0.70
IV	530	385.1	1.38	IV 1.28
2012		—	—	
I	520	437.4	1.19	
II	420	489.6	0.86	
III	400	541.9	0.74	
IV	700	594.2	1.18	

We can compute the 2013 forecast including trend and seasonal factors (FITS) as follows:

$$\text{FITS}_t = \text{FIT} \times \text{Seasonal}$$
$$\text{I—2013 FITS}_9 = [176.1 + 52.3(9)]1.25 = 808$$
$$\text{II—2013 FITS}_{10} = [176.1 + 52.3(10)]0.79 = 552$$
$$\text{III—2013 FITS}_{11} = [176.1 + 52.3(11)]0.70 = 526$$
$$\text{IV—2013 FITS}_{12} = [176.1 + 52.3(12)]1.28 = 1{,}029$$

Note, these numbers were calculated using Excel, so your numbers may differ slightly due to rounding.

Decomposition Using Least Squares Regression This procedure is different from the previous one and in some cases may give better results. The approach described in Example 18.3 started by fitting a regression line, and given the line, the seasonal indexes are calculated. With this approach, we start by calculating seasonal indexes. Then, using data that have been "deseasonalized," we estimate a trend line using linear regression. More formally, the process is:

1. Decompose the time series into its components.
   a. Find seasonal component.
   b. Deseasonalize the demand.
   c. Find trend component.

Exhibit 18.11

Deseasonalized Demand

(1) Period (t)	(2) Quarter	(3) Actual Demand (y)	(4) Average of the Same Quarters of Each Year	(5) Seasonal Factor	(6) Deseasonalized Demand (y_d) Col. (3) ÷ Col. (5)	(7) t^2 (Col. 1)^2	(8) $t \times y_d$ Col. (1) × Col. (6)
1	I	600	(600 + 2,400 + 3,800)/3 = 2,266.7	0.82	735.7	1	735.7
2	II	1,550	(1,550 + 3,100 + 4,500)/3 = 3,050	1.10	1,412.4	4	2,824.7
3	III	1,500	(1,500 + 2,600 + 4,000)/3 = 2,700	0.97	1,544.0	9	4,631.9
4	IV	1,500	(1,500 + 2,900 + 4,900)/3 = 3,100	1.12	1,344.8	16	5,379.0
5	I	2,400		0.82	2,942.6	25	14,713.2
6	II	3,100		1.10	2,824.7	36	16,948.4
7	III	2,600		0.97	2,676.2	49	18,733.6
8	IV	2,900		1.12	2,599.9	64	20,798.9
9	I	3,800		0.82	4,659.2	81	41,932.7
10	II	4,500		1.10	4,100.4	100	41,004.1
11	III	4,000		0.97	4,117.3	121	45,290.1
12	IV	4,900		1.12	4,392.9	144	52,714.5
78		33,350*		12.03	33,350.1*	650	265,706.9

$$\bar{t} = \frac{78}{12} = 6.5 \quad b = \frac{\sum t y_d - n\bar{t}\bar{y}_d}{\sum t^2 - n\bar{t}^2} = \frac{265{,}706.9 - 12(6.5)2{,}779.2}{650 - 12(6.5)^2} = 342.2$$

$$\bar{y}_d = 33{,}350/12 = 2{,}779.2 \quad a = \bar{y}_d - b\bar{t} = 2{,}779.2 - 342.2(6.5) = 554.9$$

Therefore, $Y = a + bt = 554.9 + 342.2t$

*Column 3 and column 6 totals should be equal at 33,350. Differences are due to rounding. Column 5 was rounded to two decimal places.

2. Forecast future values of each component.
   a. Project trend component into the future.
   b. Multiply trend component by seasonal component.

Exhibit 18.11 shows the decomposition of a time series using least squares regression and the same basic data we used in our first regression example. Each data point corresponds to using a single three-month quarter of the three-year (12-quarter) period. Our objective is to forecast demand for the four quarters of the fourth year.

Step 1. Determine the seasonal factor (or index). Exhibit 18.11 summarizes the calculations needed. Column 4 develops an average for the same quarters in the three-year period. For example, the first quarters of the three years are added together and divided by three. A seasonal factor is then derived by dividing that average by the general average for all 12 quarters $\left(\frac{33,350}{12}, \text{ or } 2,779\right)$. For example, this first quarter seasonal factor is $\frac{2,266.7}{2,779} = 0.82$. These are entered in column 5. Note that the seasonal factors are identical for similar quarters in each year.

Step 2. Deseasonalize the original data. To remove the seasonal effect on the data, we divide the original data by the seasonal factor. This step is called the deseasonalization of demand and is shown in column 6 of Exhibit 18.11.

Step 3. Develop a least squares regression line for the deseasonalized data. The purpose here is to develop an equation for the trend line *Y*, which we then modify with the seasonal factor. The procedure is the same as we used before:

$$Y = a + bt$$

where

y_d = Deseasonalized demand (see Exhibit 18.11)
t = Quarter
Y = Demand computed using the regression equation $Y = a + bt$
a = Y intercept
b = Slope of the line

The least squares calculations using columns 1, 7, and 8 of Exhibit 18.11 are shown in the lower section of the exhibit. The final deseasonalized equation for our data is $Y = 554.9 + 342.2t$. This straight line is shown in Exhibit 18.12.

EXHIBIT 18.12

Straight Line Graph of Deseasonalized Equation

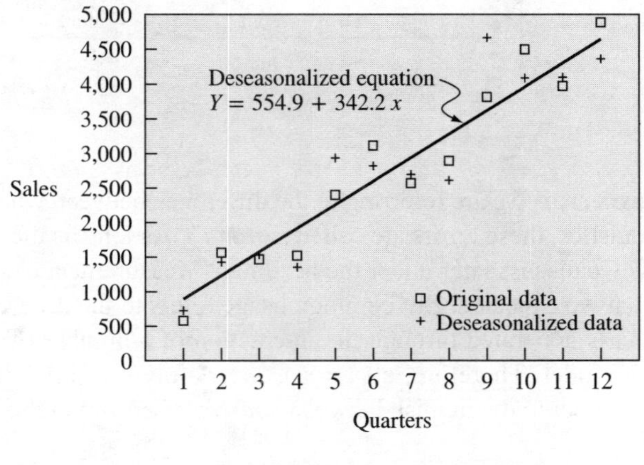

Step 4. Project the regression line through the period to be forecast. Our purpose is to forecast periods 13 through 16. We start by solving the equation for Y at each of these periods (shown in step 5, column 3).

Step 5. Create the final forecast by adjusting the regression line by the seasonal factor. Recall that the Y equation has been deseasonalized. We now reverse the procedure by multiplying the quarterly data we derived by the seasonal factor for that quarter:

Period	Quarter	*Y* from Regression Line	Seasonal Factor	Forecast ($Y \times$ Seasonal Factor)
13	1	5,003.5	0.82	4,102.87
14	2	5,345.7	1.10	5,880.27
15	3	5,687.9	0.97	5,517.26
16	4	6,030.1	1.12	6,753.71

Our forecast is now complete.

When a straight line is fitted through data points and then used for forecasting, errors can come from two sources. First, there are the usual errors similar to the standard deviation of any set of data. Second, there are errors that arise because the line is wrong. Exhibit 18.13 shows this error range. Instead of developing the statistics here, we will briefly show why the range broadens. First, visualize that one line is drawn that has some error such that it slants too steeply upward. Standard errors are then calculated for this line. Now visualize another line that slants too steeply downward. It also has a standard error. The total error range, for this analysis, consists of errors resulting from both lines, as well as all other possible lines. We included this exhibit to show how the error range widens as we go further into the future.

EXHIBIT 18.13

Prediction Intervals for Linear Trend

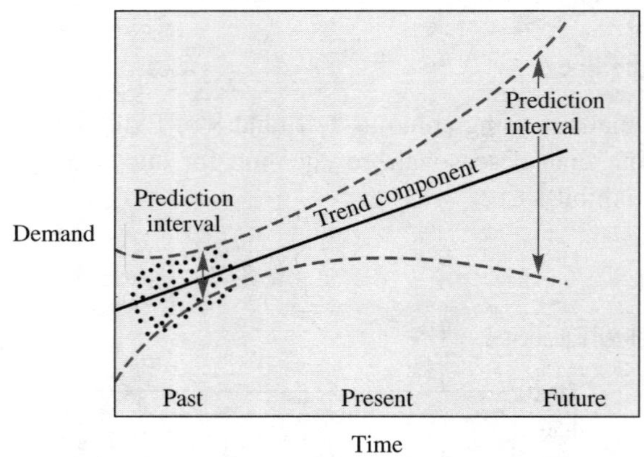

Forecast Errors

Forecast error
The difference between actual demand and what was forecast.

In using the term **forecast error**, we are referring to the difference between what actually occurred and what was forecast. In statistics, these errors are called *residuals.* As long as the forecast value is within the confidence limits, as we discuss later under the heading, "Measurement of Error," this is not really an error because it is what we expected. But common usage refers to the difference as an error.

Demand for a product is generated through the interaction of a number of factors too complex to describe accurately in a model. Therefore, all forecasts certainly contain some error. In discussing forecast errors, it is convenient to distinguish between *sources of error* and the *measurement of error.*

Sources of Error Errors can come from a variety of sources. One common source that many forecasters are unaware of is projecting past trends into the future. For example, when we talk about statistical errors in regression analysis, we are referring to the deviations of observations from our regression line. It is common to attach a confidence band (that is, statistical control limits) to the regression line to reduce the unexplained error. But when we then use this regression line as a forecasting device by projecting it into the future, the error may not be correctly defined by the projected confidence band. This is because the confidence interval is based on past data; it may not hold for projected data points and therefore cannot be used with the same confidence. In fact, experience has shown that the actual errors tend to be greater than those predicted from forecast models.

Analytics

Errors can be classified as bias or random. *Bias errors* occur when a consistent mistake is made. Sources of bias include the failure to include the right variables; the use of the wrong relationships among variables; employing the wrong trend line; a mistaken shift in the seasonal demand from where it normally occurs; and the existence of some undetected secular trend. *Random errors* can be defined as those that cannot be explained by the forecast model being used.

Measurement of Error Several common terms used to describe the degree of error are *standard error, mean squared error* (or *variance*), and *mean absolute deviation.* In addition, tracking signals may be used to indicate any positive or negative bias in the forecast.

Standard error is discussed in the section on linear regression in this chapter. Because the standard error is the square root of a function, it is often more convenient to use the function itself. This is called the mean squared error, or variance.

The **mean absolute deviation (MAD)** was in vogue in the past but subsequently was ignored in favor of standard deviation and standard error measures. In recent years, MAD has made a comeback because of its simplicity and usefulness in obtaining tracking signals. MAD is the average error in the forecasts, using absolute values. It is valuable because MAD, like the standard deviation, measures the dispersion of some observed value from some expected value.

Mean absolute deviation (MAD)
The average of the absolute value of the actual forecast error.

MAD is computed using the differences between the actual demand and the forecast demand without regard to sign. It equals the sum of the absolute deviations divided by the number of data points or, stated in equation form,

$$\text{MAD} = \frac{\sum_{t=1}^{n}|A_t - F_t|}{n} \qquad [18.11]$$

where

t = Period number
A_t = Actual demand for the period t
F_t = Forecast demand for the period t
n = Total number of periods
$||$ = A symbol used to indicate the absolute value disregarding positive and negative signs

When the errors that occur in the forecast are normally distributed (the usual case), the mean absolute deviation relates to the standard deviation of the error terms as

$$1 \text{ standard deviation} \approx \sqrt{\frac{\pi}{2}} \times \text{MAD, or approximately } 1.25 \text{ MAD}$$

Conversely,

1 MAD is approximately 0.8 standard deviation

The standard deviation is the larger measure. If the MAD of a set of points was found to be 60 units, then the standard deviation would be approximately 75 units. In the usual statistical manner, if control limits were set at plus or minus 3 standard deviations (or ±3.75 MADs), then 99.7 percent of the points would fall within these limits.

An additional measure of error that is often useful is the **mean absolute percent error (MAPE)**. This measure gauges the error relative to the demand as a percentage. For example, if the error is 10 units and actual demand is 20 units, the error is 50 percent $\left(\frac{10}{20} = .50\right)$ In the case of an average demand of 1,000 units, the MAPE would be only 1 percent $\left(\frac{10}{1{,}000} = .01\right)$ MAPE is the average of the percent error. MAPE is calculated as follows:

Mean absolute percent error (MAPE)
The average error measured as a percentage of average demand.

$$\text{MAPE} = \frac{100}{n}\sum_{t=1}^{n}\left[\frac{|A_t - F_t|}{A_t}\right] \qquad [18.12]$$

This is a useful measure because it is an estimate of how much error to expect with a forecast. The real value of the MAPE is that it allows you to compare forecasts between products that have very different average demand. If you used the MAD, the product with the higher demand would have the higher MAD even if it was a better forecast.

Tracking signal
A measure of whether the forecast is keeping pace with any genuine upward or downward changes in demand. This is used to detect forecast bias.

A **tracking signal** is a measurement that indicates whether the forecast average is keeping pace with any genuine upward or downward changes in demand. When a forecast is consistently low or high, it is referred to as a *biased* forecast. Exhibit 18.14 shows a normal distribution with a mean of 0 and a MAD equal to 1. Thus, if we compute the tracking signal and find it equal to minus 2, we can see that the forecast model is providing forecasts that are quite a bit above the mean of the actual occurrences.

A tracking signal (TS) can be calculated using the arithmetic sum of forecast deviations divided by the mean absolute deviation:

$$\text{TS} = \frac{\text{RSFE}}{\text{MAD}} \qquad [18.13]$$

where

RSFE = The running sum of forecast errors, considering the nature of the error. (For example, negative errors cancel positive errors and vice versa.)

MAD = The average of all the forecast errors (disregarding whether the deviations are positive or negative). It is the average of the absolute deviations.

Exhibit 18.14

A Normal Distribution with Mean = 0 and MAD = 1

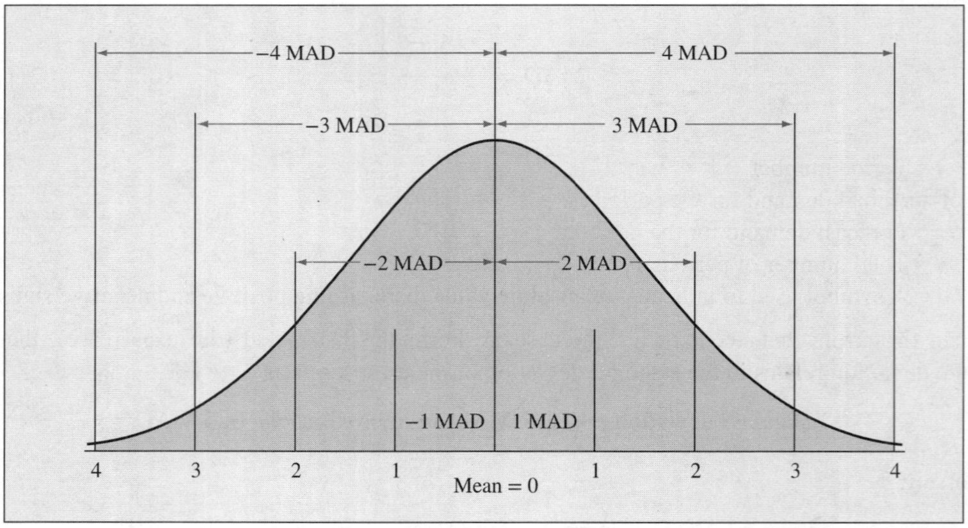

Exhibit 18.15 illustrates the procedure for computing MAD and the tracking signal for a six-month period where the forecast had been set at a constant 1,000 and the actual demands that occurred are as shown. In this example, the forecast, on the average, was off by 66.7 units and the tracking signal was equal to 3.3 mean absolute deviations.

We can get a better feel for what the MAD and tracking signal mean by plotting the points on a graph. Though this is not completely legitimate from a sample-size standpoint, we plotted each month in Exhibit 18.15 to show the drift of the tracking signal. Note that it drifted from minus 1 MAD to plus 3.3 MADs. This happened because actual demand was greater than the forecast in four of the six periods. If the actual demand does not fall below the forecast to offset the continual positive RSFE, the tracking signal would continue to rise and we would conclude that assuming a demand of 1,000 is a bad forecast.

Aggregate Forecast Improves Forecasting Accuracy

The case pertains to the time when power distribution was mainly through State Electricity Boards (SEB) in India. Every state in India had to meet the demand of electricity for their three categories of consumers: domestic, commercial and industrial. In a particular state, the department, which is responsible for electricity planning, used to come up with forecast for electricity requirement from its different directorates, which were individually responsible for one category of consumers. Based on the future requirements for the three categories of consumers, the Central Planning Unit (CPU), headed by a Senior Director, used to plan the electricity purchase from other SEBs, National Thermal Power Corporation (NTPC), etc. This step was necessary to bridge a possible deficit in total power generation in the power plants under local SEB.

The Central Planning Unit of the state always complained that the forecasts of the three different types of consumers had huge error due to vast difference with between forecast and actual requirements. This aspect was unfolding too late - only when the actual requirements were known. Consumers, were highly demanding and never liked a disruption in the power supply. Due to forecasting error, at the time of actual consumption, too many adjustments were made to fulfil the immediate requirement of the different consumers.

The following hypothetical data-set presents the demand pattern of electricity demand during ten year study period for three different types of consumers: domestic, commercial and industrial.

Year	1997-98	1998-99	1999-00	2000-01	2001-02	2002-03	2003-04	2004-05	2005-06	2006-07
Domestic	3020	2000	1234	2456	3963	5004	678	5994	2000	6825
Commercial	1000	500	7000	1292	120	1991	2312	190	3251	3730
Industrial	1866	2424	2292	200	3035	100	1681	2161	2383	200

Everybody was blaming the forecasting error as the main reason for poor planning in power procurement and distribution. We need to improve the forecasting accuracy.

First of all, the forecast and its accuracy should be calculated using an appropriate method. For illustration purpose, let us use "three period moving average" (3 PMA) method of forecasting. Absolute value of forecasting error (ABS) is calculated. This is the basis to judge the 'goodness of forecasting'. For example, the forecasting error for domestic consumers is calculated as follows.

Percent Error in Forecast = 100 * (Total Absolute Error in All Forecasted Periods)/(Total Demand in the Corresponding Period).

$$=100*(371.3+2066.3+2453+3129.7+2779+1892+3934.3)/(2456+3963+5004+678+5994+2000+6825)$$

$$=61.759\ \%$$

Percent Accuracy of Forecast = 100 - Percent Error in Forecast

$$=100-61.759=38.24\%.$$

Similarly, we can calculate for other categories of consumers. Forecasting accuracy for commercial and industrial consumers are 11.9% and 5.7%, respectively. These Forecasting accuracies are horrible!

We assume that from the power generation side suppliers, same electricity is purchased for all the three consumers of this case. Almost at the last minute, at the time of distribution, the voltage, amperage etc. are changed as per the consumer's need. Therefore, at the time of purchase, individual and disaggregated forecast is meaningless. Instead, one can use the aggregate forecast by adding the past demands of three consumers in each year and with this total demand data-set, same forecasting method (3 PMA in this case) is applied.

F15 =100*F14/SUM(C7:C13)

CASE: ELECTRICITY REQUIREMENT

Year	Domestic	3 PMA	Error	ABS	Commercial	3 PMA	Error	ABS	Industrial	3 PMA	Error	ABS	Total	3 PMA	Error	ABS
1997-98	3020				1000				1866				5886			
1998-99	2000				500				2424				4924			
1999-00	1234				7000				2292				10526			
2000-01	2456	2085	-371.3	371.33	1292	2833.33	1541.3	1541.3	200	2194	1994	1994	3948	7112	3164	3164
2001-02	3963	1897	-2066	2066.3	120	2930.67	2810.7	2810.7	3035	1638.7	-1396	1396	7118	6466	-652	652
2002-03	5004	2551	-2453	2453	1919	2804	885	885	100	1842.3	1742.3	1742	7023	7197.3	174.33	174.33
2003-04	678	3808	3129.7	3129.7	2312	1110.33	-1202	1201.7	1681	1111.7	-569.3	569.3	4671	6029.7	1358.7	1358.7
2004-05	5994	3215	-2779	2779	190	1450.33	1260.3	1260.3	2161	1605.3	-555.7	555.7	8345	6270.7	-2074	2074.3
2005-06	2000	3892	1892	1892	3251	1473.67	-1777	1777.3	2383	1314	-1069	1069	7634	6679.7	-954.3	954.33
2006-07	6825	2891	-3934	3934.3	3730	1917.67	-1812	1812.3	200	2075	1875	1875	10755	6883.3	-3872	3871.7
Σ				16626				11289				9202				12249
% Error				61.7595				88.0964				94.279				24.7491
% Accuracy				**38.24**				**11.904**				**5.721**				**75.251**

Note: Case Freapered for Illustration Purpose Only

Using the same "three period moving average" (3 PMA) forecasting method, the overall forecasting accuracy for power purchase improves to 75.25%. This is a significant improvement as compared to disaggregate forecast. The learning of this illustrative example can be articulated with an interesting *guru-mantra* (golden-rule), "Aggregate forecast is more accurate than the disaggregate forecast."

Exhibit 18.15

Computing the Mean Absolute Deviation (MAD), the Running Sum of Forecast Errors (RSFE), and the Tracking Signal (TS) from Forecast and Actual Data

Month	Demand Forecast	Actual	Deviation	RSFE	Abs. Dev.	Sum of Abs. Dev.	MAD (% Error)*	$TS = \frac{RSFE†}{MAD}$
1	1,000	950	−50	−50	50	50	50 (5.26%)	−1
2	1,000	1,070	+70	+20	70	120	60 (5.61%)	.33
3	1,000	1,100	+100	+120	100	220	73.3 (6.67%)	1.64
4	1,000	960	−40	180	40	260	65 (6.77%)	1.2
5	1,000	1,090	+90	+170	90	350	70 (6.42%)	2.4
6	1,000	1,050	+50	+220	50	400	66.7 (6.35%)	3.3

*Overall, MAD = 400 ÷ 6 = 66.7. MAPE = (5.26 + 5.61 + 6.67 + 6.77 + 6.42 + 6.35)/6 = 6.18%

†Overall, $TS = \frac{RSFE}{MAD} = \frac{220}{66.7} = 3.3$ MADs.

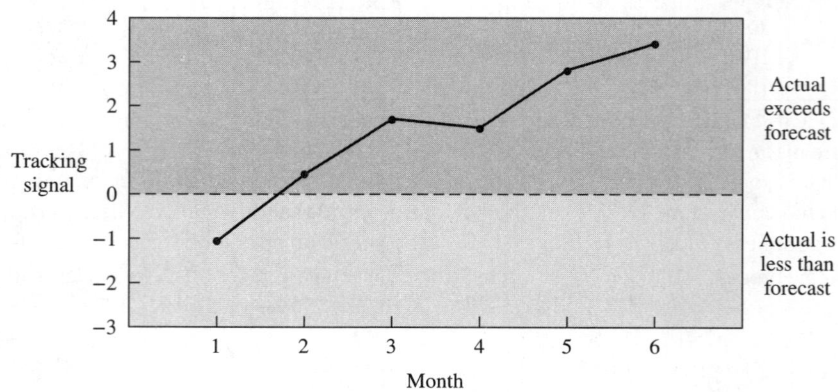

Causal Relationship Forecasting

Causal relationship forecasting
Forecasting using independent variables other than time to predict future demand.

Causal relationship forecasting involves using independent variables other than time to predict future demand. To be of value for the purpose of forecasting, any independent variable must be a leading indicator. For example, we can expect that an extended period of rain will increase sales of umbrellas and raincoats. The rain causes the sale of rain gear. This is a causal relationship, where one occurrence causes another. If the causing element is known far enough in advance, it can be used as a basis for forecasting.

Often, leading indicators are not causal relationships, but in some indirect way they may suggest that some other things might happen. Other noncausal relationships just seem to exist as a coincidence. The following shows one example of a forecast using a causal relationship.

Analytics

EXAMPLE 18.5 Forecasting Using a Causal Relationship

The Carpet City Store in Carpenteria has kept records of its sales (in square yards) each year, along with the number of permits for new houses in its area.

Number of Housing Starts

Year	Permits	Sales (in Sq. Yds.)
1	18	13,000
2	15	12,000

(Contd.)

Number of Housing Starts		
Year	Permits	Sales (in Sq. Yds.)
3	12	11,000
4	10	10,000
5	20	14,000
6	28	16,000
7	35	19,000
8	30	17,000
9	20	13,000

Carpet City's operations manager believes forecasting sales is possible if housing starts are known for that year. First, the data are plotted in Exhibit 18.16, with

x = Number of housing start permits

y = Sales of carpeting

EXHIBIT 18.16

Causal Relationship: Sales to Housing Starts

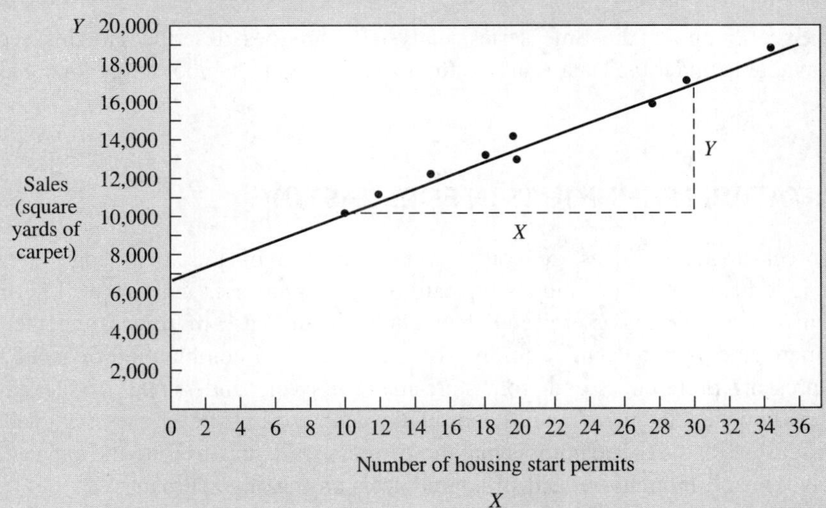

Because the points appear to be in a straight line, the manager decides to use the linear relationship $Y = a + bx$.

SOLUTION

An easy way to solve this problem is to use the SLOPE and INTERCEPT functions in Excel. Given the data in the table, the SLOPE is equal to 344.2211 and the INTERCEPT is equal to 6698.492.

The manager interprets the slope as the average number of square yards of carpet sold for each new house built in the area. The forecasting equation is therefore

$$Y = 6698.492 + 344.2211x$$

Now suppose that there are 25 permits for houses to be built next year. The sales forecast would therefore be

$$6{,}698.492 + 344.2211(25) = 15{,}304.02 \text{ square yards}$$

In this problem, the lag between filing the permit with the appropriate agency and the new home owner coming to Carpet City to buy carpet makes a causal relationship feasible for forecasting.

Multiple Regression Analysis Another forecasting method is multiple regression analysis, in which a number of variables are considered, together with the effects of each on the item of interest. For example, in the home furnishings field, the effects of the number of marriages, housing starts, disposable income, and the trend can be expressed in a multiple regression equation as

$$S = A + B_m(M) + B_h(H) + B_i(I) + B_t(T)$$

where

S = Gross sales for year
A = Base sales, a starting point from which other factors have influence
M = Marriages during the year
H = Housing starts during the year
I = Annual disposable personal income
T = Time trend (first year = 1, second = 2, third = 3, and so forth)

B_m, B_h, B_i, and B_t represent the influence on expected sales of the numbers of marriages and housing starts, income, and trend.

Forecasting by multiple regression is appropriate when a number of factors influence a variable of interest—in this case, sales. Its difficulty lies with collecting all the additional data that is required to produce the forecast, especially data that comes from outside the firm. Fortunately, standard computer programs for multiple regression analysis are available, relieving the need for tedious manual calculation.

Microsoft Excel supports the time series analysis techniques described in this section. These functions are available under the Data Analysis tools for exponential smoothing, moving averages, and regression.

LO 18-3

Apply qualitative techniques to forecast demand*

QUALITATIVE TECHNIQUES IN FORECASTING

Qualitative forecasting techniques generally take advantage of the knowledge of experts and require much judgment. These techniques typically involve processes that are well defined to those participating in the forecasting exercise. For example, in the case of forecasting the demand for new fashion merchandise in a retail store, the firm can include a combination of input from typical customers expressing preferences and from store managers who understand product mix and store volumes, where they view the merchandise and run through a series of exercises designed to bring the group to a consensus estimate. The point is that these are no wild guesses as to the expected demand—rather, it involves a well-thought-out and structured decision-making approach.

These techniques are most useful when the product is new or there is little experience with selling into a new region. Here such information as knowledge of similar products, the habits of customers in the area, and how the product will be advertised and introduced may be important to estimate demand successfully. In some cases, it may even be useful to consider industry data and the experience of competing firms in making estimates of expected demand.

The following are samples of qualitative forecasting techniques.

Market Research

Firms often hire outside companies that specialize in *market research* to conduct this type of forecasting. You may have been involved in market surveys through a marketing class. Certainly, you have not escaped telephone calls asking you about product preferences, your income, habits, and so on.

Market research is used mostly for product research in the sense of looking for new product ideas, likes and dislikes about existing products, which competitive products within a particular class are preferred, and so on. Again, the data collection methods are primarily surveys and interviews.

Panel Consensus

In a *panel consensus,* the idea that two heads are better than one is extrapolated to the idea that a panel of people from a variety of positions can develop a more reliable forecast than a narrower group. Panel forecasts are developed through open meetings with a free exchange of ideas from all levels of management and individuals. The difficulty with this open style is that lower-level employees are intimidated by higher levels of management. For example, a salesperson in a particular product line may have a good estimate of future product demand but may not speak up to refute a much different estimate given by the vice president of marketing. The Delphi technique (which we discuss shortly) was developed to try to correct this impairment to free exchange.

When decisions in forecasting are at a broader, higher level (as when introducing a new product line or concerning strategic product decisions such as new marketing areas), the term *executive judgment* is generally used. The term is self-explanatory: a higher level of management is involved.

Historical Analogy

In trying to forecast demand for a new product, an ideal situation would be one where an existing product or generic product could be used as a model. There are many ways to classify such analogies—for example, complementary products, substitutable or competitive products, and products as a function of income. Again, you have surely gotten a deluge of mail advertising products in a category similar to a product purchased via catalog, the Internet, or mail order. If you buy a DVD through the mail, you will receive more mail about new DVDs and DVD players. A causal relationship would be that demand for compact discs is caused by demand for DVD players. An analogy would be forecasting the demand for digital videodisc players by analyzing the historical demand for VCRs. The products are in the same general category of electronics and may be bought by consumers at similar rates. A simpler example would be toasters and coffeepots. A firm that already produces toasters and wants to produce coffeepots could use the toaster history as a likely growth model.

Delphi Method

As we mentioned under panel consensus, a statement or opinion of a higher-level person will likely be weighted more than that of a lower-level person. The worst case is where lower-level people feel threatened and do not contribute their true beliefs. To prevent this problem, the *Delphi method* conceals the identity of the individuals participating in the study. Everyone has the same weight. Procedurally, a moderator creates a questionnaire and distributes it to participants. Their responses are summed and given back to the entire group along with a new set of questions.

The step-by-step procedure for the Delphi method is:

1. Choose the experts to participate. There should be a variety of knowledgeable people in different areas.
2. Through a questionnaire (or e-mail), obtain forecasts (and any premises or qualifications for the forecasts) from all participants.
3. Summarize the results, and redistribute them to the participants along with appropriate new questions.
4. Summarize again, refining forecasts and conditions, and again develop new questions.
5. Repeat step 4 if necessary. Distribute the final results to all participants.

The Delphi technique can usually achieve satisfactory results in three rounds. The time required is a function of the number of participants, how much work is involved for them to develop their forecasts, and their speed in responding.

LO 18-4

Apply collaborative techniques to forecast demand

WEB-BASED FORECASTING: COLLABORATIVE PLANNING, FORECASTING, AND REPLENISHMENT (CPFR)

Collaborative planning, forecasting, and replenishment (CPFR)

An Internet tool to coordinate forecasting, production, and purchasing in a firm's supply chain.

Collaborative planning, forecasting, and replenishment (CPFR) is a Web-based tool used to coordinate demand forecasting, production and purchase planning, and inventory replenishment between supply chain trading partners. CPFR is being used as a means of integrating all members of an *n*-tier supply chain, including manufacturers, distributors, and retailers. As depicted in Exhibit 18.17, the ideal point of collaboration utilizing CPFR is the retail-level demand forecast, which is successively used to synchronize forecasts, production, and replenishment plans upstream through the supply chain.

Although the methodology is applicable to any industry, CPFR applications to date have largely focused on the food, apparel, and general merchandise industries. The potential benefits of sharing information for enhanced planning visibility in any supply chain are enormous. Various estimates for cost savings attributable to improved supply chain coordination have been proposed, including $30 billion annually in the food industry alone.

Exhibit 18.17

n-Tier Supply Chain with Retail Activities

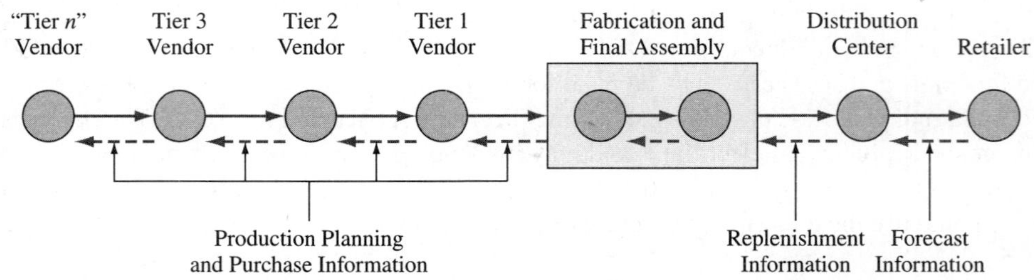

Note: Solid arrows represent material flows; dashed arrows represent information flows.

CPFR's objective is to exchange selected internal information on a shared Web server in order to provide for reliable, longer-term future views of demand in the supply chain. CPFR uses a cyclic and iterative approach to derive consensus supply chain forecasts. It consists of the following five steps:

Process

Step 1. Creation of a front-end partnership agreement. This agreement specifies (1) objectives (e.g., inventory reductions, lost sales elimination, lower product obsolescence) to be gained through collaboration, (2) resource requirements (e.g., hardware, software, performance metrics) necessary for the collaboration, and (3) expectations of confidentiality concerning the prerequisite trust necessary to share sensitive company information, which represents a major implementation obstacle.

Step 2. Joint business planning. Typically, partners create partnership strategies, design a joint calendar identifying the sequence and frequency of planning activities to follow that affect product flows, and specify exception criteria for handling planning variances between the trading partners' demand forecasts.

Step 3. Development of demand forecasts. Forecast development may follow preexisting company procedures. Retailers should play a critical role because shared *point-of-sale* (*POS*) data permit the development of more accurate and timely expectations (compared with extrapolated warehouse withdrawals or aggregate store orders) for both retailers and vendors. Given the frequency of forecast generation and the potential for vast numbers of items requiring forecast preparation, a simple forecast procedure such as a moving average is commonly used within CPFR. Simple techniques are easily used in conjunction with expert knowledge of promotional or pricing events to modify forecast values accordingly.

Step 4. Sharing forecasts. Retailer (order forecasts) and vendor (sales forecasts) then electronically post their latest forecasts for a list of products on a shared server. The server examines pairs of corresponding forecasts and issues an exception notice for any forecast pair where the difference exceeds a preestablished safety margin (e.g., 5 percent). If the safety margin is exceeded, planners from both firms may collaborate electronically to derive a consensus forecast.

Step 5. Inventory replenishment. Once the corresponding forecasts are in agreement, the order forecast becomes an actual order, which commences the replenishment process. Each of these steps is then repeated iteratively in a continuous cycle, at varying times, by individual products, and the calendar of events is established between trading partners. For example, partners may review the front-end partnership agreement annually, evaluate the joint business plans quarterly, develop forecasts weekly to monthly, and replenish daily.

The early exchange of information between trading partners provides for reliable, longer-term future views of demand in the supply chain. The forward visibility based upon information sharing leads to a variety of benefits within supply chain partnerships.

As with most new corporate initiatives, there is skepticism and resistance to change. One of the largest hurdles hindering collaboration is the lack of trust over complete information sharing between supply chain partners. The conflicting objective between the profit-maximizing vendor and the cost-minimizing customer gives rise to adversarial supply chain relationships. Sharing sensitive operating data may enable one trading partner to take advantage of the other. Similarly, there is the potential loss of control as a barrier to implementation. Some companies are rightfully concerned about the idea of placing strategic data such as financial reports, manufacturing schedules, and inventory values online. Companies open themselves up to security breaches. However, front-end partnership agreements, nondisclosure agreements, and limited information access may help overcome these fears.

CONCEPT CONNECTIONS

LO 18–1 Understand how forecasting is essential to supply chain planning

Summary

Forecasts are essential to every business organization. It is important to consider the purpose of the forecast before selecting the technique.

- Strategic forecasts are typically longer term and usually involve forecasting demand for a group of products.
- Tactical forecasts would cover only a short period of time, at most a few weeks in the future, and would typically be for individual items.

Forecasts are used in many different problems studied in this book.

Key Terms

Strategic forecasts Medium and long-term forecasts that are used for decisions related to strategy and aggregate demand.

Tactical forecasts Short-term forecasts used for making day-to-day decisions related to meeting demand.

LO 18–2 Evaluate demand using quantitative forecasting models

Summary

In this chapter, the focus is on time series analysis techniques. With a time series analysis, past demand data are used to predict future demand.

- Demand can be broken down or "decomposed" into basic elements, such as trend, seasonality, and random variation (there are other elements, but these are the ones considered in this chapter).

- Four different time series models are evaluated: simple moving average, weighted moving average, exponential smoothing, and linear regression.
- Trend and seasonal components are analyzed for these problems.
- Causal relationship forecasting is different from time series (but commonly used) because it uses data other than past demand in making the forecast.
- The quality of a forecast is measured based on its error. Various measures exist, including the average error, percentage of error, and bias. Bias occurs when a forecast is consistently higher or lower than actual demand.

Key Terms

Time series analysis A forecast in which past demand data is used to predict future demand.

Moving average A forecast based on average past demand.

Weighted moving average A forecast made with past data where more recent data is given more significance than older data.

Exponential smoothing A time series forecasting technique using weights that decrease exponentially $(1 - \alpha)$ for each past period.

Smoothing constant alpha (α) The parameter in the exponential smoothing equation that controls the speed of reaction to differences between forecasts and actual demand.

Smoothing constant delta (δ) An additional parameter used in an exponential smoothing equation that includes an adjustment for trend.

Linear regression forecasting A forecasting technique that fits a straight line to past demand data.

Decomposition The process of identifying and separating time series data into fundamental components such as trend and seasonality.

Forecast error The difference between actual demand and what was forecast.

Mean absolute deviation (MAD) The average of the absolute value of the actual forecast error.

Mean absolute percent error (MAPE) The average error measured as a percentage of average demand.

Tracking signal A measure of whether the forecast is keeping pace with any genuine upward or downward changes in demand. This is used to detect forecast bias.

Causal relationship forecasting Forecasting using independent variables other than time to predict future demand.

Key Formulae

[18.1] $$F_t = \frac{A_{t-1} + A_{t-2} + A_{t-3} + \ldots + A_{t-n}}{n}$$

[18.2] $$F_t = w_1 A_{t-1} + w_2 A_{t-2} + \ldots + w_n A_{t-n}$$

[18.3] $$F_t = F_{t-1} + \alpha(A_{t-1} - F_{t-1})$$

[18.4] $$F_t = \text{FIT}_{t-1} + \alpha(A_{t-1} - \text{FIT}_{t-1})$$

[18.5] $$T_t = T_{t-1} + \delta(F_t - \text{FIT}_{t-1})$$

[18.6] $$\text{FIT}_t = F_t + T_t$$

[18.7] $$Y = a + bt$$

[18.8] $$b = \frac{\sum ty - n\bar{t} \cdot \bar{y}}{\sum t^2 - n\bar{t}^2}$$

$$a = \bar{y} - b\bar{t}$$ [18.9]

$$S_{yt} = \sqrt{\frac{\sum_{i=1}^{n} (y_i - Y_i)^2}{n-2}}$$ [18.10]

$$\text{MAD} = \frac{\sum_{t=1}^{n} |A_t - F_t|}{n}$$ [18.11]

$$\text{MAPE} = \frac{100}{n} \sum_{t=1}^{n} \left[\frac{|A_t - F_t|}{A_t} \right]$$ [18.12]

$$\text{TS} = \frac{\text{RSFE}}{\text{MAD}}$$ [18.13]

LO 18–3 Apply qualitative techniques to forecast demand

Summary

- Qualitative techniques depend more on judgment or the opinions of experts and can be useful when past demand data are not available.
- These techniques typically involve a structured process so that experience can be acquired and accuracy assessed.

LO 18–4 Apply collaborative techniques to forecast demand

Summary

- Collaboration between supply chain partners, such as the manufacturer and the retailer selling a product, can be useful.
- Typically, Web-based technology is used to derive a forecast that is a consensus of all the participants. There are often great benefits to all participants due to the sharing of information and future planning visibility offered through the system.

Key Terms

Collaborative Planning, Forecasting, and Replenishment (CPFR) An Internet tool to coordinate forecasting, production, and purchasing in a firm's supply chain.

SOLVED PROBLEMS

LO 18–2 SOLVED PROBLEM 1

Sunrise Baking Company markets doughnuts through a chain of food stores. It has been experiencing overproduction and underproduction because of forecasting errors. The following data are its demand in dozens of doughnuts for the past four weeks. Doughnuts are made for the following day; for example, Sunday's doughnut production is for Monday's sales, Monday's production is for Tuesday's sales, and so forth. The bakery is closed Saturday, so Friday's production must satisfy demand for both Saturday and Sunday.

	4 Weeks Ago	3 Weeks Ago	2 Weeks Ago	Last Week
Monday	2,200	2,400	2,300	2,400
Tuesday	2,000	2,100	2,200	2,200
Wednesday	2,300	2,400	2,300	2,500
Thursday	1,800	1,900	1,800	2,000
Friday	1,900	1,800	2,100	2,000
Saturday	(closed on Saturday)			
Sunday	2,800	2,700	3,000	2,900

Make a forecast for this week based on the following:

a. Daily, using a simple four-week moving average.

b. Daily, using a weighted moving average with weights of 0.40, 0.30, 0.20, and 0.10 (most recent to oldest week).

c. Sunrise is also planning its purchases of ingredients for bread production. If bread demand had been forecast for last week at 22,000 loaves and only 21,000 loaves were actually demanded, what would Sunrise's forecast be for this week using exponential smoothing with $\alpha = 0.10$?

d. Suppose, with the forecast made in *c,* this week's demand actually turns out to be 22,500. What would the new forecast be for the next week?

Solution

a. Simple moving average, four-week.

$$\text{Monday}\ \frac{2{,}400+2{,}300+2{,}400+2{,}200}{4}=\frac{9{,}300}{4}=2{,}325\text{ doz.}$$

$$\text{Tuesday}\qquad =\frac{8{,}500}{4}=2{,}125\text{ doz.}$$

$$\text{Wednesday}\qquad =\frac{9{,}500}{4}=2{,}375\text{ doz.}$$

$$\text{Thursday}\qquad =\frac{7{,}500}{4}=1{,}875\text{ doz.}$$

$$\text{Friday}\qquad =\frac{7{,}800}{4}=1{,}950\text{ doz.}$$

$$\text{Saturday and Sunday}\qquad =\frac{11{,}400}{4}=2{,}850\text{ doz.}$$

b. Weighted average with weights of .40, .30, .20, and .10.

	(.10)		(.20)		(.30)		(.40)		
Monday	220	+	480	+	690	+	960	=	2,350
Tuesday	200	+	420	+	660	+	880	=	2,160
Wednesday	230	+	480	+	690	+	1,000	=	2,400
Thursday	180	+	380	+	540	+	800	=	1,900
Friday	190	+	360	+	630	+	800	=	1,980
Saturday and Sunday	280	+	540	+	900	+	1,160	=	2,880

c. Exponentially smoothed forecast for bread demand

$$\begin{aligned} F_t &= F_{t-1}+\alpha(A_{t-1}-F_{t-1}) \\ &= 22{,}000+0.10(21{,}000-22{,}000) \\ &= 22{,}000-100=21{,}900\text{ loaves} \end{aligned}$$

d. Exponentially smoothed forecast

$$\begin{aligned} F_{t+1} &= 21{,}900+.10(22{,}500-21{,}900) \\ &= 21{,}900+.10(600)=21{,}960\text{ loaves} \end{aligned}$$

SOLVED PROBLEM 2

Given the following information, make a forecast for May using exponential smoothing with trend and linear regression.

Month	January	February	March	April
Demand	700	760	780	790

For exponential smoothing with trend, assume that the previous forecast (for April) including trend (FIT) was 800 units, and the previous trend component (T) was 50 units. Also, alpha (α) = .3 and delta(δ) = .1.

For linear regression, use the January-through-April demand data to fit the regression line. Use the Excel regression functions SLOPE and INTERCEPT to calculate these values.

Solution

Exponential smoothing with trend

Use the following three steps to update the forecast for each period:

1 Forecast without Trend $F_t = \text{FIT}_{t-1} + \alpha(A_{t-1} - \text{FIT}_{t-1})$

2 Update Trend estimate $T_t = T_{t-1} + \delta(F_t - \text{FIT}_{t-1})$

3 New Forecast including Trend $\text{FIT}_t = F_t + T_t$

$$\text{Given}\quad \text{FIT}_{April} = 800$$
$$\text{and } T_{April} = 50$$
$$\text{Then}\quad F_{May} = 800 + .3(790 - 800) = 797$$
$$T_{May} = 50 + .1(797 - 800) = 49.7$$
$$\text{FIT}_{May} = 797 + 49.7 = 846.7$$

Linear regression

1 Set up the problem and calculate the slope and intercept as shown here.
2 Forecast using linear regression

$$F_t = a + bt$$

where a is the "Slope" and b is the "Intercept," and t for May is 5 (the index for month 5).

$$\text{Then}\quad F_{May} = 685 + 29(5) = 830$$

	A	B	C	D	E
1	Month	Demand			
2	1	700			
3	2	760			
4	3	780			
5	4	790			
6	Intercept	685	=INTERCEPT(B2:B5,A2:A5)		
7	Slope	29	=SLOPE(B2:B5,A2:A5)		
8					

SOLVED PROBLEM 3

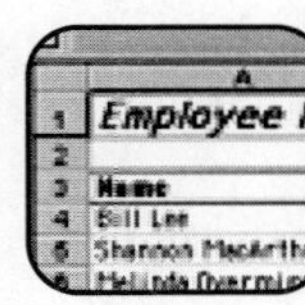

The following are quarterly data for the past two years. From these data, prepare a forecast for the upcoming year using decomposition.

Period	Actual	Period	Actual
1	300	5	416
2	540	6	760
3	885	7	1,191
4	580	8	760

Solution

(Note that the values you obtain may be slightly different due to rounding. The values given here were obtained using an Excel spreadsheet.)

(1) Period x	(2) Actual y	(3) Period average	(4) Seasonal factor	(5) Deseasonalized demand y_d
1	300	358	0.527	568.99
2	540	650	0.957	564.09
3	885	1,038	1.529	578.92
4	580	670	0.987	587.79
5	416		0.527	789.01
6	760		0.957	793.91
7	1,191		1.529	779.08
8	760		0.987	770.21
Total	5,432	2,716	8.0	
Average	679	679	1	

Column 3 is seasonal average. For example, the first-quarter average is

$$\frac{300 + 416}{2} = 358$$

Column 4 is the quarter average (column 3) divided by the overall average (679). Column 5 is the actual data divided by the seasonal index. To determine t^2 and ty, we can construct a table as follows:

	Period t	Deseasonalized Demand (y_d)	t^2	ty_d
	1	568.99	1	569.0
	2	564.09	4	1,128.2
	3	578.92	9	1,736.7
	4	587.79	16	2,351.2
	5	789.01	25	3,945.0
	6	793.91	36	4,763.4
	7	779.08	49	5,453.6
	8	770.21	64	6,161.7
Sums	36	5,432	204	26,108.8
Average	4.5	679		

Now we calculate regression results for deseasonalized data.

$$b = \frac{(26108.8) - (8)(4.5)(679)}{(204) - (8)(4.5)^2} = 39.64$$

$$a = \bar{y}_d - b\bar{t}$$

$$a = 679 - 39.64(4.5) = 500.6$$

Therefore, the deseasonalized regression results are

$$Y = 500.6 + 39.64t$$

Period	Trend Forecast		Seasonal Factor		Final Forecast
9	857.4	×	0.527	=	452.0
10	897.0	×	0.957	=	858.7
11	936.7	×	1.529	=	1,431.9
12	976.3	×	0.987	=	963.4

SOLVED PROBLEM 4

A specific forecasting model was used to forecast demand for a product. The forecasts and the corresponding demand that subsequently occurred are shown as follows. Use the MAD, tracking signal technique, and MAPE to evaluate the accuracy of the forecasting model.

	Actual	Forecast
October	700	660
November	760	840
December	780	750
January	790	835
February	850	910
March	950	890

Solution

Evaluate the forecasting model using the MAD, the tracking signal, and MAPE.

	Actual Demand	Forecast Demand	Actual Deviation	Cumulative Deviation (RSFE)	Tracking Signal	Absolute Deviation (% Deviation)
October	700	660	40	40	1.00	40 (5.71%)
November	760	840	−80	−40	0.67	80 (10.53%)
December	780	750	30	−10	0.20	30 (3.85%)
January	790	835	−45	−55	1.13	45 (5.70%)
February	850	910	−60	−115	2.25	60 (7.06%)
March	950	890	60	−55	1.05	60 (6.32%)
Average demand = 805						Total dev. = 315

$$\text{MAD} = \frac{315}{6} = 52.5$$

$$\text{Tracking signal} = \frac{-55}{52.5} = -1.05$$

$$\text{MAPE} = \frac{5.71 + 10.53 + 3.85 + 5.70 + 7.06 + 6.32}{6} = 6.53\%$$

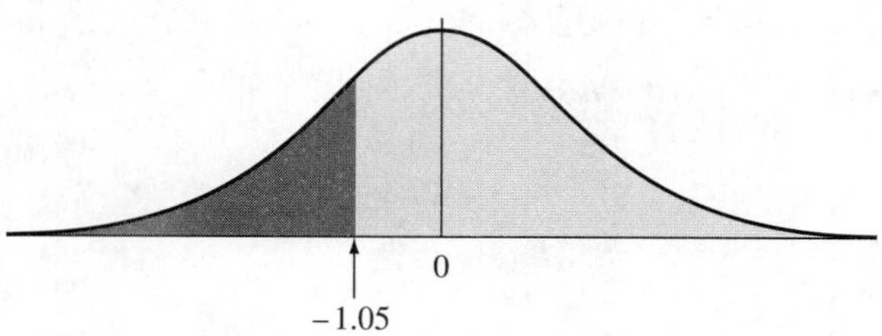

There is not enough evidence to reject the forecasting model, so we accept its recommendations.

DISCUSSION QUESTIONS

1. Why is forecasting necessary in OSCM? **LO 18–1**
2. It is a common saying that the only thing certain about a forecast is that it will be wrong. What is meant by this?
3. From the choice of the simple moving average, weighted moving average, exponential smoothing, and linear regression analysis, which forecasting technique would you consider the most accurate? Why? **LO 18–2**
4. All forecasting methods using exponential smoothing, adaptive smoothing, and exponential smoothing including trend require starting values to get the equations going. How would you select the starting value for, say, F_{t-1}?
5. How is a seasonal index computed from a regression line analysis?
6. Discuss the basic differences between the mean absolute deviation and mean absolute percent error.
7. What implications do forecast errors have for the search for ultrasophisticated statistical forecasting models?
8. Causal relationships are potentially useful for which component of a time series?
9. Let's say you work for a company that makes prepared breakfast cereals like corn flakes. Your company is planning to introduce a new hot breakfast product made from whole grains that would require some minimal preparation by the consumer. This would be a completely new product for the company. How would you propose forecasting initial demand for this product? **LO 18–3**

LO 18–4 10. How has the development of the Internet affected the way companies forecast in support of their supply chain planning process?

11. What sorts of risks do you see in reliance on the Internet in the use of collaborative planning, forecasting, and replenishment (CPFR)?

OBJECTIVE QUESTIONS

LO 18–1 1. What is the term for forecasts used for making day-to-day decisions about meeting demand?

2. What category of forecasting techniques uses managerial judgment in lieu of numerical data?

LO 18–2 3. Given the following history, use a three-quarter moving average to forecast the demand for the third quarter of this year. Note, the 1st quarter is Jan, Feb, and Mar; 2nd quarter Apr, May, Jun; 3rd quarter Jul, Aug, Sep; and 4th quarter Oct, Nov, Dec.

	Jan	Feb	Mar	Apr	May	Jun	Jul	Aug	Sep	Oct	Nov	Dec
Last year	100	125	135	175	185	200	150	140	130	200	225	250
This year	125	135	135	190	200	190						

4. Here are the data for the past 21 months for actual sales of a particular product:

	Last Year	This Year		Last Year	This Year
January	300	275	July	400	350
February	400	375	August	300	275
March	425	350	September	375	350
April	450	425	October	500	
May	400	400	November	550	
June	460	350	December	500	

Develop a forecast for the fourth quarter using a three-quarter, weighted moving average. Weight the most recent quarter 0.5, the second most recent 0.25, and the third 0.25. Do the problem using quarters, as opposed to forecasting separate months. (Answer in Appendix D)

5. The following table contains the number of complaints received in a department store for the first six months of operation.

Month	Complaints	Month	Complaints
January	36	April	90
February	45	May	108
March	81	June	144

If a three-month moving average is used to smooth this series, what would have been the forecast for May?

6. The following tabulations are actual sales of units for six months and a starting forecast in January. (Answers in Appendix D)

a. Calculate forecasts for the remaining five months using simple exponential smoothing with $\alpha = 0.2$.

b. Calculate MAD for the forecasts.

	Actual	Forecast
January	100	80
February	94	
March	106	
April	80	
May	68	
June	94	

7. The following table contains the demand from the last 10 months.

Month	Actual Demand	Month	Actual Demand
1	31	6	36
2	34	7	38
3	33	8	40
4	35	9	40
5	37	10	41

   a. Calculate the single exponential smoothing forecast for these data using an α of 0.30 and an initial forecast (F_1) of 31.
   b. Calculate the exponential smoothing with trend forecast for these data using an α of 0.30, a δ of 0.30, an initial trend forecast (T_1) of 1, and an initial exponentially smoothed forecast (F_1) of 30.
   c. Calculate the mean absolute deviation (MAD) for each forecast. Which is best?
8. Actual demand for a product for the past three months was

Three months ago	400 units
Two months ago	350 units
Last month	325 units

   a. Using a simple three-month moving average, make a forecast for this month.
   b. If 300 units were actually demanded this month, what would your forecast be for next month?
   c. Using simple exponential smoothing, what would your forecast be for this month if the exponentially smoothed forecast for three months ago was 450 units and the smoothing constant was 0.20?
9. Assume an initial starting F_t of 300 units, a trend (T_t) of eight units, an alpha of 0.30, and a delta of 0.40. If actual demand turned out to be 288, calculate the forecast for the next period.
10. The number of cases of merlot wine sold by the Connor Owen winery in an eight-year period is as follows.

Year	Cases of Merlot Wine	Year	Cases of Merlot Wine
1	270	5	358
2	356	6	500
3	398	7	410
4	456	8	376

   Using an exponential smoothing model with an alpha value of 0.20, estimate the smoothed value calculated as of the end of year 8. Use the average demand for years 1 through 3 as your initial forecast, and then smooth the forecast forward to year 8.
11. Not all the items in your office supply store are evenly distributed as far as demand is concerned, so you decide to forecast demand to help plan your stock. Past data for legal-sized yellow tablets for the month of August are

Week 1	300
Week 2	400
Week 3	600
Week 4	700

   a. Using a three-week moving average, what would you forecast the next week to be?
   b. Using exponential smoothing with $\alpha = 0.20$, if the exponential forecast for week 3 was estimated as the average of the first two weeks [(300 + 400)/2 = 350], what would you forecast week 5 to be?

12. Assume that your stock of sales merchandise is maintained based on the forecast demand. If the distributor's sales personnel call on the first day of each month, compute your forecast sales by each of the three methods requested here.

	Actual
June	140
July	180
August	170

a. Using a simple three-month moving average, what is the forecast for September?
b. Using a weighted moving average, what is the forecast for September with weights of 0.20, 0.30, and 0.50 for June, July, and August, respectively?
c. Using single exponential smoothing and assuming that the forecast for June had been 130, forecast sales for September with a smoothing constant alpha of 0.30.

13. Historical demand for a product is as follows.

	Demand		Demand
April	60	July	60
May	55	August	80
June	75	September	75

a. Using a simple four-month moving average, calculate a forecast for October.
b. Using single exponential smoothing with $\alpha = 0.2$ and a September forecast = 65, calculate a forecast for October.
c. Using simple linear regression, calculate the trend line for the historical data. Let's say the X axis is April = 1, May = 2, and so on, while the Y axis is demand.
d. Calculate a forecast for October using your regression formula.

14. Demand for stereo headphones and MP3 players for joggers has caused Nina Industries to grow almost 50 percent over the past year. The number of joggers continues to expand, so Nina expects demand for headsets to also expand, because, as yet, no safety laws have been passed to prevent joggers from wearing them. Demand for the players for last year was as follows.

Month	Demand (units)	Month	Demand (units)
January	4,200	July	5,300
February	4,300	August	4,900
March	4,000	September	5,400
April	4,400	October	5,700
May	5,000	November	6,300
June	4,700	December	6,000

a. Using linear regression analysis, what would you estimate demand to be for each month next year? Using a spreadsheet, follow the general format in Exhibits 18.7 and 18.8. Compare your results to those obtained by using the forecast spreadsheet function.
b. To be reasonably confident of meeting demand, Nina decides to use three standard errors of estimate for safety. How many additional units should be held to meet this level of confidence?

15. Historical demand for a product is

	Demand
January	12
February	11
March	15
April	12
May	16
June	15

a. Using a weighted moving average with weights of 0.60, 0.30, and 0.10, find the July forecast.
b. Using a simple three-month moving average, find the July forecast.
c. Using single exponential smoothing with $\alpha = 0.2$ and a June forecast = 13, find the July forecast. Make whatever assumptions you wish.
d. Using simple linear regression analysis, calculate the regression equation for the preceding demand data.
e. Using the regression equation in *d,* calculate the forecast for July.

16. The tracking signals computed using past demand history for three different products are as follows. Each product used the same forecasting technique.

	TS 1	TS 2	TS 3
1	−2.70	1.54	0.10
2	−2.32	−0.64	0.43
3	−1.70	2.05	1.08
4	−1.10	2.58	1.74
5	−0.87	−0.95	1.94
6	−0.05	−1.23	2.24
7	0.10	0.75	2.96
8	0.40	−1.59	3.02
9	1.50	0.47	3.54
10	2.20	2.74	3.75

Discuss the tracking signals for each and what the implications are.

17. Here are the actual tabulated demands for an item for a nine-month period (January through September). Your supervisor wants to test two forecasting methods to see which method was better over this period.

Month	Actual	Month	Actual
January	110	June	180
February	130	July	140
March	150	August	130
April	170	September	140
May	160		

a. Forecast April through September using a three-month moving average.
b. Use simple exponential smoothing with an alpha of 0.3 to estimate April through September, using the average of January through March as the initial forecast for April.
c. Use MAD to decide which method produced the better forecast over the six-month period.

18. A particular forecasting model was used to forecast a six-month period. Here are the forecasts and actual demands that resulted:

	Forecast	Actual
April	250	200
May	325	250
June	400	325
July	350	300
August	375	325
September	450	400

Find the tracking signal and state whether you think the model being used is giving acceptable answers.

19. Harlen Industries has a simple forecasting model: Take the actual demand for the same month last year and divide that by the number of fractional weeks in that month. This gives the average weekly demand for that month. This weekly average is used as the weekly forecast for the same

month this year. This technique was used to forecast eight weeks for this year, which are shown as follows, along with the actual demand that occurred.

The following eight weeks show the forecast (based on last year) and the demand that actually occurred:

Week	Forecast Demand	Actual Demand
1	140	137
2	140	133
3	140	150
4	140	160
5	140	180
6	150	170
7	150	185
8	150	205

a. Compute the MAD of forecast errors.
b. Using the RSFE, compute the tracking signal.
c. Based on your answers to parts (*a*) and (*b*), comment on Harlen's method of forecasting.

20. In this problem, you are to test the validity of your forecasting model. Here are the forecasts for a model you have been using and the actual demands that occurred:

Week	Forecast	Actual
1	800	900
2	850	1,000
3	950	1,050
4	950	900
5	1,000	900
6	975	1,100

Use the method stated in the text to compute MAD and the tracking signal. Then, decide whether the forecasting model you have been using is giving reasonable results.

21. The following table shows predicted product demand using your particular forecasting method along with the actual demand that occurred. (Answers in Appendix D)

Forecast	Actual
1,500	1,550
1,400	1,500
1,700	1,600
1,750	1,650
1,800	1,700

a. Compute the tracking signal using the mean absolute deviation and running sum of forecast errors.
b. Discuss whether your forecasting method is giving good predictions.

22. Your manager is trying to determine what forecasting method to use. Based upon the following historical data, calculate the following forecast and specify what procedure you would utilize.

Month	Actual Demand	Month	Actual Demand
1	62	7	76
2	65	8	78
3	67	9	78
4	68	10	80
5	71	11	84
6	73	12	85

a. Calculate the simple three-month moving average forecast for periods 4 to 12.
b. Calculate the weighted three-month moving average using weights of 0.50, 0.30, and 0.20 for periods 4 to 12.
c. Calculate the single exponential smoothing forecast for periods 2 to 12 using an initial forecast (F_1) of 61 and an α of 0.30.
d. Calculate the exponential smoothing with trend component forecast for periods 2 to 12 using an initial trend forecast (T_1) of 1.8, an initial exponential smoothing forecast (F_1) of 60, an α of 0.30, and a δ of 0.30.
e. Calculate the mean absolute deviation (MAD) for the forecasts made by each technique in periods 4 to 12. Which forecasting method do you prefer?

23. After using your forecasting model for six months, you decide to test it using MAD and a tracking signal. Here are the forecast and actual demands for the six-month period:

Period	Forecast	Actual
May	450	500
June	500	550
July	550	400
August	600	500
September	650	675
October	700	600

a. Find the tracking signal.
b. Decide whether your forecasting routine is acceptable.

24. Zeus Computer Chips, Inc. used to have major contracts to produce the Centrino-type chips. The market has been declining during the past three years because of the quad-core chips, which it cannot produce, so Zeus has the unpleasant task of forecasting next year. The task is unpleasant because the firm has not been able to find replacement chips for its product lines. Here is the demand over the past 12 quarters:

Two Years Ago		Last Year		This Year	
I	4,800	I	3,500	I	3,200
II	3,500	II	2,700	II	2,100
III	4,300	III	3,500	III	2,700
IV	3,000	IV	2,400	IV	1,700

Use the decomposition technique to forecast the demand for the next four quarters.

25. The sales data for two years are as follows. Data are aggregated with two months of sales in each "period."

Months	Sales	Months	Sales
January–February	109	January–February	115
March–April	104	March–April	112
May–June	150	May–June	159
July–August	170	July–August	182
September–October	120	September–October	126
November–December	100	November–December	106

a. Plot the data.
b. Fit a simple linear regression model to the sales data.
c. In addition to the regression model, determine multiplicative seasonal index factors. A full cycle is assumed to be a full year.
d. Using the results from parts (*b*) and (*c*), prepare a forecast for the next year.

26. The following table shows the past two years of quarterly sales information. Assume that there are both trend and seasonal factors and that the seasonal cycle is one year. Use time series decomposition to forecast quarterly sales for the next year.

Quarter Last Year	Sales	Quarter This Year	Sales
I	215	I	160
II	240	II	195
III	205	III	150
IV	190	IV	140

27. Tucson Machinery, Inc. manufactures numerically controlled machines, which sell for an average price of $0.5 million each. Sales for these NCMs for the past two years were as follows.

Quarter	Quantity (Units)	Quarter	Quantity (Units)
Last Year		This Year	
I	12	I	16
II	18	II	24
III	26	III	28
IV	16	IV	18

a. Find a line using regression in Excel.
b. Find the trend and seasonal factors.
c. Forecast sales for next year.

28. Use regression analysis on deseasonalized demand to forecast next summer's demand, given the following historical demand data.

Year	Season	Actual Demand
2 years ago	Spring	205
	Summer	140
	Fall	375
	Winter	575
Last year	Spring	475
	Summer	275
	Fall	685
	Winter	965

29. The following are earnings per share for two companies by quarter from the first quarter three years ago through the second quarter of this year. Forecast earnings per share for the rest of this year and next year. Use exponential smoothing to forecast the third period of this year, and the time series decomposition method to forecast the last two quarters of this year and all four quarters of next year. (It is much easier to solve this problem on a computer spreadsheet so you can see what is happening.)

		Earnings per Share	
	Quarter	Company A	Company B
3 years ago	I	$1.67	$0.17
	II	2.35	0.24
	III	1.11	0.26
	IV	1.15	0.34
2 years ago	I	1.56	0.25
	II	2.04	0.37
	III	1.14	0.36
	IV	0.38	0.44
Last year	I	0.29	0.33
	II	−0.18 (loss)	0.40
	III	−0.97 (loss)	0.41
	IV	0.20	0.47
This year	I	−1.54 (loss)	0.30
	II	0.38	0.47

a. For the exponential smoothing method, choose the first quarter of three years ago as the beginning forecast. Make two forecasts: one with $\alpha = 0.10$ and one with $\alpha = 0.30$.
b. Using the MAD method of testing the forecasting model's performance, plus actual data from three years ago through the second quarter of this year, how well did the model perform?
c. Using the decomposition of a time series method of forecasting, forecast earnings per share for the last two quarters of this year and all four quarters of next year. Is there a seasonal factor in the earnings?
d. Using your forecasts, comment on each company.

30. Mark Price, the new productions manager for Speakers and Company, needs to find out which variable most affects the demand for their line of stereo speakers. He is uncertain whether the unit price of the product or the effects of increased marketing are the main drivers in sales and wants to use regression analysis to figure out which factor drives more demand for its particular market. Pertinent information was collected by an extensive marketing project that lasted over the past 12 years (year 1 is data from 12 years ago) and was reduced to the data that follow.

Year	Sales/Unit (thousands)	Price/Unit	Advertising ($000)
1	400	280	600
2	700	215	835
3	900	211	1,100
4	1,300	210	1,400
5	1,150	215	1,200
6	1,200	200	1,300
7	900	225	900
8	1,100	207	1,100
9	980	220	700
10	1,234	211	900
11	925	227	700
12	800	245	690

a. Perform a regression analysis based on these data using Excel. Answer the following questions based on your results.
b. Which variable, price or advertising, has a larger effect on sales and how do you know?
c. Predict average yearly speaker sales for Speakers and Company based on the regression results if the price was $300 per unit and the amount spent on advertising (in thousands) was $900.

31. Sales by quarter for last year and the first three quarters of this year were as follows.

	Quarter			
	I	II	III	IV
Last year	$23,000	$27,000	$18,000	$9,000
This year	19,000	24,000	15,000	

Using a procedure that you develop that captures the change in demand from last year to this year and also the seasonality in demand, forecast expected sales for the fourth quarter of this year.

32. The following are sales revenues for a large utility company for years 1 through 11. Forecast revenue for years 12 through 15. Because we are forecasting four years into the future, you will need to use linear regression as your forecasting method.

Year	Revenue (millions)
1	$4,865.9
2	5,067.4
3	5,515.6
4	5,728.8
5	5,497.7
6	5,197.7
7	5,094.4
8	5,108.8
9	5,550.6
10	5,738.9
11	5,860.0

LO 18–3

33. What forecasting technique makes use of written surveys or telephone interviews?
34. Which qualitative forecasting technique was developed to ensure that the input from every participant in the process is weighted equally?
35. When forecasting demand for new products, sometimes firms will use demand data from similar existing products to help forecast demand for the new product. What technique is this an example of?

LO 18–4

36. Often, firms will work with their partners across the supply chain to develop forecasts and execute production and distribution between the partners. What technique does this describe?
37. How many steps are there in collaborative planning, forecasting, and replenishment (CPFR)?
38. What is the first step in CPFR?

ANALYTICS EXERCISE: FORECASTING SUPPLY CHAIN DEMAND—STARBUCKS CORPORATION (LO 18–2)

As we discussed at the beginning of the chapter, Starbucks has a large, global supply chain that must efficiently supply over 17,000 stores. Although the stores might appear to be very similar, they are actually very different. Depending on the location of the store, its size, and the profile of the customers served, Starbucks management configures the store offerings to take maximum advantage of the space available and customer preferences.

Starbucks' actual distribution system is much more complex, but for the purpose of our exercise let's focus on a single item that is currently distributed through five distribution centers in the United States. Our item is a logo-branded coffeemaker that is sold at some of the larger retail stores. The coffeemaker has been a steady seller over the years due to its reliability and rugged construction. Starbucks does not consider this a seasonal product, but there is some variability in demand. Demand for the product over the past 13 weeks is shown in the following table.

The demand at the distribution centers (DCs) varies between about 40 units, on average, per week in Atlanta and 48 units in Dallas. The current quarter's data are pretty close to the demand shown in the table.

Management would like you to experiment with some forecasting models to determine what should be used in a new system to be implemented. The new system is programmed to use one of two forecasting models: simple moving average or exponential smoothing.

Week	1	2	3	4	5	6	7	8	9	10	11	12	13	Average
Atlanta	33	45	37	38	55	30	18	58	47	37	23	55	40	40
Boston	26	35	41	40	46	48	55	18	62	44	30	45	50	42
Chicago	44	34	22	55	48	72	62	28	27	95	35	45	47	47
Dallas	27	42	35	40	51	64	70	65	55	43	38	47	42	48
LA	32	43	54	40	46	74	40	35	45	38	48	56	50	46
Total	162	199	189	213	246	288	245	204	236	257	174	248	229	222

Questions

1. Consider using a simple moving average model. Experiment with models using five weeks' and three weeks' past data. The past data in each region are given as follows (week −1 is the week before week

1 in the table, −2 is two weeks before week 1, etc.). Evaluate the forecasts that would have been made over the 13 weeks using the overall (at the end of the 13 weeks) mean absolute deviation, mean absolute percent error, and tracking signal as criteria.

Week	−5	−4	−3	−2	−1
Atlanta	45	38	30	58	37
Boston	62	18	48	40	35
Chicago	62	22	72	44	48
Dallas	42	35	40	64	43
LA	43	40	54	46	35
Total	254	153	244	252	198

2. Next, consider using a simple exponential smoothing model. In your analysis, test two alpha values, 0.2 and 0.4. Use the same criteria for evaluating the model as in part 1. When using an alpha value of 0.2, assume that the forecast for week 1 is the past three-week average (the average demand for periods −3, −2, and −1). For the model using an alpha of 0.4, assume that the forecast for week 1 is the past five-week average.
3. Starbucks is considering simplifying the supply chain for their coffeemaker. Instead of stocking the coffeemaker in all five distribution centers, they are considering only supplying it from a single location. Evaluate this option by analyzing how accurate the forecast would be based on the demand aggregated across all regions. Use the model that you think is best from your analysis of parts 1 and 2. Evaluate your new forecast using mean absolute deviation, mean absolute percent error, and the tracking signal.
4. What are the advantages and disadvantages of aggregating demand from a forecasting view? Are there other things that should be considered when going from multiple DCs to a DC?

PRACTICE EXAM

In each of the following, name the term defined or answer the question. Answers are listed at the bottom.

1. This is a type of forecast used to make long-term decisions, such as where to locate a warehouse or how many employees to have in a plant next year.
2. This is the type of demand that is most appropriate for using forecasting models.
3. This is a term used for actually influencing the sale of a product or service.
4. These are the six major components of demand.
5. This type of analysis is most appropriate when the past is a good predictor of the future.
6. This is identifying and separating time series data into components of demand.
7. If the demand in the current week was 102 units and we had forecast it to be 125, what would be next week's forecast using an exponential smoothing model with an alpha of 0.3?
8. Assume you are using exponential smoothing with an adjustment for trend. Demand is increasing at a very steady rate of about five units per week. Would you expect your alpha and delta parameters to be closer to one or zero?
9. Your forecast is, on average, incorrect by about 10 percent. The average demand is 130 units. What is the MAD?
10. If the tracking signal for your forecast was consistently positive, you could then say this about your forecasting technique.
11. What would you suggest to improve the forecast described in question 10?
12. You know that sales are greatly influenced by the amount your firm advertises in the local paper. What forecasting technique would you suggest trying?
13. What forecasting tool is most appropriate when closely working with customers dependent on your products?

Answers to Practice Exam 1. Strategic forecast 2. Independent demand 3. Demand management 4. Average demand for the period, trend, seasonal elements, cyclical elements, random variation, and autocorrelation 5. Time series analysis 6. Decomposition 7. 118 units 8. Zero 9. 13 10. Biased, consistently too low 11. Add a trend component 12. Causal relationship forecasting (using regression) 13. Collaborative planning, forecasting, and replenishment (CPFR)

For PowerPoint lecture slides, Solutions Manual, Test Bank, Data files for solved examples, Excel Templates, Step-by-Step Solved Examples in video format, Tutorial Videos and many more, scan the adjacent **QR code**, or **visit http://www.mhhe.com/sie-chase15e**

Chapter 19

Sales and Operations Planning

LEARNING OBJECTIVES

LO19-1 Understand what sales and operations planning is and how it coordinates manufacturing, logistics, service, and marketing plans

LO19-2 Construct and evaluate aggregate plans that employ different strategies for meeting demand

LO19-3 Explain yield management and why it is an important strategy

Consider the dilemma of the executive staff at Southwest Manufacturing Company at their monthly planning meeting. Things are tough and it seems that everyone is complaining.

- The president has been reviewing reports from marketing. "We keep running out of product. How can we sell stuff if we don't have it when the customer wants it? And the response time on customer questions is terrible. It is often days between when the question comes in and when we get around to responding. This cannot continue."
- The supply chain executive responds, "Our forecast from marketing was terrible last month. They sold 30 percent more than they had forecast. How do you expect us to keep this stuff in stock?"

© Lane Oatey/Getty Images RF

- Marketing chimes in with, "We had a great month, what are you complaining about? We told you mid-month that things were going well." The plant manager replies, "There is no way that we can react that quickly. What are you expecting from us? Our schedules are fixed six weeks into the future. You want us to be efficient, don't you?"
- The president asks, "Should we just bump everything up 30 percent for next month? I sure don't want to run out again."
- Marketing responds, "Only if you are willing to keep running that 2-for-1 deal that we

were running last month. Our customers pass that discount on to their customers and that keeps sales going. I am not sure that we are making much money when we discount like that."

- This wakes up the finance guy, "Oh, so now I understand why we have such a big negative revenue variance. We can't give the stuff away anymore."

This struggle between those selling the product, those supplying the product, and those keeping track of the money goes on month after month. The problem is one of matching supply with demand at a price that makes the firm profitable. It is a difficult balancing act and one that plays out at most companies.

Today, many companies are using a business process called sales and operations planning (S&OP) to help avoid such problems. This chapter defines S&OP and discusses how to make it work.

WHAT IS SALES AND OPERATIONS PLANNING?

LO 19-1

Understand what sales and operations planning is and how it coordinates manufacturing, logistics, service, and marketing plans

In this chapter, we focus on the **aggregate operations plan**, which translates annual and quarterly business plans into broad labor and output plans for the intermediate term (3 to 18 months). The objective of the aggregate operations plan is to minimize the cost of resources required to meet demand over that period.

Aggregate operations plan
A plan for labor and production for the intermediate term with the objective to minimize the cost of resources needed to meet demand.

Sales and operations planning is a process that helps firms provide better customer service, lower inventory, shorten customer lead times, stabilize production rates, and give top management a handle on the business. The process is designed to coordinate the key business activities related to marketing and sales with the operations and supply chain activities that are required to meet demand over time. Depending on the situation, business activities may include the timing of newspaper advertisements, volume discounting of discontinued items, and major direct sales promotions, for example. The process is designed to help a company get demand and supply in balance and keep them in balance over time. The process requires teamwork among marketing and sales, distribution and logistics, operations, finance, and product development.

The sales and operations planning process consists of a series of meetings, finishing with a high-level meeting where key intermediate-term decisions are made. The end goal is an agreement between various departments on the best course of action to achieve the optimal balance between supply and demand. The idea is to put the operational plan in line with the business plan.

This balance must occur at an aggregate level and also at the detailed individual product level. By *aggregate* we mean at the level of major groups of products. Over time, we need to ensure that we have enough total capacity. Because demand is often quite dynamic, it is important that we monitor our expected needs 3 to 18 months or further into the future. When planning this far into the future, it is difficult to know exactly how many of a particular product we will need, but we should be able to know how a larger group of similar products should sell. The term *aggregate* refers to this group of products. Given that we have enough aggregate capacity, our individual product schedulers, working within aggregate capacity constraints, can handle the daily and weekly launching of individual product orders to meet short-term demand.

An Overview of Sales and Operations Planning Activities

Exhibit 19.1 positions sales and operations planning relative to other major operations planning activities. The term **sales and operations planning** was coined by companies to refer to the process that helps firms keep demand and supply in balance. In operations management, this process traditionally was called *aggregate planning.* The new terminology is meant to capture the importance of cross-functional work. Typically, this activity requires an integrated effort with cooperation from sales, distribution and logistics, operations, finance, and product development.

Sales and operations planning
The process that companies use to keep demand and supply in balance by coordinating manufacturing, distribution, marketing, and financial plans.

EXHIBIT 19.1

Overview of Major Operations and Supply Planning Activities

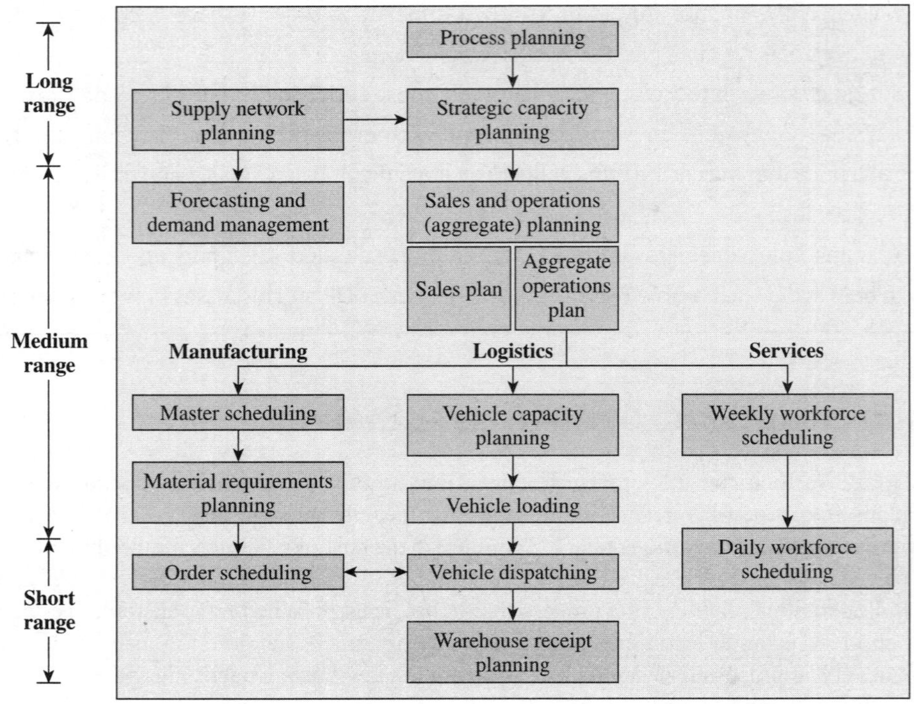

Product family of similar earphones produced by the same company.

Within sales and operations planning, marketing develops a sales plan that extends through the next 3 to 18 months. This sales plan typically is stated in units of aggregate product groups and often is tied into sales incentive programs and other marketing activities. The operations side develops an operations plan as an output of the process, which is discussed in depth in this chapter. By focusing on aggregate product and sales volumes, the marketing and operations functions are able to develop plans for the way demand will be met. This is a particularly difficult task when there are significant changes in demand over time as a result of market trends or other factors.

Aggregation on the supply side is done by product families, and on the demand side it is done by groups of customers. Individual product production schedules and matching customer orders can be handled more readily as a result of the sales and operations planning process. Typically, sales and operations planning occurs on a monthly cycle. Sales and operations planning links a company's strategic plans and business plan to its detailed operations and supply processes. These detailed processes include manufacturing, logistics, and service activities, as shown in Exhibit 19.1.

Long-range planning
One year or more.

Intermediate-range planning
Involves a time period of usually 3 to 18 months.

Short-range planning
From a day to six months.

In Exhibit 19.1, the time dimension is shown as long, intermediate, and short range. **Long-range planning** generally is done annually, focusing on a horizon greater than one year. **Intermediate-range planning** usually covers a period from 3 to 18 months, with time increments that are weekly, monthly, or sometimes quarterly. **Short-range planning** covers a period from one day to six months, with daily or weekly time increments.

Long-range planning activities are done in two major areas. The first is the design of the manufacturing and service processes that produce the products of the firm, and the second is the design of the logistics activities that deliver products to the customer. Process planning deals with determining the specific technologies and procedures required to produce a product or service. Strategic capacity planning deals with determining the long-term capabilities (such as size and scope) of the production systems. Similarly, from a logistics point of view, supply network planning determines how the product will be distributed to the customer on the outbound side, with decisions relating to the location of warehouses and the types of transportation systems to be used. On the inbound side, supply network planning involves decisions relating to outsourcing production, the selection of parts and component suppliers, and related decisions.

Intermediate-term activities include forecasting and demand management, as well as sales and operations planning. The determination of expected demand is the focus of forecasting and demand management. From these data, detailed sales and operations plans for meeting these requirements are made. The sales plans are inputs to sales force activities, which are the focus of marketing books. The operations plan provides input into the manufacturing, logistics, and service planning activities of the firm. Master scheduling and material requirements planning are designed to generate detailed schedules that indicate when parts are needed for manufacturing activities. Coordinated with these plans are the logistics plans needed to move the parts and finished products through the supply chain.

Short-term details are focused mostly on scheduling production and shipment orders. These orders need to be coordinated with the actual vehicles that transport material through the supply chain. On the service side, short-term scheduling of employees is needed to ensure that adequate customer service is provided and fair worker schedules are maintained.

The Aggregate Operations Plan

The aggregate operations plan is concerned with setting production rates by product group or other broad categories for the intermediate term (3 to 18 months). Note again from Exhibit 19.1 that the aggregate plan precedes the master schedule. *The main purpose of the aggregate plan is to specify the optimal combination of production rate, workforce level, and inventory on hand.* **Production rate** refers to the number of units completed per unit of time (such as per hour or per day). **Workforce level** is the number of workers needed for production (production = production rate × workforce level). **Inventory on hand** is unused inventory carried over from the previous period.

Production rate
Number of units completed per unit of time.

Workforce level
Number of workers needed in a period.

Inventory on hand
Inventory carried from the previous period.

Here is a formal statement of the aggregate planning problem: Given the demand forecast F_t for each period t in the planning horizon that extends over T periods, determine the production level P_t, inventory level I_t, and workforce level W_t for periods $t = 1, 2, \ldots, T$ that minimize the relevant costs over the planning horizon.

The form of the aggregate plan varies from company to company. In some firms, it is a formalized report containing planning objectives and the planning premises on which it is based. In other companies, particularly smaller ones, the owner may make simple calculations of workforce needs that reflect a general staffing strategy.

The process by which the plan itself is derived also varies. One common approach is to derive it from the corporate annual plan, as shown in Exhibit 19.1. A typical corporate plan contains a section on manufacturing that specifies how many units in each major product line need to be produced over the next 12 months to meet the sales forecast. The planner takes this information and attempts to determine how best to meet these requirements with available resources. Alternatively, some organizations combine output requirements into equivalent units and use this as the basis for the aggregate plan. For example, a division of General Motors may be asked to produce a certain number of cars of all types at a particular facility. The production planner would then take the average labor hours required for all models as a basis for the overall aggregate plan. Refinements to this plan, specifically model types to be produced, would be reflected in shorter-term production plans.

Another approach is to develop the aggregate plan by simulating various master production schedules and calculating corresponding capacity requirements to see if adequate labor and equipment exist at each workcenter. If capacity is inadequate, additional requirements for overtime, subcontracting, extra workers, and so forth are specified for each product line and combined into a rough-cut plan. This plan is then modified by cut-and-try or mathematical methods to derive a final and (one hopes) lower-cost plan.

EXHIBIT 19.2

Required Inputs to the Production Planning System

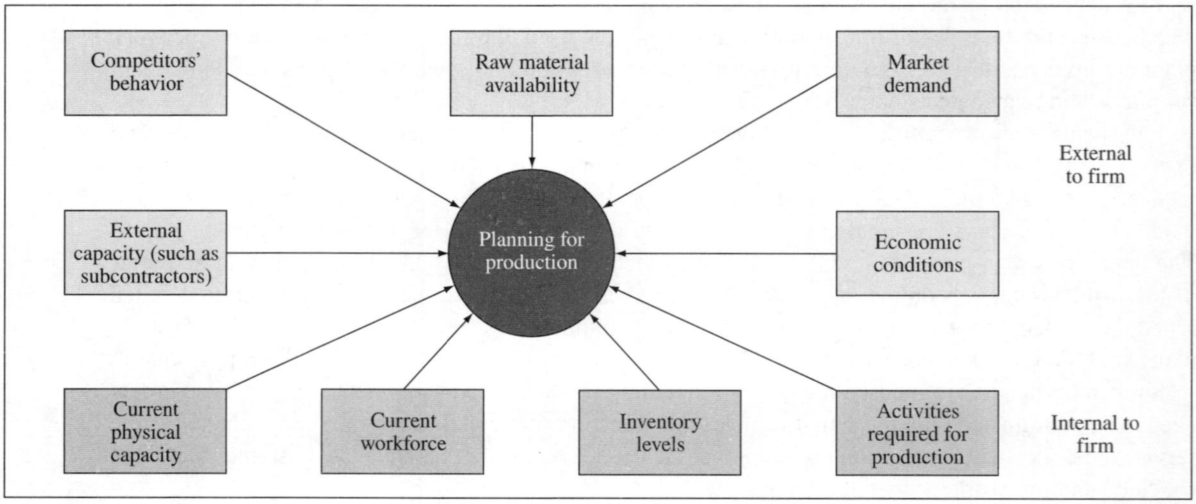

The Production Planning Environment Exhibit 19.2 illustrates the internal and external factors that constitute the production planning environment. In general, the external environment is outside the production planner's direct control, but in some firms, demand for the product can be managed. Through close cooperation between marketing and operations, promotional activities and price cutting can be used to build demand during slow periods. Conversely, when demand is strong, promotional activities can be curtailed and prices raised to maximize the revenues from those products or services that the firm has the capacity to provide. The current practices in managing demand will be discussed later in the section titled "Yield Management."

Complementary products may work for firms facing cyclical demand fluctuations. For instance, lawnmower manufacturers will have strong demand for spring and summer, but weak demand during fall and winter. Demands on the production system can be smoothed out by producing a complementary product with high demand during fall and winter, and low demand during spring and summer (for instance, snowmobiles, snowblowers, or leafblowers). With services, cycles are more often measured in hours than months. Restaurants with strong demand during lunch and dinner will often add a breakfast menu to increase demand during the morning hours.

But even so, there are limits to how much demand can be controlled. Ultimately, the production planner must live with the sales projections and orders promised by the marketing function, leaving the internal factors as variables that can be manipulated in deriving a production plan. A new approach to facilitate managing these internal factors is termed *accurate response.* This entails refined measurement of historical demand patterns blended with expert judgment to determine when to begin production of particular items. The key element of the approach is clearly identifying those products for which demand is relatively predictable from those for which demand is relatively unpredictable.

Production planning strategies
Plans for meeting demand that involve trade-offs in the number of workers employed, work hours, inventory, and shortages.

The internal factors themselves differ in their controllability. Current physical capacity (plant and equipment) is usually nearly fixed in the short run; union agreements often constrain what can be done in changing the workforce; physical capacity cannot always be increased; and top management may limit the amount of money that can be tied up in inventories. Still, there is always some flexibility in managing these factors, and production planners can implement one or a combination of the **production planning strategies** discussed here.

Production Planning Strategies There are essentially three production planning strategies. These strategies involve trade-offs among the workforce size, work hours, inventory, and backlogs.

1. **Chase strategy.** Match the production rate to the order rate by hiring and laying off employees as the order rate varies. The success of this strategy depends on having a pool of easily trained

© Ingram Publishing/SuperStock RF

© Pixtal/AGE fotostock RF

Water skis and snow skis are examples of complementary products.

applicants to draw on as order volumes increase. There are obvious motivational impacts. When order backlogs are low, employees may feel compelled to slow down out of fear of being laid off as soon as existing orders are completed.

2. **Stable workforce—variable work hours.** Vary the output by varying the number of hours worked through flexible work schedules or overtime. By varying the number of work hours, you can match production quantities to orders. This strategy provides workforce continuity and avoids many of the emotional and tangible costs of hiring and firing associated with the chase strategy.

Strategy

3. **Level strategy.** Maintain a stable workforce working at a constant output rate. Shortages and surpluses are absorbed by fluctuating inventory levels, order backlogs, and lost sales. Employees benefit from stable work hours at the costs of potentially decreased customer service levels and increased inventory costs. Another concern is the possibility of inventoried products becoming obsolete.

When just one of these variables is used to absorb demand fluctuations, it is termed a **pure strategy**; two or more used in combination constitute a **mixed strategy**. As you might suspect, mixed strategies are more widely applied in industry.

Pure strategy
A simple strategy that uses just one option, such as hiring and firing workers, for meeting demand.

Mixed strategy
A more complex strategy that combines options for meeting demand.

Subcontracting In addition to these strategies, managers also may choose to subcontract some portion of production. This strategy is similar to the chase strategy, but hiring and laying off are translated into subcontracting and not subcontracting. Some level of subcontracting can be desirable to accommodate demand fluctuations. However, unless the relationship with the supplier is particularly strong, a manufacturer can lose some control over schedule and quality.

Relevant Costs Four costs are relevant to the aggregate production plan. These relate to the production cost itself, as well as the cost to hold inventory and to have unfilled orders. More specifically, these are

1. **Basic production costs** These are the fixed and variable costs incurred in producing a given product type in a given time period. Included are direct and indirect labor costs and regular as well as overtime compensation.
2. **Costs associated with changes in the production rate** Typical costs in this category are those involved in hiring, training, and laying off personnel. Hiring temporary help is a way of avoiding these costs.

OSCM AT WORK

It's All in the Planning

You're sitting anxiously in the suddenly assembled general manager's staff meeting. Voices are nervously subdued. The rumor mill is in high gear about another initiative-of-the-month about to be loosed among the leery survivors of the last purge. The meeting begins. Amid the tricolor visuals and 3D spreadsheets, the same old message is skeptically received by managers scrambling for politically correct responses in an endless game of shoot the messenger.

This is a familiar scene in corporations around the world. But interestingly, firms such as Advanced Optical Components, a division of Finisar, formerly VCSEL, have learned how to manage the process of successfully matching supply and demand. Advanced Optical Components has developed a new semiconductor laser used in computing, networking, and sensing applications. Forecasting and managing production capacity is a unique challenge for companies with a stream of new and innovative products coming to market. Using a monthly sales and operations planning process, Advanced Optical Components has been able to improve its short- and long-term forecasting accuracy from 60 percent to consistently hitting 95 percent or better. The specific steps within its plan focus the executive team on (1) the demand opportunities for current and new products and (2) the constraints on the organization's ability to produce product to meet this demand. The plan, developed in a monthly sales and operations planning executive meeting, ensures that demand is synchronized with supply, so customers get the product they want, when they want it, while inventory and costs are kept to a minimum.

Advanced Optical Components managers indicated that a critical step was getting the general manager to champion the process. The second step was achieving a complete understanding of required behavior from the team, including committing to a balanced and synchronized demand/supply plan, being accountable for meeting the performance standards, having open and honest communication, not promising what cannot be delivered, and making the decisions needed to address the identified opportunities and constraints.

3. **Inventory holding costs** A major component is the cost of capital tied up in inventory. Other components are storing, insurance, taxes, spoilage, and obsolescence.
4. **Backordering costs** Usually, these are very hard to measure and include costs of expediting, loss of customer goodwill, and loss of sales revenues resulting from backordering.

Budgets To receive funding, operations managers are generally required to submit annual, and sometimes quarterly, budget requests. The aggregate plan is key to the success of the budgeting process. Recall that the goal of the aggregate plan is to minimize the total production-related costs over the planning horizon by determining the optimal combination of workforce levels and inventory levels. Thus, the aggregate plan provides justification for the requested budget amount. Accurate medium-range planning increases the likelihood of (1) receiving the requested budget and (2) operating within the limits of the budget.

In the next section, we provide an example of medium-range planning in a manufacturing setting. This example illustrates the trade-offs associated with different production planning strategies.

LO 19-2

Construct and evaluate aggregate plans that employ different strategies for meeting demand

AGGREGATE PLANNING TECHNIQUES

Companies commonly use simple cut-and-try charting and graphic methods to develop aggregate plans. A cut-and-try approach involves costing out various production planning alternatives and selecting the one that is best. Elaborate spreadsheets are developed to facilitate the decision process. Sophisticated approaches involving linear programming and simulation are often incorporated into these spreadsheets. In the following, we demonstrate a spreadsheet approach to evaluate four strategies for meeting demand for the JC Company. Later, we discuss more sophisticated approaches using linear programming (see Appendix A).

A Cut-and-Try Example: The JC Company

A firm with pronounced seasonal variation normally plans production for a full year to capture the extremes in demand during the busiest and slowest months. But we can illustrate the general principles involved with a shorter horizon. Suppose we wish to set up a production plan for the JC Company's Chinese manufacturing plant for the next six months. We are given the following information.

Analytics

Demand and Working Days

	January	February	March	April	May	June	Totals
Demand forecast	1,800	1,500	1,100	900	1,100	1,600	8,000
Number of working days	22	19	21	21	22	20	125

Costs

Materials	$100.00/unit
Inventory holding cost	$1.50/unit/month
Marginal cost of stock out	$5.00/unit/month
Marginal cost of subcontracting	$20.00/unit ($120 subcontracting cost less $100 material savings)
Hiring and training cost	$200.00/worker
Layoff cost	$250.00/worker
Labor hours required	5/unit
Straight-time cost (first eight hours each day)	$4.00/hour
Overtime cost (time and a half)	$6.00/hour

Inventory

Beginning inventory	400 units
Safety stock	25% of month demand

In solving this problem, we can exclude the material costs. We could have included this $100 cost in all our calculations, but if we assume that a $100 cost is common to each demanded unit, then we need only concern ourselves with the marginal costs. Because the subcontracting cost is $120, our marginal cost that does not include materials is $20.

Note that many costs are expressed in a different form than typically found in the accounting records of a firm. Therefore, do not expect to obtain all these costs directly from such records, but obtain them indirectly from management personnel, who can help interpret the data.

Inventory at the beginning of the first period is 400 units. Because the demand forecast is imperfect, the JC Company has determined that a *safety stock* (buffer inventory) should be established to reduce the likelihood of stock outs. For this example, assume the safety stock should be one-quarter of the demand forecast. (Chapter 20 covers this topic in depth.)

Before investigating alternative production plans, it is often useful to convert demand forecasts into *production requirements,* which take into account the safety stock estimates. In Exhibit 19.3, note that these requirements implicitly assume that the safety stock is never actually used, so that the ending

EXHIBIT 19.3

Aggregate Production Planning Requirements

	January	February	March	April	May	June
Beginning inventory	400	450	375	275	225	275
Demand forecast	1,800	1,500	1,100	900	1,100	1,600
Safety stock (.25 × Demand forecast)	450	375	275	225	275	400
Production requirement (Demand forecast + Safety stock − Beginning inventory)	1,850	1,425	1,000	850	1,150	1,725
Ending inventory (Beginning inventory + Production requirement − Demand forecast)	450	375	275	225	275	400

inventory each month equals the safety stock for that month. For example, the January safety stock of 450 (25 percent of January demand of 1,800) becomes the inventory at the end of January. The production requirement for January is demand plus safety stock minus beginning inventory (1,800 + 450 – 400 = 1,850).

Now we must formulate alternative production plans for the JC Company. Using a spreadsheet, we investigate four different plans with the objective of finding the one with the lowest total cost.

Plan 1. Produce to exact monthly production requirements using a regular eight-hour day by varying workforce size.

Plan 2. Produce to meet expected average demand over the next six months by maintaining a constant workforce. This constant number of workers is calculated by finding the average number of workers required each day over the horizon. Take the total production requirements and multiply by the time required for each unit. Then divide by the total time that one person works over the horizon [(8,000 units × 5 hours per unit) ÷ (125 days × 8 hours per day) = 40 workers]. Inventory is allowed to accumulate, with shortages filled from next month's production by backordering. Negative beginning inventory balances indicate that demand is backordered. In some cases, sales may be lost if demand is not met. The lost sales can be shown with a negative ending inventory balance followed by a zero beginning inventory balance in the next period. Notice that in this plan we use our safety stock in January, February, March, and June to meet expected demand.

Plan 3. Produce to meet the minimum expected demand (April) using a constant workforce on regular time. Subcontract to meet additional output requirements. The number of workers is calculated by locating the minimum monthly production requirement and determining how many workers would be needed for that month [(850 units × 5 hours per unit) ÷ (21 days × 8 hours per day) = 25 workers] and subcontracting any monthly difference between requirements and production.

Plan 4. Produce to meet expected demand for all but the first two months using a constant workforce on regular time. Use overtime to meet additional output requirements. The number of workers is more difficult to compute for this plan, but the goal is to finish June with an ending inventory as close as possible to the June safety stock. By trial and error it can be shown that a constant workforce of 38 workers is the closest approximation.

Key Idea

In practice, there are often many different types of special requirements. These can be due to union contracts, or other factors relating to worker availability, for example.

The next step is to calculate the cost of each plan. This requires the series of simple calculations shown in Exhibit 19.4. Note that the headings in each row are different for each plan because each is a different problem requiring its own data and calculations.

The final step is to tabulate and graph each plan and compare their costs. From Exhibit 19.5 we can see that using subcontractors resulted in the lowest cost (Plan 3). Exhibit 19.6 shows the effects of the four plans. This is a cumulative graph illustrating the expected results on the total production requirement.

Note that we have made one other assumption in this example: The plan can start with any number of workers with no hiring or layoff cost. This usually is the case because an aggregate plan draws on existing personnel, and we can start the plan that way. However, in an actual application, the availability of existing personnel transferable from other areas of the firm may change the assumptions.

Plan 1 is the "S" curve when we chase demand by varying workforce. Plan 2 has the highest average production rate (the line representing cumulative demand has the greatest slope). Using subcontracting in Plan 3 results in it having the lowest production rate. Limits on the amount of overtime available results in Plan 4 being similar to Plan 2.

Each of these four plans focused on one particular cost, and the first three were simple pure strategies. Obviously, there are many other feasible plans, some of which would use a combination of workforce changes, overtime, and subcontracting. The problems at the end of this chapter include examples of such mixed strategies. In practice, the final plan chosen would come from searching a variety of alternatives and future projections beyond the six-month planning horizon we have used.

Keep in mind that the cut-and-try approach does not guarantee finding the minimum-cost solution. However, spreadsheet programs, such as Microsoft Excel, can perform cut-and-try cost estimates in seconds and have elevated this kind of "what if" analysis to a fine art. More sophisticated programs can generate much better solutions without the user having to intercede, as in the cut-and-try method.

EXHIBIT 19.4

Costs of Four Production Plans

Production Plan 1: Exact Production; Vary Workforce							
	January	February	March	April	May	June	Total
Production requirement (from Exhibit 19.3)	1,850	1,425	1,000	850	1,150	1,725	
Production hours required (Production requirement × 5 hr/unit)	9,250	7,125	5,000	4,250	5,750	8,625	
Working days per month	22	19	21	21	22	20	
Hours per month per worker (Working days × 8 hr/day)	176	152	168	168	176	160	
Workers required (Production hours required/Hours per month per worker)	53	47	30	26	33	54	
New workers hired (assuming opening workforce equal to first month's requirement of 53 workers)	0	0	0	0	7	21	
Hiring cost (New workers hired × $200)	$0	$0	$0	$0	$1,400	$4,200	$5,600
Workers laid off	0	6	17	4	0	0	
Layoff cost (Workers laid off × $250)	$0	$1,500	$4,250	$1,000	$0	$0	$6,750
Straight-time cost (Production hours required × $4)	$37,000	$28,500	$20,000	$17,000	$23,000	$34,500	$160,000
						Total cost	$172,350

Production Plan 2: Constant Workforce; Vary Inventory and Stock out							
	January	February	March	April	May	June	Total
Beginning inventory	400	8	−276	−32	412	720	
Working days per month	22	19	21	21	22	20	
Production hours available (Working days per month × 8 hr/day × 40 workers)*	7,040	6,080	6,720	6,720	7,040	6,400	
Actual production (Production hours available/5 hr/unit)	1,408	1,216	1,344	1,344	1,408	1,280	
Demand forecast (from Exhibit 19.3)	1,800	1,500	1,100	900	1,100	1,600	
Ending inventory (Beginning inventory + Actual production − Demand forecast)	8	−276	−32	412	720	400	
Shortage cost (Units short × $5)	$0	$1,380	$160	$0	$0	$0	$1,540
Safety stock (from Exhibit 19.3)	450	375	275	225	275	400	
Units excess (Ending inventory − Safety stock) only if positive amount	0	0	0	187	445	0	
Inventory cost (Units excess × $1.50)	$0	$0	$0	$281	$668	$0	$948
Straight-time cost (Production hours available × $4)	$28,160	$24,320	$26,880	$26,880	$28,160	$25,600	$160,000
						Total cost	$162,488

*(Sum of production requirement in Exhibit 19.3 × 5 hr/unit)/(Sum of production hours available × 8 hr/day) = (8,000 × 5)/(125 × 8) = 40.

Aggregate Planning Applied to Services: Tucson Parks and Recreation Department

Charting and graphic techniques are also useful for aggregate planning in service applications. The following example shows how a city's parks and recreation department could use the alternatives of full-time employees, part-time employees, and subcontracting to meet its commitment to provide a service to the city.

EXHIBIT 19.4

Costs of Four Production Plans *(concluded)*

Production Plan 3: Constant Low Workforce; Subcontract							
	January	February	March	April	May	June	Total
Production requirement (from Exhibit 19.3)	1,850	1,425	1,000	850	1,150	1,725	
Working days per month	22	19	21	21	22	20	
Production hours available (Working days × 8 hr/day × 25 workers)*	4,400	3,800	4,200	4,200	4,400	4,000	
Actual production (Production hours available/5 hr per unit)	880	760	840	840	880	800	
Units subcontracted (Production requirement – Actual production)	970	665	160	10	270	925	
Subcontracting cost (Units subcontracted × $20)	$19,400	$13,300	$3,200	$200	$5,400	$18,500	$60,000
Straight-time cost (Production hours available × $4)	$17,600	$15,200	$16,800	$16,800	$17,600	$16,000	$100,000
						Total cost	$160,000

*Minimum production requirement. In this example, April is minimum of 850 units. Number of workers required for April is (850 × 5)/(21 × 8) = 25.

Productio Plan 4: Constant Workforce Overtime							
	January	February	March	April	May	June	Total
Beginning inventory	400	0	0	177	554	792	
Working days per month	22	19	21	21	22	20	
Production hours available (Working days × 8 hr/day × 38 workers)*	6,688	5,776	6,384	6,384	6,688	6,080	
Regular shift production (Production hours available/5 hr/unit)	1,338	1,155	1,277	1,277	1,338	1,216	
Demand forecast (from Exhibit 19.3)	1,800	1,500	1,100	900	1,100	1,600	
Units available before overtime (Beginning inventory + Regular shift production – Demand forecast). This number has been rounded to the nearest integer.	–62	–345	177	554	792	408	
Units overtime	62	375	0	0	0	0	
Overtime cost (Units overtime × 5 hr/unit × $6/hr.)	$1,860	$10,350	$0	$0	$0	$0	$12,210
Safety stock (from Exhibit 19.3)	450	375	275	225	275	400	
Units excess (Units available before overtime – Safety stock) only if positive amount	0	0	0	329	517	8	
Inventory cost (Units excessive × $1.50)	$0	$0	$0	$494	$776	$12	$1,281
Straight-time cost (Production hours available × $4)	$26,752	$23,104	$25,536	$25,536	$26,752	$24,320	$152,000
						Total cost	$165,491

*Workers determined by trial and error. See text for explanation.

EXHIBIT 19.5

Comparison of Four Plans

Costs	Plan 1: Exact Production; Vary Workforce	Plan 2: Constant Workforce; Vary Inventory and Stock out	Plan 3: Constant Low Workforce; Subcontract	Plan 4: Constant Workforce; Overtime
Hiring	$ 5,600	$ 0	$ 0	$ 0
Layoff	6,750	0	0	0
Excess inventory	0	948	0	1,281
Shortage	0	1,540	0	0
Subcontract	0	0	60,000	0
Overtime	0	0	0	12,210
Straight time	160,000	160,000	100,000	152,000
	$172,350	$162,488	$160,000	$165,491

EXHIBIT 19.6

Four Plans for Satisfying a Production Requirement over the Number of Production Days Available

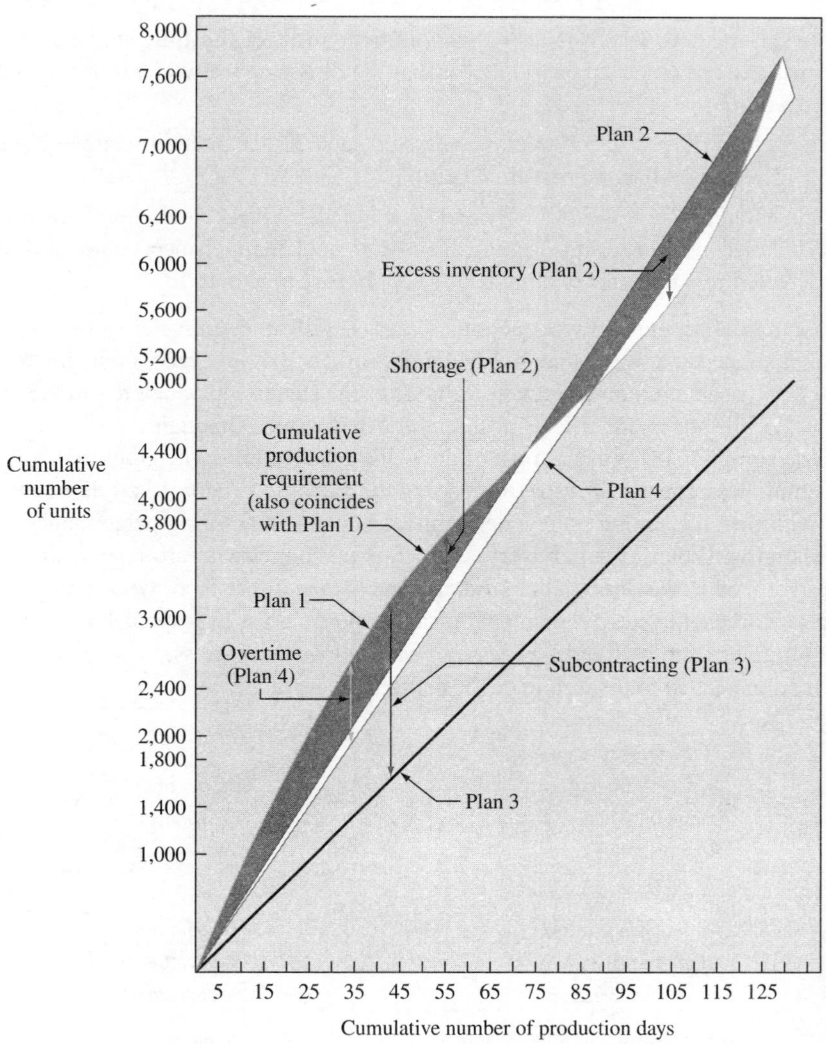

Analytics

Tucson Parks and Recreation Department has an operation and maintenance budget of $9,760,000. The department is responsible for developing and maintaining open space, all public recreational programs, adult sports leagues, golf courses, tennis courts, pools, and so forth. There are 336 full-time-equivalent employees (FTEs). Of these, 216 are full-time permanent personnel who provide the administration and year-round maintenance to all areas. The remaining 120 FTE positions are staffed with part-timers; about three-quarters of them are used during the summer, and the remaining quarter in the fall, winter, and spring seasons. The three-fourths (or 90 FTE positions) show up as approximately 800 part-time summer jobs: lifeguards, baseball umpires, and instructors in summer programs for children. Eight hundred part-time jobs came from 90 FTEs because many last only for a month or two, while the FTE positions are a year long.

Currently, the only parks and recreation work subcontracted amounts to less than $100,000. This is for the golf and tennis pros and for grounds maintenance at the libraries and veterans' cemetery.

Key Ideas

With services, inventory is typically not an issue. Sometimes a few extra employees are added as a buffer to cover employee vacations and other needs.

Because of the nature of city employment, the probable bad public image, and civil service rules, the option to hire and fire full-time help daily or weekly to meet seasonal demand is out of the question. However, temporary part-time help is authorized and traditional. Also, it is virtually impossible to have regular (full-time) staff for all the summer jobs. During the summer months, the approximately 800 part-time employees are staffing many programs that occur simultaneously, prohibiting level scheduling over a normal 40-hour week. A wider variety of skills are required (such as umpires, coaches, lifeguards, and teachers of ceramics, guitar, karate, belly dancing, and yoga) than can be expected from full-time employees.

Three options are open to the department in its aggregate planning:

1. The present method, which is to maintain a medium-level full-time staff and schedule work during off-seasons (such as rebuilding baseball fields during the winter months) and to use part-time help during peak demands.
2. Maintain a lower level of staff over the year and subcontract all additional work presently done by full-time staff (still using part-time help).
3. Maintain an administrative staff only and subcontract all work, including part-time help. (This would entail contracts to landscaping firms and pool maintenance companies as well as to newly created private firms to employ and supply part-time help.)

The common unit of measure of work across all areas is full-time-equivalent jobs or employees. For example, assume in the same week that 30 lifeguards worked 20 hours each, 40 instructors worked 15 hours each, and 35 baseball umpires worked 10 hours each. This is equivalent to $(30 \times 20) + (40 \times 15) + (35 \times 10) = 1{,}550 \div 40 = 38.75$ FTE positions for that week. Although a considerable amount of workload can be shifted to off-season, most of the work must be done when required.

Full-time employees consist of three groups: (1) the skeleton group of key department personnel coordinating with the city, setting policy, determining budgets, measuring performance, and so forth; (2) the administrative group of supervisory and office personnel who are responsible for or whose jobs are directly linked to the direct-labor workers; and (3) the direct-labor workforce of 116 full-time positions. These workers physically maintain the department's areas of responsibility, such as cleaning up, mowing golf greens and ballfields, trimming trees, and watering grass.

Cost information needed to determine the best alternative strategy is

Full-time direct-labor employees	
Average wage rate	$8.90 per hour
Fringe benefits	17% of wage rate
Administrative costs	20% of wage rate
Part-time employees	
Average wage rate	$8.06 per hour
Fringe benefits	11% of wage rate
Administrative costs	25% of wage rate
Subcontracting all full-time jobs	$3.2 million
Subcontracting all part-time jobs	$3.7 million

EXHIBIT 19.7

Actual Demand Requirement for Full-Time Direct Employees and Full-Time-Equivalent (FTE) Part-Time Employees

	Jan.	Feb.	Mar.	Apr.	May	June	July	Aug.	Sept.	Oct.	Nov.	Dec.	Total
Days	22	20	21	22	21	20	21	21	21	23	18	22	252
Full-time employees	66	28	130	90	195	290	325	92	45	32	29	60	
Full-time days*	1,452	560	2,730	1,980	4,095	5,800	6,825	1,932	945	736	522	1,320	28,897
Full-time-equivalent part-time employees	41	75	72	68	72	302	576	72	0	68	84	27	
FTE days	902	1,500	1,512	1,496	1,512	6,040	12,096	1,512	0	1,564	1,512	594	30,240

*Full-time days are derived by multiplying the number of days in each month by the number of workers.

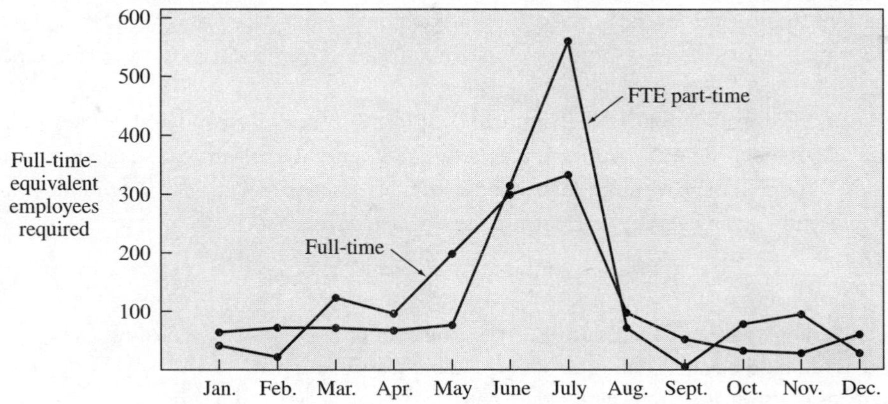

June and July are the peak demand seasons in Tucson. Exhibit 19.7 shows the high requirements for June and July personnel. The part-time help reaches 576 FTE positions (although, in actual numbers, this is approximately 800 different employees). After a low fall and winter staffing level, the demand shown as "full-time direct" reaches 130 in March (when grounds are reseeded and fertilized) and then increases to a high of 325 in July. The present method levels this uneven demand over the year to an average of 116 full-time year-round employees by early scheduling of work. Note that the actual requirement is 115 (28,897/252 = 114.67), but an extra employee has been added as a safety measure. As previously mentioned, no attempt is made to hire and lay off full-time workers to meet this uneven demand.

Exhibit 19.8 shows the cost calculations for all three alternatives and compares the total costs for each alternative. From this analysis, it appears that the department is already using the lowest-cost alternative (Alternative 1).

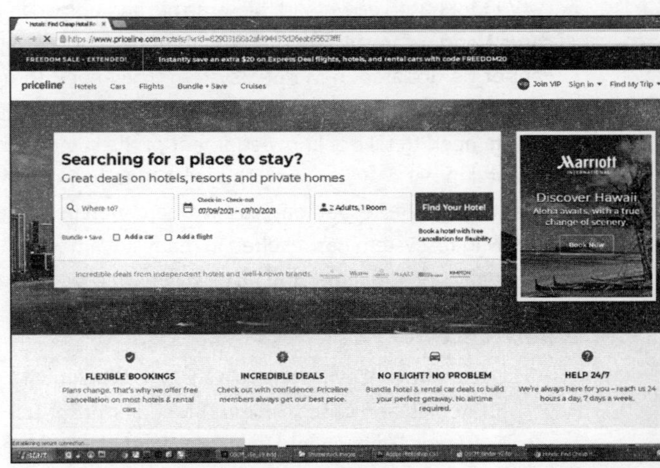

Many Hotel Chains Use Priceline to Sell Excess Capacity at a Discount.

YIELD MANAGEMENT

LO 19-3

Explain yield management and why it is an important strategy

Why is it that the guy sitting next to you on the plane paid half the price you paid for your ticket? Why was a hotel room you booked more expensive when you booked it six months in advance than when you checked in without a reservation (or vice versa)? The answers lie in the practice known as yield management. **Yield management** can be defined as the process of allocating the right type of capacity to the right type of customer at the right price and time to maximize revenue or yield. Yield management can be a powerful approach to making demand more predictable, which is important to aggregate planning.

Yield management

Given limited capacity, the process of allocating it to customers at the right price and time to maximize profit.

OSCM AT WORK

eNagare System in Maruti

Maruti Suzuki India Limited (MSIL), fondly called as Maruti, uses Electronic Nagare (eNagare) system, which helps Maruti to collaborate with its vendors to achieve just-in-time objectives in its inbound side of supply chain. In this approach, MSIL electronically shares its plan with those vendors who are located in or around NCR (National Capital Region) of Delhi, which includes Gurgaon, Faridabad, Ghaziabad, Sohna, etc. This system was implemented in January 2003 to tackle the problem of material accumulation due to multiple sourcing, losses of procurement information, and sub-model variations, and to help to achieve systematic levelized production with synchronized supplies [1]. A similar system was later adopted by Suzuki Japan as the *Jumbiki System*.

A typical planning system in a discrete part manufacturing environment like that of in Maruti involves making plans at three important levels: (i) an annual production plan, (ii) a fortnight production plan involving a plan each on 1st and 15th of the month followed by a firm delivery schedule sent to suppliers for the 5th and 20th of the month, respectively and (iii) a firm daily schedule. An e-Nagare system is useful for planning and scheduling a large set of voluminous items from local vendors where transit time is just a few hours.

In this system, an eNagare, which works like an electronic kanban (refer to Chapter 12), is posted everyday at 06:00 AM for a period of "05:30 PM of the same day till 05:30 PM of the next day." Maruti operates in two shifts and normally the last delivery time is around 23:00 Hrs. Once given an authorization through password, a vendor can login from his place to Maruti's site. Maruti provides following information in a file, which is generally uploaded everyday on Maruti's site.

- Part code
- Quantity to deliver
- Delivery location in Maruti (all unloading and usage points are given unique code)
- Date and Time of delivery—date is required because it may be of one and half day rolling plan
- A unique 12 digit code to be send as bar code form to facilitate gate entry /material receipt and payment.

Vendor has to download the same file and upload in its ERP or computer system to generate the dispatch plan, invoice and receipt cards. Vendors are allowed to enter material at Maruti gate slightly ahead (say 59 minutes) of delivery time and before that material cannot be updated in Maruti's system. They need to upload back its invoice details to Maruti's site and generate a bar-code with details of eNagare number in two parts. First, when material is delivered to specified location, vendor representative or driver of the vehicle need to take acknowledgment of the same and put the card into automatic bar code reader, where half of the card is being retained in bar code scanner. The remaining half of the card is returned to the vendor as POD (Proof of Delivery). Maruti adjusts its inventory on the second day, as any fluctuation in production of Nth day is getting adjusted in (N+2)nd days delivery.

e-Nagare system has resulted in many advantages such as JIT supply, low inventory, less human intervention. Therefore, chances of error are very minimal and faster payment processing is also possible, etc. [2].

References:

1. David Simchi-Levi, Philip Kaminsky, Edith Simchi-Levi and Ravi Shankar, Designing and Managing the Supply Chain: Concepts, Strategies, and Case studies (Third Edition: Special Indian Edition), Tata McGraw-Hill Publishing Company Ltd, New Delhi (2008).
2. G. Trivedi, IT on wheels, Real CIO World, Vol. 2, Issue 15, pp. 26-32 (2007).

Yield management has existed as long as there has been limited capacity for serving customers. However, its widespread scientific application began with American Airlines' computerized reservation system (SABRE), introduced in the mid-1980s. The system allowed the airline to change ticket prices on any routes instantaneously as a function of forecast demand. People Express, a no-frills, low-cost competitor airline, was one of the most famous victims of American's yield management system. Basically, the system enabled hour-by-hour updating on competing routes so that American could match or better prices wherever People Express was flying. The president of People Express realized that the game was lost when his mother flew on American to People's hub for a lower price than People could offer!

From an operational perspective, yield management is most effective when

1. Demand can be segmented by customer.

EXHIBIT 19.8

Three Possible Plans for the Parks and Recreation Department

Alternative 1: Maintain 116 full-time regular direct workers. Schedule work during off-seasons to level workload throughout the year. Continue to use 120 full-time-equivalent (FTE) part-time employees to meet high demand periods.

Costs	Days per Year (Exhibit 19.7)	Hours (Employees × Days × 8 Hours)	Wages (Full-Time, $8.90; Part-Time, $8.06)	Fringe Benefits (Full-Time, 17%; Part-Time, 11%)	Administrative Cost (Full-Time, 20%; Part-Time, 25%)
116 full-time regular employees	252	233,856	$2,081,318	$353,824	$416,264
120 part-time employees	252	241,920	$1,949,875	$214,486	$487,469
Total cost = $5,503,236			$4,031,193	$568,310	$903,733

Alternative 2: Maintain 50 full-time regular direct workers and the present 120 FTE part-time employees. Subcontract jobs, releasing 66 full-time regular employees. Subcontract cost, $2,200,000.

Cost	Days per Year (Exhibit 19.7)	Hours (Employees × Days × 8 Hours)	Wages (Full-Time, $8.90; Part-Time, $8.06)	Fringe Benefits (Full-Time, 17%; Part-Time, 11%)	Administrative Cost (Full-Time, 20%; Part-Time, 25%)	Subcontract Cost
50 full-time employees	252	100,800	$ 897,120	$152,510	$179,424	
120 FTE part-time employees	252	241,920	$1,949,875	$214,486	$487,469	
Subcontracting cost						$2,200,000
Total cost = $6,080,884			$2,846,995	$366,996	$666,893	$2,200,000

Alternative 3: Subcontract all jobs previously performed by 116 full-time regular employees. Subcontract cost $3,200,000. Subcontract all jobs previously performed by 120 FTE part-time employees. Subcontract cost $3,700,000.

Cost	Subcontract Cost
0 full-time employees	
0 part-time employees	
Subcontract full-time jobs	$3,200,000
Subcontract part-time jobs	$3,700,000
Total cost	$6,900,000

2. Fixed costs are high and variable costs are low.
3. Inventory is perishable.
4. Product can be sold in advance.
5. Demand is highly variable.

Hotels illustrate these five characteristics well. They offer one set of rates during the week for the business traveler and another set during the weekend for the vacationer. The variable costs associated with a room (such as cleaning) are low in comparison to the cost of adding rooms to the property. Available rooms cannot be transferred from night to night, and blocks of rooms can be sold to conventions or tours. Finally, potential guests may cut short their stay or not show up at all.

Strategy

Most organizations (such as airlines, rental car agencies, cruise lines, and hotels) manage yield by establishing decision rules for opening or closing rate classes as a function of expected demand and available supply. The methodologies for doing this can be quite sophisticated. A common approach is to forecast demand over the planning horizon and then use marginal analysis to determine the rates that will be charged if demand is forecast as being above or below set control limits around the forecast mean.

Operating Yield Management Systems

A number of interesting issues arise in managing yield. One is that pricing structures must appear logical to the customer and justify the different prices. Such justification, commonly called *rate fences,* may have either a physical basis (such as a room with a view) or a nonphysical basis (like unrestricted access to the Internet). Pricing also should relate to addressing specific capacity problems. If capacity is sufficient for peak demand, price reductions to stimulate off-peak demand should be the focus. If capacity is insufficient, offering deals to customers who arrive during non-peak periods (or creating alternative service locations) may enhance revenue generation.

A second issue is handling variability in arrival or starting times, duration, and time between customers. This entails employing maximally accurate forecasting methods (the greater the accuracy in forecasting demand, the more likely yield management will succeed); coordinated policies on overbooking, deposits, and no-show or cancellation penalties; and well-designed service processes that are reliable and consistent.

A third issue relates to managing the service process. Some strategies include scheduling additional personnel to meet peak demand, increasing customer self-service, creating adjustable capacity, utilizing idle capacity for complementary services, and cross-training employees to create reserves for peak periods.

The fourth and perhaps most critical issue is training workers and managers to work in an environment where overbooking and price changes are standard occurrences that directly impact the customer. Companies have developed creative ways of mollifying overbooked customers. A golf course company offers $100 putters to players who have been overbooked at a popular tee time. Airlines, of course, frequently give overbooked passengers free tickets for other flights.

CONCEPT CONNECTIONS

LO 19–1 Understand what sales and operations planning is and how it coordinates manufacturing, logistics, service, and marketing plans

Summary

- The output of the sales and operation planning process is the aggregate plan.
- The aggregate plan is a high-level operational plan that can be executed by the operations and supply chain functions.
- The process brings together marketing and sales, distribution and logistics, operations, finance, and product development to agree on the best plan to match supply with demand.
- The input into the process is the sales plan developed by marketing.
- Typically, aggregation is done by product families and by groups of customers, and the plan is completed using these aggregate supply and demand quantities.
- Outputs of the plan are planned production rates, aggregate labor requirements, and expected finished good levels.
- Cost minimization is typically a major driver when finding a plan.

Key Terms

Aggregate operations plan A plan for labor and production for the intermediate term with the objective to minimize the cost of resources needed to meet demand.

Sales and operations planning The process that companies use to keep demand and supply in balance by coordinating manufacturing, distribution, marketing, and financial plans.

Long-range planning One year or more.

Intermediate-range planning Involves a time period of usually 3 to 18 months.

Short-range planning From a day to six months.

Production rate Number of units completed per unit of time.

Workforce level Number of workers needed in a period.

Inventory on hand Inventory carried from the previous period.

Production planning strategies Plans for meeting demand that involve trade-offs in the number of workers employed, work hours, inventory, and shortages.

Pure strategy A simple strategy that uses just one option, such as hiring and firing workers, for meeting demand.

Mixed strategy A more complex strategy that combines options for meeting demand.

LO 19–2 Construct and evaluate aggregate plans that employ different strategies for meeting demand

Summary

- Companies commonly use simple cut-and-try (trial-and-error) techniques for analyzing aggregate planning problems. Sophisticated mathematical programming techniques can also be used.
- Strategies vary greatly depending on the situation faced by the company. Plans are typically evaluated based on cost, but it is important to consider the feasibility of the plan (that overtime is not excessive, for example).

LO 19–3 Explain yield management and why it is an important strategy

Summary

- Yield management occurs when a firm adjusts the price of its product or service in order to influence demand. Usually, it is done to make future demand more predictable, which is important to successful sales and operations planning.
- This practice is commonly used in the airline, hotel, casino, and auto retail industries, for example.
- Policies that involve overbooking, requiring deposits, and no-show or cancellation penalties are coordinated with the different pricing scheme.

Key Term

Yield management Given limited capacity, the process of allocating it to customers at the right price and time to maximize profit.

SOLVED PROBLEMS

LO19–2

Jason Enterprises (JE) produces video telephones for the home market. Quality is not quite as good as it could be at this point, but the selling price is low and Jason can study market response while spending more time on R&D.

At this stage, however, JE needs to develop an aggregate production plan for the six months from January through June. You have been commissioned to create the plan. The following information should help.

Demand and Working Days

	January	February	March	April	May	June	Totals
Demand forecast	500	600	650	800	900	800	4,250
Number of working days	22	19	21	21	22	20	125

Costs

Materials	$100.00/unit
Inventory holding cost	$10.00/unit/month
Marginal cost of stock out	$20.00/unit/month
Marginal cost of subcontracting	$100.00/unit ($200 subcontracting cost less $100 material savings)
Hiring and training cost	$50.00/worker
Layoff cost	$100.00/worker
Labor hours required	4/unit
Straight-time cost (first eight hours each day)	$12.50/hour
Overtime cost (time and a half)	$18.75/hour

Inventory

Beginning inventory	200 units
Safety stock required	0% of month demand

What is the cost of each of the following production strategies?

a. Produce exactly to meet demand; vary workforce (assuming opening workforce equal to first month's requirements).
b. Constant workforce; vary inventory and allow shortages only (assuming a workforce of 10).
c. Constant workforce of 10; use subcontracting.

Solution

Aggregate Production Planning Requirements

	January	February	March	April	May	June	Total
Beginning inventory	200	0	0	0	0	0	
Demand forecast	500	600	650	800	900	800	
Safety stock (0.0 × Demand forecast)	0	0	0	0	0	0	
Production requirement (Demand forecast + Safety stock − Beginning inventory)	300	600	650	800	900	800	
Ending inventory (Beginning inventory + Production requirement − Demand forecast)	0	0	0	0	0	0	

Production Plan 1: Exact Production; Vary Workforce

	January	February	March	April	May	June	Total
Production requirement	300	600	650	800	900	800	
Production hours required (Production requirement × 4 hr/unit)	1,200	2,400	2,600	3,200	3,600	3,200	
Working days per month	22	19	21	21	22	20	
Hours per month per worker (Working days × 8 hr/day)	176	152	168	168	176	160	

(continued)

Production Plan 1: Exact Production; Vary Workforce

	January	February	March	April	May	June	Total
Workers required (Production hours required/Hours per month per worker)	7	16	15	19	20	20	
New workers hired (assuming opening workforce equal to first month's requirement of 7 workers)	0	9	0	4	1	0	
Hiring cost (New workers hired × $50)	$0	$450	$0	$200	$50	$0	$700
Workers laid off	0	0	1	0	0	0	
Layoff cost (Workers laid off × $100)	$0	$0	$100	$0	$0	$0	$100
Straight-time cost (Production hours required × $12.50)	$15,000	$30,000	$32,500	$40,000	$45,000	$40,000	$202,500
							Total cost $203,300

Production Plan 2: Constant Workforce; Vary Inventory and Stock Out

	January	February	March	April	May	June	Total
Beginning inventory	200	140	−80	−310	−690	−1150	
Working days per month	22	19	21	21	22	20	
Production hours available (Working days per month × 8 hr/day × 10 workers)*	1,760	1,520	1,680	1,680	1,760	1,600	
Actual production (Production hours available/4 hr/unit)	440	380	420	420	440	400	
Demand forecast	500	600	650	800	900	800	
Ending inventory (Beginning inventory + Actual production − Demand forecast)	140	−80	−310	−690	−1,150	−1,550	
Shortage cost (Units short × $20)	$0	$1,600	$6,200	$13,800	$23,000	$31,000	$75,600
Safety stock	0	0	0	0	0	0	
Units excess (Ending inventory − Safety stock; only if positive amount)	140	0	0	0	0	0	
Inventory cost (Units excess × $10)	$1,400	$0	$0	$0	$0	$0	$1,400
Straight-time cost (Production hours available × $12.50)	$22,000	$19,000	$21,000	$21,000	$22,000	$20,000	$125,000
							Total cost $202,000

*Assume a constant workforce of 10.

Production Plan 3: Constant Workforce; Subcontract

	January	February	March	April	May	June	Total
Production requirement	300	460†	650	800	900	800	
Working days per month	22	19	21	21	22	20	
Production hours available (Working days × 8 hr/day × 10 workers)*	1,760	1,520	1,680	1,680	1,760	1,600	

(continued)

Production Plan 3: Constant Workforce; Subcontract

	January	February	March	April	May	June	Total
Actual production (Production hours available/4 hrs per unit)	440	380	420	420	440	400	
Units subcontracted (Production requirements – Actual production)	0	80	230	380	460	400	
Subcontracting cost (Units subcontracted × $100)	$0	$8,000	$23,000	$38,000	$46,000	$40,000	$155,000
Straight-time cost (Production hours available × $12.50)	$22,000	$19,000	$21,000	$21,000	$22,000	$20,000	$125,000
							Total cost $280,000

*Assume a constant workforce of 10.
†600 – 140 units of beginning inventory in February.

Summary

Plan Description	Hiring	Layoff	Subcontract	Straight Time	Shortage	Excess Inventory	Total Cost
1. Exact production; vary workforce	$700	$100		$202,500			$203,300
2. Constant workforce; vary inventory and shortages				$125,000	$75,600	$1,400	$202,000
3. Constant workforce; subcontract			$155,000	$125,000			$280,000

DISCUSSION QUESTIONS

LO19–1 1. What are the basic controllable variables of a production planning problem? What are the four major costs?

LO19–2 2. Distinguish between pure and mixed strategies in production planning.

3. What are the major differences between aggregate planning in manufacturing and aggregate planning in services?
4. How does forecast accuracy relate, in general, to the practical application of the aggregate planning models discussed in the chapter?
5. In what way does the time horizon chosen for an aggregate plan determine whether it is the best plan for the firm?

LO19–3 6. Define yield management. How does it differ from the pure strategies in production planning?

7. How would you apply yield management concepts to a barbershop? A soft drink vending machine?

OBJECTIVE QUESTIONS

LO19–1 1. Major operations and supply planning activities can be grouped into categories based on the relevant time range of the activity. Into what time range category does sales and operations planning fit?

2. What category of planning covers a period from a day to six months, with daily or weekly time increments?

3. In the agriculture industry, migrant workers are commonly employed to pick crops ready for harvest. They are hired as needed and are laid off once the crops are picked. The realities of the industry make this approach necessary. Which production planning strategy best describes this approach?
4. What is the term for a more complex production strategy that combines approaches from more than one basic strategy?
5. List at least three of the four costs relevant to the aggregate production plan.
6. Which of the four costs relevant to aggregate production planning is the most difficult to accurately measure?
7. Develop a production plan and calculate the annual cost for a firm whose demand forecast is fall, 10,000; winter, 8,000; spring, 7,000; summer, 12,000. Inventory at the beginning of fall is 500 units. At the beginning of fall, you currently have 30 workers, but you plan to hire temporary workers at the beginning of summer and lay them off at the end of summer. In addition, you have negotiated with the union an option to use the regular workforce on overtime during winter or spring if overtime is necessary to prevent stock outs at the end of those quarters. Overtime is *not* available during the fall. Relevant costs are hiring, $100 for each temp; layoff, $200 for each worker laid off; inventory holding, $5 per unit-quarter; backorder, $10 per unit; straight time, $5 per hour; overtime, $8 per hour. Assume that the productivity is 0.5 unit per worker hour, with eight hours per day and 60 days per season. (Answer in Appendix D) **LO19-2**
8. Plan production for a four-month period: February through May. For February and March, you should produce to exact demand forecast. For April and May, you should use overtime and inventory with a stable workforce; *stable* means that the number of workers needed for March will be held constant through May. However, government constraints put a maximum of 5,000 hours of overtime labor per month in April and May (zero overtime in February and March). If demand exceeds supply, then backorders occur. There are 100 workers on January 31. You are given the following demand forecast: February, 80,000; March, 64,000; April, 100,000; May, 40,000. Productivity is four units per worker hour, eight hours per day, 20 days per month. Assume zero inventory on February 1. Costs are: hiring, $50 per new worker; layoff, $70 per worker laid off; inventory holding, $10 per unit-month; straight-time labor, $10 per hour; overtime, $15 per hour; backorder, $20 per unit. Find the total cost of this plan.
9. Plan production for the next year. The demand forecast is: spring, 20,000; summer, 10,000; fall, 15,000; winter, 18,000. At the beginning of spring you have 70 workers and 1,000 units in inventory. The union contract specifies that you may lay off workers only once a year, at the beginning of summer. Also, you may hire new workers only at the end of summer to begin regular work in the fall. The number of workers laid off at the beginning of summer and the number hired at the start of fall should result in planned production levels for summer and fall that equal the demand forecasts for summer and fall, respectively. If demand exceeds supply, use overtime in spring only, which means that backorders could occur in winter. You are given these costs: hiring, $100 per new worker; layoff, $200 per worker laid off; holding, $20 per unit-quarter; backorder cost, $8 per unit; straight-time labor, $10 per hour; overtime, $15 per hour. Productivity is 0.5 unit per worker hour, eight hours per day, 50 days per quarter. Find the total cost.
10. DAT, Inc., needs to develop an aggregate plan for its product line. Relevant data are

Production time	1 hour per unit	Beginning inventory	500 units
Average labor cost	$10 per hour	Safety stock	One-half month
Workweek	5 days, 8 hours each day	Shortage cost	$20 per unit per month
Days per month	Assume 20 workdays per month	Carrying cost	$5 per unit per month

The forecast for next year is

Jan.	Feb.	Mar.	Apr.	May	June	July	Aug.	Sept.	Oct.	Nov.	Dec.
2,500	3,000	4,000	3,500	3,500	3,000	3,000	4,000	4,000	4,000	3,000	3,000

Management prefers to keep a constant workforce and production level, absorbing variations in demand through inventory excesses and shortages. Demand not met is carried over to the following month.

Develop an aggregate plan that will meet the demand and other conditions of the problem. Do not try to find the optimum; just find a good solution and state the procedure you might use to test for a better solution. Make any necessary assumptions. (Answer in Appendix D)

11. Old Pueblo Engineering Contractors creates six-month "rolling" schedules, which are recomputed monthly. For competitive reasons (it would need to divulge proprietary design criteria, methods, and so on), Old Pueblo does not subcontract. Therefore, its only options to meet customer requirements are (1) work on regular time; (2) work on overtime, which is limited to 30 percent of regular time; (3) do customers' work early, which would cost an additional \$5 per hour per month; and (4) perform customers' work late, which would cost an additional \$10 per hour per month penalty, as provided by their contract.

    Old Pueblo has 25 engineers on its staff at an hourly rate of \$30. The overtime rate is \$45. Customers' hourly requirements for the six months from January to June are

January	February	March	April	May	June
5,000	4,000	6,000	6,000	5,000	4,000

    Develop an aggregate plan using a spreadsheet. Assume 20 working days in each month.

12. Alan Industries is expanding its product line to include three new products: A, B, and C. These are to be produced on the same production equipment, and the objective is to meet the demands for the three products using overtime where necessary. The demand forecast for the next four months, in hours required to make each product, is

Product	April	May	June	July
A	800	600	800	1,200
B	600	700	900	1,100
C	700	500	700	850

    Because the products deteriorate rapidly, there is a high loss in quality and, consequently, a high carrying cost when a product is made and carried in inventory to meet future demand. Each hour's production carried into future months costs \$3 per production hour for A, \$4 for Model B, and \$5 for Model C.

    Production can take place either during regular working hours or during overtime. Regular time is paid at \$4 when working on A, \$5 for B, and \$6 for C. The overtime premium is 50 percent of the regular time cost per hour.

    The number of production hours available for regular time and overtime is

	April	May	June	July
Regular time	1,500	1,300	1,800	2,000
Overtime	700	650	900	1,000

    Set up the problem in a spreadsheet and an optimal solution using the Excel Solver. Appendix A describes how to use the Excel Solver.

13. Shoney Video Concepts produces a line of video streaming servers that are linked to computers for storing movies. These devices have very fast access and large storage capacity.

    Shoney is trying to determine a production plan for the next 12 months. The main criterion for this plan is that the employment level is to be held constant over the period. Shoney is continuing in its R&D efforts to develop new applications and prefers not to cause any adverse feelings with the local workforce. For the same reason, all employees should put in full workweeks, even if that is not the lowest-cost alternative. The forecast for servers for the next 12 months is

Month	Forecast Demand	Month	Forecast Demand
January	600	July	200
February	800	August	200
March	900	September	300
April	600	October	700
May	400	November	800
June	300	December	900

Manufacturing cost is $200 per server, equally divided between materials and labor. Inventory storage cost is $5 per month. A shortage of servers results in lost sales and is estimated to cost an overall $20 per unit short.

The inventory on hand at the beginning of the planning period is 200 units. Ten labor hours are required per DVD player. The workday is eight hours.

Develop an aggregate production schedule for the year using a constant workforce. For simplicity, assume 22 working days each month except July, when the plant closes down for three weeks' vacation (leaving seven working days). Assume that total production capacity is greater than or equal to total demand.

14. Develop a production schedule to produce the exact production requirements by varying the workforce size for the following problem. Use the example in the chapter as a guide (Plan 1).

    The monthly forecasts for Product X for January, February, and March are 1,000, 1,500, and 1,200, respectively. Safety stock policy recommends that half of the forecast for that month be defined as safety stock. There are 22 working days in January, 19 in February, and 21 in March. Beginning inventory is 500 units.

    Manufacturing cost is $200 per unit, storage cost is $3 per unit per month, standard pay rate is $6 per hour, overtime rate is $9 per hour, cost of stock out is $10 per unit per month, marginal cost of subcontracting is $10 per unit, hiring and training cost is $200 per worker, layoff cost is $300 per worker, and worker productivity is 0.1 unit per hour. Assume that you start off with 50 workers and that they work 8 hours per day.

15. Helter Industries, a company that produces a line of women's bathing suits, hires temporaries to help produce its summer product demand. For the current four-month rolling schedule, there are three temps on staff and 12 full-time employees. The temps can be hired when needed and can be used as needed, whereas the full-time employees must be paid whether they are needed or not. Each full-time employee can produce 205 suits, while each temporary employee can produce 165 suits per month.

    Demand for bathing suits for the next four months is as follows:

May	June	July	August
3,200	2,800	3,100	3,000

Beginning inventory in May is 403 bathing suits. Bathing suits cost $40 to produce and carrying cost is 24 percent per year.

Develop an aggregate plan that uses the 12 full-time employees each month and a minimum number of temporary employees. Assume that all employees will produce at their full potential each month. Calculate the inventory carrying cost associated with your plan using planned end of month levels.

16. The widespread scientific application of yield management began within what industry? LO19-3
17. Under what type of demand is yield management most effective?
18. In a yield managment system, pricing differences must appear logical and justified to the customer. What is the basis for this justification commonly called?
19. The essence of yield management is the ability to manage what?

ANALYTICS EXERCISE: DEVELOPING AN AGGREGATE PLAN—BRADFORD MANUFACTURING

The Situation

You are the operations manager for a manufacturing plant that produces pudding food products. One of your important responsibilities is to prepare an aggregate plan for the plant. This plan is an important input into the annual budget process. The plan provides information on production rates, manufacturing labor requirements, and projected finished goods inventory levels for the next year.

You make those little boxes of pudding mix on packaging lines in your plant. A packaging line has a number of machines that are linked by conveyors. At the start of the line, the pudding is mixed; it is then placed in small packets. These packets are inserted into the small pudding boxes, which are collected and placed in cases that hold 48 boxes of pudding. Finally, 160 cases are collected and put on a pallet. The pallets are staged in a shipping area from which they are sent to four distribution centers. Over the years, the technology of the packaging lines has improved so that all the different flavors can be made in relatively small batches with no setup time to switch between flavors. The plant has 15 of these lines, but currently only 10 are being used. Six employees are required to run each line.

The demand for this product fluctuates from month to month. In addition, there is a seasonal component, with peak sales before Thanksgiving, Christmas, and Easter each year. To complicate matters, at the end of the first quarter of each year the marketing group runs a promotion in which special deals are made for large purchases. Business is going well, and the company has been experiencing a general increase in sales.

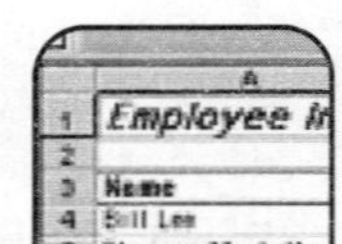

The plant sends product to four large distribution warehouses strategically located in the United States. Trucks move product daily. The amounts shipped are based on maintaining target inventory levels at the warehouses. These targets are calculated based on anticipated weeks of supply at each warehouse. Current targets are set at two weeks of supply.

In the past, the company has had a policy of producing very close to what it expects sales to be because of limited capacity for storing finished goods. Production capacity has been adequate to support this policy.

A sales forecast for next year has been prepared by the marketing department. The forecast is based on quarterly sales quotas, which are used to set up an incentive program for the salespeople. Sales are mainly to the large U.S. retail grocers. The pudding is shipped to the grocers from the distribution warehouses based on orders taken by the salespeople.

Forecast Demand by Quarter (1,000 Case Units)

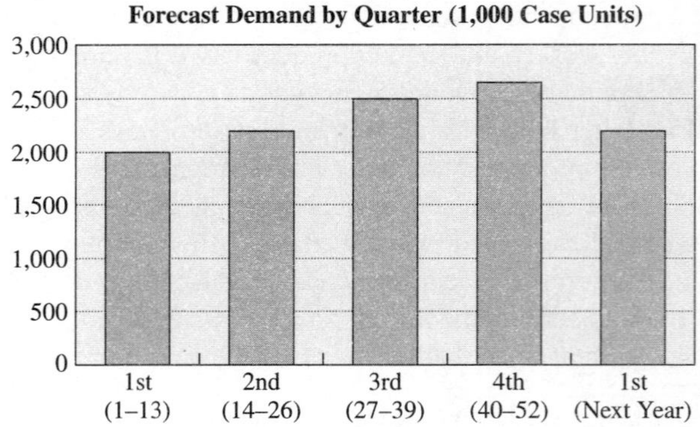

Your immediate task is to prepare an aggregate plan for the coming year. The technical and economic factors that must be considered in this plan are shown next.

Technical and Economic Information

1. The plant runs 5 days each week, and currently is running 10 lines with no overtime. Each line requires six people to run. For planning purposes, the lines are run for 7.5 hours each normal shift. Employees, though, are paid for eight hours' work. It is possible to run up to two hours of overtime each day, but it must be scheduled for a week at a time, and all the lines must run overtime when it is scheduled. Workers are paid \$20.00/hour during a regular shift and \$30.00/hour on overtime. The standard production rate for each line is 450 cases/hour.
2. The marketing forecast for demand is as follows: Q1—2,000; Q2—2,200; Q3—2,500; Q4—2,650; and Q1 (next year)—2,200. These numbers are in 1,000-case units. Each number represents a 13-week forecast.
3. Management has instructed manufacturing to maintain a two-week safety stock supply of pudding inventory in the warehouses. The two-week supply should be based on future expected sales. The following are ending inventory target levels to comply with the safety stock requirement for each quarter: Q1—338; Q2—385; Q3—408; Q4—338.
4. Inventory carrying cost is estimated by accounting to be \$1.00 per case per year. This means that if a case of pudding is held in inventory for an entire year, the cost to just carry that case in inventory is \$1.00. If a case is carried for only one week, the cost is \$1.00/52, or \$0.01923. The cost is proportional to the time carried in inventory. There are 200,000 cases in inventory at the beginning of Q1 (this is 200 cases in the 1,000-case units that the forecast is given in).

5. If a stock out occurs, the item is backordered and shipped at a later date. The cost when a backorder occurs is $2.40 per case due to the loss of goodwill and the high cost of emergency shipping.
6. The human resource group estimates that it costs $5,000 to hire and train a new production employee. It costs $3,000 to lay off a production worker.
7. Make the following assumptions in your cost calculations:

- Inventory costs are based on inventory in excess of the safety stock requirement.
- Backorder costs are incurred on the negative deviation from the planned safety stock requirement, even though planned inventory may be positive.
- Overtime must be used over an entire quarter and should be based on hours per day over that time.

Questions

1. Prepare an aggregate plan for the coming year, assuming that the sales forecast is perfect. Use the worksheet "Bradford Manufacturing" that is in the "19 Sales and Operations Planning" spreadsheet. In the worksheet, an area has been designated for your aggregate plan solution. Supply the number of packaging lines to run and the number of overtime hours for each quarter. You will need to set up the cost calculations in the spreadsheet.

   You may want to try using the Excel Solver to find a low-cost solution. Remember that your final solution needs an integer number of lines and an integer number of overtime hours for each quarter. (Solutions that require 8.9134 lines and 1.256 hours of overtime are not feasible.)

   It is important that your spreadsheet calculations are set up so that any values in the number of lines and overtime hours rows evaluates correctly. Your spreadsheet will be evaluated based on this.
2. Find a solution to the problem that goes beyond just minimizing cost. Prepare a short write-up that describes the process you went through to find your solution and that justifies why you think it is a good solution.

PRACTICE EXAM

In each of the following, name the term defined or answer the question. Answers are listed at the bottom.
1. Term used to refer to the process a firm uses to balance supply and demand.
2. When doing aggregate planning, these are the three general operations–related variables that can be adjusted.
3. A strategy where the production rate is set to match expected demand.
4. When overtime is used to meet demand and avoid the costs associated with hiring and firing.
5. A strategy that uses inventory and backorders as part of the strategy to meet demand.
6. Sometimes a firm may choose to have all or part of the work done by an outside vendor. This is the term used for the approach.
7. If expected demand during the next four quarters is 150, 125, 100, and 75 thousand units, and each worker can produce 1,000 units per quarter, how many workers should be used if a level strategy is being employed?
8. Given the data from question 7, how many workers would be needed for a chase strategy?
9. In a service setting, what general operations–related variable is not available compared to a production setting?
10. The practice of allocating capacity and manipulating demand to make it more predictable.

Answers to Practice Exam 1. Sales and operations planning 2. Production rate, workforce level, inventory 3. Chase 4. Stable workforce – Variable work hours 5. Level strategy 6. Subcontracting 7. 113 8. 150, 125, 100, 75 9. Inventory 10. Yield management

For PowerPoint lecture slides, Solutions Manual, Test Bank, Data files for solved examples, Excel Templates, Step-by-Step Solved Examples in video format, Tutorial Videos and many more, scan the adjacent **QR code**, or **visit http://www.mhhe.com/sie-chase15e**

Chapter 20

Inventory Management

LEARNING OBJECTIVES

LO 20-1 Explain how inventory is used and understand what it costs

LO 20-2 Analyze how different inventory control systems work

LO 20-3 Analyze inventory using the *Pareto principle*

WILL WAREHOUSES BE NEEDED IN THE FUTURE?

Logistics visionaries have talked for years about eliminating—or at least drastically reducing—the role of inventory in modern supply chains. The most efficient, slack-free supply chains, after all, wouldn't require any inventory buffer because supply and demand would be in perfect sync. This vision certainly has its appeal: The death of inventory would mean dramatically reduced logistics costs and simplified fulfillment.

There's no need to write a eulogy for inventory just yet. Most companies haven't honed their networks and technologies well enough to eliminate the need for at least minimal inventory. Logistics managers have to perform a daily, delicate act balancing:

- Transportation costs against fulfillment speed
- Inventory costs against the cost of stock outs
- Customer satisfaction against the cost to serve
- New capabilities against profitability

What's more, two accelerating business trends are making it even harder to synchronize supply chains.

First, global sourcing is forcing supply chains to stretch farther across borders. The goods people consume are increasingly made in some other part of the world, particularly in Asia. This acceleration in global sourcing changes the logistics equation. When goods cross borders, considerations such as fulfillment speed (these are the activities performed once an order is received) and inventory costs get more complicated. Second, powerful retailers and other end customers with clout are starting to push value-added supply chain responsibilities further up the supply chain. More customers are asking manufacturers or third-party logistics providers to label and prepare individual items so the products are ready to go directly to store shelves. With added responsibilities, of course, come added costs. Upstream suppliers are always looking for ways to squeeze more costs out of other areas of the supply chain, such as transportation and distribution.

A growing number of companies are overcoming these barriers by taking a more direct approach to global fulfillment. This direct-to-store approach—also known as distribution center bypass or direct distribution—keeps inventory moving from manufacturer to end customer by eliminating stops at warehouses along the way. Because companies can shrink the fulfillment cycle and eliminate inventory costs, direct-to-store can offer a good balance between fulfillment speed and logistics costs.

Internet-enabled electronic links between supply chain partners have allowed better coordination and collaboration among the various supply chain segments. Meanwhile, at the front of the supply chain, increasingly sophisticated point-of-sale systems can capture product demand patterns. This information can then be fed up the supply chain to manufacturers and components suppliers. More accurate sales-forecasting tools take some of the guesswork out of production and reduce the need for large inventory safety stocks. Tracking and tracing tools are also available to follow orders across borders and through the hands of different supply partners.

In short, companies no longer need as much inventory gathering dust in warehouses because they can better synchronize production and distribution with demand. Direct-to-store lets them keep inventory in motion—across borders and around the world.

You should visualize inventory as stacks of money sitting on forklifts, on shelves, and in trucks and planes while in transit. That's what inventory is—money. For many businesses, inventory is the largest asset on the balance sheet at any given time, even though it is often not very liquid. It is a good idea to try to get your inventory down as far as possible.

The economic benefit from inventory reduction is evident from the following statistics: The average cost of inventory in the United States is 30 to 35 percent of its value. For example, if a firm carries an inventory of $20 million, it costs the firm more than $6 million per year. These costs are due mainly to obsolescence, insurance, and opportunity costs. If the amount of inventory could be reduced to $10 million, for instance, the firm would save over $3 million, which goes directly to the bottom line; that is, the savings from reduced inventory results in increased profit.

UNDERSTANDING INVENTORY MANAGEMENT

LO 20-1 Explain how inventory is used and understand what it costs

This chapter and Chapter 21 present techniques designed to manage inventory in different supply chain settings. In this chapter, the focus is on settings where the desire is to maintain a stock of inventory that can be delivered to our customers on demand. Recall in Chapter 7 the concept of the *customer order decoupling point,* which is a point where inventory is positioned to allow processes or entities in the supply chain to operate independently. For example, if a product is stocked at a retailer, the customer pulls the item from the shelf and the manufacturer never sees a customer order. In this case, inventory acts as a buffer to separate the customer from the manufacturing process. Selection of decoupling points is a strategic decision that determines customer lead times and can greatly impact inventory investment. The closer this point is to the customer, the quicker the customer can be served.

The techniques described in this chapter are suited for managing the inventory at these decoupling points. Typically, there is a trade-off where quicker response to customer demand comes at the expense of greater inventory investment. This is because finished goods inventory is more expensive than raw material inventory. In practice, the idea of a single decoupling point in a supply chain is unrealistic. There may actually be multiple points where buffering takes place.

Key Ideas

A decoupling point is where inventory is carried and allows the "upstream" part of the supply chain to operate relatively independent of the "downstream" part.

Good examples of where the models described in this chapter are used include retail stores, grocery stores, wholesale distributors, hospital suppliers, and suppliers of repair parts needed to fix or maintain equipment quickly. Situations in which it is necessary to have the item "in-stock" are ideal candidates for the models described in this chapter. A distinction that needs to be made with the models included in this chapter is whether this is a one-time purchase—for example, for a seasonal item or for use at a special event—or whether the item will be stocked on an ongoing basis.

Exhibit 20.1 depicts different types of supply chain inventories that would exist in a make-to-stock environment, typical of items directed at the consumer. In the upper echelons of the supply chain, which are supply points closer to the customer, stock usually is kept so that an item can be delivered quickly when a customer need occurs. Of course, there are many exceptions, but in general this is the

EXHIBIT 20.1

Supply Chain Inventories—Make-to-Stock Environment

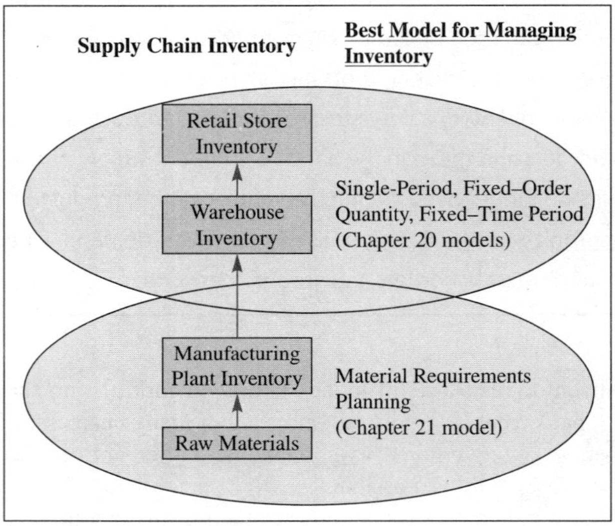

case. The raw materials and manufacturing plant inventory held in the lower echelon potentially can be managed in a special way to take advantage of the planning and synchronization that are needed to efficiently operate this part of the supply chain. In this case, the models in this chapter are most appropriate for the upper echelon inventories (retail and warehouse), and the lower echelon should use the material requirements planning (MRP) technique that will be described in Chapter 21. The applicability of these models could be different for other environments, such as when we produce directly to customer order as in the case of an aircraft manufacturer.

Strategy

The techniques described here are most appropriate when demand is difficult to predict with great precision. In these models, we characterize demand by using a probability distribution and maintain stock so that the risk associated with stockout is managed. For these applications, the following three models are discussed:

1. **The single-period model.** This is used when we are making a one-time purchase of an item. An example might be purchasing T-shirts to sell at a one-time sporting event.
2. **Fixed–order quantity model.** This is used when we want to maintain an item "in-stock," and when we resupply the item, a certain number of units must be ordered each time. Inventory for the item is monitored until it gets down to a level where the risk of stocking out is great enough that we are compelled to order.

3. **Fixed–time period model.** This is similar to the fixed–order quantity model, and is used when the item should be in-stock and ready to use. In this case, rather than monitoring the inventory level and ordering when the level gets down to a critical quantity, the item is ordered at certain intervals of time, for example, every Friday morning. This is often convenient when a group of items is ordered together. An example is the delivery of different types of bread to a grocery store. The bakery supplier may have 10 or more products stocked in a store, and rather than delivering each product individually at different times, it is much more efficient to deliver all 10 together at the same time and on the same schedule.

In this chapter, we want to show not only the mathematics associated with great inventory control but also the "art" of managing inventory. Ensuring accuracy in inventory records is essential to running an efficient inventory control process. Techniques such as ABC analysis and cycle counting are essential to the actual management of the system because they focus attention on the high-value items and ensure the quality of the transactions that affect the tracking of inventory levels.

Inventory is the stock of any item or resource used in an organization. An *inventory system* is the set of policies and controls that monitor levels of inventory and determine what levels should be maintained, when stock should be replenished, and how large orders should be.

Inventory (Goldratt's definition)
All the money that the system has invested in purchasing things it intends to sell (Goldratt's definition).

By convention, *manufacturing inventory* generally refers to items that contribute to or become part of a firm's product output. Manufacturing inventory is typically classified into *raw materials, finished products, component parts, supplies,* and *work-in-process.* In distribution, inventory is classified as *in-transit,* meaning that it is being moved in the system, and *warehouse,* which is inventory in a warehouse or distribution center. Retail sites carry inventory for immediate sale to customers. In services, *inventory* generally refers to the tangible goods to be sold and the supplies necessary to administer the service.

The basic purpose of inventory analysis, whether in manufacturing, distribution, retail, or services, is to specify (1) when items should be ordered and (2) how large the order should be. Many firms are tending to enter into longer-term relationships with vendors to supply their needs for perhaps the entire year. This changes the "when" and "how many to order" to "when" and "how many to deliver."

Purposes of Inventory

All firms (including JIT operations) keep a supply of inventory for the following reasons:

Key Ideas
Every individual item in inventory should be there for a specific purpose. Also, when you see an item in inventory, put a dollar sign on it. Inventory is like piles of money sitting in a warehouse.

1. **To maintain independence of operations.** A supply of materials at a work center allows that center flexibility in operations. For example, because there are costs for making each new production setup, this inventory allows management to reduce the number of setups.

   Independence of workstations is desirable on assembly lines as well. The time it takes to do identical operations will naturally vary from one unit to the next. Therefore, it is desirable to have a cushion of several parts within the workstation so that shorter performance times can compensate for longer performance times. This way, the average output can be fairly stable.

2. **To meet variation in product demand.** If the demand for the product is known precisely, it may be possible (though not necessarily economical) to produce the product to exactly meet the demand. Usually, however, demand is not completely known, and a safety or buffer stock must be maintained to absorb variation.

3. **To allow flexibility in production scheduling.** A stock of inventory relieves the pressure on the production system to get the goods out. This causes longer lead times, which permit production planning for smoother flow and lower-cost operation through larger lot-size production. High setup costs, for example, favor producing a larger number of units once the setup has been made.

4. **To provide a safeguard for variation in raw material delivery time.** When material is ordered from a vendor, delays can occur for a variety of reasons: a normal variation in shipping time, a shortage of material at the vendor's plant causing backlogs, an unexpected strike at the vendor's plant or at one of the shipping companies, a lost order, or a shipment of incorrect or defective material.

Elevated view of a large distribution warehouse
© Alistair Berg/Getty Images RF

5. **To take advantage of economic purchase order size.** There are costs to place an order: labor, phone calls, typing, postage, and so on. Therefore, the larger each order is, the fewer the orders that need be written. Also, shipping costs favor larger orders—the larger the shipment, the lower the per-unit cost.
6. **Many other domain-specific reasons.** Depending on the situation, inventory may need to be carried. For example, in-transit inventory is material being moved from the suppliers to customers and depends on the order quantity and the transit lead time. Another example is inventory that is bought in anticipation of price changes such as fuel for jet planes or semiconductors for computers. There are many other examples.

For each of the preceding reasons (especially for items 3, 4, and 5), be aware that inventory is costly and large amounts are generally undesirable. Long cycle times are caused by large amounts of inventory, which are undesirable as well.

Inventory Costs

In making any decision that affects inventory size, the following costs must be considered:

1. **Holding (or carrying) costs.** This broad category includes the costs for storage facilities, handling, insurance, pilferage, breakage, obsolescence, depreciation, taxes, and the opportunity cost of capital. Obviously, high holding costs tend to favor low inventory levels and frequent replenishment.
2. **Setup (or production change) costs.** To make each different product involves obtaining the necessary materials, arranging specific equipment setups, filling out the required papers, appropriately charging time and materials, and moving out the previous stock of material.

   If there were no costs or loss of time in changing from one product to another, many small lots would be produced. This would reduce inventory levels, with a resulting savings in cost. One challenge today is to try to reduce these setup costs to permit smaller lot sizes. (This is the goal of a JIT system.)
3. **Ordering costs.** These costs refer to the managerial and clerical costs to prepare the purchase or production order. Ordering costs include all the details, such as counting items and calculating order quantities. The costs associated with maintaining the system needed to track orders are also included in ordering costs.

4. **Shortage costs.** When the stock of an item is depleted, an order for that item must either wait until the stock is replenished or be canceled. When the demand is not met and the order is canceled, this is referred to as a stock out. A backorder is when the order is held and filled at a later date when the inventory for the item is replenished. There is a trade-off between carrying stock to satisfy demand and the costs resulting from stock outs and backorders. This balance is sometimes difficult to obtain because it may not be possible to estimate lost profits, the effects of lost customers, or lateness penalties. Frequently, the assumed shortage cost is little more than a guess, although it is usually possible to specify a range of such costs.

Establishing the correct quantity to order from vendors or the size of lots submitted to the firm's productive facilities involves a search for the minimum total cost resulting from the combined effects of four individual costs: holding costs, setup costs, ordering costs, and shortage costs. Of course, the timing of these orders is a critical factor that may impact inventory cost.

Independent versus Dependent Demand

In inventory management, it is important to understand the trade-offs involved in using different types of inventory control logic. Exhibit 20.2 is a framework that shows how characteristics of demand, transaction cost, and the risk of obsolete inventory map into different types of systems. The systems in the upper left of the exhibit are described in this chapter, and those in the lower right in Chapter 21.

EXHIBIT 20.2

Inventory-Control-System Design Matrix: Framework Describing Inventory Control Logic

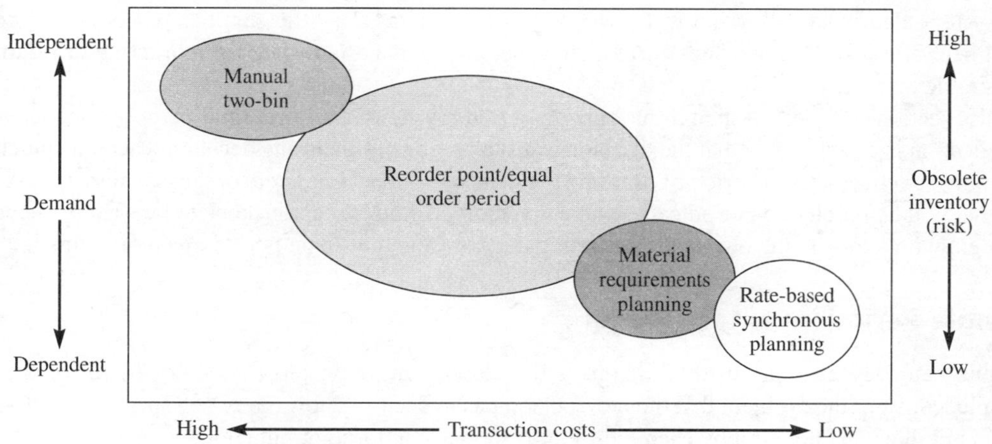

Transaction cost is dependent on the level of integration and automation incorporated in the system. Manual systems such as simple *two-bin* logic depend on human posting of the transactions to replenish inventory, which is relatively expensive compared to using a computer to automatically detect when an item needs to be ordered. Integration relates to how connected systems are. For example, it is common for orders for material to be automatically transferred to suppliers electronically and for these orders to be automatically captured by the supplier inventory control system. This type of integration greatly reduces transaction cost.

The risk of obsolescence is also an important consideration. If an item is used infrequently or only for a very specific purpose, there is considerable risk in using inventory control logic that does not track the specific source of demand for the item. Further, items that are sensitive to technical obsolescence, such as computer memory chips and processors, need to be managed carefully based on actual need to reduce the risk of getting stuck with inventory that is outdated.

An important characteristic of demand relates to whether demand is derived from an end item or is related to the item itself. We use the terms **independent demand** and **dependent demand** to describe this characteristic. Briefly, the distinction between independent and dependent demand is

Independent demand
The demands for these items are unrelated to each other, or to activities that can be predicted with certainty.

Dependent demand
The need for an item is a direct result of the need for some other item, usually an item of which it is a part. Also, when the demand for the item can be predicted with accuracy due to a schedule or specific activitity.

this: In independent demand, the demands for various items are unrelated to each other. For example, a workstation may produce many parts that are unrelated but that meet some external demand requirement. In dependent demand, the need for any one item is a direct result of the need for some other item, usually a higher-level item of which it is part.

In concept, dependent demand is a relatively straightforward computational problem. Required quantities of a dependent-demand item are simply computed, based on the number needed in each higher-level item in which it is used. For example, if an automobile company plans on producing 500 cars per day, then obviously it will need 2,000 wheels and tires (plus spares). The number of wheels and tires needed is *dependent* on the production levels and is not derived separately. The demand for cars, on the other hand, is *independent*—it comes from many sources external to the automobile firm and is not a part of other products; it is unrelated to the demand for other products.

To determine the quantities of independent items that must be produced, firms usually turn to their sales and market research departments. They use a variety of techniques, including customer surveys, forecasting techniques, and economic and sociological trends, as we discussed in Chapter 18 on forecasting. Because independent demand is uncertain, extra units must be carried in inventory. This chapter presents models to determine how many units need to be ordered, and how many extra units should be carried to reduce the risk of stocking out.

LO 20-2

Analyze how different inventory control systems work

INVENTORY CONTROL SYSTEMS

An inventory system provides the organizational structure and the operating policies for maintaining and controlling goods to be stocked. The system is responsible for ordering and receipt of goods: timing the order placement and keeping track of what has been ordered, how much, and from whom. The system also must follow up to answer such questions as: Has the supplier received the order? Has it been shipped? Are the dates correct? Are the procedures established for reordering or returning undesirable merchandise?

This section divides systems into single-period systems and multiple-period systems. The classification is based on whether the decision is just a one-time purchasing decision where the purchase is designed to cover a fixed period of time and the item will not be reordered, or the decision involves an item that will be purchased periodically where inventory should be kept in stock to be used on demand. We begin with a look at the one-time purchasing decision and the single-period inventory model.

A Single-Period Inventory Model

Single-period problem
Answers the question of how much to order when an item is purchased only one time and it is expected that it will be used and then not reordered.

Certainly, an easy example to think about is the classic **single-period** (newsperson) **problem**. For example, consider the problem that the newsperson has in deciding how many newspapers to put in the sales stand outside a hotel lobby each morning. If the person does not put enough papers in the stand, some customers will not be able to purchase a paper and the newsperson will lose the profit associated with these sales. On the other hand, if too many papers are placed in the stand, the newsperson will have paid for papers that were not sold during the day, lowering profit for the day.

Actually, this is a very common type of problem. Consider the person selling T-shirts promoting a championship basketball or football game. This is especially difficult, because the person must wait to learn what teams will be playing. The shirts can then be printed with the proper team logos. Of course, the person must estimate how many people will actually want the shirts. The shirts sold prior to the game can probably be sold at a premium price, whereas those sold after the game will need to be steeply discounted.

A simple way to think about this is to consider how much risk we are willing to take for running out of inventory. Let's consider that the newsperson selling papers in the sales stand had collected data over a few months and had found that, on average, each Monday 90 papers were sold with a standard deviation of 10 papers (assume that during this time the papers were purposefully overstocked in order not to run out, so they would know what "real" demand was). With these data, our newsperson could simply state a service rate that is felt to be acceptable. For example, the newsperson might want to be 80 percent sure of not running out of papers each Monday.

Recall from your study of statistics, assuming that the probability distribution associated with the sales of the paper is normal, that if we stocked exactly 90 papers each Monday morning, the risk of stocking out would be 50 percent, because 50 percent of the time we expect demand to be less than 90 papers and 50 percent of the time we expect demand to be greater than 90. To be 80 percent sure of not stocking out, we need to carry a few more papers. From the cumulative standard normal distribution table given in Appendix G, we see that we need approximately 0.85 standard deviation of extra papers to be 80 percent sure of not stocking out. A quick way to find the exact number of standard deviations needed for a given probability of stocking out is with the NORMSINV(probability) function in Microsoft Excel (NORMSINV(0.8) = 0.84162). Given our result from Excel, which is more accurate than what we can get from the tables, the number of extra papers would be $0.84162 \times 10 = 8.416$, or 9 papers (There is no way to stock 0.4 paper!).

Analytics

To make this more useful, it would be good to actually consider the potential profit and loss associated with stocking either too many or too few papers on the stand. Let's say that our newspaper person pays \$0.20 for each paper and sells the papers for \$0.50. In this case, the marginal cost associated with underestimating demand is \$0.30, the lost profit. Similarly, the marginal cost of overestimating demand is \$0.20, the cost of buying too many papers. The optimal stocking level, using marginal analysis, occurs at the point where the expected benefits derived from carrying the next unit are less than the expected costs for that unit. Keep in mind that the specific benefits and costs depend on the problem.

In symbolic terms, define

$$C_o = \text{Cost per unit of demand overestimated}$$
$$C_u = \text{Cost per unit of demand underestimated}$$

By introducing probabilities, the expected marginal cost equation becomes

$$P(C_o) \le (1 - P)C_u$$

where P is the probability that the unit will not be sold and $1 - P$ is the probability of it being sold because one or the other must occur. (The unit is sold or is not sold.)[1]

Then, solving for P, we obtain

$$P \le \frac{C_u}{C_o + C_u} \qquad [20.1]$$

This equation states that we should continue to increase the size of the order so long as the probability of selling what we order is equal to or less than the ratio $C_u/(C_o + C_u)$.

Returning to our newspaper problem, our cost of overestimating demand (C_o) is \$0.20 per paper and the cost of underestimating demand (C_u) is \$0.30. The probability therefore is $0.3/(0.2 + 0.3) = 0.6$. Now we need to find the point on our demand distribution that corresponds to the cumulative probability of 0.6. Using the NORMSINV function to get the number of standard deviations (commonly referred to as the Z-score) of extra newspapers to carry, we get 0.253, which means we should stock 0.253(10) = 2.53 or 3 extra papers. The total number of papers for the stand each Monday morning, therefore, should be 93 papers.

Single-period inventory models are useful for a wide variety of service and manufacturing applications. Consider the following:

1. **Overbooking of airline flights.** It is common for customers to cancel flight reservations for a variety of reasons. Here, the cost of underestimating the number of cancellations is the revenue lost due to an empty seat on a flight. The cost of overestimating cancellations is the awards, such as free flights or cash payments, that are given to customers unable to board the flight.
2. **Ordering of fashion items.** A problem for a retailer selling fashion items is that often only a single order can be placed for the entire season. This is often caused by long lead times and the limited life of the merchandise. The cost of underestimating demand is the lost profit due to sales not made. The cost of overestimating demand is the cost that results when it is discounted.
3. **Any type of one-time order.** For example, ordering T-shirts for a sporting event or printing maps that become obsolete after a certain period of time.

EXAMPLE 20.1 Hotel Reservations

A hotel near the university always fills up on the evening before football games. History has shown that when the hotel is fully booked, the number of last-minute cancellations has a mean of 5 and a standard deviation of 3. The average room rate is \$80. When the hotel is overbooked, the policy is to find a room in a nearby hotel and to pay for the room for the customer. This usually costs the hotel approximately \$200 because rooms booked on such late notice are expensive. How many rooms should the hotel overbook?

SOLUTION

The cost of underestimating the number of cancellations is \$80 and the cost of overestimating cancellations is \$200.

$$P \leq \frac{C_u}{C_o + C_u} = \frac{\$80}{\$200 + \$80} = 0.2857$$

Using NORMSINV(.2857) from Excel gives a *Z*-score of –0.56599. The negative value indicates that we should overbook by a value less than the average of 5. The actual value should be –0.56599(3) = –1.69797, or 2 reservations less than 5. The hotel should overbook three reservations on the evening prior to a football game.

Another common method for analyzing this type of problem is with a discrete probability distribution found using actual data and marginal analysis. For our hotel, consider that we have collected data and our distribution of no-shows is as follows.

Number of No-Shows	Probability	Cumulative Probability
0	0.05	0.05
1	0.08	0.13
2	0.10	0.23
3	0.15	0.38
4	0.20	0.58
5	0.15	0.73
6	0.11	0.84
7	0.06	0.90
8	0.05	0.95
9	0.04	0.99
10	0.01	1.00

Using these data, we can create a table showing the impact of overbooking. Total expected cost of each overbooking option is then calculated by multiplying each possible outcome by its probability and summing the weighted costs. The best overbooking strategy is the one with minimum cost.

		Number of Reservations Overbooked										
No-Shows	Probability	0	1	2	3	4	5	6	7	8	9	10
0	0.05	0	200	400	600	800	1,000	1,200	1,400	1,600	1,800	2,000
1	0.08	80	0	200	400	600	800	1,000	1,200	1,400	1,600	1,800
2	0.1	160	80	0	200	400	600	800	1,000	1,200	1,400	1,600
3	0.15	240	160	80	0	200	400	600	800	1,000	1,200	1,400
4	0.2	320	240	160	80	0	200	400	600	800	1,000	1,200
5	0.15	400	320	240	160	80	0	200	400	600	800	1,000
6	0.11	480	400	320	240	160	80	0	200	400	600	800
7	0.06	560	480	400	320	240	160	80	0	200	400	600
8	0.05	640	560	480	400	320	240	160	80	0	200	400
9	0.04	720	640	560	480	400	320	240	160	80	0	200
10	0.01	800	720	640	560	480	400	320	240	160	80	0
Expected cost		337.6	271.6	228	212.4	238.8	321.2	445.6	600.8	772.8	958.8	1,156

From the table, the minimum total cost is when three extra reservations are taken. This approach, using discrete probability, is useful when valid historic data are available.

Multiperiod Inventory Systems

There are two general types of multiperiod inventory systems: **fixed–order quantity models** (also called the *economic order quantity,* EOQ, and **Q-model**) and **fixed–time period models** (also referred to variously as the *periodic* system, *periodic review* system, *fixed–order interval* system, and **P-model**). Multiperiod inventory systems are designed to ensure that an item will be available on an ongoing basis throughout the year. Usually, the item will be ordered multiple times throughout the year where the logic in the system dictates the actual quantity ordered and the timing of the order.

Fixed–time period model (P-model)
An inventory control model that specifies inventory is ordered at the end of a predetermined time period. The interval of time between orders is fixed and the order quantity varies.

The basic distinction is that fixed–order quantity models are "event triggered" and fixed–time period models are "time triggered." That is, a fixed–order quantity model initiates an order when the event of reaching a specified reorder level occurs. This event may take place at any time, depending on the demand for the items considered. In contrast, the fixed–time period model is limited to placing orders at the end of a predetermined time period; only the passage of time triggers the model.

To use the fixed–order quantity model (which places an order when the remaining inventory drops to a predetermined order point, *R*), the inventory remaining must be continually monitored. Thus, the fixed–order quantity model is a *perpetual* system, which requires that every time a withdrawal from inventory or an addition to inventory is made, records must be updated to reflect whether the reorder point has been reached. In a fixed–time period model, counting takes place only at the review period. (We will discuss some variations of systems that combine features of both.)

Fixed–order quantity model (Q-model)
An inventory control model where the amount requisitioned is fixed and the actual ordering is triggered by inventory dropping to a specified level of inventory.

Some additional differences tend to influence the choice of systems (also see Exhibit 20.3):

- The fixed–time period model has a larger average inventory because it must also protect against stockout during the review period, *T;* the fixed–order quantity model has no review period.
- The fixed–order quantity model favors more expensive items because average inventory is lower.
- The fixed–order quantity model is more appropriate for important items such as critical repair parts because there is closer monitoring and therefore quicker response to potential stockout.
- The fixed–order quantity model requires more time to maintain because every addition or withdrawal is logged.

EXHIBIT 20.3

Fixed–Order Quantity and Fixed–Time Period Differences

Feature	*Q-Model* Fixed–Order Quantity Model	*P-Model* Fixed–Time Period Model
Order quantity	*Q*—constant (the same amount ordered each time)	*q*—variable (varies each time order is placed)
When to place order	*R*—when the inventory position drops to the reorder level	*T*—when the review period arrives
Recordkeeping	Each time a withdrawal or addition is made	Counted only at review period
Size of inventory	Less than fixed–time period model	Larger than fixed–order quantity model
Time to maintain	Higher due to perpetual recordkeeping	Efficient, because multiple items can be ordered at the same time
Type of items	Higher-priced, critical, or important items	Typically used with lower-cost items

EXHIBIT 20.4

Comparison of Fixed–Order Quantity and Fixed–Time Period Reordering Inventory Systems

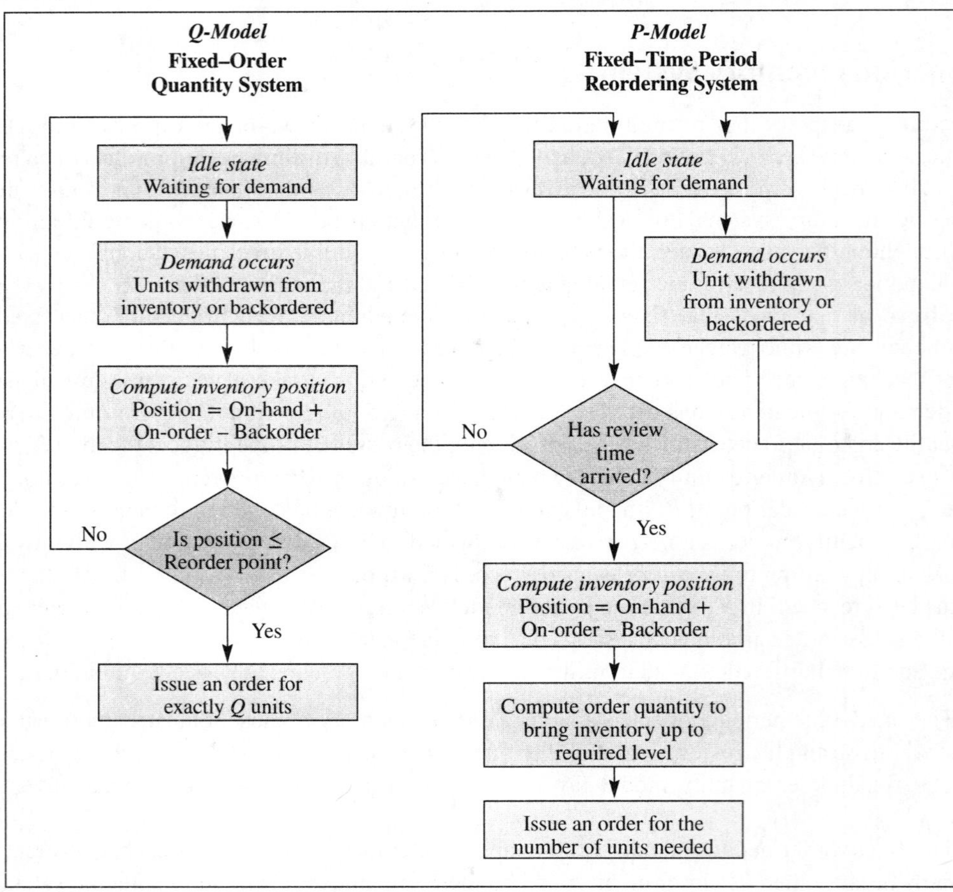

Exhibit 20.4 shows what occurs when each of the two models is put into use and becomes an operating system. As we can see, the fixed–order quantity system focuses on order quantities and reorder points. Procedurally, each time a unit is taken out of stock, the withdrawal is logged and the

amount remaining in inventory is immediately compared to the reorder point. If it has dropped to this point, an order for Q items is placed. If it has not, the system remains in an idle state until the next withdrawal.

In the fixed–time period system, a decision to place an order is made after the stock has been counted or reviewed. Whether an order is actually placed depends on the inventory position at that time.

Fixed–Order Quantity Models

Fixed–order quantity models attempt to determine the specific point, R, at which an order will be placed and the size of that order, Q. The order point, R, is always a specified number of units. An order of size Q is placed when the inventory available (currently in stock and on order) reaches the point R. **Inventory position** is defined as the on-hand plus on-order minus backordered quantities. The solution to a fixed–order quantity model may stipulate something like this: When the inventory position drops to 36, place an order for 57 more units.

Inventory position
The amount on hand plus on-order minus backordered quantities. In the case where inventory has been allocated for special purposes, the inventory position is reduced by these allocated amounts.

The simplest models in this category occur when all aspects of the situation are known with certainty. If the annual demand for a product is 1,000 units, it is precisely 1,000—not 1,000 plus or minus 10 percent. The same is true for setup costs and holding costs. Although the assumption of complete certainty is rarely valid, it provides a good basis for our coverage of inventory models.

Exhibit 20.5 and the discussion about deriving the optimal order quantity are based on the following characteristics of the model. These assumptions are unrealistic, but they represent a starting point and allow us to use a simple example.

EXHIBIT 20.5

Basic Fixed–Order Quantity Model

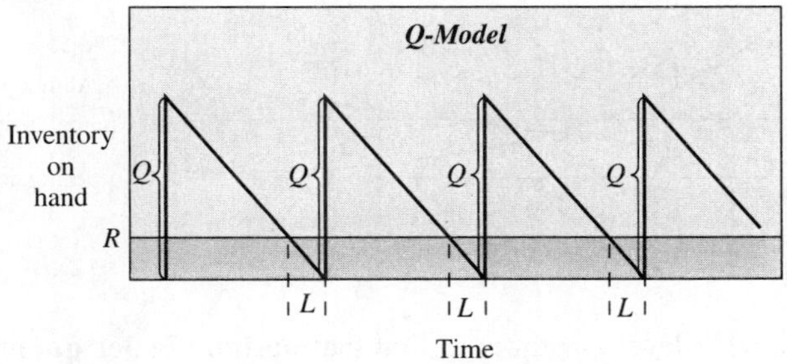

- Demand for the product is constant and uniform throughout the period.
- Lead time (time from ordering to receipt) is constant.
- Price per unit of product is constant.
- Inventory holding cost is based on average inventory.
- Ordering or setup costs are constant.
- All demands for the product will be satisfied. (No backorders are allowed.)

Analytics

The "sawtooth effect" relating Q and R in Exhibit 20.5 shows that when the inventory position drops to point R, a reorder is placed. This order is received at the end of time period L, which does not vary in this model.

In constructing any inventory model, the first step is to develop a functional relationship between the variables of interest and the measure of effectiveness. In this case, because we are concerned with cost, the following equation becomes:

$$\begin{pmatrix}\text{Total}\\ \text{annual cost}\end{pmatrix} = \begin{pmatrix}\text{Annual}\\ \text{purchase cost}\end{pmatrix} + \begin{pmatrix}\text{Annual}\\ \text{ordering cost}\end{pmatrix} + \begin{pmatrix}\text{Annual}\\ \text{holding cost}\end{pmatrix}$$

or

$$TC = DC + \frac{D}{Q}S + \frac{Q}{2}H \qquad [20.2]$$

where

TC = Total annual cost
D = Demand (annual)
C = Cost per unit
Q = Quantity to be ordered (the optimal amount is termed the *economic order quantity*—EOQ—or Q_{opt})
S = Setup cost or cost of placing an order
R = Reorder point
L = Lead time
H = Annual holding and storage cost per unit of average inventory (often, holding cost is taken as a percentage of the cost of the item, such as $H = iC$, where i is the percent carrying cost)

On the right side of the equation, DC is the annual purchase cost for the units, $(D/Q)S$ is the annual ordering cost (the actual number of orders placed, D/Q, times the cost of each order, S), and $(Q/2)H$ is the annual holding cost (the average inventory, $Q/2$, times the cost per unit for holding and storage, H). These cost relationships are graphed in Exhibit 20.6.

EXHIBIT 20.6

Annual Product Costs, Based on Size of the Order

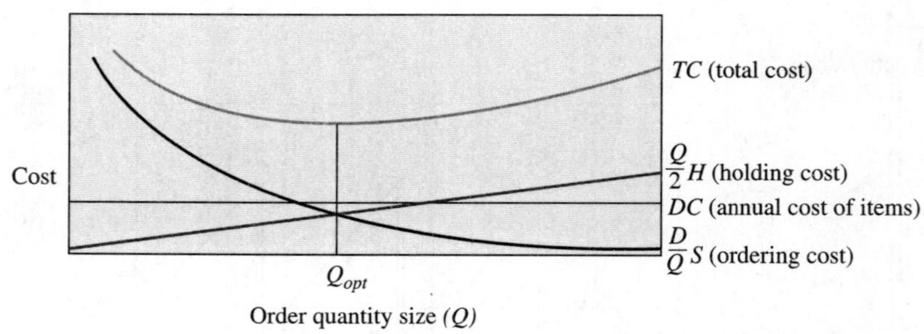

Optimal order quantity (Q_{opt})
This order size minimizes total annual cost.

The second step in model development is to find that **optimal order quantity Q_{opt}** at which total cost is a minimum. In Exhibit 20.6, the total cost is minimal at the point where the slope of the curve is zero. Using calculus, we take the derivative of total cost with respect to Q and set this equal to zero. For the basic model considered here, the calculations are

$$TC = DC + \frac{D}{Q}S + \frac{Q}{2}H$$

$$\frac{dTC}{dQ} = 0 + \left(\frac{-DS}{Q^2}\right) + \frac{H}{2} = 0$$

$$Q_{\text{opt}} = \sqrt{\frac{2DS}{H}} \qquad [20.3]$$

Because this simple model assumes constant demand and lead time, neither safety stock nor stockout cost is necessary, and the **reorder point, R,** is simply

Reorder point (R)
An order is placed when inventory drops to this level.

$$R = \bar{d}L \qquad [20.4]$$

where

$\bar{d}$ = Average daily demand (constant)
L = Lead time in days (constant)

EXAMPLE 20.2 Economic Order Quantity and Reorder Point

Find the economic order quantity and the reorder point, given

$$\begin{aligned} \text{Annual demand } (D) &= 1{,}000 \text{ units} \\ \text{Average daily demand } (\bar{d}) &= 1{,}000/365 \\ \text{Ordering cost } (S) &= \$5 \text{ per order} \\ \text{Holding cost } (H) &= \$1.25 \text{ per unit per year} \\ \text{Lead time } (L) &= 5 \text{ days} \\ \text{Cost per unit } (C) &= \$12.50 \end{aligned}$$

What quantity should be ordered?

SOLUTION

The optimal order quantity is

$$Q_{opt} = \frac{\sqrt{2DS}}{H} = \sqrt{\frac{2(1{,}000)5}{1.25}} = \sqrt{8{,}000} = 89.4 \text{ units}$$

The reorder point is

$$R = \bar{d}L = \frac{1{,}000}{365}(5) = 13.7 \text{ units}$$

Rounding to the nearest unit, the inventory policy is as follows: When the inventory position drops to 14, place an order for 89 more.

The total annual cost will be

$$\begin{aligned} TC &= DC + \frac{D}{Q}S + \frac{Q}{2}H \\ &= 1{,}000\left(12.50\right) + \frac{1{,}000}{89}(5) + \frac{89}{2}(1.25) \\ &= \$12{,}611.80 \end{aligned}$$

Note that the total ordering cost $(1{,}000/89) \times 5 = \$56.18$ and the total carrying cost $(89/2) \times 1.25 = \$55.625$ are very close but not exactly the same due to rounding Q to 89.

Note that, in this example, the purchase cost of the units was not required to determine the order quantity and the reorder point because the cost was constant and unrelated to order size.

Establishing Safety Stock Levels The previous model assumed that demand was constant and known. In the majority of cases, though, demand is not constant but varies from day to day. Safety stock must therefore be maintained to provide some level of protection against stock outs. **Safety stock** can be defined as the amount of inventory carried in addition to the expected demand. In a normal distribution, this would be the mean. For example, if our average monthly demand is 100 units and we expect next month to be the same, if we carry 120 units, then we have 20 units of safety stock.

Safety stock
The amount of inventory carried in addition to the expected demand.

Safety stock can be determined based on many different criteria. A common approach is for a company to simply state that a certain number of weeks of supply needs to be kept in safety stock. It is better, though, to use an approach that captures the variability in demand.

For example, an objective may be something like "set the safety stock level so that there will only be a 5 percent chance of stocking out if demand exceeds 300 units." We call this approach to setting safety stock the probability approach.

The Probability Approach Using the probability criterion to determine safety stock is pretty simple. With the models described in this chapter, we assume that the demand over a period of time is normally distributed with a mean and a standard deviation. *Again, remember that this approach considers only the probability of running out of stock, not how many units we are short.* To determine the probability of stocking out over the time period, we can simply plot a normal distribution for the expected demand and note where the amount we have on hand lies on the curve.

Let's take a few simple examples to illustrate this. Say we expect demand to be 100 units over the next month, and we know that the standard deviation is 20 units. If we go into the month with just 100 units, we know that our probability of stocking out is 50 percent. Half of the months we would expect demand to be greater than 100 units; half of the months we would expect it to be less than 100 units. Taking this further, if we ordered a month's worth of inventory of 100 units at a time and received it at the beginning of the month, over the long run we would expect to run out of inventory in six months of the year.

If running out this often was not acceptable, we would want to carry extra inventory to reduce this risk of stocking out. One idea might be to carry an extra 20 units of inventory for the item. In this case, we would still order a month's worth of inventory at a time, but we would schedule delivery to arrive when we still have 20 units remaining in inventory. This would give us that little cushion of safety stock to reduce the probability of stocking out. If the standard deviation associated with our demand was 20 units, we would then be carrying one standard deviation worth of safety stock. Looking at the cumulative standard normal distribution (Appendix G), and moving one standard deviation to the right of the mean, gives a probability of 0.8413. So approximately 84 percent of the time we would not expect to stock out, and 16 percent of the time we would. Now, if we order every month, we would expect to stock out approximately two months per year ($0.16 \times 12 = 1.92$). For those using Excel, given a z value, the probability can be obtained with the NORMSDIST function.

It is common for companies using this approach to set the probability of not stocking out at 95 percent. This means we would carry about 1.64 standard deviations of safety stock, or 33 units ($1.64 \times 20 = 32.8$) for our example. Once again, keep in mind that this does not mean that we would order 33 units extra each month. Rather, it means that we would still order a month's worth each time, but we would schedule the receipt so that we could expect to have 33 units in inventory when the order arrives. In this case, we would expect to stock out approximately 0.6 month per year, or that stockouts would occur in 1 of every 20 months.

Analytics

Fixed–Order Quantity Model with Safety Stock A fixed–order quantity system perpetually monitors the inventory level and places a new order when stock reaches some level, R. The danger of stockout in this model occurs only during the lead time, between the time an order is placed and the time it is received. As shown in Exhibit 20.7, an order is placed when the inventory position drops to the reorder point, R. During this lead time, L, a range of demands is possible. This range is determined either from an analysis of past demand data or from an estimate (if past data are not available).

EXHIBIT 20.7

Fixed–Order Quantity Model

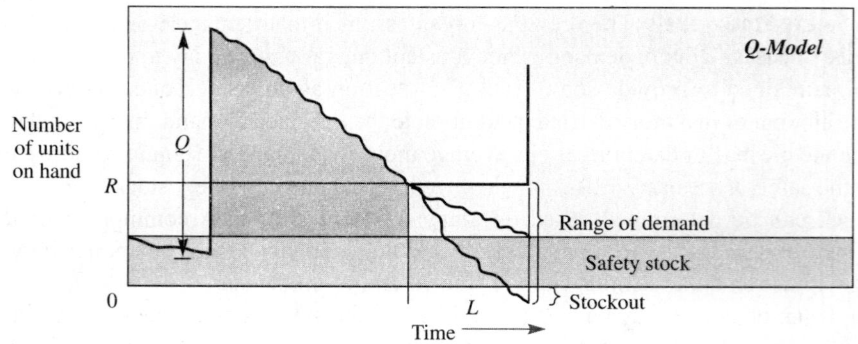

The amount of safety stock depends on the service level desired, as previously discussed. The quantity to be ordered, Q, is calculated in the usual way considering the demand, shortage cost, ordering cost, holding cost, and so forth. A fixed–order quantity model can be used to compute Q, such as the simple Q_{opt} model previously discussed. The reorder point is then set to cover the expected demand during the lead time plus a safety stock determined by the desired service level. Thus, *the key difference between a fixed–order quantity model where demand is known and one where demand*

is uncertain is in computing the reorder point. The order quantity is the same in both cases. The uncertainty element is taken into account in the safety stock.

The reorder point is

$$R = \bar{d}L + z\sigma_L \quad [20.5]$$

where

R = Reorder point in units

$\bar{d}$ = Average daily demand

L = Lead time in days (time between placing an order and receiving the items)

z = Number of standard deviations for a specified service probability

σ_L = Standard deviation of usage during lead time

The term $z\sigma_L$ is the amount of safety stock. Note that if safety stock is positive, the effect is to place a reorder sooner. That is, R without safety stock is simply the average demand during the lead time. If lead time usage was expected to be 20, for example, and safety stock was computed to be 5 units, then the order would be placed sooner, when 25 units remained. The greater the safety stock, the sooner the order is placed.

Computing d, σ_L, and z Demand during the replenishment lead time is really an estimate or forecast of expected use of inventory from the time an order is placed to when it is received. It may be a single number (for example, if the lead time is a month, the demand may be taken as the previous year's demand divided by 12), or it may be a summation of expected demands over the lead time (such as the sum of daily demands over a 30-day lead time). For the daily demand situation, d can be a forecast demand using any of the models in Chapter 18 on forecasting. For example, if a 30-day period was used to calculate d, then a simple average would be

$$\bar{d} = \frac{\sum_{i=1}^{n} d_i}{n}$$

$$= \frac{\sum_{i=1}^{30} d_i}{30} \quad [20.6]$$

where n is the number of days.

The standard deviation of the daily demand is

$$\sigma_d = \frac{\sqrt{\sum_{i=1}^{n} (d_i - \bar{d})^2}}{n}$$

$$= \frac{\sqrt{\sum_{i=1}^{30} (d_i - \bar{d})^2}}{30} \quad [20.7]$$

Because σ_d refers to one day, if lead time extends over several days, we can use the statistical premise that the standard deviation of a series of independent occurrences is equal to the square root of the sum of the variances. That is, in general,

$$\sigma_L = \sqrt{\sigma_1^2 + \sigma_2^2 + \ldots + \sigma_L^2}$$

For example, suppose we computed the standard deviation of demand to be 10 units per day. If our lead time to get an order is five days, the standard deviation for the five-day period, assuming each day can be considered independent, is

$$\sigma_5 = \sqrt{(10)^2 + (10)^2 + (10)^2 + (10)^2 + (10)^2} = 22.36$$

Next we need to find z, the number of standard deviations of safety stock.

Suppose we wanted our probability of not stocking out during the lead time to be 0.95. The z value associated with a 95 percent probability of not stocking out is 1.64 (see Appendix G or use the Excel NORMSINV function). Given this, safety stock is calculated as follows:

$$\begin{aligned} SS &= z\sigma_L \\ &= 1.64 \times 22.36 \\ &= 36.67 \end{aligned} \qquad [20.9]$$

We now compare two examples. The difference between them is that in the first, the variation in demand is stated in terms of standard deviation over the entire lead time, while in the second, it is stated in terms of standard deviation per day.

EXAMPLE 20.3 Reorder Point

Consider an economic order quantity case where annual demand $D = 1{,}000$ units, economic order quantity $Q = 200$ units, the desired probability of not stocking out $P = .95$, the standard deviation of demand during lead time $\sigma_L = 25$ units, and lead time $L = 15$ days. Determine the reorder point. Assume that demand is over a 250-workday year.

SOLUTION

In our example,

$\bar{d} = \dfrac{1{,}000}{250} = 4$, and lead time is 15 days. We use the equation

$$\begin{aligned} R &= \bar{d}L + z\sigma_L \\ &= 4(15) + z(25) \end{aligned}$$

In this case, z is 1.64.

Completing the solution for R, we have

$$R = 4(15) + 1.64(25) = 60 + 41 = 101 \text{ units}$$

This says that when the stock on hand gets down to 101 units, order 200 more.

EXAMPLE 20.4 Order Quantity and Reorder Point

Daily demand for a certain product is normally distributed, with a mean of 60 and a standard deviation of 7. The source of supply is reliable and maintains a constant lead time of six days. The cost of placing the order is $10 and annual holding costs are $0.50 per unit. There are no stock-out costs, and unfilled orders are filled as soon as the order arrives. Assume sales occur over the entire 365 days of the year. Find the order quantity and reorder point to satisfy a 95 percent probability of not stocking out during the lead time.

SOLUTION

In this problem we need to calculate the order quantity Q as well as the reorder point R.

$$\begin{array}{ll} \bar{d} = 60 & S = \$10 \\ \sigma_d = 7 & H = \$0.50 \\ D = 60(365) & L = 6 \end{array}$$

The optimal order quantity is

$$Q_{opt} = \sqrt{\frac{2DS}{H}} = \sqrt{\frac{2(60)365(10)}{0.50}} = \sqrt{876{,}000} = 936 \text{ units}$$

To compute the reorder point, we need to calculate the amount of product used during the lead time and add this to the safety stock.

The standard deviation of demand during the lead time of six days is calculated from the variance of the individual days. Because each day's demand is independent,[2]

$$\sigma_L = \sqrt{\sum_{i=1}^{L} \sigma_d^2} = \sqrt{6(7)^2} = 17.15$$

Once again, z is 1.64.

$$R = \bar{d}L + z\sigma_L = 60(6) + 1.64(17.15) = 388 \text{ units}$$

To summarize the policy derived in this example, an order for 936 units is placed whenever the number of units remaining in inventory drops to 388.

Fixed–Time Period Models

In a fixed–time period system, inventory is counted only at particular times, such as every week or every month. Counting inventory and placing orders periodically are desirable in situations such as when vendors make routine visits to customers and take orders for their complete line of products, or when buyers want to combine orders to save transportation costs. Other firms operate on a fixed time period to facilitate planning their inventory count; for example, Distributor X calls every two weeks and employees know that all Distributor X's product must be counted.

Fixed–time period models generate order quantities that vary from period to period, depending on the usage rates. These generally require a higher level of safety stock than a fixed–order quantity system. The fixed–order quantity system assumes continual tracking of inventory on hand, with an order immediately placed when the reorder point is reached. In contrast, the standard fixed–time period models assume that inventory is counted only at the time specified for review. It is possible that some large demand will draw the stock down to zero right after an order is placed. This condition could go unnoticed until the next review period. Then, the new order, when placed, still takes time to arrive. Thus, it is possible to be out of stock throughout the entire review period, T, and order lead time, L. Safety stock, therefore, must protect against stock outs during the review period itself, as well as during the lead time from order placement to order receipt.

Analytics

Fixed–Time Period Model with Safety Stock In a fixed–time period system, reorders are placed at the time of review (T), and the safety stock that must be reordered is

$$\text{Safety stock} = z\sigma_{T+L} \qquad [20.10]$$

Exhibit 20.8 shows a fixed–time period system with a review cycle of T and a constant lead time of L. In this case, demand is randomly distributed about a mean d. The quantity to order, q, is

$$\begin{array}{ccccccc} \text{Order quantity} & = & \left(\begin{array}{c}\text{Average demand}\\ \text{over the}\\ \text{vulnerable period}\end{array}\right) & + & \left(\begin{array}{c}\text{Safety}\\ \text{stock}\end{array}\right) & - & \left(\begin{array}{c}\text{Inventory currently}\\ \text{on hand (plus on}\\ \text{order, if any)}\end{array}\right) \\ q & = & \bar{d}(T+L) & + & z\sigma_{T+L} & - & I \end{array} \qquad [20.11]$$

where

q = Quantity to be ordered

T = The number of days between reviews

L = Lead time in days (time between placing an order and receiving it)

$\bar{d}$ = Forecast average daily demand

z = Number of standard deviations for a specified service probability

EXHIBIT 20.8

Fixed–Time Period Inventory Model

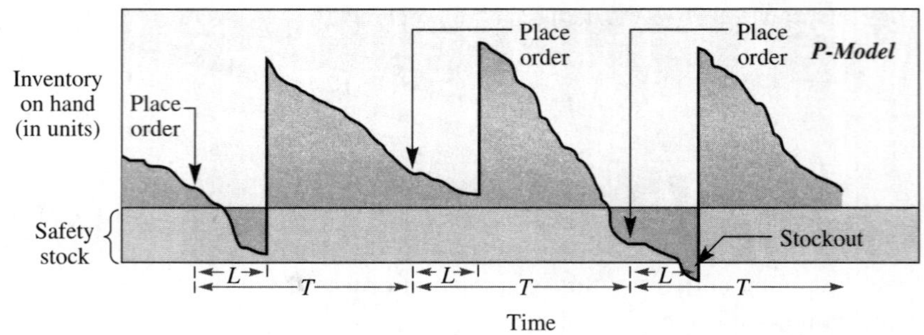

Note: The demand, lead time, review period, and so forth can be any time units such as days, weeks, or years so long as they are consistent throughout the equation.

σ_{T+L} = Standard deviation of demand over the review and lead time

I = Current inventory level (includes items on order)

In this model, demand ($\bar{d}$) can be forecast and revised each review period if desired, or the yearly average may be used if appropriate. We assume that demand is normally distributed.

The value of z is dependent on the probability of stocking out and can be found using Appendix G or by using the Excel NORMSINV function.

EXAMPLE 20.5 Quantity to Order

Daily demand for a product is 10 units, with a standard deviation of 3 units. The review period is 30 days, and the lead time is 14 days. Management has set a policy of satisfying 98 percent of demand from items in stock. At the beginning of this review period, there are 150 units in inventory.

How many units should be ordered?

SOLUTION

The quantity to order is

$$q = \bar{d}(T+L) + z\sigma_{T+L} - I$$
$$= 10(30+14) + z\sigma_{T+L} - 150$$

Before we can complete the solution, we need to find σ_{TIL} and z. To find σ_{TIL}, we use the notion, as before, that the standard deviation of a sequence of independent random variables equals the square root of the sum of the variances. Therefore, the standard deviation during the period $T + L$ is the square root of the sum of the variances for each day:

$$\sigma_{T+L} = \sqrt{\sum_{i=1}^{T+L} \sigma_d^2}$$

Because each day is independent and σ_d is constant,

$$\sigma_{T+L} = \sqrt{(T+L)\sigma_d^2} = \sqrt{(30+14)(3)^2} = 19.90$$

The z value for $P = 0.98$ is 2.05.

The quantity to order, then, is

$$q = \bar{d}(T+L) + z\sigma_{T+L} - I = 10(30+14) + 2.05(19.90) - 150 = 331 \text{ units}$$

To ensure a 98 percent probability of not stocking out, order 331 units at this review period.

Inventory Turn Calculation

It is important for managers to realize that how they run items using inventory control logic relates directly to the financial performance of the firm. A key measure that relates to company performance is inventory turn. Recall that **inventory turn** is calculated as follows:

$$\text{Inventory turn} = \frac{\text{Cost of goods sold}}{\text{Average inventory value}}$$

Inventory turn
A measure of the expected number of times inventory is replaced over a year.

So what is the relationship between how we manage an item and the inventory turn for that item? Here, let us simplify things and consider just the inventory turn for an individual item or a group of items. First, if we look at the numerator, the cost of goods sold for an individual item relates directly to the expected yearly demand (D) for the item. Given a cost per unit (C) for the item, the cost of goods sold is just D times C. Recall this is the same as what was used in our total cost equation when calculating. Next, consider average inventory value. Recall from EOQ that the average inventory is $Q/2$, which is true if we assume that demand is constant. When we bring uncertainty into the equation, safety stock is needed to manage the risk created by demand variability. The fixed–order quantity model and fixed–time period model both have equations for calculating the safety stock required for a given probability of stocking out. In both models, we assume that, when going through an order cycle, half the time we need to use the safety stock and half the time we do not. So, on average, we expect the safety stock (SS) to be on hand. Given this, the average inventory is equal to the following:

$$\text{Average inventory value} = (Q/2 + SS)C \tag{20.13}$$

The inventory turn for an individual item then is

$$\text{Inventory turn} = \frac{DC}{(Q/2 + SS)C} = \frac{D}{Q/2 + SS} \tag{20.14}$$

EXAMPLE 20.6 **Average Inventory Calculation—Fixed–Order Quantity Model**

Suppose the following item is being managed using a fixed–order quantity model with safety stock.

Annual demand (D) = 1,000 units
Order quantity (Q) = 300 units
Safety stock (SS) = 40 units

What are the average inventory level and inventory turn for the item?

SOLUTION

$$\text{Average inventory} = Q/2 + SS = 300/2 + 40 = 190 \text{ units}$$

$$\text{Inventory turn} = \frac{D}{Q/2 + SS} = \frac{1{,}000}{190} = 5.263 \text{ turns per year}$$

EXAMPLE 20.7 **Average Inventory Calculation—Fixed–Time Period Model**

Consider the following item that is being managed using a fixed–time period model with safety stock.

Weekly demand (d) = 50 units
Review cycle (T) = 3 weeks
Safety stock (SS) = 30 units

What are the average inventory level and inventory turn for the item?

SOLUTION

Here we need to determine how many units we expect to order each cycle. If we assume that demand is fairly steady, then we would expect to order the number of units that we expect demand to be during the review cycle. This expected demand is equal to dT if we assume there is no trend or seasonality in the demand pattern.

$$\text{Average inventory} = dT/2 + SS = 50(3)/2 + 30 = 105 \text{ units}$$

$$\text{Inventory turn} = \frac{52d}{dT/2 + SS} = \frac{52(50)}{105} = 24.8 \text{ turns per year}$$

Here we assume the firm operates 52 weeks in the year.

Price-Break Model

Price-break model
This model is useful for finding the order quantity of an item when the price of the item varies with the order size.

The **price-break model** deals with the fact that, generally, the selling price of an item varies with the order size. This is a discrete or step change rather than a per-unit change. For example, wood screws may cost $0.02 each for 1 to 99 screws, $1.60 per 100, and $13.50 per 1,000. To determine the optimal quantity of any item to order, we simply solve for the economic order quantity for each price and at the point of price change. But not all of the economic order quantities determined by the formula are feasible. In the wood screw example, the Q_{opt} formula might tell us that the optimal decision at the price of 1.6 cents is to order 75 screws. This would be impossible, however, because 75 screws would cost 2 cents each.

In general, to find the lowest-cost order quantity, we need to calculate the economic order quantity for each possible price and check to see whether the quantity is feasible. It is possible that the economic order quantity that is calculated is either higher or lower than the range to which the price corresponds. Any feasible quantity is a potential candidate for order quantity. We also need to calculate the cost at each of the price-break quantities, because we know that price is feasible at these points and the total cost may be lowest at one of these values.

The calculations can be simplified a little if holding cost is based on a percentage of unit price (they will be in all the examples and problems given in this book). In this case, we only need to look at a subset of the price-break quantities. The following two-step procedure can be used:

Step 1. Sort the prices from lowest to highest and then, beginning with the lowest price, calculate the economic order quantity for each price level until a feasible economic order quantity is found. By feasible, we mean that the quantity is in the correct corresponding range for that price.

EXHIBIT 20.9

Curves for Three Separate Order Quantity Models in a Three-Price-Break Situation (red line depicts feasible range of purchases)

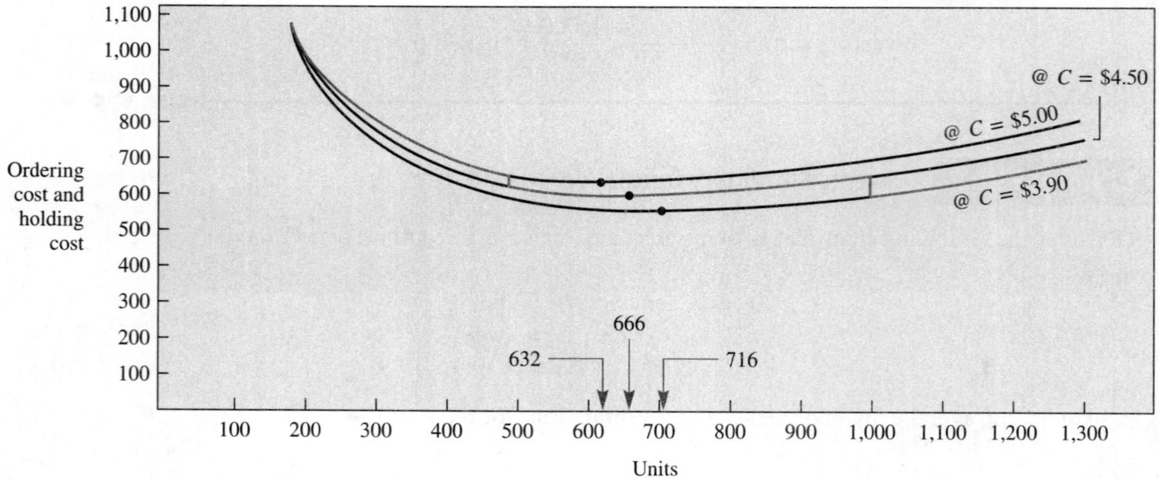

Step 2. If the first feasible economic order quantity is for the lowest price, this quantity is best and you are finished. Otherwise, calculate the total cost for the first feasible economic order quantity (you did these from lowest to highest price) and also calculate the total cost at each price break lower than the price associated with the first feasible economic order quantity. This is the lowest order quantity at which you can take advantage of the price break. The optimal Q is the one with the lowest cost.

Looking at Exhibit 20.9, we see that order quantities are solved from right to left, or from the lowest unit price to the highest, until a valid Q is obtained. Then, the order quantity at each *price break* above this Q is used to find which order quantity has the least cost—the computed Q or the Q at one of the price breaks.

EXAMPLE 20.8 Price Break

Consider the following case, where

$D = 10{,}000$ units (annual demand)

$S = \$20$ to place each order

$i = 20$ percent of cost (annual carrying cost, storage, interest, obsolescence, etc.)

$C =$ Cost per unit (according to the order size; orders of 0 to 499 units, \$5.00 per unit; 500 to 999, \$4.50 per unit; 1,000 and up, \$3.90 per unit)

What quantity should be ordered?

SOLUTION

The appropriate equations from the basic fixed–order quantity case are

$$TC = DC + \frac{D}{Q}S + \frac{Q}{2}iC$$

and

$$Q = \sqrt{\frac{2DS}{iC}} \qquad [10.15]$$

Exhibit 20.10

Relevant Costs in a Three-Price-Break Model

	$Q = 632$ Where $c = \$5$	$Q = 667$ Where $c = \$4.50$	$Q = 716$ Where $c = \$3.90$	Price Break 1,000
Holding cost $\left(\frac{Q}{2}iC\right)$		$\frac{667}{2}(0.20)4.50 = \$300.15$		$\frac{1{,}000}{2}(0.20)3.90 = \$390$
Ordering cost $\left(\frac{D}{Q}S\right)$	Not feasible	$\frac{10{,}000(20)}{667} = \$299.85$	Not feasible	$\frac{10{,}000(20)}{1{,}000} = \$200$
Holding and ordering cost		\$600.00		\$590
Item cost (DC)		10,000(4.50)		10,000(3.90)
Total cost		\$45,600		\$39,590

Solving for the economic order size, we obtain

@ $C = \$3.90$,	$Q = 716$	Not feasible
@ $C = \$4.50$,	$Q = 667$	Feasible, cost = \$45,600
Check $Q = 1{,}000$,	Cost = \$39,590	Optimal solution

In Exhibit 20.9, which displays the cost relationship and order quantity range, note that most of the order quantity–cost relationships lie outside the feasible range and that only a single, continuous range results. This should be readily apparent because, for example, the first order quantity specifies buying 632 units at \$5.00 per unit. However, if 632 units are ordered, the price is \$4.50, not \$5.00. The same holds true for the third order quantity, which specifies an order of 716 units at \$3.90 each. This \$3.90 price is not available on orders of less than 1,000 units.

Exhibit 20.10 itemizes the total costs at the economic order quantities and at the price breaks. The optimal order quantity is shown to be 1,000 units.

One practical consideration in price-break problems is that the price reduction from volume purchases frequently makes it seemingly economical to order amounts larger than the Q_{opt}. Thus, when applying the model, we must be particularly careful to obtain a valid estimate of product obsolescence and warehousing costs.

LO 20-3

Analyze inventory using the *Pareto principle*

INVENTORY PLANNING AND ACCURACY

Maintaining inventory through counting, placing orders, receiving stock, and so on takes personnel time and costs money. When there are limits on these resources, the logical move is to try to use the available resources to control inventory in the best way. In other words, focus on the most important items in inventory.

Strategy

In the nineteenth century, Villefredo Pareto, in a study of the distribution of wealth in Milan, found that 20 percent of the people controlled 80 percent of the wealth. This logic of the few having the greatest importance and the many having little importance has been broadened to include many situations and is termed the *Pareto principle.*[3] This is true in our everyday lives (most of our decisions are relatively unimportant, but a few shape our future) and is certainly true in inventory systems (where a few items account for the bulk of our investment).

ABC inventory classification

Divides inventory into dollar volume categories that map into strategies appropriate for the category.

Any inventory system must specify when an order is to be placed for an item and how many units to order. Most inventory control situations involve so many items that it is not practical to model and give thorough treatment to each item. To get around this problem, the **ABC inventory classification** scheme divides inventory items into three groupings: high dollar volume (A), moderate dollar volume (B), and low dollar volume (C). Dollar volume is a measure of importance; an item low in cost but high in volume can be more important than a high-cost item with low volume.

ABC Classification

If the annual usage of items in inventory is listed according to dollar volume, generally, the list shows that a small number of items account for a large dollar volume and that a large number of items account for a small dollar volume. Exhibit 20.11A illustrates the relationship.

Analytics

The ABC approach divides this list into three groupings by value: A items constitute roughly the top 15 percent of the items, B items the next 35 percent, and C items the last 50 percent. From observation, it appears that the list in Exhibit 20.11A can be meaningfully grouped with A including 20 percent (2 of the 10), B including 30 percent, and C including 50 percent. These points show clear delineations between sections. The result of this segmentation is shown in Exhibit 20.11B and plotted in Exhibit 20.11C.

Segmentation may not always occur so neatly. The objective, though, is to try to separate the important from the unimportant. Where the lines actually break depends on the particular inventory

EXHIBIT 20.11

A. Annual Usage of Inventory by Value

Item Number	Annual Dollar Usage	Percentage of Total Value
22	$ 95,000	40.69%
68	75,000	32.13
27	25,000	10.71
03	15,000	6.43
82	13,000	5.57
54	7,500	3.21
36	1,500	0.64
19	800	0.34
23	425	0.18
41	225	0.10
	$233,450	100.00%

B. ABC Grouping of Inventory Items

Classification	Item Number	Annual Dollar Usage	Percentage of Total
A	22, 68	$170,000	72.8%
B	27, 03, 82	53,000	22.7
C	54, 36, 19, 23, 41	10,450	4.5
		$233,450	100.0%

C. ABC Inventory Classification (inventory value for each group versus the group's portion of the total list)

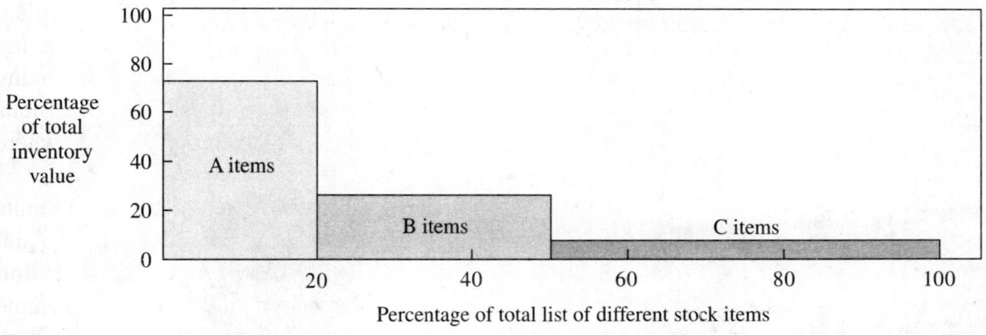

under question and on how much personnel time is available. (With more time, a firm could define larger A or B categories.)

The purpose of classifying items into groups is to establish the appropriate degree of control over each item. On a periodic basis, for example, class A items may be more clearly controlled with weekly ordering, B items may be ordered biweekly, and C items may be ordered monthly or bimonthly. Note that the unit cost of items is not related to their classification. An A item may have a high dollar volume through a combination of either low cost and high usage or high cost and low usage. Similarly, C items may have a low dollar volume because of either low demand or low cost. In an automobile service station, gasoline would be an A item with daily or weekly replenishment; tires, batteries, oil, grease, and transmission fluid may be B items and ordered every two to four weeks; and C items would consist of valve stems, windshield wiper blades, radiator caps, hoses, fan belts, oil and gas additives, car wax, and so forth. C items may be ordered every two or three months or even be allowed to run out before reordering because the penalty for stockout is not serious.

Sometimes an item may be critical to a system if its absence creates a sizable loss. In this case, regardless of the item's classification, sufficiently large stocks should be kept on hand to prevent runout. One way to ensure closer control is to designate this item an A or a B, forcing it into the category even if its dollar volume does not warrant such inclusion.

Inventory Accuracy and Cycle Counting

Inventory records usually differ from the actual physical count; inventory accuracy refers to how well the two agree. Companies such as Walmart understand the importance of inventory accuracy and expend considerable effort ensuring it. The question is, "How much error is acceptable?" If the record shows a balance of 683 of part X, and an actual count shows 652, is this within reason? Suppose the actual count shows 750, an excess of 67 over the record. Is this any better?

Every production system must have agreement, within some specified range, between what the record says is in inventory and what actually is in inventory. There are many reasons why records and inventory may not agree. For example, an open stockroom area allows items to be removed for both legitimate and unauthorized purposes. The legitimate removal may have been done in a hurry and simply not recorded. Sometimes parts are misplaced, turning up months later. Parts are often stored in several locations, but records may be lost or the location recorded incorrectly. Sometimes stock replenishment orders are recorded as received, when in fact they never were. Occasionally, a group of parts is recorded as removed from inventory, but the customer order is canceled and the parts are replaced in inventory without canceling the record. To keep the production system flowing smoothly without parts shortages and efficiently without excess balances, records must be accurate.

How can a firm keep accurate, up-to-date records? Using bar codes and RFID tags is important to minimizing errors caused by inputting wrong numbers in the system. It is also important to keep the storeroom locked. If only storeroom personnel have access, and one of their measures of performance for personnel evaluation and merit increases is record accuracy, there is a strong motivation to comply. Every location of inventory storage, whether in a locked storeroom or on the production floor, should have a recordkeeping mechanism. A second way is to convey the importance of accurate records to all personnel and depend on them to assist in this effort. (It all boils down to this: Put a fence that goes all the way to the ceiling around the storage area so that workers cannot climb over to get parts; put a lock on the gate and give one person the key. Nobody can pull parts without having the transaction authorized and recorded.)

A sales clerk at department store reads an RFID tag on clothes to check stock.

Another way to ensure accuracy is to count inventory frequently and match this against records. A widely used method is called *cycle counting.*

Cycle counting a physical inventory-taking technique in which inventory is counted frequently rather than once or twice a year. The key to effective cycle counting and, therefore, to accurate records lies in deciding which items are to be counted, when, and by whom.

Cycle counting
A physical inventory-taking technique in which inventory is counted on a frequent basis rather than once or twice a year.

Virtually all inventory systems these days are computerized. The computer can be programmed to produce a cycle count notice in the following cases:

1. When the record shows a low or zero balance on hand. (It is easier to count fewer items.)
2. When the record shows a positive balance but a backorder was written (indicating a discrepancy).
3. After some specified level of activity.
4. To signal a review based on the importance of the item (as in the ABC system) such as in the following table:

Annual Dollar Usage	Review Period
$10,000 or more	30 days or less
$3,000–$10,000	45 days or less
$250–$3,000	90 days or less
Less than $250	180 days or less

The easiest time for stock to be counted is when there is no activity in the stockroom or on the production floor. This means on the weekends or during the second or third shift, when the facility is less busy. If this is not possible, more careful logging and separation of items are required to count inventory while production is going on and transactions are occurring.

The counting cycle depends on the available personnel. Some firms schedule regular stockroom personnel to do the counting during lulls in the regular working day. Other companies hire private firms that come in and count inventory. Still other firms use full-time cycle counters who do nothing but count inventory and resolve differences with the records. Although this last method sounds expensive, many firms believe that it is actually less costly than the usual hectic annual inventory count generally performed during the two- or three-week annual vacation shutdown.

The question of how much error is tolerable between physical inventory and records has been much debated. Some firms strive for 100 percent accuracy, whereas others accept a 1, 2, or 3 percent error. The accuracy level often recommended by experts is ±0.2 percent for A items, ±1 percent for B items, and ±5 percent for C items. Regardless of the specific accuracy decided on, the important point is that the level be dependable so that safety stocks may be provided as a cushion. Accuracy is important for a smooth production process so that customer orders can be processed as scheduled and not held up because of unavailable parts.

CONCEPT CONNECTIONS

LO 20–1 Explain how inventory is used and understand what it costs

Summary

- Inventory is expensive mainly due to storage, obsolescence, insurance, and the value of the money invested.
- This chapter explains models for controlling inventory that are appropriate when it is difficult to predict exactly what demand will be for an item in the future and it is desired to have the item available from "stock."
- The basic decisions that need to be made are: (1) when should an item be ordered, and (2) how large should the order be.

- The main costs relevant to these models are: (1) the cost of the item itself, (2) the cost to hold an item in inventory, (3) setup costs, (4) ordering costs, and (5) costs incurred when an item runs short.

Key Terms

Inventory The stock of any item or resource used in an organization.

Independent demand The demands for these items are unrelated to each other, or to activities that can be predicted with certainty.

Dependent demand The need for an item is a direct result of the need for some other item, usually an item of which it is a part. Also, when the demand for the item can be predicted with accuracy due to a schedule or specific activity.

LO 20–2 Analyze how different inventory control systems work

Summary

- An inventory system provides a specific operating policy for managing items to be in stock. Other than defining the timing and sizing of orders, the system needs to track the exact status of these orders (Have the orders been received by the supplier? Have they been shipped? On which date is each expected? And so on.).
- Single-period model—When an item is purchased only one time and it is expected that it will be used and then not reordered, the single-period model is appropriate.
- Multiple-period models—When the item will be reordered and the intent is to maintain the item in stock, multiple-period models are appropriate.
- There are two basic types of multiple-period models, with the key distinction being what triggers the timing of the order placement.
- With the fixed–order quantity model, an order is placed when inventory drops to a low level called the reorder point.
- With the fixed–time period model, orders are placed at fixed intervals of time, say, every two weeks. The order quantity varies for each order.
- Safety stock is extra inventory that is carried for protection in case the demand for an item is greater than expected. Statistics are used to determine an appropriate amount of safety stock to carry based on the probability of stocking out.
- Inventory turn measures the expected number of times that average inventory is replaced over a year. It can be calculated in aggregate using average inventory levels or on an individual item basis.

Key Terms

Single-period problem Answers the question of how much to order when an item is purchased only one time and it is expected that it will be used and then not reordered.

Fixed–order quantity model (Q-model) An inventory control model where the amount requisitioned is fixed and the actual ordering is triggered by inventory dropping to a specified level of inventory.

Fixed–time period model (P-model) An inventory control model that specifies inventory is ordered at the end of a predetermined time period. The interval of time between orders is fixed and the order quantity varies.

Inventory position The amount on hand plus on-order minus backordered quantities. In the case where inventory has been allocated for special purposes, the inventory position is reduced by these allocated amounts.

Optimal order quantity (Q_{opt}) This order size minimizes total annual cost.

Reorder point (*R*) An order is placed when inventory drops to this level.

Safety stock The amount of inventory carried in addition to the expected demand.

Inventory turn The cost of goods sold divided by the total average value of inventory. A measure of the expected number of times that inventory is replaced each year.

Price-break model This model is useful for finding the order quantity of an item when the price of the item varies with the order size.

Key Formulas

$$P \le \frac{C_u}{C_o + C_u} \quad [20.1]$$

Inventory position = On-hand + On-order – Back-order [20.2]

$$TC = DC + \frac{D}{Q}S + \frac{Q}{2}H \quad [20.3]$$

$$Q_{opt} = \sqrt{\frac{2DS}{H}} \quad [20.4]$$

$$R = \bar{d}L \quad [20.5]$$

$$R = \bar{d}L + z\sigma_L \quad [20.6]$$

$$\bar{d} = \frac{\sum_{i=1}^{n} d_i}{n} \quad [20.7]$$

$$\bar{d} = \frac{\sqrt{\sum_{i=1}^{n} (d_i - \bar{d})^2}}{n} \quad [20.8]$$

$$\sigma_L = \sqrt{\sigma_1^2 + \sigma_2^2 + \ldots + \sigma_L^2} \quad [20.9]$$

$$\text{Safety stock} = z\sigma_{T+L} \quad [20.10]$$

Order quantity	=	Average demand over the vulnerable period	+	Safety stock	–	Inventory currently on hand (plus on order, if any)	[20.11]
q	=	$\bar{d}(T+L)$	+	$z\sigma$	–	I	

$$\sigma_{T+L} = \sqrt{\sum_{i=1}^{T+L} \sigma_d^2} \quad [20.12]$$

Average inventory value= $(Q/2 + SS)C$ [20.13]

$$\text{Inventory turn} = \frac{DC}{(Q/2 + SS)C} = \frac{D}{Q/2 + SS} \quad [20.14]$$

$$Q = \sqrt{\frac{2DS}{iC}} \quad [20.15]$$

LO 20–3 Analyze inventory using the *Pareto principle*

Summary

- Most inventory control systems are so large that it is not practical to model and give a thorough treatment to each item. In these cases, it is useful to categorize items according to their yearly dollar value.
- A simple A, B, C categorization where A items are the high annual dollar value items, B items are the medium dollar value items, and C items are the low dollar value items is useful. This categorization can be used as a measure of the relative importance of an item.
- Typically, A items are roughly the top 15 percent of the items and represent 80 percent of the yearly dollar value. B items would be the next 35 percent and make up around 15 percent of the yearly dollar value. The C items would be the last 50 percent of the item, and have only 5 percent of the yearly dollar value.
- Cycle counting is a useful method for scheduling the audit of each item carried in inventory. Companies audit their inventory at least yearly to ensure accuracy of the records.

Key Terms

ABC inventory classification Divides inventory into dollar volume categories that map into strategies appropriate for the category.

Cycle counting A physical inventory-taking technique in which inventory is counted on a frequent basis rather than once or twice a year.

SOLVED PROBLEMS

LO 20–2 SOLVED PROBLEM 1

A product is priced to sell at \$100 per unit, and its cost is constant at \$70 per unit. Each unsold unit has a salvage value of \$20. Demand is expected to range between 35 and 40 units for the period; 35 definitely can be sold and no units over 40 will be sold. The demand probabilities and the associated cumulative probability distribution (P) for this situation are shown as follows.

Number of Units Demanded	Probability of This Demand	Cumulative Probability
35	0.10	0.10
36	0.15	0.25
37	0.25	0.50
38	0.25	0.75
39	0.15	0.90
40	0.10	1.00

How many units should be ordered?

Solution

The cost of underestimating demand is the loss of profit, or C_u = \$100 – \$70 = \$30 per unit. The cost of overestimating demand is the loss incurred when the unit must be sold at salvage value, C_o = \$70 – \$20 = \$50.

The optimal probability of not being sold is

$$P \leq \frac{C_u}{C_o + C_u} = \frac{30}{50 + 30} = .375$$

From the distribution data given, this corresponds to the 37th unit.

The following is a full marginal analysis for the problem. Note that the minimum cost occurs when 37 units are purchased.

		Number of Units Purchased					
Units Demanded	Probability	35	36	37	38	39	40
35	0.1	0	50	100	150	200	250
36	0.15	30	0	50	100	150	200
37	0.25	60	30	0	50	100	150
38	0.25	90	60	30	0	50	100
39	0.15	120	90	60	30	0	50
40	0.1	150	120	90	60	30	0
Total cost		75	53	43	53	83	125

SOLVED PROBLEM 2

Items purchased from a vendor cost \$20 each, and the forecast for next year's demand is 1,000 units. If it costs \$5 every time an order is placed for more units, and the storage cost is \$4 per unit per year, answer the following questions.

a. What quantity should be ordered each time?

b. What is the total ordering cost for a year?

c. What is the total storage cost for a year?

Solution

a. The quantity to be ordered each time is

$$Q = \sqrt{\frac{2DS}{H}} = \sqrt{\frac{2(1{,}000)5}{4}} = 50 \text{ units}$$

b. The total ordering cost for a year is

$$\frac{D}{Q}S = \frac{1{,}000}{50}(\$5) = \$100$$

c. The storage cost for a year is

$$\frac{Q}{2}H = \frac{50}{2}(\$4) = \$100$$

SOLVED PROBLEM 3

Daily demand for a product is 120 units, with a standard deviation of 30 units. The review period is 14 days and the lead time is 7 days. At the time of review, 130 units are in stock. If only a 1 percent risk of stocking out is acceptable, how many units should be ordered?

Solution

$$\sigma_{T+L} = \sqrt{(14+7)(30)^2} = \sqrt{18{,}900} = 137.5$$

$$z = 2.33$$

$$q = \bar{d}(T+L) + z\sigma_{T+L} - I$$

$$= 120(14+7) + 2.33(137.5) - 130$$

$$= 2{,}710 \text{ units}$$

SOLVED PROBLEM 4

A company currently has 200 units of a product on-hand that it orders every two weeks when the salesperson visits the premises. Demand for the product averages 20 units per day with a standard deviation of 5 units. Lead time for the product to arrive is seven days. Management has a goal of a 95 percent probability of not stocking out for this product.

The salesperson is due to come in late this afternoon when 180 units are left in stock (assuming that 20 are sold today). How many units should be ordered?

Solution

Give $I = 180$, $T = 14$, $L = 7$, $d = 20$

$$\sigma_{T+L} = \sqrt{21(5)^2} = 23$$

$$z = 1.64$$

$$q = \bar{d}(T+L) + z\sigma_{T+L} - I$$

$$= 20(14+7) + 1.64(23) - 180$$

$$q = 278 \text{ units}$$

SOLVED PROBLEM 5

Sheet Metal Industries Inc. (SMI) is a Tier 1 supplier to various industries that use components made from sheet metal in their final products. Manufacturers of desktop computers and electronic devices are its primary customers. SMI orders a relatively small number of different raw sheet metal products in very large quantities. The purchasing department is trying to establish an ordering policy that will minimize total costs while meeting the needs of the firm. One of the highest volume items it purchases comes in precut sheets direct from the steel processor. Forecasts based on historical data indicate that SMI will need to purchase 200,000 sheets of this product on an annual basis. The steel producer has a minimum order quantity of 1,000 sheets, and offers a sliding price scale based on the quantity in each order, as follows.

Order Quantity	Unit Price
1,000–9,999	$2.35
10,000–29,999	$2.20
30,000 +	$2.15

The purchasing department estimates that it costs $300 to process each order, and SMI has an inventory carrying cost equal to 15 percent of the value of inventory.

Based on this information, use the price-break model to determine an optimal order quantity.

Solution

The first step is to take the information in the problem and assign it to the proper notation in the model.

D = 200,000 units (annual demand)
S = $300 to place and process each order
I = 15 percent of the item cost
C = cost per unit, based on the order quantity Q, as shown in the table

Next, solve the economic order size at each price point starting with the lowest unit price. Stop when you reach a feasible Q.

$$Q_{\$2.15} = \sqrt{\frac{2*200{,}000*300}{.15*2.15}} = 19{,}290 \text{ (infeasible)}$$

The EOQ at $2.15 is not feasible for that price point. The best quantity to order at that price point is therefore the minimum feasible quantity of 30,000.

$$Q_{\$2.20} = \sqrt{\frac{2*200{,}000*300}{.15*2.20}} = 19{,}069 \text{ (feasible)}$$

The EOQ at $2.20 is feasible, therefore the best quantity to order at that price point is the EOQ of 19,069. Because we found a feasible EOQ at this price point, we do not need to consider any higher price points. The two ordering policies to consider are: Order 30,000 sheets each time at $2.15 apiece, or order 19,069 sheets each time at $2.20 each. The question is whether the purchase price savings at the $2.15 price point will offset the higher holding costs that would result from the higher ordering quantity. To answer this question, compute the total cost of each option.

$$TC_{Q=30{,}000} = 200{,}000*\$2.15 + \frac{200{,}000}{30{,}000}(\$300) + \frac{30{,}000}{2}(.15)(\$2.15) \approx \$436{,}837$$

$$TC_{Q=19{,}069} = 200{,}000*\$2.20 + \frac{200{,}000}{19{,}069}(\$300) + \frac{19{,}069}{2}(.15)(\$2.20) \approx \$446{,}293$$

The lowest total annual cost comes when ordering 30,000 units at $2.15, so that would be the best ordering policy. Are you surprised that the 5-cent difference in unit price would make such a difference in total cost? When dealing in large volumes, even tiny price changes can have a significant impact on the big picture.

DISCUSSION QUESTIONS

1. Distinguish between dependent and independent demand in a McDonald's restaurant, in an integrated manufacturer of personal copiers, and in a pharmaceutical supply house. **LO20–1**
2. Distinguish between in-process inventory, safety stock inventory, and seasonal inventory.
3. Discuss the nature of the costs that affect inventory size. For example:
   a. How does shrinkage (stolen stock) contribute to the cost of carrying inventory? How can this cost be reduced?
   b. How does obsolescence contribute to the cost of carrying inventory? How can this cost be reduced?
4. Under which conditions would a plant manager elect to use a fixed–order quantity model as opposed to a fixed–time period model? What are the disadvantages of using a fixed–time period ordering system? **LO20–2**
5. What two basic questions must be answered by an inventory control decision rule?
6. Discuss the assumptions that are inherent in production setup cost, ordering cost, and carrying costs. How valid are they?
7. "The nice thing about inventory models is that you can pull one off the shelf and apply it so long as your cost estimates are accurate." Comment.
8. Which type of inventory system would you use in the following situations?
   a. Supplying your kitchen with fresh food
   b. Obtaining a daily newspaper
   c. Buying gas for your car

   To which of these items do you impute the highest stock-out cost?
9. What is the purpose of classifying items into groups, as the ABC classification does? **LO20–3**
10. When cycle counting inventory, why do experts recommend a lower acceptable error tolerance for A items than B or C items?

OBJECTIVE QUESTIONS

1. What is the term used to refer to inventory while in distribution—that is, being moved within the supply chain? **LO20–1**
2. Almost certainly you have seen vending machines being serviced on your campus and elsewhere. On a predetermined schedule, the vending company checks each machine and fills it with various products. This is an example of which category of inventory model?
3. To support the manufacture of desktop computers for its customers, Dell needs to order all the parts that go into the computer, such as hard drives, motherboards, and memory modules. Obviously, the demand for these items is driven by the production schedule for the computers. What is the term used to describe demand for these parts?
4. The local supermarket buys lettuce each day to ensure really fresh produce. Each morning, any lettuce that is left from the previous day is sold to a dealer that resells it to farmers who use it to feed their animals. This week, the supermarket can buy fresh lettuce for $4.00 a box. The lettuce is sold for $10.00 a box and the dealer that sells old lettuce is willing to pay $1.50 a box. Past history says that tomorrow's demand for lettuce averages 250 boxes with a standard deviation of 34 boxes. How many boxes of lettuce should the supermarket purchase tomorrow? (Answer available in Appendix D) **LO20–2**
5. Next week, Super Discount Airlines has a flight from New York to Los Angeles that will be booked to capacity. The airline knows from past history that an average of 25 customers (with a standard deviation of 15) cancel their reservation or do not show for the flight. Revenue from a ticket on the flight is $125. If the flight is overbooked, the airline has a policy of getting the customer on the next available flight and giving the person a free round-trip ticket on a future

flight. The cost of this free round-trip ticket averages \$250. Super Discount considers the cost of flying the plane from New York to Los Angeles a sunk cost. By how many seats should Super Discount overbook the flight?

6. Solve the newsperson problem. What is the optimal order quantity?

Probability	0.2	0.1	0.1	0.2	0.3	0.1
Value	1	2	3	4	5	6

Purchase cost $c = 15$
Selling price $p = 25$
Salvage value $v = 10$

7. Wholemark is an Internet order business that sells one popular New Year's greeting card once a year. The cost of the paper on which the card is printed is \$0.05 per card, and the cost of printing is \$0.15 per card. The company receives \$2.15 per card sold. Because the cards have the current year printed on them, unsold cards have no salvage value. Its customers are from the four areas: Los Angeles, Santa Monica, Hollywood, and Pasadena. Based on past data, the number of customers from *each* of the four regions is normally distributed with a mean of 2,000 and a standard deviation of 500. (Assume these four are independent.) What is the optimal production quantity for the card?
8. Lakeside Bakery bakes fresh pies every morning. The daily demand for its apple pies is a random variable with (discrete) distribution, based on past experience, given by

Demand	5	10	15	20	25	30
Probability	10%	20%	25%	25%	15%	5%

Each apple pie costs the bakery \$6.75 to make and is sold for \$17.99. Unsold apple pies at the end of the day are purchased by a nearby soup kitchen for 99 cents each. Assume no goodwill cost.
   a. If the company decided to bake 15 apple pies each day, what would be its expected profit?
   b. Based on the demand distribution given, how many apple pies should the company bake each day to maximize its expected profit?
9. Sally's Silk Screening produces specialty T-shirts that are primarily sold at special events. She is trying to decide how many to produce for an upcoming event. During the event, Sally can sell T-shirts for \$20 a piece. However, when the event ends, any unsold T-shirts are sold for \$4 each. It costs Sally \$8 to make a specialty T-shirt. Sally's estimate of demand is the following:

Demand	Probability
300	.05
400	.10
500	.40
600	.30
700	.10
800	.05

   a. What is the service rate (or optimal fractile)?
   b. How many T-shirts should she produce for the upcoming event?
10. You are a newsvendor selling the *San Pedro Times* every morning. Before you get to work, you go to the printer and buy the day's paper for \$0.25 a copy. You sell a copy of the *San Pedro Times* for \$1.00. Daily demand is distributed normally with mean = 250 and standard deviation = 50. At the end of each morning, any leftover copies are worthless and they go to a recycle bin.
   a. How many copies of the *San Pedro Times* should you buy each morning?
   b. Based on part (*a*), what is the probability that you will run out of stock?
11. Famous Albert prides himself on being the Cookie King of the West. Small, freshly baked cookies are the specialty of his shop. Famous Albert has asked for help to determine the number of cookies

he should make each day. From an analysis of past demand, he estimates demand for cookies as the following:

Demand	Probability of Demand
1,800 dozen	0.05
2,000	0.10
2,200	0.20
2,400	0.30
2,600	0.20
2,800	0.10
3,000	0.05

Each dozen sells for $0.69 and costs $0.49, which includes handling and transportation. Cookies that are not sold at the end of the day are reduced to $0.29 and sold the following day as day-old merchandise.

a. Construct a table showing the profits or losses for each possible quantity.
b. What is the optimal number of cookies to make?
c. Solve this problem by using marginal analysis.

12. Ray's Satellite Emporium wishes to determine the best order size for its best-selling satellite dish (Model TS111). Ray has estimated the annual demand for this model at 1,000 units. His cost to carry one unit is $100 per year per unit, and he has estimated that each order costs $25 to place. Using the EOQ model, how many should Ray order each time?
13. Dunstreet's Department Store would like to develop an inventory ordering policy with a 95 percent probability of not stocking out. To illustrate your recommended procedure, use as an example the ordering policy for white percale sheets.

    Demand for white percale sheets is 5,000 per year. The store is open 365 days per year. Every two weeks (14 days) inventory is counted and a new order is placed. It takes 10 days for the sheets to be delivered. Standard deviation of demand for the sheets is 5 per day. There are currently 150 sheets on-hand.

    How many sheets should you order?
14. Charlie's Pizza orders all of its pepperoni, olives, anchovies, and mozzarella cheese to be shipped directly from Italy. An American distributor stops by every four weeks to take orders. Because the orders are shipped directly from Italy, they take three weeks to arrive.

    Charlie's Pizza uses an average of 150 pounds of pepperoni each week, with a standard deviation of 30 pounds. Charlie's prides itself on offering only the best-quality ingredients and a high level of service, so it wants to ensure a 98 percent probability of not stocking out on pepperoni.

    Assume that the sales representative just walked in the door and there are currently 500 pounds of pepperoni in the walk-in cooler. How many pounds of pepperoni would you order? (Answer in Appendix D)
15. Given the following information, formulate an inventory management system. The item is demanded 50 weeks a year.

Parameter	Value
Item cost	$10.00
Order cost	$250.00/order
Annual holding cost	33% of item cost
Annual demand	25,750 units
Average weekly demand	515/week
Standard deviation of weekly demand	25 units
Lead time	1 week
Service probability	95%

a. State the order quantity and reorder point.
b. Determine the annual holding and order costs.
c. If a price break of $50 per order was offered for purchase quantities of over 2,000, would you take advantage of it? How much would you save annually?

16. Lieutenant Commander Data is planning to make his monthly (every 30 days) trek to Gamma Hydra City to pick up a supply of isolinear chips. The trip will take Data about two days. Before he leaves, he calls in the order to the GHC Supply Store. He uses chips at an average rate of 5 per day (seven days per week) with a standard deviation of demand of 1 per day. He needs a 98 percent service probability. If he currently has 35 chips in inventory, how many should he order? What is the most he will ever have to order?
17. Jill's Job Shop buys two parts (Tegdiws and Widgets) for use in its production system from two different suppliers. The parts are needed throughout the entire 52-week year. Tegdiws are used at a relatively constant rate and are ordered whenever the remaining quantity drops to the reorder level. Widgets are ordered from a supplier who stops by every three weeks. Data for both products are as follows: (Answers in Appendix D)

Item	Tegdiw	Widget
Annual demand	10,000	5,000
Holding cost (% of item cost)	20%	20%
Setup or order cost	$150.00	$25.00
Lead time	4 weeks	1 week
Safety stock	55 units	5 units
Item cost	$10.00	$2.00

a. What is the inventory control system for Tegdiws? That is, what is the reorder quantity and what is the reorder point?
b. What is the inventory control system for Widgets?

18. Demand for an item is 1,000 units per year. Each order placed costs $10; the annual cost to carry items in inventory is $2 each. In what quantities should the item be ordered?
19. The annual demand for a product is 15,600 units. The weekly demand is 300 units with a standard deviation of 90 units. The cost to place an order is $31.20, and the time from ordering to receipt is four weeks. The annual inventory carrying cost is $0.10 per unit. Find the reorder point necessary to provide a 98 percent service probability.

    Suppose the production manager is asked to reduce the safety stock of this item by 50 percent. If she does so, what will the new service probability be?
20. Daily demand for a product is 100 units, with a standard deviation of 25 units. The review period is 10 days and the lead time is 6 days. At the time of review, there are 50 units in stock. If 98 percent service probability is desired, how many units should be ordered?
21. Item X is a standard item stocked in a company's inventory of component parts. Each year, the firm, on a random basis, uses about 2,000 of item X, which costs $25 each. Storage costs, which include insurance and cost of capital, amount to $5 per unit of average inventory. Every time an order is placed for more of item X, it costs $10.
    a. Whenever item X is ordered, what should the order size be?
    b. What is the annual cost for ordering item X?
    c. What is the annual cost for storing item X?
22. Annual demand for a product is 13,000 units; weekly demand is 250 units with a standard deviation of 40 units. The cost of placing an order is $100, and the time from ordering to receipt is four weeks. The annual inventory carrying cost is $0.65 per unit. To provide a 98 percent service probability, what must the reorder point be?

    Suppose the production manager is told to reduce the safety stock of this item by 100 units. If this is done, what will the new service probability be?
23. Gentle Ben's Bar and Restaurant uses 5,000 quart bottles of an imported wine each year. The effervescent wine costs $3 per bottle and is served only in whole bottles because it loses its bubbles

quickly. Ben figures that it costs $10 each time an order is placed, and holding costs are 20 percent of the purchase price. It takes three weeks for an order to arrive. Weekly demand is 100 bottles (closed two weeks per year) with a standard deviation of 30 bottles.

Ben would like to use an inventory system that minimizes inventory cost and will provide a 95 percent service probability.

a. What is the economic quantity for Ben to order?

b. At what inventory level should he place an order?

24. Retailers Warehouse (RW) is an independent supplier of household items to department stores. RW attempts to stock enough items for a 98 percent service probability.

A stainless steel knife set is one item it stocks. Demand (2,400 sets per year) is relatively stable over the entire year. Whenever new stock is ordered, a buyer must ensure that numbers are correct for stock on-hand and then phone in a new order. The total cost involved to place an order is about $5. RW figures that holding inventory in stock and paying for interest on borrowed capital, insurance, and so on, add up to about $4 holding cost per unit per year.

Analysis of the past data shows that the standard deviation of demand from retailers is about four units per day for a 365-day year. Lead time to get the order is seven days.

a. What is the economic order quantity?

b. What is the reorder point?

25. Daily demand for a product is 60 units with a standard deviation of 10 units. The review period is 10 days, and lead time is 2 days. At the time of review, there are 100 units in stock. If 98 percent service probability is desired, how many units should be ordered?

26. University Drug Pharmaceuticals orders its antibiotics every two weeks (14 days) when a salesperson visits from one of the pharmaceutical companies. Tetracycline is one of its most prescribed antibiotics, with an average daily demand of 2,000 capsules. The standard deviation of daily demand was derived from examining prescriptions filled over the past three months and was found to be 800 capsules. It takes five days for the order to arrive. University Drug would like to satisfy 99 percent of the prescriptions. The salesperson just arrived, and there are currently 25,000 capsules in stock.

How many capsules should be ordered?

27. Sarah's Muffler Shop has one standard muffler that fits a large variety of cars. Sarah wishes to establish a reorder point system to manage inventory of this standard muffler. Use the following information to determine the best order size and the reorder point.

Annual demand	3,500 mufflers	Ordering cost	$50 per order
Standard deviation of daily demand	6 mufflers per working day	Service probability	90%
Item cost	$30 per muffler	Lead time	2 working days
Annual holding cost	25% of item value	Working days	300 per year

28. After graduation, you decide to go into a partnership in an office supply store that has existed for a number of years. Walking through the store and stockrooms, you find a great discrepancy in service levels. Some spaces and bins for items are completely empty; others have supplies that are covered with dust and have obviously been there a long time. You decide to take on the project of establishing consistent levels of inventory to meet customer demands. Most of your supplies are purchased from just a few distributors that call on your store once every two weeks.

You choose, as your first item for study, computer printer paper. You examine the sales records and purchase orders and find that demand for the past 12 months was 5,000 boxes. Using your calculator, you sample some days' demands and estimate that the standard deviation of daily demand is 10 boxes. You also search out these figures:

Cost per box of paper: $11

Desired service probability: 98 percent

Store is open every day.

Salesperson visits every two weeks.

Delivery time following visit is three days.

Using your procedure, how many boxes of paper would be ordered if, on the day the salesperson calls, 60 boxes are on-hand?

29. A distributor of large appliances needs to determine the order quantities and reorder points for the various products it carries. The following data refer to a specific refrigerator in its product line.

Cost to place an order	\$100/order
Holding cost	20 percent of product cost per year
Cost of refrigerator	\$500/unit
Annual demand	500 units
Standard deviation of demand during lead time	10 units
Lead time	7 days

Consider an even daily demand and a 365-day year.

a. What is the economic order quantity?

b. If the distributor wants a 97 percent service probability, what reorder point, *R*, should be used?

30. It is your responsibility, as the new head of the automotive section of Nichols Department Store, to ensure that reorder quantities for the various items have been correctly established. You decide to test one item and choose Michelin tires, XW size 185 × 14 BSW. A perpetual inventory system has been used, so you examine this, as well as other records, and come up with the following data.

Cost per tire	\$35 each
Holding cost	20 percent of tire cost per year
Demand	1,000 per year
Ordering cost	\$20 per order
Standard deviation of daily demand	3 tires
Delivery lead time	4 days

Because customers generally do not wait for tires but go elsewhere, you decide on a service probability of 98 percent. Assume the demand occurs 365 days per year.

a. Determine the order quantity.

b. Determine the reorder point.

31. UA Hamburger Hamlet (UAHH) places a daily order for its high-volume items (hamburger patties, buns, milk, and so on). UAHH counts its current inventory on-hand once per day and phones in its order for delivery 24 hours later. Determine the number of hamburgers UAHH should order for the following conditions:

Average daily demand	600
Standard deviation of demand	100
Desired service probability	99%
Hamburger inventory	800

32. A local service station is open 7 days per week, 365 days per year. Sales of 10W40 grade premium oil average 20 cans per day. Inventory holding costs are \$0.50 per can per year. Ordering costs are \$10 per order. Lead time is two weeks. Backorders are not practical—the motorist drives away.

a. Based on these data, choose the appropriate inventory model and calculate the economic order quantity and reorder point. Describe in a sentence how the plan would work. *Hint:* Assume demand is deterministic.

b. The boss is concerned about this model because demand really varies. The standard deviation of demand was determined from a data sample to be 6.15 cans per day. The manager wants a 99.5 percent service probability. Determine a new inventory plan based on this information and the data in part (*a*). Use Q_{opt} from part (*a*).

33. Dave's Auto Supply custom mixes paint for its customers. The shop performs a weekly inventory count of the main colors used for mixing paint. Determine the amount of white paint that should be ordered using the following information:

Average weekly demand	20 gallons
Standard deviation of demand	5 gallons/week
Desired service probability	98%
Current inventory	25 gallons
Lead time	1 week

34. SY Manufacturers (SYM) is producing T-shirts in three colors: red, blue, and white. The monthly demand for each color is 3,000 units. Each shirt requires 0.5 pound of raw cotton that is imported from Luft-Geshfet-Textile (LGT) Company in Brazil. The purchasing price per pound is \$2.50 (paid only when the cotton arrives at SYM's facilities) and transportation cost by sea is \$0.20 per pound. The traveling time from LGT's facility in Brazil to the SYM facility in the United States is two weeks. The cost of placing a cotton order, by SYM, is \$100 and the annual interest rate that SYM is facing is 20 percent.
    a. What is the optimal order quantity of cotton?
    b. How frequently should the company order cotton?
    c. Assuming that the first order is needed on April 1, when should SYM place the order?
    d. How many orders will SYM place during the next year?
    e. What is the resulting annual holding cost?
    f. What is the resulting annual ordering cost?
    g. If the annual interest cost is only 5 percent, how will it affect the annual number of orders, the optimal batch size, and the average inventory? (You are not expected to provide a numerical answer to this question. Just describe the direction of the change and explain your answer.)
35. Demand for a book at Amazon.com is 250 units per week. The product is supplied to the retailer from a factory. The factory pays \$10 per unit, while the total cost of a shipment from the factory to the retailer when the shipment size is Q is given by

$$\text{Shipment cost} = \$50 + 2Q$$

Assume the annual inventory carrying cost is 20 percent.
    a. What is the cost per shipment and annual holding cost per book?
    b. What is the optimal shipment size?
    c. What is the average throughput time?
36. Palin's Muffler Shop has one standard muffler that fits a large variety of cars. The shop wishes to establish a *periodic review* system to manage inventory of this standard muffler. Use the information in the following table to determine the optimal inventory target level (or order-up-to level).

Annual demand	3,000 mufflers	Ordering cost	\$50 per order
Standard deviation of daily demand	6 mufflers per working day	Service probability	90%
Item cost	\$30 per muffler	Lead time	2 working days
Annual holding cost	25% of item value	Working days	300 per year
Review period	15 working days		

    a. What is the optimal target level (order-up-to level)?
    b. If the service probability requirement is 95 percent, the optimal target level [your answer in part (*a*)] will (select one):
        I. Increase.
        II. Decrease.
        III. Stay the same.
37. Daily demand for a certain product is normally distributed, with a mean of 100 and a standard deviation of 15. The supplier is reliable and maintains a constant lead time of 5 days. The cost of placing an order is \$10 and the cost of holding inventory is \$0.50 per unit per year. There are no stock-out costs, and unfilled orders are filled as soon as the order arrives. Assume sales occur over 360 days of the year.

Your goal here is to find the order quantity and reorder point to satisfy a 90 percent probability of not stocking out during the lead time.

a. What type of system is the company using?

b. Find the order quantity.

c. Find the reorder point.

38. A particular raw material is available to a company at three different prices, depending on the size of the order:

Less than 100 pounds	$20 per pound
100 pounds to 1,000 pounds	$19 per pound
More than 1,000 pounds	$18 per pound

The cost to place an order is $40. Annual demand is 3,000 units. The holding (or carrying) cost is 25 percent of the material price.

What is the economic order quantity to buy each time?

39. CU, Incorporated (CUI), produces copper contacts that it uses in switches and relays. CUI needs to determine the order quantity, *Q*, to meet the annual demand at the lowest cost. The price of copper depends on the quantity ordered. Here are price-break and other data for the problem:

Price of copper	$0.82 per pound up to 2,499 pounds
	$0.81 per pound for orders between 2,500 and 5,000 pounds
	$0.80 per pound for orders greater than 5,000 pounds
Annual demand	50,000 pounds per year
Holding cost	20 percent per unit per year of the price of the copper
Ordering cost	$30.00

Which quantity should be ordered?

LO 20-3 40. In the past, Taylor Industries has used a fixed–time period inventory system that involved taking a complete inventory count of all items each month. However, increasing labor costs are forcing Taylor Industries to examine alternative ways to reduce the amount of labor involved in inventory stockrooms, yet without increasing other costs, such as shortage costs. Here is a random sample of 20 of Taylor's items.

Item Number	Annual Usage	Item Number	Annual Usage
1	$1,500	11	$13,000
2	12,000	12	600
3	2,200	13	42,000
4	50,000	14	9,900
5	9,600	15	1,200
6	750	16	10,200
7	2,000	17	4,000
8	11,000	18	61,000
9	800	19	3,500
10	15,000	20	2,900

a. What would you recommend Taylor do to cut back its labor cost? (Illustrate using an ABC plan.)

b. Item 15 is critical to continued operations. How would you recommend it be classified?

41. Alpha Products, Inc., is having a problem trying to control inventory. There is insufficient time to devote to all its items equally. The following is a sample of some items stocked, along with the annual usage of each item expressed in dollar volume.

Item	Annual Dollar Usage	Item	Annual Dollar Usage
a	$ 7,000	k	$80,000
b	1,000	l	400
c	14,000	m	1,100
d	2,000	n	30,000
e	24,000	o	1,900
f	68,000	p	800
g	17,000	q	90,000
h	900	r	12,000
i	1,700	s	3,000
j	2,300	t	32,000

a. Can you suggest a system for allocating control time?
b. Specify where each item from the list would be placed.

42. DAT, Inc., produces digital audiotapes to be used in the consumer audio division. DAT lacks sufficient personnel in its inventory supply section to closely control each item stocked, so it has asked you to determine an ABC classification. Here is a sample from the inventory records:

Item	Average Monthly Demand	Price per Unit	Item	Average Monthly Demand	Price per Unit
1	700	$ 6.00	6	100	$10.00
2	200	4.00	7	3,000	2.00
3	2,000	12.00	8	2,500	1.00
4	1,100	20.00	9	500	10.00
5	4,000	21.00	10	1,000	2.00

Develop an ABC classification for these 10 items.

CASE: Inventory Management at the Onset of Economic Depression in India

The global economic depression struck India in September-October 2008. There was a slump in the market due to depressed demands. Customers were not ready to spend. Other countries, like the USA, etc have also witnessed similar depressions in the market on different occasions. During economic downturn in India in 2008, the supply chains of auto sector started getting choked with raw-material, work-in-process inventory, and finished vehicles at different stages. Sources within a leading auto manufacturer of India said, "it has been observed in the month of October (2008) across the industry that unavailability of finance coupled with high interest rate is forcing the customers to postpone purchases."

Tata Motors understood it well that immediate step must be taken to match demand with supply and avoid unnecessary build-up of inventories in the company or with its dealers. Therefore, to tackle the slump in demand, it decided to shut down its Jamshedpur plant, which produces commercial vehicles. The process started initially for three days, starting from November 6 and again for five days, starting from November 25. In another plant at Pune, which has a strong well-trained workforce of over 10,000, "Tata Motors" produces passenger cars like Indica, Indigo, Safari and Sumo and also light, medium and heavy commercial vehicles. This plant was temporarily planned to stop production during November 21 to 26. Similarly, the Lucknow plant of Tata Motors manufactures a range of buses including low-floor CNG, and high capacity buses. This plant took a similar block closure from November 10 to November 15, 2008.

Other auto manufactures were no way different. The Hinduja Group's Ashok Leyland also started feeling the pinch of high inventory due to slump in the market. It decided to bring down the manufacturing at its Chennai plant to just three days per week. Almost all manufacturing sectors in India went through this phase at that point of time.

Government suggestion to the industry was quite interesting. According to the then Finance Minister, Mr. P. Chidambaram, this situation was entirely manageable and within industry's control as he further said in an interview that cutting down the production by planned closure of manufacturing is a short-sighted approach. There is a need to stimulate the demand by cutting down the price and providing liquidity in the market.

Source: *Business Standard*, 23 November 2008.

Questions

1. Other than planned closure of manufacturing units, what are the other ways to flush out inventory from a supply chain?
2. Economic depression in India was not too sudden as there were warning signals coming from USA economy. Then, why did Indian auto sector still struggle with the unplanned inventory?
3. Why did the then Finance Minister advocate a solution other than closure of manufacturing? Do you expect a cascading effect of economic depression due to planned closures?

ANALYTICS EXERCISE: INVENTORY MANAGEMENT AT BIG10SWEATERS.COM

Big10Sweaters.com is a new company started last year by two recent college graduates. The idea behind the company was simple. It will sell premium logo sweaters for Big Ten colleges with one major, unique feature. This unique feature is a special large monogram that has the customer's name, major, and year of graduation. The sweater is the perfect gift for graduating students and alumni, particularly avid football fans who want to show support during the football season. The company is off to a great start and had a successful first year while selling to only a few schools. This year it plans to expand to a few more schools and target the entire Big Ten Conference within three years.

You have been hired by Big10Sweaters.com and need to make a good impression by making good supply chain decisions. This is your big opportunity with a startup. There are only two people in the firm and you were hired with the prospect of possibly becoming a principal in the future. You majored in supply chain (operations) management in school and had a great internship at a big retailer that was getting into Internet sales. The experience was great, but now you are on your own and have none of the great support that the big company had. You need to find and analyze your own data and make some big decisions. Of course, Rhonda and Steve, the partners who started the company, are knowledgeable about this venture and they are going to help along the way.

Rhonda had the idea to start the company two years ago and talked her friend from business school, Steve, into joining her. Rhonda is into Web marketing, has a degree in computer science, and has been working on completing an online MBA. She is as much an artist as a techie. She can really make the Website sing.

Steve majored in accounting and likes to pump the numbers. He has done a great job of keeping the books and selling the company to some small venture capital people in the area. Last year, he was successful in getting them to invest $2,000,000 in the company (a onetime investment). There were some significant strings attached to this investment in that it stipulated that only $100,000 per year could go toward paying the salary of the two principals. The rest had to be spent on the Website, advertising, and inventory. In addition, the venture capital company gets 25 percent of the company profits, before taxes, during the first four years of operation, assuming the company makes a profit.

Your first job is to focus on the firm's inventory. The company is centered on selling the premium sweaters to college football fans through a Website. Your analysis is important since a significant portion of the company's assets is the inventory that it carries.

The business is cyclic, and sales are concentrated during the period leading up to the college football season, which runs between late August and the end of each year. For the upcoming season, the firm wants to sell sweaters to only a few of the largest schools in the Midwest region of the United States. In particular, it is targeting the Ohio State University (OSU), University of Michigan (UM), Michigan State University (MSU), Purdue University (PU), and Indiana University (IU). These five schools have major football programs and a loyal fan base.

The firm has considered the idea of making the sweaters in its own factory, but for now it purchases them from a supplier in China. The prices are great, but service is a problem because the supplier has a 20-week lead time for each order and the minimum order size is 5,000 sweaters. The order can consist of a mix of the different logos, such as 2,000 for OSU, 1,500 for UM, 750 for MSU, 500 for PU, and 250 for IU. Within each logo sublot, sizes are allocated based on percentages, and the supplier suggests 20 percent X-large, 50 percent large, 20 percent medium, and 10 percent small based on its historical data.

Once an order is received, a local subcontractor applies the monograms and ships the sweaters to the customer. The subcontractor stores the inventory of sweaters for the company in a small warehouse area located at their site.

This is the company's second year of operation. Last year, it sold sweaters for only three of the schools, OSU, MU, and PU. It ordered the minimum 5,000 sweaters and sold all of them, but the experience was painful because the company had too many MU sweaters and not enough for OSU fans. Last year, it ordered 2,300 OSU, 1,800 MU, and 900 PU sweaters. Of the 5,000 sweaters, 342 had to be sold at a steep discount on eBay after the season. The company was hoping not to do this again.

For the next year, you have collected some data relevant to the decision. Exhibit 20.12 shows cost information for the product when purchased from the supplier in China. Here we see that the cost for each sweater, delivered to the warehouse of our monogramming subcontractor, is $60.88. This price is valid for any quantity we order above 5,000 sweaters. This order can be a mix of sweaters for each of the five schools we are targeting. The supplier needs 20 weeks to process the order, so the order needs to be placed around April 1 for the upcoming football season.

EXHIBIT 20.12

Cost Information for Big10Sweaters.com

Item	Cost	
Material	$32.00	
Labor	10.50	
Overhead	1.25	
Transportation within China	1.00	
Supplier profit	8.95	
Agent's fee	2.68	
Freight (ocean carrier)	1.50	
Duty, insurance, etc.	3.00	
Total China supplier cost		$60.88
Monogram material	5.00	
Labor	8.00	
Total subcontractor cost		$13.00
Total (per sweater)		$73.88

Our monogramming subcontractor gets $13 for each sweater. Shipping cost is paid by the customer when the order is placed.

In addition to the cost data, you also have some demand information, as shown in Exhibit 20.13. The exact sales numbers for last year are given. Sweaters sold at full retail price were sold for $120 each. Sweaters left over at the end of the season were sold through eBay for $50 each and these sweaters were not monogrammed by our subcontractor. Keep in mind that the retail sales numbers do not accurately reflect actual demand because they stocked out of the OSU sweaters toward the end of the season.

As for advertising the sweaters for next season, Rhonda is committed to using the same approach used last year. The firm placed ads in the football program sold at each game. These worked very well for reaching those attending the games, but she realized there may be ways to advertise that may open sales to more alumni. She has hired a market research firm to help identify other advertising outlets but has decided to wait at least another year to try something different.

Forecasting demand is a major problem for the company. You have asked Rhonda and Steve to predict what they think sales might be next year. You have also asked the market research firm to apply their forecasting tools. Data on these forecasts are given in Exhibit 20.13. To generate some statistics, you have averaged the forecasts and calculated the standard deviation for each school and in total.

Based on advice from the market research firm, you have decided to use the aggregate demand forecast and standard deviation for the aggregate demand. The aggregate demand was calculated by adding the average forecast for each item. The aggregate standard deviation was calculated by squaring the standard deviation for each item (this is the variance), summing the variance for each item, and then taking the square root of this sum. This assumes that the demand for each school is independent, meaning that the demand for Ohio State is totally unrelated to the demand at Michigan and the other schools.

You will allocate your aggregate order to the individual schools based on their expected percentage of total demand. You discussed your analysis with Rhonda and Steve and they are OK with your analysis. They would like to see what the order quantities would be if each school was considered individually.

EXHIBIT 20.13

Forecast Data for Big10Sweaters.com

	Average Football Game Attendance	Last Year's Actual Sales (full price)	Rhonda's Forecast for Next Year	Steve's Forecast for Next Year	Market Research Forecast for Next Year	Average Forecast	Standard Deviation
Ohio State	105,261	2,300	2,500	2,200	2,800	2,500	300
Michigan	108,933	1,468	1,800	1,500	2,000	1,767	252
Purdue	50,457	890	1,000	900	1,100	1,000	100
Michigan State	74,741	—	1,750	1,500	1,600	1,617	126
Indiana	41,833	—	600	500	450	517	76
Penn State	107,008						
Wisconsin	80,109						
Iowa	70,214						
Illinois	59,545						
Minnesota	50,805						
Northwestern	24,190						
Nebraska	85,071						
Total		4,658*	7,650	6,600	7,950	7,400	430**

*342 sweaters were sold through eBay for $50 each (the customer pays shipping on all orders).

**Calculated assuming the demand at each school is independent $\sqrt{\sum_{i=1}^{N} \sigma_i^2}$

You have a spreadsheet set up with all the data from the exhibits called Big10Sweater.xls and you are ready to do some calculations.

Questions

1. You are curious as to how much Rhonda and Steve made in their business last year. You do not have all the data, but you know that most of their expenses relate to buying the sweaters and having them monogrammed. You know they paid themselves $50,000 each and you know the rent, utilities, insurance, and a benefit package for the business was about $20,000. About how much do you think they made "before taxes" last year? If they must make their payment to the venture capital firm, and then pay 50 percent in taxes, what was their increase in cash last year?
2. What was your reasoning behind using the aggregate demand forecast when determining the size of your order rather than the individual school forecasts? Should you rethink this or is there a sound basis for doing it this way?
3. How many sweaters should you order this year? Break down your order by individual school. Document your calculations in your spreadsheet. Calculate this based on the aggregate forecast and also the forecast by individual school.
4. What do you think they could make this year? They are paying you $40,000 and you expect your benefit package addition would be about $1,000 per year. Assume that they order based on the aggregate forecast.
5. How should the business be developed in the future? Be specific and consider changes related to your supplier, the monogramming subcontractor, target customers, and products.

PRACTICE EXAM

In each of the following, name the term defined or answer the question. Answers are listed at the bottom.

1. The model most appropriate for making a one-time purchase of an item.
2. The model most appropriate when inventory is replenished only in fixed intervals of time—for example, on the first Monday of each month.

3. The model most appropriate when a fixed amount must be purchased each time an order is placed.
4. Based on an EOQ-type ordering criterion, what cost must be taken to zero if the desire is to have an order quantity of a single unit?
5. Term used to describe demand that can be accurately calculated to meet the need of a production schedule, for example.
6. Term used to describe demand that is uncertain and needs to be forecast.
7. We are ordering T-shirts for the spring party and are selling them for twice what we paid for them. We expect to sell 100 shirts and the standard deviation associated with our forecast is 10 shirts. How many shirts should we order?
8. We have an item that we stock in our store that has fairly steady demand. Our supplier insists that we buy 1,200 units at a time. The lead time is very short on the item because the supplier is only a few blocks away and we can pick up another 1,200 units when we run out. How many units do you expect to have in inventory, on average?
9. For the item described in question 8, if we expect to sell approximately 15,600 units next year, how many trips will we need to make to the supplier over the year?
10. If we decide to carry 10 units of safety stock for the item described in questions 8 and 9, and we implemented this by going to our supplier when we had 10 units left, how much inventory would you expect to have, on average, now?
11. We are being evaluated based on the percentage of total demand met in a year (not the probability of stocking out as used in the chapter). Consider an item that we are managing using a fixed–order quantity model with safety stock. We decide to double the order quantity but leave the reorder point the same. Would you expect the percent of total demand met next year to go up or down? Why?
12. Consider an item for which we have 120 units currently in inventory. The average demand for the item is 60 units per week. The lead time for the item is exactly 2 weeks and we carry 16 units for safety stock. What is the probability of running out of the item if we order right now?
13. If we take advantage of a quantity discount, would you expect your average inventory to go up or down? Assume that the probability of stocking out criterion stays the same.
14. This is an inventory auditing technique where inventory levels are checked more frequently than one time a year.

Answers to Practice Exam 1. Single-period model 2. Fixed–time period model 3. Fixed–order quantity model 4. Setup or ordering cost 5. Dependent demand 6. Independent demand 7. 100 shirts 8. 600 units 9. 13 trips 10. 610 units 11. Go up (we are taking fewer chances of running out) 12. 50 percent 13. Will probably go up if the probability of stocking out stays the same 14. Cycle counting

Footnotes

1. *P* is actually a cumulative probability because the sale of the *n*th unit depends not only on exactly *n* being demanded but also on the demand for any number greater than *n*.
2. As previously discussed, the standard deviation of a sum of independent variables equals the square root of the sum of the variances.
3. The Pareto principle is also widely applied in quality problems through the use of Pareto charts. (See Chapter 12.)

For PowerPoint lecture slides, Solutions Manual, Test Bank, Data files for solved examples, Excel Templates, Step-by-Step Solved Examples in video format, Tutorial Videos and many more, scan the adjacent **QR code**, or **visit http://www.mhhe.com/sie-chase15e**

Chapter 21

Material Requirements Planning

LEARNING OBJECTIVES

LO 21-1 Explain what material requirements planning (MRP) is

LO 21-2 Understand how the MRP system is structured

LO 21-3 Analyze an MRP problem

LO 21-4 Evaluate and compare MRP lot-sizing techniques

INSIDE THE IPAD

© Aleksey Boldin/123RF

So what does it cost for Apple Computer to build an iPad?

A good estimate can be made by taking one apart and evaluating the cost of each component. There are many analysts who look at this each time a new model iPad is introduced. Looking at many of these reports, an estimate of the major costs for an iPad 3 with 64GB of memory is the following:

Memory $80
Touchscreen and display $130
Processor $23
Cameras $12
Wi-Fi and sensors $15
Battery and power management $42
Other items $50
Box and charger $6
Manufacturing cost $10

So, for a total cost of about $368, Apple can build an iPad that it sells for about $700. Of course, this does not include the cost to transport the iPad and other support costs, but a profit of $332 is not bad.

UNDERSTANDING MATERIAL REQUIREMENTS PLANNING

LO 21-1

Explain what material requirements planning (MRP) is

Our emphasis in this chapter is on **material requirements planning (MRP)**, which is the key piece of logic that ties the production functions together from a material planning and control view. MRP has been installed almost universally in manufacturing firms, even those considered small companies. The reason is that MRP is a logical, easily understandable approach to the problem of determining the number of parts, components, and materials needed to produce each end item. MRP also provides the schedule specifying when each of these items should be ordered or produced.

Material requirements planning (MRP)
The logic for determining the number of parts, components, and materials needed to produce a product.

MRP is based on dependent demand. Dependent demand is caused by the demand for a higher-level item. Tires, wheels, and engines are dependent demand items based on the demand for automobiles, for example.

Determining the number of dependent demand items needed is essentially a straightforward multiplication process. If one Part A takes five parts of B to make it, then five parts of A require 25 parts of B. The basic difference in independent demand, covered in Chapter 20, and dependent demand covered in this chapter, is as follows: If Part A is sold outside the firm, the amount of Part A that we sell is uncertain. We need to create a forecast using past data or do something like a market analysis. Part A is an independent item. However, Part B is a dependent part and its use depends on Part A. The number of B needed is simply the number of A times five. As a result of this type of multiplication, the requirements of other dependent demand items tend to become more and more lumpy as we go farther down into the product creation sequence. Lumpiness means that the requirements tend to bunch or lump rather than having an even dispersal. This is also caused by the way manufacturing is done. When manufacturing occurs in lots (or batches), items needed to produce the lot are withdrawn from inventory in quantities (perhaps all at once) rather than one at a time.

Strategy

Where MRP Can Be Used

MRP is most valuable in industries where a number of products are made in batches using the same productive equipment. The list in Exhibit 21.1 includes examples of different industry types and the expected benefit from MRP. As you can see in the exhibit, MRP is most valuable to companies involved in assembly operations and least valuable to those in make-to-order fabrication. One more point to note: MRP does not work well in companies that produce a low number of units annually. Especially for companies producing complex, expensive products requiring advanced research and design, experience has shown that lead times tend to be too long and too uncertain, and the product configuration too complex. Such companies need the control features that network scheduling techniques offer. These project management methods are covered in Chapter 4.

An employee performs the final quality control check for the make-to-stock company making automobile tires.

EXHIBIT 21.1

Industry Applications and Expected Benefits of MRP

Industry Type	Examples	Expected Benefits
Assemble-to-stock	Combines multiple component parts into a finished product, which is then stocked in inventory to satisfy customer demand. Examples: watches, tools, appliances.	High
Make-to-stock	Items are manufactured by machine rather than assembled from parts. These are standard stock items carried in anticipation of customer demand. Examples: piston rings, electrical switches.	Medium
Assemble-to-order	A final assembly is made from standard options that the customer chooses. Examples: trucks, generators, motors.	High
Make-to-order	Items are manufactured by machine to customer order. These are generally industrial orders. Examples: bearings, gears, fasteners.	Low
Engineer-to-order	Items are fabricated or assembled completely to customer specification. Examples: turbine generators, heavy machine tools.	High
Process	Includes industries such as foundries, rubber and plastics, specialty paper, chemicals, paint, drug, food processors.	Medium

Master Production Scheduling

Generally, the master production schedule deals with end items (typically finished goods items sold to customers) and is a major input to the MRP process. If the end item is quite large or quite expensive, however, the master schedule may schedule major subassemblies or components instead.

Process

All production systems have limited capacity and limited resources. This presents a challenging job for the master scheduler. Although the aggregate plan provides the general range of operation, the master scheduler must specify exactly what is to be produced. These decisions are made while responding to pressures from various functional areas such as the sales department (meet the customer's promised due date), finance (minimize inventory), management (maximize productivity and customer service, minimize resource needs), and manufacturing (have level schedules and minimize setup time).

To determine an acceptable, feasible schedule to be released to the shop, trial master production schedules are run through the MRP program, which is described in the next section. The resulting planned order releases (the detailed production schedules) are checked to make sure that resources are available and that the completion times are reasonable. What appears to be a feasible master schedule may turn out to require excessive resources once the required materials, parts, and components from lower levels are determined. If this does happen (the usual case), the master production schedule is then modified with these limitations and the MRP program is run again. To ensure good master scheduling, the master scheduler (the human being) must

- Include all demands from product sales, warehouse replenishment, spares, and interplant requirements.
- Never lose sight of the aggregate plan.
- Be involved with customer order promising.
- Be visible to all levels of management.
- Objectively trade off manufacturing, marketing, and engineering conflicts.
- Identify and communicate all problems.

The upper portion of Exhibit 21.2 shows an aggregate plan for the total number of mattresses planned per month, without regard for mattress type. The lower portion shows a master production schedule specifying the exact type of mattress and the quantity planned for production by week. In month 1, for example, a total of 900 mattresses are scheduled: 600 model 327s, 200 model 538s, and 100 model 749s. The next level down (not shown) would be the MRP program that develops detailed schedules showing when cotton batting, springs, and hardwood are needed to make the mattresses.

Exhibit 21.2

The Aggregate Plan and the Master Production Schedule for Mattresses

Aggregate Production Plan for Mattresses

Month	1	2
Mattress production	900	950

Master Production Schedule for Mattress Models

	Week 1	2	3	4	5	6	7	8
Model 327	200			400		200	100	
Model 538		100	100		150		100	
Model 749			100			200		200

To again summarize the planning sequence, the aggregate operations plan, discussed in Chapter 19, specifies product groups. It does not specify exact items. The next level down in the planning process is the master production schedule. The **master production schedule (MPS)** is the time-phased plan specifying how many of each end item the firm plans to build and when. For example, the aggregate plan for a furniture company may specify the total volume of mattresses it plans to produce over the next month or next quarter. The MPS goes the next step down and identifies the exact size of the mattresses and their qualities and styles. All of the mattresses sold by the company would be specified by the MPS. The MPS also states period by period (usually weekly) how many and when each of these mattress types is needed.

Master production schedule (MPS)
A time-phased plan specifying how many of each end item the firm plans to build and when.

Still further down the disaggregation process is the MRP program, which calculates and schedules all raw materials, parts, and supplies needed to make the mattress specified by the MPS.

Time Fences The question of flexibility within a master production schedule depends on several factors: production lead time, commitment of parts and components to a specific end item, relationship between the customer and vendor, amount of excess capacity, and the reluctance or willingness of management to make changes.

The purpose of time fences is to maintain a reasonably controlled flow through the production system. Unless some operating rules are established and adhered to, the system could be chaotic and filled with overdue orders and constant expediting.

Exhibit 21.3 shows an example of a master production schedule time fence. Management defines *time fences* as periods of time having some specified level of opportunity for the customer to make changes. (The customer may be the firm's own marketing department, which may be considering product promotions, broadening variety, or the like.) Note in the exhibit that for the next eight weeks, this particular master schedule is frozen. Each firm has its own time fences and operating rules. Under these rules, *frozen* could be defined as anything from absolutely no changes in one company to only the most minor of changes in another. *Slushy* may allow changes in specific products within a product group so long as parts are available. *Liquid* may allow almost any variations in products, with the provisions that capacity remains about the same and that there are no long lead time items involved.

Some firms use a feature known as **available to promise** for items that are master scheduled. This feature identifies the difference between the number of units currently included in the master schedule and firm customer orders. For example, assume the master schedule indicates that 100 units of Model 538 mattress are going to be made during week seven. If firm customer orders now only indicate that 65 of those mattresses have actually been sold, the sales group has another 35 mattresses "available to promise" for delivery during that week. This can be a powerful tool for coordinating sales and production activities.

Available to promise
A feature of MRP systems that identifies the difference between the number of units currently included in the master schedule and the actual (firm) customer orders.

EXHIBIT 21.3

Master Production Schedule Time Fences

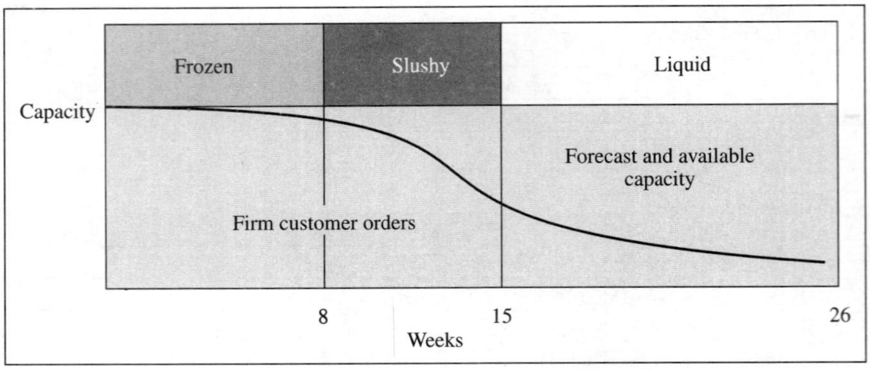

LO 21-2

Understand how the MRP system is structured

MATERIAL REQUIREMENTS PLANNING SYSTEM STRUCTURE

The material requirements planning portion of manufacturing activities most closely interacts with the master schedule, bill-of-materials file, inventory records file, and output reports as shown in Exhibit 21.4.

Each facet of Exhibit 21.4 is detailed in the following sections, but essentially the MRP system works as follows: The master production schedule states the number of items to be produced during specific time periods. A *bill-of-materials* file identifies the specific materials used to make each item and the correct quantities of each. The inventory records file contains data such as the number of units on hand and on order. These three sources—master production schedule, bill-of-materials file, and inventory records file—become the data sources for the material requirements program, which expands the production schedule into a detailed order scheduling plan for the entire production sequence.

Process

Demand for Products

Product demand for end items comes primarily from two main sources. The first is known customers who have placed specific orders, such as those generated by sales personnel, or from interdepartment transactions. These orders usually carry promised delivery dates. There is no forecasting involved in these orders—simply add them up. The second source is the aggregate production plan (described in Chapter 19). The aggregate plan reflects the firm's strategy for meeting demand in the future. The strategy is implemented through the detailed master production schedule.

In addition to the demand for end products, customers also order specific parts and components either as spares or for service and repair. These demands are not usually part of the master production schedule; instead, they are fed directly into the material requirements planning program at the appropriate levels. That is, they are added in as a gross requirement for that part or component.

Bill-of-Materials

Bill-of-Materials (BOM)

The complete product description, listing the materials, parts, and components; the quantity of each item; and also the sequence in which the product is created.

The **bill-of-materials (BOM)** file contains the complete product description, listing the materials, parts, and components; the quantity of each item; and also the sequence in which the product is created. This BOM file is one of the three main inputs to the MRP program. (The other two are the master schedule and the inventory records file.)

The BOM file is often called the *product structure file* or *product tree* because it shows how a product is put together. It contains the information to identify each item and the quantity used per unit of the item of which it is a part. To illustrate this, consider Product A shown in Exhibit 21.5A. Product A is made of two units of Part B and three units of Part C. Part B is made of one unit of Part D and four units of Part E. Part C is made of two units of Part F, five units of Part G, and four units of Part H.

EXHIBIT 21.4

Overall View of the Inputs to a Standard Material Requirements Planning Program and the Reports Generated by the Program

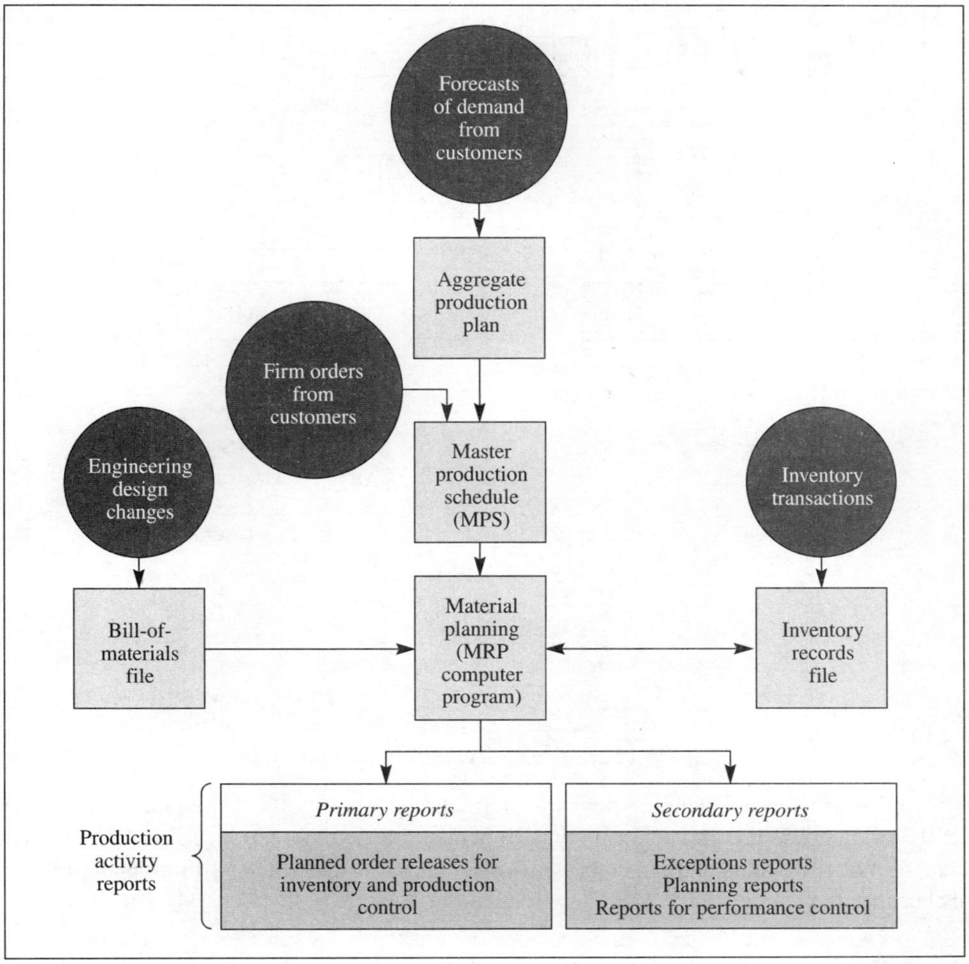

Bill-of-materials files often list parts using an indented structure. This clearly identifies each item and the manner in which it is assembled because each indentation signifies the components of the item. A comparison of the indented parts in Exhibit 21.5B with the item structure in Exhibit 21.5A shows the ease of relating the two displays. From a computer standpoint, however, storing items in indented parts lists is very inefficient. To compute the amount of each item needed at the lower levels, each item would need to be expanded ("exploded") and summed. A more efficient procedure is to store parts data in simple single-level lists. That is, each item and component is listed showing only its parent and the number of units needed per unit of its parent. This avoids duplication because it includes each assembly only once. Exhibit 21.5B shows both the indented parts list and the single-level parts list for Product A.

A *modular* bill-of-materials is the term for a buildable item that can be produced and stocked as a subassembly. It is also a standard item with no options within the module. Many end items that are large and expensive are better scheduled and controlled as modules (or subassemblies). It is particularly advantageous to schedule subassembly modules when the same subassemblies appear in different end items. For example, a manufacturer of cranes can combine booms, transmissions, and engines in a variety of ways to meet a customer's needs. Using a modular bill-of-materials simplifies the scheduling and control and also makes it easier to forecast the use of different modules. Another benefit in using modular bills is that if the same item is used in a number of products, then the total inventory investment can be minimized.

Exhibit 21.5

A. Bill-of-Materials (Product Structure Tree) for Product A

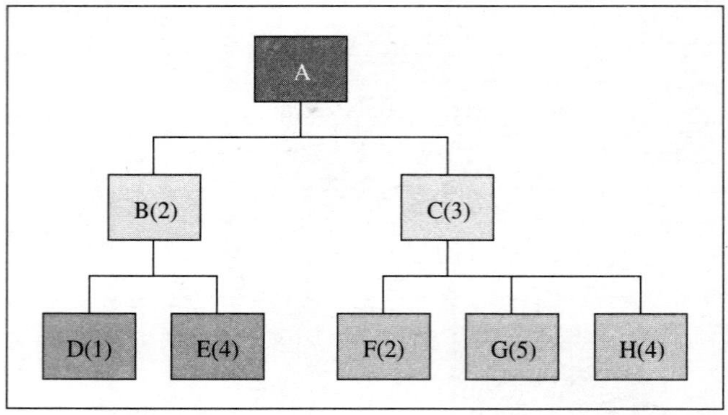

B. Parts List in an Indented Format and in a Single-Level List

Indented Parts List		
A		
	B(2)	
		D(1)
		E(4)
	C(3)	
		F(2)
		G(5)
		H(4)

Single-Level Parts List	
A	
	B(2)
	C(3)
B	
	D(1)
	E(4)
C	
	F(2)
	G(5)
	H(4)

A *super* bill-of-materials includes items with fractional options. (A super bill can specify, for example, 0.3 of a part. What that means is that 30 percent of the units produced contain that part and 70 percent do not.) Modular and super bills-of-materials are often referred to as planning bills-of-materials because they simplify the planning process.

Low-Level Coding If all identical parts occur at the same level for each end product, the total number of parts and materials needed for a product can be computed easily. Consider Product L shown in Exhibit 21.6A. Notice that Item N, for example, occurs both as an input to L and as an input to M. Item N, therefore, needs to be lowered to level 2 (Exhibit 21.6B) to bring all Ns to the same level. If all

Exhibit 21.6

Product L Hierarchy in (A) Expanded to the Lowest Level of Each Item in (B)

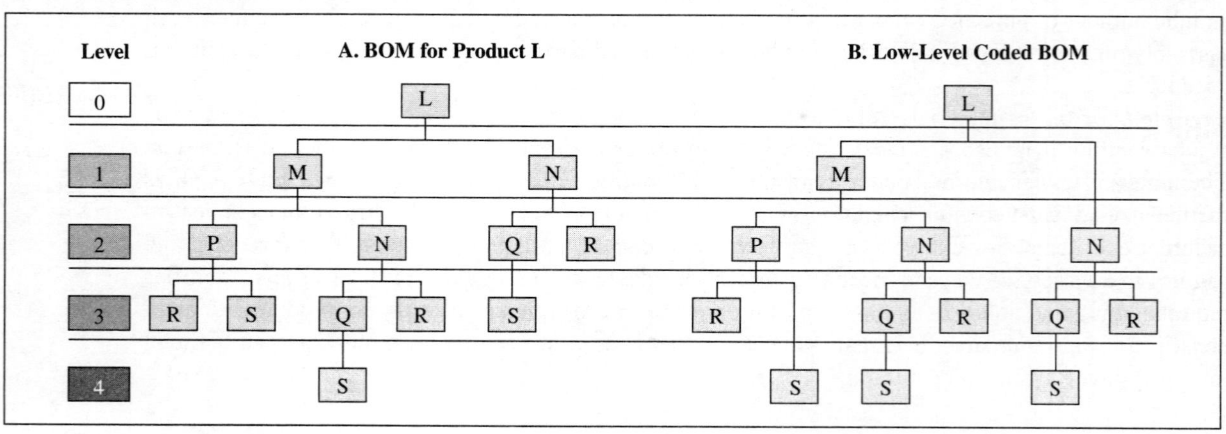

identical items are placed at the same level, it becomes a simple matter for the computer to scan across each level and summarize the number of units of each item required.

Inventory Records

The inventory records file can be quite lengthy. Exhibit 21.7 shows the variety of information contained in the inventory records. The MRP program accesses the *status* segment of the record according to specific time periods (called *time buckets* in MRP slang). These records are accessed as needed during the program run.

EXHIBIT 21.7

The Inventory Status Record for an Item in Inventory

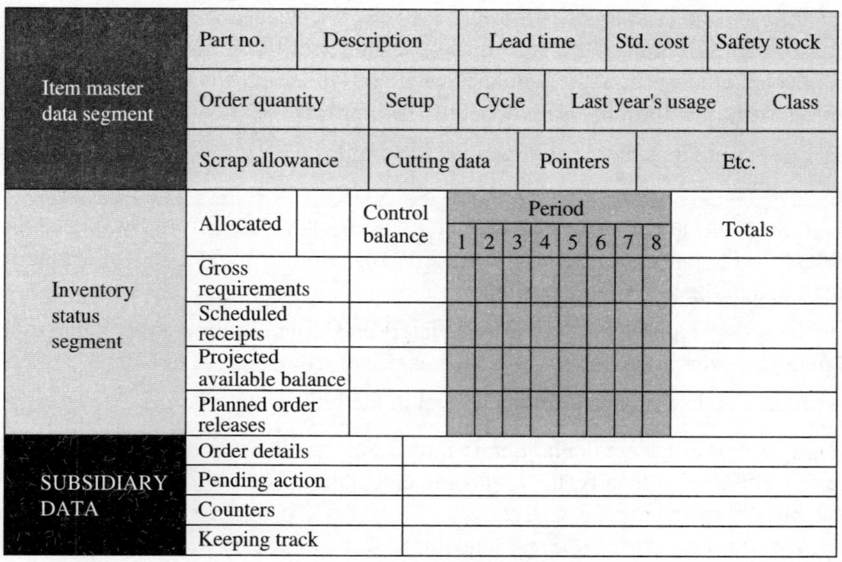

As we will see, the MRP program performs its analysis from the top of the product structure downward, calculating requirements level by level. There are times, however, when it is desirable to identify the parent item that caused the material requirement. For example, we may want to know what subassemblies are generating the requirement for a part that we order from a supplier. The MRP program allows the creation of a *peg record* file either separately or as part of the inventory record file. Pegging requirements allows us to retrace a material requirement upward in the product structure through each level, identifying each parent item that created the demand.

Inventory Transactions File The inventory status file is kept up-to-date by posting inventory transactions as they occur. These changes occur because of stock receipts and disbursements, scrap losses, wrong parts, canceled orders, and so forth.

MRP Computer Program

The material requirements planning program operates using information from the inventory records, the master schedule, and the bill-of-materials. The process of calculating the exact requirements for each item managed by the system is often referred to as the "explosion" process. Working from the top level downward in the bill-of-materials, requirements from parent items are used to calculate the requirements for component items. Consideration is taken of current on-hand balances and orders that are scheduled for receipt in the future.

Key Ideas

MRP programs are integrated into ERP systems offered by companies such as SAP and Oracle.

The following is a general description of the MRP explosion process:

1. The requirements for level 0 items, typically referred to as *end items,* are retrieved from the master schedule. These requirements are referred to as *gross requirements* by the MRP program. Typically, the gross requirements are scheduled in weekly time buckets.
2. Next, the program uses the current on-hand balance together with the schedule of orders that will be received in the future to calculate the *net requirements*. Net requirements are the amounts needed week by week in the future over and above what is currently on hand or committed to through an order already released and scheduled.
3. Using net requirements, the program calculates when orders should be received to meet these requirements. This can be a simple process of just scheduling orders to arrive according to the exact net requirements or a more complicated process where requirements are combined for multiple periods. This schedule of when orders should arrive is referred to as *planned-order receipts*.
4. Because there is typically a lead time associated with each order, the next step is to find a schedule for when orders are actually released. Offsetting the planned-order receipts by the required lead time does this. This schedule is referred to as the *planned-order release.*
5. After these four steps have been completed for all the level zero items, the program moves to level 1 items.
6. The gross requirements for each level 1 item are calculated from the planned-order release schedule for the parents of each level 1 item. Any additional independent demand also needs to be included in the gross requirements.
7. After the gross requirements have been determined, net requirements, planned-order receipts, and planned-order releases are calculated as described in steps 2 to 4.
8. This process is then repeated for each level in the bill-of-materials.

Net change systems
MRP systems that calculate the impact of a change in the MRP data (the inventory status, BOM, or master schedule) immediately.

The process of doing these calculations is much simpler than the description, as you will see in the example that follows. Typically, the explosion calculations are performed each week or whenever changes have been made to the master schedule. Some MRP programs have the option of generating immediate schedules, called *net change* schedules. **Net change systems** are "activity" driven and requirements and schedules are updated whenever a transaction is processed that has an impact on the item. Net change enables the system to reflect in real time the exact status of each item managed by the system.

LO 21-3
Analyze an MRP problem

AN EXAMPLE USING MRP

Ampere, Inc., produces a line of electric meters installed in residential buildings by electric utility companies to measure power consumption. Meters used on single-family homes are of two basic types for different voltage and amperage ranges. In addition to complete meters, some subassemblies are sold separately for repair or for changeovers to a different voltage or power load. The problem for the MRP system is to determine a production schedule to identify each item, the period when it is needed, and the appropriate quantities. The schedule is then checked for feasibility, and the schedule is modified if necessary.

Forecasting Demand

Process

Demand for the meters and components originates from two sources: regular customers that place firm orders in advance based on the needs of their projects and other, typically smaller, customers that buy these items as needed. The smaller customer requirements were forecast using one of the usual techniques described in Chapter 18 and past demand data. Exhibit 21.8 shows the requirements for meters A and B and subassembly D for a three-month period (Months 3 through 5). There are some "other parts" used to make the meters. In order to keep our example manageable, we are not including them in this example.

EXHIBIT 21.8

Future Requirements for Meters A and B and Subassembly D Stemming from Specific Customer Orders and from Forecasts

	Meter A		Meter B		Subassembly D	
Month	Known	Forecast	Known	Forecast	Known	Forecast
3	1,000	250	410	60	200	70
4	600	250	300	60	180	70
5	300	250	500	60	250	70

Developing a Master Production Schedule

For the meter and component requirements specified in Exhibit 21.8, assume that the quantities to satisfy the known and random demands must be available during the first week of the month. This assumption is reasonable because management (in our example) prefers to produce meters in a single batch each month rather than a number of batches throughout the month.

Exhibit 21.9 shows the trial master schedule that we use under these conditions, with demand for Months 3, 4, and 5 listed in the first week of each month, or as Weeks 9, 13, and 17. For brevity, we will work with demand through Week 9. The schedule we develop should be examined for resource availability, capacity availability, and so on, and then revised and run again. We will stop with our example at the end of this one schedule, however.

EXHIBIT 21.9

A Master Schedule to Satisfy Demand Requirements as Specified in Exhibit 21.8

	Week								
	9	10	11	12	13	14	15	16	17
Meter A	1,250				850				550
Meter B	470				360				560
Subassembly D	270				250				320

Bill-of-Materials (Product Structure)

The product structure for meters A and B is shown in Exhibit 21.10A in the typical way using low-level coding, in which each item is placed at the lowest level at which it appears in the structure hierarchy. Meters A and B consist of a common subassembly C and some parts that include part D. To keep things simple, we will focus on only one of the parts, part D, which is a transformer.

From the product structure, notice that part D (the transformer) is used in subassembly C (which is used in both meters A and B). In the case of meter A, an additional part D (transformer) is needed. The "2" in parentheses next to D when used to make a C indicates that two Ds are required for every C that is made. The product structure, as well as the indented parts list in Exhibit 21.10B, indicates how the meters are actually made. First, subassembly C is made, and potentially these are carried in inventory. In a final assembly process, meters A and B are put together, and in the case of meter A an additional part D is used.

Exhibit 12.10B shows the subassemblies and parts that make up the meters and shows the numbers of units required per unit of parent in parentheses.

Inventory Records

The inventory records data would be similar to those shown in Exhibit 21.7. As shown earlier in the chapter, additional data such as vendor identity, cost, and lead time also would be included in these

EXHIBIT 21.10

A. Product Structure for Meters A and B

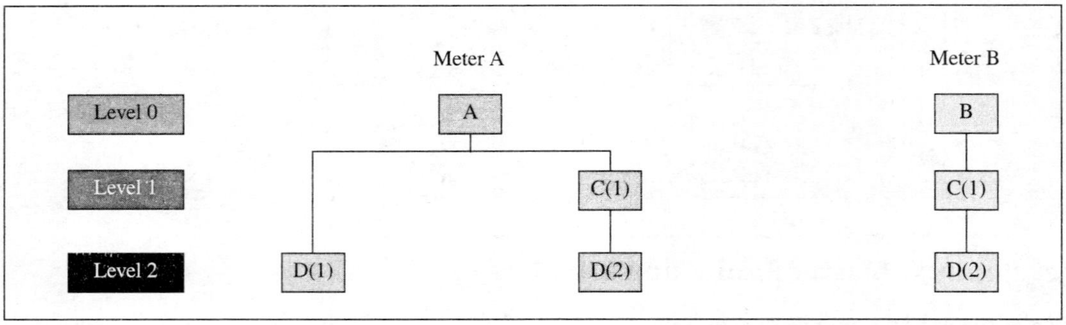

B. Indented Parts List for Meter A and Meter B, with the Required Number of Items per Unit of Parent Listed in Parentheses

Meter A	Meter B
A	B
D(1)	
C(1)	C(1)
D(2)	D(2)

data. For this example, the pertinent data include the on-hand inventory at the start of the program run, safety stock requirements, and the current status of orders that have already been released (see Exhibit 21.11). Safety stock is a minimum amount of inventory that we always want to keep on hand for an item. For example, for subassembly C, we never want the inventory to get below 5 units. We also see that we have an order for 10 units of meter B that is scheduled for receipt at the beginning of Week 5. Another order for 100 units of part D (the transformer) is scheduled to arrive at the beginning of Week 4.

EXHIBIT 21.11

Number of Units On Hand and Lead Time Data that Would Appear on the Inventory Record File

Item	On-Hand Inventory	Lead Time (Weeks)	Safety Stock	On Order
A	50	2	0	
B	60	2	0	10 (Week 5)
C	40	1	5	
D	200	1	20	100 (Week 4)

Performing the MRP Calculations

Conditions are now set to perform the MRP calculations: End-item requirements have been presented in the master production schedule, while the status of inventory and the order lead times are available, and we also have the pertinent product structure data. The MRP calculations (often referred to as an explosion) are done level by level, in conjunction with the inventory data and data from the master schedule.

Exhibit 21.12 shows the details of these calculations. The following analysis explains the logic in detail. We will limit our analysis to the problem of meeting the gross requirements for 1,250 units of meter A, 470 units of meter B, and 270 units of transformer D, all in Week 9.

An MRP record is kept for each item managed by the system. The record contains *gross requirements, scheduled receipts, projected available balance, net requirements, planned order receipts,* and *planned order releases* data. *Gross requirements* are the total amount required for a particular item.

Exhibit 21.12

Material Requirements Planning Schedule for Meters A and B, and Subassemblies C and D

		Week					
Item		4	5	6	7	8	9
A							
LT = 2 weeks	Gross requirements						1,250
On hand = 50	Scheduled receipts						
Safety stock = 0	Projected available balance	50	50	50	50	50	0
Order qty = lot-for-lot	Net requirements						1,200
	Planned order receipts						1,200
	Planned order releases				1,200		
B							
LT = 2 weeks	Gross requirements						470
On hand = 60	Scheduled receipts		10				
Safety stock = 0	Projected available balance	60	70	70	70	70	0
Order qty = lot-for-lot	Net requirements						400
	Planned order receipts						400
	Planned order releases				400		
C					400+		
LT = 1 week	Gross requirements				1,200		
On hand = 40	Scheduled receipts						
Safety stock = 5	Projected available balance	35	35	35	435	435	435
Order qty = 2,000	Net requirements				1,565		
	Planned order receipts				2,000		
	Planned order releases			2,000			
D							
LT = 1 week	Gross requirements			4,000	1,200		270
On hand = 200	Scheduled receipts	100					
Safety stock = 20	Projected available balance	280	280	1,280	80	80	4,810
Order qty = 5,000	Net requirements			3,720			190
	Planned order receipts			5,000			5,000
	Planned order releases		5,000			5,000	

These requirements can be from external customer demand and also from demand calculated due to manufacturing requirements. *Scheduled receipts* represent orders that have already been released and that are scheduled to arrive as of the beginning of the period. Once the paperwork on an order has been released, what was a "planned" order prior to that event now becomes a *scheduled receipt. Projected available balance* is the amount of inventory expected as of the end of a period. This can be calculated as follows:

Analytics

$$\text{Projected available balance}_t = \text{Projected available balance}_{t-1} - \text{Gross requirements}_t + \text{Scheduled receipts}_t + \text{Planned order receipts}_t$$

One thing that needs to be considered is the initial projected available balance. In the case where safety stock is needed, the on-hand balance needs to be reduced by the safety stock. So projected available balance in period zero is on hand minus the safety stock.

A *net requirement* is the amount needed when the *projected available balance* plus the *scheduled receipts* in a period are not sufficient to cover the *gross requirement.* The *planned order receipt* is the amount of an order that is required to meet a net requirement in the period. Finally, the *planned order release* is the planned order receipt offset by the lead time.

EXAMPLE 21.1 MRP Explosion Calculations

Juno Lighting makes special lights that are popular in new homes. Juno expects demand for two popular lights to be the following over the next eight weeks.

	Week							
	1	2	3	4	5	6	7	8
VH1-234	34	37	41	45	48	48	48	48
VH2-100	104	134	144	155	134	140	141	145

A key component in both lights is a socket that the bulb is screwed into in the base fixture. Each light has one of these sockets. Given the following information, plan the production of the lights and purchases of the socket.

	VH1-234	VH2-100	Light Socket
On hand	85	358	425
Q	200 (the production lot size)	400 (the production lot size)	500 (purchase quantity)
Lead time	1 week	1 week	3 weeks
Safety stock	0 units	0 units	20 units

SOLUTION

Item		Week 1	2	3	4	5	6	7	8
VH1-234	Gross requirement	34	37	41	45	48	48	48	48
$Q = 200$	Scheduled receipts								
$LT = 1$	Projected available balance	51	14	173	128	80	32	184	136
$OH = 85$	Net requirements			27				16	
$SS = 0$	Planned order receipts			200				200	
	Planned order releases		200				200		
VH2-100	Gross requirement	104	134	144	155	134	140	141	145
$Q = 400$	Scheduled receipts								
$LT = 1$	Projected available balance	254	120	376	221	87	347	206	61
$OH = 358$	Net requirements			24			53		
$SS = 0$	Planned order receipts			400			400		
	Planned order releases		400			400			
Socket	Gross requirement		600			400	200		
$Q = 500$	Scheduled receipts	500							
$LT = 3$	Projected available balance	905	305	305	305	405	205	205	205
$OH = 425$	Net requirements					95			
$SS = 20$	Planned order receipts					500			
	Planned order releases		500						

The best way to proceed is to work period by period by focusing on the projected available balance calculation. Whenever the available balance goes below zero, a net requirement is generated. When this happens, plan an order receipt to meet the requirement. For example, for VH1 we start with 85 units in inventory and need 34 to meet Week 1 production requirements. This brings our available balance at the end of Week 1 to 51 units. Another 37 units are used during Week 2, dropping inventory to 14. In Week 3, our projected balance drops to 0 and we have a net requirement of 27 units that needs to be covered with an order scheduled to be received in Week 3. Because the lead time is one week, this order needs to be released in Week 2. Week 4 projected available balance is 128, calculated by taking the 200 units received in Week 3 and subtracting the Week 3 net requirement of 27 units and the 45 units needed for Week 4.

Because sockets are used in both VH1 and VH2, the gross requirements come from the planned order releases for these items: 600 are needed in Week 2 (200 for VH1s and 400 for VH2s), 400 in Week 5, and 200 in Week 6. Projected available balance is beginning inventory of 425 plus the scheduled receipts of 500 units minus the 20 units of safety stock.

Beginning with meter A, the projected available balance is 50 units and there are no net requirements until Week 9. In Week 9, an additional 1,200 units are needed to cover the demand of 1,250 generated from the order scheduled through the master schedule. The order quantity is designated "lot-for-lot," which means that we can order the exact quantity needed to meet net requirements. An order, therefore, is planned for receipt of 1,200 units for the beginning of Week 9. Because the lead time is two weeks, this order must be released at the beginning of Week 7.

Meter B is similar to A, although an order for 10 units is scheduled for receipt in period 5. We project that 70 units will be available at the end of Week 5. There is a net requirement for 400 additional units to meet the gross requirement of 470 units in Week 9. This requirement is met with an order for 400 units that must be released at the beginning of Week 7.

Item C is the subassembly used in both meters A and B. We only need additional Cs when either A or B is being made. Our analysis of A indicates that an order for 1,200 will be released in Week 7. An order for 400 Bs also will be released in Week 7, so total demand for C is 1,600 units in Week 7. The projected available balance is the 40 units on hand minus the safety stock of 5 units that we have specified, or 35 units. In Week 7, the net requirement is 1,565 units. The order policy for C indicates an order quantity of 2,000 units, so an order receipt for 2,000 is planned for Week 7. This order needs to be released in Week 6 due to the one-week lead time. Assuming this order is actually processed in the future, the projected available balance is 435 units in Weeks 7, 8, and 9.

Item D, the transformer, has demand from three different sources. The demand in Week 6 is due to the requirement to put Ds into subassembly C. In this case, two Ds are needed for every C, or 4,000 units (the product structure indicates this two-to-one relationship). In the seventh week, 1,200 Ds are needed for the order for 1,200 As that are scheduled to be released in Week 7. Another 270 units are needed in Week 9 to meet the independent demand scheduled through the master schedule. Projected available balance at the end of Week 4 is 280 units (200 on hand plus the scheduled receipt of 100 units minus the safety stock of 20 units) and 280 units in Week 5. There is a net requirement for an additional 3,720 units in Week 6, so we plan to receive an order for 5,000 units (the order quantity). This results in a projected balance of 1,280 in Week 6 and 80 in Week 7 because 1,200 are used to meet demand. Eighty units are projected to be available in Week 8. Due to the demand for 270 in Week 9, a net requirement of 190 units in Week 9 results in planning the receipt of an additional 5,000-unit order in Week 9.

LOT SIZING IN MRP SYSTEMS

LO 21-4

Evaluate and compare MRP lot-sizing techniques

The determination of lot sizes in an MRP system is a complicated and difficult problem. Lot sizes are the part quantities issued in the planned order receipt and planned order release sections of an MRP schedule. For parts produced in-house, lot sizes are the production quantities of batch sizes. For purchased parts, these are the quantities ordered from the supplier. Lot sizes generally meet part requirements for one or more periods.

Analytics

Most lot-sizing techniques deal with how to balance the setup or order costs and holding costs associated with meeting the net requirements generated by the MRP planning process. Many MRP systems have options for computing lot sizes based on some of the more commonly used techniques. The use of lot-sizing techniques increases the complexity of running MRP schedules in a plant. In an attempt to save setup costs, the inventory generated with the larger lot sizes needs to be stored, making the logistics in the plant much more complicated.

Next we explain four lot-sizing techniques using a common example. The lot-sizing techniques presented are lot-for-lot (L4L), economic order quantity (EOQ), least total cost (LTC), and least unit cost (LUC).

Consider the following MRP lot-sizing problem; the net requirements are shown for eight scheduling weeks:

Cost per item				$10.00			
Order or setup cost				$47.00			
Inventory carrying cost/week				0.5%			
Weekly net requirements:							
1	2	3	4	5	6	7	8
50	60	70	60	95	75	60	55

Lot-for-Lot

Lot-for-lot (L4L) is the most common technique. It

- Sets planned orders to exactly match the net requirements.
- Produces exactly what is needed each week with no inventory carried over into future periods.
- Minimizes carrying cost.
- Does not take into account setup costs or capacity limitations.

Exhibit 21.13 shows the lot-for-lot calculations. The net requirements are given in column 2. Because the logic of lot-for-lot says the production quantity (column 3) will exactly match the required quantity (column 2), there will be no inventory left at the end (column 4). Without any inventory to carry over into the next week, there is zero holding cost (column 5). However, lot-for-lot requires a setup cost each week (column 6). Incidentally, there is a setup cost each week because this is a workcenter where a variety of items are worked on each week. This is not a case where the workcenter is committed to one product and sits idle when it is not working on that product (in which case only one setup would result). Lot-for-lot causes high setup costs.

EXHIBIT 21.13

Lot-for-Lot Run Size for an MRP Schedule

(1) Week	(2) Net Requirements	(3) Production Quantity	(4) Ending Inventory	(5) Holding Cost	(6) Setup Cost	(7) Total Cost
1	50	50	0	$0.00	$47.00	$ 47.00
2	60	60	0	0.00	47.00	94.00
3	70	70	0	0.00	47.00	141.00
4	60	60	0	0.00	47.00	188.00
5	95	95	0	0.00	47.00	235.00
6	75	75	0	0.00	47.00	282.00
7	60	60	0	0.00	47.00	329.00
8	55	55	0	0.00	47.00	376.00

Economic Order Quantity

In Chapter 20, we discussed the EOQ model that explicitly balances setup and holding costs. In an EOQ model, either fairly constant demand must exist or safety stock must be kept to provide for demand variability. The EOQ model uses an estimate of total annual demand, the setup or order cost, and the annual holding cost. EOQ was not designed for a system with discrete time periods such as MRP. The lot-sizing techniques used for MRP assume that part requirements are satisfied at the start of the period. Holding costs are then charged only to the ending inventory for the period, not to the average inventory as in the case of the EOQ model. EOQ assumes that parts are used continuously during the period. The lot sizes generated by EOQ do not always cover the entire number of periods.

For example, the EOQ might provide the requirements for 4.6 periods. Using the same data as in the lot-for-lot example, the economic order quantity is calculated as follows:

$$\text{Annual demand based on the 8 weeks} = D = \frac{525}{8} \times 52 = 3{,}412.5 \text{ units}$$

$$\text{Annual holding cost} = H = 0.5\% \times \$10 \times 52 \text{ weeks} = \$2.60 \text{ per unit}$$

$$\text{Setup cost} = S = \$47(\text{given})$$

$$\text{EOQ}=\sqrt{\frac{2DS}{H}} = \sqrt{\frac{2(3{,}412.5)(\$47)}{\$2.60}} = 351 \text{ units}$$

Exhibit 21.14 shows the MRP schedule using an EOQ of 351 units. The EOQ lot size in Week 1 is enough to meet requirements for Weeks 1 through 5 and a portion of Week 6. Then, in Week 6 another EOQ lot is planned to meet the requirements for Weeks 6 through 8. Notice that the EOQ plan leaves some inventory at the end of Week 8 to carry forward into Week 9.

EXHIBIT 21.14

Economic Order Quantity Run Size for an MRP Schedule

Week	Net Requirements	Production Quantity	Ending Inventory	Holding Cost	Setup Cost	Total Cost
1	50	351	301	$15.05	$47.00	$62.05
2	60	0	241	12.05	0.00	74.10
3	70	0	171	8.55	0.00	82.65
4	60	0	111	5.55	0.00	88.20
5	95	0	16	0.80	0.00	89.00
6	75	351	292	14.60	47.00	150.60
7	60	0	232	11.60	0.00	162.20
8	55	0	177	8.85	0.00	171.05

Least Total Cost

The least total cost method (LTC) is a dynamic lot-sizing technique that calculates the order quantity by comparing the carrying cost and the setup (or ordering) costs for various lot sizes and then selects the lot in which these are most nearly equal.

The top half of Exhibit 21.15 shows the least cost lot size results. The procedure to compute least total cost lot sizes is to compare order costs and holding costs for various numbers of weeks. For example, costs are compared for producing in Week 1 to cover the requirements for Week 1; producing in Week 1 for Weeks 1 and 2; producing in Week 1 to cover Weeks 1, 2, and 3; and so on. The correct selection is the lot size where the ordering costs and holding costs are approximately equal. In Exhibit 21.15, the best lot size is 335 because a $38 carrying cost and a $47 ordering cost are closer than $56.75 and $47 ($9 versus $9.75). This lot size covers requirements for Weeks 1 through 5. Unlike EOQ, the lot size covers only whole numbers of periods.

Based on the Week 1 decision to place an order to cover five weeks, we are now located in Week 6, and our problem is to determine how many weeks into the future we can provide for from here. Exhibit 21.15 shows that holding and ordering costs are closest in the quantity that covers requirements for Weeks 6 through 8. Notice that the holding and ordering costs here are far apart. This is because our example extends only to Week 8. If the planning horizon were longer, the lot size planned for Week 6 would likely cover more weeks into the future beyond Week 8. This brings up one of the limitations of both LTC and LUC (discussed below). Both techniques are influenced by the length of the planning horizon. The bottom half of Exhibit 21.15 shows the final run size and total cost.

EXHIBIT 21.15

Least Total Cost Run Size for an MRP Schedule

Weeks	Quantity Ordered	Carrying Cost	Order Cost	Total Cost	
1	50	$ 0.00	$47.00	$ 47.00	
1–2	110	3.00	47.00	50.00	
1–3	180	10.00	47.00	57.00	
1–4	240	19.00	47.00	66.00	1st order
1–5	335	38.00	47.00	85.00	← Least total cost
1–6	410	56.75	47.00	103.75	
1–7	470	74.75	47.00	121.75	
1–8	525	94.00	47.00	141.00	
6	75	0.00	47.00	47.00	
6–7	135	3.00	47.00	50.00	2nd order
6–8	190	8.50	47.00	55.50	← Least total cost

Week	Net Requirements	Production Quantity	Ending Inventory	Holding Cost	Setup Cost	Total Cost
1	50	335	285	$14.25	$47.00	$ 61.25
2	60	0	225	11.25	0.00	72.50
3	70	0	155	7.75	0.00	80.25
4	60	0	95	4.75	0.00	85.00
5	95	0	0	0.00	0.00	85.00
6	75	190	115	5.75	47.00	137.75
7	60	0	55	2.75	0.00	140.50
8	55	0	0	0.00	0.00	140.50

Least Unit Cost

The least unit cost method is a dynamic lot-sizing technique that adds ordering and inventory carrying cost for each trial lot size and divides by the number of units in each lot size, picking the lot size with the lowest unit cost. The top half of Exhibit 21.16 calculates the unit cost for ordering lots to meet the needs of Weeks 1 through 8. Note that the minimum occurred when the quantity 410, ordered in Week 1, was sufficient to cover Weeks 1 through 6. The lot size planned for Week 7 covers through the end of the planning horizon.

The least unit cost run size and total cost are shown in the bottom half of Exhibit 21.16.

Choosing the Best Lot Size

Using the lot-for-lot method, the total cost for the eight weeks is $376; the EOQ total cost is $171.05; the least total cost method is $140.50; and the least unit cost is $153.50. The lowest cost was obtained using the least total cost method of $140.50. If there were more than eight weeks, the lowest cost could differ.

The advantage of the least unit cost method is that it is a more complete analysis and would take into account ordering or setup costs that might change as the order size increases. If the ordering or setup costs remain constant, the lowest total cost method is more attractive because it is simpler and easier to compute, yet it would be just as accurate under that restriction.

EXHIBIT 21.16

Least Total Cost Run Size for an MRP Schedule

Weeks	Quantity Ordered	Carrying Cost	Order Cost	Total Cost	Unit Cost	
1	50	$ 0.00	$47.00	$ 47.00	$0.9400	
1–2	110	3.00	47.00	50.00	0.4545	
1–3	180	10.00	47.00	57.00	0.3167	
1–4	240	19.00	47.00	66.00	0.2750	
1–5	335	38.00	47.00	85.00	0.2537	1st order
1–6	410	56.75	47.00	103.75	0.2530	← Least unit cost
1–7	470	74.75	47.00	121.75	0.2590	
1–8	525	94.00	47.00	141.00	0.2686	
?	60	0.00	47.00	47.00	0.7833	2nd order
7–8	115	2.75	47.00	49.75	0.4326	← Least unit cost

Week	Net Requirements	Production Quantity	Ending Inventory	Holding Cost	Setup Cost	Total Cost
1	50	410	360	$18.00	$47.00	$ 65.00
2	60	0	300	15.00	0.00	80.00
3	70	0	230	11.50	0.00	91.50
4	60	0	170	8.50	0.00	100.00
5	95	0	75	3.75	0.00	103.75
6	75	0	0	0	0	103.75
7	60	115	55	2.75	47.00	153.50
8	55	0	0	0	0	$153.50

CONCEPT CONNECTIONS

LO 21–1 Explain what material requirements planning (MRP) is

Summary

- An enterprise resource planning (ERP) system integrates application programs in accounting, sales, manufacturing, and the other functions in a firm. MRP is typically an application within the ERP system.
- MRP is the logic that calculates the number of parts, components, and other materials needed to produce a product.
- MRP determines detailed schedules that show exactly what is needed over time.
- MRP is most useful in industries where standard products are made in batches from common components and parts.
- The master production schedule (MPS) is a plan that specifies what will be made by a production system in the future.
- The items scheduled in the MPS are referred to as "end items" and represent the products that drive the requirements for the MRP system.
- The MPS is a plan for meeting all the demands for the end items, including customer demand, the demand for replacements, and any other demands that might exist.
- Often, "time fences" are used in the MPS to make the schedules calculated by the MRP system stable and ensure their feasibility. When the MPS is based on forecast demand, rather than actual demand, a feature known as "available to promise" is often used that identifies the difference between the number of units included in the MPS and current actual customer orders (these may be different because the forecast may be different than actual customer demand). This can be useful for coordinating sales and production activities.

Key Terms

Enterprise resource planning (ERP) A computer system that integrates application programs in accounting, sales, manufacturing, and the other functions in a firm. This integration is accomplished through a database shared by all the application programs.

Material requirements planning (MRP) The logic for determining the number of parts, components, and materials needed to produce a product.

Master production schedule (MPS) A time-phased plan specifying how many of each end item the firm plans to build and when.

Available to promise A feature of MRP systems that identifies the difference between the number of units currently included in the master schedule and the actual (firm) customer orders.

LO 21–2 Understand how the MRP system is structured

Summary

- The MRP system uses three sources of information:
  1. Demand comes from the master schedule.
  2. The bill-of-materials identifies exactly what is needed to make each end item.
  3. The current inventory status of the items managed by the system (units currently on-hand, expected receipts in the future, and how long it takes to replenish an item).
- Using the three sources of information, the MRP system produces schedules for each item it manages.
- The MRP system can be updated in real time or periodically, depending on the application.

Key Terms

Bill-of-Materials (BOM) The complete product description, listing the materials, parts, and components; the quantity of each item; and also the sequence in which the product is created.

Net change systems MRP systems that calculate the impact of a change in the MRP data (the inventory status, BOM, or master schedule) immediately.

LO 21–3 Analyze an MRP problem

Summary

- The logic used by MRP is often referred to as explosion calculations because the requirements shown in the MPS are "exploded" into detailed schedules for each item managed by the system.
- The basic logic is that the projected available balance in this period is calculated by taking the balance from the last period, subtracting the gross requirements from this period, and adding in scheduled and planned receipts.

LO 21–4 Evaluate and compare MRP lot-sizing techniques

Summary

- Lot sizes are the production (or purchasing) quantities used by the MRP system.
- Lot-for-lot is the simplest case and is when the system schedules exactly what is needed in each period.
- When setup cost is significant or other constraints force different quantities, lot-for-lot might not be the best method to use.
- Lot-size techniques are used to balance the fixed and variable costs that vary according to the production lot size.

SOLVED PROBLEMS

LO 21–3 SOLVED PROBLEM 1

Product X is made of two units of Y and three of Z. Y is made of one unit of A and two units of B. Z is made of two units of A and four units of C.

Lead time for X is one week; Y, two weeks; Z, three weeks; A, two weeks; B, one week; and C, three weeks.

a. Draw the bill-of-materials (product structure tree).

b. If 100 units of X are needed in week 10, develop a planning schedule showing when each item should be ordered and in what quantity. Assume we have no inventory in any of the items to start.

Solution

a.

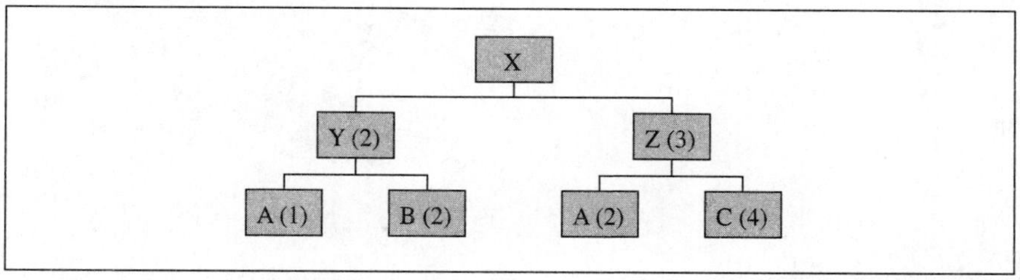

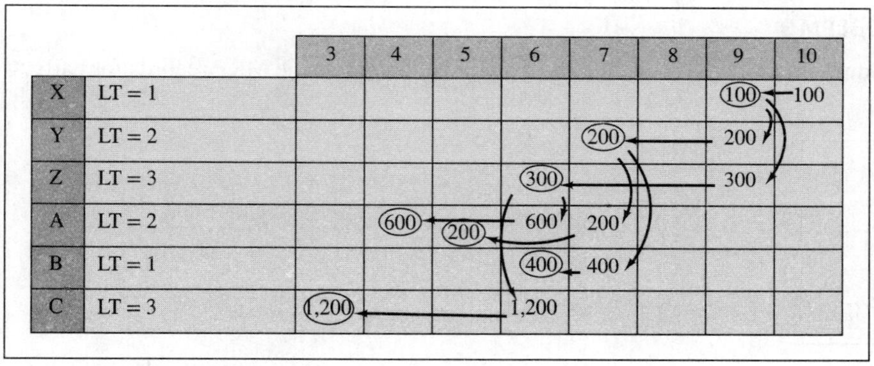

b. The orders are circled.

SOLVED PROBLEM 2

Product M is made of two units of N and three of P. N is made of two units of R and four units of S. R is made of one unit of S and three units of T. P is made of two units of T and four units of U.

a. Show the bill-of-materials (product structure tree).

b. If 100 Ms are required, how many units of each component are needed?

c. Show both a single-level parts list and an indented parts list.

Solution

a.

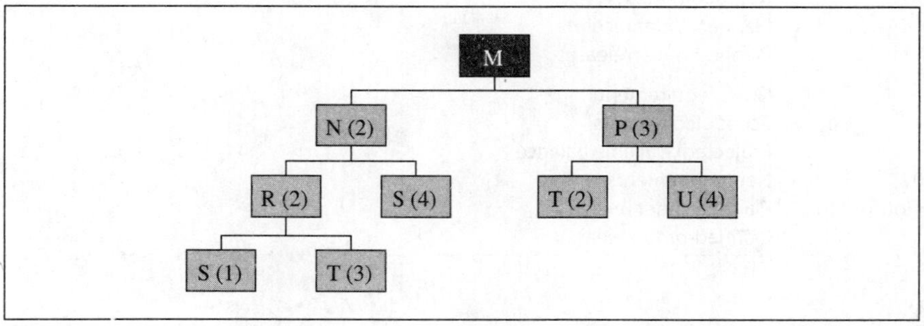

b. M = 100 S = 800 + 400 = 1,200
N = 200 T = 600 + 1,200 = 1,800
P = 300 U = 1,200
R = 400

c.

Single-Level Parts List		Indented Parts List		
		M		
	N (2)	N(2)		
	P (3)		R(2)	
N				S (1)
	R (2)			T (3)
	S (4)		S (4)	
R		P (3)		
	S (1)		T (2)	
	T (3)		U (4)	
P				
	T (2)			
	U (4)			

SOLVED PROBLEM 3

Given the product structure diagram, and the data given, complete the MRP records for parts A, B, and C.

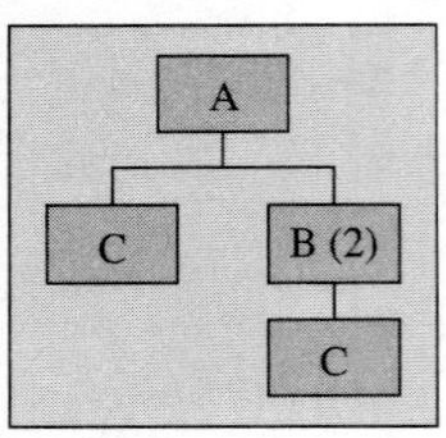

Item		Week 1	2	3	4	5	6
A	Gross requirements	5	15	18	8	12	22
LT = 1 week	Scheduled receipts						
On-hand = 21	Projected available balance						
Safety stock = 0	Net requirements						
Order quantity = 20	Planned-order receipts						
	Planned-order releases						
B	Gross requirements						
LT = 2 weeks	Scheduled receipts	32					
On-hand = 20	Projected available balance						
Safety stock = 0	Net requirements						
Order quantity = 40	Planned-order receipts						
	Planned-order releases						
C	Gross requirements						
LT = 1 week	Scheduled receipts						
On-hand = 70	Projected available balance						
Safety Stock = 10	Net requirements						
Order quantity = lot-for-lot	Planned-order receipts						
	Planned-order releases						

Solution

Item		Week 1	2	3	4	5	6
A	Gross requirements	5	15	18	8	12	22
LT = 1 week	Scheduled receipts						
On-hand = 21	Projected available balance	16	1	3	15	3	1
Safety stock = 0	Net requirements			17	5		19
Order quantity = 20	Planned-order receipts			20	20		20
	Planned-order releases		20	20		20	
B	Gross requirements		40	40		40	
LT = 2 weeks	Scheduled receipts	32					
On-hand = 20	Projected available balance	52	12	12	12	12	12
Safety stock = 0	Net requirements			28		28	
Order quantity = 40	Planned-order receipts			40		40	
	Planned-order releases	40		40			
C	Gross requirements	40	20	60		20	
LT = 1 week	Scheduled receipts						
On-hand = 70	Projected available balance	20	0	0	0	0	0
Safety Stock = 10	Net requirements			60		20	
Order quantity = lot-for-lot	Planned-order receipts			60		20	
	Planned-order releases		60		20		

Notes:

1. For item A, start by calculating the projected available balance through week 2. In week 3, there is a net requirement for 17 units, so we plan to receive an order for 20 units. Projected available balance for week 3 is three units and a net requirement for five in week 4, so we plan another order to be received in week 4. Projected available balance for week 4 is 15 units, with three in week 5 and a net requirement for 19 in week 6. We need to plan one more order for receipt in week 6.
2. The gross requirements for B are based on two times the planned order releases for A. We need to account for the scheduled receipt in week 1 of 32 units, resulting in a projected available balance of 52 at the end of week 1.
3. The gross requirements for C are based on the planned order releases for items A and B because C is used in both items. The projected available balance is calculated by subtracting out the safety stock because this inventory is kept in reserve. In week 1, for example, projected available balance is 70 units on-hand − 40 units gross requirements − 10 units safety stock = 20 units.

LO 21–4 SOLVED PROBLEM 4

Consider the following data relevant to an MRP lot-sizing problem:

Item cost per unit	$25
Setup cost	$100
Inventory carrying cost per year	20.8%

Weekly Net Requirements

1	2	3	4	5	6	7	8
105	80	130	50	0	200	125	100

Use the four lot-sizing rules in the chapter to propose an MRP schedule under each rule. Assume there is no beginning inventory.

Solution

Lot-for-Lot

The lot-for-lot rule is very commonly used because it is so simple and intuitive. The planned-order quantities are equal to the net requirements each week.

Week	Requirements Net	Production Quantity	Ending Inventory	Holding Cost	Setup Cost	Total Cost
1	105	105	0	$0.00	$100.00	$100.00
2	80	80	0	0.00	100.00	200.00
3	130	130	0	0.00	100.00	300.00
4	50	50	0	0.00	100.00	400.00
5	0	0	0	0.00	0.00	400.00
6	200	200	0	0.00	100.00	500.00
7	125	125	0	0.00	100.00	600.00
8	100	100	0	0.00	100.00	700.00

Economic Order Quantity

We need *D, S,* and *H* in the EOQ formula. We will estimate annual demand based on average weekly demand over these 8 weeks.

$$D = \text{Annual demand} = \frac{105 + 80 + 130 + 50 + 0 + 200 + 125 + 100}{8} \times 52 = 5,135$$

$$H = \text{Annual holding cost} = .208 \times \$25.00 = \$5.20$$

$$S = \text{Setup cost} = \$100 \quad (\text{given})$$

$$EOQ = \sqrt{\frac{2DS}{H}} = \sqrt{\frac{2(5135)(100)}{5.20}} = 444$$

In computing holding costs per week, divide H by 52. Weekly holding cost is $0.10 per unit. We can now develop an order schedule based on EOQ lot sizing.

Week	Net Requirements	Production Quantity	Ending Inventory	Holding Cost	Setup Cost	Total Cost
1	105	444	339	$33.90	$100.00	$133.90
2	80	0	259	25.90	0.00	159.80
3	130	0	129	12.90	0.00	172.70
4	50	0	79	7.90	0.00	180.60
5	0	0	79	7.90	0.00	188.50
6	200	444	323	32.30	100.00	320.80
7	125	0	198	19.80	0.00	340.60
8	100	0	98	9.80	0.00	350.40

Least Total Cost (LTC)

Similar to the example in Exhibit 21.15, we can create the following table comparing costs for ordering 1 through 8 weeks' demand in the first order.

Weeks	Net Requirements	Production Quantity	Holding Cost	Setup Cost	Total Cost
1	105	105	$ 0.00	$100.00	$100.00
1–2	80	185	8.00	100.00	108.00
1–3	130	315	34.00	100.00	134.00
1–4	50	365	49.00	100.00	149.00
1–5	0	365	49.00	100.00	149.00
1–6	**200**	**565**	**149.00**	**100.00**	**249.00**
1–7	125	690	224.00	100.00	324.00
1–8	100	790	294.00	100.00	394.00
7	125	125	0.00	100.00	100.00
7–8	**100**	**225**	**10.00**	**100.00**	**110.00**

For the first order, the difference between holding and setup costs is least when ordering for weeks 1 through 6, so the first order should be for 565 units, enough for weeks 1 through 6. For the second order, we need to consider only weeks 7 and 8. The difference between holding and setup costs is least when placing a second order to cover demand during weeks 7 through 8, so the second order should be for 225 units. Note that as we move through time and net requirements for weeks 9 and beyond become known, we would revisit the second order based on those new requirements. It is likely that the best second order will end up being for more than just weeks 7 and 8. For now, we can develop an order schedule based on the data we have available.

Week	Net Requirements	Production Quantity	Ending Inventory	Holding Cost	Setup Cost	Total Cost
1	105	565	460	$46.00	$100.00	$146.00
2	80	0	380	38.00	0.00	184.00
3	130	0	250	25.00	0.00	209.00
4	50	0	200	20.00	0.00	229.00
5	0	0	200	20.00	0.00	249.00
6	200	0	0	0.00	0.00	249.00
7	125	225	100	10.00	100.00	359.00
8	100	0	0	0.00	0.00	359.00

Least Unit Cost (LUC)

The LUC method uses calculations from the LTC method, dividing each option's total cost by the order quantity to determine a unit cost. Most of the following table is copied from the LTC method, with one additional column to calculate the unit costs.

Week	Net Requirements	Production Quantity	Holding Cost	Setup Cost	Total Cost	Unit Cost
1	105	105	$ 0.00	$100.00	$100.00	$0.9524
1–2	80	185	8.00	100.00	108.00	0.5838
1–3	130	315	34.00	100.00	134.00	0.4254
1–4	**50**	**365**	**49.00**	**100.00**	**149.00**	**0.4082**
1–5	**0**	**365**	**49.00**	**100.00**	**149.00**	**0.4082**
1–6	200	565	149.00	100.00	249.00	0.4407
1–7	125	690	224.00	100.00	324.00	0.4696
1–8	100	790	294.00	100.00	394.00	0.4987
6	200	200	0.00	100.00	100.00	0.5000
6–7	125	325	12.50	100.00	112.50	0.3462
6–8	**100**	**425**	**32.50**	**100.00**	**132.50**	**0.3118**

For the first order, the least unit cost results from ordering enough to cover weeks 1 through 5, so our first order would be for 365 units. (This example can be a bit tricky—we have to use a little common sense.) Ordering for weeks 1 through 4 has the same low unit cost because there is no demand for week 5. We will say we are ordering for weeks 1 through 5 so that we don't place an unnecessary order in week 5 to cover demand for weeks 5 through 8. For the second order, the lowest unit cost comes from ordering for weeks 6 through 8, so we would plan for an order of 425 units. As with the LTC example, our second order might change as we learn net requirements for weeks 9 and beyond. Based on these orders, we can now develop an order schedule based on LUC.

Week	Net Requirements	Production Quantity	Ending Inventory	Holding Cost	Setup Cost	Total Cost
1	105	365	260	$26.00	$100.00	$126.00
2	80	0	180	18.00	0.00	144.00
3	130	0	50	5.00	0.00	149.00
4	50	0	0	0.00	0.00	149.00

5	0	0	0	0.00	0.00	149.00
6	200	425	225	22.50	100.00	271.50
7	125	0	100	10.00	0.00	281.50
8	100	0	0	0.00	0.00	281.50

Best Lot Size Method

Based on the data we have available, the total costs for each lot-sizing method are lot-for-lot, \$700.00; EOQ, \$350.40; LTC, \$359.00; and LUC, \$281.50. The relatively high setup cost in this example makes lot-for-lot an unwise choice. LUC has the lowest total cost by a significant margin. It works so well here because it minimizes holding costs across the planning horizon.

DISCUSSION QUESTIONS

LO 21-1

1. What do we mean when we say that MRP is based on dependent demand?
2. Discuss the importance of the master production schedule in an MRP system.
3. Explain the need for *time fences* in the master production schedule.

LO 21-2

4. "MRP just prepares shopping lists. It does not do the shopping or cook the dinner." Comment.
5. What are the sources of demand in an MRP system? Are these dependent or independent, and how are they used as inputs to the system?
6. State the types of data that would be carried in the bill-of-materials file and the inventory record file.

LO 21-3

7. Discuss the meaning of MRP terms such as *planned order release* and *scheduled order receipt.*
8. Why is the MRP process referred to as an "explosion"?
9. Many practitioners currently update MRP weekly or biweekly. Would it be more valuable if it were updated daily? Discuss.
10. Should safety stock be necessary in an MRP system with dependent demand? If so, why? If not, why do firms carry it anyway?
11. Contrast the significance of the term *lead time* in the traditional EOQ context and in an MRP system.

LO 21-4

12. Planning orders using a lot-for-lot (L4L) technique is commonly done because it is simple and intuitive. It also helps minimize holding costs because you are only ordering what is needed when it is needed. So far, it sounds like a good idea. Are there any disadvantages to this approach?
13. What is meant when we say that the least total cost (LTC) and least unit cost (LUC) methods are dynamic lot-sizing techniques?

OBJECTIVE QUESTIONS

LO 21-1

1. Match the industry type to the expected benefits from an MRP system as High, Medium, or Low.

Industry Type	Expected Benefit (High, Medium, or Low)
Assemble-to-stock	
Assemble-to-order	
Make-to-stock	
Make-to-order	
Engineer-to-order	
Process	

2. MRP is based on what type of demand?
3. Which scheduling process drives requirements in the MRP process?
4. What term is used to identify the difference between the number of units of an item listed on the master schedule and the number of firm customer orders?
5. What are the three primary data sources used by the MRP system? **LO 21–2**
6. What is another common name for the bill-of-materials?
7. What is the process used to ensure that all of the needs for a particular item are calculated at the same time in the MRP process?
8. What is the MRP term for the time periods used in planning?

Note: For these problems, to simplify data handling to include the receipt of orders that have actually been placed in previous periods, the following six-level scheme can be used. (A number of different techniques are used in practice, but the important issue is to keep track of what is on-hand, what is expected to arrive, what is needed, and what size orders should be placed.) One way to calculate the numbers is as follows: **LO 21–3**

	Week					
Gross requirements						
Scheduled receipts						
Projected available balance						
Net requirements						
Planned-order receipt						
Planned-order release						

9. Semans is a manufacturer that produces bracket assemblies. Demand for bracket assemblies (X) is 130 units. The following is the BOM in indented form:

Item	Description	Usage
X	Bracket assembly	1
A	Wall board	4
B	Hanger subassembly	2
D	Hanger casting	3
E	Ceramic knob	1
C	Rivet head screw	3
F	Metal tong	4
G	Plastic cap	2

The following is a table indicating current inventory levels:

Item	X	A	B	C	D	E	F	G
Inventory	25	16	60	20	180	160	1,000	100

a. Using Excel, create the MRP using the information provided.
b. What are the net requirements of each item in the MPS?

10. In the following MRP planning schedule for item J, indicate the correct net requirements, planned-order receipts, and planned-order releases to meet the gross requirements. Lead time is one week.

	Week Number					
Item J	**0**	**1**	**2**	**3**	**4**	**5**
Gross requirements			75		50	70
On-hand	40					
Net requirements						
Planned-order receipt						
Planned-order release						

11. Assume that product Z is made of two units of A and four units of B. A is made of three units of C and four of D. D is made of two units of E.

    Lead times for the purchase or fabrication of each unit to final assembly are: Z takes two weeks; A, B, C, and D take one week each; and E takes three weeks.

    Fifty units are required in period 10. (Assume that there is currently no inventory on-hand of any of these items.)

    a. Show the bill-of-materials (product structure tree). (Answer in Appendix D)

    b. Develop an MRP planning schedule showing gross and net requirements and order release and order receipt dates.

12. One unit of A is made of three units of B, one unit of C, and two units of D. B is composed of two units of E and one unit of D. C is made of one unit of B and two units of E. E is made of one unit of F.

    Items B, C, E, and F have one-week lead times; A and D have lead times of two weeks.

    Assume that lot-for-lot (L4L) lot sizing is used for items A, B, and F; lots of size 50, 50, and 200 are used for Items C, D, and E, respectively. Items C, E, and F have on-hand (beginning) inventories of 10, 50, and 150, respectively; all other items have zero beginning inventory. We are scheduled to receive 10 units of A in week 2, 50 units of E in week 1, and also 50 units of F in week 1. There are no other scheduled receipts. If 30 units of A are required in week 8, use the low-level-coded bill-of-materials to find the necessary planned-order releases for all components.

13. One unit of A is made of two units of B, three units of C, and two units of D. B is composed of one unit of E and two units of F. C is made of two units of F and one unit of D. E is made of two units of D. Items A, C, D, and F have one-week lead times; B and E have lead times of two weeks. Lot-for-lot (L4L) lot sizing is used for items A, B, C, and D; lots of size 50 and 180 are used for items E and F, respectively. Item C has an on-hand (beginning) inventory of 15; D has an on-hand inventory of 50; all other items have zero beginning inventories. We are scheduled to receive 20 units of item E in week 2; there are no other scheduled receipts.

    Construct simple and low-level-coded bill-of-materials (product structure tree) and indented and summarized parts lists.

    If 20 units of A are required in week 8, use the low-level-coded bill-of-materials to find the necessary planned-order releases for all components.

14. One unit of A is made of one unit of B and one unit of C. B is made of four units of C and one unit each of E and F. C is made of two units of D and one unit of E. E is made of three units of F. Item C has a lead time of one week; items A, B, E, and F have two-week lead times; and item D has a lead time of three weeks. Lot-for-lot (L4L) lot sizing is used for items A, D, and E; lots of size 50, 100, and 50 are used for items B, C, and F, respectively. Items A, C, D, and E have on-hand (beginning) inventories of 20, 50, 100, and 10, respectively; all other items have zero beginning inventory. We are scheduled to receive 10 units of A in week 1, 100 units of C in week 1, and 100 units of D in week 3; there are no other scheduled receipts. If 50 units of A are required in week 10, use the low-level-coded bill-of-materials (product structure tree) to find the necessary planned-order releases for all components.

15. One unit of A is made of two units of B and one unit of C. B is made of three units of D and one unit of F. C is composed of three units of B, one unit of D, and four units of E. D is made of one unit of E. Item C has a lead time of one week; items A, B, E, and F have two-week lead times; and item D has a lead time of three weeks. Lot-for-lot (L4L) lot sizing is used for items C, E, and F; lots of size 20, 40, and 160 are used for items A, B, and D, respectively. Items A, B, D, and E have on-hand (beginning) inventories of 5, 10, 100, and 100, respectively; all other items have zero beginning inventories. We are scheduled to receive 10 units of A in week 3, 20 units of B in week 7, 40 units of F in week 5, and 60 units of E in week 2; there are no other scheduled receipts. If 20 units of A are required in week 10, use the low-level-coded bill-of-materials (product structure tree) to find the necessary planned order releases for all components.

16. One unit of A is composed of two units of B and three units of C. Each B is composed of one unit of F. C is made of one unit of D, one unit of E, and two units of F. Items A, B, C, and D have 20, 50, 60, and 25 units of on-hand inventory, respectively. Items A, B, and C use lot-for-lot (L4L) as their lot-sizing technique, while D, E, and F require multiples of 50, 100, and 100, respectively, to

be purchased. B has scheduled receipts of 30 units in period 1. No other scheduled receipts exist. Lead times are one period for items A, B, and D, and two periods for items C, E, and F. Gross requirements for A are 20 units in period 1, 20 units in period 2, 60 units in period 6, and 50 units in period 8. Find the planned order releases for all items.

17. Each unit of A is composed of one unit of B, two units of C, and one unit of D. C is composed of two units of D and three units of E. Items A, C, D, and E have on-hand inventories of 20, 10, 20, and 10 units, respectively. Item B has a scheduled receipt of 10 units in period 1, and C has a scheduled receipt of 50 units in period 1. Lot-for-lot (L4L) lot sizing is used for items A and B. Item C requires a minimum lot size of 50 units. D and E are required to be purchased in multiples of 100 and 50, respectively. Lead times are one period for items A, B, and C, and two periods for items D and E. The gross requirements for A are 30 in period 2, 30 in period 5, and 40 in period 8. Find the planned-order releases for all items.
18. Product A is an end item and is made from two units of B and four of C. B is made of three units of D and two of E. C is made of two units of F and two of E.

    A has a lead time of one week. B, C, and E have lead times of two weeks, and D and F have lead times of three weeks.

    a. Show the bill-of-materials (product structure tree).

    b. If 100 units of A are required in week 10, develop the MRP planning schedule, specifying when items are to be ordered and received. There are currently no units of inventory on-hand.
19. Audio Products, Inc., produces two AM/FM/CD players for cars. The radio/CD units are identical, but the mounting hardware and finish trim differ. The standard model fits intermediate and full-sized cars, and the sports model fits small sports cars.

    Audio Products handles the production in the following way. The chassis (radio/CD unit) is assembled in Mexico and has a manufacturing lead time of two weeks. The mounting hardware is purchased from a sheet steel company and has a three-week lead time. The finish trim is purchased as prepackaged units consisting of knobs and various trim pieces from a Taiwan electronics company with offices in Los Angeles. Trim packages have a two-week lead time. Final assembly time may be disregarded because adding the trim package and mounting are performed by the customer.

    Audio Products supplies wholesalers and retailers, which place specific orders for both models up to eight weeks in advance. These orders, together with enough additional units to satisfy the small number of individual sales, are summarized in the following demand schedule.

	Week							
Model	**1**	**2**	**3**	**4**	**5**	**6**	**7**	**8**
Standard model				300				400
Sports model					200			100

    There are currently 50 radio/CD units on-hand but no trim packages or mounting hardware.

    Prepare a material requirements plan to meet the demand schedule exactly. Specify the gross and net requirements, on-hand amounts, and the planned order release and receipt periods for the radio/CD chassis, the standard trim and sports car model trim, and the standard mounting hardware and the sports car mounting hardware.

20. The MRP gross requirements for item A are shown here for the next 10 weeks. Lead time for A is three weeks and setup cost is $10. There is a carrying cost of $0.01 per unit per week. Beginning inventory is 90 units. **LO 21–4**

	Week									
	1	**2**	**3**	**4**	**5**	**6**	**7**	**8**	**9**	**10**
Gross requirements	30	50	10	20	70	80	20	60	200	50

Use the least total cost or the least unit cost lot-sizing method to determine when and for what quantity the first order should be released.

21. The MRP gross requirements for item X are shown here for the next 10 weeks. Lead time for A is two weeks, and setup cost is $9. There is a carrying cost of $0.02 per unit per week. Beginning inventory is 70 units.

	Week									
	1	2	3	4	5	6	7	8	9	10
Gross requirements	20	10	15	45	10	30	100	20	40	150

Use the least total cost or the least unit cost lot-sizing method to determine when and for what quantity the first order should be released. (Answer in Appendix D)

22. Product A consists of two units of subassembly B, three units of C, and one unit of D. B is composed of four units of E and three units of F. C is made of two units of H and three units of D. H is made of five units of E and two units of G.
   a. Construct a simple bill-of-materials (product structure tree).
   b. Construct a product structure tree using low-level coding.
   c. Construct an indented parts list.
   d. To produce 100 units of A, determine the number of units of B, C, D, E, F, G, and H required.

ANALYTICS EXERCISE: AN MRP EXPLOSION—BRUNSWICK MOTORS

Recently, Phil Harris, the production control manager at Brunswick, read an article on time-phased requirements planning. He was curious about how this technique might work in scheduling Brunswick's engine assembly operations and decided to prepare an example to illustrate the use of time-phased requirements planning.

Phil's first step was to prepare a master schedule for one of the engine types produced by Brunswick: the Model 1000 engine. This schedule indicates the number of units of the Model 1000 engine to be assembled each week during the last 12 weeks and is shown on the next page. Next, Phil decided to simplify his requirements planning example by considering only two of the many components needed to complete the assembly of the Model 1000 engine. These two components, the gear box and the input shaft, are shown in the product structure diagram shown below. Phil noted that the gear box is assembled by the Subassembly Department and subsequently is sent to the main engine assembly line. The input shaft is one of several component parts manufactured by Brunswick needed to produce a gear box subassembly. Thus, levels 0, 1, and 2 are included in the product structure diagram to indicate the three manufacturing stages involved in producing an engine: the Engine Assembly Department, the Subassembly Department, and the Machine Shop.

The manufacturing lead times required to produce the gear box and input shaft components are also indicated in the bill-of-materials diagram. Note that two weeks are required to produce a batch of gear boxes and that all the gear boxes must be delivered to the assembly line parts stockroom before Monday morning of the week in which they are to be used. Likewise, it takes three weeks to produce a lot of input shafts, and all the shafts needed for the production of gear boxes in a given week must be delivered to the Subassembly Department stockroom before Monday morning of that week.

In preparing the MRP example, Phil planned to use the worksheets shown on the next page and to make the following assumptions:

Model 1000 master schedule

Week	1	2	3	4	5	6	7	8	9	10	11	12
Demand	15	5	7	10		15	20	10		8	2	16

Model 1000 product structure

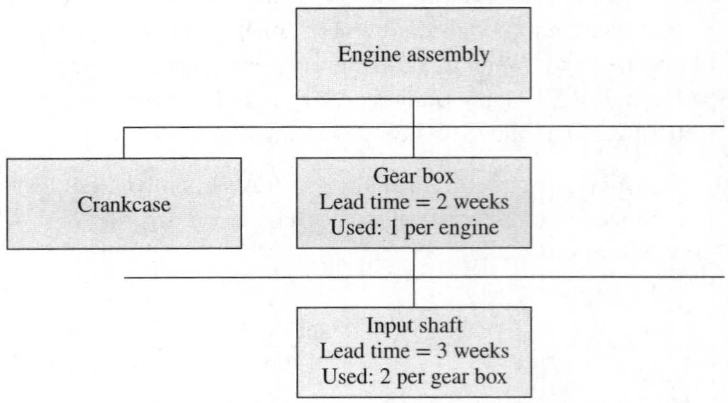

1. Seventeen gear boxes are on-hand at the beginning of week 1, and five gear boxes are currently on order to be delivered at the start of week 2.
2. Forty input shafts are on-hand at the start of week 1, and 22 are scheduled for delivery at the beginning of week 2.

Assignment

1. Initially, assume that Phil wants to minimize his inventory requirements. Assume that each order will be only for what is required for a single period. Using the following forms, calculate the net requirements and planned order releases for the gear boxes and input shafts. Assume that lot sizing is done using lot-for-lot.
2. Phil would like to consider the costs that his accountants are currently using for inventory carrying and setup for the gear boxes and input shafts. These costs are as follows:

Part	Cost
Gear Box	Setup = $90/order
	Inventory carrying cost = $2/unit/week
Input Shaft	Setup = $45/order
	Inventory carrying cost = $1/unit/week

   Given the cost structure, evaluate the cost of the schedule from (1). Assume inventory is valued at the end of each week.
3. Find a better schedule by reducing the number of orders and carrying some inventory. What are the cost savings with this new schedule?

Engine assembly master schedule

Week	1	2	3	4	5	6	7	8	9	10	11	12
Quantity												

Gear box requirements

Week	1	2	3	4	5	6	7	8	9	10	11	12
Gross requirements												
Scheduled receipts												
Projected available balance												
Net requirements												
Planned order release												

Input shaft requirements

Week	1	2	3	4	5	6	7	8	9	10	11	12
Gross requirements												
Scheduled receipts												
Projected available balance												
Net requirements												
Planned order release												

PRACTICE EXAM

In each of the following, name the term defined or answer the question. Answers are listed at the bottom.

1. Term used for a computer system that integrates application programs for the different functions in a firm.
2. Logic used to calculate the needed parts, components, and other materials needed to produce an end item.
3. This drives the MRP calculations and is a detailed plan for how we expect to meet demand.
4. Period of time during which a customer has a specified level of opportunity to make changes.
5. This identifies the specific materials used to make each item and the correct quantities of each.
6. If an item is used in two places in a bill-of-materials, say level 3 and level 4, what low-level code would be assigned to the item?
7. One unit of part C is used in item A and in item B. Currently, we have 10 As, 20 Bs, and 100 Cs in inventory. We want to ship 60 As and 70 Bs. How many additional Cs do we need to purchase?
8. These are orders that have already been released and are to arrive in the future.
9. This is the total amount required for a particular item.
10. This is the amount needed after considering what we currently have in inventory and what we expect to arrive in the future.
11. The planned-order receipt and planned-order release are offset by this amount of time.
12. These are the part quantities issued in the planned-order release section of an MRP report.
13. The term for ordering exactly what is needed each period without regard to economic considerations.
14. None of the techniques for determining order quantity consider this important noneconomic factor that could make the order quantity infeasible.

Answers to Practice Exam 1. Enterprise resource planning (ERP) 2. Material requirements planning (MRP) 3. Master production schedule 4. Time fence 5. Bill-of-materials 6. Level 4 7. Zero 8. Scheduled receipts 9. Gross requirements 10. Net requirements 11. Lead time 12. Lot sizes 13. Lot-for-lot ordering 14. Capacity

For PowerPoint lecture slides, Solutions Manual, Test Bank, Data files for solved examples, Excel Templates, Step-by-Step Solved Examples in video format, Tutorial Videos and many more, scan the adjacent **QR code**, or **visit http://www.mhhe.com/sie-chase15e**

Chapter 22

Workcenter Scheduling

LEARNING OBJECTIVES

LO22-1 Explain workcenter scheduling

LO22-2 Analyze scheduling problems using priority rules and more specialized techniques

LO22-3 Apply scheduling techniques to the manufacturing shop floor

LO22-4 Analyze employee schedules in the service sector

Hospitals Cut ER Waits—New "Fast Track" Units, High-Tech IDs Speed Visits

A few years ago, Oakwood Hospital and Medical Center in Dearborn, Michigan, promised that anybody taken to the emergency department would be seen by a doctor within 30 minutes—or they would get a written apology and two free movie passes. It sounded like a cheap marketing ploy. Some employees cringed.

The 30-minute guarantee has been a huge success. All four of Oakwood Healthcare System's hospitals rolled it out, and patient satisfaction levels soared. Less than 1 percent of the patients asked for free tickets.

Patients in a hospital waiting room.

© Heath Korvola/Getty Images RF

Recently, the center announced a zero-wait program in the four hospital emergency departments and at Oakwood's health care center. Success with this precedent-setting service is not yet known, but processes were redesigned and some tricky scheduling of staff is being employed.

A growing number of hospitals are putting patients with relatively minor ailments—who previously would be left to languish in the waiting room—into "fast track" units to get them in and out of emergency beds quickly. Others are using sophisticated computer systems to give administrators a complete up-to-the-minute status report on every patient in every emergency bed. In some areas, medical identification cards are being used that can be swiped into a computer to speed up patient registrations and produce instant vital information to emergency doctors and nurses. Other changes needed to slash waiting times require reengineering billing, records, and laboratory operations; upgrading technical staff; and replacing the emergency physician group with a new crew willing to work longer hours.

LO 22-1

Explain workcenter scheduling

WORKCENTER SCHEDULING

Keep in mind that workflow equals cash flow, and scheduling lies at the heart of the process. A schedule is a timetable for performing activities, utilizing resources, or allocating facilities. In this chapter, we discuss short-run scheduling and control of orders with an emphasis on workcenters. We also introduce some basic approaches to short-term scheduling of workers in services.

Manufacturing Execution System (MES)
An information system that schedules, dispatches, tracks, monitors, and controls production on the factory floor.

Operations scheduling is at the heart of what is currently referred to as **Manufacturing Execution Systems (MES)**. An MES is an information system that schedules, dispatches, tracks, monitors, and controls production on the factory floor. Such systems also provide real-time linkages to MRP systems, product and process planning, and systems that extend beyond the factory, including supply chain management, ERP, sales, and service management. A number of software specialty houses develop and implement MESs as part of a suite of software tools.

Similar to an MES, a Service Execution System (SES) is an information system that links, schedules, dispatches, tracks, monitors, and controls the customer's encounters with the service organization and its employees. Obviously, the extent to which each of these elements is brought into play is determined by the extent of the customer's physical involvement with the service organization, the number of stages in the service, and whether the service is standardized (e.g., a scheduled airline flight) or customized (e.g., a hospital visit). The common features of any large system are a central database that contains all the relevant information on resource availability and customers, and a management control function that integrates and oversees the process.

The Nature and Importance of Workcenters

Workcenter
Often referred to as a job shop, a process structure suited for low-volume production of a great variety of nonstandard products. Workcenters sometimes are referred to as departments and are focused on a particular type of operation.

A **workcenter** is an area in a business in which productive resources are organized and work is completed. The workcenter may be a single machine, a group of machines, or an area where a particular type of work is done. These workcenters can be organized according to function in a workcenter configuration or by-product in a flow, assembly line, or group technology cell (GT cell) configuration. Recall from the discussion in Chapter 8 that many firms have moved from the workcenter configuration to GT cells.

In the case of the workcenter, jobs need to be routed between functionally organized workcenters to complete the work. When a job arrives at a workcenter—for example, the drilling department in a factory that makes custom-printed circuit boards—it enters a queue to wait for a drilling machine that can drill the required holes. Scheduling, in this case, involves determining the order for running the jobs, and also assigning a machine that can be used to make the holes.

Infinite loading
Work is assigned to a workcenter based on what is needed over time. Capacity is not considered.

A characteristic that distinguishes one scheduling system from another is how capacity is considered in determining the schedule. Scheduling systems can use either infinite or finite loading. **Infinite loading** occurs when work is assigned to a workcenter simply based on what is needed over time. No consideration is given directly to whether there is sufficient capacity at the resources required to complete the work, nor is the actual sequence of the work as done by each resource in the workcenter considered. Often, a simple check is made of key resources to see if they are overloaded in an aggregate sense. This is done by calculating the amount of work required over a period (usually a week) using setup and run time standards for each order. When using an infinite loading system, lead time is estimated by taking a multiple of the expected operation time (setup and run time) plus an expected queuing delay caused by material movement and waiting for the order to be worked on.

A **finite loading** approach actually schedules in detail each resource using the setup and run time required for each order. In essence, the system determines exactly what will be done by each resource at every moment during the working day. If an operation is delayed due to a part(s) shortage, the order will sit in the queue and wait until the part is available from a preceding operation. Theoretically, all schedules are feasible when finite loading is used.

Finite loading
Each resource is scheduled in detail using the setup and run time required for each order. The system determines exactly what will be done by each resource at every moment during the working day.

Another characteristic that distinguishes scheduling systems is whether the schedule is generated forward or backward in time. For this forward–backward dimension, the most common is forward scheduling. **Forward scheduling** refers to the situation in which the system takes an order and then schedules each operation that must be completed forward in time. A system that forward schedules can tell the earliest date that an order can be completed. Conversely, **backward scheduling** starts from some date in the future (possibly a due date) and schedules the required operations in reverse sequence. This tells the latest time when an order can be started so that it is completed by a specific date.

Forward scheduling
Schedules from now into the future to tell the earliest that an order can be completed.

Backward scheduling
Starts from some date in the future (typically the due date) and schedules the required operations in reverse sequence. Tells the latest time when an order can be started so that it is completed by a specific date.

A material requirements planning (MRP) system is an example of an infinite loading, backward scheduling system for materials. With simple MRP, each order has a due date sometime in the future. In this case, the system calculates parts needs by backward scheduling the time that the operations will be run to complete the orders. The time required to make each part (or batch of parts) is estimated based on historical data. The scheduling systems addressed in this chapter are intended for the processes required to actually make those parts and subassemblies.

Thus far, the term *resources* has been used in a generic sense. In practice, we need to decide what we are going to actually schedule. Commonly, processes are referred to as either machine limited or labor limited. In a **machine-limited process**, equipment is the critical resource that is scheduled. Similarly, in a **labor-limited process**, people are the key resource that is scheduled. Most actual processes are either labor limited or machine limited but, luckily, not both.

Machine-limited process
Equipment is the critical resource that is scheduled.

Labor-limited process
People are the key resource that is scheduled.

At kaiten sushi restaurants, sushi is circulated to customers on a conveyor belt. In order to monitor the quality of the product, some Kaiten Sushi restaurants use RFID tagging.

© sozaijiten/Datacraft/Getty Images RF

Exhibit 22.1 describes the scheduling approaches typically used for different manufacturing processes. Whether capacity is considered depends on the actual process. Available computer technology allows generation of very detailed schedules such as scheduling each job on each machine and assigning a specific worker to the machine at a specific point in time. Systems that capture the

EXHIBIT 22.1

Types of Manufacturing Processes and Scheduling Approaches

Type	Product	Characteristics	Typical Scheduling Approach
Continuous process	Chemicals, steel, wire and cables, liquids (beer, soda), canned goods	Full automation, low labor content in product costs, facilities dedicated to one product	Finite forward scheduling of the process; machine limited
High-volume manufacturing	Automobiles, telephones, fasteners, textiles, motors, household fixtures	Automated equipment, partially automated handling, moving assembly lines, most equipment in line	Finite forward scheduling of the line (a production rate is typical); machine limited; parts are pulled to the line using just-in-time (kanban) system
Mid-volume manufacturing	Industrial parts, high-end consumer products	GT cells, focused minifactories	Infinite forward scheduling typical: priority control; typically labor limited, but often machine limited; often responding to just-in-time orders from customers or MRP due dates
Low-volume workcenters	Custom or prototype equipment, specialized instruments, low-volume industrial products	Machining centers organized by manufacturing function (not in line), high labor content in product cost, general-purpose machinery with significant changeover time, little automation of material handling, large variety of product	Infinite, forward scheduling of jobs: usually labor limited, but certain functions may be machine limited (a heat-treating process or a precision machining center, for example); priorities determined by MRP due dates

exact state of each job and each resource are also available. Using RFID or bar-coding technology, these systems can efficiently capture all of this detailed information.

Typical Scheduling and Control Functions

The following functions must be performed in scheduling and controlling an operation:

1. Allocating jobs, equipment, and personnel to workcenters or other specified locations. Essentially, this is short-run capacity planning.
2. Determining the sequence of order performance (that is, establishing job priorities).
3. Initiating performance of the scheduled work. This is commonly termed the **dispatching** of jobs.
4. Shop-floor control (or production activity control) involving:
   a. Reviewing the status and controlling the progress of jobs as they are being worked on.
   b. Expediting late and critical jobs.

Dispatching
The activity of initiating scheduled work.

A simple workcenter scheduling process is shown in Exhibit 22.2. At the start of the day, the scheduler (in this case, a production control person assigned to this department) selects and sequences available jobs to be run at individual workstations. The scheduler's decisions would be based on the operations and routing requirements of each job, the status of existing jobs at each workcenter, the queue of work before each workcenter, job priorities, material availability, anticipated job orders to be released later in the day, and workcenter resource capabilities (labor and/or machines).

To help organize the schedule, the scheduler would draw on job status information from the previous day, external information provided by central production control, process engineering, and so on. The scheduler also would confer with the supervisor of the department about the feasibility of the schedule, especially workforce considerations and potential bottlenecks. The details of the schedule are communicated to workers via dispatch lists shown on computer terminals, in hard-copy printouts, or by posting a list of what should be worked on in central areas. Visible schedule boards are highly effective ways to communicate the priority and current status of work.

Exhibit 22.2

Typical Scheduling Process

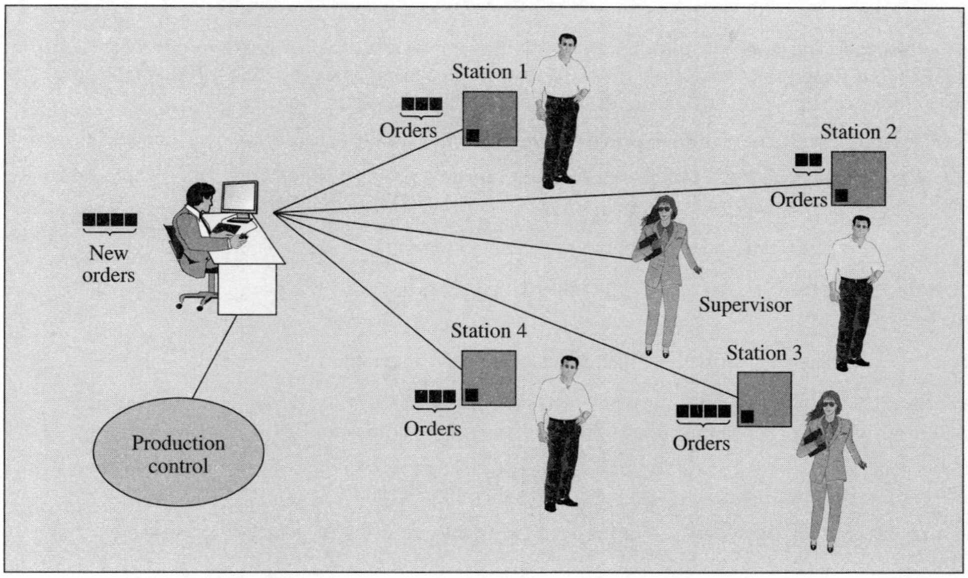

Objectives of Workcenter Scheduling

The objectives of workcenter scheduling are to (1) meet due dates, (2) minimize lead time, (3) minimize setup time or cost, (4) minimize work-in-process inventory, and (5) maximize machine or labor utilization. It is unlikely, and often undesirable, to simultaneously satisfy all of these objectives. For example, keeping all equipment and/or employees busy may result in having to keep too much inventory. Or, as another example, it is possible to meet 99 out of 100 of your due dates but still have a major schedule failure if the one due date that was missed was for a critical job or key customer. The important point, as is the case with other production activities, is to maintain a systems perspective to assure that workcenter objectives are in sync with the operations strategy of the organization.

Job Sequencing

The process of determining the job order on some machine or in some workcenter is known as **sequencing** or priority sequencing. **Priority rules** are the rules used in obtaining a job sequence. These can be very simple, requiring only that jobs be sequenced according to one piece of data, such as processing time, due date, or order of arrival. Other rules, though equally simple, may require several pieces of information, typically to derive an index number such as the least slack rule and the critical ratio rule (both defined later). Still others, such as Johnson's rule (also discussed later), apply to job scheduling on a sequence of machines and require a computational procedure to specify the order of performance. Eight of the more common priority rules are shown in Exhibit 22.3.

Sequencing
The process of determining which job to start first on a machine or workcenter.

Priority rules
The logic used to determine the sequence of jobs in a queue.

The following standard measures of schedule performance are used to evaluate priority rules:

1. Meeting due dates of customers or downstream operations.
2. Minimizing the flow time (the time a job spends in the process).
3. Minimizing work-in-process inventory.
4. Minimizing the idle time of machines or workers.

Exhibit 22.3

Priority Rules for Job Sequencing

1. **FCFS** (first come, first served). Orders are run in the order they arrive in the department.
2. **SOT** (shortest operating time). Run the job with the shortest completion time first, next-shortest second, and so on. This is sometimes also referred to as SPT (shortest processing time). This rule is often combined with a lateness rule to prevent jobs with longer times from being delayed too long.
3. **EDD** (earliest due date first). Run the job with the earliest due date first.
4. **STR** (slack time remaining). This is calculated as the time remaining before the due date minus the processing time remaining. Orders with the shortest slack time remaining (STR) are run first.

   STR = Time remaining before due date — Remaining processing time

5. **STR/OP** (slack time remaining per operation). Orders with the shortest slack time per number of operations are run first.

   STR/OP = STR/Number of remaining operations

6. **CR** (critical ratio). This is calculated as the difference between the due date and the current date divided by the number of work days remaining. Orders with the smallest CR are run first.
7. **LCFS** (last come, first served). This rule occurs frequently by default. As orders arrive, they are placed on the top of the stack; the operator usually picks up the order on top to run first.
8. **Random** order or whim. The supervisors or the operators usually select whichever job they feel like running.

LO 22-2

Analyze scheduling problems using priority rules and more specialized techniques

PRIORITY RULES AND TECHNIQUES

Scheduling *n* Jobs on One Machine

Let's look at some of the eight priority rules compared in a static scheduling situation involving four jobs on one machine. (In scheduling terminology, this class of problems is referred to as an "*n* job—one-machine problem" or simply "*n*/1.") The theoretical difficulty of scheduling problems increases as more machines are considered rather than as more jobs must be processed; therefore, the only restriction on *n* is that it be a specified, finite number. Consider the following example.

EXAMPLE 22.1 ***n* Jobs on One Machine**

Mike Morales is the supervisor of Legal Copy-Express, which provides copy services for downtown Los Angeles law firms. Five customers submitted their orders at the beginning of the week. Specific scheduling data are as follows:

Job (in Order of Arrival)	Processing Time (Days)	Due Date (Days Hence)
A	3	5
B	4	6
C	2	7
D	6	9
E	1	2

All orders require the use of the only color copy machine available; Morales must decide on the processing sequence for the five orders. The evaluation criterion is minimum flow time. Suppose that Morales decides to use the FCFS rule in an attempt to make Legal Copy-Express appear fair to its customers.

SOLUTION

FCFS RULE: The FCFS rule results in the following flow times:

FCFS Schedule

Job Sequence	Processing Time (Days)	Due Date (Days Hence)	Flow Time (Days)
A	3	5	0 + 3 = 3
B	4	6	3 + 4 = 7
C	2	7	7 + 2 = 9
D	6	9	9 + 6 = 15
E	1	2	15 + 1 = 16

Total flow time = 3 + 7 + 9 + 15 + 16 = 50 days

Average flow time = $\frac{50}{5}$ = 10 days

Comparing the due date of each job with its flow time, we observe that only Job A will be on time. Jobs B, C, D, and E will be late by 1, 2, 6, and 14 days, respectively. On average, a job will be late by (0 + 1 + 2 + 6 + 14)/5 = 4.6 days.

SOLUTION

SOT RULE: Let's now consider the SOT rule. Here, Morales gives the highest priority to the order that has the shortest processing time. The resulting flow times are

SOT Schedule

Job Sequence	Processing Time (Days)	Due Date (Days Hence)	Flow Time (Days)
E	1	2	0 + 1 = 1
C	2	7	1 + 2 = 3
A	3	5	3 + 3 = 6
B	4	6	6 + 4 = 10
D	6	9	10 + 6 = 16

Total flow time = 1 + 3 + 6 + 10 + 16 = 36 days

Average flow time = $\frac{36}{5}$ = 7.2 days

SOT results in a lower average flow time than the FCFS rule. In addition, Jobs E and C will be ready before the due date, and Job A is late by only one day. On average, a job will be late by (0 + 0 + 1 + 4 + 7)/5 = 2.4 days.

SOLUTION

EDD RULE: If Morales decides to use the EDD rule, the resulting schedule is

EDD Schedule

Job Sequence	Processing Time (Days)	Due Date (Days Hence)	Flow Time (Days)
E	1	2	0 + 1 = 1
A	3	5	1 + 3 = 4
B	4	6	4 + 4 = 8
C	2	7	8 + 2 = 10
D	6	9	10 + 6 = 16

Total flow time 1 + 4 + 8 + 10 + 16 = 39 days

Average flow time = 7.8 days

In this case, Jobs B, C, and D will be late. On average, a job will be late by (0 + 0 + 2 + 3 + 7)/5 = 2.4 days.

SOLUTION

LCFS, RANDOM, and STR RULES: Here are the resulting flow times of the LCFS, random, and STR rules:

Job Sequence	Processing Time (Days)	Due Date (Days Hence)	Flow Time (Days)	
LCFS Schedule				
E	1	2	0 + 1 = 1	
D	6	9	1 + 6 = 7	
C	2	7	7 + 2 = 9	
B	4	6	9 + 4 = 13	
A	3	5	13 + 3 = 16	
Total flow time = 46 days				
Average flow time = 9.2 days				
Average lateness = 4.0 days				
Random Schedule				
D	6	9	0 + 6 = 6	
C	2	7	6 + 2 = 8	
A	3	5	8 + 3 = 11	
E	1	2	11 + 1 = 12	
B	4	6	12 + 4 = 16	
Total flow time = 53 days				
Average flow time = 10.6 days				
Average lateness = 5.4 days				
STR Schedule				*Slack*
E	1	2	0 + 1 = 1	2 − 1 = 1
A	3	5	1 + 3 = 4	5 − 3 = 2
B	4	6	4 + 4 = 8	6 − 4 = 2
D	6	9	8 + 6 = 14	9 − 6 = 3
C	2	7	14 + 2 = 16	7 − 2 = 5
Total flow time = 43 days				
Average flow time = 8.6 days				
Average lateness = 3.2 days				

Comparison of Priority Rules

Here are some of the results summarized for the rules that Morales examined:

Rule	Total Flow Time (Days)	Average Flow Time (Days)	Average Lateness (Days)
FCFS	50	10	4.6
SOT	36	7.2	2.4
EDD	39	7.8	2.4
LCFS	46	9.2	4.0
Random	53	10.6	5.4
STR	43	8.6	3.2

Here, SOT is better than the other rules in terms of average flow time. Moreover, it can be shown mathematically that the SOT rule yields an optimal solution in the $n/1$ case for average flow time and performs well relative to average lateness as well. In fact, so powerful is this simple rule that it has been termed the most important concept in the entire aspect of sequencing. It does have its shortcomings, however. The main one is that longer jobs may never be started if short jobs keep arriving at the scheduler's desk. To avoid this, companies may invoke what is termed a *truncated* SOT rule whereby jobs waiting for a specified time period are automatically moved to the front of the line.

Scheduling *n* Jobs on Two Machines

The next step up in complexity is the *n*/2 flow-shop case, where two or more jobs must be processed on two machines in a common sequence. As in the *n*/1 case, there is an approach that leads to an optimal solution according to certain criteria. The objective of this approach, termed **Johnson's rule** or *Johnson's method* (after its developer), is to minimize the flow time from the beginning of the first job until the finish of the last. Johnson's rule consists of the following steps:

Johnson's rule
A sequencing rule used for scheduling any number of jobs on two machines. The rule is designed to minimize the time required to complete all the jobs.

1. List the operation time for each job on both machines.
2. Select the shortest operation time.
3. If the shortest time is on the first machine, do the job first; if it is on the second machine, do the job last. In the case of a tie, do the job on the first machine.
4. Repeat Steps 2 and 3 for each remaining job until the schedule is complete.

EXAMPLE 22.2 *n* Jobs on Two Machines

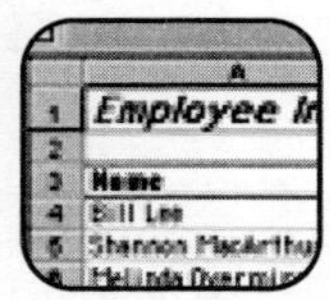

We can illustrate this procedure by scheduling four jobs through two machines.

SOLUTION

Step 1: List operation times.

Job	Operation Time on Machine 1	Operation Time on Machine 2
A	3	2
B	6	8
C	5	6
D	7	4

Steps 2 and 3: Select the shortest operation time and assign. Job A is shortest on Machine 2 and is assigned first and performed last. (Once assigned, Job A is no longer available to be scheduled.)

Step 4: Repeat Steps 2 and 3 until completion of the schedule. Select the shortest operation time among the remaining jobs. Job D is second-shortest on Machine 2, so it is performed second to last. (Remember, Job A is last.) Now Jobs A and D are not available for scheduling. Job C is the shortest on Machine 1 among the remaining jobs. Job C is performed first. Now only Job B is left with

EXHIBIT 22.4

Optimal Schedule of Jobs Using Johnson's Rule

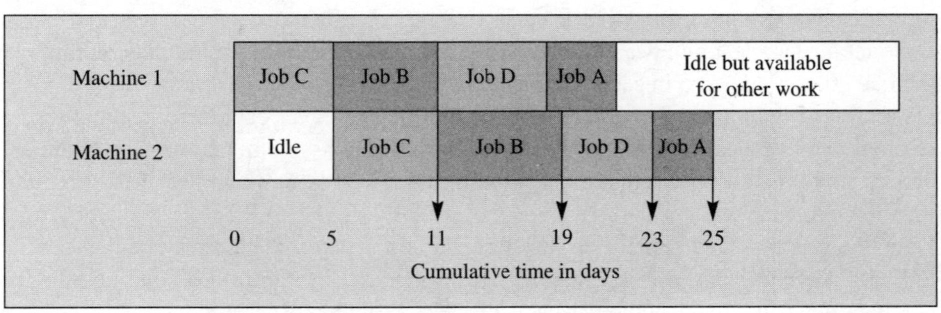

the shortest operation time on Machine 1. Thus, according to Step 3, it is performed first among the remaining, or second overall. (Job C was already scheduled first.)

In summary, the solution sequence is C → B → D → A and the flow time is 25 days, which is a minimum. Also minimized are total idle time and mean idle time. The final schedule appears in Exhibit 22.4.

These steps result in scheduling the jobs having the shortest time in the beginning and end of the schedule. As a result, the concurrent operating time for the two machines is maximized, thus minimizing the total operating time required to complete the jobs.

Johnson's method has been extended to yield an optimal solution for the $n/3$ case. When flow-shop scheduling problems larger than $n/3$ arise (and they generally do), analytical solution procedures leading to optimality are not available. The reason for this is that, even though the jobs may arrive in static fashion at the first machine, the scheduling problem becomes dynamic, and waiting lines start to form in front of machines downstream. At this point, it becomes a multistage queuing problem, which is generally solved using simulation techniques such as those discussed in Chapter 10.

Scheduling a Set Number of Jobs on the Same Number of Machines

Some workcenters have enough of the right kinds of machines to start all jobs at the same time. Here, the problem is not which job to do first, but rather which particular assignment of individual jobs to individual machines will result in the best overall schedule. In such cases, we can use the assignment method.

Assignment method
A special case of the transportation method of linear programming that is used to allocate a specific number of jobs to the same number of machines.

The **assignment method** is a special case of the transportation method of linear programming. It can be applied to situations where there are n supply sources and n demand uses (such as five jobs on five machines) and the objective is to minimize or maximize some measure of effectiveness. This technique is convenient in applications involving the allocation of jobs to workcenters, people to jobs, and so on. The assignment method is appropriate in solving problems that have the following characteristics:

1. There are n "things" to be distributed to n "destinations."
2. Each thing must be assigned to one and only one destination.
3. Only one criterion can be used (minimum cost, maximum profit, or minimum completion time, for example).

EXAMPLE 22.3 Assignment Method

Suppose that a scheduler has five jobs that can be performed on any of five machines ($n = 5$). The cost of completing each job–machine combination is shown in Exhibit 22.5. The scheduler would like to devise a minimum-cost assignment. (There are 5!, or 120, possible assignments.)

SOLUTION

This problem may be solved by the assignment method, which consists of four steps (note that this also can be solved using the Excel Solver):

1. Subtract the smallest number in each *row* from itself and all other numbers in that row. (There will then be at least one zero in each row.)
2. Subtract the smallest number in each *column* from all other numbers in that column. (There will then be at least one zero in each column.)
3. Determine if the *minimum* number of lines required to cover each zero is equal to n. If so, an optimal solution has been found, because job machine assignments must be made at the zero entries, and this test proves that this is possible. If the minimum number of lines required is less than n, go to Step 4.
4. Draw the least possible number of lines through all the zeros. (These may be the same lines used in Step 3.) Subtract the smallest number not covered by lines from itself and all other uncovered numbers, and add it to the number at each intersection of lines. Repeat Step 3.

EXHIBIT 22.5

Assignment Matrix Showing Machine Processing Costs for Each Job

	Machine				
Job	A	B	C	D	E
I	$5	$6	$4	$8	$3
II	6	4	9	8	5
III	4	3	2	5	4
IV	7	2	4	5	3
V	3	6	4	5	5

For the example problem, the steps listed in Exhibit 22.6 would be followed.

EXHIBIT 22.6

Procedure to Solve an Assignment Matrix

Step 1: Row reduction—the smallest number is subtracted from each row.

	Machine				
Job	A	B	C	D	E
I	2	3	1	5	0
II	2	0	5	4	1
III	2	1	0	3	2
IV	5	0	2	3	1
V	0	3	1	2	2

Step 2: Column reduction—the smallest number is subtracted from each column.

	Machine				
Job	A	B	C	D	E
I	2	3	1	3	0
II	2	0	5	2	1
III	2	1	0	1	2
IV	5	0	2	1	1
V	0	3	1	0	2

Step 3: Apply line test—the number of lines to cover all zeros is 4; because 5 are required, go to step 4.

	Machine				
Job	A	B	C	D	E
I	2	3	1	3	0
II	2	0	5	2	1
III	2	1	0	1	2
IV	5	0	2	1	1
V	0	3	1	0	2

Step 4: Subtract smallest uncovered number and add to intersection of lines. Using lines drawn in Step 3, smallest uncovered number is 1.

	Machine				
Job	A	B	C	D	E
I	1	3	0	2	0
II	1	0	4	1	1
III	2	2	0	1	3
IV	4	0	1	0	1
V	0	4	1	0	3

Optimal solution—by "line test."

	Machine				
Job	A	B	C	D	E
I	1	3	0	2	0
II	1	0	4	1	1
III	2	2	0	1	3
IV	4	0	1	0	1
V	0	4	1	0	3

Optimal assignments and their costs.

Job I to Machine E	$ 3
Job II to Machine B	4
Job III to Machine C	2
Job IV to Machine D	5
Job V to Machine A	3
Total cost	$17

Note that even though there are two zeros in three rows and three columns, the solution shown in Exhibit 22.6 is the only one possible for this problem because Job III must be assigned to Machine C to meet the "assign to zero" requirement. Other problems may have more than one optimal solution, depending, of course, on the costs involved.

The nonmathematical rationale of the assignment method is one of minimizing opportunity costs. For example, if we decided to assign Job I to Machine A instead of to Machine E, we would be sacrificing the opportunity to save $2 ($5 – $3). The assignment algorithm in effect performs such comparisons for the entire set of alternative assignments by means of row and column reduction, as described in Steps 1 and 2. It makes similar comparisons in Step 4. Obviously, if assignments are made to zero cells, no opportunity cost, with respect to the entire matrix, occurs.

Scheduling *n* Jobs on *m* Machines

Complex workcenters are characterized by multiple machine centers processing a variety of different jobs arriving at the machine centers intermittently throughout the day. If there are n jobs to be processed on m machines and all jobs are processed on all machines, then there are $(n!)^m$ alternative schedules for this job set. Because of the large number of schedules that exist for even small workcenters, computer simulation (see Chapter 10) is the only practical way to determine the relative merits of different priority rules in such situations.

Which Priority Rule Should Be Used? We believe that the needs of most manufacturers are reasonably satisfied by a relatively simple priority scheme that embodies the following principles:

1. It should be dynamic; that is, computed frequently during a job to reflect changing conditions.
2. It should be based in one way or another on slack (the difference between the work remaining to be done on a job and the time remaining to do it).

Current approaches used by companies combine simulation with human schedulers to create schedules.

LO 22-3

Apply scheduling techniques to the manufacturing shop floor

SHOP-FLOOR CONTROL

Shop-floor (production activity) control
A system for utilizing data from the shop floor to maintain and communicate status information on shop orders and workcenters.

Scheduling job priorities is just one aspect of **shop-floor control** (now often called **production activity control**). The *APICS Dictionary* defines a *shop-floor control system* as

> A system for utilizing data from the shop floor as well as data processing files to maintain and communicate status information on shop orders and workcenters.

The major functions of shop-floor control are

- Assigning the priority of each shop order.
- Maintaining work-in-process quantity information.
- Conveying shop-order status information to the office.
- Providing actual output data for capacity control purposes.
- Providing quantity by location by shop order for WIP inventory and accounting purposes.
- Measuring efficiency, utilization, and productivity of manpower and machines.

Gantt Charts

Smaller job shops and individual departments of large ones employ the venerable Gantt chart to help plan and track jobs. As described in Chapter 4, the Gantt chart is a type of bar chart that plots tasks against time. Gantt charts are used for project planning and to coordinate a number of scheduled activities. The example in Exhibit 22.7 indicates that Job A is behind schedule by about four hours, Job B is ahead of schedule, and Job C has been completed, after a delayed start for equipment maintenance. Note that whether the job is ahead of schedule or behind schedule is based on where it stands compared to where we are now. In Exhibit 22.7, we are at the end of Wednesday, and Job A should have been completed. Job B has already had some of Thursday's work completed.

EXHIBIT 22.7

Gantt Chart

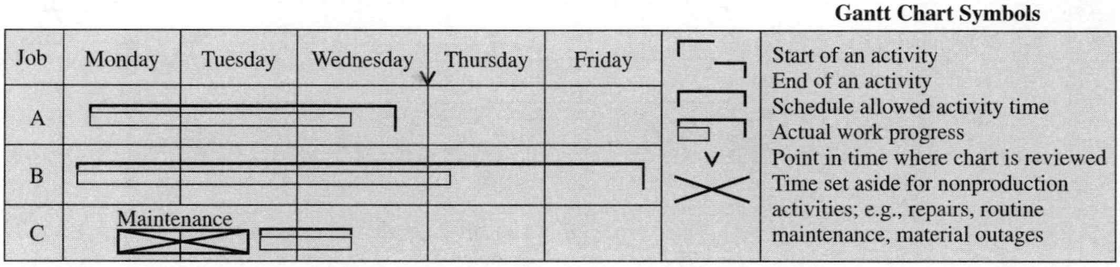

Tools of Shop-Floor Control

The basic tools of shop-floor control are

1. The *daily dispatch list,* which tells the supervisor which jobs are to be run, their priority, and how long each will take. (See Exhibit 22.8A.)
2. Various *status and exception reports,* including
   a. The anticipated delay report, made out by the shop planner once or twice a week and reviewed by the chief shop planner to see if there are any serious delays that could affect the master schedule. (See Exhibit 22.8B.)
   b. Scrap reports.
   c. Rework reports.
   d. Performance summary reports giving the number and percentage of orders completed on schedule, the lateness of unfilled orders, the volume of output, and so on.
   e. Shortage list.
3. An *input/output control report,* which is used by the supervisor to monitor the workload–capacity relationship for each workstation. (See Exhibit 22.8C.)

Input/Output Control **Input/output (I/O) control** is a major feature of a manufacturing planning and control system. Its major precept is that the planned work input to a workcenter should never exceed the planned work output. When the input exceeds the output, backlogs build up at the workcenter, which in turn increases the lead time estimates for jobs upstream. Moreover, when jobs pile up at the workcenter, congestion occurs, processing becomes inefficient, and the flow of work to downstream workcenters becomes sporadic. (The water flow analogy to shop capacity control in Exhibit 22.9 illustrates the general phenomenon.) Exhibit 22.8C shows an I/O report for a downstream workcenter. Looking first at the lower or output half of the report, we see that output is far below plan. It would seem that a serious capacity problem exists for this workcenter. However, a look at the input part of the plan makes it apparent that the serious capacity problem exists at an upstream workcenter feeding this workcenter. The control process would entail finding the cause of upstream problems and adjusting capacity and inputs accordingly. The basic solution is simple: Either increase capacity at the bottleneck station or reduce the input to it. (Input reduction at bottleneck workcenters, incidentally, is usually the first step recommended by production control consultants when job shops get into trouble.)

Input/output (I/O) control
Work being released into a workcenter should never exceed the planned work output. When the input exceeds the output, backlogs build up at the workcenter that increase the lead time.

Data Integrity Shop-floor control systems in most modern plants are now computerized, with job status information entered directly into a computer as the job enters and leaves a workcenter. Many plants have gone heavily into bar coding and optical scanners to speed up the reporting process and to cut down on data entry errors. As you might guess, the key problems in shop-floor control are data inaccuracy and lack of timeliness. When these occur, data fed back to the overall planning system are wrong, and incorrect production decisions are made. Typical results are excess inventory, stockout problems, or both; missed due dates; and inaccuracies in job costing.

Of course, maintaining data integrity requires that a sound data-gathering system be in place. More importantly, however, it requires adherence to the system by everybody interacting with it. Most

EXHIBIT 22.8

Some Basic Tools of Shop-Floor Control

A. Dispatch List

Workcenter 1501—Day 205

Start date	Job #	Description	Run time
201	15131	Shaft	11.4
203	15143	Stud	20.6
205	15145	Spindle	4.3
205	15712	Spindle	8.6
207	15340	Metering rod	6.5
208	15312	Shaft	4.6

B. Anticipated Delay Report

Dept. 24 April 8

Part #	Sched. date	New date	Cause of delay	Action
17125	4/10	4/15	Fixture broke	Toolroom will return on 4/15
13044	4/11	5/1	Out for plating—plater on strike	New lot started
17653	4/11	4/14	New part holes don't align	Engineering laying out new jig

C. Input/Output Control Report

Workcenter 0162

Week ending	505	512	519	526
Planned input	210	210	210	210
Actual input	110	150	140	130
Cumulative deviation	–100	–160	–230	–310
Planned output	210	210	210	210
Actual output	140	120	160	120
Cumulative deviation	–70	–160	–210	–300

firms recognize this, but maintaining what is variously referred to as *shop discipline, data integrity,* or *data responsibility* is not always easy. And despite periodic drives to publicize the importance of careful shop-floor reporting by creating data integrity task forces, inaccuracies can still creep into the system in many ways: A line worker drops a part under the workbench and pulls a replacement from stock without recording either transaction. An inventory clerk makes an error in a cycle count. A manufacturing engineer fails to note a change in the routing of a part. A department supervisor decides to work jobs in a different order than specified in the dispatch list.

Principles of Workcenter Scheduling

Much of our discussion of workcenter scheduling systems can be summarized in the following principles:

1. There is a direct equivalence between workflow and cash flow.
2. The effectiveness of any shop should be measured by speed of flow through the shop.

EXHIBIT 22.9

Shop Capacity Control Load Flow

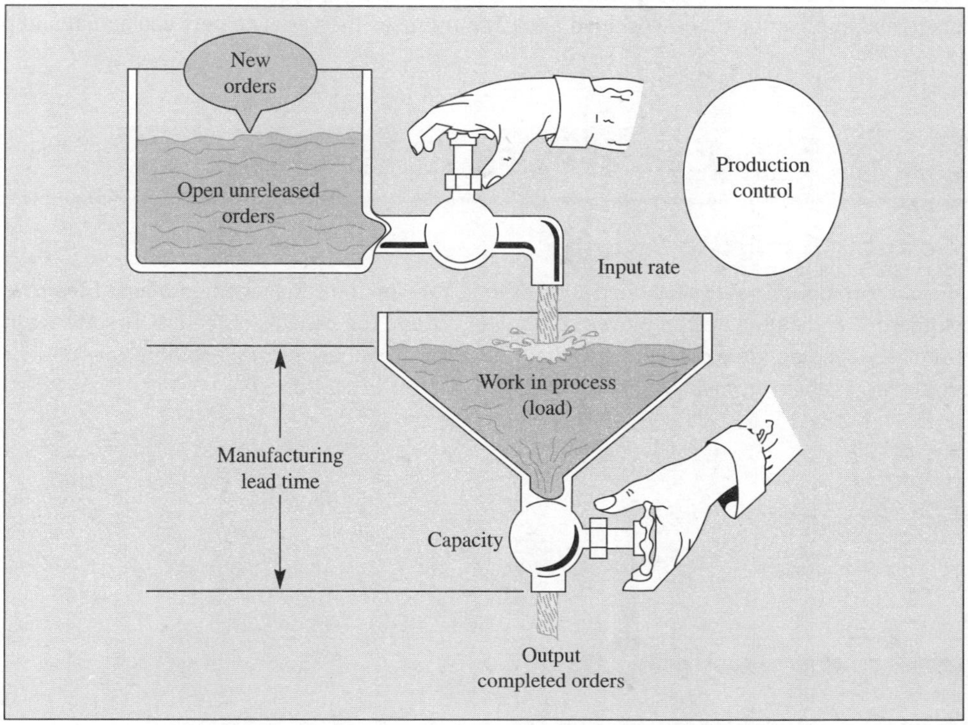

3. Schedule jobs as a string, with process steps back to back.
4. Once started, a job should not be interrupted.
5. Speed of flow is most efficiently achieved by focusing on bottleneck workcenters and jobs.
6. Reschedule every day.
7. Obtain feedback each day on jobs that are not completed at each workcenter.
8. Match workcenter input information to what the worker can actually do.
9. When seeking improvement in output, look for incompatibility between engineering design and process execution.
10. Certainty of standards, routings, and so forth, is not possible in´ a shop, but always work toward achieving it.

An assembly line supervisor taking notes as he observes employees.

© Corbis Super RF/Alamy RF

PERSONNEL SCHEDULING IN SERVICES

LO 22-4

Analyze employee schedules in the service sector

The scheduling problem in most service organizations revolves around setting weekly, daily, and hourly personnel schedules. In this section, we present a simple analytical approach for developing such schedules.

Scheduling Daily Work Times

We now show how bank clearinghouses and back-office operations of large bank branches establish daily work times. Basically, management wants to derive a staffing plan that (1) requires the fewest workers to accomplish the daily workload and (2) minimizes the variance between actual and planned output.

OSCM AT WORK

Employee Scheduling Software Applied to Security

ScheduleSource Inc. of Broomfield, Colorado, offers an integrated suite of tools for workforce management named TeamWork. At the heart of TeamWork is a customizable and automated employee scheduling system. The benefits of TeamWork software include features such as Web-based, optimized schedules; zero conflict scheduling; time and attendance recordkeeping; e-mail notifications; audit trails; advanced reporting; and accessibility from anywhere anytime. The way it works is this:

Step 1: Define labor requirements.

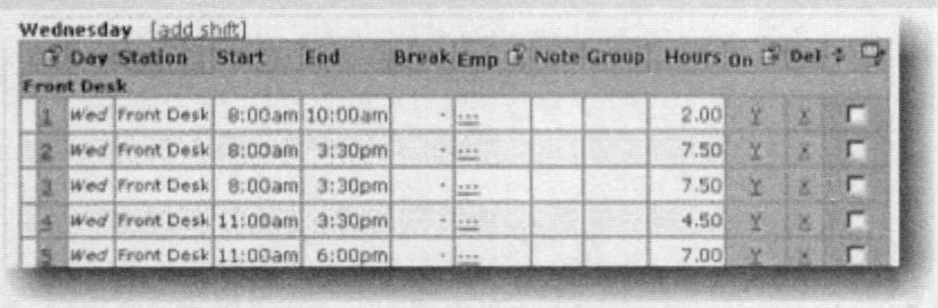

McGraw-Hill Education, Inc

Step 2: Establish employee availability.

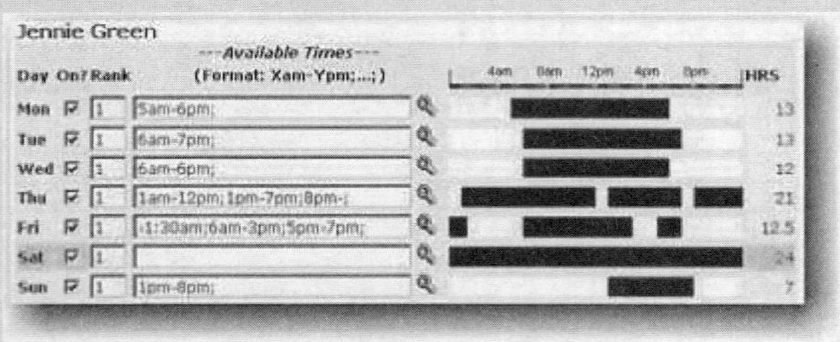

McGraw-Hill Education, Inc

Step 3: Assign employees to particular skill sets and rank an employee's skill set level from 1 to 10 (1 being novice, 5 being average, and 10 being superlative).

Step 4: The TeamWork software automatically builds a schedule.

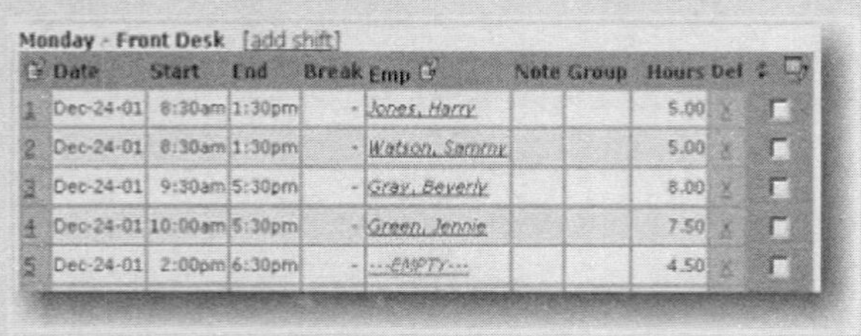

McGraw-Hill Education, Inc

ScheduleSource customers include the Transportation Security Administration (TSA). ScheduleSource was successfully implemented to generate schedules for more than 44,000 federal airport security personnel at 429 airports. Over 30,000,000 individual shifts were scheduled in the airport security deployment.

EXHIBIT 22.10

Daily Staff Hours Required to Schedule Daily Work Times

		Function								
		Receive		Preprocess		Microfilm		Verify		Totals
Product	Daily Volume	*P/H*	H_{std}	*P/H*	H_{std}	*P/H*	H_{std}	*P/H*	H_{std}	H_{std}
Checks	2,000	1,000	2.0	600	3.3	240	8.3	640	3.1	16.8
Statements	1,000	—	—	600	1.7	250	4.0	150	6.7	12.3
Notes	200	30	6.7	15	13.3		—			20.0
Investments	400	100	4.0	50	8.0	200	2.0	150	2.7	16.7
Collections	500	300	1.7			300	1.7	60	8.4	11.7
Total hours required			14.3		26.3		16.0		20.8	77.5
Times 1.25 (absences and vacations)			17.9		32.9		20.0		26.0	
Divided by 8 hours equals staff required			2.2		4.1		2.5		3.2	12.1

Note: *P/H* indicates production rate per hour; H_{std} indicates required hours.

In structuring the problem, bank management defines inputs (checks, statements, investment documents, and so forth) as *products,* which are routed through different processes or *functions* (receiving, sorting, encoding, and so forth).

To solve the problem, a daily demand forecast is made by product for each function. This is converted to labor hours required per function, which in turn is converted to workers required per function. These figures are then tabulated, summed, and adjusted by an absence and vacation factor to give planned hours. They are then divided by the number of hours in the workday to yield the number of workers required. This yields the daily staff hours required. (See Exhibit 22.10.) This becomes the basis for a departmental staffing plan that lists the workers required, workers available, variance, and managerial action to deal with the variance. (See Exhibit 22.11.)

EXHIBIT 22.11

Staffing Plan

Function	Staff Required	Staff Available	Variance (±)	Management Actions
Receive	2.3	2.0	−0.3	Use overtime.
Preprocess	4.1	4.0	−0.1	Use overtime.
Microfilm	2.5	3.0	+0.5	Use excess to verify.
Verify	3.3	3.0	−0.3	Get 0.3 from microfilm.

Scheduling Hourly Work Times

Services such as restaurants face changing requirements from hour to hour. More workers are needed for peak hours, and fewer are needed in between. Management must continuously adjust to this changing requirement. This kind of personnel scheduling situation can be approached by applying a simple rule, the *"first-hour" principle.* This procedure can be best explained using the following example. Assume that each worker works continuously for an eight-hour shift. The first-hour rule says that for the first hour, we assign a number of workers equal to the requirement in that period. For each subsequent period, assign the exact number of additional workers to meet the requirements. When in a period one or more workers come to the end of their shifts, add more workers only if they are needed

OSCM AT WORK

Nurse Scheduling Problem

The administration of a leading hospital in Bangalore wants to schedule the duties for nurses under different shifts. As a routine practice, the hospital administration assesses the work-load and accordingly the number of nurses needed during each shift. The hospital has Nurses' residence facility in the campus and they can join the hospital duty at the beginning of eight shifts as listed in the table below. Although every shift is for three hours duration, a nurse who joins a shift will have to work for six hours at a stretch.

The hospital administration would like to schedule the nurse duty and for this they will first like to know the minimum number of nurses needed to do the job every day. For the roster-duty, it is important to know the minimum number of nurses, who would join every shift.

	PERIOD							
	1	2	3	4	5	6	7	8
SHIFT	07AM-10AM	10AM-01PM	01PM-04PM	04AM-07PM	07PM-10PM	10PM-01AM	01AM-04AM	04AM-07AM
NURSES NEEDED	80	65	40	45	65	35	25	45

To solve this optimization problem, we should first decide the decision variables. There are eight decision variables, X1, X2, X3, X4, X5, X6, X7 and X8, which indicate the number of nurses joining at the beginning of first shift, second shift, and so on.

Next step is to formulate the objective function, which need to be minimized. The objective function, therefore, is to minimize (X1 + X2 + X3 + X4 + X5 + X6 + X7 + X8).

Last step of formulation in a linear programming problem is deciding the constraints. For the first shift, the minimum number of nurses that is needed should be 80, which forms the right hand side (RHS) of corresponding constraint. Then, who are the nurses working in the first shift? The answer is: those, who joined at 07 AM as well as those who joined at 04 AM. This is because, nurses joining at 04 AM will stay till next six hours, i.e. up to 10 AM. Therefore, the constraint for the first shift is: "$X1 + X8 \geq 80$."

Similarly, other seven constraints are formulated. Also, there are non-negativity constraints, as decision variables X1, X2, ... are non-negative due to the fact that negative number of nurses cannot join a shift.

The complete formulation of the nurse scheduling problem is as follows:

LINEAR PROGRAMMING FORMULATION OF NURSE SCHEDULING PROBLEM

MINIMIZE!

$X1 + X2 + X3 + X4 + X5 + X6 + X7 + X8$

SUBJECT TO!

$X1 + X8 \geq 80$

$X2 + X1 \geq 65$

$X3 + X2 \geq 40$

$X4 + X3 \geq 45$

$X5 + X4 \geq 65$

$X6 + X5 \geq 35$

$X7 + X6 \geq 25$

$X8 + X7 \geq 45$

$X1, X2, X3, X4, X5, X6, X7, X8 \geq 0.$

The solution, using Linear Programming (LP) approach is as follows. Refer to "Appendix A" for using Solver. One may also use standard LP Package like LINDO (www.lindo.com) etc.

SOLUTION OF THE NURSE SCEDULING PROBLEM

OBJECTIVE FUNCTION VALUE = 210

VARIABLES VALUE IS:

X1 = 60, X2 = 5, X3 = 35, X4 = 30, X5 = 35, X6 = 0, X7 = 25, X8 = 20.

One can check that this scheduling results into minimum requirement for nurses; of course, there are 20 extra nurses in Shift-4. A prudent approach could be to assign these extra nurses of Shift-4 to do some maintenance or record updating work.

to meet the requirement. The following table shows the worker requirements for the first 12 hours in a 24-hour restaurant:

	Period											
	10 A.M.	11 A.M.	Noon	1 P.M	2 P.M.	3 P.M.	4 P.M.	5 P.M.	6 P.M.	7 P.M.	8 P.M.	9 P.M.
Requirement	4	6	8	8	6	4	4	6	8	10	10	6

The schedule shows that four workers are assigned at 10 A.M., two are added at 11 A.M., and another two are added at noon to meet the requirement. From noon to 5 P.M. we have eight workers on duty. Note the overstaffing between 2 P.M. and 6 P.M. The four workers assigned at 10 A.M. finish their eight-hour shifts by 6 P.M., and four more workers are added to start their shifts. The two workers starting at 11 A.M. leave by 7 P.M., and the number of workers available drops to six. Therefore, four new workers are assigned at 7 P.M. At 9 P.M., there are 10 workers on duty, which is more than the requirement, so no worker is added. This procedure continues as new requirements are given.

	Period											
	10 A.M.	11 A.M.	Noon	1 P.M.	2 P.M.	3 P.M.	4 P.M.	5 P.M.	6 P.M.	7 P.M.	8 P.M.	9 P.M.
Requirement	4	6	8	8	6	4	4	6	8	10	10	6
Assigned	4	2	2	0	0	0	0	0	4	4	2	0
On duty	4	6	8	8	8	8	8	8	8	10	10	10

Another option is splitting shifts. For example, the worker can come in, work for four hours, then come back two hours later for another four hours. The impact of this option in scheduling is essentially similar to that of changing the lot size in production. When workers start working, they have to log in, change uniforms, and probably get necessary information from workers in the previous shift. This preparation can be considered as the "setup cost" in a production scenario. Splitting shifts is like having smaller production lot sizes and thus more preparation (more setups). This is a complex problem that can be solved by specialized linear programming methods.

CONCEPT CONNECTIONS

LO 22–1 Explain workcenter scheduling

Summary

- A schedule is a timetable for performing work that indicates how resources are to be used over time.
- This chapter focuses on short-term schedules showing what is to be done over the next few days or weeks.
- One characteristic of a scheduling system is whether capacity is directly considered or not (finite versus infinite loading). Another characteristic is whether jobs are scheduled forward, from now and into the future, or backward from a due date.

- Typically, either labor or equipment is scheduled, depending on what is the most limiting resource in a process.
- Typically, work is done in workcenters and the main focus of the chapter is on scheduling jobs through these areas. This process involves (1) allocating jobs to resources, (2) sequencing the jobs at each resource, (3) releasing (dispatching) the jobs, and (4) monitoring the status of the jobs.
- Jobs are often sequenced (ordered) using priority rules based on processing time, due dates, or order of arrival. This entire process is often done using a comprehensive software package known as a manufacturing execution system.

Key Terms

Manufacturing Execution System (MES) An information system that schedules, dispatches, tracks, monitors, and controls production on the factory floor.

Workcenter Often referred to as a job shop, a process structure suited for low-volume production of a great variety of non-standard products. Workcenters sometimes are referred to as departments and are focused on a particular type of operation.

Infinite loading Work is assigned to a workcenter based on what is needed over time. Capacity is not considered.

Finite loading Each resource is scheduled in detail using the setup and run time required for each order. The system determines exactly what will be done by each resource at every moment during the working day.

Forward scheduling Schedules from now into the future to tell the earliest that an order can be completed.

Backward scheduling Starts from some date in the future (typically the due date) and schedules the required operations in reverse sequence. Tells the latest time when an order can be started so that it is completed by a specific date.

Machine-limited process Equipment is the critical resource that is scheduled.

Labor-limited process People are the key resource that is scheduled.

Dispatching The activity of initiating scheduled work.

Sequencing The process of determining which job to start first on a machine or workcenter.

Priority rules The logic used to determine the sequence of jobs in a queue.

LO 22–2 Analyze scheduling problems using priority rules and more specialized techniques

Summary

- Many different techniques are available for scheduling jobs. Three of the most common approaches are analyzed in this section.
- Priority rules are used when there are a number of jobs that need to be run on a single machine.
- A special case is when a set of jobs needs to be run on only two machines. In this case, a technique called "Johnson's rule" can be used to minimize the time to complete all jobs.
- Another special case is when there are exactly the same number of jobs as machines available, and the jobs each need to be assigned to a unique machine (not all of the machines are equally efficient). In this case, the assignment method can be used.
- These different techniques are mixed and matched to real-world scheduling situations.

Key Terms

Johnson's rule A sequencing rule used for scheduling any number of jobs on two machines. The rule is designed to minimize the time required to complete all the jobs.

Assignment method A special case of the transportation method of linear programming that is used to allocate a specific number of jobs to the same number of machines.

LO 22–3 Apply scheduling techniques to the manufacturing shop floor

Summary

- The job of actually managing work in a manufacturing environment is called shop-floor or production activity control.
- The system consists of computer-based tracking and decision support, augmented with visual charts and lists to quickly convey information to workers.

- An important feature of the system is acquiring the ability to manage the inflow of work so the system is not overloaded. This is called input/output control, and recognizes that production systems have limited capacity.

Key Terms

Shop-floor (production activity) control A system for utilizing data from the shop floor to maintain and communicate status information on shop orders and workcenters.

Input/output (I/O) control Work being released into a workcenter should never exceed the planned work output. When the input exceeds the output, backlogs build up at the workcenter that increase the lead time.

LO 22–4 Analyze employee schedules in the service sector

Summary

- Service sector scheduling focuses on setting detailed personnel schedules. It answers the questions of when and where each employee will be working in the short term.
- These techniques are driven by daily worker requirements that may vary considerably by hour and day.

SOLVED PROBLEMS

LO 22–2 SOLVED PROBLEM 1

Consider the following data on jobs waiting to be processed on a *single machine* in a job shop. They are listed here in order of their arrival at the machine:

Job	Processing Time (days)	Due Date (days hence)
A	5	8
B	3	5
C	4	12
D	7	14
E	2	11

Develop a schedule for these jobs based on the following rules: FCFS, SOT, and EDD. In each schedule, list the flow time and lateness for each job (the lateness of a job that is done early equals zero), as well as the mean for each measure.

Solution

FCFS Schedule

Job Sequence	Processing Time (days)	Due Date (days hence)	Flow Time (days)	Lateness (days)
A	5	8	0 + 5 = 5	5 − 8 = 0
B	3	5	5 + 3 = 8	8 − 5 = 3
C	4	12	8 + 4 = 12	12 − 12 = 0
D	7	14	12 + 7 = 19	19 − 14 = 5
E	2	11	19 + 2 = 21	21 − 11 = 10

$$\text{Average flow time} = \frac{5 + 8 + 12 + 19 + 21}{5} = \mathbf{13.0}$$

$$\text{Average flow time} = \frac{0 + 3 + 0 + 5 + 10}{5} = \mathbf{3.6}$$

SOT Schedule

Job Sequence	Processing Time (days)	Due Date (days hence)	Flow Time (days)	Lateness (days)
E	2	11	$0+2=2$	$2-11=0$
B	3	5	$2+3=5$	$5-5=0$
C	4	12	$5+4=9$	$9-12=0$
A	5	8	$9+5=14$	$14-8=6$
D	7	14	$14+7=21$	$21-14=7$

$$\text{Average flow time} = \frac{2+5+9+14+21}{5} = \mathbf{10.2}$$

$$\text{Average flow time} = \frac{0+0+0+6+7}{5} = \mathbf{2.6}$$

EDD Schedule

Job Sequence	Processing Time (days)	Due Date (days hence)	Flow Time (days)	Lateness (days)
B	3	5	$0+3=3$	$3-5=0$
A	5	8	$3+5=8$	$8-8=0$
E	2	11	$8+2=10$	$10-11=0$
C	4	12	$10+4=14$	$14-12=2$
D	7	14	$14+7=21$	$21-14=7$

$$\text{Average flow time} = \frac{3+8+10+14+21}{5} = \mathbf{11.2}$$

$$\text{Average flow time} = \frac{0+0+0+2+7}{5} = \mathbf{1.8}$$

SOLVED PROBLEM 2

Joe's Auto Seat Cover and Paint Shop is bidding on a contract to do all the custom work for Smiling Ed's used car dealership. One of the main requirements in obtaining this contract is rapid delivery time, because Ed—for reasons we shall not go into here—wants the cars face-lifted and back on his lot in a hurry. Ed has said that if Joe can refit and repaint five cars that Ed has just received in 24 hours or less, the contract will be his. The following is the time (in hours) required in the refitting shop and the paint shop for each of the five cars. Assuming that cars go through the refitting operations before they are repainted, can Joe meet the time requirements and get the contract?

Car	Refitting Time (hours)	Repainting Time (hours)
A	6	3
B	0	4
C	5	2
D	8	6
E	2	1

Solution

This problem can be viewed as a two-machine flow shop and can be easily solved using Johnson's rule. The final schedule is B–D–A–C–E.

Manually, the problem is solved as follows:

	Original Data		Johnson's Rule	
Car	**Refitting Time (hours)**	**Repainting Time (hours)**	**Order of Selection**	**Position in Sequence**
A	6	3	4	3
B	0	4	1	1
C	5	2	3	4
D	8	6	5	2
E	2	1	2	5

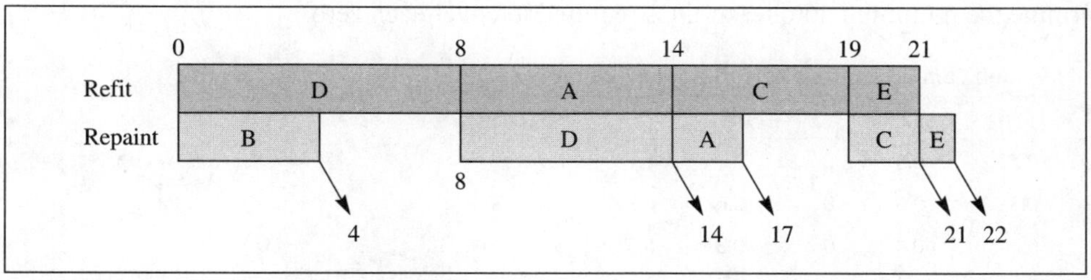

SOLVED PROBLEM 3

The production scheduler for Marion Machine Shop has six jobs ready to be processed that can each be assigned to any of six different workstations. Due to the characteristics of each job and the different equipment and skills at the workstations, the time to complete a job depends on the station it is assigned to. The following is data on the jobs and the time it would take to do each job at each workstation.

	Job Completion Time at Workstation (hours)					
Job	**1**	**2**	**3**	**4**	**5**	**6**
A	3.2	3.5	2.9	3	4	3.6
B	2.7	2.9	2.3	3	3.1	3.7
C	3.8	4	4.3	4.5	4.1	3.6
D	2.8	2.1	2.9	2.5	3	2.2
E	6.1	6.5	6.7	7	6	6.2
F	1.5	1.3	1.9	2.9	4	3.6

Assign each job to a machine in order to minimize total processing time.

SOLUTION

Use the assignment method following Example 22.3.

a. Subtract the smallest number in each row from itself and all other numbers in that row.

	Job Completion Time at Workstation (hours)					
Job	**1**	**2**	**3**	**4**	**5**	**6**
A	0.3	0.6	0	0.1	1.1	0.7
B	0.4	0.6	0	0.7	0.8	1.4
C	0.2	0.4	0.7	0.9	0.5	0
D	0.7	0	0.8	0.4	0.9	0.1
E	0.1	0.5	0.7	1	0	0.2
F	0.2	0	0.6	1.6	2.7	2.3

b. Subtract the smallest number in each column from itself and all other numbers in that column.

	Job Completion Time at Workstation (hours)					
Job	**1**	**2**	**3**	**4**	**5**	**6**
A	0.2	0.6	0	0	1.1	0.7
B	0.3	0.6	0	0.6	0.8	1.4
C	0.1	0.4	0.7	0.8	0.5	0
D	0.6	0	0.8	0.3	0.9	0.1
E	0	0.5	0.7	0.9	0	0.2
F	0.1	0	0.6	1.5	2.7	2.3

c. Determine the minimum number of lines required to cover each zero.

	Job Completion Time at Workstation (hours)					
Job	**1**	**2**	**3**	**4**	**5**	**6**
A	0.2	0.6	0	0	1.1	0.7
B	0.3	0.6	0	0.6	0.8	1.4
C	0.1	0.4	0.7	0.8	0.5	0
D	0.6	0	0.8	0.3	0.9	0.1
E	0	0.5	0.7	0.9	0	0.2
F	0.1	0	0.6	1.5	2.7	2.3

d. We can cover every zero with just five lines. Subtract the smallest number not covered by lines (0.1) from itself and every other uncovered number, and add it to the number at each intersection of lines. Repeat part (*c*).

	Job Completion Time at Workstation (hours)					
Job	**1**	**2**	**3**	**4**	**5**	**6**
A	0.2	0.7	0.1	0	1.1	0.8
B	0.2	0.6	0	0.5	0.7	1.4
C	0	0.4	0.7	0.7	0.4	0
D	0.5	0	0.8	0.2	0.8	0.1
E	0	0.6	0.8	0.9	0	0.3
F	0	0	0.6	1.4	2.6	2.3

e. It now takes six lines to cover all zeroes. Make job assignments at zero entries, starting with those jobs that have just one zero entry. Then, move to jobs that have more than one zero entry, but only one zero remaining that has not been assigned to another job yet, and so on. The job assignments and times are as follows:

Job	Machine	Time
A	4	3.0
B	3	2.3
D	2	2.1
F	1	1.5
C	6	3.6
E	5	6.0
	Total:	18.5

LO 22–4 SOLVED PROBLEM 4

Albert's Downtown Café is a very popular restaurant in Indianapolis that serves breakfast, lunch, and dinner six days a week. The restaurant needs its wait staff in varying numbers throughout the day to serve customers. Analysis of past data indicates that Albert has the following staffing needs throughout the day.

	6:00	7:00	8:00	9:00	10:00	11:00	Noon	1:00	2:00	3:00	4:00	5:00	6:00	7:00	8:00	9:00
Servers needed	3	6	5	3	2	4	7	5	3	3	4	6	7	7	4	2

Currently, servers work 8-hour shifts. They eat when they can so there are no scheduled lunch hours.

a. Use the *first-hour principle* to develop a schedule showing how many workers start a shift in each hour, how many servers are on duty each hour, and how many excess servers are on duty each hour. Comment on your results.

b. Albert has noticed that during slow periods he often has far too many servers on duty. Also, the wait staff has been complaining about the long hours in the current policy. Therefore, Albert is considering shortening the shifts to either 6 hours or 4 hours. The current wait staff would prefer 6-hour shifts. Using the *first-hour principle,* develop schedules based on both 6-hour and 4-hour shifts. Comment on each.

c. Assume that servers at Albert's are paid $7.50 per hour. Cost out each of the schedules you have developed and compare the costs.

Solution

a.

	6:00	7:00	8:00	9:00	10:00	11:00	Noon	1:00	2:00	3:00	4:00	5:00	6:00	7:00	8:00	9:00
Servers needed	3	6	5	3	2	4	7	5	3	3	4	6	7	7	4	2
Start shift	3	3	0	0	0	0	1	0	0	2	1	2	1	0	0	0
Off shift	0	0	0	0	0	0	0	0	3	3	0	0	0	0	1	0
On duty	3	6	6	6	6	6	7	7	4	3	4	6	7	7	6	6
Excess staff	0	0	1	3	4	2	0	2	1	0	0	0	0	0	2	4

There is an excess of staff during the morning lull and at the end of the workday. Due to the 8-hour shifts, the early morning staff end their shifts during the afternoon lull, so that the slow period is fairly well staffed. You should also note that the workers who start at 3:00 P.M. and later will not be able to finish their 8-hour shift by the 10:00 P.M. closing time. Obviously, using only 8-hour shifts is not practical for the evenings.

b.

6-Hour Shifts

	6:00	7:00	8:00	9:00	10:00	11:00	Noon	1:00	2:00	3:00	4:00	5:00	6:00	7:00	8:00	9:00
Servers needed	3	6	5	3	2	4	7	5	3	3	4	6	7	7	4	2
Start shift	3	3	0	0	0	0	4	1	0	0	0	1	5	1	0	0
Off shift	0	0	0	0	0	0	3	3	0	0	0	0	4	1	0	0
On duty	3	6	6	6	6	6	7	5	5	5	5	6	7	7	7	7
Excess staff	0	0	1	3	4	2	0	0	2	2	1	0	0	0	3	5

Again we're bringing on people at the end of the day that will not be able to finish out their full shift. We haven't seemed to improve on the excess staff much, if at all, here either.

4-Hour Shifts

	6:00	7:00	8:00	9:00	10:00	11:00	Noon	1:00	2:00	3:00	4:00	5:00	6:00	7:00	8:00	9:00
Servers needed	3	6	5	3	2	4	7	5	3	3	4	6	7	7	4	2
Start shift	3	3	0	0	0	4	3	0	0	0	4	2	1	0	1	0
Off shift	0	0	0	0	3	3	0	0	0	4	3	0	0	0	4	2
On duty	3	6	6	6	3	4	7	7	7	3	4	6	7	7	4	2
Excess staff	0	0	1	3	1	0	0	2	4	0	0	0	0	0	0	0

This schedule seems to do a much better job matching staff to needs, and we only start one employee too late to finish the 4-hour shift.

c. In costing out the schedules, simply sum the numbers on duty each hour throughout the day and multiply by $7.50.

Schedule	Worker-Hours	Cost
8-hour	90	$675.00
6-hour	94	705.00
4-hour	82	615.00

Because the 4-hour shift policy better matches servers to demand, it has the lower daily labor cost. This policy will require us to have the largest number of employees, though, so Albert will have to do some hiring. He should also consider the impact on morale of current employees if he cuts their hours in half. They would like a 6-hour shift policy, but given the restaurant's demand patterns, and using the first-hour scheduling principle, that would result in the least efficient schedule.

Clearly, scheduling workers in a service business is not a simple task! There are costs as well as human issues to consider. For Albert, the best solution will likely contain a mix of different length shifts—ideally, he'll be able to match employees with shifts they will be happy with.

DISCUSSION QUESTIONS

LO22-1 1. What are the objectives of workcenter scheduling?
2. Distinguish between a workcenter, a GT cell, and an assembly line.

LO22-2 3. What practical considerations are deterrents to using the SOT rule?
4. What priority rule do you use in scheduling your study time for midterm examinations?
5. If you have five exams to study for, how many alternative schedules exist?
6. The SOT rule provides an optimal solution in a number of evaluation criteria. Should the manager of a bank use the SOT rule as a priority rule? Why?
7. Why does batching cause so much trouble in workcenters?
8. What job characteristics would lead you to schedule jobs according to "longest processing time first"?
9. Why is managing bottlenecks so important in workcenter scheduling?
10. Under what conditions is the assignment method appropriate?

LO22-3 11. The chapter discusses the use of Gantt charts in shop floor control. You were introduced to Gantt charts in Chapter 4, "Project Management." Projects and workcenter processes are rather different in nature. Why is it that the same tool can be used in both projects and workcenters?
12. Why is it desired to have smooth, continuous flow on the shop floor?

13. Data integrity is a big deal in industry. Why?
14. Explain why scheduling personnel in a service operation can be challenging. **LO22-4**
15. How might planning for a special customer affect the personnel schedule in a service?

OBJECTIVE QUESTIONS

1. What is the term used for an information system that links, schedules, dispatches, tracks, monitors, and controls customer encounters with a service organization? **LO22-1**
2. What do we generally call an area in a business where productive resources are organized and work is completed?
3. What type of inventory are we trying to minimize as the result of workcenter scheduling?
4. A key part of workcenter scheduling is job sequencing—deciding in what order jobs are scheduled to start/complete. What is the term for the simple rules used to aid this process using a single piece of data about the jobs?
5. The following table gives the operation times and due dates for five jobs that are to be processed on a machine. Assign the jobs according to the shortest operation time and calculate the mean flow time. (Answer in Appendix D) **LO22-2**

Job	Processing Time	Due Date (Days Hence)
101	6 days	5
102	7 days	3
103	4 days	4
104	9 days	7
105	5 days	2

6. The MediQuick lab has three lab technicians available to process blood samples and three jobs that need to be assigned. Each technician can do only one job. The following table represents the lab's estimate (in dollars) of what it will cost for each job to be completed. Assign the technicians to the jobs to minimize costs.

Job	Tech A	Tech B	Tech C
J-432	11	14	6
J-487	8	10	11
J-492	9	12	7

7. Christine has three cars that must be overhauled by her ace mechanic, Megan. Given the following data about the cars, use the least slack per remaining operation to determine Megan's scheduling priority for each car. (Answer in Appendix D)

Car	Customer Pick-Up Time (hours hence)	Remaining Overhaul Time (hours)	Remaining Operation
A	10	4	Painting
B	17	5	Wheel alignment, painting
C	15	1	Chrome plating, painting, seat repair

8. The following list of jobs in a critical department includes estimates of their required times.

Job	Required T (days)	Days to Delivery Promise	Slack
A	8	12	4
B	3	9	6
C	7	8	1
D	1	11	10
E	10	−10 (late)	−20
F	6	10	4
G	5	−8 (late)	−13
H	4	6	2

a. Use the shortest operation time rule to schedule these jobs.
What is the schedule?
What is the mean flow time?

b. The boss does not like the schedule in part (*a*). Jobs E and G must be done first, for obvious reasons. (They are already late.) Reschedule and do the best you can while scheduling Jobs E and G first and second, respectively.
What is the new schedule?
What is the new mean flow time?

9. A manufacturing facility has five jobs to be scheduled into production. The following table gives the processing times plus the necessary wait times and other necessary delays for each of the jobs. Assume that today is April 3, that the facility will work every day between now and the due dates, and the jobs are due on the dates shown:

Job	Days of Actual Processing Time Required	Days of Necessary Delay Time	Total Time Required	Date Job Due
1	2	12	14	April 30
2	5	8	13	April 21
3	9	15	24	April 28
4	7	9	16	April 29
5	4	22	26	April 27

Determine *two* schedules, stating the order in which the jobs are to be done. Use the critical ratio priority rule for one. You may use any other rule for the second schedule as long as you state what it is. (Answer in Appendix D)

10. The following table contains information regarding jobs that are to be scheduled through one machine.

Job	Processing Time	Due Date
A	4	20
B	12	30
C	2	15
D	11	16
E	10	18
F	3	5
G	6	9

a. What is the first-come, first-served (FCFS) schedule?
b. What is the shortest operating time (SOT) schedule?
c. What is the slack time remaining (STR) schedule?
d. What is the earliest due date (EDD) schedule?
e. What are the mean flow times for each of the schedules above?

11. Bill Edstrom, managing partner at a biomedical consulting firm, has requested your expert advice in devising the best schedule for the following consulting projects, starting on February 2.

	Description of Consultation		Call Received		Due Date
Task	Length	Company	Date	Time	(close of business)
I	3 days	Novartis Corp.	February 1	9 A.M.	February 5
II	1 day	Reardon Biotech Corp.	February 1	10 A.M.	February 6
III	2 days	Vertex Pharmaceuticals	February 1	11 A.M.	February 8
IV	2 days	OSI Pharmaceuticals	February 1	1 P.M.	February 7

The consulting firm charges a flat rate of $4,000 per day. All four firms impose fines for lateness. Reardon Biotech charges a $500-per-day fine for each day that the completion of the consulting work is past the due date; Vertex Pharmaceuticals, Novartis, and OSI Pharmaceuticals all charge a fine of $1,500 per day for each day late.

Prepare alternative schedules based on the following priority rules: SOT, FCFS, EDD, STR, and another rule—longest processing time (LPT), which orders jobs according to longest assigned first, second-longest assigned second, and so on. For the sake of simplicity, assume that consulting work is performed seven days a week. Which rule provides Bill with the best schedule? Why?

12. Seven jobs must be processed in two operations: A and B. All seven jobs must go through A and B in that sequence—A first, then B. Determine the optimal order (shortest flow time to complete all the jobs) in which the jobs should be sequenced through the process using these times:

Job	Process A Time	Process B Time
1	9	6
2	8	5
3	7	7
4	6	3
5	1	2
6	2	6
7	4	7

13. Jobs A, B, C, D, and E must go through Processes I and II in that sequence (Process I first, then Process II). Use Johnson's rule to determine the optimal sequence in which to schedule the jobs to minimize the total required time.

Job	Required Processing Time on I	Required Processing Time on II
A	4	5
B	16	14
C	8	7
D	12	11
E	3	9

14. Joe is the production scheduler in a brand-new custom refinishing auto service shop located near the border. This system is capable of handling 10 cars per day. The sequence is customizing first, followed by repainting.

Car	Customizing Time (hours)	Painting (hours)	Car	Customizing Time (hours)	Painting (hours)
1	3.0	1.2	6	2.1	0.8
2	2.0	0.9	7	3.2	1.4
3	2.5	1.3	8	0.6	1.8
4	0.7	0.5	9	1.1	1.5
5	1.6	1.7	10	1.8	0.7

In what sequence should Joe schedule the cars to minimize the time needed to complete all the cars?

15. Schedule the following six jobs through two machines in sequence to minimize the flow time using Johnson's rule.

	Operations Time	
Job	Machine 1	Machine 2
A	5	2
B	16	15
C	1	9
D	13	11
E	17	3
F	18	7

16. The following matrix shows the costs in thousands of dollars for assigning Individuals A, B, C, and D to Jobs 1, 2, 3, and 4. Solve the problem showing your final assignments in order to minimize cost. Assume that each job will be assigned to one individual.

	Jobs			
Individuals	1	2	3	4
A	7	9	3	5
B	3	11	7	6
C	4	5	6	2
D	5	9	10	12

17. In a workcenter, six machinists were uniquely qualified to operate any one of the five machines in the shop. The workcenter had considerable backlog, and all five machines were kept busy at all times. The one machinist not operating a machine was usually occupied doing clerical or routine maintenance work. Given the following value schedule for each machinist on each of the five machines, develop the optimal assignments. Assume only one machinist will be assigned to each machine. (*Hint:* Add a dummy column with zero cost values, and solve using the assignment method.)

	Machine				
Machinist	1	2	3	4	5
A	65	50	60	55	80
B	30	75	125	50	40
C	75	35	85	95	45
D	60	40	115	130	110
E	90	85	40	80	95
F	145	60	55	45	85

18. Joe has achieved a position of some power in the institution in which he currently resides and works. In fact, things have gone so well that he has decided to divide the day-to-day operations of his business activities among four trusted subordinates: Big Bob, Dirty Dave, Baby Face Nick,

and Tricky Dick. The question is how he should do this in order to take advantage of his associates' unique skills and to minimize the costs from running all areas for the next year. The following matrix summarizes the costs that arise under each possible combination of men and areas.

	Area			
Associate	**1**	**2**	**3**	**4**
Big Bob	$1,400	$1,800	$ 700	$1,000
Dirty Dave	600	2,200	1,500	1,300
Baby Face Nick	800	1,100	1,200	500
Tricky Dick	1,000	1,800	2,100	1,500

19. The following matrix contains the costs (in dollars) associated with assigning Jobs A, B, C, D, and E to Machines 1, 2, 3, 4, and 5. Assign jobs to machines to minimize costs.

	Machines				
Jobs	**1**	**2**	**3**	**4**	**5**
A	6	11	12	3	10
B	5	12	10	7	9
C	7	14	13	8	12
D	4	15	16	7	9
E		13	17	11	12

20. What is another common term for shop-floor control? **LO 22–3**
21. Which graphical tool commonly used in project management is also very useful in shop-floor control?
22. What shop-floor control document tells the supervisor which jobs are to be run, in what order, and how long each will take?
23. What feature of manufacturing planning and control systems operates under the premise that the planned work input to a workcenter should never exceed the planned work output?
24. A hotel has to schedule its receptionists according to hourly loads. Management has identified the number of receptionists needed to meet the hourly requirement, which changes from day to day. Assume each receptionist works a four-hour shift. Given the following staffing requirement in a certain day, use the first-hour principle to find the personnel schedule: **LO 22–4**

	Period											
	8 A.M.	**9 A.M.**	**10 A.M.**	**11 A.M.**	**Noon**	**1 P.M.**	**2 P.M.**	**3 P.M.**	**4 P.M.**	**5 P.M.**	**6 P.M.**	**7 P.M.**
Requirement	2	3	5	8	8	6	5	8	8	6	4	3
Assigned												
On duty												

25. The following wait staff members are needed at a restaurant. Use the first-hour principle to generate a personnel schedule. Assume a four-hour shift.

	Period										
	11 A.M.	**Noon**	**1 P.M.**	**2 P.M.**	**3 P.M.**	**4 P.M.**	**5 P.M.**	**6 P.M.**	**7 P.M.**	**8 P.M.**	**9 P.M.**
Requirements	4	8	5	3	2	3	5	7	5	4	2
Assigned											
On duty											

26. Which simple scheduling concept can be applied to help schedule workers for a service operation with changing staffing requirements throughout the day?

CASE: Keep Patients Waiting? Not in My Office

Good doctor–patient relations begin with both parties being punctual for appointments. I am Dr. Schafer, and being punctual is particularly important in my specialty: pediatrics. Mothers whose children have only minor problems don't like them to sit in the waiting room with really sick ones, and the sick kids become fussy if they have to wait long.

But lateness—no matter who's responsible for it—can cause problems in any practice. Once you've fallen more than slightly behind, it may be impossible to catch up that day. And although it's unfair to keep someone waiting who may have other appointments, the average office patient cools his heels for almost 20 minutes, according to one recent survey. Patients may tolerate this, but they don't like it.

I don't tolerate that in my office, and I don't believe you have to in yours. I see patients *exactly* at the appointed hour more than 99 times out of 100. So there are many GPs (grateful patients) in my busy solo practice. Parents often remark to me, "We really appreciate your being on time. Why can't other doctors do that, too?" My answer is "I don't know, but I'm willing to tell them how I do it."

Booking Appointments Realistically

The key to successful scheduling is to allot the proper amount of time for each visit, depending on the services required, and then stick to it. This means that the physician must pace her- or himself carefully, receptionists must be corrected if they stray from the plan, and patients must be taught to respect their appointment times.

By actually timing a number of patient visits, I found that they break down into several categories. We allow half an hour for any new patient, 15 minutes for a well-baby checkup or an important illness, and either 5 or 10 minutes for a recheck on an illness or injury, an immunization, or a minor problem like warts. You can, of course, work out your own time allocations, geared to the way you practice.

When appointments are made, every patient is given a specific time, such as 10:30 or 2:40. It's an absolute no-no for anyone in my office to say to a patient, "Come in 10 minutes" or "Come in a half-hour." People often interpret such instructions differently, and nobody knows just when they'll arrive.

There are three examining rooms that I use routinely, a fourth that I reserve for teenagers, and a fifth for emergencies. With that many rooms, I don't waste time waiting for patients, and they rarely have to sit in the reception area. In fact, some of the younger children complain that they don't get time to play with the toys and puzzles in the waiting room before being examined, and their mothers have to let them play awhile on the way out.

On a light day, I see 20 to 30 patients between 9 A.M. and 5 P.M. But our appointment system is flexible enough to let me see 40 to 50 patients in the same number of hours if I have to. Here's how we tighten the schedule:

My two assistants (three on the busiest days) have standing orders to keep a number of slots open throughout each day for patients with acute illnesses. We try to reserve more such openings in the winter months and on the days following weekends and holidays, when we're busier than usual.

Initial visits, for which we allow 30 minutes, are always scheduled on the hour or the half-hour. If I finish such a visit sooner than planned, we may be able to squeeze in a patient who needs to be seen immediately. And, if necessary, we can book two or three visits in 15 minutes between well-checks. With these cushions to fall back on, I'm free to spend an extra 10 minutes or so on a serious case, knowing that the lost time can be made up quickly.

Parents of new patients are asked to arrive in the office a few minutes before they're scheduled in order to get the preliminary paperwork done. At that time, the receptionist informs them, "The doctor always keeps an accurate appointment schedule." Some already know this and have chosen me for that very reason. Others, however, don't even know that there *are* doctors who honor appointment times, so we feel it's best to warn them on the first visit.

Fitting in Emergencies

Emergencies are the excuse doctors most often give for failing to stick to their appointment schedules. Well, when a child comes in with a broken arm or the hospital calls with an emergency Caesarean section, naturally I drop everything else. If the interruption is brief, I may just scramble to catch up. If it's likely to be longer, the next few patients are given the choice of waiting or making new appointments. Occasionally, my assistants have to reschedule all appointments for the next hour or two. Most such interruptions, though, take no more than 10 to 20 minutes, and the patients usually choose to wait. I then try to fit them into the spaces we've reserved for acute cases that require last-minute appointments.

Source: W. B. Schafer, "Keep Patients Waiting? Not in My Office," *Medical Economics,* May 12, 1986, pp. 137–41. Copyright © by Medical Economics. Reprinted by permission. Medical Economics is a copyrighted publication of Advanstar Communications, Inc. All rights reserved.

The important thing is that emergencies are never allowed to spoil my schedule for the whole day. Once a delay has been adjusted for, I'm on time for all later appointments. The only situation I can imagine that would really wreck my schedule is simultaneous emergencies in the office and at the hospital—but that has never occurred.

When I return to the patient I've left, I say, "Sorry to have kept you waiting, I had an emergency—a bad cut" (or whatever). A typical reply from the parent: "No problem, Doctor. In all the years I've been coming here, you've never made me wait before. And I'd surely want you to leave the room if *my* kid were hurt."

Emergencies aside, I get few walk-ins, because it's generally known in the community that I see patients only by appointment except in urgent circumstances. A nonemergency walk-in is handled as a phone call would be. The receptionist asks whether the visitor wants advice or an appointment. If the latter, he or she is offered the earliest time available for nonacute cases.

Taming the Telephone

Phone calls from patients can sabotage an appointment schedule if you let them. I don't. Unlike some pediatricians, I don't have a regular telephone hour, but my assistants will handle calls from parents at any time during office hours. If the question is a simple one, such as "How much aspirin do you give a one-year-old?" the assistant will answer it. If the question requires an answer from me, the assistant writes it in the patient's chart and brings it to me while I'm seeing another child. I write the answer in—or she enters it in the chart. Then, she relays it to the caller.

What if the caller insists on talking with me directly? The standard reply is "The doctor will talk with you personally if it won't take more than one minute. Otherwise, you'll have to make an appointment and come in." I'm rarely called to the phone in such cases, but if the mother is very upset, I prefer to talk with her. I don't always limit her to one minute; I may let the conversation run two or three. But the caller knows I've left a patient to talk with her, so she tends to keep it brief.

Dealing with Latecomers

Some people are habitually late; others have legitimate reasons for occasional tardiness, such as a flat tire or "He threw up on me." Either way, I'm hard-nosed enough not to see them immediately if they arrive at my office more than 10 minutes behind schedule, because to do so would delay patients who arrived on time. Anyone who is less than 10 minutes late is seen right away, but is reminded of what the appointment time was.

When it's exactly 10 minutes past the time reserved for a patient and he hasn't appeared at the office, a receptionist phones his home to arrange a later appointment. If there's no answer and the patient arrives at the office a few minutes later, the receptionist says pleasantly, "Hey, we were looking for you. The doctor's had to go ahead with his other appointments, but we'll squeeze you in as soon as we can." A note is then made in the patient's chart showing the date, how late he was, and whether he was seen that day or given another appointment. This helps us identify the rare chronic offender and take stronger measures if necessary.

Most people appear not to mind waiting if they know they themselves have caused the delay. And I'd rather incur the anger of the rare person who *does* mind than risk the ill will of the many patients who would otherwise have to wait after coming in on schedule. Although I'm prepared to be firm with parents, this is rarely necessary. My office in no way resembles an army camp. On the contrary, most people are happy with the way we run it, and tell us so frequently.

Coping with No-Shows

What about the patient who has an appointment, doesn't turn up at all, and can't be reached by telephone? Those facts, too, are noted in the chart. Usually there's a simple explanation, such as being out of town and forgetting about the appointment. If it happens a second time, we follow the same procedure. A third-time offender, though, receives a letter reminding him that time was set aside for him and he failed to keep three appointments. In the future, he's told, he'll be billed for such wasted time.

That's about as tough as we ever get with the few people who foul up our scheduling. I've never dropped a patient for doing so. In fact, I can't recall actually billing a no-show; the letter threatening to do so seems to cure them. And when they come back—as nearly all of them do—they enjoy the same respect and convenience as my other patients.

Questions

1. What features of the appointment scheduling system were crucial in capturing "many grateful patients"?
2. What procedures were followed to keep the appointment system flexible enough to accommodate the emergency cases, and yet be able to keep up with the other patients' appointments?
3. How were the special cases such as latecomers and no-shows handled?

4. Prepare a schedule starting at 9 A.M. for the following patients of Dr. Schafer:

   Johnny Appleseed, a splinter on his left thumb.
   Mark Borino, a new patient.
   Joyce Chang, a new patient.
   Amar Gavhane, 102.5 degree (Fahrenheit) fever.
   Sarah Goodsmith, an immunization.
   Tonya Johnston, well-baby checkup.
   JJ Lopez, a new patient.
   Angel Ramirez, well-baby checkup.
   Bobby Toolright, recheck on a sprained ankle.
   Rebecca White, a new patient.

   Dr. Schafer starts work promptly at 9 A.M. and enjoys taking a 15-minute coffee break around 10:15 or 10:30 A.M.

   Apply the priority rule that maximizes scheduling efficiency. Indicate whether or not you see an exception to this priority rule that might arise. Round up any times listed in the case study (e.g., if the case study stipulates 5 or 10 minutes, then assume 10 minutes for the sake of this problem).

PRACTICE EXAM

In each of the following, name the term defined or answer the question. Answers are listed at the bottom.

1. This is the currently used term for a system that schedules, dispatches, tracks, monitors, and controls production.
2. This is when work is assigned to workcenters based simply on when it is needed. Resources required to complete the work are not considered.
3. This is when detailed schedules are constructed that consider the setup and run times required for each order.
4. This is when work is scheduled from a point in time and out into the future, in essence telling the earliest the work can be completed.
5. This is when work is scheduled in reverse from a future due date, to tell the time original work must be started.
6. If we were to coin the phrase "dual constrained" relative to the resources being scheduled, we would probably be referring to what two resources?
7. For a single machine scheduling problem, what priority rule guarantees that the average flow time is minimized?
8. Consider the following three jobs that need to be run on two machines in sequence: A(3 1), B(2 2), and C(1 3), where the run times on the first and second machine are given in parenthesis. In what order should the jobs be run to minimize the total time to complete all three jobs?
9. According to APICS, this is a system for utilizing data from the shop as well as data processing files to maintain and communicate status information on shop orders and workcenters.
10. A resource that limits the output of a process by limiting capacity is called this.

Answers to Practice Exam 1. Manufacturing Execution System 2. Infinite scheduling 3. Finite scheduling 4. Forward scheduling 5. Backward scheduling 6. Labor and equipment (machines) 7. Shortest operating time 8. C B A 9. Shop-floor (or production activity) control 10. Bottleneck

For PowerPoint lecture slides, Solutions Manual, Test Bank, Data files for solved examples, Excel Templates, Step-by-Step Solved Examples in video format, Tutorial Videos and many more, scan the adjacent **QR code**, or **visit http://www.mhhe.com/sie-chase15e**

Chapter 23

Theory of Constraints

LEARNING OBJECTIVES

LO 23-1 Explain the Theory of Constraints (TOC)

LO 23-2 Analyze bottleneck resources and apply TOC principles to controlling a process

LO 23-3 Compare TOC to conventional approaches

LO 23-4 Evaluate bottleneck scheduling problems by applying TOC principles

This chapter is about the ideas of management guru Eli Goldratt. He proposed the idea that managing "constraints" is the key to maximizing the throughput and efficiency of business processes. He argued that a manager should focus on managing the resource that most limits the process from achieving its goal. This resource is called the "bottleneck" and nothing can be achieved beyond the capability of the bottleneck. He suggests a simple repetitive cycle for improving a process. Step 1: Find the weakest step in the process, the step that is limiting performance the most. Step 2: Improve that weakest step so that it is no longer limiting performance. Step 3: Repeat steps 1 and 2 over and over again making the process better with each cycle.

To explain his ideas in an easy to understand way, Goldratt wrote a book titled *The Goal*. The book tracks the life of Alex Rogo, a plant manager struggling with keeping his plant on schedule, reducing inventory, meeting quality goals, and cutting costs. Alex's job is on the line and his boss has given him three months to make the plant productive, otherwise it will be closed.

The most insightful analogy in the book is the description of a 20-mile overnight hike that Alex takes with his son. Alex is leading his son's Boy Scout troop on a hike that will take them to a site 10 miles away where they will spend the night. The troop will then return the following morning after breakfast.

© dolgachov/123RF

The analogy starts by describing the hike out to the campsite. They are way behind schedule and the line of scouts is spread out over a long distance. The fastest kids are up front, and poor Herbie, the slowest kid, lags way behind at the end of the line. The goal is to get all the kids to the campsite as quickly as possible so they can get the tents setup, have dinner, and enjoy some camp fire fun. Nothing can happen until all the kids make it to the campsite.

Alex analyzes the situation and can see that Andy, the first kid in line is trying to set a speed record. Herbie, who is way in the back, is the bottleneck. Herbie just cannot move fast enough to keep up with Andy. Alex checks the speed of Andy and finds his pace is three miles per hour and that compared to the speed of Herbie he will be two miles ahead in less than an hour. In two hours, the stragglers will be four miles behind! The plan had been to cover the 10 miles in five hours. Something needed to be done, and quickly.

Alex stops the leaders and tells everyone in the troop to hold hands with the person before and after him, and to not let go. He then takes Herbie, who is in the back, and leads him to the front of the line. He keeps walking with Herbie turning the troop around so that Herbie, the slowest, is now leading and Andy, the fastest, is now at the end. Alex tells the troop that the goal of the hike is not to get there the fastest, but to get there together. The troop is a team—not a bunch of individuals.

And so the troop moves on with Herbie in the lead. The line is now tight with no gaps between the scouts. The scouts in the back of the line begin complaining that they want to go faster. Alex tells the troop they if they want to go faster, they need to figure out a way Herbie can go faster.

When the scouts check out Herbie they find that he is carrying a backpack much heavier than the others. He has soda, cans of spaghetti, candy bars, and all kinds of other stuff that the others are not carrying. No wonder he is so much slower. So the others decide to take some of the load off Herbie by carrying some of his stuff. Now Herbie can really move, since most of the weight in his pack is removed. The troop is now moving at twice the speed it was before and they are still staying together.

That night Alex thought about the analogy between the troop hike and his plant. Most of his machines were fast, but the slowest one always kept the jobs from getting done. This causes inventory in the plant to keep increasing, and lead-time to increase as well. He needed to tie all the processes in his plant together; there is no reason for any of them to process any faster than that slow bottleneck process. Then he needed to figure out how he could get more output from that bottleneck. Possibly, he could buy another machine, or run some overtime on that machine. Only in this way could he decrease his inventory, and increase throughput. Alex had learned a lot on his son's camping trip.

LO 23-1

Explain the Theory of Constraints (TOC)

ELI GOLDRATT'S THEORY OF CONSTRAINTS

The story of Herbie is an analogy to the problems facing plant manager Alex Rogo and comes from a best-selling novel, *The Goal,* by Dr. Eli Goldratt. Around 1980, Goldratt contended that manufacturers were not doing a good job in scheduling and controlling their resources and inventories. To solve this problem, Goldratt and his associates, at a company named Creative Output, developed software that scheduled jobs through manufacturing processes, taking into account limited facilities, machines, personnel, tools, materials, and any other constraints that would affect a firm's ability to adhere to a schedule.

EXHIBIT 23.1

Goldratt's Rules of Production Scheduling

1. Do not balance capacity—balance the flow.
2. The level of utilization of a nonbottleneck resource is determined not by its own potential but by some other constraint in the system.
3. Utilization and activation of a resource are not the same.
4. An hour lost at a bottleneck is an hour lost for the entire system.
5. An hour saved at a nonbottleneck is a mirage.
6. Bottlenecks govern both throughput and inventory in the system.
7. The transfer batch may not, and many times should not, be equal to the process batch.
8. A process batch should be variable both along its route and in time.
9. Priorities can be set only by examining the system's constraints. Lead time is a derivative of the schedule.

This was called *optimized production technology (OPT)*. The schedules were feasible and accurate and could be run on a computer in a fraction of the time needed by an MRP system. This was because the scheduling logic was based on the separation of bottleneck and nonbottleneck operations. To explain the principles behind the OPT scheduling logic, Goldratt described nine production scheduling rules (see Exhibit 23.1). After approximately 100 large firms had installed this software, Goldratt went on to promote the logic of the approach rather than the software.

In broadening his scope, Goldratt developed his "Theory of Constraints" (TOC), which has become popular as a problem-solving approach that can be applied to many business areas. Exhibit 23.2 lists the "Five Focusing Steps of TOC." His Goldratt Institute (www.goldratt.com) teaches courses in improving production, distribution, and project management. The common thread through all of these courses is Goldratt's TOC concepts.

EXHIBIT 23.2

Goldratt's Theory of Constraints (TOC)

1. Identify the system constraints. (No improvement is possible unless the constraint or weakest link is found.)
2. Decide how to exploit the system constraints. (Make the constraints as effective as possible.)
3. Subordinate everything else to that decision. (Align every other part of the system to support the constraints even if this reduces the efficiency of nonconstraint resources.)
4. Elevate the system constraints. (If output is still inadequate, acquire more of this resource so it no longer is a constraint.)
5. If, in the previous steps, the constraints have been broken, go back to Step 1, but do not let inertia become the system constraint. (After this constraint problem is solved, go back to the beginning and start over. This is a continuous process of improvement: identifying constraints, breaking them, and then identifying the new ones that result.)

Before we go into detail on the theory of constraints, it is useful to compare it with two other popular approaches to continuous improvement: Six Sigma and lean manufacturing. Both Six Sigma and lean approaches focus on cost reduction through the elimination of waste and the reduction of variability at every step in a process or in view of every component of a system. In contrast, the TOC five-step approach is more focused in its application. It concentrates its improvement efforts only on the operation that is constraining a critical process or on the weakest component that is limiting the performance of the system as a whole. If these elements are effectively managed, then it follows that better overall performance of the system relative to its goal is more likely to be achieved.

In this chapter, we focus on Goldratt's approach to manufacturing. To correctly treat the topic, we decided to approach it in the same way that Goldratt did: that is, by first defining some basic issues about firms—purposes, goals, and performance measures—and then dealing with scheduling, providing buffer inventories, focusing on the influences of quality, and looking at interactions with marketing and accounting.

Synchronous manufacturing
A production process coordinated to work in harmony to achieve the goals of the firm.

Underlying Goldratt's work is the notion of **synchronous manufacturing**, which refers to the entire production process working in harmony to achieve the profit goal of the firm. When manufacturing is truly synchronized, its emphasis is on total system performance, not on localized measures such as labor or machine utilization.

The Goal of the Firm

Goldratt has a very straightforward idea about the goal of any firm:

THE GOAL OF A FIRM IS TO MAKE MONEY.

Goldratt argues that although an organization may have many purposes—providing jobs, consuming raw materials, increasing sales, increasing share of the market, developing technology, or producing high-quality products—these do not guarantee long-term survival of the firm. They are means to achieve the goal, not the goal itself. If the firm makes money—and only then—it will prosper. When a firm has money, it can place more emphasis on other objectives.

Performance Measurements

To adequately measure a firm's performance, two sets of measurements must be used: one from the financial point of view and the other from the operations point of view.

Financial Measurements We have three measures of the firm's ability to make money:

1. *Net profit*—an absolute measurement in dollars.
2. *Return on investment*—a relative measure based on investment.
3. *Cash flow*—a survival measurement.

All three measurements must be used together. For example, a *net profit* of $10 million is important as one measurement, but it has no real meaning until we know how much investment was needed to generate that $10 million. If the investment was $100 million, this is a 10 percent *return on investment. Cash flow* is important because cash is necessary to pay bills for day-to-day operations; without cash, a firm can go bankrupt even though it is very sound in normal accounting terms. A firm can have a high profit and a high return on investment but still be short on cash if, for example, profit is invested in new equipment or tied up in inventory.

Throughput
The rate at which money is generated by the system through sales (Goldratt's definition).

Operational Measurements Financial measurements work well at the higher level, but they cannot be used at the operational level. We need another set of measurements that will give us guidance:

1. **Throughput**—the rate at which money is generated by the system through sales.
2. **Inventory**—all the money that the system has invested in purchasing things it intends to sell.
3. **Operating expenses**—all the money that the system spends to turn inventory into throughput.

Inventory (Goldratt's definition)
All the money that the system has invested in purchasing things it intends to sell.

Operating expenses
All the money that the system spends to turn inventory into throughput (Goldratt's definition).

Throughput is specifically defined as goods *sold.* An inventory of finished goods is not throughput, but inventory. Actual sales must occur. It is specifically defined this way to prevent the system from continuing to produce under the illusion that the goods *might* be sold. Such action simply increases costs, builds inventory, and consumes cash. Inventory that is carried (whether work-in-process or finished goods) is valued only at the cost of the materials it contains. Labor cost and machine hours are ignored. (In traditional accounting terms, money spent is called *value added.*)

Although this is often an arguable point, using only the raw material cost is a conservative view. When the value-added method (which includes all costs of production) is used, inventory is inflated and presents some serious income and balance sheet problems. Consider, for example, work-in-process or finished-goods inventory that has become obsolete, or for which a contract was canceled. A management decision to declare large amounts of inventory as scrap is difficult because it is often carried on the books as an asset even though it may really have no value. Using just raw materials cost also avoids the problem of determining which costs are direct and which are indirect.

Operating expenses include production costs (such as direct labor, indirect labor, inventory carrying costs, equipment depreciation, and materials and supplies used in production) and administrative costs. The key difference here is that there is no need to separate direct and indirect labor.

As shown in Exhibit 23.3, the objective of a firm is to treat all three measurements simultaneously and continually; this achieves the goal of making money.

From an operations standpoint, the goal of the firm is to

> INCREASE THROUGHPUT WHILE SIMULTANEOUSLY REDUCING INVENTORY AND REDUCING OPERATING EXPENSE.

Exhibit 23.3

Operational Goal

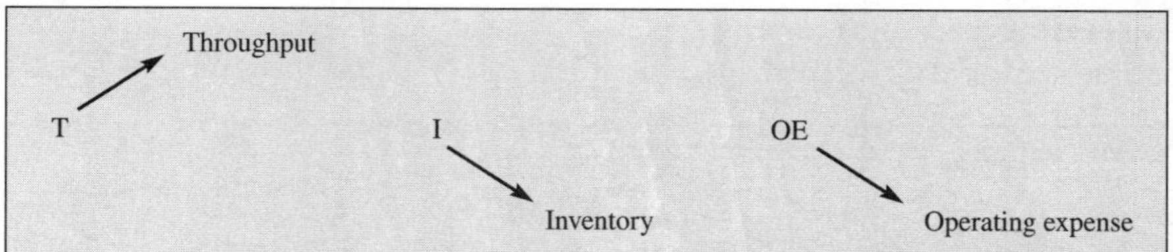

The operational goal of a firm is to increase throughput while reducing inventory and operating expense.

Productivity Typically, **productivity** is measured in terms of output per labor hour. However, this measurement does not ensure that the firm will make money (for example, when extra output is not sold but accumulates as inventory). To test whether productivity has increased, we should ask these questions: Has the action taken increased throughput? Has it decreased inventory? Has it decreased operational expense? This leads us to a new definition:

> PRODUCTIVITY IS ALL THE ACTIONS THAT BRING A COMPANY CLOSER TO ITS GOALS.

Productivity
A measure of how well resources are used. According to Goldratt's definition (see Chapter 23), all the actions that bring a company closer to its goals.

Unbalanced Capacity

Historically (and still typically in most firms), manufacturers have tried to balance capacity across a sequence of processes in an attempt to match capacity with market demand. However, this is the wrong thing to do—*unbalanced capacity* is better. The vignette at the beginning of this chapter is an example of unbalanced capacity. Some Boy Scouts were fast walkers, whereas Herbie was very slow. The challenge is to use this difference advantageously.

Consider a simple process line with several stations, for example. Once the output rate of the line has been established, production people try to make the capacities of all stations the same. This is done by adjusting machines or equipment used, workloads, skill and type of labor assigned, tools used, overtime budgeted, and so on.

In synchronous manufacturing thinking, however, making all capacities the same is viewed as a bad decision. Such a balance would be possible only if the output times of all stations were constant or had a very narrow distribution. A normal variation in output times causes downstream stations to have idle time when upstream stations take longer to process. Conversely, when upstream stations process in a shorter time, inventory builds up between the stations. The effect of the statistical variation is cumulative. The only way that this variation can be smoothed is by increasing work-in-process to absorb the variation (a bad choice because we should be trying to reduce work-in-process) or increasing capacities downstream to be able to make up for the longer upstream times. The rule here is that capacities within the process sequence should not be balanced to the same levels. Rather, attempts should be made to balance the flow of product through the system. When flow is balanced, capacities are unbalanced. This idea is further explained in the next section.

Dependent Events and Statistical Fluctuations The term *dependent events* refers to a process sequence. If a process flows from A to B to C to D, and each process must be completed before passing on to the next step, then B, C, and D are dependent events. The ability to do the next process is dependent on the preceding one.

Statistical fluctuation refers to the normal variation about a mean or average. When statistical fluctuations occur in a dependent sequence without any inventory between workstations, there is no opportunity to achieve the average output. When one process takes longer than the average, the next process cannot make up the time. We follow through an example of this to show what could happen.

Suppose we wanted to process five items that could come from the two distributions in Exhibit 23.4. The processing sequence is from A to B, with no space for inventory in between. Process A has a mean of 10 hours and a standard deviation of 2 hours. This means we would expect 95.5 percent of the processing time to be between 6 hours and 14 hours (plus or minus 2 sigma). Process B has a constant processing time of 10 hours.

Exhibit 23.4

Processing and Completion Times, Process A to Process B

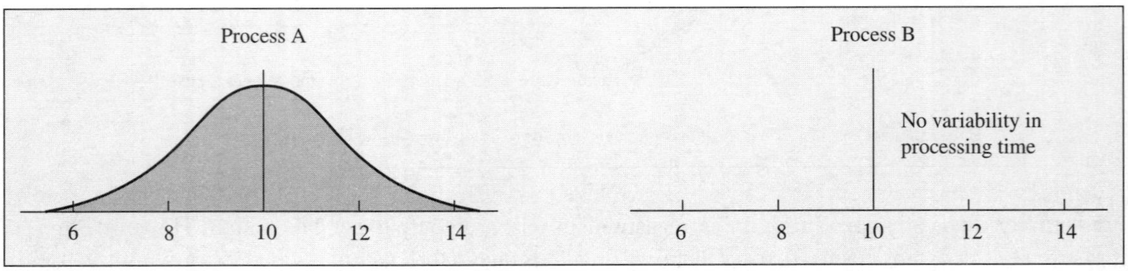

Item Number	Start Time	Processing Time	Finish Time
1	0 hrs	14 hrs	14 hrs
2	14	12	26
3	26	10	36
4	36	8	44
5	44	6	50
		Average = 10 hours	

Item Number	Start Time	Processing Time	Finish Time
1	14 hrs	10 hrs	24 hrs
2	26	10	36
3	36	10	46
4	46	10	56
5	56	10	66
		Average = 10 hours	

Here the flow is from Process A (on the left) to Process B (on the right). Process A has a mean of 10 hours and a standard deviation of 2 hours; Process B has a constant 10-hour processing time.

We see that the last item was completed in 66 hours, for an average of 13.2 hours per item, although the expected time of completion was 60, for an average of 12 hours per item (taking into account the waiting time for the first unit by Process B).

Suppose we reverse the processes—B feeds A. To illustrate the possible delays, we also reverse A's performance times. (See Exhibit 23.5.) Again, the completion time of the last item is greater than the average (13.2 hours rather than 12 hours). Process A and Process B have the same average performance time of 10 hours, and yet performance is late. In neither case could we achieve the expected average output rate. Why? Because the time lost when the second process is idle cannot be made up.

This example is intended to challenge the theory that capacities should be balanced to an average time. *Rather than capacities being balanced, the flow of product through the system should be balanced.*

OSCM AT WORK

Ratan Tata: Mastering the Art of "Theory of Constraints"

Mr. Ratan Naval Tata is a well known figure in Indian corporate world, who was the Chairman of Tata Sons till a few years back. Tata Group is India's largest conglomerate founded by Jamsetji Tata and consolidated and expanded by later generations of his family. During the tenure of Mr. Ratan Tata, the group's revenues have grown nearly 13-fold [1].

For Ratan Tata, constraints were opportunity to outperform competitors. In December 1998, when Tata Indica was launched, it became the first indigenously designed and produced car of India. In 1995, the specifications of this car were designed around the following requirements [2]:

- The inside space of an Ambassador (the most traditional car by Hindustan Motors for Indian market) and the external dimensions of a Zen (the most recent car from Maruti Udyog Limited).
- Easy entry and exit for passengers; this meant a higher suspension and raised back seats.
- World-class standards of safety.
- The fuel economy of a typical diesel engine.
- Price approximating the Maruti 800 (the cheapest family car in Indian market).
- Contemporary design.

With a support from 700 engineers, the Indica project was completed in record 31 months. With a total developmental cost of ₹1700 crore, the project involved 3885 specially developed components, 740 specially designed dies and 4010 fixtures. Tata bought an unused Nissan Motor plant at Australia, which was still in prime condition for ₹103 crore. Tata Engineering moved 4,800 tonnes of the useable part of this plant to India in 582 containers through 16 shipments over six months. Tata Engineering involved its vendors right from the concept stage. According to Mr. Ratan Tata, over 300 vendors supplied some 1,360 parts of the Indica to Tata Engineering, which comprised 77 per cent of the vehicle's cost [2]. Success of first indigenous car Indica is a true demonstration of converting constraints into possibility.

Tata Indica is not the only example. In the year 2000, Tata struck an astonishing $435 million deal for Tetley, the world's second largest manufacturer and distributor of tea. According to Ratan Tata, "The strategy is to acquire a brand with an international presence. Tetley has a strong position in tea bags, and we have a strong position in tea. So it enables us to promote our product through a brand that is known in the Western world. It would have taken much more effort and much more money to create the same level of awareness for the Tata Tea brand overseas [3]." In the financial year 2005-06, the group made 14 acquisitions (worth nearly $1.5 bn). [4]

Another most talked about acquisition by Tata took place on January 31, 2007. Corus Group, an Anglo-Dutch steel and aluminum producer was acquired at $12.1 billion. As quoted by Ratan Tata, "I think it's a moment of great fulfilment for all of us in India because Tata Steel, as an Indian steel company, now has global scale with a footprint in Europe. I think, it is the commencement of Tata Steel's global strategy. It also elevates Tata Steel to the fifth largest steel company in the world." [5]. According to Mr. Philippe Varin, Chief Executive of Corus, "The value creation for the new company has to come from three areas. One is what we call synergies. It is about sharing of manufacturing practices, shared services and purchasing — these are the traditional type of synergies in any merger. The second area is about sharing our complementary strengths. For example, Corus has strong R&D and product development capabilities for value-added products in the auto, construction and packaging markets, which will complement what Tata Steel is doing in the fast-growing Asian markets. The third is linked to the option for the future to bring low-cost slabs once Tata Steel has completed its greenfield projects." [6] Ratan Tata is also credited for leading the revamp operations of Tata Steel and making it one of the lowest-cost producers in the world. [4]

On March 26, 2008, Tata Motors, under the leadership of Ratan Tata, bought Jaguar & Land Rover from Ford Motor Company. The acquisition of these two iconic British brands was at £1.15 billion ($2.3 billion). According to Mr. Ratan Tata, "This is a momentous time for all of us at Tata Motors. Jaguar and Land Rover are two iconic British brands with worldwide growth prospects. Tata Group have been using this strategy of acquisitions very effectively either to expand their global footprints or to diversify into a new industry segment."

In the year 2009, Tata Motors rolled out its most awaited indigenous low cost car Tata Nano car at a price tag of around ₹1,00,000. According to Mr. Tata, "It was never meant to be a ₹1 lakh car; that happened by circumstance. I was interviewed by the [British newspaper] *Financial Times* at the Geneva Motor Show and I talked about this future product as a low-cost car. I was asked how much it would cost and I said about ₹1 lakh. The next day the *Financial Times* had a headline to the effect that the Tatas are to produce a ₹100,000 car. My immediate reaction was to issue a rebuttal, to clarify that that was not exactly what I had said. Then I thought, I did say it would be around that figure, so why don't we just take that as a target. When I came back our people were aghast, but we had our goal." [6,7] This demonstrates Mr. Tata's mindset and business acumen to use the "*art of possibility*" which is needed to convert constraints into opportunities. Nano schedule suffered a major setback due to its re-location from Singur in West Bengal. Still Mr. Tata ensured to meet the deadline.

There are numerous other occasions when Mr. Tata showed that business excellence requires a continuous search for possibilities to convert constraints into opportunities. For example, recently launched low cost water purifier, "Tata Swach" is the result of collaborative innovations by group companies like TCS, Tata Chemicals and Titan. It is an example of the philanthropic cum dream projects of Mr. Ratan Tata, which has the potential to cover millions in rural India, who are deprived of portable drinking water. [8]

In recognition to the service to nation, on 26 January 2008, Mr. Ratan Tata was conferred Padma Vibhushan, the second highest civilian decoration in India [9].

References

1 http://www.tata.com/aboutus/articles/inside.aspx?artid=uBZjT+/ooH8= (Accessed on 10 January 2014).
2 http://www.tata.com/aboutus/articles/inside.aspx?artid=bPF2afb3P0E= (Accessed on 10 January 2014).
3 http://www.accenture.com/Global/Research_and_Insights/Outlook/By_Alphabet/InterviewSons.htm (Interview of Ratan Tata: Accessed on 10 January 2014)
4 http://news.bbc.co.uk/2/hi/south_asia/6071090.stm (Accessed on 21 January 2014).
5 http://www.rediff.com/money/2007/feb/01corus5.htm (Accessed on 10 January 2014).
6 http://www.businessworld.in/index.php/interview-ratan-tata.html (Accessed on 10 January 2014).
7 http://www.tata.com/aboutus/articles/inside.aspx?artid=Sd75BUBmzSM= (Accessed on 10 January 2014).
8 http://www.deccanherald.com/content/40000/tata-launches-swach-water-filters.html (Accessed on 21 January 2014).
9 *The Hindu*, Tata Sons Chairman Ratan Tata receives Padma Vibhushan, 11 May 2008.

EXHIBIT 23.5

Processing and Completion Times, Process A to Process B

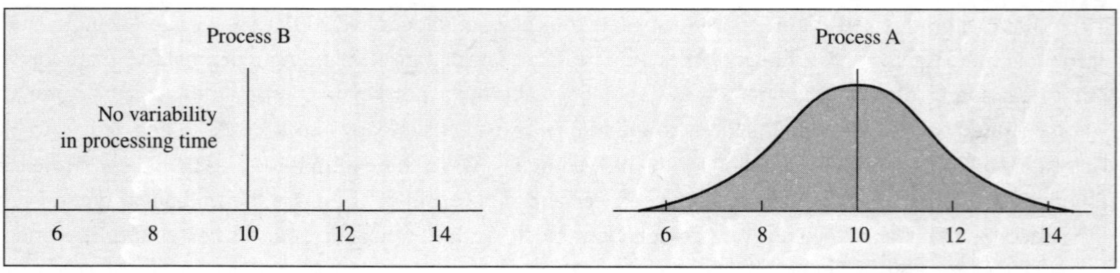

Item Number	Start Time	Processing Time	Finish Time
1	0 hrs	10 hrs	10 hrs
2	10	10	20
3	20	10	30
4	30	10	40
5	40	10	50
Average = 10 hours			

Item Number	Start Time	Processing Time	Finish Time
1	10 hrs	6 hrs	16 hrs
2	20	8	28
3	30	10	40
4	40	12	52
5	52	14	66
Average = 10 hours			

This is similar to Exhibit 23.4. However, the processing sequence has been reversed, as well as the order of the Process A times.

BOTTLENECKS, CAPACITY-CONSTRAINED RESOURCES, AND SYNCHRONOUS MANUFACTURING

LO 23-2

Analyze bottleneck resources and apply TOC principles to controlling a process

A **bottleneck** is defined as any resource whose capacity is less than the demand placed upon it. A bottleneck is a constraint within the system that limits throughput. It is that point in the manufacturing process where flow thins to a narrow stream. A bottleneck may be a machine, scarce or highly skilled labor, or a specialized tool. Observations in industry have shown that most plants have very few bottleneck operations.

If there is no bottleneck, then excess capacity exists and the system should be changed to create a bottleneck (such as more setups or reduced capacity), which we will discuss later.

Capacity is defined as the available time for production. This excludes maintenance and other downtime. A **nonbottleneck** is any resource whose capacity is greater than the demand placed on it. A nonbottleneck, therefore, should not be working constantly because it can produce more than is needed. A nonbottleneck contains idle time.

A **capacity-constrained resource (CCR)** is one whose utilization is close to capacity and could be a bottleneck if it is not scheduled carefully. For example, a CCR may be receiving work in a job-shop environment from several sources. If these sources schedule their flow in a way that causes occasional idle time for the CCR in excess of its unused capacity time, the CCR becomes a bottleneck when the surge of work arrives at a later time. This can happen if batch sizes are changed or if one of the upstream operations is not working for some reason and does not feed enough work to the CCR.

Bottleneck
A resource that limits the capacity or maximum output of the process.

Nonbottleneck
Any resource whose capacity is greater than the demand placed on it (Goldratt's definition).

Capacity-constrained resource (CCR)
A resource whose utilization is close to capacity and could be a bottleneck if not scheduled carefully (Goldratt's definition).

Basic Manufacturing Building Blocks

All manufacturing processes and flows can be simplified to four basic configurations, as shown in Exhibit 23.6. In configuration A of Exhibit 23.6, product that flows through Process X feeds into Process Y. In configuration B, Y is feeding X. In C, Process X and Process Y are creating subassemblies, which are then combined, say, to feed the market demand. In D, Process X and Process Y are independent of each other and are supplying their own markets. The last column in the exhibit shows possible sequences of nonbottleneck resources, which can be grouped and displayed as Y to simplify the representation.

EXHIBIT 23.6

The Basic Building Blocks of Manufacturing Derived by Grouping Process Flows

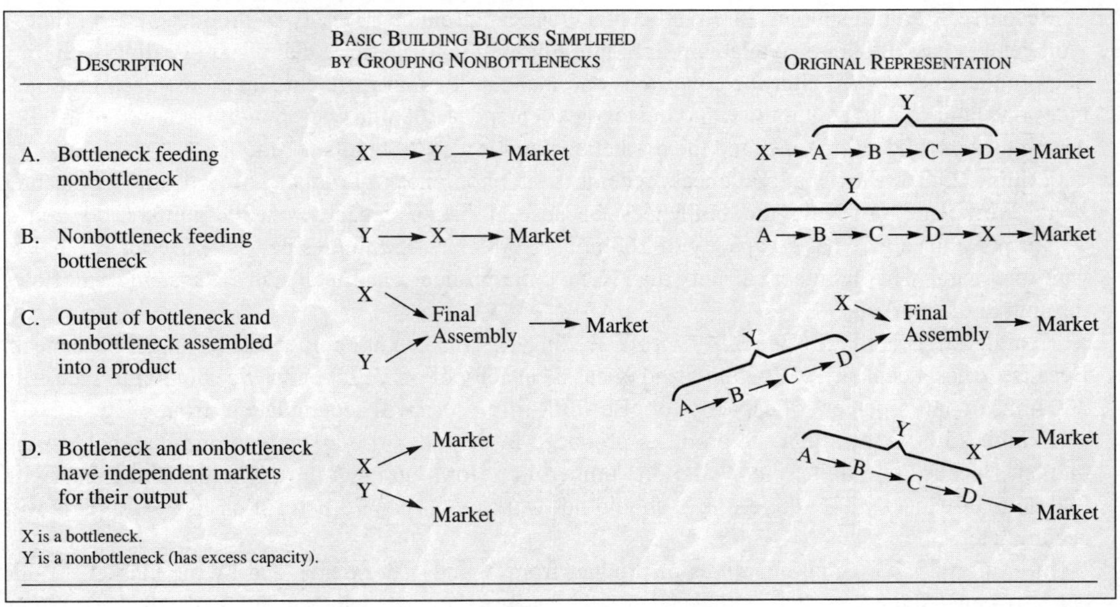

The value in using these basic building blocks is that a production process can be greatly simplified for analysis and control. Rather than track and schedule all of the steps in a production sequence through nonbottleneck operations, for example, attention can be placed at the beginning and end points of the building block groupings.

Methods for Synchronous Control

Exhibit 23.7 shows how bottleneck and nonbottleneck resources should be managed.

Exhibit 23.7

Product Flow through Bottlenecks and Nonbottlenecks

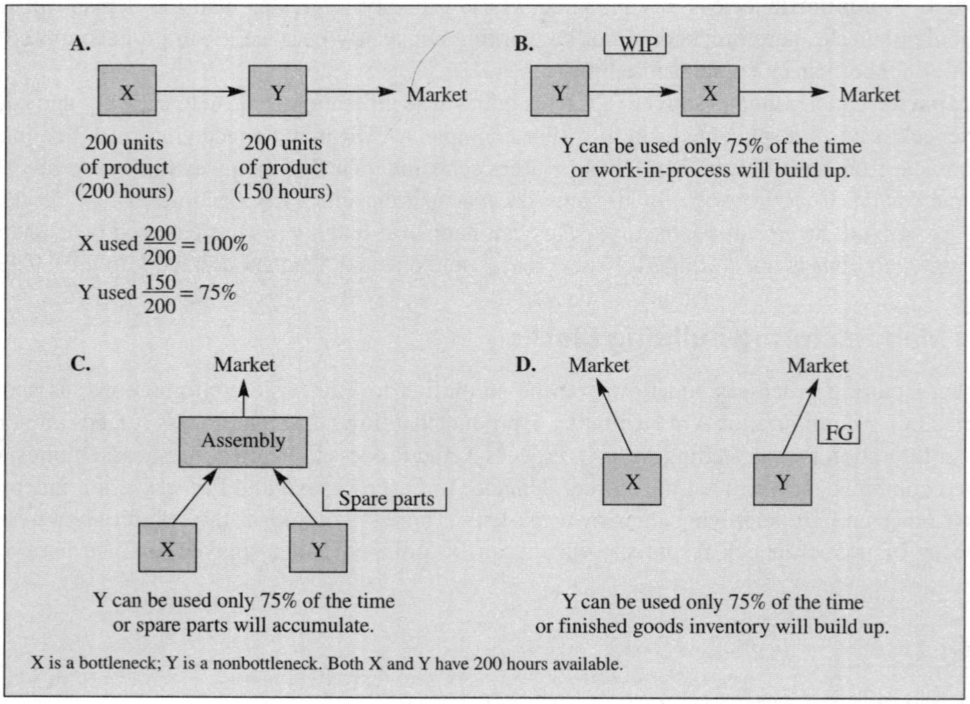

Resource X and Resource Y are workcenters that can produce a variety of products. Each of these workcenters has 200 hours available per month. For simplicity, assume that we are dealing with only one product and we will alter the conditions and makeup for four different situations. Each unit of X takes one hour of production time, and the market demand is 200 units per month. Each unit of Y takes 45 minutes of production time, and the market demand is also 200 units per month.

Exhibit 23.7A shows a bottleneck feeding a nonbottleneck. Product flows from Workcenter X to Workcenter Y. X is the bottleneck because it has a capacity of 200 units (200 hours/1 hour per unit) and Y has a capacity of 267 units (200 hours/45 minutes per unit). Because Y has to wait for X, and Y has a higher capacity than X, no extra product accumulates in the system. It all flows through to the market.

Exhibit 23.7B is the reverse of A, with Y feeding X. This is a nonbottleneck feeding a bottleneck. Because Y has a capacity of 267 units and X has a capacity of only 200 units, we should produce only 200 units of Y (75 percent of capacity) or else work-in-process will accumulate in front of X.

Exhibit 23.7C shows that the products produced by X and Y are assembled and then sold to the market. Because one unit from X and one unit from Y form an assembly, X is the bottleneck with 200 units of capacity and, therefore, Y should not work more than 75 percent or else extra parts will accumulate.

In Exhibit 23.7D, equal quantities of product from X and Y are demanded by the market. In this case, we can call these products "finished goods" because they face independent demands. Here, Y has access to material independent of X and, with a higher capacity than needed to satisfy the market (in essence, the market is the bottleneck), it can produce more product than the market will take. However, this would create an inventory of unneeded finished goods.

The four situations just discussed demonstrate bottleneck and nonbottleneck resources and their relationships to production and market demand. They show that the industry practice of using resource utilization as a measure of performance can encourage the overuse of nonbottlenecks and result in excess inventories.

Time Components The following kinds of time make up production cycle time:

1. *Setup time*—the time that a part spends waiting for a resource to be set up to work on this same part.
2. *Processing time*—the time that the part is being processed.
3. *Queue time*—the time that a part waits for a resource while the resource is busy with something else.
4. *Wait time*—the time that a part waits not for a resource but for another part so that they can be assembled together.
5. *Idle time*—the unused time; that is, the cycle time minus the sum of the setup time, processing time, queue time, and wait time.

For a part waiting to go through a bottleneck, queue time is usually the greatest. As we discuss later in this chapter, this is because the bottleneck has a fairly large amount of work to do in front of it (to make sure it is always working). For a nonbottleneck, wait time is usually the greatest. The part is just sitting there waiting for the arrival of other parts so that an assembly can take place.

Schedulers are tempted to save setup times. Suppose that the batch sizes are doubled to save half the setup times. Then, with a double batch size, all of the other times (processing time, queue time, and wait time) increase twofold. Because these times are doubled while saving only half of the setup time, the net result is that the work-in-process is approximately doubled, as is the investment in inventory.

Finding the Bottleneck There are two ways to find the bottleneck (or bottlenecks) in a system. One is to run a capacity resource profile; the other is to use our knowledge of the particular plant, look at the system in operation, and talk with supervisors and workers.

A capacity resource profile is obtained by looking at the loads placed on each resource by the products that are scheduled through them. In running a capacity profile, we assume that the data are reasonably accurate, although not necessarily perfect. As an example, consider that products have been routed through Resources M1 through M5. Suppose that our first computation of the resource loads on each resource caused by these products shows the following:

M1 130 percent of capacity
M2 120 percent of capacity
M3 105 percent of capacity
M4 95 percent of capacity
M5 85 percent of capacity

For this first analysis, we can disregard any resources at lower percentages because they are nonbottlenecks and should not be a problem. With this list in hand, we should physically go to the facility and check all five operations. Note that M1, M2, and M3 are overloaded; that is, they are scheduled above their capacities. We would expect to see large quantities of inventory in front of M1. If this is not the case, errors must exist somewhere—perhaps in the bill of materials or in the routing sheets. Let's say that our observations and discussions with shop personnel showed that there were errors in M1, M2, M3, and M4. We tracked them down, made the appropriate corrections, and ran the capacity profile again:

M1 115 percent of capacity
M2 110 percent of capacity
M3 105 percent of capacity
M4 90 percent of capacity
M5 85 percent of capacity

M1, M2, and M3 are still showing a lack of sufficient capacity, but M2 is the most serious. If we now have confidence in our numbers, we use M2 as our bottleneck. If the data contain too many errors for a reliable data analysis, it may not be worth spending time (it could take months) making all the corrections.

Saving Time Recall that a bottleneck is a resource whose capacity is less than the demand placed on it. Because we focus on bottlenecks as restricting *throughput* (defined as *sales*), a bottleneck's capacity is less than the market demand. There are a number of ways we can save time on a bottleneck (better tooling, higher-quality labor, larger batch sizes, reduction in setup times, and so forth), but how valuable is the extra time? Very, very valuable!

AN HOUR SAVED AT THE BOTTLENECK ADDS AN EXTRA HOUR TO THE ENTIRE PRODUCTION SYSTEM.

How about time saved on a nonbottleneck resource?

AN HOUR SAVED AT A NONBOTTLENECK IS A MIRAGE AND ONLY ADDS AN HOUR TO ITS IDLE TIME.

Because a nonbottleneck has more capacity than the system needs for its current throughput, it already contains idle time. Implementing any measures to save more time does not increase throughput but only serves to increase its idle time.

Avoid Changing a Nonbottleneck into a Bottleneck When nonbottleneck resources are scheduled with larger batch sizes, this action could create a bottleneck that we certainly would want to avoid. Consider the case in Exhibit 23.8, where Y_1, Y_2, and Y_3 are nonbottleneck resources. Y_1 currently produces Part A, which is routed to Y_3, and Part B, which is routed to Y_2. To produce Part A, Y_1 has a 200-minute setup time and a processing time of 1 minute per part. Part A is currently produced in batches of 500 units. To produce Part B, Y_1 has a setup time of 150 minutes and 2 minutes' processing time per part. Part B is currently produced in batches of 200 units. With this sequence, Y_2 is utilized 70 percent of the time and Y_3 is utilized 80 percent of the time.

Because setup time is 200 minutes for Y_1 on Part A, both worker and supervisor mistakenly believe that more production can be gained if fewer setups are made. Let's assume that the batch size is increased to 1,500 units and see what happens. The illusion is that we have saved 400 minutes of setup. (Instead of three setups taking 600 minutes to produce three batches of 500 units each, there is just one setup with a 1,500-unit batch.)

EXHIBIT 23.8

Nonbottleneck Resources

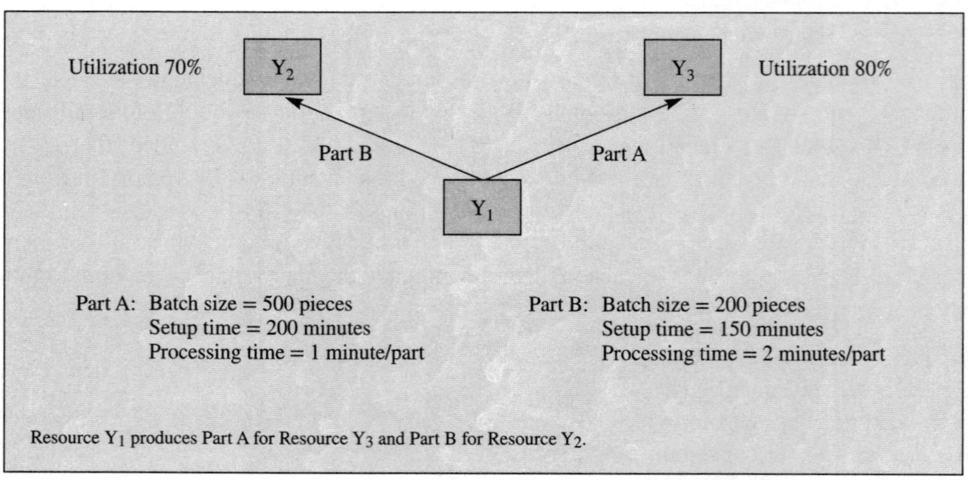

The problem is that the 400 minutes saved served no purpose, but this delay did interfere with the production of Part B because Y_1 produces Part B for Y_2. The sequence before any changes were made was Part A (700 minutes), Part B (550 minutes), Part A (700 minutes), Part B (550 minutes), and so on. Now, however, when the Part A batch is increased to 1,500 units (1,700 minutes), Y_2 and Y_3 could well be starved for work and have to wait more time than they have available (30 percent idle time for Y_2 and 20 percent for Y_3). The new sequence would be Part A (1,700 minutes), Part B (1,350 minutes), and so on. Such an extended wait for Y_2 and Y_3 could be disruptive. Y_2 and Y_3 could become temporary bottlenecks and lose throughput for the system.

Drum, Buffer, Rope Every production system needs some control point or points to control the flow of product through the system. If the system contains a bottleneck, the bottleneck is the best place for control. This control point is called the *drum* because it strikes the beat that the rest of the system (or those parts that it influences) uses to function. Recall that a *bottleneck* is defined as a resource that does not have the capacity to meet demand. Therefore, a bottleneck is working all the time, and one reason for using it as a control point is to make sure that the operations upstream do not overproduce and build up excess work-in-process inventory that the bottleneck cannot handle.

If there is no bottleneck, the next-best place to set the drum would be a capacity-constrained resource (CCR). A capacity-constrained resource, remember, is one that is operating near capacity but, on average, has adequate capability as long as it is not incorrectly scheduled (for example, with too many setups, causing it to run short of capacity, or producing too large a lot size, thereby starving downstream operations).

If neither a bottleneck nor a CCR is present, the control point can be designated anywhere. The best position would generally be at some divergent point where the output of the resource is used in several downstream operations.

Dealing with the bottleneck is most critical, and our discussion focuses on ensuring that the bottleneck always has work to do. Exhibit 23.9 shows a simple linear flow A through G. Suppose that Resource D, which is a machine center, is a bottleneck. This means the capacities are greater both upstream and downstream from it. If this sequence is not controlled, we would expect to see a large amount of inventory in front of Workcenter D and very little anywhere else. There would be little finished goods inventory because (by the definition of the term *bottleneck*) all the product produced would be taken by the market.

EXHIBIT 23.9

Linear Flow of Product with a Bottleneck

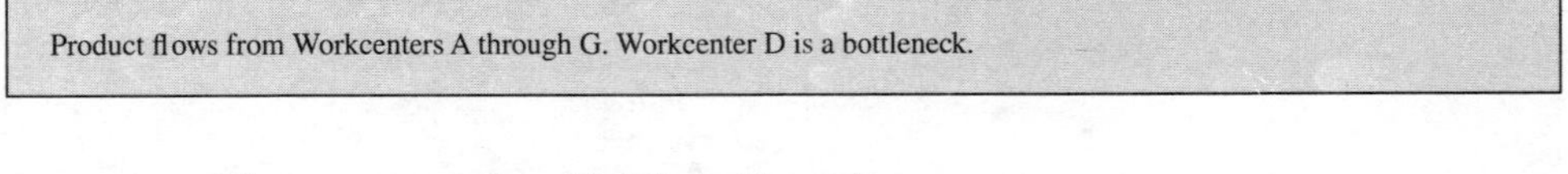

Product flows from Workcenters A through G. Workcenter D is a bottleneck.

There are two things we must do with this bottleneck:

1. Keep a *buffer* inventory in front of it to make sure it always has something to work on. Because it is a bottleneck, its output determines the throughput of the system.
2. Communicate back upstream to A what D has produced so that A provides only that amount. This keeps inventory from building up. This communication is called the *rope*. It can be formal (such as a schedule) or informal (such as daily discussion).

EXHIBIT 23.10

Capacity Profile of Workcenter D (showing assigned jobs A through P over a period of four 24-hour days)

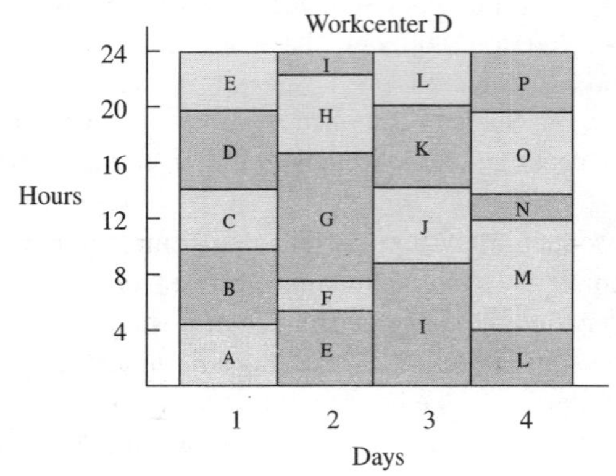

The buffer inventory in front of a bottleneck operation is a *time buffer*. We want to make sure that Workcenter D always has work to do, and it does not matter which of the scheduled products are worked on. We might, for example, provide 96 hours of inventory in the buffer as shown in the sequence A through P in Exhibit 23.10. Jobs A through about half of E are scheduled during the 24 hours of Day 1; Jobs E through a portion of Job I are scheduled during the second 24-hour day; Jobs I through part of L are scheduled during the third 24-hour day; and Jobs L through P are scheduled during the fourth 24-hour day, for a total of 96 hours. This means that through normal variation, or if something happens upstream and the output has been temporarily stalled, D can work for another 96 hours, protecting the throughput. (The 96 hours of work, incidentally, include setups and processing times contained in the job sheets, which usually are based on engineering standard times.)

We might ask, How large should the time buffer be? The answer: As large as it needs to be to ensure that the bottleneck continues to work. By examining the variation of each operation, we can make a guess. Theoretically, the size of the buffer can be computed statistically by examining past performance data, or the sequence can be simulated. In any event, precision is not critical. We could start with an estimate of the time buffer as one-fourth of the total lead time of the system. Say, the sequence A to G in our example (Exhibit 23.9) took a total of 16 days. We could start with a buffer of four days in front of D. If, during the next few days or weeks, the buffer runs out, we need to increase the buffer size. We do this by releasing extra material to the first operation, A. On the other hand, if we find that our buffer never drops below three days, we might want to hold back releases to A and reduce the time buffer to three days. Experience is the best determination of the final buffer size.

If the drum is not a bottleneck but a CCR (and thus it can have a small amount of idle time), we might want to create two buffer inventories: one in front of the CCR and the second at the end as finished goods. (See Exhibit 23.11.) The finished-goods inventory protects the market, and the time

EXHIBIT 23.11

Linear Flow of Product with a Capacity-Constrained Resource

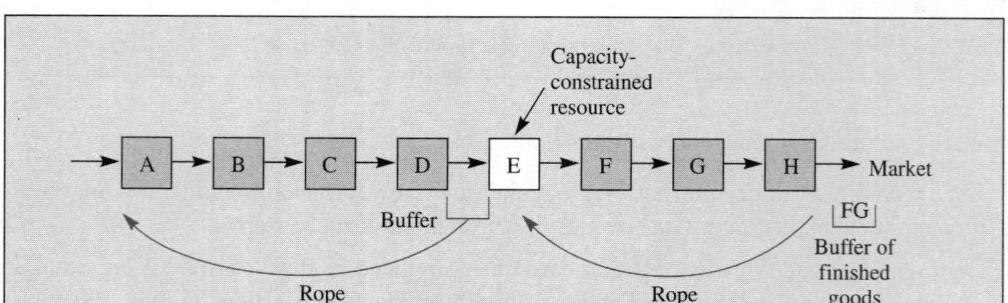

Product flows through Workcenters A through H. Workcenter E is capacity constrained.

buffer in front of the CCR protects throughput. For this CCR case, the market cannot take all that we can produce, so we want to ensure that finished goods are available when the market does decide to purchase.

We need two ropes in this case: (1) a rope communicating from finished-goods inventory back to the drum to increase or decrease output and (2) a rope from the drum back to the material release point, specifying how much material is needed.

Exhibit 23.12 is a more detailed network flow showing one bottleneck. Inventory is provided not only in front of that bottleneck but also after the nonbottleneck sequence of processes that feed the subassembly. This ensures that the flow of product is not slowed down by having to wait after it leaves the bottleneck.

Exhibit 23.12

Network Flow with One Bottleneck

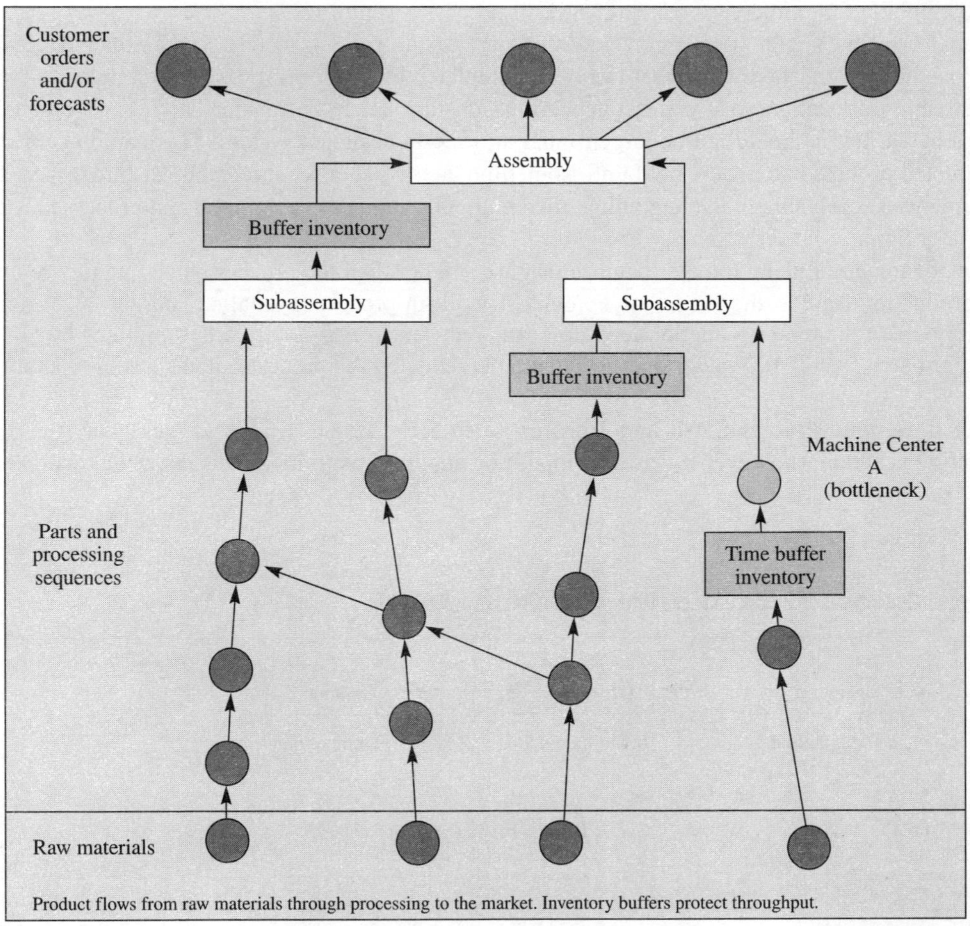

Importance of Quality An MRP system allows for rejects by building a larger batch than actually needed. A JIT system cannot tolerate poor quality because JIT success is based on a balanced capacity. A defective part or component can cause a JIT system to shut down, thereby losing throughput of the total system. Synchronous manufacturing, however, has excess capacity throughout the system, except for the bottleneck. If a bad part is produced upstream of the bottleneck, the result is that there is a loss of material only. Because of the excess capacity, there is still time to do another operation to replace the one just scrapped. For the bottleneck, however, extra time does not exist, so there should be a quality control inspection just prior to the bottleneck to ensure that the bottleneck works only on good product. Also, there needs to be assurance downstream from the bottleneck that the passing product is not scrapped—that would mean lost throughput.

Batch Sizes In an assembly line, what is the batch size? Some would say "one" because one unit is moved at a time; others would say "infinity" because the line continues to produce the same item. Both answers are correct, but they differ in their point of view. The first answer, "one," in an assembly line focuses on the *part* transferred one unit at a time. The second focuses on the *process*. From the point of view of the resource, the process batch is infinity because it is continuing to run the same units. Thus, in an assembly line, we have a *process batch* of infinity (or all the units until we change to another process setup) and a *transfer batch* of one unit.

Setup costs and carrying costs were treated in depth in Chapter 20, "Inventory Management." In the present context, setup costs relate to the process batch and carrying costs relate to the transfer batch.

A process batch is of a size large enough or small enough to be processed in a particular length of time. From the point of view of a resource, two times are involved: setup time and processing run time (ignoring downtime for maintenance or repair). Larger process batch sizes require fewer setups and therefore can generate more processing time and more output. For bottleneck resources, larger batch sizes are desirable. For nonbottleneck resources, smaller process batch sizes are desirable (by using up the existing idle time), thereby reducing work-in-process inventory.

Transfer batches refer to the movement of part of the process batch. Rather than wait for the entire batch to be finished, work that has been completed by that operation can be moved to the next downstream workstation so it can begin working on that batch. A transfer batch can be equal to a process batch, but it should not be larger under a properly designed system. This could occur only if a completed process batch were held until sometime later when a second batch was processed. If this later time was acceptable in the beginning, then both jobs should be combined and processed together at the later time.

The advantage of using transfer batches that are smaller than the process batch quantity is that the total production time is shorter so the amount of work-in-process is smaller. Exhibit 23.13 shows a situation where the total production lead time was reduced from 2,100 to 1,310 minutes by (1) using a transfer batch size of 100 rather than 1,000 and (2) reducing the process batch sizes of Operation 2.

How to Determine Process Batch and Transfer Batch Sizes Logic would suggest that the master production schedule (however it was developed) be analyzed as to its effect on various workcenters.

Exhibit 23.13

Effect of Changing the Process Batch Sizes on Production Lead Time for a Job Order of 1,000 Units

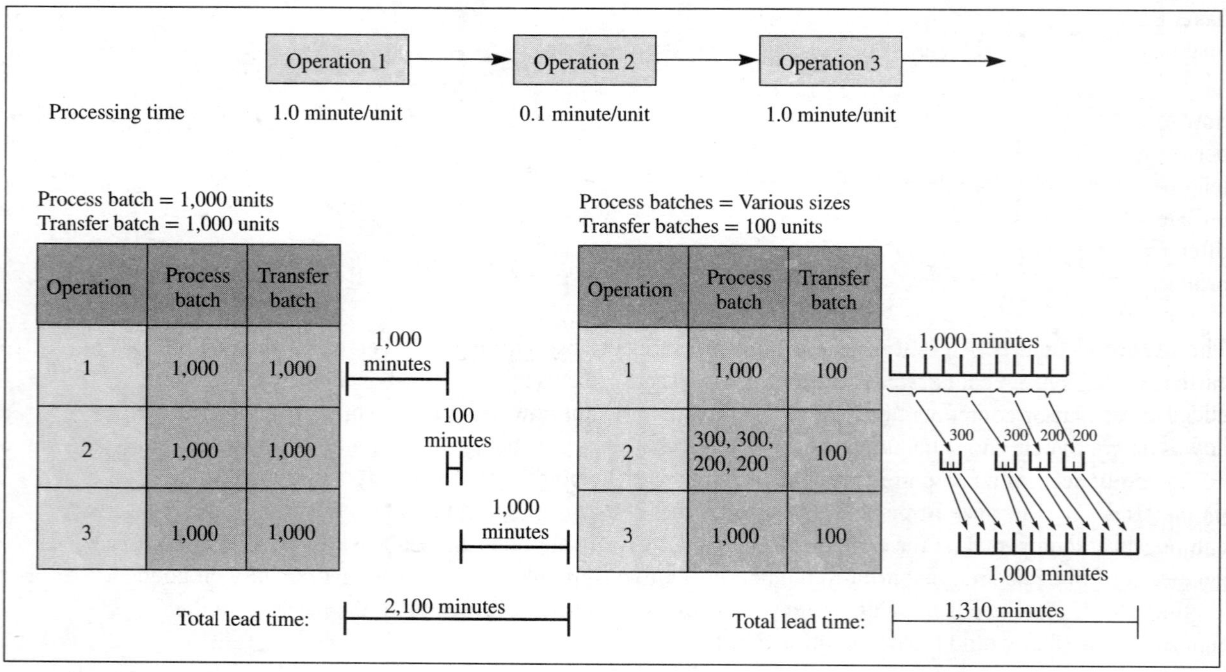

In an MRP system, this means that the master production schedule should be run through the MRP and the CRP (capacity requirements planning program) to generate a detailed load on each workcenter. From this report, probable CCRs and bottlenecks can be identified. There should be only one (or a few), and they should be reviewed by managers so that they understand which resources are actually controlling their plant. These resources set the drumbeat.

Rather than try to adjust the master production schedule to change resource loads, it is more practical to control the flow at each bottleneck or CCR to bring the capacities in line. The process batch sizes and transfer batch sizes are changed after comparing past performances in meeting due dates.

Smaller transfer batches give lower work-in-process inventory and faster product flow (and consequently shorter lead time). More material handling is required, however. Larger transfer batches give longer lead times and higher inventories, but there is less material handling. Therefore, the transfer batch size is determined by a trade-off of production lead times, inventory reduction benefits, and costs of material movement.

When trying to control the flow at CCRs and bottlenecks, there are four possible situations:

1. A bottleneck (no idle time) with no setup time required when changing from one product to another.
2. A bottleneck with setup time required to change from one product to another.
3. A capacity-constrained resource with a small amount of idle time, with no setup time required to change from one product to another.
4. A CCR with setup time required when changing from one product to another.

In the first case (a bottleneck with no setup time to change products), jobs should be processed in the order of the schedule so that delivery is on time. Without setups, only the sequence is important. In the second case, when setups are required, larger batch sizes combine separate similar jobs in the sequence. This means reaching ahead into future time periods. Some jobs will therefore be done early. Because this is a bottleneck resource, larger batches save setups and thereby increase throughput. (The setup time saved is used for processing.) The larger process batches may cause the early-scheduled jobs to be late. Therefore, frequent small transfer batches are necessary to try to shorten the lead time.

Situations 3 and 4 include a CCR without a setup and a CCR with setup time requirements, respectively. Handling the CCR would be similar to handling a nonbottleneck, though more carefully. That is, a CCR has some idle time. It would be appropriate here to cut the size of some of the process batches so that there can be more frequent changes of product. This would decrease lead time, and jobs would be more likely to be done on time. In a make-to-stock situation, cutting process batch sizes has a much more profound effect than increasing the number of transfer batches. This is because the resulting product mix is much greater, leading to reduced WIP and production lead time.

How to Treat Inventory The traditional view of inventory is that its only negative impact on a firm's performance is its carrying cost. We now realize inventory's negative impact also comes from lengthening lead times and creating problems with engineering changes. (When an engineering change on a product comes through, which commonly occurs, product still within the production system often must be modified to include the changes. Therefore, less work-in-process reduces the amount of product rework necessary.)

From a constraint management perspective, inventory is a loan given to the manufacturing unit. The value of the loan is based only on the purchased items that are part of the inventory. As we stated earlier, inventory is treated in this chapter as material cost only, without any accounting-type value added from production. If inventory is carried as a loan to manufacturing, we need a way to measure how long the loan is carried. One measurement is dollar days.

Dollar Days A useful performance measurement is the concept of *dollar days,* a measurement of the value of inventory and the time it stays within an area. To use this measure, we could simply multiply the total value of inventory by the number of days inventory spends within a department.

Suppose Department X carries an average inventory of $40,000, and, on average, the inventory stays within the department five days. In dollar days, Department X is charged with $40,000 times five

OSCM AT WORK

Critical Chain Project Management

Critical Chain Project Management is the name of the approach that Eli Goldratt developed for scheduling and managing projects. The approach borrows many ideas from those used for manufacturing processes. The conventional critical path method was covered in Chapter 4, and Goldratt goes beyond those ideas by considering resource constraints and special time buffers in the project. The following are specific ideas included in his Critical Chain Project Management approach:

1. Schedules are level-loaded based on the limitations of available resources (constraints). This produces the "critical chain"—the longest set of sequential tasks (due to both task dependency and resource contention)—which dictates the shortest overall project duration.
2. Time buffers are inserted at strategic locations in the plan—at the end of the critical chain and at every point where a task enters the critical chain—to absorb the adverse effects of uncertainty without damaging performance. To create the buffers, some of the slack time built into tasks in planning is repositioned to these strategic locations.
3. Projects are "pipelined" or staged based on resource availability to combat the cascade effect of shared resources across projects and create viable multiproject plans.
4. Buffer management is used to dynamically set task priorities in execution. As uncertainty changes the original plan, tasks are prioritized based on the buffer burn rate (the amount of buffer consumed versus the percentage of the work complete). Tasks with critical buffer penetration take precedence over those with lower burn rates.

days, or $200,000 dollar days of inventory. At this point, we cannot say the $200,000 is high or low, but it does show where the inventory is located. Management can then see where it should focus attention and determine acceptable levels. Techniques can be instituted to try to reduce the number of dollar days while being careful that such a measure does not become a local objective (that is, minimizing dollar days) and hurt the global objectives (such as increasing ROI, cash flow, and net profit).

Dollar days could be beneficial in a variety of ways. Consider the current practice of using efficiencies or equipment utilization as a performance measurement. To get high utilization, large amounts of inventory are held to keep everything working. However, high inventories would result in a high number of dollar days, which would discourage high levels of work-in-process. Dollar day measurements also could be used in other areas:

- Marketing—to discourage holding large amounts of finished-goods inventory. The net result would be to encourage the sales of finished products.
- Purchasing—to discourage placing large purchase orders that on the surface appear to take advantage of quantity discounts. This would encourage just-in-time purchasing.
- Manufacturing—to discourage large work-in-process and producing earlier than needed. This would promote rapid flow of material within the plant.
- Project management—to quantify a project's limited resource investments as a function of time. This promotes the proper allocation of resources to competing projects. See the OSCM at Work box titled "Critical Chain Project Management" for Goldratt's ideas on scheduling projects.

LO 22-3 Compare TOC to conventional approaches

COMPARING SYNCHRONOUS MANUFACTURING (TOC) TO TRADITIONAL APPROACHES

MRP and JIT

MRP uses *backward scheduling* after having been fed a master production schedule. MRP schedules production through a bill of materials explosion in a backward manner—working backward in time from the desired completion date. As a secondary procedure, MRP, through its capacity resource planning module, develops capacity utilization profiles of workcenters. When workcenters are overloaded, either the master production schedule must be adjusted or enough slack capacity must be left unscheduled in the system so that work can be smoothed at the local level (by workcenter supervisors or the workers themselves). Trying to smooth capacity using MRP is so difficult and would

OSCM AT WORK

Tata Steel Rides on "Theory of Constraint"

Since 1868, Tata Group is now around 150 years old. Under its umbrella, there are 98 companies, which are supported by over 350,000 committed employees worldwide. It is undoubtedly the most global Indian business group and one of the best known Indian corporate brands across the globe. Tata Steel is its flagship company, which has provided leadership role in the corporate world of India. It is one of the leading steel producing companies of the world.

In the year 2001, mainly due to a slowdown in Indian economy, Tata Steel witnessed one of the toughest business environments in its history of existence. It was being called as the sunset industry. Indian steel companies were apparently at a brink of bankruptcy and Tata Steel was no exception.

Consequently, a new vision was created in 2002, which involved two aspects:

1. **EVA Positive Company**: EVA stands for "Economic-Value-Added", which is the difference between "return on invested capital" and "weighted average cost of capital." This part of new vision involved:

- Value creating partnerships with customers and suppliers,
- Moving from commodities to brands, and
- Developing EVA positive core business.

The challenge to become EVA-positive despite offering average steel prices was very difficult and no steel company has ever achieved it in the past. Tata Steel launched a new programme, called "ASPIRE", to help it in making an EVA-positive growth.

2. **Improve the *quality of life*:** The second important aspect of the new vision was to improve the *quality of life* of its employees and the communities that are being served. Broadly, this involved:

- Enthused and happy employees, and
- Sustainable growth.

The Improvement Philosophy of Tata Steel [2]

The three major weaknesses in the operating practices of organizations on continuous improvement path were:

(i) Approach towards continuous improvement was generally inward looking and relatively lesser attention was paid on distinctly differentiating the offerings to the customers,

(ii) The objectives may not be aspirational (challenging),

(iii) There was not much effort on testing the situations of causality during the journey of continuous improvement, i.e. the means are not checked for necessary and sufficiency conditions to meet the desired objective. Failure to test interventions against appropriate causality led to making the 'one size fits all' approach to target setting as well as the choice of tools and techniques.

To overcome these weaknesses, the ASPIRE (ASPirational Initiatives to Retain Excellence) Program was designed to first set goals and then choose the appropriate tools for delivering these goals. Certain parts of the planned improvements were checked for causality, explored for means (causes) and then the implementations were carried out using differentiated tools and techniques. For the remaining parts of the aspirational goals, the means were innovated during the implementation journey [2].

In November 2006, Tata Steel came out with "ASPIRE-T3" initiative, which aimed at motivating the employees in dedicating themselves to 3 T's, i.e., TOC (Theory of constraints), TQM (Total Quality Management), and Technology, for making the company a world leader in steel business [3]. TQM and Technology helped in achieving superior product quality through process consistency, process capability and technological capability. Similarly, TOC implementation helped it in improving the service quality [4,5,6]. To overcome many constraints in superior performance, ASPIRE-T3 is playing a major role.

"The focus on TOC, TQM and technology has been captured at Aspire with T3 ('Teen se jeet'). The synergy and integration in the efforts of the employees through TOC, TQM and technology initiatives will help TATA Steel in becoming one of the top steel companies in the world not only in size but in any other ways like corporate governance, human resources, product and service quality and so on..."

—B. Muthuraman, MD, Tata Steel on launch of Aspire T3, November 02, 2006

Opportunities

The ASPIRE-T3 evolves round the philosophy of setting aspirations (which may be beyond the current capability), then getting determined about reaching these aspirations, mustering required resources, which leads to achievement, and thus the self confidence to aspire for more. It was launched in the presence of Dr. Eliyahu M Goldratt, who explained the fundamentals of TOC to Tata Steel and explained that the TOC approach looks at business problems at a system level, in contrast to some other methods that are focused on specific processes. Focusing on viable vision implementations, using TOC, industrial organizations could achieve unprecedented improvements in their bottom-line performances. He emphasized the need to identify and capitalize on those few elements that govern an organizational system and are constraining in the goal of the organizational performance indicators.

TOC approach has helped Tata Steel in its major restructuring of supply chain and replenishment process. Due to very high dependency on the demands from industrial clusters and other major institutional clients, its goal of making profit is adversely affected due to high inventory and stock-outs. In the language of TOC, major constraint for inferior SCM performance is demand uncertainty. To deal with this constraint, marketing and sales teams of Tata Steel are using replenishment-offers to distributors while vendor managed inventory (VMI)-offers to original equipment (OEM) customers, and rapid-response-offers to some other selected customers [2]. Backed by a product portfolio covered under these offers, reliable replenishments, warehousing, inventory management, and end-to-end communications for better planning and decision making, Tata Steel has started making considerable achievements from ASPIRE-T3. It has helped bringing down the average distributor inventory of cold rolled sheets and galvanized sheets by as much as 20 per cent [2, 3]. The ASPIRE program is thus successful in supporting an accelerated pace of growth and making Tata Steel an EVA positive on a sustainable basis.

References

1 http://www.tatasteel.com/investors/annual-report-2008-09/html/financial_highlights.html (Accessed on 12 May 2010).
2 http://www.tatasteel.com/investors/annualreport-2007-08/html/process_improvement.html (Accessed on 02 March 2014).
3 http://www.tata.com/article.aspx?artid=cllfRf+toMc= (Accessed on 09 May 2010).
4 http://www.indiaprwire.com/pressrelease/mining-metals/20061102908.htm (Accessed on 02 March 2014).
5 Business Line Article on 'Tata Steel Revamping Supply Chain Management' by Santanu Sanyal, 22nd Jul 2006 available on http://www.blonnet.com/2006/07/22/stories/2006072202080700.htm (Accessed on 12 May 2010).
6 http://www.tata.com/company/Articles/inside.aspx?artid=7VXdehaS0IY= (accessed on 12 May 2010).

require so many computer runs that capacity overloads and underloads are best left to local decisions, such as at the machine centers. An MRP schedule becomes invalid just days after it was created.

The synchronous manufacturing approach uses *forward scheduling* because it focuses on the critical resources. These are scheduled forward in time, ensuring that loads placed on them are within capacity. The noncritical (or nonbottleneck) resources are then scheduled to support the critical resources. This can be done backward to minimize the length of time that inventories are held. This procedure ensures a feasible schedule. To help reduce lead time and work-in-process, in synchronous manufacturing the process batch size and transfer batch size are varied—a procedure that MRP is not able to do.

Comparing JIT to synchronous manufacturing, JIT does an excellent job of reducing lead times and work-in-process, but it has several drawbacks:

1. JIT is most often used in repetitive manufacturing environments.
2. JIT requires a stable production level (usually about a month long).
3. JIT does not allow very much flexibility in the products produced. (Products must be similar with a limited number of options.)

4. JIT still requires work-in-process when used with kanbans so that there is "something to pull." This means that completed work must be stored on the downstream side of each workstation to be pulled by the next workstation.
5. Vendors need to be located nearby because the system depends on smaller, more frequent deliveries.

Because synchronous manufacturing uses a schedule to assign work to each workstation, there is no need for more work-in-process other than that being worked on. The exception is for inventory specifically placed in front of a bottleneck to ensure continual work, or at specific points downstream from a bottleneck to ensure flow of product.

Concerning continual improvements to the system, JIT is a trial-and-error procedure applied to a real system. In synchronous manufacturing, the system can be programmed and simulated on a computer because the schedules are realistic (can be accomplished) and computer run time is short.

Relationship with Other Functional Areas

The production system must work closely with other functional areas to achieve the best operating system. This section briefly discusses accounting and marketing—areas where conflicts can occur and where cooperation and joint planning should occur.

Accounting's Influence Sometimes we are led into making decisions to suit the measurement system rather than to follow the firm's goals. Consider the following example: Suppose that two old machines are currently being used to produce a product. The processing time for each is 20 minutes per part and, because each has the capacity of three parts per hour, they have the combined capacity of six per hour, which exactly meets the market demand of six parts per hour. Suppose that engineering finds a new machine that produces parts in 12 minutes rather than 23. However, the capacity of this one machine is only five per hour, which does not meet the market demand. Logic would seem to dictate that the supervisor should use an old machine to make up the lacking of one unit per hour. However, the system does not allow this. The standard has been changed from 20 minutes each to 12 minutes each and performance would look very bad on paper because the variance would be 67 percent [(20 – 12)/12] for units made on the old machines. The supervisor, therefore, would work the new machine on overtime.

Problems in Cost Accounting Measurements Cost accounting is used for performance measurement, cost determinations, investment justification, and inventory valuation. Two sets of accounting performance measurements are used for evaluation: (1) global measurements, which are financial statements showing net profit, return on investment, and cash flow (with which we agree); and (2) local cost accounting measurements showing efficiencies (as variances from standard) or utilization rate (hours worked/hours present).

From the cost accounting (local measurement) viewpoint, then, performance has traditionally been based on cost and full utilization. This logic forces supervisors to activate their workers all the time, which leads to excess inventory. The cost accounting measurement system also can instigate other problems. For example, attempting to use the idle time to increase utilization can create a bottleneck, as we discussed earlier in this chapter. Any measurement system should support the objectives of the firm and not stand in the way. Fortunately, the cost accounting measurement philosophy is changing.

Marketing and Production Marketing and production should communicate and conduct their activities in close harmony. In practice, however, they act very independently. There are many reasons for this. The difficulties range from differences in personalities and cultures to unlike systems of merits and rewards in the two functions. Marketing people are judged on the growth of the company in terms of sales, market share, and new products introduced. Marketing is sales oriented. Manufacturing people are evaluated on cost and utilization. Therefore, marketing wants a variety of products to increase the company's position, whereas manufacturing is trying to reduce cost.

Data used for evaluating marketing and manufacturing are also quite different. Marketing data are "soft" (qualitative); manufacturing data are "hard" (quantitative). The orientation and experiences of marketing and production people also differ. Those in marketing management have likely come up through sales and a close association with customers. Top manufacturing managers have likely progressed through production operations and therefore have plant performance as a top objective.

Cultural differences also can be important in contrasting marketing and manufacturing personnel. Marketing people tend to have a greater ego drive and are more outgoing. Manufacturing personnel tend to be more meticulous and perhaps more introverted (at least less extroverted than their marketing counterparts).

The solution to coping with these differences is to develop an equitable set of measurements to evaluate performance in each area and to promote strong lines of communication so they both contribute to reaching the firm's goals.

LO 23-4

Evaluate bottleneck scheduling problems by applying TOC principles

THEORY OF CONSTRAINTS—PROBLEMS ABOUT WHAT TO PRODUCE

We now present three examples to show that different objectives and measurement criteria can lead to the wrong decisions. These examples also show that, even though you may have all the data required, you still may not be able to solve the problem—unless you know how!

EXAMPLE 23.1 What to Produce?

In this first example, three products (A, B, and C) are sold in the market at $50, $75, and $60 per unit, respectively. The market will take all that can be supplied.

Three workcenters (X, Y, and Z) process the three products as shown in Exhibit 23.14. Processing times for each workcenter also are shown. Note that each workcenter works on all three products. Raw materials, parts, and components are added at each workcenter to produce each product. The per unit cost of these materials is shown as RM.

Which product or products should be produced?

SOLUTION

Three different objectives could exist that lead to different conclusions:

1. Maximize sales revenue because marketing personnel are paid commissions based on total revenue.
2. Maximize per unit gross profit.
3. Maximize total gross profit.

In this example, we use gross profit as selling price less materials. We also could include other expenses such as operating expenses, but we left them out for simplicity. (We include operating expenses in our next example.)

Objective 1: Maximize sales commission. Sales personnel in this case are unaware of the processing time required so, therefore, they will try to sell only B at $75 per unit and none of A or C. Maximum revenue is determined by the limiting resource as follows:

Product	Limiting Resource	Time Required	Number Produced per Hour	Selling Price	Sales Revenue per Hour
A	Y	10 min	6	$50	$300
B	X	6 min	10	75	750
C	Z	5 min	12	60	720

EXHIBIT 23.14

Prices and Production Requirements for Three Products and Three Workcenters

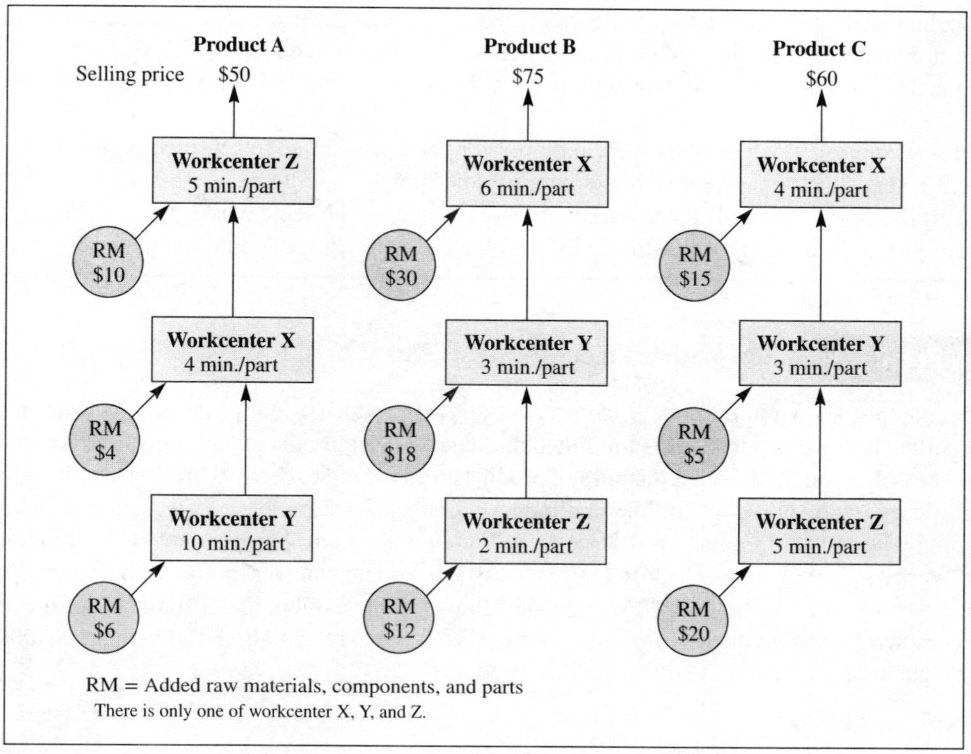

Objective 2: Maximize per unit gross profit.

(1) Product	(2) Selling Price	(3) Raw Material Cost	(4) Gross Profit per Unit (2) – (3)
A	$50	$20	$30
B	$75	$60	$15
C	$60	$40	$20

The decision would be to sell only Product A, which has a $30 per unit gross profit.

Objective 3: Maximize total gross profit. We can solve this problem by finding either total gross profit for the period or the rate at which profit is generated. We use rate to solve the problem both because it is easier and because it is a more appropriate measure. We use profit per hour as the rate.

Note that each product has a different workcenter that limits its output. The rate at which the product is made is then based on this bottleneck workcenter.

(1) Product	(2) Limiting Work Center	(3) Processing Time per Unit (Minutes)	(4) Product Output Rate (per Hour)	(5) Selling Price	(6) Raw Material Cost	(7) Profit per Unit	(8) Profit per Hour (4) × (7)
A	Y	10	6	$50	$20	$30	$180
B	X	6	10	75	60	15	150
C	Z	5	12	60	40	20	240

From our calculations, and if we only consider a single product, Product C provides the highest profit of $240 per hour. Note that we get three different answers:

1. We choose B to maximize sales revenue.
2. We choose A to maximize profit per unit.
3. We choose C to maximize total profit.

Choosing Product C is obviously the correct answer for the firm if we restrict ourselves to making a single product. Profit can be improved to $280/hour by producing a mix of A-3, B-2, and C-8 units each hour. This solution can be obtained by solving the "product mix" problem described in Appendix A (see Example A.1).

In this example, all workcenters were required for each product and each product had a different workcenter as a constraint. We did this to simplify the problem and to ensure that only one product would surface as the answer. If there were more workcenters or the same workcenter constraint in different products, the problem could still easily be solved using linear programming (as in Appendix A).

EXAMPLE 23.2 How Much to Produce?

In this example, shown in Exhibit 23.15, two workers are producing four products. The plant works three shifts. The market demand is unlimited and takes all the products that the workers can produce. The only stipulation is that the ratio of products sold cannot exceed 10 to 1 between the maximum sold of any one product and the minimum of another. For example, if the maximum number sold of any one of the products is 100 units, the minimum of any other cannot be fewer than 10 units. Workers 1 and 2, on each shift, are not cross-trained and can work only on their own operations. The time and raw material (RM) costs are shown in the exhibit, and a summary of the costs and times involved is on the lower portion of the exhibit. Weekly operating expenses are $3,000.

What quantities of A, B, C, and D should be produced?

EXHIBIT 23.15

The Production Requirements and Selling Price of Four Products

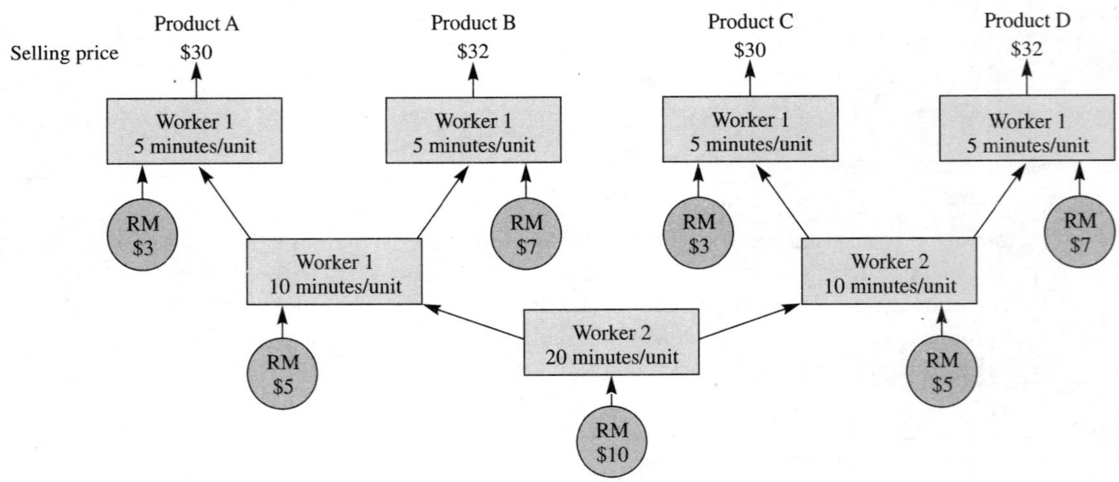

RM = Raw materials

Product	Selling price	Processing time per unit: Worker 1	Processing time per unit: Worker 2	Raw material cost per unit
A	$30(each)	15 min.	20 min.	$18
B	32	15	20	22
C	30	5	30	18
D	32	5	30	22

One Worker 1 and one Worker 2 operate on each shift. Three shifts. Five days per week. Eight hours per shift. Operating expenses $3,000 per week.

SOLUTION

As in the previous example, there are three answers to this question, depending on each of the following objectives:

1. Maximize revenue for sales personnel, who are paid on commission.
2. Maximize per unit gross profit.
3. Maximize the utilization of the bottleneck resource (leading to maximum gross profit).

Objective 1: Maximize sales commission on sales revenue. Sales personnel prefer to sell B and D (selling price $32) rather than A and C (selling price $30). Weekly operating expenses are $3,000.

The ratio of units sold will be: 1A : 10B : 1C : 10D.

Worker 2 on each shift is the bottleneck and therefore determines the output. Note that if this truly is a bottleneck with an unlimited market demand, this should be a seven-day-per-week operation, not just a five-day workweek.

$$5 \text{ days per week} \times 3 \text{ shifts} \times 8 \text{ hours} \times 60 \text{ minutes} = 7{,}200 \text{ minutes per week available}$$

Worker 2 spends these times on each unit:

A 20 minutes B 20 minutes C 30 minutes D 30 minutes

The ratio of output units is 1 : 10 : 1 : 10. Therefore,

$$1x(20) + 10x(20) + 1x(30) + 10x(30) = 7,200$$
$$550x = 7,200$$
$$x = 13.09$$

Therefore, the numbers of units produced are

A = 13 B = 131 C = 13 D = 131

Total revenue is

$$13(30) + 131(32) + 13(30) + 131(32) = \$9,164 \text{ per week}$$

For comparison with Objectives 2 and 3, we will compute gross profit per week.

Gross profit per week (selling price less raw material less weekly expenses) is

$$13(30-18) + 131(32-22) + 13(30-18) + 131(32-22) - 3,000$$
$$= 156 + 1,310 + 156 + 1,310 - 3,000$$
$$= (\$68)\text{loss}$$

Objective 2: Maximize per unit gross profit.

	Gross Profit	=	Selling Price	–	Raw Material Cost
A	12	=	30	–	18
B	10	=	32	–	22
C	12	=	30	–	18
D	10	=	32	–	22

A and C have the maximum gross profit, so the ratio will be 10 : 1 : 10 : 1 for A, B, C, and D. Worker 2 is the constraint and has

$$5 \text{ days} \times 3 \text{ shifts} \times 8 \text{ hours} \times 60 \text{ minutes} = 7{,}200 \text{ minutes available per week}$$

As before, A and B take 20 minutes, while C and D take 30 minutes. Thus

$$10x(20) + 1x(20) + 10x(30) + 1x(30) = 7,200$$
$$550x = 7,200$$
$$x = 13$$

Therefore, the number of units produced is

$$A = 131 \quad B = 13 \quad C = 131 \quad D = 13$$

Gross profit (selling price less raw materials less $3,000 weekly expense) is

$$\begin{aligned} &131(30 - 18) + 13(32 - 22) + 131(30 - 18) + 13(32 - 22) - 3,000 \\ &\quad = 1,572 + 130 + 1,572 + 130 - 3,000 \\ &\quad = \$404 \text{ profit} \end{aligned}$$

Objective 3: Maximize the use of the bottleneck resource, Worker 2. For every hour Worker 2 works, the following numbers of products and gross profits result.

(1) Product	(2) Production Time	(3) Units Produced per Hour	(4) Selling Price Each	(5) Raw Material Cost per Unit	(6) Gross Profit per Hour (3) × [(4) – (5)]
A	20 minutes	3	$30	$18	$36
B	20	3	32	22	30
C	30	2	30	18	24
D	30	2	32	22	20

Product A generates the greatest gross profit per hour of Worker 2 time, so the ratio is 10 : 1 : 1 : 1 for A, B, C, and D.

Available time for Worker 2 is the same as before:

$$3 \text{ shifts} \times 5 \text{ days} \times 8 \text{ hours} \times 60 \text{ minutes} = 7{,}200 \text{ minutes}$$

Worker 2 should produce 10 As for every 1 B, 1 C, and 1 D. Worker 2's average production rate is

$$\begin{aligned} 10x(20) + 1x(20) + 1x(30) + 1x(30) &= 7,200 \\ 280x &= 7,200 \\ x &= 25.7 \end{aligned}$$

Therefore, the number of units that should be produced is

$$A = 257 \quad B = 25.7 \quad C = 25.7 \quad D = 25.7$$

Gross profit (price less raw materials less $3,000 weekly expenses) is

$$\begin{aligned} &257(30 - 18) + 25.7(32 - 22) + 25.7(30 - 18) + 25.7(32 - 22) - 3,000 \\ &\quad = 3,084 + 257 + 308.4 + 257 - 3,000 \\ &\quad = \$906.40 \end{aligned}$$

In summary, using three different objectives to decide how many of each product to make gave us three different results:

1. Maximizing sales commission resulted in a $68 loss in gross profit.
2. Maximizing gross profit gave us a profit of $404.
3. Maximizing the use of the capacity-constrained worker gave us the best gross profit: $906.40.

Both examples demonstrate that production and marketing need to interact. Marketing should sell the most profitable use of available capacity. However, to plan capacity, production needs to know from marketing what products could be sold.

EXAMPLE 23.3 TOC Applied to Bank Loan Application Processing[3]

In this example, Goldratt's Theory of Constraints five-step approach (see Exhibit 23.2) to removing bottlenecks is applied to a bank loan application process. As can be seen through the example, the ideas can be applied to all types of applications, including service processes.

Step 1: Identify the system constraint. Assume that the bank is a private-sector institution and that its goal is to make more money now and in the future. Furthermore, suppose that the initial constraint is internal, namely, the loan officers are unable to carry out all of their responsibilities in a timely manner. That is, given the current demand for bank loan application processing, the loan officers are unable to perform all of the steps in the loan approval process in a responsive manner that is viewed as satisfactory by its customers.

Step 2: Decide how to exploit the system constraint. Once a constraint is identified, management must effectively maximize the usage of the constraint's capacity and capability to fulfill the system's goal. By calculating the throughput yield per unit of time at the constraining resource, management has the information necessary to prioritize the work performed at the constraint. For example, the loan department manager could measure the throughput yield associated with each hour spent working on each type of loan request, such as home mortgage, automobile, and small business. The sequence of loans processed at the constraint would then be established by the "profitability" of the different types of loans so that the bank's goal can be expeditiously met. An optional approach to exploitation that complements prioritization is assuring that the constraint is always being effectively utilized. Thus, it may be possible to redesign the loan approval process so that some of the loan officers' current workload is offloaded to available personnel who are currently only being partially utilized.

Step 3: Subordinate everything else to the preceding decisions. Subordination involves aligning all of the nonconstraint resources in support of maximizing the performance of the constraint resource. In this case, the bank management would want to schedule appointments for potential customers seeking to complete their loan applications with bank agents so that there was always an abundant supply of completed loan requests waiting for the loan officers to process. Also, the manager of the bank's loan approval process would control the release of loan applications into the approval process so that the loan officers were not overwhelmed. Finally, the bank would have a non–fully occupied clerk assure that each application was complete and met process quality standards prior to being given to the loan officers. (Note that having a supply of finished applications available assured a highly productive usage of loan officer time; this approach to subordination would produce only a small increase in throughput. It would move the bank toward its goal; the constraint would remain with the loan officers.)

Step 4: Elevate the constraint. Elevating the constraining resource means adding enough new capacity so that the current constraint no longer limits system throughput. In contrast to the previous two steps, elevation often requires a monetary outlay or investment for new resources or capabilities. In the bank's loan subsystem illustration, despite increases in loan officer productivity that were presumed to result from steps 2 and 3, the system constraint has remained with the bank's loan officers. Thus, because these improvements were insufficient to break the constraint, it is necessary to address the constraining factor directly. The obvious step is to hire an additional loan officer. This action elevates the existing constraint by providing more than sufficient capacity to meet existing demand for processing loan applications. While this decision would produce a sizable increase in operating expenses, it could be justified by management as the best approach to meeting their process goal as well as the bank's overall goal.

Step 5: Return to step 1, but do not allow inertia to cause a system constraint. After the original constraint has been overcome in step 4, it is necessary to revisit all of the changes made in steps 2 and 3 to determine if they are still appropriate to effective process and system performance. In the loan example, a review of the implemented changes in step 2 might show that offloading the responsibilities for assembling the loan package and some of the credit checking activities to bank clerical personnel was working well and that there is no need to go back to the original procedure. With regard to step 3, although the bank might still seek to aggressively schedule bank agents to meet with customers to help them complete their loan applications, it might not be possible to have a large inventory of loan requests in progress because the constraint in the loan application and approval process had shifted to the marketplace. Thus, it is appropriate to return to step 1 of the five-step focusing process.

Extending the process. Exhibit 23.16 shows how the application of the five-step focusing process might realistically unfold in managing the bank's loan application process over the next couple of years. Elevating the capacity of the original approval process constraint by hiring a new loan officer leads to a new constraint. This time it resides in the marketplace. Suppose this new constraint turns out to be a policy constraint, namely, bank management does not extend consumer loans to clients who do not use the bank's credit card services. Reconsideration of this policy leads to an exemption for a bank customer who has had any type of an account at the bank for at least the past year. Next, because there are insufficient monetary reserves to fund all of the approved loads, the new system constraint resides in the supply of capital. To address this new constraint, assume that the bank negotiates for additional funds from a wholesale lender and is now able to provide more loans than customers are currently demanding. Now, a new market constraint develops because the monetary supply of funds is greater than the demand in the marketplace. With some effort, the bank marketing team is able to break this constraint by creating a special loan product-service bundle to serve the needs of local university students. Finally in this example, the constraint shifts back inside the bank's loan approval process, where the loan officers and bank clerks are unable to process applications fast enough to keep up with demand. Bank management purchases a new software package that has been designed to augment loan application processing and fully trains the loan officer staff and clerical assistants on its use.

Exhibit 23.16

Sequential Application of the Five-Step Focusing Process in Managing the Bank's Loan Subsystem

Constraint Location	Constraint Type	Constraint Identification	Approach to Constraint Alleviation
Bank loan application process	Physical	Loan officers and bank clerks are unable to process all customer loan applications in a timely manner.	Some loan officer tasks offloaded to clerks and additional loan officers hired. Now sufficient capacity exists in the loan application process.
Marketplace	Policy	Current bank policy: If a loan applicant does not have a credit card account with the bank, then he or she is not eligible to apply for a consumer loan.	New bank policy: Every loan applicant must have some type of active account with the bank. Now demand for loans increases because more potential applicants qualify.
Supply	Physical	The availability of funds is insufficient to meet all approved customer loan requests.	Bank negotiates for additional funds from wholesale lenders. Now capital reserves are greater than customers are demanding.
Marketplace	Policy	Loan markets are saturated relative to current loan products, and excess funds are available to loan to qualified customers.	Bank develops new loan product designed for local college students. Now total demand for loans in the marketplace increases.
Bank loan application process	Physical	Loan officers and bank clerks are unable to process all customer loan applications in a timely manner.	Bank invests in the acquisition of a new software package to facilitate loan application processing. Now process capacity exceeds demand.

Source: Richard A. Reid, "Applying the TOC Five-Step Focusing Process in the Service Sector: A Banking Subsystem," *Managing Service Quality* 17, no. 2 (2007), pp. 209–234. Copyright © 2007 Emerald Group Publishing Ltd.

CONCEPT CONNECTIONS

LO 23–1 Explain the Theory of Constraints (TOC)

Summary

- Eli Goldratt developed his Theory of Constraints as an alternative way to think about improving processes. His ideas have stimulated thought by practitioners due to their applicability to many areas, including production, distribution, and project management.
- His underlying philosophy is that it is essential to concentrate on system limitations imposed by capacity-constrained resources, and for a firm to make money, it must systematically remove these limitations.
- He argues that, to do this, the firm must simultaneously increase throughput, reduce inventory, and reduce operating expenses. He argues that improving labor productivity will not necessarily make money for the firm, and will only do so when it increases throughput, reduces inventory, or reduces operating expenses.
- Goldratt argues that trying to maintain perfectly balanced capacity leads to many problems because this makes every resource dependent on every other. Since statistical fluctuations are inherent in any process, perfect balance leads to disruptions. He argues that not capacity, but flow through the process, should be balanced.

Key Terms

Synchronous manufacturing A production process coordinated to work in harmony to achieve the goals of the firm.

Throughput The rate at which money is generated by the system through sales (Goldratt's definition).

Inventory All the money that the system has invested in purchasing things it intends to sell (Goldratt's definition).

Operating expenses All the money that the system spends to turn inventory into throughput (Goldratt's definition).

Productivity A measure of how well resources are used. According to Goldratt's definition (see Chapter 23), all the actions that bring a company closer to its goals.

LO 23–2 Analyze bottleneck resources and apply TOC principles to controlling a process

Summary

- Managing the flow through the bottlenecks is essential to the TOC synchronous manufacturing approach.
- Bottlenecks are identified by calculating the expected utilization (percentage of capacity used) for each resource.
- Saving time on a bottleneck resource is the only way to increase throughput.
- A technique that paces work through the system according to the speed of the bottleneck is used to manage flow through the system.

Key Terms

Bottleneck A resource that limits the capacity or maximum output of the process.

Nonbottleneck Any resource whose capacity is greater than the demand placed on it (Goldratt's definition).

Capacity-constrained resource (CCR) A resource whose utilization is close to capacity and could be a bottleneck if not scheduled carefully (Goldratt's definition).

LO 23–3 Compare TOC to traditional approaches

- MRP uses a backward scheduling approach and is oriented toward meeting due dates and maximizing the use of capacity.
- JIT pulls material based on need, but does not allow much flexibility for changes, particularly when capacity is tight.
- Synchronous manufacturing (TOC) is more flexible and focused on maximizing flow through the system while minimizing cost.

- In order for TOC to be successfully applied, the firm must recognize how it can be in conflict with conventional accounting and marketing/sales thought. Traditional cost accounting is based on a goal of fully utilizing resources and minimizing cost. This can be in direct conflict with TOC goals, which include maximizing profit by improving throughput.

LO 23–4 Evaluate bottleneck scheduling problems by applying TOC principles

Summary

- TOC can be used to schedule production. The solutions are often very different compared to those using conventional rules such as discussed in Chapter 22.

SOLVED PROBLEMS

LO23–4

Here is the process flow for Products A, B, and C. Products A, B, and C sell for $20, $25, and $30, respectively. There are only one Resource X and one Resource Y, which are used to produce A, B, and C for the numbers of minutes stated on the diagram. Raw materials are needed at the process steps as shown, with the costs in dollars per unit of raw material. (One unit is used for each product.)

The market will take all that you can produce.

a. Which product would you produce to maximize gross margin per unit?

b. If sales personnel are paid on commission, which product or products would they sell and how many could they sell?

c. Which and how many product or products should you produce to maximize gross profit for one week?

d. From part (*c*), how much gross profit would there be for the week?

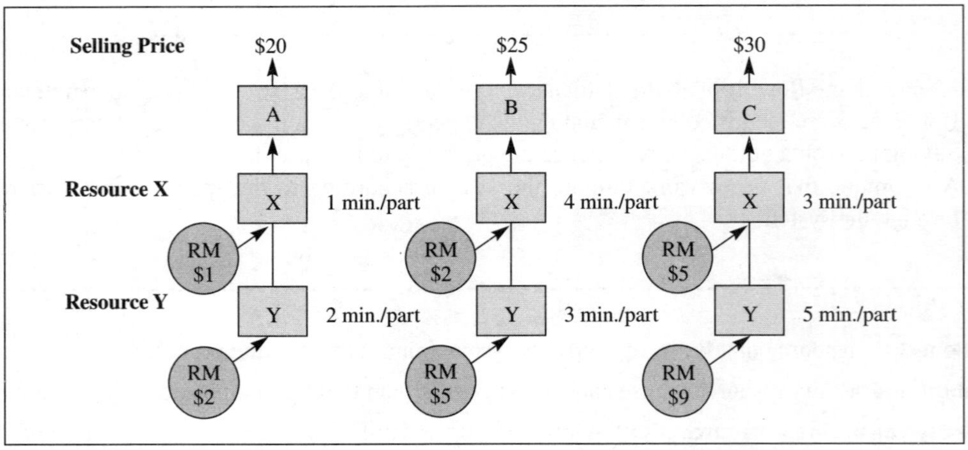

Solution

a. Maximizing gross margin per unit:

	Gross Margin	=	Selling Price	–	Raw Material Cost
A	17	=	20	–	3
B	18	=	25	–	7
C	16	=	30	–	14

Product B will be produced.

b. Maximizing sales commission: Sales personnel would sell the highest-priced product, C (unless they knew the market and capacity limitations). If we assume the market will take all that we can make, then we would work 7 days/week, 24 hours/day. Y is the constraint in producing C. The number of C we can make in a week is

$$C = \frac{24 \text{ hours/day} \times 7 \text{ days/week} \times 60 \text{ minutes/hour}}{5 \text{ minutes/part}}$$

$$= 2,016 \text{ units}$$

c. To maximize profit, we need to compare profits per hour for each product:

(1) Product	(2) Constraint Resource	(3) Production Time on Resource	(4) Number of Units Output per Hour	(5) Selling Price ($)	(6) RM Cost ($)	(7) Gross Profit per Hour (4) × (5 − 6)
A	Y	2	30	20	3	$510
B	X	4	15	25	7	270
C	Y	5	12	30	14	192

If the constraining resource were the same for all three products, our problem would be solved and the answer would be to produce just A, and as many as possible. However, X is the constraint for B, so the answer could be a combination of A and B. To test this, we can see that the value of each hour of Y while producing B is

$$\frac{60 \text{ minutes/hour}}{3 \text{ minutes/unit}} \times (\$25 - 7) = \$360/\text{hour}$$

This is less than the $510 per hour producing A, so we would produce only A. The number of units of A produced during the week is

$$\frac{60 \text{ minutes/hour} \times 24 \text{ hours/day} \times 7 \text{ days/week}}{2 \text{ minutes/unit}} = 5,040$$

d. Gross profit for the week is 5,040 × $17 = $85,680.
Solved using profit per hour: $510 × 24 × 7 = $85,680.

DISCUSSION QUESTIONS

1. How does Goldratt's Theory of Constraints (TOC) differ from other current approaches to continuous improvement in organizations? How is it similar? **LO 23–1**
2. State the global performance measurements and operational performance measurements and briefly define each. How do these differ from traditional accounting measurements?
3. Most manufacturing firms try to balance capacity for their production sequences. Some believe this is an invalid strategy. Explain why balancing capacity does not work.
4. Individually or in a small group, examine your own experiences either working in a company or as a customer of a company. Describe an instance where TOC was successfully applied to improve a process, or where you saw the potential for TOC to improve the process. **LO 23–2**
5. Discuss why transfer batches and process batches often may not and should not be equal.
6. Discuss process batches and transfer batches. How might you determine what the sizes should be?
7. Define and explain the cause or causes of a moving bottleneck.

8. Explain how a nonbottleneck can become a bottleneck.
9. Discuss the concept of "drum–buffer–rope."

LO23-3

10. Compare and contrast JIT, MRP, and synchronized manufacturing, stating their main features, such as where each is or might be used, amounts of raw materials and work-in-process inventories, production lead times and cycle times, and methods for control.
11. Compare the importance and relevance of quality control in JIT, MRP, and synchronous manufacturing.
12. Discuss how a production system is scheduled using MRP logic, JIT logic, and synchronous manufacturing logic.
13. Discuss what is meant by forward loading and backward loading.
14. Define *process batch* and *transfer batch* and their meaning in each of these applications: MRP, JIT, and bottleneck or constrained resource logic.
15. From the standpoint of the scheduling process, how are resource limitations treated in an MRP application? How are they treated in a synchronous manufacturing application?
16. What are operations people's primary complaints against the accounting procedures used in most firms? Explain how such procedures can cause poor decisions for the total company.

LO23-4

17. As an individual or small group, visit your favorite fast-food restaurant during lunch period. As you order, and while you are eating, observe as much of the process as you can. Where are the bottlenecks in the system? What recommendations can you come up with to relieve them?
18. When making decisions about what product(s) to produce in a manufacturing system, why is it not enough to simply consider the selling prices and demands for different items?

OBJECTIVE QUESTIONS

LO23-1

1. What is the name of the software Goldratt developed to implement his idea of TOC?
2. What are the three financial measurements necessary to adequately measure a firm's performance?
3. What is the term that refers to the entire production process working in harmony to achieve the profit goals of the firm?
4. What classic operational measurement does Goldratt redefine as "all the actions that bring a company closer to its goals"?

LO23-2

5. The following production flow shows Parts O, Q, and T; Subassembly U; and the final assembly for Product V.

   M to N to O
   P to Q
   R to S to T
   O and Q to U
   U and T to V

   N involves a bottleneck operation, and S involves a capacity-constrained resource. Draw the process flow.
6. For the four basic configurations that follow, assume that the market is demanding product that must be processed by both Resource X and Resource Y for Cases I, II, and III. For Case IV, both resources supply separate but dependent markets; that is, the number of units of output from both X and Y must be equal.

   Plans are being made to produce a product that requires 40 minutes on Resource X and 30 minutes on Resource Y. Assume that there is only one of each of these resources and that market demand is 1,400 units per month.

How many hours of production time would you schedule for X and Y? What would happen if both were scheduled for the same number of hours? (Answer in Appendix D)

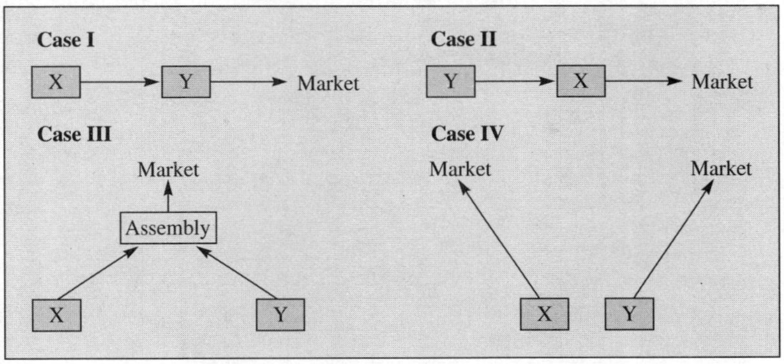

7. Following are the process flow sequences for three products: A, B, and C. There are two bottleneck operations—on the first leg and fourth leg—marked with an X. Boxes represent processes, which may be either machine or manual. Suggest the location of the drum, buffer, and ropes.

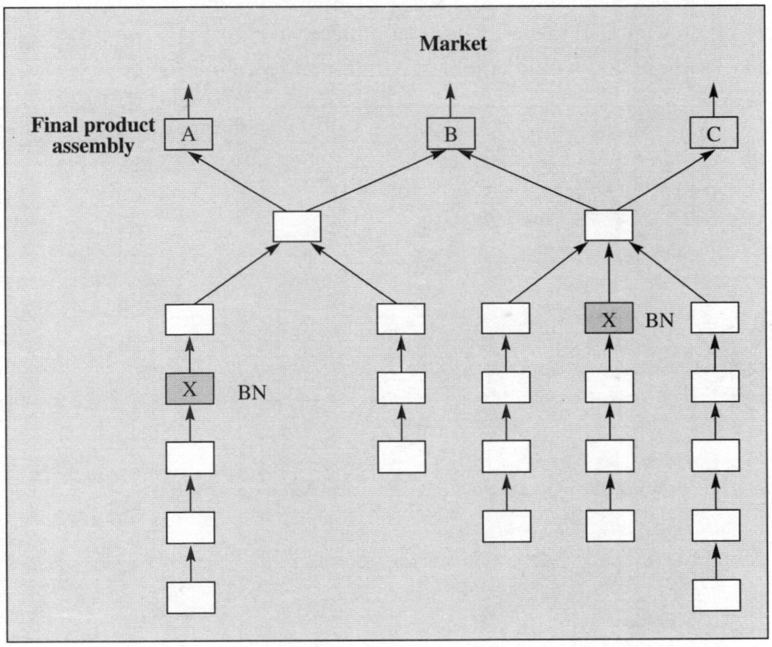

8. Willard Lock Company is losing market share because of horrendous due-date performance and long delivery lead times. The company's inventory level is high and includes many finished goods that do not match the short-term orders. Material control analysis shows that purchasing has ordered on time, the vendors have delivered on time, and the scrap/rework rates have been as expected. However, the buildable mix of components and subassemblies does not generally match the short-term and past-due requirements at final assembly. End-of-month expediting and overtime are the rule, even though there is idle time early in the month. Overall efficiency figures are around 70 percent for the month. These figures are regarded as too low.

   You have just been hired as a consultant and must come up with recommendations. Help the firm understand its problems. State some specific actions it should take. The product flow is shown in the following diagram.

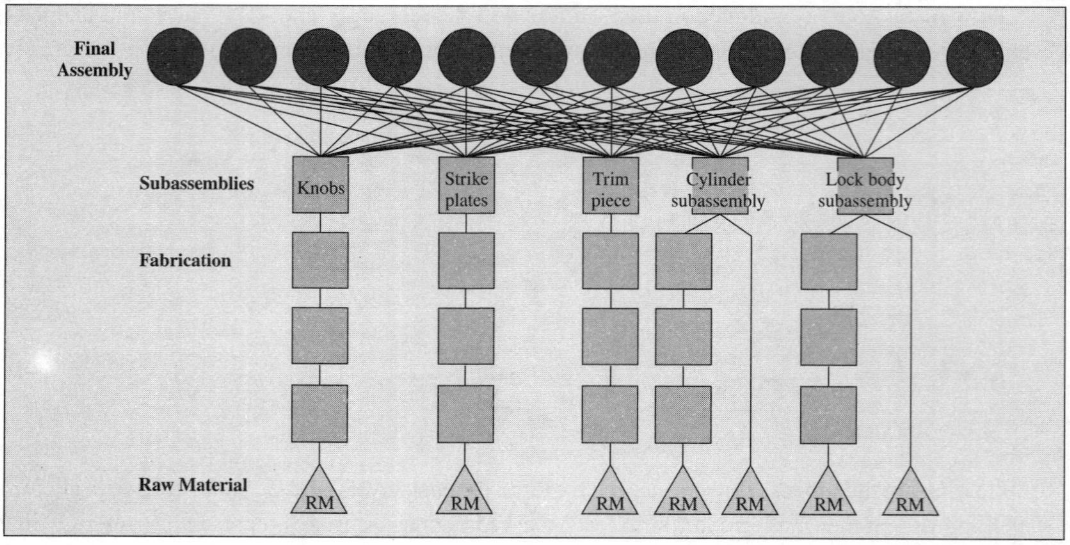

9. The accompanying figure shows a production network model with the parts and processing sequences. State clearly on the figure (1) where you would place inventory; (2) where you would perform inspection; and (3) where you would emphasize high-quality output.

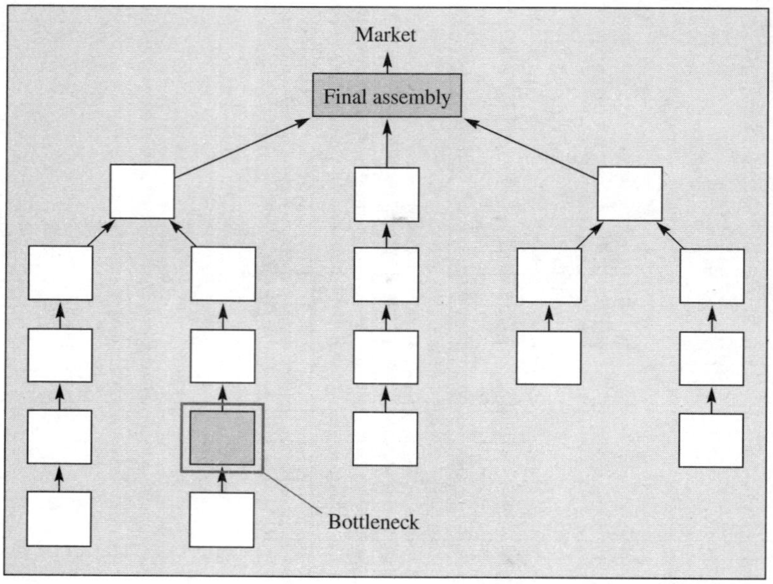

10. The following production flow shows Parts E, I, and N; Subassembly O; and the final assembly for Product P.

    A to B to C to D to E
    F to G to H to I
    J to K to L to M to N
    E and I to O
    N and O to P

    B involves a bottleneck operation, and M involves a CCR.

    a. Draw the process flow.
    b. Where would you locate buffer inventories?
    c. Where would you place inspection points?
    d. Where would you stress the importance of quality production?

11. Here are average process cycle times for several workcenters. State which are bottlenecks, non-bottlenecks, and capacity-constrained resources.

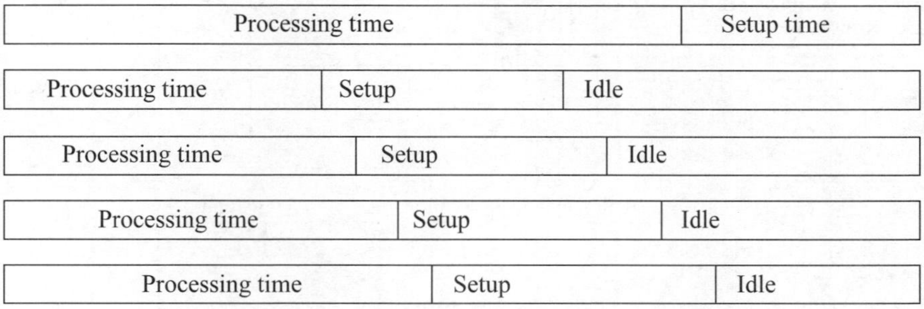

12. The following diagram shows the flow process, raw material costs, and machine processing time for three products: A, B, and C. There are three machines (W, X, and Y) used in the production of these products; the times shown are in required minutes of production per unit. Raw material costs are shown in cost per unit of product. The market will take all that can be produced.
    a. Assuming that sales personnel are paid on a commission basis, which product should they sell?
    b. On the basis of maximizing gross profit per unit, which product should be sold?
    c. To maximize total profit for the firm, which product should be sold?

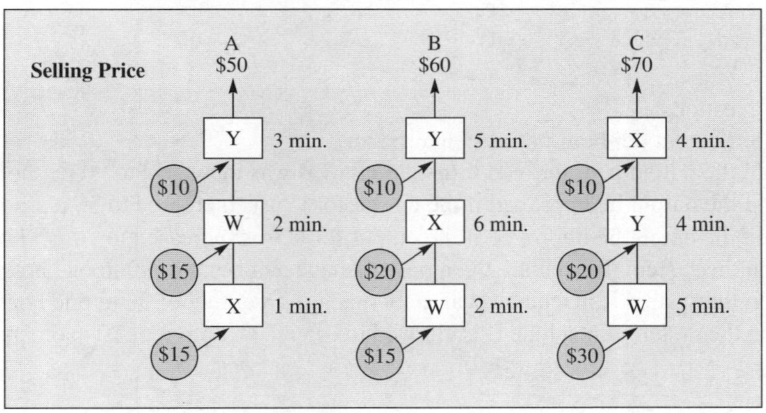

13. How does synchronous manufacturing differ from MRP with respect to scheduling? **LO 23–3**
14. JIT is limited to what type of manufacturing environment?
15. Cost accounting logic can lead managers to keep their resources busy all the time, increasing productivity with no regard to demand. What is the negative result from this effect?
16. The solution to coping with natural differences between marketing and production functions is to do what two things?
17. The M–N plant manufactures two different products: M and N. Selling prices and weekly market demands are shown in the following diagram. Each product uses raw materials with costs as shown. The plant has three different machines: A, B, and C. Each performs different tasks and can work on only one unit of material at a time. **LO 23–4**

    Process times for each task are shown in the diagram. Each machine is available 2,400 minutes per week. There are no "Murphys" (major opportunities for the system to foul up). Setup and transfer times are zero. Demand is constant.

    Operating expenses (including labor) total a constant $12,000 per week. Raw materials are not included in weekly operating expenses. (Answers in Appendix D)
    a. Where is the constraint in this plant?
    b. What product mix provides the highest profit?
    c. What is the maximum weekly profit this plant can earn?

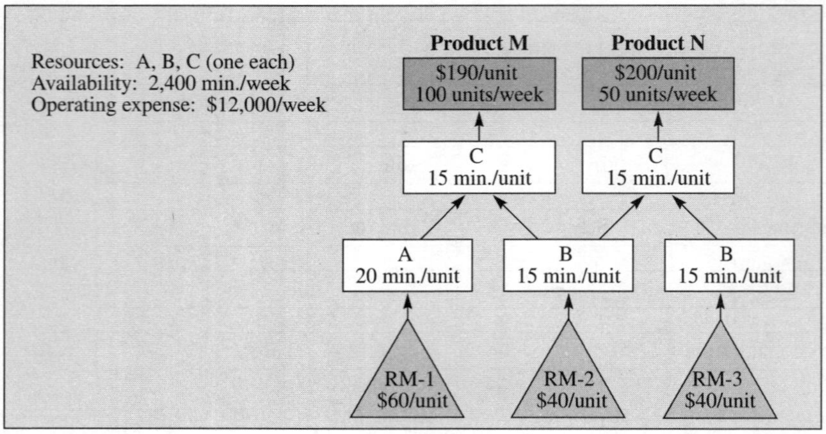

18. A steel product is manufactured by starting with raw material (carbon steel wire) and then processing it sequentially through five operations using machines A to E, respectively (see following table). This is the only use that the five machines are put to. The hourly rates for each machine are given in the table.

Operation:	1	2	3	4	5
Machine:	A	B	C	D	E
Hourly unit output rate:	100	80	40	60	90

Consider the following questions.

a. What is the maximum output per hour of the steel product?
b. By how much would the output be improved if the output of B was increased to 90 per hour?
c. By how much would the output be improved if the output for C was increased to 50 per hour?
d. By how much would the output be improved if the output for C was increased to 70 per hour?
e. What is the effect on the system if machine A can only manage an output of 90 in one hour?
f. What is the effect on the system if machine C can only manage an output of 30 in one hour?
g. What is the effect on the system if machine B is allowed to drop to an output of 30 in one hour?

PRACTICE EXAM

In each of the following, name the term defined or answer the question. Answers are listed at the bottom.

1. According to Goldratt, the goal of a firm is to do what?
2. At the operational level, Goldratt suggests that these three measures should guide decisions.
3. The goal related to these three measures is this.
4. Goldratt argues that, rather than capacity, this should be balanced.
5. This is any resource whose capacity is less than the demand placed on it.
6. Goldratt suggests that a production system should be controlled using these three mechanisms.
7. A bottleneck should have this placed in front of it to ensure it never runs out of work.
8. A rope is used for this purpose in controlling a production system.
9. To pace the production system, this is used.
10. This is a measure of the value of inventory and the time it stays within an area.

Answers to Practice Exam 1. Make money 2. Throughput, inventory, operating expenses 3. Increase throughput while simultaneously reducing inventory and reducing operating expense 4. Flow 5. Bottleneck 6. Drum, buffer, and rope 7. Buffer 8. Communication 9. Drum 10. Dollar days

For PowerPoint lecture slides, Solutions Manual, Test Bank, Data files for solved examples, Excel Templates, Step-by-Step Solved Examples in video format, Tutorial Videos and many more, scan the adjacent **QR code**, or **visit http://www.mhhe.com/sie-chase15e**

SECTION FIVE

Special Topics

IT'S NOT JUST APPLICABLE TO MANUFACTURING AND SERVICES

In this section of the book, we include chapters that show how the operations and supply chain management (OSCM) concepts that were developed in the rest of the book can be applied to specific industries. Concepts such as lean manufacturing, waste elimination, value chain analysis, and all others are applicable to all types of businesses, not just pure manufacturing or service companies.

Many of you may be interested in jobs in the financial industry, for example. Many of the processes used in this industry are repetitive, just like manufacturing processes. Take, for example, sending out a mutual fund prospectus to investors. These documents need to be prepared and printed, are stored in a warehouse with thousands of similar documents, and are then mailed to actual and potential investors at the proper time. Given the volume sent by a large company, such as Fidelity Investments, this process needs to be done quickly, in response to the needs of investors, and efficiently. This process has manufacturing and logistics elements, and companies can draw on the ideas studied here to minimize cost while delivering the documents quickly.

We study two specific industries: health care and consulting. We selected these because we know that many of you may be interested in pursuing careers in these areas. Part of the process of becoming a business professional is applying what you learn in new and different ways that go beyond the specific examples you studied in the classroom. These chapters are designed to help you develop this expertise.

Chapter 24

Health Care

LEARNING OBJECTIVES

LO 24-1 Understand health care operations and contrast these operations to manufacturing and service operations

LO 24-2 Exemplify performance measures used in health care

LO 24-3 Illustrate future trends in health care

THE INSTITUTE FOR HEALTH CARE OPTIMIZATION

The Institute for Health Care Optimization (IHO) is dedicated to applying the tools and methodologies that have been used in operations and supply chain management for years to the health care industry. Businesses have used tools such as queuing models and simulation to design operations and material flow to minimize cost and maximize quality. These same tools have not usually been applied for similar effect in the health care setting. The Institute for Health Care Optimization has been built on a multidisciplinary foundation that will bring together the science of operations management, clinical knowledge, analytical skills, and an understanding of organizational behavior in the health care field.

IHO Variability Methodology™ services are based on a unique three-phase approach for patient flow redesign for hospitals and other health care delivery organizations: **Phase 1**—Separate homogenous groups, such as elective versus nonelective and inpatient versus outpatient flows. The purpose is to reduce waiting times for urgent/emergency cases, increase throughput in the operating rooms and cath labs, decrease overtime, and decrease delays for scheduled cases. **Phase 2**—Smooth the flow of electively scheduled cases by decreasing the competition between unscheduled emergency procedures and elective scheduled procedures. The goal is to increase hospital-wide throughput, achieve consistent nurse-to-patient staffing, and increase patient placement in appropriate units. **Phase 3**—Estimate resource (e.g., beds, ORs, MRIs, staff) needs for each type of flow to ensure the right care at the right time and place for every patient.

Source: From the Institute for Health Care Optimization Website: www.ihoptimize.org.

A hospital is a combination care facility, hotel, restaurant, and store staffed by highly skilled professionals supported by semiskilled and low-skilled workers, using state-of-the-art technology and employing precise discipline to perform work of zero-defect quality on a heterogeneous population, all while trying to be affordable.

It's not easy . . .

Health care is the most intensive of service industries in the range of service activities and the impact these activities have on the customer. Nowhere is this more evident than in a hospital, where operational excellence is central to the clinical treatment of patients, the quality of their experience, and, of course, cost. This is particularly critical in the United States, where more than $2 trillion is spent on health care each year. It's not just high cost alone—recent surveys show that more than 55 percent of all Americans said they were dissatisfied with the quality of health care. Nevertheless, numerous health care organizations are innovative and excel in their operations performance. In this chapter, we will discuss some of the unique features of hospitals and health care centers and how OSCM concepts and tools are used to achieve outstanding results in this critical service industry.

LO 24-1

Understand health care operations and contrast these operations to manufacturing and service operations

THE NATURE OF HEALTH CARE OPERATIONS

Health care operations management may be defined as the design, management, and improvement of the systems that deliver health care services. Health care as a service is characterized by extensive customer contact, a wide variety of providers, and literally life or death as potential outcomes.

Health care operations management
The design, management, and improvement of the systems that create and deliver health care services.

The focus of our discussion of health care operations is the hospital, although everything here is also applicable to the smaller health care clinic. The standard definition of a **hospital** is a facility whose staff provides services relating to observation, diagnosis, and treatment to cure or lessen the suffering of patients. Observation involves studying patients and conducting tests to arrive at a diagnosis; diagnosis is the medical expert's explanation of the cause of a patient's symptoms; and treatment is the course of action to be followed based upon the diagnosis. All of the services provided in a hospital are generally organized around at least one of these three areas.

Hospital
A facility whose staff provides services relating to observation, diagnosis, and treatment to cure or lessen the suffering of patients.

The following are important factors that set hospitals' operations apart from other organizations:

- The key operators in the core processes are highly trained professionals (medical specialists) who generate requests for service (orders) but are also involved in delivering the service.
- The relationship between the prices that can be charged and actual performance is not as direct as in most other production environments. Quality and service measures are largely based on opinion rather than hard evidence.
- Hospitals do not have a simple line of command, but are characterized by a delicate balance of power between different interest groups (management, medical specialists, nursing staff, and referring doctors), each of them having ideas about what should be targets for operations performance.
- Production control approaches presuppose complete and explicit specifications of end product requirements and delivery requirements; in hospitals product specifications are often subjective and vague.
- Hospital care is not a commodity that can be stocked; the hospital is a resource-oriented service organization.

Classification of Hospitals

The American Hospital Association classifies hospitals as follows:

- *General hospital/emergency room*—Provides a broad range of services for multiple conditions.
- *Specialty*—Provides services for a specific medical condition; for example, cardiology (heart conditions).

- *Psychiatric*—Provides care for behavioral and mental disorders.
- *Rehabilitation*—Provides services focused on restoring health.

As in other industries, the complexity of hospital operations has a major impact on performance. In Exhibit 24.1, we have arrayed these four types of hospitals in a product–process framework matching range of health care product lines with complexity of operations. The inherent complexity of general hospitals is magnified by their need for physical size and extensive technology to handle a wide range of patient needs. Chris Hani Baragwanath Hospital is the largest hospital in the world, occupying 173 acres, with 3,200 beds and 6,760 staff members. The hospital is in the Soweto area of Johannesburg, South Africa. Specialty hospital facilities may be large as well, but they tend to have a narrower range of medical skills and technology onsite. An example would be the Johns Hopkins Hospital in Baltimore, which focuses on cancer patients. Psychiatric hospitals are in a sense specialty hospitals, but because their clinical focus is on the mind rather than the body, they are generally less technology-intense than those focusing on physical illnesses. An example of a psychiatric hospital is McLean Hospital, affiliated with Harvard University. It is well known for its patient list of famous people. Rehabilitation facilities are seen as least complex because, although they use technology, the type of work done is more custodial compared to the active treatment found in other hospitals. Veterans Administration hospitals are representative of this category.

EXHIBIT 24.1

Hospital Product–Process Framework

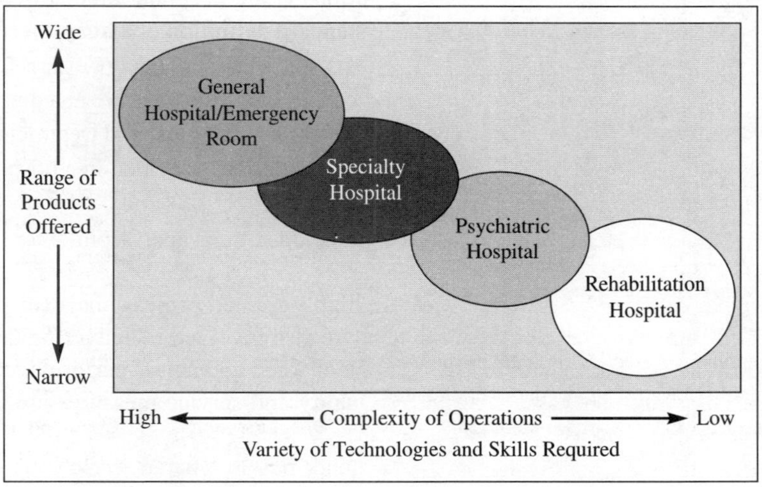

Hospital Layout and Care Chains

The layout sets the physical constraints on a hospital's operations. The goal of hospital layout is to move patients and resources through the units and floors to minimize wait and transport times. The layout can be determined using software models that minimize the total combined costs of travel of patients and staff. For those situations where the numerical flow of patients and staff does not reveal quantitative factors, manual methods such as systematic layout planning (discussed in the layout chapter) may be more appropriate.

A general rule for the design of a hospital is to separate patient and guest traffic flows from staff flows. Use of separate elevators and dedicated resource corridors is particularly important in avoiding congestion and delays. The principal element of the overall layout of a hospital is the nursing station, which is the area support staff work from. Many nursing stations are located in the hospital to support the various patient areas. Nursing stations today tend to be more compact shapes than the elongated rectangles of the past. Compact rectangles, modified triangles, or even circles have been used in an attempt to shorten the distance between the nursing station and the patient's bed. The choice depends on such issues as the organization of the nursing program, number of beds to a nursing unit, and number of beds to a patient room. The growth of more holistic, patient-centered treatment and environments is leading to modifications in layout to include providing small medical libraries and computer terminals so patients can research their conditions and treatments, and locating kitchens and dining areas in patient units so family members can prepare food for patients and families to eat together.

Care chain
The flow of work through a hospital consisting of the services for patients provided by various medical specialties and functions, within and across departments.

Decoupling points
Stages in the process where waiting takes place, either before or after the procedure is performed.

The flow of work through a hospital is sometimes referred to as a **care chain**, consisting of the services for patients provided by various medical specialties and functions, within and across departments. Exhibit 24.2 lists typical characteristics of care chain processes for key patient groups within general surgery. A major distinction among health care processes shown in the exhibit is the extent to which access to medical treatment and resources can be scheduled efficiently. Emergency situations such as trauma must be dealt with immediately, require rapid access to medical staff, and, as a result, are inherently inefficient. Elective procedures, on the other hand, can be scheduled to achieve more efficient use of resources. The number of steps, the time of each step, and whether the care chain has a definite end affects resource use and schedule complexity. A chronic condition, for example, may lack a clearly identifiable ending. Complexity is also increased by the need for rapid diagnostics, extensive consultation, and the need to work with other specialties. **Decoupling points** are steps in the process where waiting takes place, either before or after the procedure is performed. For many operations, it is after diagnosis; for trauma cases, it might be after the emergency treatment and when the patient is transferred from the recovery room to a ward.

Exhibit 24.2

Characteristics of Processes/Care Chain in a Typical General Surgery Unit

Characteristic of Process/Care Chain	Trauma Patients	Cancer (Oncology) Patients	Joint Replacement Patients
Emergency or elective	Emergency	Elective	Elective
Urgency	High	Moderate	Low
Volume	High	Medium	High
Short, long, or chronic treatment	Short	Chronic	Short
Diagnostic requirements	Immediate	Ongoing	Ongoing
Consultation requirements	Limited time possible	Involved	Little
Number of specialties involved	Depends on situation	Many	Few
Bottleneck	Operating room	Operating room	Operating room
Decoupling point	After surgery	Diagnosis	Diagnosis

A work flow diagram of a care chain is shown in Exhibit 24.3. It focuses on the contacts between the patient and the provider for surgery such as a hip replacement. The actual flow can be lengthier, as when the patient wants a second opinion, and we have left out recuperation at home. Also omitted are process flow modifications resulting from, say, the patient's medical tests indicating a particular issue like a drop in blood pressure. In this case, the patient can either be processed serially by different specialties (e.g., blood pressure first and hip replacement second), in parallel (blood pressure and hip replacement at the same time with one specialty assisting the other), or as a team (both specialties present in the operating room to work at the same time).

Tracking of Workflow Using RFID Radio frequency identification uses electronic tags that can store, send, and receive data over wireless frequencies. They are now being used in a few of the more progressive hospitals to track the location of patients, medical staff, and physical assets as they move through the hospital. Among the benefits of using RFID for patient flow are improvement of

EXHIBIT 24.3

Care Chain Diagram of Hip Replacement Surgery

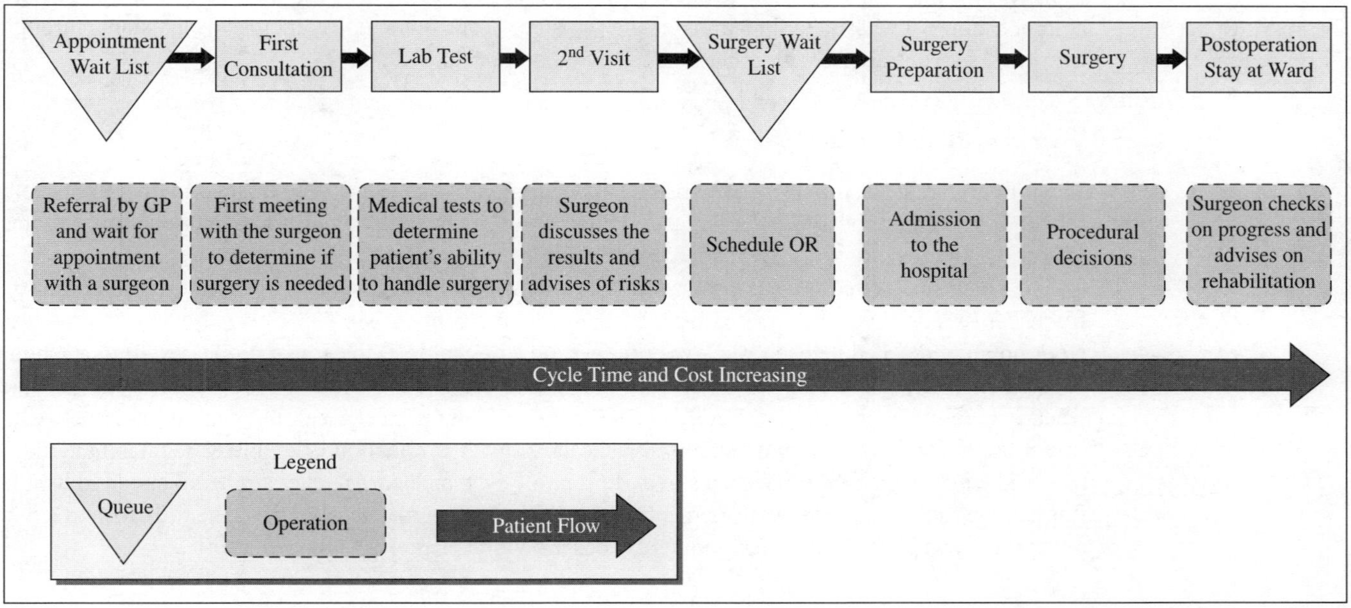

the patient check-in process and tighter links between patient and medical records. For example, RFID readers placed on doors throughout the hospital can automatically detect patients as they pass through. With this knowledge, clerks can determine where bottlenecks are likely to occur and redirect patients to other treatment areas if the process is not sequence dependent. Thus, for example, rather than waiting in the cardiology department for a cardiogram, a hip replacement patient could be sent to X-ray for a required test where there is no waiting. With regard to physical assets, RFID can pinpoint the location of equipment such as gurneys, portable X-ray machines, and wheelchairs to help get them to the patient when needed. In addition, knowing where each piece of equipment is can save hours that are spent at the end of the day conducting "equipment round-ups."

Capacity Planning

Capacity planning entails matching an organization's resources to current and future demand. Determination of the resource requirements is primarily a function of the number of customers in the hospital's local market and the length of stay. Length of stay can be shortened by technologies and process management, which can increase patient throughput. In health care, capacity is measured in terms of multiple resources including beds, clinics, and treatment rooms; availability of physicians, nurses, and other providers, medical technologies, and equipment such as X-ray machines; facility space such as hallways and elevators; and various support services such as cafeteria and parking.

The starting point in developing a capacity plan is determining the effective capacity of a resource over some period of time. This is accomplished by multiplying design capacity (which is the capacity if the resource is operated continuously) by the average utilization rate. The formula is

$$\text{Effective capacity} = \text{Design capacity} \times \text{Utilization}$$

For example, if average utilization is 70 percent on an X-ray machine that could operate 24 hours per day, 7 days a week, then its effective capacity per day is 16.8 hours per day (24 hours × 0.7 = 16.8 hours). It should be noted that the 70 percent utilization figure is in line with the 70 percent utilization target common to companies seeking a high level of service. The subsequent steps consist of (1) forecasting patient demand by hour, location, specialty, and so on; (2) translating this demand, adjusted by productivity estimates, into capacity requirements; (3) determining the current capacity level in terms of hours of staff, facilities, and equipment; (4) calculating the gap between demand and capacity on a per-hour basis; and (5) developing a strategy to close the gap. This can be done by several common approaches, including transferring capacity from other units, increasing capacity through overtime, subcontracting with other hospitals, and bottleneck reduction.

Workforce Scheduling

The primary areas of importance in hospital scheduling are nurse shift scheduling and operating room scheduling. Nurses constitute the largest component of the hospital's workforce, and operating rooms (or surgical suites) are typically the largest revenue-generating centers.

The nurse shift schedules can be classified as either permanent (cyclical) or flexible (discretionary). In *cyclical scheduling,* the work is usually planned for a four- to six-week period, where employees work on a fixed schedule each week over the period (for example, the conventional fixed, five 8-hour days each week). Several types of *flexible scheduling* are used, but the most popular is the flexible week, where nurses maintain 8-hour days and average 40 hours per week but can alternate between, say, 8 hours for four days and 8 hours for six days. Both cyclical and flexible schedules have their pros and cons, though the edge seems to go to flexible systems because they are better suited to handle fluctuations in demand, as well as meeting the desires of nurses to change from full- to part-time. Several personnel scheduling techniques are described in Chapter 22.

Quality Management and Process Improvement

Ever since the work of Florence Nightingale (see the OSCM at Work box later in this section), hospitals have been seeking ways to achieve quality and process improvement. TQM approaches have been a staple for decades, and within the past few years Six Sigma and lean concepts are being instituted in many hospitals. Hospital personnel are well suited to analytics of TQM because so much of health care involves precise measuring of patient responses to drugs and clinical procedures.

Gap Errors and Bottlenecks Two problems that get frequent attention in quality programs are dealing with gap errors and bottlenecks. *Gap errors* are information mistakes that arise when a task is transferred or handed off between people or groups. Many professional routines, such as formal handoff procedures between shifts of nurses and physicians are designed to bridge gaps. Handoffs may be as significant a source of serious patient harm as are medication-related events. In a study of formal handoff procedures, 94 percent of the handoffs were conducted face-to-face, more than half of the 161 residents surveyed reported that they were rarely done in a quiet, private setting, and over a third reported frequent interruptions. One successful approach to managing handoffs is the SBAR (Situation-Background-Assessment-Recommendation) checklist technique for communicating information about a patient's condition between members of the health care team. Adapted from a program used to provide quick briefings of nuclear submariners during a change in command, SBAR is an easy-to-remember tool for framing any conversation requiring a clinician's immediate attention and action.

As discussed elsewhere in the book, a *bottleneck* is that part of the system that has the smallest capacity relative to the demand on it. Bottlenecks frequently result from individual departments optimizing their own throughput—the number of patients or procedures per hour—without considering the effects on upstream or downstream departments. If changes are made to improve parts of a system without addressing the constraint, the changes may not result in a reduction of delays and waiting times for the entire system. To identify the constraint, observe where the work is piling up or where lines are forming, and perform some simple calculations. For example, Exhibit 24.4 shows the capacity of the five processes in a preoperative clinic at Beth Israel Deaconess Medical Center in Boston. (Note that nursing is the bottleneck.)

The handbook provides suggestions for eliminating bottlenecks. These are presented in Exhibit 24.5.

OSCM AT WORK

Florence Nightingale, Hospital Quality Improvement Pioneer

Long before Deming, Crosby, and the other industrial quality gurus, Britain's Florence Nightingale was leading a quality revolution in hospitals. During the Crimean War, the British public was shocked by reports of the terrible conditions of British hospitals, and Nightingale, founder of the modern profession of nursing, was sent to Scutari, Turkey, to improve them. In addition to overseeing the introduction of nurses to the hospitals, she also led the effort to improve sanitary conditions in the hospitals. Central to her approach was collecting, tabulating, interpreting, and graphically displaying data relating to process care changes on outcomes. (She is credited as being the developer of the pie chart.) For example, to quantify the overcrowding of hospitals, she compared the amount of space per patient in London hospitals, 1,600 square feet, to that in Scutari, 400 square feet. She also developed a standard statistical form to enable the collection of data for analysis and comparison. The results of these innovations were astounding: The mortality of patients decreased from 42 percent in February 1855 to 2.2 percent in June of that year. Nightingale's approach, termed *evidence-based medicine,* underlies current approaches to medical practices.

EXHIBIT 24.4

Pre-op Clinical Capacity at Beth Israel Deaconess Medical Center

	Anesthesia	Nursing	Phlebotomy	EXG	X-ray
Total process (minutes including paperwork)	15	18	8	10	9
Estimated capacity (number of visits per day) with breaks, calls, lunch	48	36	58	42	On-call
Range of visits per day (4-day period)	27–45	23–11	22–41	11–30	7–21
Average number of visits per day (4-day period)	35	27	29	20	14

EXHIBIT 24.5

Diagnoses and Remedies for Eliminating Bottlenecks

How to Manage the Constraint	Diagnoses (Dxs)	Remedies (Rxs)
Constraints should not have idle time.	The doctor is in the exam room waiting to see the first patient of the day while the patient is being registered.	Register the patient after the exam.
If experts are the constraint, they should be doing only work for which an expert is needed.	In preoperative testing, patients are backed up waiting for the nurse (the constraint in the process).	The receptionist or assistant assumes tasks that are being done by the nurse but that do not require nursing skills.
Put inspection in front of a constraint.	On the day of the surgery, key X-rays are not available.	One person coordinates and expedites all necessary information on the day of the surgery.

Service Quality Hospitals, like other customer contact businesses, have been raising the level of their customer service to improve the patient experience. This has been shown to save money through reductions in malpractice suits, reductions in no-shows, and lower nurse turnover. The standard philosophy is an end-to-end customer focus. An example of this focus is at Good Samaritan Hospital in Los Angeles. When patients arrive at "Good Sam" for an appointment, rather than having to sit in a waiting room they are greeted at a modern hotel-like lobby and escorted directly to the unit of the hospital where they are to be treated. During their stay, efforts are made to ensure that their comfort needs are anticipated (such as having an extra pillow in the room), and before leaving a patient, every employee is to ask, "Is there anything else I can do for you?" In addition, hospital patients can use the Red Carpet Hospitality Program, which provides concierge-like services such as the ordering-in of meals from local restaurants and providing information about local accommodations and spas for families.

Health Care Supply Chains

Hospital Supply Chains Exhibit 24.6 presents a hospital supply chain, showing the flow of three essential resources: information, funds, and goods and services. Goods and services move downstream from manufacturers to distributors/third-party logistics providers (3PL) and retailers to the hospital warehouse to receiving to central stores, and then to nursing and patients. Cash/funds flow upstream. On a day-to-day basis, hospital supply chain management focuses on medical supplies and pharmaceutical supplies. Traditionally, these activities are operated as separate organizational units. The medical-surgical supplies are complex, and are ordered from multiple vendors and from manufacturers. For the pharmacy, the vast majority of medications come directly from the distributors. Very few ship directly from the manufacturer. Current approaches involve merging of the two procurement operations within one department to reduce the number of vendors and to get better transparency.

EXHIBIT 24.6

Health Care Supply Chain

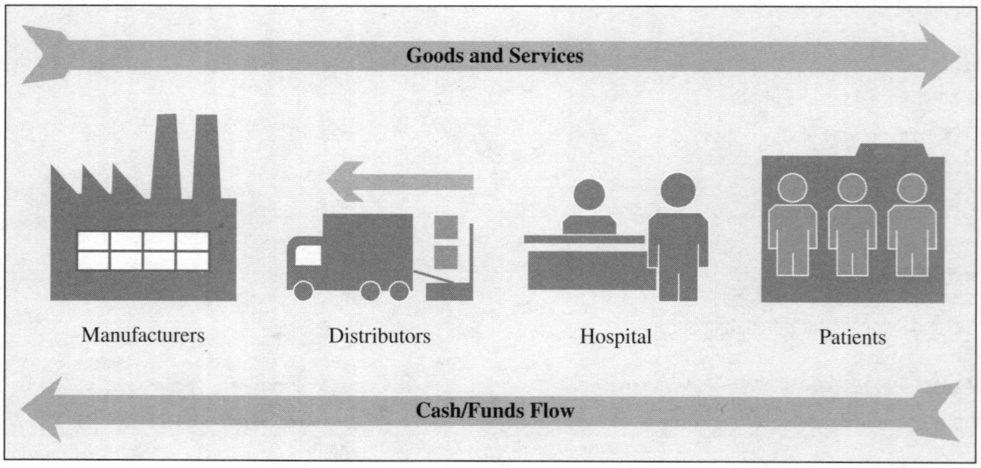

Physician-Driven Service Chains The widespread use of computerized physician order entry (CPOE) systems for prescriptions has led experts to propose broadening their application to include scheduling all resources needed by physicians to treat their individual patients. Called "event management," the way it works is that the admission order for a patient—for example, for a surgery procedure—triggers a series of follow-up events that are automatically entered into the information system (see Exhibit 24.7). The information system then initiates an admission date and books an operating room date, a surgical team (including an anesthesiologist and nurses), recovery room, and lab tests. These activities and processes are linked as well. For example, an electronically issued lab order for blood work is routed directly to the phlebotomist, who then draws and ships blood to the lab for analysis. Lab managers use the information to batch orders. Behind the scenes, accounting transactions are generated for billing insurance companies, recording copayments, placing purchase orders for supplies, and so on.

EXHIBIT 24.7

Supply Chain Event Management

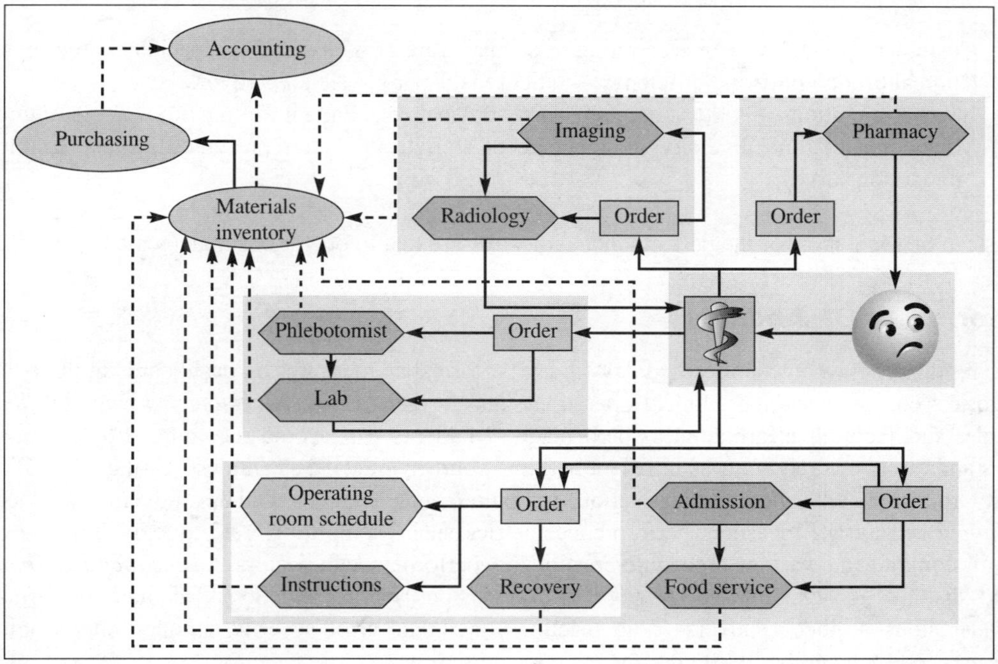

Inventory Management

Average inventory for medium-size hospitals is about \$3.5 million. It represents 5 to 15 percent of current assets and 2 to 4 percent of total assets; typically, inventory is the largest working capital requirement. The cost of inventory is directly related to the hospital's case mix. A case-mix index is calculated based on classifications such as **diagnosis-related groups (DRGs)**.

Diagnosis-related groups (DRGs)
Homogeneous units of hospital activity for planning and costing surgeries—essentially a bill of labor and materials.

DRGs classify patients by diagnosis or surgical procedure (sometimes including age) into major diagnostic categories (each containing specific diseases, disorders, or procedures) based on the premise that treatment of similar medical diagnoses generate similar costs. Over 1,000 DRGs have been developed for Medicare as part of the payment system.

Hospital inventory management systems can be broken down into two general categories: push systems, consisting of fixed–order quantity systems and fixed–time period systems (covered in Chapter 20), and pull systems, using just-in-time delivery (covered in Chapter 14). The basic difference between the two categories is that push systems either place reorders for a set amount in anticipation of need (fixed–order quantity systems) or count inventory at set time periods and place orders to bring inventory to a predetermined level (fixed–time period systems). Pull systems, by contrast, have mechanisms called pull signals to supply inventory just-in-time (JIT) for use. Push systems make sense when a hospital owns its own inventory or buys in bulk and then breaks it down to distribute to nursing units or floors when required. JIT makes sense for expensive items such as implants, which are supplied by a partner vendor on a pull-system basis.

A major distinction between health care inventory management and that of other businesses is planning safety stock. The standard calculation of safety stock is predicated on trading off the cost of carrying an additional unit of inventory with the cost of being out of stock. In a department store, we can easily balance the cost of holding too many pairs of jeans with the cost (or lost profit) caused by running out of them. In hospitals, such trade-offs are much trickier when faced with balancing the cost of holding, say, a unit of type A blood with the cost of running out of it. The problem with estimating the cost of a stockout in a hospital is that consequences such as prolonged patient pain or even (though rarely) a threat to the life of the patient may be an issue. For critical items, backup contingency plans such as borrowing from a nearby hospital are often developed.

LO 24-2

Exemplify performance measures used in health care

PERFORMANCE MEASURES

The following are typical indicators used to measure performance at a health care clinic:

- Customer satisfaction—Survey rating of primary care provided and subspecialty care provided.
- Clinical productivity and efficiency—Patient visits per physician per workday.
- Internal operations—Patient complaints per 1,000 patients. Patient waiting time for appointments.
- Mutual respect and diversity—Percentage of staff from underrepresented groups. Employee satisfaction survey.

As can be seen, most of the performance indicators are tied to operations management.

Performance Dashboards

Current practice is to present detailed day-to-day performance measures on dashboards in three major categories: customer service, clinical operations, and key processes. A *customer service dashboard* provides such scoring information as percentage of patients who would recommend the hospital to others and rating of such items as inpatient parking, courtesy of staff, cleanliness, caring of staff, meal quality, follow-up education and instruction, and pain management, as well as an overall satisfaction. A *clinical dashboard* measures performance metrics such as mortality rate, quality improvement, readmission rate, and various procedure-specific key performance indicators. A *key process dashboard* would display, for example, percentage of transfusions having reactions, accurate performance of transfusions protocols, adverse drug reactions, medicine error severity, autopsy rate, employee exposures to blood and bodily fluids, and code response times.

LO 24-3

Illustrate future trends in health care

TRENDS IN HEALTH CARE

Among the major trends in health care that relate to OSCM are the following.

Evidence-based medicine (EBM): EBM is the application of the scientific method to evaluate alternative treatment methods and create guidelines for similar clinical situations. Essentially, it is the development of standard methods for therapeutic interventions.

Integrated medical care: Developed by the Mayo Clinic, this approach has a number of philosophical as well as operational features, including staff/team work with multispecialty integration, unhurried examination with time to listen to the patient, the hospital physician taking personal responsibility for directing patient care over time in a partnership with the local physician, and integrated medical records with common support services for all patients.

Electronic medical records: Digital technologies are revolutionizing the way patient records are gathered and stored. For example, emergency department doctors and nurses at Kaiser Permanente in Oakland carry flat computer tablets that can access every patient's entire medical record. These tablets also enable doctors and nurses to call up medical test records and X-rays right at the patient's bedside. Similar technologies are now within the reach of smaller medical practices with handheld tablet PCs for medical records being sold by Walmart.

Health information exchanges (HIEs): HIEs provide the capability to electronically move clinical information over various kinds of information systems while maintaining the meaning of the information being exchanged. For example, the Indiana Health Information Exchange (IHIE) allows physicians to track in real time those patients who are due for preventive screenings and chronic disease follow-up care.

Computer-assisted diagnosis: This approach uses expert system software programs to arrive at a diagnosis. Suppose the doctor with a child patient who has pain in the joints wants to determine its most likely cause. The expert system matches the child's symptoms with the criteria tables for each type of illness and reaches diagnostic conclusions at three different levels of certainty: definite,

OSCM AT WORK

Remote Doctor Consultation!

You broke your ankle playing tennis yesterday afternoon. What a mess—the whole joint dislocated and three broken bones. The doctor says that it might be a year before you are back to normal. Your surgery was performed last night. No pain right now, but the medication coming through that tube connected to your arm may be the reason for that.

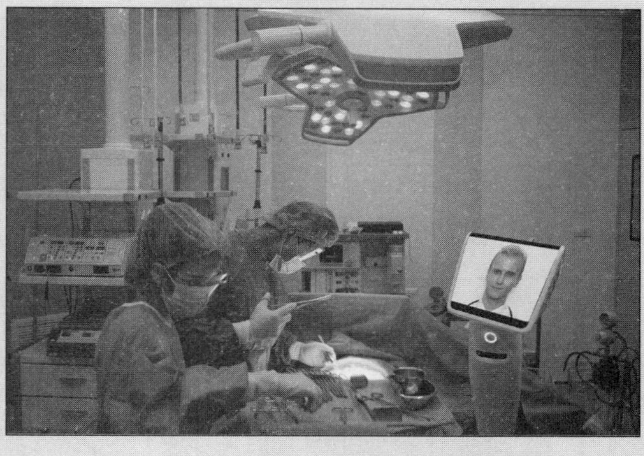

The Remote Presence Robot (RP-7) is a mobile telemedicine unit that connects doctors and specialists in real time through computers equipped with cameras and microphones.

The doctor wanted to get the surgery done last night since he was leaving for vacation early this morning. Just prior to going under the knife, he assured you that everything would be fine and that he would talk to you in the morning. He is 700 miles away by now, so how could this be?

The nurse comes in and asks how things are going. She says the doctor wants to talk and asks if I am up for that. "Sure," I say, but I am still unsure how this can be done. "No problem, I'll be right in with the doctor" says the nurse. The nurse rolls in a device like I had never seen before. It looks to be a little over 5 feet high and has a computer monitor on top.

I hear a voice say, "Hi, how are you doing?" I look up and sure enough there is my doctor on the screen. He tells me about how well the surgery went. He describes how he put a plate in my ankle and seven screws to hold everything together. He explains that it is going to take time for all of this to heal and that after six months he would probably do another surgical procedure and take the plate and screws out. It is all part of the process. He said he would check in with me again tomorrow morning and that it might be four or five days before I could leave the hospital. Also, I should let the nurses know if I am feeling any pain. He assured me that he was connected to the gadget through an app and that the nurses could contact him quickly, even better than if he were at the local office.

This type of electronic physician assistant gives the doctor direct access to current data related to the patient—heart rate, blood pressure, sleep and active periods, and current drugs being administered. In many ways, this is even better than the old way of doing hospital rounds. Everything is at the doctor's finger tips; the information is in real-time and accurate.

The "Remote Presence Robot" is a reality and is being used by many hospitals today. Physician-to-patient communication is now possible regardless of whether a physician is out of town or out of the country. Doctors can now make rounds off-site or from their office any time of the day via an app on the physician's cell phone. Patients are still monitored by the hospital nursing staff, but now they have a direct link to the doctor via the app with real-time ability to communicate.

Many patients are impressed with the new technology as it gives doctors the ability to provide better coverage to patients, rather than everything being done face-to-face. For example, the doctor is now able to connect and see the patient when family members are visiting. This is so much better when the need to communicate with the family is critical.

probable, and possible. If the diagnosis is suggested at the "possible" level, the system recommends looking for further clues to exclude or include it.

Remote diagnosis: Called *telemedicine,* it uses electronic devices for measuring blood pressure, heart rate, blood oxygen levels, and so on, for diagnosing patients who are far from the hospital. This is especially valuable in areas where few specialists are available to rapidly diagnose a patient's problem.

Robots: Robots are being used in the operating room for a range of illnesses that include breast cancer and gall bladder removal. In using robots, surgeons employ a tiny camera to guide them as they manipulate the robot's instruments from a console. Benefits of robots are that their "hands" are steady and they have a wide range of motions, which can result in less pain and blood loss than with manual surgery. An interesting low-tech robotic application is Mr. Rounder, described in the OSCM at Work box.

CONCEPT CONNECTIONS

LO 24–1 Understand health care operations and contrast these operations to manufacturing and service operations

Summary

- Health care is an industry that requires operational excellence. The focus of this discussion was hospitals, but these ideas are also applicable to more specialized clinics.
- Hospitals are categorized in a manner similar to the way production processes are, using the product/process matrix. Layouts, capacity management, quality and process improvement, supply chains, and inventory, all in the context of hospitals, are described.

Key Terms

Health care operations management The design, management, and improvement of the systems that create and deliver health care services.

Hospital A facility whose staff provides services relating to observation, diagnosis, and treatment to cure or lessen the suffering of patients.

Care chain The flow of work through a hospital consisting of the services for patients provided by various medical specialties and functions, within and across departments.

Decoupling points Stages in the process where waiting takes place, either before or after the procedure is performed.

Diagnosis-related groups (DRGs) Homogeneous units of hospital activity for planning and costing surgeries—essentially a bill of labor and materials.

LO 24–2 Exemplify performance measures used in health care

Summary

- A diverse set of performance measures are used in health care.
- In addition to traditional customer satisfaction and worker (physician) productivity measures, other ways to capture patient mortality, and follow-ups from the administration of procedures, for example, may be used.

LO 24–3 Illustrate future trends in health care

Summary

- The application of new technologies drives change in the health care area.
- The integration of information, remote and computer-assisted diagnosis, and the use of remotely controlled robots have all resulted in dramatic changes in productivity, while improving the quality of patient care.

DISCUSSION QUESTIONS

1. Where would you place Shouldice Hospital on the product–process framework (see the Chapter 5 case, "Shouldice Hospital—A Cut Above")? What are the implications of adding a specialty such as cosmetic surgery? **LO24–1**
2. Think about your latest trip to a hospital/health care facility. How many different handoffs did you encounter? How would you rate the quality of the service relative to the patient experience and relative to that of the friends and family?
3. Some have argued that, for hospitals, both medical schools and nursing schools should be considered part of the supply chain. Do you agree?
4. Hospitals are major users of poka-yoke (fail-safe) devices. Which ones can you think of that would apply?
5. Could a hospital or physician offer a service guarantee? Explain.
6. How does a physician-driven supply chain differ from a typical materials supply chain?
7. What could a hospital learn from benchmarking a Ritz-Carlton Hotel? Southwest Airlines? Disneyland?
8. As in manufacturing, productivity and capacity utilization are important performance measures in health care operations. What are the similarities and differences in how these measures might be used in the two different industries? **LO24–2**
9. What would you consider to be the most important performance measure in a hospital? Explain.
10. As the "baby-boomer" generation ages, the percentage of the U.S. population over age 65 will grow at a faster rate than the size of the workforce paying taxes and health insurance premiums. How do you expect that to impact health care operations and supply chain management? **LO24–3**

OBJECTIVE QUESTIONS

1. In manufacturing, quality measures are largely based on hard evidence. In health care, what are quality and service measures largely based on? **LO24–1**
2. A general rule of designing hospital layouts is to separate patient/visitor flow from what? (Answer in Appendix D)
3. What is the term used to refer to the flow of work through a hospital?
4. What inventory-related term is used to refer to points in a health care process where waiting takes place, either before or after treatment takes place?
5. What type of worker constitutes the largest component of the hospital's workforce?
6. In hospitals, dashboards are often used to display performance measures on a routine basis. What type of dashboard tracks metrics such as mortality rate, quality improvement, and readmission rates? (Answer in Appendix D) **LO24–2**
7. What dashboard would display metrics such as accurate performance of transfusion protocols and code response time?
8. Remote diagnosis uses electronic devices for diagnosing patients at a distance. What is another term used to refer to this practice? **LO24–3**
9. What is the term used to describe arrangements to move clinical information across various information systems while still maintaining the meaning of the information being exchanged?
10. What is the term used to refer to the application of the scientific method to evaluate alternative treatment methods and create guidelines for similar clinical situations?

CASE: Managing Patient Wait Times at a Family Clinic

You have a job assisting the Medical Director at a Family Medical Clinic in New York City. The Medical Director is concerned about the long wait times of patients visiting the clinic and would like to improve operations. The following are facts about the clinic:

- The patients are seen in the clinic between the hours of 9:00 A.M. and 12:00 P.M. and between 1:00 and 5:00 P.M.
- On average the clinic sees 150 patients per day.
- Nine physicians are usually on duty to see patients at the clinic. Physicians arrive at 9:00 A.M. and are on duty until 5:00 P.M. with a one-hour break during the day.
- They are supported by seven medical assistants who take vital signs and put patients in exam rooms.
- Four registration clerks are present to register patients, enroll them in federal and local aid programs, prep their medical records, and collect copayments.
- There are three coordinators who make follow-up appointments and arrange referrals. Coordinators see patients from 9:00 A.M. until 5:30 P.M., with a one-hour break during the day.
- There is one security guard who is available from 7 A.M. to 6 P.M.
- There is one pharmacist, and two pharmacy technicians. The pharmacy is open from 9:00 A.M. to 5:30 P.M., with a lunch break from noon to 1:00.
- The facility itself has a security window at the front door with a guard-controlled entry door, a large waiting area, five registration windows, 11 provider rooms (3 of which are used for taking vitals and 8 by physicians for exams), and four coordinator's desks.

Patient Flow Through the Clinic

An average of 120 patients have appointments at the clinic each day. An additional 30 patients come for prescription refills each day.

Step 1—Security/Check-in
When patients arrive, they all must first pass through security. Often, there is a small wait outside at the door. The average wait time at security is 10 minutes, while the average processing time is 2 minutes. The guard at the door double-checks the appointment time and issues the patient a colored card with a number on it—either red or yellow. Red cards are reserved for patients without appointments who need only medication refills. These patients must pass through registration but do not need to see a provider.

Step 2—Registration
All patients then proceed to the waiting room where they wait for their color and number to be called. This wait can often be quite long, but on average takes 24 minutes.

Once patients are called by a registration clerk, their information is verified. This process can take anywhere from 1 minute up to 40 minutes if the patient is new and needs to be enrolled in several programs. On average, eight new patients come per day. The average time to complete registration is 7 minutes for returning patients and 22 minutes for new patients, with an overall average registration time of 8 minutes. Patients seeking medication refills (with red cards) proceed directly to the pharmacy (step 6) after registration.

Step 3—Vitals
The yellow card patients return to the waiting area and wait another 15 minutes to be called by a medical assistant to have their vital signs taken. This takes 6 minutes, after which they return again to the waiting area.

Step 4—Doctor Visit
Patients wait 8 minutes more in the waiting room and are then called back to a provider room. Once in a provider room, the patient waits 17 minutes, on average, for the provider (doctor) to arrive. Providers spend approximately 20 minutes with each patient.

Step 5—Coordinator/Follow-up
After the patient has seen the doctor, the patient's chart goes to a coordinator. The patient waits 25 minutes to be called by a coordinator who schedules further laboratory tests, get referrals to specialists, and makes follow-up appointments, which takes an additional 7 minutes.

On average, 50 percent of patients with appointments (yellow cards) continue onto the pharmacy following their medical visit.

Step 6—Pharmacy

If the patient needs a prescription, the wait is 13 minutes before the pharmacy calls them to process the prescription, with an average of 11 minutes spent filling the prescription. Each pharmacy technician works independently and fills the prescription after consulting the pharmacist.

In general, patient satisfaction with the quality of medical services at VFC remains high, but there are still complaints each day about the waiting times for these services. Wait times are critical for these patients, because they often directly lead to lost income during the hours spent waiting.

The Physicians' Workflow

Each physician is assigned to a team; A, B, or C. These groups of two or three physicians all see the same patients, helping to ensure continuity for the patients. Each patient, therefore, will see one of the team's physicians at any given visit and has a higher likelihood of seeing the same doctor each time.

Physicians arrive at 9:00 A.M. and wait for their first patients to arrive. Often, due to the lag at registration and the wait for open rooms for the medical assistants to take vitals, patients are not in the exam rooms until well after 9:30.

In addition, because of the team system, one provider may have three patients waiting, while another is still waiting for his or her first patient to check in at registration. The registration desk has no communication link to the physicians' area or other form of coordination; so clerks may check in three patients in a row for one team, but none for another. Added to this, new patients are randomly assigned to teams regardless of who is busiest that day.

Once a patient is in an exam room, the chart is placed in a rack for the physician to review prior to seeing the patient. If key lab report or X-ray results are missing, the physician must call for medical records or call outside facilities and wait for the results to be faxed or called in before seeing the patient. This happens 60 to 70 percent of the time, causing a 10-minute delay per patient. These challenges often lead to inefficient use of the provider's time.

After seeing a patient, the physician will either have the patient wait in the waiting room to see the coordinator or have the patient wait in the exam room for further testing or nursing procedures. Rarely, if no follow-up or prescriptions are needed, the patient is free to leave the clinic.

The physicians generally are extremely committed to the clinic's mission but are frustrated with their patients' long wait times, the incomplete medical records, and the disorganized patient flow through the clinic.

The Registration Clerks' Workflow

At the start of each day, the four registration clerks prepare by printing out copies of that day's scheduled appointments. Charts of patients with appointments are pulled the night before and placed within easy reach of the clerks. The four clerks work from 8:30 until 11:00 A.M. and close the registration windows until 12:30 P.M. During this time, in addition to eating lunch, the clerks pull the charts for the afternoon clinic and finish up paperwork. At 12:30, the registration windows are reopened for the afternoon clinic and patients are checked in until 4:00 P.M.

Questions

1. Draw two process flow diagrams. One for the pharmacy customers, and another for the regular and new patients.
2. Calculate the capacity and utilization of each resource (people, rooms) and identify bottlenecks.
3. Calculate the average wait and time in service for patients with appointments (new and returning) and for those seeking a prescription refill.
4. What are your recommendations for improvement?

PRACTICE EXAM

In each of the following, name the term defined or answer the question. Answers are listed at the bottom.

1. A hospital consists of these three basic services. What are these?
2. The most complex type of health care facility.
3. The type of schedule where workers work on a fixed schedule each week over a four- to six-week period.
4. The hospital quality pioneer who is credited as the developer of the pie chart.

5. A term used to refer to information mistakes at handoffs.
6. A checklist technique developed by submariners that is now used in hospitals.
7. A widely used case-mix index classification scheme.
8. Use of the scientific method to develop standard methods for therapeutic interventions.
9. The two general categories of hospital inventory management systems.
10. A nickname for InTouch Health's RP-6 for Remote Presence.
11. Stage in a health care process where waiting takes place.

Answers to Practice Exam 1. Observation, diagnosis, and treatment 2. General hospital/emergency room 3. Cyclical schedule 4. Florence Nightingale 5. Gap error 6. SBAR (Situation-Background-Assessment-Recommendation) 7. Diagnosis-related groups 8. Evidence-based medicine 9. Push systems and pull systems 10. Mr. Rounder 11. Decoupling point

For PowerPoint lecture slides, Solutions Manual, Test Bank, Data files for solved examples, Excel Templates, Step-by-Step Solved Examples in video format, Tutorial Videos and many more, scan the adjacent **QR code**, or **visit http://www.mhhe.com/sie-chase15e**

Chapter 25

Operations Consulting

LEARNING OBJECTIVES

LO 25-1 Explain operations consulting and how money is made in the industry

LO 25-2 Illustrate the operations analysis tools used in the consulting industry

LO 25-3 Analyze processes using business process reengineering concepts

Pittiglio Rabin Todd & McGrath (PRTM)— A Leading Operations Consulting Company

Good business strategy plots changes in where a company is going. A winning operational strategy translates that direction into operational reality, creating strategic competitive advantage in the process. PRTM is a leading company specializing in finding ways to structure business operations to create breakout results in top-line growth, earnings, and valuation.

Today's operational CEOs realize that brilliant business strategies and operational strategies are interconnected. Business strategies drive the need for new operational capabilities, and evolving operational capabilities shape the future business strategies. PRTM Consultants focus on the following six essential ingredients of operational strategy:

- **Transform market forces into operational advantage.** This is the kind of insight that Black & Decker used to turn a regulatory requirement for double-insulated power tools into a new modular product platform that redefined cost and performance in category after category. The same type of insight helped Progressive Insurance transform automobile claims from an unproductive part of its cost structure into a far more economical and valued source of competitive advantage.
- **Do one thing extraordinarily well.** Consider the case of Apple iTunes. Its gigantic share of the digital music player market is fueled by Apple's relentless pursuit of ease of use as a basis of competition. Companies like Walmart are all about cost leadership, attaining the lowest end-to-end operational cost, and the highest productivity.

- **Think end-to-end, continuous, real time, and horizontally.** Every organization has a set of core operational domains that make up its operational model. For most, these comprise some combination of the product development chain, the supply chain, and the customer chain. Operational strategy configures these operational domains to deliver against business strategy, and create advantage in their own right.
- **Think and execute globally.** Due to global markets for products and the global availability of supply, many companies need to consider strategies that best position the firm to compete in this domain. Global opportunities are often the key driver to changes to both business and operational strategies.
- **Drive innovation in your operations and business model.** Peter Drucker defined innovation as change that creates a new dimension of performance. He also stated that a key accountability of the CEO is innovation. Too often, innovation is perceived to be a technical or product-oriented activity. The reality is that operational innovation is creating the commanding leaders today.
- **Execute relentlessly.** A complete operational strategy requires a commitment to execution. Companies with commanding leads in their markets execute relentlessly, informed by their global marketplace insight, and are aligned to a singular competitive focus, emboldened by a clear innovation intent, and guided by a sound operational model aligned with business strategy and business economics.

In the twenty-first century, companies that make all aspects of their operations a source of strategic innovation will dominate their markets, delivering unparalleled revenue growth, earnings performance, and shareholder return.

Source: Adapted from a statement by Tom Godward and Mark Deck, partners in PRTM's Worldwide Operational Strategy Practice, www.prtm.com.

Operations consulting has become one of the major areas of employment for business school graduates. The page cited from the PRTM Website nicely summarizes the importance of operations on bottom-line performance. In this chapter, we discuss how one goes about consulting for operations, as well as the nature of the consulting business in general. We also survey the tools and techniques used in operations consulting and provide an overview of business process reengineering because much OSCM consulting entails this activity.

LO 25-1 Explain operations consulting and how money is made in the industry

WHAT IS OPERATIONS CONSULTING?

Operations consulting Assisting clients in developing operations strategies and improving production processes.

Operations consulting deals with assisting clients in developing operations strategies and improving production processes. In strategy development, the focus is on analyzing the capabilities of operations in light of the firm's competitive strategy. It has been suggested that market leadership can be attained in one of three ways: through product leadership, through operational excellence, or through customer intimacy. Each of these strategies may well call for different operations capabilities and focus. The operations consultant must be able to assist management in understanding these differences and be able to define the most effective combination of technology and systems to execute the strategy. In process improvement, the focus is on employing analytical tools and methods to help operating managers enhance performance of their departments. Deloitte & Touche Consulting lists the actions to improve processes as follows: refine/revise processes, revise activities, reconfigure flows, revise policies/procedures, change outputs, and realign structure. We say more about both strategy issues and tools later. Regardless of where one focuses, *an effective job of operations consulting results in an alignment between strategy and process dimensions that enhances the business performance of the client.*

The Management Consulting Industry

The management consulting industry can be categorized in three ways: by size, by specialization, and by in-house and external consultants. Most consulting firms are small, generating less than $1 million in annual revenue. Relative to specialization, although all large firms provide a variety of services, they also may specialize by function, such as operations management, or by industry, such as manufacturing. Most large consulting companies are built on information technology (IT) and accounting work. The third basis for segmentation, in-house versus external, refers to whether a company maintains its own consulting organization or buys consulting services from the outside. Internal consulting arms are common in large companies and are often affiliated with planning departments.

Consulting firms are also frequently characterized according to whether their primary skill is in strategic planning or in tactical analysis and implementation. McKinsey & Company and the Boston Consulting Group are standard examples of strategy-type companies, whereas Gemini Consulting and A. T. Kearney focus rather extensively on tactical and implementation projects. The big accounting firms and Accenture are known for providing a wide range of services. The major new players in the consulting business are the large information technology firms such as Infosys Technology, Computer Sciences Corporation (CSC), Electronic Data Systems (EDS), and IBM. Consultancies are faced with problems similar to those of their clients: the need to provide a global presence, the need to computerize to coordinate activities, and the need to continually recruit and train their workers. This has led consultancies to make the hard choice of being very large or being a boutique firm. Being in the middle creates problems of lack of scale economies on the one hand and lack of focus and flexibility on the other.

The hierarchy of the typical consulting firm can be viewed as a pyramid. At the top of the pyramid are the partners or seniors, whose primary function is sales and client relations. In the middle are managers, who manage consulting projects or "engagements." At the bottom are juniors, who carry out the consulting work as part of a consulting team. There are gradations in rank within each of these categories (such as senior partners). The three categories are frequently referred to colloquially as the **finders** (of new business), the **minders** (or managers) of the project teams, and the **grinders** (the consultants who do the work). Consulting firms typically work in project teams, selected according to client needs and the preferences of the project managers and the first-line consultants themselves. Getting oneself assigned to interesting, high-visibility projects with good co-workers is an important career strategy of most junior consultants. Being in demand for team membership and obtaining quality consulting experiences are critical for achieving long-term success with a consulting firm (or being attractive to another firm within or outside consulting).

Finders
Partners or senior consultants whose primary function is sales and client relations.

Minders
Managers of a consulting firm whose primary function is managing consulting projects.

Grinders
Junior consultants whose primary function is to do the work.

Economics of Consulting Firms

The economics of consulting firms have been written about extensively by David H. Maister. In his classic article "Balancing the Professional Service Firm," he draws the analogy of the consulting firm as a job shop, where the right kinds of "machines" (professional staff) must be correctly allocated to the right kinds of jobs (consulting projects). As in any job shop, the degree of job customization and attendant complexity is critical. The most complex projects, which Maister calls *brain surgery* projects, require innovation and creativity. Next come *gray hair* projects, which require a great deal of experience but little in the way of innovation. A third type of project is the *procedures* project, where the general nature of the problem is well known and the activities necessary to complete it are similar to those performed on other projects.

Because consulting firms are typically partnerships, the goal is to maximize profits for the partners. This, in turn, is achieved by leveraging the skills of the partners through the effective use of midlevel and junior consultants. This is often presented as a ratio of partners to midlevel and junior consultants for the average project. (See Exhibit 25.1 for a numerical example of how profitability is calculated for a hypothetical consulting firm, Guru Associates.) Because most consulting firms

EXHIBIT 25.1

The Economics of Guru Associates

Level	No.	Target Utilization	Target Billable Hours @ 2,000 Hours per Person per Year	Billing Rate	Fees	Salary per Individual	Total Salaries
Partner (senior)	4	75%	6,000	$400	$2,400,000	(see calculations below)	
Middle	8	75%	12,000	$200	$2,400,000	$150,000	$1,200,000
Junior	20	90%	36,000	$100	$3,600,000	$ 64,000	$1,280,000
Totals					$8,400,000		$2,480,000
			Fees		$8,400,000		
			Salaries		(2,480,000)		
			Contributions		$5,920,000		
			Overhead*		$2,560,000		
			Partner profits		$3,360,000		
			Per partner		$ 840,000		

*Assume overhead costs of $80,000 per professional.

are engaged in multiple projects simultaneously, the percentage of billable employee hours assigned to all projects (target utilization) will be less than 100 percent. A practice that specializes in cutting-edge, high-client risk (brain surgery) work must be staffed with a high partner-to-junior ratio because lower-level people will not be able to deliver the quality of services required. In contrast, practices that deal with more procedural, low-risk work will be inefficient if they do not have a lower ratio of partners to juniors because high-priced staff should not be doing low-value tasks.

The most common method for improving efficiency is the use of uniform approaches to each aspect of a consulting job. Accenture, the company most famous for this approach, sends its new consultants through a boot camp at its St. Charles, Illinois, training facility. At this boot camp, it provides highly refined, standardized methods for such common operations work as systems design, process reengineering, and continuous improvement, and for the project management and reporting procedures by which such work is carried out. Of course, other large consulting firms have their own training methods and step-by-step procedures for selling, designing, and executing consulting projects.

When Operations Consulting Is Needed

The following are some of the major strategic and tactical areas where companies typically seek operations consulting. Looking first at manufacturing consulting areas (grouped under what could be called the *5 Ps of production*), we have

- *Plant:* Adding and locating new plants; expanding, contracting, or refocusing existing facilities.
- *People:* Quality improvement, setting/revising work standards, learning curve analysis.
- *Parts:* Make or buy decisions, vendor selection decisions.
- *Processes:* Technology evaluation, process improvement, reengineering.
- *Planning and control systems:* Supply chain management, ERP, MRP, shop-floor control, warehousing, distribution.

Obviously, many of these issues are interrelated, calling for systemwide solutions. Examples of common themes reflecting this are developing manufacturing strategy; designing and implementing JIT systems; implementing MRP or proprietary ERP software such as SAP; and systems integration involving client–server technology. Typical questions addressed are: How can the client cut lead times? How can inventory be reduced? How can better control be maintained over the shop floor?

Among the hot areas of manufacturing strategy consulting are sustainability, outsourcing, supply chain management, and global manufacturing networks. At the tactical level, there is a huge market for consulting in e-operations, product development, ISO 9000 quality certification, and design and implementation of decentralized production control systems.

Turning to services, while consulting firms in manufacturing may have broad specialties in process industries on the one hand and assembly or discrete product manufacture on the other, service operations consulting typically has a strong industry or sector focus. A common consulting portfolio of specialties in services (and areas of consulting need) would include the following:

Financial services (staffing, automation, quality studies)

Health care (staffing, billing, office procedures, phone answering, layout)

Transportation (route scheduling and shipping logistics for goods haulers, reservation systems, and baggage handling for airlines)

Hospitality (reservations, staffing, cost containment, quality programs)

For both manufacturing and service industries, the current hot area for consultants, as well as in-house teams, is Lean Six Sigma. The reason is companies have reached their limit on how much can be done by downsizing and are thus focusing on rigorously measuring and perfecting various processes. Pharmaceutical companies, large retailers, and food companies are examples of industries with heavy demand for consultants who specialize in such programs.

When Are Operations Consultants Needed? Companies typically seek out operations consultants when they are faced with major investment decisions or when they believe they are not getting maximum effectiveness from their productive capacity. As an example of the first type of situation, consider the following:

> A national pie restaurant chain retained consultants to determine if a major addition to its freezer storage capacity was needed at its pie-making plant. Its lease had run out on a nearby freezer warehouse, so the firm had to make a decision rather quickly. The pie plant manager wanted to spend $500,000 for a capacity increase. After analysis of the demand for various types of pies, the distribution system, and the contractual arrangement with the shipper, the consultant concluded that management could avoid all but a $30,000 investment in capacity if they did the following: Run a mixed-model production schedule for pies according to a forecast for each of 10 kinds of pies (for example, 20 percent strawberry, 30 percent cherry, 30 percent apple, and 20 percent other pies each two-day pie production cycle). To do this, more timely information about pie demand at each of the chain restaurants had to be obtained. This in turn required that information links for pie requirements go directly to the factory. Previously the distributor bought the pies and resold them to the restaurants. Finally, the company renegotiated pickup times from the pie plant to enable just-in-time delivery at the restaurants. The company was in a much stronger bargaining situation than it had been five years previously, and the distributor was willing to make reasonable adjustments.

The lesson from this is that few investment decisions in operations are all or nothing, and good solutions can be obtained by simply applying standard OSCM concepts of production planning, forecasting, and scheduling. The solution recognized that the problem must be viewed at a systemwide level to see how better planning and distribution could substitute for brick-and-mortar capacity.

THE OPERATIONS CONSULTING PROCESS

LO 25-2

Illustrate the operations analysis tools used in the consulting industry

The broad steps in the operations consulting process (see Exhibit 25.2) are roughly the same as for any type of management consulting. The major differences exist in the nature of the problem to be

Exhibit 25.2

Stages in the Operations Consulting Process

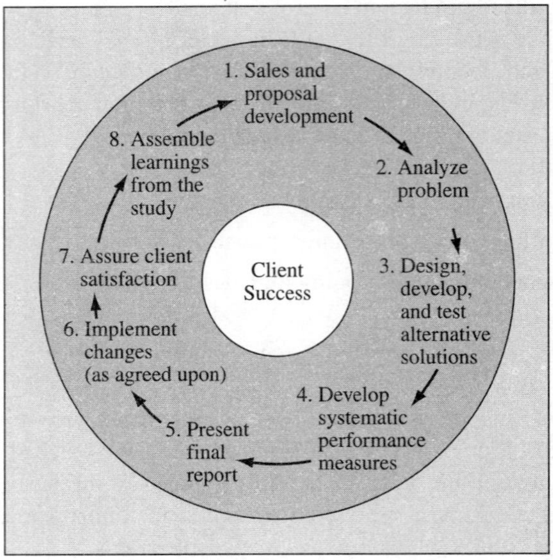

analyzed and the kinds of analytical methods to be employed. Like general management consulting, operations consulting may focus on the strategic level or tactical level, and the process itself generally requires extensive interviewing of employees, managers, and, frequently, customers. If there is one large difference, it is that operations consulting leads to changes in physical or information processes whose results are measurable immediately. General management consulting usually calls for changes in attitudes and culture, which take longer to yield measurable results. The roles in which consultants find themselves range from an *expert,* to a *pair of hands,* to a *collaborative or process consultant.* Generally, the collaborative or process consultation role is most effective in operations management consulting projects. Some consulting firms now provide the expert role online.

The steps in a typical operations consulting process are summarized in Exhibit 25.2. A book by Ethan M. Rasiel on the McKinsey & Company approach offers some practical guidelines for conducting consulting projects:

- Be careful what you promise in structuring an engagement. *Underpromise and overdeliver* is a good maxim.
- Get the team mix right. You can't just throw four random people at a problem and expect them to solve it. Think about what sorts of skills and personalities work best for the project at hand, and choose your teammates accordingly.
- The 80–20 rule is a management truth. Eighty percent of sales come from 20 percent of the sales force; 80 percent of your time is taken up with 20 percent of your job; and so on.
- Don't boil the ocean. Don't try to analyze everything—be selective in what you investigate.
- Use the elevator test. If you know your solution so well that you can explain it clearly and precisely to your client in a 30-second elevator ride, you are doing well enough to sell it to the client.
- Pluck the low-hanging fruit. If you can make an immediate improvement even though you are in the middle of a project, do it. It boosts morale and gives credibility to your analysis.
- Make a chart every day. Commit your learning to paper; it will help push your thinking and assure that you won't forget it.
- Hit singles. You can't do everything, so don't try. It's better to get to first base consistently than to try to hit a home run and strike out 9 times out of 10.
- Don't accept "I have no idea." Clients and their staff always know something, so probe them for some educated guesses.

- Engage the client in the process. If the client doesn't support you, the project will stall. Keep your clients engaged by keeping them involved.
- Get buy-in throughout the organization. If your solution is to have lasting impact on your client, you have to get support for it throughout the organization.
- Be rigorous about implementation. Making change happen takes a lot of work. Be rigorous and thorough. Make sure someone takes responsibility for getting the job done.

Operations Consulting Tool Kit

Operations consulting tools can be categorized as tools for *problem definition, data gathering, data analysis and solution development, cost impact and payoff analysis, and implementation.* These—along with some tools from strategic management, marketing, and information systems that are commonly used in OSCM consulting—are noted in Exhibit 25.3 and are described next. Note that several of these tools are used in more than one stage of a project.

EXHIBIT 25.3

Operations Consulting Tool Kit

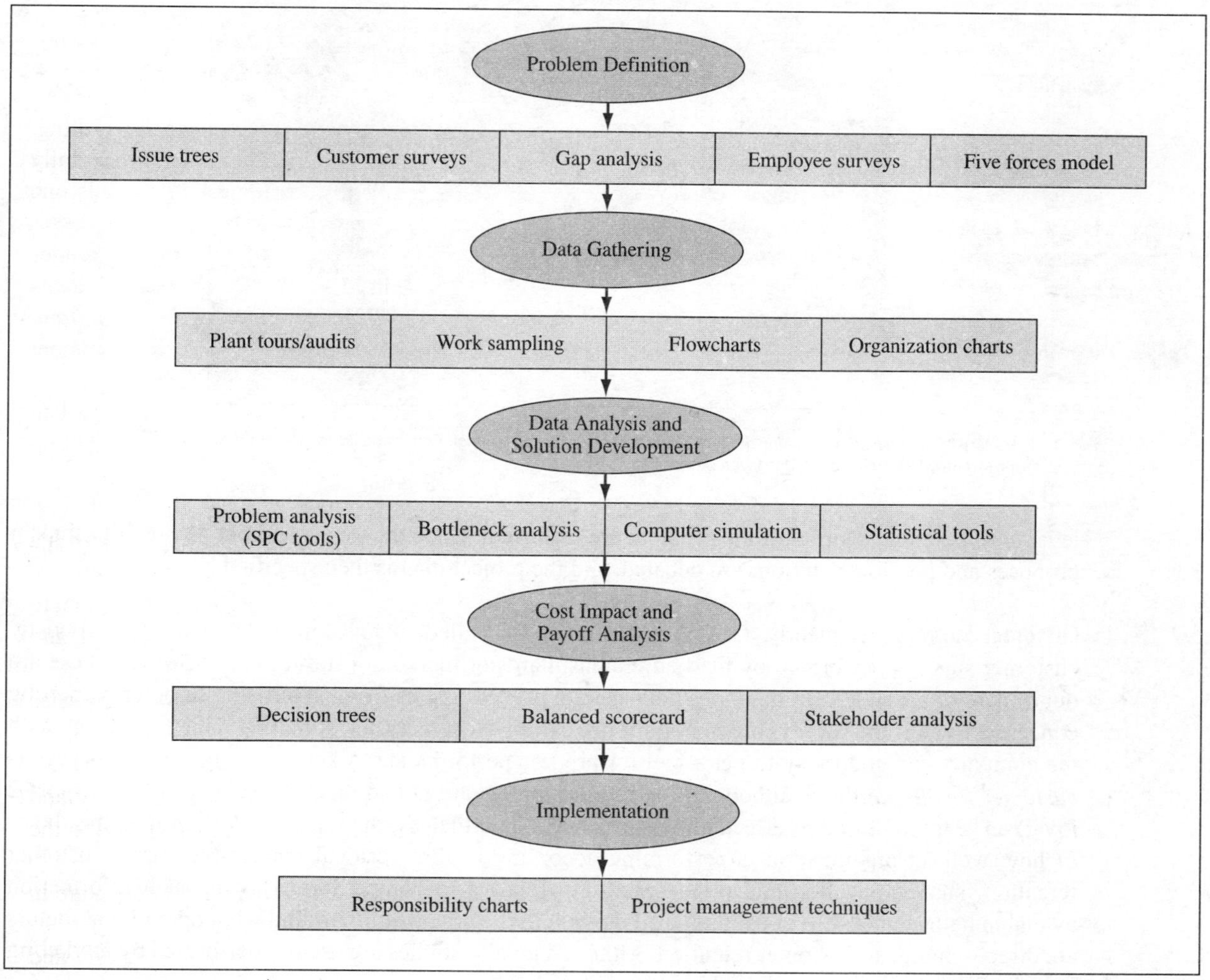

Problem Definition Tools

Issue Trees Issue trees are used by McKinsey to structure or map the key problems to be investigated and provide a working initial hypothesis as to the likely solution to these problems. As can be seen in Exhibit 25.4, a tree starts with the general problem (increase widget sales) and then goes level by

EXHIBIT 25.4

Issue Tree for Acme Widgets

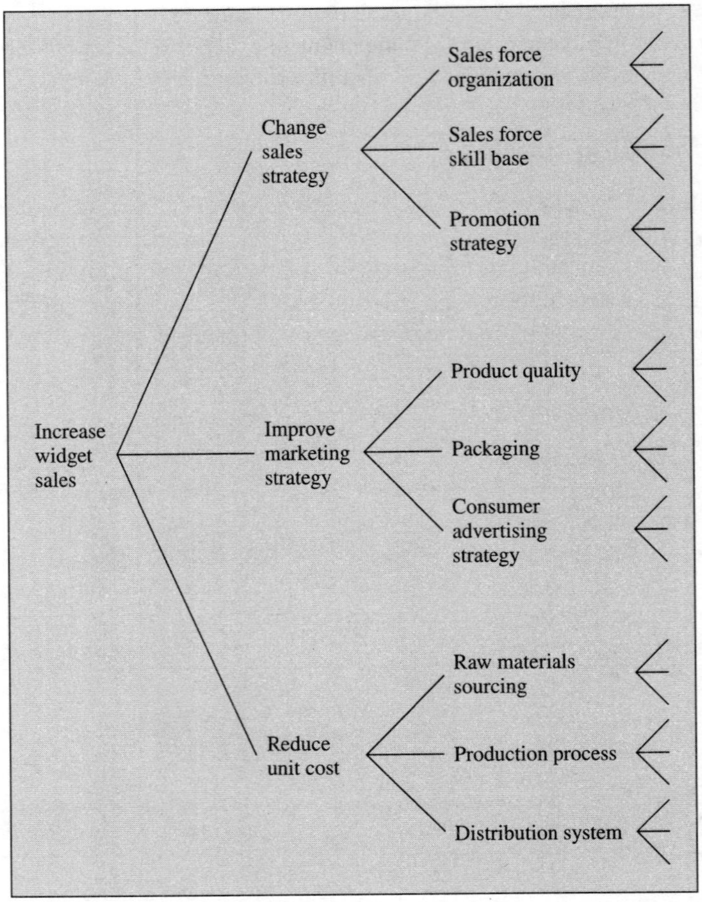

E. M. Rasiel, *The McKinsey Way: Using the Techniques of the World's Top Strategic Consultants to Help You and Your Business,* (New York, McGraw-Hill, 1998), p. 12. Used with permission.

level until potential sources of the problem are identified. Once the tree is laid out, the relationships it proposes and possible solutions are debated, and the project plan is then specified.

Customer Surveys Frequently, OSCM consultants are called in to address problems identified by customer surveys performed by marketing consultants or marketing staff. Often, however, these are out of date or are in a form that does not separate process issues from advertising or other marketing concerns. Even if the surveys are in good form, calling customers and soliciting their experience with the company is a good way to get a feel for process performance. A key use of customer surveys is *customer loyalty analysis,* although in reality customers are not so much "loyal" (your dog, Spot, is loyal) as "earned" through effective performance. Nevertheless, the term *loyalty* captures the flavor of how well an organization is performing according to three critical market measures: customer retention, share of wallet, and price sensitivity relative to competitors. Having such information available helps the OSCM consultant drill down into the organization to find what operational factors are directly linked to customer retention. Although loyalty studies are usually performed by marketing groups, OSCM consultants should be aware of their importance.

Gap Analysis Gap analysis is used to assess the client's performance relative to the expectations of its customers, or relative to the performance of its competitors. An example is shown in Exhibit 25.5.

EXHIBIT 25.5

Issue Tree for Acme Widgets

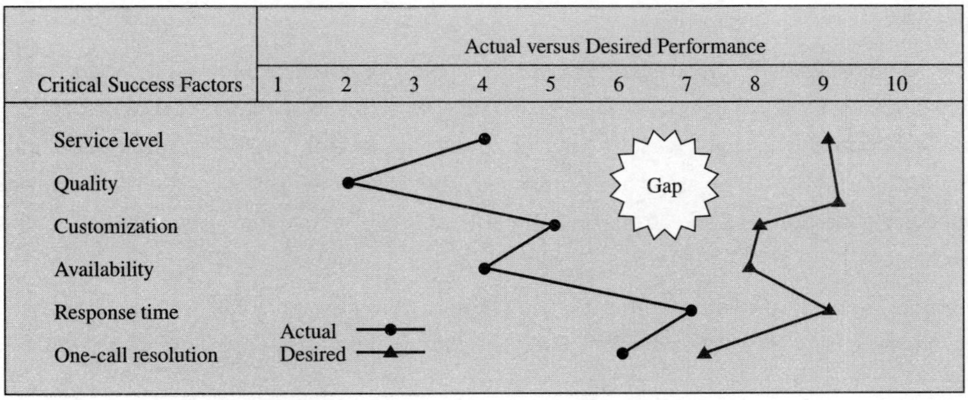

Source: Deloitte & Touche Consulting Group

Another form of gap analysis is benchmarking particular client company processes against exemplars in the process and measuring the differences. For example, if one is interested in billing process accuracy and problem resolution, American Express would be the benchmark; for timeliness and efficiency in railway transportation, Japanese Railways; for order entry in catalog sales, it would be L.L.Bean.

Employee Surveys Such surveys range from employee satisfaction surveys to suggestion surveys. A key point to remember is if the consultant requests employee suggestions, such information must be carefully evaluated and acted upon by management. A few years ago, Singapore Airlines distributed a questionnaire to its flight personnel, but made the mistake of not following through to address their concerns. As a result, the employees were more critical of the company than if the survey had not been taken, and to this day the company does not use this form of evaluation.

The Five Forces Model This is one of the better-known approaches to evaluating a company's competitive position in light of the structure of its industry. The five forces are buyer power, potential entrants, raw material suppliers, substitute products, and industry rivals. The consultant applies the model by developing a list of factors that fit under each of these headings. Some examples of where a client's competitive position might be strong are when buyers have limited information, there are major barriers to potential entrants, there are many alternative suppliers, there are few substitute products (or services), or there are few industry rivals.

Often used with the five forces model is the *value chain,* such as shown in Exhibit 25.6. The value chain provides a structure to capture the linkage of organizational activities that create value for the customer and profit for the firm. It is particularly useful to get across the notion that operations and the other activities must work cross-functionally for optimal organizational performance (and avoid the dreaded "functional silo" syndrome).

A tool similar to the five forces model is *SWOT analysis.* This is a somewhat more general method of evaluating an organization and has the advantage of being easy to remember: *S*trengths of the client, *W*eaknesses of the client, *O*pportunities for the client in the industry, and *T*hreats from competitors or the economic and market environment.

Data Gathering

Plant Tours/Audits These can be classified as manufacturing tours/audits and service facility tours/audits. Full manufacturing audits are a major undertaking, entailing measurement of all aspects of the production facility and processes, as well as support activities such as maintenance and inventory stockkeeping. Frequently these require several weeks, utilizing checklists developed explicitly for the

OSCM AT WORK

Quick Plant Assessment

1. **Customer focus.** A customer-oriented workforce will take pride in satisfying both external and internal customers. The extent of this orientation should be apparent even in a brief plant tour. For example, when asked about the next step in the process, customer-aware employees will respond by giving a person's name or product, rather than saying that they just put it on the pallet and it's moved later. Cordiality to the touring group and posted quality and customer satisfaction ratings are other signs of a customer-oriented workforce. (Questions 1, 2, and 20 on the QPA questionnaire relate to this measure. This questionnaire is included at the end of this chapter.)
2. **Safety, cleanliness, and order.** The physical environment of a plant is important to operating effectiveness. Cleanliness, low noise levels, good lighting, and air quality are obvious things to look for. Labeling and tracking of all inventory items, not just expensive ones, should be in evidence. (Not having the required nuts and bolts can be as disruptive to production as lacking a major component.) (Questions 3–5 and 20)
3. **Visual management/Scheduling.** Production management tools such as work instructions, kanban schedules, and quality and productivity charts should be easily visible. Posted workflow diagrams linking each stage of a process are particularly effective visual cues. In addition, scheduling typically involves some mechanism for pacing of the workflow based on demand. (Questions 2, 4, 6–10, 11, and 20)
4. **Use of space, movement efficiency, and product line flow.** Good indicators of efficient space utilization are minimum material movement over short distances, use of efficient containers; materials stored at the point of use, not in separate inventory storage areas; tooling kept near the machines; and product flow layout rather than process layout. (Questions 7, 12, 13, and 20)
5. **Teamwork.** Discussions with workers and visible indicators of teamwork such as names of teams over a work area and productivity award banners are quick ways of determining how the workforce feels about their jobs, the company, and their co-workers. (Questions 9, 14, 15, and 20)
6. **Maintenance of equipment.** Purchase dates and equipment costs should be stenciled on the side of machinery, and maintenance records should be posted nearby. Asking people on the factory floor how things are working and whether they are involved in purchasing tools and equipment is also indicative of the extent to which workers are encouraged to address these issues. (Questions 16 and 20)
7. **Management of complexity and variability.** This depends greatly on the type of industry. Obviously, industries with narrow product lines have less difficulty handling complexity and variability. Indicators to watch for in general are the number of people manually recording data and the number of keyboards available for data entry. (Questions 8, 17, and 20)
8. **Supply chain integration.** It is generally desirable to work closely with a relatively small number of dedicated and supportive suppliers. A rough estimate of the number of suppliers can be ascertained by looking at container labels to see what supplier names appear on containers. Containers that appear to be designed and labeled specifically for customized parts shipped to a plant indicate the extent to which a strong supplier partnership exists. A sign of poor supply chain integration is lots of paperwork on the receiving dock. This indicates lack of a smooth pull system where plants pull the materials from their suppliers as if it was just another link in the pull system for each product line. (Questions 18 and 20)
9. **Quality commitment.** Attention to quality is evidenced in many ways, including posting of quality awards, quality scorecards, and quality goal statements. Quality is reflected in many of the other plant activities such as product development and startups. (Questions 8, 9, 15, 17, 19, and 20)

Modified from R. Eugene Goodson, "Read a Plant—Fast," *Harvard Business Review* 80, no. 5 (May 2002), pp. 105–13.

Exhibit 25.6

Value Chain

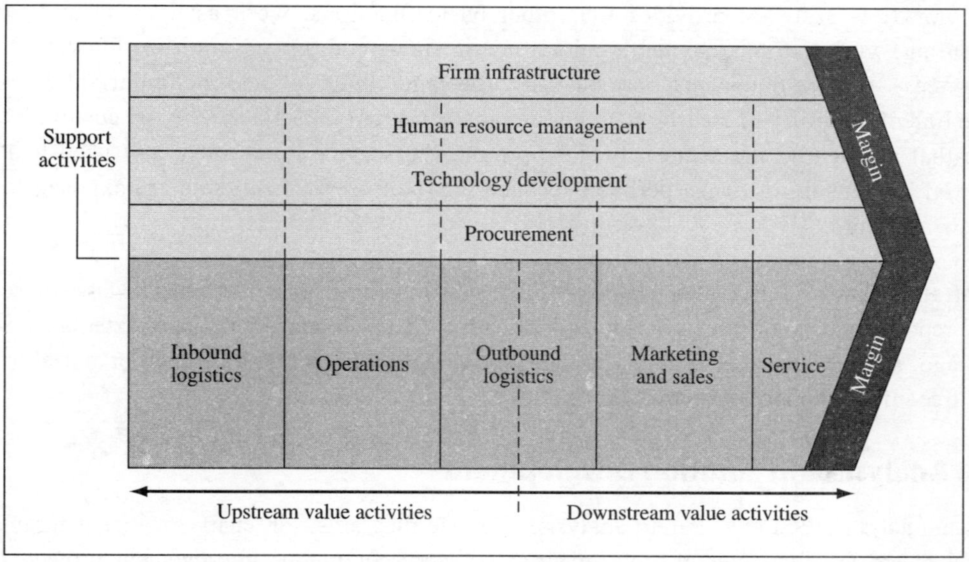

Based on Harvard Business School Press. From M. E. Porter, *Competition in Global Industries,* (Boston,MA, 1986), p. 24.

client's industry. Plant tours, on the other hand, are usually much less detailed and can be done in a half day. The purpose of the tour is to get a general understanding of the manufacturing process before focusing on a particular problem area. To collect consistent information, the members of the study team in a tour use the same generic checklist or general questions.

The quick plant assessment (QPA) tour is designed to enable a study team to determine the "leanness" of a plant in just 45 minutes. The approach uses a 20-item questionnaire and an 9-category item rating sheet (see "Quick Plant Assessment" Exercise at the end of the chapter). During the tour, team members talk with workers and managers and look for evidence of best practices. At the end of the tour, members discuss their impressions and fill out the worksheets. The categories are key to the tour. Their features are summarized in the nearby OSCM at Work box, "Quick Plant Assessment."

Complete service facility audits are also a major undertaking, but they differ from manufacturing audits in that, when properly done, they focus on the customer's experience as much as on the utilization of resources. Typical questions in a service audit address time to get service, the cleanliness of the facility, staff sizing, and customer satisfaction. A service facility tour or walk-through can often be done as a mystery shopper, where the consultant actually partakes of the service and records his or her experiences.

Work Sampling Work sampling entails random sampling observations of work activities, designed to give a statistically valid picture of how time is spent by a worker or the utilization of equipment. Diary studies are another way to collect activity data. These are used by consultants to get an understanding of specific tasks being performed by the workforce. In these, the employee simply writes down the activities he or she performs during the week as they occur. This avoids the problem of having analysts look over a worker's shoulder to gather data. Examples of where these studies are used include library front desks, nursing, and knowledge work.

Flowcharts Flowcharts can be used in both manufacturing and services to track materials, information, and people flows. Workflow software such as Optima! and BPR Capture are widely used for process analysis. In addition to providing capabilities for defining a process, most workflow software provides four other basic functions: work assignment and routing, scheduling, work list management, and automatic status and process metrics. Flowcharts used in services—service blueprints—are basically the same thing, but add the important distinction of the line of visibility to clearly differentiate activities that take place with the customer versus those that are behind the scenes. In our opinion, the service blueprint is not used to its full potential by consulting firms, perhaps because relatively few consultants are exposed to them in their training.

Organization Charts Organization charts are often subject to change, so care must be taken to see who really reports to whom. Some companies are loath to share organization charts externally. Several years ago, a senior manager from a large electronics firm told us that a detailed organization chart gives free information to the competition.

Data Analysis and Solution Development

Problem Analysis (SPC Tools) Pareto analysis, fishbone diagrams, run charts, scatter diagrams, and control charts are fundamental tools in virtually every continuous improvement project. *Pareto analysis* is applied to inventory management under the heading of ABC analysis. Such ABC analysis is still the standard starting point of production control consultants when examining inventory management problems. *Fishbone diagrams* (or cause-and-effect diagrams) are a great way to organize one's first cut at a consulting problem (and they make a great impression when used to analyze, for example, a case study as part of the employment selection process for a consulting firm). *Run charts, scatter diagrams,* and *control charts* are tools that one is simply expected to know when doing operations consulting.

Bottleneck Analysis Resource bottlenecks appear in most OSCM consulting projects. In such cases, the consultant has to specify how available capacity is related to required capacity for some product or service in order to identify and eliminate the bottleneck. This isn't always evident, and abstracting the relationships calls for the same kind of logical analysis used in the classic "word problems" you loved in high school algebra.

Computer Simulation Computer simulation analysis has become a very common tool in OSCM consulting. The most common general-purpose simulation packages are Extend and Crystal Ball. SimFactory and ProModel (for manufacturing systems), MedModel (hospital simulation), and Service Model are examples of specialized packages. For smaller and less complex simulation, consultants often use Excel. Chapter 10 introduces the topic of simulation in this book.

A growing interest in simulation is in the analysis of "system dynamics." System dynamics is a language that helps us see the patterns that underlie complex situations. These complex situations are modeled using causal loop diagrams that are useful when factors either enhance or degrade system performance. Causal loops are of two types: reinforcing loops and balancing loops. *Reinforcing loops* are positive feedback loops driving positive values in criteria important to the system. *Balancing loops* reflect the mechanisms that counter reinforcing loops, thereby driving the system toward equilibrium. By way of example, with reference to Exhibit 25.7, suppose you have a quality goal that is reflected in a quality standard. The reinforcing loop (R) indicates that the standard, if left unmodified, would yield an ever-increasing (or decreasing) level of actual quality. In reality, what happens is that the balancing

EXHIBIT 25.7

Causal Loop Analysis

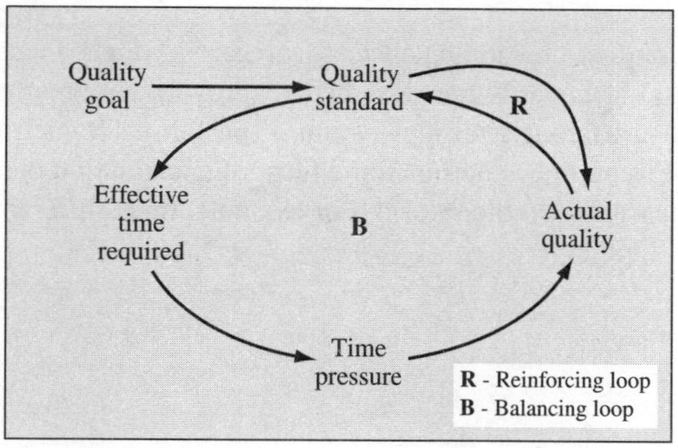

loop (B) comes into play. Effective time required to meet the standard determines time pressure (on the workers), which, in turn, modifies the actual quality achieved and ultimately achievement of the quality standard itself. An obvious use of the system shown here would be to hypothesize the consequences of raising the quality goal, or raising or lowering the values of the other variables in the system. In addition to its use in problem analysis, causal loop analysis simulations are often used by consultants to help client companies become more effective learning organizations.

Statistical Tools *Correlation analysis* and *regression analysis* are expected skills for consulting in OSCM. The good news is that these types of analyses are easily performed with spreadsheets. *Hypothesis testing* is mentioned frequently in the consulting firm methodology manuals, and one should certainly be able to perform Chi-square and *t*-tests in analyzing data. Two other widely used tools that use statistical analysis are *queuing theory* and *forecasting.* Consultants frequently use queuing theory to investigate how many service channels are needed to handle customers in person or on the phone. Forecasting problems likewise arise continually in OSCM consulting (such as forecasting the incoming calls to a call center).

A newly emerging tool (not shown on our exhibit) is *data envelopment analysis.* DEA is a linear programming technique used to measure the relative performance of branches of multisite service organizations such as banks, franchise outlets, and public agencies. A DEA model compares each branch with all other branches and computes an efficiency rating based on the ratio of resource inputs to product or service outputs. The key feature of the approach is that it permits using multiple inputs such as materials and labor hours, and multiple outputs such as products sold and repeat customers, to get an efficiency ratio. This feature provides a more comprehensive and reliable measure of efficiency than a set of operating ratios or profit measures.

Cost Impact and Payoff Analysis

Decision Trees Decision trees represent a fundamental tool from the broad area of risk analysis. They are widely used in examining plant and equipment investments and R&D projects. Decision trees are built into various software packages such as TreeAge (www.treeage.com).

Stakeholder Analysis Most consulting projects impact in some way each of five types of stakeholders: customers, stockholders, employees, suppliers, and the community. The importance of considering the interest of all stakeholders is reflected in the mission statements of virtually all major corporations and, as such, provides guidance for consultants in formulating their recommendations.

Balanced Scorecard In an attempt to reflect the particular needs of each stakeholder group in a performance measurement system, accountants have developed what is termed a *balanced scorecard.* (Balanced refers to the fact that the scorecard looks at more than just the bottom line or one or two other performance measures.) The Bank of Montreal has used the balanced scorecard notion in setting specific goals and measures for customer service, employee relations, return to owners, and community relations. A key feature of the system is that it is tailored to what senior management and branch-level management can control.

Process Dashboards In contrast to the balanced scorecard, which focuses on organizationwide performance data, process dashboards are designed to provide summary performance updates for specific processes. Dashboards consist of a selection of performance metrics presented in graphical form with color-coding of trend lines, alarms in the form of exclamation marks, and so forth, to show when key indicators are nearing a problem level. For example, three different dials on a dashboard for suppliers are shown in Exhibit 25.8.

Exhibit 25.8

Dashboard for Suppliers

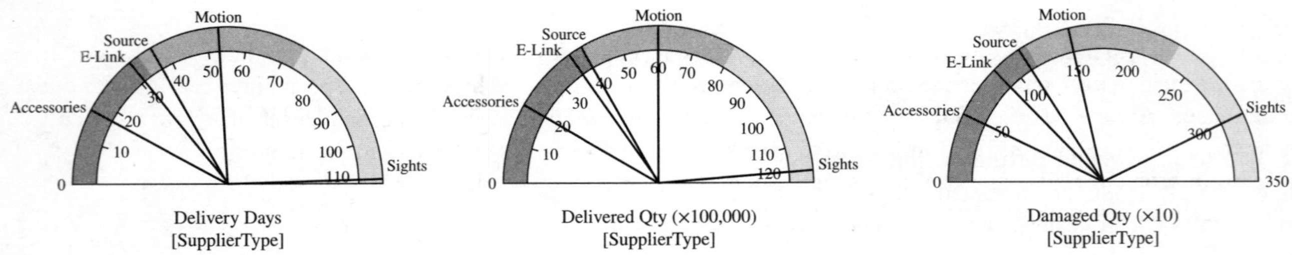

Implementation

Responsibility Charts A responsibility chart is used in planning the task responsibilities for a project. It usually takes the form of a matrix with tasks listed across the top and project team members down the side. The goal is to make sure that a checkmark exists in each cell to assure that a person is assigned to each task.

Project Management Techniques Consulting firms use the project management techniques of CPM/PERT and Gantt charts to plan and monitor the entire portfolio of consulting engagements of the firm, as well as individual consulting projects. Microsoft Project and Primavera Project Planner are examples of commonly used software to automate such tools. Evolve Software has developed a software suite for professional service firms, modeled on ERP for manufacturing, that allows management to integrate opportunity management (the selling process), resource management, and delivery management. It should be emphasized that these planning tools are very much secondary to the people management skills needed to successfully execute a consulting project. This admonition is likewise true for all of the tools we have discussed in this section.

LO 25-3 Analyze processes using business process reengineering concepts

BUSINESS PROCESS REENGINEERING (BPR)

Business process **reengineering** is the radically restructuring of business processes to significantly improve customer service, reduce cost, and become competitive. It uses many of the tools just discussed to achieve these goals.

Reengineering
The radically resturcturing of business processes to significantly improve customer service, reduce cost, and become competitive.

The concept of reengineering has been around for nearly two decades and was implemented in a piecemeal fashion in organizations. Production organizations have been in the vanguard without knowing it. They have undertaken reengineering by implementing concurrent engineering, lean production, cellular manufacturing, group technology, and pull-type production systems. These represent a fundamental rethinking of the manufacturing process.

Reengineering is often compared to total quality management (TQM), a topic covered in Chapter 12. Some people have said that the two are, in fact, the same, whereas others have even argued that they are incompatible. Both concepts are centered on a customer focus. The concepts of teamwork, worker participation and empowerment, cross-functionality, process analysis and measurement, supplier involvement, and benchmarking are significant contributions from quality management. In addition, the need for a "total" view of the organization has been reemphasized by quality management in an era of extensive functionalization of business. Quality management has also influenced company culture and values by exposing organizations to the need for change. The basic difference between the two is that quality management has emphasized continuous and incremental improvement of processes that are in control, whereas reengineering is about radical, discontinuous change through process innovation. Thus, a given process is enhanced by TQM until its useful lifetime is over, at which point it is reengineered. Then, enhancement is resumed and the entire cycle starts again. As business circumstances change in major ways, so must process designs.

Principles of Reengineering

Reengineering is about achieving a significant improvement in processes so that contemporary customer requirements of quality, speed, innovation, customization, and service are met. The following are seven principles or rules for reengineering and integration that can be used to guide a process reengineering project.

Rule 1. Organize around Outcomes, Not Tasks Several specialized tasks previously performed by different people should be combined into a single job. This could be performed by an individual "case worker" or by a "case team." The new job created should involve all the steps in a process that creates a well-defined outcome. Organizing around outcomes eliminates the need for handoffs, resulting in greater speed, productivity, and customer responsiveness. It also provides a single knowledgeable point of contact for the customer.

Rule 2. Have Those Who Use the Output of the Process Perform the Process In other words, work should be carried out where it makes the most sense to do it. This results in people closest to the process actually performing the work, which shifts work across traditional intra- and interorganizational boundaries. For instance, employees can make some of their own purchases without going through purchasing, customers can perform simple repairs themselves, and suppliers can be asked to manage parts inventories. Relocating work in this fashion eliminates the need to coordinate the performers and users of a process.

Rule 3. Merge Information-Processing Work into the Real Work that Produces the Information This means that people who collect information should also be responsible for processing it. It minimizes the need for another group to reconcile and process that information, and greatly reduces errors by cutting the number of external contact points for a process. A typical accounts payable department that reconciles purchase orders, receiving notices, and supplier invoices is a case in point. By eliminating the need for invoices by processing orders and receiving information online, much of the work done in the traditional accounts payable function becomes unnecessary.

Rule 4. Treat Geographically Dispersed Resources as Though They Were Centralized Information technology now makes the concept of hybrid centralized/decentralized operations a reality. It facilitates the parallel processing of work by separate organizational units that perform the same job, while improving the company's overall control. For instance, centralized databases and telecommunication networks now allow companies to link with separate units or individual field personnel, providing them with economies of scale while maintaining their individual flexibility and responsiveness to customers.

Rule 5. Link Parallel Activities Instead of Integrating Their Results The concept of integrating only the outcomes of parallel activities that must eventually come together is the primary cause for rework, high costs, and delays in the final outcome of the overall process. Such parallel activities should be linked continually and coordinated during the process.

OSCM AT WORK

e-Governance Projects in India Need BPR

Business Process Reengineering (BPR) is a very powerful concept that has helped businesses in bringing radical changes in operations along with quantum jump in critical performance parameters such as cost, delivery and effectiveness. Reengineering of governance processes, involving government-to-citizen (G2C) activities, needs administrative acumen and political will. Main characteristics of these G2C systems are:

- Involvement of legacy processes, which are often driven by administrative/legislative guidelines
- Institutional mechanism, which is unable to respond fast enough to the need of globalization and liberalization
- Large user-base which is less friendly with computer-based systems
- System complexity
- Stringent hierarchy, role and reporting system, which are typically interwoven with red-tapes and corruption.

Being the biggest institutional mechanism, government institutions are often deeply engraved in the old rigid processes. Changes are talked about, but they barely scratch the surface [1]. There is a close link between inefficiency and costly delivery of services, which also include opportunity cost of not serving the purpose for which these G2C activities are meant. Traditional government departments are designed for the convenience of the government and its employees [2]. Public services are organized around the structure of the providers rather than the users [3].

Why We Need e-Governance Projects

Vertical organization of the departments and complex collaboration among employees across departments can sometimes, if not always, create problems for the citizens, who are interested in getting their work done and not in the internal structure of the government agencies. Therefore, unless governance processes are modernized and departments are redesigned according to the convenience of the users, quality of services will be distant dream. There is a need to create cost-effective, efficient and user-friendly delivery mechanism through e-governance by cutting through tiers of existing layers of in-efficient and in-effective system of governance [4]. This requires radical changes in processes involved in governance.

The Information Technology (IT) Action Plan Part-II of the Government of India (GoI) furnishes 84 policy instruments for the Development, Manufacture and Export of IT hardware. The strategic policies for Long Term National IT Policy is defined in IT Action Plan (Part III) where it specifies the need for Reengineering of Government Processes (recommendation 54) as: 'Reengineering of the existing government processes and procedures will be implemented to bring about transparency in working, reducing constraining controls, increasing efficiency and productivity, reducing cost of service delivery, etc. Integration of projects across various departments to provide a single point of contact for citizens for delivery of services electronically will be put in place.'

One of the priorities of GoI is to improve the functioning of its different arms, such as tax collection, passport issue, rural employment, etc,. and on the top of these; there is an urgency to downsize government, which should be more citizen-friendly and free from corruption. This requires transparency, speed of execution, citizen involvement, and ease in the use of technology. Current governance processes generally lack the capability to deliver in the present scenario and therefore require reengineering before going for automation using information technology tools.

GoI Initiatives

In 1999, Government of India (GoI) declared important policy measures such as setting up of a separate Ministry of Information Technology (MIT). Then, there was Information Technology Act 2000, allocation of 2-3 percent of budget for IT in every government department, and most importantly the announcement of National e-Governance Plan (NeGP) in 2006. NeGP originally stipulated a budget of ₹33,000 crores, with planning for 100,000 Community Services Centers (CSC), covering one CSC for every six villages, State Data Centers (SDC), State Wide Area Networks (SWAN) and several mission mode projects in the critical areas of government functioning, such as Police, Customs, Income Tax, Justice, Treasury, etc [5]. NeGP offered great opportunity of provisioning intensive re-engineering through e-Government projects along with administrative reforms, and recasting of the structure and functioning of administrative departments to facilitate adaptation to IT. This exercise is intended to achieve creation of integrated databanks, removal of redundancies, resource optimization and rationalization of rules and procedures to bring about transparency in working and enhancing efficiency and providing a single point of contact to citizens for electronic delivery of services.

GOI Approach Towards PPP

Many e-Government projects in India are functioning under Public Private Partnership (PPP) mode. For example, in PPP model, government may extend the provision of a royalty-free right as an incentive for attracting investments into setting up high-speed optical fibre networks. Companies such as IBM, Tata Consultancy Services (TCS), CMC Limited, 3i Infotech, e-Govservices, etc are extensively engaged in such arrangements. One of the largest and most successful projects MCA-21 (Ministry of Corporate Affairs) is developed and maintained by TCS. Similarly, other companies are participating in the areas such as Agriculture, Commercial Taxes, e-District, Employment Exchange, Land Records, Municipalities, Panchayats, Police, Property Registration, Road Transport and Treasuries. Besides these projects, there are other integrated PPP initiatives in the following areas: e-Courts, e-Procurement, National e-governance Service Delivery Gateway and India Portal [6].

Few e-Governance Initiatives

There are many successful e-government initiatives in India, for example, citizen service project 'e-Seva' of Andhra Pradesh, 'Setu' in Maharashtra, Land record project 'Bhoomi' in Karnataka,, 'Old Age Pension System' of Thiruvarur District of Tamil Nadu, public grievance project 'Lokvani' in Uttar Pradesh, grand G-B project MCA-21 (Ministry of Corporate Affairs), etc. These initiatives bear strong testimony to how IT is being conceived as an important agenda of public administration in India.

There are also quite a few other projects, such as 'Gyandoot' in the state of 'Madhya Pradesh' in India, which are not so successful despite having much hype. Another similar project is 'Community Information Centre (CIC)' started by the Ministry of Information Technology in Assam and the North-East states in year 2002 with a budget of ₹200 crore.

Why BPR for e-Governance Projects

Government processes are often very sluggish and bureaucratic in nature. There is no point automating these processes in the form as they have existed in past. Inefficient bureaucratic process, if automated, will create more problems for the citizen. Therefore, a thorough re-engineering is needed to make these processes aligned with citizens' need. Also, seamless integration of databases would be needed.

References

1. Gellman, R. (2000), Taming the privacy monster: a proposal for a non-regulatory privacy agency, Government Information Quarterly, 17, 3, 235-241.
2. Choi, Y. Sung-Don H. and Seung-Hwan M. (1999), Electronic government in South Korea: Conceptual problems, Government Information Quarterly 16, 3, 277–285.
3. Gupta, M. P., Kumar, P. and Bhattacharya, J. (2005), Government Online: Opportunities and Challenges, McGraw-Hill, New Delhi.
4. Bertot, J.C., and Paul T. Jaeger P.T. (2006), User-centered e-government: Challenges and benefits for government Web sites, Government Information Quarterly, 23, 2, 163-168.
5. http://www.i4donline.net/articles/current-article.asp?articleid=764&typ=News
6. www.india.gov.in

Rule 6. Put the Decision Point Where the Work Is Performed, and Build Control into the Process Decision making should be made part of the work performed. This is possible today with a more educated and knowledgeable workforce plus decision-aiding technology. Controls are now made part of the process. The vertical compression that results produces flatter, more responsive organizations.

Rule 7. Capture Information Once—at the Source Information should be collected and captured in the company's online information system only once—at the source where it was created. This approach avoids erroneous data entries and costly reentries.

Guidelines for Implementation

The principles of business process reengineering just enumerated are based on a common platform of the innovative use of information technology. But creating a new process and sustaining the improvement requires more than a creative application of information technology. A detailed study of reengineering

The British retailer Marks & Spencer has gone through company reengineering, producing Plan A, a 100-point eco-plan. It is reducing how much of its clothing and packaging ends up as landfill by improving packaging, recycling more, and using fewer plastic bags.

applications in 765 hospitals yielded the following three managerial guidelines that apply to almost every organization contemplating reengineering:

1. **Codification of reengineering.** Organizationwide change programs such as reengineering are complex processes whose implementation may be separated by space and time. Middle managers are often left to implement significant portions of reengineering proposals. Codifying provides guidance and direction for consistent, efficient implementation.
2. **Clear goals and consistent feedback.** Goals and expectations must be clearly established, preapplication baseline data gathered, and the results monitored and fed back to employees. Without clear feedback, employees often became dissatisfied and their perceptions of reengineering success can be quite different from actual outcomes. For example, the hospital researchers found that, at 10 hospitals they studied in depth, most employees in 4 of them felt that the reengineering program had done little to change costs, even though their costs had actually dropped 2 to 12 percent relative to their competitors'. On the other hand, 4 hospitals in which most felt that reengineering had lowered costs actually experienced an increase in relative costs and a deterioration of their cost position.
3. **High executive involvement in process changes.** A high level of involvement by the chief executive officer in major process changes (procedure changes in hospitals, for example) improves reengineering outcomes. Changes that require reductions of managers and employees are certainly less popular and more difficult. It is better that these be done using a more long-term plan.

CONCEPT CONNECTIONS

LO 25–1 Explain operations consulting and how money is made in the industry

Summary

- Consulting firms specializing in operations and supply chain management focus on improving a firm's competitiveness by improving processes.
- These firms can bring expertise that the client firm does not have. The consultant can do specialized analysis, such as simulation and optimization.
- A consulting firm makes money by charging for services, typically based on a set of rates that depend on the relative experience of the consultant. The most experienced consultants run the projects and are billed at the highest rates. Partners share the profits of the consulting practice.

Key Terms

Operations consulting Assisting clients in developing operations strategies and improving production processes.

Finders Partners or senior consultants whose primary function is sales and client relations.

Minders Managers of a consulting firm whose primary function is managing consulting projects.

Grinders Junior consultants whose primary function is to do the work.

LO 25–2 Illustrate the operations analysis tools used in the consulting industry

Summary

- The consulting firm uses tools to aid in understanding problems, collecting data, developing solutions, analyzing the payoff from proposed changes, and implementing recommendations.
- These tools provide structure to the consulting practice and are matched to the needs of the client. Many of these tools have already been discussed in earlier chapters of this book.

LO 25–3 Analyze processes using business process reengineering concepts

Summary

- Compared to the approach normally taken to improve a process, reengineering is different. Here the idea is to radically rethink how business processes are done with the goal of achieving a dramatic improvement in performance.

Key Terms

Reengineering The radically resturcturing of business processes to significantly improve customer service, reduce cost, and become competitive.

DISCUSSION QUESTIONS

1. Check the Websites of the consulting companies listed in the chapter. Which ones impressed you most as a potential client and as a potential employee? **LO 25–1**
   Boston Consulting Group (www.bcg.com)
   Deloitte Touche Tohmatsu (www.deloitte.com)
   McKinsey & Co. (www.McKinsey.com)
2. What does it take to be a good consultant? Is this the career for you?
3. In discussing characteristics of efficient plants, Goodson, developer of rapid plant assessments (see the OSCM at Work box), suggests that numerous forklifts are a sign of poor space utilization. What do you think is behind this observation? **LO25–2**
4. Think about the registration process at your university. Develop a flowchart to understand it. How would you radically redesign this process? **LO25–3**
5. Have you driven a car lately? Try not to think of the insurance claim settlement process while you drive! How would you reengineer your insurance company's claim process?

OBJECTIVE QUESTIONS

1. In what three ways can market leadership be obtained? **LO25–1**
2. The process of running a consulting firm is analogous to what type of manufacturing process structure?

3. What are the *5 Ps of production* in which firms typically seek operations consulting?
4. What is the current "hot area" for operations consultants in both manufacturing and services?

LO25-2
5. What methodology is used to assess a client's performance relative to the expectations of its customers or the performance of its competitors?
6. What type of plant tour is designed to determine the "leanness" of a plant in just 30 minutes?
7. What tool is used to reflect the particular needs of each stakeholder group in a performance measurement system? (Answer in Appendix D)
8. What tool is used to ensure that all tasks in a project have the right mix of project team members assigned?

LO25-3
9. An equipment manufacturer has the following steps in its order entry process:
   a. Take the order and fax it to order entry.
   b. Enter the order into the system (10 percent unclear or incorrect).
   c. Check stock availability (stock not available for 15 percent of orders).
   d. Check customer credit (10 percent of orders have credit questions).
   e. Send bill of materials to warehouse.

   The order receipt to warehouse cycle time is typically 48 hours; 80 percent of the orders are handled without error; and order-handling costs are 6 percent of order revenue. Should you reengineer this process or is continuous improvement the appropriate approach? If you choose to reengineer, how would you go about it?
10. Is the business reengineering process more gradual, more radical, or about the same as the TQM process?
11. What concept provides guidance and direction for consistent, efficient implementation of BPR projects? (Answer in Appendix D)

EXERCISE: QUICK PLANT ASSESSMENT

This exercise is designed to support a plant tour event conducted as part of a class.

This questionnaire is focused on assessing the "leanness" of a manufacturing plant. It might be useful to review the material on "lean" processes in Chapter 14 where the concepts considered in the questionnaire are described.

The questionnaire can be modified for non-manufacturing type processes, for example services or warehouses, depending on the facility that is being visited.

We would suggest working with a team of two to four people and taking at least a 45-minute tour of a plant. It would be most useful if your tour guide were knowledgeable about the operation of the plant and willing to answer questions. At the conclusion of the tour, rate what you observed using the Quick Plant Assessment (QPA) questionnaire and Score Sheet.

In class, discuss those areas where leanness is generally lacking across the plant(s) visited.

Additional analysis for a consulting report:

1. Use the results from filling out the QPA Questionnaire in Exhibit 25.9 and your team's observations to develop a consensus score for each Assessment Category in the QPA Score Sheet.
2. Prioritize targets of opportunity for management.
3. Develop a two-page action plan that you would present to management to help them make improvements.

PRACTICE EXAM

In each of the following, name the term defined or answer the question. Answers are listed at the bottom.

1. Name the three categories of consultants.
2. This type of project requires a great deal of experience but little innovation.
3. Accenture is well known for this type of approach to training consultants.
4. Target utilization is usually highest for which level of consultant?

EXHIBIT 25.9

Quick Plant Assessment Questionnaire

	Yes	No
1. Are visitors welcome to the plant and given information about how the plant operates, the workforce, customers, and products?		
2. Are ratings for product quality and customer satisfaction displayed for the workforce and customers to view?		
3. Is the plant clean, orderly, and well lit? Is the air quality good, and are noise levels low?		
4. Is a visual labeling system used to identify inventory locations, storage places for tools, process areas, and movement lanes?		
5. Does it appear that everything has a specific place, and everything is stored in its place?		
6. Are performance measures and goals for these measures prominently posted and up to date?		
7. Are production materials brought to and stored near where they are used rather than in separate remote storage areas?		
8. Are specific instructions for how work is to be done and quality specifications visible at all workstations?		
9. Are up to date charts that show productivity, quality, and safety visible in all process areas?		
10. Is each process area scheduled using some type of pacing mechanism so workers can see real-time status against the schedule?		
11. Can the current state of the plant be viewed from a central control room, on a status board, or online computer display?		
12. Is material moved only once and as short a distance as possible? Is material moved efficiently in appropriate containers?		
13. Is the plant laid out in continuous product line flows rather than in "shops"?		
14. Are workers organized in teams and are they trained and empowered to engage in problem solving and ongoing improvements?		
15. Do employees seem committed to continuously improving processes?		
16. Is there a formal plan for equipment preventive maintenance and improvement of tools and processes?		
17. Is there a process for managing projects (especially new product start-ups), with cost and timing goals?		
18. Is there a supplier certification process with measures for delivery, cost, and quality performance? Are these measures shared with suppliers frequently?		
19. Are fail-safe methods used in the processes to prevent common product quality problems?		
20. Would you buy the products this plant produces?		

EXHIBIT 25.10

QPA Score Sheet

Assessment category	Relevant Questions	Number of Yes's	Ratio of Yes's to Number of Relevant Questions
Customer focus	1, 2, 20		
Safety, cleanliness, and order	3, 4, 5, 20		
Visual management/Scheduling	2, 4, 6, 7, 8, 9, 10, 11, 20		
Use of space, movement efficiency, and product line flow	7, 12, 13, 20		
Teamwork	9, 14, 15, 20		
Maintenance of equipment	16, 20		
Management of complexity and variability	8, 17, 20		
Supply chain integration	18, 20		
Quality commitment	8, 9, 15, 17, 19, 20		

5. McKinsey uses these to structure or map the key problems to be investigated.
6. These are the five forces of the five forces model.
7. Gap analysis measures the difference between these two factors.
8. Rapid plant assessment is used to measure this variable.
9. An accounting approach to reflect the needs of each stakeholder is called this.
10. In contrast to TQM, this approach seeks radical change through innovation.

Answers to Practice Exam 1. Finders, minders, and grinders 2. Gray hair 3. Uniform approaches 4. Junior level 5. Issue trees 6. Buyer power, potential entrants, suppliers, substitute products, and industry rivals 7. Actual and desired performance 8. Leanness of a plant 9. Balanced scorecard 10. Business process reengineering

For PowerPoint lecture slides, Solutions Manual, Test Bank, Data files for solved examples, Excel Templates, Step-by-Step Solved Examples in video format, Tutorial Videos and many more, scan the adjacent **QR code**, or **visit http://www.mhhe.com/sie-chase15e**

Linear Programming Using the Excel Solver

The key to profitable operations is making the best use of available resources of people, material, plant and equipment, and money. Today's manager has a powerful mathematical modeling tool available for this purpose with linear programming. In this appendix, we will show how the use of the Microsoft Excel Solver to solve LP problems opens a whole new world to the innovative manager and provides an invaluable addition to the technical skill set for those who seek careers in consulting. In this appendix, we use a product-planning problem to introduce this tool. Here we find the optimal mix of products that have different costs and resource requirements. This problem is certainly relevant to today's competitive market. Extremely successful companies provide a mix of products, from standard to high-end luxury models. All these products compete for the use of limited production and other capacity. Maintaining the proper mix of these products over time can significantly bolster earnings and the return on a firm's assets.

LO A-1

Use Microsoft Excel Solver to solve a linear programming problem.

We begin with a quick introduction to linear programming and conditions under which the technique is applicable. Then, we solve a simple product-mix problem. Other linear programming applications appear throughout the rest of the book.

Linear programming (or simply **LP**) refers to several related mathematical techniques used to allocate limited resources among competing demands in an optimal way. LP is the most widely used of the approaches falling under the general heading of mathematical optimization techniques and has been applied to many operations management problems. The following are typical applications:

Linear programming (LP)
Refers to several related mathematical techniques used to allocate limited resources among competing demands in an optimal way.

Aggregate sales and operations planning: Finding the minimum-cost production schedule. The problem is to develop a three- to six-month plan for meeting expected demand given constraints on expected production capacity and workforce size. Relevant costs considered in the problem include regular and overtime labor rates, hiring and firing, subcontracting, and inventory carrying cost.

Service/manufacturing productivity analysis: Comparing how efficiently different service and manufacturing outlets are using their resources compared to the best-performing unit. This is done using an approach called data envelopment analysis.

Product planning: Finding the optimal product mix where several products have different costs and resource requirements. Examples include finding the optimal blend of chemicals for gasoline, paints, human diets, and animal feeds. Examples of this problem are covered in this chapter.

Product routing: Finding the optimal way to produce a product that must be processed sequentially through several machine centers, with each machine in the center having its own cost and output characteristics.

Vehicle/crew scheduling: Finding the optimal way to use resources such as aircraft, buses, or trucks and their operating crews to provide transportation services to customers and materials to be moved between different locations.

Process control: Minimizing the amount of scrap material generated by cutting steel, leather, or fabric from a roll or sheet of stock material.

Inventory control: Finding the optimal combination of products to stock in a network of warehouses or storage locations.

Distribution scheduling: Finding the optimal shipping schedule for distributing products between factories and warehouses or between warehouses and retailers.

Plant location studies: Finding the optimal location of a new plant by evaluating shipping costs between alternative locations and supply and demand sources.

Material handling: Finding the minimum-cost routings of material-handling devices (such as fork-lift trucks) between departments in a plant, or, for example, hauling materials from a supply yard to work sites by trucks. Each truck might have different capacities and performance capabilities.

Linear programming is gaining wide acceptance in many industries due to the availability of detailed operating information and the interest in optimizing processes to reduce cost. Many software vendors offer optimization options to be used with enterprise resource planning systems. Some firms refer to these as *advanced planning option, synchronized planning,* and *process optimization.*

For linear programming to pertain in a problem situation, five essential conditions must be met. First, there must be *limited resources* (such as a limited number of workers, equipment, finances, and material); otherwise, there would be no problem. Second, there must be an *explicit objective* (such as maximize profit or minimize cost). Third, there must be *linearity* (two is twice as much as one; if three hours are needed to make a part, then two parts would take six hours and three parts would take nine hours). Fourth, there must be *homogeneity* (the products produced on a machine are identical, or all the hours available from a worker are equally productive). Fifth, there must be *divisibility:* Normal linear programming assumes products and resources can be subdivided into fractions. If this subdivision is not possible (such as flying half an airplane or hiring one-fourth of a person), a modification of linear programming, called *integer programming,* can be used.

When a single objective is to be maximized (like profit) or minimized (like costs), we can use linear programming. When multiple objectives exist, *goal programming* is used. If a problem is best solved in stages or time frames, *dynamic programming* is employed. Other restrictions on the nature of the problem may require that it be solved by other variations of the technique, such as *nonlinear programming* or *quadratic programming.*

The Linear Programming Model

Stated formally, the linear programming problem entails an optimizing process in which nonnegative values for a set of decision variables $X_1, X_2, \ldots, X_n$ are selected so as to maximize (or minimize) an objective function in the form

$$\text{Maximize (minimize) } Z = C_1X_1 + C_2X_2 + \ldots + C_nX_n$$

subject to resource constraints in the form

$$\begin{gathered} A_{11}X_1 + A_{12}X_2 + \ldots + A_{1n}X_n \leq B_1 \\ A_{21}X_1 + A_{22}X_2 + \ldots + A_{2n}X_n \leq B_2 \\ \cdot \\ \cdot \\ \cdot \\ A_{m1}X_1 + A_{m2}X_2 + \ldots + A_{mn}X_n \leq B_m \end{gathered}$$

where C_n, A_{mn}, and B_m are given constants.

Depending on the problem, the constraints also may be stated with equal signs (=) or greater-than-or-equal-to signs (≥).

EXAMPLE A.1 Puck and Pawn Company

We describe the steps involved in solving a simple linear programming model in the context of a sample problem, that of Puck and Pawn Company, which manufactures hockey sticks and chess sets. Each hockey stick yields an incremental profit of \$2, and each chess set, \$4. A hockey stick requires 4 hours of processing at machine center A and 2 hours at machine center B. A chess set requires 6 hours at machine center A, 6 hours at machine center B, and 1 hour at machine center C. Machine center A has a maximum of 120 hours of available capacity per day, machine center B has 72 hours, and machine center C has 10 hours.

If the company wishes to maximize profit, how many hockey sticks and chess sets should be produced per day?

SOLUTION

Formulate the problem in mathematical terms. If H is the number of hockey sticks and C is the number of chess sets, to maximize profit the objective function may be stated as

$$\text{Maximize } Z = \$2H + \$4C$$

The maximization will be subject to the following constraints:

$$\begin{aligned} 4H + 6C &\leq 120 \text{ (machine center A constraint)} \\ 2H + 6C &\leq 72 \text{ (machine center B constraint)} \\ 1C &\leq 10 \text{ (machine center C constraint)} \\ H, C &\leq 0 \end{aligned}$$

This formulation satisfies the five requirements for standard LP stated in the first section of this appendix:

1. There are limited resources (a finite number of hours available at each machine center).
2. There is an explicit objective function (we know what each variable is worth and what the goal is in solving the problem).
3. The equations are linear (no exponents or cross-products).
4. The resources are homogeneous (everything is in one unit of measure, machine hours).
5. The decision variables are divisible and nonnegative (we can make a fractional part of a hockey stick or chess set; however, if this were deemed undesirable, we would have to use integer programming).

Graphical Linear Programming

Graphical linear programming
Provides a quick insight into the nature of linear programming.

Though limited in application to problems involving two decision variables (or three variables for three-dimensional graphing), **graphical linear programming** provides a quick insight into the nature of linear programming. We describe the steps involved in the graphical method in the context of Puck and Pawn Company. The following steps illustrate the graphical approach.

1. **Formulate the problem in mathematical terms.** The equations for the problem are given previously.
2. **Plot constraint equations.** The constraint equations are easily plotted by letting one variable equal zero and solving for the axis intercept of the other. (The inequality portions of the restrictions are disregarded for this step.) For the machine center A constraint equation, when $H = 0$, $C = 20$, and when $C = 0$, $H = 30$. For the machine center B constraint equation, when $H = 0$, $C = 12$, and when $C = 0$, $H = 36$. For the machine center C constraint equation, $C = 10$ for all values of H. These lines are graphed in Exhibit A.1.
3. **Determine the area of feasibility.** The direction of inequality signs in each constraint determines the area where a feasible solution is found. In this case, all inequalities are of the less-than-or-equal-to variety, which means it would be impossible to produce any combination of products

EXHIBIT A.1

Graph of Hockey Stick and Chess Set Problem

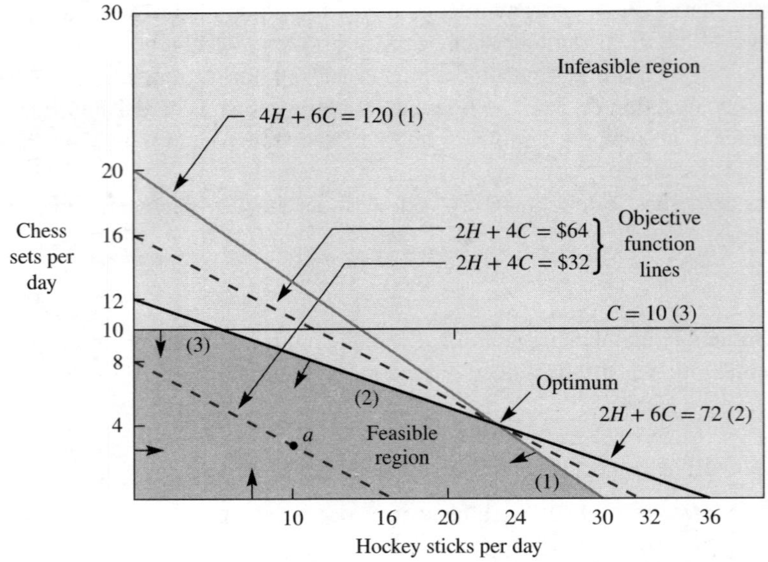

that would lie to the right of any constraint line on the graph. The region of feasible solutions is unshaded on the graph and forms a convex polygon. A convex polygon exists when a line drawn between any two points in the polygon stays within the boundaries of that polygon. If this condition of convexity does not exist, the problem is either incorrectly set up or is not amenable to linear programming.

4. **Plot the objective function.** The objective function may be plotted by assuming some arbitrary total profit figure and then solving for the axis coordinates, as was done for the constraint equations. Other terms for the objective function when used in this context are the *iso-profit* or *equal contribution line,* because it shows all possible production combinations for any given profit figure. For example, from the dotted line closest to the origin on the graph, we can determine all possible combinations of hockey sticks and chess sets that yield \$32 by picking a point on the line and reading the number of each product that can be made at that point. The combination yielding \$32 at point *a* would be 10 hockey sticks and three chess sets. This can be verified by substituting $H = 10$ and $C = 3$ in the objective function:

$$\$2(10) + \$4(3) = \$20 + \$12 = \$32$$

H	*C*	Explanation
0	120/6 = 20	Intersection of Constraint (1) and *C* axis
120/4 = 30	0	Intersection of Constraint (1) and *H* axis
0	72/6 = 12	Intersection of Constraint (2) and *C* axis
72/2 = 36	0	Intersection of Constraint (2) and *H* axis
0	10	Intersection of Constraint (3) and *C* axis
0	32/4 = 8	Intersection of \$32 iso-profit line (objective function) and *C* axis
32/2 = 16	0	Intersection of \$32 iso-profit line and *H* axis
0	64/4 = 16	Intersection of \$64 iso-profit line and *C* axis
64/2 = 32	0	Intersection of \$64 iso-profit line and *H* axis

5. **Find the optimum point.** It can be shown mathematically that the optimal combination of decision variables is always found at an extreme point (corner point) of the convex polygon. In Exhibit A.1, there are four corner points (excluding the origin), and we can determine which one is the optimum by either of two approaches. The first approach is to find the values of the various corner

solutions algebraically. This entails simultaneously solving the equations of various pairs of intersecting lines and substituting the quantities of the resultant variables in the objective function. For example, the calculations for the intersection of $2H + 6C = 72$ and $C = 10$ are as follows:

Substituting $C = 10$ in $2H + 6C = 72$ gives $2H + 6(10) = 72$, $2H = 12$, or $H = 6$. Substituting $H = 6$ and $C = 10$ in the objective function, we get

$$\begin{aligned}\text{Profit} &= \$2H + \$4C = \$2(6) + \$4(10)\\ &= \$12 + \$40 = \$52\end{aligned}$$

A variation of this approach is to read the H and C quantities directly from the graph and substitute these quantities into the objective function, as shown in the previous calculation. The drawback in this approach is that, in problems with a large number of constraint equations, there will be many possible points to evaluate, and the procedure of testing each one mathematically is inefficient.

The second and generally preferred approach entails using the objective function or iso-profit line directly to find the optimum point. The procedure involves simply drawing a straight line *parallel* to any arbitrarily selected initial iso-profit line so the iso-profit line is farthest from the origin of the graph. (In cost minimization problems, the objective would be to draw the line through the point closest to the origin.) In Exhibit A.1, the dashed line labeled $\$2H + \$4C = \$64$ intersects the most extreme point. Note that the initial arbitrarily selected iso-profit line is necessary to display the slope of the objective function for the particular problem. (Note, the slope of the objective function is –2. If P = profit, $P = \$2H + \$4C$; $\$2H = P + \$4C$; $H = P/2 - 2C$. Thus, the slope is –2.) This is important because a different objective function (try Profit = $3H + 3C$) might indicate that some other point is farthest from the origin. Given that $\$2H + \$4C = \$64$ is optimal, the amount of each variable to produce can be read from the graph: 24 hockey sticks and four chess sets. No other combination of the products yields a greater profit.

Linear Programming Using Microsoft Excel

Spreadsheets can be used to solve linear programming problems. Microsoft Excel has an optimization tool called *Solver* that we will demonstrate by solving the hockey stick and chess problem. We invoke the Solver from the Data tab. A dialogue box requests information required by the program. The following example describes how our sample problem can be solved using Excel.

If the Solver option does not appear in your Data tab, click on File → Options → Add-Ins → Go (Manage Excel Add-Ins) → Select the Solver Add-in. Solver should then be available directly from the Data tab for future use.

In the following example, we work in a step-by-step manner, setting up a spreadsheet and then solving our Puck and Pawn Company problem. Our basic strategy is to first define the problem within the spreadsheet. Following this, we invoke the Solver and feed it required information. Finally, we execute the Solver and interpret results from the reports provided by the program.

Step 1: Define Changing Cells A convenient starting point is to identify cells to be used for the decision variables in the problem. These are H and C, the number of hockey sticks and the number of chess sets to produce. Excel refers to these cells as changing cells in Solver. Referring to our Excel screen (Exhibit A.2), we have designated B4 as the location for the number of hockey sticks to produce and C4 for the number of chess sets. Note that we have set these cells equal to two initially. We could set these cells to anything, but a value other than zero will help verify that our calculations are correct.

Step 2: Calculate Total Profit (or Cost) This is our objective function and is calculated by multiplying profit associated with each product by the number of units produced. We have placed the profits in cells B5 and C5 ($2 and $4), so the profit is calculated by the following equation: B4*B5 + C4*C5, which is calculated in cell D5. Solver refers to this as the Target Cell, and it corresponds to the objective function for a problem.

Exhibit A.2

Microsoft Excel Screen for Puck and Pawn Company

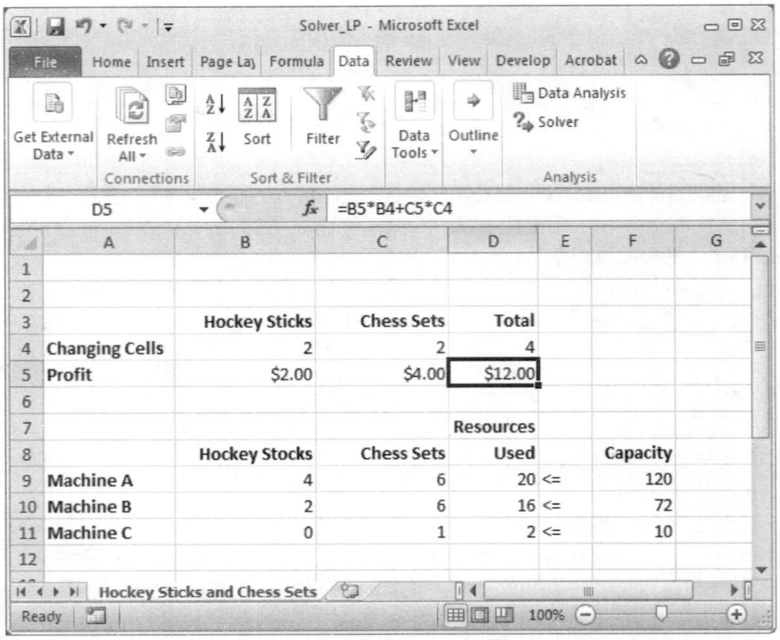

© McGraw-Hill Education

Step 3: Set Up Resource Usage Our resources are machine centers A, B, and C as defined in the original problem. We have set up three rows (9, 10, and 11) in our spreadsheet, one for each resource constraint. For machine center A, 4 hours of processing time are used for each hockey stick produced (cell B9) and 6 hours for each chess set (cell C9). For a particular solution, the total amount of the machine center A resource used is calculated in D9 (B9*B4 + C9*C4). We have indicated in cell E9 that we want this value to be less than the 120-hour capacity of machine center A, which is entered in F9. Resource usage for machine centers B and C is set up in the exact same manner in rows 10 and 11.

Step 4: Set Up Solver Go to the Data tab and select the Solver option.

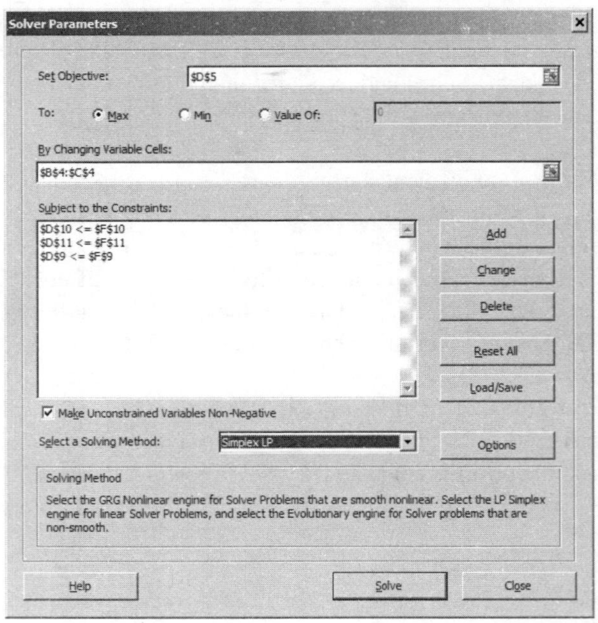

1. Set Objective: is set to the location where the value that we want to optimize is calculated. This is the profit calculated in D5 in our spreadsheet.
2. To: is set to Max because the goal is to maximize profit.
3. By Changing Variable Cells: are the cells that Solver can change to maximize profit. Cells B4 through C4 are the changing cells in our problem.
4. Subject to the Constraints: corresponds to our machine center capacity. Here we click on Add and indicate that the total used for a resource is less than or equal to the capacity available. A sample for machine center A follows. Click OK after each constraint is specified.

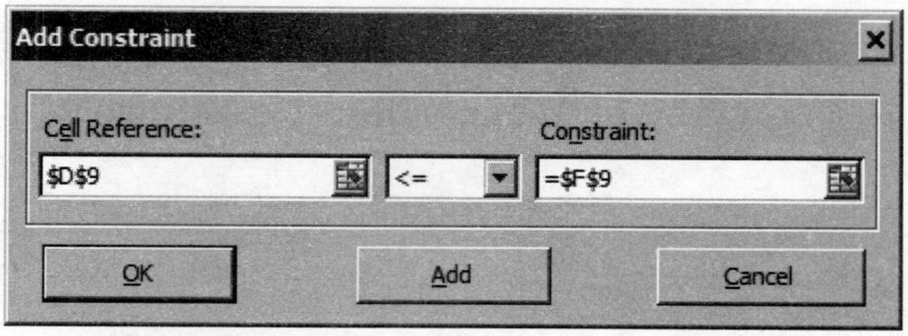

5. Select a Solving Method allows us to tell Solver what type of problem we want it to solve and how we want it solved. Solver has numerous options, but we will need to use only a few.

Most of the options relate to how Solver attempts to solve nonlinear problems. These can be very difficult to solve, and optimal solutions difficult to find. Luckily, our problem is a linear problem. We know this because our constraints and our objective function are all calculated using linear equations. Select Simplex LP to tell Solver that we want to use the linear programming option for solving the problem. In addition, we know our changing cells (decision variables) must be numbers that are greater than or equal to zero because it makes no sense to create a negative number of hockey sticks or chess sets. We indicate this by selecting Make Unconstrained Variables Non-Negative as an option. We are now ready to actually solve the problem.

Step 5: Solve the Problem Click Solve. We immediately get a Solver Results acknowledgment like that shown as follows.

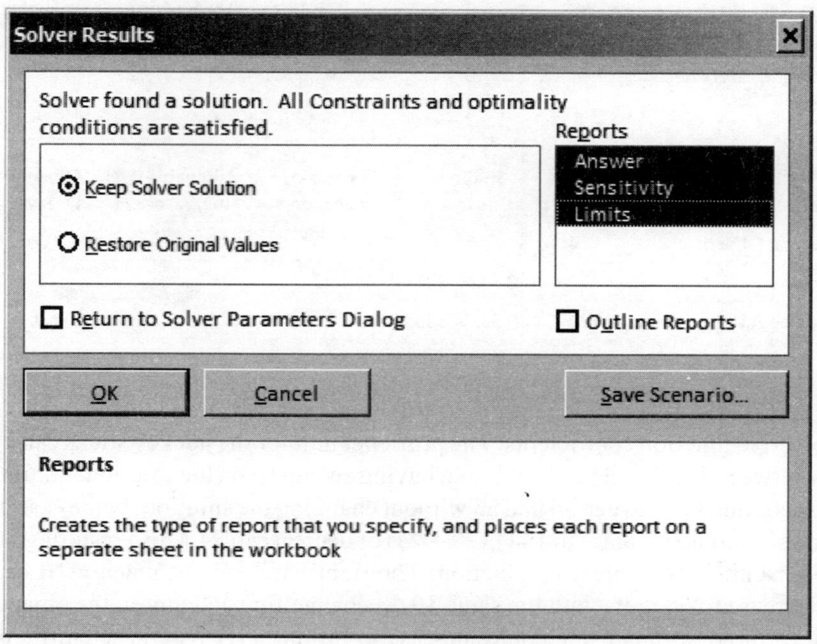

Solver acknowledges that a solution was found that appears to be optimal. On the right side of this box are options for three reports: an Answer Report, a Sensitivity Report, and a Limits Report. Click on each report to have Solver provide these. After highlighting the reports, click OK to exit back to the spreadsheet. Three new tabs have been created that correspond to these reports.

The most interesting reports for our problem are the Answer Report and the Sensitivity Report, both of which are shown in Exhibit A.3. The Answer Report shows the final answers for the total profit ($64) and the amounts produced (24 hockey sticks and 4 chess sets). In the constraints section of the Answer Report, the status of each resource is given. All of machine A and machine B are used, and there are six units of slack for machine C.

EXHIBIT A.3

Excel Solver Answer and Sensitivity Reports

Answer Report

Target Cell (Max)

Cell	Name	Original Value	Final Value
$D$5	Profit Total	$12	$64

Adjustable Cells

Cell	Name	Original Value	Final Value
$B$4	Changing Cells Hockey Sticks	2	24
$C$4	Changing Cells Chess Sets	2	4

Constraints

Cell	Name	Cell Value	Formula	Status	Slack
$D$11	Machine C Used	4	$D$1<=$F$11	Not Binding	6
$D$10	Machine B Used	72	$D$10<=$F$10	Binding	0
$D$9	Machine A Used	120	$D$9<=$F$9	Binding	0

Sensitivity Report

Adjustable Cells

Cell	Name	Final Value	Reduced Cost	Objective Coefficient	Allowable Increase	Allowable Decrease
$B$4	Changing Cells Hockey Sticks	24	0	2	0.666666667	0.666666667
$C$4	Changing Cells Chess Sets	4	0	4	2	1

Constraints

Cell	Name	Final Value	Shadow Price	Constraint R.H. Side	Allowable Increase	Allowable Decrease
$D$11	Machine C Used	4	0	10	1E + 30	6
$D$10	Machine B Used	72	0.333333333	72	18	12
$D$9	Machine A Used	120	0.333333333	120	24	36

The Sensitivity Report is divided into two parts. The first part, titled "Adjustable Cells," corresponds to objective function coefficients. The profit per unit for the hockey sticks can be either up or down $0.67 (between $2.67 and $1.33) without having an impact on the solution. Similarly, the profit of the chess sets could be between $6 and $3 without changing the solution. In the case of machine A, the right-hand side could increase to 144 (120 + 24) or decrease to 84 with a resulting $0.33 increase or decrease per unit in the objective function. The right-hand side of machine B can increase to 90 units or decrease to 60 units with the same $0.33 change for each unit in the objective function. For machine C, the right-hand side could increase to infinity (1E + 30 is scientific notation for a very large number) or decrease to 4 units with no change in the objective function.

CONCEPT CONNECTIONS

LO A–1 Use Microsoft Excel Solver to solve a linear programming problem.

Summary

- Linear programming is a powerful tool for today's business because it allows managers to make the best use of the available resources of material, plant, and equipment.
- Using Microsoft Excel Solver, we can solve linear programming problems dealing with aggregate sales and operations planning, service/manufacturing productivity analysis, product planning, product routing, and more.
- Linear programming problems can be solved in Microsoft Excel Solver using the following steps: (1) Define changing cells; (2) Calculate total profit (or cost); (3) Set up resource usage; (4) Set up the Solver; (5) Solve the problem.

Key Terms

Linear programming (LP) Refers to several related mathematical techniques used to allocate limited resources among competing demands in an optimal way.

Graphical linear programming Provides a quick insight into the nature of linear programming.

SOLVED PROBLEM

SOLVED PROBLEM 1

A furniture company produces three products: end tables, sofas, and chairs. These products are processed in five departments: the saw lumber, fabric cutting, sanding, staining, and assembly departments. End tables and chairs are produced from raw lumber only, and the sofas require lumber and fabric. Glue and thread are plentiful and represent a relatively insignificant cost that is included in operating expense. The specific requirements for each product are as follows.

Resource or Activity (quantity available per month)	Required per End Table	Required per Sofa	Required per Chair
Lumber (4,350 board feet)	10 board feet @ \$10/foot = \$100/table	7.5 board feet @ \$10/foot = \$75	4 board feet @ \$10/foot = \$40
Fabric (2,500 yards)	None	10 yards @ \$17.50/yard = \$175	None
Saw lumber (280 hours)	30 minutes	24 minutes	30 minutes
Cut fabric (140 hours)	None	24 minutes	None
Sand (280 hours)	30 minutes	6 minutes	30 minutes
Stain (140 hours)	24 minutes	12 minutes	24 minutes
Assemble (700 hours)	60 minutes	90 minutes	30 minutes

The company's direct labor expenses are \$75,000 per month for the 1,540 hours of labor, at \$48.70 per hour. Based on current demand, the firm can sell 300 end tables, 180 sofas, and 400 chairs per month. Sales prices are \$400 for end tables, \$750 for sofas, and \$240 for chairs. Assume that labor cost is fixed and the firm does not plan to hire or fire any employees over the next month.

Required:

1. What is the most limiting resource to the furniture company?

2. Determine the product mix needed to maximize profit at the company. What is the optimal number of end tables, sofas, and chairs to produce each month?

Solution

Define X_1 as the number of end tables, X_2 as the number of sofas, and X_3 as the number of chairs to produce each month. Profit is calculated as the revenue for each item minus the cost of materials (lumber and fabric), minus the cost of labor. Because labor is fixed, we subtract this out as a total sum. Mathematically, we have $(400 - 100)X_1 + (750 - 75 - 175)X_2 + (240 - 40)X_3 - 75{,}000$. Profit is calculated as follows:

$$\text{Profit} = 300X_1 + 500X_2 + 200X_3 - 75{,}000$$

Constraints are the following:

Lumber:	$10X_1 + 7.5X_2 + 4X_3 \le 4{,}350$
Fabric:	$10X_2 \le 2{,}500$
Saw:	$.5X_1 + .4X_2 + .5X_3 \le 280$
Cut:	$.4X_2 \le 140$
Sand:	$.5X_1 + .1X_2 + .5X_3 \le 280$
Stain:	$.4X_1 + .2X_2 + .4X_3 \le 140$
Assemble:	$1X_1 + 1.5X_2 + .5X_3 \le 700$
Demand:	
Table:	$X_1 \le 300$
Sofa:	$X_2 \le 180$
Chair:	$X_3 \le 400$

Step 1: Define Changing Cells These are B3, C3, and D3. Note that these cells have been set equal to zero.

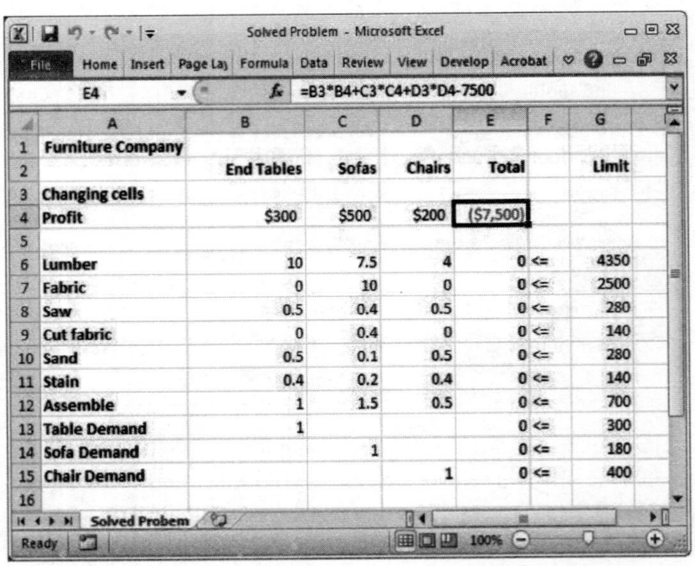

	A	B	C	D	E	F	G
1	Furniture Company						
2		End Tables	Sofas	Chairs	Total		Limit
3	Changing cells						
4	Profit	$300	$500	$200	($7,500)		
5							
6	Lumber	10	7.5	4	0	<=	4350
7	Fabric	0	10	0	0	<=	2500
8	Saw	0.5	0.4	0.5	0	<=	280
9	Cut fabric	0	0.4	0	0	<=	140
10	Sand	0.5	0.1	0.5	0	<=	280
11	Stain	0.4	0.2	0.4	0	<=	140
12	Assemble	1	1.5	0.5	0	<=	700
13	Table Demand	1			0	<=	300
14	Sofa Demand		1		0	<=	180
15	Chair Demand			1	0	<=	400
16							

Step 2: Calculate Total Profit This is E4 (this is equal to B3 times the $300 revenue associated with each end table, plus C3 times the $500 revenue for each sofa, plus D3 times the $200 revenue associated

with each chair). Note the $75,000 fixed expense that has been subtracted from revenue to calculate profit.

Step 3: Set Up Resource Usage In cells E6 through E15, the usage of each resource is calculated by multiplying B3, C3, and D3 by the amount needed for each item and summing the product (for example, E6 = B3*B6 + C3*C6 + D3*D6). The limits on these constraints are entered in cells G6 to G15.

Step 4: Set Up Solver Go to Tools and select the Solver option.

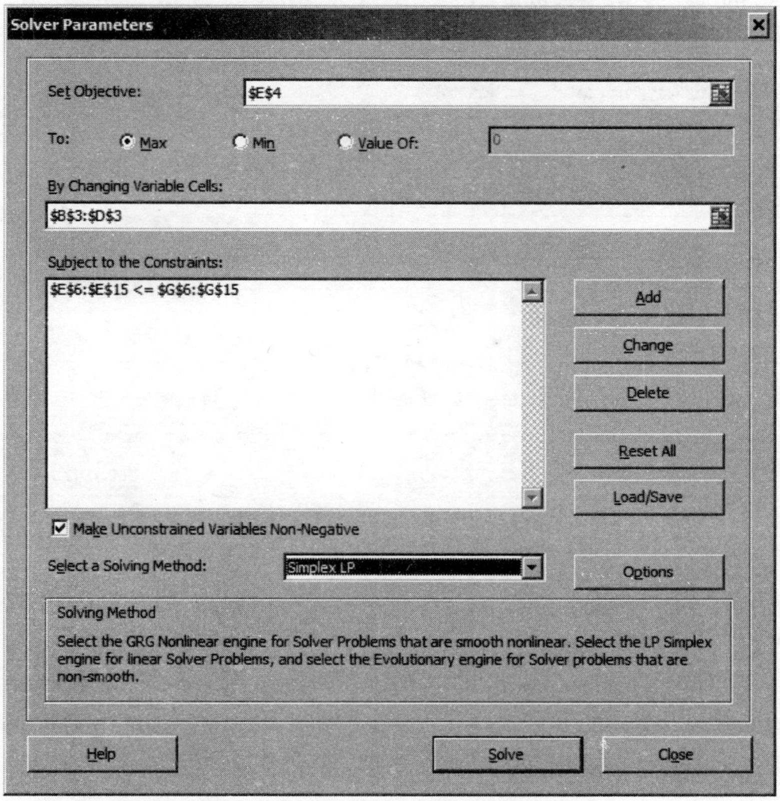

a. Set Objective: is set to the location where the value that we want to optimize is calculated. This is the profit calculated in E4 in this spreadsheet.
b. To: is set to Max because the goal is to maximize profit.
c. By Changing Variable Cells: are the cells that Solver can change to maximize profit (cells B3 through D3 in this problem).
d. Subject to the Constraints: is where a constraint set is added; we indicate that the range E6 to E15 must be less than or equal to G6 to G15.

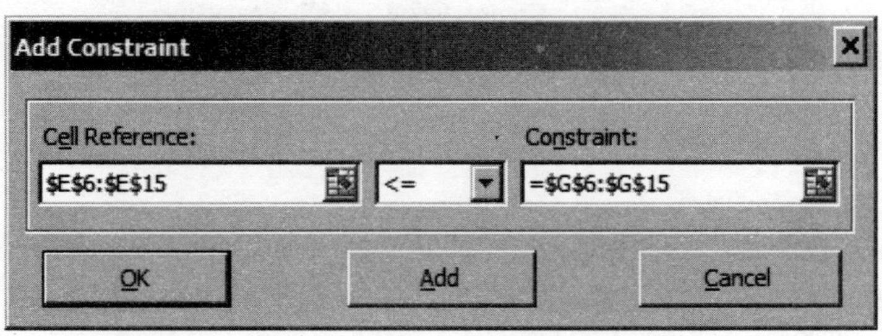

Step 5: Select a Solving Method There are a few options here, but for our purposes we just need to indicate Simplex LP and Make Unconstrained Variables Non-Negative. Simplex LP means all of our formulas are simple linear equations. Make Unconstrained Variables Non-Negative indicates that changing cells must be greater than or equal to zero.

Step 6: Solve the Problem Click Solve. We can see the solution and two special reports by highlighting items on the Solver Results acknowledgment that is displayed after a solution is found. Note that in the following report, Solver indicates that it has found a solution and all constraints and optimality conditions are satisfied. In the Reports box on the right, the Answer, Sensitivity, and Limits options have been highlighted, indicating we would like to see these items. After highlighting the reports, click OK to exit back to the spreadsheet.

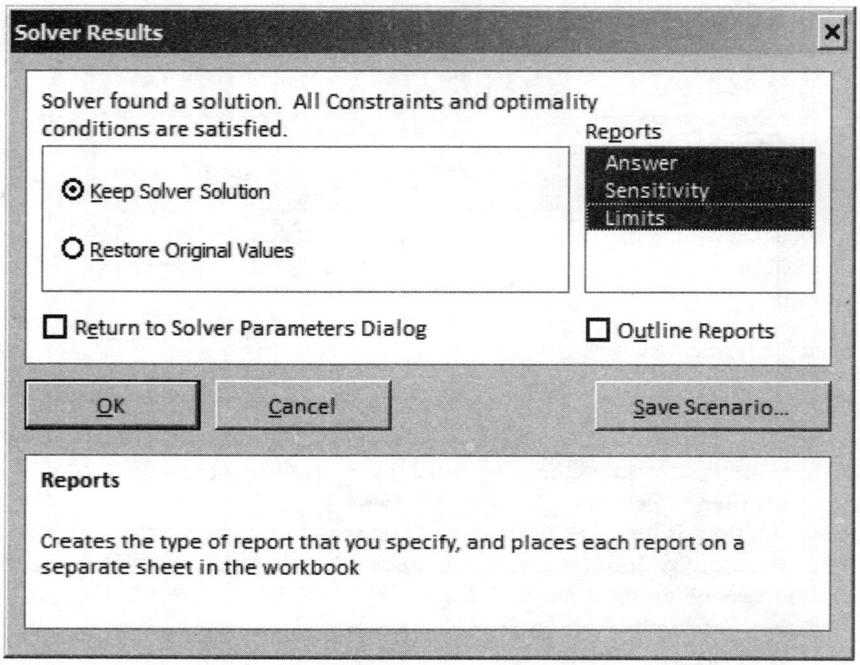

Note that three new tabs have been created: an Answer Report, a Sensitivity Report, and a Limits Report. The Answer Report indicates in the Target Cell section that the profit associated with this solution is $93,000 (we started at –$75,000). From the Target Cell section, we should make 260 end tables, 180 sofas, and no chairs. From the Constraints section, notice that the only constraints limiting profit are the staining capacity and the demand for sofas. We can see this from the column indicating whether a constraint is binding or nonbinding. Nonbinding constraints have slack, as indicated in the last column.

Target Cell (Max)

Cell	Name	Original Value	Final Value
$E$4	Profit Total	–$75,000	$93,000

Adjustable Cells

Cell	Name	Original Value	Final Value
$B$3	Changing cells End Tables	0	260
$C$3	Changing cells Sofas	0	180
$D$3	Changing cells Chairs	0	0

Constraints

Cell	Name	Cell Value	Formula	Status	Slack
$E$6	Lumber Total	3950	$E$6<=$G$6	Not Binding	400
$E$7	Fabric Total	1800	$E$7<=$G$7	Not Binding	700
$E$8	Saw Total	202	$E$8<=$G$8	Not Binding	78
$E$9	Cut fabric Total	72	$E$9<=$G$9	Not Binding	68
$E$10	Sand Total	148	$E$10<=$G$10	Not Binding	132
$E$11	Stain Total	140	$E$1<=$G$11	Binding	0
$E$12	Assemble Total	530	$E$12<=$G$12	Not Binding	170
$E$13	Table Demand Total	260	$E$13<=$G$13	Not Binding	40
$E$14	Sofa Demand Total	180	$E$14<=$G$14	Binding	0
$E$15	Chair Demand Total	0	$E$15<=$G$15	Not Binding	400

Of course, we may not be too happy with this solution because we are not meeting all the demand for tables, and it may not be wise to totally discontinue the manufacturing of chairs.

The Sensitivity Report (shown as follows) gives additional insight into the solution. The Adjustable Cells section of this report shows the final value for each cell and the reduced cost. The reduced cost indicates how much the target cell value would change if a cell that was currently set to zero were brought into the solution. Because the end tables (B3) and sofas (C3) are in the current solution, their reduced cost is zero. For each chair (D3) we make, our target cell would be reduced $100 (just round these numbers for interpretation purposes). The final three columns in the adjustable cells section of the report are the Objective Coefficient from the original spreadsheet and columns titled Allowable Increase and Allowable Decrease. Allowable Increase and Decrease show by how much the value of the corresponding coefficient could change so there would not be a change in the changing cell values (of course, the target cell value would change). For example, revenue for each end table could be as high as $1,000 ($300 + $700) or as low as $200 ($300 – $100), and we would still want to produce 260 end tables. Keep in mind that these values assume nothing else is changing in the problem. For the allowable increase value for sofas, note the value 1E + 30. This is a very large number, essentially infinity, represented in scientific notation.

Adjustable Cells

Cell	Name	Final Value	Reduced Cost	Objective Coefficient	Allowable Increase	Allowable Decrease
$B$3	Changing cells End Tables	260	0	299.9999997	700.0000012	100.0000004
$C$3	Changing cells Sofas	180	0	500.0000005	1E+30	350.0000006
$D$3	Changing cells Chairs	0	−100.0000004	199.9999993	100.0000004	1E+30

Constraints

Cell	Name	Final Value	Shadow Price	Constraint R.H. Side	Allowable Increase	Allowable Decrease
$E$6	Lumber Total	3950	0	4350	1E + 30	400
$E$7	Fabric Total	1800	0	2500	1E + 30	700
$E$8	Saw Total	202	0	280	1E + 30	78
$E$9	Cut fabric Total	72	0	140	1E + 30	68
$E$10	Sand Total	148	0	280	1E + 30	132
$E$11	Stain Total	140	749.9999992	140	16	104

(*Contd.*)

$E$12	Assemble Total	530	0	700	1E + 30	170
$E$13	Table Demand Total	260	0	300	1E + 30	40
$E$14	Sofa Demand Total	180	350.0000006	180	70	80
$E$15	Chair Demand Total	0	0	400	1E + 30	400

For the Constraints section of the report, the actual final usage of each resource is given in Final Value. The Shadow Price is the value to our target cell for each unit increase in the resource. If we could increase staining capacity, it would be worth $750 per hour. The Constraint Right-Hand Side is the current limit on the resource. Allowable Increase is the amount the resource could be increased while the shadow price is still valid. Another 16 hours' work of staining capacity could be added with a value of $750 per hour. Similarly, the Allowable Decrease column shows the amount the resource could be reduced without changing the shadow price. There is some valuable information available in this report.

The Limits Report provides additional information about our solution.

Cell	Target Name	Value
$E$4	Profit Total	$93,000

Cell	Adjustable Name	Value	Lower Limit	Target Result	Upper Limit	Target Result
$B$3	Changing cells End Tables	260	0	15000	260.0000002	93000
$C$3	Changing cells Sofas	180	0	3000	180	93000
$D$3	Changing cells Chairs	0	0	93000	0	93000

Total profit for the current solution is $93,000. Current value for B3 (end tables) is 260 units. If this were reduced to 0 units, profit would be reduced to $15,000. At an upper limit of 260, profit is $93,000 (the current solution). Similarly, for C3 (sofas), if this were reduced to 0, profit would be reduced to $3,000. At an upper limit of 180, profit is $93,000. For D3 (chairs), if this were reduced to 0, profit is $93,000 (current solution), and in this case the upper limit on chairs is also 0 units.

Acceptable answers to the questions are as follows:

1. *What is the most limiting resource to the furniture company?*

   In terms of our production resources, staining capacity is really hurting profit at this time. We could use another 16 hours of capacity.
2. *Determine the product mix needed to maximize profit at the furniture company.*

   The product mix would be to make 260 end tables, 180 sofas, and no chairs.

Of course, we have only scratched the surface with this solution. We could actually experiment with increasing staining capacity. This would give insight into the next most limiting resource. We also could run scenarios where we are required to produce a minimum number of each product, which is probably a more realistic scenario. This could help us determine how we could possibly reallocate the use of labor in our shop.

SOLVED PROBLEM 2

It is 2:00 on Friday afternoon and Joe Bob, the head chef (grill cook) at Bruce's Diner, is trying to decide the best way to allocate the available raw material to the four Friday night specials. The decision has to be made in the early afternoon because three of the items must be started now (Sloppy Joes, Tacos, and Chili). The following table contains the information on the food in inventory and the amounts required for each item.

Food	Cheeseburgers	Sloppy Joes	Tacos	Chili	Available
Ground Beef (lbs.)	0.3	0.25	0.25	0.4	100 lbs.
Cheese (lbs.)	0.1	0	0.3	0.2	50 lbs.
Beans (lbs.)	0	0	0.2	0.3	50 lbs.
Lettuce (lbs.)	0.1	0	0.2	0	15 lbs.
Tomato (lbs.)	0.1	0.3	0.2	0.2	50 lbs.
Buns	1	1	0	0	80 buns
Taco Shells	0	0	1	0	80 shells

One other fact relevant to Joe Bob's decision is the estimated market demand and selling price.

	Cheeseburgers	Sloppy Joes	Tacos	Chili
Demand	75	60	100	55
Selling Price	$2.25	$2.00	$1.75	$2.50

Joe Bob wants to maximize revenue because he has already purchased all the materials that are sitting in the cooler.

Required:

1. What is the best mix of the Friday night specials to maximize Joe Bob's revenue?
2. If a supplier offered to provide a rush order of buns at $1.00 a bun, is it worth the money?

SOLUTION

Define X_1 as the number of Cheeseburgers, X_2 as the number of Sloppy Joes, X_3 as the number of Tacos, and X_4 as the number of bowls of Chili made for the Friday night specials.

$$\text{Revenue} = \$2.25\,X_1 + \$2.00\,X_2 + \$1.75\,X_3 + \$2.50\,X_4$$

Constraints are the following:

Ground Beef:	$0.30\,X_1 + 0.25\,X_2 + 0.25\,X_3 + 0.40\,X_4 \leq 100$
Cheese:	$0.10\,X_1 + 0.30\,X_3 + 0.20\,X_4 \leq 50$
Beans:	$0.20\,X_3 + 0.30\,X_4 \leq 50$
Lettuce:	$0.10\,X_1 + 0.20\,X_3 \leq 15$
Tomato:	$0.10\,X_1 + 0.30\,X_2 + 0.20\,X_3 + 0.20\,X_4 \leq 50$
Buns:	$X_1 + X_2 \leq 80$
Taco Shells:	$X_3 \leq 80$
Demand	
Cheeseburger	$X_1 \leq 75$
Sloppy Joes	$X_2 \leq 60$
Tacos	$X_3 \leq 100$
Chili	$X_4 \leq 55$

Step 1: Define the Changing Cells These are B3, C3, D3, and E3. Note the values in the changing cell are set to 10 each so the formulas can be checked.

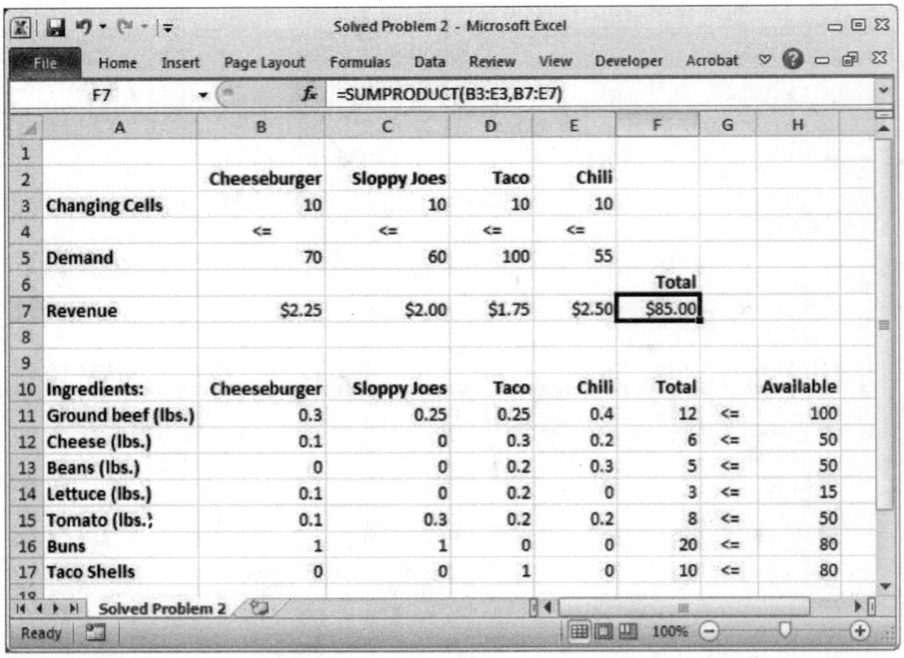

	A	B	C	D	E	F	G	H
1								
2		Cheeseburger	Sloppy Joes	Taco	Chili			
3	Changing Cells	10	10	10	10			
4		<=	<=	<=	<=			
5	Demand	70	60	100	55			
6						Total		
7	Revenue	$2.25	$2.00	$1.75	$2.50	$85.00		
8								
9								
10	Ingredients:	Cheeseburger	Sloppy Joes	Taco	Chili	Total		Available
11	Ground beef (lbs.)	0.3	0.25	0.25	0.4	12	<=	100
12	Cheese (lbs.)	0.1	0	0.3	0.2	6	<=	50
13	Beans (lbs.)	0	0	0.2	0.3	5	<=	50
14	Lettuce (lbs.)	0.1	0	0.2	0	3	<=	15
15	Tomato (lbs.)	0.1	0.3	0.2	0.2	8	<=	50
16	Buns	1	1	0	0	20	<=	80
17	Taco Shells	0	0	1	0	10	<=	80

Step 2: Calculate Total Revenue This is in cell F7 (this is equal to B3 times the $2.25 for each Cheeseburger, plus C3 times the $2.00 for a Sloppy Joe, plus D3 times the $1.75 for each Taco, plus E3 times the $2.50 for each bowl of Chili; the SUMPRODUCT function in Excel was used to make this calculation faster). Note that the current value is $85, which is a result of selling 10 of each item.

Step 3: Set Up the Usage of the Food In cells F11 to F17, the usage of each food is calculated by multiplying the changing cells row times the per item use in the table and then summing the result. The limits on each of these food types are given in H11 through H17.

Step 4: Set Up Solver and Select the Solver Option

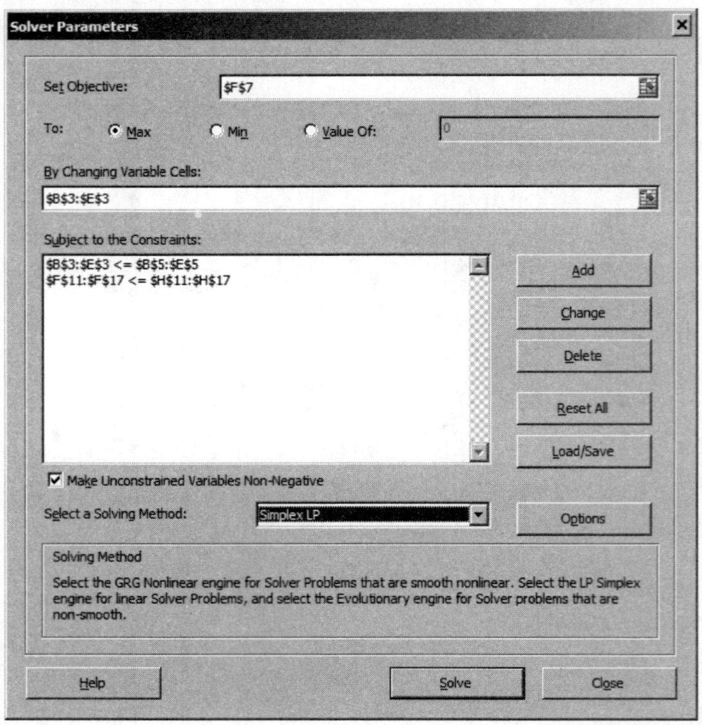

a. Set Objective: is set to the location where the value that we want to optimize is calculated. The revenue is calculated in F7 in this spreadsheet.
b. To: is set to Max because the goal is to maximize revenue.
c. By Changing Variable Cells: are the cells that tell how many of each special to produce.
d. Subject to the Constraints: is where we add two separate constraints, one for demand and one for the usage of food.

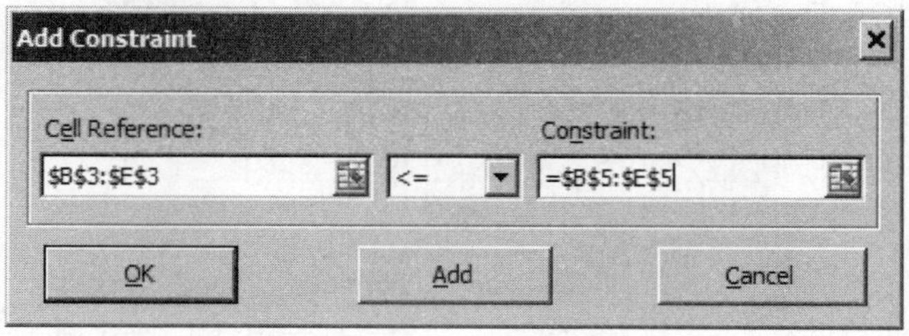

Step 5: Select a Solving Method We will leave all the settings as the default values and only make sure of two changes: (1) Simplex LP option and (2) check the Make Unconstrained Variables Non-Negative. These two options make sure that Solver knows that this is a linear programming problem and that all changing cells should be nonnegative.

Step 6: Solve the Problem Click Solve. We will get a Solver Results box. Make sure it says it has the following statement: "Solver found a solution. All constraints and optimality conditions are satisfied."

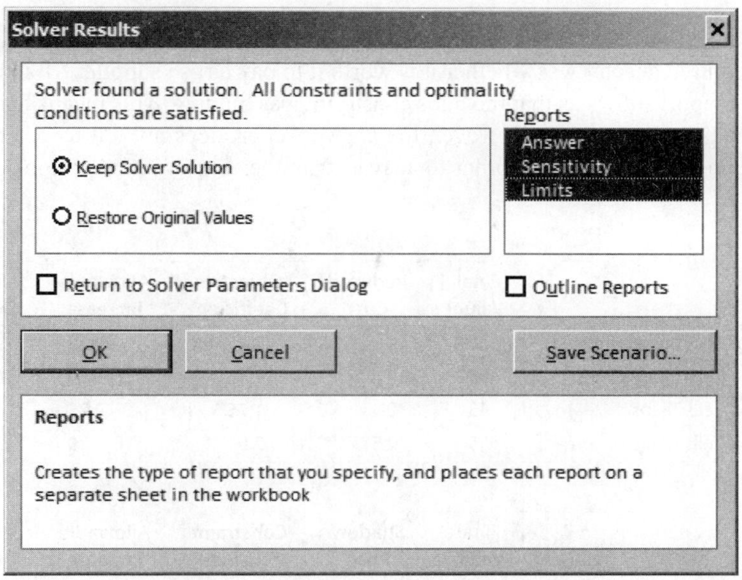

On the right-hand side of the box, there is an option for three reports: Answer, Sensitivity, and Limit. Click on all three reports and then click OK. This will exit you back to the spreadsheet, but you will have three new worksheets in your workbook.

The answer report indicates that the target cell has a final solution of $416.25 and started at $85. From the adjustable cells area, we can see that we should make 20 Cheeseburgers, 60 Sloppy Joes, 65 Tacos, and 55 bowls of Chili. This answers the first requirement from the problem of what the mix of Friday night specials should be.

Target Cell (Max)

Cell	Name	Original Value	Final Value
$F$7	Revenue Total	$85.00	$416.25

Adjustable Cells

Cell	Name	Original Value	Final Value
$B$3	Changing Cells Cheeseburgers	10	20
$C$3	Changing Cells Sloppy Joes	10	60
$D$3	Changing Cells Tacos	10	65
$E$3	Changing Cells Chili	10	55

Constraints

Cell	Name	Cell Value	Formula	Status	Slack
$F$11	Ground Beef (lbs.) Total	59.25	$F$11<=$H$11	Not Binding	40.75
$F$12	Cheese (lbs.) Total	32.50	$F$12<=$H$12	Not Binding	17.5
$F$13	Beans (lbs.) Total	29.50	$F$13<=$H$13	Not Binding	20.5
$F$14	Lettuce (lbs.) Total	15.00	$F$14<=$H$14	Binding	0
$F$15	Tomato (lbs.) Total	44.00	$F$15<=$H$15	Not Binding	6
$F$16	Buns Total	80.00	$F$16<=$H$16	Binding	0
$F$17	Taco Shells Total	65.00	$F$17<=$H$17	Not Binding	15
$B$3	Changing Cells Cheeseburgers	20	$B$3<=$B$5	Not Binding	55
$C$3	Changing Cells Sloppy Joes	60	$C$3<=$C$5	Binding	0
$D$3	Changing Cells Tacos	65	$D$3<=$D$5	Not Binding	35
$E$3	Changing Cells Chili	55	$E$3<=$E$5	Binding	0

The second required answer was whether it is worth it to pay a rush supplier $1 a bun for additional buns. The answer report shows us that the buns constraint was binding. This means that if we had more buns, we could make more money. However, the answer report does not tell us whether a rush order of buns at $1 a bun is worthwhile. In order to answer that question, we have to look at the sensitivity report.

Adjustable Cells

Cell	Name	Final Value	Reduced Cost	Objective Coefficient	Allowable Increase	Allowable Decrease
$B$3	Changing Cells Cheeseburgers	20	0	2.25	0.625	1.375
$C$3	Changing Cells Sloppy Joes	60	0.625	2	1E + 30	0.625
$D$3	Changing Cells Tacos	65	0	1.75	2.75	1.25
$E$3	Changing Cells Chili	55	2.5	2.5	1E + 30	2.5

Constraints

Cell	Name	Final Value	Shadow Price	Constraint R.H. Side	Allowable Increase	Allowable Decrease
$F$11	Ground Beef (lbs.) Total	59.25	0.00	100	1E + 30	40.75
$F$12	Cheese (lbs.) Total	32.50	0.00	50	1E + 30	17.5
$F$13	Beans (lbs.) Total	29.50	0.00	50	1E + 30	20.5
$F$14	Lettuce (lbs.) Total	15.00	8.75	15	3	13
$F$15	Tomato (lbs.) Total	44.00	0.00	50	1E + 30	6
$F$16	Buns Total	80.00	1.38	80	55	20
$F$17	Taco Shells Total	65.00	0.00	80	1E + 30	15

We have highlighted the buns row to answer the question. We can see that buns have a shadow price of $1.38. This shadow price means that each additional bun will generate $1.38 of profit. We also can see that other foods such as ground beef have a shadow price of $0. The items with a shadow price of

$0 add nothing to profit because we are currently not using all that we have now. The other important piece of information that we have on the buns is that they are only worth $1.38 up until the next 55 buns, and that is why the allowable increase is 55. We also can see that a pound of lettuce is worth $8.75. It might be wise to also look for a rush supplier of lettuce so we can increase our profit on Friday nights.

Acceptable answers to the questions are as follows:

1. *What is the best mix of the Friday night specials to maximize Joe Bob's revenue?*
   20 Cheeseburgers, 60 Sloppy Joes, 65 Tacos, and 55 bowls of Chili
2. *If a supplier offered to provide a rush order of buns at $1.00 a bun, is it worth the money?*
   Yes, each additional bun brings in $1.38, so if they cost us $1, then we will net $0.38 per bun. However, this is true only up to 55 additional buns.

OBJECTIVE QUESTIONS

1. Solve the following problem with Excel Solver:

$$
\begin{aligned}
\text{Maximize Z } &= 3X + Y. \\
12X + 14Y &\le 85 \\
3X + 2Y &\le 18 \\
Y &\le 4
\end{aligned}
$$

2. Solve the following problem with Excel Solver: (Answer in Appendix D)

$$
\begin{aligned}
\text{Maximize Z } &= 2A + 4B. \\
4A + 6B &\ge 120 \\
2A + 6B &\ge 72 \\
B &\ge 10
\end{aligned}
$$

3. A manufacturing firm has discontinued production of a certain unprofitable product line. Considerable excess production capacity was created as a result. Management is considering devoting this excess capacity to one or more of three products: X_1, X_2, and X_3.
   Machine hours required per unit are:

	Product		
Machine Type	X_1	X_2	X_3
Milling machine	8	2	3
Lathe	4	3	0
Grinder	2	0	1

The available time in machine hours per week is:

	Machine Hours per Week
Milling machines	800
Lathes	480
Grinders	320

The salespeople estimate they can sell all the units of X_1 and X_2 that can be made. But the sales potential of X_3 is 80 units per week maximum.

Unit profits for the three products are:

	Unit Profits
X_1	\$20
X_2	6
X_3	8

a. Set up the equations that can be solved to maximize the profit per week.
b. Solve these equations using the Excel Solver.
c. What is the optimal solution? How many of each product should be made, and what should the resultant profit be?
d. What is this situation with respect to the machine groups? Would they work at capacity, or would there be unused available time? Will X_3 be at maximum sales capacity?
e. Suppose an additional 200 hours per week can be obtained from the milling machines by using staff overtime. The incremental cost would be \$1.50 per hour. Would you recommend doing this? Explain how you arrived at your answer.

4. A diet is being prepared for the University of Arizona dorms. The objective is to feed the students at the least cost, but the diet must have between 1,800 and 3,600 calories. No more than 1,400 calories can be starch, and no fewer than 400 can be protein. The varied diet is to be made of two foods: *A* and *B*. Food *A* costs \$0.75 per pound and contains 600 calories, 400 of which are protein and 200 starch. No more than two pounds of food *A* can be used per resident. Food *B* costs \$0.15 per pound and contains 900 calories, of which 700 are starch, 100 are protein, and 100 are fat. (Answers in Appendix D)
   a. Write the equations representing this information.
   b. Solve the problem graphically for the amounts of each food that should be used.
5. Repeat problem 4 with the added constraint that not more than 150 calories shall be fat and that the price of food has escalated to \$1.75 per pound for food *A* and \$2.50 per pound for food *B*.
6. Logan Manufacturing wants to mix two fuels, *A* and *B*, for its trucks to minimize cost. It needs no fewer than 3,000 gallons to run its trucks during the next month. It has a maximum fuel storage capacity of 4,000 gallons. There are 2,000 gallons of fuel *A* and 4,000 gallons of fuel *B* available. The mixed fuel must have an octane rating of no less than 80.

   When fuels are mixed, the amount of fuel obtained is just equal to the sum of the amounts put in. The octane rating is the weighted average of the individual octanes, weighted in proportion to the respective volumes.

   The following is known: Fuel *A* has an octane of 90 and costs \$1.20 per gallon. Fuel *B* has an octane of 75 and costs \$0.90 per gallon.
   a. Write the equations expressing this information.
   b. Solve the problem using the Excel Solver, giving the amount of each fuel to be used. State any assumptions necessary to solve the problem.
7. You are trying to create a budget to optimize the use of a portion of your disposable income. You have a maximum of \$1,500 per month to be allocated to food, shelter, and entertainment. The amount spent on food and shelter combined must not exceed \$1,000. The amount spent on shelter alone must not exceed \$700. Entertainment cannot exceed \$300 per month. Each dollar spent on food has a satisfaction value of 2, each dollar spent on shelter has a satisfaction value of 3, and each dollar spent on entertainment has a satisfaction value of 5.

   Assuming a linear relationship, use the Excel Solver to determine the optimal allocation of your funds.
8. C-Town Brewery brews two beers: Expansion Draft and Burning River. Expansion Draft sells for \$20 per barrel, while Burning River sells for \$8 per barrel. Producing a barrel of Expansion Draft takes 8 pounds of corn and 4 pounds of hops. Producing a barrel of Burning River requires 2 pounds of corn, 6 pounds of rice, and 3 pounds of hops. The brewery has 500 pounds of corn, 300 pounds of rice, and 400 pounds of hops. Assuming a linear relationship, use Excel Solver to determine the optimal mix of Expansion Draft and Burning River that maximizes C-Town's revenue.
9. BC Petrol manufactures three chemicals at its chemical plant in Kentucky: BCP1, BCP2, and BCP3. These chemicals are produced in two production processes known as zone and man.

Running the zone process for an hour costs \$48 and yields three units of BCP1, one unit of BCP2, and one unit of BCP3. Running the man process for one hour costs \$24 and yields one unit of BCP1 and one unit of BCP2. To meet customer demands, at least 20 units of BCP1, 10 units of BCP2, and 6 units of BCP3 must be produced daily. Assuming a linear relationship, use Excel Solver to determine the optimal mix of processes zone and man to minimize costs and meet BC Petrol daily demands.

10. A farmer in Wood County has 900 acres of land. She is going to plant each acre with corn, soybeans, or wheat. Each acre planted with corn yields a \$2,000 profit; each with soybeans yields \$2,500 profit; and each with wheat yields \$3,000 profit. She has 100 workers and 150 tons of fertilizer. The following table shows the requirement per acre of each of the crops. Assuming a linear relationship, use Excel Solver to determine the optimal planting mix of corn, soybeans, and wheat to maximize her profits.

	Corn	Soybeans	Wheat
Labor (workers)	0.1	0.3	0.2
Fertilizer (tons)	0.2	0.1	0.4

Appendix B

Operations Technology

LO B-1

Explain how the application of operations technology has affected manufacturing.

Much of the recent growth in productivity has come from the application of operations technology. In services, this comes primarily from soft technology—information processing. In manufacturing, it comes from a combination of soft and hard (machine) technologies. Given that most readers of this book have covered information technologies in services in MIS courses, our focus in this supplement is on manufacturing.

Technologies in Manufacturing

Some technological advances in recent decades have had a significant, widespread impact on manufacturing firms in many industries. These advances, which are the topic of this section, can be categorized in two ways: hardware systems and software systems.

Hardware technologies have generally resulted in greater automation of processes; they perform labor-intensive tasks originally performed by humans. Examples of these major types of hardware technologies are numerically controlled machine tools, machining centers, industrial robots, automated materials handling systems, and flexible manufacturing systems. These are all computer-controlled devices that can be used in the manufacturing of products. Software-based technologies aid in the design of manufactured products and in the analysis and planning of manufacturing activities. These technologies include computer-aided design and automated manufacturing planning and control systems. Each of these technologies will be described in greater detail in the following sections.

Hardware Systems *Numerically controlled (NC) machines* are comprised of (1) a typical machine tool used to turn, drill, or grind different types of parts and (2) a computer that controls the sequence of processes performed by the machine. NC machines were first adopted by U.S. aerospace firms in the 1960s, and they have since proliferated to many other industries. In more recent models, feedback control loops determine the position of the machine tooling during the work, constantly compare the actual location with the programmed location, and correct as needed. This is often called *adaptive control.*

Machining centers represent an increased level of automation and complexity relative to NC machines. Machining centers not only provide automatic control of a machine, they also may carry many tools that can be automatically changed depending on the tool required for each operation. In addition, a single machine may be equipped with a shuttle system so that a finished part can be unloaded and an unfinished part loaded while the machine is working on a part. To help you visualize a machining center, we have included a diagram in Exhibit B.1A.

Industrial robots are used as substitutes for workers for many repetitive manual activities and tasks that are dangerous, dirty, or dull. A robot is a programmable, multifunctional machine that may be equipped with an end effector. Examples of end effectors include a gripper to pick things up or a tool such as a wrench, a welder, or a paint sprayer. Exhibit B.1B examines the human motions a robot can reproduce. Advanced capabilities have been designed into robots to allow vision, tactile sensing, and hand-to-hand coordination. In addition, some models can be "taught" a sequence of motions in a three-dimensional pattern. As a worker moves the end of the robot arm through the required motions,

EXHIBIT B.1

A. The CNC Machining Center

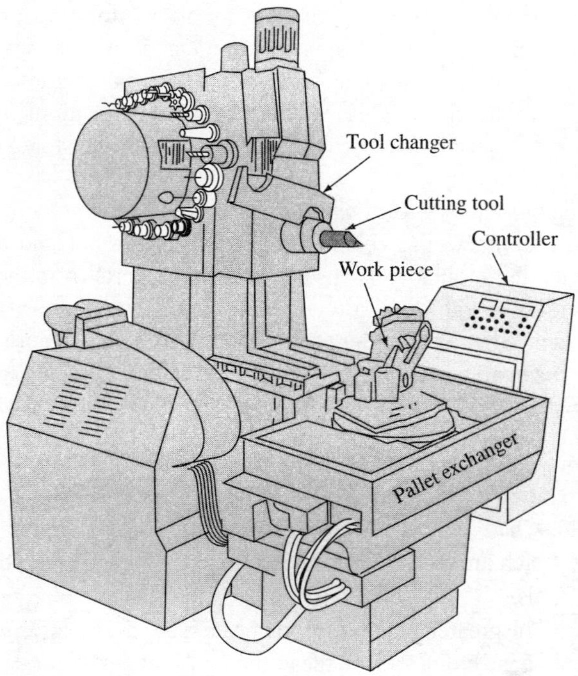

B. Typical Robot Axes of Motion

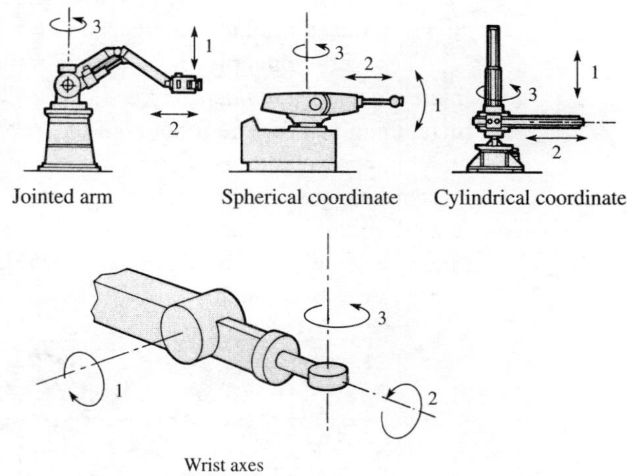

J. T. Black, *The Design of the Factory with a Future* (New York: McGraw-Hill, 1991), p. 39, with permission of The McGraw-Hill Companies.

L. V. Ottinger, "Robotics for the IE: Terminology, Types of Robots," *Industrial Engineering*, November 1981, p. 30.

OSCM AT WORK

Formula for Evaluating a Robot Investment

Many companies use the following modification of the basic payback formula in deciding if a robot should be purchased:

$$P = \frac{I}{L - E + q(L + Z)}$$

where

P = Payback period in years
I = Total capital investment required in robot and accessories
L = Annual labor costs replaced by the robot (wage and benefit costs per worker times the number of shifts per day)
E = Annual maintenance cost for the robot
q = Fractional speedup (or slowdown) factor
Z = Annual depreciation

Example:

I = \$50,000
L = \$60,000 (two workers × \$20,000 each working one of two shifts; overhead is \$10,000 each)
E = \$9,600 (\$2/hour × 4,800 hours/year)
q = 1.5 (robot works 150 percent as fast as a worker)
Z = \$10,000

then

$$P = \frac{\$50{,}000}{\$60{,}000 - \$9{,}600 + 1.5(\$60{,}000 + \$10{,}000)}$$
$$= 1/3 \text{ year}$$

the robot records this pattern in its memory and repeats it on command. Newer robotic systems can conduct quality control inspections and then transfer, via mobile robots, those parts to other robots downstream. As shown in the OSCM at Work box "Formula for Evaluating a Robot Investment," robots are often justified based on labor savings.

Automated materials handing (AMH) systems improve efficiency of transportation, storage, and retrieval of materials. Examples are computerized conveyors and automated storage and retrieval systems (AS/RS) in which computers direct automatic loaders to pick and place items. Automated guided vehicle (AGV) systems use embedded floor wires to direct driverless vehicles to various locations in the plant. Benefits of AMH systems include quicker material movement, lower inventories and storage space, reduced product damage, and higher labor productivity.

These individual pieces of automation can be combined to form *manufacturing cells* or even complete *flexible manufacturing systems (FMS)*. A manufacturing cell might consist of a robot and a machining center. The robot could be programmed to automatically insert and remove parts from the machining center, thus allowing unattended operation. An FMS is a totally automated manufacturing system that consists of machining centers with the automated loading and unloading of parts, an automated guided vehicle system for moving parts between machines, and other automated elements to allow the unattended production of parts. In an FMS, a comprehensive computer control system is used to run the entire system.

One of the four large machining centers (see Exhibit B.2) that are part of the flexible manufacturing systems at Cincinnati Milacron's Mt. Orab, Ohio, Plant.

Courtesy of Cincinnati Milacron, Mt. Orab, Ohio plant

A good example of an FMS is the Cincinnati Milacron facility in Mt. Orab, Ohio, which has been in operation for over 30 years. Exhibit B.2 is a layout of this FMS. In this system, parts are loaded onto standardized fixtures (these are called "risers"), which are mounted on pallets that can be moved by the AGVs. Workers load and unload tools and parts onto the standardized fixtures at the workstations shown on the right side of the diagram. Most of this loading and unloading is done during a single shift. The system can operate virtually unattended for the other two shifts each day.

Within the system there are areas for the storage of tools (Area 7) and for parts (Area 5). This system is designed to machine large castings used in the production of the machine tools made by Cincinnati Milacron. The machining is done by the four CNC machining centers (Area 1). When the machining has been completed on a part, it is sent to the parts washing station (Area 4), where it is cleaned. The part is then sent to the automated inspection station (Area 6) for a quality check. The system is capable of producing hundreds of different parts.

Exhibit B.2

The Cincinnati Milacron Flexible Manufacturing System

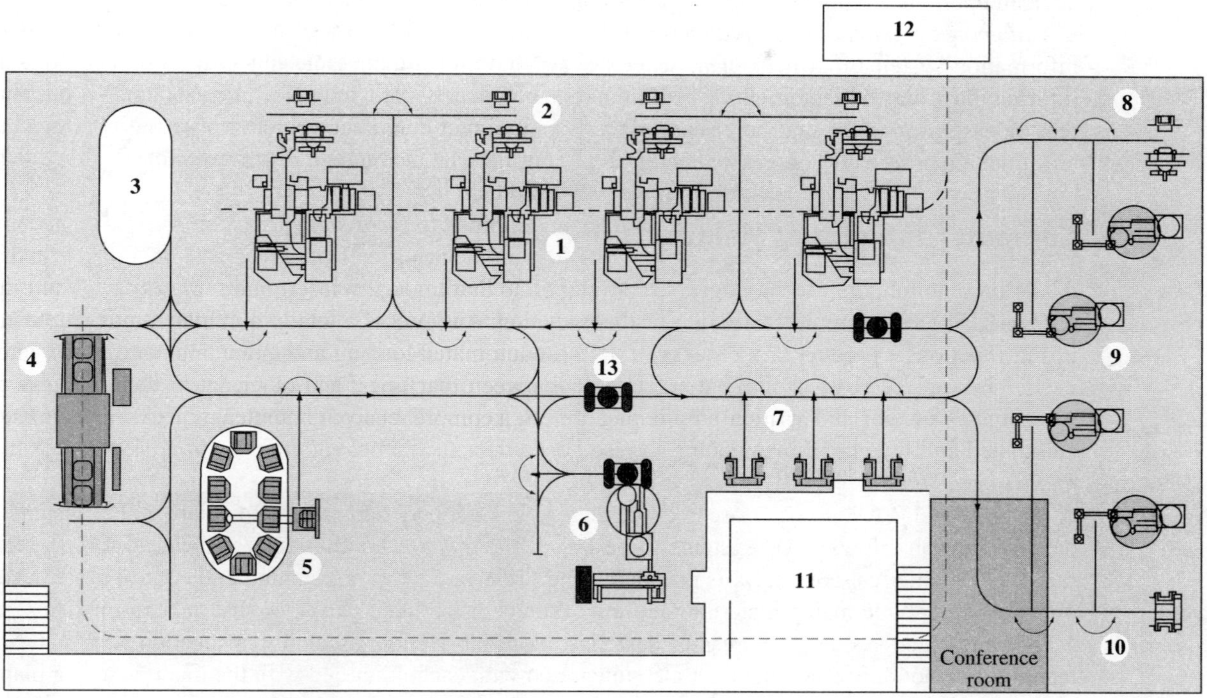

Key:

1 Four Milacron T-30 CNC Machining Centers.
2 Four tool interchange stations, one per machine, for tool storage chain delivery via computer-controlled cart.
3 Cart maintenance station. Coolant monitoring and maintenance area.
4 Parts wash station, automatic handling.
5 Automatic Workchanger (10 pallets) for online pallet queue.
6 One inspection module—horizontal type coordinate measuring machine.
7 Three queue stations for tool delivery chains.
8 Tool delivery chain load/unload stations.
9 Four part load/unload stations.
10 Pallet/fixture build station.
11 Control center, computer room (elevated).
12 Centralized chip/coolant collection/recovery system (----flume path).
13 Three computer-controlled carts, with wire-guided path.
⌒ Cart turnaround station (up to 360° around its own axis)

Source: A tour brochure from the plant

Software Systems *Computer-aided design (CAD)* is an approach to product and process design that utilizes the power of the computer. CAD covers several automated technologies, such as *computer graphics* to examine the visual characteristics of a product and *computer-aided engineering (CAE)* to evaluate its engineering characteristics. Rubbermaid used CAD to refine dimensions of its ToteWheels to meet airline requirements for checked baggage. CAD also includes technologies associated with the manufacturing process design, referred to as *computer-aided process planning (CAPP).* CAPP is used to design the computer part programs that serve as instructions to computer-controlled machine tools and to design the programs used to sequence parts through the machine centers and other processes (such as the washing and inspection) needed to complete the part. These programs are referred to as *process plans.* Sophisticated CAD systems also are able to do on-screen tests, replacing the early phases of prototype testing and modification.

CAD has been used to design everything from computer chips to potato chips. Frito-Lay, for example, used CAD to design its O'Grady's double-density, ruffled potato chip. The problem in designing such a chip is that if it is cut improperly, it may be burned on the outside and soggy on the inside, be too brittle (and shatter when placed in the bag), or display other characteristics that make it unworthy for, say, a guacamole dip. However, through the use of CAD, the proper angle and number of ruffles were determined mathematically; the O'Grady's model passed its stress test in the infamous Frito-Lay "crusher" and made it to your grocer's shelf. But despite some very loyal fans, O'Grady's has been discontinued, presumably due to lack of sales.

CAD is now being used to custom-design swimsuits. Measurements of the wearer are fed into the CAD program, along with the style of suit desired. Working with the customer, the designer modifies the suit design as it appears on a human-form drawing on the computer screen. Once the design is decided upon, the computer prints out a pattern, and the suit is cut and sewn on the spot.

Automated manufacturing planning and control systems (MP&CS) are simply computer-based information systems that help plan, schedule, and monitor a manufacturing operation. They obtain information from the factory floor continuously about work status, material arrivals, and so on, and they release production and purchase orders. Sophisticated manufacturing and planning control systems include order-entry processing, shop-floor control, purchasing, and cost accounting.

Computer-Integrated Manufacturing (CIM)

All of these automation technologies are brought together under *computer-integrated manufacturing (CIM)*. CIM is the automated version of the manufacturing process, where the three major manufacturing functions—product and process design, planning and control, and the manufacturing process itself—are replaced by the automated technologies just described. Further, the traditional integration mechanisms of oral and written communication are replaced by computer technology. Such highly automated and integrated manufacturing also goes under the names *total factory automation* and the *factory of the future*.

All of the CIM technologies are tied together using a network and integrated database. For instance, data integration allows CAD systems to be linked to *computer-aided manufacturing (CAM),* which consists of numerical-control parts programs; and the manufacturing planning and control system can be linked to the automated material handling systems to facilitate parts pick list generation. Thus, in a fully integrated system, the areas of design, testing, fabrication, assembly, inspection, and material handling are not only automated but also integrated with each other and with the manufacturing planning and scheduling function.

Evaluation of Technology Investments Modern technologies such as flexible manufacturing systems or computerized order processing systems represent large capital investments. Hence, a firm has to carefully assess its financial and strategic benefits from a technology before acquiring it. Evaluating such investments is especially hard because the purpose of acquiring new technologies is not just to reduce labor costs but also to increase product quality and variety, to shorten production lead times, and to increase the flexibility of an operation. Some of these benefits are intangible relative to labor cost reduction, so justification becomes difficult. Further, rapid technological change renders new equipment obsolete in just a few years, making the cost–benefit evaluation more complex.

But never assume that new automation technologies are always cost-effective. Even when there is no uncertainty about the benefits of automation, it may not be worthwhile to adopt it. For instance, many analysts predicted that integrated CAD/CAM systems would be the answer to all manufacturing problems. But a number of companies investing in such systems lost money in the process. The idea was to take a lot of skilled labor out of the process of tooling up for new or redesigned products and to speed up the process. However, it can take less time to mill complex, low-volume parts than to program the milling machine, and programmer time is more expensive than the milling operator time. Also, it may not always be easy to transfer all the expert knowledge and experience that a milling operator has gained over the years into a computer program. CAD/CAM integration software has attained sufficient levels of quality and cost-effectiveness that it is now routinely utilized even in high-variety low-volume manufacturing environments.

Benefits of Technology Investments The typical benefits from adopting new manufacturing technologies are both tangible and intangible. The tangible benefits can be used in traditional modes of financial analysis such as discounted cash flow to make sound investment decisions. Specific benefits can be summarized as follows:

Cost Reduction

Labor costs. Replacing people with robots, or enabling fewer workers to run semiautomatic equipment.

Material costs. Using existing materials more efficiently, or enabling the use of high-tolerance materials.

Inventory costs. Fast changeover equipment allowing for JIT inventory management.

Quality costs. Automated inspection and reduced variation in product output.

Maintenance costs. Self-adjusting equipment.

Other Benefits

Increased product variety. Scope economies due to flexible manufacturing systems.

Improved product features. Ability to make things that could not be made by hand (e.g., microprocessors).

Shorter cycle times. Faster setups and changeovers.

Greater product output.

Risks in Adopting New Technologies Although there may be many benefits in acquiring new technologies, several types of risk accompany the acquisition of new technologies. These risks have to be evaluated and traded off against the benefits before the technologies are adopted. Some of these risks are described next.

Technological Risks

An early adopter of a new technology has the benefit of being ahead of the competition, but he or she also runs the risk of acquiring an untested technology whose problems could disrupt the firm's operations. There is also the risk of obsolescence, especially with electronics-based technologies where change is rapid and when the fixed cost of acquiring new technologies or the cost of upgrades is high. Also, alternative technologies may become more cost-effective in the future, negating the benefits of a technology today.

Operational Risks

There also could be risks in applying a new technology to a firm's operations. Installation of a new technology generally results in significant disruptions, at least in the short run, in the form of plantwide reorganization, retraining, and so on. Further risks are due to the delays and errors introduced in the production process and the uncertain and sudden demands on various resources.

Organizational Risks

Firms may lack the organizational culture and top management commitment required to absorb the short-term disruptions and uncertainties associated with adopting a new technology. In such organizations, there is a risk that the firm's employees or managers may quickly abandon the technology when there are short-term failures or they will avoid major changes by simply automating the firm's old, inefficient process and therefore not obtain the benefits of the new technology.

Environmental or Market Risks

In many cases, a firm may invest in a particular technology only to discover a few years later that changes in some environmental or market factors make the investment worthless. For instance, in environmental issues, auto firms have been reluctant to invest in technology for making electric cars because they are uncertain about future emission standards of state and federal governments, the potential for decreasing emissions from gasoline-based cars, and the potential for significant improvements in battery technology. Typical examples of market risks are fluctuations in currency exchange rates and interest rates.

CONCEPT CONNECTIONS

LO B–1 Explain how the application of operations technology has affected manufacturing.

Summary

- Technology has played the dominant role in the productivity growth of most nations and has provided the competitive edge to firms that have adopted it early and implemented it successfully.
- Although each of the manufacturing and information technologies described here is a powerful tool by itself and can be adopted separately, their benefits grow exponentially when they are integrated with each other. This is particularly the case with CIM technologies.
- With more modern technologies, the benefits are not entirely tangible and many benefits may be realized only on a long-term basis. Thus, typical cost accounting methods and standard financial analysis may not adequately capture all the potential benefits of technologies such as CIM. Hence, we must take into account the strategic benefits in evaluating such investments. Further, because capital costs for many modern technologies are substantial, the various risks associated with such investments have to be carefully assessed.
- Implementing flexible manufacturing systems or complex decision support systems requires a significant commitment for most firms. Such investments may even be beyond the reach of small to medium-size firms. However, as technologies continue to improve and are adopted more widely, their costs may decline and place them within the reach of smaller firms. Given the complex, integrative nature of these technologies, the total commitment of top management and all employees is critical for the successful implementation of these technologies.

DISCUSSION QUESTIONS

1. Do robots have to be trained? Explain.
2. How does the axiom used in industrial selling "You don't sell the product; you sell the company" pertain to manufacturing technology?
3. List three analytical tools (other than financial analysis) covered elsewhere in the book that can be used to evaluate technological alternatives.
4. The Belleville, Ontario, Canada, subsidiary of Atlanta-based Interface Inc., one of the world's largest makers of commercial flooring, credits much of its profitability to "green manufacturing" or "eco-efficiency." What do you believe these terms mean, eh? And how could such practices lead to cost reduction?
5. Give two examples each of recent process and product technology innovations.
6. What is the difference between an NC machine and a machining center?
7. The major auto companies are planning to invest millions of dollars in developing new product and process technologies required to make electric cars. Describe briefly why they are investing in these technologies. Discuss the potential benefits and risks involved in these investments.

Appendix C

Financial Analysis

In this appendix, we review the basic concepts and tools of financial analysis for OSCM. These include the types of cost (fixed, variable, sunk, opportunity, avoidable), risk and expected value, and depreciation (straight line, sum-of-the-years'-digits, declining balance, double-declining-balance, and depreciation-by-use). We also discuss activity-based costing and cost-of-capital calculations. Our focus is on capital investment decisions.

LO C-1

Evaluate capital investments using the various types of cost, risk and expected value, and depreciation.

Concepts and Definitions

We begin with some basic definitions.

Fixed Costs A *fixed cost* is any expense that remains constant regardless of the level of output. Although no cost is truly fixed, many types of expense are virtually fixed over a wide range of output. Examples are rent, property taxes, most types of depreciation, insurance payments, and salaries of top management.

Variable Costs *Variable costs* are expenses that fluctuate directly with changes in the level of output. For example, each additional unit of sheet steel produced by USx requires a specific amount of material and labor. The incremental cost of this additional material and labor can be isolated and assigned to each unit of sheet steel produced. Many overhead expenses are also variable because utility bills, maintenance expense, and so forth, vary with the production level.

Exhibit C.1 illustrates the fixed and variable cost components of total cost. Note that total cost increases at the same rate as variable costs because fixed costs are constant.

Sunk Costs *Sunk costs* are past expenses or investments that have no salvage value and therefore should not be taken into account in considering investment alternatives. Sunk costs also could be current costs that are essentially fixed such as rent on a building. For example, suppose an ice cream manufacturing

EXHIBIT C.1

Fixed and Variable Cost Components of Total Cost

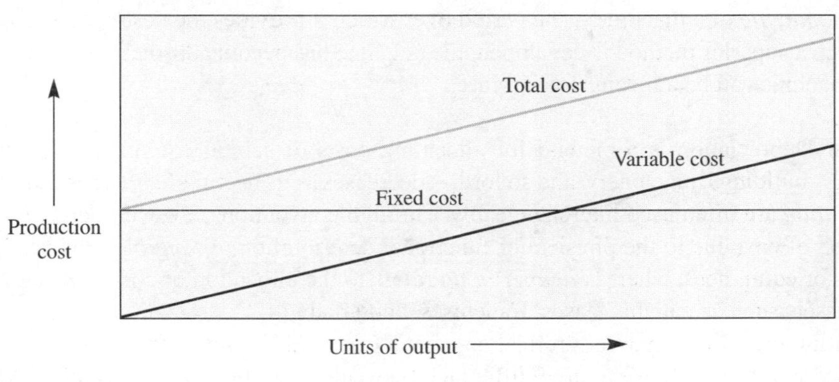

firm occupies a rented building and is considering making sherbet in the same building. If the company enters sherbet production, its cost accountant will assign some of the rental expense to the sherbet operation. However, the building rent remains unchanged and therefore is not a relevant expense to be considered in making the decision. The rent is *sunk;* that is, it continues to exist and does not change in amount regardless of the decision.

Opportunity Costs *Opportunity cost* is the benefit *forgone,* or advantage *lost,* that results from choosing one action over the *best-known alternative* course of action.

Suppose a firm has $100,000 to invest and then two alternatives of comparable risk present themselves, each requiring a $100,000 investment. Investment A will net $25,000; Investment B will net $23,000. Investment A is clearly the better choice, with a $25,000 net return. If the decision is made to invest in B instead of A, the opportunity cost of B is $2,000, which is the benefit forgone.

Avoidable Costs *Avoidable costs* include any expense that is *not* incurred if an investment is made but that *must* be incurred if the investment is *not* made. Suppose a company owns a metal lathe that is not in working condition but is needed for the firm's operations. Because the lathe must be repaired or replaced, the repair costs are avoidable if a new lathe is purchased. Avoidable costs reduce the cost of a new investment because they are not incurred if the investment is made. Avoidable costs are an example of how it is possible to "save" money by spending money.

Expected Value Risk is inherent in any investment because the future can never be predicted with absolute certainty. To deal with this uncertainty, mathematical techniques such as expected value can help. Expected value is the expected outcome multiplied by the probability of its occurrence. Recall that in the preceding example the expected outcome of Alternative A was $25,000 and B, $23,000. Suppose the probability of A's actual outcome is 80 percent while B's probability is 90 percent. The expected values of the alternatives are determined as follows:

$$\begin{matrix}\text{Expected} \\ \text{outcome}\end{matrix} \times \begin{matrix}\text{Probability that actual} \\ \text{outcome will be the} \\ \text{expected outcome}\end{matrix} = \begin{matrix}\text{Expected} \\ \text{value}\end{matrix}$$

$$\text{Investment A: } \$25{,}000 \times 0.80 = \$20{,}000$$
$$\text{Investment B: } \$23{,}000 \times 0.90 = \$20{,}700$$

Investment B is now seen to be the better choice, with a net advantage over A of $700.

Economic Life and Obsolescence When a firm invests in an income-producing asset, the productive life of the asset is estimated. For accounting purposes, the asset is depreciated over this period. It is assumed that the asset will perform its function during this time and then be considered obsolete or worn out, and replacement will be required. This view of asset life rarely coincides with reality.

Assume that a machine expected to have a productive life of 10 years is purchased. If at any time during the ensuing 10 years a new machine is developed that can perform the same task more efficiently or economically, the old machine has become obsolete. Whether or not it is "worn out" is irrelevant.

The *economic life* of a machine is the period over which it provides the best method for performing its task. When a superior method is developed, the machine has become obsolete. Thus, the stated *book value* of a machine can be a meaningless figure.

Depreciation Depreciation is a method for allocating costs of capital equipment. The value of any capital asset—buildings, machinery, and so forth—decreases as its useful life is expended. *Amortization* and *depreciation* are often used interchangeably. Through convention, however, *depreciation* refers to the allocation of cost due to the physical or functional deterioration of *tangible* (physical) assets such as buildings or equipment, whereas *amortization* refers to the allocation of cost over the useful life of *intangible* assets such as patents, leases, franchises, and goodwill.

Depreciation procedures may not reflect an asset's true value at any point in its life because obsolescence may at any time cause a large difference between true value and book value. Also, because depreciation rates significantly affect taxes, a firm may choose a particular method from the several alternatives with more consideration for its effect on taxes than its ability to make the book value of an asset reflect the true resale value.

Next we describe five commonly used methods of depreciation.

Straight-Line Method

Under this method, an asset's value is reduced in uniform annual amounts over its estimated useful life. The general formula is

$$\text{Annual amount to be depreciated} = \frac{\text{Cost} - \text{Salvage value}}{\text{Estimated useful life}}$$

A machine costing \$10,000 with an estimated salvage value of \$0 and an estimated life of 10 years would be depreciated at the rate of \$1,000 per year for each of the 10 years. If its estimated salvage value at the end of the 10 years is \$1,000, the annual depreciation charge is

$$\frac{\$10,000 - \$1,000}{10} = \$900$$

Sum-of-the-Years'-Digits (SYD) Method

The purpose of the SYD method is to reduce the book value of an asset rapidly in early years and at a lower rate in the later years of its life.

Suppose that the estimated useful life is five years. The numbers add up to 15: $1 + 2 + 3 + 4 + 5 = 15$. Therefore, we depreciate the asset by $5 \div 15$ after the first year, $4 \div 15$ after the second year, and so on, down to $1 \div 15$ in the last year.

Declining-Balance Method

This method also achieves an accelerated depreciation. The asset's value is decreased by reducing its book value by a constant percentage each year. The percentage rate selected is often the one that just reduces book value to salvage value at the end of the asset's estimated life. In any case, the asset should never be reduced below estimated salvage value. Use of the declining-balance method and allowable rates are controlled by Internal Revenue Service regulations. As a simplified illustration, the preceding example is used in the next table with an arbitrarily selected rate of 40 percent. Note that depreciation is based on full cost, *not* cost minus salvage value.

Year	Depreciation Rate	Beginning Book Value	Depreciation Charge	Accumulated Depreciation	Ending Book Value
1	0.40	\$17,000	\$6,800	\$ 6,800	\$10,200
2	0.40	10,200	4,080	10,880	6,120
3	0.40	6,120	2,448	13,328	3,672
4	0.40	3,672	1,469	14,797	2,203
5		2,203	203	15,000	2,000

In the fifth year, reducing book value by 40 percent would have caused it to drop below salvage value. Consequently, the asset was depreciated by only \$203, which decreased book value to salvage value.

Double-Declining-Balance Method

Again, for tax advantages, the double-declining-balance method offers higher depreciation early in the life span. This method uses a percentage twice the straight line for the life span of the item but applies this rate to the undepreciated original cost. The method is the same as the declining-balance method, but the term *double-declining balance* means double the straight-line rate. Thus, equipment with a 10-year life span would have a straight-line depreciation rate of 10 percent per year and a double-declining-balance rate (applied to the undepreciated amount) of 20 percent per year.

Depreciation-by-Use Method

The purpose of this method is to depreciate a capital investment in proportion to its use. It is applicable, for example, to a machine that performs the same operation many times. The life of the machine is estimated not in years but rather in the total number of operations it may reasonably be expected to perform before wearing out. Suppose that a metal-stamping press has an estimated life of one million stamps and costs \$100,000. The charge for depreciation per stamp is then \$100,000 ÷ 1,000,000, or \$0.10. Assuming a \$0 salvage value, the depreciation charges are as shown in the following table.

Year	Total Yearly Stamps	Cost per Stamp	Yearly Depreciation Charge	Accumulated Depreciation	Ending Book Value
1	150,000	0.10	\$15,000	\$ 15,000	\$85,000
2	300,000	0.10	30,000	45,000	55,000
3	200,000	0.10	20,000	65,000	35,000
4	200,000	0.10	20,000	85,000	15,000
5	100,000	0.10	10,000	95,000	5,000
6	50,000	0.10	5,000	100,000	0

The depreciation-by-use method is an attempt to gear depreciation charges to actual use and thereby coordinate expense charges with productive output more accurately. Also, because a machine's resale value is related to its remaining productive life, it is hoped that book value will approximate resale value. The danger, of course, is that technological improvements will render the machine obsolete, in which case book value will not reflect true value.

Activity-Based Costing

To know the costs incurred to make a certain product or deliver a service, some method of allocating overhead costs to production activities must be applied. The traditional approach is to allocate overhead costs to products on the basis of direct labor dollars or hours. By dividing the total estimated overhead costs by total budgeted direct labor hours, an overhead rate can be established. The problem with this approach is that direct labor as a percentage of total costs has fallen dramatically over the past decade. For example, the introduction of advanced manufacturing technology and other productivity improvements has driven direct labor to as low as 7 to 10 percent of total manufacturing costs in many industries. As a result, overhead rates of 600 percent or even 1,000 percent are found in some highly automated plants.

This traditional accounting practice of allocating overhead to direct labor can lead to questionable investment decisions. For example, automated processes may be chosen over labor-intensive processes based on a comparison of projected costs. Unfortunately, overhead does not disappear when the equipment is installed and overall costs may actually be lower with the labor-intensive process. It also can lead to wasted effort because an inordinate amount of time is spent tracking direct labor hours. For example, one plant spent 65 percent of computer costs tracking information about direct labor transactions even though direct labor accounted for only 4 percent of total production costs.

Activity-based costing techniques have been developed to alleviate these problems by refining the overhead allocation process to more directly reflect actual proportions of overhead consumed by the production activity. Causal factors, known as *cost drivers,* are identified and used as the means for allocating overhead. These factors might include machine hours, beds occupied, computer time, flight hours, or miles driven. The accuracy of overhead allocation, of course, depends on the selection of appropriate cost drivers.

Activity-based costing involves a two-stage allocation process, with the first stage assigning overhead costs to *cost activity pools.* These pools represent activities such as performing machine setups, issuing purchase orders, and inspecting parts. In the second stage, costs are assigned from these pools to activities based on the number or amount of pool-related activity required in their completion. Exhibit C.2 compares traditional cost accounting and activity-based costing.

Consider the example of activity-based costing in Exhibit C.3. Two products, A and B, are produced using the same number of direct labor hours. The same number of direct labor hours produces 5,000 units of Product A and 20,000 units of Product B. Applying traditional costing, identical overhead costs would be charged to each product. By applying activity-based costing, traceable costs are assigned to specific activities. Because each product required a different amount of transactions, different overhead amounts are allocated to these products from the pools.

EXHIBIT C.2

Traditional and Activity-Based Costing

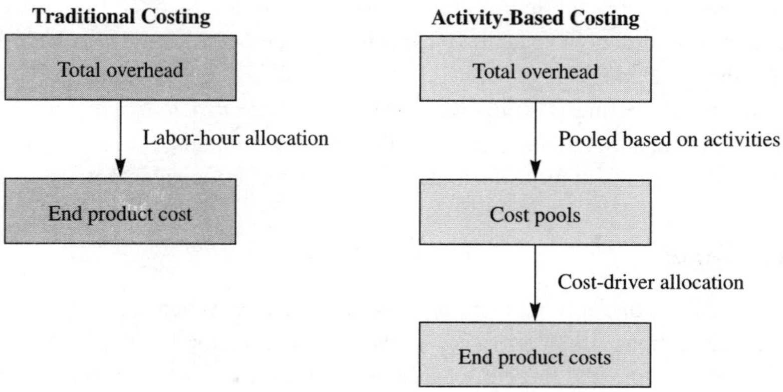

EXHIBIT C.3

Overhead Allocations by an Activity Approach

Basic Data

Activity	Traceable Costs	Events of Transactions: Total	Product A	Product B
Machine setups	$230,000	5,000	3,000	2,000
Quality inspections	160,000	8,000	5,000	3,000
Production orders	81,000	600	200	400
Machine-hours worked	314,000	40,000	12,000	28,000
Material receipts	90,000	750	150	600
Number of units produced		25,000	5,000	20,000
	$875,000			

Overhead Rates by Activity

Activity	(*a*) Traceable Costs	(*b*) Total Events or Transactions	(*a*) ÷ (*b*) Rate per Event or Transaction
Machine setups	$230,000	5,000	$46/setups
Quality inspections	160,000	8,000	$20/inspection
Production orders	81,000	600	$135/order
Machine-hours worked	314,000	40,000	$7.85/hour
Material receipts	90,000	750	$120/receipt

Overhead Cost per Unit of Product

	Product A: Events or Transactions	Product A: Amount	Product B: Events or Transactions	Product B: Amount
Machine setups, at $46/setup	3,000	$138,000	2,000	$ 92,000
Quality inspections, at $20/inspection	5,000	100,000	3,000	60,000
Product orders, at $135/order	200	27,000	400	54,000
Machine-hours worked, at $7.85/hour	12,000	94,200	28,000	219,800
Material receipts, at $120/receipt	150	18,000	600	72,000
Total overhead cost assigned		$377,200		$497,800
Number of units produced		5,000		20,000
		$ 75.44		$24.89

Note: See R. Garrison, *Managerial Accounting,* 12th ed. (New York: McGraw-Hill, 2007).

As stated earlier, activity-based costing overcomes the problem of cost distortion by creating a cost pool for each activity or transaction that can be identified as a cost driver, and by assigning overhead cost to products or jobs on a basis of the number of separate activities required for their completion. Thus, in the previous situation, the low-volume product would be assigned the bulk of the costs for machine setup, purchase orders, and quality inspections, thereby showing it to have high unit costs compared to the other product.

Finally, activity-based costing is sometimes referred to as *transactions costing*. This transactions focus gives rise to another major advantage over other costing methods: It improves the traceability of overhead costs and thus results in more accurate unit cost data for management.

The Effects of Taxes

Tax rates and the methods of applying them occasionally change. When analysts evaluate investment proposals, tax considerations often prove to be the deciding factor because depreciation expenses directly affect taxable income and therefore profit. The ability to write off depreciation in early years provides an added source of funds for investment. Before 1986, firms could employ an investment tax credit, which allowed a direct reduction in tax liability. But tax laws change, so it is crucial to stay on top of current tax laws and try to predict future changes that may affect current investments and accounting procedures.

Choosing among Investment Proposals

The capital investment decision has become highly rationalized, as evidenced by the variety of techniques available for its solution. In contrast to pricing or marketing decisions, the capital investment decision can usually be made with a higher degree of confidence because the variables affecting the decision are relatively well known and can be quantified with fair accuracy.

Investment decisions may be grouped into six general categories:

1. Purchase of new equipment or facilities.
2. Replacement of existing equipment or facilities.
3. Make-or-buy decisions.
4. Lease-or-buy decisions.
5. Temporary shutdowns or plant abandonment decisions.
6. Addition or elimination of a product or product line.

Investment decisions are made with regard to the lowest acceptable rate of return on investment. As a starting point, the lowest acceptable rate of return may be considered to be the cost of investment capital needed to underwrite the expenditure. Certainly, an investment will not be made if it does not return at least the cost of capital.

Investments are generally ranked according to the return they yield in excess of their cost of capital. In this way, a business with only limited investment funds can select investment alternatives that yield the highest net returns. (*Net return* is the earnings an investment yields after gross earnings have been reduced by the cost of the funds used to finance the investment.) In general, investments should not be made unless the return in funds exceeds the marginal cost of investment capital. (*Marginal cost* is the incremental cost of each new acquisition of funds from outside sources.)

Determining the Cost of Capital The cost of capital is calculated from a weighted average of debt and equity security costs. This average will vary depending on the financing strategy employed by the company. The most common sources of financing are short-term debt, long-term debt, and equity securities. A bank loan is an example of short-term debt. Bonds normally provide long-term debt.

Finally, stock is a common form of equity financing. In the following, we give a short example of each form of financing, and then show how they are combined to find the weighted average cost of capital.

The cost of short-term debt depends on the interest rate on the loan and whether the loan is discounted. Remember that interest is a tax-deductible expense for a company.

$$\text{Cost of short-term debt} = \frac{\text{Interest paid}}{\text{Proceeds received}}$$

If a bank discounts a loan, interest is deducted from the face of the loan to get the proceeds. When a compensating balance is required (that is, a percentage of the face value of the loan is held by the bank as collateral), proceeds are also reduced. In either case, the effective or real interest rate on the loan is higher than the face interest rate owing to the proceeds received from the loan being less than the amount (face value) of the loan.

Example of Short-Term Debt

A company takes a \$150,000, one-year, 13 percent loan. The loan is discounted, and a 10 percent compensating balance is required. The effective interest rate is computed as follows:

$$\frac{13\% \times \$150,000}{\$115,500} = \frac{\$19,500}{\$115,500} = 16.89\%$$

Proceeds received equal

Face of loan	\$150,000
Less interest	(19,500)
Compensating balance (10% × \$150,000)	(15,000)
Proceeds	\$115,500

Notice how the effective cost of the loan is significantly greater than the stated interest rate.

Long-term debt is normally provided through the sale of corporate bonds. The real cost of bonds is obtained by computing two types of yield: simple (face) yield and yield to maturity (effective interest rate). The first involves an easy approximation, but the second is more accurate. The nominal interest rate equals the interest paid on the face (maturity value) of the bond and is always stated on a per-annum basis. Bonds are generally issued in \$1,000 denominations and may be sold above face value (at a premium) or below (at a discount, termed original issue discount, or OID). A bond is sold at a discount when the interest rate is below the going market rate. In this case, the yield will be higher than the nominal interest rate. The opposite holds for bonds issued at a premium.

The issue price of a bond is the par (or face value) times the premium (or discount).

$$\text{Simple yield} = \frac{\text{Nominal interest}}{\text{Issue price of bond}}$$

$$\text{Yield to maturity} = \frac{\text{Nominal interest} + \dfrac{\text{Discount(or premium)}}{\text{Years}}}{\dfrac{\text{Issue price} + \text{Maturity value}}{2}}$$

Example of Long-Term Debt

A company issues a \$400,000, 12 percent, 10-year bond for 97 percent of face value. Yield computations are as follows:

$$\begin{aligned}\text{Nominal annual payment} &= 12\% \times \$400,000 \\ &= \$48,000 \\ \text{Bond proceeds} &= 97\% \times \$400,000 \\ &= \$388,000\end{aligned}$$

$$\text{Bond discount} = 3\% \times \$400,000$$
$$= \$12,000$$
$$\text{Simple yield} = \frac{12\% \times \$400,000}{97\% \times \$400,000} = \frac{\$48,000}{\$388,000} = 12.4\%$$
$$\text{Yield to maturity} = \frac{\$48,000 + \dfrac{\$12,000}{10}}{\dfrac{\$388,000 + \$400,000}{2}} = \frac{\$48,000 + \$1,200}{\$394,000} = 12.5\%$$

Note that because the bonds were sold at a discount, the yield exceeds the nominal interest rate (12 percent). Bond interest is tax deductible to the corporation.

The actual cost of equity securities (stocks) comes in the form of dividends, which are not tax deductible to the corporation.

$$\text{Cost of common stock} = \frac{\text{Dividends per share}}{\text{Value per share}} + \text{Growth rate of dividends}$$

Here the value per share equals the market price per share minus flotation costs (that is, the cost of issuing securities such as brokerage fees and printing costs). It should be noted that this valuation does not consider what the investor expects in market price appreciation. This expectation is based on the expected growth in earnings per share and the relative risk taken by purchasing the stock. The capital asset pricing model (CAPM) can be used to capture this impact.

Example of the Cost of Common Stock

A company's dividend per share is \$10, net value is \$70 per share, and the dividend growth rate is 5 percent.

$$\text{Cost of the stock} = \frac{\$10}{\$70} + 0.05 = 19.3\%$$

To compute the weighted average cost of capital, we consider the percentage of the total capital that is being provided by each financing alternative. We then calculate the after-tax cost of each financing alternative. Finally, we weight these costs in proportion to their use.

Example of Calculating the Weighted Average Cost of Capital

Consider a company that shows the following figures in its financial statements:

Short-term bank loan (13%)	\$1 million
Bonds payable (16%)	\$4 million
Common stock (10%)	\$5 million

For our example, assume that each of the percentages given represents the cost of the source of capital. In addition to this, we need to consider the tax rate of the firm because the interest paid on the bonds and on the short-term loan is tax deductible. Assume a corporate tax rate of 40 percent.

	Percent	After-Tax Cost	Weighted Average Cost
Short-term bank loan	10%	13% × 60% = 7.8%	.78%
Bonds payable	40%	16% × 60% = 9.6%	3.84%
Common stock	50%	10%	5%
Total	100%		9.62%

Keep in mind that in developing this section we have made many assumptions in these calculations. When these ideas are applied to a specific company, many of these assumptions may change. The basic concepts, though, are the same; keep in mind that the goal is to simply calculate the after-tax cost of the capital used by the company. We have shown the cost of capital for the entire company, though often only the capital employed for a specific project is used in the calculation.

Interest Rate Effects There are two basic ways to account for the effects of interest accumulation. One is to compute the total amount created over the time period into the future as the *compound value.* The other is to remove the interest rate effect over time by reducing all future sums to present-day dollars, or the *present value.*

Compound Value of a Single Amount Albert Einstein was quoted as saying that compound interest is the eighth wonder of the world. After reviewing this section showing compound interest's dramatic growth effects over a long time, you might wish to propose a new government regulation: On the birth of a child, the parents must put, say, \$1,000 into a retirement fund for that child, available at age 65. This might reduce the pressure on Social Security and other state and federal pension plans. Although inflation would decrease the value significantly, there would still be a lot left over. At a 14 percent return on investment, our \$1,000 would increase to \$500,000 after subtracting the \$4.5 million for inflation. That is still a 500-fold increase. (Many mutual funds today have long-term performances in excess of 14 percent per year.)

Spreadsheets and calculators make such computation easy. The OSCM at Work box titled "Using a Spreadsheet" shows the most useful financial functions. However, many people still refer to tables for compound values. Using Appendix I, Table I.1 (compound sum of \$1), for example, we see that the value of \$1 at 10 percent interest after three years is \$1.331. Multiplying this figure by \$10 gives \$13.31.

Compound Value of an Annuity An *annuity* is the receipt of a constant sum each year for a specified number of years. Usually an annuity is received at the end of a period and does not earn interest during that period. Therefore, an annuity of \$10 for three years would bring in \$10 at the end of the first year (allowing the \$10 to earn interest if invested for the remaining two years), \$10 at the end of the second year (allowing the \$10 to earn interest for the remaining one year), and \$10 at the end of the third year (with no time to earn interest). If the annuity receipts were placed in a bank savings account at 5 percent interest, the total or compound value of the \$10 at 5 percent for the three years would be

Year	Receipt at End of Year		Compound Interest Factor $(1 + i)^n$		Value at End of Third Year
1	\$10.00	×	$(1 + 0.05)^2$	=	\$11.02
2	10.00	×	$(1 + 0.05)^1$	=	10.50
3	10.00	×	$(1 + 0.05)^0$	=	10.00
					\$31.52

The general formula for finding the compound value of an annuity is

$$S_n = R[(1 + i)^{n-1} + (1 + i)^{n-2} + \ldots + (1 + i)^1 + 1]$$

where

S_n = Compound value of an annuity
R = Periodic receipts in dollars
n = Length of the annuity in years

Applying this formula to the preceding example, we get

$$S_n = R[(1 + i)^2 + (1 + i) + 1]$$
$$= \$10[(1 + 0.05)^2 + (1 + 0.05) + 1] = \$31.52$$

In Appendix I, Table I.2 lists the compound value factor of \$1 for 5 percent after three years as 3.152. Multiplying this factor by \$10 yields \$31.52.

In a fashion similar to our previous retirement investment example, consider the beneficial effects of investing \$2,000 each year, just starting at the age of 21. Assume investments in AAA-rated bonds are available today yielding 9 percent. From Table I.2 in Appendix I, after 30 years (at age 51) the

OSCM AT WORK

Using a Spreadsheet

We hope you are doing these calculations using a spreadsheet program. Even though the computer makes these calculations simple, it is important that you understand what the computer is actually doing. Further, you should check your calculations manually to make sure you have the formulas set up correctly in your spreadsheet. There are many stories of the terrible consequences of making a wrong decision based on a spreadsheet with errors!

For your quick reference, the following are the financial functions you will find most useful. These are from the Microsoft Excel help screens.

PV (rate, nper, pmt)—Returns the present value of an investment. The present value is the total amount that a series of future payments is worth now. For example, when you borrow money, the loan amount is the present value to the lender. Rate is the interest rate per period. For example, if you obtain an automobile loan at a 10% annual interest rate and make monthly payments, your interest rate per month is 10%/12, or .83%. You would enter 10%/12, or .83%, or .0083, in the formula as the rate. Nper is the total number of payment periods in an annuity. For example, if you get a four-year car loan and make monthly payments, your loan has 4*12 (or 48) periods. You would enter 48 into the formula for nper. Pmt is the payment made each period and cannot change over the life of the annuity. Typically, this includes principal and interest but no other fees or taxes. For example, the monthly payment on a $10,000, four-year car loan at 12% is $263.33. You would enter 263.33 into the formula as pmt.

FV (rate, nper, pmt)—Returns the future value of an investment based on periodic, constant payments and a constant interest rate. Rate is the interest rate per period. Nper is the total number of payment periods in an annuity. Pmt is the payment made each period; it cannot change over the life of the annuity. Typically, pmt contains principal and interest but no other fees or taxes.

NPV (rate, value1, value2, . . .)—Returns the net present value of an investment based on a series of periodic cash flows and a discount rate. The net present value of an investment is today's value of a series of future payments (negative values) and income (positive values). Rate is the rate of discount over the length of one period. Value1, value2. . ., must be equally spaced in time and occur at the end of each period.

IRR(values)—Returns the internal rate of return for a series of cash flows represented by the numbers in values. (Values is defined as follows.) These cash flows do not have to be even, as they would be for an annuity. The internal rate of return is the interest rate received for an investment consisting of payments (negative values) and income (positive values) that occur at regular periods. *Values* is an array or a reference to cells that contain numbers for which you want to calculate the internal rate of return. Values must contain at least one positive value and one negative value to calculate the internal rate of return. IRR uses the order of values to interpret the order of cash flows. Be sure to enter your payment and income values in the sequence you want.

Source: From Microsoft Excel. Copyright © 2016 Microsoft Corporation.

investment is worth 136.3 times $2,000, or $272,600. Fourteen years later (at age 65) this would be worth $963,044 (using a hand calculator, because the table goes only to 30 years, and assuming the $2,000 is deposited at the end of each year)! But what 21-year-old thinks about retirement?

Present Value of a Future Single Payment Compound values are used to determine future value after a specific period has elapsed; present value (PV) procedures accomplish just the reverse. They are used to determine the current value of a sum or stream of receipts expected to be received in the future. Most investment decision techniques use present value concepts rather than compound values. Because decisions affecting the future are made in the present, it is better to convert future returns into their present value at the time the decision is being made. In this way, investment alternatives are placed in better perspective in terms of current dollars.

An example makes this more apparent. If a rich uncle offers to make you a gift of $100 today or $250 after 10 years, which should you choose? You must determine whether the $250 in 10 years will be worth more than the $100 now. Suppose that you base your decision on the rate of inflation in the economy and believe that inflation averages 10 percent per year. By deflating the $250, you can compare its relative purchasing power with $100 received today. Procedurally, this is accomplished by solving the compound formula for the present sum, P, where V is the future amount of $250 in 10 years at 10 percent. The compound value formula is

$$V = P(1 + i)^n$$

Dividing both sides by $(1 + i)^n$ gives

$$P = \frac{V}{(1 + i)^n}$$

$$= \frac{250}{(1 + 0.10)^{10}} = \$96.39$$

This shows that, at a 10 percent inflation rate, $250 in 10 years will be worth $96.39 today. The rational choice, then, is to take the $100 now.

The use of tables is also standard practice in solving present value problems. With reference to Appendix I, Table I.3, the present value factor for $1 received 10 years hence is 0.386. Multiplying this factor by $250 yields $96.50.

Present Value of an Annuity The present value of an annuity is the value of an annual amount to be received over a future period expressed in terms of the present. To find the value of an annuity of $100 for three years at 10 percent, find the factor in the present value table that applies to 10 percent in *each* of the three years in which the amount is received and multiply each receipt by this factor. Then sum the resulting figures. Remember that annuities are usually received at the end of each period.

Year	Amount Received at End of Year		Present Value Factor at 10%		Present Value
1	$100	×	0.909	=	$ 90.90
2	100	×	0.826	=	82.60
3	100	×	0.751	=	75.10
Total receipts	$300		Total present value	=	$248.60

The general formula used to derive the present value of an annuity is

$$A_n = R\left[\frac{1}{(1+i)} + \frac{1}{(1+i)^2} + \ldots + \frac{1}{(1+i)^n}\right]$$

where

A_n = Present value of an annuity of n years
R = Periodic receipts
n = Length of the annuity in years

Applying the formula to the preceding example gives

$$A_n = \$100\left[\frac{1}{(1+0.10)} + \frac{1}{(1+0.10)^2} + \frac{1}{(1+0.10)^3}\right]$$

$$= \$100(2.487) = \$248.70$$

In Appendix I, Table I.4 contains present values of an annuity for varying maturities. The present value factor for an annuity of $1 for three years at 10 percent (from Table I.4) is 2.487. Given that our sum is $100 rather than $1, we multiply this factor by $100 to arrive at $248.70.

When the stream of future receipts is uneven, the present value of each annual receipt must be calculated. The present values of the receipts for all years are then summed to arrive at total present value. This process can sometimes be tedious, but it is unavoidable.

Discounted Cash Flow The term *discounted cash flow* refers to the total stream of payments that an asset will generate in the future discounted to the present time. This is simply present value analysis that includes all flows: single payments, annuities, and all others.

Methods of Ranking Investments

Net Present Value The net present value method is commonly used in business. With this method, decisions are based on the amount by which the present value of a projected income stream exceeds the cost of an investment.

A firm is considering two alternative investments. The first costs $30,000 and the second, $50,000. The expected yearly cash income streams are shown in the following table.

	Cash Inflow	
Year	Alternative A	Alternative B
1	$10,000	$15,000
2	10,000	15,000
3	10,000	15,000
4	10,000	15,000
5	10,000	15,000

To choose between Alternatives A and B, find which has the higher net present value. Assume an 8 percent cost of capital.

Alternative A		Alternative B	
3.993 (PV factor) × $10,000	= $39,930	3.993 (PV factor) × $15,000	= $59,895
Less cost of investment	= 30,000	Less cost of investment	= 50,000
Net present value	= $ 9,930	Net present value	= $ 9,895

Investment A is the better alternative. Its net present value exceeds that of Investment B by $35 ($9,930 – $9,895 = $35).

Payback Period The payback method ranks investments according to the time required for each investment to return earnings equal to the cost of the investment. The rationale is that the sooner the investment capital can be recovered, the sooner it can be reinvested in new revenue-producing projects. Thus, supposedly, a firm will be able to get the most benefit from its available investment funds.

Consider two alternatives requiring a $1,000 investment each. The first will earn $200 per year for six years; the second will earn $300 per year for the first three years and $100 per year for the next three years.

If the first alternative is selected, the initial investment of $1,000 will be recovered at the end of the fifth year. The income produced by the second alternative will total $1,000 after only four years. The second alternative will permit reinvestment of the full $1,000 in new revenue-producing projects one year sooner than the first.

Though the payback method is declining in popularity as the sole measure in investment decisions, it is still frequently used in conjunction with other methods to indicate the time commitment of funds. The major problems with payback are that it does not consider income beyond the payback period and it ignores the time value of money. A method that ignores the time value of money must be considered questionable.

Internal Rate of Return The internal rate of return may be defined as the interest rate that equates the present value of an income stream with the cost of an investment. There is no procedure or formula that may be used directly to compute the internal rate of return—it must be found by interpolation or iterative calculation.

Suppose we wish to find the internal rate of return for an investment costing $12,000 that will yield a cash inflow of $4,000 per year for four years. We see that the present value factor sought is

$$\frac{\$12,000}{\$4,000} = 3.000$$

and we seek the interest rate that will provide this factor over a four-year period. The interest rate must lie between 12 and 14 percent because 3.000 lies between 3.037 and 2.914 (in the fourth row of Appendix I, Table I.4). Linear interpolation between these values, according to the equation

$$I = 12 + (14 - 12)\frac{(3.037 - 3.000)}{(3.037 - 2.914)}$$

$$= 12 + 0.602 = 12.602\%$$

gives a good approximation to the actual internal rate of return.

When the income stream is discounted at 12.6 percent, the resulting present value closely approximates the cost of investment. Thus, the internal rate of return for this investment is 12.6 percent. The cost of capital can be compared with the internal rate of return to determine the net rate of return on the investment. If, in this example, the cost of capital were 8 percent, the net rate of return on the investment would be 4.6 percent.

The net present value and internal rate of return methods involve procedures that are essentially the same. They differ in that the net present value method enables investment alternatives to be compared in terms of the dollar value in excess of cost, whereas the internal rate of return method permits comparison of rates of return on alternative investments. Moreover, the internal rate of return method occasionally encounters problems in calculation, as multiple rates frequently appear in the computation.

Ranking Investments with Uneven Lives When proposed investments have the same life expectancy, comparison among them using the preceding methods will give a reasonable picture of their relative value. When lives are unequal, however, there is the question of how to relate the two different time periods. Should replacements be considered the same as the original? Should productivity for the shorter-term unit that will be replaced earlier be considered higher? How should the cost of future units be estimated?

No estimate dealing with investments unforeseen at the time of decision can be expected to reflect a high degree of accuracy. Still, the problem must be dealt with, and some assumptions must be made in order to determine a ranking.

Sample Problems: Investment Decisions

EXAMPLE C.1 An Expansion Decision

William J. Wilson Ceramic Products, Inc., leases plant facilities in which firebrick is manufactured. Because of rising demand, Wilson could increase sales by investing in new equipment to expand output. The selling price of $10 per brick will remain unchanged if output and sales increase. Based on engineering and cost estimates, the accounting department provides management with the following cost estimates based on an annual increased output of 100,000 bricks.

Cost of new equipment having an expected life of five years	$500,000
Equipment installation cost	20,000
Expected salvage value	0
New operation's share of annual lease expense	40,000
Annual increase in utility expenses	40,000
Annual increase in labor costs	160,000
Annual additional cost for raw materials	400,000

The sum-of-the-years'-digits method of depreciation will be used, and taxes are paid at a rate of 40 percent. Wilson's policy is not to invest capital in projects earning less than a 20 percent rate of return. Should the proposed expansion be undertaken?

SOLUTION

Compute the cost of investment:

Acquisition cost of equipment	$500,000
Equipment installation costs	20,000
Total cost of investment	$520,000

Determine yearly cash flows throughout the life of the investment.

The lease expense is a sunk cost. It will be incurred whether or not the investment is made and is therefore irrelevant to the decision and should be disregarded. Annual production expenses to be considered are utility, labor, and raw materials. These total $600,000 per year.

Annual sales revenue is $10 × 100,000 units of output, which totals $1,000,000. Yearly income before depreciation and taxes is thus $1,000,000 gross revenue, less $600,000 expenses, or $400,000.

Next, determine the depreciation charges to be deducted from the $500,000 income each year using the SYD method (sum-of-years'-digits = 1 + 2 + 3 + 4 + 5 = 15).

Year	Proportion of $500,000 to Be Depreciated		Depreciation Charge
1	5/15 × 500,000	=	$166,667
2	4/15 × 500,000	=	133,333
3	3/15 × 500,000	=	100,000
4	2/15 × 500,000	=	66,667
5	1/15 × 500,000	=	33,333
	Accumulated depreciation		$500,000

Find each year's cash flow when taxes are 40 percent. Cash flow for only the first year is illustrated:

Earnings before depreciation and taxes		$400,000
Deduct: Taxes at 40% (40% × 400,000)	$160,000	
Tax benefit of depreciation expense (0.4 × 166,667)	66,667	93,333
Cash flow (first year)		$306,667

Determine the present value of the cash flow. Because Wilson demands at least a 20 percent rate of return on investments, multiply the cash flows by the 20 percent present value factor for each year. The factor for each respective year must be used because the cash flows are not an annuity.

Year	Present Value Factor		Cash Flow		Present Value
1	0.833	×	$306,667	=	$255,454
2	0.694	×	293,333	=	203,573
3	0.579	×	280,000	=	162,120
4	0.482	×	266,667	=	128,533
5	0.402	×	253,334	=	101,840
	Total present value of cash flows (discounted at 20%)			=	$851,520

Now find whether net present value is positive or negative:

Total present value of cash flows	$851,520
Total cost of investment	520,000
Net present value	$331,520

Net present value is positive when returns are discounted at 20 percent. Wilson will earn an amount in excess of 20 percent on the investment. The proposed expansion should be undertaken.

EXAMPLE C.2 A Replacement Decision

For five years, Bennie's Brewery has been using a machine that attaches labels to bottles. The machine was purchased for \$4,000 and is being depreciated over 10 years to a \$0 salvage value using straight-line depreciation. The machine can be sold now for \$2,000. Bennie can buy a new labeling machine for \$6,000 that will have a useful life of five years and cut labor costs by \$1,200 annually. The old machine will require a major overhaul in the next few months at an estimated cost of \$300. If purchased, the new machine will be depreciated over five years to a \$500 salvage value using the straight-line method. The company will invest in any project earning more than the 12 percent cost of capital. The tax rate is 40 percent. Should Bennie's Brewery invest in the new machine?

SOLUTION

Determine the cost of investment:

Price of the new machine		\$6,000
Less: Sale of old machine	\$2,000	
Avoidable overhaul costs	300	2,300
Effective cost of investment		\$3,700

Determine the increase in cash flow resulting from investment in the new machine:

Yearly cost savings = \$1,200
Differential depreciation
Annual depreciation on old machine:

$$\frac{\text{Cost} - \text{Salvage}}{\text{Expected life}} = \frac{\$4{,}000 - \$0}{10} = \$400$$

Annual depreciation on new machine:

$$\frac{\text{Cost} - \text{Salvage}}{\text{Expected life}} = \frac{\$6{,}000 - \$500}{5} = \$1{,}100$$

Differential depreciation = \$1,100 – \$400 = \$700

Yearly net increase in cash flow into the firm:

Cost savings		\$1,200
Deduct: Taxes at 40%	\$480	
Add: Advantage of increase in depreciation (0.4 × \$700)	280	200
Yearly increase in cash flow		\$1,000

The five-year cash flow of \$1,000 per year is an annuity.
Discounted at 12 percent, the cost of capital, the present value is
3.605 × \$1,000 = \$3,605.
The present value of the new machine, if sold at its salvage value of \$500 at the end of the fifth year, is
0.567 × \$500 = \$284
Total present value of the expected cash flows is
\$3,605 + \$284 = \$3,889

Determine whether net present value is positive:

Total present value	\$3,889
Cost of investment	3,700
Net present value	\$ 4189

Bennie's Brewery should make the purchase because the investment will return slightly more than the cost of capital.

Note: The importance of depreciation has been shown in this example. The present value of the yearly cash flow resulting from operations is

$$(\text{Cost saving} - \text{Taxes}) \times (\text{Present value factor})$$

$$(\$1,200 - \$480) \quad \times \quad (3.605) \qquad = \$2,596$$

This figure is $1,104 less than the $3,700 cost of the investment. Only a very large depreciation advantage makes this investment worthwhile. The total present value of the advantage is $1,009:

$$(\text{Tax rate} \times \text{Differential depreciation}) \times (\text{PV factor})$$

$$(0.4 \times \$700) \qquad \times \quad (3.605) = \$1,009$$

EXAMPLE C.3 **A Make-or-Buy Decision**

Triple X Company manufactures and sells refrigerators. It makes some of the parts for the refrigerators and purchases others. The engineering department believes it might be possible to cut costs by manufacturing one of the parts currently being purchased for $8.25 each. The firm uses 100,000 of these parts each year. The accounting department compiles the following list of costs based on engineering estimates:

Fixed costs will increase by $50,000.
Labor costs will increase by $125,000.
Factory overhead, currently running $500,000 per year, may be expected to increase 12 percent.
Raw materials used to make the part will cost $600,000.

Given the preceding estimates, should Triple X make the part or continue to buy it?

SOLUTION

Find the total cost incurred if the part were manufactured:

Additional fixed costs	$ 50,000
Additional labor costs	125,000
Raw materials cost	600,000
Additional overhead costs = 0.12 × $500,000	60,000
Total cost to manufacture	$835,000

Find the cost per unit to manufacture:

$$\frac{\$835,000}{100,000} = \$8.35 \text{ per unit}$$

Triple X should continue to buy the part. Manufacturing costs exceed the present cost to purchase by $0.10 per unit.

CONCEPT CONNECTIONS

LO C–1 **Evaluate capital investment decisions using the various types of cost, risk and expected value, and depreciation.**

Summary

- Financial analysis is essential to OSCM because many management decisions relate to major capital investments. In this appendix, we discuss basic concepts that are most useful in OSCM.
- Understanding how costs are categorized and the most common techniques for depreciating assets are reviewed. We use activity-based costing to allocate common and overhead costs relative to OSCM activities.
- A medium- to long-term time horizon is used when choosing among alternative investments. When this is the case, consideration of the time value of money by present value analysis is useful. These decisions are modeled using spreadsheets.

Appendix D

Answers to Selected Objective Questions

Chapter 1

1. Strategy, Processes, and Analytics
9. *a.* Receivable turnover ratio = 5.453, *b.* inventory turnover ratio = 4.383, *c.* asset turnover ratio = 2.306

Chapter 2

1. Triple bottom line
17. Productivity (hours), Deluxe = 0.20, Limited = 0.20; Productivity (dollars), Deluxe = 133.33, Limited = 135.71

Chapter 3

1. Testing and refinement
9. Time to market, productivity, and quality

Chapter 4

7. *b.* A-C-F-G-I and A-D-F-G-I, 18 weeks; *c.* C: one week, D: one week, G: one week; *d.* Two paths: A-C-F-G-I and A-D-F-G-I, 16 weeks.
12. *a.* A-E-G-C-D; *b.* 26 weeks; *c.* No difference in completion date.

Chapter 5

1. Capacity utilization rate = 89.1%
8. NPV – Small factory = $4.8 million; NPV – Large factory = $2.6 million. Therefore, build small factory.
10. Capacity utilization rate = 75%. They are in the critical zone on these nights.

Chapter 6

5. 4,710 hours
7. Learning rate – Labor = 80%, Learning rate – Parts = 90%; Labor = 11,556 hours, Parts = $330,876

Chapter 7

9. Break-even = 7,500 units
16. 80 units/hour

Chapter 8

5. *b.* 120 seconds/unit; *c.* station 1 (AD), station 2 (BC), station 3 (EF), station 4 (GH); *d.* 87.5%
10. *a.* 33.6 seconds/unit; *b.* 3.51 → 4 workstations; *d.* station 1 (AB), station 2 (DF), station 3 (C), station 4 (EF), station 5 (H); *e.* 70.2%; *f.* Reduce cycle time to 32 seconds and work 6.67 minutes overtime; *g.* 1.89 hours overtime, may be better to rebalance.

Chapter 9

1. Service package
4. Face-to-face tight specs

Chapter 10

6. *a.* 33.33%, *b.* 1/3 hour or 20 minutes, *c.* 1.33 students, *d.* 44.44%
21. *a.* .2333 minutes or 14 seconds; *b.* 2.083 cars in queue, 2.92 cars in the system

Chapter 11

10. Traditional method = 40 minutes, alternative method = 51 minutes. Traditional method is best.
12. *a.* The market can only be served at 3 gal/hour and in 50 hours the bathtub will overflow; *b.* The average amount being serviced is 2.5 gal/hour, so that is the output rate.

Chapter 12

6. DPMO = 15,333; this is not very good.
11. Opportunity flow diagram

Chapter 13

1. *a.* Cost when not inspecting = \$20/hr, cost to inspect = \$9/hr, therefore inspect; *b.* \$0.18 each; *c.* \$0.22 per unit.
6. *a.* .333, *b.* No, the machine is not capable of high enough quality.
9. UCL = 1014.965, LCL = 983.235 for *X*-bar chart; UCL = 49.552, LCL = 0.00 for the *R*-chart.

Chapter 14

10. Five kanban card sets
14. Five kanban card sets

Chapter 15

9. Total cost \$1,056.770; *b.* Should consider closing the Philadelphia plant because we are using very little of the capacity from that plant.
10. $C_x = 373.8$, $C_y = 356.9$

Chapter 16

11. Buy NPV = \$143,226.27, make NPV = \$84,442.11, we should accept the bid.
16. Inventory turn = 148.6, weeks of supply = .350 (1/3 of a week's supply on hand)

Chapter 17

5. Manufacturing and logistics
11. 9.61 days

Chapter 18

3. 3rd most recent = 1,000, 2nd most recent = 1,175, most recent = 975
6. *a.* February 84, March 86, April 90, May 88, June 84; *b.* MAD = 15
21. *a.* MAD = 90, TS = –1.67; *b.* TS acceptable for now, but is trending downward.

Chapter 19

7. Total cost = \$416,600
10. Total cost = \$413,750

Chapter 20

4. Purchase 268 boxes of lettuce.
14. $q = 713$
17. *a.* $Q = 1{,}225$, $R = 824$; *b.* $q = 390 - I$

Chapter 21

11. *a.*

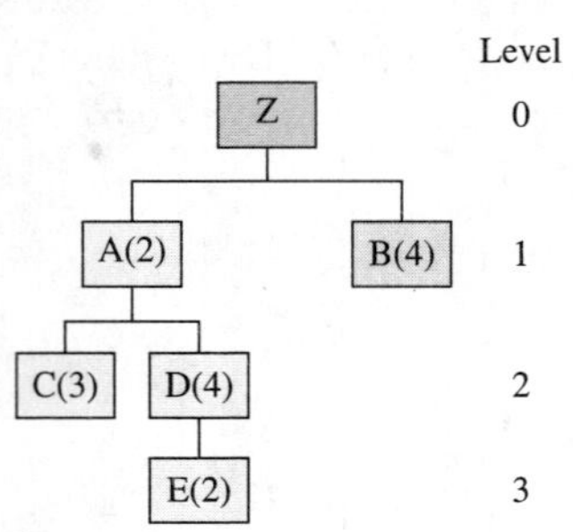

21. Least total cost order 180 to cover periods 4 through 8. Least unit cost is tied for ordering 180 for periods 4 through 8, or order 220 units to cover 4 through 9.

Chapter 22

5. Run the jobs in the following order: 103, 105, 101, 102, 104. Mean flow time = 16.2 days.
7. Select car C first, then A and B tie for second.
9. Critical ratio schedule: 5, 3, 2, 4, 1; Earliest due date schedule: 2, 5, 3, 4, 1; Shortest processing time: 2, 1, 4, 3, 5

Chapter 23

6. Case I: X used = 933.3 hours, Y used = 700 hours
   Case II: X used = 933.3 hours, Y used = 700 hours
   Case III: X used = 933.3 hours, Y used = 700 hours
   Case IV: X used = 933.3 hours, Y used = 700 hours

With no restrictions.
   Case I: No problem
   Case II: Excess WIP
   Case III: Excess spare parts
   Case IV: Excess finished goods

17. *a.* Machine B is the constraint; *b.* All 100 of M, as many N as possible; *c.* $600 (100 M and 30 N)

Chapter 24

2. Staff flows
6. Clinical dashboard

Chapter 25

7. Balanced scorecard
11. Codification of reengineering

Appendix A

2. Optimal combination is $B = 10$, $A = 15$, and $Z = 70$.
4. (a) $600A + 900B < = 3,600$
   $600A + 900B > = 1,800$
   $200A + 700B < = 1,400$
   $400A + 100B > = 400$
   $A < = 2$
   Minimize $.75A + .15B$

   (b) A = 0.54
   B = 1.85
   Obj = 0.68

Appendix E

Present Value Table

EXHIBIT E.1

Costs of Four Production Plans

Year	1%	2%	3%	4%	5%	6%	7%	8%	9%	10%	12%	14%	15%
1	.990	.980	.971	.962	.952	.943	.935	.926	.917	.909	.893	.877	.870
2	.980	.961	.943	.925	.907	.890	.873	.857	.842	.826	.797	.769	.756
3	.971	.942	.915	.889	.864	.840	.816	.794	.772	.751	.712	.675	.658
4	.961	.924	.889	.855	.823	.792	.763	.735	.708	.683	.636	.592	.572
5	.951	.906	.863	.822	.784	.747	.713	.681	.650	.621	.567	.519	.497
6	.942	.888	.838	.790	.746	.705	.666	.630	.596	.564	.507	.456	.432
7	.933	.871	.813	.760	.711	.665	.623	.583	.547	.513	.452	.400	.376
8	.923	.853	.789	.731	.677	.627	.582	.540	.502	.467	.404	.351	.327
9	.914	.837	.766	.703	.645	.592	.544	.500	.460	.424	.361	.308	.284
10	.905	.820	.744	.676	.614	.558	.508	.463	.422	.386	.322	.270	.247
11	.896	.804	.722	.650	.585	.527	.475	.429	.388	.350	.287	.237	.215
12	.887	.788	.701	.625	.557	.497	.444	.397	.356	.319	.257	.208	.187
13	.879	.773	.681	.601	.530	.469	.415	.368	.326	.290	.229	.182	.163
14	.870	.758	.661	.577	.505	.442	.388	.340	.299	.263	.205	.160	.141
15	.861	.743	.642	.555	.481	.417	.362	.315	.275	.239	.183	.140	.123
16	.853	.728	.623	.534	.458	.394	.339	.292	.252	.218	.163	.123	.107
17	.844	.714	.605	.513	.436	.371	.317	.270	.231	.198	.146	.108	.093
18	.836	.700	.587	.494	.416	.350	.296	.250	.212	.180	.130	.095	.081
19	.828	.686	.570	.475	.396	.331	.276	.232	.194	.164	.116	.083	.070
20	.820	.673	.554	.456	.377	.312	.258	.215	.178	.149	.104	.073	.061
25	.780	.610	.478	.375	.295	.233	.184	.146	.116	.092	.059	.038	.030
30	.742	.552	.412	.308	.231	.174	.131	.099	.075	.057	.033	.020	.015

Year	16%	18%	20%	24%	28%	32%	36%	40%	50%	60%	70%	80%	90%
1	.862	.847	.833	.806	.781	.758	.735	.714	.667	.625	.588	.556	.526
2	.743	.718	.694	.650	.610	.574	.541	.510	.444	.391	.346	.309	.277
3	.641	.609	.579	.524	.477	.435	.398	.364	.296	.244	.204	.171	.146
4	.552	.516	.482	.423	.373	.329	.292	.260	.198	.153	.120	.095	.077
5	.476	.437	.402	.341	.291	.250	.215	.186	.132	.095	.070	.053	.040
6	.410	.370	.335	.275	.227	.189	.158	.133	.088	.060	.041	.029	.021
7	.354	.314	.279	.222	.178	.143	.116	.095	.059	.037	.024	.016	.011

8	.305	.266	.233	.179	.139	.108	.085	.068	.039	.023	.014	.009	.006
9	.263	.226	.194	.144	.108	.082	.063	.048	.026	.015	.008	.005	.003
10	.227	.191	.162	.116	.085	.062	.046	.035	.017	.009	.005	.003	.002
11	.195	.162	.135	.094	.066	.047	.034	.025	.012	.006	.003	.002	.001
12	.168	.137	.112	.076	.052	.036	.025	.018	.008	.004	.002	.001	.001
13	.145	.116	.093	.061	.040	.027	.018	.013	.005	.002	.001	.001	.000
14	.125	.099	.078	.049	.032	.021	.014	.009	.003	.001	.001	.000	.000
15	.108	.084	.065	.040	.025	.016	.010	.006	.002	.001	.000	.000	.000
16	.093	.071	.054	.032	.019	.012	.007	.005	.002	.001	.000	.000	
17	.080	.060	.045	.026	.015	.009	.005	.003	.001	.000	.000		
18	.069	.051	.038	.021	.012	.007	.004	.002	.001	.000	.000		
19	.060	.043	.031	.017	.009	.005	.003	.002	.000	.000			
20	.051	.037	.026	.014	.007	.004	.002	.001	.000	.000			
25	.024	.016	.010	.005	.002	.001	.000	.000					
30	.012	.007	.004	.002	.001	.000	.000						

Using Microsoft Excel, these are calculated with the equation: $(1 + \text{interest})^{-\text{years}}$.

Appendix F

Negative Exponential Distribution: Values of e^{-x}

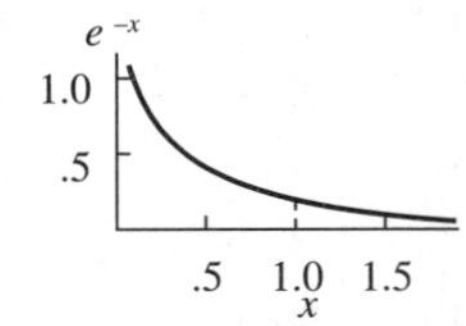

X	e^{-x} (VALUE)	X	e^{-x} (VALUE)	X	e^{-x} (VALUE)	X	e^{-x} (VALUE)
0.00	1.00000	0.51	.60050	1.01	.36422	1.51	.22091
0.01	.99005	0.52	.59452	1.02	.36060	1.52	.21871
0.02	.98020	0.53	.58860	1.03	.35701	1.53	.21654
0.03	.97045	0.54	.58275	1.04	.35345	1.54	.21438
0.04	.96079	0.55	.57695	1.05	.34994	1.55	.21225
0.05	.95123	0.56	.57121	1.06	.34646	1.56	.21014
0.06	.94176	0.57	.56553	1.07	.34301	1.57	.20805
0.07	.93239	0.58	.55990	1.08	.33960	1.58	.20598
0.08	.92312	0.59	.55433	1.09	.33622	1.59	.20393
0.09	.91393	0.60	.54881	1.10	.33287	1.60	.20190
0.10	.90484	0.61	.54335	1.11	.32956	1.61	.19989
0.11	.89583	0.62	.53794	1.12	.32628	1.62	.19790
0.12	.88692	0.63	.53259	1.13	.32303	1.63	.19593
0.13	.87809	0.64	.52729	1.14	.31982	1.64	.19398
0.14	.86936	0.65	.52205	1.15	.31664	1.65	.19205
0.15	.86071	0.66	.51685	1.16	.31349	1.66	.19014
0.16	.87514	0.67	.51171	1.17	.31037	1.67	.18825
0.17	.84366	0.68	.50662	1.18	.30728	1.68	.18637
0.18	.83527	0.69	.50158	1.19	.30422	1.69	.18452
0.19	.82696	0.70	.49659	1.20	.30119	1.70	.18268
0.20	.81873	0.71	.49164	1.21	.29820	1.71	.18087
0.21	.81058	0.72	.48675	1.22	.29523	1.72	.17907
0.22	.80252	0.73	.48191	1.23	.29229	1.73	.17728
0.23	.79453	0.74	.47711	1.24	.28938	1.74	.17552
0.24	.78663	0.75	.47237	1.25	.28650	1.75	.17377
0.25	.77880	0.76	.46767	1.26	.28365	1.76	.17204
0.26	.77105	0.77	.46301	1.27	.28083	1.77	.17033
0.27	.76338	0.78	.45841	1.28	.27804	1.78	.16864
0.28	.75578	0.79	.45384	1.29	.27527	1.79	.16696
0.29	.74826	0.80	.44933	1.30	.27253	1.80	.16530
0.30	.74082	0.81	.44486	1.31	.26982	1.81	.16365
0.31	.73345	0.82	.44043	1.32	.26714	1.82	.16203
0.32	.72615	0.83	.43605	1.33	.26448	1.83	.16041
0.33	.71892	0.84	.43171	1.34	.26185	1.84	.15882
0.34	.71177	0.85	.42741	1.35	.25924	1.85	.15724
0.35	.70469	0.86	.42316	1.36	.25666	1.86	.15567
0.36	.69768	0.87	.41895	1.37	.25411	1.87	.15412
0.37	.69073	0.88	.41478	1.38	.25158	1.88	.15259
0.38	.68386	0.89	.41066	1.39	.24908	1.89	.15107
0.39	.67706	0.90	.40657	1.40	.24660	1.90	.14957
0.40	.67032	0.91	.40252	1.41	.24414	1.91	.14808
0.41	.66365	0.92	.39852	1.42	.24171	1.92	.14661
0.42	.65705	0.93	.39455	1.43	.23931	1.93	.14515
0.43	.65051	0.94	.39063	1.44	.23693	1.94	.14370
0.44	.64404	0.95	.38674	1.45	.23457	1.95	.14227
0.45	.63763	0.96	.38289	1.46	.23224	1.96	.14086
0.46	.63128	0.97	.37908	1.47	.22993	1.97	.13946
0.47	.62500	0.98	.37531	1.48	.22764	1.98	.13807
0.48	.61878	0.99	.37158	1.49	.22537	1.99	.13670
0.49	.61263	1.00	.36788	1.50	.22313	2.00	.13534
0.50	.60653						

Using Microsoft Excel, these values are calculated with the equation: 1 – EXPONDIST(x, 1, TRUE).

Appendix G

Areas of the Cumulative Standard Normal Distribution

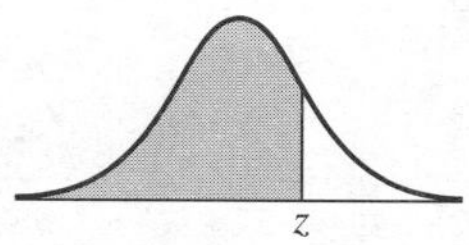

An entry in the table is the proportion under the curve cumulated from the negative tail.

z	G(z)	z	G(z)	z	G(z)	z	G(z)
−4.00	0.00003	−1.95	0.02559	0.10	0.53983	2.15	0.98422
−3.95	0.00004	−1.90	0.02872	0.15	0.55962	2.20	0.98610
−3.90	0.00005	−1.85	0.03216	0.20	0.57926	2.25	0.98778
−3.85	0.00006	−1.80	0.03593	0.25	0.59871	2.30	0.98928
−3.80	0.00007	−1.75	0.04006	0.30	0.61791	2.35	0.99061
−3.75	0.00009	−1.70	0.04457	0.35	0.63683	2.40	0.99180
−3.70	0.00011	−1.65	0.04947	0.40	0.65542	2.45	0.99286
−3.65	0.00013	−1.60	0.05480	0.45	0.67364	2.50	0.99379
−3.60	0.00016	−1.55	0.06057	0.50	0.69146	2.55	0.99461
−3.55	0.00019	−1.50	0.06681	0.55	0.70884	2.60	0.99534
−3.50	0.00023	−1.45	0.07353	0.60	0.72575	2.65	0.99598
−3.45	0.00028	−1.40	0.08076	0.65	0.74215	2.70	0.99653
−3.40	0.00034	−1.35	0.08851	0.70	0.75804	2.75	0.99702
−3.35	0.00040	−1.30	0.09680	0.75	0.77337	2.80	0.99744
−3.30	0.00048	−1.25	0.10565	0.80	0.78814	2.85	0.99781
−3.25	0.00058	−1.20	0.11507	0.85	0.80234	2.90	0.99813
−3.20	0.00069	−1.15	0.12507	0.90	0.81594	2.95	0.99841
−3.15	0.00082	−1.10	0.13567	0.95	0.82894	3.00	0.99865
−3.10	0.00097	−1.05	0.14686	1.00	0.84134	3.05	0.99886
−3.05	0.00114	−1.00	0.15866	1.05	0.85314	3.10	0.99903
−3.00	0.00135	−0.95	0.17106	1.10	0.86433	3.15	0.99918
−2.95	0.00159	−0.90	0.18406	1.15	0.87493	3.20	0.99931
−2.90	0.00187	−0.85	0.19766	1.20	0.88493	3.25	0.99942
−2.85	0.00219	−0.80	0.21186	1.25	0.89435	3.30	0.99952
−2.80	0.00256	−0.75	0.22663	1.30	0.90320	3.35	0.99960
−2.75	0.00298	−0.70	0.24196	1.35	0.91149	3.40	0.99966
−2.70	0.00347	−0.65	0.25785	1.40	0.91924	3.45	0.99972
−2.65	0.00402	−0.60	0.27425	1.45	0.92647	3.50	0.99977
−2.60	0.00466	−0.55	0.29116	1.50	0.93319	3.55	0.99981
−2.55	0.00539	−0.50	0.30854	1.55	0.93943	3.60	0.99984
−2.50	0.00621	−0.45	0.32636	1.60	0.94520	3.65	0.99987
−2.45	0.00714	−0.40	0.34458	1.65	0.95053	3.70	0.99989
−2.40	0.00820	−0.35	0.36317	1.70	0.95543	3.75	0.99991
−2.35	0.00939	−0.30	0.38209	1.75	0.95994	3.80	0.99993
−2.30	0.01072	−0.25	0.40129	1.80	0.96407	3.85	0.99994
−2.25	0.01222	−0.20	0.42074	1.85	0.96784	3.90	0.99995
−2.20	0.01390	−0.15	0.44038	1.90	0.97128	3.95	0.99996
−2.15	0.01578	−0.10	0.46017	1.95	0.97441	4.00	0.99997
−2.10	0.01786	−0.05	0.48006	2.00	0.97725		
−2.05	0.02018	0.00	0.50000	2.05	0.97982		
−2.00	0.02275	0.05	0.51994	2.10	0.98214		

Using Microsoft Excel, these probabilities are generated with the NORMSDIST(z) function.

Appendix H

Uniformly Distributed Random Digits

56970	10799	52098	04184	54967	72938	50834	23777	08392
83125	85077	60490	44369	66130	72936	69848	59973	08144
55503	21383	02464	26141	68779	66388	75242	82690	74099
47019	06683	33203	29603	54553	25971	69573	83854	24715
84828	61152	79526	29554	84580	37859	28504	61980	34997
08021	31331	79227	05748	51276	57143	31926	00915	45821
36458	28285	30424	98420	72925	40729	22337	48293	86847
05752	96045	36847	87729	81679	59126	59437	33225	31280
26768	02513	58454	56958	20575	76746	40878	06846	32828
42613	72456	43030	58085	06766	60227	96414	32671	45587
95457	12176	65482	25596	02678	54592	63607	82096	21913
95276	67524	63564	95958	39750	64379	46059	51666	10433
66954	53574	64776	92345	95110	59448	77249	54044	67942
17457	44151	14113	02462	02798	54977	48340	66738	60184
03704	23322	83214	59337	01695	60666	97410	55064	17427
21538	16997	33210	60337	27976	70661	08250	69509	60264
57178	16730	08310	70348	11317	71623	55510	64750	87759
31048	40058	94953	55866	96283	40620	52087	80817	74533
69799	83300	16498	80733	96422	58078	99643	39847	96884
90595	65017	59231	17772	67831	33317	00520	90401	41700
33570	34761	08039	78784	09977	29398	93896	78227	90110
15340	82760	57477	13898	48431	72936	78160	87240	52710
64079	07733	36512	56186	99098	48850	72527	08486	10951
63491	84886	67118	62063	74958	20946	28147	39338	32109
92003	76568	41034	28260	79708	00770	88643	21188	01850
52360	46658	66511	04172	73085	11795	52594	13287	82531
74622	12142	68355	65635	21828	39539	18988	53609	04001
04157	50070	61343	64315	70836	82857	35335	87900	36194
86003	60070	66241	32836	27573	11479	94114	81641	00496
41208	80187	20351	09630	84668	42486	71303	19512	50277
06433	80674	24520	18222	10610	05794	37515	48619	62866
39298	47829	72648	37414	75755	04717	29899	78817	03509
89884	59651	67533	68123	17730	95862	08034	19473	63971
61512	32155	51906	61662	64430	16688	37275	51262	11569
99653	47635	12506	88535	36553	23757	34209	55803	96275
95913	11085	13772	76638	48423	25018	99041	77529	81360
55804	44004	13122	44115	01601	50541	00147	77685	58788
35334	82410	91601	40617	72876	33967	73830	15405	96554
57729	88646	76487	11622	96297	24160	09903	14047	22917
86648	89317	63677	70119	94739	25875	38829	68377	43918
30574	06039	07967	32422	76791	30725	53711	93385	13421
81307	13114	83580	79974	45929	85113	72268	09858	52104
02410	96385	79067	54939	21410	86980	91772	93307	34116
18969	87444	52233	62319	08598	09066	95288	04794	01534
87863	80514	66860	62297	80198	19347	73234	86265	49096
08397	10538	15438	62311	72844	60203	46412	65943	79232
28520	45247	58729	10854	99058	18260	38765	90038	94209
44285	09452	15867	70418	57012	72122	36634	97283	95943
86299	22510	33571	23309	57040	29285	67870	21913	72958
84842	05748	90894	61658	15001	94005	36308	41161	37341

Interest Tables

Exhibit I.1

Compound Sum of $1

Year	1%	2%	3%	4%	5%	6%	7%	8%	9%
1	1.010	1.020	1.030	1.040	1.050	1.060	1.070	1.080	1.090
2	1.020	1.040	1.061	1.082	1.102	1.124	1.145	1.166	1.188
3	1.030	1.061	1.093	1.125	1.158	1.191	1.225	1.260	1.295
4	1.041	1.082	1.126	1.170	1.216	1.262	1.311	1.360	1.412
5	1.051	1.104	1.159	1.217	1.276	1.338	1.403	1.469	1.539
6	1.062	1.126	1.194	1.265	1.340	1.419	1.501	1.587	1.677
7	1.072	1.149	1.230	1.316	1.407	1.504	1.606	1.714	1.828
8	1.083	1.172	1.267	1.369	1.477	1.594	1.718	1.851	1.993
9	1.094	1.195	1.305	1.423	1.551	1.689	1.838	1.999	2.172
10	1.105	1.219	1.344	1.480	1.629	1.791	1.967	2.159	2.367
11	1.116	1.243	1.384	1.539	1.710	1.898	2.105	2.332	2.580
12	1.127	1.268	1.426	1.601	1.796	2.012	2.252	2.518	2.813
13	1.138	1.294	1.469	1.665	1.886	2.133	2.410	2.720	3.066
14	1.149	1.319	1.513	1.732	1.980	2.261	2.579	2.937	3.342
15	1.161	1.346	1.558	1.801	2.079	2.397	2.759	3.172	3.642
16	1.173	1.373	1.605	1.873	2.183	2.540	2.952	3.426	3.970
17	1.184	1.400	1.653	1.948	2.292	2.693	3.159	3.700	4.328
18	1.196	1.428	1.702	2.026	2.407	2.854	3.380	3.996	4.717
19	1.208	1.457	1.754	2.107	2.527	3.026	3.617	4.316	5.142
20	1.220	1.486	1.806	2.191	2.653	3.207	3.870	4.661	5.604
25	1.282	1.641	2.094	2.666	3.386	4.292	5.427	6.848	8.623
30	1.348	1.811	2.427	3.243	4.322	5.743	7.612	10.063	13.268
Year	**10%**	**12%**	**14%**	**15%**	**16%**	**18%**	**20%**	**24%**	**28%**
1	1.100	1.120	1.140	1.150	1.160	1.180	1.200	1.240	1.280
2	1.210	1.254	1.300	1.322	1.346	1.392	1.440	1.538	1.638
3	1.331	1.405	1.482	1.521	1.561	1.643	1.728	1.907	2.067
4	1.464	1.574	1.689	1.749	1.811	1.939	2.074	2.364	2.684
5	1.611	1.762	1.925	2.011	2.100	2.288	2.488	2.932	3.436
6	1.772	1.974	2.195	2.313	2.436	2.700	2.986	3.635	4.398
7	1.949	2.211	2.502	2.660	2.826	3.185	3.583	4.508	5.629
8	2.144	2.476	2.853	3.059	3.278	3.759	4.300	5.590	7.206
9	2.358	2.773	3.252	3.518	3.803	4.435	5.160	6.931	9.223
10	2.594	3.106	3.707	4.046	4.411	5.234	6.192	8.594	11.806
11	2.853	3.479	4.226	4.652	5.117	6.176	7.430	10.657	15.112
12	3.138	3.896	4.818	5.350	5.936	7.288	8.916	13.216	19.343
13	3.452	4.363	5.492	6.153	6.886	8.599	10.699	16.386	24.759
14	3.797	4.887	6.261	7.076	7.988	10.147	12.839	20.319	31.691
15	4.177	5.474	7.138	8.137	9.266	11.974	15.407	25.196	40.565
16	4.595	6.130	8.137	9.358	10.748	14.129	18.488	31.243	51.923
17	5.054	6.866	9.276	10.761	12.468	16.672	22.186	38.741	66.461
18	5.560	7.690	10.575	12.375	14.463	19.673	26.623	48.039	85.071
19	6.116	8.613	12.056	14.232	16.777	23.214	31.948	59.568	108.89
20	6.728	9.646	13.743	16.367	19.461	27.393	38.338	73.864	139.38
25	10.835	17.000	26.462	32.919	40.874	62.669	95.396	216.542	478.90
30	17.449	29.960	50.950	66.212	85.850	143.371	237.376	634.820	1645.5

Using Microsoft Excel, these are calculated with the equation: $(1 + \text{interest})^{\text{years}}$.

EXHIBIT I.2

Sum of an Annuity of $1 for *N* Years

Year	1%	2%	3%	4%	5%	6%	7%	8%
1	1.000	1.000	1.000	1.000	1.000	1.000	1.000	1.000
2	2.010	2.020	2.030	2.040	2.050	2.060	2.070	2.080
3	2.030	3.060	3.019	3.122	3.152	3.184	3.215	3.246
4	4.060	4.122	4.184	4.246	4.310	4.375	4.440	4.506
5	5.101	5.204	5.309	5.416	5.526	5.637	5.751	5.867
6	6.152	6.308	6.468	6.633	6.802	6.975	7.153	7.336
7	7.214	7.434	7.662	7.898	8.142	8.394	8.654	8.923
8	8.286	8.583	8.892	9.214	9.549	9.897	10.260	10.637
9	9.369	9.755	10.159	10.583	11.027	11.491	11.978	12.488
10	10.462	10.950	11.464	12.006	12.578	13.181	13.816	14.487
11	11.567	12.169	12.808	13.486	14.207	14.972	15.784	16.645
12	12.683	13.412	14.192	15.026	15.917	16.870	17.888	18.977
13	13.809	14.680	15.618	16.627	17.713	18.882	20.141	21.495
14	14.947	15.974	17.086	18.292	19.599	21.051	22.550	24.215
15	16.097	17.293	18.599	20.024	21.579	23.276	25.129	27.152
16	17.258	18.639	20.157	21.825	23.657	25.673	27.888	30.324
17	18.430	20.012	21.762	23.698	25.840	28.213	30.840	33.750
18	19.615	21.412	23.414	25.645	28.132	30.906	33.999	37.450
19	20.811	22.841	25.117	27.671	30.539	33.760	37.379	41.446
20	22.019	24.297	26.870	29.778	33.066	36.786	40.995	45.762
25	28.243	32.030	36.459	41.646	47.727	54.865	63.249	73.106
30	34.785	40.568	47.575	56.085	66.439	79.058	94.461	113.283

Year	9%	10%	12%	14%	16%	18%	20%	24%
1	1.000	1.000	1.000	1.000	1.000	1.000	1.000	1.000
2	2.090	2.100	2.120	2.140	2.160	2.180	2.200	2.240
3	3.278	3.310	3.374	3.440	3.506	3.572	3.640	3.778
4	4.573	4.641	4.770	4.921	5.066	5.215	5.368	5.684
5	5.985	6.105	6.353	6.610	6.877	7.154	7.442	8.048
6	7.523	7.716	8.115	8.536	8.977	9.442	9.930	10.980
7	9.200	9.487	10.089	10.730	11.414	12.142	12.916	14.615
8	11.028	11.436	12.300	13.233	14.240	15.327	16.499	19.123
9	13.021	13.579	14.776	16.085	17.518	19.086	20.799	24.712
10	15.193	15.937	17.549	19.337	21.321	23.521	25.959	31.643
11	17.560	18.531	20.655	23.044	25.733	28.755	32.150	40.238
12	20.141	21.384	24.133	27.271	30.850	34.931	39.580	50.985
13	22.953	24.523	28.029	32.089	36.786	42.219	48.497	64.110
14	26.019	27.975	32.393	37.581	43.672	50.818	59.196	80.496
15	29.361	31.772	37.280	43.842	51.660	60.965	72.035	100.815
16	33.003	35.950	42.753	50.980	60.925	72.939	87.442	126.011
17	36.974	40.545	48.884	59.118	71.673	87.068	105.931	157.253
18	41.301	45.599	55.750	68.394	84.141	103.740	128.117	195.994
19	46.018	51.159	63.440	78.969	98.603	123.414	154.740	244.033
20	51.160	57.275	72.052	91.025	115.380	146.628	186.688	303.601
25	84.701	93.347	133.334	181.871	249.214	342.603	471.981	898.092
30	136.308	164.494	241.333	356.787	530.312	790.948	1181.882	2640.916

Using Microsoft Excel, these are calculated with the function: FV(interest, years, −1).

EXHIBIT I.3

Present Value of $1

Year	1%	2%	3%	4%	5%	6%	7%	8%	9%	10%	12%	14%	15%
1	.990	.980	.971	.962	.952	.943	.935	.926	.917	.909	.893	.877	.870
2	.980	.961	.943	.925	.907	.890	.873	.857	.842	.826	.797	.769	.756
3	.971	.942	.915	.889	.864	.840	.816	.794	.772	.751	.712	.675	.658
4	.961	.924	.889	.855	.823	.792	.763	.735	.708	.683	.636	.592	.572
5	.951	.906	.863	.822	.784	.747	.713	.681	.650	.621	.567	.519	.497
6	.942	.888	.838	.790	.746	.705	.666	.630	.596	.564	.507	.456	.432
7	.933	.871	.813	.760	.711	.665	.623	.583	.547	.513	.452	.400	.376
8	.923	.853	.789	.731	.677	.627	.582	.540	.502	.467	.404	.351	.327
9	.914	.837	.766	.703	.645	.592	.544	.500	.460	.424	.361	.308	.284
10	.905	.820	.744	.676	.614	.558	.508	.463	.422	.386	.322	.270	.247
11	.896	.804	.722	.650	.585	.527	.475	.429	.388	.350	.287	.237	.215
12	.887	.788	.701	.625	.557	.497	.444	.397	.356	.319	.257	.208	.187
13	.879	.773	.681	.601	.530	.469	.415	.368	.326	.290	.229	.182	.163
14	.870	.758	.661	.577	.505	.442	.388	.340	.299	.263	.205	.160	.141
15	.861	.743	.642	.555	.481	.417	.362	.315	.275	.239	.183	.140	.123
16	.853	.728	.623	.534	.458	.394	.339	.292	.252	.218	.163	.123	.107
17	.844	.714	.605	.513	.436	.371	.317	.270	.231	.198	.146	.108	.093
18	.836	.700	.587	.494	.416	.350	.296	.250	.212	.180	.130	.095	.081
19	.828	.686	.570	.475	.396	.331	.276	.232	.194	.164	.116	.083	.070
20	.820	.673	.554	.456	.377	.312	.258	.215	.178	.149	.104	.073	.061
25	.780	.610	.478	.375	.295	.233	.184	.146	.116	.092	.059	.038	.030
30	.742	.552	.412	.308	.231	.174	.131	.099	.075	.057	.033	.020	.015
Year	**16%**	**18%**	**20%**	**24%**	**28%**	**32%**	**36%**	**40%**	**50%**	**60%**	**70%**	**80%**	**90%**
1	.862	.847	.833	.806	.781	.758	.735	.714	.667	.625	.588	.556	.526
2	.743	.718	.694	.650	.610	.574	.541	.510	.444	.391	.346	.309	.277
3	.641	.609	.579	.524	.477	.435	.398	.364	.296	.244	.204	.171	.146
4	.552	.516	.482	.423	.373	.329	.292	.260	.198	.153	.120	.095	.077
5	.476	.437	.402	.341	.291	.250	.215	.186	.132	.095	.070	.053	.040
6	.410	.370	.335	.275	.227	.189	.158	.133	.088	.060	.041	.029	.021
7	.354	.314	.279	.222	.178	.143	.116	.095	.059	.037	.024	.016	.011
8	.305	.266	.233	.179	.139	.108	.085	.068	.039	.023	.014	.009	.006
9	.263	.226	.194	.144	.108	.082	.063	.048	.026	.015	.008	.005	.003
10	.227	.191	.162	.116	.085	.062	.046	.035	.017	.009	.005	.003	.002
11	.195	.162	.135	.094	.066	.047	.034	.025	.012	.006	.003	.002	.001
12	.168	.137	.112	.076	.052	.036	.025	.018	.008	.004	.002	.001	.001
13	.145	.116	.093	.061	.040	.027	.018	.013	.005	.002	.001	.001	.000
14	.125	.099	.078	.049	.032	.021	.014	.009	.003	.001	.001	.000	.000
15	.108	.084	.065	.040	.025	.016	.010	.006	.002	.001	.000	.000	.000
16	.093	.071	.054	.032	.019	.012	.007	.005	.002	.001	.000	.000	
17	.080	.060	.045	.026	.015	.009	.005	.003	.001	.000	.000		
18	.069	.051	.038	.021	.012	.007	.004	.002	.001	.000	.000		
19	.060	.043	.031	.017	.009	.005	.003	.002	.000	.000			
20	.051	.037	.026	.014	.007	.004	.002	.001	.000	.000			
25	.024	.016	.010	.005	.002	.001	.000	.000					
30	.012	.007	.004	.002	.001	.000	.000						

Using Microsoft Excel, these are calculated with the equation: $(1 + \text{interest})^{-\text{years}}$.

Exhibit I.4

Present Value of an Annuity of $1

Year	1%	2%	3%	4%	5%	6%	7%	8%	9%	10%
1	0.990	0.980	0.971	0.962	0.952	0.943	0.935	0.926	0.917	0.909
2	1.970	1.942	1.913	1.886	1.859	1.833	1.808	1.783	1.759	1.736
3	2.941	2.884	2.829	2.775	2.723	2.673	2.624	2.577	2.531	2.487
4	3.902	3.808	3.717	3.630	3.546	3.465	3.387	3.312	3.240	3.170
5	4.853	4.713	4.580	4.452	4.329	4.212	4.100	3.993	3.890	3.791
6	5.795	5.601	5.417	5.242	5.076	4.917	4.766	4.623	4.486	4.355
7	6.728	6.472	6.230	6.002	5.786	5.582	5.389	5.206	5.033	4.868
8	7.652	7.325	7.020	6.733	6.463	6.210	6.971	5.747	5.535	5.335
9	8.566	8.162	7.786	7.435	7.108	6.802	6.515	6.247	5.985	5.759
10	9.471	8.983	8.530	8.111	7.722	7.360	7.024	6.710	6.418	6.145
11	10.368	9.787	9.253	8.760	8.306	7.887	7.449	7.139	6.805	6.495
12	11.255	10.575	9.954	9.385	8.863	8.384	7.943	7.536	7.161	6.814
13	12.134	11.348	10.635	9.986	9.394	8.853	8.358	7.904	7.487	7.103
14	13.004	12.106	11.296	10.563	9.899	9.295	8.745	8.244	7.786	7.367
15	13.865	12.849	11.938	11.118	10.380	9.712	9.108	8.559	8.060	7.606
16	14.718	13.578	12.561	11.652	10.838	10.106	9.447	8.851	8.312	7.824
17	15.562	14.292	13.166	12.166	11.274	10.477	9.763	9.122	8.544	8.022
18	16.398	14.992	13.754	12.659	11.690	10.828	10.059	9.372	8.756	8.201
19	17.226	15.678	14.324	13.134	12.085	11.158	10.336	9.604	8.950	8.365
20	18.046	16.351	14.877	13.590	12.462	11.470	10.594	9.818	9.128	8.514
25	22.023	19.523	17.413	15.622	14.094	12.783	11.654	10.675	9.823	9.077
30	25.808	22.397	19.600	17.292	15.373	13.765	12.409	11.258	10.274	9.427

Year	12%	14%	16%	18%	20%	24%	28%	32%	36%
1	0.893	0.877	0.862	0.847	0.833	0.806	0.781	0.758	0.735
2	1.690	1.647	1.605	1.566	1.528	1.457	1.392	1.332	1.276
3	2.402	2.322	2.246	2.174	2.106	1.981	1.868	1.766	1.674
4	3.037	2.914	2.798	2.690	2.589	2.404	2.241	2.096	1.966
5	3.605	3.433	3.274	3.127	2.991	2.745	2.532	2.345	2.181
6	4.111	3.889	3.685	3.498	3.326	3.020	2.759	2.534	2.339
7	4.564	4.288	4.039	3.812	3.605	3.242	2.937	2.678	2.455
8	4.968	4.639	4.344	4.078	3.837	3.421	3.076	2.786	2.540
9	5.328	4.946	4.607	4.303	4.031	3.566	3.184	2.868	2.603
10	5.650	5.216	4.833	4.494	4.193	3.682	3.269	2.930	2.650
11	5.988	5.453	5.029	4.656	4.327	3.776	3.335	2.978	2.683
12	6.194	5.660	5.197	4.793	4.439	3.851	3.387	3.013	2.708
13	6.424	5.842	5.342	4.910	4.533	3.912	3.427	3.040	2.727
14	6.628	6.002	5.468	5.008	4.611	3.962	3.459	3.061	2.740
15	6.811	6.142	5.575	5.092	4.675	4.001	3.483	3.076	2.750
16	6.974	6.265	5.669	5.162	4.730	4.033	3.503	3.088	2.758
17	7.120	6.373	5.749	5.222	4.775	4.059	3.518	3.097	2.763
18	7.250	6.467	5.818	5.273	4.812	4.080	3.529	3.104	2.767
19	7.366	6.550	5.877	5.316	4.844	4.097	3.539	3.109	2.770
20	7.469	6.623	5.929	5.353	4.870	4.110	3.546	3.113	2.772
25	7.843	6.873	6.097	5.467	4.948	4.147	3.564	3.122	2.776
30	8.055	7.003	6.177	5.517	4.979	4.160	3.569	3.124	2.778

Using Microsoft Excel, these are calculated with the function: PV(interest, years, −1).

Index